QGIS: Becomin
Power Use

Master data management, visualization, and spatial analysis techniques in QGIS and become a GIS power user

A course in three modules

Packt>

BIRMINGHAM - MUMBAI

QGIS:Becoming a GIS Power User

Published on: February 2017

Production reference: 1210217

Published by Packt Publishing Ltd.
Livery Place
35 Livery Street
Birmingham B3 2PB, UK.

ISBN 978-1-78829-972-5

www.packtpub.com

Credits

Authors

Anita Graser,

Ben Mearns,

Alex Mandel,

Víctor Olaya Ferrero,

Alexander Bruy

Reviewers

Cornelius Roth

Ujaval Gandhi

Fred Gibbs

Gergely Padányi-Gulyás

Abdelghaffar KHORCHANI

Pablo Pardo

Mats Töpel

Jorge Arévalo

Olivier Dalang

Ben Mearns

Content Development Editor

Aishwarya Pandere

Production Coordinator

Aparna Bhagat

Credits

Authors

Anita Graser,

Ben Mearns,

Alex Mandel,

Víctor Olaya Ferrero,

Alexander Bruy

Reviewers

Cornelius Roth

Ujaval Gandhi

Fred Gibbs

Gergely Padányi-Gulyás

Abdelghaffar KHORCHANI

Pablo Pardo

Mats Töpel

Jorge Arévalo

Olivier Dalang

Ben Mearns

Content Development Editor

Aishwarya Pandere

Production Coordinator

Aparna Bhagat

Preface

QGIS is a crossing point of the free and open source geospatial world. While there are a great many tools in QGIS, it is not one massive application that does everything, and it was never really designed to be that from the beginning. It is rather a visual interface to much of the open source geospatial world. You can load data from proprietary and open formats into spatial databases of various flavors and then analyze the data with well-known analytical backends before creating a printed or web-based map to display and interact with your results. What's QGIS's role in all this? It's the place where you check your data along the way, build and queue the analysis, visualize the results, and develop cartographic end products.

This learning path will teach you all that and more, in a hands-on learn-by-doing manner. Become an expert in QGIS with this useful companion.

What this learning path covers

Module 1, Learning QGIS, Third edition, covers important features that enable us to create great maps. Then, we will cover labeling using examples of labeling point locations as well as creating more advanced road labels with road shield graphics. We will also cover how to tweak labels manually. We will get to know the print composer and how to use it to create printable maps and map books. Finally, we will cover solutions to present your maps on the Web.

Module 2, QGIS Blueprints, will demonstrate visualization and analytical techniques to explore relationships between place and time and between places themselves. You will work with demographic data from a census for election purposes through a timeline controlled animation.

Module 3, QGIS 2 Cookbook, deals with converting data into the formats you need for analysis, including vector to and from raster, transitioning through different types of vectors, and cutting your data to just the important areas. It also shows you how to take QGIS beyond the out-of-the-box features with plugins, customization, and add-on tools.

What you need for this learning path

Module 1:

To follow the exercises in this book, you need QGIS 2.14. QGIS installation is covered in the first chapter and download links for the exercise data are provided in the respective chapters.

Module 2:

You will need:

- QGIS 2.10
- A computer running OS X, Windows, or Linux

Module 3:

We recommend installing QGIS 2.8 or later; you will need at least QGIS 2.4. During the writing of this book, several new versions were released, approximately every 4 months, and most recently, 2.14 was released. Most of the recipes will work on older versions, but some may require 2.6 or newer. In general, if you can, upgrade to the latest stable release or Long Term Support (LTS) version.

There are also a lot of side interactions with other software throughout many of these

recipes, including — but not limited to — Postgis 2+, GRASS 6.4+, SAGA 2.0.8+, and Spatialite 4+. On Windows, most of these can be installed using OSGeo4W; on Mac, you may need some additional frameworks from Kyngchaos, or if you're familiar with Brew, you can use the OSGeo4Mac Tap. For Linux users, in particular Ubuntu and Debian, refer to the UbuntuGIS PPA and the DebianGIS blend.

Does all of this sound a little too complicated? If yes, then consider using a virtual machine that runs OSGeo-Live (http://live.osgeo.org). All the software is preinstalled for you and is known to work together.

Lastly, you will need data. For the most part, we've provided a lot of free and open data from a variety of sources, including the OSGeo Educational dataset (North Carolina), Natural Earth Data, OpenFlights, Wake County, City of Davis, and Armed Conflict Location & Event Data Project (ACLED). A full list of our data sources is provided here if you would like additional data.

We recommend that you try methods with the sample data first, only because we tested it.

Feel free to try using your own data to test many of the recipes; however, just remember that you might need to alter the structure to make it work. After all, that's what you'll be working with normally.

The following are the data sources for this book:

OSGeo Educational Data: `http://grass.osgeo.org/download/sample-data/`

Wake County, USA: `http://www.wakegov.com/gis/services/pages/data.aspx`

Natural Earth Data: `http://www.naturalearthdata.com/`

City of Davis, USA: `http://maps.cityofdavis.org/library`

Stamen Designs: `http://stamen.com/`

Armed Conflict Location & Event Data Project: `http://www.acleddata.com/`

Who this learning path is for

If you are a user, developer, or consultant and want to know how to use QGIS to achieve the results you are used to from other types of GIS, then this learning path is for you. You are expected to be comfortable with core GIS concepts. This Learning Path will make you an expert with QGIS by showing you how to develop more complex, layered map applications. It will launch you to the next level of GIS users.

Reader feedback

Feedback from our readers is always welcome. Let us know what you think about this course—what you liked or disliked. Reader feedback is important for us as it helps us develop titles that you will really get the most out of.

To send us general feedback, simply e-mail `feedback@packtpub.com`, and mention the course's title in the subject of your message.

If there is a topic that you have expertise in and you are interested in either writing or contributing to a course, see our author guide at `www.packtpub.com/authors`.

Customer support

Now that you are the proud owner of a Packt course, we have a number of things to help you to get the most from your purchase.

Downloading the example code

You can download the example code files for this course from your account at `http://www.packtpub.com`. If you purchased this course elsewhere, you can visit `http://www.packtpub.com/support` and register to have the files e-mailed directly to you.

You can download the code files by following these steps:

1. Log in or register to our website using your e-mail address and password.
2. Hover the mouse pointer on the **SUPPORT** tab at the top.
3. Click on **Code Downloads & Errata**.
4. Enter the name of the course in the **Search** box.
5. Select the course for which you're looking to download the code files.
6. Choose from the drop-down menu where you purchased this course from.
7. Click on **Code Download**.

You can also download the code files by clicking on the **Code Files** button on the course's webpage at the Packt Publishing website. This page can be accessed by entering the course's name in the **Search** box. Please note that you need to be logged in to your Packt account.

Once the file is downloaded, please make sure that you unzip or extract the folder using the latest version of:

*   WinRAR / 7-Zip for Windows
*   Zipeg / iZip / UnRarX for Mac
*   7-Zip / PeaZip for Linux

The code bundle for the course is also hosted on GitHub at `https://github.com/PacktPublishing/QGIS-Becoming-a-GIS-Power-User`.

We also have other code bundles from our rich catalog of books, videos and courses available at `https://github.com/PacktPublishing/`. Check them out!

Errata

Although we have taken every care to ensure the accuracy of our content, mistakes do happen. If you find a mistake in one of our books—maybe a mistake in the text or the code—we would be grateful if you could report this to us. By doing so, you can save other readers from frustration and help us improve subsequent versions of this course. If you find any errata, please report them by visiting `http://www.packtpub.com/submit-errata`, selecting your course, clicking on the **Errata Submission Form** link, and entering the details of your errata. Once your errata are verified, your submission will be accepted and the errata will be uploaded to our website or added to any list of existing errata under the Errata section of that title.

To view the previously submitted errata, go to `https://www.packtpub.com/books/content/support` and enter the name of the book in the search field. The required information will appear under the **Errata** section.

Piracy

Piracy of copyrighted material on the Internet is an ongoing problem across all media. At Packt, we take the protection of our copyright and licenses very seriously. If you come across any illegal copies of our works in any form on the Internet, please provide us with the location address or website name immediately so that we can pursue a remedy.

Please contact us at `copyright@packtpub.com` with a link to the suspected pirated material.

We appreciate your help in protecting our authors and our ability to bring you valuable content.

Questions

If you have a problem with any aspect of this course, you can contact us at `questions@packtpub.com`, and we will do our best to address the problem.

Module 1: Learning QGIS, Third Edition

Module 2: QGIS Blueprints

Module 3: QGIS 2 Cookbook

Module 1

Learning QGIS, Third Edition

*The latest guide to using QGIS 2.14 to create great maps and
perform geoprocessing tasks with ease*

Getting Started with QGIS

In this chapter, we will install and configure the **QGIS** geographic information system. We will also get to know the user interface and how to customize it. By the end of this chapter, you will have QGIS running on your machine and be ready to start with the tutorials.

Installing QGIS

QGIS runs on **Windows**, various **Linux** distributions, **Unix**, **Mac OS X**, and **Android**. The QGIS project provides ready-to-use packages as well as instructions to build from the source code at `http://download.qgis.org`. We will cover how to install QGIS on two systems, Windows and Ubuntu, as well as how to avoid the most common pitfalls.

> Further installation instructions for other supported operating systems are available at `http://www.qgis.org/en/site/forusers/alldownloads.html`.

Like many other open source projects, QGIS offers you a choice between different releases. For the tutorials in this book, we will use the **QGIS 2.14 LTR** version. The following options are available:

- **Long-term release (LTR)**: The LTR version is recommended for corporate and academic use. It is currently released once per year in the end of February. It receives bug fix updates for at least a year, and the features and user interface remain unchanged. This makes it the best choice for training material that should not become outdated after a few months.

- **Latest release (LR)**: The LR version contains newly developed and tested features. It is currently released every four months (except when an LTR version is released instead). Use this version if you want to stay up to date with the latest developments, including new features and user interface changes, but are not comfortable with using the DEV version.

- **Developer version (DEV, master, or testing)**: The cutting-edge DEV version contains the latest and greatest developments, but be warned that on some days, it might not work as reliably as you want it to.

> You can find more information about the releases as well as the schedule for future releases at http://www.qgis.org/en/site/getinvolved/development/roadmap.html#release-schedule.
>
> For an overview of the changes between releases, check out the visual change logs at http://www.qgis.org/en/site/forusers/visualchangelogs.html.

Installing QGIS on Windows

On Windows, we have two different options to install QGIS, the standalone installer and the **OSGeo4W** installer:

- The **standalone installer** is one big file to download (approximately 280 MB); it contains a QGIS release, the **Geographic Resources Analysis Support System (GRASS)** GIS, as well as the **System for Automated Geoscientific Analyses (SAGA)** GIS in one package.

- The **OSGeo4W installer** is a small, flexible installation tool that makes it possible to download and install QGIS and many more OSGeo tools with all their dependencies. The main advantage of this installer over the standalone installer is that it makes updating QGIS and its dependencies very easy. You can always have access to both the current release and the developer versions if you choose to, but, of course, you are never forced to update. That is why I recommend that you use **OSGeo4W**. You can download the 32-bit and 64-bit OSGeo4W installers from http://osgeo4w.osgeo.org (or directly from http://download.osgeo.org/osgeo4w/osgeo4w-setup-x86.exe for the 32-bit version or http://download.osgeo.org/osgeo4w/osgeo4w-setup-x86_64.exe if you have a 64-bit version of Windows). Download the version that matches your operating system and keep it! In the future, whenever you want to change or update your system, just run it again.

> Regardless of the installer you choose, make sure that you avoid special characters such as German umlauts or letters from alphabets other than the default Latin ones (for details, refer to https://en.wikipedia.org/wiki/ISO_basic_Latin_ alphabet) in the installation path, as they can cause problems later on, for example, during plugin installation.

When the OSGeo4W installer starts, we get to choose between **Express Desktop Install**, **Express Web-GIS Install**, and **Advanced Install**. To install the QGIS LR version, we can simply select the **Express Desktop Install** option, and the next dialog will list the available desktop applications, such as **QGIS, uDig**, and **GRASS GIS**. We can simply select **QGIS**, click on **Next**, and confirm the necessary dependencies by clicking on **Next** again. Then the download and installation will start automatically. When the installation is complete, there will be desktop shortcuts and start menu entries for OSGeo4W and QGIS.

To install QGIS LTR (or DEV), we need to go through the **Advanced Install** option, as shown in the following screenshot:

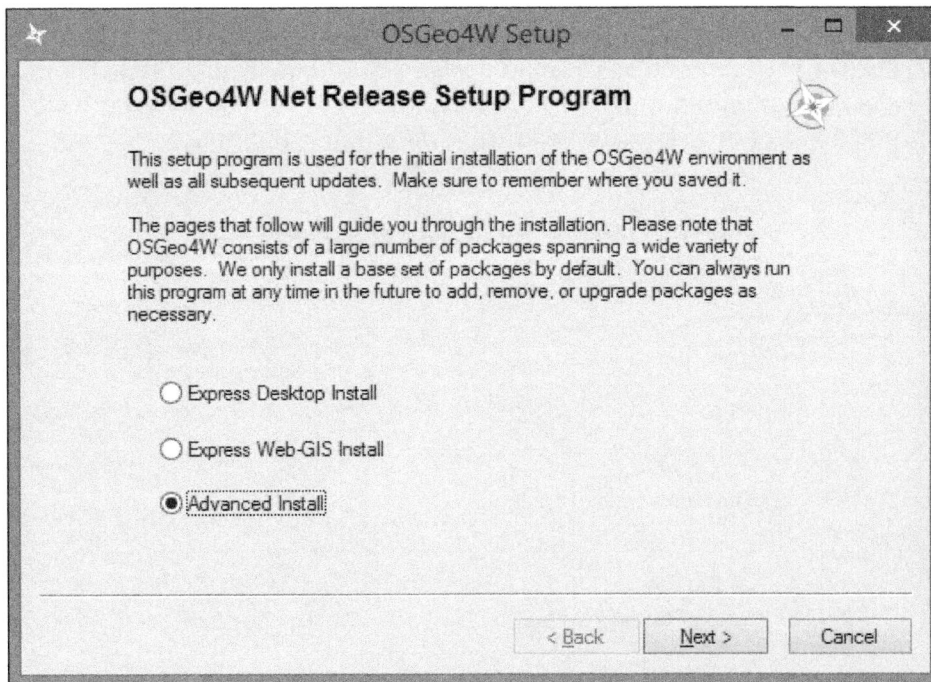

This installation path offers many options, such as **Download Without Installing** and **Install from Local Directory**, which can be used to download all the necessary packages on one machine and later install them on machines without Internet access. We just select **Install from Internet**, as shown in this screenshot:

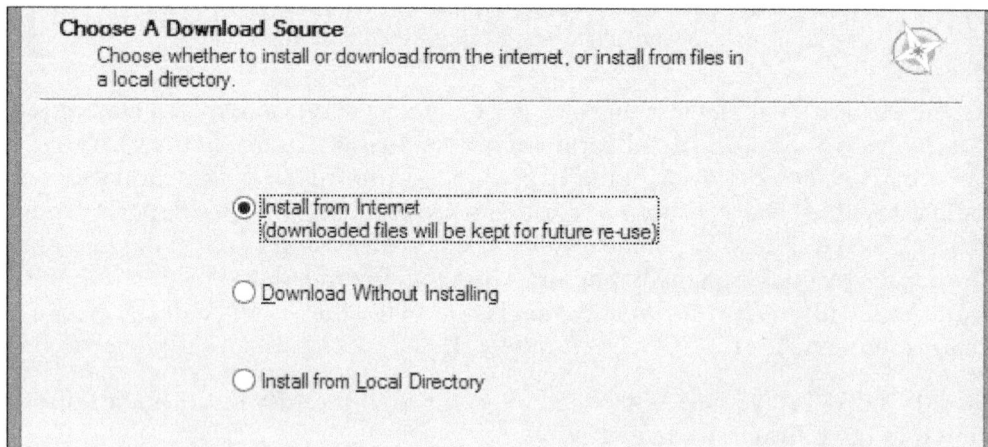

Choose A Download Source
Choose whether to install or download from the internet, or install from files in a local directory.

○ Install from Internet
   (downloaded files will be kept for future re-use)

○ Download Without Installing

○ Install from Local Directory

When selecting the installation **Root Directory**, as shown in the following screenshot, avoid special characters such as German umlauts or letters from alphabets other than the default Latin ones in the installation path (as mentioned before), as they can cause problems later on, for example, during plugin installation:

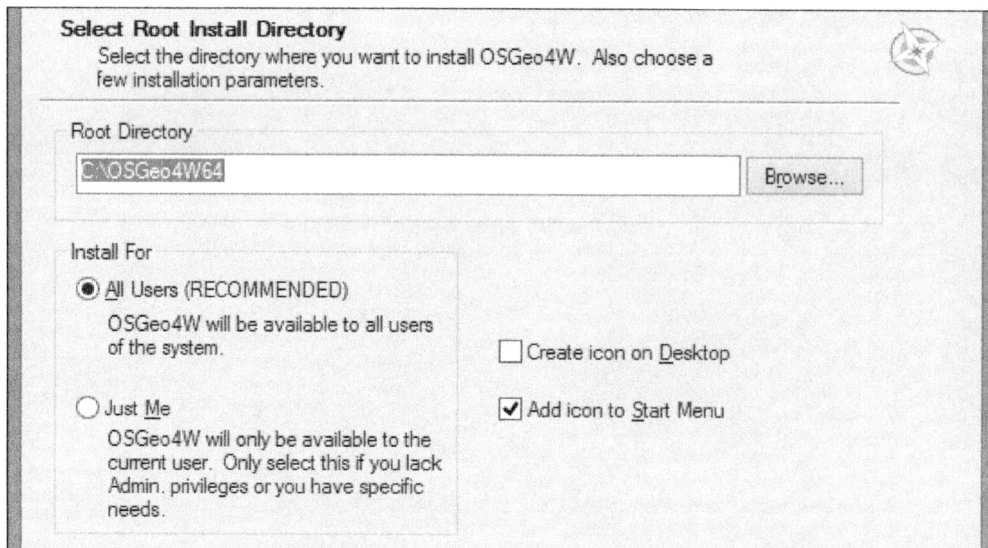

Select Root Install Directory
Select the directory where you want to install OSGeo4W. Also choose a few installation parameters.

Root Directory

C:\OSGeo4W64   Browse...

Install For

○ All Users (RECOMMENDED)
   OSGeo4W will be available to all users
   of the system.   ☐ Create icon on Desktop

○ Just Me   ☑ Add icon to Start Menu
   OSGeo4W will only be available to the
   current user. Only select this if you lack
   Admin. privileges or you have specific
   needs.

Then you can specify the folder (**Local Package Directory**) where the setup process will store the installation files as well as customize **Start menu name**. I recommend that you leave the default settings similar to what you can see in this screenshot:

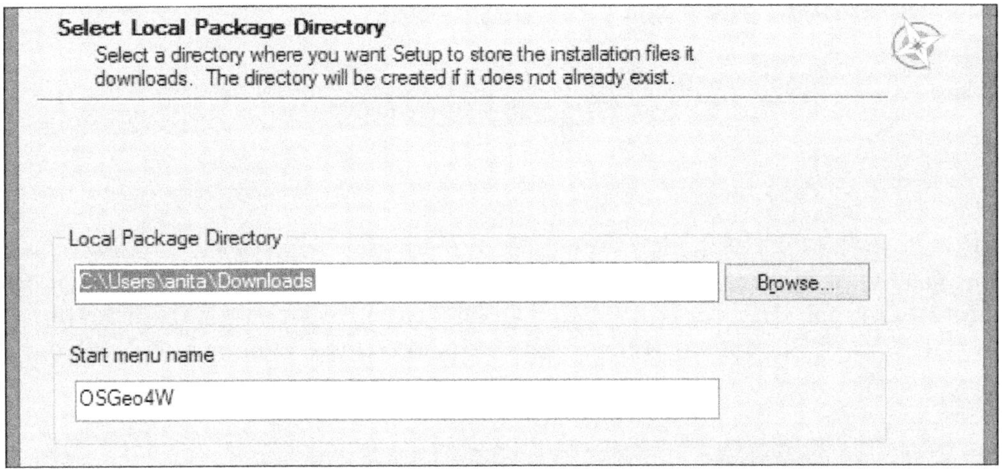

In the Internet connection settings, it is usually not necessary to change the default settings, but if your machine is, for example, hidden behind a **proxy**, you will be able to specify it here:

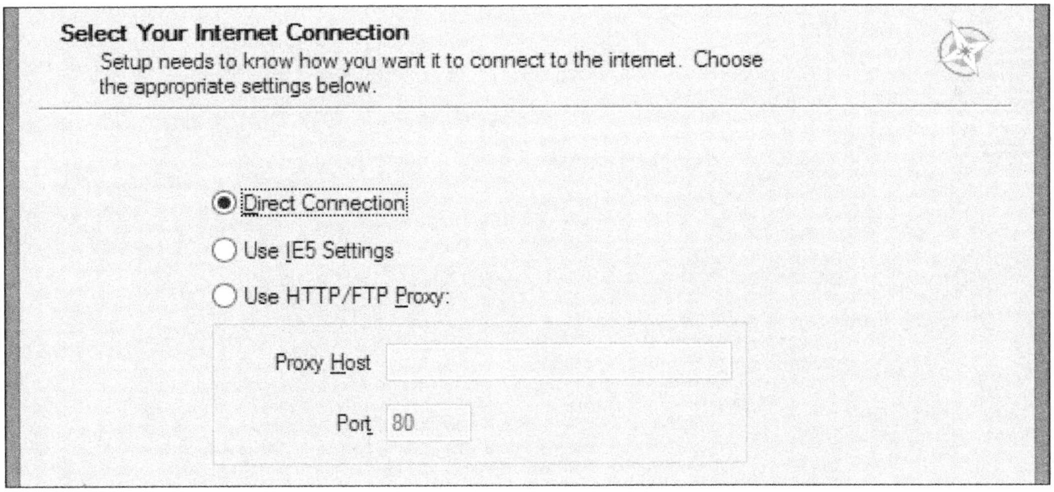

Then we can pick the *download site*. At the time of writing this book, there is only one download server available, anyway, as you can see in the following screenshot:

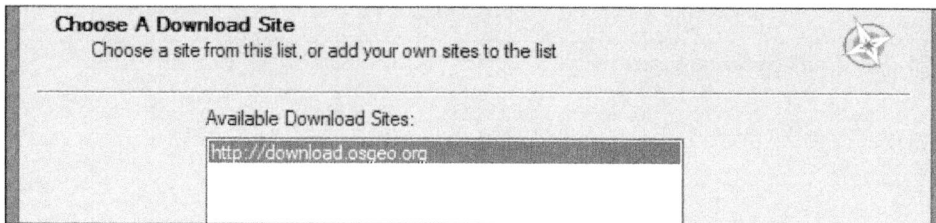

Choose A Download Site
Choose a site from this list, or add your own sites to the list

Available Download Sites:
http://download.osgeo.org

After the installer fetches the latest package information from OSGeo's servers, we get to pick the packages for installation. QGIS LTR is listed in the desktop category as **qgis-ltr** (and the DEV version is listed as **qgis-dev**). To select the LTR version for installation, click on the text that reads **Skip**, and it will change and display the version number, as shown in this screenshot:

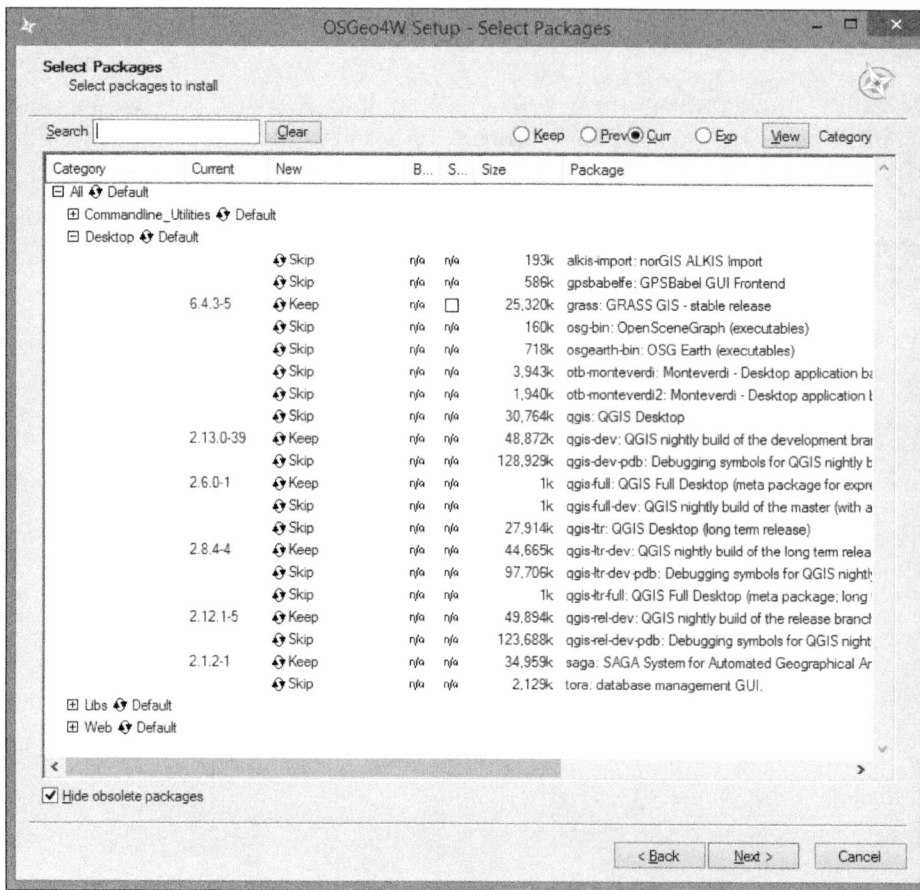

OSGeo4W Setup - Select Packages

Select Packages
Select packages to install

Search [ ]   [Clear]   ○ Keep ○ Prev ● Curr ○ Exp   [View] Category

Category	Current	New	B...	S...	Size	Package
⊟ All ✪ Default						
⊞ Commandline_Utilities ✪ Default						
⊟ Desktop ✪ Default						
		✪ Skip	n/a	n/a	193k	alkis-import: norGIS ALKIS Import
		✪ Skip	n/a	n/a	586k	gpsbabelfe: GPSBabel GUI Frontend
	6.4.3-5	✪ Keep	n/a	☐	25,320k	grass: GRASS GIS - stable release
		✪ Skip	n/a	n/a	160k	osg-bin: OpenSceneGraph (executables)
		✪ Skip	n/a	n/a	718k	osgearth-bin: OSG Earth (executables)
		✪ Skip	n/a	n/a	3,943k	otb-monteverdi: Monteverdi - Desktop application ba
		✪ Skip	n/a	n/a	1,940k	otb-monteverdi2: Monteverdi - Desktop application b
		✪ Skip	n/a	n/a	30,764k	qgis: QGIS Desktop
	2.13.0-39	✪ Keep	n/a	n/a	48,872k	qgis-dev: QGIS nightly build of the development bra
		✪ Skip	n/a	n/a	128,929k	qgis-dev-pdb: Debugging symbols for QGIS nightly b
	2.6.0-1	✪ Keep	n/a	n/a	1k	qgis-full: QGIS Full Desktop (meta package for expr
		✪ Skip	n/a	n/a	1k	qgis-full-dev: QGIS nightly build of the master (with a
		✪ Skip	n/a	n/a	27,914k	qgis-ltr: QGIS Desktop (long term release)
	2.8.4-4	✪ Keep	n/a	n/a	44,665k	qgis-ltr-dev: QGIS nightly build of the long term relea
		✪ Skip	n/a	n/a	97,706k	qgis-ltr-dev-pdb: Debugging symbols for QGIS nightl
		✪ Skip	n/a	n/a	1k	qgis-ltr-full: QGIS Full Desktop (meta package; long
	2.12.1-5	✪ Keep	n/a	n/a	49,894k	qgis-rel-dev: QGIS nightly build of the release branc
		✪ Skip	n/a	n/a	123,688k	qgis-rel-dev-pdb: Debugging symbols for QGIS night
	2.1.2-1	✪ Keep	n/a	n/a	34,959k	saga: SAGA System for Automated Geographical Ar
		✪ Skip	n/a	n/a	2,129k	tora: database management GUI.
⊞ Libs ✪ Default						
⊞ Web ✪ Default						

☑ Hide obsolete packages

[< Back] [Next >] [Cancel]

As you can see in the following screenshot, the installer will automatically select all the necessary dependencies (such as GDAL, SAGA, OTB, and GRASS), so we don't have to worry about this:

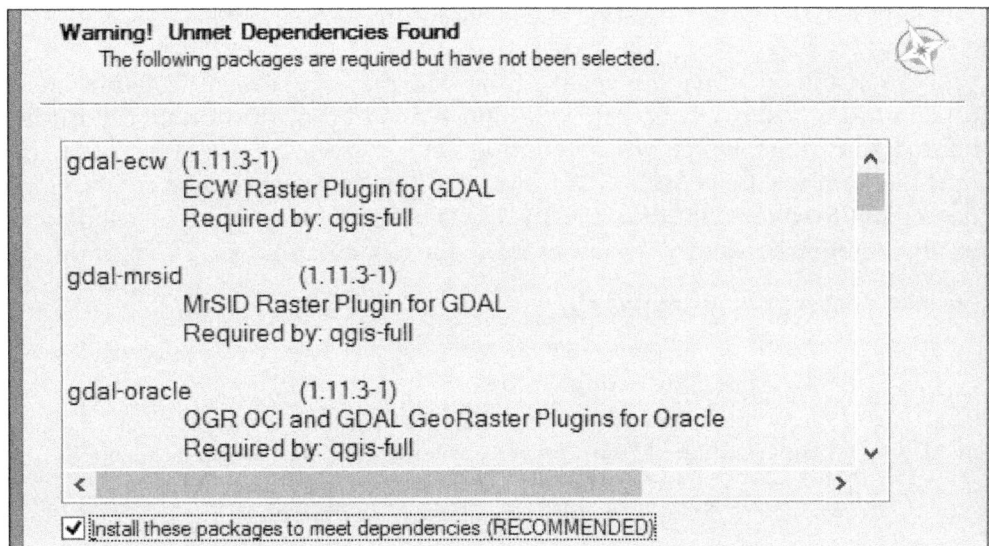

Warning! Unmet Dependencies Found
The following packages are required but have not been selected.

gdal-ecw (1.11.3-1)
          ECW Raster Plugin for GDAL
          Required by: qgis-full

gdal-mrsid   (1.11.3-1)
          MrSID Raster Plugin for GDAL
          Required by: qgis-full

gdal-oracle   (1.11.3-1)
          OGR OCI and GDAL GeoRaster Plugins for Oracle
          Required by: qgis-full

☑ Install these packages to meet dependencies (RECOMMENDED)

After you've clicked on **Next**, the download and installation starts automatically, just as in the Express version.

You have probably noticed other available QGIS packages called **qgis-ltr-dev** and **qgis-rel-dev**. These contain the latest changes (to the LTR and LR versions, respectively), which will be released as bug fix versions according to the release schedule. This makes these packages a good option if you run into an issue with a release that has been fixed recently but the bug fix version release is not out yet.

> If you try to run QGIS and get a popup that says, **The procedure entry point <some-name> could not be located in the dynamic link library <dll-name>.dll**, it means that you are facing a common issue on Windows systems — a *DLL conflict*. This error is easy to fix; just copy the DLL file mentioned in the error message from C:\OSGeo4W\bin\ to C:\OSGeo4W\apps\qgis\bin\ (adjust the paths if necessary).

Installing on Ubuntu

On Ubuntu, the QGIS project provides packages for the LTR, LR, and DEV versions. At the time of writing this book, the Ubuntu versions Precise, Trusty, Vivid, and Wily are supported, but you can find the latest information at http://www.qgis.org/en/site/forusers/alldownloads.html#debian-ubuntu. Be aware, however, that you can install only one version at a time. The packages are not listed in the default Ubuntu repositories. Therefore, we have to add the appropriate repositories to Ubuntu's source list, which you can find at /etc/apt/sources.list. You can open the file with any text editor. Make sure that you have super user rights, as you will need them to save your edits. One option is to use gedit, which is installed in Ubuntu by default. To edit the sources.list file, use the following command:

```
sudo gedit /etc/apt/sources.list
```

> **Downloading the example code**
>
> You can download the example code files for this book from your account at http://www.packtpub.com. If you purchased this book elsewhere, you can visit http://www.packtpub.com/support and register to have the files e-mailed directly to you.

Make sure that you add only one of the following package-source options to avoid conflicts due to incompatible packages. The specific lines that you have to add to the source list depend on your Ubuntu version:

1. *The first option*, which is also the default one, is to install the LR version. To install the QGIS LR release on Trusty, add the following lines to your file:

   ```
   deb      http://qgis.org/debian trusty main
   deb-src http://qgis.org/debian trusty main
   ```

   > If necessary, replace trusty with precise, vivid, or wily to fit your system. For an updated list of supported Ubuntu versions, check out http://www.qgis.org/en/site/forusers/alldownloads.html#debian-ubuntu.

2. *The second option* is to install QGIS LTR by adding the following lines to your file:

   ```
   deb      http://qgis.org/debian-ltr trusty main
   deb-src http://qgis.org/debian-ltr trusty main
   ```

3. *The third option* is to install QGIS DEV by adding these lines to your file:

```
deb       http://qgis.org/debian-nightly trusty main
deb-src http://qgis.org/debian-nightly trusty main
```

> The preceding versions depend on other packages such as GDAL and proj4, which are available in the Ubuntu repositories. It is worth mentioning that these packages are often quite old.

4. *The fourth option* is to install QGIS LR with updated dependencies, which are provided by the ubuntugis repository. Add these lines to your file:

```
deb       http://qgis.org/ubuntugis trusty main
deb-src http://qgis.org/ubuntugis trusty main
deb       http://ppa.launchpad.net/ubuntugis/ubuntugis-unstable/
ubuntu trusty main
```

5. *The fifth option* is QGIS LTR with updated dependencies. Add these lines to your file:

```
deb       http://qgis.org/ubuntugis-ltr trusty main
deb-src http://qgis.org/ubuntugis-ltr trusty main
deb       http://ppa.launchpad.net/ubuntugis/ubuntugis-unstable/
ubuntu trusty main
```

6. *The sixth option* is the QGIS master with updated dependencies. Add these lines to your file:

```
deb       http://qgis.org/ubuntugis-nightly trusty main
deb-src http://qgis.org/ubuntugis-nightly trusty main
deb       http://ppa.launchpad.net/ubuntugis/ubuntugis-unstable/
ubuntu trusty main
```

> To follow the tutorials in this book, it is recommended that you install QGIS 2.14 LTR with updated dependencies (the fifth option).

After choosing the repository, we will add the qgis.org repository's public key to our apt keyring. This will avoid the warnings that you might otherwise get when installing from a non-default repository. Run the following command in the terminal:

```
sudo apt-key adv --keyserver keyserver.ubuntu.com --recv-key
3FF5FFCAD71472C4
```

[　By the time this book goes to print, the key information might have
changed. Refer to http://www.qgis.org/en/site/forusers/
alldownloads.html#debian-ubuntu for the latest updates.　]

Finally, to install QGIS, run the following commands:

```
sudo apt-get update
sudo apt-get install qgis python-qgis qgis-plugin-grass
```

Running QGIS for the first time

When you install QGIS, you will get two applications: **QGIS Desktop** and **QGIS
Browser**. If you are familiar with **ArcGIS**, you can think of QGIS Browser as
something similar to **ArcCatalog**. It is a small application used to preview spatial data
and related metadata. For the remainder of this book, we will focus on QGIS Desktop.

By default, QGIS will use the operating system's default language. To follow the
tutorials in this book, I advise you to change the language to English by going to
Settings | Options | Locale.

On the first run, the way the toolbars are arranged can hide some buttons. To be
able to work efficiently, I suggest that you rearrange the toolbars (for the sake of
completeness, I have enabled all toolbars in **Toolbars**, which is in the **View** menu). I
like to place some toolbars on the left and right screen borders to save vertical screen
estate, especially on wide-screen displays.

Additionally, we will activate the file browser by navigating to **View | Panels |
Browser Panel**. It will provide us with quick access to our spatial data. At the end,
the QGIS window on your screen should look similar to the following screenshot:

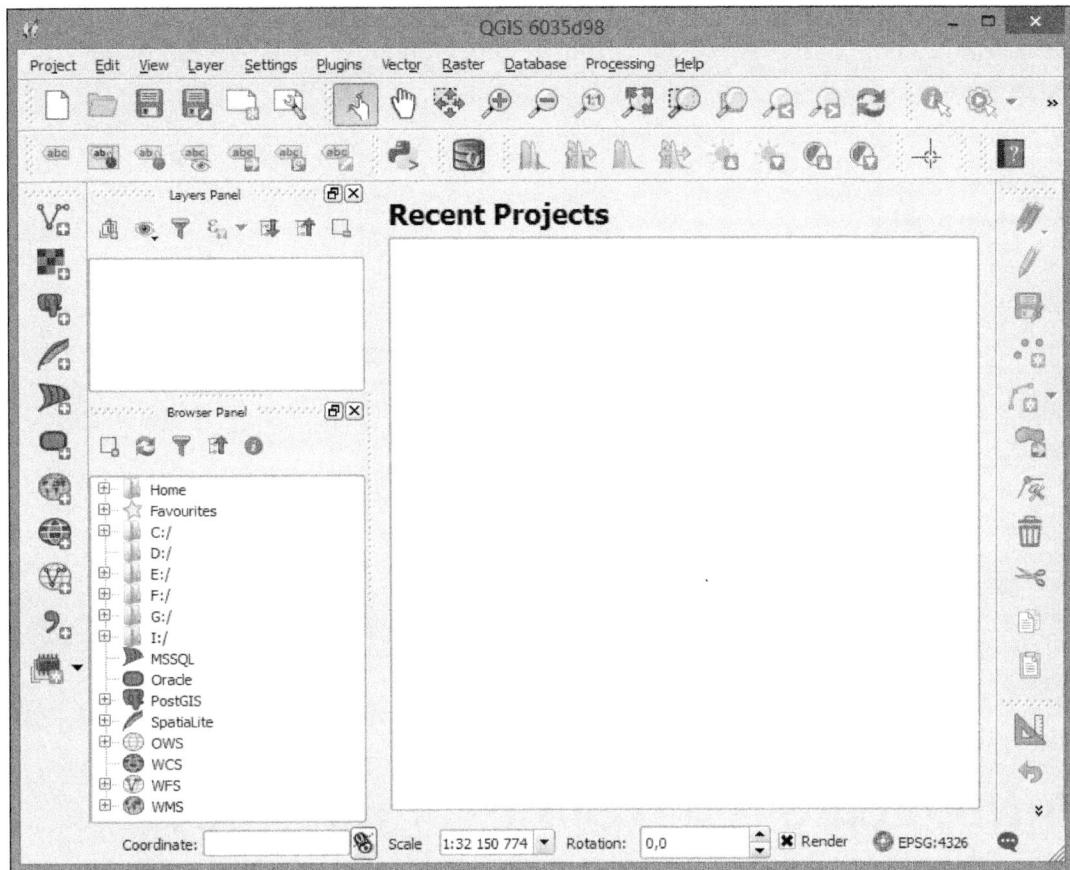

Next, we will activate some must-have plugins by navigating to **Plugins | Manage and Install Plugins**. Plugins are activated by ticking the checkboxes beside their names. To begin with, I will recommend the following:

- **Coordinate Capture**: This plugin is useful for picking coordinates in the map
- **DB Manager**: This plugin helps you manage the SpatiaLite and PostGIS databases
- **fTools**: This plugin offers vector analysis and management tools
- **GdalTools**: This plugin offers raster analysis and management tools
- **Processing**: This plugin provides access to many useful raster and vector analysis tools, as well as a model builder for task automation

To make it easier to find specific plugins, we can filter the list of plugins using the **Search** input field at the top of the window, which you can see in the following screenshot:

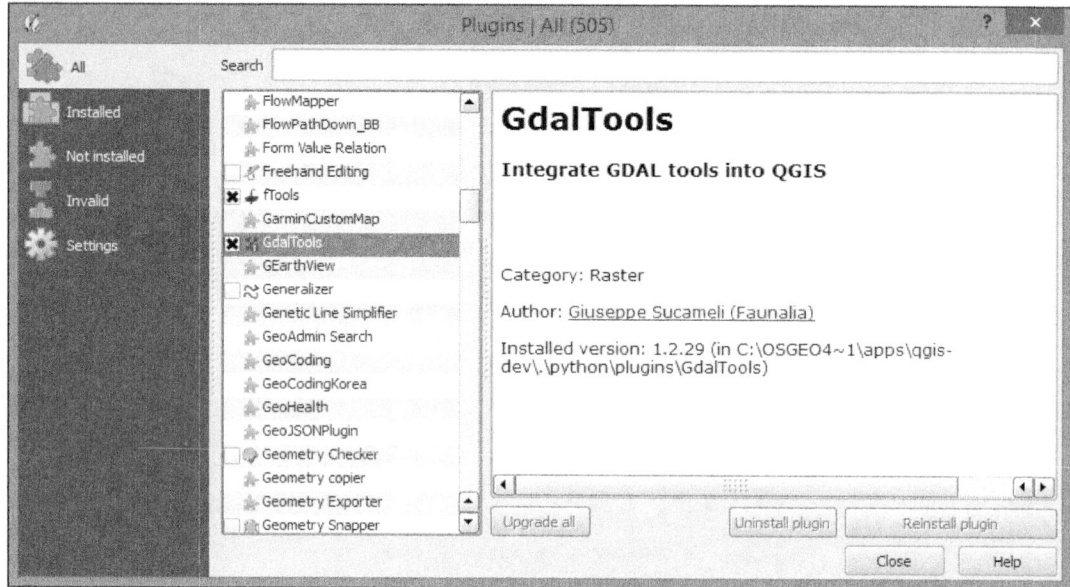

Introducing the QGIS user interface

Now that we have set up QGIS, let's get accustomed to the interface. As we have already seen in the screenshot presented in the *Running QGIS for the first time* section, the biggest area is reserved for the map. To the left of the map, there are the **Layers** and **Browser** panels. In the following screenshot, you can see how the **Layers Panel** looks once we have loaded some layers (which we will do in the upcoming *Chapter 2, Viewing Spatial Data*). To the left of each layer entry, you can see a preview of the layer style. Additionally, we can use **layer group** to structure the layer list. The **Browser Panel** (on the right-hand side in the following screenshot) provides us with quick access to our spatial data, as you will soon see in the following chapter:

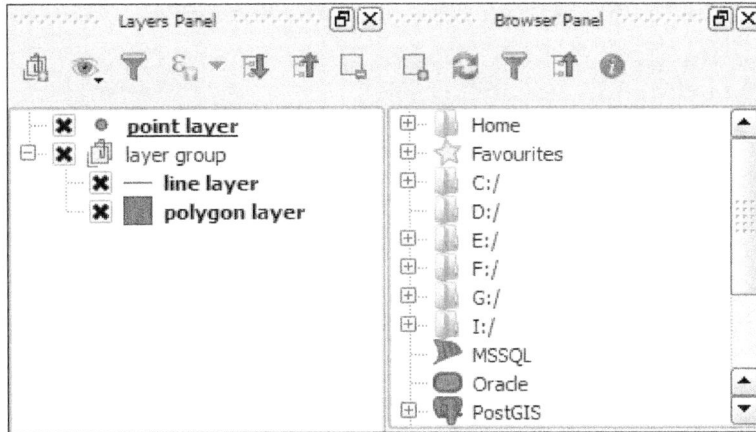

Below the map, we find important information such as (from left to right) the current map **Coordinate**, map **Scale**, and the (currently inactive) project **coordinate reference system (CRS)**, for example, **EPSG:4326** in this screenshot:

Next, there are multiple toolbars to explore. If you arrange them as shown in the previous section, the top row contains the following toolbars:

- **File**: This toolbar contains the tools needed to **Create**, **Open**, **Save**, and **Print projects**
- **Map Navigation**: This toolbar contains the pan and zoom tools
- **Attributes**: These tools are used to *identify*, *select*, *open attribute tables*, *measure*, and so on, and looks like this:

The second row contains the following toolbars:

- **Label**: These tools are used to add, configure, and modify labels
- **Plugins**: This currently only contains the **Python Console** tool, but will be filled in by additional Python plugins
- **Database**: Currently, this toolbar only contains DB Manager, but other database-related tools (for example, the **OfflineEditing** plugin, which allows us to edit offline and synchronize with databases) will appear here when they are installed

- **Raster**: This toolbar includes histogram stretch, brightness, and contrast control
- **Vector**: This currently only contains the **Coordinate Capture** tool, but it will be filled in by additional Python plugins
- **Web**: This is currently empty, but it will also be filled in by additional Python plugins
- **Help**: This toolbar points to the option for downloading the user manual and looks like this:

On the left screen border, we place the **Manage Layers** toolbar. This toolbar contains the tools for adding layers from the *vector or raster files*, *databases*, *web services*, and *text files* or *create new layers*:

Finally, on the right screen border, we have two more toolbars:

- **Digitizing**: The tools in this toolbar **enable editing**, basic feature creation, and editing
- **Advanced Digitizing**: This toolbar contains the **Undo/Redo** option, **advanced editing tools**, **the geometry-simplification tool**, and so on, which look like this:

> All digitizing tools (except the **Enable advanced digitizing tools** button) are currently inactive. They will turn active only once we start editing a vector layer.

Toolbars and panels can be activated and deactivated via the **View** menu's **Panels** and **Toolbars** entries, as well as by right-clicking on a menu or toolbar, which will open a context menu with all the available toolbars and panels. All the tools on the toolbars can also be accessed via the menu. If you deactivate the **Manage Layers Toolbar**, for example, you will still be able to add layers using the **Layer** menu.

As you might have guessed by now, QGIS is highly customizable. You can increase your productivity by assigning shortcuts to the tools you use regularly, which you can do by going to **Settings | Configure Shortcuts**. Similarly, if you realize that you never use a certain toolbar button or menu entry, you can hide it by going to **Settings | Customization**. For example, if you don't have access to an Oracle Spatial database, you might want to hide the associated buttons to remove clutter and save screen estate, as shown in the following screenshot:

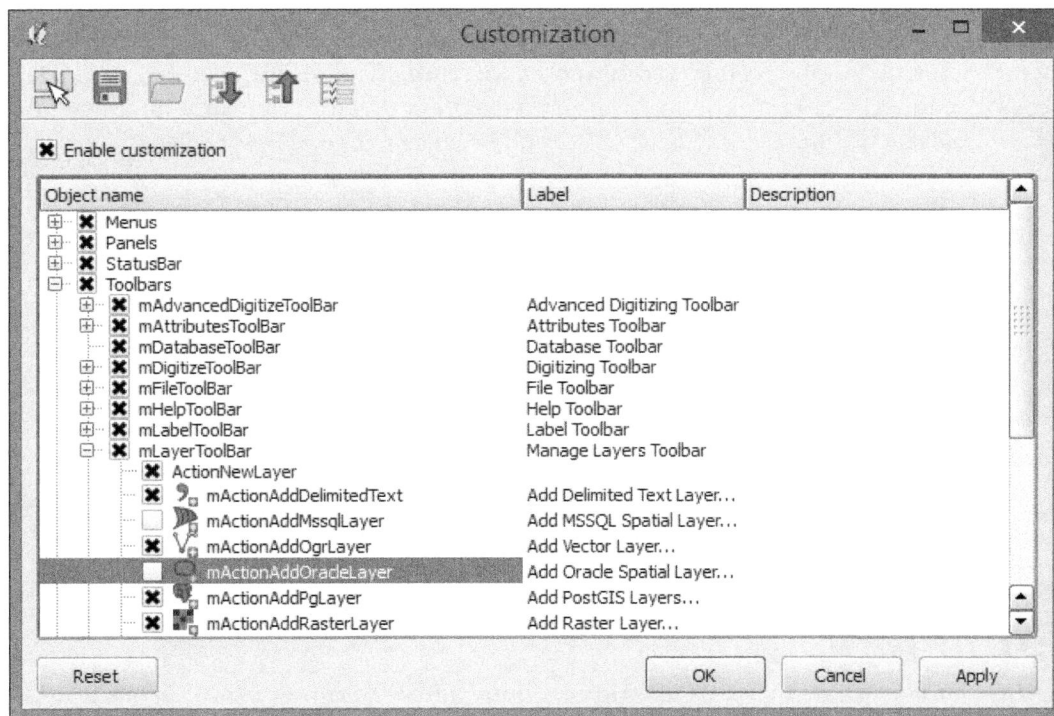

Finding help and reporting issues

The QGIS community offers a variety of different community-based support options. These include the following:

- **GIS StackExchange**: One of the most popular support channels is `http://gis.stackexchange.com/`. It's a general-purpose GIS question-and-answer site. If you use the tag `qgis`, you will see all QGIS-related questions and answers at `http://gis.stackexchange.com/questions/tagged/qgis`.

- **Mailing lists**: The most important mailing list for user questions is `qgis-user`. For a full list of available mailing lists and links to sign up, visit `http://www.qgis.org/en/site/getinvolved/mailinglists.html#qgis-mailinglists`. To comfortably search for existing mailing list threads, you can use Nabble (`http://osgeo-org.1560.x6.nabble.com/Quantum-GIS-User-f4125267.html`).

- **Chat**: A lot of developer communication runs through IRC. There is a `#qgis` channel on `www.freenode.net`. You can visit it using, for example, the web interface at `http://webchat.freenode.net/?channels=#qgis`.

> Before contacting the community support, it's recommended to first take a look at the documentation at `http://docs.qgis.org`.

If you prefer commercial support, you can find a list of companies that provide support and custom development at `http://www.qgis.org/en/site/forusers/commercial_support.html#qgis-commercial-support`.

If you find a bug, please report it because the QGIS developers can only fix the bugs that they are aware of. For details on how to report bugs, visit `http://www.qgis.org/en/site/getinvolved/development/bugreporting.html`.

Summary

In this chapter, we installed QGIS and configured it by selecting useful defaults and arranging the user interface elements. Then we explored the panels, toolbars, and menus that make up the QGIS user interface, and you learned how to customize them to increase productivity. In the following chapter, we will use QGIS to view spatial data from different data sources such as files, databases, and web services in order to create our first map.

2
Viewing Spatial Data

In this chapter, we will cover how to view spatial data from different data sources. QGIS supports many file and database formats as well as standardized **Open Geospatial Consortium (OGC)** Web Services. We will first cover how we can load layers from these different data sources. We will then look into the basics of styling both vector and raster layers and will create our first map, which you can see in the following screenshot:

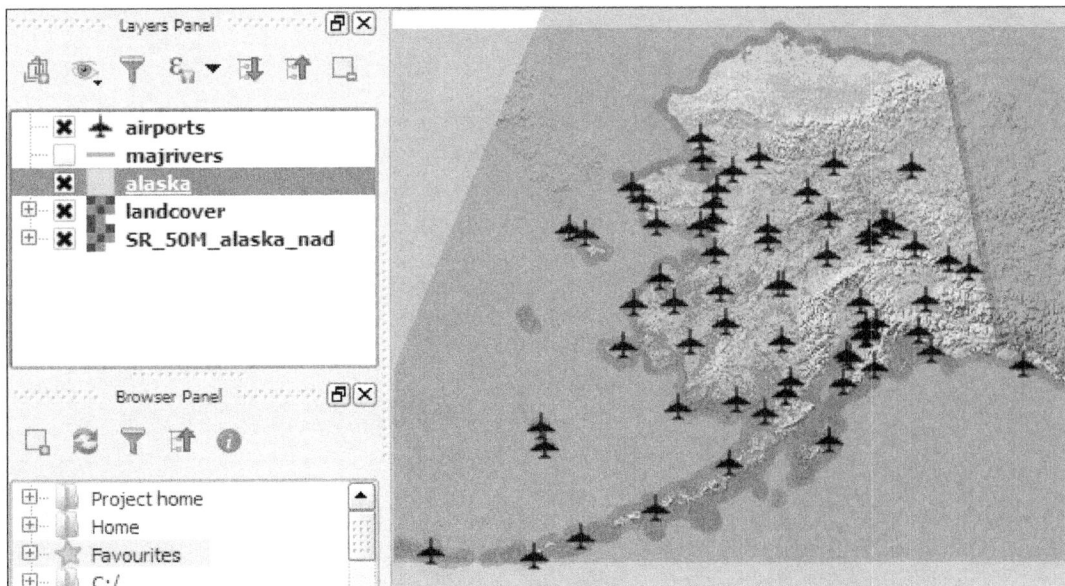

We will finish this chapter with an example of loading background maps from online services.

> For the examples in this chapter, we will use the sample data provided by the QGIS project, which is available for download from http://qgis.org/downloads/data/qgis_sample_data.zip (21 MB). Download and unzip it.

Loading vector data from files

In this section, we will talk about loading vector data from GIS file formats, such as **shapefiles**, as well as from text files.

We can load vector files by going to **Layer | Add Layer | Add Vector Layer** and also using the **Add Vector Layer** toolbar button. If you like shortcuts, use *Ctrl + Shift + V*. In the **Add vector layer** dialog, which is shown in the following screenshot, we find a drop-down list that allows us to specify the encoding of the input file. This option is important if we are dealing with files that contain special characters, such as German umlauts or letters from alphabets different from the default Latin ones.

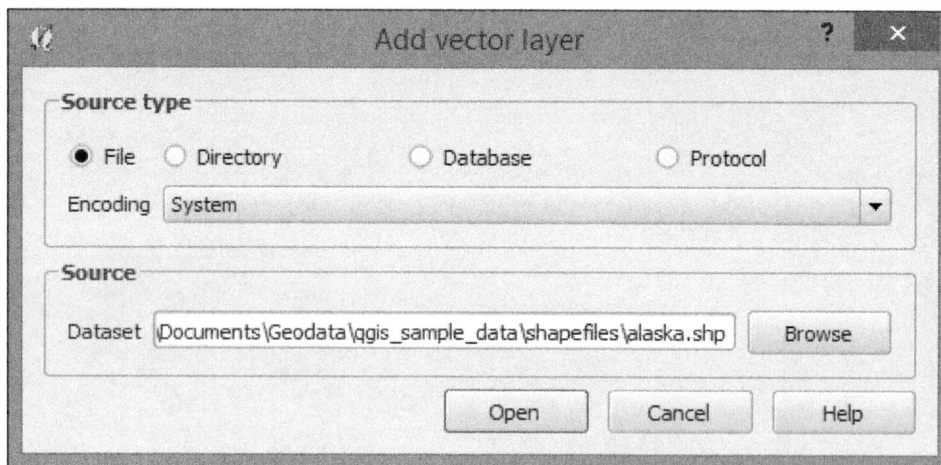

What we are most interested in now is the **Browse** button, which opens the file-opening dialog. Note the file type filter drop-down list in the bottom-right corner of the dialog. We can open it to see a list of supported vector file types. This filter is useful to find specific files faster by hiding all the files of a different type, but be aware that the filter settings are stored and will be applied again the next time you open the file opening dialog. This can be a source of confusion if you try to find a different file later and it happens to be hidden by the filter, so remember to check the filter settings if you are having trouble locating a file.

We can load more than one file in one go by selecting multiple files at once (holding down *Ctrl* on Windows/Ubuntu or *cmd* on Mac). Let's give it a try:

1.   First, we select `alaska.shp` and `airports.shp` from the `shapefiles` sample data folder.

2.   Next, we confirm our selection by clicking on **Open**, and we are taken back to the **Add vector layer** dialog.

3.   After we've clicked on **Open** once more, the selected files are loaded. You will notice that each vector layer is displayed in a random color, which is most likely different from the color that you see in the following screenshot. Don't worry about this now; we'll deal with layer styles later in this chapter.

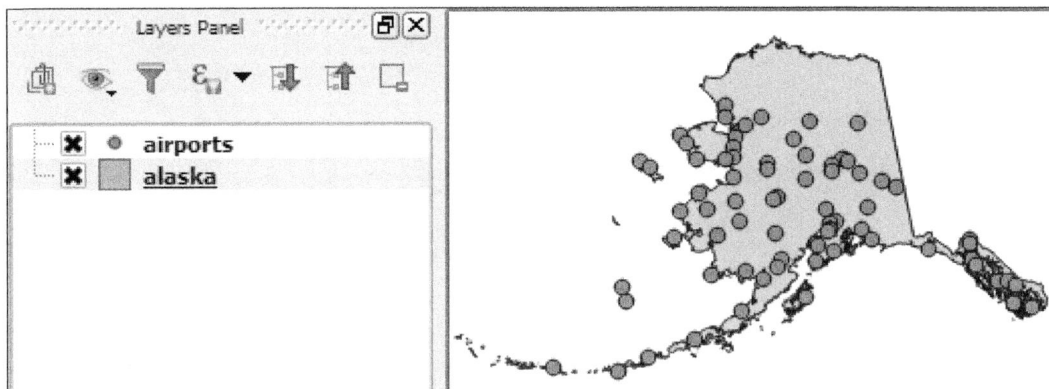

Even without us using any spatial analysis tools, these simple steps of visualizing spatial datasets enable us to find, for example, the southernmost airport on the Alaskan mainland.

> There are multiple tricks that make loading data even faster; for example, you can simply drag and drop files from the operating system's file browser into QGIS.
>
> Another way to quickly access your spatial data is by using QGIS's built-in file *browser*. If you have set up QGIS as shown in *Chapter 1, Getting Started with QGIS*, you'll find the browser on the left-hand side, just below the layer list. Navigate to your `data` folder, and you can again drag and drop files from the browser to the map.
>
> Additionally, you can mark a folder as *favorite* by right-clicking on it and selecting **Add as a favorite**. In this way, you can access your data folders even faster, because they are added in the **Favorites** section right at the top of the browser list.

Another popular source of spatial data is **delimited text (CSV)** files. QGIS can load CSV files using the **Add Delimited Text Layer** option available via the menu entry by going to **Layer | Add Layer | Add Delimited Text Layer** or the corresponding toolbar button. Click on **Browse** and select `elevp.csv` from the sample data. CSV files come with all kinds of delimiters. As you can see in the following screenshot, the plugin lets you choose from the most common ones (**Comma, Tab**, and so on), but you can also specify any other plain or regular-expression delimiter:

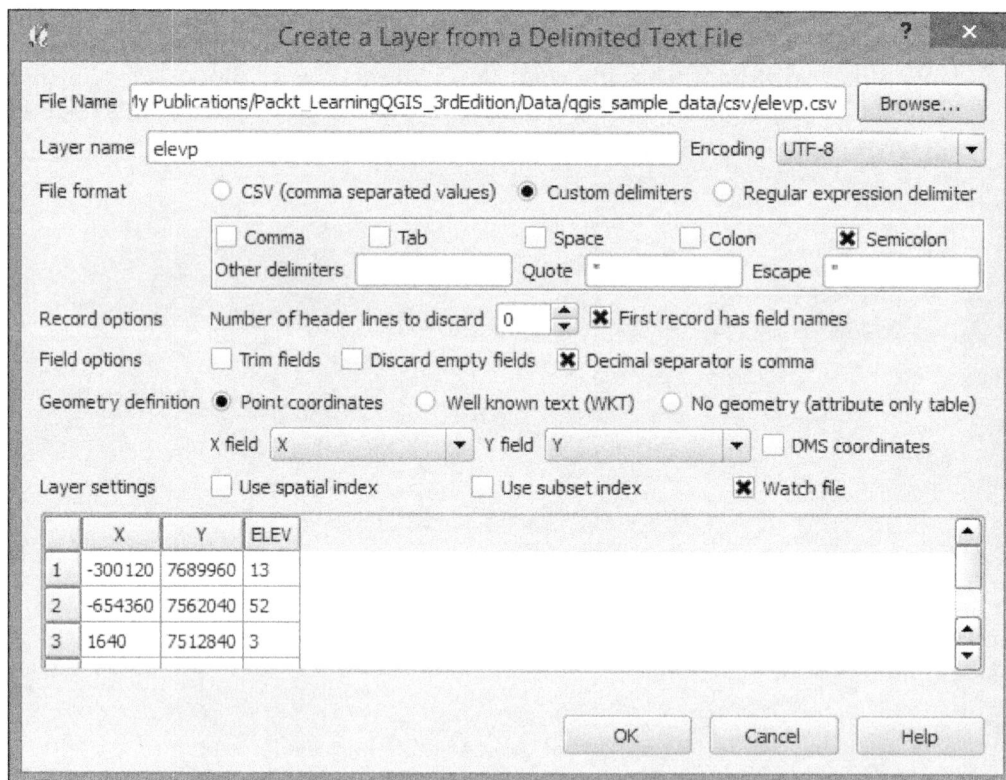

If your CSV file contains quotation marks such as, " or ', you can use the **Quote** option to have them removed. The **Number of header lines to discard** option allows us to skip any potential extra lines at the beginning of the text file. The following **Field options** include functionality for trimming extra spaces from field values or redefine the decimal separator to a comma. The spatial information itself can be provided either in the two columns that contain the coordinates of points X and Y, or using the **Well known text (WKT)** format. A WKT field can contain points, lines, or polygons. For example, a point can be specified as POINT (30 10), a simple line with three nodes would be LINESTRING (30 10, 10 30, 40 40), and a polygon with four nodes would be POLYGON ((30 10, 40 40, 20 40, 10 20, 30 10)).

> Note that the first and last coordinate pair in a polygon has to be identical.
>
> WKT is a very useful and flexible format. If you are unfamiliar with the concept, you can find a detailed introduction with examples at http://en.wikipedia.org/wiki/Well-known_text.

After we've clicked on **OK**, QGIS will prompt us to specify the layer's **coordinate reference system (CRS)**. We will talk about handling CRS next.

Dealing with coordinate reference systems

Whenever we load a data source, QGIS looks for usable CRS information, for example, in the shapefile's .prj file. If QGIS cannot find any usable information, by default, it will ask you to specify the CRS manually. This behavior can be changed by going to **Settings | Options | CRS** to always use either the project CRS or a default CRS.

The QGIS **Coordinate Reference System Selector** offers a filter that makes finding a CRS easier. It can filter by name or ID (for example, the EPSG code). Just start typing and watch how the list of potential CRS gets shorter. There are actually two separate lists; the upper one contains the CRS that we recently used, while the lower list is much longer and contains all the available CRS. For the elevp.csv file, we select **NAD27 / Alaska Albers**. With the correct CRS, the elevp layer will be displayed as shown in this screenshot:

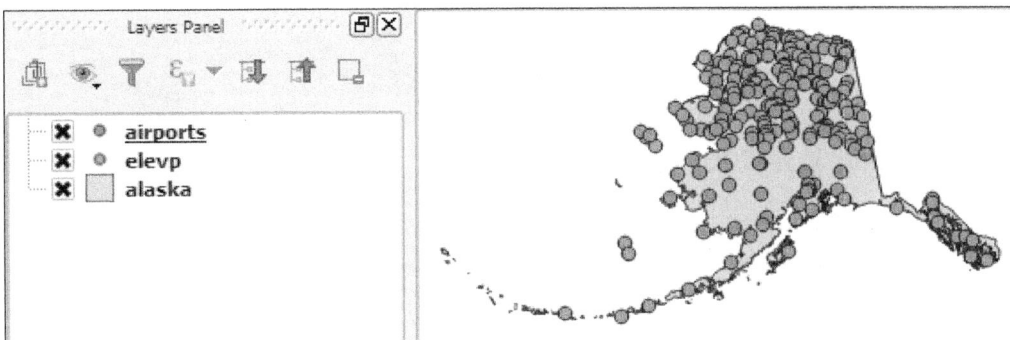

If we want to check a layer's CRS, we can find this information in the layer properties' **General** section, which can be accessed by going to **Layer | Properties** or by double-clicking on the layer name in the layer list. If you think that QGIS has picked the wrong CRS or if you have made a mistake in specifying the CRS, you can correct the CRS settings using **Specify CRS**. Note that this does not change the underlying data or reproject it. We'll talk about reprojecting vectors and raster files in *Chapter 3, Data Creation and Editing*.

In QGIS, we can create a map out of multiple layers even if each dataset is stored with a different CRS. QGIS handles the necessary reprojections automatically by enabling a mechanism called **on the fly reprojection**, which can be accessed by going to **Project | Project Properties**, as shown in the following screenshot. Alternatively, you can click on the **CRS status** button (with the globe symbol and the EPSG code right next to it) in the bottom-right corner of the QGIS window to open this dialog:

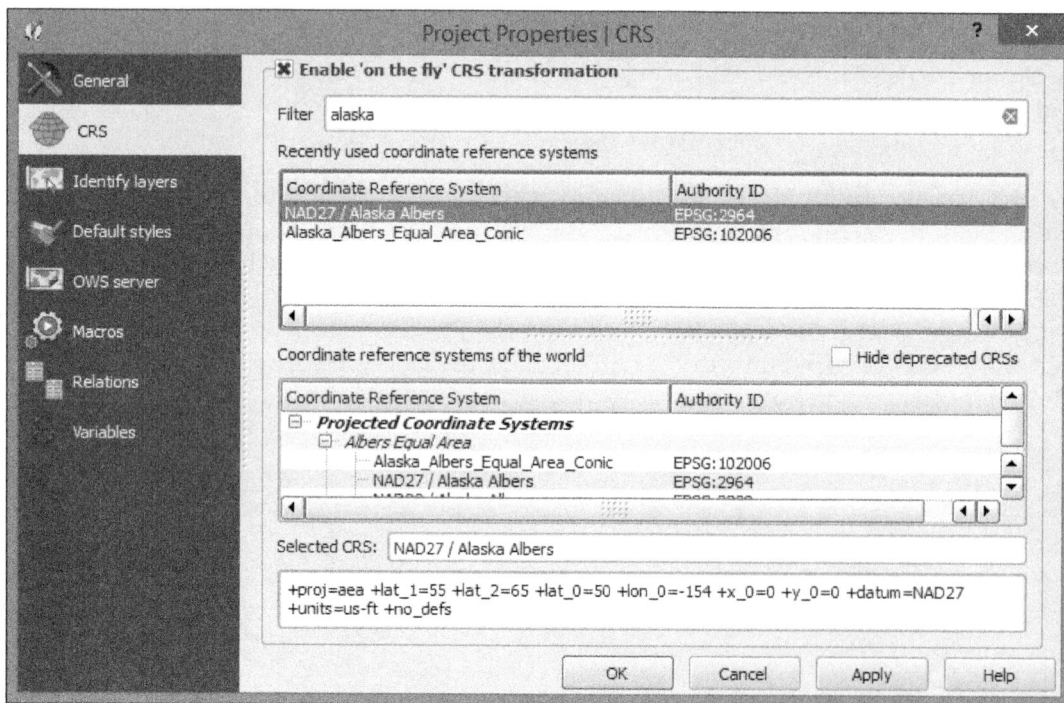

All layers are reprojected to the project CRS on the fly, which means that QGIS calculates these reprojections dynamically and only for the purpose of rendering the map. This also means that it can slow down your machine if you are working with big datasets that have to be reprojected. The underlying data is not changed and spatial analyses are not affected. For example, the following image shows Alaska in its default NAD27 / Alaska Albers projection (on the left-hand side), a reprojection on the fly to WGS84 EPSG:4326 (in the middle), and Web Mercator EPSG:3857 (on the right-hand side). Even though the map representation changes considerably, the analysis results for each version are identical since the on the fly reprojection feature does not change the data.

In some cases, you might have to specify a CRS that is not available in the QGIS CRS database. You can add CRS definitions by going to **Settings | Custom CRS**. Click on the **Add new CRS** button to create a new entry, type in a name for the new CRS, and paste the proj4 definition string in the **Parameters** input field. This definition string is used by the **Proj4** projection engine to determine the correct coordinate transformation. Just close the dialog by clicking on **OK** when you are done.

> If you are looking for a specific projection proj4 definition, http://spatialreference.org is a good source for this kind of information.

Loading raster files

Loading raster files is not much different from loading vector files. Going to **Layer | Add Layer | Add Raster Layer**, clicking on the **Add Raster Layer** button, or pressing the *Ctrl + Shift + R* shortcut will take you directly to the file-opening dialog. Again, you can check the file type filter to see a list of supported file types.

Let's give it a try and load `landcover.img` from the `raster` sample data folder. Similarly to vector files, you can load rasters by dragging them into QGIS from the operating system or the built-in file browser. The following screenshot shows the loaded raster layer:

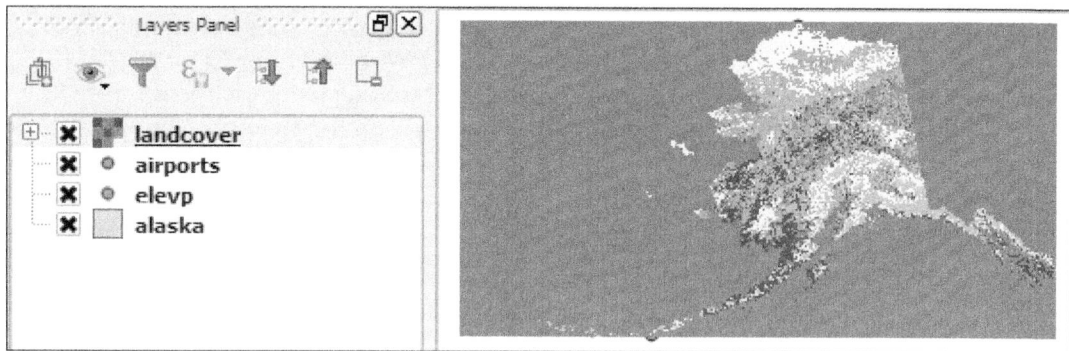

> Support for all of these different vector and raster file types in QGIS is handled by the powerful GDAL/OGR package. You can check out the full list of supported formats at www.gdal.org/formats_list.html (for rasters) and http://www.gdal.org/ogr_formats.html (for vectors).

Georeferencing raster maps

Some raster data sources, such as simple scanned maps, lack proper spatial referencing, and we have to georeference them before we can use them in a GIS. In QGIS, we can georeference rasters using the **Georeferencer** GDAL plugin, which can be accessed by going to **Raster | Georeferencer**. (Enable it by going to **Plugins | Manage and Install Plugins** if you cannot find it in the **Raster** menu).

The Georeferencer plugin covers the following use cases:

- We can create a world file for a raster file without altering the original raster.
- If we have a map image that contains points with known coordinates, we can set **ground control points** (GCPs) and enter the known coordinates.
- Finally, if we don't know the coordinates of any points on the map, we still have the chance to place GCPs manually using a second, and already georeferenced, map of the same area. We can use objects that are visible in both maps to pick points on the map that we want to georeference and work out their coordinates from the reference map.

After loading a raster into Georeferencer by going to **File | Open raster** or using the **Open raster** toolbar button, we are asked to specify the CRS of the ground control points that we are planning to add. Next, we can start adding ground control points by going to **Edit | Add point**. We can use the pan and zoom tools to navigate, and we can place GCPs by clicking on the map. We are then prompted to insert the coordinates of the new point or pick them from the reference map in the main QGIS window. The placed GCPs are displayed as red circles in both **Georeferencer** and the QGIS window, as you can see in the following screenshot:

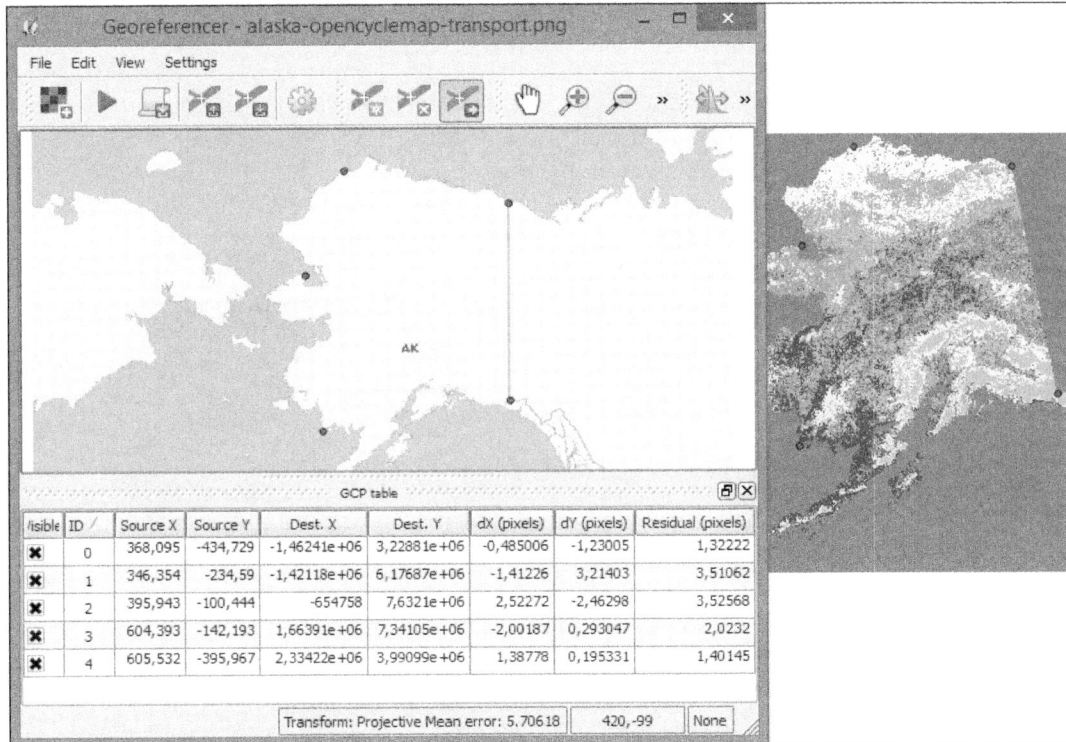

Georeferencer shows a screenshot of the OCM Landscape map © Thunderforest, Data © OpenStreetMap contributors (http://www.opencyclemap.org/?zoom=4&lat=62.50806&lon=-145.01953&layers=0B000)

After placing the GCPs, we can define the transformation algorithm by going to **Settings | Transformation Settings**. Which algorithm you choose depends on your input data and the level of geometric distortion you want to allow. The most commonly used algorithms are polynomial 1 to 3. A **first-order polynomial transformation** allows scaling, translation, and rotation only.

A **second-order polynomial transformation** can handle some curvature, and a **third-order polynomial transformation** consequently allows for even higher degrees of distortion. The **thin-plate spline** algorithm can handle local deformations in the map and is therefore very useful while working with very low-quality map scans. **Projective** transformation offers rotation and translation of coordinates. The **linear** option, on the other hand, is only used to create world files, and as mentioned earlier, this does not actually transform the raster.

The **resampling method** depends on your input data and the result you want to achieve. Cubic resampling creates smooth results, but if you don't want to change the raster values, choose the nearest neighbor method.

Before we can start the georeferencing process, we have to specify the output filename and target CRS. Make sure that the **Load in QGIS when done** option is active and activate the **Use 0 for transparency when needed** option to avoid black borders around the output image. Then, we can close the **Transformation Settings** dialog and go to **File | Start Georeferencing**. The georeferenced raster will automatically be loaded into the main map window of QGIS. In the following screenshot, you can see the result of applying projective transformation using the five specified GCPs:

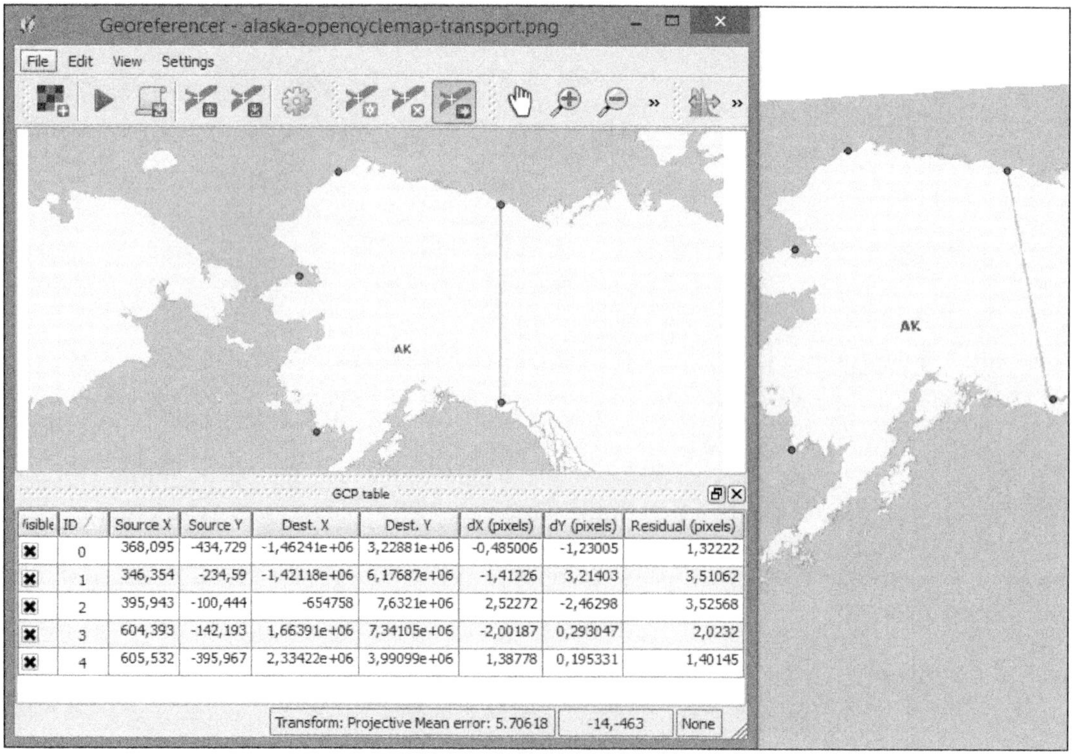

Loading data from databases

QGIS supports **PostGIS**, **SpatiaLite**, **MSSQL**, and **Oracle Spatial** databases. We will cover two open source options: SpatiaLite and PostGIS. Both are available cross-platform, just like QGIS.

SpatiaLite is the spatial extension for SQLite databases. SQLite is a self-contained, server-less, zero-configuration, and transactional SQL database engine (`www.sqlite.org`). This basically means that a SQLite database, and therefore also a SpatiaLite database, doesn't need a server installation and can be copied and exchanged just like any ordinary file.

You can download an example database from `www.gaia-gis.it/spatialite-2.3.1/test-2.3.zip` (4 MB). Unzip the file; you will be able to connect to it by going to **Layer | Add Layer | Add SpatiaLite Layer**, using the **Add SpatiaLite Layer** toolbar button, or by pressing *Ctrl + Shift + L*. Click on **New** to select the `test-2.3.sqlite` database file. QGIS will save all the connections and add them to the drop-down list at the top. After clicking on **Connect**, you will see a list of layers stored in the database, as shown in this screenshot:

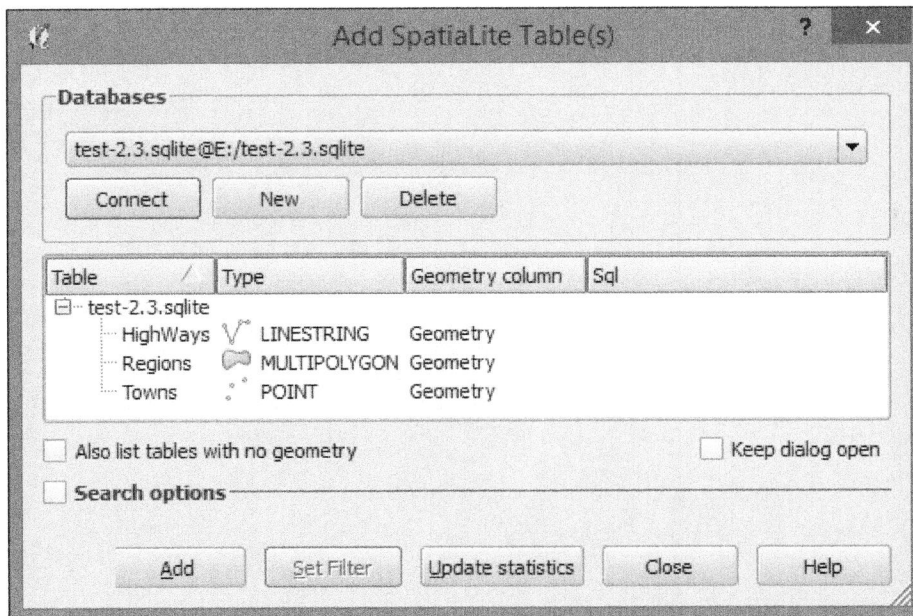

As with files, you can select one or more tables from the list and click on **Add** to load them into the map. Additionally, you can use **Set Filter** to only load specific features.

> Filters in QGIS use SQL-like syntax, for example,
> `"Name" = 'EMILIA-ROMAGNA'` to select only the region called
> EMILIA-ROMAGNA or `"Name" LIKE 'ISOLA%'` to select all regions
> whose names start with ISOLA. The filter queries are passed on to the
> underlying data provider (for example, SpatiaLite or OGR). The provider
> syntax for basic filter queries is consistent over different providers but
> can vary when using more exotic functions. You can read the details of
> OGR SQL at `http://www.gdal.org/ogr_sql.html`.

In *Chapter 4, Spatial Analysis*, we will use this database to explore how we can take advantage of the spatial analysis capabilities of SpatiaLite.

PostGIS is the spatial extension of the PostgreSQL database system. Installing and configuring the database is out of the scope of this book, but there are installers for Windows and packages for many Linux distributions as well as for Mac (for details, visit `http://www.postgresql.org/download/`). To load data from a PostGIS database, go to **Layers | Add Layer | Add PostGIS Layer**, use the **Add PostGIS Layer** toolbar button, or press *Ctrl + Shift + D*.

When using a database for the first time, click on **New** to establish a new database connection. This opens the dialog shown in the following screenshot, where you can create a new connection, for example, to a database called `postgis`:

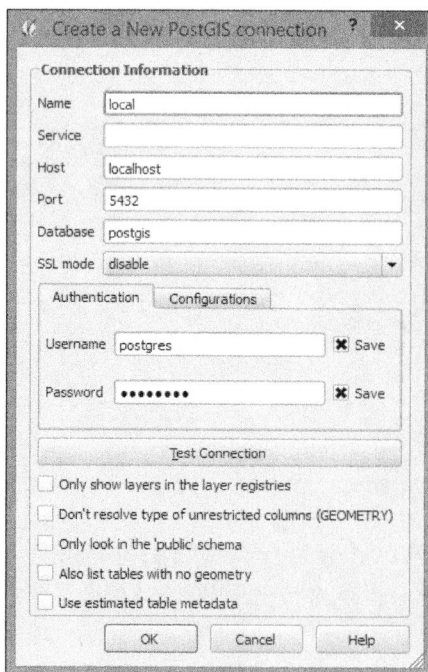

The fields that have to be filled in are as follows:

- **Name**: Insert a name for the new connection. You can use any name you like.
- **Host**: The server's IP address is inserted in this field. You can use `localhost` if PostGIS is running locally.
- **Port**: The PostGIS default port is `5432`. If you have trouble reaching a database, it is recommended that you check the server's firewall settings for this port.
- **Database**: This is the name of the PostGIS database that you want to connect to.
- **Username** and **Password**: For convenience, you can tell QGIS to save these.

After the connection is established, you can load and filter tables, just as we discussed for SpatiaLite.

Loading data from OGC web services

More and more data providers offer access to their datasets via OGC-compliant web services such as **Web Map Services (WMS)**, **Web Coverage Services (WCS)**, or **Web Feature Services (WFS)**. QGIS supports these services out of the box.

> If you want to learn more about the different OGC web services available, visit `http://live.osgeo.org/en/standards/standards.html` for an overview.

You can load **WMS** layers by going to **Layer | Add WMS/WMTS Layer**, clicking on the **Add WMS/WMTS Layer** button, or pressing *Ctrl + Shift + W*. If you know a WMS server, you can connect to it by clicking on **New** and filling in a name and the URL. All other fields are optional. Don't worry if you don't know of any WMS servers, because you can simply click on the **Add default servers** button to get access information about servers whose administrators collaborate with the QGIS project. One of these servers is called **Lizardtech server**. Select **Lizardtech server** or any of the other servers from the drop-down box, and click on **Connect** to see the list of layers available through the server, as shown here:

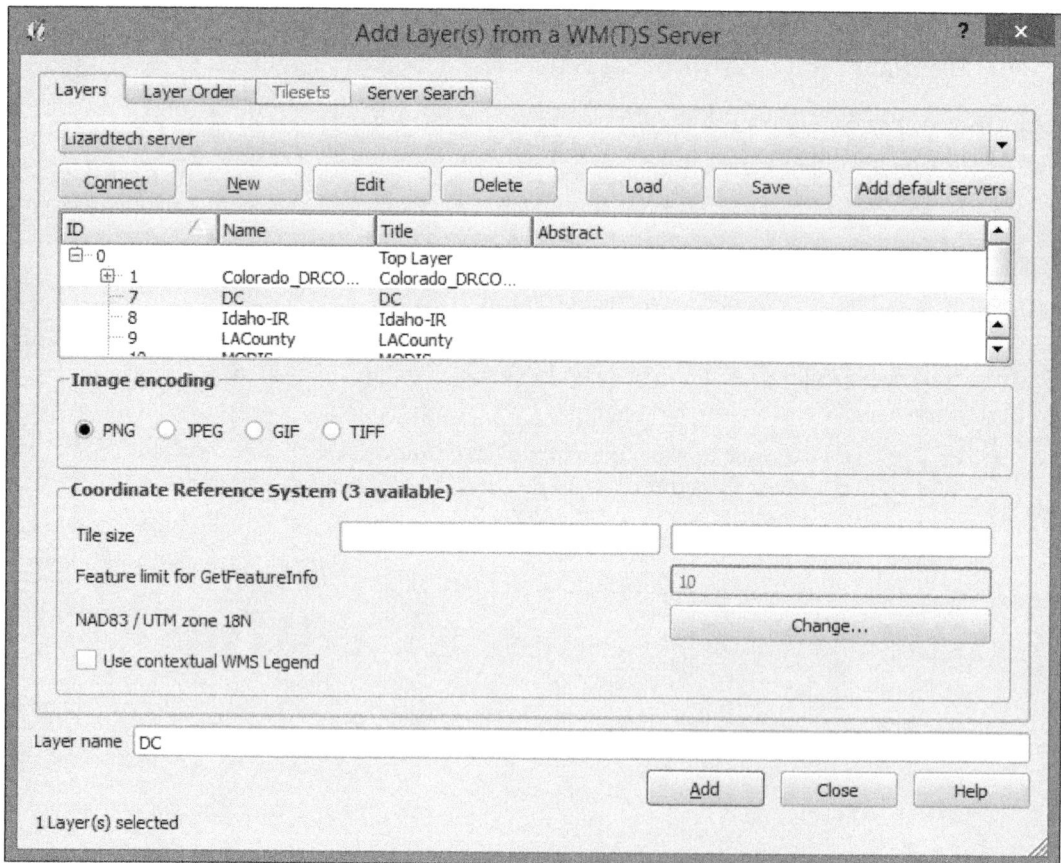

From the layer list, you can now select one or more layers for download. It is worth noting that the order in which you select the layers matters, because the layers will be combined on the server side and QGIS will only receive the combined image as the resultant layer. If you want to be able to use the layers separately, you will have to download them one by one. The data download starts once you click on **Add**. The dialog will stay open so that you can add more layers from the server.

Many WMS servers offer their layers in multiple, different CRS. You can check out the list of available CRS by clicking on the **Change** button at the bottom of the dialog. This will open a CRS selector dialog, which is limited to the WMS server's CRS capabilities.

Loading data from **WCS** or **WFS** servers works in the same way, but public servers are quite rare. One of the few reliable public WFS servers is operated by the city of Vienna, Austria. The following screenshot shows how to configure the connection to the data.wien.gv.at WFS, as well as the list of available datasets that is loaded when we click on the **Connect** button:

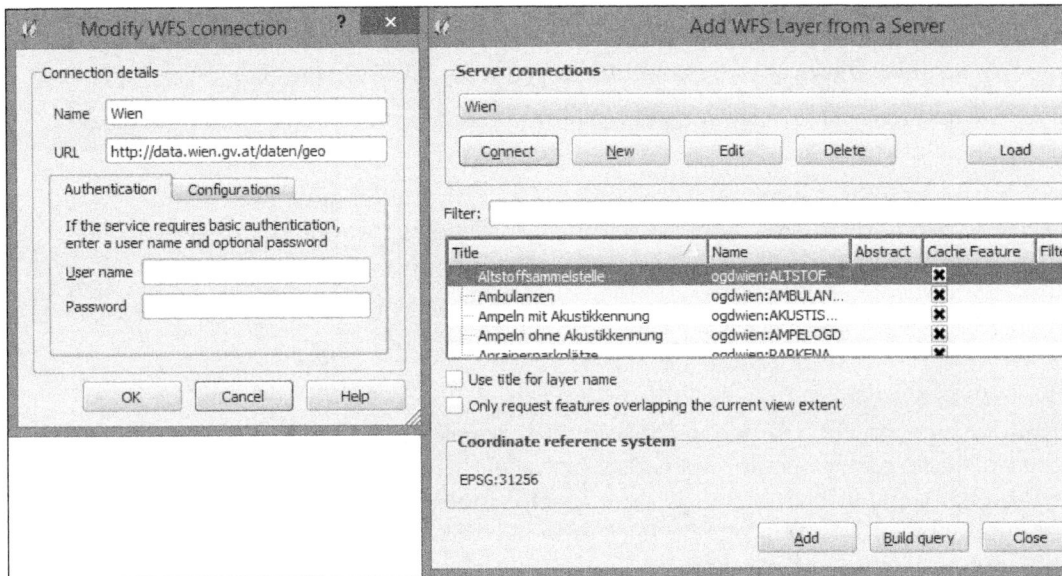

> The main advantage of using a **WFS** rather than a **WMS** is that the **Web Feature Service** returns vector features, including all their attributes, instead of only an image of a map. Of course, this also means that WFS layers usually take longer to download and cause more load on the server.

Styling raster layers

After this introduction to data sources, we can create our first map. We will build the map from the bottom up by first loading some background rasters (hillshade and land cover), which we will then overlay with point, line, and polygon layers.

Let's start by loading a land cover and a hillshade from `landcover.img` and `SR_50M_alaska_nad.tif`, and then opening the **Style** section in the layer properties (by going to **Layer | Properties** or double-clicking on the layer name). QGIS automatically tries to pick a reasonable default render type for both raster layers. Besides these defaults, the following style options are available for raster layers:

- **Multiband color**: This style is used if the raster has several bands. This is usually the case with satellite images with multiple bands.

- **Paletted**: This style is used if a single-band raster comes with an indexed palette.

- **Singleband gray**: If a raster has neither multiple bands nor an indexed palette (this is the case with, for example, elevation model rasters or hillshade rasters), it will be rendered using this style.

- **Singleband pseudocolor**: Instead of being limited to gray, this style allows us to render a raster band using a color map of our choice.

The `SR_50M_alaska_nad.tif` hillshade raster is loaded with **Singleband gray Render type**, as you can see in the following screenshot. If we want to render the hillshade raster in color instead of grayscale, we can change **Render type** to **Singleband pseudocolor**. In the pseudocolor mode, we can create color maps either manually or by selecting one of the premade color ramps. However, let's stick to **Singleband gray** for the hillshade for now.

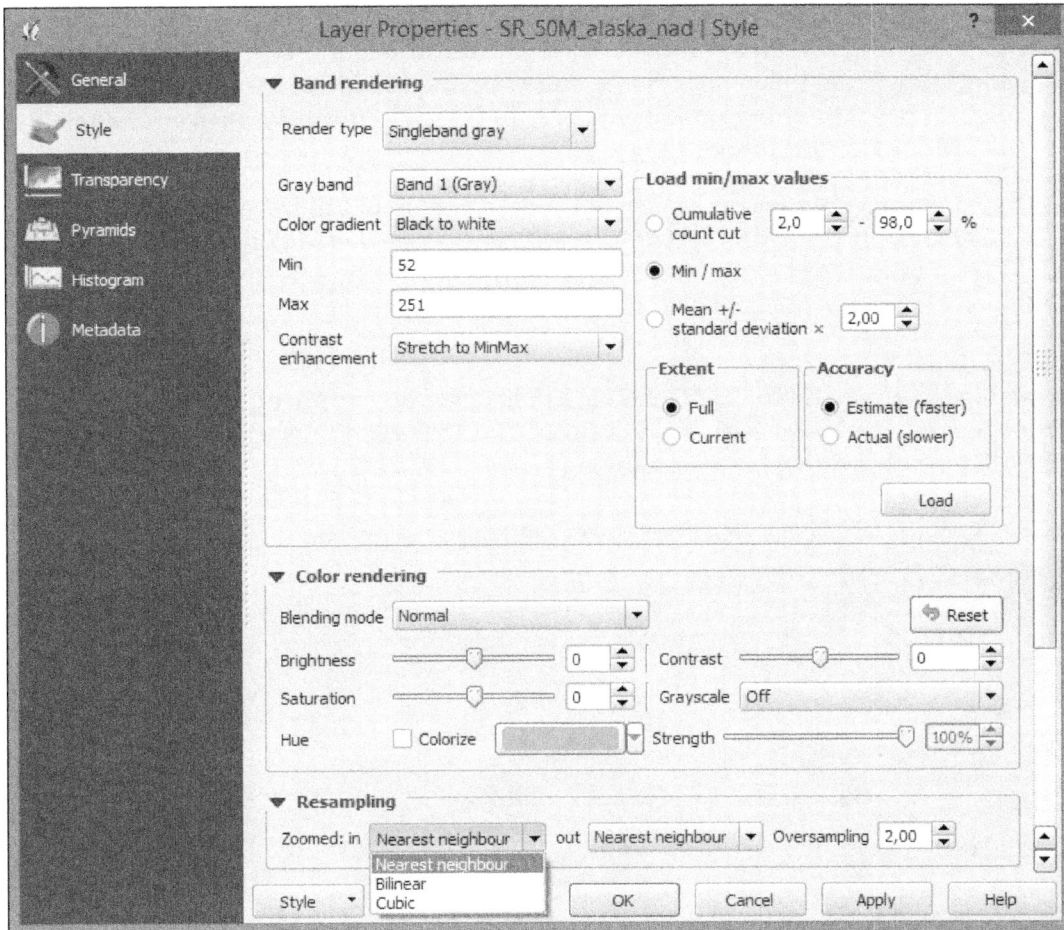

The **Singleband gray** renderer offers a **Black to white Color gradient** as well as a **White to black** gradient. When we use the **Black to white** gradient, the minimum value (specified in **Min**) will be drawn black and the maximum value (specified in **Max**) will be drawn in white, with all the values in between in shades of gray. You can specify these minimum and maximum values manually or use the **Load min/max values** interface to let QGIS compute the values.

> Note that QGIS offers different options for computing the values from either the complete raster (**Full Extent**) or only the currently visible part of the raster (**Current Extent**). A common source of confusion is the **Estimate (faster)** option, which can result in different values than those documented elsewhere, for example, in the raster's metadata. The obvious advantage of this option is that it is faster to compute, so use it carefully!

Below the color settings, we find a section with more advanced options that control the raster **Resampling**, **Brightness**, **Contrast**, **Saturation**, and **Hue**—options that you probably know from image processing software. By default, resampling is set to the fast **Nearest neighbour** option. To get nicer and smoother results, we can change to the **Bilinear** or **Cubic** method.

Click on **OK** or **Apply** to confirm. In both cases, the map will be redrawn using the new layer style. If you click on **Apply**, the **Layer Properties** dialog stays open, and you can continue to fine-tune the layer style. If you click on **OK**, the **Layer Properties** dialog is closed.

The landcover.img raster is a good example of a paletted raster. Each cell value is mapped to a specific color. To change a color, we can simply double-click on the **Color** preview and a color picker will open. The style section of a paletted raster looks like what is shown in the following screenshot:

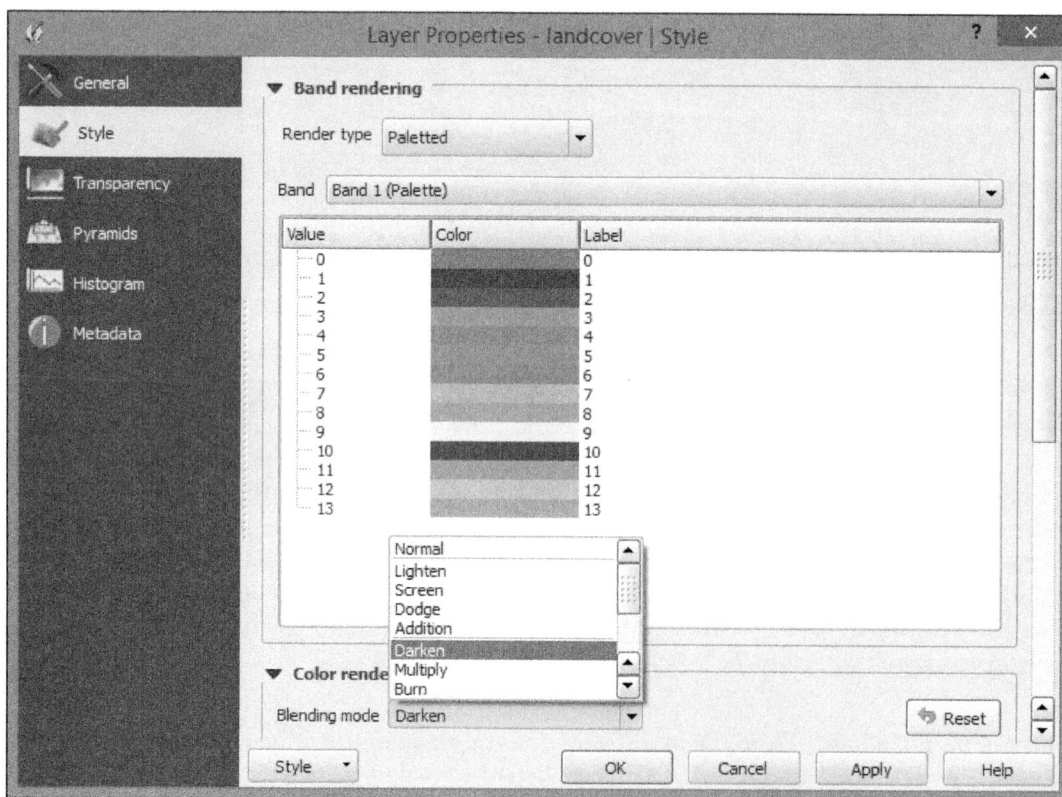

If we want to combine hillshade and land cover into one aesthetically pleasing background, we can use a combination of **Blending mode** and layer **Transparency**. Blending modes are another feature commonly found in image processing software. The main advantage of blending modes over transparency is that we can avoid the usually dull, low-contrast look that results from combining rasters using transparency alone. If you haven't had any experience with blending, take some time to try the different effects. For this example, I used the **Darken** blending mode, as highlighted in the previous screenshot, together with a global layer transparency of **50** %, as shown in the following screenshot:

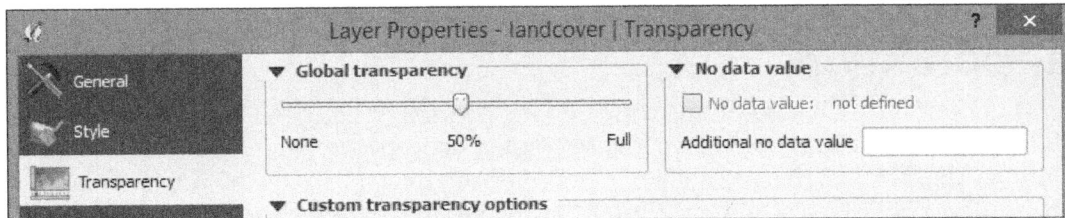

Styling vector layers

When we load vector layers, QGIS renders them using a default style and a random color. Of course, we want to customize these styles to better reflect our data. In the following exercises, we will style point, line, and polygon layers, and you will also get accustomed to the most common vector styling options.

Regardless of the layer's geometry type, we always find a drop-down list with the available style options in the top-left corner of the **Style** dialog. The following style options are available for vector layers:

- **Single Symbol**: This is the simplest option. When we use a **Single Symbol** style, all points are displayed with the same symbol.

- **Categorized**: This is the style of choice if a layer contains points of different categories, for example, a layer that contains locations of different animal sightings.

- **Graduated**: This style is great if we want to visualize numerical values, for example, temperature measurements.

- **Rule-based**: This is the most advanced option. Rule-based styles are very flexible because they allow us to write multiple rules for one layer.

- **Point displacement**: This option is available only for point layers. These styles are useful if you need to visualize point layers with multiple points at the same coordinates, for example, students of a school living at the same address.

- **Inverted polygons**: This option is available for polygon layers only. By using this option, the defined symbology will be applied to the area outside the polygon borders instead of filling the area inside the polygon.

- **Heatmap**: This option is available only for point layers. It enables us to create a dynamic heatmap style.

- **2.5D**: This option is available only for polygon layers. It enables us to create extruded polygons in 2.5 dimensions.

Creating point styles – an example of an airport style

Let's get started with a point layer! Load `airport.shp` from your sample data. In the top-left corner of the **Style** dialog, below the drop-down list, we find the symbol preview. Below this, there is a list of symbol layers that shows us the different layers the symbol consists of. On the right-hand side, we find options for the symbol size and size units, color and transparency, as well as rotation. Finally, the bottom-right area contains a preview area with saved symbols.

Point layers are, by default, displayed using a simple circle symbol. We want to use a symbol of an airplane instead. To change the symbol, select the **Simple marker** entry in the symbol layers list on the left-hand side of the dialog. Notice how the right-hand side of the dialog changes. We can now see the options available for simple markers: **Colors**, **Size**, **Rotation**, **Form**, and so on. However, we are not looking for circles, stars, or square symbols—we want an airplane. That's why we need to change the **Symbol layer type** option from **Simple marker** to **SVG marker**. Many of the options are still similar, but at the bottom, we now find a selection of SVG images that we can choose from. Scroll through the list and pick the airplane symbol, as shown in the following screenshot:

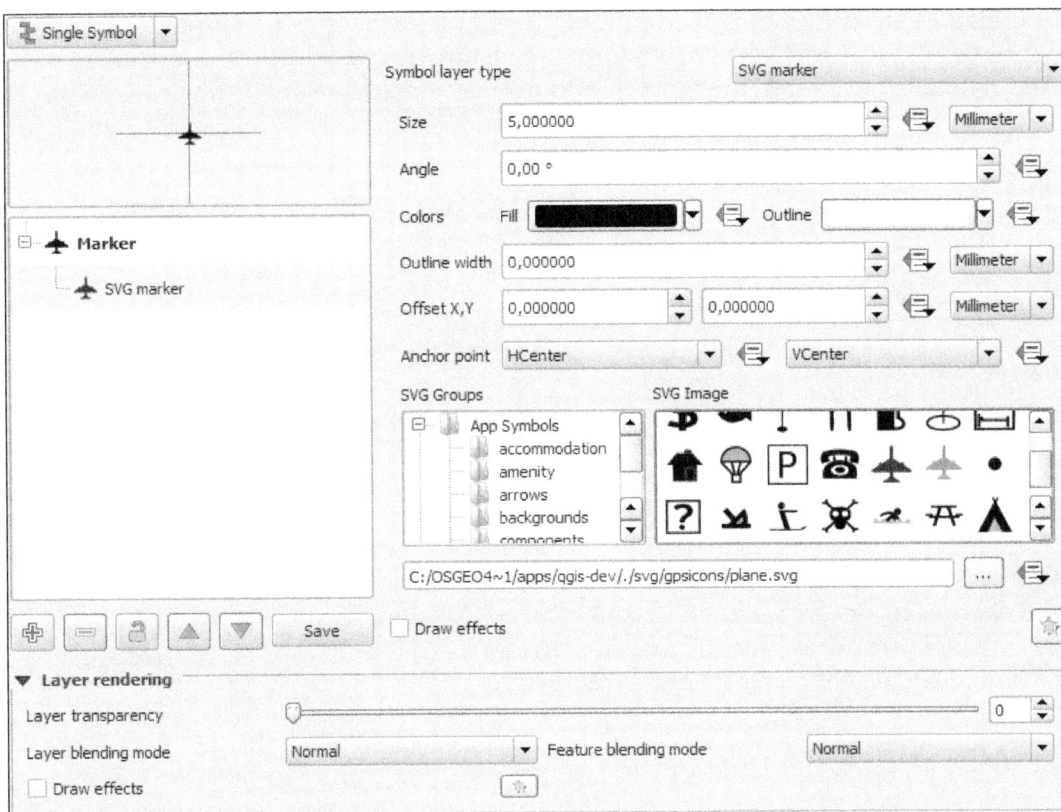

Before we move on to styling lines, let's take a look at the other symbol layer types for points, which include the following:

- **Simple marker**: This includes geometric forms such as circles, stars, and squares

- **Font marker**: This provides access to your symbol fonts

- **SVG marker**: Each QGIS installation comes with a collection of default SVG symbols; add your own folders that contain SVG images by going to **Settings | Options | System | SVG Paths**

- **Ellipse marker**: This includes customizable ellipses, rectangles, crosses, and triangles

- **Vector Field marker**: This is a customizable vector-field visualization tool

- **Geometry Generator**: This enables us to manipulate geometries and even create completely new geometries using the built-in expression engine

Simple marker layers can have different geometric forms, sizes, outlines, and angles (orientation), as shown in the following screenshot, where we create a red square without an outline (using the **No Pen** option):

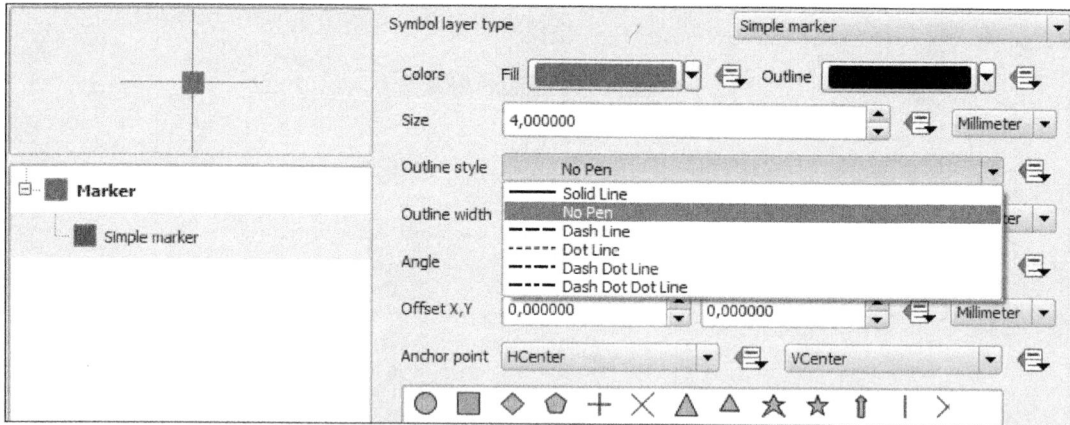

Font marker layers are useful for adding letters or other symbols from fonts that are installed on your computer. This screenshot, for example, shows how to add the yin-and-yang character from the **Wingdings** font:

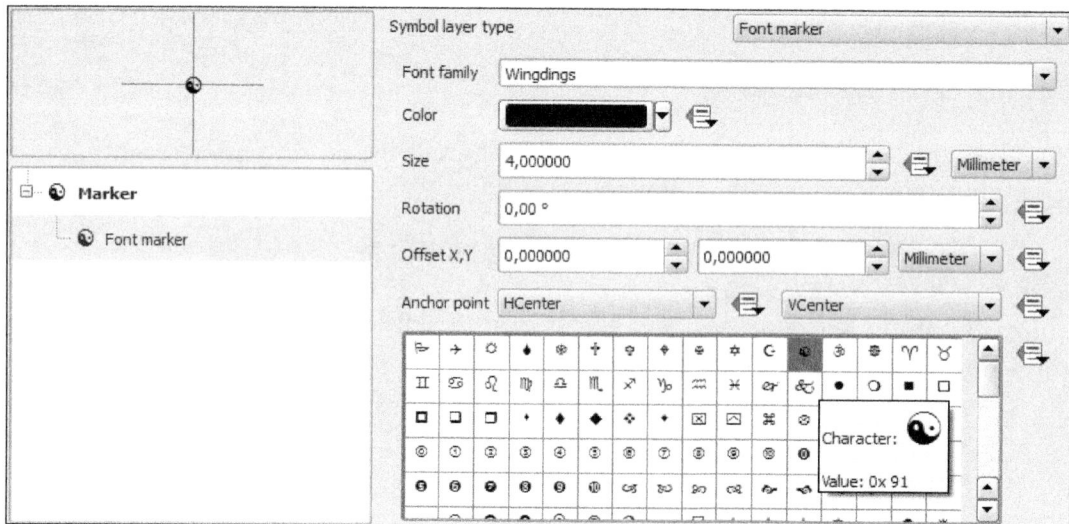

Ellipse marker layers make it possible to draw different ellipses, rectangles, crosses, and triangles, where both the width and height can be controlled separately. This symbol layer type is especially useful when combined with *data-defined overrides*, which we will discuss later. The following screenshot shows how to create an ellipse that is 5 millimeters long, 2 millimeters high, and rotated by 45 degrees:

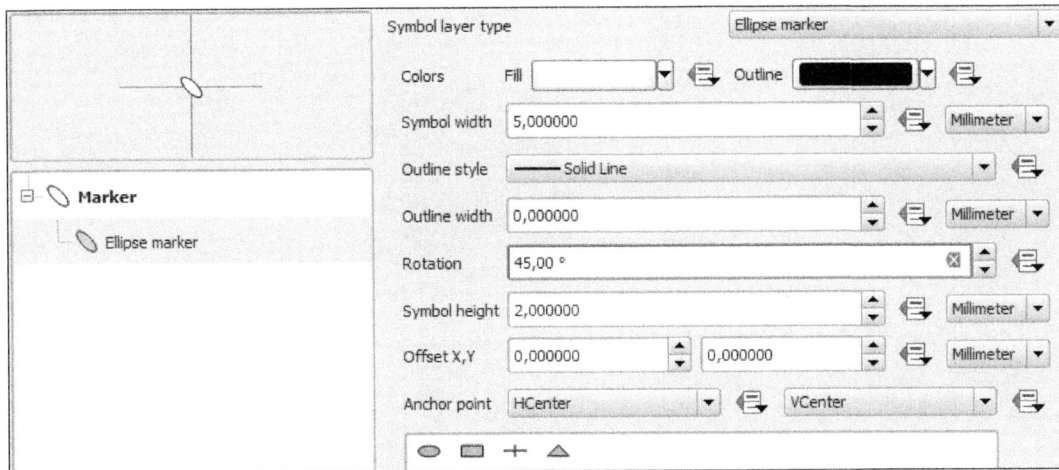

Creating line styles – an example of river or road styles

In this exercise, we create a river style for the `majriver.shp` file in our sample data. The goal is to create a line style with two colors: a fill color for the center of the line and an outline color. This technique is very useful because it can also be used to create road styles.

To create such a style, we combine two simple lines. The default symbol is one simple line. Click on the green **+** symbol located below the symbol layers list in the bottom-left corner to add another simple line. The lower line will be our outline and the upper one will be the fill. Select the upper simple line and change the color to blue and the width to 0.3 millimeters. Next, select the lower simple line and change its color to gray and width to 0.6 millimeters, slightly wider than the other line. Check the preview and click on **Apply** to test how the style looks when applied to the river layer.

You will notice that the style doesn't look perfect yet. This is because each line feature is drawn separately, one after the other, and this leads to a rather disconnected appearance. Luckily, this is easy to fix; we only need to enable the so-called symbol levels. To do this, select the **Line** entry in the symbol layers list and tick the checkbox in the **Symbol Levels** dialog of the **Advanced** section (the button in the bottom-right corner of the style dialog), as shown in the following screenshot. Click on **Apply** to test the results.

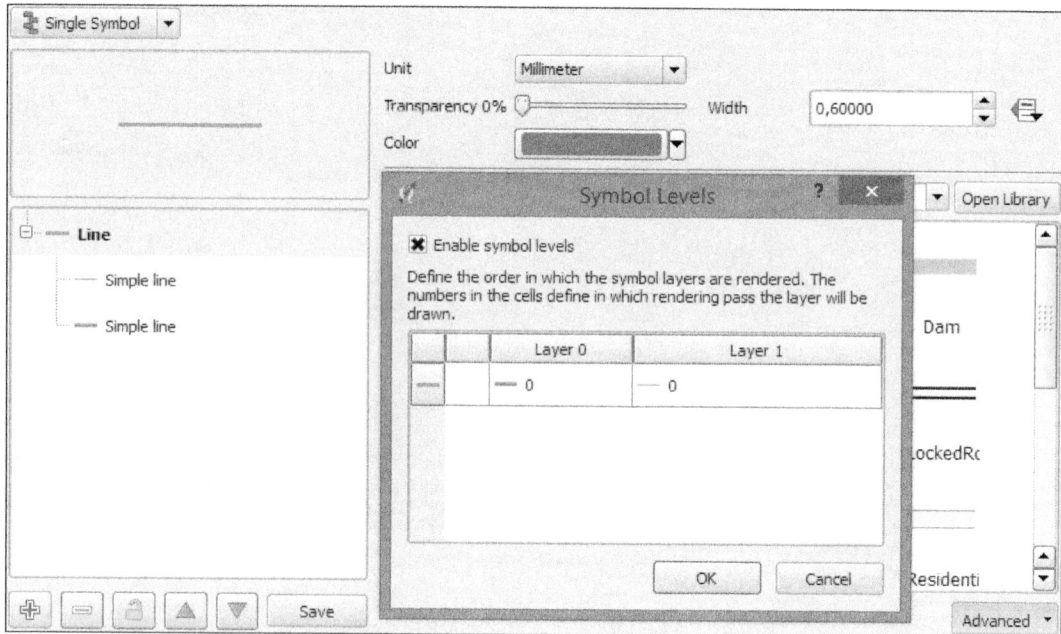

Before we move on to styling polygons, let's take a look at the other symbol layer types for lines, which include the following:

- **Simple line**: This is a solid or dashed line
- **Marker line**: This line is made up of point markers located at line vertices or at regular intervals
- **Geometry Generator**: This enables us to manipulate geometries and even create completely new geometries using the built-in expression engine.

A common use case for **Marker line** symbol layers are train track symbols; they often feature repeating perpendicular lines, which are abstract representations of railway sleepers. The following screenshot shows how we can create a style like this by adding a marker line on top of two simple lines:

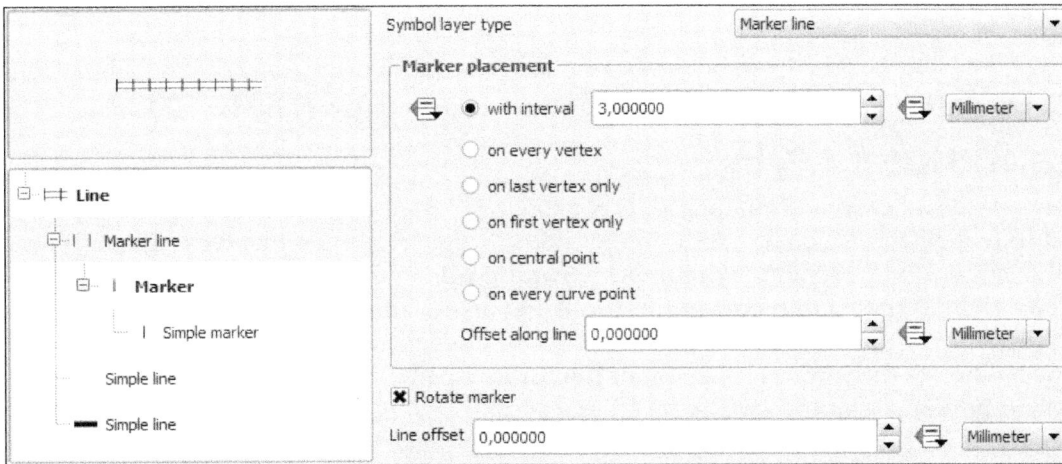

Another common use case for **Marker line** symbol layers is arrow symbols. The following screenshot shows how we can create a simple arrow by combining **Simple line** and **Marker line**. The key to creating an arrow symbol is to specify that **Marker placement** should be **last vertex only**. Then we only need to pick a suitable arrow head marker and the arrow symbol is ready.

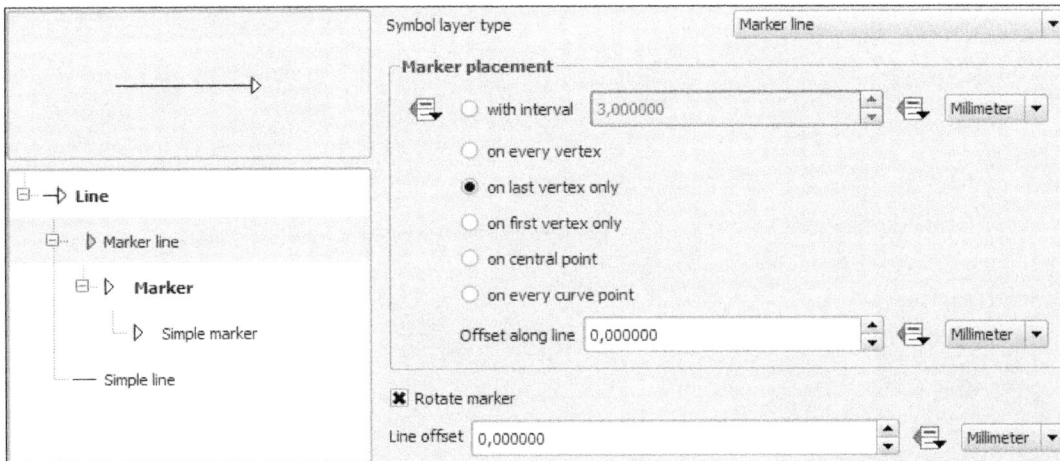

> Whenever we create a symbol that we might want to reuse in other maps, we can save it by clicking on the **Save** button under the symbol preview area. We can assign a name to the new symbol, and after we save it, it will be added to the saved symbols preview area on the right-hand side.

Creating polygon styles – an example of a landmass style

In this exercise, we will create a style for the `alaska.shp` file. The goal is to create a simple fill with a blue halo. As in the previous river style example, we will combine two symbol layers to create this style: a **Simple fill** layer that defines the main fill color (white) with a thin border (in gray), and an additional **Simple line** outline layer for the (light blue) halo. The halo should have nice rounded corners. To achieve these, change the **Join style** option of the **Simple line** symbol layer to **Round**. Similar to the previous example, we again enable symbol levels; to prevent this landmass style from blocking out the background map, we select the **Multiply** blending mode, as shown in the following screenshot:

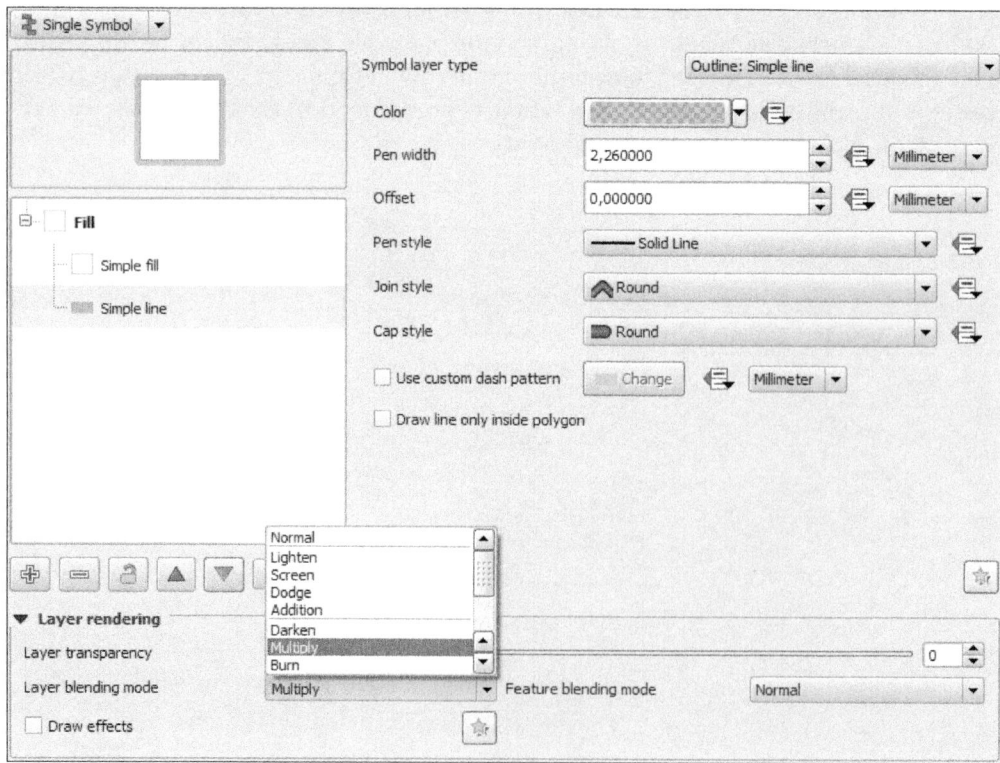

Before we move on, let's take a look at the other symbol layer types for polygons, which include the following:

- **Simple fill**: This defines the fill and outline colors as well as the basic fill styles
- **Centroid fill**: This allows us to put point markers at the centers of polygons
- **Line/Point pattern fill**: This supports user-defined line and point patterns with flexible spacing
- **SVG fill**: This fills the polygon using SVGs
- **Gradient fill**: This allows us to fill polygons with linear, radial, or conical gradients
- **Shapeburst fill**: This creates a gradient that starts at the polygon border and flows towards the center
- **Outline: Simple line** or **Marker line**: This makes it possible to outline areas using line styles
- **Geometry Generator**: This enables us to manipulate geometries and even create completely new geometries using the built-in expression engine.

A common use case for **Point pattern fill** symbol layers is topographic symbols for different vegetation types, which typically consist of a **Simple fill** layer and **Point pattern fill**, as shown in this screenshot:

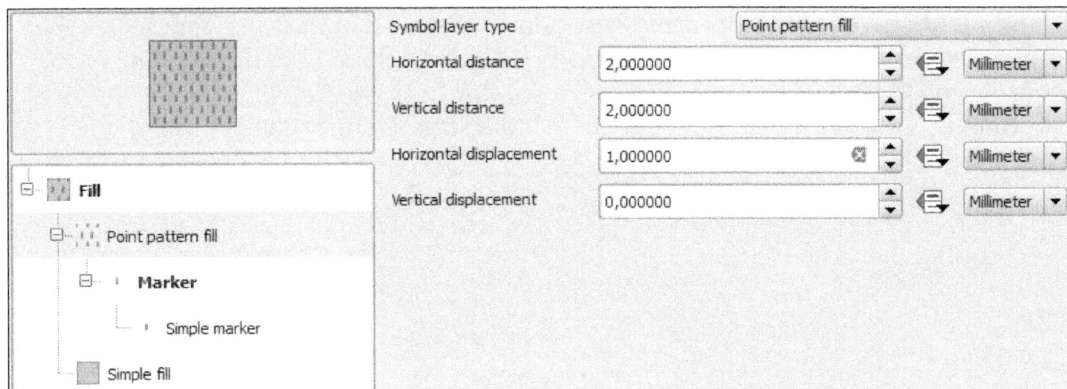

When we design point pattern fills, we are, of course, not restricted to simple markers. We can use any other marker type. For example, the following screenshot shows how to create a polygon fill style with a **Font marker** pattern that shows repeating alien faces from the **Webdings** font:

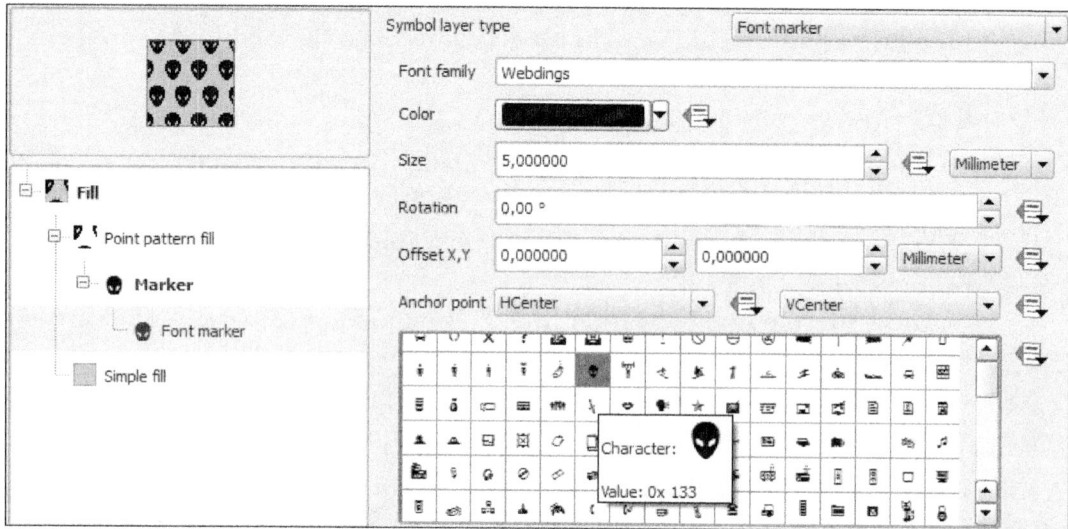

As an alternative to simple fills with only one color, we can create **Gradient fill** symbol layers. Gradients can be defined by **Two colors**, as shown in the following screenshot, or by a **Color ramp** that can consist of many different colors. Usually, gradients run from the top to the bottom, but we can change this to, for example, make the gradient run from right to left by setting **Angle** to 270 degrees, as shown here:

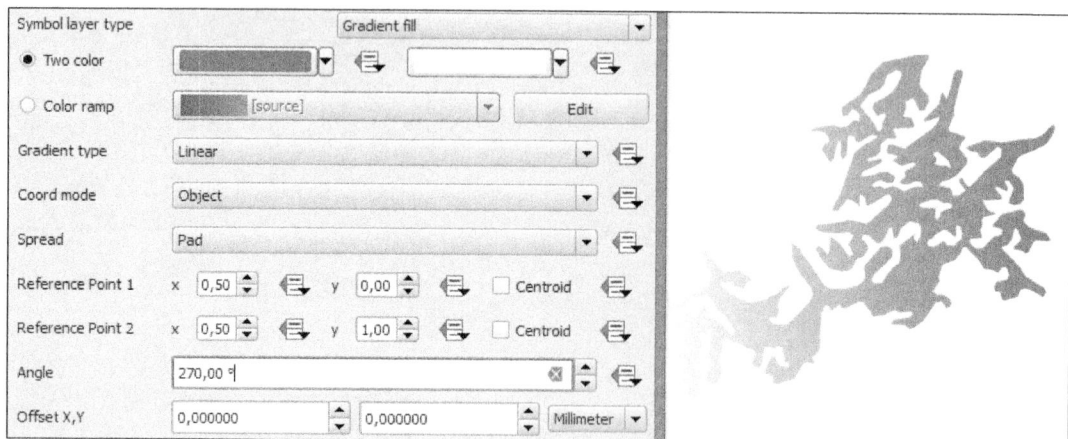

The **Shapeburst fill** symbol layer type, also known as a "buffered" gradient fill, is often used to style water areas with a smooth gradient that flows from the polygon border inwards. The following screenshot shows a fixed-distance shading using the **Shade to a set distance** option. If we select **Shade whole shape** instead, the gradient will be drawn all the way from the polygon border to the center.

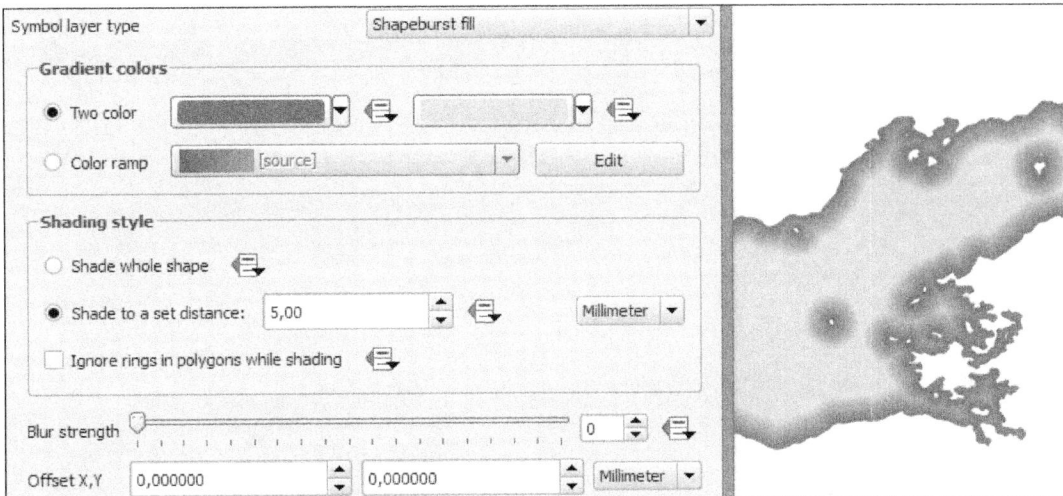

Loading background maps

Background maps are very useful for quick checks and to provide orientation, especially if you don't have access to any other base layers. Adding background maps is easy with the help of the **QuickMapServices** plugin. It provides access to satellite, street, and hybrid maps by different providers.

To install the **QuickMapServices** plugin, go to **Plugins | Manage and Install Plugins**. Wait until the list of available plugins has finished loading. Use the filter to look for the **QuickMapServices** option, as shown in the following screenshot. Select it from the list and click on **Install plugin**. This is going to take a moment. Once it's done, you will see a short confirmation message. You can then close the installer, and the **QuickMapServices** plugin will be available through the **Web** menu.

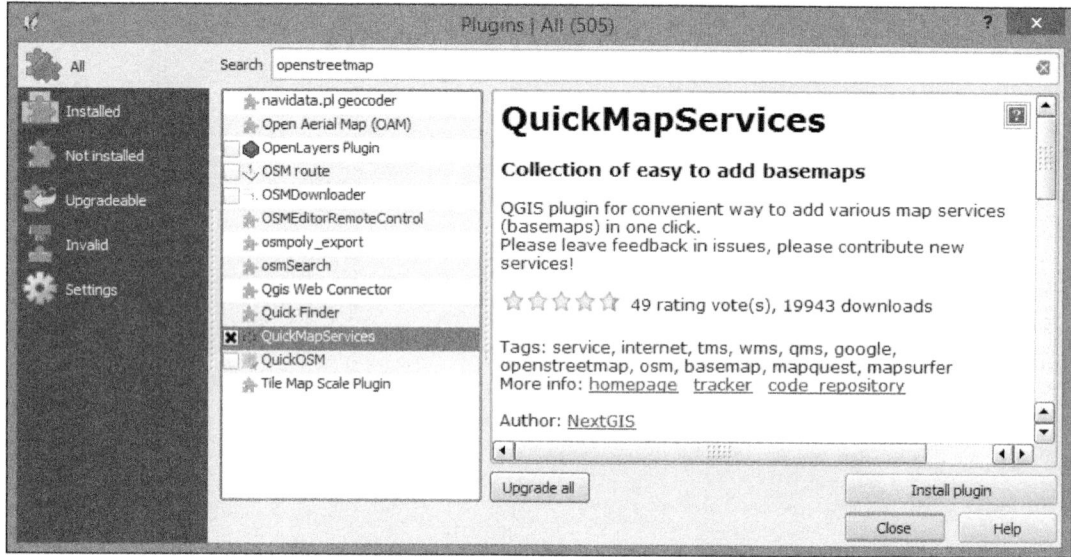

[Note that you have to be online to use these services.]

Another fact worth mentioning is that all of these services provide their maps only in Pseudo Mercator (EPSG: 3857). You should change your project CRS to Pseudo Mercator when using background maps from **QuickMapServices**, particularly if the map contains labels that would otherwise show up distorted.

[Background maps added using the **QuickMapServices** plugin are not suitable for printing due to their low resolution.]

If you load the **OSM TF Landscape** layer, your map will look like what is shown in this screenshot:

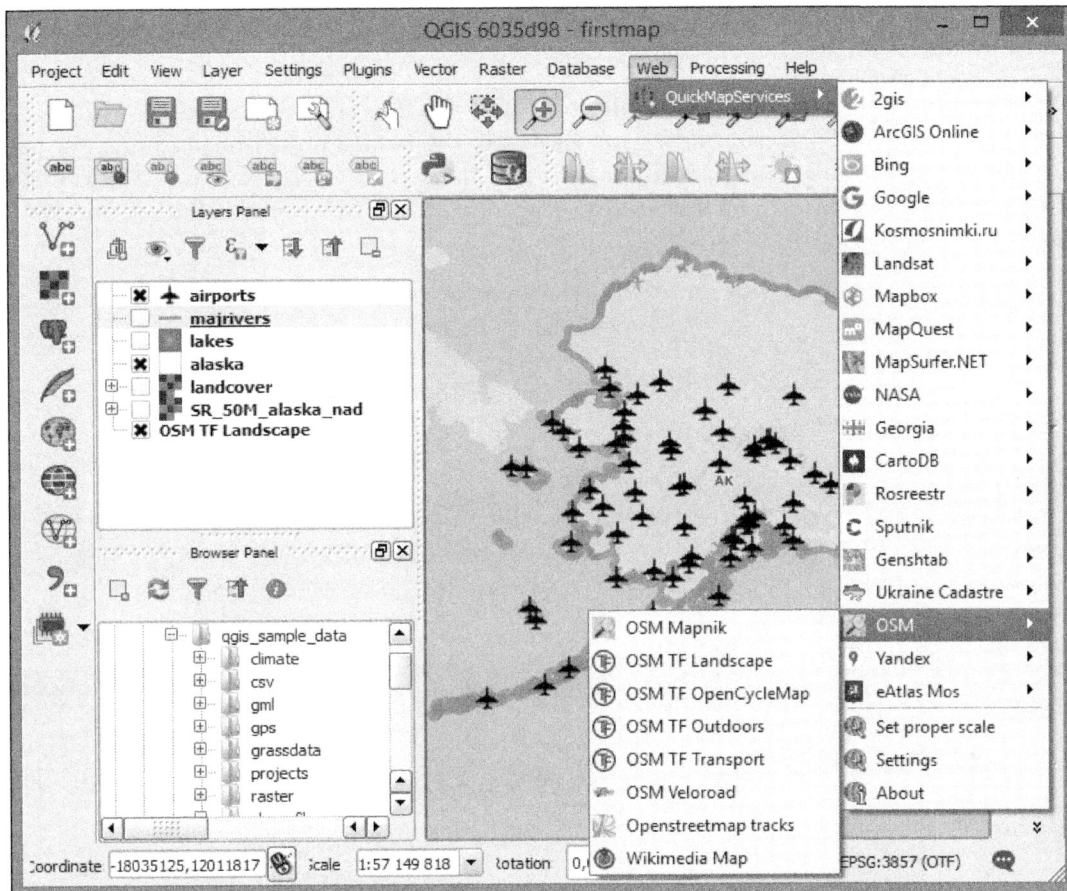

> An alternative to the **QuickMapServices** plugin is **OpenLayers Plugin**, which provides very similar functionality but offers fewer different background maps.

Dealing with project files

QGIS project files are human-readable XML files with the filename ending with `.qgs`. You can open them in any text editor (such as **Notepad++** on Windows or **gedit** on Ubuntu) and read or even change the file contents.

When you save a project file, you will notice that QGIS creates a second file with the same name and a `.qgs~` ending, as shown in the next screenshot. This is a simple backup copy of the project file with identical content. If your project file gets *corrupted* for any reason, you can simply copy the *backup* file, remove the ~ from the file ending, and continue working from there.

Name	Date modified	Type	Size
firstmap.qgs	12.12.2015 15:10	QGS File	84 KB
firstmap.qgs~	12.12.2015 15:07	QGS~ File	84 KB

By default, QGIS stores the **relative path** to the datasets in the project file. If you move a project file (without its associated data files) to a different location, QGIS won't be able to locate the data files anymore and will therefore display the following **Handle bad layers** dialog:

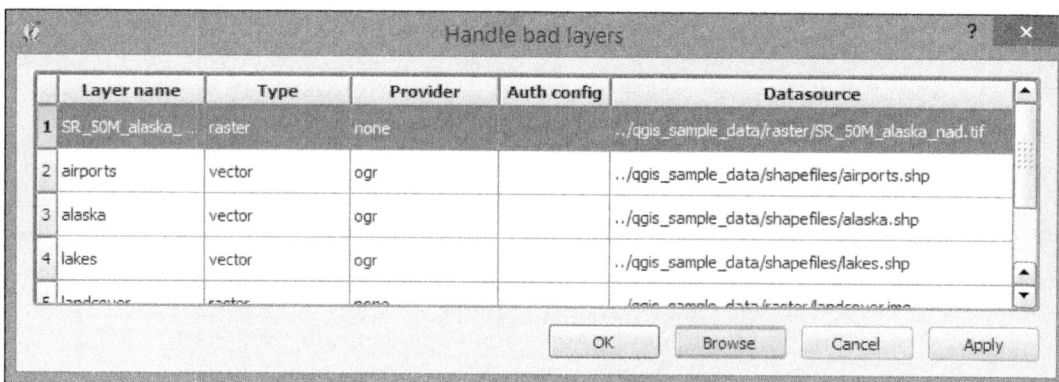

	Layer name	Type	Provider	Auth config	Datasource
1	SR_50M_alaska_	raster	none		../qgis_sample_data/raster/SR_50M_alaska_nad.tif
2	airports	vector	ogr		../qgis_sample_data/shapefiles/airports.shp
3	alaska	vector	ogr		../qgis_sample_data/shapefiles/alaska.shp
4	lakes	vector	ogr		../qgis_sample_data/shapefiles/lakes.shp
5	landcover	raster	none		../qgis_sample_data/raster/landcover.img

OK   Browse   Cancel   Apply

> If you are working with data files that are stored on a **network drive** rather than locally on your machine, it can be useful to change from storing **relative paths** to storing **absolute paths** instead. You can change this setting by going to **Project | Project Properties | General**.

To fix the layers, you need to correct the path in the **Datasource** column. This can be done by double-clicking on the path text and typing in the correct path, or by pressing the **Browse** button at the bottom of the dialog and selecting the new file location in the file dialog that opens up.

> A comfortable way to copy QGIS projects to other computers or share QGIS projects and associated files with other users is provided by the **QConsolidate** plugin. This plugin collects all the datasets used in the project and saves them in one directory, which you can then move around easily without breaking any paths.

Summary

In this chapter, you learned how to load spatial data from files, databases, and web services. We saw how QGIS handles coordinate reference systems and had an introduction to styling vector and raster layers, a topic that we will cover in more detail in *Chapter 5, Creating Great Maps*. We also installed our first Python plugin, the QuickMapServices plugin, and used it to load background maps into our project. Finally, we took a look at QGIS project files and how to work with them efficiently. In the following chapter, we will go into more detail and see how to create and edit raster and vector data.

3
Data Creation and Editing

In this chapter, we will first create some new vector layers and explain how to select features and take measurements. We will then continue with editing feature geometries and attributes. After that, we will reproject vector and raster data and convert between different file formats. We will also discuss how to join data from text files and spreadsheets to our spatial data and how to use temporary scratch layers for quick editing work. Moreover, we will take a look at common geometry topology issues and how to detect and fix them, before we end this chapter on how to add data to spatial databases.

Creating new vector layers

In this exercise, we'll create a new layer from scratch. QGIS offers a wide range of functionalities to create different layers. The **New** menu under **Layer** lists the functions needed to create new Shapefile and SpatiaLite layers, but we can also create new database tables using the DB Manager plugin. The interfaces differ slightly in order to accommodate the features supported by each format.

Let's create some new Shapefiles to see how it works:

1. **New Shapefile layer**, which can be accessed by going to **Layer | Create Layer** or by pressing *Ctrl + Shift + N*, opens the **New Vector Layer** dialog with options for different geometry types, CRS, and attributes.

   ○ Creating a new Shapefile is really fast because all the mandatory fields already have default values. By default, the tool will create a new point layer in WGS84 (EPSG:4326) CRS (unless specified otherwise in **Settings | Options | CRS**) and one integer field called **id**.

2. Leaving everything at the default values, we can simply click on **OK** and specify a filename. This creates a new Shapefile, and the new point layer appears in the layer list.

3. Next, we also create one line and one polygon layer. We'll add some extra fields to these layers. Besides integer fields (for whole numbers only), Shapefiles also support strings (for text), decimal numbers (also referred to as real), and dates (in ISO 8601 format, that is, 2016-12-24 for Christmas eve 2016).

4. To add a field, we only need to insert a name, select a type and width, and click on **Add to fields list**.

> For decimal numbers, we also have to define the **Precision** value, which determines the number of digits after the comma. A **Length** value of 3 with a **Precision** value of 1 will allow a value range from -99.9 to +99.9.

5. The left-hand side of the following screenshot shows the **New Vector Layer** dialog that was used to create my example polygon layer, which I called new_polygons:

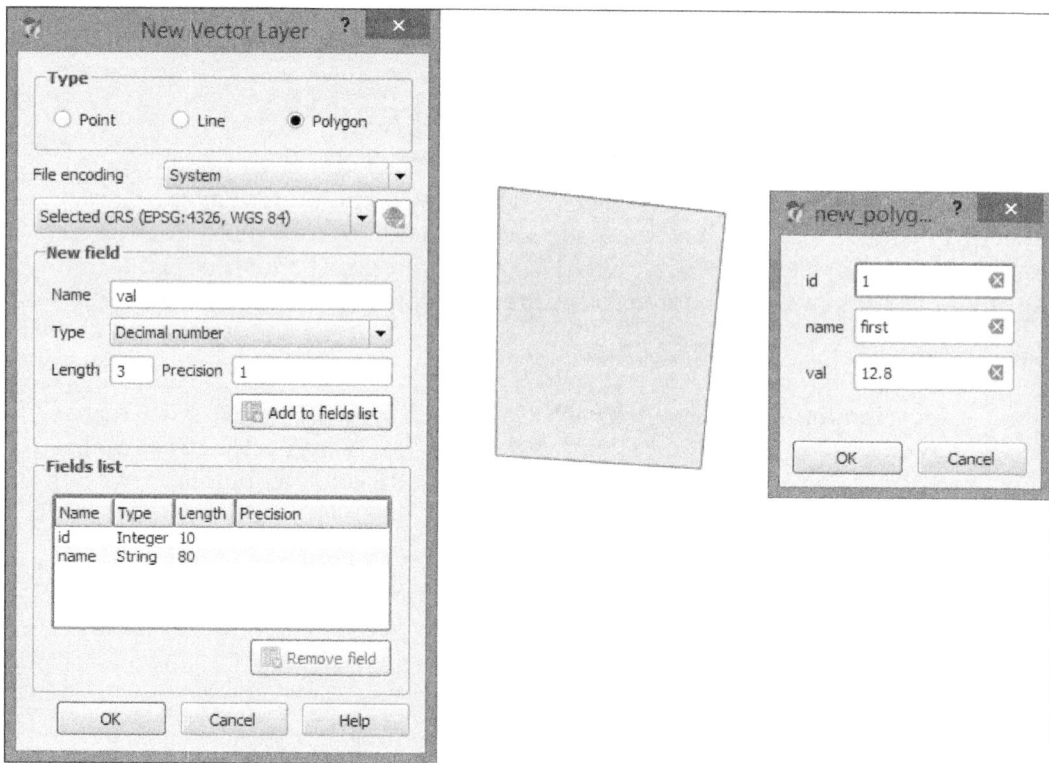

6. All the new layers are empty so far, but we will create some features now. If we want to add features to a layer, we first have to enable editing for that particular layer. Editing can be turned on and off by any one of these ways: going to **Layer | Toggle editing**, using **Toggle editing** in the layer name context menu, or clicking on the **Toggle editing** button in the **Digitizing** toolbar.

> You will notice that the layer's icon in the layer list changes to reflect whether editing is on or off. When we turn on editing for a layer, QGIS automatically enables the digitizing tools suitable for the layer's geometry type.

7. Now, we can use the **Add Feature** tool in the editing toolbar to create new features. To place a point, we can simply click on the map. We are then prompted to fill in the attribute form, which you can see on the right-hand side of the previous screenshot, and once we click on **OK**, the new feature is created.

8. As with points, we can create new lines and polygons by placing nodes on the map. To finish a line or polygon, we simply right-click on the map. Create some features in each layer and then save your changes. We can reuse these test layers in upcoming exercises.

> New features and feature edits are saved permanently only after we've clicked on the **Save Layer Edits** button in the **Digitizing** toolbar, or once we have finished editing and confirmed that we want to save the changes.

Working with feature selection tools

Selecting features is one of the core functions of any GIS, and it is useful to know them before we venture into editing geometries and attributes. Depending on the use case, **selection tools** come in many different flavors. QGIS offers three different kinds of tools to select features using the mouse, an expression, or another layer.

Selecting features with the mouse

The first group of tools in the **Attributes** toolbar allows us to select features on the map using the mouse. The following screenshot shows the **Select Feature(s)** tool. We can select a single feature by clicking on it, or select multiple features by drawing a rectangle. The other tools can be used to select features by drawing different shapes (polygons, freehand areas, or circles) around the features. All features that intersect with the drawn shape are selected.

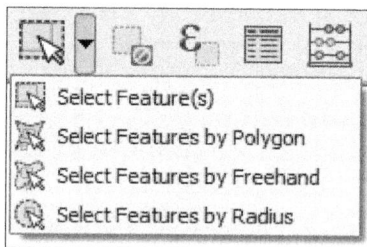

Selecting features with expressions

The second type of select tool is called **Select by Expression**, and it is also available in the **Attribute** toolbar. It selects features based on expressions that can contain references and functions that use feature attributes and/or geometry. The list of available functions in the center of the dialog is pretty long, but we can use the search box at the top of the list to filter it by name and find the function we are looking for faster. On the right-hand side of the window, we find the function help, which explains the functionality and how to use the function in an expression. The function list also shows the layer attribute fields, and by clicking on **all unique** or **10 samples**, we can easily access their content. We can choose between creating a new selection or adding to or deleting from an existing selection. Additionally, we can choose to only select features from within an existing selection. Let's take a look at some example expressions that you can build on and use in your own work:

- Using the `lakes.shp` file in our sample data, we can, for example, select lakes with an area greater than 1,000 square miles by using a simple `"AREA_MI" > 1000.0` attribute query, as shown in the following screenshot. Alternatively, we can use geometry functions such as `$area > (1000.0 * 27878400)`. Note that the `lakes.shp` CRS uses feet, and therefore we have to multiply by 27,878,400 to convert square feet to square miles.

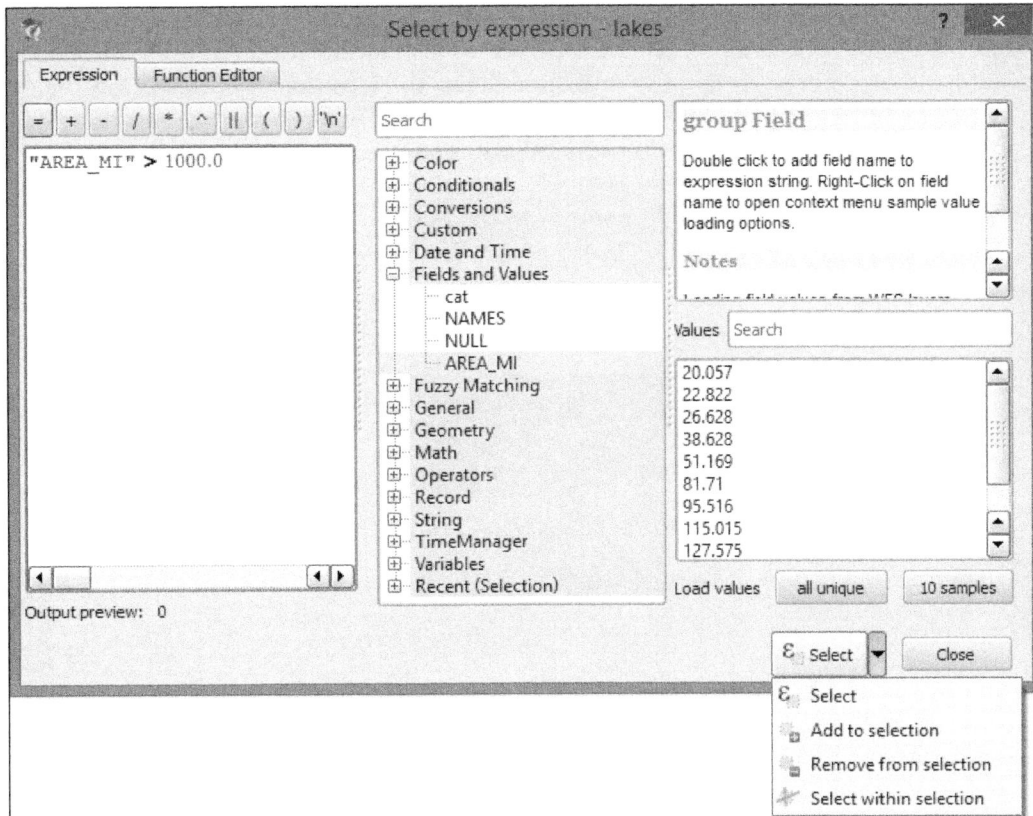

- We can also work with string functions, for example, to find lakes with long names (such as `length("NAMES") > 12`) or lakes with names that contain s or S (such as `lower("NAMES") LIKE '%s%'`); this function first converts the names to lowercase and then looks for any appearance of s.

Selecting features using spatial queries

The third type of tool is called **Spatial Query** and allows us to select features in one layer based on their location relative to features in a second layer. These tools can be accessed by going to **Vector | Research Tools | Select by location** and **Vector | Spatial Query | Spatial Query**. Enable it in **Plugin Manager** if you cannot find it in the **Vector** menu. In general, we want to use the Spatial Query plugin as it supports a variety of spatial operations such as **Crosses**, **Equals**, **Intersects**, **Is disjoint**, **Overlaps**, **Touches**, and **Contains**, depending on the layer geometry type.

Let's test the Spatial Query plugin using `railroads.shp` and `pipelines.shp` from the sample data. For example, we might want to find all railroad features that cross a pipeline; therefore, we select the **railroads** layer, the **Crosses** operation, and the **pipelines** layer. After we've clicked on **Apply**, the plugin presents us with the query results. There is a list of IDs of the result features on the right-hand side of the window, as you can see in the next screenshot. Below this list, we can check the **Zoom to item** box, and QGIS will zoom into the feature that belongs to the selected ID. Additionally, the plugin offers buttons for direct saving of all the resulting features to a new layer:

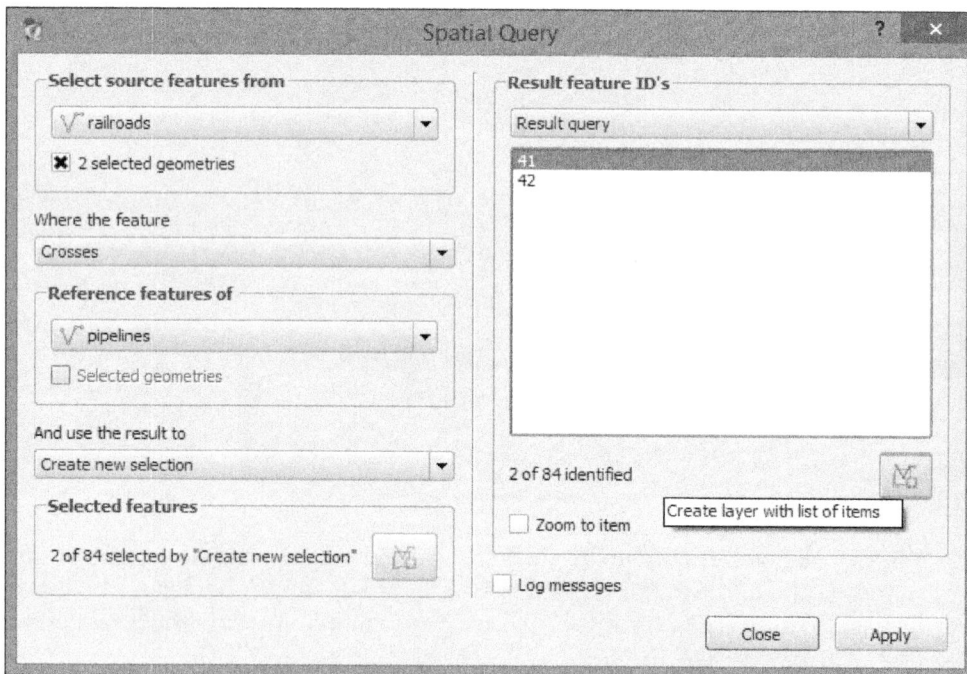

Editing vector geometries

Now that we know how to create and select features, we can take a closer look at the other tools in the **Digitizing** and **Advanced Digitizing** toolbars.

Using basic digitizing tools

This is the basic **Digitizing** toolbar:

The **Digitizing** toolbar contains tools that we can use to create and move features and nodes as well as delete, copy, cut, and paste features, as follows:

- The **Add Feature** tool allows us to create new features by placing feature nodes on the map, which are connected by straight lines.

- Similarly, the **Add Circular String** tool allows us to create features where consecutive nodes are connected by curved lines.

- With the **Move Feature(s)** tool, it is easy to move one or more features at once by dragging them to the new location.

- Similarly, the **Node Tool** feature allows us to move one or more nodes of the same feature. The first click activates the feature, while the second click selects the node. Hold the mouse key down to drag the node to its new location. Instead of moving only one node, we can also move an edge by clicking and dragging the line. Finally, we can select and move multiple nodes by holding down the *Ctrl* key.

- The **Delete Selected**, **Cut Features**, and **Copy Features** tools are active only if one or more layer features are selected. Similarly, **Paste Features** works only after a feature has been cut or copied.

Using advanced digitizing tools

The **Advanced Digitizing** toolbar offers very useful **Undo** and **Redo** functionalities as well as additional tools for more involved geometry editing, as shown in the following screenshot:

The **Advanced Digitizing** tools include the following:

- **Rotate Feature(s)** enables us to rotate one or more selected features around a central point.

- Using the **Simplify Feature** tool, we can simplify/generalize feature geometries by simply clicking on the feature and specifying a desired tolerance in the pop-up window, as shown in the following screenshot, where you can see the original geometry on the left-hand side and the simplified geometry on the right-hand side:

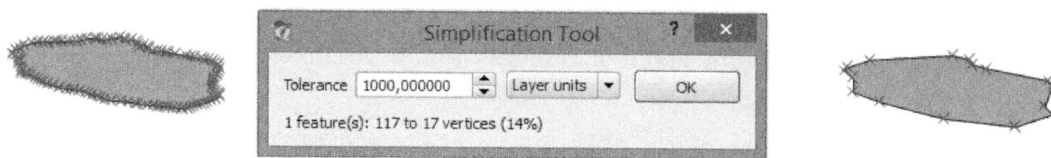

- The following tools can be used to modify polygons. They allow us to add rings, also known as *holes*, into existing polygons or add parts to them. The **Fill Ring** tool is similar to **Add Ring**, but instead of just creating a hole, it also creates a new feature that fills the hole. Of course, there are tools to delete rings and parts well.

- The **Reshape Features** tool can be used to alter the geometry of a feature by either cutting out or adding pieces. You can control the behavior by starting to draw the new form inside the original feature to add a piece, or by starting outside to cut out a piece, as shown in this example diagram:

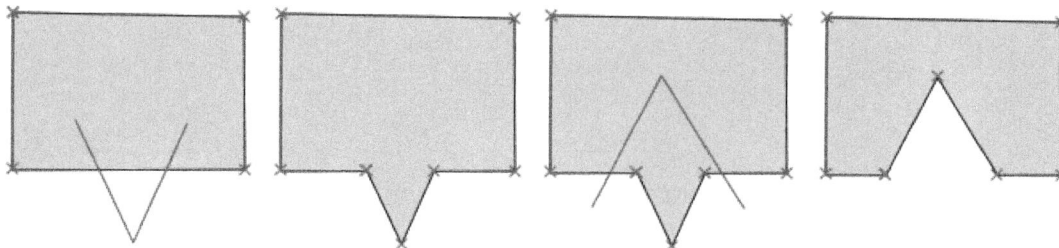

- The **Offset Curve** tool is only available for lines and allows us to displace a line geometry by a given offset.

- The **Split Features** tool allows us to split one or more features into multiple features along a cut line. Similarly, **Split Parts** allows us to split a feature into multiple parts that still belong to the same multipolygon or multipolyline.

- The **Merge Selected Features** tool enables us to merge multiple features while keeping control over which feature's attributes will be available in the output feature.

- Similarly, **Merge Attributes of Selected Features** also lets us combine the attributes of multiple features but without merging them into one feature. Instead, all the original features remain as they were; the attribute values are updated.

- Finally, **Rotate Point Symbols** is available only for point layers with the **Rotation field** feature enabled (we will cover this feature in *Chapter 5, Creating Great Maps*).

Using snapping to enable topologically correct editing

One of the challenges of digitizing features by hand is avoiding undesired gaps or overlapping features. To make it easier to avoid these issues, QGIS offers a **snapping** functionality. To configure snapping, we go to **Settings | Snapping options**. The following screenshot shows how to enable snapping for the **Current layer**. Similarly, you can choose snapping modes for **All layers** or the **Advanced** mode, where you can control the settings for each layer separately. In the example shown in the following screenshot, we enable snapping **To vertex**. This means that digitizing tools will automatically snap to vertices/nodes of existing features in the current layer. Similarly, you can enable snapping **To segment** or **To vertex and segment**. When snapping is enabled during digitizing, you will notice bold cross-shaped markers appearing whenever you go close to a vertex or segment that can be snapped to:

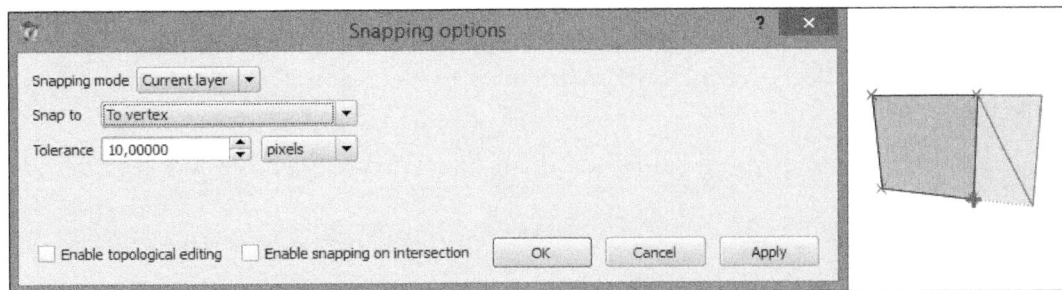

Using measuring tools

Another core functionality of any GIS is provided by **measurement tools**. In QGIS, we find the tools needed to measure lines, areas, and angles in the **Attribute** toolbar, as shown in this screenshot:

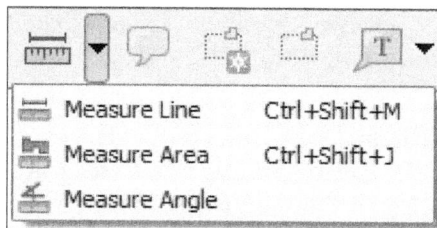

The measurements are updated continuously while we draw measurement lines, areas, or angles. When we draw a line with multiple segments, the tool shows the length of each segment as well as the total length of all the segments put together. To stop measuring, we can just right-click. If we want to change the measurement units from meters to feet or from degrees to radians, we can do this by going to **Settings | Options | Map Tools**.

Editing attributes

There are three main use cases of attribute editing:

- First, we might want to edit the attributes of a specific feature, for example, to fix a wrong name
- Second, we might want to edit the attributes of a group of features
- Third, we might want to change the attributes of all features within a layer

Editing attributes in the attribute table

All three use cases are covered by the functionality available through the **attribute table**. We can access it by going to **Layer | Open Attribute Table**, using the **Open Attribute Table** button present in the **Attributes** toolbar, or in the layer name context menu.

1. To change an attribute value, we always have to enable editing first.

2. Then, we can double-click on any cell in the attribute table to activate the input mode, as shown in the upper dialog of the following screenshot, where I am editing NAME_2 of the first feature:

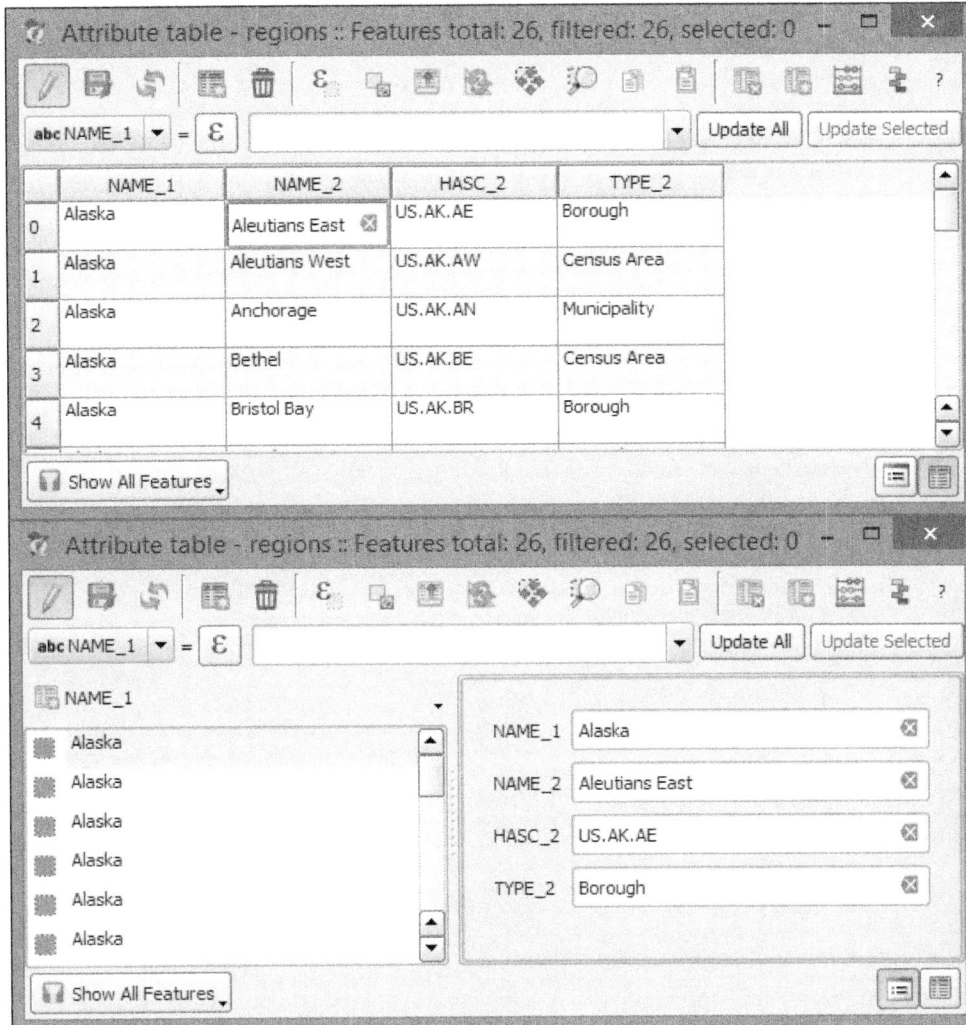

3. Pressing the *Enter* key confirms the change, but to save the new value permanently, we also have to click on the **Save Edit(s)** button or press *Ctrl + S*.

Besides the classic attribute table view, QGIS also supports a **form view**, which you can see in the lower dialog of the previous image. You can switch between these two views using the buttons in the bottom-right corner of the attribute table dialog.

In the attribute table, we also find tools for handling selections (from left to right, starting at the fourth button): **Delete selected features, Select features using an expression, Unselect all, Move selection to top, Invert selection, Pan map to the selected rows, Zoom map to the selected rows**, and **Copy selected rows to clipboard**. Another way to select features in the attribute table is by clicking on the row number.

The next two buttons allow us to add and remove columns. When we click on the **Delete column** button, we get a list of columns to choose from. Similarly, the **New column** button brings up a dialog that we can use to specify the name and data type of the new column.

Editing attributes in the feature form

Another option to edit the attributes of one feature is to open the **attribute form** directly by clicking on the feature on the map using the **Identify tool**. By default, the **Identify tool** displays the attribute values in read mode, but we can enable the **Auto open form** option in the **Identify Results** panel, as shown here:

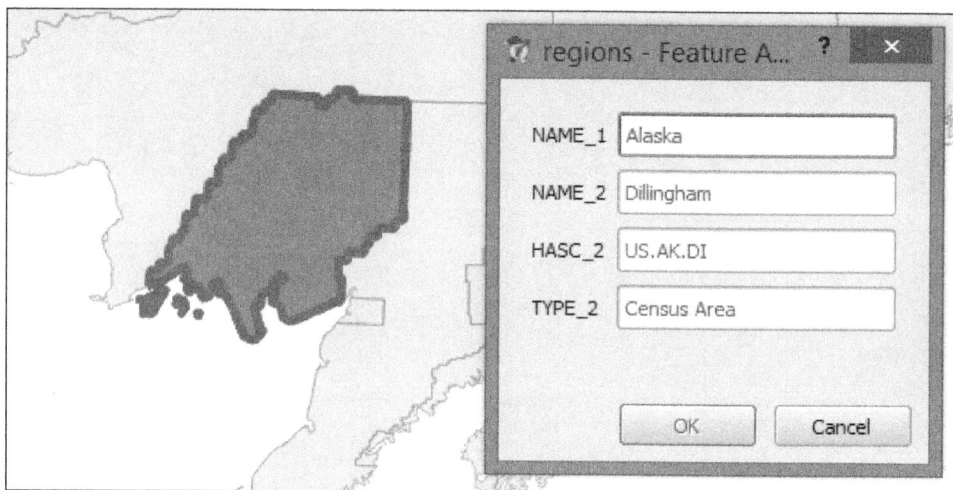

What you can see in the previous screenshot is the default feature attributes form that QGIS creates automatically, but we are not limited to this basic form. By going to **Layer Properties | Fields** section, we can configure the look and feel of the form in greater detail. The **Attribute editor layout** options are (in an increasing level of complexity) **autogenerate, Drag and drop designer**, and providing a .ui file. These options are described in detail as follows.

Creating a feature form using autogenerate

Autogenerate is the most basic option. You can assign a specific **Edit widget** and **Alias** for each field; this will replace the default input field and label in the form. For this example, we use the following edit widget types:

- **Text Edit** supports inserting one or more lines of text.

- **Unique Values** creates a drop-down list that allows the user to select one of the values that have already been used in the attribute table. If the **Editable** option is activated, the drop-down list is replaced by a text edit widget with autocompletion support.

- **Range** creates an edit widget for numerical values from a specific range.

> For the complete list of available *Edit widget* types, refer to the user manual at http://docs.qgis.org/2.2/en/ docs/user_manual/working_with_vector/vector_ properties.html#fields-menu.

Designing a feature form using drag and drop designer

This allows more control over the form layout. As you can see in the next screenshot, the designer enables us to create tabs within the form and also makes it possible to change the order of the form fields. The workflow is as follows:

1. Click on the plus button to add one or more tabs (for example, a **Region** tab, as shown in the following screenshot).

2. On the left-hand side of the dialog, select the field that you want to add to the form.

3. On the right-hand side, select the tab to which you want to add the field.

4. Click on the button with the icon of an arrow pointing to the right to add the selected field to the selected tab.

5. You can reorder the fields in the form using the up and down arrow buttons or, as the name suggests, by dragging and dropping the fields up or down:

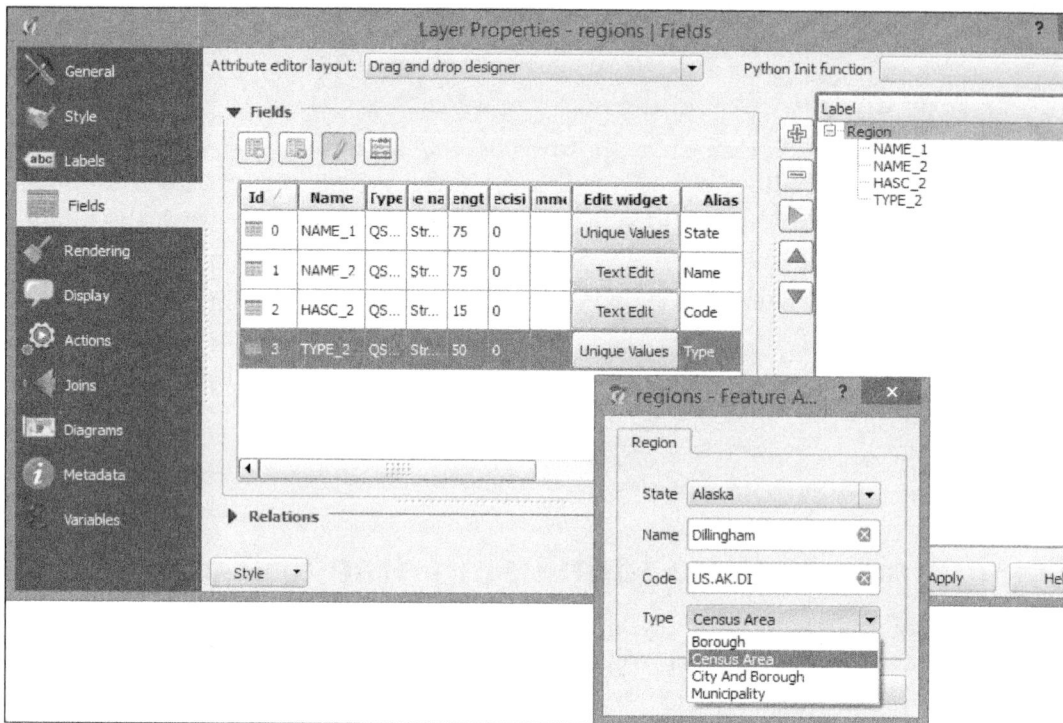

Designing a feature form using a .ui file

This is the most advanced option. It enables you to use a Qt user interface designed using, for example, the Qt Designer software. This allows a great deal of freedom in designing the form layout and behavior.

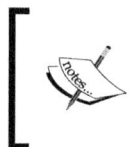

> Creating .ui files is out of the scope of this book, but you can find more information about it at http://docs.qgis.org/2.2/en/docs/training_manual/create_vector_data/forms.html#hard-fa-creating-a-new-form.

Calculating new attribute values

If we want to change the attributes of multiple or all features in a layer, editing them manually usually isn't an option. This is what the **Field calculator** is good for. We can access it using the **Open field calculator** button in the attribute table, or by pressing *Ctrl + I*. In the **Field calculator**, we can choose to update only the selected features or update all the features in the layer. Besides updating an existing field, we can also create a new field. The function list is the same one that we explored when we selected features by expression. We can use any of the functions and variables in this list to populate a new field or update an existing one. Here are some example expressions that are often used:

- We can create a sequential id column using the @row_number variable, which populates a column with row numbers, as shown in the following screenshot:

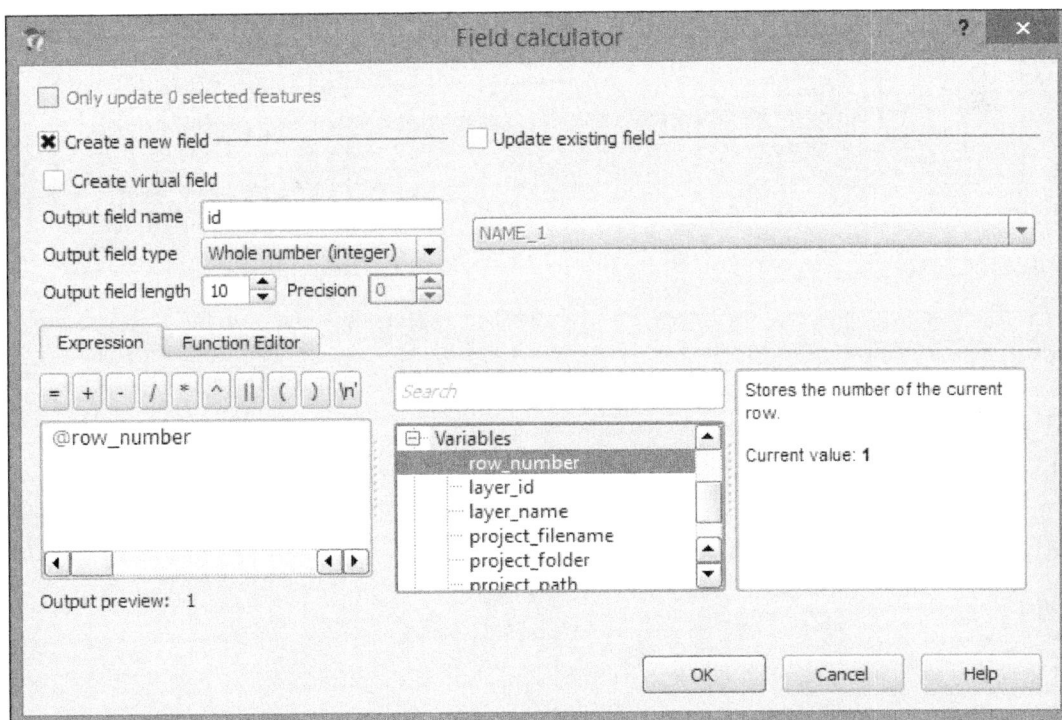

- Another common use case is calculating a line's length or a polygon's area using the $length and $area geometry functions, respectively
- Similarly, we can get point coordinates using $x and $y
- If we want to get the start point or end point of a line, we can use $x_at(0) and $y_at(0), or $x_at(-1) and $y_at(-1), respectively

An alternative to the **Field calculator** — especially if you already know the formula you want to use — is the field calculator bar, which you can find directly in the **Attribute table** dialog right below the toolbar. In the next screenshot, you can see an example that calculates the area of all census areas (use the **New Field** button to add a **Decimal number field** called CENSUSAREA first). This example uses a CASE WHEN – THEN – END expression to check whether the value of TYPE_2 is Census Area:

```
CASE WHEN TYPE_2 = 'Census Area' THEN $area / 27878400 END
```

> An alternative solution would be to use the if() function instead. If you use the CENSUSAREA attribute as the third parameter (which defines the value that is returned if the condition evaluates to false), the expression will only update those rows in which TYPE_2 is Census Area and leave the other rows unchanged:
>
> ```
> if(TYPE_2 = 'Census Area', $area / 27878400,
> CENSUSAREA)
> ```
>
> Alternatively, you can use NULL as a third parameter which will overwrite all rows where TYPE_2 does not equal Census Area with NULL:
>
> ```
> if(TYPE_2 = 'Census Area', $area / 27878400, NULL)
> ```

Enter the formula and click on the **Update All** button to execute it:

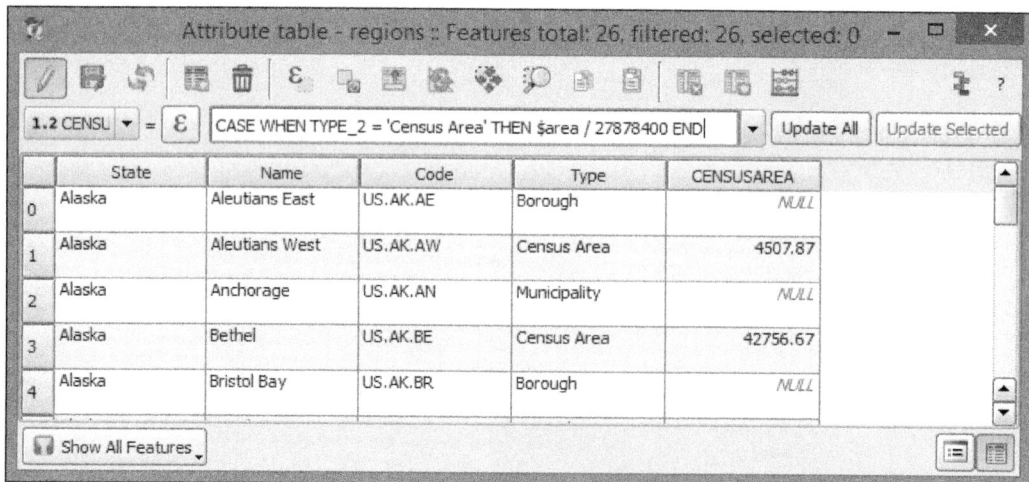

Since it is not possible to directly *change a field data type* in a Shapefile or SpatiaLite attribute table, the field calculator and calculator bar are also used to create new fields with the desired properties and then populate them with the values from the original column.

Reprojecting and converting vector and raster data

In *Chapter 2, Viewing Spatial Data*, we talked about CRS and the fact that QGIS offers on the fly reprojection to display spatial datasets, which are stored in different CRS, in the same map. Still, in some cases, we might want to permanently reproject a dataset, for example, to geoprocess it later on.

In QGIS, reprojecting a vector or raster layer is done by simply saving it with a new CRS. We can save a layer by going to **Layer | Save as...** or using **Save as...** in the layer name context menu. Pick a target file format and filename, and then click on the **Select CRS** button beside the CRS drop-down field to pick a new CRS.

Besides changing the CRS, the main use case of the **Save vector/raster layer** dialog, as depicted in the following screenshot, is conversion between different file formats. For example, we can load a Shapefile and export it as GeoJSON, MapInfo MIF, CSV, and so on, or the other way around.

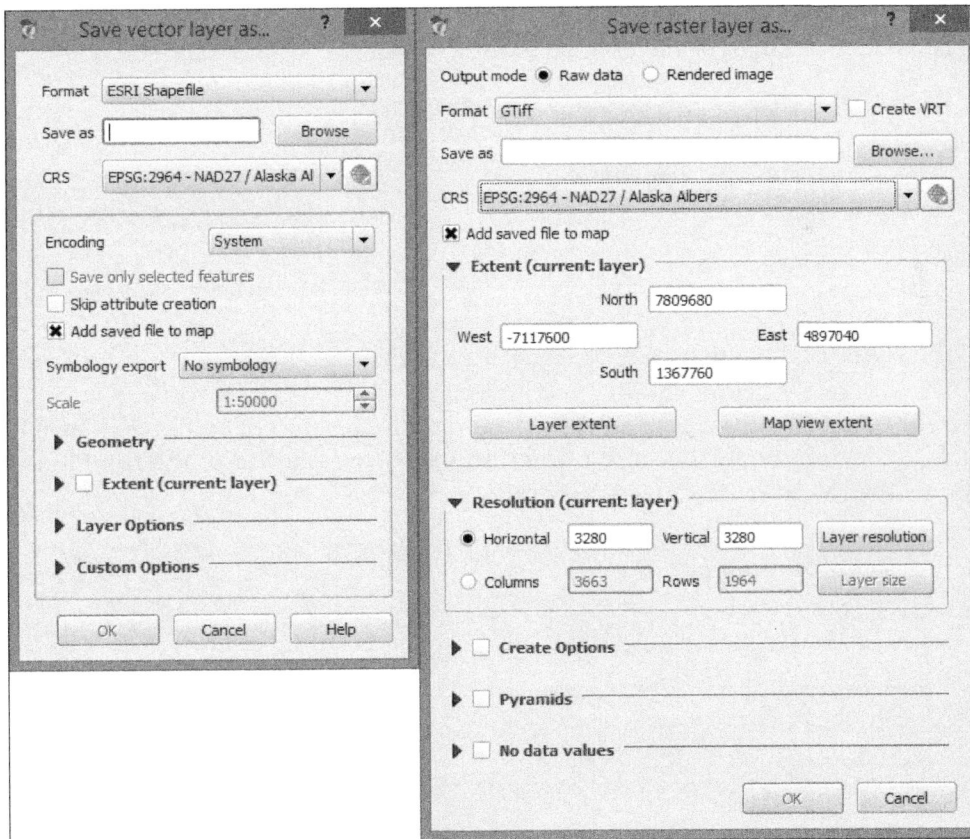

The **Save raster layer** dialog is also a convenient way to clip/crop rasters by a bounding box, since we can specify which **Extent** we want to save.

Furthermore, the **Save vector layer** dialog features a **Save only selected features** option, which enables us to save only selected features instead of all features of the layer (this option is active only if there are actually some selected features in the layer).

> Enabling **Add saved file to map** is very convenient because it saves us the effort of going and loading the new file manually after it has been saved.

Joining tabular data

In many real-life situations, we get additional non-spatial data in the form of spreadsheets or text files. The good news is that we can load XLS files by simply dragging them into QGIS from the file browser or using **Add Vector Layer**. Don't let the wording fool you! It really works without any geometry data in the file. The file can even contain more than one table. You will see the following dialog, which lets you choose which table (or tables) you want to load:

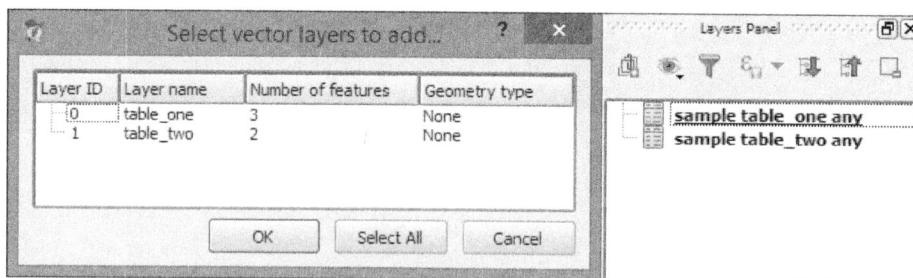

QGIS will automatically recognize the names and data types of columns in an XLS table. It's quite easy to tell because numerical values are aligned to the right in the attribute table, as shown in this screenshot:

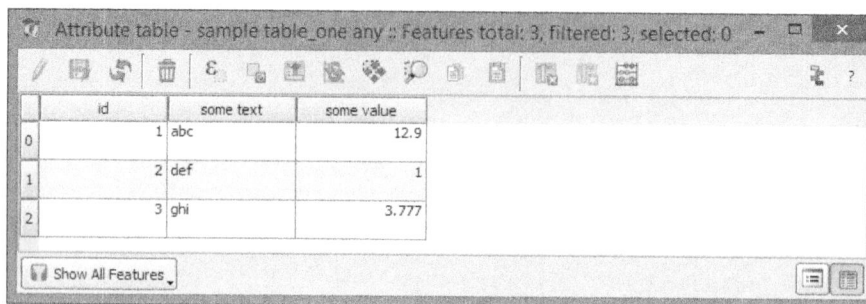

We can also load tabular data from delimited text files, as we saw in *Chapter 2, Viewing Spatial Data*, when we loaded a point layer from a delimited text file. To load a delimited text file that contains only tabular data but no geometry information, we just need to enable the **No geometry (attribute table only)** option.

Setting up a join in Layer Properties

After loading the tabular data from either the spreadsheet or text file, we can continue to join this non-spatial data to a vector layer (for instance, our `airports.shp` dataset, as shown in the following example). To do this, we go to the vector's **Layer Properties | Joins** section. Here, we can add a new join by clicking on the green plus button. All we have to do is select the tabular **Join layer** and **Join field** (of the tabular layer), which will contain values that match those in the **Target field** (of the vector layer). Additionally, we can—if we want to—select a subset of the fields to be joined by enabling the **Choose which fields are joined** option. For example, the settings shown in the following screenshot will add only the `some value` field. Additionally, we use a **Custom field name prefix** instead of using the entire join layer name, which would be the default option.

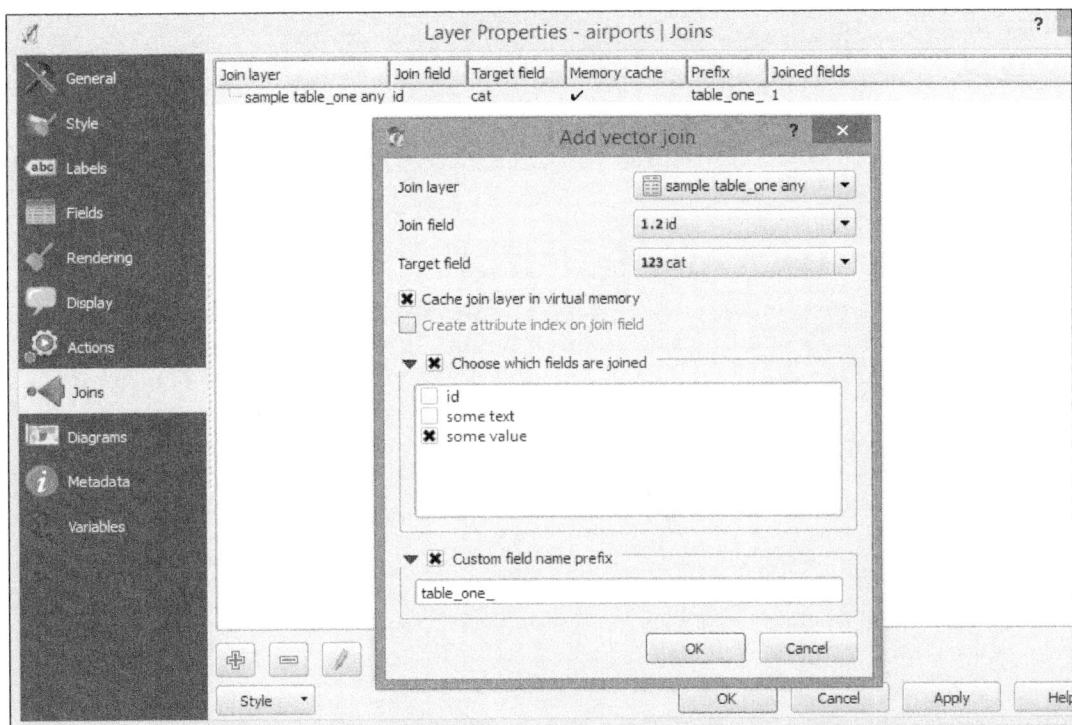

Checking join results in the attribute table

Once the join is added, we can see the extended attribute table and use the new appended attributes (as shown in the following screenshot) for styling and labeling. The way joins work in QGIS is as follows: the join layer's attributes are appended to the original layer's attribute table. The number of features in the original layer is not changed. Whenever there is a match between the join and the target field, the attribute value is filled in; otherwise, you see **NULL** entries.

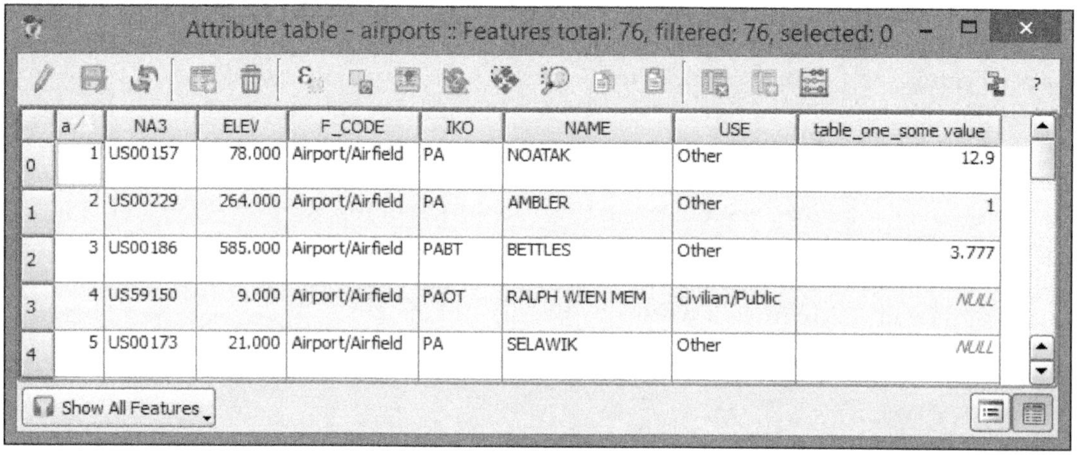

	a	NA3	ELEV	F_CODE	IKO	NAME	USE	table_one_some value
0	1	US00157	78.000	Airport/Airfield	PA	NOATAK	Other	12.9
1	2	US00229	264.000	Airport/Airfield	PA	AMBLER	Other	1
2	3	US00186	585.000	Airport/Airfield	PABT	BETTLES	Other	3.777
3	4	US59150	9.000	Airport/Airfield	PAOT	RALPH WIEN MEM	Civilian/Public	NULL
4	5	US00173	21.000	Airport/Airfield	PA	SELAWIK	Other	NULL

You can save the joined layer permanently using **Save as...** to create the new file.

Using temporary scratch layers

When you just want to quickly draw some features on the map, **temporary scratch layers** are a great way of doing that without having to worry about file formats and locations for your temporary data. Go to **Layer** | **Create Layer** | **New Temporary Scratch Layer...** to create a new temporary scratch layer. As you can see in the following screenshot, all we need to do to configure this temporary layer is pick a **Type** for the geometry, a **Layer name**, and a CRS. Once the layer is created, we can add features and attributes as we would with any other vector layer:

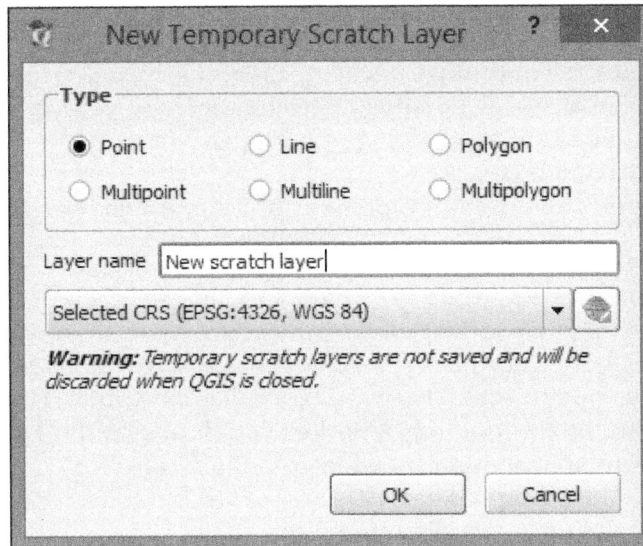

As the name suggests, temporary scratch layers are temporary. This means that they will vanish when you close the project.

> If you want to preserve the data of your temporary layers, you can either use **Save as...** to create a file or install the **Memory Layer Saver** plugin, which will make layers with memory data providers (such as temporary scratch layers) persistent so that they are restored when a project is closed and reopened. The memory provider data is saved in a portable binary format that is saved with the .mldata extension alongside the project file.

Checking for topological errors and fixing them

Sometimes, the data that we receive from different sources or data that results from a chain of spatial processing steps can have problems. Topological errors can be particularly annoying, since they can lead to a multitude of different problems when using the data for analysis and further spatial processing. Therefore, it is important to have tools that can check data for topological errors and to know ways to fix discovered errors.

Finding errors with the Topology Checker

In QGIS, we can use the **Topology Checker** plugin; it is installed by default and is accessible via the **Vector** menu **Topology Checker** entry (if you cannot find the menu entry, you might have to enable the plugin in **Plugin Manager**). When the plugin is activated, it adds a **Topology Checker Panel** to the QGIS window. This panel can be used to configure and run different topology checks and will list the detected errors.

To see the **Topology Checker** in action, we create a temporary scratch layer with polygon geometries and digitize some polygons, as shown in the following screenshot. Make sure you use snapping to create polygons that touch but don't overlap. These could, for example, represent a group of row houses. When the polygons are ready, we can set up the topology rules we want to check for. Click on the **Configure** button in **Topology Checker Panel** to open the **Topology Rule Settings** dialog. Here, we can manage all the topology rules for our project data. For example, in the following screenshot, you can see the rules we might want to configure for our polygon layer, including these:

- Polygons *must not overlap* each other
- There must not be gaps between polygons
- There shouldn't be any duplicate geometries

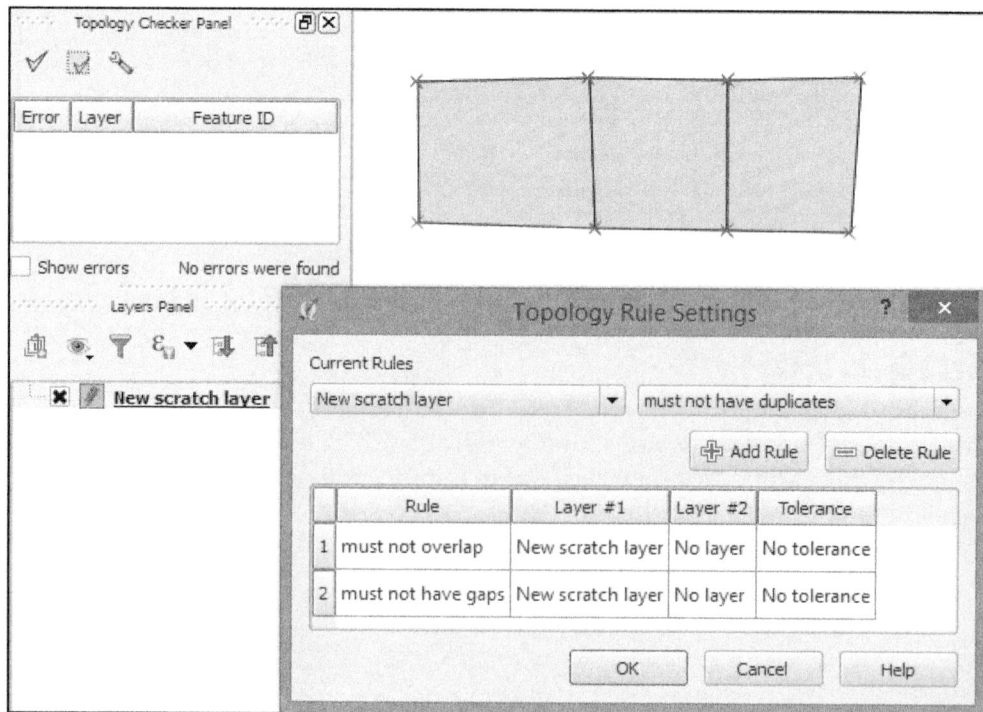

Once the rules are set up, we can close the settings dialog and click on the **Validate All** button in **Topology Checker Panel** to start running the **topology rule** checks. If you have been careful while creating the polygons, the checker will not find any errors and the status at the bottom of **Topology Checker Panel** will display this message: **0 errors were found**. Let's change that by introducing some **topology errors**.

For example, if we move one vertex so that two polygons end up overlapping each other and then click on **Validate All**, we get the error shown in the next screenshot. Note that the error type and the affected layer and feature are displayed in **Topology Checker Panel**. Additionally, since the **Show errors** option is enabled, the problematic geometry part is highlighted in red on the map:

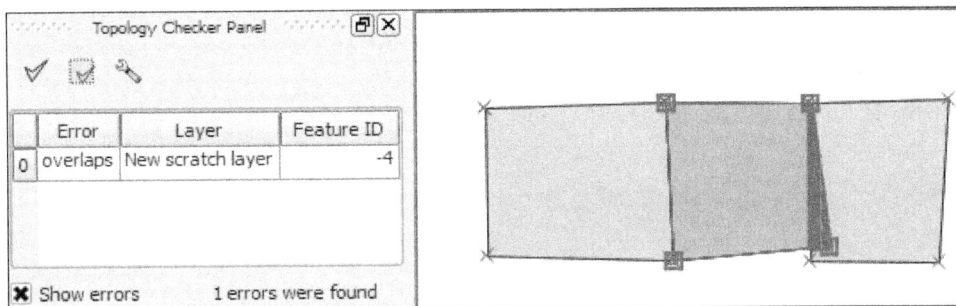

Of course, it is also possible to create rules that describe the relationship between features in different layers. For example, the following screenshot shows a point and a polygon layer where the rules state that each point should be inside a polygon and each polygon should contain a point:

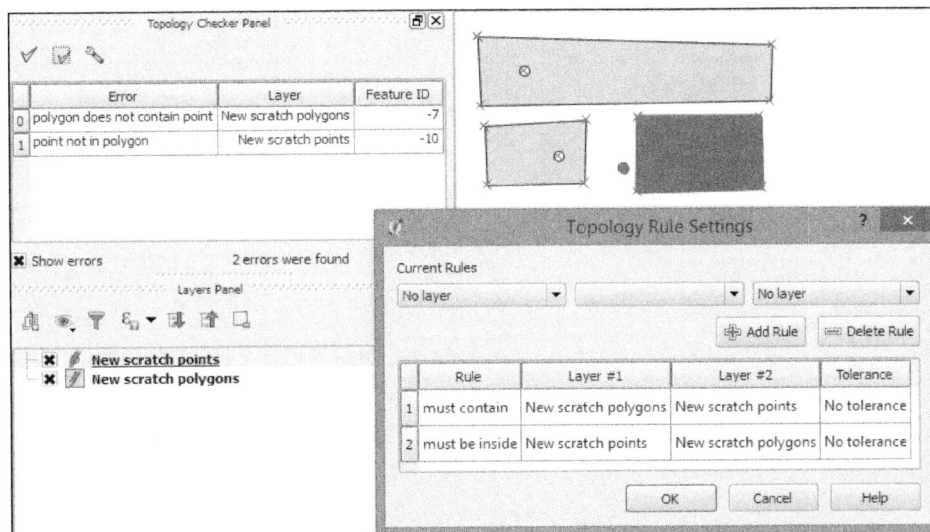

Selecting an error from the list of errors in the panel centres the map on the problematic location so that we can start fixing it, for example, by moving the lone point into the empty polygon.

Fixing invalid geometry errors

Sometimes, fixing all errors manually can be a lot of work. Luckily, certain errors can be addressed automatically. For example, the common error of **self-intersecting polygons**, which cause *invalid geometry* errors (as illustrated in the following screenshot), is often the result of intersecting polygon nodes or edges. These issues can often be resolved using a buffer tool (for example, **Fixed distance buffer** in the **Processing Toolbox**, which we will discuss in more detail in *Chapter 4, Spatial Analysis*) with the buffer **Distance** set to 0. Buffering will, for example, fix the self-intersecting polygon on the left-hand side of the following screenshot by removing the self-intersecting nodes and constructing a valid polygon with a hole (as depicted on the right-hand side):

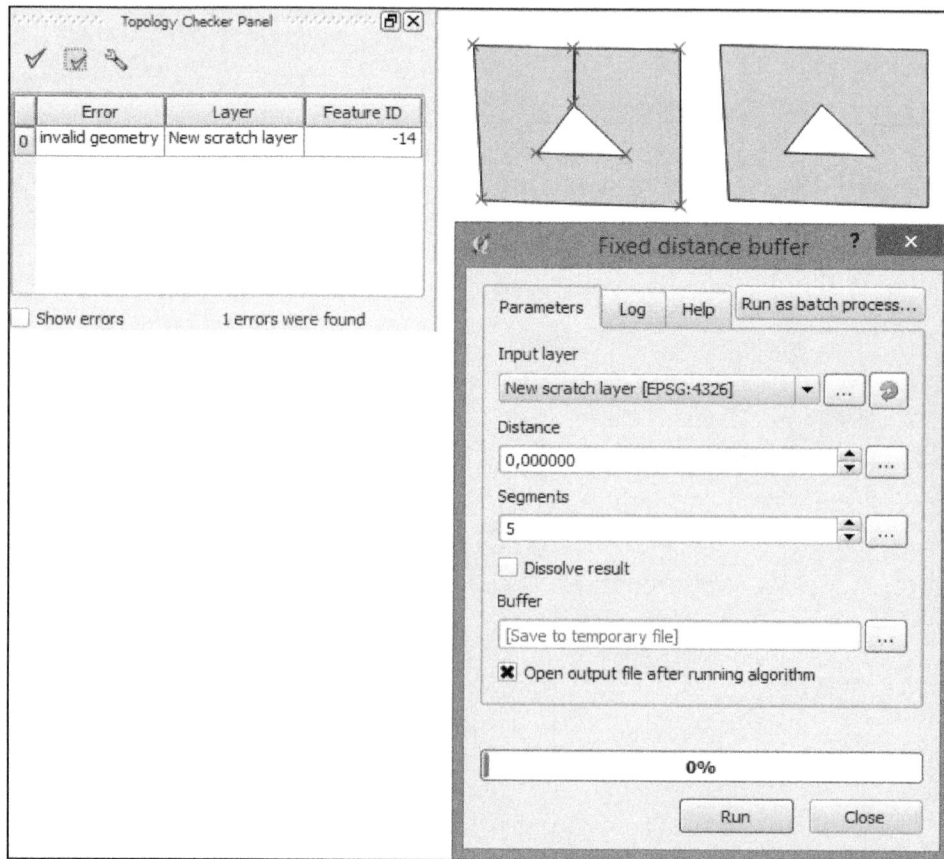

Another common issue that can be fixed automatically is so-called **sliver polygons**. These are small, and often quite thin, polygons that can be the result of spatial processes such as intersection operations. To get rid of these sliver polygons, we can use the **v.clean** tool with the **Cleaning tool** option set to **rmarea** (meaning "remove area"), which is also available through the **Processing Toolbox**. In the example shown in this screenshot, the **Threshold** value of 10000 tells the tool to remove all polygons with an area less than 10,000 square meters by merging them with the neighboring polygon with the longest common boundary:

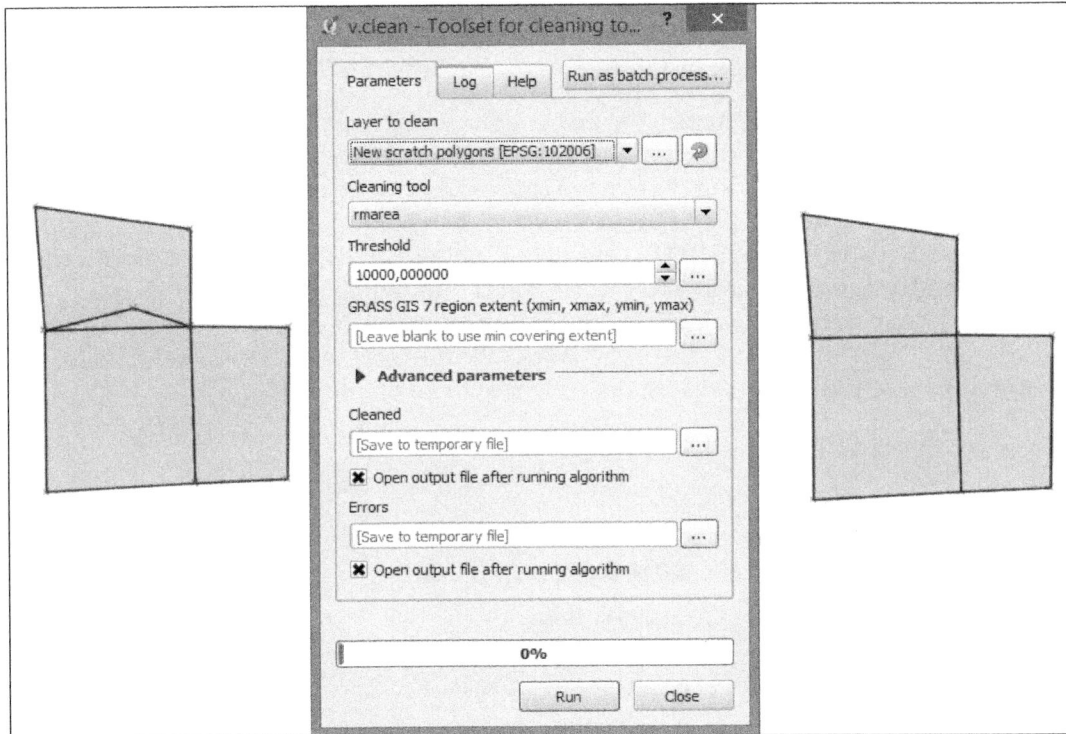

For a thorough introduction and more details on the **Processing Toolbox**, refer to *Chapter 4, Spatial Analysis*.

Adding data to spatial databases

In *Chapter 2, Viewing Spatial Data*, we saw how to view data from spatial databases. Of course, we also want to be able to add data to our databases. This is where the **DB Manager** plugin comes in handy. **DB Manager** is installed by default, and you can find it in the **Database** menu (if **DB Manager** is not visible in the **Database** menu, you might need to activate it in **Plugin Manager**).

The **Tree** panel on the left-hand side of the **DB Manager** dialog lists all available database connections that have been configured so far. Since we have added a connection to the test-2.3.sqlite SpatiaLite database in *Chapter 2, Viewing Spatial Data*, this connection is listed in **DB Manager**, as shown in the next screenshot.

To add new data to this database, we just need to select the connection from the list of available connections and then go to **Table | Import layer/file**. This will open the **Import vector layer** dialog, where we can configure the import settings, such as the name of the **Table** we want to create as well as additional options, including the input data CRS (the **Source SRID** option) and table CRS (the **Target SRID** option). By enabling these CRS options, we can reproject data while importing it. In the example shown in the following screenshot, we import urban areas from a Shapefile and reproject the data from EPSG:4326 (WGS84) to EPSG:32632 (WGS 84 / UTM zone 32N), since this is the CRS used by the already existing tables:

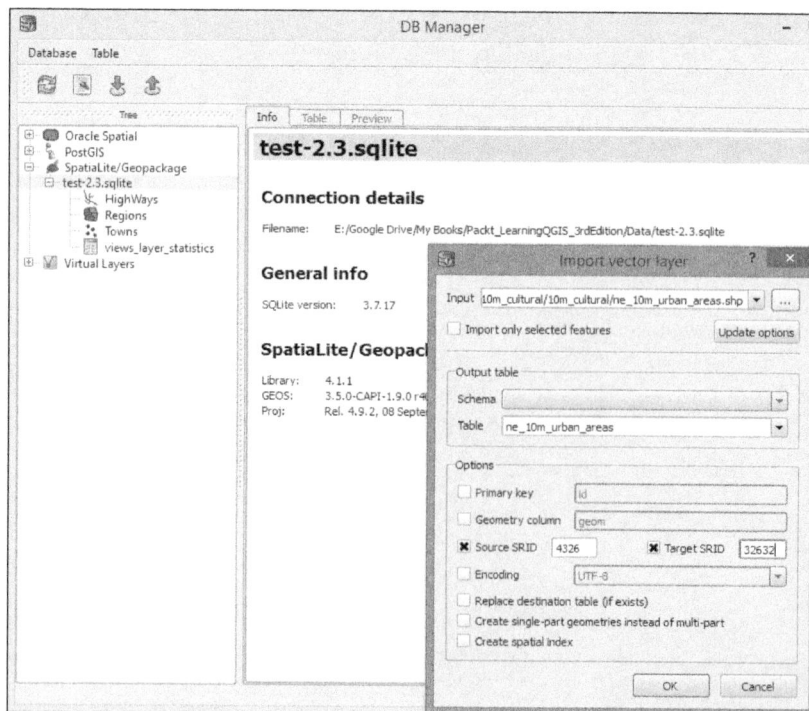

A handy shortcut for importing data into databases is by directly dragging and dropping files from the main window **Browser** panel to a database listed in **DB Manager**. This even works for multiple selected files at once (hold down *Ctrl* on Windows/Ubuntu or *cmd* on Mac to select more than one file in the **Browser** panel). When you drop the files onto the desired database, an **Import vector layer** dialog will appear, where you can configure the import.

Summary

In this chapter, you learned how to create new layers from scratch. We used a selection of tools to create and edit feature geometries in different ways. Then, we went into editing attributes of single features, feature selections, and whole layers. Next, we reprojected both vector and raster layers, and you learned how to convert between different file formats. We also covered tabular data and how it can be loaded and joined to our spatial data. Furthermore, we explored the use of temporary scratch layers and discussed how to check for topological errors in our data and fix them. We finished this chapter with an example of importing new data into a database.

In the following chapter, we will put our data to good use and see how to perform different kinds of spatial analysis on raster and vector data. We will also take a closer look at the **Processing Toolbox**, which has made its first appearance in this chapter. You will learn how to use the tools and combine them to create automated workflows.

4
Spatial Analysis

In this chapter, we will use QGIS to perform many typical geoprocessing and spatial analysis tasks. We will start with raster processing and analysis tasks such as clipping and terrain analysis. We will cover the essentials of converting between raster and vector formats, and then continue with common vector geoprocessing tasks, such as generating heatmaps and calculating area shares within a region. We will also use the Processing modeler to create automated geoprocessing workflows. Finally, we will finish the chapter with examples of how to use the power of spatial databases to analyze spatial data in QGIS.

Analyzing raster data

Raster data, including but not limited to elevation models or remote sensing imagery, is commonly used in many analyses. The following exercises show common raster processing and analysis tasks such as clipping to a certain extent or mask, creating relief and slope rasters from digital elevation models, and using the raster calculator.

Clipping rasters

A common task in raster processing is clipping a raster with a polygon. This task is well covered by the **Clipper** tool located in **Raster | Extraction | Clipper**. This tool supports clipping to a specified **extent** as well as clipping using a polygon **mask** layer, as follows:

- **Extent** can be set manually or by selecting it in the map. To do this, we just click and drag the mouse to open a rectangle in the map area of the main QGIS window.

- A mask layer can be any polygon layer that is currently loaded in the project or any other polygon layer, which can be specified using **Select...**, right next to the **Mask layer** drop-down list.

> If we only want to clip a raster to a certain extent (the current map view extent or any other), we can also use the raster **Save as...** functionality, as shown in *Chapter 3, Data Creation and Editing*.

For a quick exercise, we will clip the hillshade raster (SR_50M_alaska_nad.tif) using the Alaska Shapefile (both from our sample data) as a mask layer. At the bottom of the window, as shown in the following screenshot, we can see the concrete gdalwarp command that QGIS uses to clip the raster. This is very useful if you also want to learn how to use **GDAL**.

> In *Chapter 2, Viewing Spatial Data*, we discussed that GDAL is one of the libraries that QGIS uses to read and process raster data. You can find the documentation of gdalwarp and all other GDAL utility programs at http://www.gdal.org/gdal_utilities.html.

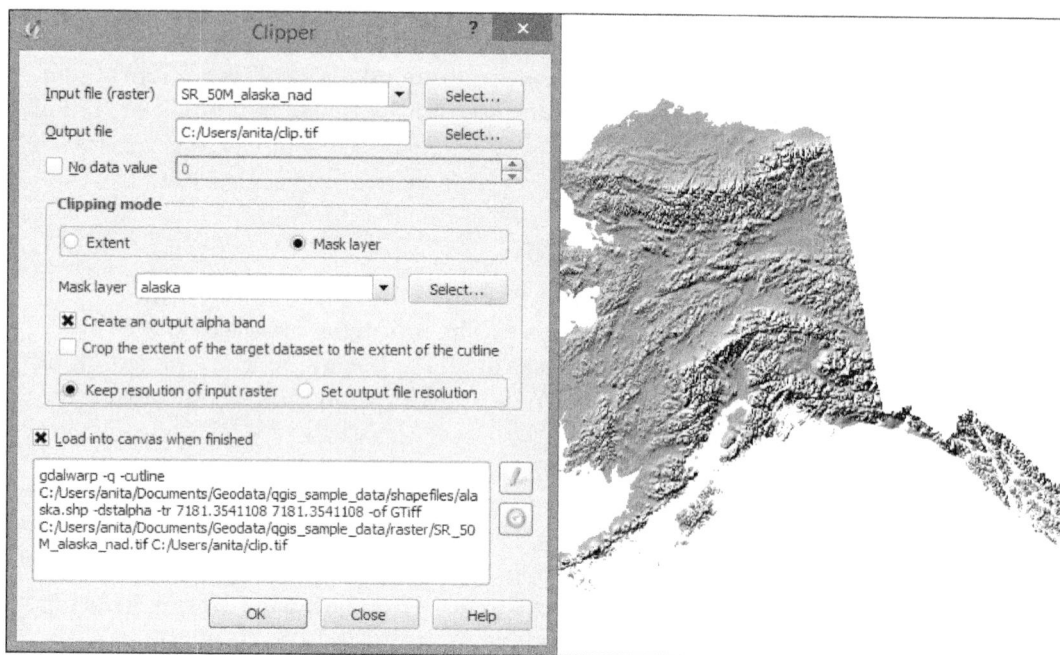

The default **No data value** is the no data value used in the input dataset or **0** if nothing is specified, but we can override it if necessary. Another good option is to **Create an output alpha band**, which will set all areas outside the mask to transparent. This will add an extra band to the output raster that will control the transparency of the rendered raster cells.

A common source of error is forgetting to add the file format extension to the **Output file** path (in our example, .tif for GeoTIFF). Similarly, you can get errors if you try to overwrite an existing file. In such cases, the best way to fix the error is to either choose a different filename or delete the existing file first.

The resulting layer will be loaded automatically, since we have enabled the **Load into canvas when finished** option. QGIS should also automatically recognize the alpha layer that we created, and the raster areas that fall outside the Alaska landmass should be transparent, as shown on the right-hand side in the previous screenshot. If, for some reason, QGIS fails to automatically recognize the alpha layer, we can enable it manually using the **Transparency band** option in the **Transparency** section of the raster layer's properties, as shown in the following screenshot. This dialog is also the right place to specify any **No data value** that we might want to be used:

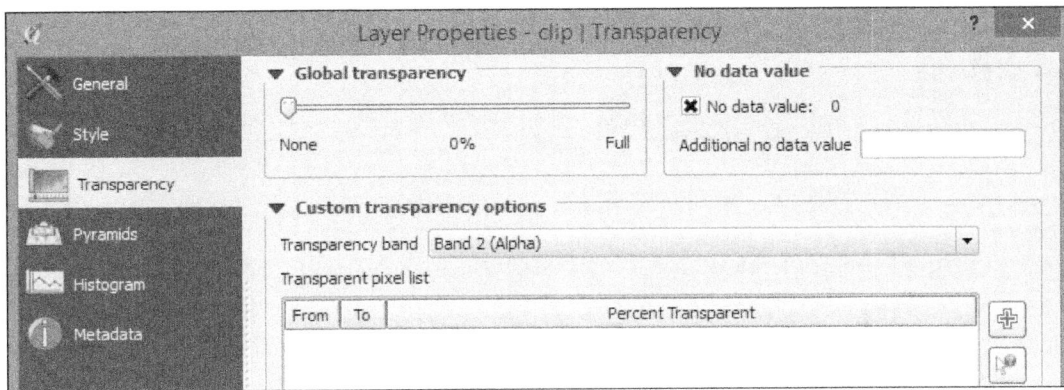

Analyzing elevation/terrain data

To use **terrain analysis tools**, we need an elevation raster. If you don't have any at hand, you can simply download a dataset from the NASA **Shuttle Radar Topography Mission (SRTM)** using http://dwtkns.com/srtm/ or any of the other SRTM download services.

If you want to replicate the results in the following exercise exactly, then get the dataset called srtm_05_01.zip, which covers a small part of Alaska.

Raster **Terrain Analysis** can be used to calculate **Slope**, **Aspect**, **Hillshade**, **Ruggedness Index**, and **Relief** from elevation rasters. These tools are available through the **Raster Terrain Analysis** plugin, which comes with QGIS by default, but we have to enable it in the Plugin Manager in order to make it appear in the **Raster** menu, as shown in the following screenshot:

Terrain Analysis includes the following tools:

- **Slope**: This tool calculates the slope angle for each cell in degrees (based on the first-order derivative estimation).

- **Aspect**: This tool calculates the exposition (in degrees and counterclockwise, starting with 0 for north).

- **Hillshade**: This tool creates a basic hillshade raster with lighted areas and shadows.

- **Relief**: This tool creates a shaded relief map with varying colors for different elevation ranges.

- **Ruggedness Index**: This tool calculates the ruggedness of a terrain, which describes how flat or rocky an area is. The index is computed for each cell using the algorithm presented by Riley and others (1999) by summarizing the elevation changes within a 3 x 3 cell grid.

> The results of terrain analysis steps depend on the resolution of the input elevation data. It is recommendable to use small scale elevation data, with for example, 30 meters x/y resolution, particularly when computing ruggedness.

An important element in all terrain analysis tools is the **Z factor**. The Z factor is used if the x/y units are different from the z (elevation) unit. For example, if we try to create a relief from elevation data where x/y are in degrees and z is in meters, the resulting relief will look grossly exaggerated. The values for the z factor are as follows:

- If x/y and z are either all in meters or all in feet, use the default z factor, 1.0
- If x/y are in degrees and z is in feet, use the z factor 370,400
- If x/y are in degrees and z is in meters, use the z factor 111,120

Since the SRTM rasters are provided in WGS84 EPSG:4326, we need to use a **Z factor** of 111,120 in our exercise. Let's create a relief! The tool can calculate relief color ranges automatically; we just need to click on **Create automatically**, as shown in the following screenshot. Of course, we can still edit the elevation ranges' upper and lower bounds as well as the colors by double-clicking on the respective list entry:

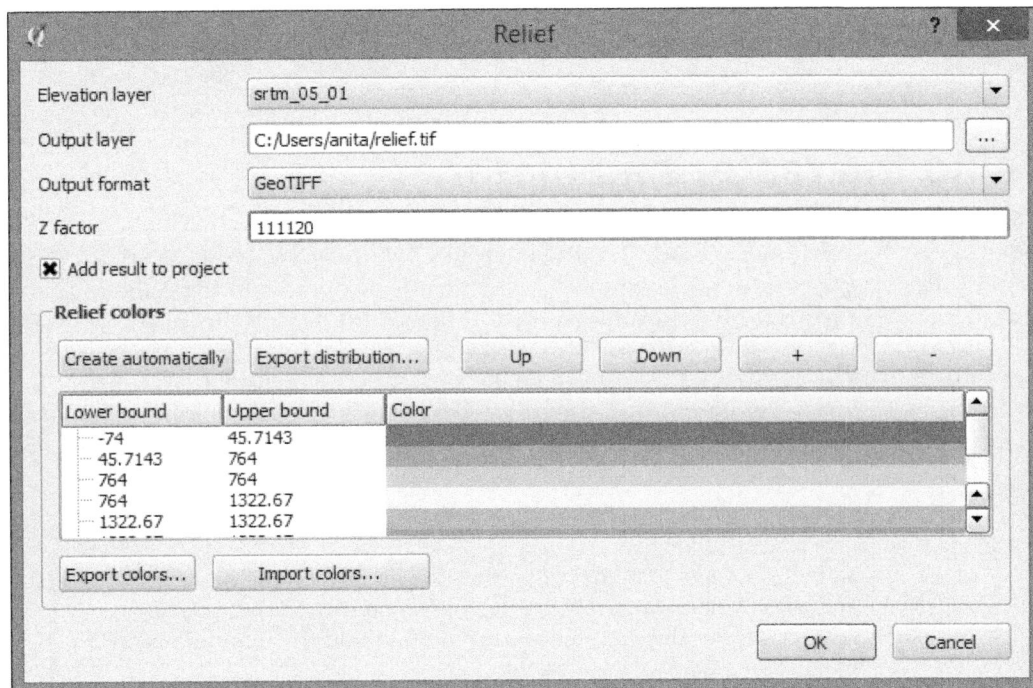

While relief maps are three-banded rasters, which are primarily used for visualization purposes, slope rasters are a common intermediate step in spatial analysis workflows. We will now create a slope raster that we can use in our example workflow through the following sections. The resulting slope raster will be loaded in grayscale automatically, as shown in this screenshot:

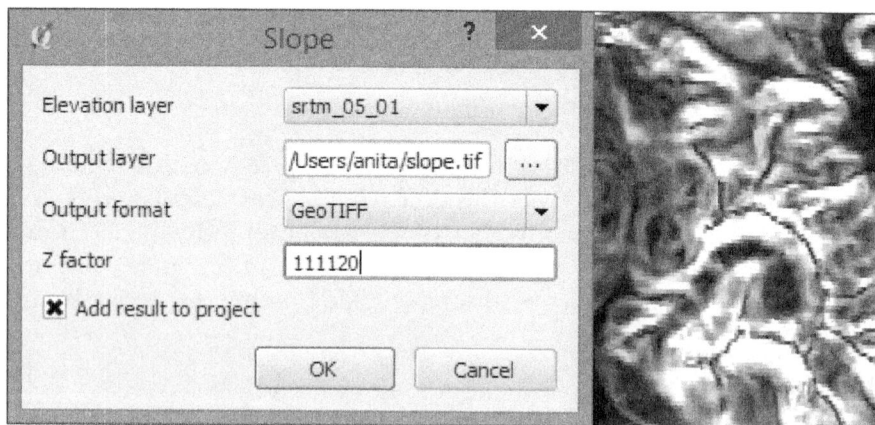

Using the raster calculator

With the **Raster calculator**, we can create a new raster layer based on the values in one or more rasters that are loaded in the current QGIS project. To access it, go to **Raster | Raster Calculator**. All available raster bands are presented in a list in the top-left corner of the dialog using the `raster_name@band_number` format.

Continuing from our previous exercise in which we created a slope raster, we can, for example, find areas at elevations above 1,000 meters and with a slope of less than 5 degrees using the following expression:

```
"srtm_05_01@1" > 1000 AND "slope@1" < 5
```

> You might have to adjust the values depending on the dataset you are using. Check out the *Accessing raster and vector layer statistics* section later in this chapter to learn how to find the minimum and maximum values in your raster.

Cells that meet both criteria of high elevation and evenness will be assigned a value of 1 in the resulting raster, while cells that fail to meet even one criterion will be set to 0. The only bigger areas with a value of 1 are found in the southern part of the raster layer. You can see a section of the resulting raster (displayed in black over the relief layer) to the right-hand side of the following screenshot:

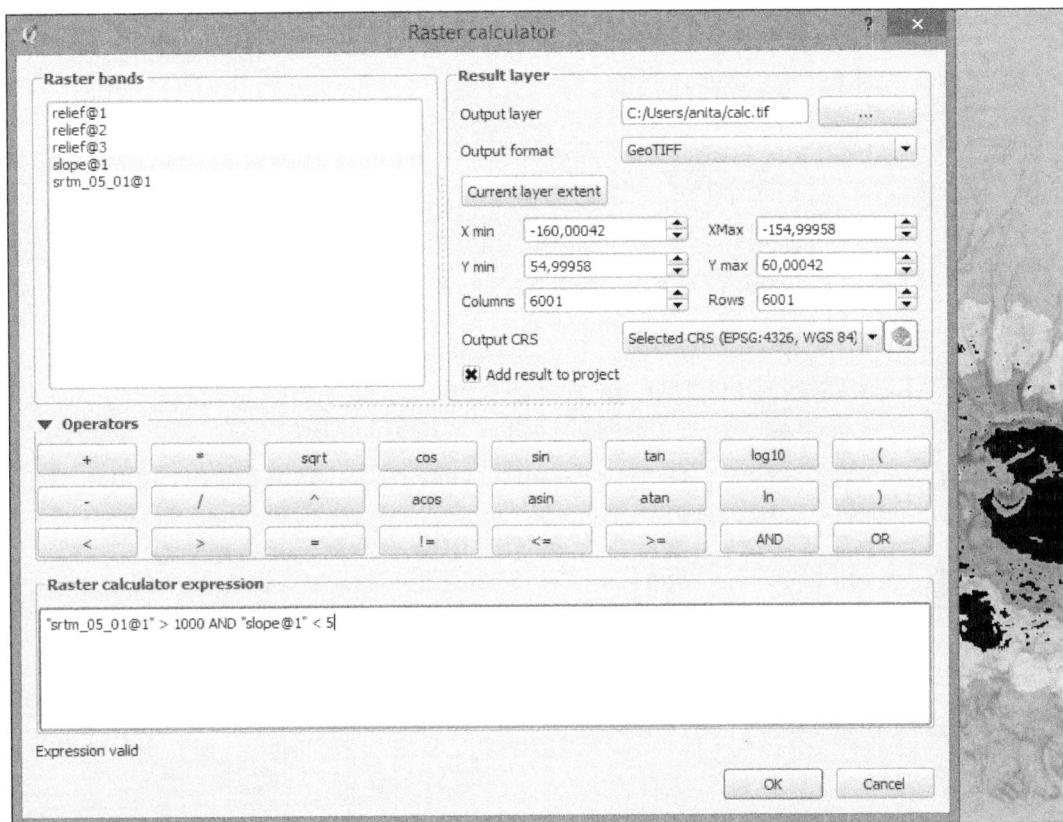

Another typical use case is reclassifying a raster. For example, we might want to reclassify the landcover.img raster in our sample data so that all areas with a landcover class from 1 to 5 get the value 100, areas from 6 to 10 get 101, and areas over 11 get a new value of 102. We will use the following code for this:

```
("landcover@1" > 0 AND "landcover@1" <= 6 ) * 100
+ ("landcover@1" >= 7 AND "landcover@1" <= 10 ) * 101
+ ("landcover@1" >= 11 ) * 102
```

The preceding raster calculator expression has three parts, each consisting of a check and a multiplication. For each cell, only one of the three checks can be true, and true is represented as 1. Therefore, if a `landcover` cell has a value of 4, the first check will be true and the expression will evaluate to `1*100 + 0*101 + 0*102 = 100`.

Combining raster and vector data

Some analyses require a combination of raster and vector data. In the following exercises, we will use both raster and vector datasets to explain how to convert between these different data types, how to access layer and zonal statistics, and finally how to create a raster heatmap from points.

Converting between rasters and vectors

Tools for converting between raster and vector formats can be accessed by going to **Raster | Conversion**. These tools are called **Rasterize (Vector to raster)** and **Polygonize (Raster to vector)**. Like the raster clipper tool that we used before, these tools are also based on **GDAL** and display the command at the bottom of the dialog.

Polygonize converts a raster into a polygon layer. Depending on the size of the raster, the conversion can take some time. When the process is finished, QGIS will notify us with a popup. For a quick test, we can, for example, convert the reclassified `landcover` raster to polygons. The resulting vector polygon layer contains multiple polygonal features with a single attribute, which we name `lc`; it depends on the original raster value, as shown in the following screenshot:

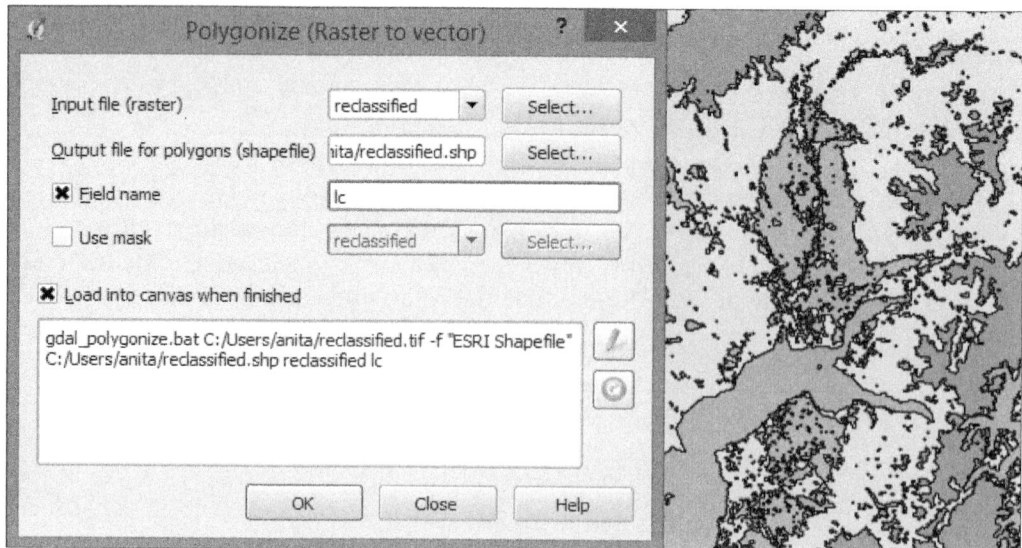

Using the **Rasterize** tool is very similar to using the **Polygonize** tool. The only difference is that we get to specify the size of the resulting raster in pixels/cells. We can also specify the attribute field, which will provide input for the raster cell value, as shown in the next screenshot. In this case, the **cat** attribute of our `alaska.shp` dataset is rather meaningless, but you get the idea of how the tool works:

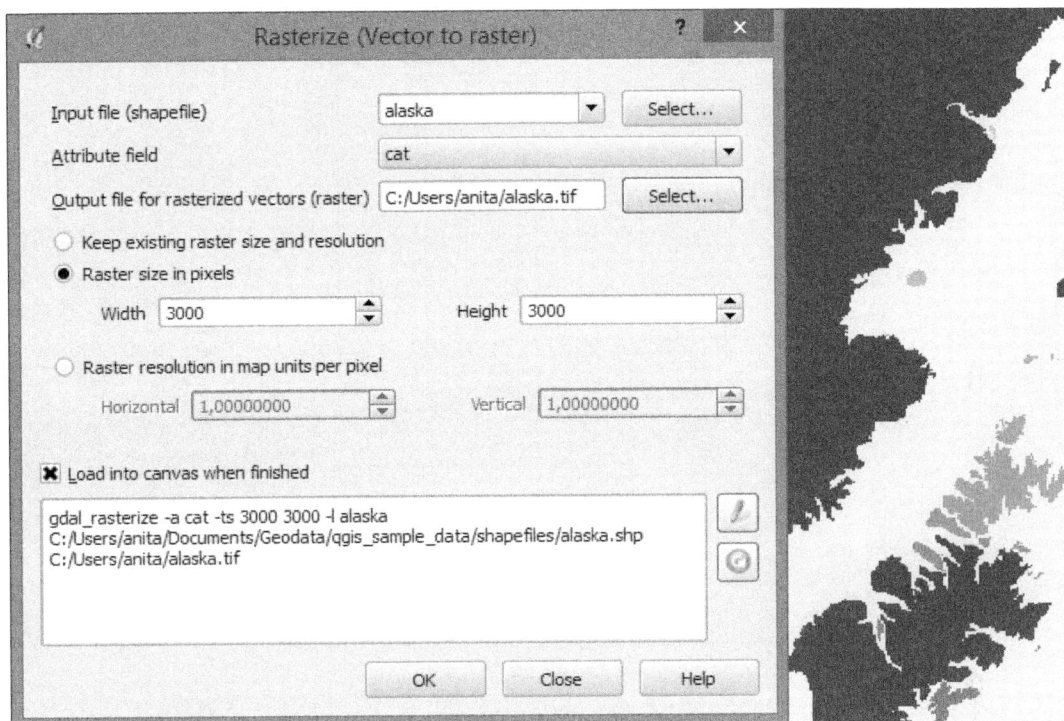

Accessing raster and vector layer statistics

Whenever we get a new dataset, it is useful to examine the layer statistics to get an idea of the data it contains, such as the minimum and maximum values, number of features, and much more. QGIS offers a variety of tools to explore these values.

Raster layer statistics are readily available in the **Layer Properties** dialog, specifically in the following tabs:

- **Metadata**: This tab shows the minimum and maximum cell values as well as the mean and the standard deviation of the cell values.

- **Histogram**: This tab presents the distribution of raster values. Use the mouse to zoom into the histogram to see the details. For example, the following screenshot shows the zoomed-in version of the histogram for our `landcover` dataset:

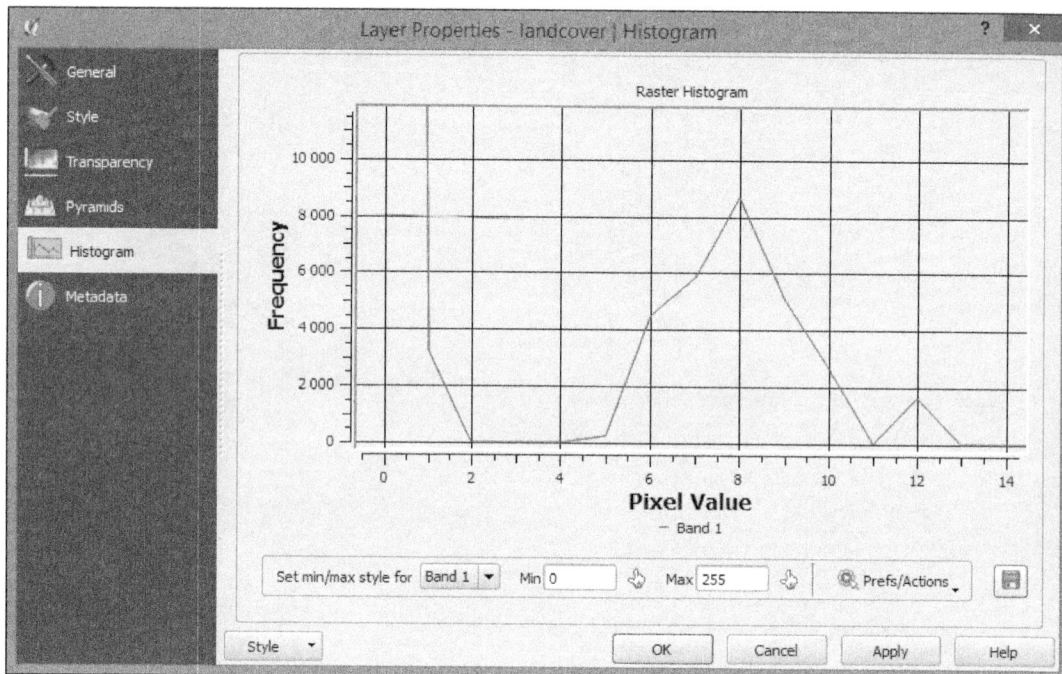

For **vector layers**, we can get summary statistics using two tools in **Vector | Analysis Tools**:

- **Basics statistics** is very useful for numerical fields. It calculates parameters such as mean and median, min and max, the feature count n, the number of unique values, and so on for all features of a layer or for selected features only.

- **List unique values** is useful for getting all unique values of a certain field.

In both tools, we can easily copy the results using *Ctrl + C* and paste them in a text file or spreadsheet. The following image shows examples of exploring the contents of our `airports` sample dataset:

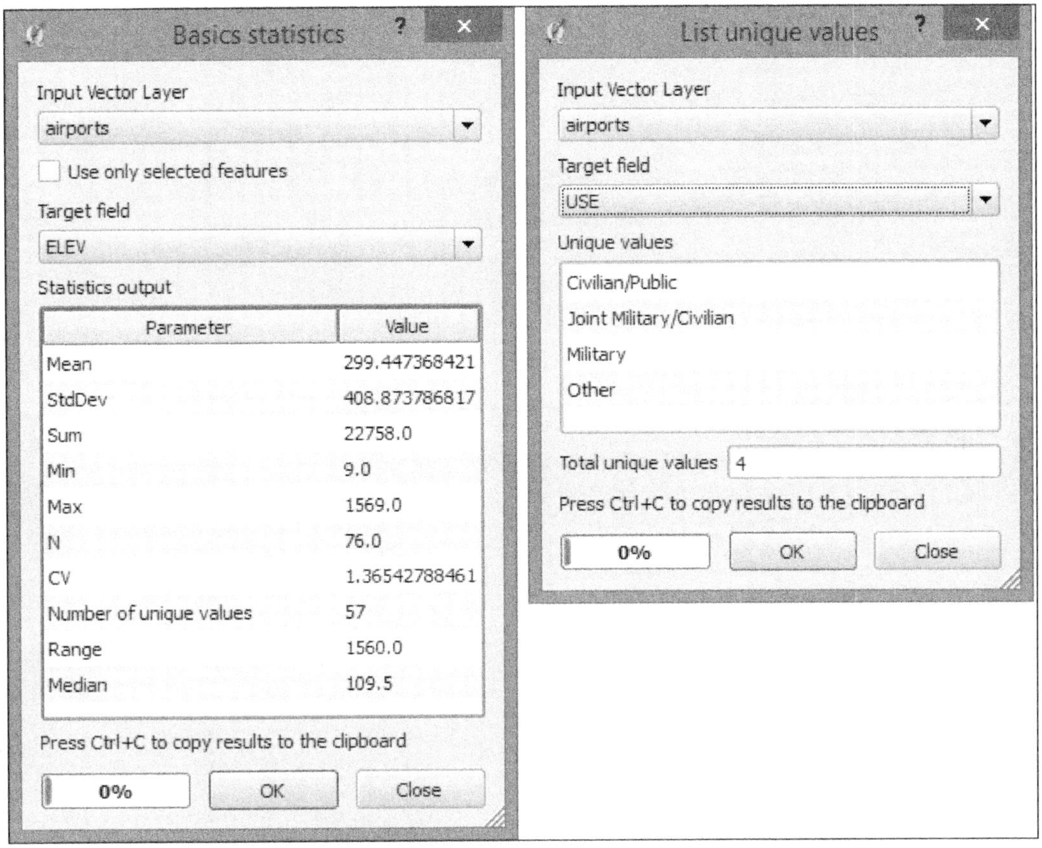

An alternative to the **Basics statistics** tool is the **Statistics Panel**, which you can activate by going to **View | Panels | Statistics Panel**. As shown in the following screenshot, this panel can be customized to show exactly those statistics that you are interested in:

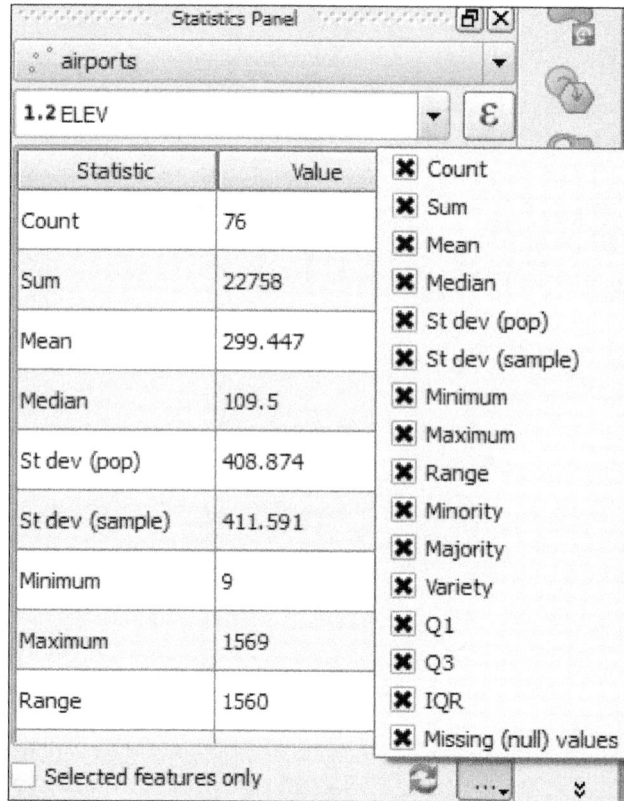

Computing zonal statistics

Instead of computing raster statistics for the entire layer, it is sometimes necessary to compute statistics for selected regions. This is what the **Zonal statistics plugin** is good for. This plugin is installed by default and can be enabled in the **Plugin Manager**.

For example, we can compute elevation statistics for areas around each airport using srtm_05_01.tif and airports.shp from our sample data:

1. First, we create the analysis areas around each airport using the **Vector | Geoprocessing Tools | Buffer(s)** tool and a buffer size of 10,000 feet.

2. Before we can use the **Zonal statistics plugin**, it is important to notice that the buffer layer and the elevation raster use two different **CRS** (short for **Coordinate Reference System**). If we simply went ahead, the resulting statistics would be either empty or wrong. Therefore, we need to reproject the buffer layer to the raster CRS (WGS84 EPSG:4326, for details on how to change a layer CRS, see *Chapter 3, Data Creation and Editing*, in the *Reprojecting and converting vector and raster data* section).

3. Now we can compute the statistics for the analysis areas using the **Zonal Statistics** tool, which can be accessed by going to **Raster | Zonal statistics**. Here, we can configure the desired **Output column prefix** (in our example, we have chosen `elev`, which is short for elevation) and the **Statistics to calculate** (for example, `Mean`, `Minimum`, and `Maximum`), as shown in the following screenshot:

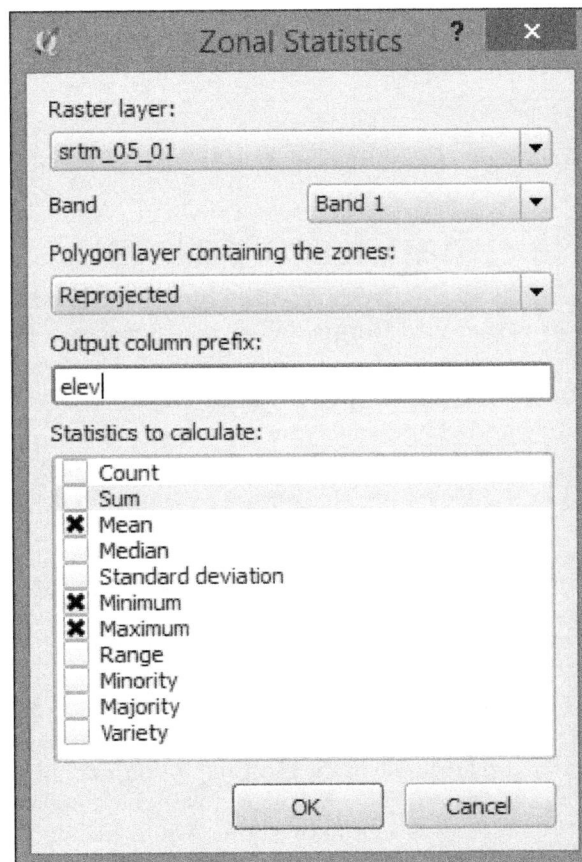

4. After you click on **OK**, the selected statistics are appended to the polygon layer attribute table, as shown in the following screenshot. We can see that **Big Mountain AFS** is the airport with the highest mean elevation among the four airports that fall within the extent of our elevation raster:

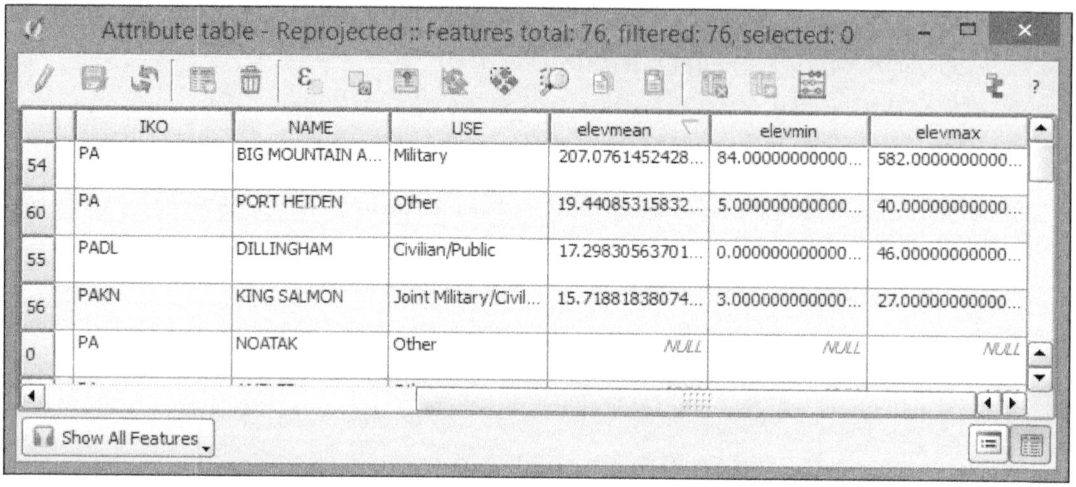

	IKO	NAME	USE	elevmean	elevmin	elevmax
54	PA	BIG MOUNTAIN A...	Military	207.0761452428...	84.00000000000...	582.0000000000...
60	PA	PORT HEIDEN	Other	19.44085315832...	5.000000000000...	40.00000000000...
55	PADL	DILLINGHAM	Civilian/Public	17.29830563701...	0.000000000000...	46.00000000000...
56	PAKN	KING SALMON	Joint Military/Civil...	15.71881838074...	3.000000000000...	27.00000000000...
0	PA	NOATAK	Other	*NULL*	*NULL*	*NULL*

Attribute table - Reprojected :: Features total: 76, filtered: 76, selected: 0

Show All Features

Creating a heatmap from points

Heatmaps are great for visualizing a distribution of points. To create them, QGIS provides a simple-to-use **Heatmap Plugin**, which we have to activate in the **Plugin Manager**, and then we can access it by going to **Raster** | **Heatmap** | **Heatmap**. The plugin offers different **Kernel shapes** to choose from. The kernel is a moving window of a specific size and shape that moves over an area of points to calculate their local density. Additionally, the plugin allows us to control the output heatmap raster size in cells (using the **Rows** and **Columns** settings) as well as the cell size.

> **Radius** determines the distance around each point at which the point will have an influence. Therefore, smaller radius values result in heatmaps that show finer and smaller details, while larger values result in smoother heatmaps with fewer details.
>
> Additionally, **Kernel shape** controls the rate at which the influence of a point decreases with increasing distance from the point. The kernel shapes that are available in the **Heatmap plugin** are listed in the following screenshot. For example, a Triweight kernel creates smaller hotspots than the Epanechnikov kernel. For formal definitions of the kernel functions, refer to http://en.wikipedia.org/wiki/Kernel_(statistics).

The following screenshot shows us how to create a heatmap of our `airports.shp` sample with a kernel radius of 300,000 layer units, which in the case of our airport data is in feet:

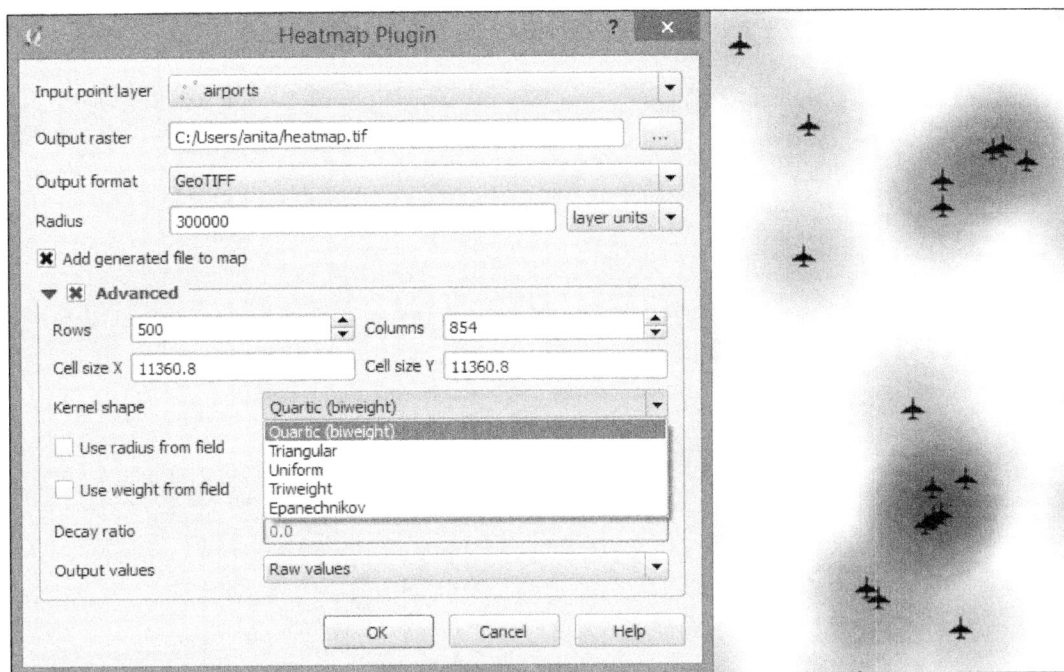

By default, the heatmap output will be rendered using the **Singleband gray** render type (with low raster values in black and high values in white). To change the style to something similar to what you saw in the previous screenshot, you can do the following:

1. Change the heatmap raster layer render type to **Singleband pseudocolor**.

2. In the **Generate new color map section** on the right-hand side of the dialog, select a color map you like, for example, the **PuRd** color map, as shown in the next screenshot.

3. You can enter the **Min** and **Max** values for the color map manually, or have them computed by clicking on **Load** in the **Load min/max values** section.

> When loading the raster min/max values, keep an eye on the settings. To get the actual min/max values of a raster layer, enable **Min/max**, **Full Extent**, and **Actual (slower) Accuracy**. If you only want the min/max values of the raster section that is currently displayed on the map, use **Current Extent** instead.

4. Click on **Classify** to add the color map classes to the list on the left-hand side of the dialog.

5. Optionally, we can change the color of the first entry (for value 0) to white (by double-clicking on the color in the list) to get a smooth transition from the white map background to our heatmap.

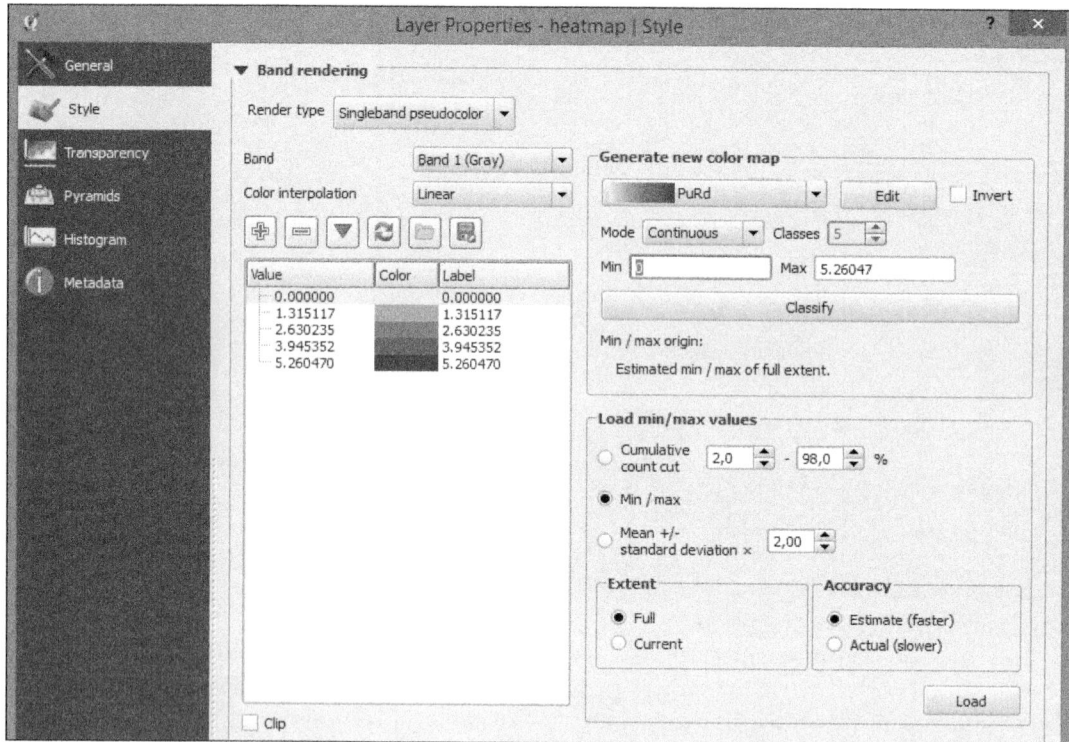

Vector and raster analysis with Processing

The most comprehensive set of spatial analysis tools is accessible via the **Processing plugin**, which we can enable in the **Plugin Manager**. When this plugin is enabled, we find a **Processing** menu, where we can activate the **Toolbox**, as shown in the following screenshot. In the toolbox, it is easy to find spatial analysis tools by their name thanks to the dynamic **Search** box at the top. This makes finding tools in the toolbox easier than in the **Vector** or **Raster** menu. Another advantage of getting accustomed to the Processing tools is that they can be automated in Python and in geoprocessing models.

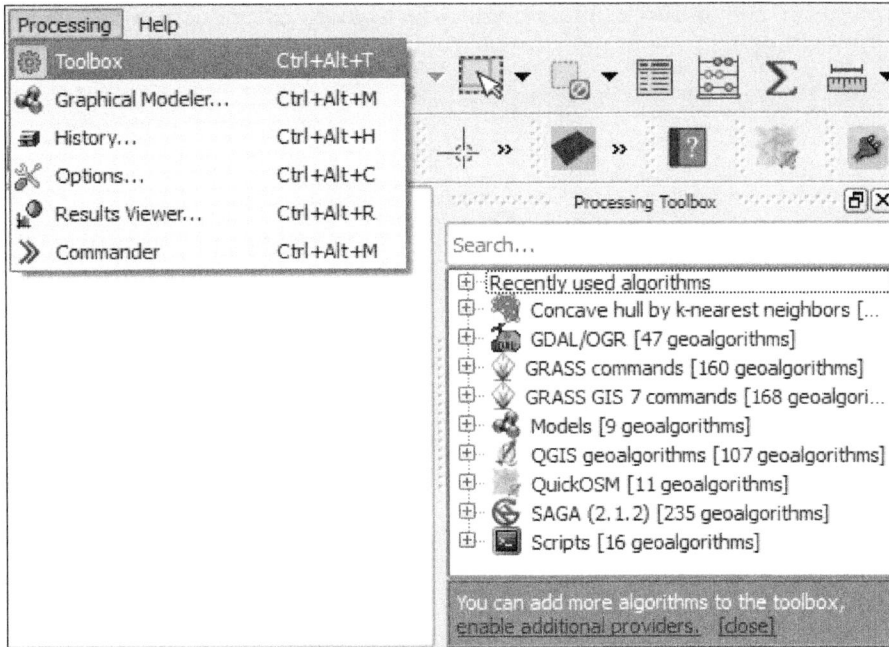

In the following sections, we will cover a selection of the available geoprocessing tools and see how we can use the modeler to automate our tasks.

Finding nearest neighbors

Finding **nearest neighbors**, for example, the airport nearest to a populated place, is a common task in geoprocessing. To find the nearest neighbor and create connections between input features and their nearest neighbor in another layer, we can use the **Distance to nearest hub** tool.

As shown in the next screenshot, we use the populated places as **Source points layer** and the airports as the **Destination hubs layer**. The **Hub layer name attribute** will be added to the result's attribute table to identify the nearest feature. Therefore, we select NAME to add the airport name to the populated places. There are two options for **Output shape type**:

- **Point**: This option creates a point output layer with all points of the source point layer, with new attributes for the nearest hub feature and the distance to it

- **Line to hub**: This option creates a line output layer with connections between all points of the source point layer and their corresponding nearest hub feature

It is recommended that you use **Layer units** as **Measurement unit** to avoid potential issues with wrong measurements:

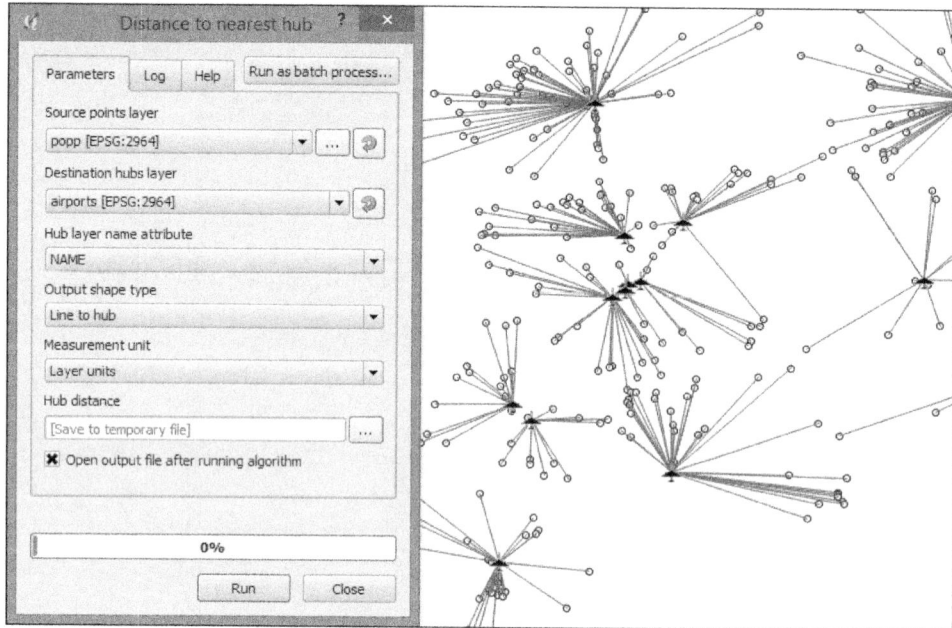

Converting between points, lines, and polygons

It is often necessary to be able to convert between points, lines, and polygons, for example, to create lines from a series of points, or to extract the nodes of polygons and create a new point layer out of them. There are many tools that cover these different use cases. The following table provides an overview of the tools that are available in the Processing toolbox for conversion between points, lines, and polygons:

	To points	To lines	To polygons
From points		Points to path	Convex hull
			Concave hull
From lines	Extract nodes		Lines to polygons
			Convex hull
From polygons	Extract nodes	Polygons to lines	
	Polygon centroids		
	(Random points inside a polygon)		

In general, it is easier to convert more complex representations to simpler ones (polygons to lines, polygons to points, or lines to points) than conversion in the other direction (points to lines, points to polygons, or lines to polygons). Here is a short overview of these tools:

- **Extract nodes**: This is a very straightforward tool. It takes one input layer with lines or polygons and creates a point layer that contains all the input geometry nodes. The resulting points contain all the attributes of the original line or polygon feature.

- **Polygon centroids**: This tool creates one centroid per polygon or multipolygon. It is worth noting that it does not ensure that the centroid falls within the polygon. For concave polygons, multipolygons, and polygons with holes, the centroid can therefore fall outside the polygon.

- **Random points inside polygon**: This tool creates a certain number of points at random locations inside the polygon.

- **Points to path**: To be able to create lines from points, the point layer needs attributes that identify the line (**Group field**) and the order of points in the line (**Order field**), as shown in this screenshot:

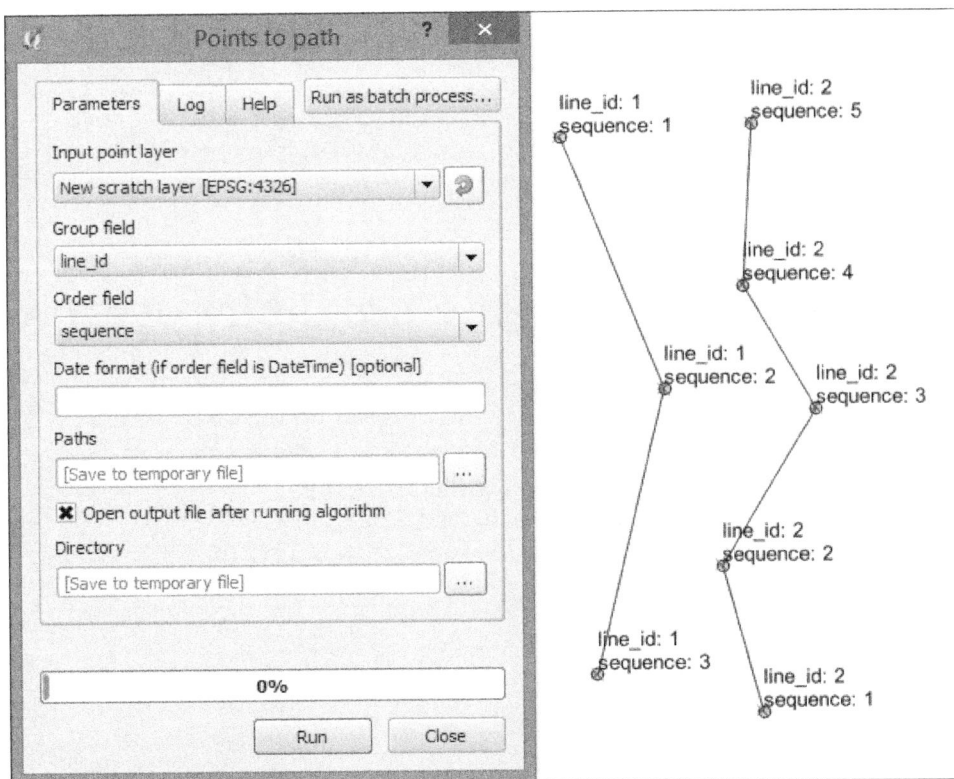

- **Convex hull**: This tool creates a convex hull around the input points or lines. The convex hull can be imagined as an area that contains all the input points as well as all the connections between the input points.

- **Concave hull**: This tool creates a concave hull around the input points. The concave hull is a polygon that represents the area occupied by the input points. The concave hull is equal to or smaller than the convex hull. In this tool, we can control the level of detail of the concave hull by changing the **Threshold** parameter between 0 (very detailed) and 1 (which is equivalent to the convex hull). The following screenshot shows a comparison between convex and concave hulls (with the threshold set to 0.3) around our airport data:

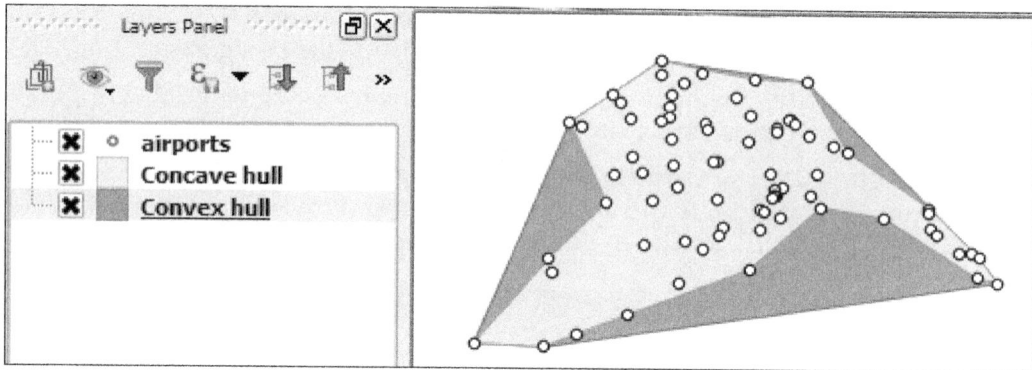

- **Lines to polygon**: Finally, this tool can create polygons from lines that enclose an area. Make sure that there are no gaps between the lines. Otherwise, it will not work.

Identifying features in the proximity of other features

One common spatial analysis task is to identify features in the proximity of certain other features. One example would be to find all airports near rivers. Using `airports.shp` and `majrivers.shp` from our sample data, we can find `airports` within 5,000 feet of a river by using a combination of the **Fixed distance buffer** and **Select by location** tools. Use the search box to find the tools in the Processing Toolbox. The tool configurations for this example are shown in the following screenshot:

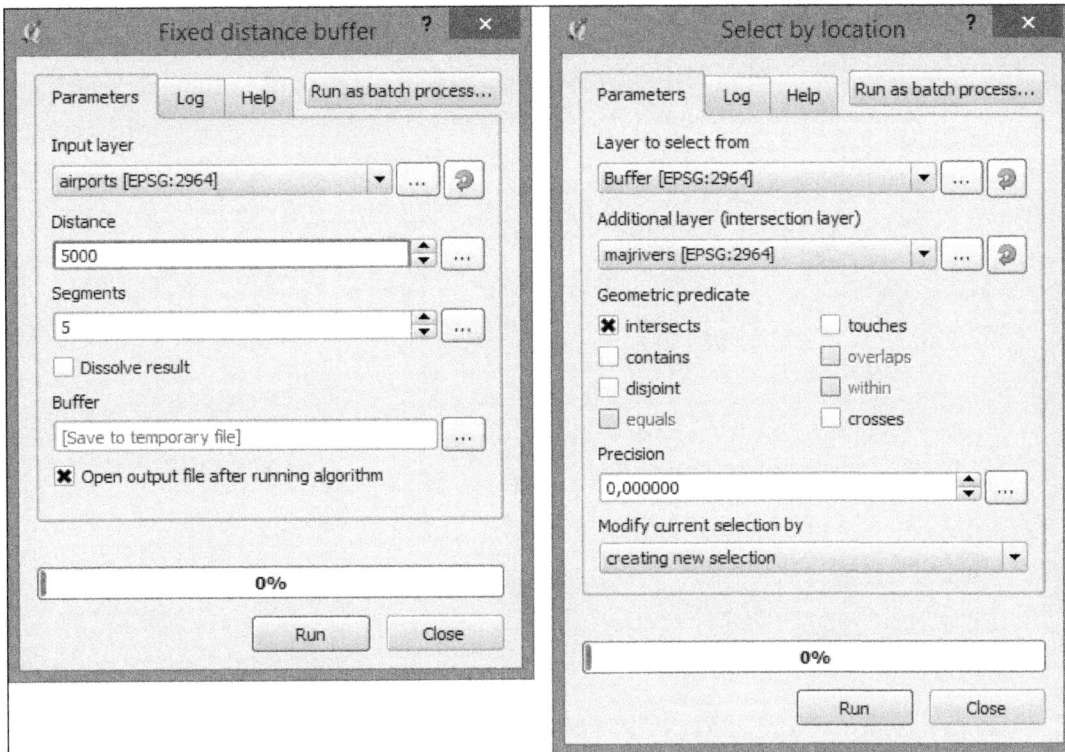

After buffering the airport point locations, the **Select by location** tool selects all the airport buffers that intersect a river. As a result, 14 out of the 76 airports are selected. This information is displayed in the information area at the bottom of the QGIS main window, as shown in this screenshot:

14 feature(s) selected on layer Buffer.

If you ever forget which settings you used or need to check whether you have used the correct input layer, you can go to **Processing** | **History**. The **ALGORITHM** section lists all the algorithms that we have been running as well as the used settings, as shown in the following screenshot:

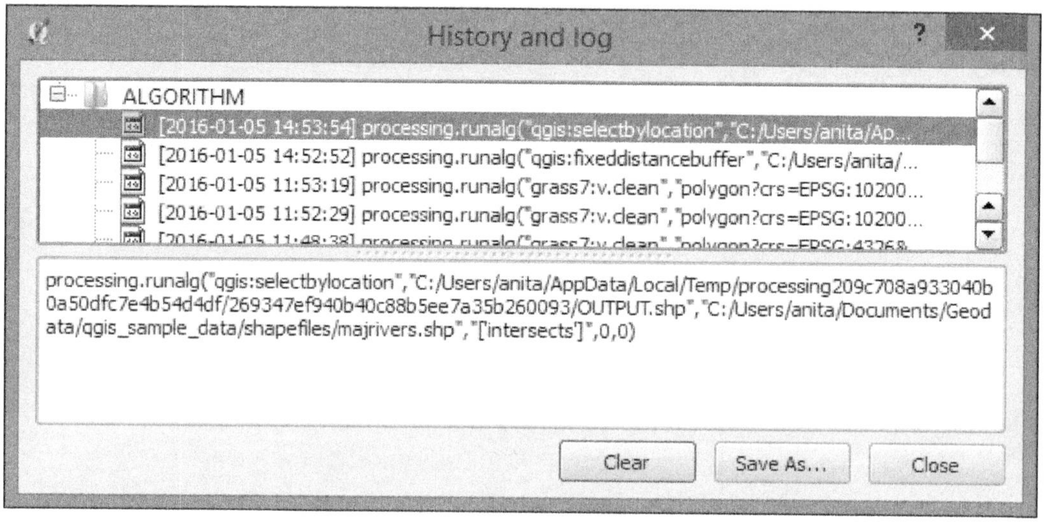

The commands listed under **ALGORITHM** can also be used to call Processing tools from the QGIS Python console, which can be activated by going to **Plugins** | **Python Console**. The Python commands shown in the following screenshot run the buffer algorithm (`processing.runalg`) and load the result into the map (`processing.load`):

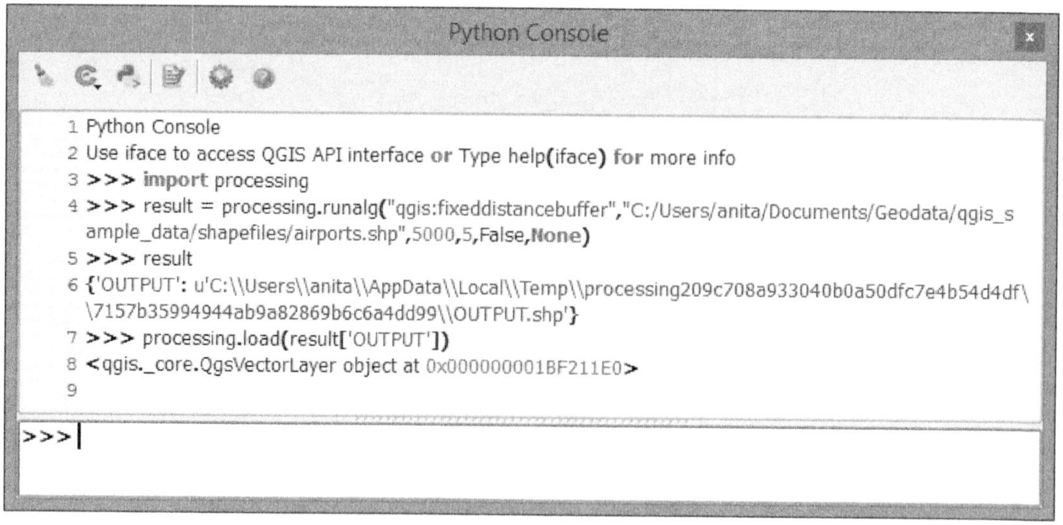

Sampling a raster at point locations

Another common task is to sample a raster at specific point locations. Using Processing, we can solve this problem with a **GRASS** tool called v.sample. To use GRASS tools, make sure that GRASS is installed and Processing is configured correctly under **Processing | Options and configuration**. On an OSGeo4W default system, the configuration will look like what is shown here:

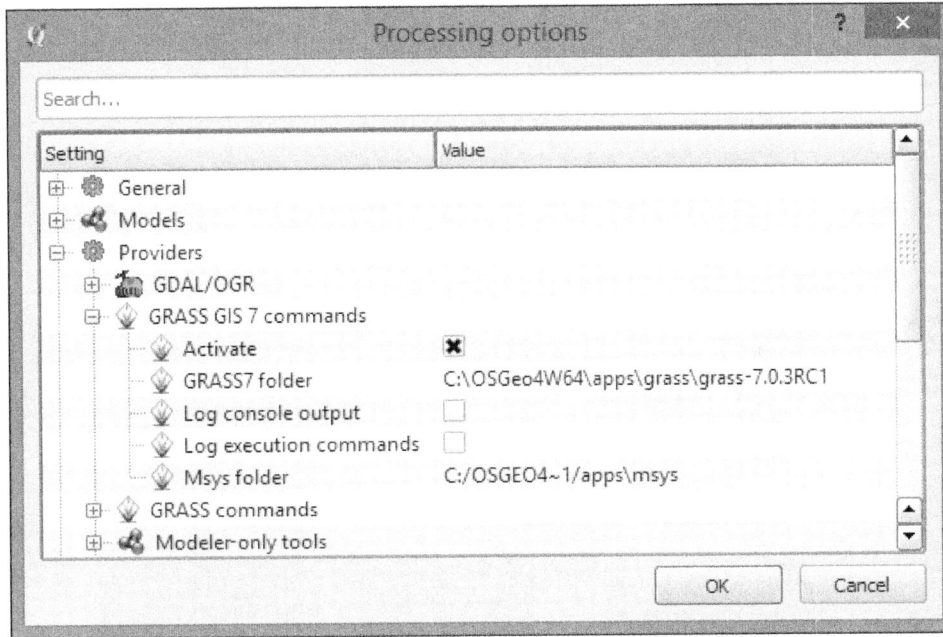

> At the time of writing this book, GRASS 7.0.3RC1 is available in OSGeo4W. As shown in the previous screenshot, there is also support for the previous GRASS version 6.x, and Processing can be configured to use its algorithms as well. In the toolbox, you will find the algorithms under **GRASS GIS 7 commands** and **GRASS commands** (for GRASS 6.x).

For this exercise, let's imagine we want to sample the **landcover** layer at the airport locations of our sample data. All we have to do is specify the vector layer containing the sample points and the raster layer that should be sampled. For this example, we can leave all other settings at their default values, as shown in the following screenshot. The tool not only samples the raster but also compares point attributes with the sampled raster value. However, we don't need this comparison in our current example:

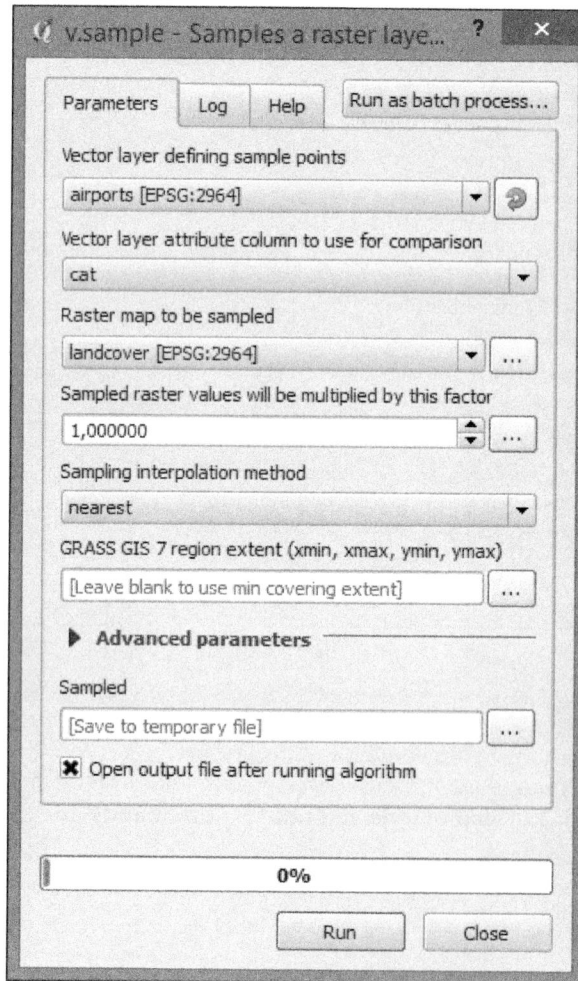

Mapping density with hexagonal grids

Mapping the density of points using a hexagonal grid has become quite a popular alternative to creating heatmaps. Processing offers us a fast way to create such an analysis. There is already a pre-made script called **Hex grid from layer bounds**, which is available through the Processing scripts collection and can be downloaded using the **Get scripts from on-line scripts collection** tool. As you can see in the following screenshot, you just need to enable the script by ticking the checkbox and clicking OK:

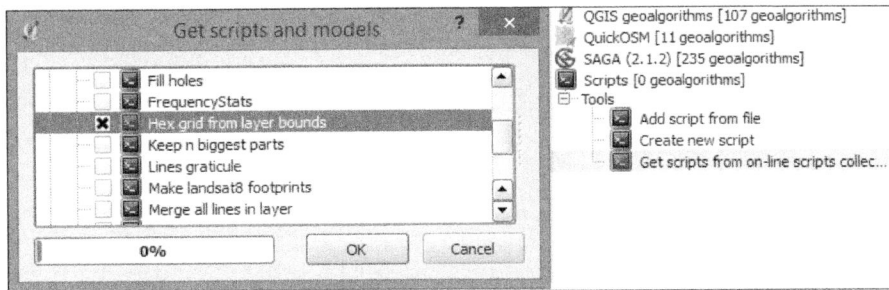

Then, we can use this script to create a hexagonal grid that covers all points in the input layer. The dataset of populated places (popp.shp), is a good sample dataset for this exercise. Once the grid is ready, we can run **Count points in polygon** to calculate the statistics. The number of points will be stored in the **NUMPOINTS** column if you use the settings shown in the following screenshot:

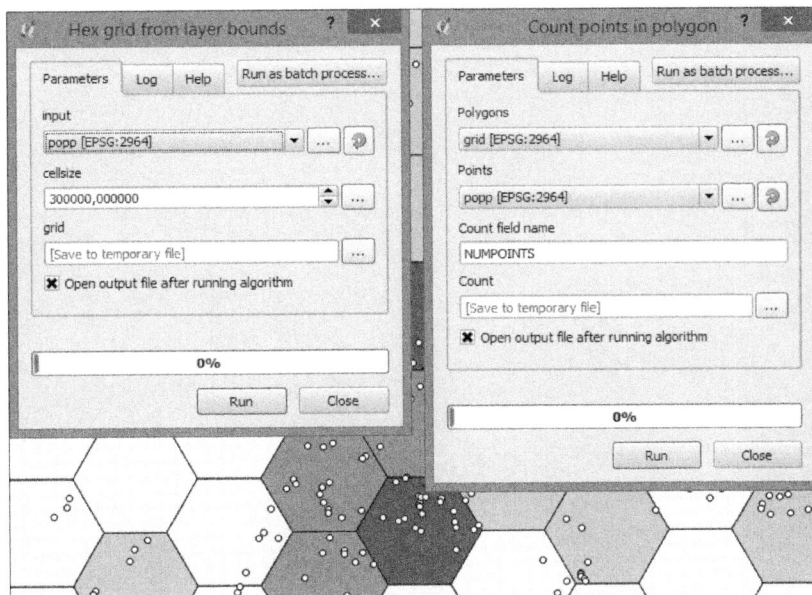

Calculating area shares within a region

Another spatial analysis task we often encounter is calculating area shares within a certain region, for example, landcover shares along one specific river. Using `majrivers.shp` and `trees.shp`, we can calculate the share of wooded area in a 10,000-foot-wide strip of land along the Susitna River:

1. We first define the analysis region by selecting the river and buffering it.

> QGIS Processing will only apply buffers to the selected features of the input layer. This default behavior can be changed under **Processing | Options and configuration** by disabling the **Use only selected features** option. For the following examples, please leave the option enabled.

   To select the Susitna River, we use the **Select by attribute** tool. After running the tool, you should see that our river of interest is selected and highlighted.

2. Then we can use the **Fixed distance buffer** tool to get the area within 5,000 feet along the river. Note that the **Dissolve result** option should be enabled to ensure that the buffer result is one continuous polygon, as shown in the following screenshot:

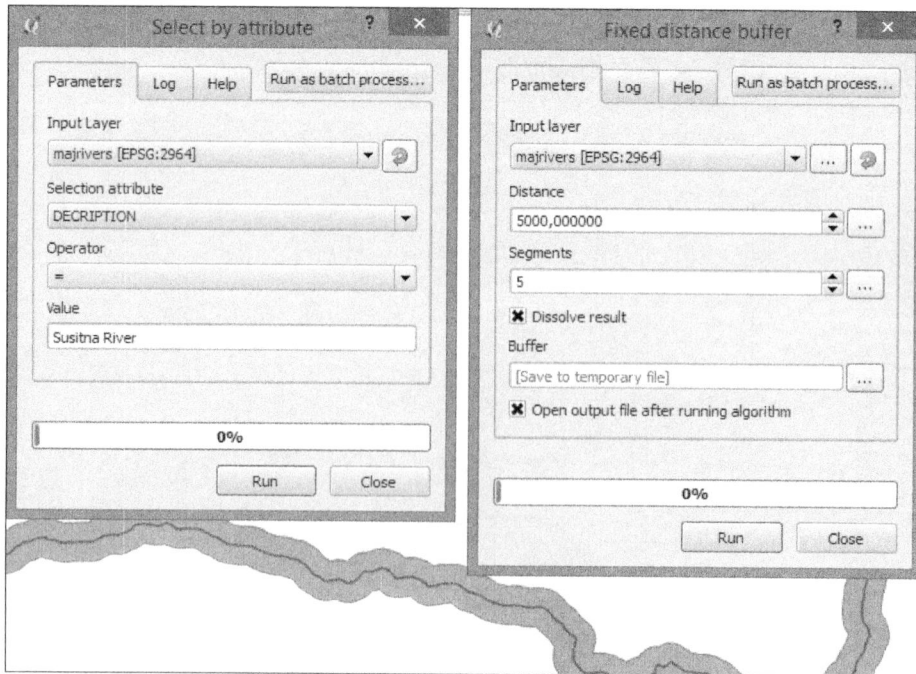

3. Next, we calculate the size of the strip of land around our river. This can be done using the **Export/Add geometry columns** tool, which adds the area and perimeter to the attribute table.

4. Then, we can calculate the **Intersection** between the area along the river and the wooded areas in `trees.shp`, as shown in the following screenshot. The result of this operation is a layer that contains only those wooded areas within the river buffer.

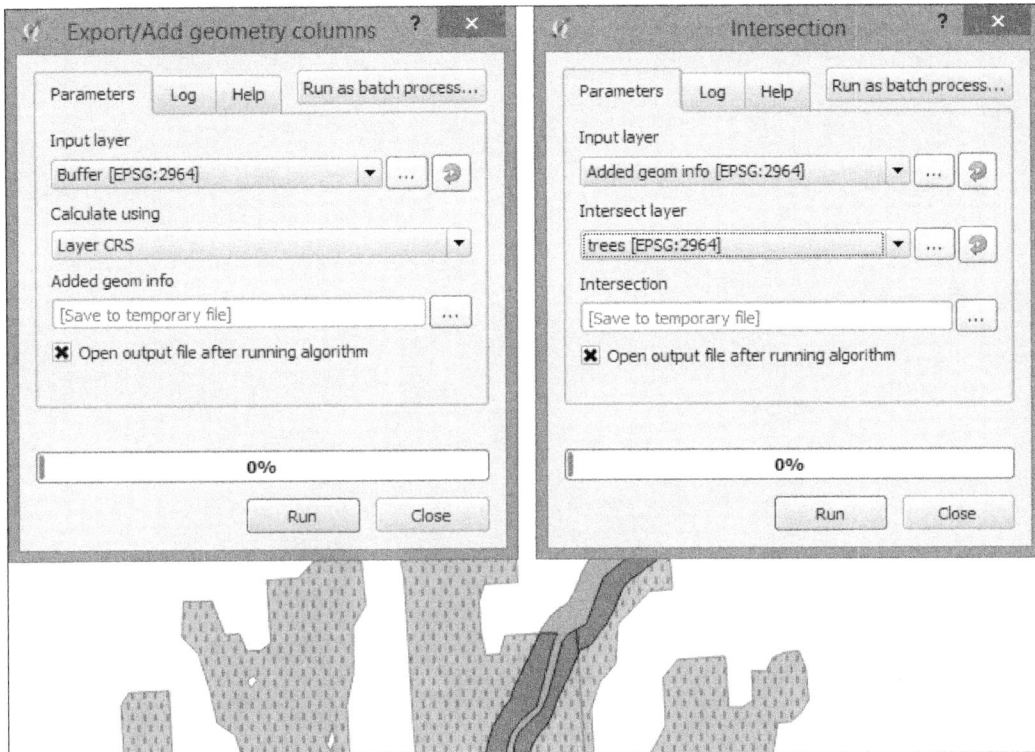

5. Using the **Dissolve** tool, we can recombine all areas from the intersection results into one big polygon that represents the total wooded area around the river. Note how we use the **Unique ID field** VEGDESC to only combine areas with the same vegetation in order not to mix deciduous and mixed trees.

6. Finally, we can calculate the final share of wooded area using the **Advanced Python field calculator**. The formula `value = $geom.area()/<area>` divides the area of the final polygon (`$geom.area()`) by the value in the `area` attribute (`<area>`), which we created earlier by running **Export/Add geometry columns**. As shown in the following screenshot, this calculation results in a wood share of **0.31601** for **Deciduous** and **0.09666** for **Mixed Trees**. Therefore, we can conclude that in total, 41.27 percent of the land along the Susitna River is wooded:

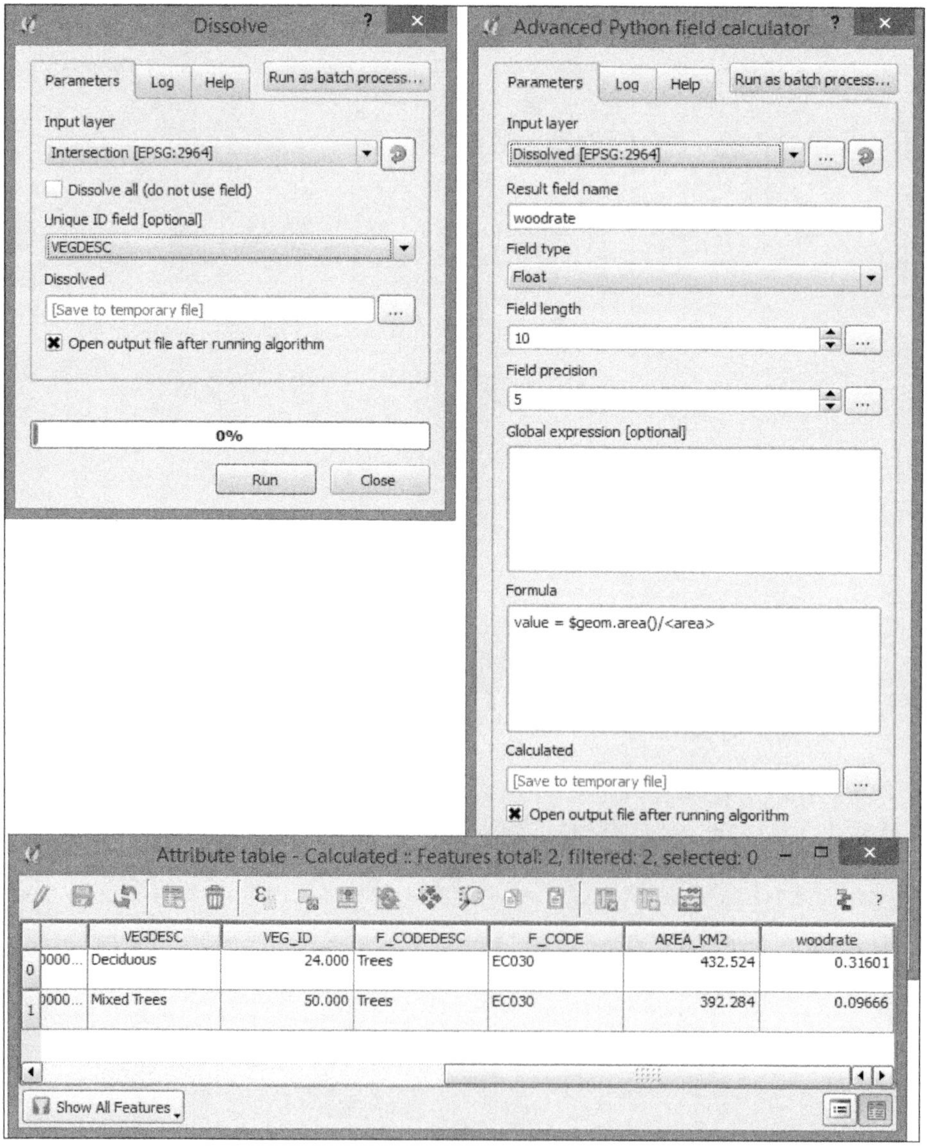

		VEGDESC	VEG_ID	F_CODEDESC	F_CODE	AREA_KM2	woodrate
0	0000...	Deciduous	24.000	Trees	EC030	432.524	0.31601
1	0000...	Mixed Trees	50.000	Trees	EC030	392.284	0.09666

Batch-processing multiple datasets

Sometimes, we want to run the same tool repeatedly but with slightly different settings. For this use case, **Processing** offers the **Batch Processing** functionality. Let's use this tool to extract some samples from our airports layer using the **Random extract** tool:

1. To access the batch processing functionality, right-click on the **Random extract** tool in the toolbox and select **Execute as batch process**. This will open the **Batch Processing** dialog.

2. Next, we configure the **Input layer** by clicking on the **...** button and selecting **Select from open layers**, as shown in the following screenshot:

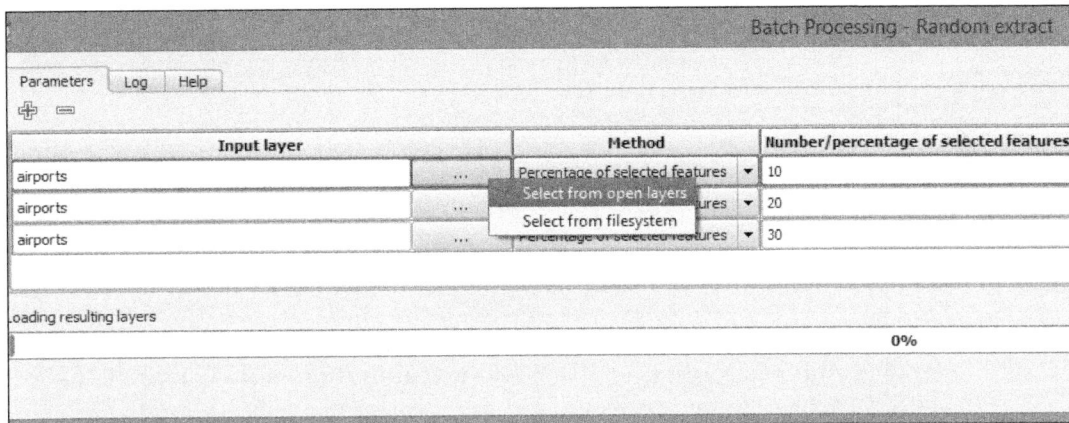

3. This will open a small dialog in which we can select the `airports` layer and click on **OK**.

4. To automatically fill in the other rows with the same input layer, we can double-click on the table header of the corresponding column (which reads **Input layer**).

5. Next, we configure the **Method** by selecting the **Percentage of selected features** option and again double-clicking on the respective table header to auto-fill the remaining rows.

6. The next parameter controls the **Number/percentage of selected features**. For our exercise, we configure **10**, **20**, and **30** percent.

7. Last but not least, we need to configure the output files in the **Extracted (random)** column. Click on the **...** button, which will open a file dialog. There, you can select the save location and filename (for example, `extract`) and click on **Save**.

8. This will open the **Autofill settings** dialog, which helps us to automatically create distinct filenames for each run. Using the **Fill with parameter values** mode with the **Number/percentage of selected features** parameter will automatically append our parameter values (**10**, **20**, and **30**, respectively) to the filename. This will result in `extract10`, `extract20`, and `extract30`, as shown in the following screenshot:

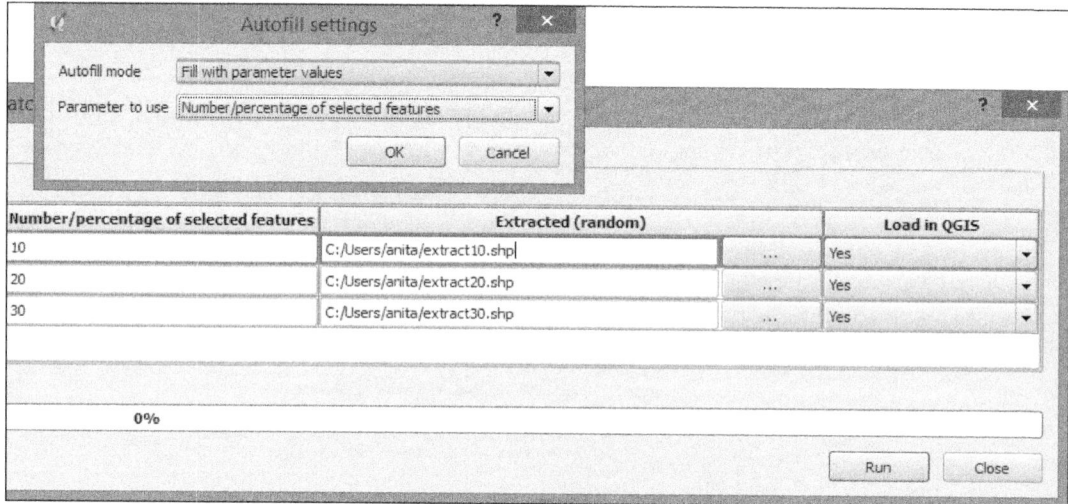

9. Once everything is configured, click on the **Run** button and wait for all the batch instructions to be processed and the results to be loaded into the project.

Automated geoprocessing with the graphical modeler

Using the graphical modeler, we can turn entire geoprocessing and analysis workflows into automated models. We can then use these models to run complex geoprocessing tasks that involve multiple different tools in one go. To create a model, we go to **Processing | Graphical modeler** to open the modeler, where we can select from different **Inputs** and **Algorithms** for our model.

Let's create a model that automates the creation of hexagonal heatmaps!

1. By double-clicking on the **Vector layer** entry in the **Inputs** list, we can add an input field for the point layer. It's a good idea to use descriptive parameter names (for example, `hex cell size` instead of just `size` for the parameter that controls the size of the hexagonal grid cells) so that we can recognize which input is first and which is later in the model. It is also useful to restrict the **Shape type** field wherever appropriate. In our example, we restrict the input to **Point** layers. This will enable Processing to pre-filter the available layers and present us only the layers of the correct type.

2. The second input that we need is a **Number** field to specify the desired hexagonal cell size, as shown in this screenshot:

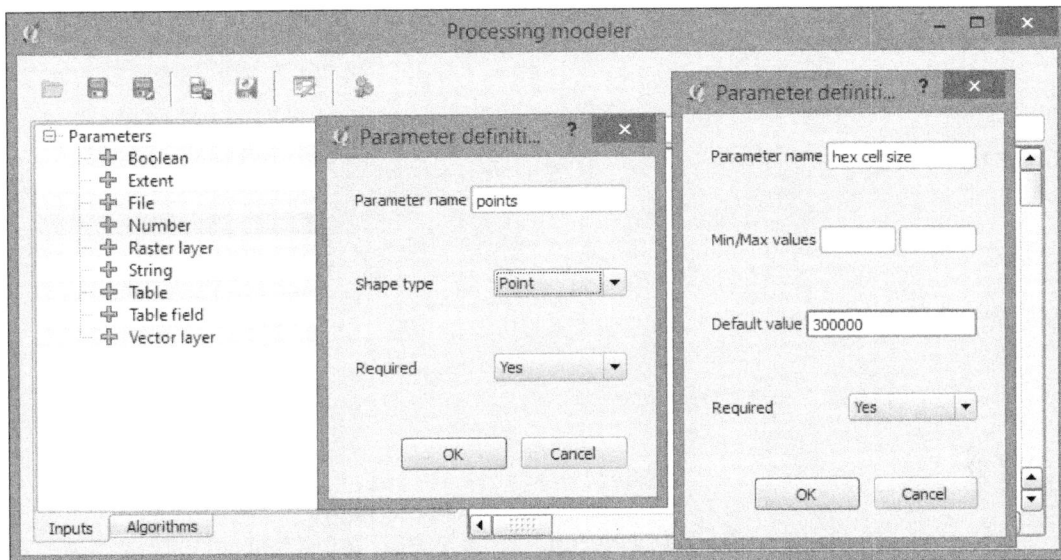

3. After adding the inputs, we can now continue creating the model by assembling the algorithms. In the **Algorithms** section, we can use the filter at the top to narrow down our search for the correct algorithm. To add an algorithm to the model, we simply double-click on the entry in the list of algorithms. This opens the algorithm dialog, where we have to specify the inputs and further algorithm-specific parameters.

4. In our example, we want to use the point vector layer as the **input** layer and the number input **hex cell size** as the **cellsize** parameter. We can access the available inputs through the drop-down list, as shown in the following screenshot. Alternatively, it's possible to hardcode parameters such as the cell size by typing the desired value in the input field:

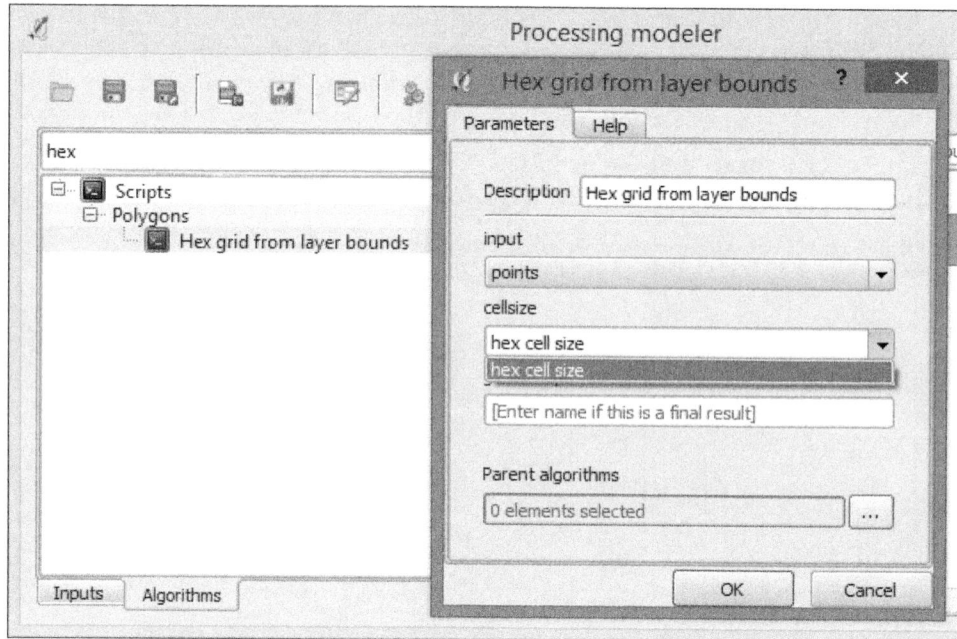

> While adding the following algorithms, it is important to always choose the correct input layer based on the previous processing step. We can verify the workflow using the connections in the model diagram that the modeler draws automatically.

5. The final model will look like this:

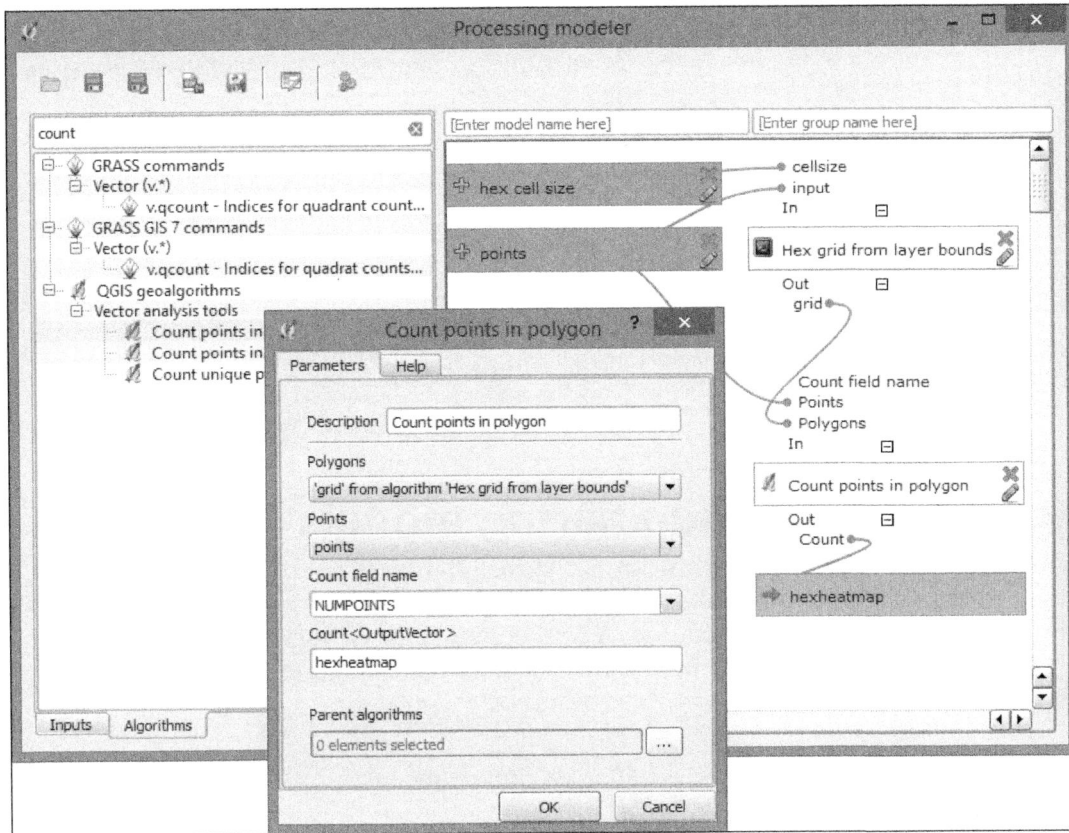

6. To finish the model, we need to enter a model name (for example, `Create hexagonal heatmap`) and a group name (for example, `Learning QGIS`). Processing will use the group name to organize all the models that we create into different toolbox groups. Once we have picked a name and group, we can save the model and then run it.

7. After closing the modeler, we can run the saved models from the toolbox like any other tool. It is even possible to use one model as a building block for another model.

Another useful feature is that we can specify a layer style that needs to be applied to the processing results automatically. This default style can be set using **Edit rendering styles for outputs** in the context menu of the created model in the toolbox, as shown in the following screenshot:

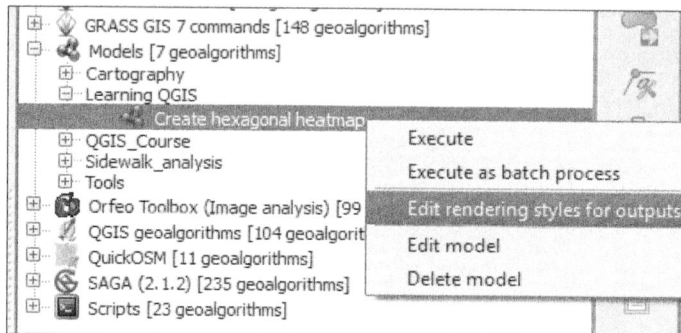

Documenting and sharing models

Models can easily be copied from one QGIS installation to another and shared with other users. To ensure the usability of the model, it is a good idea to write a short documentation. **Processing** provides a convenient **Help editor**; it can be accessed by clicking on the **Edit model help** button in the **Processing modeler**, as shown in this screenshot:

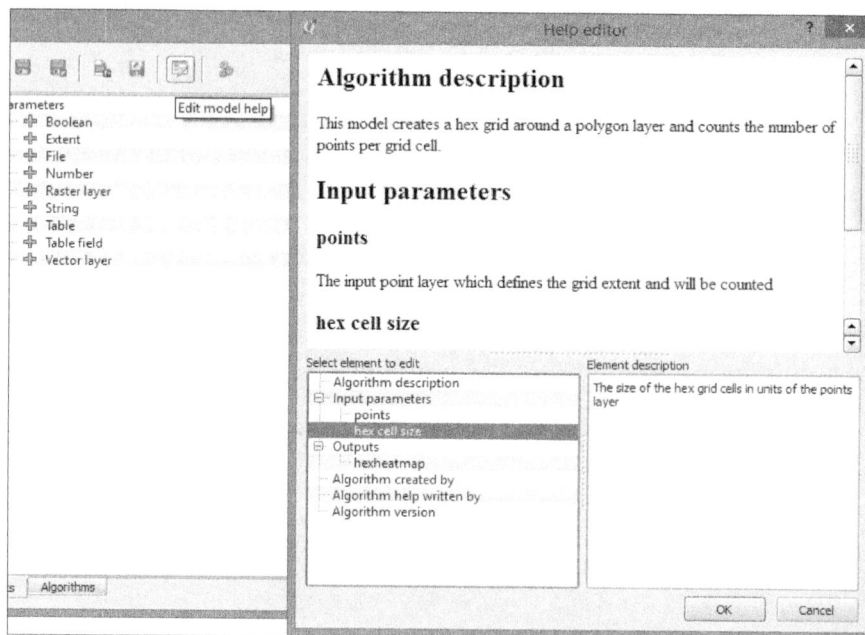

By default, the `.model` files are stored in your user directory. On Windows, it is `C:\Users\<your_user_name>\.qgis2\processing\models`, and on Linux and OS X, it is `~/.qgis2/processing/models`.

You can copy these files and share them with others. To load a model from a file, use the loading tool by going to **Models | Tools | Add model from file** in the **Processing Toolbox**.

Leveraging the power of spatial databases

Another approach to geoprocessing is to use the functionality provided by spatial databases such as PostGIS and SpatiaLite. In the *Loading data from databases* section of *Chapter 2, Viewing Spatial Data*, we discussed how to load data from a SpatiaLite database. In this exercise, we will use SpatiaLite's built-in geoprocessing functions to perform spatial analysis directly in the database and visualize the results in QGIS. We will use the same SpatiaLite database that we downloaded in *Chapter 2, Viewing Spatial Data*, from `www.gaia-gis.it/spatialite-2.3.1/test-2.3.zip` (4 MB).

Selecting by location in SpatiaLite

As an example, we will use SpatiaLite's spatial functions to get all highways that are within 1 km distance from the city of Firenze:

1. To interact with the database, we use the **DB Manager** plugin, which can be enabled in the **Plugin Manager** and is available via the **Database** menu.

   > If you have followed the *Loading data from databases* section in *Chapter 2, Viewing Spatial Data*, you will see `test-2.3.sqlite` listed under SpatiaLite in the tree on the left-hand side of the **DB Manager** dialog, as shown in the next screenshot. If the database is not listed, refer to the previously mentioned section to set up the database connection.

2. Next, we can open a **Query** tab using the **SQL window** toolbar button, by going to **Database | SQL window**, or by pressing *F2*. The following **SQL** query will select all highways that are within 1 km distance from the city of Firenze:

```
SELECT *
FROM HighWays
WHERE PtDistWithin(
  HighWays.Geometry,
```

```
(SELECT Geometry FROM Towns WHERE Name = 'Firenze'),
1000
)
```

The `SELECT Geometry FROM Towns WHERE Name = 'Firenze'` subquery
selects the point geometry that represents the city of Firenze. This point is
then used in the `PtDistWithin` function to test for each highway geometry
and check whether it is within a distance of 1,000 meters.

> An introduction to SQL is out of the scope of this book, but you can find
> a thorough tutorial on using SpatiaLite at `http://www.gaia-gis.it/`
> `gaia-sins/spatialite-cookbook/index.html`. Additionally, to
> get an overview of all the spatial functionalities offered by SpatiaLite,
> visit `http://www.gaia-gis.it/gaia-sins/spatialite-sql-`
> `4.2.0.html`.

3. When the query is entered, we can click on **Execute (F5)** to run the query. The
   query results will be displayed in a tabular form in the result section below
   the SQL query input area, as shown in the following screenshot:

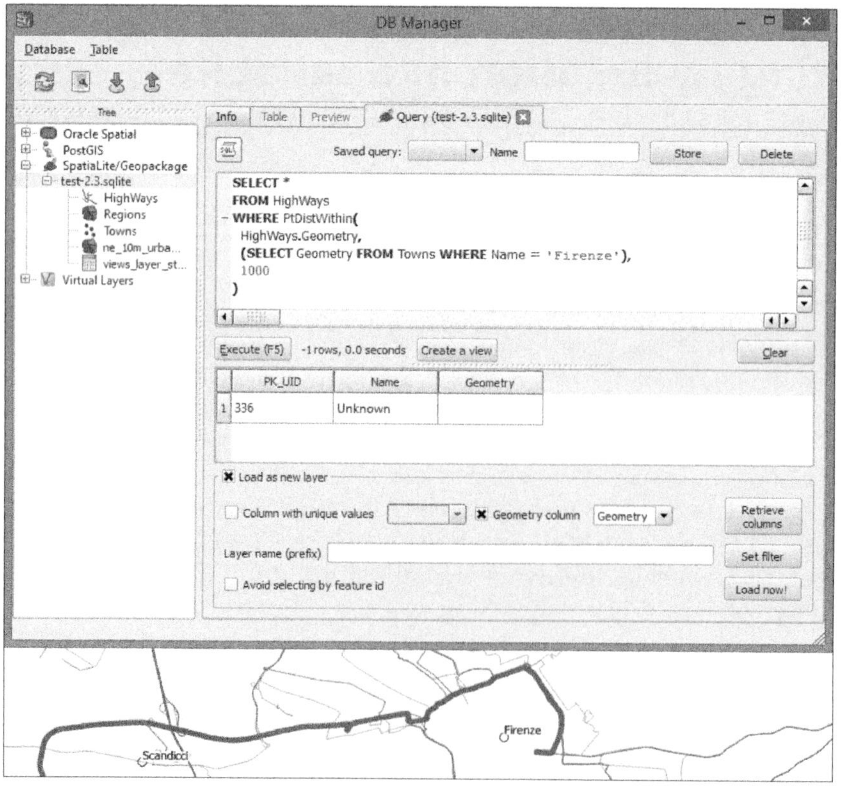

4. To display the query results on the map, we need to activate the **Load as new layer** option below the results table. Make sure you select the correct **Geometry column** (Geometry).

5. Once you have configured these settings, you can click on **Load now!** to load the query result as a new map layer. As you can see in the preceding screenshot, only one of the highways (represented by the wide blue line) is within 1 km of the city of Firenze.

Aggregating data in SpatiaLite

Another thing that databases are really good at is aggregating data. For example, the following SQL query will count the number of towns per region:

```
SELECT Regions.Name, Regions.Geometry, count(*) as Count
FROM Regions
JOIN Towns
   ON Within(Towns.Geometry,Regions.Geometry)
GROUP BY Regions.Name
```

This can be used to create a new layer of regions that includes a Count attribute. This tells the number of towns in the region, as shown in this screenshot:

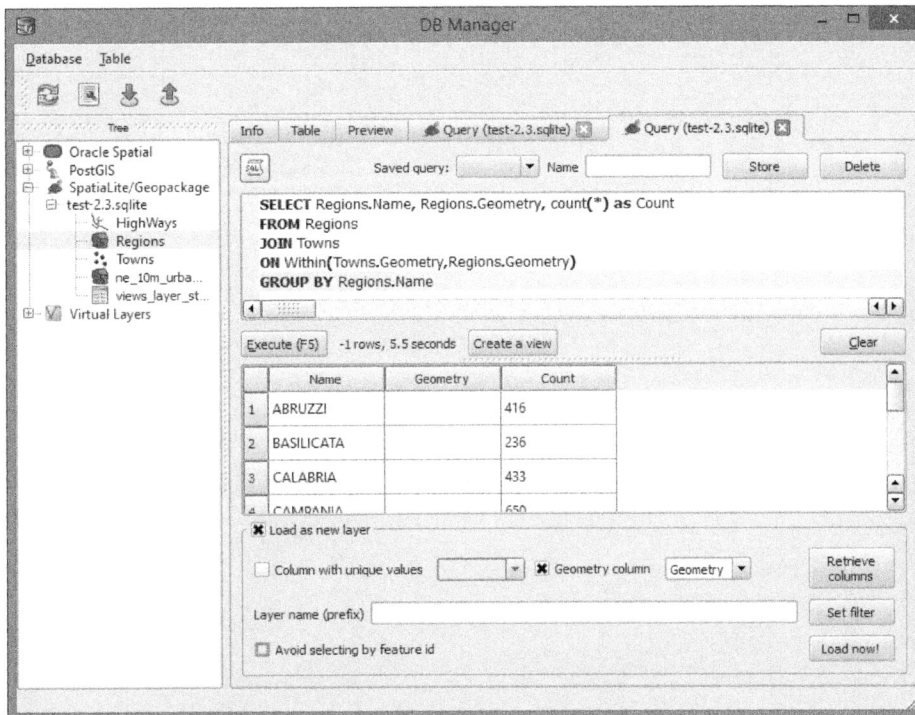

> Although we have used SpatiaLite in this example, the tools and workflow presented here work just as well with PostGIS databases. It is worth noting, however, that SpatiaLite and PostGIS often use slightly different function names. Therefore, it is usually necessary to adjust the SQL queries accordingly.

Summary

In this chapter, we covered various raster and vector geoprocessing and analysis tools and how to apply them in common tasks. We saw how to use the Processing toolbox to run individual tools as well as the modeler to create complex geoprocessing models from multiple tools. Using the modeler, we can automate our workflows and increase our productivity, especially with respect to recurring tasks. Finally, we also had a quick look at how to leverage the power of spatial databases to perform spatial analysis.

In the following chapter, we will see how to bring all our knowledge together to create beautiful maps using advanced styles and print map composition features.

5

Creating Great Maps

In this chapter, we will cover the important features that enable us to create great maps. We will first go into advanced vector styling, building on what we covered in *Chapter 2, Viewing Spatial Data*. Then, you will learn how to label features by following examples for point labels as well as more advanced road labels with road shield graphics. We will also cover how to tweak labels manually. Then, you will get to know the print composer and how to use it to create printable maps and map books. Finally, we will explain how to create web maps directly in QGIS to present our results online.

> If you want to get an idea about what kind of map you can create using QGIS, visit the QGIS Map Showcase Flickr group at `https://www.flickr.com/groups/qgis/`, which is dedicated to maps created with QGIS without any further postprocessing.

Advanced vector styling

This section introduces more advanced vector styling features, building on the basics that we covered in *Chapter 2, Viewing Spatial Data*. We will cover how to create detailed custom visualizations using the following features:

- Graduated styles
- Categorized styles
- Rule-based styles
- Data-defined styles
- Heatmap styles
- 2.5D styles
- Layer effects

Creating a graduated style

Graduated styles are great for visualizing distributions of numerical values in choropleth or similar maps. The graduated renderer supports two methods:

- **Color**: This method changes the color of the feature according to the configured attribute

- **Size**: This method changes the symbol size for the feature according to the configured attribute (this option is only available for point and line layers)

In our sample data, there is a `climate.shp` file that contains locations and mean temperature values. We can visualize this data using a graduated style by simply selecting the **T_F_MEAN** value for the **Column** field and clicking on **Classify**. Using the **Color** method, as shown in the following screenshot, we can pick a **Color ramp** from the corresponding drop-down list. Additionally, we can reverse the order of the colors within the color ramp using the **Invert** option:

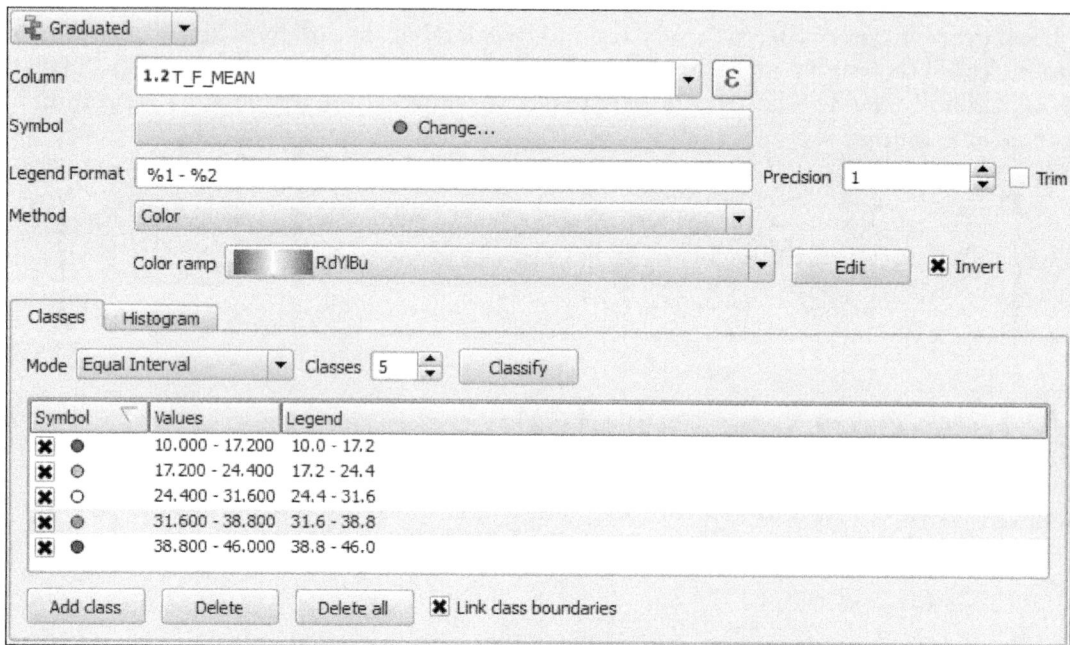

Graduated styles are available in different classification modes, as follows:

- **Equal Interval**: This mode creates classes by splitting at equal intervals between the maximum and minimum values found in the specified column.

- **Quantile (Equal Count)**: This mode creates classes so that each class contains an equal number of features.

- **Natural Breaks (Jenks)**: This mode uses the Jenks natural breaks algorithm to create classes by reducing variance within classes and maximizing variance between classes.

- **Standard Deviation**: This mode uses the column values' standard deviation to create classes.

- **Pretty Breaks**: This mode is the only classification that doesn't strictly create the specified number of classes. Instead, its main goal is to create class boundaries that are round numbers.

We can also manually edit the class values by double-clicking on the values in the list and changing the class bounds. A more convenient way to edit the classes is the **Histogram** view, as shown in the next screenshot. Switch to the **Histogram** tab and click on the **Load values** button in the bottom-right corner to enable the histogram. You can now edit the class bounds by moving the vertical lines with your mouse. You can also add new classes by adding a new vertical line, which you can do by clicking on empty space in the histogram:

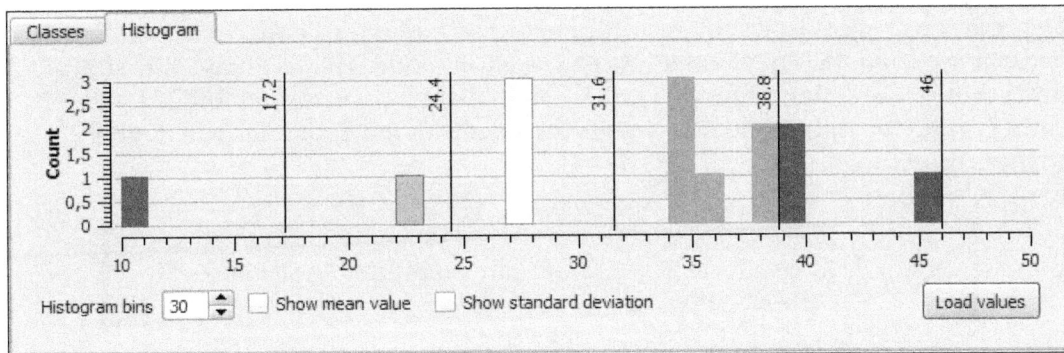

Besides the symbols that are drawn on the map, another important aspect of the styling is the **legend** that goes with it. To customize the legend, we can define **Legend Format** as well as the **Precision** (that is, the number of decimal places) that should be displayed. In the **Legend Format** string, `%1` will be replaced by the lower limit of the class and `%2` by the upper limit. You can change this string to suit your needs, for example, to this: `from %1 to %2`. If you activate the **Trim** option, excess trailing zeros will be removed as well.

When we use the **Size** method, as shown in the following screenshot, the dialog changes a little, and we can now configure the desired symbol sizes:

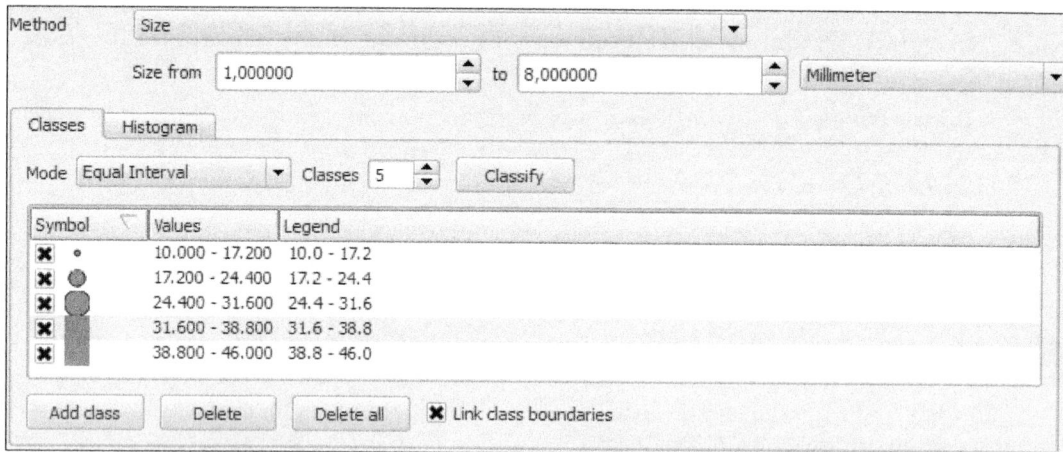

The next screenshot shows the results of using a **Graduated renderer** option with five classes using the **Equal Interval** classification mode. The left-hand side shows the results of the **Color** method (symbol color changes according to the T_F_MEAN value), while the right-hand side shows the results of the **Size** method (symbol size changes according to the T_F_MEAN value).

> Note the checkboxes besides each symbol. They can be used to selectively hide or show the features belonging to the corresponding class.

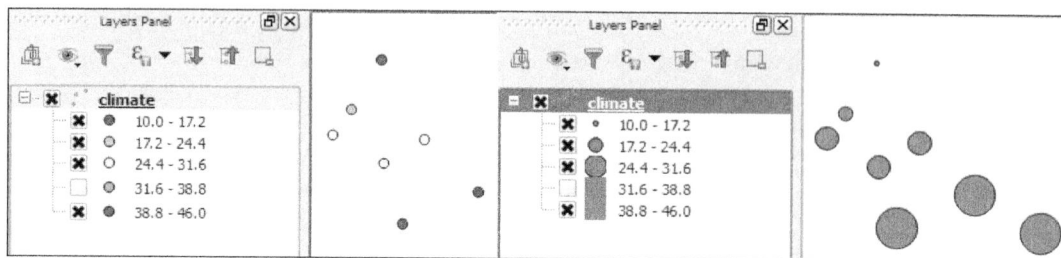

Creating and using color ramps

In the previous example, we used an existing color ramp to style our layer. Of course, we can also create our own color ramps. To create a new color ramp, we can scroll down the color ramp list to the **New color ramp...** entry. There are four different color ramp types, which we can chose from:

- **Gradient**: With this type, we can create color maps with two or more colors. The resulting color maps can be smooth gradients (using the **Continuous** type option) or distinct colors (using the **Discrete** type option), as shown in the following screenshot:

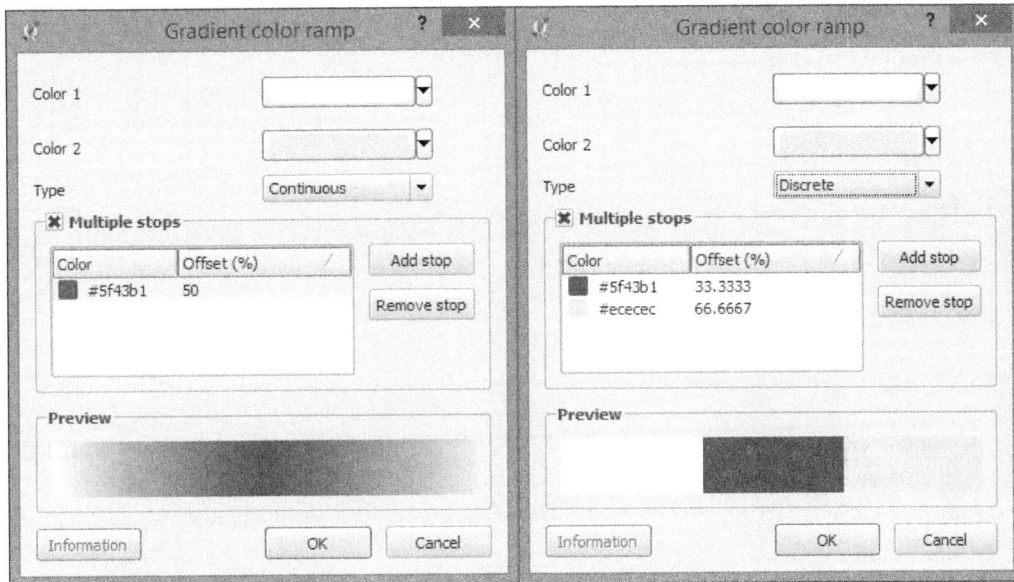

- **Random**: This type allows us to create a gradient with a certain number of random colors
- **ColorBrewer**: This type provides access to the **ColorBrewer** color schemes

- **cpt-city**: This type provides access to a wide variety of preconfigured color schemes, including schemes for typography and bathymetry, as shown in this screenshot:

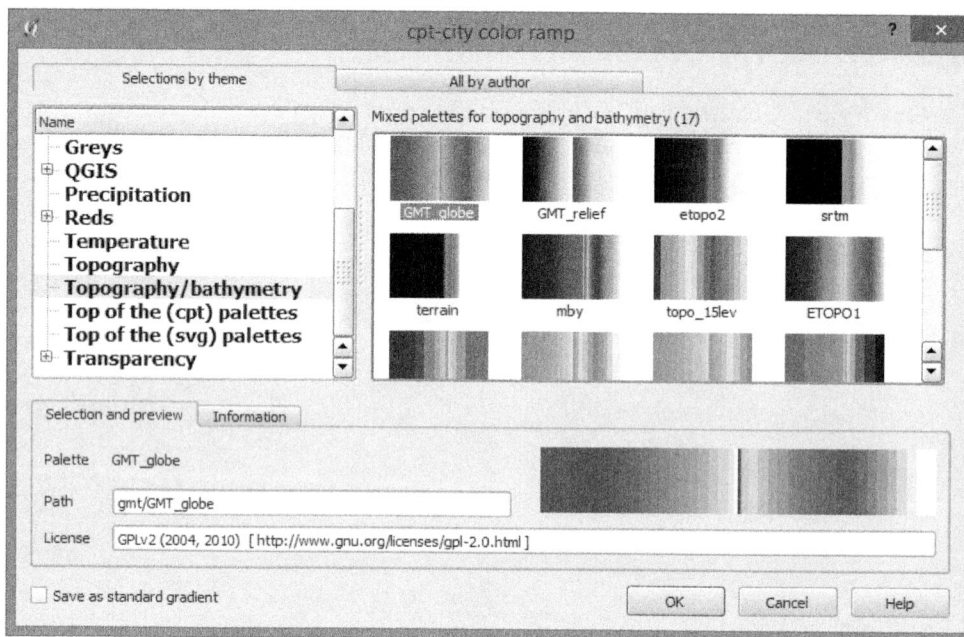

To manage all our color ramps and symbols, we can go to **Settings | Style Manager**. Here, we can add, delete, edit, export, or import color ramps and styles using the corresponding buttons on the right-hand side of the dialog, as shown in the following screenshot:

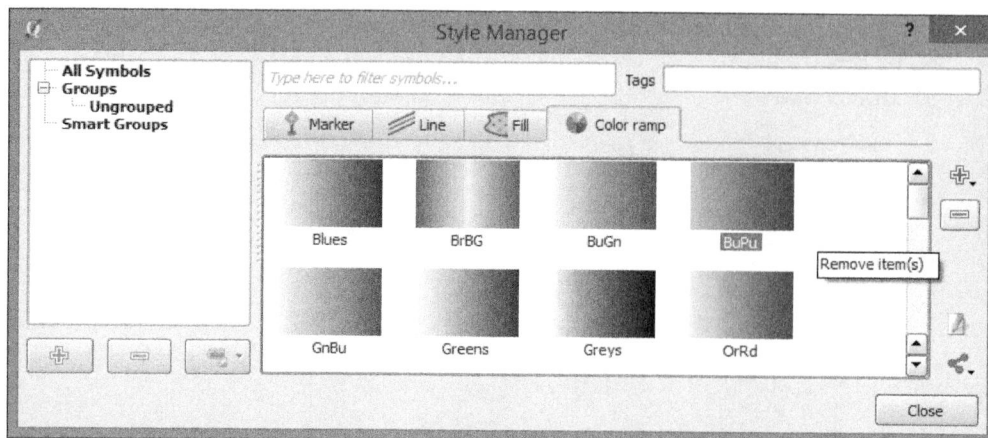

Using categorized styles for nominal data

Just as graduated styles are very useful for visualizing numeric values, categorized styles are great for text values or—more generally speaking—all kinds of values on a nominal scale. A good example for this kind of data can be found in the `trees.shp` file in our sample data. For each area, there is a **VEGDESC** value that describes the type of forest found there. Using a categorized style, we can easily generate a style with one symbol for every unique value in the **VEGDESC** column, as shown in the following screenshot. Once we click on **OK**, the style is applied to our trees layer in order to visualize the distribution of different tree types in the area:

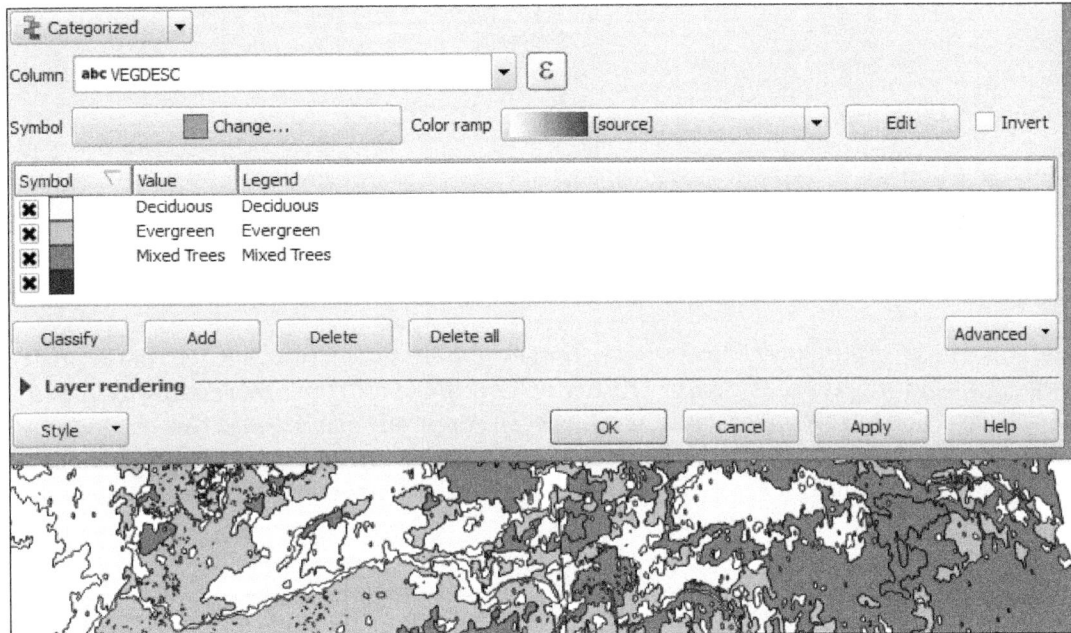

Of course, every symbol is editable and can be customized. Just double-click on the symbol preview to open the **Symbol** selector dialog, which allows you to select and combine different symbols.

Creating a rule-based style for road layers

With rule-based styles, we can create a layer style with a hierarchy of rules. Rules can take into account anything from attribute values to scale and geometry properties such as area or length. In this example, we will create a rule-based renderer for the ne_10m_roads.shp file from Natural Earth (you can download it from http://www.naturalearthdata.com/downloads/10m-cultural-vectors/roads/). As you can see here, our style will contain different road styles for major and secondary highways as well as scale-dependent styles:

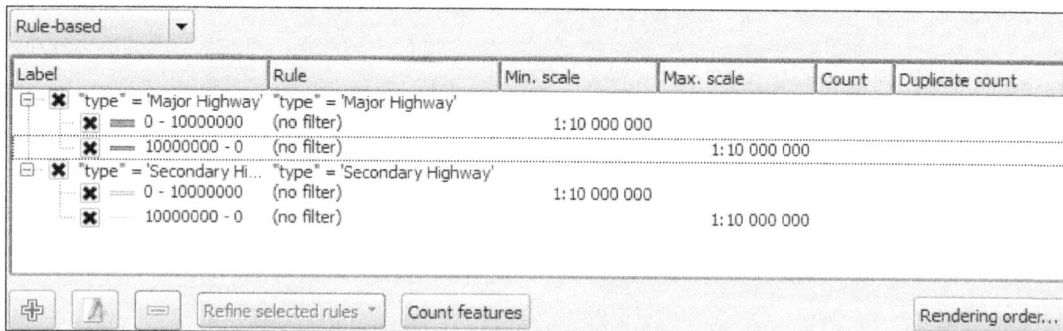

Label	Rule	Min. scale	Max. scale	Count	Duplicate count
✖ "type" = 'Major Highway'	"type" = 'Major Highway'				
✖ ▬ 0 - 10000000	(no filter)	1:10 000 000			
✖ ▬ 10000000 - 0	(no filter)		1:10 000 000		
✖ "type" = 'Secondary Hi...	"type" = 'Secondary Highway'				
✖ ▬ 0 - 10000000	(no filter)	1:10 000 000			
✖ ▬ 10000000 - 0	(no filter)		1:10 000 000		

Rule-based ▾

➕ ╱ ➖ | Refine selected rules ▾ | Count features | Rendering order...

As you can see in the preceding screenshot, on the first level of rules, we distinguish between roads of **"type" = 'Major Highway'** and those of **"type" = 'Secondary Highway'**. The next level of rules handles **scale-dependence**. To add this second layer of rules, we can use the **Refine selected rules** button and select **Add scales to rule**. We simply input one or more scale values at which we want the rule to be split.

Note that there are no symbols specified on the first rule level. If we had symbols specified on the first level as well, the renderer would draw two symbols over each other. While this can be useful in certain cases, we don't want this effect right now. Symbols can be deactivated in **Rule properties**, which is accessible by double-clicking on the rule or clicking on the edit button below the rule's tree view (the button between the plus and minus buttons).

In the following screenshot, we can see the rule-based renderer and the scale rules in action. While the left-hand side shows wider white roads with grey outlines for secondary highways, the right-hand side shows the simpler symbology with thin grey lines:

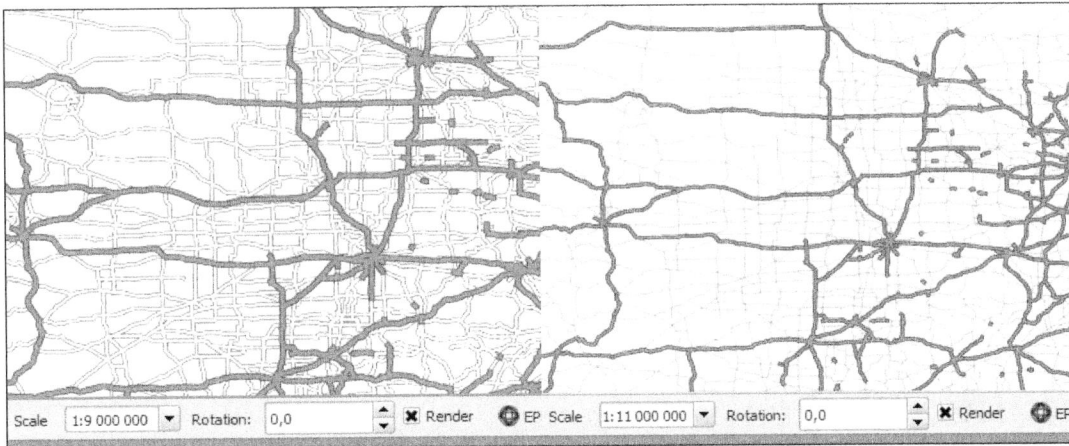

You can download the symbols used in this style by going to **Settings | Style Manager**, clicking on the sharing button in the bottom-right corner of the dialog, and selecting **Import**. The URL is `https://raw. githubusercontent.com/anitagraser/QGIS-resources/ master/qgis1.8/symbols/osm_symbols.xml`. Paste the URL in the **Location** textbox, click on **Fetch Symbols**, then click on **Select all**, and finally click on **Import**. The dialog will look like what is shown in the following screenshot:

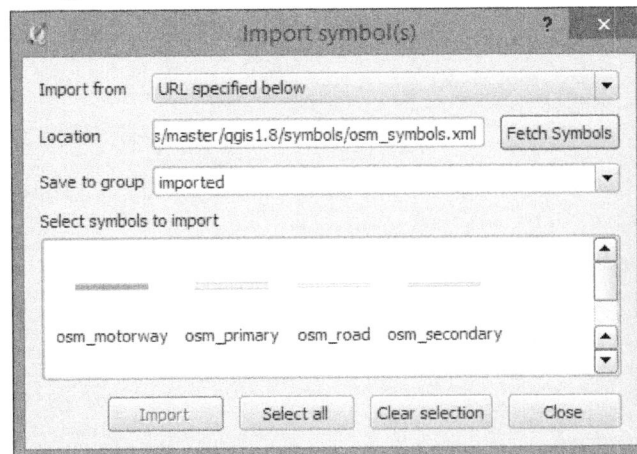

Creating data-defined symbology

In previous examples, we created categories or rules to define how features are drawn on a map. An alternative approach is to use values from the layer attribute table to define the styling. This can be achieved using a QGIS feature called **Data defined override**. These overrides can be configured using the corresponding buttons next to each symbol property, as described in the following example.

In this example, we will again use the `ne_10m_roads.shp` file from Natural Earth. The next screenshot shows a configuration that creates a style where the line's **Pen width** depends on the feature's `scalerank` and the line **Color** depends on the `toll` attribute. To set a data-defined override for a symbol property, you need to click on the corresponding button, which is located right next to the property, and choose **Edit**. The following two expressions are used:

- `CASE WHEN toll = 1 THEN 'red' ELSE 'lightgray' END`: This expression evaluates the `toll` value. If it is `1`, the line is drawn in red; otherwise, it is drawn in gray.

- `2.5 / scalerank`: This expression computes **Pen width**. Since a low scale rank should be represented by a wider line, we use a division operation instead of multiplication.

When data-defined overrides are active, the corresponding buttons are highlighted in yellow with an ε sign on them, as shown in the following screenshot:

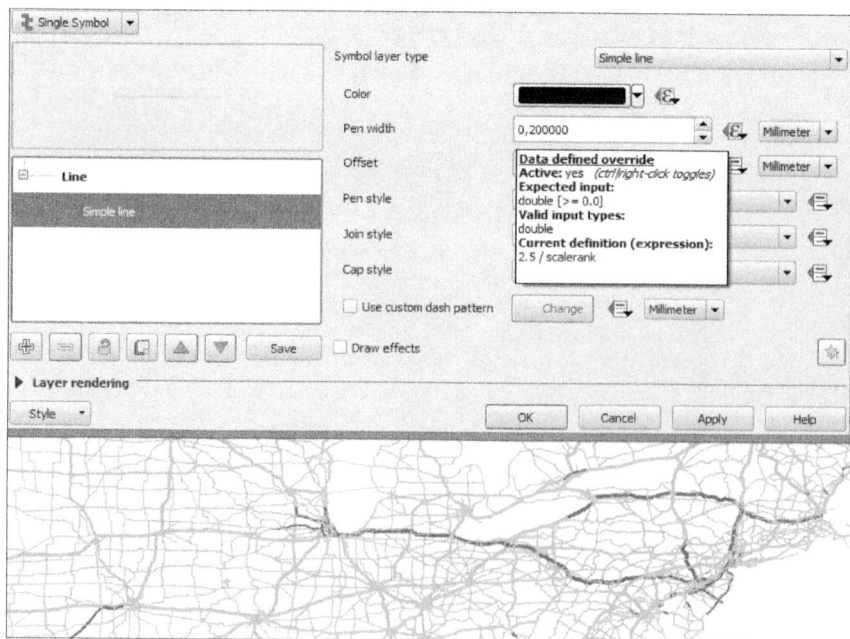

In this example, you have seen that you can specify colors using **color names** such as 'red', 'gold', and 'deepskyblue'. Another especially useful group of functions for data-defined styles is the **Color** functions. There are functions for the following **color models**:

- **RGB**: color_rgb(red, green, blue)
- **HSL**: color_hsl(hue, saturation, lightness)
- **HSV**: color_hsv(hue, saturation, value)
- **CMYK**: color_cmyk(cyan, magenta, yellow, black)

There are also functions for accessing the color ramps. Here are two examples of how to use these functions:

- ramp_color('Reds', T_F_MEAN / 46): This expression returns a color from the Reds color ramp depending on the T_F_MEAN value. Since the second parameter has to be a value between 0 and 1, we divide the T_F_MEAN value by the maximum value, 46.

> Since users can add new color ramps or change existing ones, the color ramps can vary between different QGIS installations. Therefore, the ramp_color function may return different results if the style or project file is used on a different computer.

- color_rgba(0, 0, 180, scale_linear(T_F_JUL - T_F_JAN, 20, 70, 0, 255)): This expression computes the color depending on the difference between the July and January temperatures, T_F_JUL - T_F_JAN. The difference value is transformed into a value between 0 and 255 by the scale_linear function according to the following rule: any value up to 20 will be translated to 0, any value of 70 and above will be translated to 255, and anything in between will be interpolated linearly. Bigger difference values result in darker colors because of the higher alpha parameter value.

> The alpha component in RGBA, HSLA, HSVA, and CMYKA controls the transparency of the color. It can take on an integer value from 0 (completely transparent) to 255 (opaque).

Creating a dynamic heatmap style

In *Chapter 4*, *Spatial Analysis*, you learned how to create a heatmap raster. However, there is a faster, more convenient way to achieve this look if you want a heatmap only for displaying purposes (and not for further spatial analysis) — the **Heatmap** renderer option.

The following screenshot shows a **Heatmap** renderer set up for our populated places dataset, popp.shp. We can specify a color ramp that will be applied to the resulting heatmap values between 0 and the defined **Maximum value**. If **Maximum value** is set to **Automatic**, QGIS automatically computes the highest value in the heatmap. As in the previously discussed heatmap tool, we can define point weights as well as the kernel **Radius** (for an explanation of this term, check out *Creating a heatmap from points* in *Chapter 4*, *Spatial Analysis*). The final **Rendering quality** option controls the quality of the rendered output with coarse, big raster cells for the **Fastest** option and a fine-grained look when set to **Best**:

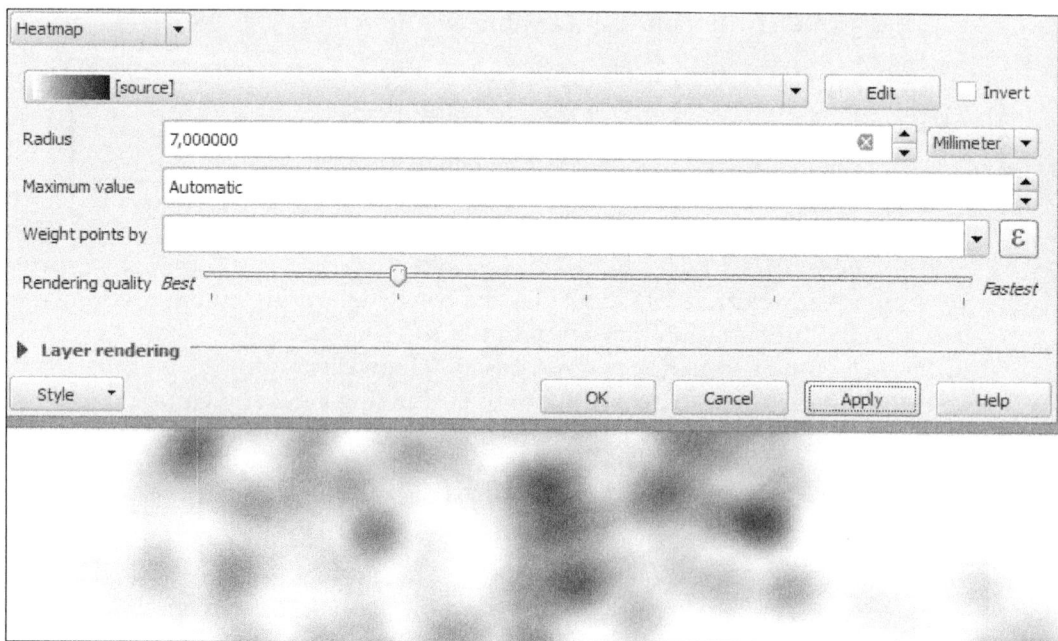

Creating a 2.5D style

If you want to create a pseudo-3D look, for example, to style building blocks or to create a thematic map, try the 2.5D renderer. The next screenshot shows the current configuration options that include controls for the feature's **Height** (in layer units), the viewing **Angle**, and colors. Since this renderer is still being improved at the time of writing this book, you might find additional options in this dialog when you see it for yourself.

Once you have configured the 2.5D renderer to your liking, you can switch to another renderer to, for example, create classified or graduated versions of symbols.

Adding live layer effects

With **layer effects**, we can change the way our symbols look even further. Effects can be added by enabling the **Draw effects** checkbox at the bottom of the symbol dialog, as shown in the following screenshot. To configure the effects, click on the Star button in the bottom-right corner of the dialog. The **Effect Properties** dialog offers access to a wide range of **Effect types**:

- **Blur**: This effect creates a blurred, fuzzy version of the symbol.

- **Colorise**: This effect changes the color of the symbol.

- **Source**: This is the original unchanged symbol.

- **Drop Shadow**: This effect creates a shadow.

- **Inner Glow**: This effect creates a glow-like gradient that extends inwards, starting from the symbol border.

- **Inner Shadow**: This effect creates a shadow that is restricted to the inside of the symbol.

- **Outer Glow**: This effect creates a glow that radiates from the symbol outwards.

- **Transform**: This effect can be used to transform the symbol. The available transformations include reflect, shear, scale, rotate, and translate:

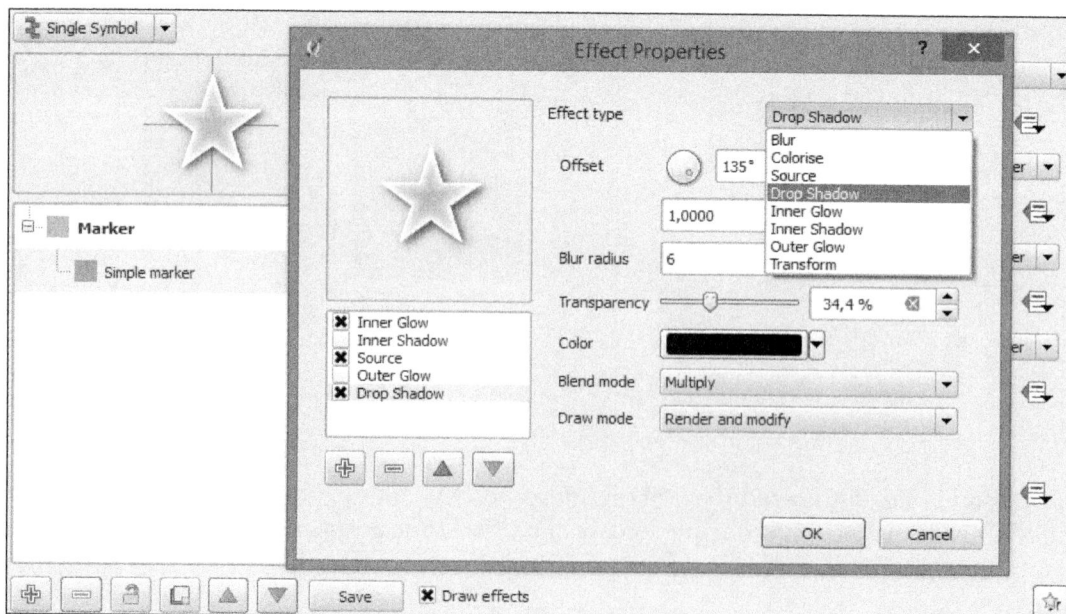

As you can see in the previous screenshot, we can combine multiple layer effects and they are organized in effect layers in the list in the bottom-left corner of the **Effect Properties** dialog.

Working with different styles

When we create elaborate styles, we might want to save them so that we can reuse them in other projects or share them with other users. To save a style, click on the **Style** button in the bottom-left corner of the style dialog and go to **Save Style | QGIS Layer Style File...**, as shown in the following screenshot. This will create a .qml file, which you can save anywhere, copy, and share with others. Similarly, to use the .qml file, click on the **Style** button and select **Load Style**:

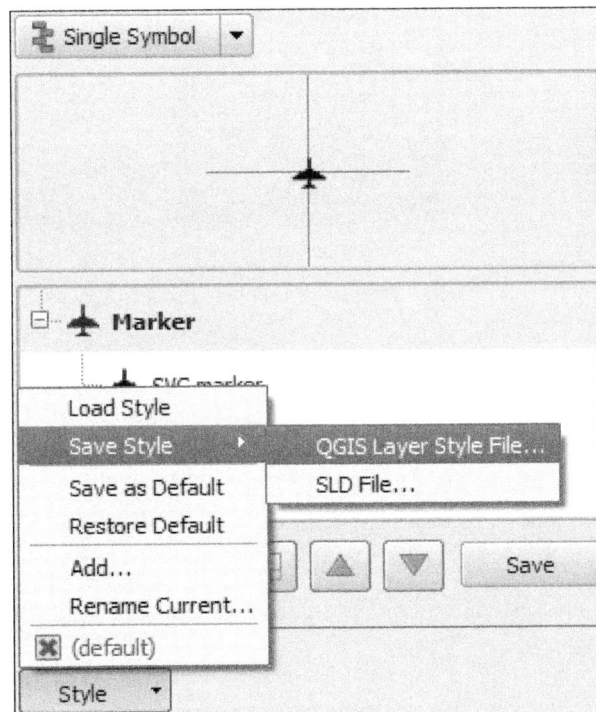

We can also save multiple different styles for one layer. For example, for our airports layer, we might want one style that displays airports using plane symbols and another style that renders a heatmap. To achieve this, we can do the following:

1. Configure the plane style.

2. Click on the **Style** button and select **Add** to add the current style to the list of styles for this layer.

3. In the pop-up dialog, enter a name for the new style, for example, `planes`.

4. Add another style by clicking on **Style** and **Add** and call it `heatmap`.

5. Now, you can change the renderer to **Heatmap** and configure it. Click on the **Apply** button when ready.

6. In the **Style** button menu, you can now see both styles, as shown in the next screenshot. Changing from one style to the other is now as simple as selecting one of the two entries from the list at the bottom of this menu:

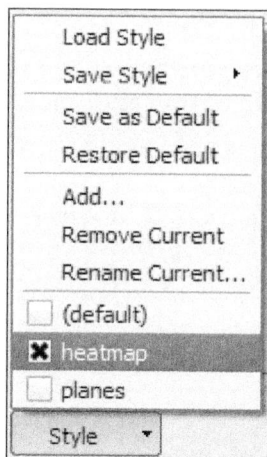

Finally, we can also access these layer styles through the layer context menu **Styles** entry in the **Layers Panel**, as shown in the following screenshot. This context menu also provides a way to copy and paste styles between layers using the **Copy Style** and **Paste Style** entries, respectively. Furthermore, this context menu provides a shortcut to quickly change the symbol color using a color wheel or by picking a color from the **Recent colors** section:

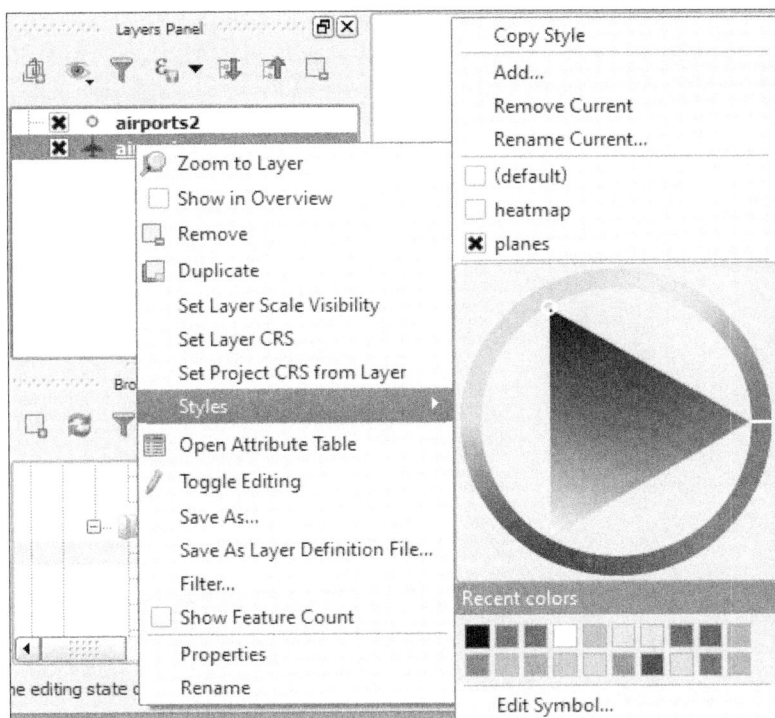

Labeling

We can activate labeling by going to **Layer Properties | Labels**, selecting **Show labels for this layer**, and selecting the attribute field that we want to **Label with**. This is all we need to do to display labels with default settings. While default labels are great for a quick preview, we will usually want to customize labels if we create visualizations for reports or standalone maps.

Using **Expressions** (the button that is right beside the attribute drop-down list), we can format the label text to suit our needs. For example, the **NAME** field in our sample `airports.shp` file contains text in uppercase. To display the airport names in mixed case instead, we can set the `title(NAME)` expression, which will reformat the name text in title case. We can also use multiple fields to create a label, for example, combining the name and elevation in brackets using the concatenation operator (| |), as follows:

```
title(NAME) || ' (' || "ELEV" || ')'
```

Note the use of simple quotation marks around text, such as ' (', and double quotation marks around field names, such as "ELEV". The dialog will look like what is shown in this screenshot:

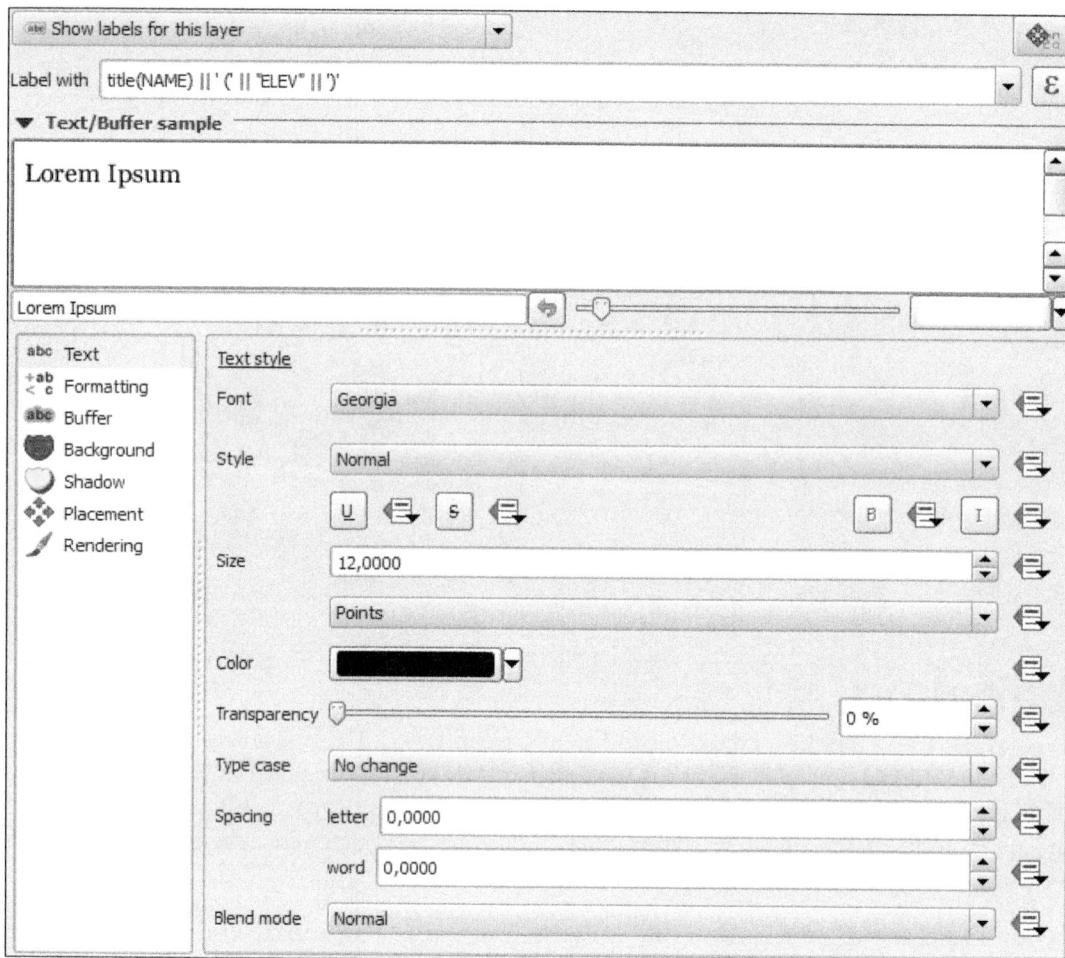

The big preview area at the top of the dialog, titled **Text/Buffer sample**, shows a preview of the current settings. The background color can be adjusted to test readability on different backgrounds. Under the preview area, we find the different label settings, which will be described in detail in the following sections.

Customizing label text styles

In the **Text** section (shown in the previous screenshot), we can configure the text style. Besides changing **Font**, **Style**, **Size**, **Color**, and **Transparency**, we can also modify the **Spacing** between **letters** and **words**, as well as **Blend mode**, which works like the layer blending mode that we covered in *Chapter 2, Viewing Spatial Data*.

Note the column of buttons on the right-hand side of every setting. Clicking on these buttons allows us to create data-defined overrides, similar to those that we discussed at the beginning of the chapter when we talked about advanced vector styling. These data-defined overrides can be used, for example, to define different label colors or change the label size depending on an individual feature's attribute value or an expression.

Controlling label formatting

In the **Formatting** section, which is shown in the following screenshot, we can enable **multiline labels** by specifying a **Wrap on character**. Additionally, we can control **Line height** and **Alignment**. Besides the typical alignment options, the QGIS labeling engine also provides a **Follow label placement** option, which ensures that multiline labels are aligned towards the same side as the symbol the label belongs to:

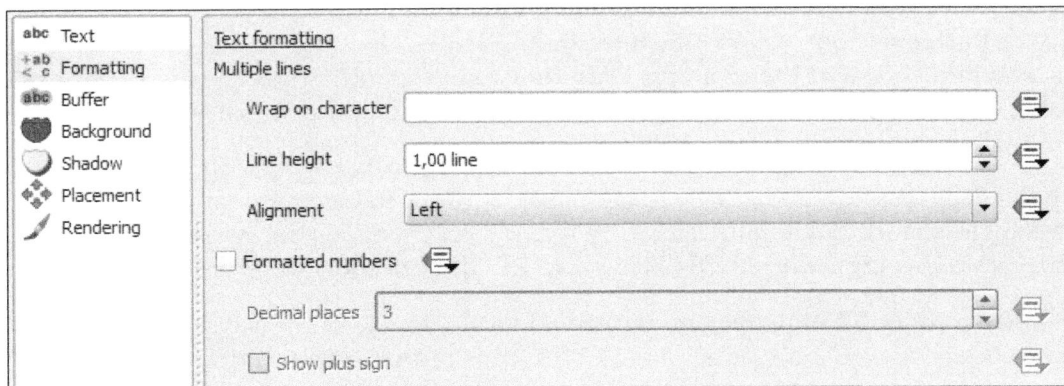

Finally, the **Formatted numbers** option offers a shortcut to format numerical values to a certain number of **Decimal places**.

An alternative to wrapping text on a certain character is the `wordwrap` function, available in expressions. It wraps the input string to a certain maximum or minimum number of characters. The following screenshot shows an example of wrapping a longer piece of text to a maximum of 22 characters per line:

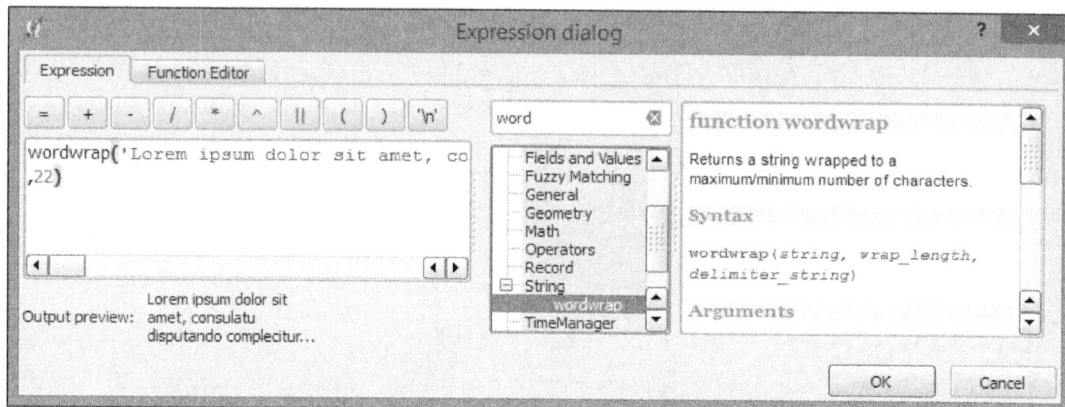

Configuring label buffers, background, and shadows

In the **Buffer** section, we can adjust the buffer **Size**, **Color**, and **Transparency**, as well as **Pen join style** and **Blend mode**. With transparency and blending, we can improve label readability without blocking out the underlying map too much, as shown in the following screenshot.

In the **Background** section, we can add a background shape in the form of a rectangle, square, circle, ellipsoid, or SVG. SVG backgrounds are great for creating effects such as **highway shields**, which we will discuss shortly.

Similarly, in the **Shadow** section, we can add a shadow to our labels. We can control everything from shadow direction to **Color**, **Blur radius**, **Scale**, and **Transparency**.

Controlling label placement

In the **Placement** section, we can configure which rules should be used to determine where the labels are placed. The available automatic label placement options depend on the layer geometry type.

Configuring point labels

For *point layers*, we can choose from the following:

- The flexible **Around point** option tries to find the best position for labels by distributing them around the points without overlaps. As you can see in the following screenshot, some labels are put in the top-right corner of their point symbol while others appear at different positions on the left (for example, **Anchorage Intl (129)**) or right (for example, **Big Lake (135)**) side.

- The **Offset from point** option forces all labels to a certain position; for example, all labels can be placed above their point symbol.

The following screenshot shows airport labels with a 50 percent transparent **Buffer** and **Drop Shadow**, placed using **Around point**. The **Label distance** is 1 mm.

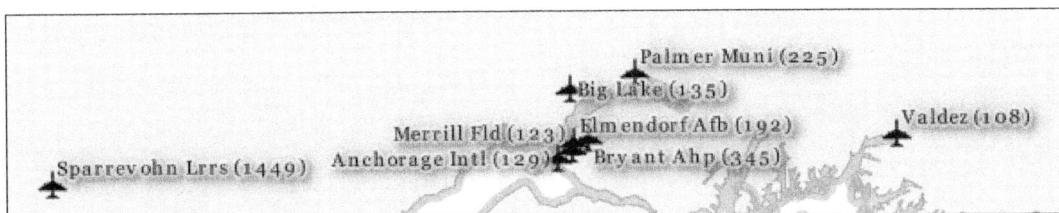

Configuring line labels

For *line layers*, we can choose from the following placement options:

- **Parallel** for straight labels that are rotated according to the line orientation
- **Curved** for labels that follow the shape of the line
- **Horizontal** for labels that keep a horizontal orientation, regardless of the line orientation

For further fine-tuning, we can define whether the label should be placed **Above line**, **On line**, or **Below line**, and how far above or below it should be placed using **Label distance**.

Configuring polygon labels

For *polygon layers*, the placement options are as follows:

- **Offset from centroid** uses the polygon centroid as an anchor and works like **Offset from point** for point layers
- **Around centroid** works in a manner similar to **Around point**

- **Horizontal** places a horizontal label somewhere inside the polygon, independent of the centroid

- **Free** fits a freely rotated label inside the polygon

- **Using perimeter** places the label on the polygon's outline

The following screenshot shows lake labels (lakes.shp) using the **Multiple lines** feature wrapping on the empty space character, **Center Alignment**, a **Letter spacing** of 2, and positioning using the **Free** option:

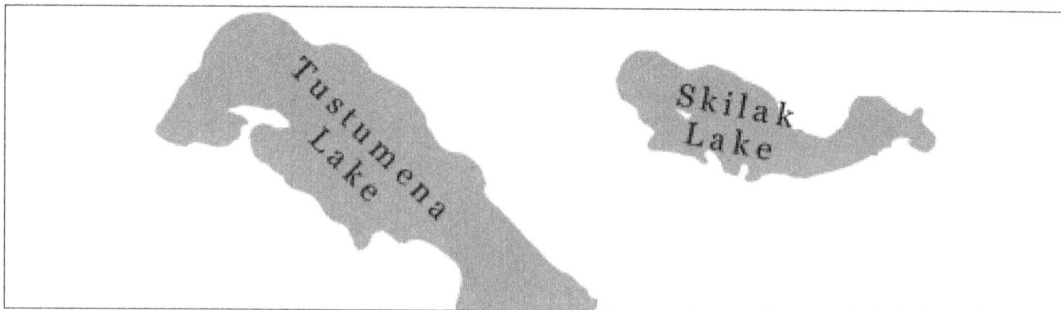

Placing labels manually

Besides automatic label placement, we also have the option to use **data-defined placement** to position labels exactly where we want them to be. In the labeling toolbar, we find tools for moving and rotating labels by hand. They are active and available only for layers that have set up data-defined placement for at least X and Y coordinates:

1. To start using the tools, we can simply add three new columns, label_x, label_y, and label_rot to, for example, the airports.shp file. We don't have to enter any values in the attribute table right now. The labeling engine will check for values, and if it finds the attribute fields empty, it will simply place the labels automatically.

2. Then, we can specify these columns in the label **Placement** section. Configure the data-defined overrides by clicking on the buttons beside **Coordinate X**, **Coordinate Y**, and **Rotation**, as shown in the following screenshot:

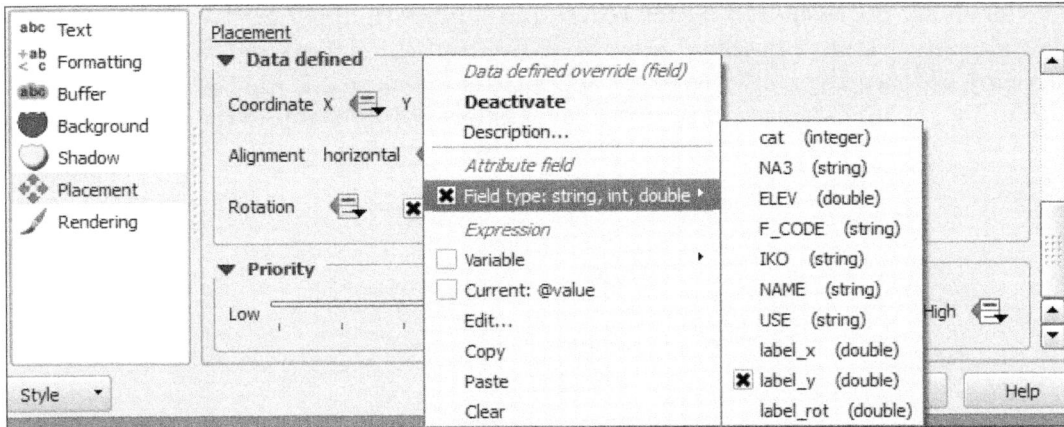

3. By specifying data-defined placement, the labeling toolbar's tools are now available (note that the editing mode has to be turned on), and we can use the **Move label** and **Rotate label** tools to manipulate the labels on the map. The changes are written back to the attribute table.

4. Try moving some labels, especially where they are placed closely together, and watch how the automatically placed labels adapt to your changes.

Controlling label rendering

In the **Rendering** section, we can define **Scale-based visibility** limits to display labels only at certain scales and **Pixel size-based visibility** to hide labels for small features. Here, we can also tell the labeling engine to **Show all labels for this layer (including colliding labels)**, which are normally hidden by default.

The following example shows labels with **road shields**. You can download a blank road shield SVG from http://upload.wikimedia.org/wikipedia/commons/c/c3/ Blank_shield.svg. Note how only Interstates are labeled. This can be achieved using the **Data defined Show label** setting in the **Rendering** section with the following expression:

```
"level" = 'Interstate'
```

The labels are positioned using the **Horizontal** option (in the **Placement** section). Additionally, **Merge connected lines to avoid duplicate labels** and **Suppress labeling of features smaller than** are activated; for example, 5 mm helps avoid clutter by not labeling pieces of road that are shorter than 5 mm in the current scale.

To set up the road shield, go to the **Background** section and select the blank shield SVG from the folder you downloaded it in. To make sure that the label fits nicely inside the shield, we additionally specify the **Size type** field as a buffer with a **Size** of 1 mm. This makes the shield a little bigger than the label it contains.

If you click on **Apply** now, you will notice that the labels are not centered perfectly inside the shields. To fix this, we apply a small **Offset** in the **Y** direction to the shield position, as shown in the following screenshot. Additionally, it is recommended that you deactivate any label buffers as they tend to block out parts of the shield, and we don't need them anyway.

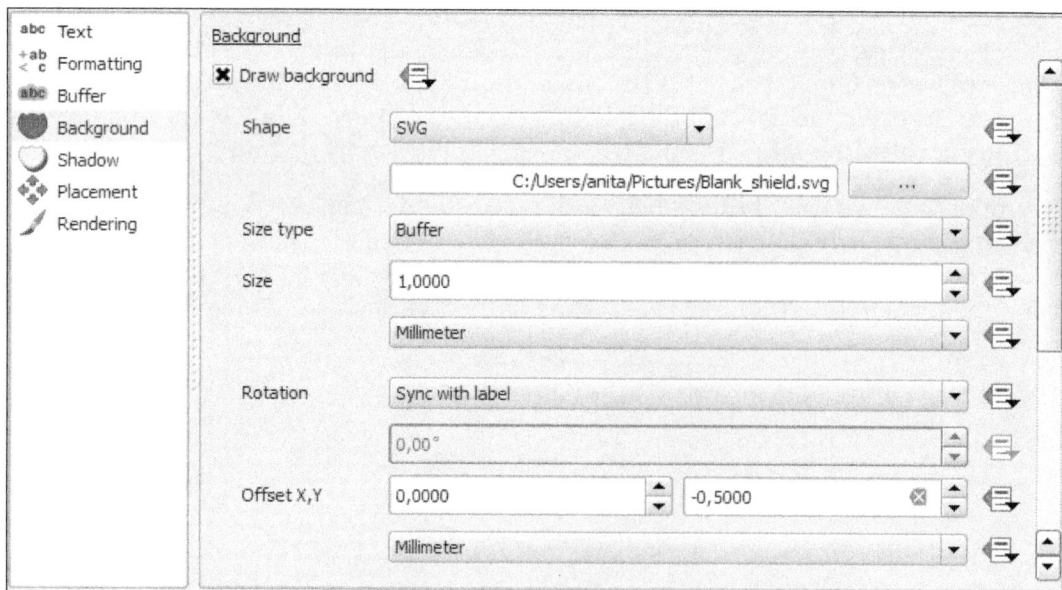

Designing print maps

In QGIS, **print maps** are designed in the print composer. A QGIS project can contain multiple composers, so it makes sense to pick descriptive names. Composers are saved automatically whenever we save the project. To see a list of all the compositions available in a project, go to **Project | Composer Manager**.

We can open a new composer by going to **Project | New Print Composer** or using *Ctrl + P*. The composer window consists of the following:

- A preview area for the map composition displaying a blank page when a new composer is created

- Panels for configuring **Composition**, **Item properties**, and **Atlas generation**, as well as a **Command history** panel for quick undo and redo actions

- Toolbars to manage, save, and export compositions; navigate in the preview area; as well as add and arrange different composer items

Once you have designed your print map the way you want it, you can save the template to a **composer template** .qpt file by going to **Composer | Save as template** and reuse it in other projects by going to **Composer | Add Items from Template**.

Creating a basic map

In this example, we will create a basic map with a scalebar, a north arrow, some explanatory text, and a legend.

When we start the print composer, we first see the **Composition** panel on the right-hand side. This panel gives us access to paper options such as size, orientation, and number of pages. It is also the place to configure snapping behavior and output resolution.

First, we add a map item to the paper using the **Add new map** button, or by going to **Layout | Add Map** and drawing the map rectangle on the paper. Click on the paper, keep the mouse button pressed down, and drag the rectangle open. We can move and resize the map using the mouse and the **Select/Move item** tools. Alternatively, it is possible to configure all the map settings in the **Item properties** panel.

The **Item properties** panel's content depends on the currently selected composition item. If a map item is selected, we can adjust the map's **Scale** and **Extents** as well as the **Position and size** tool of the map item itself. At a **Scale** of 10,000,000 (with the CRS set to EPSG:2964), we can more or less fit a map of Alaska on an A4-size paper, as shown in the following screenshot. To move the area that is displayed within the map item and change the map scale, we can use the **Move item content** tool.

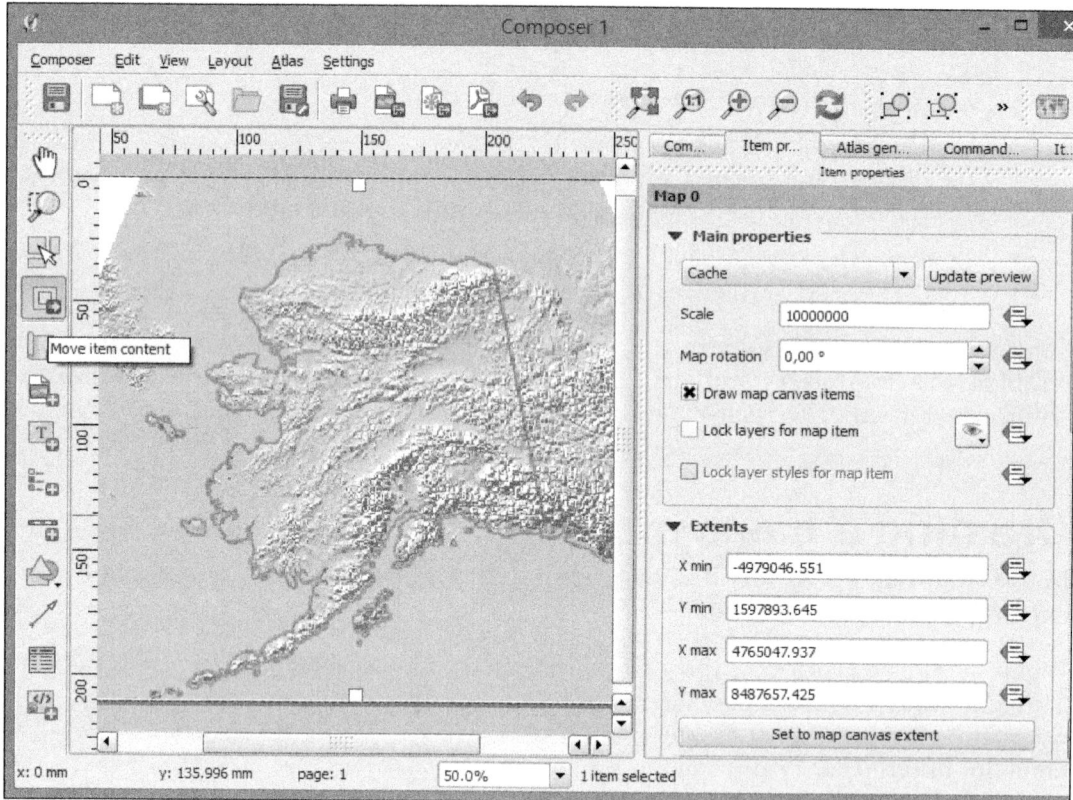

Adding a scalebar

After the map looks like what we want it to, we can add a scalebar using the **Add new scalebar** button or by going to **Layout | Add Scalebar** and clicking on the map. The **Item properties** panel now displays the scalebar's properties, which are similar to what you can see in the next screenshot. Since we can add multiple map items to one composition, it is important to specify which map the scale belongs to. The second main property is the scalebar **style**, which allows us to choose between different scalebar types, or a **Numeric** type for a simple textual representation, such as 1:10,000,000. Using the **Units** properties, we can convert the map units in feet or meters to something more manageable, such as miles or kilometers. The **Segments** properties control the number of segments and the size of a single segment in the scalebar. Further, the properties control the scalebar's color, font, background, and so on.

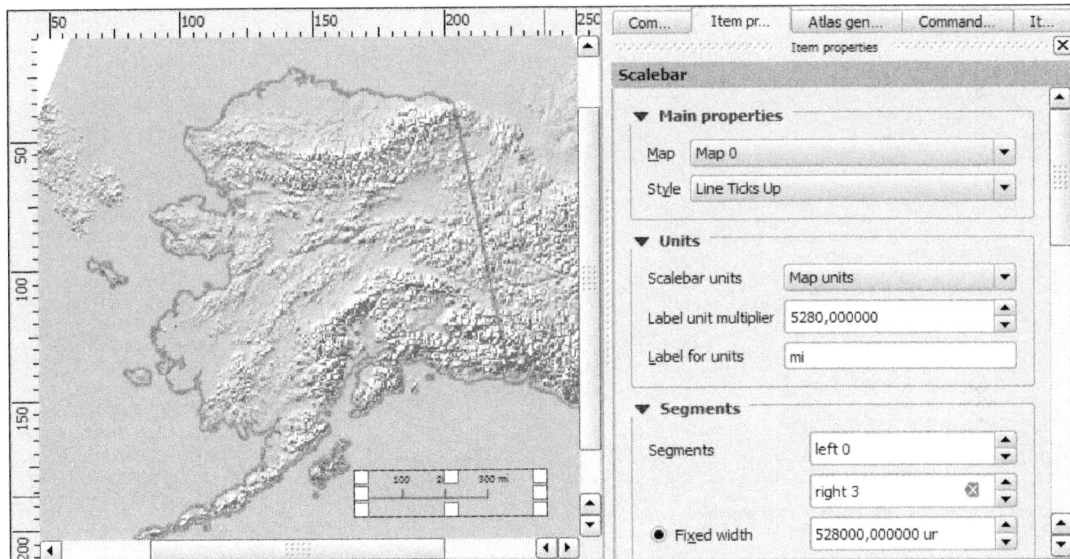

Adding a North arrow image

North arrows can be added to a composition using the **Add Image** button or by going to **Layout | Add image** and clicking on the paper. To use one of the SVGs that are part of the QGIS installation, open the **Search directories** section in the **Item properties** panel. It might take a while for QGIS to load the previews of the images in the SVG folder. You can pick a North arrow from the list of images or select your own image by clicking on the button next to the **Image source** input. More map decorations, such as arrows or rectangle, triangle, and ellipse shapes can be added using the appropriate toolbar buttons: **Add Arrow**, **Add Rectangle**, and so on.

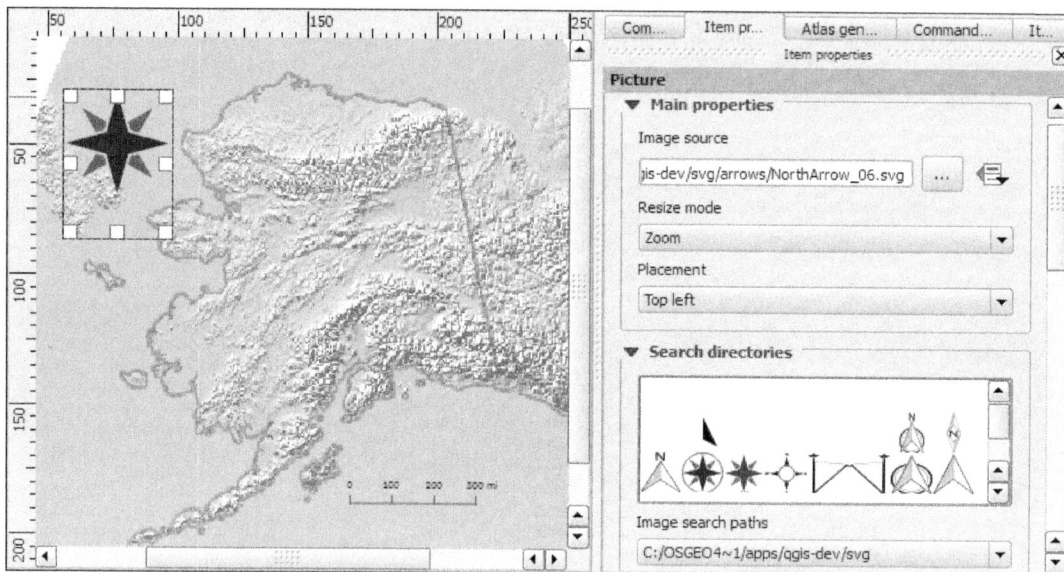

Adding a legend

Legends are another vital map element. We can use the **Add new legend** button or go to **Layout | Add legend** to add a default legend with entries for all currently visible map layers. Legend entries can be reorganized (sorted or added to groups), edited, and removed from the legend items' properties. Using the **Wrap text on** option, we can split long labels on multiple rows. The following screenshot shows the context menu that allows us to change the style (**Hidden**, **Group**, or **Subgroup**) of an entry. The corresponding font, size, and color are configurable in the **Fonts** section.

Additionally, the legend in this example is divided into three **Columns**, as you can see in the bottom-right section of the following screenshot. By default, QGIS tries to keep all entries of one layer in a single column, but we can override this behavior by enabling **Split layers**.

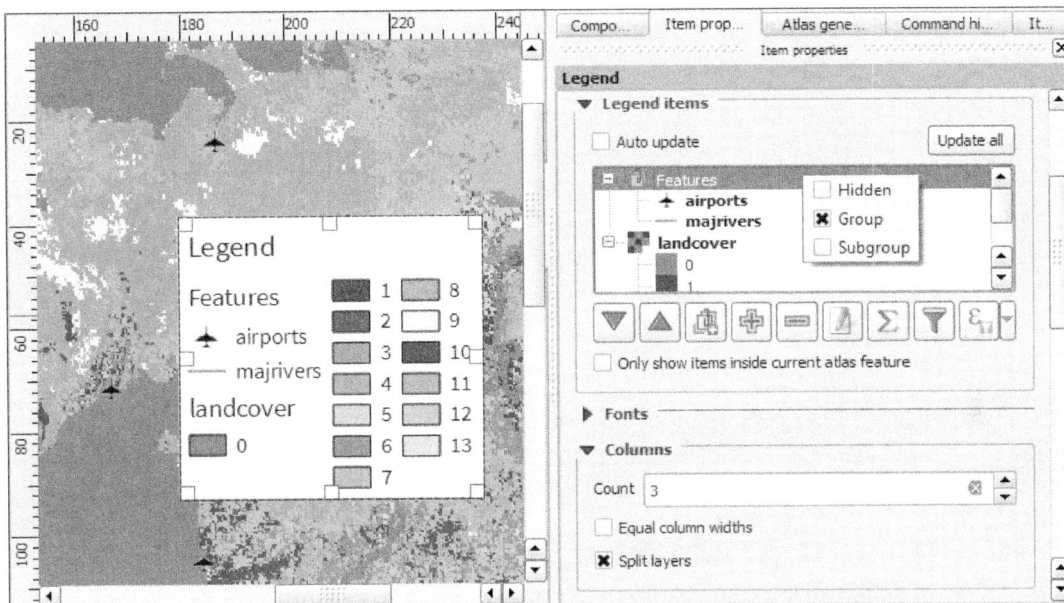

Adding explanatory text to the map

To add text to the map, we can use the **Add new label** button or go to **Layout | Add label**. Simple labels display all text using the same font. By enabling **Render as HTML**, we can create more elaborate labels with headers, lists, different colors, and highlights in bold or italics using normal HTML notation. Here is an example:

```
<h1>Alaska</h1>
<p>The name <i>"Alaska"</i> means "the mainland".</p>
<ul><li>one list entry</li><li>another entry</li></ul>
<p style="font-size:70%;">[% format_date( $now ,'yyyy-mm-dd')%]</p>
```

Labels can also contain expressions such as these:

- `[% $now %]`: This expression inserts the current timestamp, which can be formatted using the `format_date` function, as shown in the following screenshot

- `[% $page %]` of `[% $numpages %]`: This expression can be used to insert page numbers in compositions with multiple pages

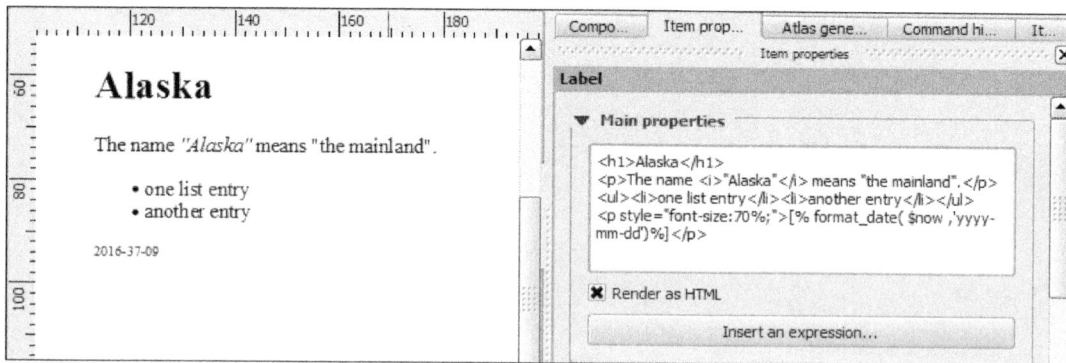

Adding map grids and frames

Other common features of maps are **grids** and **frames**. Every map item can have one or more grids. Click on the **+** button in the **Grids** section to add a grid. The **Interval** and **Offset** values have to be specified in map units. We can choose between the following **Grid types**:

- A normal **Solid** grid with customizable lines

- **Crosses** at specified intervals with customizable styles

- **Customizable Markers** at specified intervals

- **Frame and annotation only** will hide the grid while still displaying the frame and coordinate annotations

For **Grid frame**, we can select from the following **Frame styles**:

- **Zebra**, with customizable line and fill colors, as shown in the following screenshot

- **Interior ticks**, **Exterior ticks**, or **Interior and exterior ticks** for tick marks pointing inside the map, outside it, or in both directions

- **Line border** for a simple line frame

Using **Draw coordinates**, we can label the grid with the corresponding coordinates. The labels can be aligned horizontally or vertically and placed inside or outside the frame, as shown here:

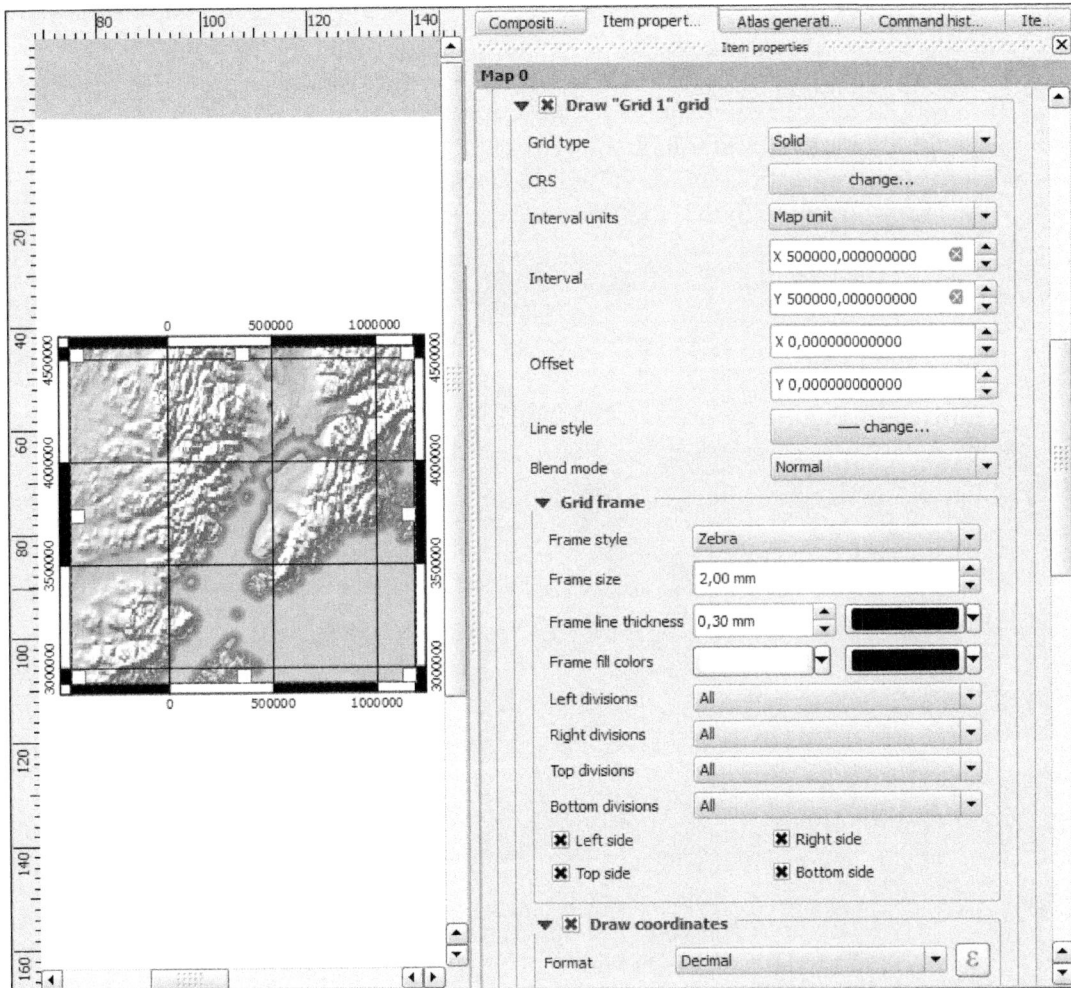

Creating overview maps

Maps that show an area close up are often accompanied by a second map that tells the reader where the area is located in a larger context. To create such an **overview map**, we add a second map item and an overview by clicking on the **+** button in the **Overviews** section. By setting the **Map frame**, we can define which detail map's extent should be highlighted. By clicking on the **+** button again, we can add more map frames to the overview map. The following screenshot shows an example with two detail maps both of which are added to an overview map. To distinguish between the two maps, the overview highlights are color-coded (by changing the overview **Frame style**) to match the colors of the frames of the detail maps.

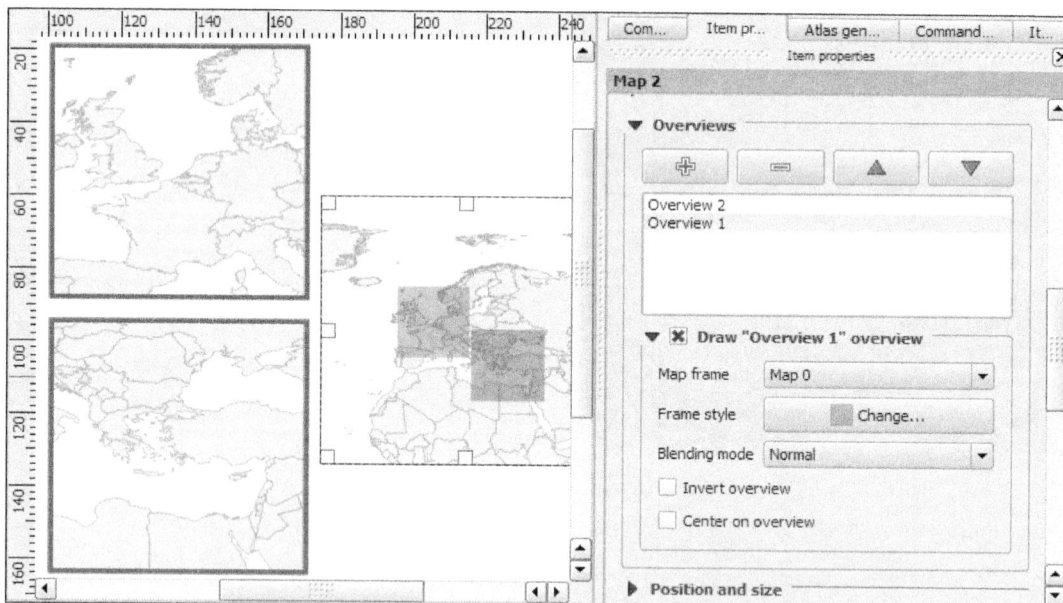

> Every map item in a composition can display a different combination of layers. Generally, map items in a composer are synced with the map in the main QGIS window. So, if we turn a layer off in the main window, it is removed from the print composer map as well. However, we can stop this automatic synchronization by enabling **Lock layers** for a map item in the map item's properties.

Adding more details with attribute tables and HTML frames

To insert additional details into the map, the composer also offers the possibility of adding an **attribute table** to the composition using the **Add attribute table** button or by going to **Layout | Add attribute table**. By enabling **Show only features visible within a map**, we can filter the table and display only the relevant results. Additional filter expressions can be set using the **Filter with** option. Sorting (by name for example, as shown in the following screenshot) and renaming of columns is possible via the **Attributes** button. To customize the header row with bold and centered text, go to the **Fonts and text styling** section and change the **Table heading** settings.

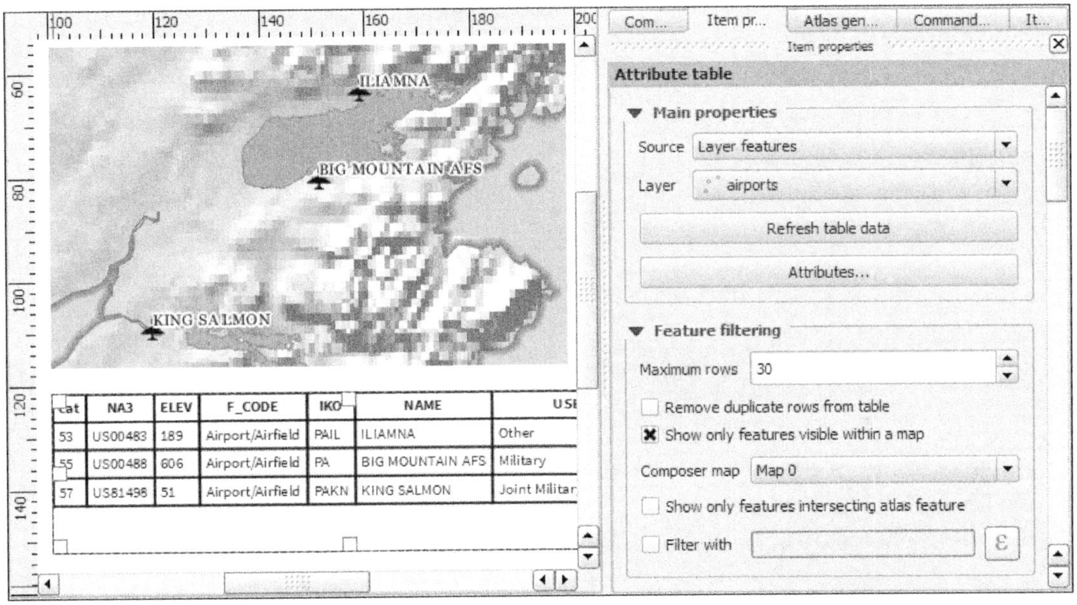

Even more advanced content can be added using the **Add html frame** button. We can point the item's URL reference to any HTML page on our local machines or online, and the content (text and images as displayed in a web browser) will be displayed on the composer page.

Creating a map series using the Atlas feature

With the print composer's Atlas feature, we can create a series of maps using one print composition. The tool will create one output (which can be image files, PDFs, or multiple pages in one PDF) for every feature in the so-called **Coverage layer**.

Atlas can control and update multiple map items within one composition. To enable Atlas for a map item, we have to enable the **Controlled by atlas** option in the **Item properties** of the map item. When we use the **Fixed scale** option in the **Controlled by atlas** section, all maps will be rendered using the same scale. If we need a more flexible output, we can switch to the **Margin around feature** option instead, which zooms to every **Coverage layer** feature and renders it in addition to the specified margin surrounding area.

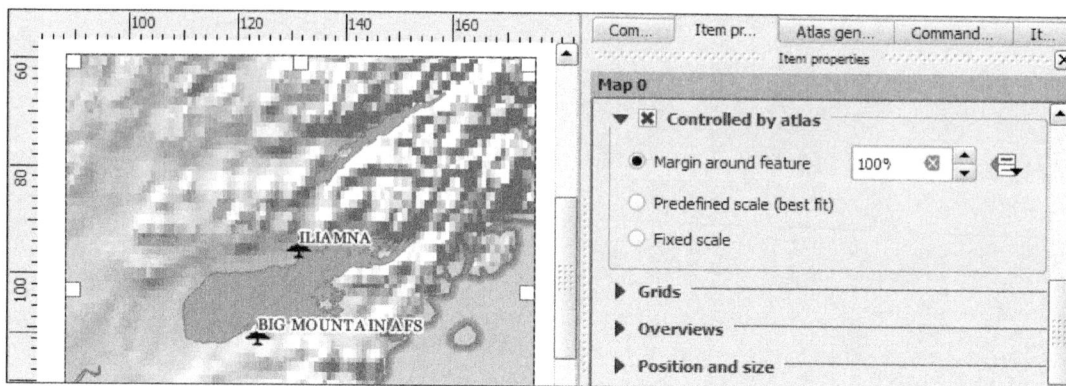

To finish the configuration, we switch to the **Atlas generation** panel. As mentioned before, Atlas will create one map for every feature in the layer configured in the **Coverage layer** dropdown. Features in the coverage layer can be displayed like regular features or hidden by enabling **Hidden coverage layer**. Adding an expression to the **Feature filtering** option or enabling the **Sort by** option makes it possible to further fine-tune the results. The **Output** field can be one image or PDF for each coverage layer feature, or you can create a multipage PDF by enabling **Single file export when possible** before going to **Composer | Export as PDF**.

Once these configurations are finished, we can preview the map series by enabling the **Preview Atlas** button, which you can see in the top-left corner of the following screenshot. The arrow buttons next to the preview button are used to navigate between the Atlas maps.

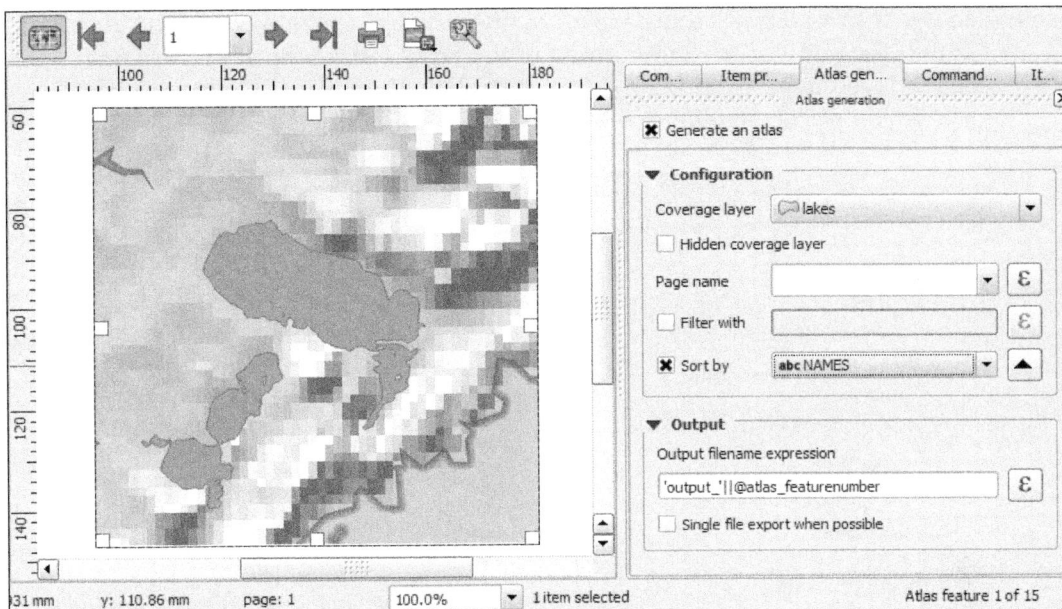

Presenting your maps online

Besides print maps, web maps are another popular way of publishing maps. In this section, we will use different QGIS plugins to create different types of web map.

Exporting a web map

To create web maps from within QGIS, we can use the **qgis2web** plugin, which we have to install using the **Plugin Manager**. Once it is installed, go to **Web | qgis2web | Create web map** to start it. **qgis2web** supports the two most popular open source **web mapping libraries**: **OpenLayers 3**, and **Leaflet**.

The following screenshot shows an example of our airports dataset. In this example, we are using the **Leaflet** library (as configured in the bottom-left corner of the following screenshot) because at the time of writing this book, only **Leaflet** supports SVG markers:

1. In the top-left corner, you can configure which layers from your project should be displayed on the web map, as well as the **Info popup content**, which is displayed when the user clicks on or hovers over a feature (depending on the **Show popups on hover** setting).

2. In the bottom-right corner, you can pick a background map for your web map. Pick one and click on the **Update preview** button to see the result.

3. In the bottom-left corner, you can further configure the web map. All available settings are documented in the **Help** tab, so the content is not reproduced here. Again, don't forget to click on the **Update preview** button when you make changes.

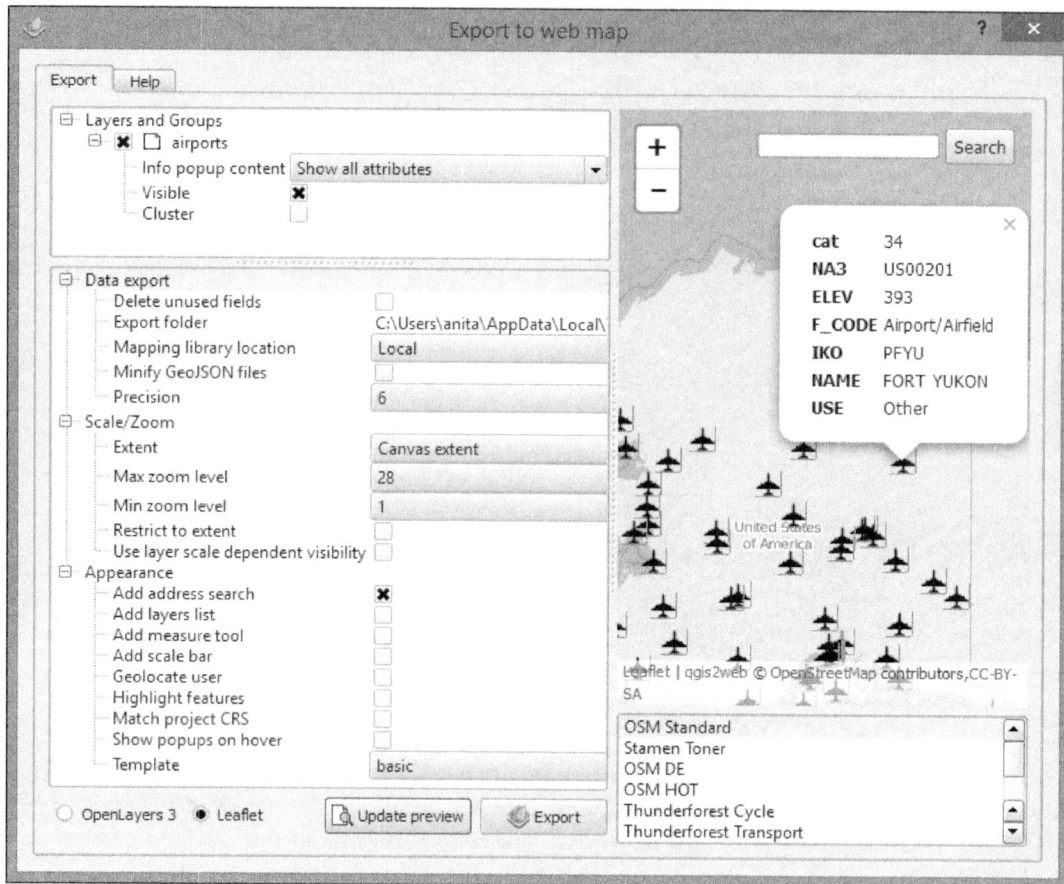

When you are happy with the configuration, click on the **Export** button. This will save the web map at the location specified as the **Export folder** and open the resulting web map in your web browser. You can copy the contents in the **Export folder** to a web server to publish the map.

Creating map tiles

Another popular way to share maps on the Web is **map tiles**. These are basically just collections of images. These image tiles are typically 256 × 256 pixels and are placed side by side in order to create an illusion of a very large, seamless map image. Each tile has a z coordinate that describes its zoom level and x and y coordinates that describe its position within a square grid for that zoom level. On zoom level 0 ($z0$), the whole world fits in one tile. From there on, each consecutive zoom level is related to the previous one by a power of 4. This means $z0$ contains 1 tile, $z1$ contains 4 tiles, and $z2$ contains 16 tiles, and so on.

In QGIS, we can use the **QTiles** plugin, which has to be installed using the **Plugin Manager**, to create map tiles for our project. Once it is installed, you can go to **Plugins | QTiles** to start it. The following screenshot shows the plugin dialog where we can configure the **Output** location, the **Extent** of the map that we want to export as tiles, as well as the **Zoom** levels we want to create tiles for.

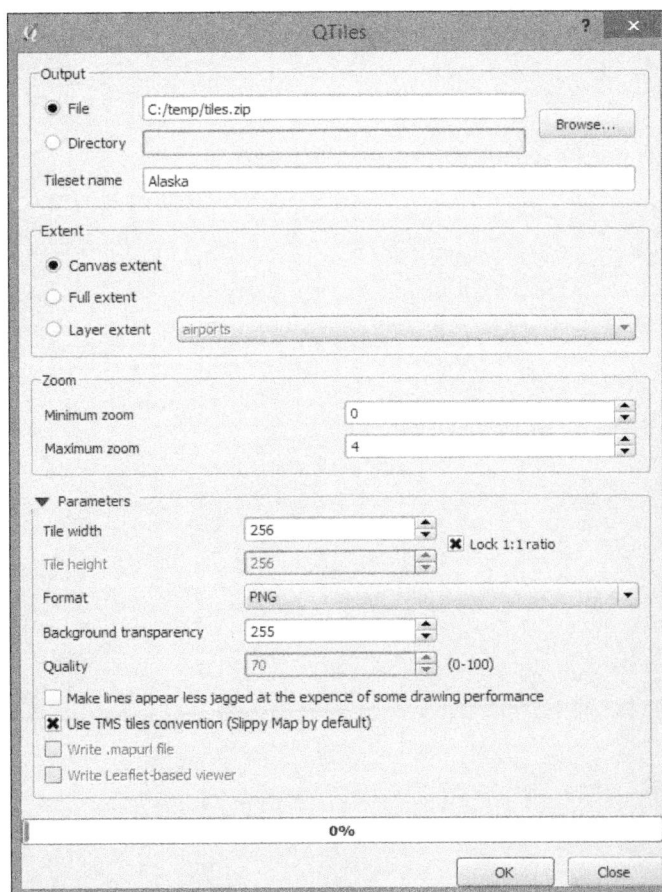

When you click on **OK**, the plugin will create a `.zip` file containing all tiles. Using map tiles in web mapping libraries is out of the scope of this book. Please refer to the documentation of your web mapping library for instructions on how to embed the tiles. If you are using Leaflet, for example, you can refer to `https://switch2osm.org/using-tiles/getting-started-with-leaflet` for detailed instructions.

Exporting a 3D web map

To create stunning **3D web maps**, we need the **Qgis2threejs** plugin, which we can install using the **Plugin Manager**.

For example, we can use our `srtm_05_01.tif` elevation dataset to create a 3D view of that part of Alaska. The following screenshot shows the configuration of **DEM Layer** in the **Qgis2threejs** dialog. By selecting **Display type** as **Map canvas image**, we furthermore define that the current map image (which is shown on the right-hand side of the dialog) will be draped over the 3D surface:

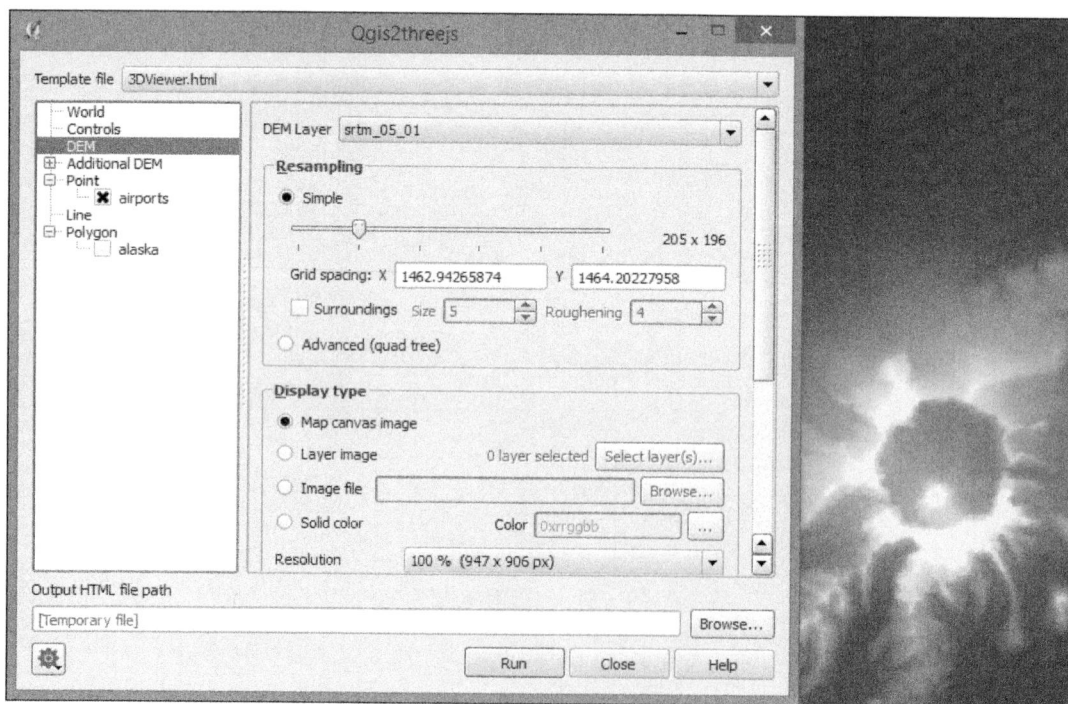

Besides creating a 3D surface, this plugin can also label features. For example, we can add our airports and label them with their names, as shown in the next screenshot. By setting **Label height** to **Height from point**, we let the plugin determine automatically where to place the label, but of course, you can manually override this by changing to **Fixed value** or one of the feature attributes.

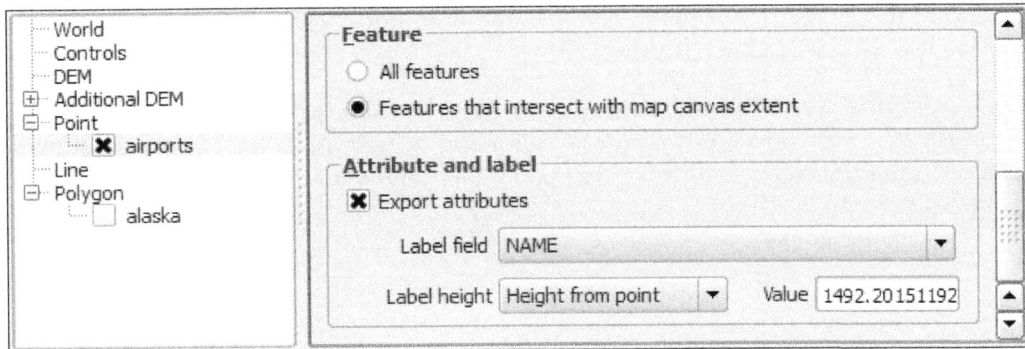

If you click on **Run** now, the plugin will create the export and open the 3D map in your web browser. On the first try, it is quite likely that the surface looks too flat. Luckily, this can be changed easily by adjusting the **Vertical exaggeration** setting in the **World** section of the plugin configuration. The following example was created with a **Vertical exaggeration** of 10:

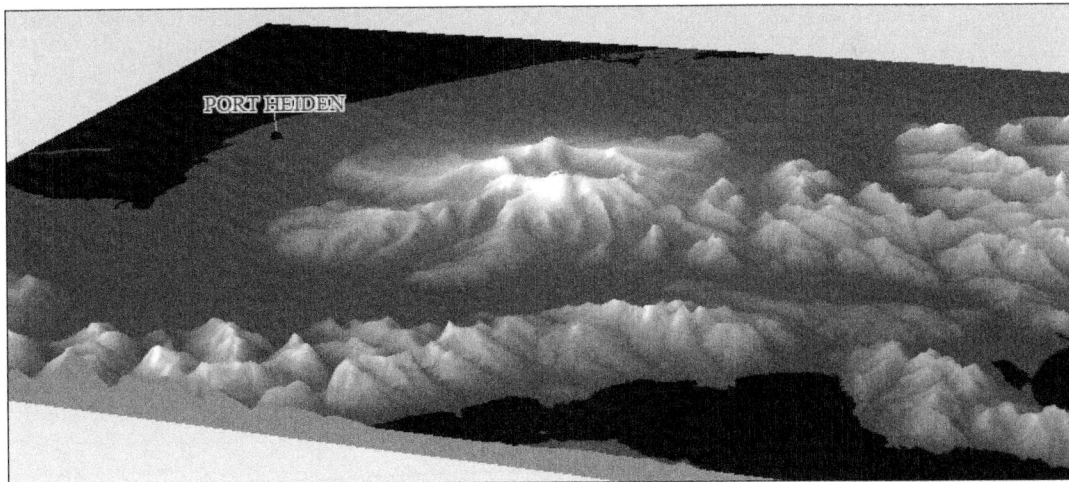

Qgis2threejs exports all files to the location specified in the **Output HTML file path**. You can copy the contents in that folder on a web server to publish the map.

Summary

In this chapter, we took a closer look at how we can create more complex maps using advanced vector layer styles, such as categorized or rule-based styles. We also covered the automatic and manual feature labeling options available in QGIS. This chapter also showed you how to create printable maps using the print composer and introduced the Atlas functionality for creating map books. Finally, we created web maps, which we can publish online.

Congratulations! In the chapters so far, you have learned how to install and use QGIS to create, edit, and analyze spatial data and how to present it in an effective manner. In the following and final chapter, we will take a look at expanding QGIS functionality using Python.

6

Extending QGIS with Python

This chapter is an introduction to scripting QGIS with Python. Of course, a full-blown Python tutorial would be out of scope for this book. The examples here therefore assume a minimum proficiency of working with Python. Python is a very accessible programming language even if you are just getting started, and it has gained a lot of popularity in both the open source and proprietary GIS world, for example, ESRI's **ArcPy** or **PyQGIS**. QGIS currently supports **Python 2.7**, but there are plans to support Python 3 in the upcoming **QGIS 3.x** series. We will start with an introduction to actions and then move on to the QGIS Python Console, before we go into more advanced development of custom tools for the *Processing Toolbox* and an explanation of how to create our own plugins.

Adding functionality using actions

Actions are a convenient way of adding custom functionality to QGIS. Actions are created for specific layers, for example, our populated places dataset, popp.shp. Therefore, to create actions, we go to **Layer Properties | Actions**. There are different types of actions, such as the following:

- **Generic actions** start external processes; for example, you run command-line applications such as ogr2ogr

> ogr2ogr is a command-line tool that can be used to convert file formats and, at the same time, perform operations such as spatial or attribute selections and reprojecting.

- **Python actions** execute Python scripts

- **Open actions** open a file using your computer's configured default application, that is, your PDF viewing application for `.pdf` files or your browser for websites

- Operating system (**Mac**, **Windows**, and **Unix**) actions work like generic actions but are restricted to the respective operating system

Configuring your first Python action

Click on the **Add default actions** button on the right-hand side of the dialog to add some example actions to your popp layer. This is really handy to get started with actions. For example, the Python action called **Selected field's value** will display the specified attribute's value when we use the action tool. All that we need to do before we can give this action a try is update it so that it accesses a valid attribute of our layer. For example, we can make it display the popp layer's TYPE attribute value in a message box, as shown in the next screenshot:

1. Select the **Selected field's value** action in **Action list**.

2. Edit the **Action** code at the bottom of the dialog. You can manually enter the attribute name or select it from the drop-down list and click on **Insert field**.

3. To save the changes, click on **Update selected action**:

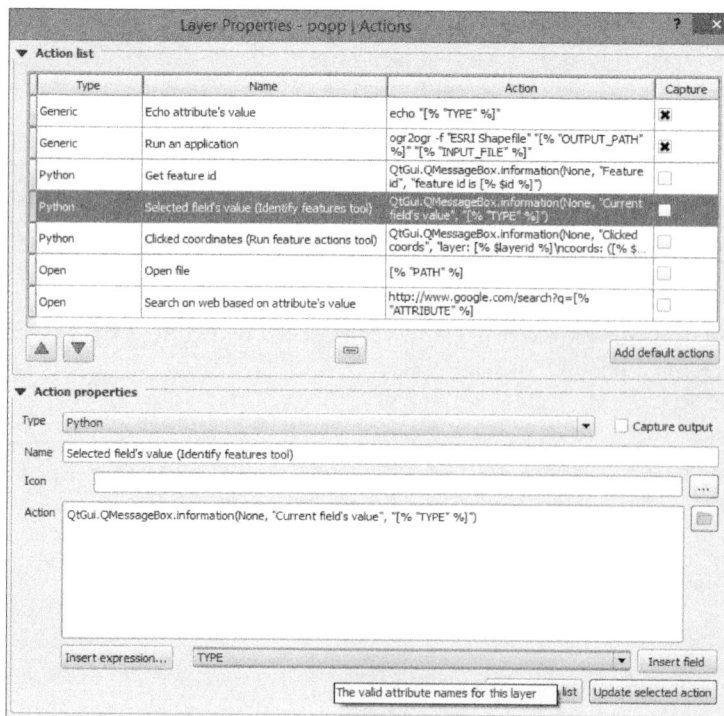

To use this action, close the **Layer Properties** dialog and click on the drop-down arrow next to the **Run Feature Action** button. This will expand the list of available layer actions, as shown in the following screenshot:

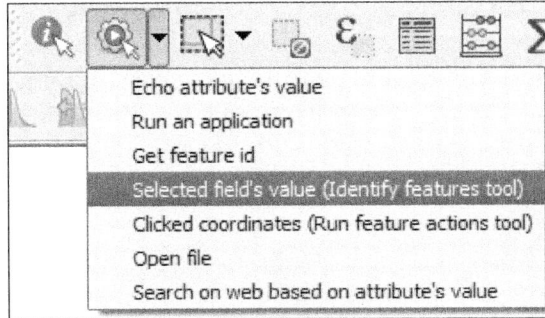

Click on the **Selected field's value** entry and then click on a layer feature. This will open a pop-up dialog in which the action will output the feature's TYPE value. Of course, we can also make this action output more information, for example, by extending it to this:

```
QtGui.QMessageBox.information(None, "Current field's value",
"Type: [% "TYPE" %] \n[% "F_CODEDESC" %]")
```

This will display the TYPE value on the first line and the F_CODEDESC value on the second line.

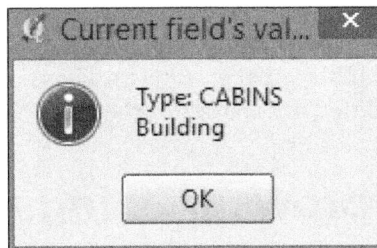

Opening files using actions

To open files directly from within QGIS, we use the **Open** actions. If you added the default actions in the previous exercise, your layer will already have an **Open file** action. The action is as simple as `[% "PATH" %]` for opening the file path specified in the layer's path attribute. Since none of our sample datasets contain a path attribute, we'll add one now to test this feature. Check out *Chapter 3, Data Creation and Editing*, if you need to know the details of how to add a new attribute. For example, the paths added in the following screenshot will open the default image viewer and PDF viewer application, respectively:

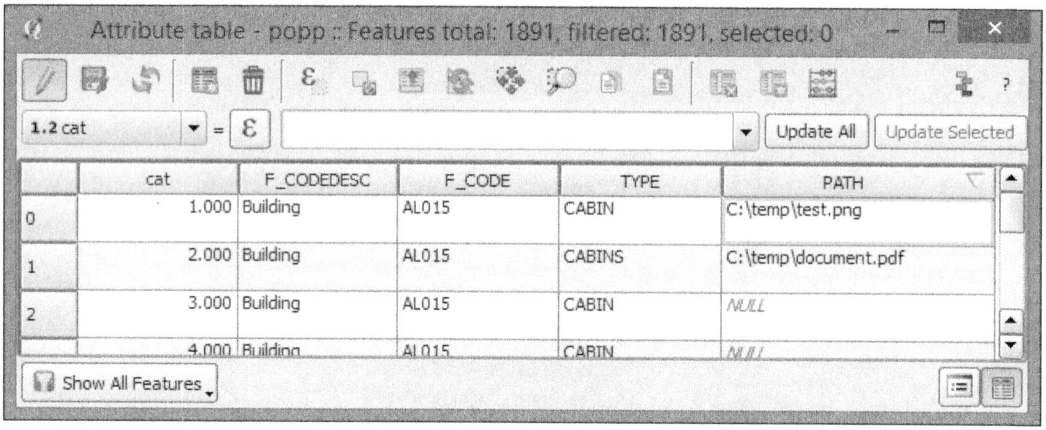

While the previous example uses absolute paths stored in the attributes, you can also use relative paths by changing the action code so that it completes the partial path stored in the attribute value; for example, you can use `C:\temp\[% "TYPE" %].png` to open `.png` files that are named according to the `TYPE` attribute values.

Opening a web browser using actions

Another type of useful **Open** action is opening the web browser and accessing certain websites. For example, consider this action:

```
http://www.google.com/search?q=[% "TYPE" %]
```

It will open your default web browser and search for the `TYPE` value using Google, and this action:.

```
https://en.wikipedia.org/w/index.php?search=[% "TYPE" %]
```

will search on Wikipedia.

Getting to know the Python Console

The most direct way to interact with the QGIS **API** (short for **Application Programming Interface**) is through the **Python Console**, which can be opened by going to **Plugins | Python Console**. As you can see in the following screenshot, the **Python Console** is displayed within a new panel below the map:

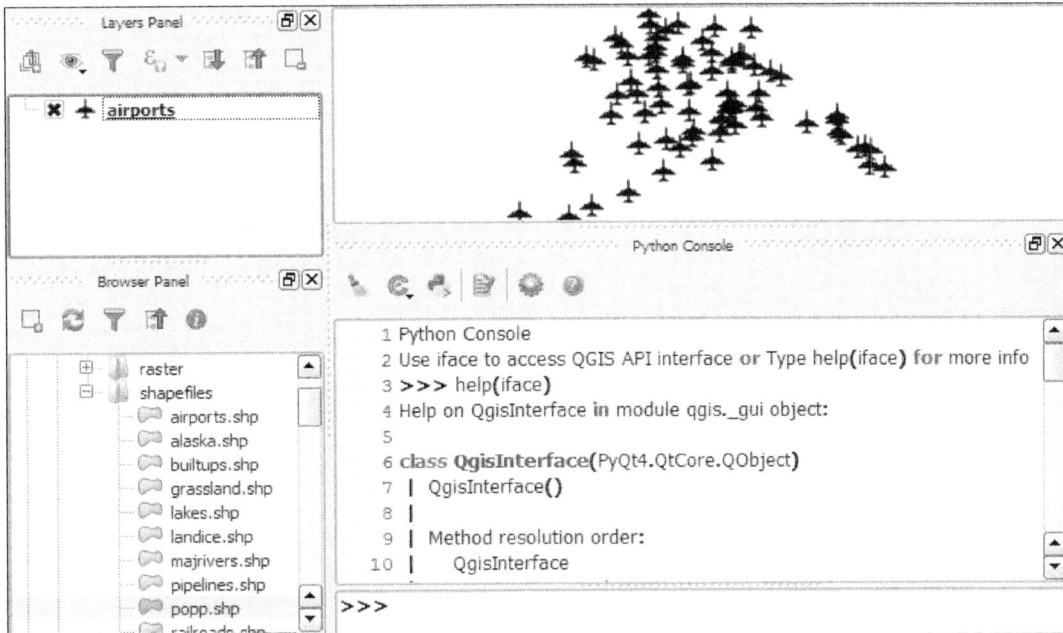

Our access point for interaction with the application, project, and data is the `iface` object. To get a list of all the functions available for `iface`, type `help(iface)`. Alternatively, this information is available online in the **API documentation** at `http://qgis.org/api/classQgisInterface.html`.

Loading and exploring datasets

One of the first things we will want to do is to load some data. For example, to load a vector layer, we use the `addVectorLayer()` function of `iface`:

```
v_layer =
iface.addVectorLayer('C:/Users/anita/Documents/Geodata/qgis_sample_
data/shapefiles/airports.shp','airports','ogr')
```

When we execute this command, `airports.shp` will be loaded using the `ogr` driver and added to the map under the layer name of `airports`. Additionally, this function returns the created `layer` object. Using this `layer` object—which we stored in `v_layer`—we can access vector layer functions, such as `name()`, which returns the layer name and is displayed in the **Layers** list:

```
v_layer.name()
```

This is the output:

```
u'airports'
```

> The u in front of the `airports` layer name shows that the name is returned as a Unicode string.

Of course, the next logical step is to look at the layer's features. The number of features can be accessed using `featureCount()`:

```
v_layer.featureCount()
```

Here is the output:

```
76L
```

This shows us that the airport layer contains 76 features. The L in the end shows that it's a numerical value of the long type. In our next step, we will access these features. This is possible using the `getFeatures()` function, which returns a `QgsFeatureIterator` object. With a simple `for` loop, we can then print the `attributes()` of all features in our layer:

```
my_features = v_layer.getFeatures()
for feature in my_features:
    print feature.attributes()
```

This is the output:

```
[1, u'US00157', 78.0, u'Airport/Airfield', u'PA', u'NOATAK' ...
[2, u'US00229', 264.0, u'Airport/Airfield', u'PA', u'AMBLER'...
[3, u'US00186', 585.0, u'Airport/Airfield', u'PABT', u'BETTL...
...
```

> When using the preceding code snippet, it is worth noting that the Python syntax requires proper indentation. This means that, for example, the content of the `for` loop has to be indented, as shown in the preceding code. If Python encounters such errors, it will raise an **Indentation Error**.

You might have noticed that `attributes()` shows us the attribute values, but we don't know the field names yet. To get the field names, we use this code:

```
for field in v_layer.fields():
    print field.name()
```

The output is as follows:

```
ID
fk_region
ELEV
NAME
USE
```

Once we know the field names, we can access specific feature attributes, for example, NAME:

```
for feature in v_layer.getFeatures():

    print feature.attribute('NAME')
```

This is the output:

```
NOATAK
AMBLER
BETTLES
...
```

A quick solution to, for example, sum up the elevation values is as follows:

```
sum([feature.attribute('ELEV') for feature in
v_layer.getFeatures()])
```

Here is the output:

```
22758.0
```

> In the previous example, we took advantage of the fact that Python allows us to create a list by writing a `for` loop inside square brackets. This is called **list comprehension**, and you can read more about it at https://docs.python.org/2/tutorial/datastructures.html#list-comprehensions.

Loading raster data is very similar to loading vector data and is done using
`addRasterLayer()`:

```
r_layer = iface.addRasterLayer('C:/Users/anita/Documents/Geodata/qgis_
sample_data/raster/SR_50M_alaska_nad.tif','hillshade')
r_layer.name()
```

The following is the output:

```
u'hillshade'
```

To get the raster layer's size in pixels we can use the `width()` and `height()`
functions, like this:

```
r_layer.width(), r_layer.height()
```

Here is the output:

```
(1754, 1394)
```

If we want to know more about the raster values, we use the layer's data provider
object, which provides access to the raster band statistics. It's worth noting that
we have to use `bandStatistics(1)` instead of `bandStatistics(0)` to access the
statistics of a single-band raster, such as our `hillshade` layer (for example, for the
maximum value):

```
r_layer.dataProvider().bandStatistics(1).maximumValue
```

The output is as follows:

```
251.0
```

Other values that can be accessed like this are `minimumValue`, `range`, `stdDev`, and
`sum`. For a full list, use this line:

```
help(r_layer.dataProvider().bandStatistics(1))
```

Styling layers

Since we now know how to load data, we can continue to style the layers. The
simplest option is to load a premade style (a `.qml` file):

```
v_layer.loadNamedStyle('C:/temp/planes.qml')
v_layer.triggerRepaint()
```

Make sure that you call `triggerRepaint()` to ensure that the map is redrawn to
reflect your changes.

> You can create `planes.qml` by saving the airport style you created in *Chapter 2, Viewing Spatial Data* (by going to **Layer Properties | Style | Save Style | QGIS Layer Style File**), or use any other style you like.

Of course, we can also create a style in code. Let's take a look at a basic single symbol renderer. We create a simple symbol with one layer, for example, a yellow diamond:

```
from PyQt4.QtGui import QColor
symbol = QgsMarkerSymbolV2()
symbol.symbolLayer(0).setName('diamond')
symbol.symbolLayer(0).setSize(10)
symbol.symbolLayer(0).setColor(QColor('#ffff00'))
v_layer.rendererV2().setSymbol(symbol)
v_layer.triggerRepaint()
```

A much more advanced approach is to create a **rule-based renderer**. We discussed the basics of rule-based renderers in *Chapter 5, Creating Great Maps*. The following example creates two rules: one for civil-use airports and one for all other airports. Due to the length of this script, I recommend that you use the **Python Console** editor, which you can open by clicking on the **Show editor** button, as shown in the following screenshot:

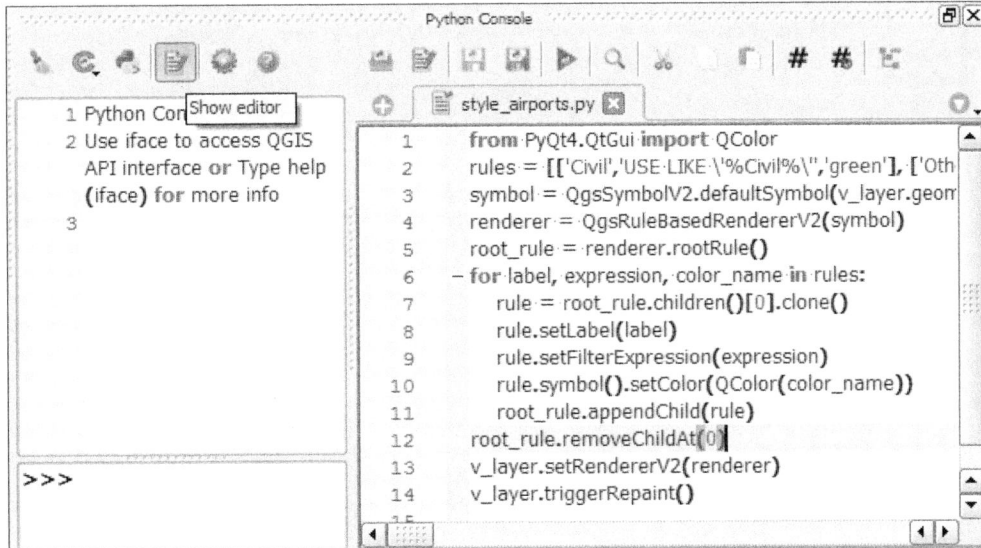

Each rule in this example has a name, a filter expression, and a symbol color. Note how the rules are appended to the renderer's root rule:

```python
from PyQt4.QtGui import QColor
rules = [['Civil','USE LIKE \'%Civil%\'','green'], ['Other','USE
NOT LIKE \'%Civil%\'','red']]
symbol = QgsSymbolV2.defaultSymbol(v_layer.geometryType())
renderer = QgsRuleBasedRendererV2(symbol)
root_rule = renderer.rootRule()
for label, expression, color_name in rules:
    rule = root_rule.children()[0].clone()
    rule.setLabel(label)
    rule.setFilterExpression(expression)
    rule.symbol().setColor(QColor(color_name))
    root_rule.appendChild(rule)
root_rule.removeChildAt(0)
v_layer.setRendererV2(renderer)
v_layer.triggerRepaint()
```

To run the script, click on the **Run script** button at the bottom of the editor toolbar.

> If you are interested in reading more about styling vector layers, I recommend Joshua Arnott's post at http://snorf.net/blog/2014/03/04/symbology-of-vector-layers-in-qgis-python-plugins/.

Filtering data

To filter vector layer features programmatically, we can specify a subset string. This is the same as defining a **Feature subset** query in in the **Layer Properties** | **General** section. For example, we can choose to display airports only if their names start with an A:

```python
v_layer.setSubsetString("NAME LIKE 'A%'")
```

To remove the filter, just set an empty subset string:

```python
v_layer.setSubsetString("")
```

Creating a memory layer

A great way to create a temporary vector layer is by using so-called **memory layers**. Memory layers are a good option for temporary analysis output or visualizations. They are the scripting equivalent of temporary scratch layers, which we used in *Chapter 3, Data Creation and Editing*. Like temporary scratch layers, memory layers exist within a QGIS session and are destroyed when QGIS is closed. In the following example, we create a memory layer and add a polygon feature to it.

Basically, a memory layer is a QgsVectorLayer like any other. However, the provider (the third parameter) is not 'ogr' as in the previous example of loading a file, but 'memory'. Instead of a file path, the first parameter is a definition string that specifies the geometry type, the CRS, and the attribute table fields (in this case, one integer field called MYNUM and one string field called MYTXT):

```
mem_layer =
QgsVectorLayer("Polygon?crs=epsg:4326&field=MYNUM:integer&field=MYTXT:
string", "temp_layer", "memory")
if not mem_layer.isValid():
    raise Exception("Failed to create memory layer")
```

Once we have created the QgsVectorLayer object, we can start adding features to its data provider:

```
mem_layer_provider = mem_layer.dataProvider()
my_polygon = QgsFeature()
my_polygon.setGeometry(
  QgsGeometry.fromRect(QgsRectangle(16,48,17,49)))
my_polygon.setAttributes([10,"hello world"])
mem_layer_provider.addFeatures([my_polygon])
QgsMapLayerRegistry.instance().addMapLayer(mem_layer)
```

> Note how we first create a blank QgsFeature, to which we then add geometry and attributes using setGeometry() and setAttributes(), respectively. When we add the layer to QgsMapLayerRegistry, the layer is rendered on the map.

Exporting map images

The simplest option for saving the current map is by using the scripting equivalent of **Save as Image** (under **Project**). This will export the current map to an image file in the same resolution as the map area in the QGIS application window:

```
iface.mapCanvas().saveAsImage('C:/temp/simple_export.png')
```

If we want more control over the size and resolution of the exported image, we need a few more lines of code. The following example shows how we can create our own QgsMapRendererCustomPainterJob object and configure to our own liking using custom QgsMapSettings for size (width and height), resolution (dpi), map extent, and map layers:

```python
from PyQt4.QtGui import QImage, QPainter
from PyQt4.QtCore import QSize
# configure the output image
width = 800
height = 600
dpi = 92
img = QImage(QSize(width, height), QImage.Format_RGB32)
img.setDotsPerMeterX(dpi / 25.4 * 1000)
img.setDotsPerMeterY(dpi / 25.4 * 1000)
# get the map layers and extent
layers = [ layer.id() for layer in
iface.legendInterface().layers() ]
extent = iface.mapCanvas().extent()
# configure map settings for export
mapSettings = QgsMapSettings()
mapSettings.setMapUnits(0)
mapSettings.setExtent(extent)
mapSettings.setOutputDpi(dpi)
mapSettings.setOutputSize(QSize(width, height))
mapSettings.setLayers(layers)
mapSettings.setFlags(QgsMapSettings.Antialiasing |
QgsMapSettings.UseAdvancedEffects |
QgsMapSettings.ForceVectorOutput | QgsMapSettings.DrawLabeling)
# configure and run painter
p = QPainter()
p.begin(img)
mapRenderer = QgsMapRendererCustomPainterJob(mapSettings, p)
mapRenderer.start()
mapRenderer.waitForFinished()
p.end()
# save the result
img.save("C:/temp/custom_export.png", "png")
```

Creating custom geoprocessing scripts using Python

In *Chapter 4, Spatial Analysis*, we used the tools of **Processing Toolbox** to analyze our data, but we are not limited to these tools. We can expand *processing* with our own scripts. The advantages of *processing* scripts over normal Python scripts, such as the ones we saw in the previous section, are as follows:

- Processing automatically generates a graphical user interface for the script to configure the script parameters
- Processing scripts can be used in **Graphical modeler** to create geoprocessing models

As the following screenshot shows, the **Scripts** section is initially empty, except for some **Tools** to add and create new scripts:

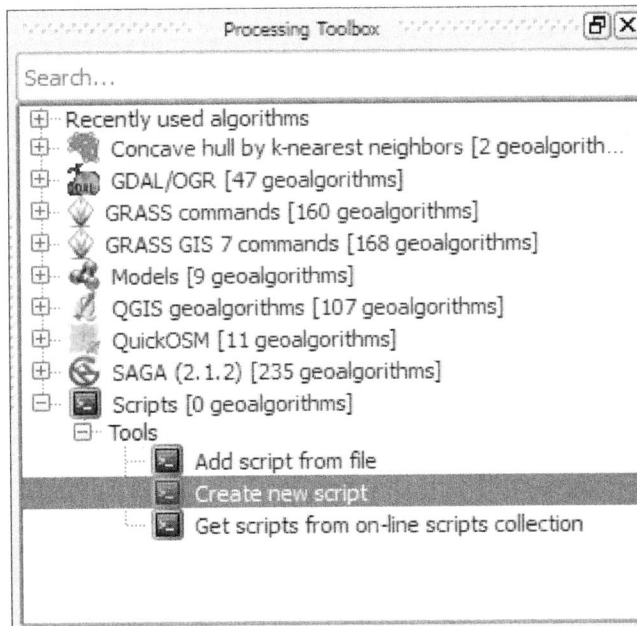

Writing your first Processing script

We will create our first simple script; which fetches some layer information. To get started, double-click on the **Create new script** entry in **Scripts | Tools**. This opens an empty **Script editor** dialog. The following screenshot shows the **Script editor** with a short script that prints the input layer's name on the **Python Console**:

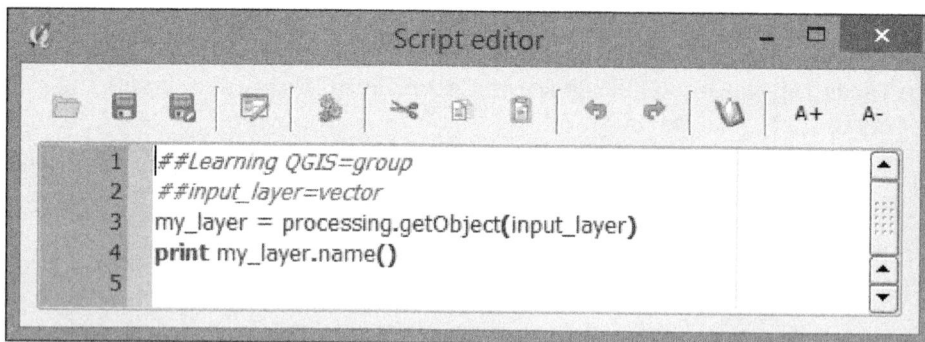

```
1  ##Learning QGIS=group
2  ##input_layer=vector
3  my_layer = processing.getObject(input_layer)
4  print my_layer.name()
5
```

The first line means our script will be put into the Learning QGIS group of scripts, as shown in the following screenshot. The double hashes (##) are Processing syntax and they indicate that the line contains Processing-specific information rather than Python code. The script name is created from the filename you chose when you saved the script. For this example, I have saved the script as my_first_script.py. The second line defines the script input, a vector layer in this case. On the following line, we use Processing's getObject() function to get access to the input layer object, and finally the layer name is printed on the **Python Console**.

You can run the script either directly from within the editor by clicking on the **Run algorithm** button, or by double-clicking on the entry in the **Processing Toolbox**. If you want to change the code, use **Edit script** from the entry context menu, as shown in this screenshot:

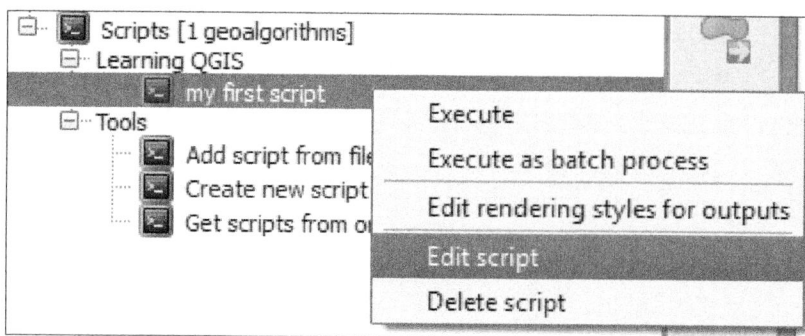

A good way of learning how to write custom scripts for Processing is to take a look at existing scripts, for example, at `https://github.com/qgis/QGIS-Processing/tree/master/scripts`. This is the official script repository, where you can also download scripts using the built-in **Get scripts from on-line scripts collection** tool in the **Processing Toolbox**.

Writing a script with vector layer output

Of course, in most cases, we don't want to just output something on the **Python Console**. That is why the following example shows how to create a vector layer. More specifically, the script creates square polygons around the points in the input layer. The numeric `size` input parameter controls the size of the squares in the `output vector` layer. The default size that will be displayed in the automatically generated dialog is set to `1000000`:

```
##Learning QGIS=group
##input_layer=vector
##size=number 1000000
##squares=output vector
from qgis.core import *
from processing.tools.vector import VectorWriter
# get the input layer and its fields
my_layer = processing.getObject(input_layer)
fields = my_layer.dataProvider().fields()
# create the output vector writer with the same fields
writer = VectorWriter(squares, None, fields, QGis.WKBPolygon,
my_layer.crs())
# create output features
feat = QgsFeature()
for input_feature in my_layer.getFeatures():
    # copy attributes from the input point feature
    attributes = input_feature.attributes()
    feat.setAttributes(attributes)
    # create square polygons
    point = input_feature.geometry().asPoint()
    xmin = point.x() - size/2
    ymin = point.y() - size/2
    square = QgsRectangle(xmin,ymin,xmin+size,ymin+size)
    feat.setGeometry(QgsGeometry.fromRect(square))
    writer.addFeature(feat)
del writer
```

In this script, we use a `VectorWriter` to write the output vector layer. The parameters for creating a `VectorWriter` object are `fileName`, `encoding`, `fields`, `geometryType`, and `crs`.

> The available geometry types are `QGis.WKBPoint`, `QGis.WKBLineString`, `QGis.WKBPolygon`, `QGis.WKBMultiPoint`, `QGis.WKBMultiLineString`, and `QGis.WKBMultiPolygon`. You can also get this list of geometry types by typing `VectorWriter.TYPE_MAP` in the **Python Console**.

Note how we use the fields of the input layer (`my_layer.dataProvider().fields()`) to create the `VectorWriter`. This ensures that the output layer has the same fields (attribute table columns) as the input layer. Similarly, for each feature in the input layer, we copy its attribute values (`input_feature.attributes()`) to the corresponding output feature.

After running the script, the resulting layer will be loaded into QGIS and listed using the output parameter name; in this case, the layer is called `squares`. The following screenshot shows the automatically generated input dialog as well as the output of the script when applied to the airports from our sample dataset:

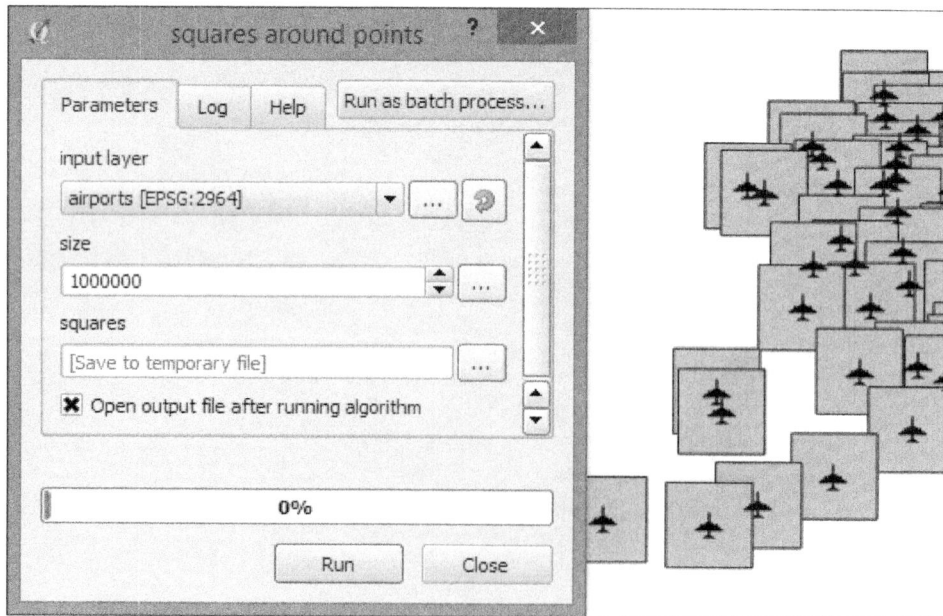

Visualizing the script progress

Especially when executing complex scripts that take a while to finish, it is good practice to display the progress of the script execution in a progress bar. To add a progress bar to the previous script, we can add the following lines of code before and inside the `for` loop that loops through the input features:

```
i = 0
n = my_layer.featureCount()
for input_feature in my_layer.getFeatures():
    progress.setPercentage(int(100*i/n))
    i+=1
```

> Note that we initialize the `i` counter before the loop and increase it inside the loop after updating the progress bar using `progress.setPercentage()`.

Developing your first plugin

When you want to implement interactive tools or very specific graphical user interfaces, it is time to look into plugin development. In the previous exercises, we introduced the QGIS Python API. Therefore, we can now focus on the necessary steps to get our first QGIS plugin started. The great thing about creating plugins for QGIS is that there is a plugin for this! It's called **Plugin Builder**. And while you are at it, also install **Plugin Reloader**, which is very useful for plugin developers. Because it lets you quickly reload your plugin without having to restart QGIS every time you make changes to the code. When you have installed both plugins, your **Plugins** toolbar will look like this:

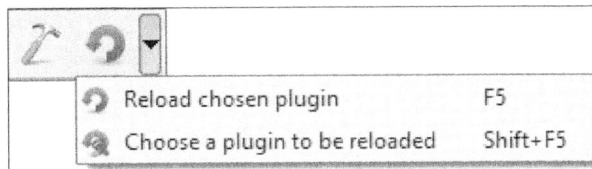

Before we can get started, we also need to install **Qt Designer**, which is the application we will use to design the user interface. If you are using Windows, I recommend **WinPython** (http://winpython.github.io/) version 2.7.10.3 (the latest version with Python 2.7 at the time of writing this book), which provides Qt Designer and **Spyder** (an integrated development environment for Python). On Ubuntu, you can install Qt Designer using `sudo apt-get install qt4-designer`. On Mac, you can get the **Qt Creator** installer (which includes Qt Designer) from http://qt-project.org/downloads.

Creating the plugin template with Plugin Builder

Plugin Builder will create all the files that we need for our plugin. To create a plugin template, follow these steps:

1. Start **Plugin Builder** and input the basic plugin information, including:

   ○ **Class name** (one word in camel case; that is, each word starts with an upper case letter)

   ○ **Plugin name** (a short description)

   ○ **Module name** (the Python module name for the plugin)

   When you hover your mouse over the input fields in the Plugin Builder dialog, it displays help information, as shown in the following screenshot:

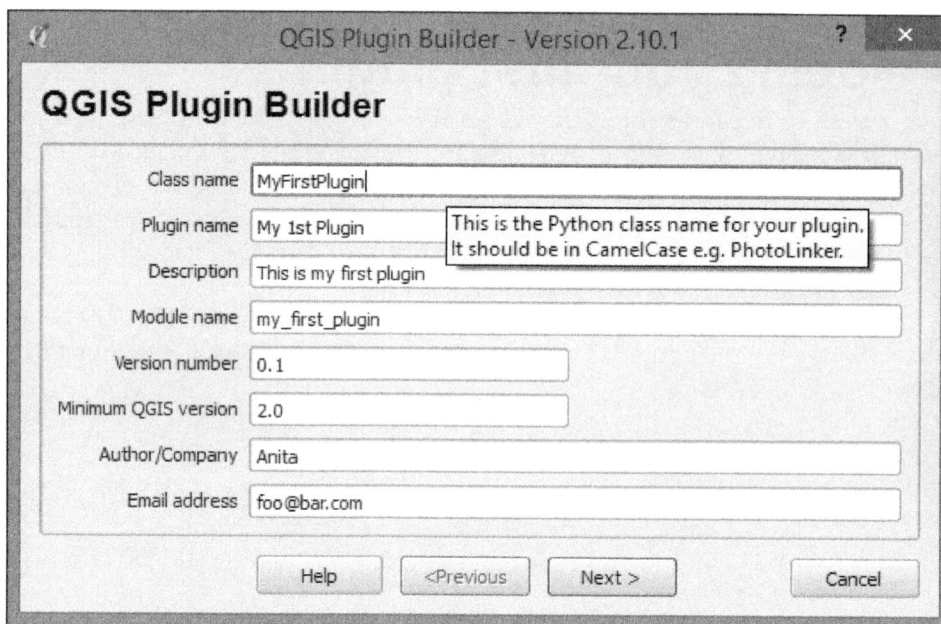

2. Click on **Next** to get to the **About** dialog, where you can enter a more detailed description of what your plugin does. Since we are planning to create the first plugin for learning purposes only, we can just put some random text here and click on **Next**.

3. Now we can select a plugin **Template** and specify a **Text for the menu item** as well as which **Menu** the plugin should be listed in, as shown in the following screenshot. The available templates include **Tool button with dialog**, **Tool button with dock widget**, and **Processing provider**. In this exercise, we'll create a **Tool button with dialog** and click on **Next**:

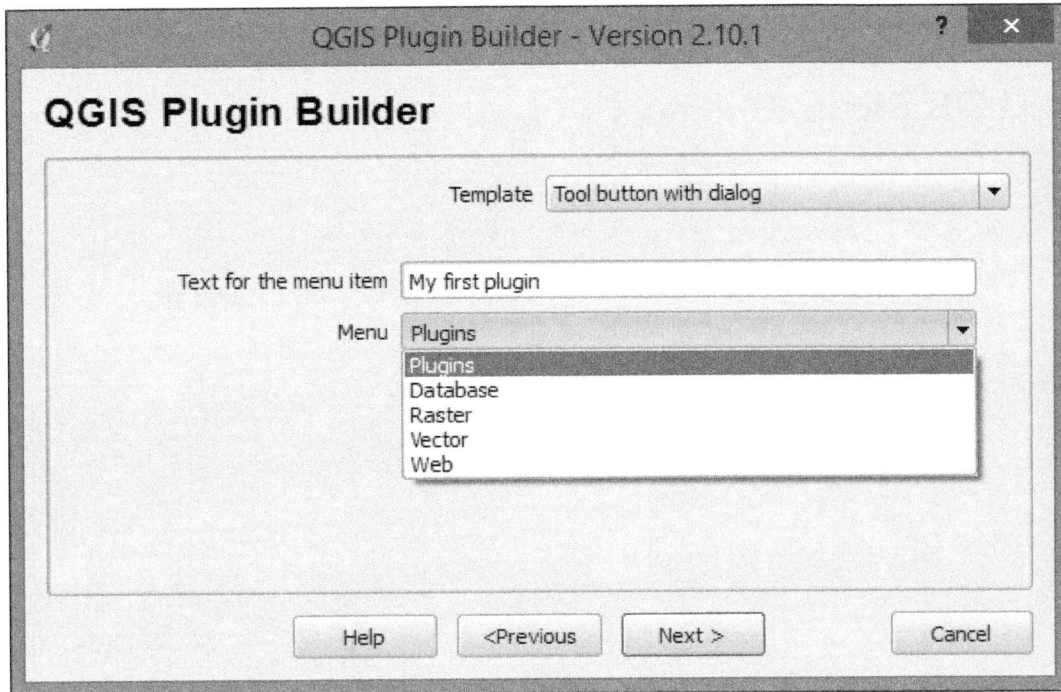

4. The following dialog presents checkboxes, where we can chose which non-essential plugin files should be created. You can select any subset of the provided options and click on **Next**.

5. In the next dialog, we need to specify the plugin **Bug tracker** and the code **Repository**. Again, since we are creating this plugin only for learning purposes, I'm just making up some URLs in the next screenshot, but you should use the appropriate trackers and code repositories if you are planning to make your plugin publicly available:

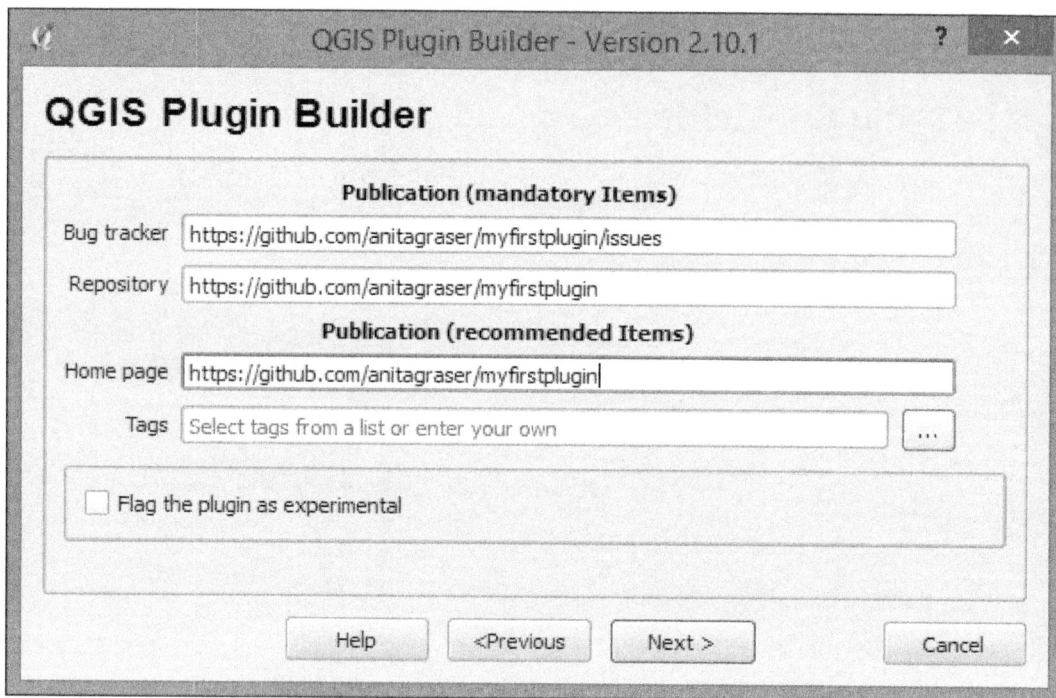

6. Once you click on **Next**, you will be asked to select a folder to store the plugin. You can save it directly in the QGIS plugin folder, `~\.qgis2\ python\plugins` on Windows, or `~/.qgis2/python/plugins` on Linux and Mac.

7. Once you have selected the plugin folder, it displays a **Plugin Builder Results** confirmation dialog, which confirms the location of your plugin folder as well as the location of your QGIS plugin folder. As mentioned earlier, I saved directly in the QGIS plugin folder, as you can see in the following screenshot. If you have saved in a different location, you can now move the plugin folder into the QGIS plugins folder to make sure that QGIS can find and load it:

Plugin Builder Results

Plugin Builder Results

Congratulations! You just built a plugin for QGIS!

Your plugin **MyFirstPlugin** was created in:
  C:\Users\anita\.qgis2\python\plugins\MyFirstPlugin

Your QGIS plugin directory is located at:
  C:/Users/anita/.qgis2/python/plugins

What's Next

1. In your plugin directory, compile the resources file using pyrcc4 (simply run **make** if you have automake or use **pb_tool**)
2. Test the generated sources using **make test** (or run tests from your IDE)
3. Copy the entire directory containing your new plugin to the QGIS plugin directory (see Notes below)
4. Test the plugin by enabling it in the QGIS plugin manager

OK

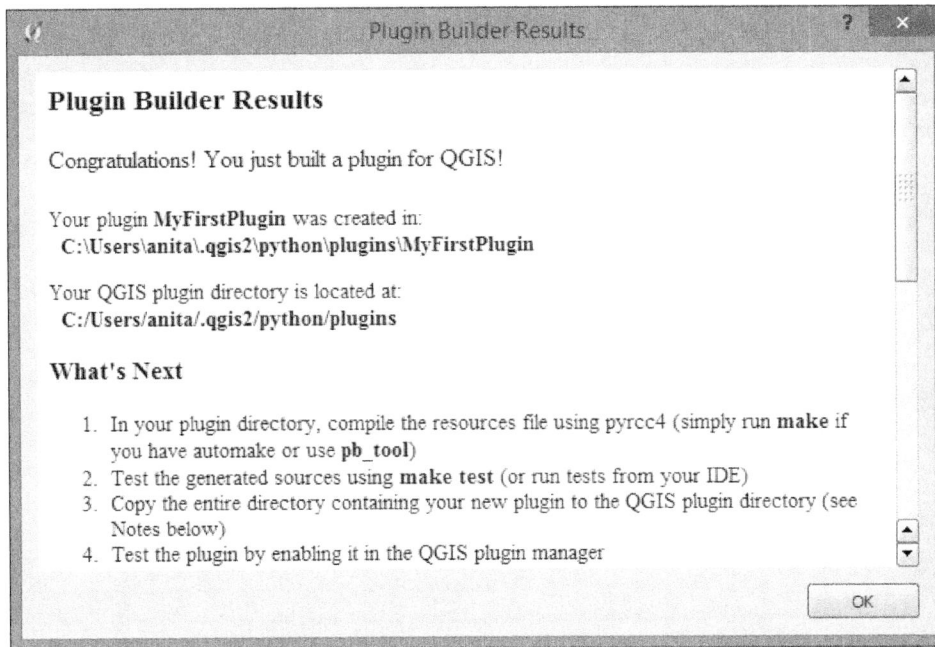

One thing we still have to do is prepare the icon for the plugin toolbar. This requires us to compile the `resources.qrc` file, which **Plugin Builder** created automatically, to turn the icon into usable Python code. This is done on the command line. On Windows, I recommend using the **OSGeo4W shell**, because it makes sure that the environment variables are set in such a way that the necessary tools can be found. Navigate to the plugin folder and run this:

```
pyrcc4 -o resources.py resources.qrc
```

> You can replace the default icon (`icon.png`) to add your own plugin icon. Afterwards, you just have to recompile `resources_rc.qrc` as shown previously.

Restart QGIS and you should now see your plugin listed in the Plugin Manager, as shown here:

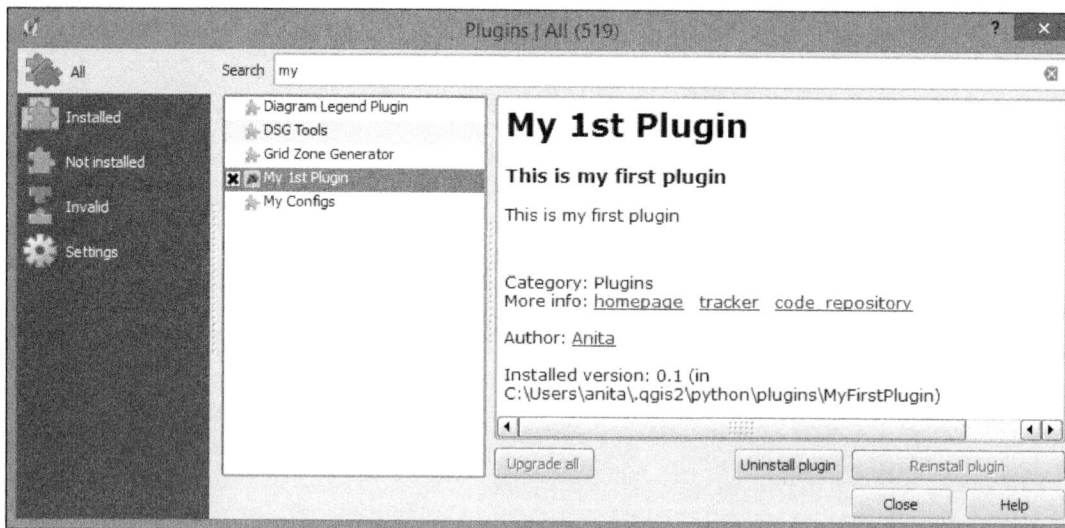

Activate your plugin in the Plugin Manager and you should see it listed in the **Plugins** menu. When you start your plugin, it will display a blank dialog that is just waiting for you to customize it.

Customizing the plugin GUI

To customize the blank default plugin dialog, we use **Qt Designer**. You can find the dialog file in the plugin folder. In my case, it is called `my_first_plugin_dialog_base.ui` (derived from the module name I specified in Plugin Builder). When you open your plugin's `.ui` file in Qt Designer, you will see the blank dialog. Now you can start adding widgets by dragging and dropping them from the **Widget Box** on the left-hand side of the Qt Designer window. In the following screenshot, you can see that I added a **Label** and a drop-down list widget (listed as **Combo Box** in the **Widgetbox**). You can change the label text to `Layer` by double-clicking on the default label text. Additionally, it is good practice to assign descriptive names to the widget objects; for example, I renamed the combobox to `layerCombo`, as you can see here in the bottom-right corner:

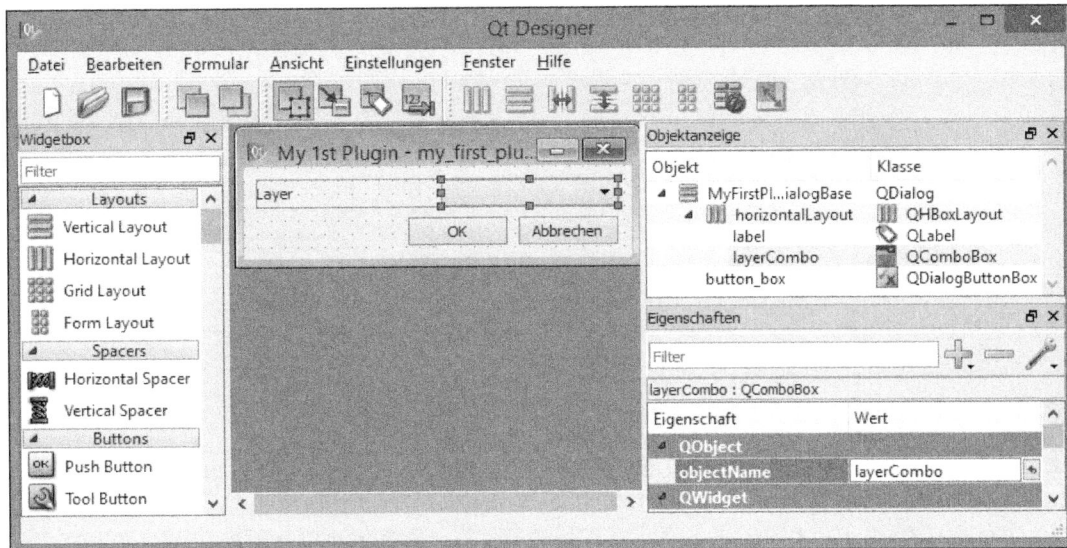

Once you are finished with the changes to the plugin dialog, you can save them. Then you can go back to QGIS. In QGIS, you can now configure **Plugin Reloader** by clicking on the **Choose a plugin to be reloaded** button in the **Plugins** toolbar and selecting your plugin. If you now click on the **Reload Plugin** button and the press your plugin button, your new plugin dialog will be displayed.

Implementing plugin functionality

As you have certainly noticed, the layer combobox is still empty. To populate the combobox with a list of loaded layers, we need to add a few lines of code to my_first_plugin.py (located in the plugin folder). More specifically, we expand the run() method:

```python
def run(self):
    """Run method that performs all the real work"""
    # show the dialog
    self.dlg.show()
    # clear the combo box to list only current layers
    self.dlg.layerCombo.clear()
    # get the layers and add them to the combo box
    layers = QgsMapLayerRegistry.instance().mapLayers().values()
    for layer in layers:
        if layer.type() == QgsMapLayer.VectorLayer:
            self.dlg.layerCombo.addItem( layer.name(), layer )
    # Run the dialog event loop
    result = self.dlg.exec_()
```

```
        # See if OK was pressed
    if result:
            # Check which layer was selected
        index = self.dlg.layerCombo.currentIndex()
        layer = self.dlg.layerCombo.itemData(index)
            # Display information about the layer
        QMessageBox.information(self.iface.mainWindow(),"Learning
QGIS","%s has %d features." %(layer.name(),layer.featureCount()))
```

You also have to add the following import line at the top of the script to avoid NameErrors concerning QgsMapLayerRegistry and QMessageBox:

```
    from qgis.core import *
    from PyQt4.QtGui import QMessageBox
```

Once you are done with the changes to my_first_plugin.py, you can save the file and use the **Reload Plugin** button in QGIS to reload your plugin. If you start your plugin now, the combobox will be populated with a list of all layers in the current QGIS project, and when you click on **OK**, you will see a message box displaying the number of features in the selected layer.

Creating a custom map tool

While the previous exercise showed how to create a custom GUI that enables the user to interact with QGIS, in this exercise, we will go one step further and implement our own custom **map tool** similar to the default **Identify tool**. This means that the user can click on the map and the tool reports which feature on the map was clicked on.

To this end, we create another **Tool button with dialog** plugin template called MyFirstMapTool. For this tool, we do not need to create a dialog. Instead, we have to write a bit more code than we did in the previous example. First, we create our custom map tool class, which we call IdentifyFeatureTool. Besides the __init__() constructor, this tool has a function called canvasReleaseEvent() that defines the actions of the tool when the mouse button is released (that is, when you let go of the mouse button after pressing it):

```
    class IdentifyFeatureTool(QgsMapToolIdentify):
        def __init__(self, canvas):
            QgsMapToolIdentify.__init__(self, canvas)
        def canvasReleaseEvent(self, mouseEvent):
            print "canvasReleaseEvent"
            # get features at the current mouse position
            results = self.identify(mouseEvent.x(),mouseEvent.y(),
                        self.TopDownStopAtFirst, self.VectorLayer)
```

```
      if len(results) > 0:
          # signal that a feature was identified
          self.emit( SIGNAL( "geomIdentified" ),
                    results[0].mLayer, results[0].mFeature)
```

You can paste the preceding code at the end of the my_first_map_tool.py code. Of course, we now have to put our new map tool to good use. In the initGui() function, we replace the run() method with a new map_tool_init() function. Additionally, we define that our map tool is checkable; this means that the user can click on the tool icon to activate it and click on it again to deactivate it:

```
def initGui(self):
    # create the toolbar icon and menu entry
    icon_path = ':/plugins/MyFirstMapTool/icon.png'
    self.map_tool_action=self.add_action(
        icon_path,
        text=self.tr(u'My 1st Map Tool'),
        callback=self.map_tool_init,
        parent=self.iface.mainWindow())
    self.map_tool_action.setCheckable(True)
```

The new map_tool_init() function takes care of activating or deactivating our map tool when the button is clicked on. During activation, it creates an instance of our custom IdentifyFeatureTool, and the following line connects the map tool's geomIdentified signal to the do_something() function, which we will discuss in a moment. Similarly, when the map tool is deactivated, we disconnect the signal and restore the previous map tool:

```
def map_tool_init(self):
    # this function is called when the map tool icon is clicked
    print "maptoolinit"
    canvas = self.iface.mapCanvas()
    if self.map_tool_action.isChecked():
        # when the user activates the tool
        self.prev_tool = canvas.mapTool()
        self.map_tool_action.setChecked( True )
        self.map_tool = IdentifyFeatureTool(canvas)
        QObject.connect(self.map_tool,SIGNAL("geomIdentified"),
                    self.do_something )
        canvas.setMapTool(self.map_tool)
        QObject.connect(canvas,SIGNAL("mapToolSet(QgsMapTool *)"),
                    self.map_tool_changed)
    else:
        # when the user deactivates the tool
```

```
        QObject.disconnect(canvas,SIGNAL("mapToolSet(QgsMapTool *)"
                                ),self.map_tool_changed)
        canvas.unsetMapTool(self.map_tool)
        print "restore prev tool %s" %(self.prev_tool)
        canvas.setMapTool(self.prev_tool)
```

Our new custom `do_something()` function is called when our map tool is used to successfully identify a feature. For this example, we simply print the feature's attributes on the **Python Console**. Of course, you can get creative here and add your desired custom functionality:

```
    def do_something(self, layer, feature):
        print feature.attributes()
```

Finally, we also have to handle the case when the user switches to a different map tool. This is similar to the case of the user deactivating our tool in the `map_tool_init()` function:

```
    def map_tool_changed(self):
        print "maptoolchanged"
        canvas = self.iface.mapCanvas()
        QObject.disconnect(canvas,SIGNAL("mapToolSet(QgsMapTool *)"),
                        self.map_tool_changed)
        canvas.unsetMapTool(self.map_tool)
        self.map_tool_action.setChecked(False)
```

You also have to add the following import line at the top of the script to avoid errors concerning `QObject`, `QgsMapTool`, and others:

```
    from qgis.core import *
    from qgis.gui import *
    from PyQt4.QtCore import *
```

When you are ready, you can reload the plugin and try it. You should have the **Python Console** open to be able to follow the plugin's outputs. The first thing you will see when you activate the plugin in the toolbar is that it prints `maptoolinit` on the console. Then, if you click on the map, it will print `canvasReleaseEvent`, and if you click on a feature, it will also display the feature's attributes. Finally, if you change to another map tool (for example, the **Pan Map** tool) it will print `maptoolchanged` on the console and the icon in the plugin toolbar will be unchecked.

Summary

In this chapter, we covered the different ways to extend QGIS using actions and Python scripting. We started with different types of actions and then continued to the **Python Console**, which offers a direct, interactive way to interact with the QGIS Python API. We also used the editor that is part of the **Python Console** panel and provides a better way to work on longer scripts containing loops or even multiple class and function definitions. Next, we applied our knowledge of PyQGIS to develop custom tools for the **Processing Toolbox**. These tools profit from Processing's automatic GUI generation capabilities, and they can be used in **Graphical modeler** to create geopreocessing models. Last but not least, we developed a basic plugin based on a **Plugin Builder** template.

With this background knowledge, you can now start your own PyQGIS experiments. There are several web and print resources that you can use to learn more about QGIS Python scripting. For the updated QGIS API documentation, check out `http://qgis.org/api/`. If you are interested in more PyQGIS recipes, take a look at *PyQGIS Developer Cookbook* at `http://docs.qgis.org/testing/en/docs/pyqgis_developer_cookbook` and QGIS programming books offered by *Packt Publishing*, as well as Gary Sherman's book *The PyQGIS Programmer's Guide, Locate Press*.

Module 2

QGIS Blueprints

Develop analytical location-based web applications with QGIS

1
Exploring Places – from Concept to Interface

How do we turn our idea into a location-based web application? If you've heard this question before or asked it yourself, you would know that this deceptively simple question can have answers posed in a limitless number of ways. In this book, we will consider the application of QGIS through specific use cases selected for their general applicability. There's a good chance that the blueprint given here will shed some light on this question and its solution for your application.

In this book, you will learn how to leverage this ecosystem, let the existing software do the heavy lifting, and build the web mapping application that serves your needs. When integrated software is seamlessly available in QGIS, it's great! When it isn't, we'll look at how to pull it in.

In this chapter, we will look at how data can be acquired from a variety of sources and formats and visualized through QGIS. We will focus on the creation of the part of our application that is relatively static: the basemap. We will use the data focused on a US city, Newark, Delaware. A collection of data, such as historical temperature by area, point data by address, and historical map images, could be used for a digital humanities project, for example, if one wanted to look at the historical evidence for lower temperatures observed in a certain part of a city.

In this chapter, we will cover the following topics:

- The software
- Extract, Transfer, and Load
- Georeference

- The table join
- Geocoding
- Orthorectification
- The spatial reference manipulation
- The spatial reference assignment
- Projection
- Transformation
- The basemap creation and configuration
- Layer scale dependency
- Labeling
- The tile creation

The development community and dependencies

As QGIS is open source, no one entity owns the project; it's supported by a well-established community. The project is guided by the QGIS **Project Steering Committee (PSC)**, which selects managers to oversee various areas of development, testing, packaging, and other infrastructure to keep the project going. The **Open Source Geospatial Foundation (OSGeo)** is a major contributor to software development, and QGIS is considered an official OSGeo project. Many of QGIS' dependencies and complimentary software are also OSGeo projects, and this collective status has served to bring some integration into what can be considered a platform. The **Open GIS Consortium (OGC)** deliberates and sets standards for the data and metadata formats. QGIS supports a range of OGC standards — from web services to data formats.

When QGIS is at its best, this rich platform provides a seamless functionality, with an ecosystem of open or simply available software ready to be tapped. At other times, the underlying dependencies and ecosystem software require more attention. Since it's an open source software, contributions are always being made, and you have the option of making customizations in code and even contributing to it!

Data format read/write

The OSGeo ecosystem provides capabilities for data format read/write through the **OGR Simple Features Library** (OGR, originally for OpenGIS Simple Features Reference Implementation) and **Geospatial Data Abstraction Library** (GDAL) libraries, which support around 220 formats.

Geospatial coordinate transformation

The models of the earth, which the coordinates refer to, are collectively known as **Coordinate Reference Systems** (**CRSs**). The spatial reference transformation between systems and projection—from a system in linear versus the one in angular coordinates—is supported by the PROJ.4 library with around 2,700 systems. These are expressed in a plain text format defined by PROJ.4 as **Well Known Text** (**WKT**). PROJ.4 WKT is actually very readable, containing the sort of information that would be familiar to the students of cartographic projection, such as meridians, spheroids, and so on.

Analysis

Analysis, or application of algorithmic functions to data is rarely handled seamlessly by QGIS. More often, it is an extension of one of the dependencies already listed before or is provided by **System for Automated Geoscientific Analyses** (**SAGA**). Many other analytical operations are provided by numerous QGIS Python plugins.

In general, these libraries will seamlessly transform to or from the formats that we require. However, in some cases, additional dependencies will need to be acquired and either be built and configured themselves or have the code built around them.

Web publishing

QGIS has the capability of publishing to web hosts through both integrated and less immediate means.

Installation

OSGeo project binaries have sometimes been bundled to ease the installation process, given the multitude of interdependencies among projects. Tutorials in this book are written based on an installation using the QGIS standalone installer for Windows.

Linux

QGIS hosts repositories with the most current versions for Debian/Ubuntu and bundled packages for other major Linux distributions; however, these repositories are generally many versions behind. You will find that this is often the case even with the extra repositories for your distribution (for example, EPEL for RHEL flavors). Seeking out other repositories is worthwhile. Another option, of course, is to attempt to build it from scratch; however, this can be very difficult.

Mac

There is no bundled package installer for Mac OS, though you should be able to install QGIS with only one or two additional installations from the binaries readily available on the Web—the KyngChaos Wiki has long been the go-to source for this.

Windows

Installation with Windows is simpler than with other platforms at this time. The most recent version of QGIS, with basic dependencies such as GDAL, is installed with a typical executable installer: the "standalone" installer. In addition, the OSGeo4W (OSGeo for Windows) package installer is very useful for the extended dependencies. You will likely find that beyond simply installing QGIS, you will return to this installer to add additional software to extend QGIS into its ecosystem. You can launch the installer from the **Setup** shortcut under the QGIS submenu in the Windows Start menu.

OSGeo-Live

The most extensive incarnation of the OSGeo software is embodied in OSGeo-Live, a Lubuntu **Virtual Machine (VM)** on which all of the OSGeo software is already installed. It is listed here separately since it will boot into its own OS, independent of the host platform.

Updates to OSGeo Live are typically released in tandem with FOSS4G, an annual global event hosted by OSGeo since 2006. Given that these events occur less regularly and are out of sync with OSGeo software development, bundled versions are usually a few releases behind. Still, OSGeo-Live is a quick way to get started.

Now that you've prepared your local machine, let's return to the idea of the generalizable web applications that will be the focus of this book. There are a few elements that we can identify in the process of developing web-mapping applications.

Acquiring data for geospatial applications

After any preliminary planning — a step that should include careful consideration of at least the use cases for our application — we must acquire data. Acquisition involves not only the physical transfer of the data, but also processing the data to a particular format and importing it into whatever data storage scheme we have developed. This is usually called **Extract, Transform, and Load** (ETL).

Though ETL is the first major step in developing a web application, it should not be taken lightly. As with any information-based project, data often comes to us in a form that's not immediately useable — whether because of nonuniform formatting, uncertain metadata, or unknown field mapping. Although any of these can affect a GIS project, as GISs are organized around cartographic coordinate systems, the principle concern is usually that data must be spatially described in a uniform way, namely by a single CRS, as referred to earlier. To that end, data often requires georeferencing and spatial reference manipulation.

For certain datasets, an ETL workflow is unnecessary because the data is already provided via web services. Using hosted data stored on the remote server and read directly from the Web by your application is a very attractive option, purely for ease of development if nothing else. However, you'll probably need to change the CRS, and possibly other formatting, of your local data to match that of the hosted data since hosted services are rarely provided in multiple CRSs. You must also consider whether the hosted data provides capabilities that support the interface of your application. You will find more information on this topic under the operational layer section of this chapter.

Producing geospatial data with georeferencing

By georeferencing, or attaching our data to coordinates, we assert the geographic location of each object in our data. Once our data is georeferenced, we can call it geospatial. Georeferencing is done according to the fields in the data and those available in some geospatial reference source.

The simplest example is when a data field actually matches a field in some existing geospatial data. This data field is often an ID number or name. This kind of georeferencing is called a **table join**.

Table join

In this example, we will take a look at a table join with some temperature data from an unknown source and census tract boundaries from the US Census. Census' TIGER/Line files are generally the first places to look for U.S. national boundary files of all sorts, not just census tabulation areas.

The temperature data to be georeferenced through a table join would be as follows:

```
tract,date,mean_temp
014501,2010-06-01,73
014402,2010-06-01,75
014703,2010-06-01,75
014100,2010-06-01,76
014502,2010-06-01,75
014403,2010-06-01,75
014300,2010-06-01,71
014200,2010-06-01,72
013610,2010-06-01,68
```

Temperature data metadata would be as follows:

```
"String","Date","Integer"
```

Downloading the example code

You can download the example code files for all Packt books you have purchased from your account at http://www.packtpub.com. If you purchased this book elsewhere, you can visit http://www.packtpub.com/support and register to have the files e-mailed directly to you.

To perform a table join, perform the following steps:

1. Copy the code from the first information box calls into a text file and save this as temperature.csv.

The CSVT format is a metadata file that accompanies a CSV file of the same name. It defines column data types.

2. Copy the code from the second information box into a text file and save this as `temperature.csvt`. Otherwise, QGIS will not know what type of data is contained in each column.

> Data for all the chapters will be found under the data directory for each chapter. You can use the included data under `c1/data/original` with the file names given earlier. Besides selecting the browse menu, you can also just drag the file into the **Layers** panel from an open operating system window. You can find examples of data output during exercises under the output directory of each chapter's data directory. This is also the directory given in the instructions as the destination directory for your output. You will probably want to create a new directory for your output and save your data there so as to not overwrite the included reference data.

3. Navigate to **Layer | Add Layer | Add Vector Layer | Browse to**, and select `temperature.csv`.

> CSV data can also be added through **Layer | Add Layer | Add Delimited Text**. This is especially useful to plot coordinates in a CSV, as you'll see later.

4. Download the **Tract** boundary data:
    1. Visit `http://www.census.gov/geo/maps-data/data/tiger-line.html`.
    2. Click on the tab for the year you wish to find.
    3. Download the web interface.
    4. This will take us to `http://www.census.gov/cgi-bin/geo/shapefiles2014/main`.
    5. Navigate to **Layer Type | Census Tracts** and click on the **submit** button. Now, select **Delaware** from the **Census Tract (2010)** dropdown. Click on **Submit** again. Now select **All counties in one state-based file** from the dropdown displayed on this page and finally click on **Download**.
    6. Unzip the downloaded folder.

5. Navigate to **Layer | Add Layer | Add Vector Layer | Browse to**, and select the `tl_2010_10_tract10.shp` file in the unzipped directory.

6. Right-click on `tl_2010_10_tract10` in the **Layer** panel, and then navigate to **Properties | Joins**. Click on the button with the green plus sign (+) to add a join.

7. Select **temperature** as the **Join layer** option, **tract** as the **Join field** option, **TRACTCE10** as the **Target field** option, and click on **OK** on this and the properties dialog:

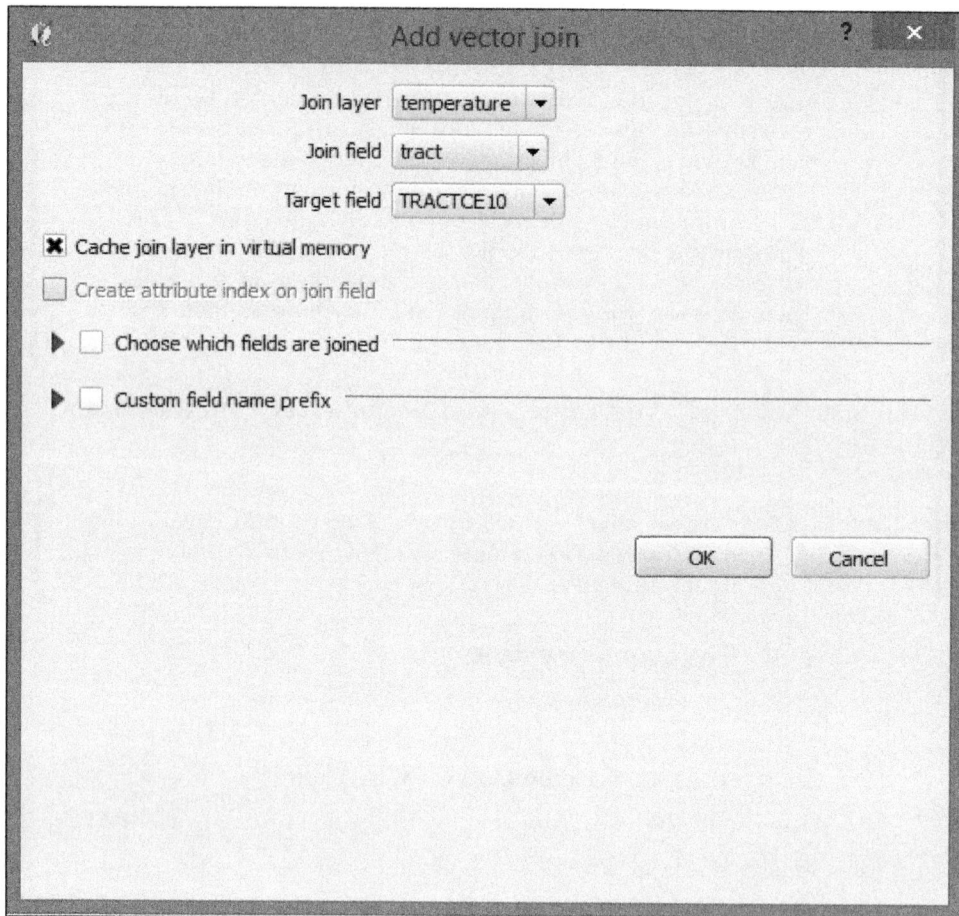

To verify that the join completed, open the attribute table of the target layer (such as the geospatial reference, in this case, `tl_2010_10`) and sort by the new `temperature_mean_temp` field. Notice that the fields and values from the join layer are now included in the target layer.

1. Select the target layer, `tl_2010_10_tract10`, from the **Layers** panel.

2. Navigate to **Layer | Open attribute table**.

3. Click on the `temperature_mean_temp` column header to sort tracts by this column. You may have to click twice to toggle the sort order from ascending to descending.

Attribute table - ti_2010_10_tract10 :: Features total: 218, filtered: 218, selected: 9

	MTFCC10	FUNCSTAT10	ALAND10	AWATER10	INTPTLAT10	INTPTLON10	temperature_date	temperature_mean_temp
168	G5020	S	2521434	0	+39.6779684	-075.7112157	2010-06-01	76
166	G5020	S	3728423	0	+39.6671809	-075.7608959	2010-06-01	75
167	G5020	S	2520725	0	+39.6691154	-075.7275330	2010-06-01	75
177	G5020	S	4196246	0	+39.6726333	-075.7439453	2010-06-01	75
180	G5020	S	1958433	0	+39.6809420	-075.7683796	2010-06-01	75
165	G5020	S	994750	0	+39.6867020	-075.7460407	2010-06-01	73
182	G5020	S	3060322	0	+39.6863968	-075.7218096	2010-06-01	72
181	G5020	S	11127440	3108	+39.7061413	-075.7641410	2010-06-01	71
184	G5020	S	17029332	0	+39.7145751	-075.7378650	2010-06-01	68
0	G5020	S	7684692	380828	+39.1768693	-075.5414576	NULL	NULL
1	G5020	S	66126748	653106	+38.9716004	-075.4728342	NULL	NULL
2	G5020	S	0	495914540	+39.1258693	-075.3111928	NULL	NULL
3	G5020	S	10466151	0	+39.1996872	-075.5439648	NULL	NULL
4	G5020	S	295718889	46394406	+39.1456274	-075.4323654	NULL	NULL
5	G5020	S	29310375	460584	+39.2124545	-075.5318450	NULL	NULL
6	G5020	S	10692748	31480	+39.1047613	-075.5560449	NULL	NULL
7	G5020	S	9731933	35860	+39.2908408	-075.6375081	NULL	NULL
8	G5020	S	59381262	1541411	+39.2858685	-075.5508359	NULL	NULL
9	G5020	S	31942633	684918	+39.2638507	-075.6184816	NULL	NULL
10	G5020	S	34337450	160924	+39.1375473	-075.6031845	NULL	NULL
11	G5020	S	7721996	45732	+38.9241318	-075.4212562	NULL	NULL
12	G5020	S	124745852	0	+39.2372835	-075.6947414	NULL	NULL
13	G5020	S	154162856	2518	+38.8949961	-075.6713506	NULL	NULL
14	G5020	S	40510840	33233	+38.9204956	-075.5779220	NULL	NULL
15	G5020	S	69732197	368153	+38.9037840	-075.5244981	NULL	NULL
16	G5020	S	147898977	542237	+38.9957512	-075.6283501	NULL	NULL
17	G5020	S	34065318	138257	+39.0786830	-075.5128103	NULL	NULL
18	G5020	S	1404255	247831	+39.1688627	-075.5258513	NULL	NULL
19	G5020	S	6077531	0	+39.1745170	-075.5639517	NULL	NULL

Show All Features

Geocode

If our data is expressed as addresses, intersections, or other well-known places, we can geocode it (that is, match it with coordinates) with a local or remote geocoder configured for our particular set of fields, such as the standard fields in an address.

In this example, we will geocode it using the remote geocoder provided by Google. Perform the following steps:

1. Install the MMQGIS plugin.
2. If you don't already have some address data to work with, you can make up a delimited file that contains some standard address fields, such as street, city, state, and county (ZIP code is not used by this plugin). The data that I'm using comes from New Castle County, Delaware's GIS site (`http://gis.nccde.org/gis_viewer/`).

3. Whether you've downloaded your address data or made up your own, make sure to create a header row. Otherwise, MMQGIS fails to geocode.

   The following is an example of MMQGIS-friendly address data:

   ```
   id,address,city,state,zip,country
   1801300170,44 W CLEVELAND AV,NEWARK,DE,19711,USA
   1801400004,85 N COLLEGE AV,NEWARK,DE,19711,USA
   1802600068,501 ACADEMY ST,NEWARK,DE,19716,USA
   ```

4. Open the MMQGIS geocode dialog by navigating to **MMQGIS | Geocode | Geocode CSV with Google/OpenStreetMap.**

5. Once you've matched your fields to the address input fields available, you have the option of choosing Google Maps or OpenStreetMap. Google Maps usually have a much higher rate of success, while OpenStreetMap has the value of not having a daily limit on the number of addresses you can geocode. At this time, the OSM geocoder produces such poor results as to not be useful.

6. You'll want to manually select or input a filesystem path for a notfound.csv file for the final input. The default file location can be problematic.

7. Once your geocode is complete, you'll see how well the geocode address text matched with our geocoder reference. You may wish to alter addresses in the notfound.csv file and attempt to geocode these again.

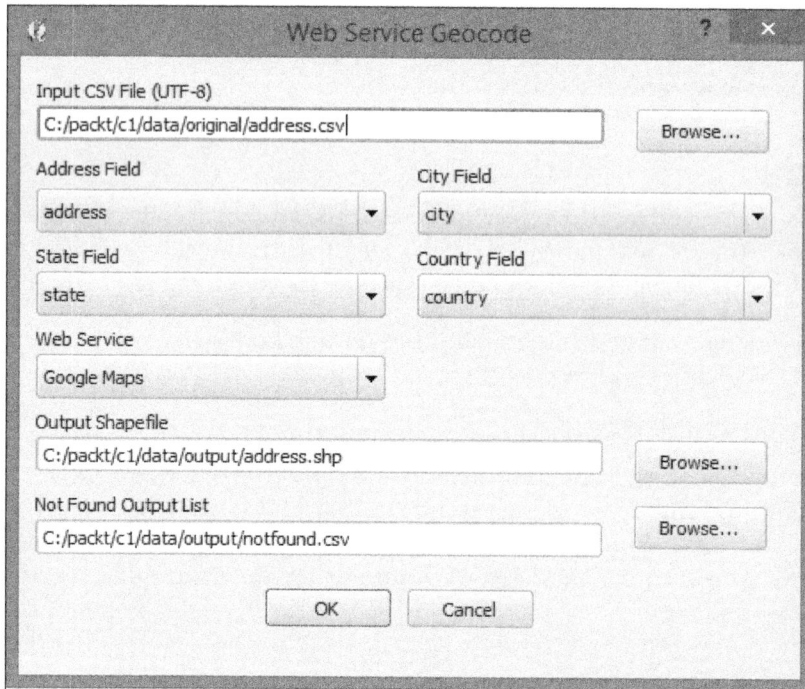

Orthorectify

Finally, if our data is an image or grid (raster), we can match up locations in the image with known locations in a reference map. The registration of these pairs and subsequent transformation of the grid is called **orthorectification** or sometimes by the more generic term, georeferencing (even though that applies to a wider range of operations).

1. Add a basemap, to be used for reference:
    1. Add the OpenLayers plugin. Navigate to **Plugins | Manage | Install Plugins**; select **OpenLayers Plugin** and click on **Install**.
    2. Navigate to **Web | OpenLayers plugin**, and select the basemap of your choice. MapQuest-OSM is a good option.

2. Obtain map image:
    1. I have downloaded a high-resolution image (c1/data/ original/4622009.jpg) from David Rumsey Map Collection, MapRank Search (http://rumsey.mapranksearch.com/), which is an excellent source for historical map images of the United States.
    2. Search by a location, filtering by time, scale, and other attributes. You can find the image we use by searching for Newark, Delaware.
    3. Once you find your map, navigate to it. Then, find **Export** in the upper right-hand corner, and export an extra high-resolution image.
    4. Unzip the downloaded folder.

3. Orthorectify/georeference the image with the following steps:
    1. Install and enable the Georeferencer GDAL plugin.
    2. Navigate to **Raster | Georeferencer | Georeferencer**.
    3. Pan and zoom the reference basemap in the canvas on a location that you recognize in the map image.
    4. Pan and zoom on the map image.
    5. Select **Add Control Point** if it is not already selected.
    6. Click on the location in the map image that you recognized in the third step.
    7. Click the **Pencil** icon to choose control point from Map Canvas.
    8. Click on the location in the reference basemap.
    9. Click on **OK**.

10. Add three of these control points, as shown in the following screenshot:

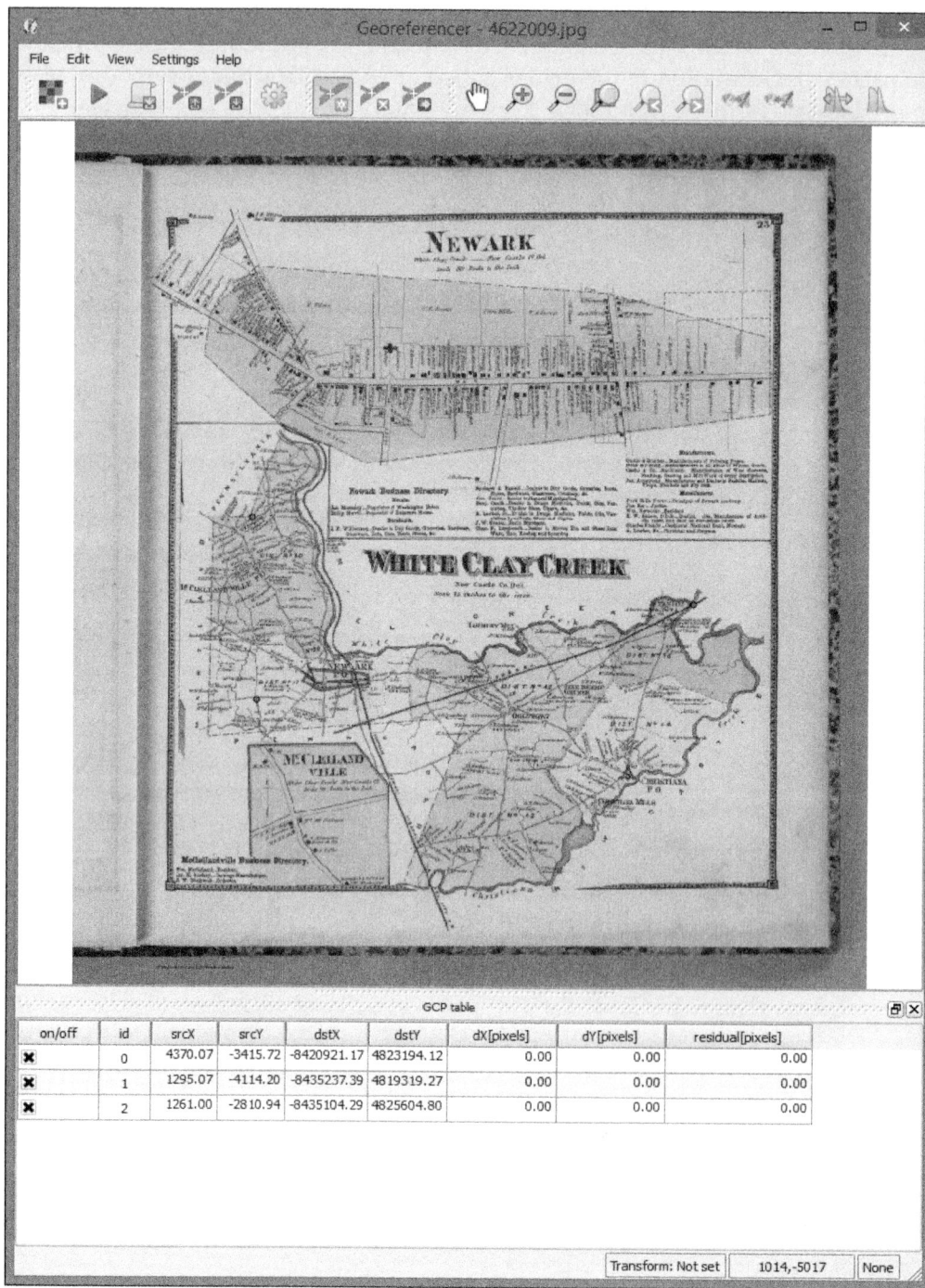

11. Start georeferencing by clicking on the **Play** button.

12. Enter the transformation settings information, as shown in the following screenshot:

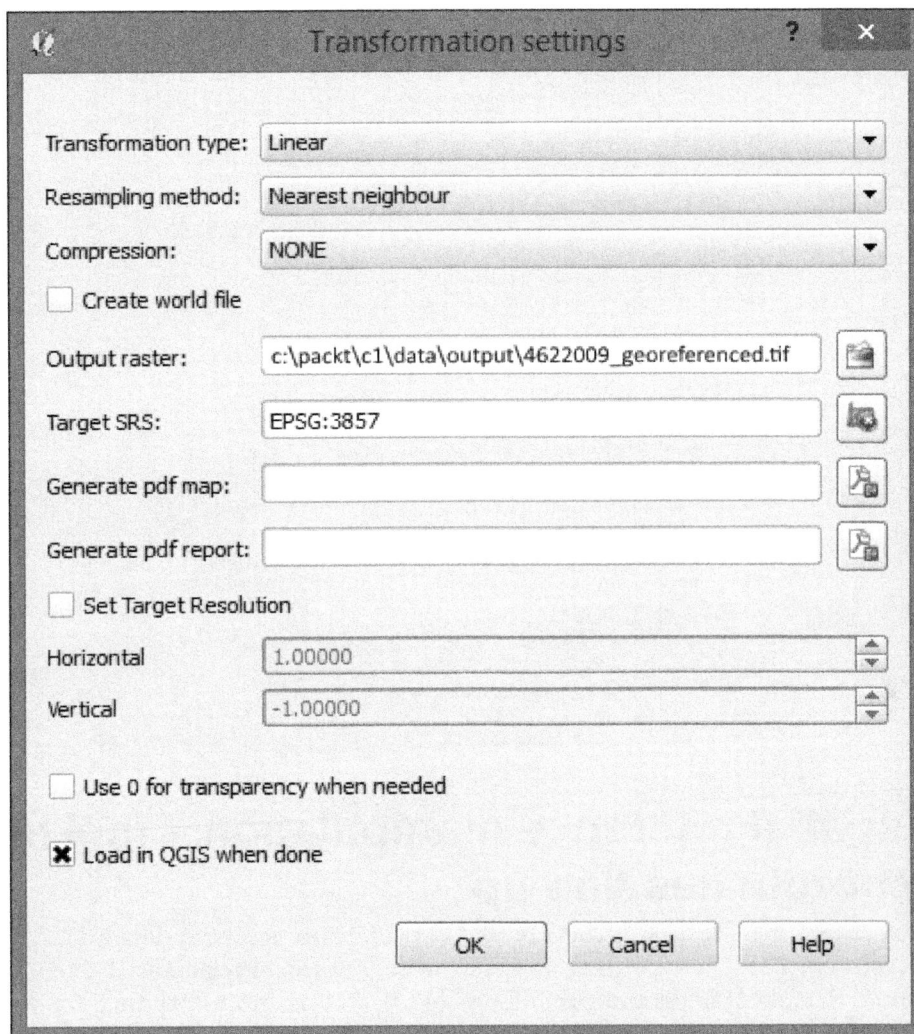

4. Now, start georeferencing by clicking on the **Play** button again.

Once your image has been georeferenced, you should see it align with the other data on your map. You can alter the layer transparency under **Layer properties | Transparency**:

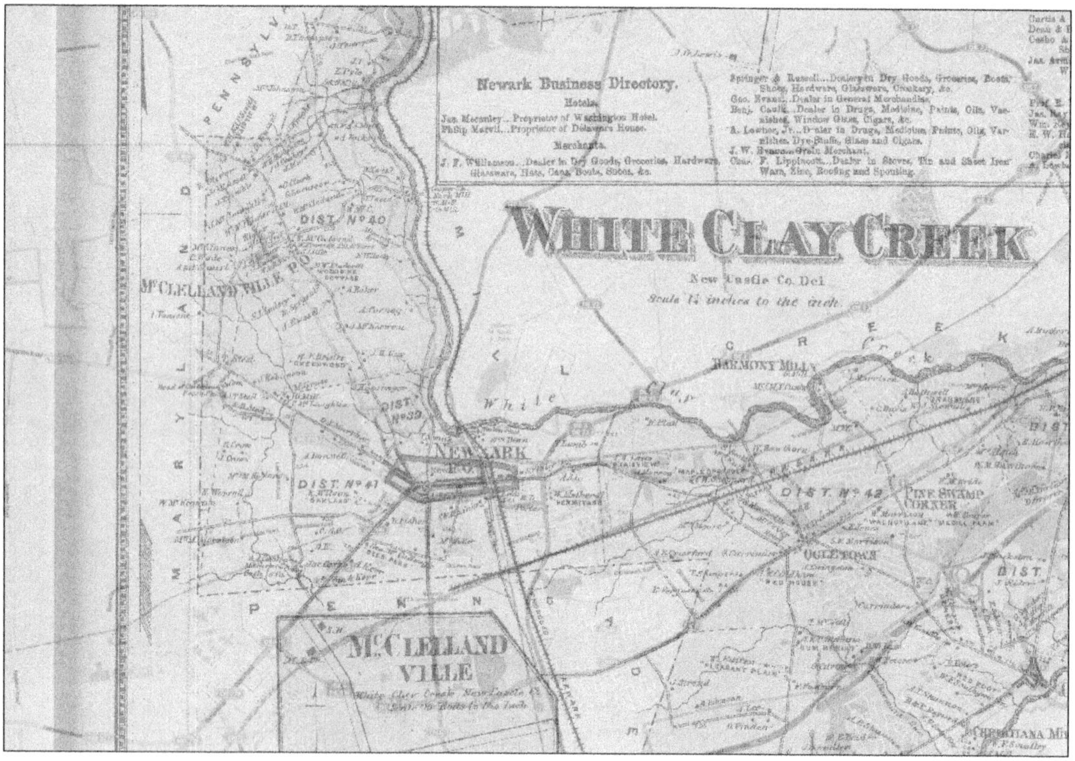

The spatial reference manipulation – making the coordinates line up

QGIS will sometimes do an **On-the-Fly (OTF)** projection of all the data added to the canvas on the project CRS (defined under **Project | Project Properties | CRS**). You will want to disable OTF projection in the projects you intend to produce for web applications, as all layers should have their own spatial reference independently defined and transformed or projected in the same CRS, if needed.

Setting CRS

When geospatial data is received with no metadata on what the spatial reference system describes its coordinates, it is necessary to assign a system. This can be by right-clicking on the layer in **Layers Panel | Save as** and selecting the new CRS.

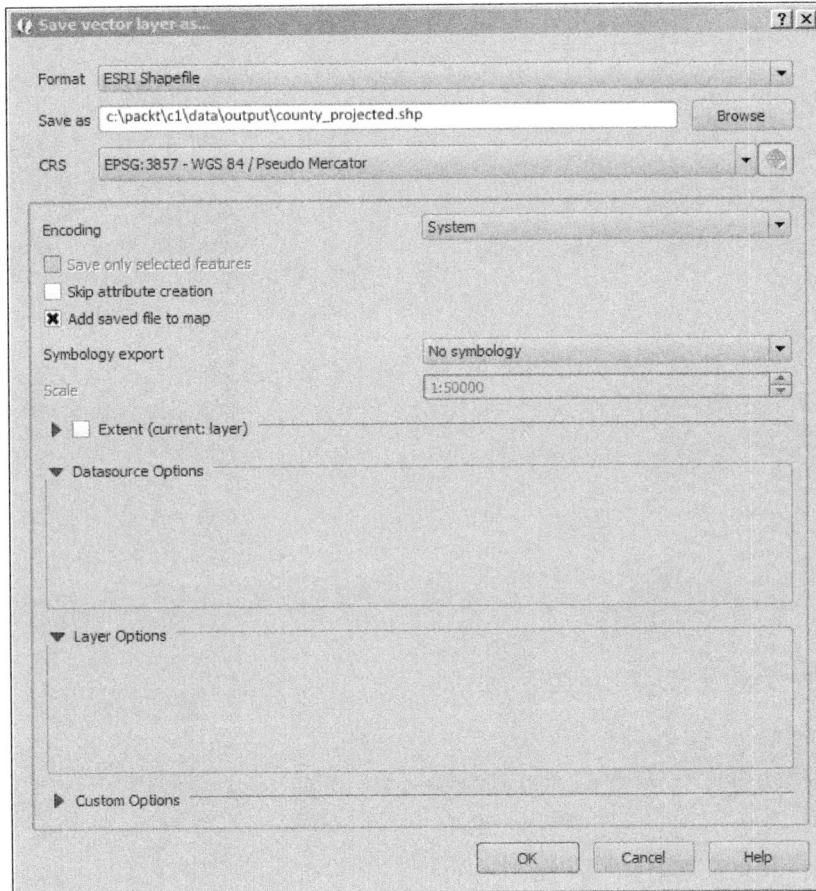

Transformation and projection

At other times, data is received with a different CRS than in the case of the other data used in the project. When CRSs differ, care should be taken to see whether to alter the CRS of the new nonconforming data or of the existing data. Of course we want to choose a system that supports our needs for accuracy or extent; at other times when we already have a suitable basemap, we will want operational layers to conform to the basemap's system. When a suitable basemap is already available to be consumed by our web application, we can often use the system of the basemap for the project. All major third-party basemap providers use **Web Mercator**, which is now known as **EPSG:3857**.

You can project data from geographic to projected coordinates or from one projection to another. This can be done in the same way as you would define a projection: by right-clicking on a layer in **Layers Panel | Save as** and selecting the new CRS. An appropriate transformation will generally be applied by default.

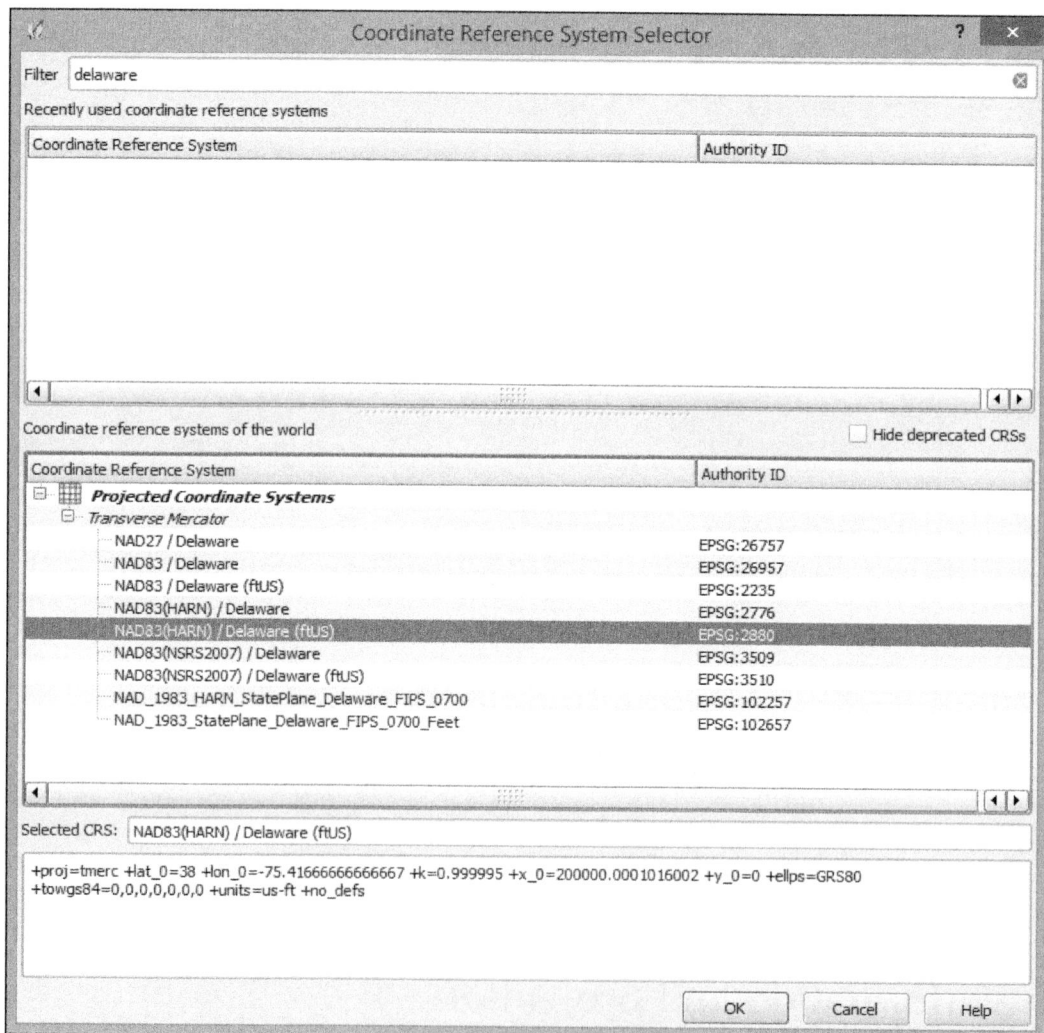

There are some features in CRS Selector that you should be aware of. By selecting from **Recently used coordinate reference systems**, you can often easily match up a new CRS with those existing in the workspace. You also have the option to search through the available systems by entering the **Filter** input. You will see the PROJ.4 WKT representation of the selected CRS at the bottom of the dialog.

Visualizing GIS data

Although the data has been added to the GIS through the ETL process, it is of limited value without adding some visualization enhancements.

The layer style

The layer style is configured through the **Styl**e tab in the **Layer Properties** dialog. The **Single Symbol** style is the default style type, and it simply shows all the geographic layer objects using the same basic symbol. This setting doesn't provide any visual differentiation between objects other than their apparent geospatial characteristics. The **Categorized** and **Graduated** style types provide different styles according to the attribute table field of your choosing. **Graduated**, which applies to quantitative data, is particularly powerful in the way the color and symbols size are mapped to a numerical scale. This is all accomplished through the **Layer Properties | Style** tab.

To configure a simple graduated layer style to the data, perform the following steps:

1. Under the **Layer Properties | Style** tab, select **Graduated** for the style type.

2. Select your quantitative field for **Column** (such as temperature_mean_temp).

3. Click on **Classify** to group your data into the number of classes specified (by default, **5**) and to select the classification mode (**Equal Interval**, by default):

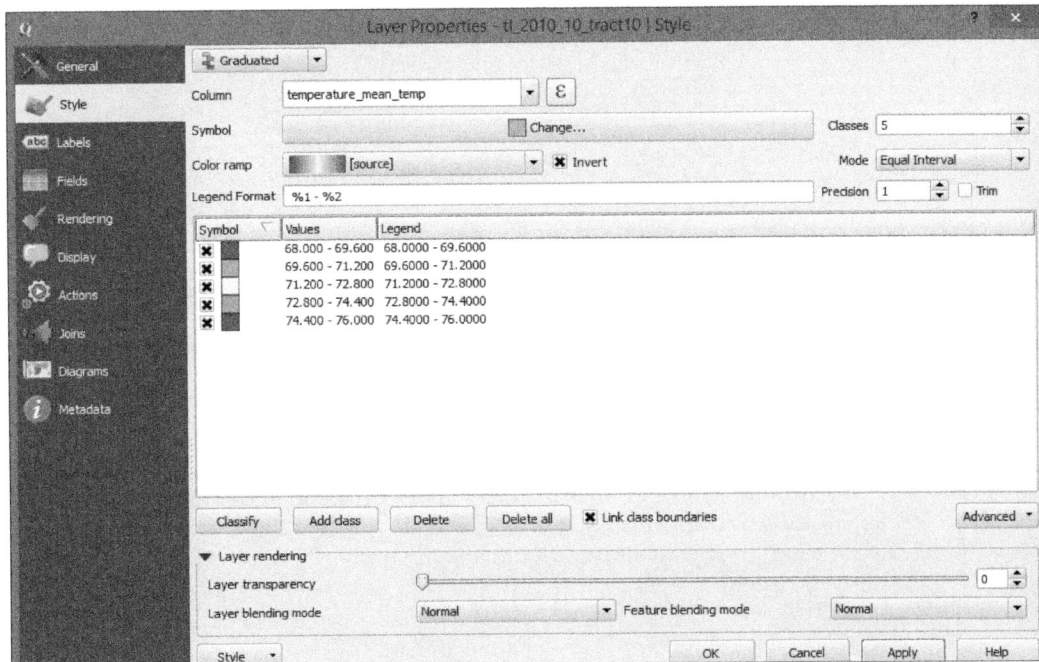

4. Now, click on **Apply**.

    If you applied the preceding steps to the joined tract/temperature layer, you'd see something similar to the following image:

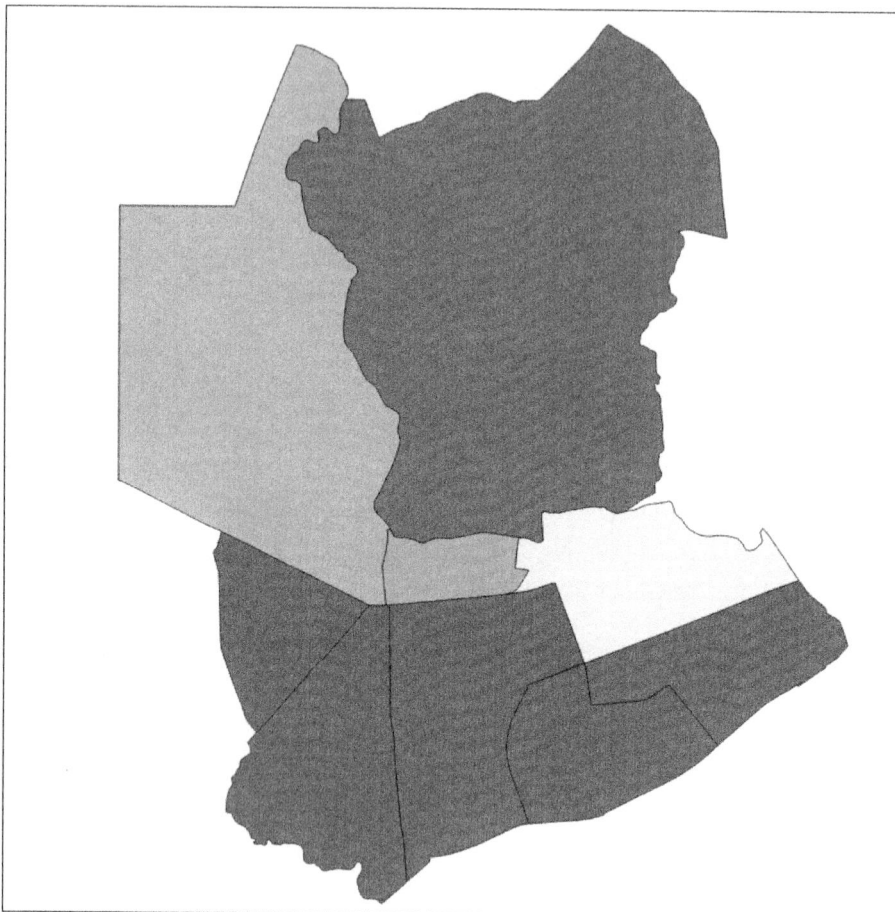

5. You can add some layer transparency here if you'd like to simultaneously view other layers. This would be appropriate if this layer were to be included in a basemap.

> You can save and load the layer style using the **Style** menu at the bottom of the **Layer Properties | Style** tab. For example, this is useful if you wish to apply the same style to different layers.

6. Now, click on **OK**.

You will now see the following output:

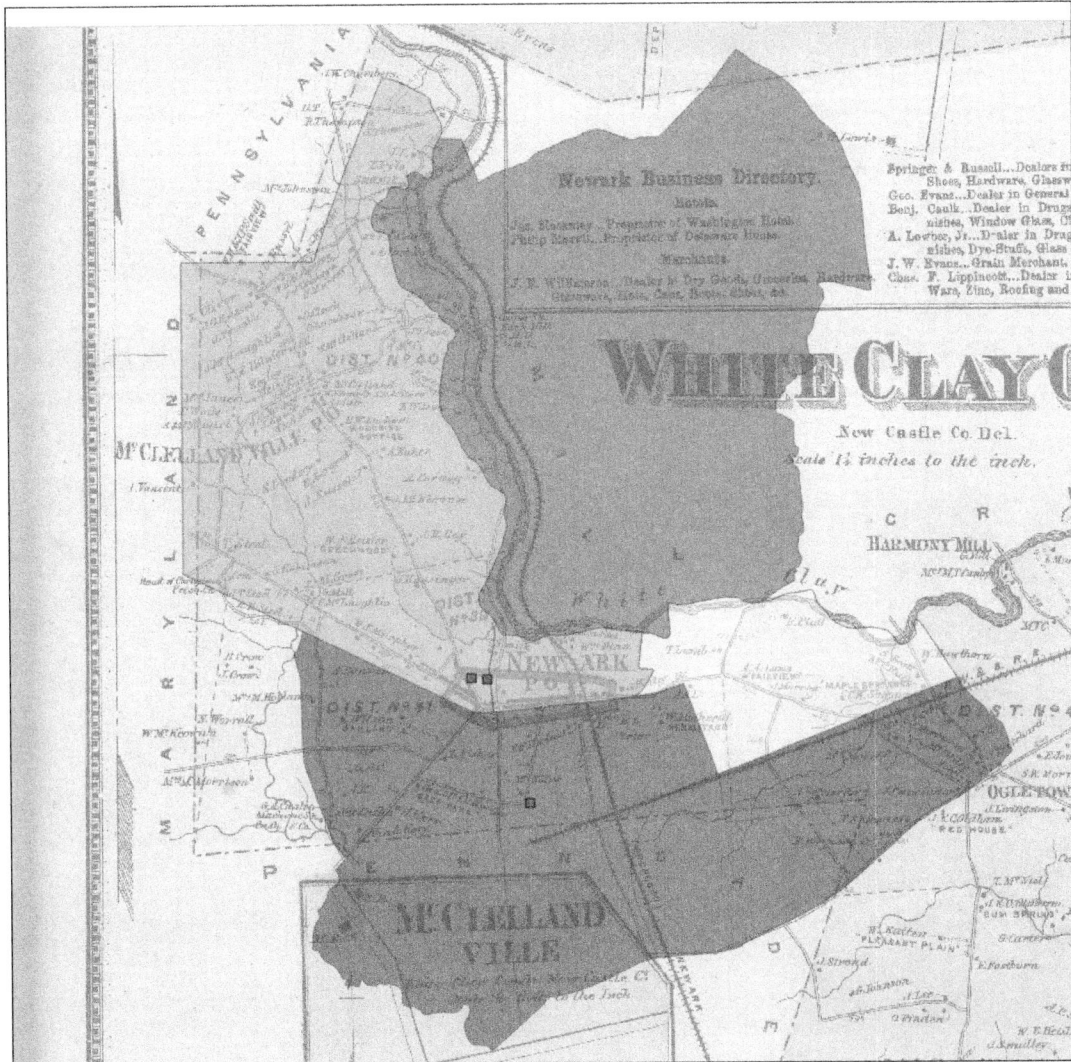

Perhaps the lower temperatures to the north of the city are related to the historical development in other parts of the city.

Labels

Labels can provide important information in a map without requiring a popup or legend. As labels are automatically placed by the software (they do not have an actual physical position in space), they are subject to particular placement issues. Also, a map with too much label text quickly becomes confusing. Sometimes, labels can be easily rendered into tiles by integrated QGIS operations. At other times, this will require an external rendering engine or a map server. These issues are discussed later on in this chapter.

To label the address points in our example, go to that layer's **Layer Properties | Labels** tab. Perform the following steps:

1. Select **address** for the **Label this layer with** field. Note that the checkbox next to this selection will be toggled. All other label style options will remain the same, as shown in the following screenshot:

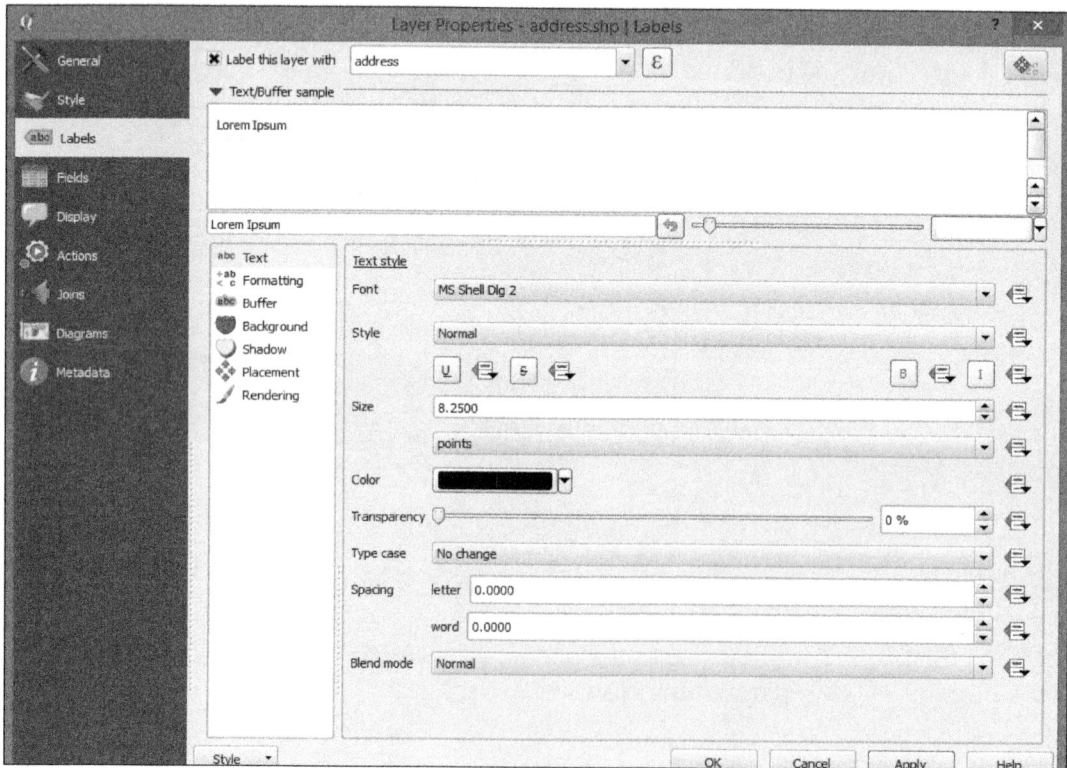

2. Open the **Buffer** subtab and toggle **Draw text buffer**:

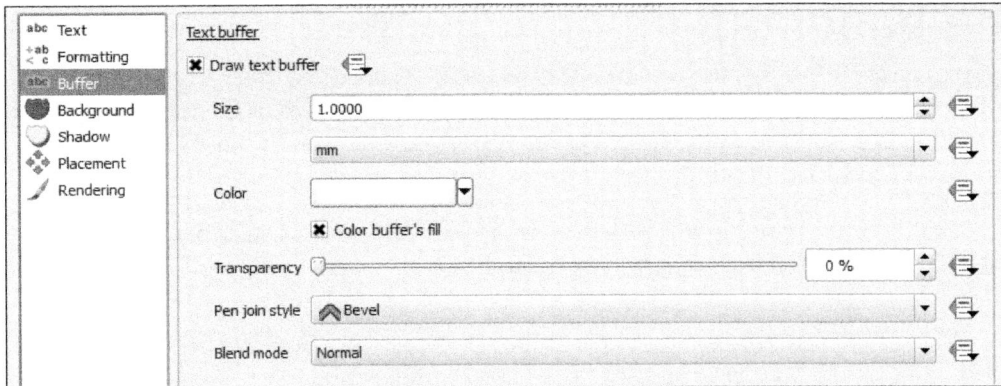

3. After you click on **OK**, you will see something similar to the following screenshot:

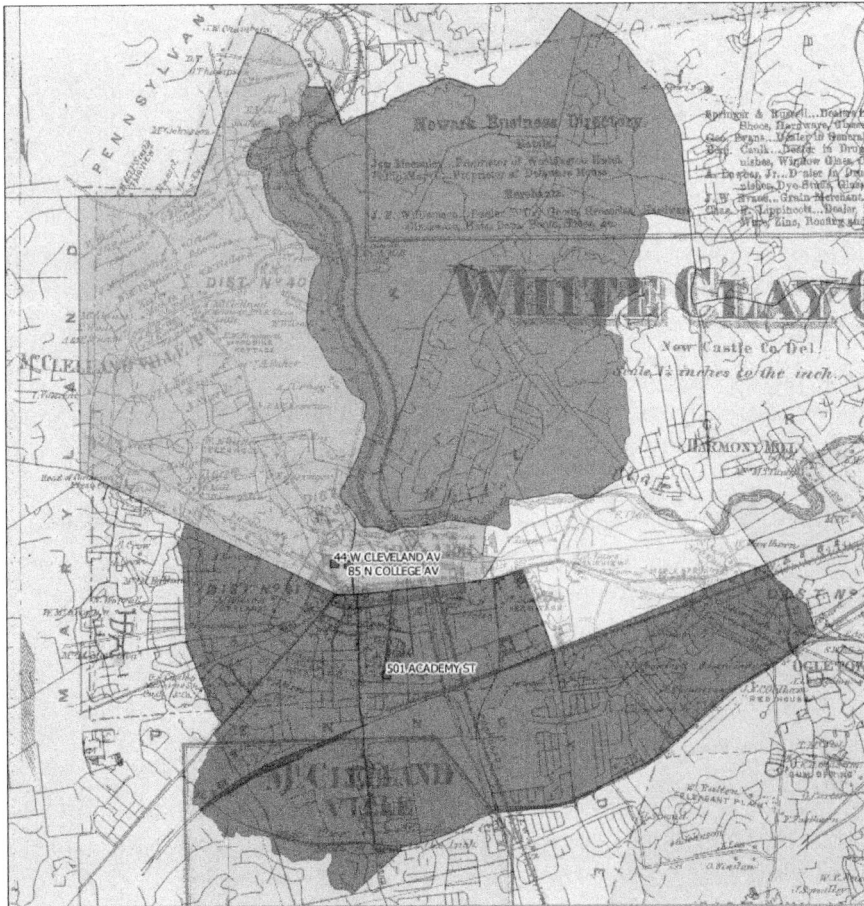

The basemap

In web map applications, the meaning of *basemap* sometimes differs from that in use for print maps; basemaps are the unchanging, often cached, layers of the map visualization that tend to appear behind the layers that support interaction. In our example, the basemap could be the georeferenced historical image, alone or with other layers.

You should consider using a public basemap service if one is suitable for your project. You can browse a selection of these in QGIS using the OpenLayers plugin.

Use a basemap service if the following conditions are fulfilled:

- The geographic features provide adequate context for your operational layer(s)
- The extent is suitable for your map interface
- Scale levels are suitable for your map interface, particularly smallest and largest
- Basemap labels and symbols don't obscure your operational layer(s)
- The map service provides terms of use consistent with your intended use
- You do not need to be able to view the basemap when disconnected from the internet

If our basemap were not available via a web service as in our example, we must turn our attention to its production. It is important to consider what a basemap is and how it differs from the operational layer.

The geographic reference features included in a basemap are selected according to the map's intended use and audience. Often, this includes certain borders, roads, topography, hydrography, and so on.

Beyond these reference features, include the geographic object class in the basemap if you do not need:

- To regularly update the geometric data
- To provide capabilities for style changes
- To permit visibility change in class objects independently of other data
- To expose objects in the class to interface controls

Assuming that we will be using some kind of caching mechanism to store and deliver the basemap, we will optimize performance by maximizing the objects included therein.

Using OpenStreetMap for the basemap data

Obtaining data for a basemap is not a trivial task. If a suitable map service is available via a web service, it would ease the task considerably. Otherwise, you must obtain supporting data from your local system and render this to a suitable cartographic format.

A challenge in creating basemaps and keeping them updated is interacting with different data providers. Different organizations tend be recognized as the provider of choice for the different classes of geographic objects. With different organizations in the mix, different data format conventions are bound to occur.

OpenStreetMap (OSM), an open data repository for geographic reference data, provides both map services and data. In addition to OSM's own map services, the data repository is a source for a number of other projects offering free basemap services.

OpenStreetMap uses a more abstract and scalable schema than most data providers. The OSM data includes a few system fields, such as `osm_id`, `user_id`, `osm_version`, and `way`. The `osm_id` field is unique to each geographic object, `user_id` is unique to the user who last modified the object, `osm_version` is unique to the versions for the object, and `way` is the geometry of the object.

By allowing a theoretically unlimited number of key value pairs along with the system fields mentioned before, the OSM data schema can potentially allow any kind of data and still maintain sanity. Keys are whatever the data editors add to the data that they upload to the repository. The well-established keys are documented on the OSM site and are compatible with the community produced rendering styles. If a community produced style does not include the key that you need or the one that you created, you can simply add it into your own rendering style. Columns are kept from overwhelming a local database during the import stage. Only keys added in a local configuration file are added to the database schema and populated.

High quality cartography with OSM data is an ongoing challenge. CloudMade has created its business on a cloud-based, albeit limited, rendering editor for OSM data, which is capable of also serving map services. CloudMade is, in fact, a fine source for cloud services for OSM data and has many visually appealing styles available. OpenMapSurfer, produced by a research group at the University of Heidelberg, shows off some best practices in high quality cartography with OSM data including sophisticated label placement, object-level scale dependency, careful color selection, and shaded topographic relief and bathymetry.

To obtain the OpenStreetMap data locally to produce your own basemap, perform the following steps:

1. Install the OpenLayers and OSMDownloader QGIS plugins if they are not already installed.
2. Create a new SpatiaLite database.
3. Turn on OSM:
   1. Navigate to **Web | OpenLayers | OpenStreetMap | OpenStreetMap**.
4. Browse your area of interest.
5. Download your area of interest:
   1. Navigate to **Vector | OpenStreetMap | Download Data**:

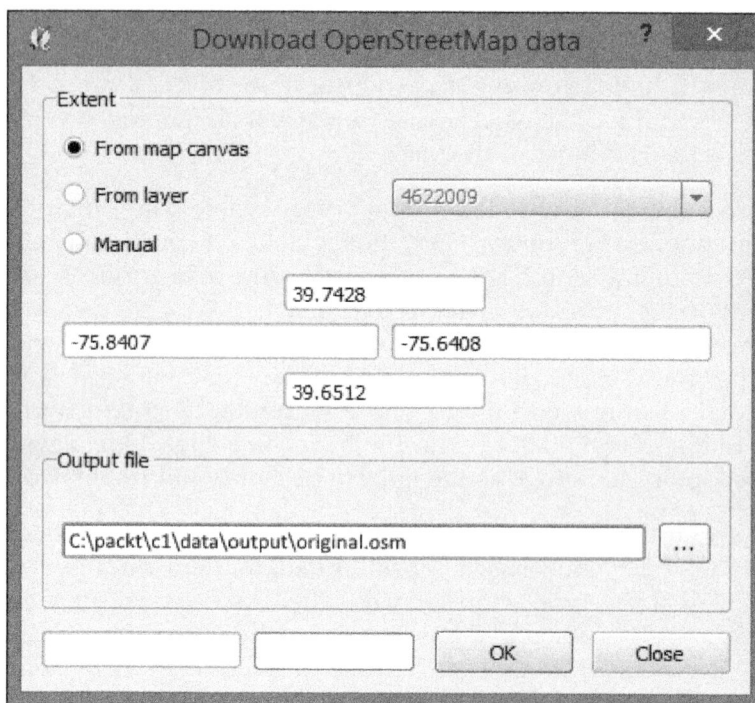

6. Import the downloaded XML data into a topological SQLite database. This does not contain SpatiaLite geographic objects; rather, it is expressed in terms of topological relationships between objects in a table. Topological relationships are explored in more depth in *Chapter 4, Finding the Best Way to Get There*, and *Chapter 5, Demonstrating Change*.

   1. Navigate to **Vector | OpenStreetMap | Import Topology** from XML.

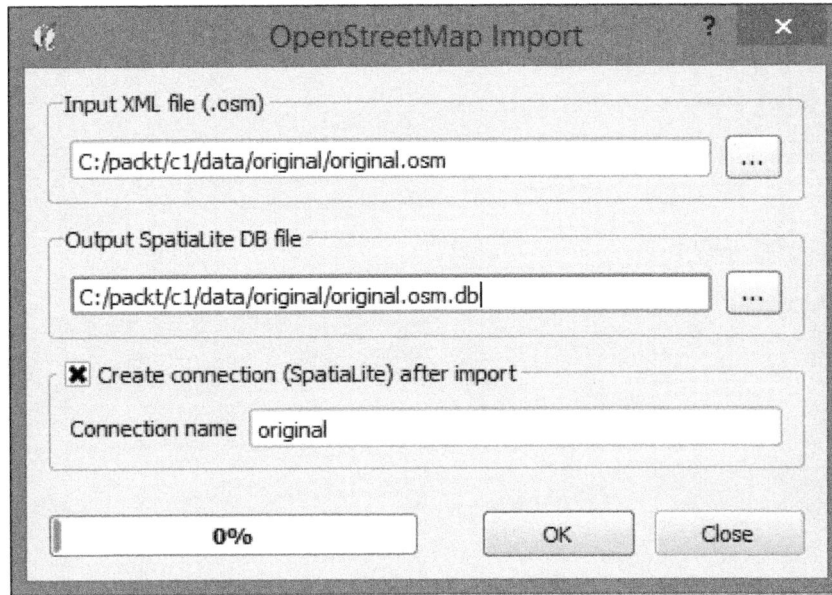

7. Convert topology to SpatiaLite spatial tables through the following steps:

   1. Navigate to **Vector | OpenStreetMap | Export Topology to Spatialite**.

   2. Select the points, polylines, or polygons to export.

   3. Then, select the fields that you may want to use for styling purposes. You can populate a list of possible fields by clicking on **Load from DB**.

4. You can repeat this step to export the additional geometry types, as shown in the following screenshot:

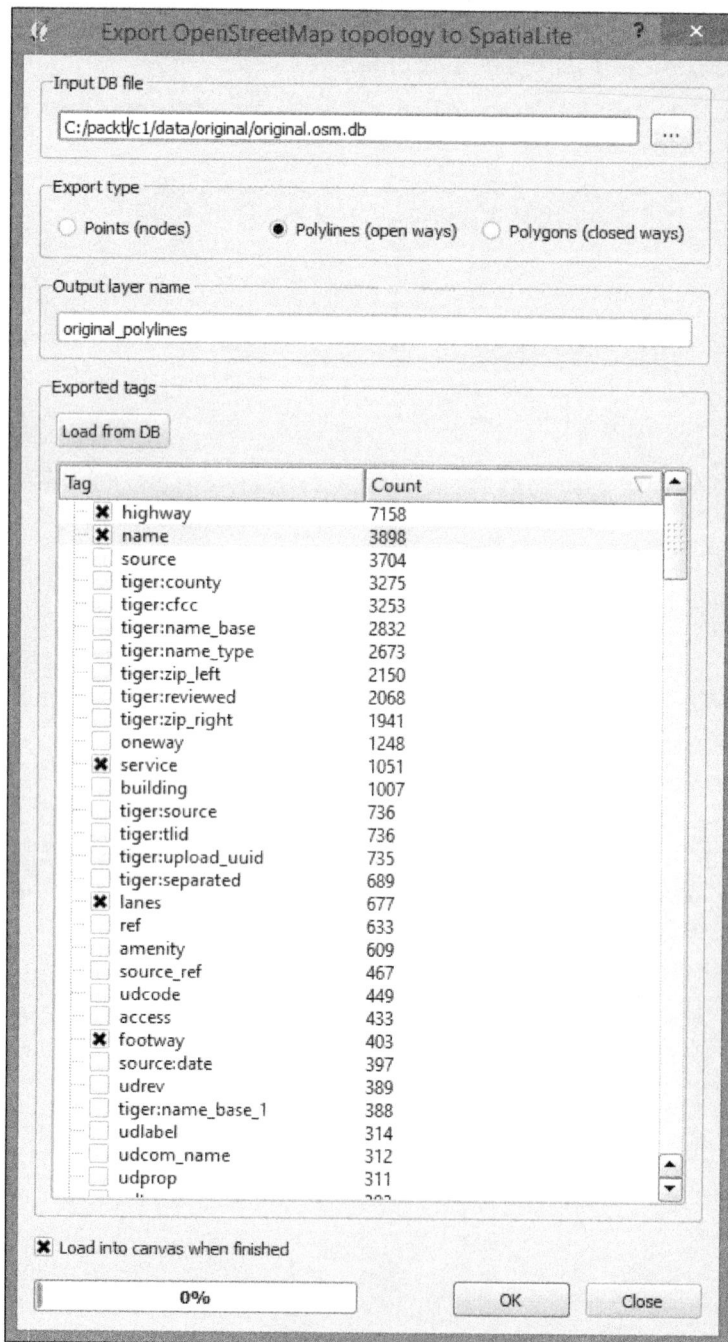

8. You can now style this as you like and export it as the tiled basemap. Then, you can save it in the `mapnik` or `sld` style for use in rendering in an external tile caching software.

Here's an example of the OSM data overlaid on our other layers with a basic, single symbol style:

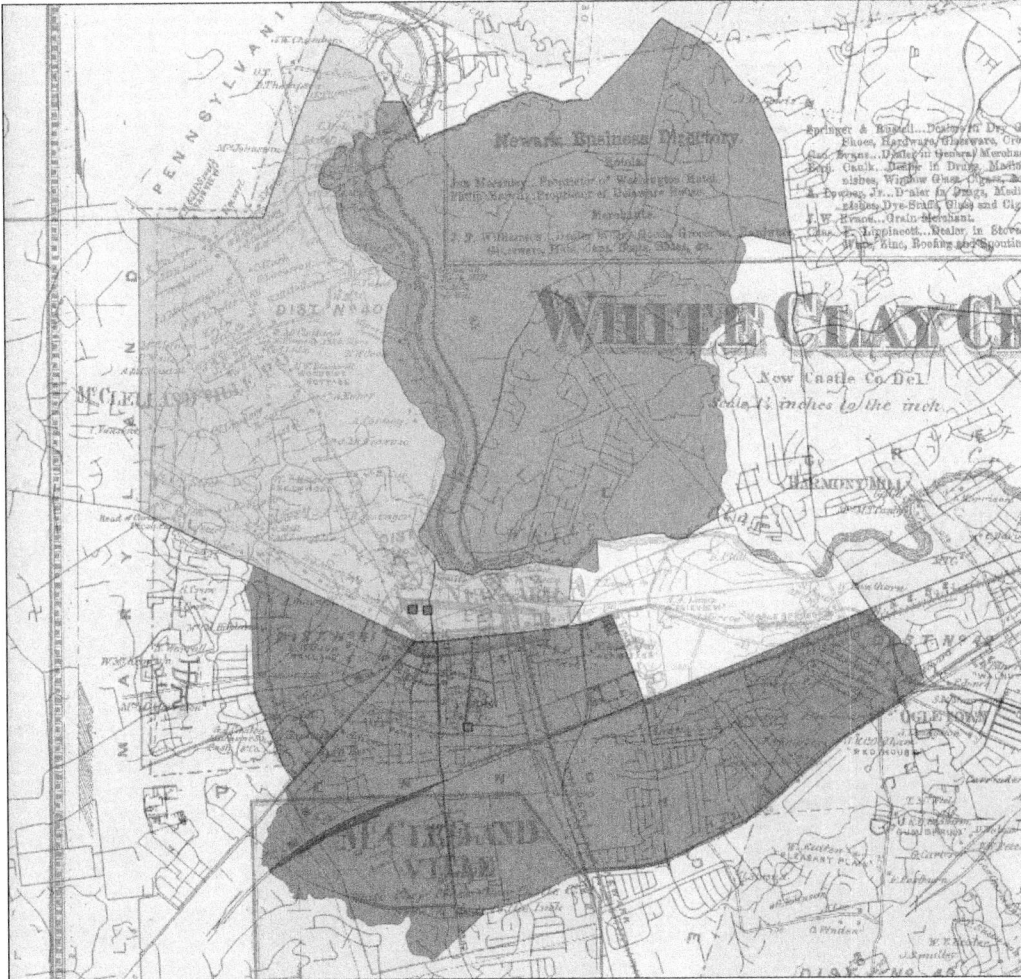

Avoiding obscurity and confusion

Of course, heaping data in the basemap is not without its drawbacks. Other than the relative loss of functionality, which occurs by design, basemaps can quickly become cluttered and otherwise unclear. The layer and label scale dependency dynamically alter the display of information to avoid the obfuscation of basemap geographic classes.

The layer scale dependency

When classes of geographic objects are unnecessary to visualize at certain scales, the whole layer scale dependency can be used to hide the layer from view. For example, in the preceding image, we can see all the layers, including the geocoded addresses, at a smaller scale even when they may not be distinctly visible. To simplify the information, we can apply the layer scale dependency so that this layer does not show these small scales.

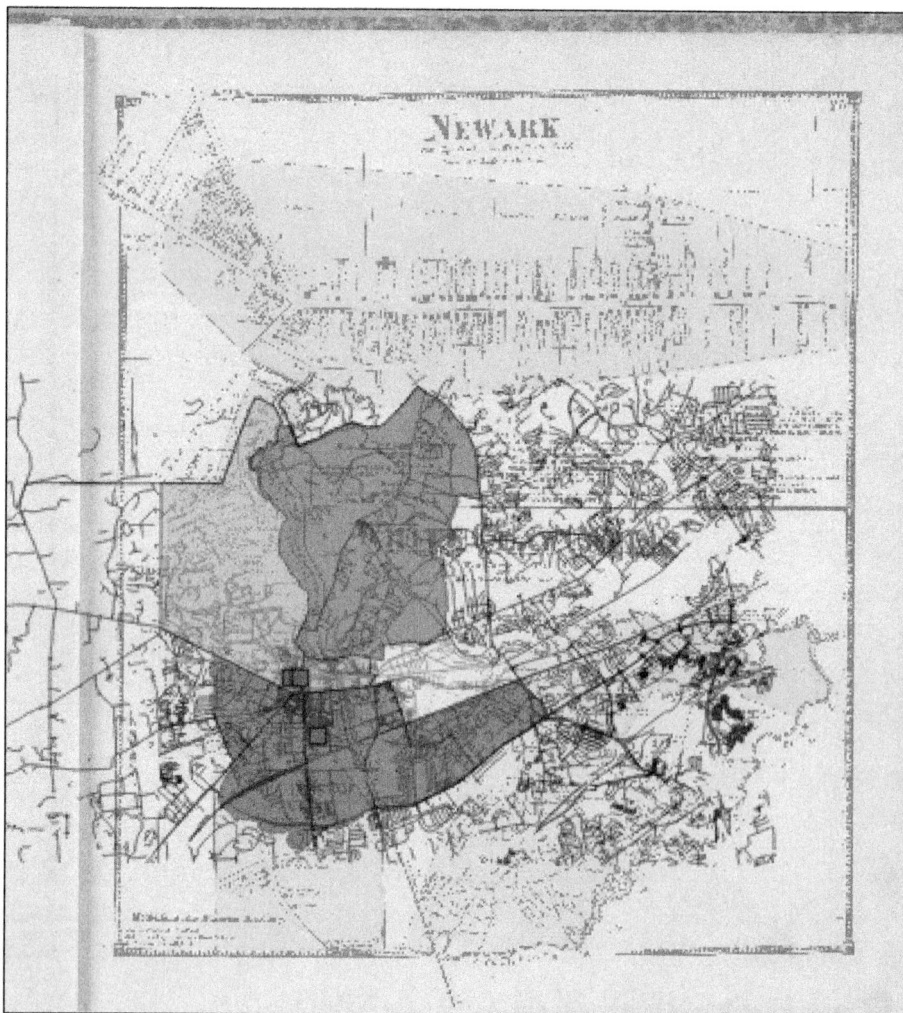

At this scale, some objects are not distinctly visible. Using the layer scale dependency, we can make these objects invisible at this scale.

It is also possible to alter visibility with scale at the geographic object level within a layer. For example, you may wish to show only the major roads at a small scale. However, this will generally require more effort to produce. Object-level visibility can be driven by attributes already existing or created for the purpose of scale dependency. It can also be defined according to the geometric characteristics of an object, such as its area. In general, smaller features should not be viewable at lower scales.

A common way to achieve layer dependency at the object level using the whole-layer dependency is to select objects that match the given criteria and create new layers from these. Scale dependency can be applied to the subsets of the object class now contained in this separate layer.

You will want to set the layer scale dependency in accordance with scale ratios that conform to those that are commonly used. These are based on some assumptions, including those about the resolution of the tiled image (96 dpi) and the size of the tile (256px x 265px).

Zoom	Object extent	Scale at 96 dpi
0	Entire planet	1 : 59165752759.16
1		1 : 295,829,355.45
2		1 : 147,914,677.73
3		1 : 73,957,338.86
4		1 : 36,978,669.43
5	Country	1 : 18,489,334.72
6		1 : 9,244,667.36
7		1 : 4,622,333.68
8	State	1 : 2,311,166.84
9		1 : 1,155,583.42
10	Metropolitan	1 : 577,791.71
11		1 : 288,895.85
12	City	1 : 144,447.93
13		1 : 72,223.96
14	Town	1 : 36,111.98
15		1 : 18,055.99
16	Minor road	1 : 9,028.00
17		1 : 4,514.00
18	Sidewalks	1 : 2,257.00

The label conflict

Labels are commonly separated from the basemap layer itself. One reason for this is that if labels are included in the basemap layer, they will be obscured by the operational layer displayed above it. Another reason is that tile caching sometimes does not properly handle labels, causing fragments of labels to be left missing. Labels should also be displayed with their own scale dependency, filtering out only the most important labels at smaller scales. If you have many layers and objects to be labeled, this may be a good use case for a map server or at least a rendering engine such as Mapnik.

The polygon label conflict resolution

To achieve conflict resolution between label layers on our map output, we will convert the geographic objects to be labeled to centroids—points in the middle of each object—which will then be displayed along with the label field as a label layer.

1. Convert objects to points through the following steps:
   1. Navigate to **Vector | Geometry Tools | Polygon Centroids**.
   2. If the polygons are in a database, create an SQL view where the polygons are stored, as shown in the following code:

```
CREATE VIEW AS
SELECT polygon_class.label, st_centroid
    (polygon_class.geography) AS geography
    FROM polygon_class;
```

2. Create a layer corresponding to the labels in the map server or renderer.
3. Add any adjustments via the SLD or whichever style markup you will use. The GeoServer implementation is particularly good at resolving conflicts and improving placement.

Chapter 7, Mapping for Enterprises and Communities, includes a more detailed blueprint for creating a labeling layer with a cartographically enhanced placement and conflict resolution using SLD in GeoServer.

The characteristics of the basemap will affect the range of interaction, panning, and zooming in the map interface. You will want a basemap that covers the extent of the area to be seen on the map interface and probably restrict the interface to a region of interest. This way, someone viewing a collection of buildings in a corner of one state does not get lost panning to the opposite corner of another state! When you cache your basemap, you will want to indicate that you wish to cache to this extent. Similarly, viewable scales will be configured at the time your basemap is cached, and you'll want to indicate which these are. This affects the incremental steps, in which the zoom tool increases or decreases the map scale.

Tile caches

The best way to cache your basemap data so that it quickly loads is to save it as individual images. Rather than requiring a potentially complicated rendering by the browser of many geometric features, a few images corresponding to the scale and extent to which they are viewed can be quickly transferred from client to server and displayed. These prerendered images are referred to as tiles because these square images will be displayed seamlessly when the basemap is requested. This is now the standard method used to prepare data for web mapping. In this book, we will cover two tools to create tile caches: QTiles plugin (*Chapter 1, Exploring Places – from Concept to Interface*) and TileMill/MBTiles (*Chapter 7, Mapping for Enterprises and Communities*).

	Configuration time	Execution time	Visual quality	Stored in a single file	Stored as image directories	Suitable for labels
QTiles Plugin	1	3	3	No	Yes	No
GDAL2Tiles.py	2	1	2	No	Yes	No
TileMill/ MBTiles	3	2	1	Yes	No	Yes
GeoServer/ GWC	3	2	1	No	No	Yes

You will need to pay some attention to the scheme for tile storage that is used. The `.mbtiles` format that TileMill uses is a SQLite database that will need to be read with a map interface that supports it, such as Leaflet. The QTiles plugin and GDAL2Tiles.py use an *XYZ* tile scheme with hierarchical directories based on row (*X*), column (*Y*), and zoom (*Z*) respectively with the origin in the top-left corner of the map. This is the most popular tiling scheme. The TMS tiling scheme sometimes used by GeoServer open source map server (which supports multiple schemes/ service specifications) and that accepted by OSGeo are almost identical; however, the origin is at the bottom-left of the map. This often leads to some confusing results. Note that zoom levels are standardized according to the tile scheme tile size and resolution (for example, 256 x 256 pixels)

Generating and testing a simple directory-based tile cache structure

We will now use the QTiles plugin to generate a directory-based *ZYX* tile scheme cache. Perform the following steps:

1. Install QTiles and the TileLayer plugin.

   ○ QTiles is listed under the experimental plugins. You must alter the plugin settings to show experimental plugins. Navigate to **Plugins | Manage and Install Plugins | Settings | "Show also experimental plugins"**.

2. Run QTiles, creating a new `mytiles` tileset with a minimum zoom of 14 and maximum of 16.

3. You'll realize the value of this directory in the next example.

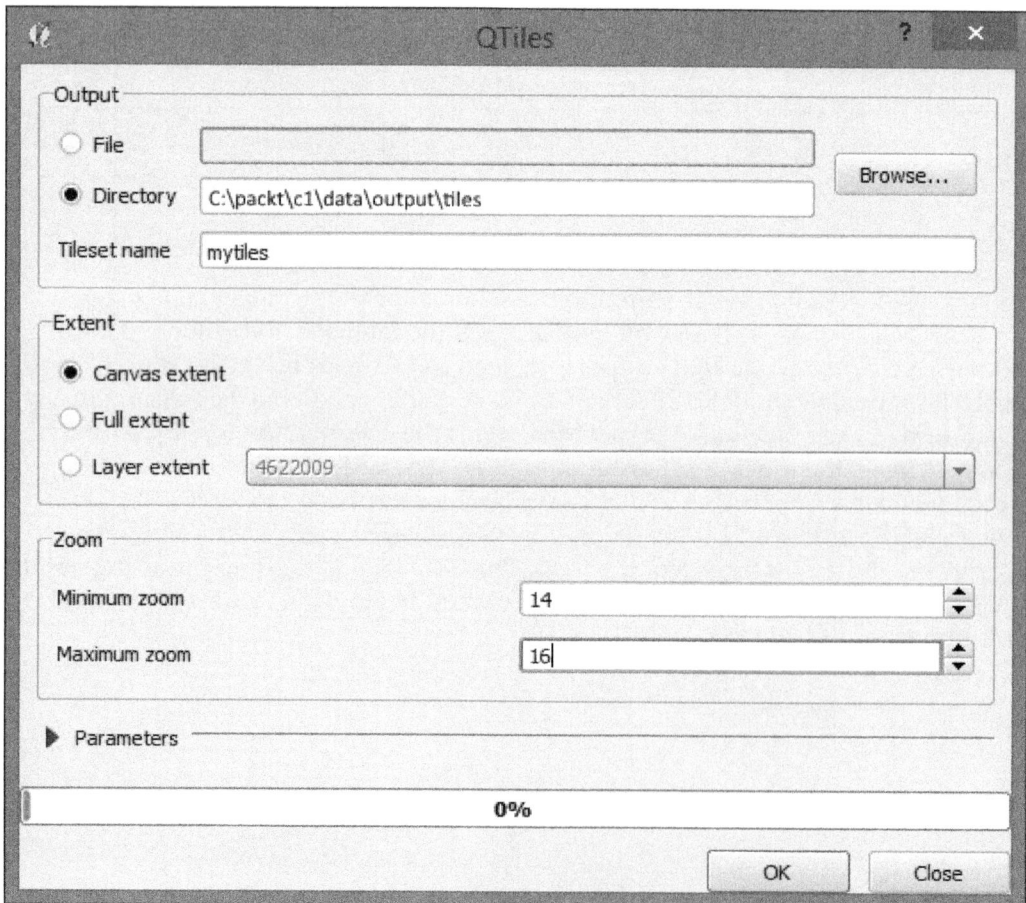

4. You can test and see whether the tiles were created by looking under the directory where you created them. They will be under the directory in the numbered subdirectories given by their *Z*, *X*, and *Y* grid positions in the tiling scheme. For example, here's a tile at 15/9489/12442.png. That's 15 zoom, 9489 longitude in the grid scheme, and 12442 latitude in the grid scheme.

You will now see the following output:

Create a layer description file for the TileLayer plugin

Create a layer description file with a `tsv` (tab delimited) extension in the UTF-8 encoding. This is a universal text encoding that is widely used on the Web and is sometimes needed for compatibility.

> Note that the last six parameters are optional and may prevent missing tiles. In the following example, I will use only the `z` parameters, `zmin` and `zmax`, related to map zoom level.

1. Add text in the following form, containing all tile parameters, to a new file:

   ```
   title credit url yOriginTop [zmin zmax xmin ymin xmax ymax]
   ```

   ○ For example, `mytiles me file:///c:/packt/c1/data/output/tiles/ mytiles/{z}/{x}/{y}.png 1 14 16`.

   ○ In the preceding example, the description file refers to a local Windows file system path, where the tiled `.png` images are stored.

2. Save `mytiles.tsv` to the following path:

```
[YOUR HOME DIRECTORY]/.qgis2///python/plugins/
    TileLayerPlugin/layers
```

  ° For me, on Windows, this was `C:\Users\[user]\.qgis2\python\plugins\TileLayerPlugin\layers`.

> Note that `.qgis2` may be a hidden directory on some systems. Make sure to show the hidden directories/files.

  ° The path for the location to save your TSV file can be found or set under **Web | TileLayer Plugin | Add Tile Layer | Settings | External layer definition directory**.

Preview it with the TileLayer plugin. You should be able to add the layer from the TilerLayerPlugin dialog. Now that the layer description file has been added to the correct location, let's go to **Web TileLayerPlugin | Add Tile Layer**:

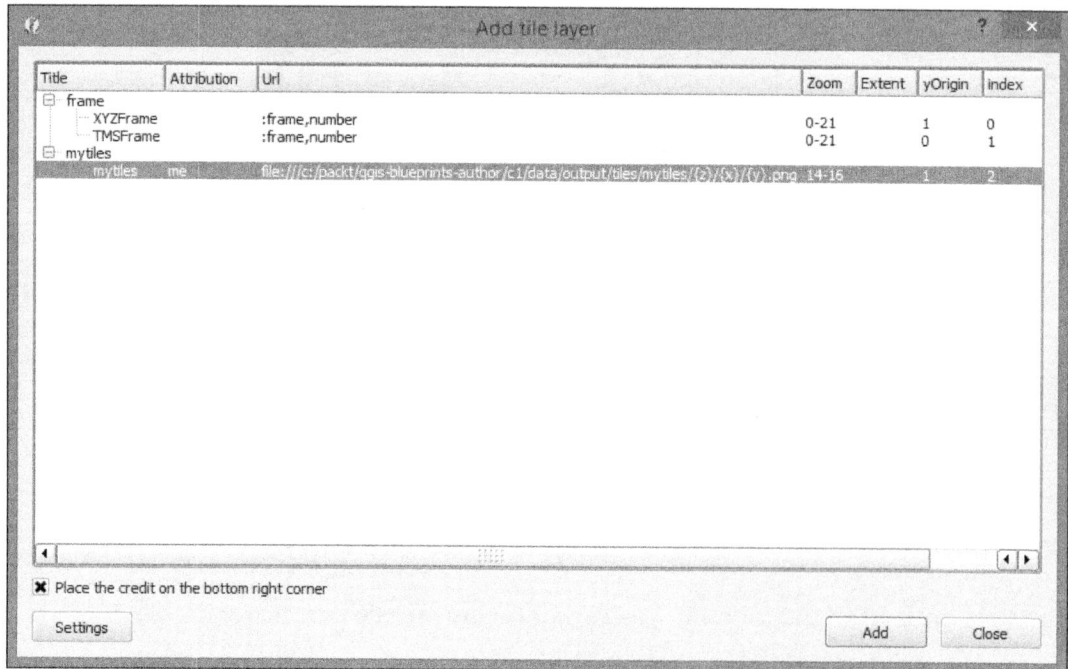

After selecting the layer, click on **Add**. Your tiles will look something like the following image:

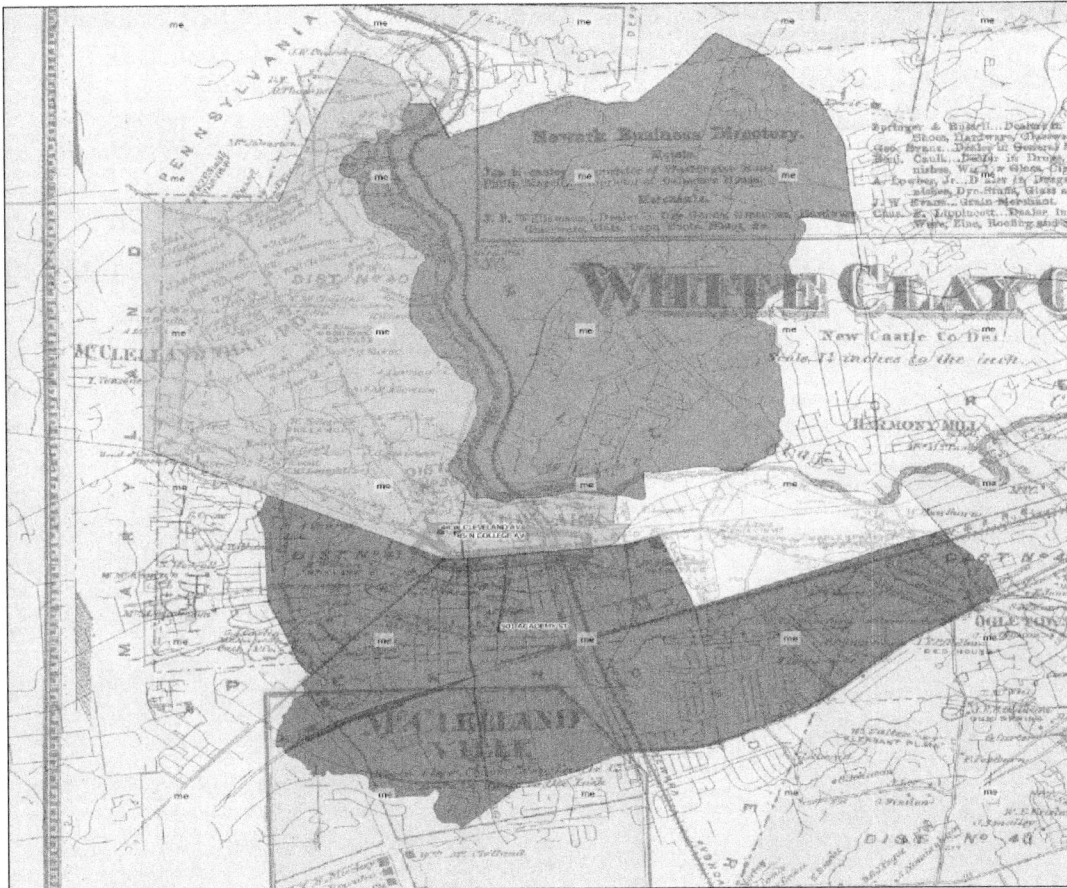

> ![notes] Note the credit value in the lower-right corner of each tile.

Summary

In this chapter, you learned the necessary background and took steps to get up and running with QGIS. We performed ETL on the location-based data to geospatially integrate it with our GIS project. You learned the fundamental GIS visualization techniques around layer style and labeling. Finally, after some consideration around the nature of basemaps, we produced a tile cache that we could preview in QGIS. In the next chapter, we will use raster analysis to produce an operational layer for interaction within a simple web map application.

2
Identifying the Best Places

In this chapter, we will take a look at how the raster data can be analyzed, enhanced, and used for map production. Specifically, you will learn to produce a grid of the suitable locations based on the criteria values in other grids using raster analysis and map algebra. Then, using the grid, we will produce a simple click-based map. The end result will be a site suitability web application with click-based discovery capabilities. We'll be looking at the suitability for the farmland preservation selection.

In this chapter, we will cover the following topics:

- Vector data ETL for raster analysis
- Batch processing
- Raster analysis concepts
- Map algebra
- Additive modeling
- Proximity analysis
- Raster data ETL for vector publication
- Leaflet map application publication with qgis2leaf

Vector data – Extract, Transform, and Load

Our suitability analysis uses map algebra and criteria grids to give us a single value for the suitability for some activity in every place. This requires that the data be expressed in the raster (grid) format. So, let's perform the other necessary ETL steps and then convert our vector data to raster.

We will perform the following actions:

- Ensure that our data has identical spatial reference systems. For example, we may be using a layer of the roads maintained by the state department of transportation and a layer of land use maintained by the department of natural resources. These layers must have identical spatial reference systems or be transformed to have identical systems.

- Extract geographic objects according to their classes as defined in some attribute table field if we want to operate on them while they're still in the vector form.

- If no further analysis is necessary, convert to raster.

Loading data and establishing the CRS conformity

It is important for the layers in this project to be transformed or projected into the same geographic or projected coordinate system. This is necessary for an accurate analysis and for publication to the web formats. Perform the following steps for this:

1. Disable 'on the fly' projection if it is turned on. Otherwise, 'on the fly' will automatically project your data again to display it with the layers that are already in the Canvas.

   1. Navigate to **Settings | Options** and configure the settings shown in the following screenshot:

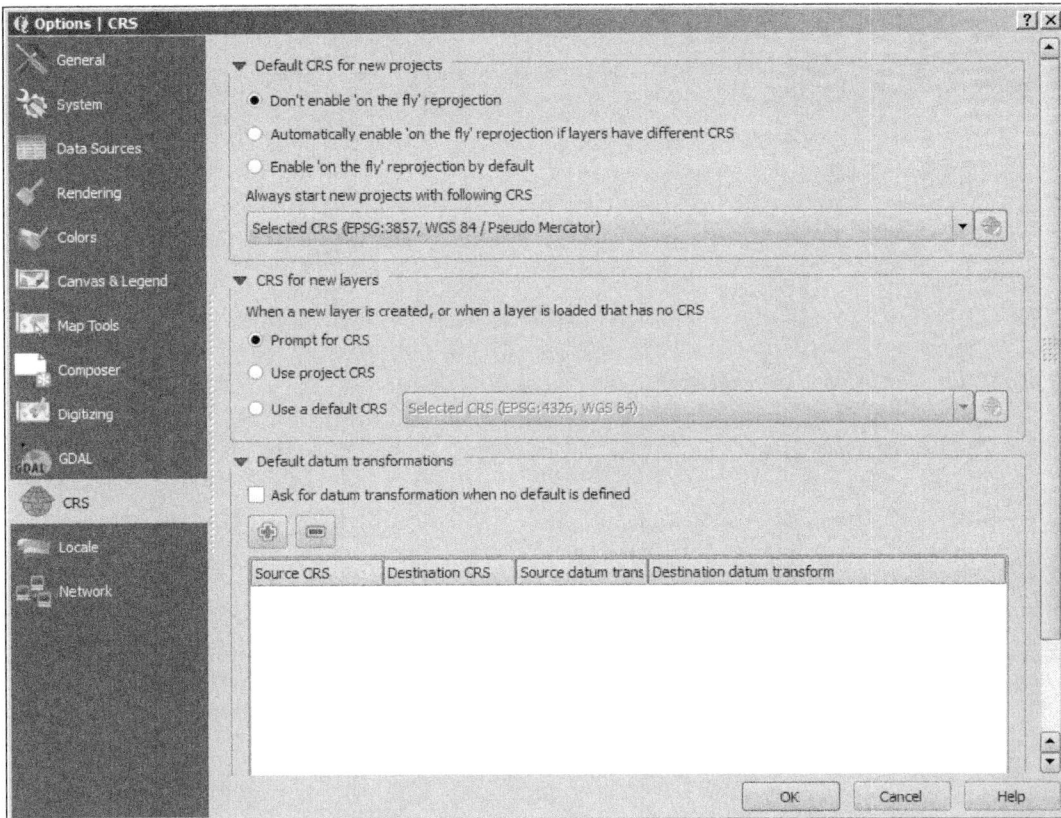

2. Add the project layers:

    2. Navigate to **Layer | Add Layer | Vector Layer**.

    3. Add the following layers from within `c2/data/original`.

       Applicants

       County

       Easements

       Land use

       Roads

You can select multiple layers to add by pressing *Shift* and clicking on the contiguous files or pressing *Ctrl* and clicking on the noncontiguous files.

3. Import the Digital Elevation Model from `c2/data/original/dem/dem.tif`.

   1. Navigate to **Layer | Add Layer | Raster Layer**.

   2. From the `dem` directory, select `dem.tif` and then click on **Open**.

4. Even though the layers are in a different CRS, QGIS does not warn us in this case. You must discover the issue by checking each layer individually. Check the CRS of the county layer and one other layer:

   1. Highlight the county layer in the **Layers** panel.

   2. Navigate to **Layer | Properties**.

   3. The CRS is displayed under the **General** tab in the **Coordinate reference system** section:

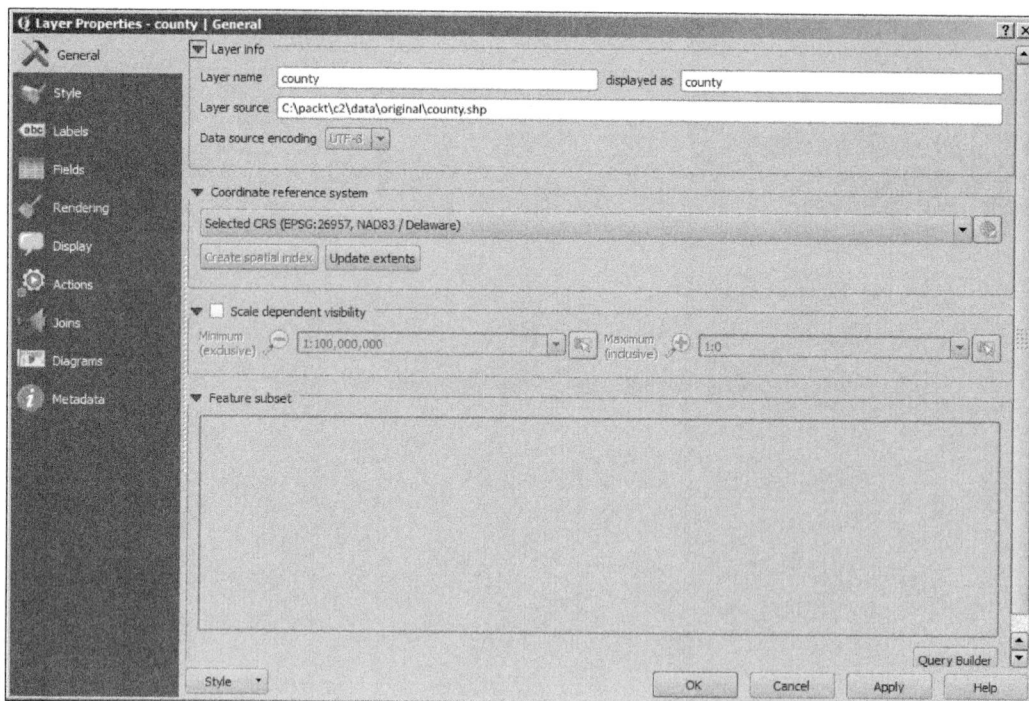

Note that the county layer is in **EPSG: 26957**, while the others are in **EPSG: 2776**.

5. Follow the steps in *Chapter 1, Exploring Places – from Concept to Interface*, for transformation and projection. We will transform the county layer from EPSG:26957 to EPSG:2776.

   1. Navigate to **Layer | Save as | Select CRS**.

   > We will save all the output from this chapter in `c2/data/output`.

To prepare the layers for conversion to raster, we will add a new generic column to all the layers populated with the number 1. This will be translated to a Boolean type raster, where the presence of the object that the raster represents (for example, roads) is indicated by a cell of 1 and all others with a zero. Follow these steps for the applicants, easements, and roads:

1. Navigate to **Layer | Toggle Editing**.
2. Then, navigate to **Layer | Open Attribute Table**.
3. Add a column with the button at the top of the **Attribute table** dialog.
4. Use `value` as the name for the new column and the following data format options:

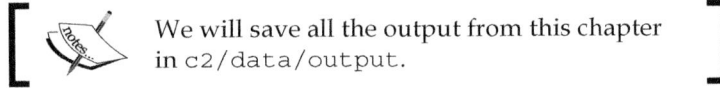

5. Select the new column from the dropdown in the **Attribute table** and enter 1 into the value box:

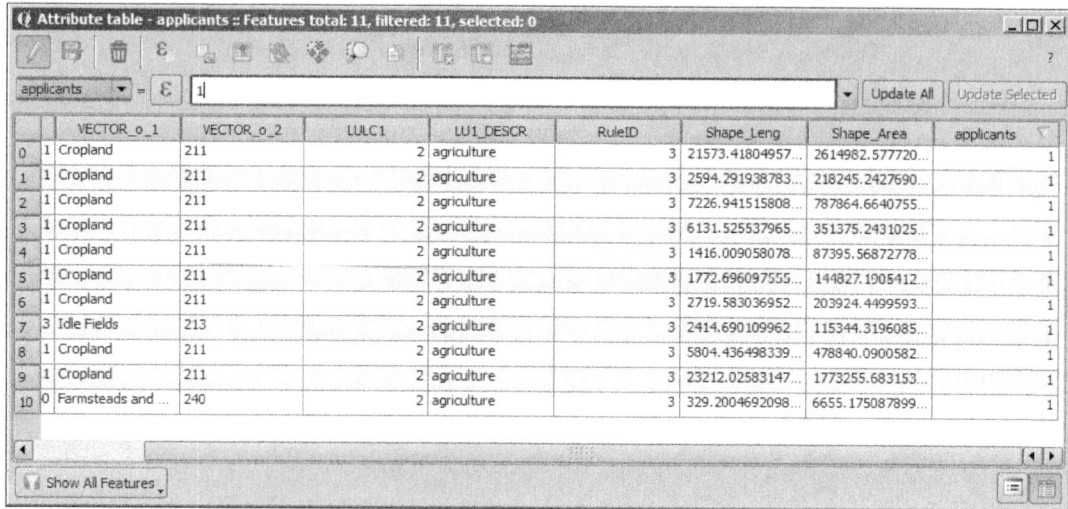

6. Click on **Update All**.
7. Navigate to **Layer | Toggle Editing**.
8. Finally, save.

The extracting (filtering) features

Let's suppose that our criteria includes only a subset of the features in our roads layer—major unlimited access roads (but not freeways), a subset of the features as determined by a **classification code** (CFCC). To temporarily extract this subset, we will do a layer query by performing the following steps:

1. Filter the major roads from the roads layer.
    1. Highlight the roads layer.
    2. Navigate to **Layer | Query**.
    3. Double-click on **CFCC** to add it to the expression.
    4. Click on the = operator to add to the expression
    5. Under the **Values** section, click on **All** to view all the unique values in the **CFCC** field.
    6. Double-click on **A21** to add this to the expression.
    7. Do this for all the codes less than A36. Include A63 for highway on-ramps.

8. Your selection code will look similar to this:

```
"CFCC" = 'A21' OR "CFCC" = 'A25' OR "CFCC" =
'A31' OR "CFCC" = 'A35' OR "CFCC" = 'A63'
```

9. Click on **OK**, as shown in the following screenshot:

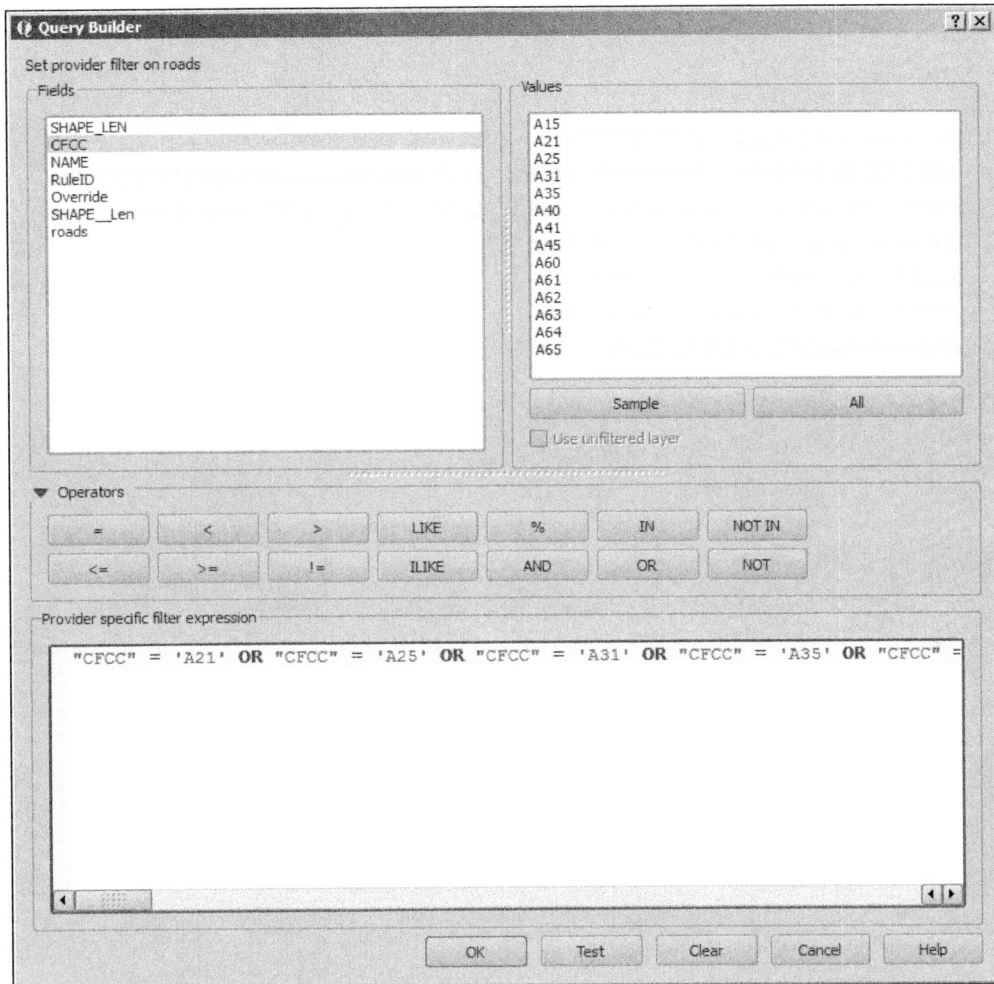

2. Save the roads layer as a new layer with only the selected features (major_roads) in c2/data/output.

> To clear a layer filter, return to the query dialog on the applied layer (highlight it in the **Layers** pane; navigate to **Layer** | **Query** and click on **Clear**).

3. Repeat these steps for the developed (LULC1 = 1) and agriculture (LULC1 = 2) land uses (separately) from the landuse layer.

Converting to raster

In this section, we will convert all the needed vector layers to raster. We will be doing this in batch, which will allow us to repeat the same operation many times over multiple layers.

Doing more at once—working in batch

The QGIS Processing Framework provides capabilities to run the same operation many times on different data. This is called **batch processing**. A batch process is invoked from an operation's context menu in the **Processing Toolbox**. The batch dialog requires that the parameters for each layer be populated for every iteration. Perform the following steps:

1. Convert the vector layers to raster.

    1. Navigate to **Processing Toolbox**.
    2. Select **Advanced Interface** from the dropdown at the bottom of **Processing Toolbox** (if it is not selected, it will show as **Simple Interface**).
    3. Type rasterize to search for the **Rasterize** tool.
    4. Right-click on the **Rasterize** tool and select **Execute as batch process**:

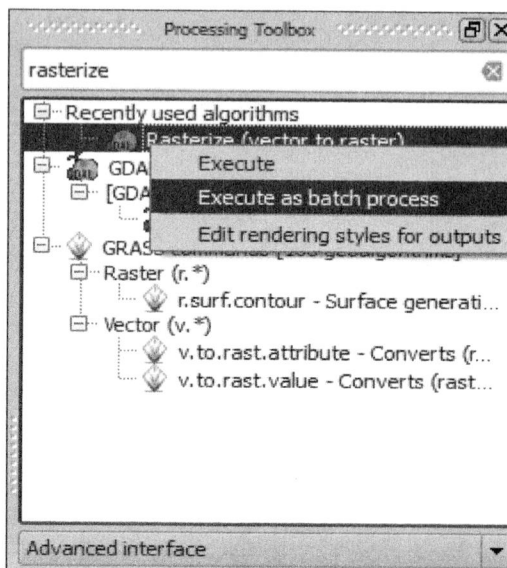

5. Fill in the **Batch Processing** dialog, making sure to specify the parameters as follows:

Parameter	Value
Input layer	(For example, `roads`)
Attribute field	`value`
Output raster size	**Output resolution in map units per pixel**
Horizontal	`30`
Vertical	`30`
Raster type	**Int16**
Output layer	(For example, `roads`)

The following images show how this will look in QGIS:

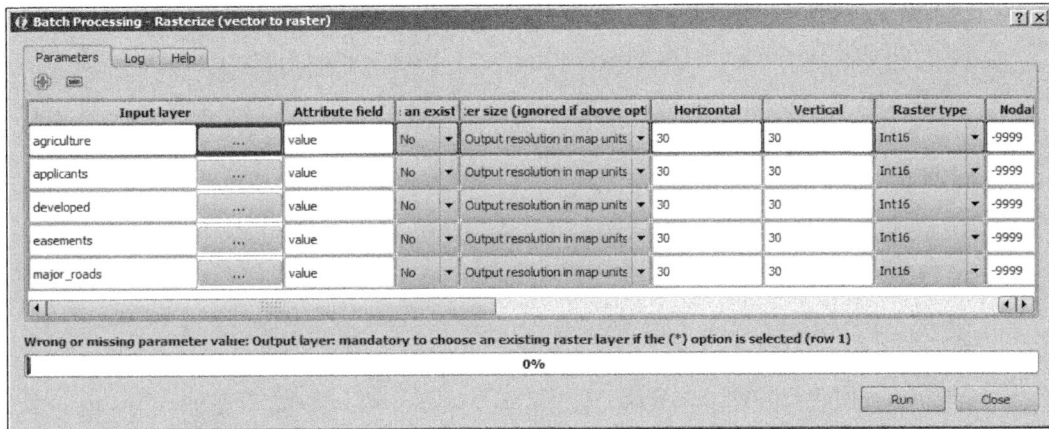

6. Scroll to the right to complete the entry of parameter values.

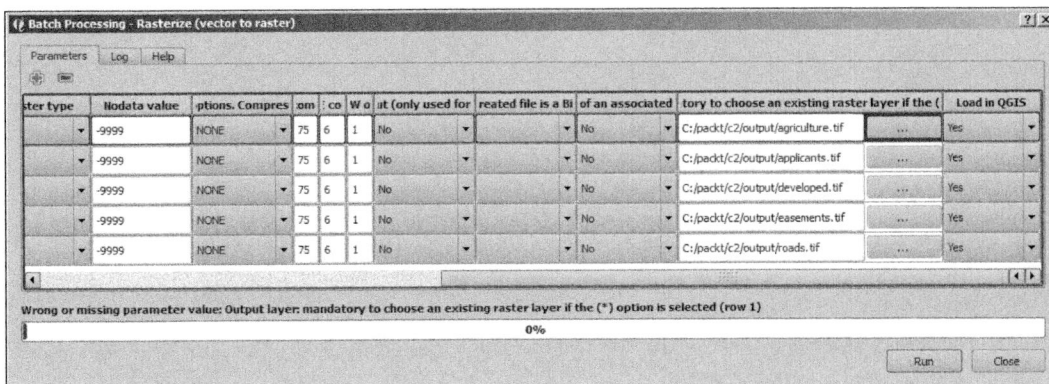

2. Organize the new layers (optional step).

   ° Batch sometimes gives unfriendly names based on some bug in the dialog box.

   ° Change the layer names by doing the following for each layer created by batch:

   1. Highlight the layer.

   2. Navigate to **Layer** | **Properties**.

   3. Change the layer name to the name of the vector layer from which this was created (for example, `applicants`). You should be able to find a hint for this value in the layer properties in the layer source (name of the `.tif` file).

   4. Group the layers:

      Press *Shift* + click on all the layers created by batch and the previous `roads` raster, in the **Layers** panel.

      Right-click on the selected layers and click on **Group selected**.

Raster analysis

Raster data, by organizing the data in uniform grids, is useful to analyze continuous phenomena or find some information at the subobject level. We will use continuous elevation and proximity data in this case, and we will look at the subapplicant object level — at the 30 meter-square cell level. You would choose a cell size depending on the resolution of the data source (for example, from sensors roughly 30 meters apart), the roughness of the analysis (regional versus local), and any hardware limitations.

First, let's make a few notes about raster data:

- Nodata refers to the cells that are included with the raster grid because a grid can't have completely undefined cells; however, these cells should really be considered *off the layer*.

- QGIS's raster renderer is more limited than in its proprietary competitors. You will want to use the **Identify** tool as well as custom styles (**Singleband Pseudocolor**) to make sense of your outputs.

- In this example, we will rely heavily on the GDAL and SAGA libraries that have been wrapped for QGIS. These are available directly through the processing framework with no additional preparation beyond the ordinary raster ETL. For additional functionality, you will want to consider the GRASS libraries. These are wrapped and provided for QGIS but require the additional preparation of a GRASS workspace.

Now that all our data is in the raster format, we can work through how to derive information from these layers and combine this information in order to select the best sites.

Map algebra

Map algebra is a useful concept to work with multiple raster layers and analysis steps, providing arithmetic operations between cells in aligned grids. These produce an output grid with the respective value of the arithmetic solution for each set of cells. We will be using map algebra in this example for additive modeling.

Additive modeling

Now that all our data is in the raster format, we can begin to model for the purpose of site selection. We want to discover which cells are best according to a set of criteria which has either been established for the domain area (for example, the agricultural conservation site selection) by convention or selected at the time of modeling. Additive modeling refers to this process of adding up all the criteria and associated weights to find the best areas, which will have the greatest value.

In this case, we have selected some criteria that are loosely known to affect the agricultural conservation site selection, as shown in the following table:

Layer	Criteria	Rule
applicants	Is applicant	
easements	Proximity	< 2000 m
landuse (agriculture)	Land use, proximity	< 100 m
dem	Slope	=> 2 and <= 5, average
landuse (developed)	Land use, proximity	> 500 m
roads	Proximity	> 100m

Proximity

The **Proximity** grid tool will generate a layer of cells with each cell having a value equal to its distance from the nearest non-nodata cell in another grid. The distance value is given in the CRS units of the other grid. It also generates direction and allocation grids with the direction and ID of the nearest nodata cell.

Creating a proximity to the easements grid

Perform the following steps:

1. Navigate to **Processing Toolbox**.

2. Search for `proximity` in this toolbox. Ensure that you have the **Advanced Interface** selected.

3. Once you've located the **Proximity** grid tool under **SAGA**, double-click on it to run it.

4. Select **easements** for the **Features** field.

5. Specify an output file for **Distance** at `c2/data/output/easements_prox.tif`.

6. Uncheck **Open output file after running algorithm** for the other two outputs, as shown in the following screenshot:

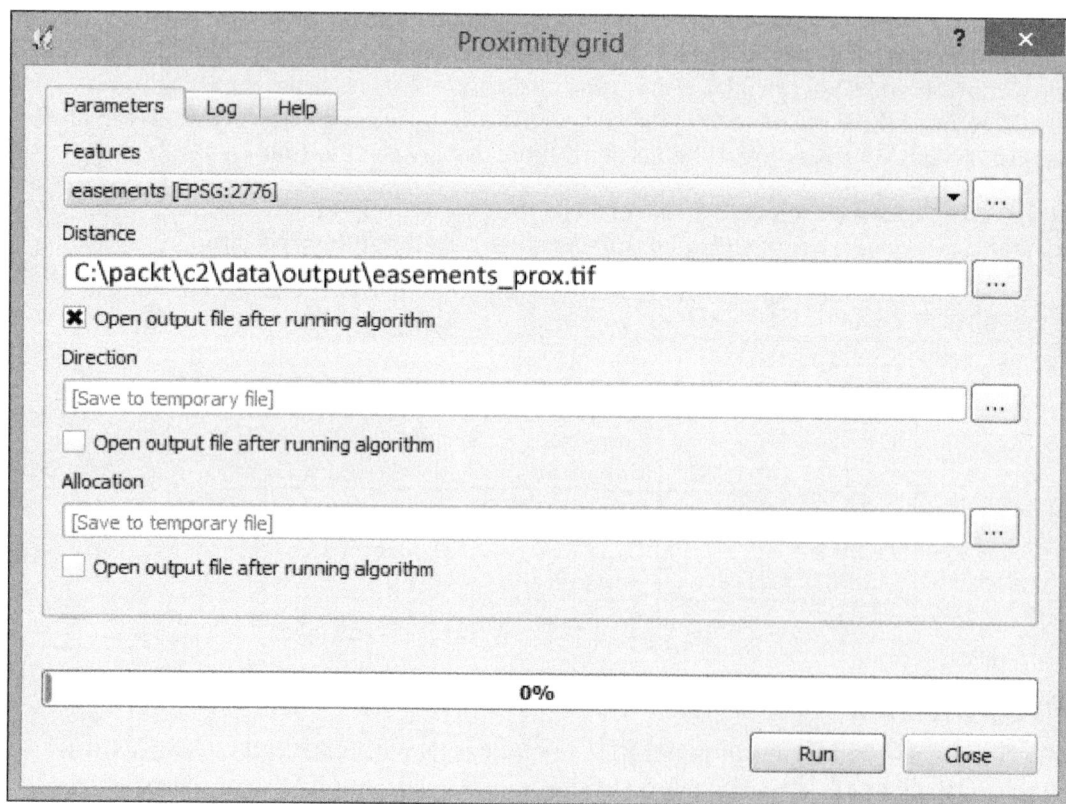

The resulting grid is of the distance to the closest easement cell.

7. Repeat these steps to create proximity grids for `agriculture`, `developed`, and `roads`. Finally, you will see the following output:

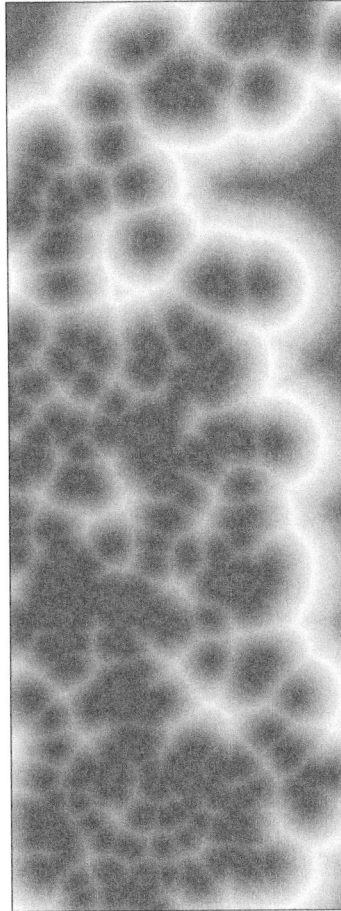

Slope

The **Slope** command creates a grid where the value of each cell is equal to the upgradient slope in percent terms. In other words, it is equal to how steep the terrain is at the current cell in the percentage of rise in elevation unit per horizontal distance unit. Perform the following steps:

1. Install and activate the Raster Terrain Analysis plugin if you have not already done so.

2. Navigate to **Raster | Terrain Analysis | Slope**.

3. Select **dem**, the Digital Elevation Model, for the **Elevation layer** field.

4. Save your output in `c2/data/output`. You can keep the other inputs as default.

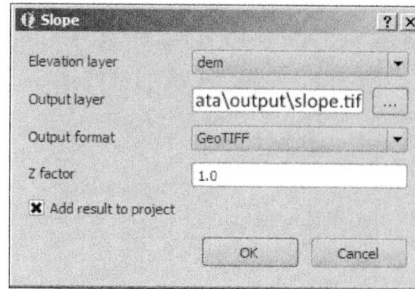

5. The output will be the steepness of each cell in the percentage of of vertical elevation over horizontal distance ("rise over run").

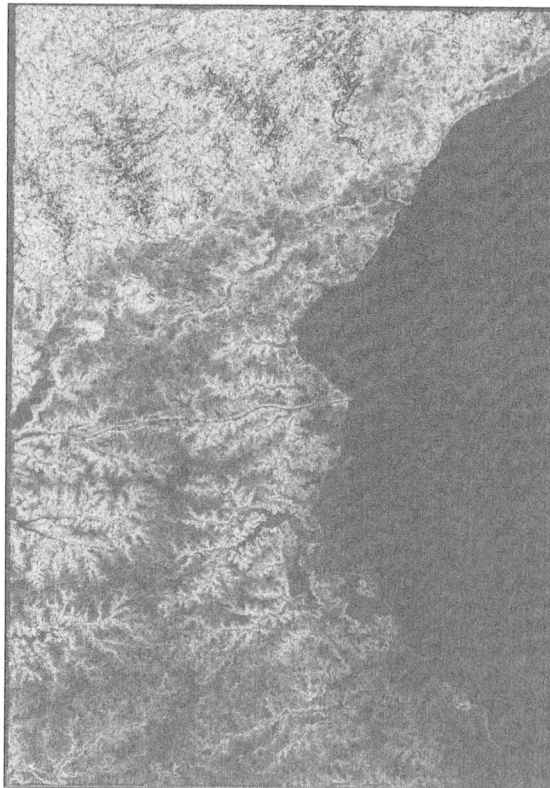

Combining the criteria with Map Calculator

1. Ensure that all the criteria grids (`proximity`, `agriculture`, `developed`, `road`, and `slope`) appear in the **Layers** panel. If they don't, add them.

2. Bring up the **Raster calculator** dialog.

    1. Navigate to **Raster | Raster calculator**

3. Enter the map algebra expression.

    ○ Add the raster layers by double-clicking on them in the **Raster bands** selection area

    ○ Add the operators by typing them out or clicking on the buttons in the operators area

    ○ The expression entered should be as follows:

    ```
    ("slope@1" < 8) + ("applicants@1" = 1) +
    ("easement_prox@1"<2000) + ("roads_prox@1">100) +
    ("developed_prox@1" > 500) + ("agriculture@1" < 100)
    ```

> @1 refers to the first and only band of the raster.

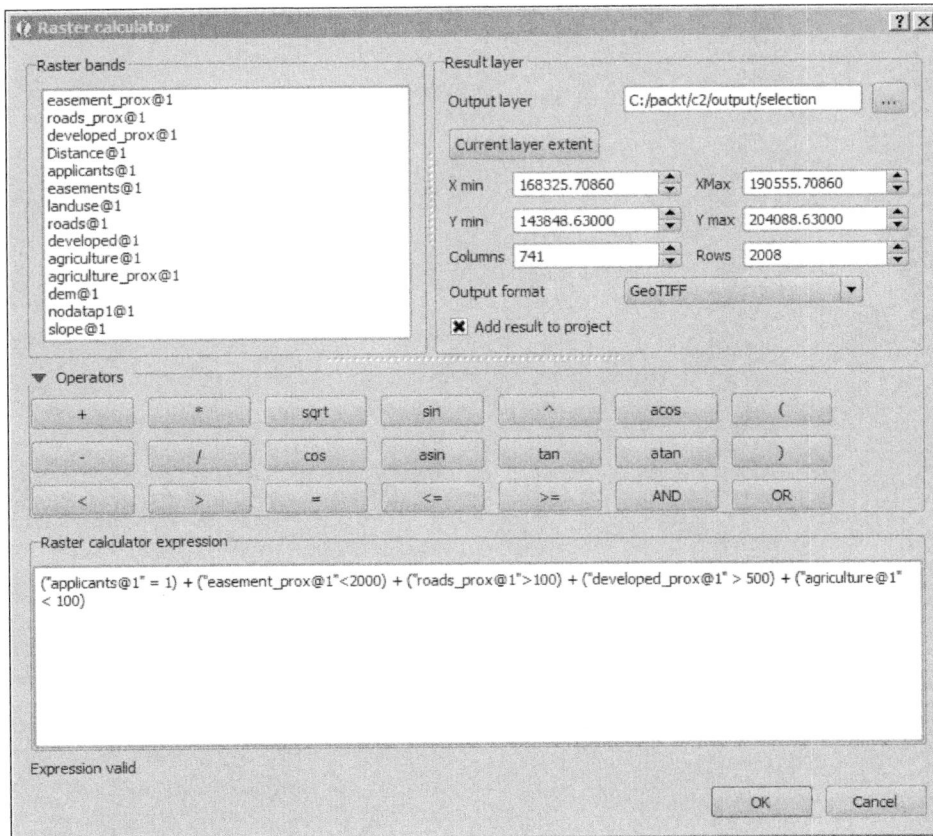

4. Add a name and path for the output file and hit *Enter*.
5. You may need to set a style if it seems like nothing happened. By default, the nonzero value is set to display in white (the same color as our background).

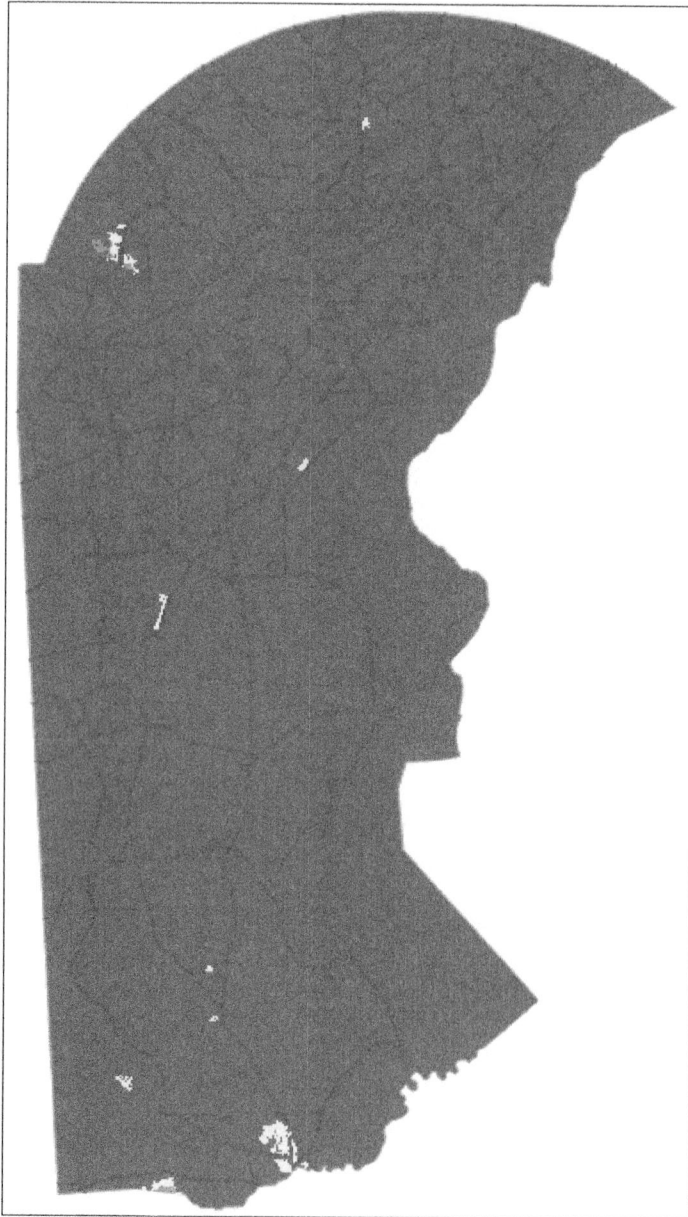

Here's a close up of the preceding map image so that you can see the variability in suitability:

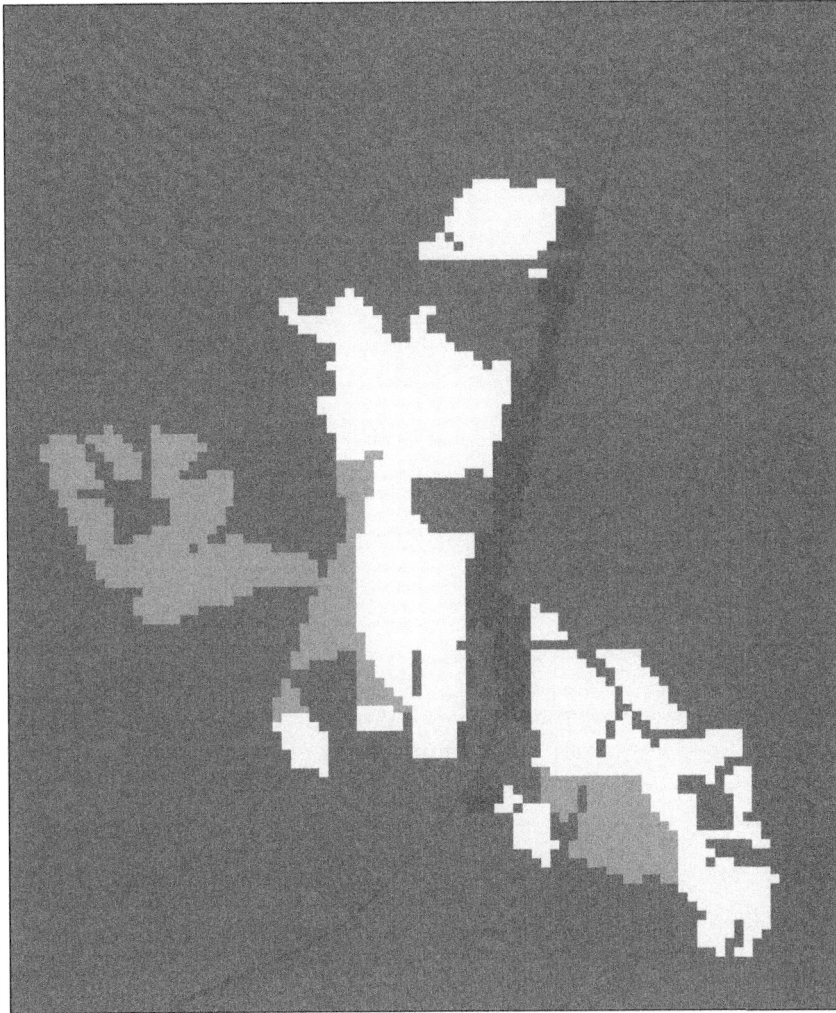

In the preceding screenshot, cells are scored as follows:

- Green = 5 (high)
- Yellow = 4 (middle)
- Red = 3 (low)

Zonal statistics

Zonal statistics are calculated from the cells that fall within polygons. Using zonal statistics, we can get a better idea of what the raster data tells us about a particular cell group, geographic object, or polygon. In this case, zonal statistics will give us an average score for a particular applicant. Perform the following steps:

1. Install and activate the Zonal Statistics plugin.

2. Navigate to **Raster | Zonal Statistics | Zonal statistics**, as shown in the following image:

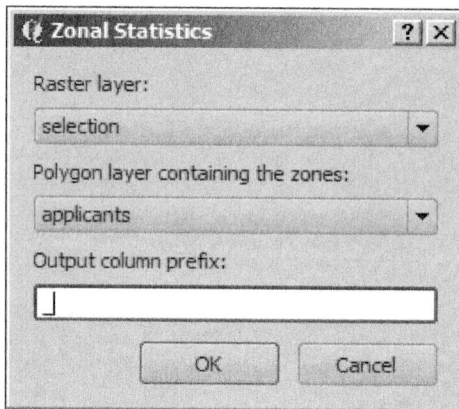

3. Input a raster layer for the values used to calculate a statistic and a polygon layer that are used to define the boundaries of the cells used. Here, we will use the applicants and land use to count the number of cells in each applicant cell group.

4. Create a `rank` field, editing each value manually according to the `_mean` field created by the zonal statistics step. This is a measure of the mean suitability per cell. We will use this field for a label to communicate the relative suitability to a general audience; so, we want a rank instead of the rough mean value.

5. Now, label the layer.

   1. Under **Layer Properties**, activate the **Labels** tab.

   2. Choose the `rank` field as the field to label.

   3. Add any other formatting, such as label placement and buffer (halo) using the inner tabs within the label tab dialog, as shown in the following screenshot:

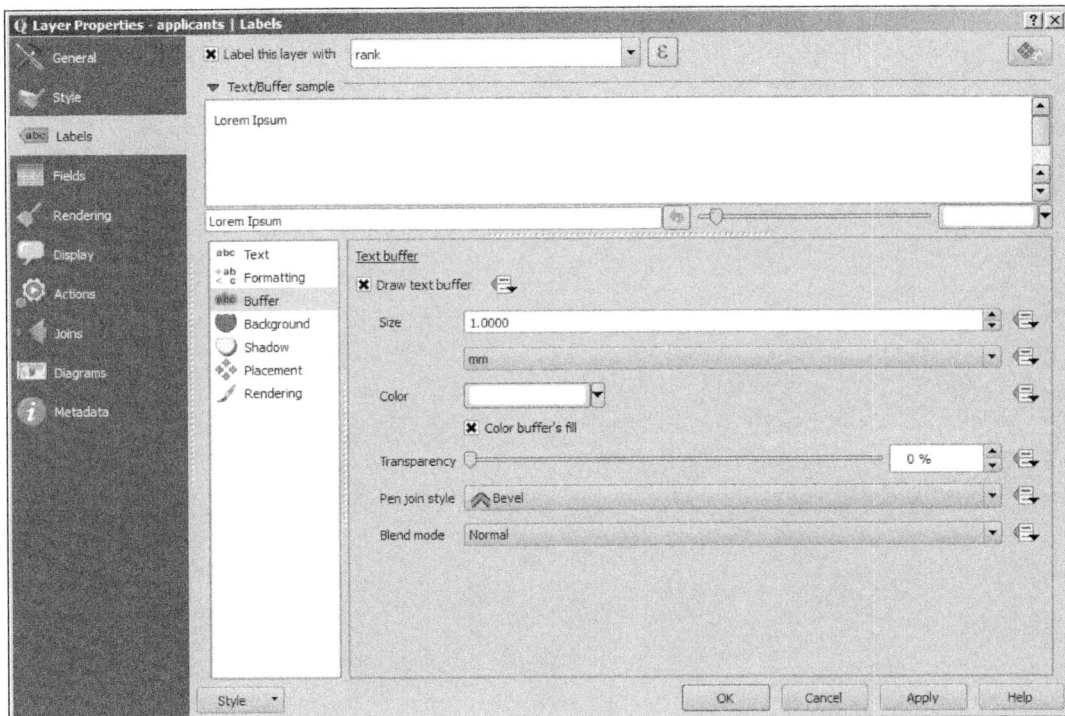

6. Add a style to the layer.

    1. Select the **Graduated** style.

    2. Select a suitable color ramp, number of classes, and classification type.

    3. Click on the **Classify** button, as shown in the following screenshot:

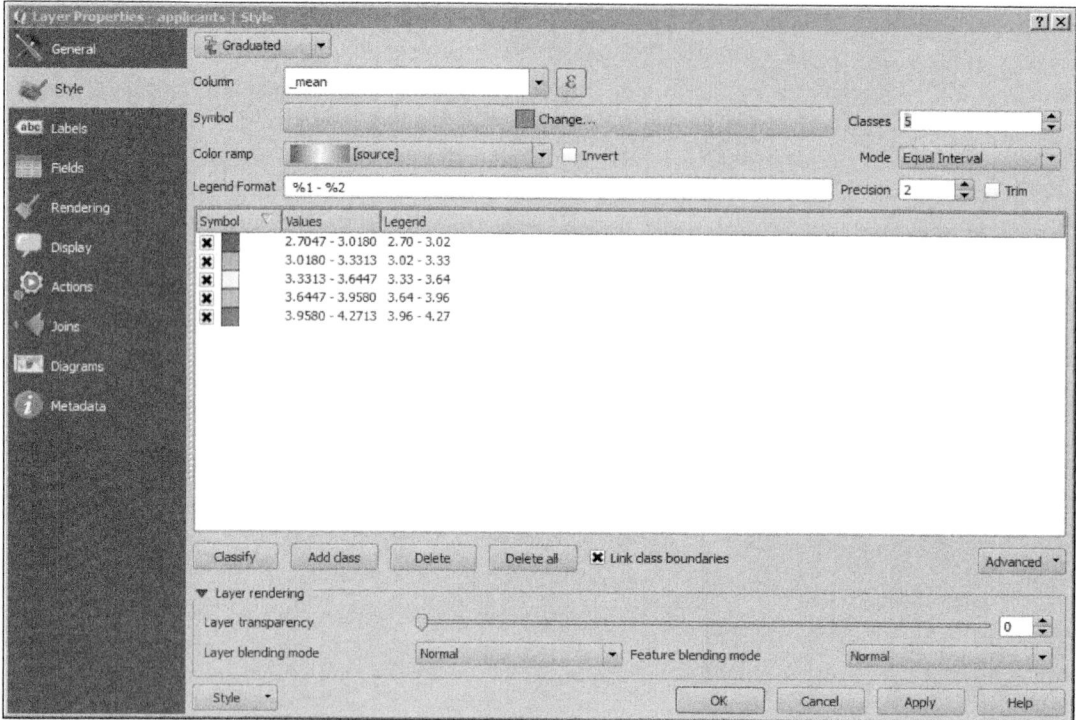

After you've completed these steps, your map will look something similar to this:

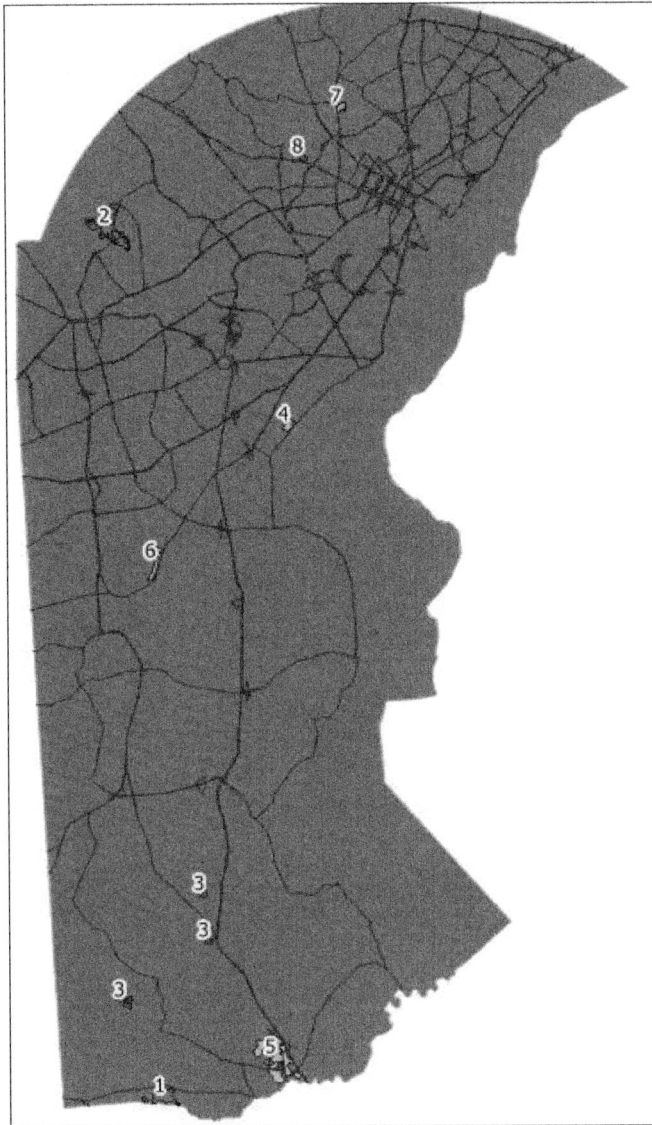

Publishing the results as a web application

Now that we have completed our modeling for the site selection of a farmland for conservation, let's take steps to publish this for the Web.

qgis2leaf

qgis2leaf allows us to export our QGIS map to web map formats (JavaScript, HTML, and CSS) using the Leaflet map API. Leaflet is a very lightweight, extensible, and responsive (and trendy) web mapping interface.

qgis2leaf converts all our vector layers to GeoJSON, which is the most common textual way to express the geographic JavaScript objects. As our operational layer is in GeoJSON, Leaflet's click interaction is supported, and we can access the information in the layers by clicking. It is a fully editable HTML and JavaScript file. You can customize and upload it to an accessible web location, as you'll understand in subsequent chapters.

qgis2leaf is very simple to use as long as the layers are prepared properly (for example, with respect to CRS) up to this point. It is also very powerful in creating a good starting application including GeoJSON, HTML, and JavaScript for our Leaflet web map. Perform the following steps:

1. Make sure to install the qgis2leaf plugin if you haven't already.

2. Navigate to **Web | qgis2leaf | Exports a QGIS Project to a working Leaflet webmap**.

3. Click on the **Get Layers** button to add the currently displayed layers to the set that qgis2leaf will export.

4. Choose a basemap and enter the additional details if so desired.

5. Select **Encode to JSON**.

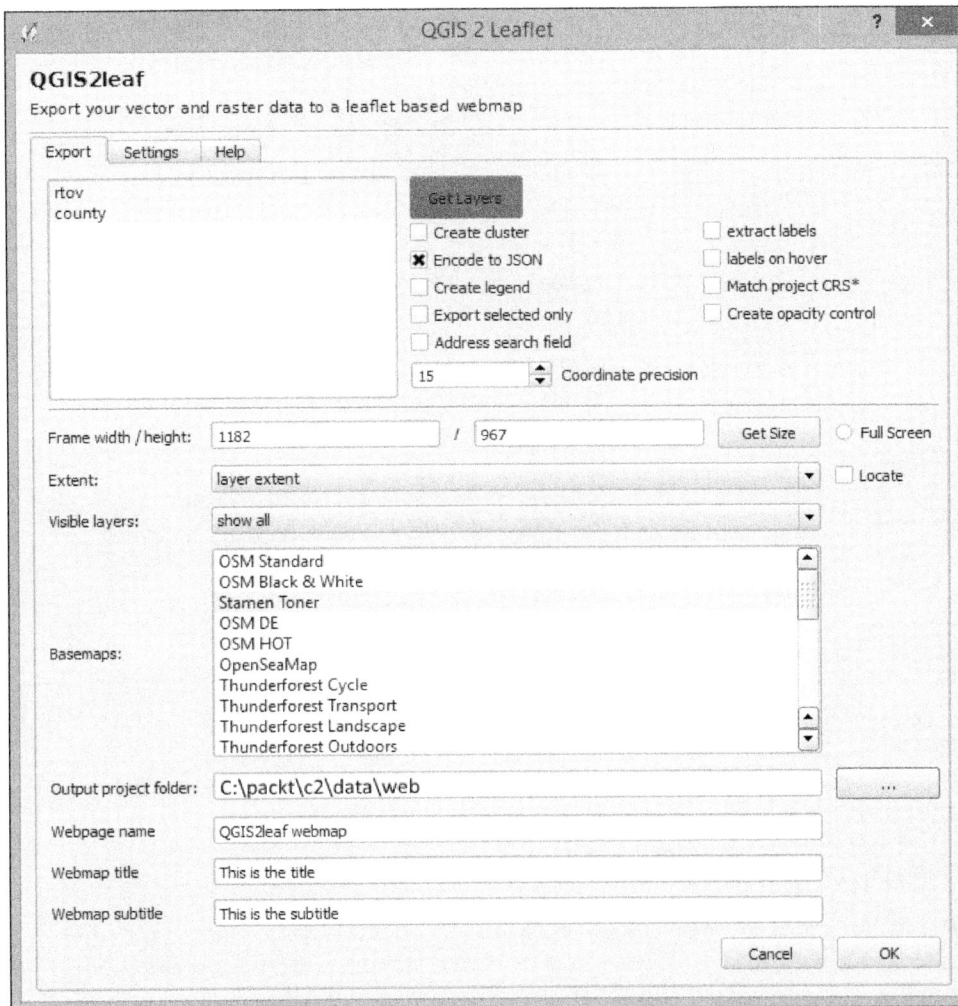

These steps will produce a map application similar to the following one. We'll take a look at how to restore the labels in the next chapter:

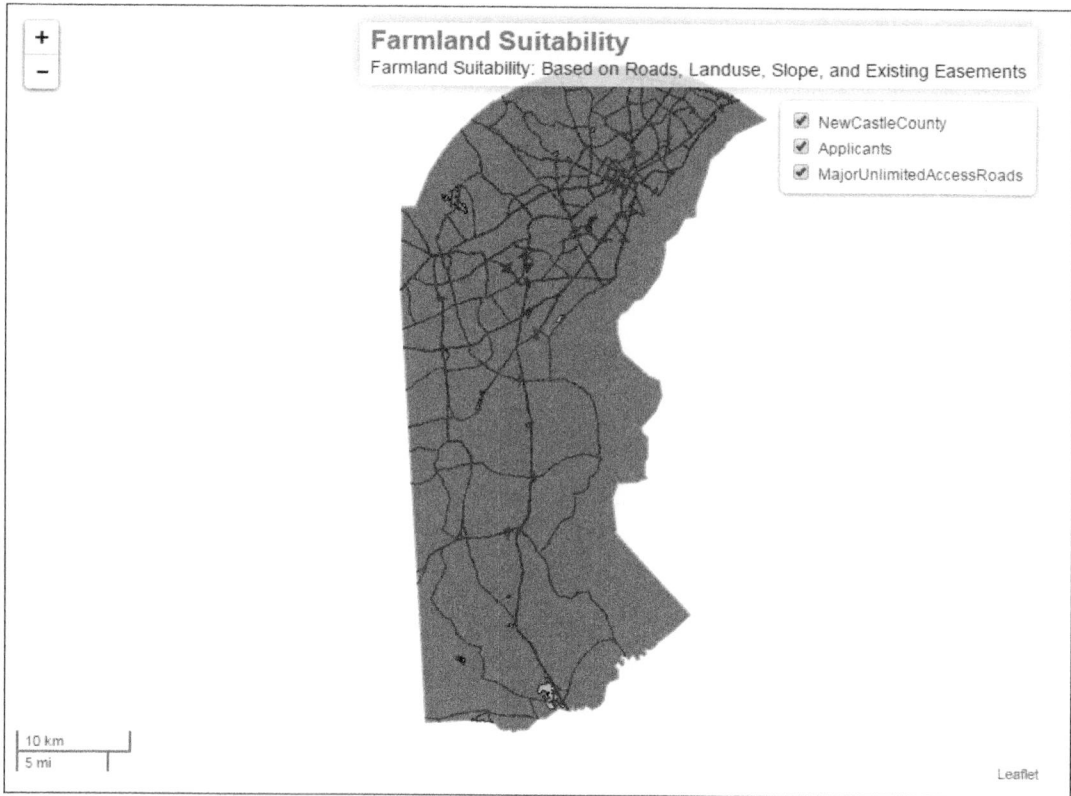

Summary

In this chapter, using the site selection example, we covered basic vector data ETL, raster analysis, and web map creation. We started with vector data, and after unifying CRS, we prepared the attribute tables. We then filtered and converted it to raster grids using batch processing. We also considered some fundamental raster concepts as we applied proximity and terrain analysis. Through map algebra, we combined these results for additive modeling site selection. We prepared these results, which required conversion to vector, styling, and labeling. Finally, we published the prepared vector output with qgis2leaf as a simple Leaflet web map application with a strong foundation for extension. In the next chapter, you will learn more about raster analysis and web application publishing with a hydrological modeling example.

3
Discovering Physical Relationships

In this chapter, we will create an application for a raster physical modeling example. First, we'll use a raster analysis to model the physical conditions for some basic hydrological analysis. Next, we'll redo these steps using a model automation tool. Then, we will attach the raster values to the vector objects for an efficient lookup in a web application. Finally, we will use a cloud platform to enable a dynamic query from the client-side application code. We will take a look at an environmental planning case, providing capabilities for stakeholders to discover the upstream toxic sites.

In this chapter, we will cover the following topics:

- Hydrological modeling
- Workflow automation with graphical models
- Spatial relationships for a performant access to information
- The NNJoin plugin
- The CartoDB cloud platform
- Leaflet SQLQueries using an external API:CartoDB

Hydrological modeling

The behavior of water is closely tied with the characteristics of the terrain's surface—particularly the values connected to elevation. In this section, we will use a basic hydrological model to analyze the location and direction of the hydrological network—streams, creeks, and rivers. To do this, we will use a digital elevation model and a raster grid, in which the value of each cell is equal to the elevation at that location. A more complex model would employ additional physical parameters (e.g., infrastructure, vegetation, etc.). These modeling steps will lay the necessary foundation for our web application, which will display the upstream toxic sites (brownfields), both active and historical, for a given location.

There are a number of different plugins and Processing Framework algorithms (operations) that enable hydrological modeling. For this exercise, we will use SAGA algorithms, of which many are available, with some help from GDAL for the raster preparation. Note that you may need to wait much longer than you are accustomed to for some of the hydrological modeling operations to finish (approximately an hour).

Preparing the data

Some work is needed to prepare the DEM data for hydrological modeling. The DEM path is `c3/data/original/dem/dem.tif`. Add this layer to the map (navigate to **Layer | Add Layer | Add Raster Layer**). Also, add the county shapefile at `c3/data/original/county.shp` (navigate to **Layer | Add Layer | Add Vector Layer**).

Filling the grid sinks

Filling the grid sinks smooths out the elevation surface to exclude the unusual low points in the surface that would cause the modeled streams to—unrealistically—drain to these local lows instead of to larger outlets. The steps to fill the grid sinks are as follows:

1. Navigate to **Processing Toolbox (Advanced Interface)**.
2. Search for **Fill Sinks** (under **SAGA | Terrain Analysis | Hydrology**).
3. Run the **Fill Sinks** tool.
4. In addition to the default parameters, define **DEM** as dem and **Filled DEM** as `c3/data/output/fill.tif`.

5. Click on **Run**, as shown in the following screenshot:

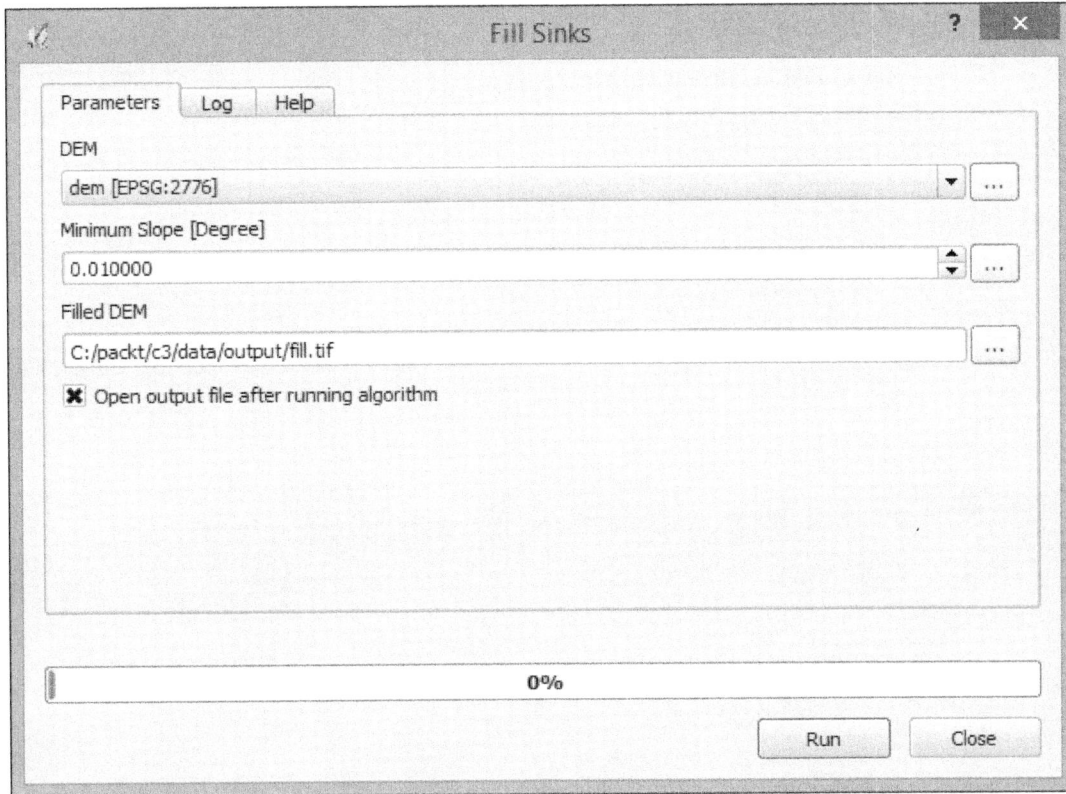

Clipping the grid to study the area by mask layer

By limiting the raster processing extent, we exclude the unnecessary data, improving the speed of the operation. At the same time, we also output a more useful grid that conforms to our extent of interest. In QGIS/SAGA, in order to limit the processing to a fixed extent or area, it is necessary to eliminate those cells from the grid—in other words, the setting cells outside the area or extent, which are sometimes referred to as **NoData** (or no-data, and so on) in raster software, to a null value.

> Unlike ArcGIS or GRASS, the SAGA package under QGIS does not have any capability to set an extent or area within which we want to limit the raster processing.

In QGIS, the raster processing's extent limitation can be accomplished using a vector polygon or a set of polygons with the **Clip raster by mask layer** tool. By following the given steps, we can achieve this:

1. Navigate to **Processing Toolbox (Advanced Interface)**.
2. Search for **Mask** (under **GDAL | Extraction**).
3. Run the **Clip raster by mask layer** tool.
4. Enter the following parameters, keeping others as default:
   - **Input layer**: This is the layer corresponding to `fill.tif`, created in the previous **Fill Sinks** section
   - **Mask layer**: `county`
   - **Output layer**: `c3/data/output/clip.tif`
5. Click on **Run**, as shown in the following screenshot:

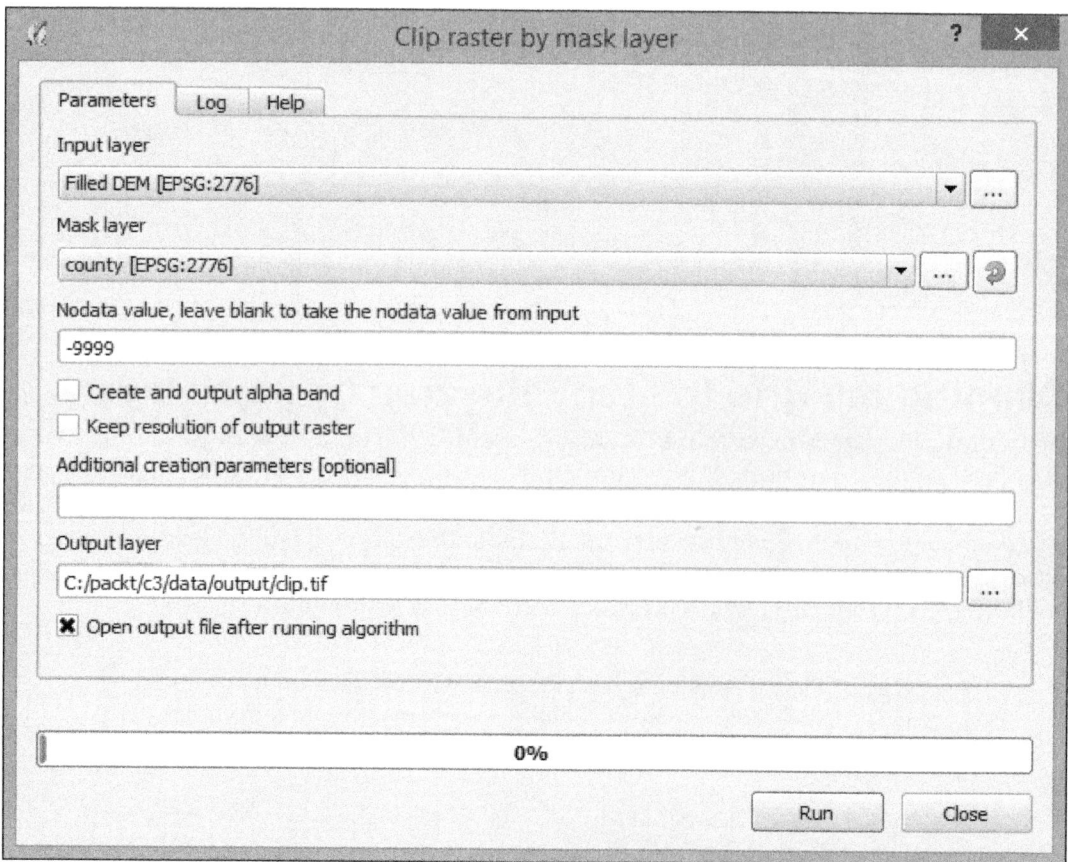

This function is not available in some versions of QGIS for Mac OS.

The output from **Clip by mask layer** tool, showing the grid clipped to the county polygon, will look similar to the following image (the black and white color gradient or mapping to a null value may be reversed):

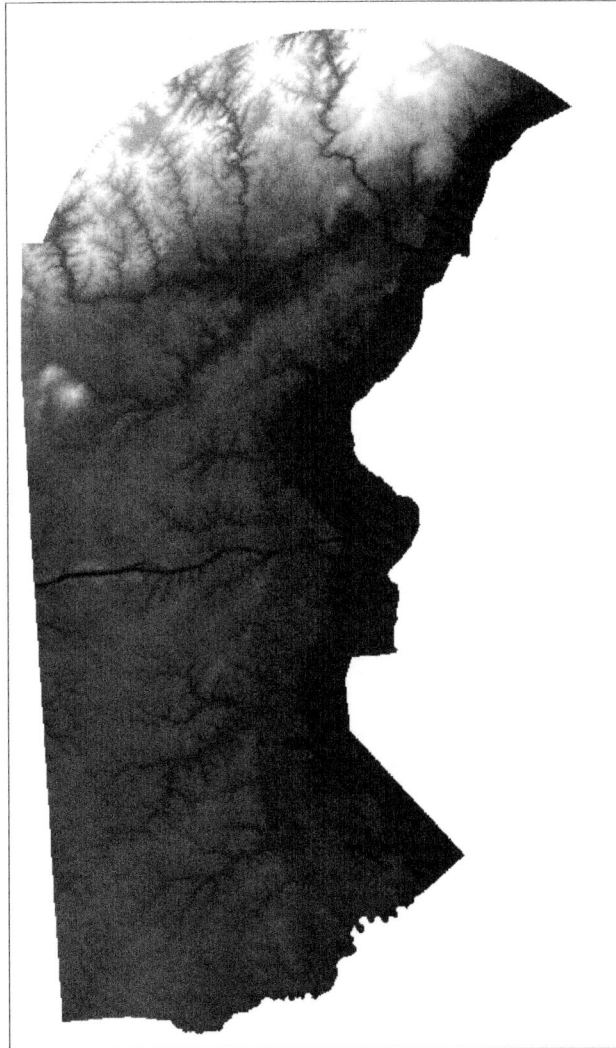

Modeling the hydrological network based on elevation

Now that our elevation grid has been prepared, it is time to actually model the hydrological network location and direction. To do this, we will use **Channel network and drainage basins**, which only requires a single input: the (filled and clipped) elevation model. This tool will produce the hydrological lines using a Strahler Order threshold, which relates to the hierarchy level of the returned streams (for example, to exclude very small ditches) The default of 5 is perfect for our purposes, including enough hydrological lines but not too many. The results look pretty realistic. This tool also produces many additional related grids, which we do not need for this project. Perform the following steps:

1. Navigate to **Processing Toolbox** (**Advanced Interface**).

2. Search for **Channel network and drainage basins** (under **SAGA | Terrain Analysis | Hydrology**).

3. Run the **Channel network and drainage basins** tool.

4. In the **Elevation** field, input the filled and clipped DEM, given as the output in the previous section.

5. In the **Threshold** field, keep it at the default value (5.0).

6. In the **Channels** field, input c3/data/output/channels.shp.

   Ensure that **Open output file after running algorithm** is selected

7. Unselect **Open output file after running algorithm** for all other outputs.

8. Click on **Run**, as shown in the following screenshot:

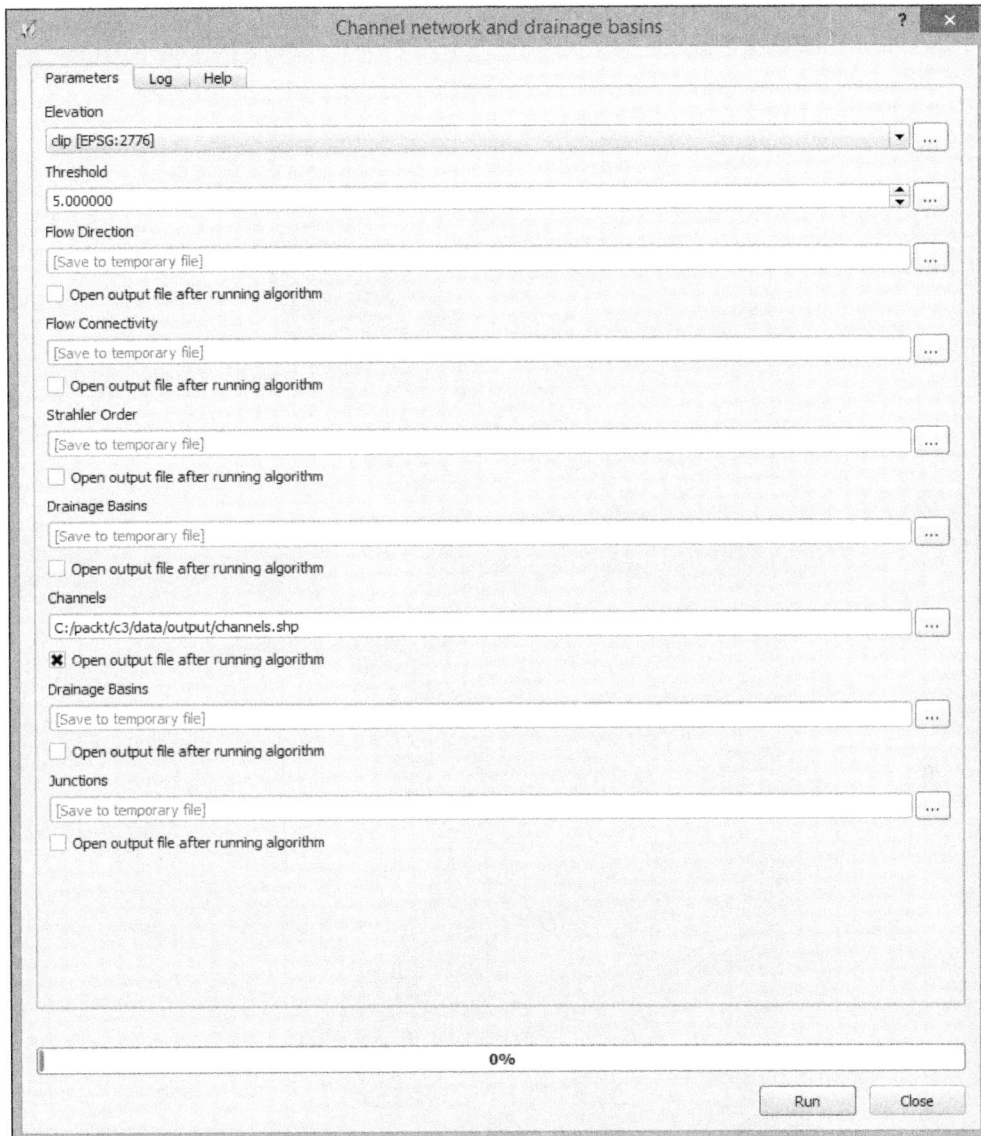

The output from the **Channel network and drainage basins**, showing the hydrological line location, will look similar to the following image:

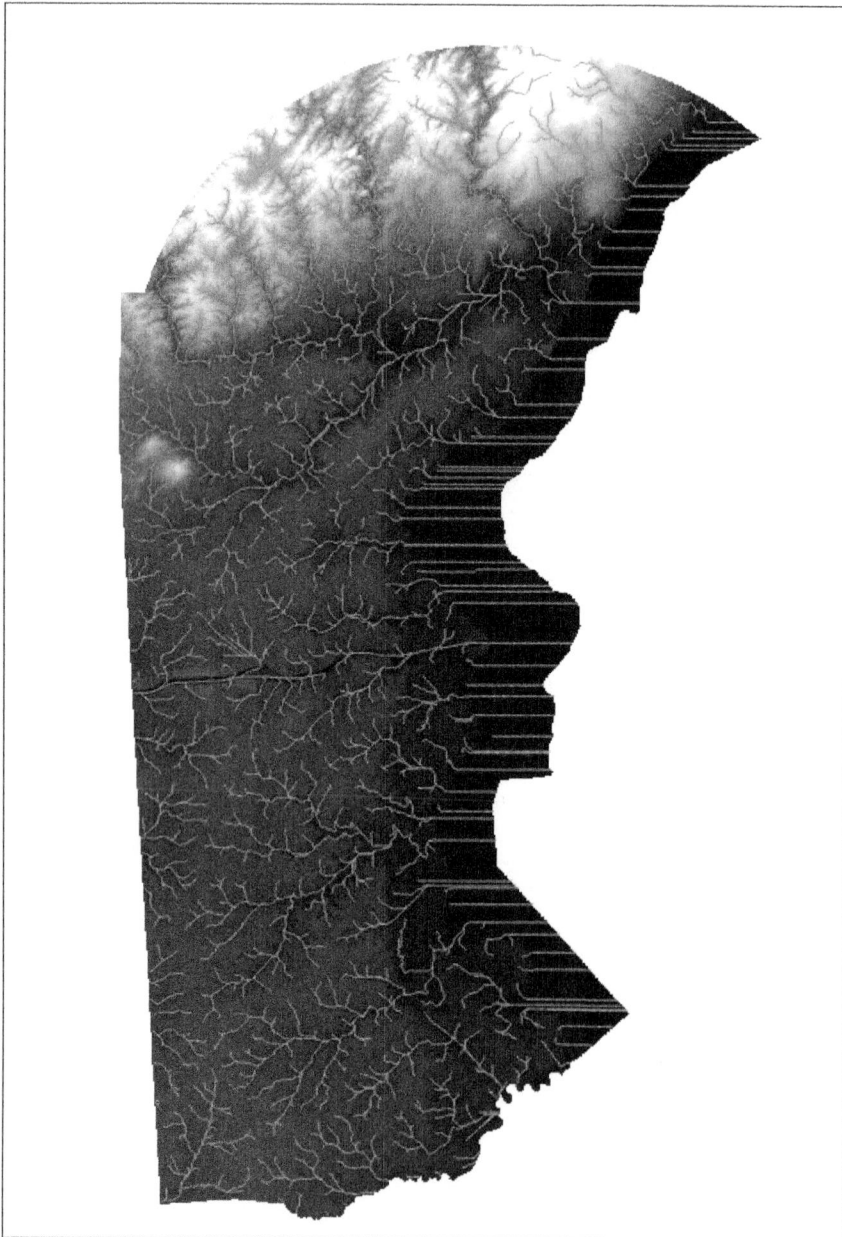

Workflow automation with the graphical models

Graphical Modeler is a tool within QGIS that is useful for modeling and automating workflows. It differs from batch processing in that you can tie together many separate operations in a processing sequence. It is considered a part of the processing framework. Graphical Modeler is particularly useful for workflows containing many steps to be repeated.

By building a graphical model, we can operationalize our hydrological modeling process. This provides a few benefits, as follows:

- Our modeling process is graphically documented and preserved
- The model can be rerun in its entirety with little to no interaction
- The model can be redistributed
- The model is parameterized so that we could rerun the same process on different data layers

Creating a graphical model

1. Bring up the **Graphical Modeler** dialog from the **Processing** menu.

    1. Navigate to **Processing | Graphical Modeler**.

2. Enter a model name and a group name.
3. Save your model under `c3/data/output/c3.model`.

    The dialog is modal and needs to be closed before you can return to other work in QGIS, so saving early will be useful.

Adding the input parameters

Some of the inputs to your model's algorithms will be the outputs of other model algorithms; for others, you will need to add a corresponding input parameter.

Adding the raster parameter – elevation

We will add the first data input parameter to the model so that it is available to the model algorithms. It is our original DEM elevation data. Perform the following steps:

1. Select the **Inputs** tab from the lower left corner of the **Processing modeler** display.
2. Drag **Raster layer** from the parameters list into the modeler pane. This parameter will represent our elevation grid (DEM).

3. Input elevation for **Parameter name**.

4. Click on **OK**, as shown in the following screenshot:

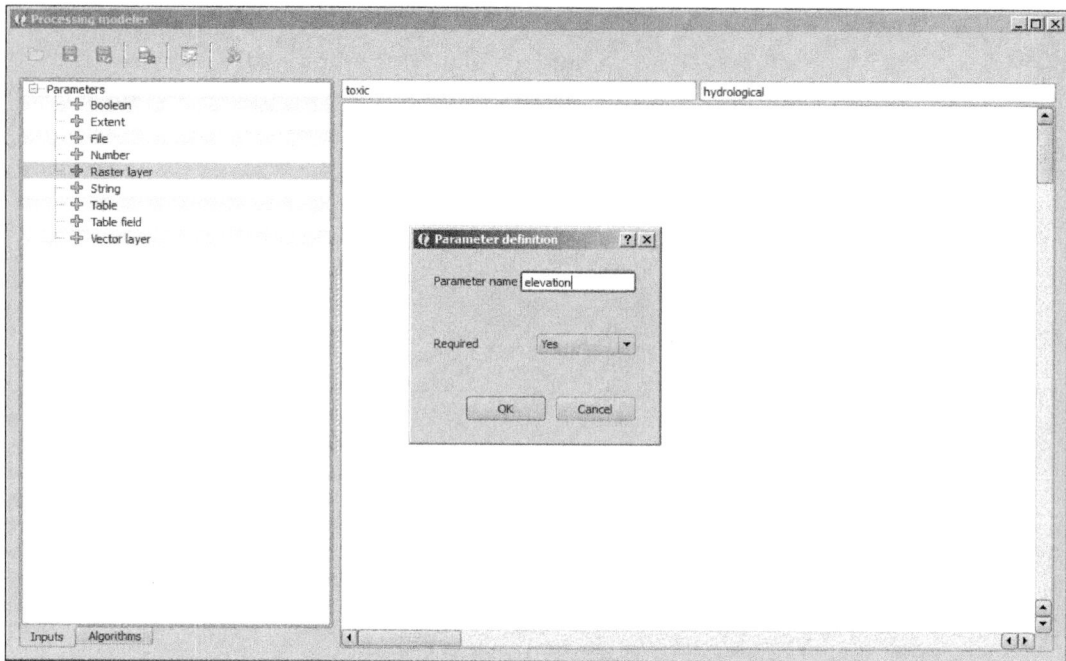

Adding the vector parameter – extent

We will add the next data input parameter to the model so that it is available to the model algorithms. It is our vector county data and the extent of our study.

1. Add a vector layer for our extent polygon (county). Make sure you select **Polygon** as the type, and call this parameter extent.

2. You will need to input a parameter name. It would be easiest to use the same layer/parameter names that we have been using so far, as shown in the following screenshot:

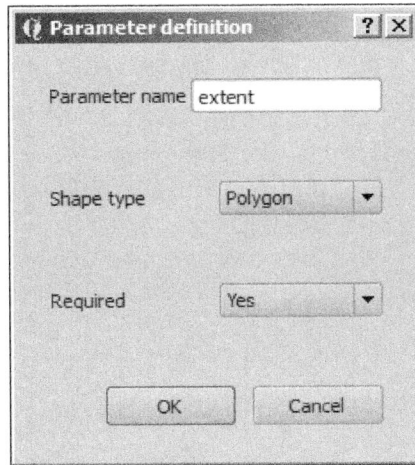

Adding the algorithms

The modeler connects the individual with their input data and their output data with the other algorithms. We will now add the algorithms.

Fill Sinks

The first algorithm we will add is **Fill Sinks**, which as we noted earlier, removes the problematic low elevations from the elevation data. Perform the following steps:

1. Select the **Algorithms** tab from the lower-left corner.

2. After you drag in an algorithm, you will be prompted to choose the parameters.

3. Use the search input to locate **Fill Sinks** and then open.

4. Select **elevation** for the DEM parameter and click on **OK**, as shown in the following screenshot:

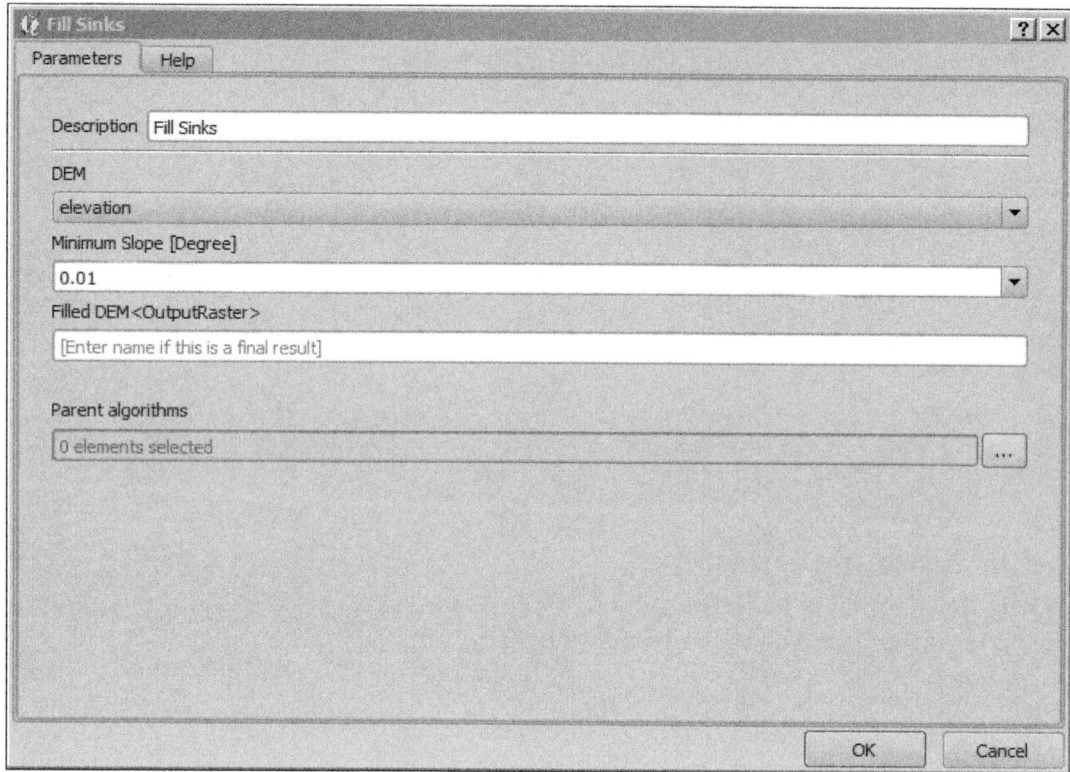

Clip raster

The next algorithm we will add is **Clip raster by mask layer**, which we've used to limit the processing extent of the subsequent raster processing. Perform the following steps:

1. Use the search input to locate **Clip raster by mask layer**.
2. Select **'Filled DEM' from algorithm 'Fill Sinks'** for the **Input layer** parameter.
3. Select **extent** for the **Mask layer** parameter.

4. Click on **OK**, accepting the other parameter defaults, as shown in the following screenshot:

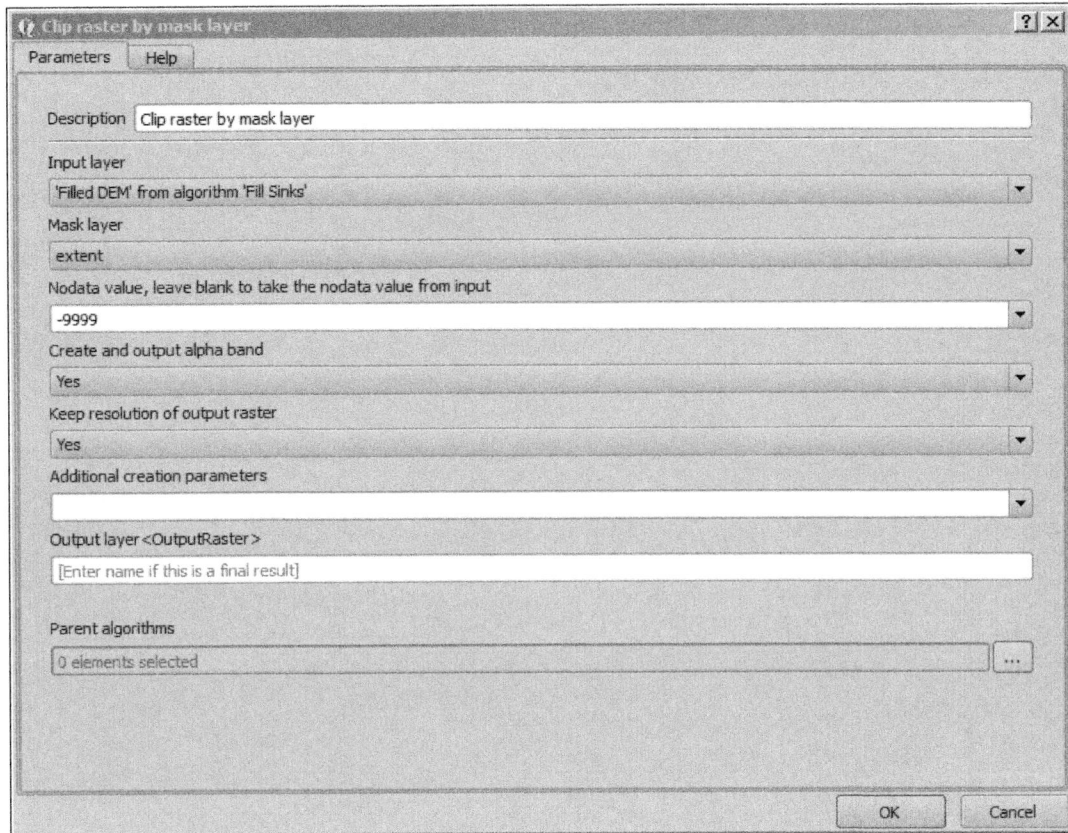

Channel network and drainage basins

The final algorithm we will add is **Channel network and drainage basins**, which produces a model of our hydrological network. Perform the following steps:

1. Use the search input to locate **Channel network and drainage basins**.

2. Select **'Output Layer' from algorithm 'Clip raster by mask layer'** for the **Elevation** parameter.

3. Click on **OK**, accepting the other parameter defaults.

4. Once you populate all the three algorithms, your model will look similar to the following image:

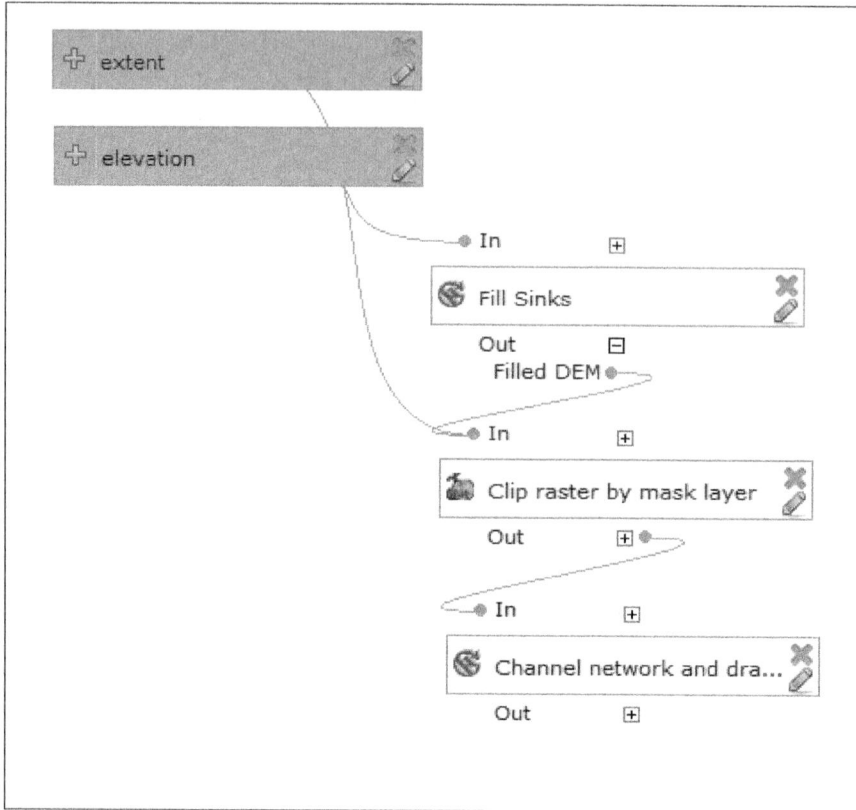

Running the model

Now that our model is complete, we can execute all the steps in an automated sequential fashion:

1. Run your model by clicking on the **Run model** button on the right-hand side of the row of buttons.

2. You'll be prompted to select values for the `elevation` and the `extent` input layer parameters you defined earlier. Select the **dem** and **county** layers for these inputs, respectively, as shown in the following screenshot:

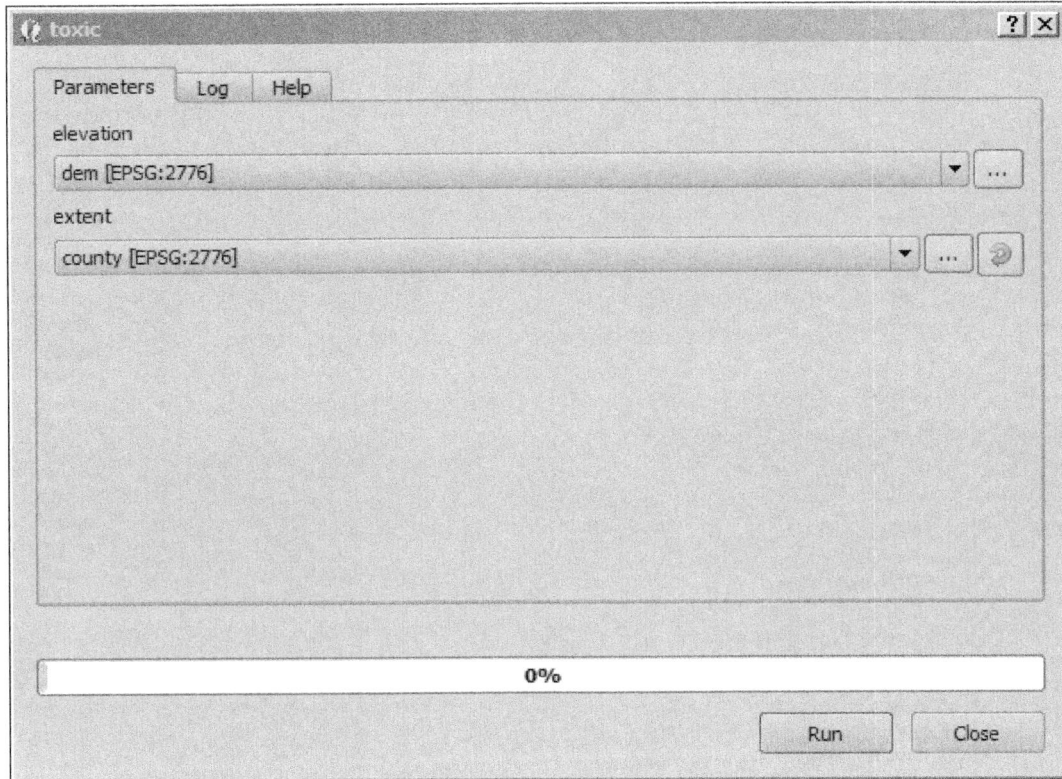

3. After you define and run your model, all the outputs you defined earlier will be produced. These will be located at the paths that you defined in the parameters dialog or in the model algorithms themselves.

> If you don't specify an output directory, the data will be saved to the `temp` directory for the processing framework, for example:
> `C:\Users\[YOURUSERNAME]\AppData\Local\Temp\processing\`

Now that we've completed the hydrological modeling, we'll look at a technique for preparing our outputs for dynamic web interaction.

Spatial join for a performant operational layer interaction

A spatial join permanently relates two layers of geographic objects based on some geographic relationship between the objects. It is wise to do a spatial join in this way, and save to disk when possible, as the spatial queries can significantly increase the time of a database request. This is especially true for the tables with a large number of records or when your request involves multiple spatial or aggregate functions. In this case, we are performing a spatial join so that the end user can do the queries of the hydrological data based on the location of their choosing.

QGIS has less extensive options for the spatial join criteria than ArcGIS. The default spatial join method in QGIS is accessible via **Vector | Data Management Tools | Join attributes by location**. However, at the time of writing, this operation was limited to the intersecting features and did not offer the functionality for nearby features. The NNJoin plugin—**NN** standing for **nearest neighbor**—achieves what we want; it joins the geographic objects in two layers based on the criteria that they are nearest to each other.

The NNJoin plugin

Perform the following steps:

1. Install the NNJoin plugin.

2. Open the NNJoin plugin from the **Vector** menu (Navigate to **Vector | NNJoin**).

3. Specify the following parameters:
    - **Input vector layer**: Select this as **toxic**—layer of toxic sites.
    - **Join vector layer**: Select this as **Channels**—hydrological lines.
    - **Output layer**: Select this as **toxic_channels**. This operation only supports the output to memory. You'll need to click on **Save as** after running it to save it to disk.

4. Click on **OK**, as shown in the following screenshot:

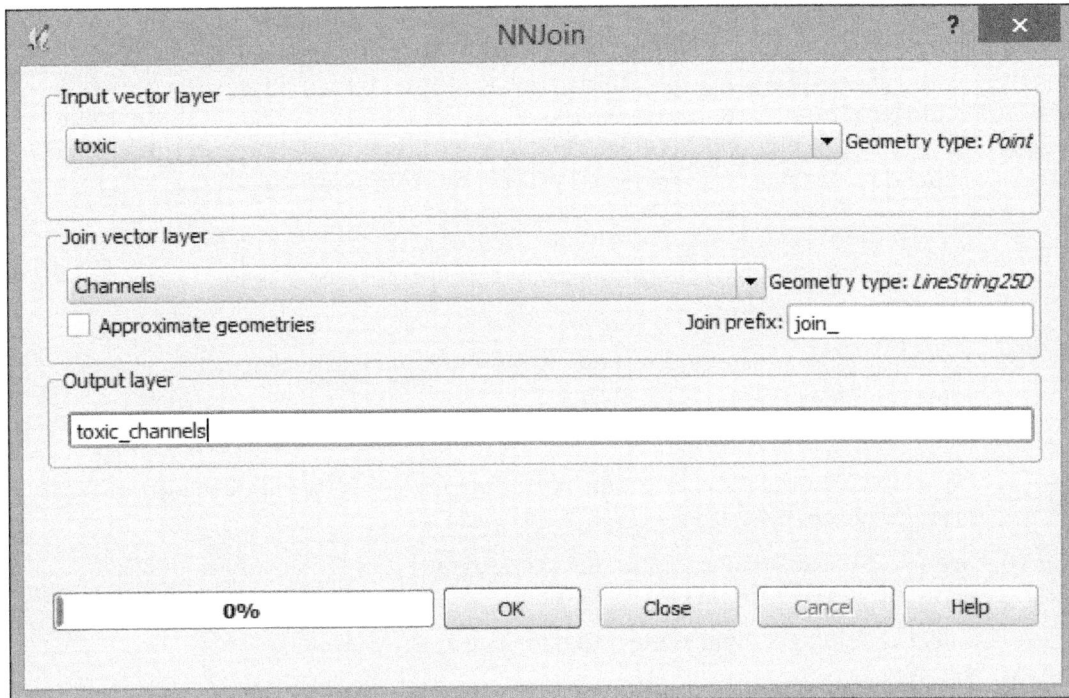

Now, in the **Layers** panel, right-click on the newly created **toxic_channels** layer and then on **Save as**. You should save this new file in the following path:

```
c3/data/output/toxic_channels.shp
```

The result of these steps will be a copy of the toxic layer with the columns from the nearest feature in the channels layer.

We've now completed all the data processing steps. It's now time to look at how we will host this data with an external cloud platform to enable the dynamic web query.

The CartoDB platform

CartoDB is a cloud-based GIS platform which provides data management, query, and visualization capabilities. CartoDB is based on Postgres/PostGIS in the backend, and one of the most exciting functions of this platform is the ability to pass spatial queries using PostGIS syntax via the URL and HTTP API.

Publishing the data to CartoDB

To publish the data to CartoDB, you'll first need to establish an account. You can easily do this with the Google Single sign-in or create your own account with a username and password. CartoDB offers free accounts, which are usable for an unlimited amount time. You are limited to 50 MB of data storage and all the data published will be publically viewable. Once you've signed up, you can upload the layer produced in the previous section. Perform the following steps:

1. Zip up the shapefile-related files, at `c3/data/output/channels.*` and `c3/data/output/toxic_channels.*`, to prepare them for upload to CartoDB.

2. Log in at `https://cartodb.com/login` if you haven't already done so.

3. You should be redirected to your dashboard page after login. Select **New Map** from this page.

4. Click on **Create New Map** to start a new map from scratch.

5. Click on **Connect dataset** under **Add dataset** to add the datasets from your local machine.

6. Browse `c3/data/output/channels.zip` and `c3/data/output/toxic_channels.zip` and add these to the map.

7. Select the datasets you would like to add to the map.

8. Select **Create Map**.

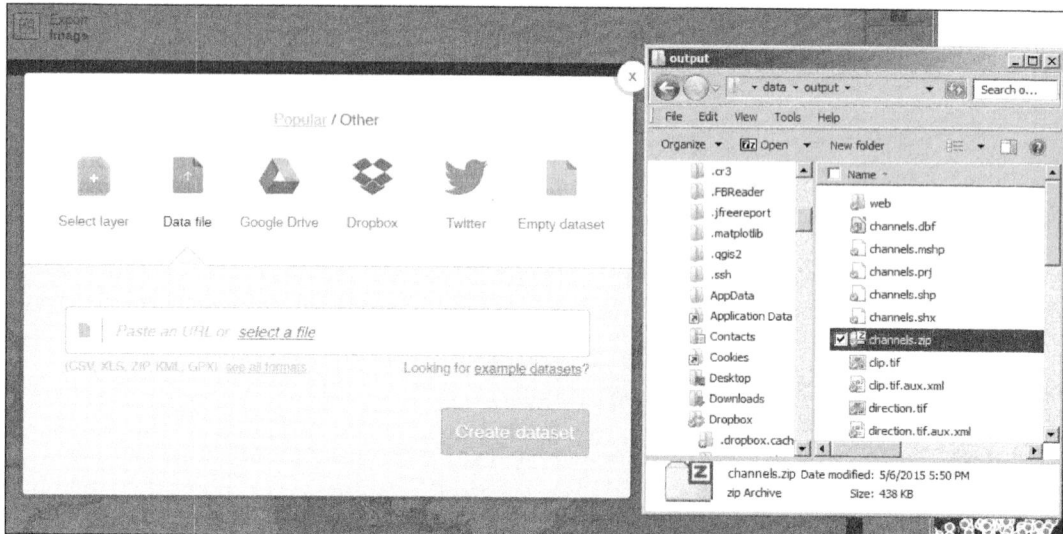

Preparing a CartoDB SQL Query

SQL is the lingua franca of database queries through which you can do anything from filtering to spatial operations to manipulating data on the database. There are slight differences in the way SQL works from one database system to the next one. The CartoDB SQL queries use valid Postgres/PostGIS syntax. For more information on Postgres/PostGIS SQL, check out the reference chapter in the manuals for Postgres (`http://www.postgresql.org/docs/9.4/interactive/reference.html`) for general functions and PostGIS (`http://postgis.net/docs/manual-2.1/reference.html`) for spatial functions.

There are a few different ways in which you can test your queries against CartoDB—each involving a different ease of input and producing a different result type.

Generating the test data

Our SQL query only requires one parameter that we do not know ahead of time: the coordinates of the user-selected click location. To simulate this interaction with QGIS and generate a coordinate pair, we will use the Coordinate Capture plugin. Perform the following steps:

1. Install the Coordinate Capture plugin if you have not already done so.

2. From the **Vector** menu, display the **Coordinate Capture** panel (navigate to **Vector** | **Coordinate Capture** | **Coordinate Capture**).

3. Select **Start capture** from the **Coordinate Capture** panel.

4. Click on a place on the map that you would expect to see upstream results for. In other words, based on the elevation surface, select a low point near a hydrological line; other hydrological objects should run down into that point, as shown in the following image:

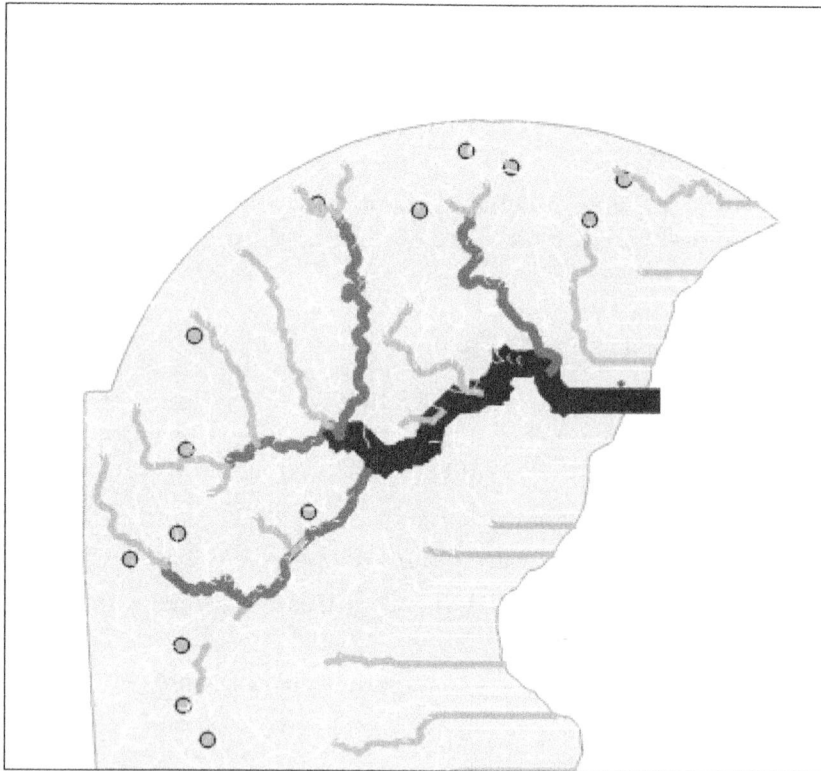

5. Record the coordinates displayed in the **Coordinate Capture** panel, as shown in the following screenshot:

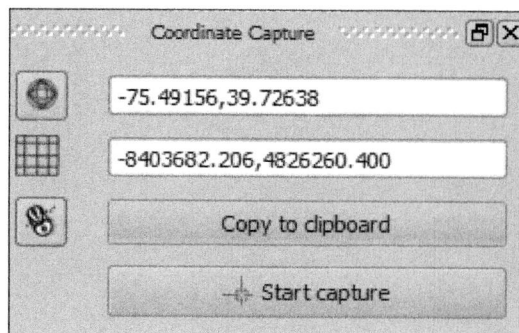

The CartoDB SQL view tab

Now, we will return to CartoDB in a web browser to run our first test.

While this method is probably the most straightforward in terms of data entry, it is limited to producing results via the map. There are no text results produced besides errors, which limits your ability to test and debug. Perform the following steps:

1. On your map, click on the tab corresponding to the **toxic_channels** layer. This is often accessed on the tab marked **2** on the right-hand side.

2. You should see the SQL view tab displayed by default with a SQL input area.

3. The SQL query given in the following section selects all the records from our joined table, which contains the location of toxic sites with their closest hydrological basin and stream order that fulfill the following criteria based on the coordinates we pass:

   ○ It is in the same hydrological basin as the passed coordinates.

   ○ It has a lower hydrological stream order than the closest stream to the passed coordinates.

   Recall that we generated test coordinates to pass with the **Coordinate Capture** plugin in the last step. Enter the following into the SQL area. This query will select all the fields from **toxic_channels** as expressed with the wildcard symbol (*) using various subqueries, joins, and spatial operations. The end result will show all the toxic sites that are upstream from the clicked point in its basin (code in c3/data/ original/query1.sql). Execute the following code:

```
SELECT toxic_channels.* FROM toxic_channels
INNER JOIN channels
ON toxic_channels.join_BASIN = channels.basin
WHERE toxic_channels.join_order <

(SELECT channels._order
FROM channels
WHERE
st_distance(the_geom, ST_GeomFromText
('POINT(-75.56111 39.72583)',4326))
IN (SELECT MIN(st_distance(the_geom,
ST_GeomFromText('POINT(-75.56111 39.72583)',4326)))
FROM channels x))

 AND toxic_channels.join_basin =

(SELECT channels.basin
FROM channels
```

```
WHERE
st_distance(the_geom, ST_GeomFromText
('POINT(-75.56111 39.72583)',4326))
IN (SELECT MIN(st_distance(the_geom,
ST_GeomFromText('POINT(-75.56111 39.72583)',4326)))
FROM channels x))
GROUP BY toxic_channels.cartodb_id
```

4. Select **Apply Query** to run the query.

If the query runs successfully, you should see an output similar to the following image:

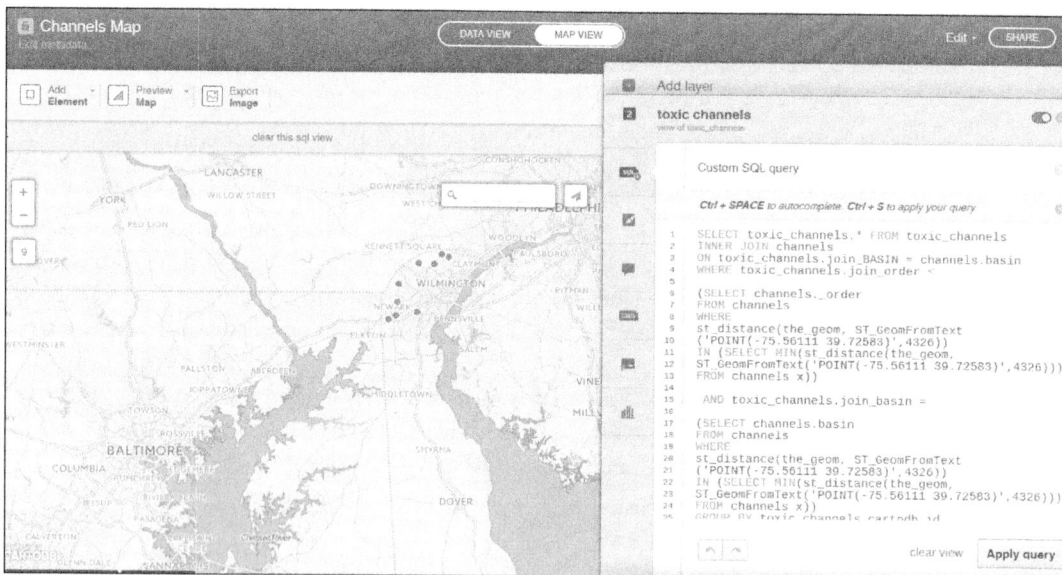

The following errors may confound the efforts to debug and test via the CartoDB SQL tab:

- **Error at the end of a statement**: A semi-colon, while valid, causes an error in this interface.
- **Does not contain cartodb_id**: The statement must explicitly contain a `cartodb_id` field so that it does not generate this error. However, this error does not typically affect the use through the API or URL parameters.
- **Does not contain the_geom**: The statement must explicitly contain a reference to the `the_geom` column even though this column is not visible within your `cartodb` table, to map the result.

Sometimes, the SQL input area is "sticky". If this happens, just "clear view".

The QGIS CartoDB plugin

Next, let's test the SQL from within QGIS using the QGIS CartoDB Plugin. Perform the following steps:

1. Install the QGIS CartoDB plugin, QGISCartoDB.

2. Open the SQL CartoDB dialog and navigate to **Web | CartoDB Plugin | Add SQL CartoDB Layer**.

3. Establish a connection to your CartoDB account:

    1. Click on **New**.

    2. Locate and enter your username and API key from your account in a browser. The query you ran earlier will be saved so you can do this in the open tab (if it is still open). Otherwise, navigate back to **CartoDB**. Your account name can be found in the URL when you are logged into CartoDB, where the username is in `username.cartodb.com/*`. You can find your API key by clicking on your avatar from your dashboard and selecting **Your API keys**.

    3. Click on **Save**, as shown in the following screenshot:

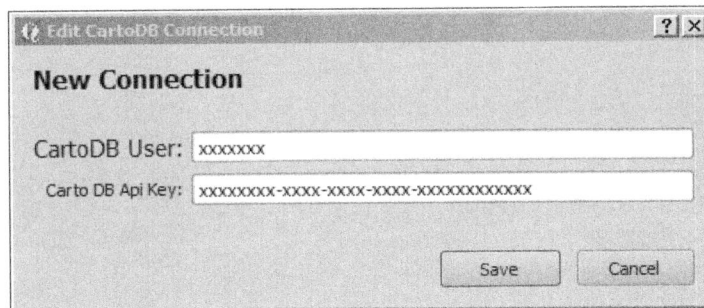

4. Now that you are connected to your CartoDB account, load tables from the CartoDB SQL Layer dialog.

5. Enter the preceding SQL statement in the SQL Query area. You can use the **Tables** section of the **Add CartoDB SQL Layer** dialog to view the field names and datatypes in your query.

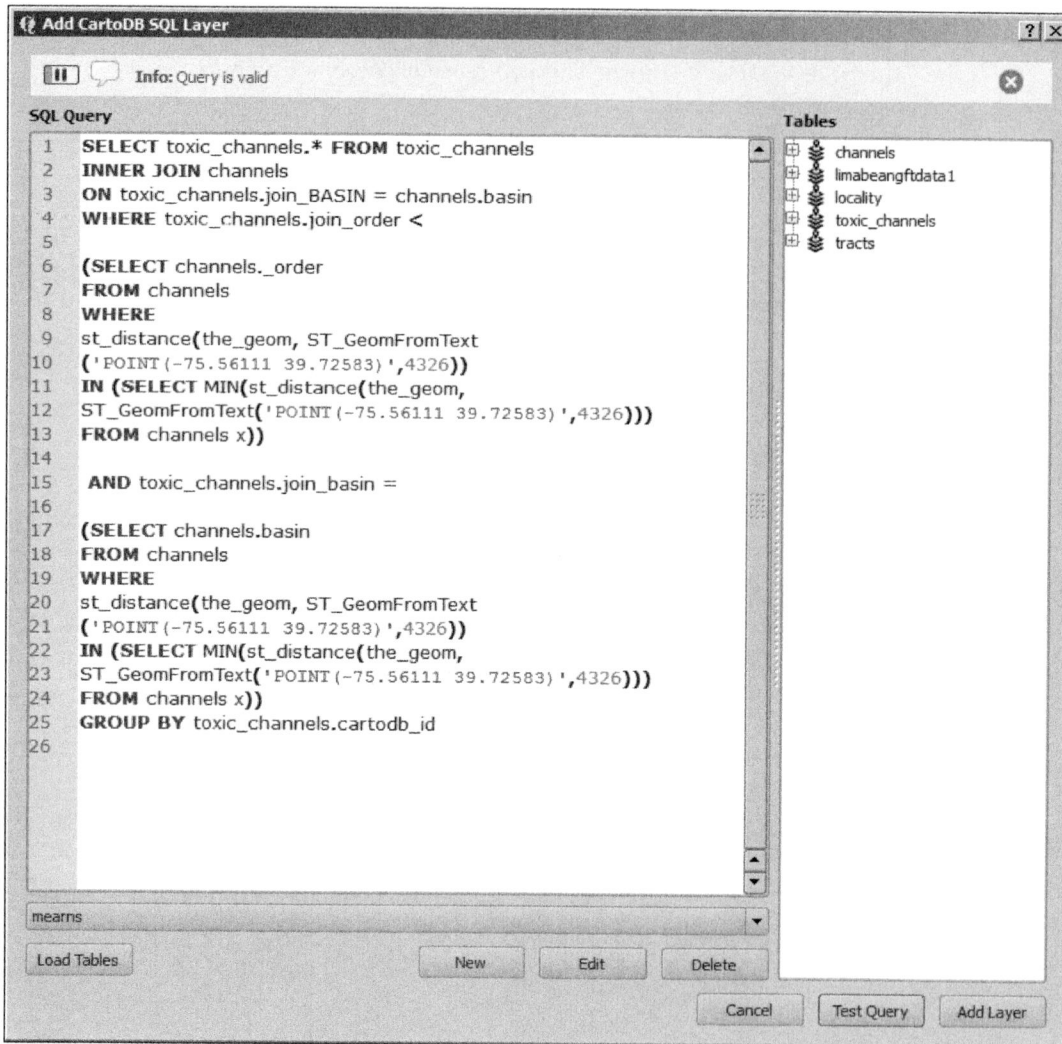

```
Add CartoDB SQL Layer                                                    ? X

    ⏸  💬   Info: Query is valid                                            ⊗

SQL Query                                                       Tables
 1   SELECT toxic_channels.* FROM toxic_channels          ▲    ⊞ ≋ channels
 2   INNER JOIN channels                                        ⊞ ≋ limabeangftdata1
 3   ON toxic_channels.join_BASIN = channels.basin              ⊞ ≋ locality
 4   WHERE toxic_channels.join_order <                          ⊞ ≋ toxic_channels
 5                                                              ⊞ ≋ tracts
 6   (SELECT channels._order
 7   FROM channels
 8   WHERE
 9   st_distance(the_geom, ST_GeomFromText
10   ('POINT(-75.56111 39.72583)',4326))
11   IN (SELECT MIN(st_distance(the_geom,
12   ST_GeomFromText('POINT(-75.56111 39.72583)',4326)))
13   FROM channels x))
14
15    AND toxic_channels.join_basin =
16
17   (SELECT channels.basin
18   FROM channels
19   WHERE
20   st_distance(the_geom, ST_GeomFromText
21   ('POINT(-75.56111 39.72583)',4326))
22   IN (SELECT MIN(st_distance(the_geom,
23   ST_GeomFromText('POINT(-75.56111 39.72583)',4326)))
24   FROM channels x))
25   GROUP BY toxic_channels.cartodb_id
26
                                                          ▲
                                                          ▼
mearns                                                              ▼

Load Tables                    New        Edit       Delete

                                      Cancel    Test Query    Add Layer
```

6. Click on **Test Query** to test the syntax against CartoDB. Refer to the info box in the previous test section for some common confounding errors you may experience with the CartoDB SQL interface.

7. Click on **Add Layer** to add the result to QGIS.

The layer added from these steps will give you the location of the toxic sites upstream from the chosen coordinate. If you symbolized these locations with stars and streams according to their upstream/downstream rank, you would see something similar to the following image:

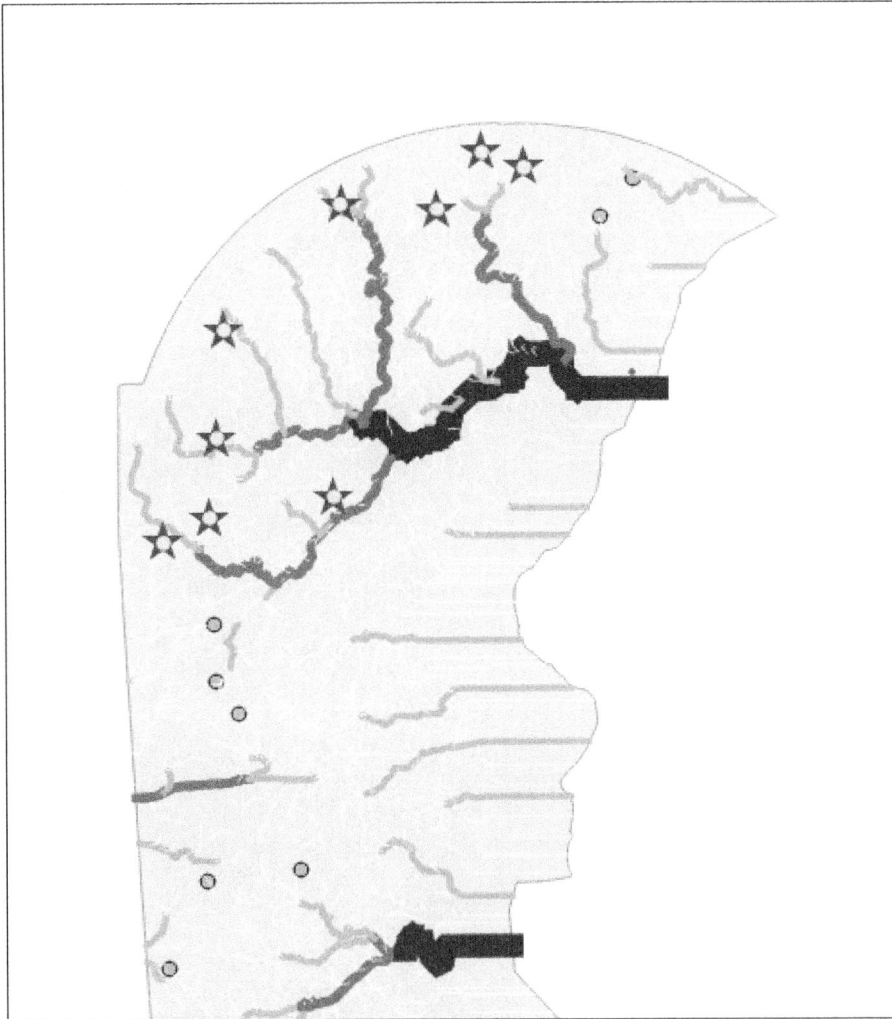

The CartoDB SQL API

If you want to see the actual contents returned by a CartoDB SQL query in the JSON format, the best way to do so is by sending your SQL statement to the CartoDB SQL API endpoint at `http://[YOURUSERNAME].cartodb.com/api/v2/sql`. This can be useful to debug issues in interaction with your web application in particular.

The browser string uses an encoded URL, which substitutes character sequences for some special characters. For example, you could use a URL encoder/decoder, which is easily found on the Web, to produce such a string.

Use the following instructions to see the result JSON returned by CartoDB given a particular SQL query. The URL string is also contained in `c3/data/original/url_query1.txt`.

1. Enter the following URL string into your browser, substituting [YOURUSERNAME] with your CartoDB user name and [YOURAPIKEY] with your API key:

```
http://[YOURUSERNAME].cartodb.com/api/v2/sql?q=%20SELECT%20
toxic_channels.*%20FROM%20toxic_channels%20INNER%20
JOIN%20channels%20ON%20toxic_channels.join_BASIN%20=%20
channels.basin%20WHERE%20toxic_channels.join_order%20%3C%20
(SELECT%20channels._order%20FROM%20channels%20WHERE%20st_
distance(the_geom,%20ST_GeomFromText%20(%27POINT(-75.56111%20
39.72583)%27,4326))%20IN%20(SELECT%20MIN(st_distance(the_geom,%20
ST_GeomFromText(%27POINT(-75.56111%2039.72583)%27,4326)))%20
FROM%20channels%20x))%20AND%20toxic_channels.join_basin%20
=%20(SELECT%20channels.basin%20FROM%20channels%20WHERE%20st_
distance(the_geom,%20ST_GeomFromText%20(%27POINT(-75.56111%20
39.72583)%27,4326))%20IN%20(SELECT%20MIN(st_distance(the_geom,%20
ST_GeomFromText(%27POINT(-75.56111%2039.72583)%27,4326)))%20
FROM%20channels%20x))%20GROUP%20BY%20toxic_channels.cartodb_id%20
&api_key=[YOURAPIKEY]
```

2. Submit the browser request.

3. You will see a result similar to the following:

```
{"rows":[{"the_geom":"0101000020E610000056099A6A64E352C0B23A9C
05D4E84340","id":13,"join_segme":1786,"join_node_":1897,"join_
nod_1":1886,"join_basin":98,"join_order":2,"join_ord_1":6,"join_
lengt":1890.6533221,"distance":150.739169156001,"cartodb_
id":14,"created_at":"2015-05-06T21:52:52Z","updated_at":"2015-
05-06T21:52:52Z","the_geom_webmercator":"0101000020110F00000B1E9
E3DB30A60C18DCB53943D765241"},{"the_geom":"0101000020E610000011
44805EA1E652C0ECE7F94B65E64340","id":3,"join_segme":1710,"join_
node_":1819,"join_nod_1":1841,"join_basin":98,"join_
order":1,"join_ord_1":5,"join_lengt":769.46323073,"distan
ce":50.1031572450681,"cartodb_id":4,"created_at":"2015-05-
06T21:52:52Z","updated_at":"2015-05-06T21:52:52Z","the_geom_webme
rcator":"0101000020110F0000181D4045730D60C1F35490178D735241"},{"t
he_geom":"0101000020E61000009449A70ACFF052C0F3916D0D41D34340","id
":17,"join_segme":1098,"join_node_":1188,"join_nod_1":1191,"join_
basin":98,"join_order":1,"join_ord_1":5,"join_lengt":1320.8328273
,"distance":260.02935238833,"cartodb_id":18,"created_at":"2015-05-
06T21:52:52Z","updated_at":"2015-05-06T21:52:52Z","the_geom_webme
```

rcator":"0101000020110F00008167DA44181660C117FA8EFC695E5241"},{"t
he_geom":"0101000020E6100000DD53F65225EA52C0966E1B86B1E64340","id
":19,"join_segme":1728,"join_node_":1839,"join_nod_1":1826,"join_
basin":98,"join_order":1,"join_ord_1":5,"join_lengt":489.2571289,
"distance":201.8453893386,"cartodb_id":20,"created_at":"2015-05-
06T21:52:52Z","updated_at":"2015-05-06T21:52:52Z","the_geom_webme
rcator":"0101000020110F00009D303E9A6F1060C1BAD6D85BE1735241"},{"t
he_geom":"0101000020E61000008868F447FAE452C02218260DC0E94340","id
":12,"join_segme":1801,"join_node_":1913,"join_nod_1":1899,"join_
basin":98,"join_order":2,"join_ord_1":6,"join_lengt":539.82994246,
"distance":232.424790511141,"cartodb_id":13,"created_at":"2015-05-
06T21:52:52Z","updated_at":"2015-05-06T21:52:52Z","the_geom_webme
rcator":"0101000020110F00003BC511F10B0C60C1D801919542775241"},{"t
he_geom":"0101000020E6100000A2EE318E20EF52C0A874919E9BD44340","id
":16,"join_segme":1151,"join_node_":1243,"join_nod_1":1195,"join_
basin":98,"join_order":1,"join_ord_1":5,"join_lengt":1585.6022332,
"distance":48.7125304167275,"cartodb_id":17,"created_at":"2015-05-
06T21:52:52Z","updated_at":"2015-05-06T21:52:52Z","the_geom_webme
rcator":"0101000020110F000055062CA8AA1460C19A29734CE85F5241"},{"t
he_geom":"0101000020E610000043356AB28DEE52C090391E3073DF4340","id
":21,"join_segme":1548,"join_node_":1650,"join_nod_1":1633,"join_
basin":98,"join_order":3,"join_ord_1":7,"join_lengt":893.68816603
,"distance":733.948566072529,"cartodb_id":22,"created_at":"2015-
05-06T21:52:52Z","updated_at":"2015-05-06T21:52:52Z","the_geom_web
mercator":"0101000020110F0000F46510EE2D1460C18C0E2241E06B5241"},{
"the_geom":"0101000020E61000009B543F2277EA52C0F3615A0BD1D54340","i
d":1,"join_segme":1198,"join_node_":1292,"join_nod_1":1293,"join_
basin":98,"join_order":1,"join_ord_1":5,"join_lengt":746.7496066,
"distance":123.258432999702,"cartodb_id":2,"created_at":"2015-05-
06T21:52:52Z","updated_at":"2015-05-06T21:52:52Z","the_geom_webme
rcator":"0101000020110F0000CFB06115B51060C1B715F2AF3D615241"},{"t
he_geom":"0101000020E610000056AEF2E2D0EE52C0305E947734D94340","id
":9,"join_segme":1336,"join_node_":1432,"join_nod_1":1391,"join_
basin":98,"join_order":1,"join_ord_1":5,"join_lengt":1143.9037155
,"distance":281.665088681164,"cartodb_id":10,"created_at":"2015-
05-06T21:52:52Z","updated_at":"2015-05-06T21:52:52Z","the_geom_we
bmercator":"0101000020110F0000D8727BFE661460C1F269C8F6FA6452
41"}],"time":0.029,"fields":{"the_geom":{"type":"geometry"},
"id":{"type":"number"},"join_segme":{"type":"number"},"join_
node_":{"type":"number"},"join_nod_1":{"type":"number"},"join_
basin":{"type":"number"},"join_order":{"type":"number"},"join_
ord_1":{"type":"number"},"join_lengt":{"type":"number"},"distan
ce":{"type":"number"},"cartodb_id":{"type":"number"},"created_
at":{"type":"date"},"updated_at":{"type":"date"},"the_geom_webmerc
ator":{"type":"geometry"}},"total_rows":9}

Leaflet and an external API: CartoDB SQL

In the first section, we created a web application using Leaflet and the local GeoJSON files containing our layers. In this section, we will use Leaflet to display data from an external API—CartoDB SQL API. Perform the following steps:

1. Open the **qgis2leaf Export** dialog (navigate to **Web | qgis2leaf | Exports**).

2. In the **qgis2leaf** dialog, you can leave the inputs as their default ones. We will be heavily modifying the output code, so this part isn't so important. You may wish to add a basemap; MapQuest Open OSM is a good choice for this.

3. Take note of the output location.

4. Click on **OK**.

5. Locate index.html in the output directory.

6. Replace the contents of index.html with the following code (also available at c3/data/web/index.html). This code is identical to the existing index.html with a few modifications. All lines after 25 and the ones below the closing script, body, and HTML tags have been removed. The getToxic function and call have been added. Look for this function to replace the existing filler text with your CartoDB account name and API key. This function carries out our CartoDB SQL query and displays the results. We will comment out a second function call, which you may want to test to see the varying results based on the different coordinate pairs passed, as follows:

```html
<!<!<!DOCTYPE html>>>>
<html>
  <head>
    <title>QGIS2leaf webmap</title>

    <meta charset="utf-8" />
    <link rel="stylesheet" href="http://cdnjs.
      cloudflare.com/ajax/libs/leaflet/0.7.3/
      leaflet.css" /> <!-- we will use this as the
      styling script for our webmap-->
    <link rel="stylesheet" href="css/MarkerCluster.css"
      />
    <link rel="stylesheet" href="css/Marker
      Cluster.Default.css" />
    <link rel="stylesheet" type="text/css"
      href="css/own_style.css"/>
    <link rel="stylesheet" href="css/label.css" />
    <script src="http://code.jquery.com/jquery-
      1.11.1.min.js"></script> <!-- this is the javascript
      file that does the magic-->
```

```html
  <script src="js/Autolinker.min.js"></script>
</head>
<body>
  <div id="map"></div> <!-- this is the initial look of
    the map. in most cases it is done externally using
    something like a map.css stylesheet where you can
    specify the look of map elements, like background
    color tables and so on.-->
  <script src="http://cdnjs.cloudflare.com/ajax/
    libs/leaflet/0.7.3/leaflet.js"></script> <!-- this
    is the javascript file that does the magic-->
  <script src="js/leaflet-hash.js"></script>
  <script src="js/label.js"></script>
  <script src="js/leaflet.markercluster.js"></script>

  <script src='data/exp_toxicchannels.js' ></script>

  <script>
    var map = L.map('map', { zoomControl:true
      }).fitBounds([[39.4194805496,-75.8685268698]
      ,[39.9951967581,-75.2662748017]]);
    var hash = new L.Hash(map); //add hashes to html
      address to easy share locations
    var additional_attrib = 'created w. <a
      href="https://github.com/geolicious/qgis2leaf"
      target ="_blank">qgis2leaf</a> by <a
      href="http://www.geolicious.de" target
      ="_blank">Geolicious</a> & contributors<br>';
    var feature_group = new L.featureGroup([]);

    var raster_group = new L.LayerGroup([]);

    var basemap_0 = L.tileLayer('http://otile1.
      mqcdn.com/tiles/1.0.0/map/{z}/{x}/{y}.jpeg', {
        attribution: additional_attrib + 'Tiles Courtesy
        of <a href="http://www.mapquest.com/">MapQuest
        </a> &mdash; Map data: &copy; <a href="
        http://openstreetmap.org">OpenStreetMap</a>
        contributors,<a href="http://creativecommons.org
        /licenses/by-sa/2.0/">CC-BY-SA</a>'});
    basemap_0.addTo(map);
    var layerOrder=new Array();
    function pop_toxicchannels(feature, layer) {
```

```
        var popupContent = '<table><tr><th
          scope="row">ID</th><td>' +
          Autolinker.link(String(feature.properties['ID']))
          + '</td></tr><tr><th
          scope="row">join_SEGME</th><td>' +
          Autolinker.link(String(feature.properties
          ['join_SEGME'])) + '</td></tr><tr><th
          scope="row">join_NODE_</th><td>' +
          Autolinker.link(String(feature.properties
          ['join_NODE_'])) + '</td></tr><tr><th
          scope="row">join_NOD_1</th><td>' +
          Autolinker.link(String(feature.properties
          ['join_NOD_1'])) + '</td></tr><tr><th
          scope="row">join_BASIN</th><td>' +
          Autolinker.link(String(feature.properties
          ['join_BASIN'])) + '</td></tr><tr><th
          scope="row">join_ORDER</th><td>' +
          Autolinker.link(String(feature.properties
          ['join_ORDER'])) + '</td></tr><tr><th
          scope="row">join_ORD_1</th><td>' +
          Autolinker.link(String(feature.properties
          ['join_ORD_1'])) + '</td></tr><tr><th
          scope="row">join_LENGT</th><td>' +
          Autolinker.link(String(feature.properties
          ['join_LENGT'])) + '</td></tr><tr><th
          scope="row">distance</th><td>' +
          Autolinker.link(String(feature.properties
          ['distance'])) + '</td></tr></table>';
        layer.bindPopup(popupContent);


    }

    var exp_toxicchannelsJSON = new L.geoJson
      (exp_toxicchannels,{
      onEachFeature: pop_toxicchannels,
      pointToLayer: function (feature, latlng) {
        return L.circleMarker(latlng, {
          radius: feature.properties.radius_qgis2leaf,
          fillColor: feature.properties.color_qgis2leaf,

          color: feature.properties.borderColor
            _qgis2leaf,
          weight: 1,
          opacity: feature.properties.transp_qgis2leaf,
          fillOpacity: feature.properties.
            transp_qgis2leaf
        })
```

```
    }
});
feature_group.addLayer(exp_toxicchannelsJSON);

layerOrder[layerOrder.length] = exp_toxic
  channelsJSON;
for (index = 0; index < layerOrder.length; index++) {
  feature_group.removeLayer(layerOrder[index]);
  feature_group.addLayer(layerOrder[index]);
}

//add comment sign to hide this layer on the map in
  the initial view.
exp_toxicchannelsJSON.addTo(map);
var title = new L.Control();
title.onAdd = function (map) {
  this._div = L.DomUtil.create('div', 'info'); //
    create a div with a class "info"
  this.update();
  return this._div;
};
title.update = function () {
  this._div.innerHTML = '<h2>This is the title</h2>
    This is the subtitle'
};
title.addTo(map);
var baseMaps = {
  'MapQuestOpen OSM': basemap_0
};
L.control.layers(baseMaps,{"toxicchannels":
  exp_toxicchannelsJSON},{collapsed:false})
  .addTo(map);
L.control.scale({options: {position:
  'bottomleft',maxWidth: 100,metric: true,imperial:
  false,updateWhenIdle: false}}).addTo(map);

/* we've inserted the following after the existing
  index.html line 83, to handle query to cartodb */

function getToxic(lon,lat)
{
  var toxicLayer = new L.GeoJSON();

    $.getJSON(
```

```
"http://YOURCARTODBACCOUNTNAMEHERE.cartodb.com/api/v2/sql?q=%20
SELECT%20toxic_channels.*%20FROM%20toxic_channels%20INNER%20
JOIN%20channels%20ON%20toxic_channels.join_BASIN%20=%20channels.
basin%20WHERE%20toxic_channels.join_order%20%3C%20(SELECT%20
channels._order%20FROM%20channels%20WHERE%20st_distance(the_
geom,%20ST_GeomFromText%20(%27POINT(" + lon + "%20" + lat +
")%27,4326))%20IN%20(SELECT%20MIN(st_distance(the_geom,%20ST_
GeomFromText(%27POINT(" + lon + "%20" + lat + ")%27,4326)))%20
FROM%20channels%20x))%20AND%20toxic_channels.join_basin%20
=%20(SELECT%20channels.basin%20FROM%20channels%20WHERE%20st_
distance(the_geom,%20ST_GeomFromText%20(%27POINT(" + lon + "%20" +
lat + ")%27,4326))%20IN%20(SELECT%20MIN(st_distance(the_geom,%20
ST_GeomFromText.(%27POINT(" + lon + "%20" + lat + ")%27,4326)))%20
FROM%20channels%20x))%20GROUP%20BY%20toxic_channels.cartodb_id%20
&api_key=YOURCARTODBAPIKEYHERE&format=geojson&callback=?",
            function(geojson) {
                $.each(geojson.features, function(i, feature)
                  {
                    toxicLayer.addData(feature);
                })
            });
            map.addLayer(toxicLayer);
        }


        getToxic(-75.56111,39.72583);

        //getToxic(-75.70993,39.69099);


    </script>
  </body>
</html>
```

Your results should look similar to the following image:

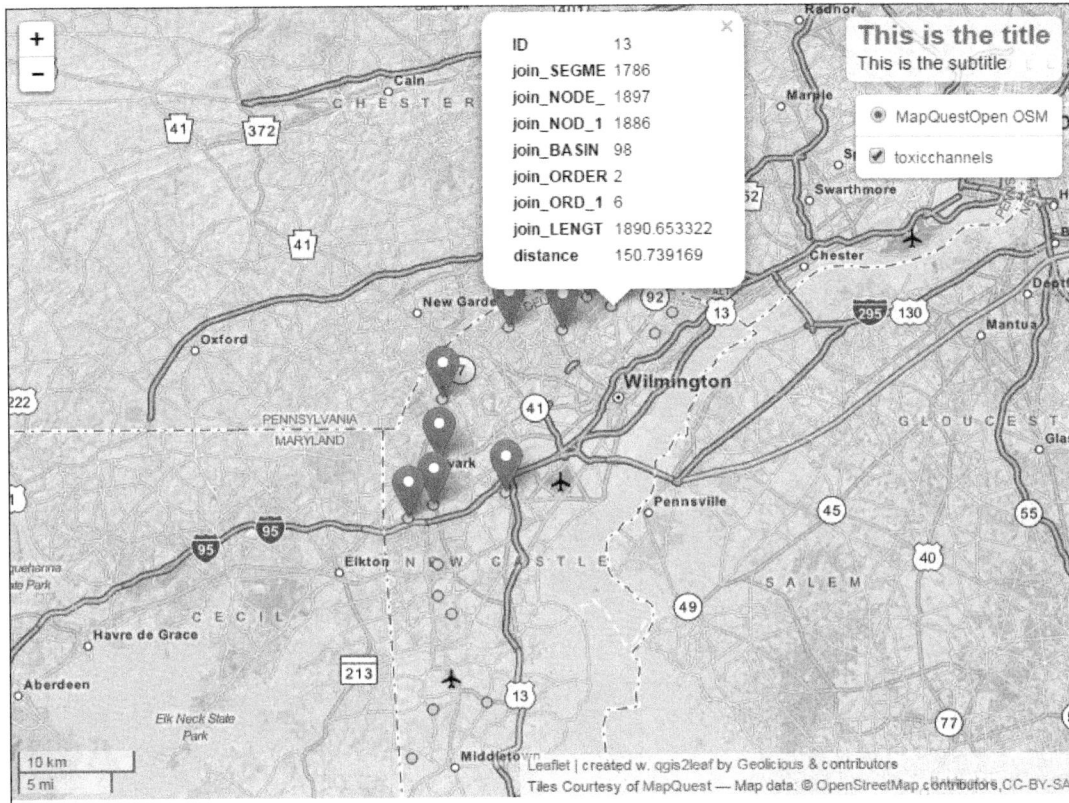

Summary

In this chapter, we produced a dynamic web application using a physical raster analysis example: hydrological analysis. To do this, we started by preparing the raster elevation data for the hydrological analysis and then performed the analysis. We took a look at how we could automate that workflow using the Modeler workflow automation tool. Next, we used NNJoin to create a spatial join between some hydrological outputs to produce a data source that would be suited to web interaction and querying. Finally, we published this data to an external cloud platform, CartoDB, and implemented their SQL API in a JavaScript function to find the toxic sites upstream from a location, given the Leaflet web client interaction. In the next chapter, we will produce a web application using network analysis and crowd sourced interaction.

4
Finding the Best Way to Get There

In this chapter, we will explore formal network-like geographic vector object relationships. Topological relationships are useful in many ways for geographical data management and analysis, but perhaps the most important application is optimal path finding. Specifically, you will learn how to make a few visualizations related to optimal paths: isochron polygons and accumulated traffic lines. With these visual elements as a background, we will incorporate social media feedback through Twitter in our web map application. The end result will be an application that communicates back and forth with the stakeholders about safe school routes.

In this chapter, we will cover the following topics:

- Downloading OpenStreetMap data
- Spatial queries
- Installing Postgres/PostGIS/pgRouting
- Building a topological network
- DB Manager
- Using the shortest path plugin to test the topology
- Generating the costs to travel to a point for each road segment
- Creating the isochron contours
- Generating the shortest paths for all students
- Adding Twitter data through Python

Postgres with PostGIS and pgRouting

Vector-based GIS, if not by definition then de facto, are organized around databases of geographic objects, storing their geometric definitions, geographic metadata, object relationships, and other attributes. Postgres is a leading open source relational database platform. Unlike SQLite, this is not a file-based system, but rather it requires a running service on an available machine, such as the localhost or an accessible server. The spatial extension to Postgres, PostGIS, provides all the functionalities around geospatial data, such as spatial references, geographic transformation, spatial relationships, and more. Most recently, PostGIS has come to support topology—the formal relationships between geometric objects. pgRouting is a topological analysis engine built around optimal path-finding. Conveniently, PostGIS now comes bundled with pgRouting. The following content applies to Postgres 9.3.

Installing Postgres/PostGIS/pgRouting

On Windows, you can use the Postgres installer to install PostGIS and pgRouting along with Postgres. On Mac, you can use the Kyngchaos binary installer found at `http://www.kyngchaos.com/software/postgres`. On Linux, you can refer to the PostGIS installation documentation for your distribution found at `http://postgis.net/install/`.

The installation instructions for Windows are as follows:

1. Download the Postgres installer from `http://www.postgresql.org/download/windows/` and start it.
2. Follow the prompt; pick a password.
3. Click on **Launch Stack Builder at exit** and then click on **Finish**.
4. In **Stack Builder**, select the PostgreSQL instance you just created.
5. Check **PostGIS 2.1** Bundle under **Spatial Extensions**.
6. Select **PostGIS** and **Create spatial database** under the **Choose Components** dialog.
7. Finish the installation, skipping the database creation steps, which are prone to failure.

Creating a new Postgres database

Now that we installed the Postgres database server with PostGIS, the pgRouting extensions, and the pgAdmin III client program, we want to create a new database where we can work. Perform the following steps:

1. Open the pgAdmin III program.
2. Right-click on the **Databases** section of the **Servers** tree and click on **New Database...** to create the database, as shown in the following screenshot:

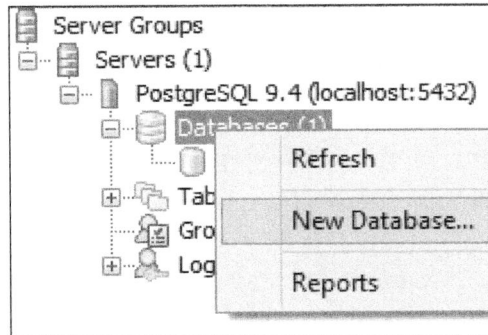

3. Enter a name for the new database, packt, and click on **OK**.

Registering the PostGIS and pgRouting extensions

Next, we need to tell Postgres that we want to use the PostGIS and pgRouting extensions with our new database. Perform the following steps:

1. Open pgAdmin III if you haven't already done so.
2. Navigate to **Tools | Query**.
3. Enter the following SQL in the **SQL Editor** area:

   ```
   CREATE EXTENSION postgis;
   CREATE EXTENSION pgrouting;
   ```

4. From the **Query** menu, choose **Execute**.

OpenStreetMap data for topology

A topological network, which specifies the formal relationships between geometric objects, requires real geographic data for it to be useful in an actual physical space. So next, we will acquire some geographic data in order to construct a network providing the shortest path between points in a physical space, following certain rules embedded in the network. A great source of data for this, and many other purposes, is OpenStreetMap.

Downloading the OSM data

Now, let's move back to QGIS to acquire the OpenStreetMap data from which we will create a topological network:

1. Navigate to **Vector | OpenStreetMap | Download Data**.
2. Select the **newark_boundaries** file as the **From layer** extent.
3. Enter c4/data/output/newark_osm.osm as the **Output file** and click on **OK**, as shown in the following screenshot:

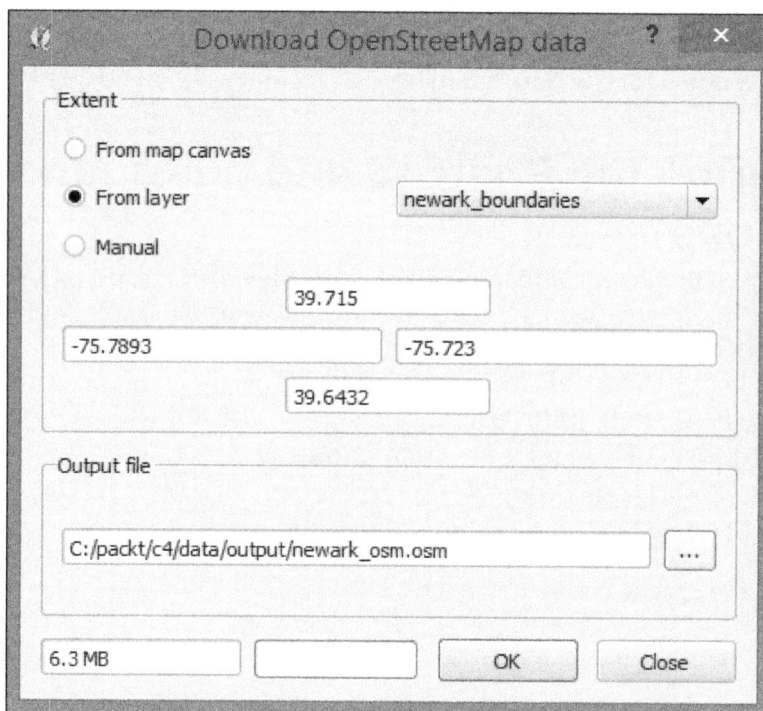

Adding the data to the map

The downloaded data must be added to the QGIS project to verify that it has been downloaded and to further work on the data from within QGIS. Perform the following steps:

1. Navigate to **Layer | Add Layer | Add Vector Layer**.

2. Select `c4/data/output/newark_osm.osm` as the **Source**.

3. Click on **Select All** from the **Select vector layers...** dialog.

4. Click on **OK**.

5. You should now see the data displayed, looking similar to the following image:

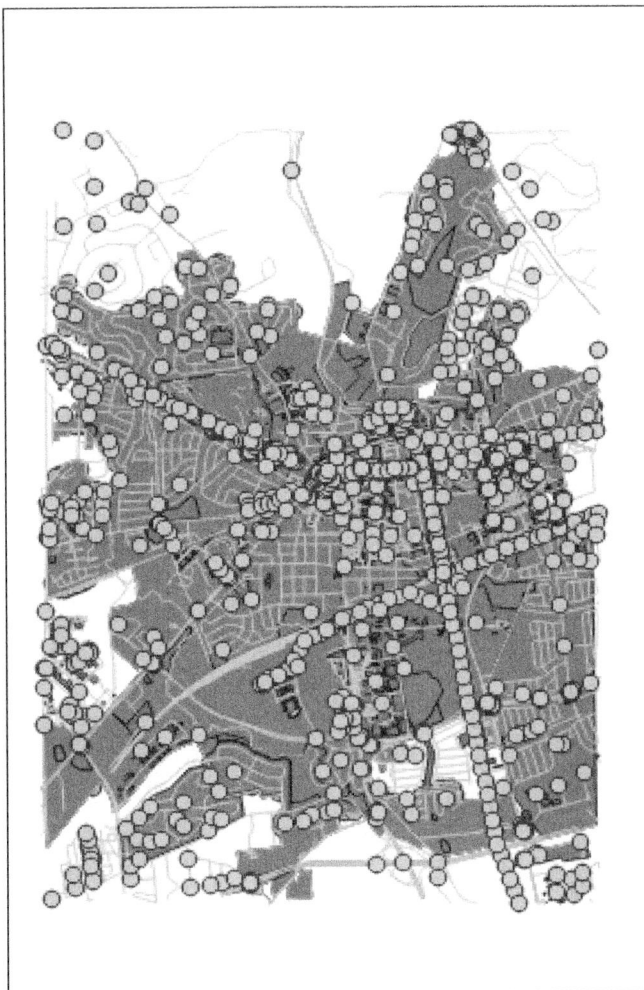

Projecting the OSM data

We will project the OSM data onto the projection used by the other data to be added to the project, which is the location of the students. We want these two datasets to use the same projection system; otherwise, we will run into trouble while building our topological network and analyzing the network. Perform the following steps:

1. Select the **lines** layer from the **Layers** panel.

2. Go to **Layer | Save as**.

3. Enter the following parameters:

    1. **Save as**: `c4/data/output/newark_osm.shp`.

    2. Select **CRS EPSG:2880** (Delaware Ft/HARN).

    3. Click on **OK**.

Splitting all the lines at intersections

It is necessary that the topological edges to be created are coterminous with the geographic data vertices. This is called a **topologically correct** dataset. We will use **Split lines with lines** to fulfill this requirement. Perform the following steps:

1. Search for **Split lines with lines** in the **Processing Toolbox** panel.

2. Select the projected OSM lines file, `c4/data/output/newark_osm.shp`, as both the **Input layer** and **Split layer**.

3. Click on **Run**, as shown in the following screenshot:

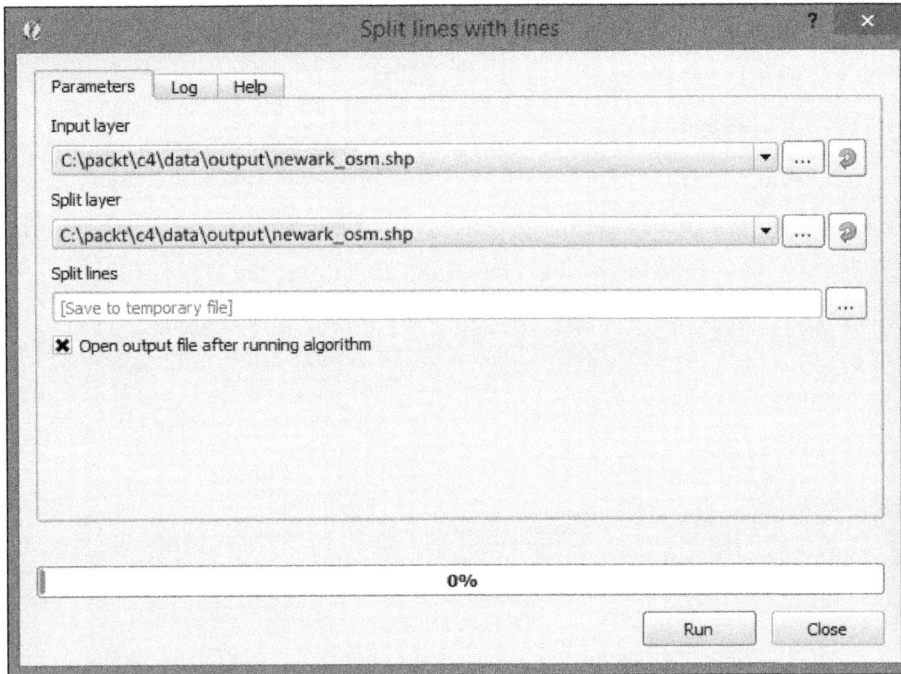

Database importing and topological relationships

Now that we've prepared the OSM data, we need to actually load it into the database. Here, we can generate the topological relationships based on geographic relationships as determined by PostGIS.

Connecting to the database

Although we will be working from the Database Manager when dealing with the database in QGIS, we will first need to connect to the database through the normal "Add Layer" dialog. Perform the following steps:

1. Navigate to **Layer | Add Layer | Add PostGIS Layers**.

2. Click on **New**.

3. In the **Create a New PostGIS connection** dialog, enter the following parameters, accepting others as their defaults:
    - **Name**: packt_c4
    - **Host**: localhost
    - **Database**: packt_c4
    - **Username/password**: As configured earlier in this chapter

4. Click on **Test Connect** to make sure you've entered the correct information.

5. You may wish to save your credentials, as shown here:

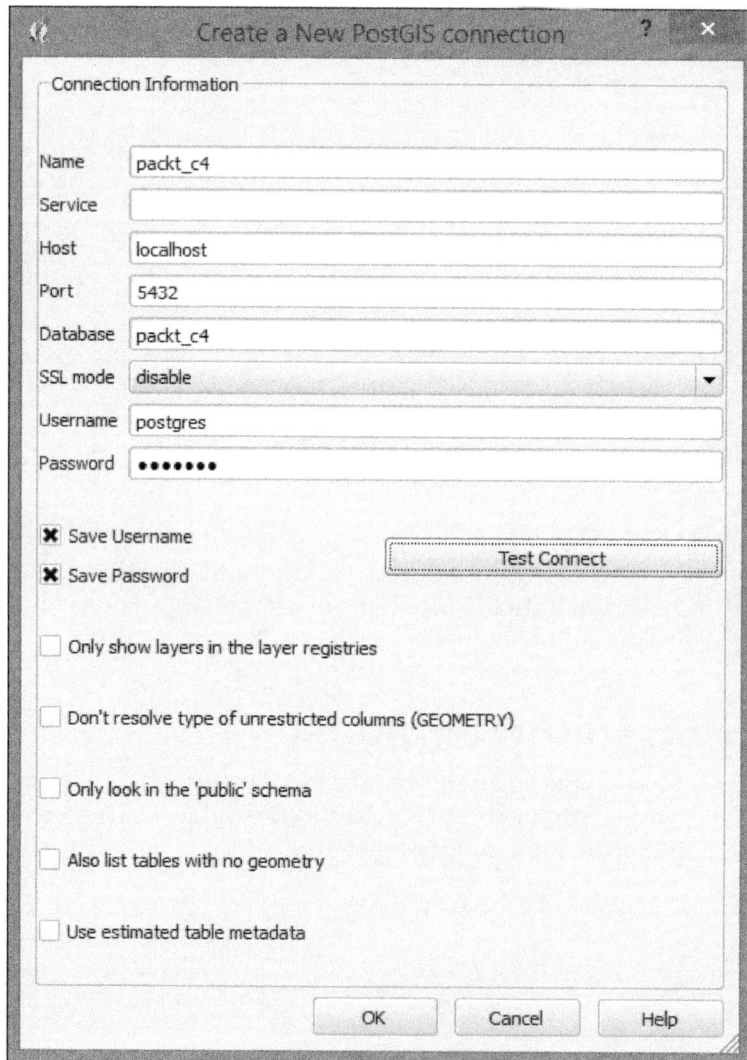

Importing into PostGIS with DB Manager

Once we've added the database connection, DB Manager is where we'll be interacting with the database. DB Manager provides query access via the SQL syntax as well as the facility to add results as a virtual (in memory, not on disk) layer. We can also use DB Manager to import or export data to/from the database when necessary. Perform the following steps:

1. Go to **Database** | **DB Manager** | **DB Manager**.

2. You may need to navigate to **Database** | **Refresh** to have a new database appear.

3. Select the database to be updated (for example, `packt_c4`). The following is an image of the Database Manager and tables, which were generated when you created your new PostGIS database:

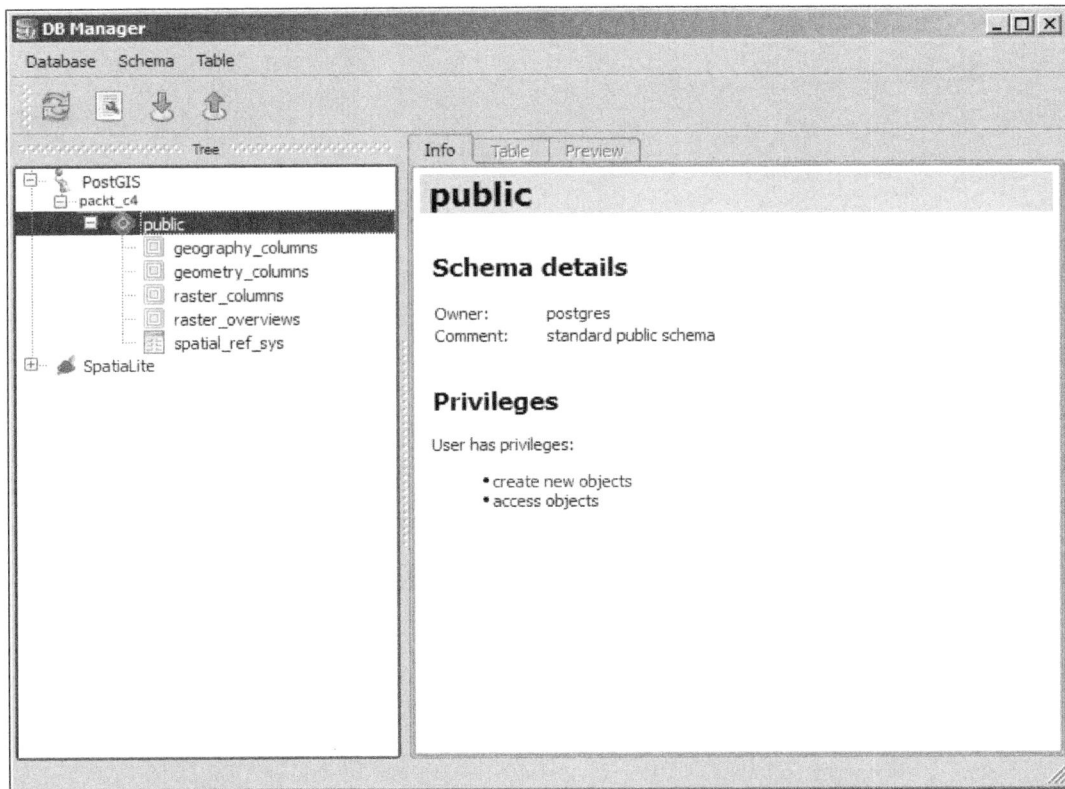

4. Navigate to **Table** | **Import layer/file**.

5. Input the following parameters:

- ° **Input**: **Split lines**
- ° **Table**: **newark_osm**
- ° **Source SRID**: 2880
- ° **Target SRID**: 2880
- ° Select **Create single-part geometries instead of multi-part**
- ° Select **Create spatial index**, as shown in the following screenshot:

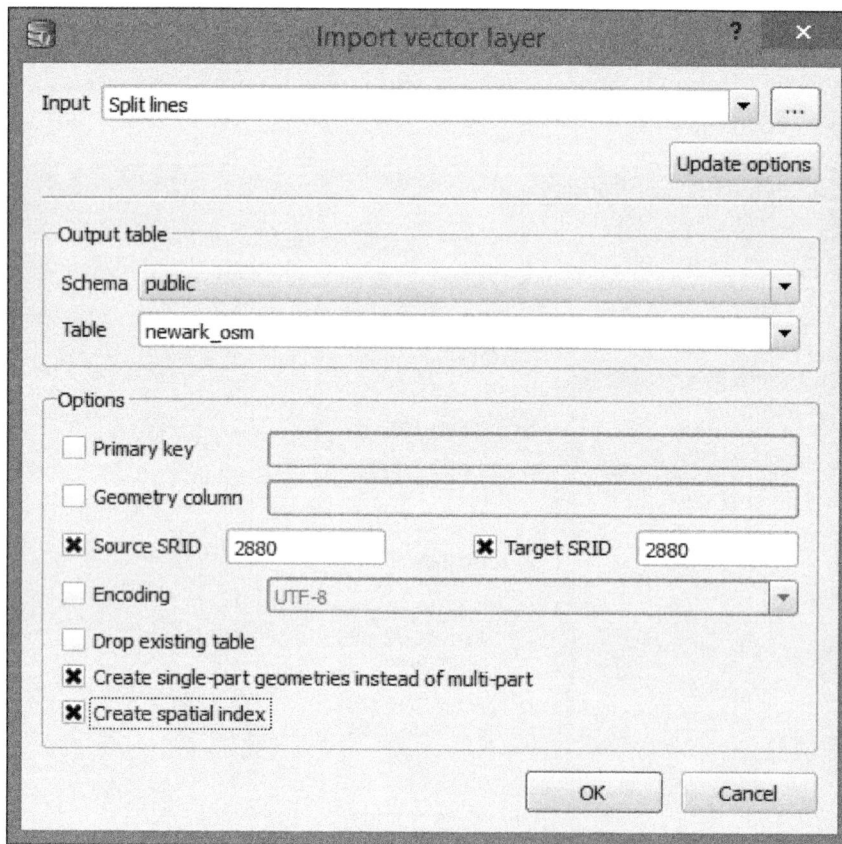

Repeat these steps with the **students** layer:

1. Add the **students** layer from `c4/data/original/students.shp`.

2. Repeat the previous **Import vector layer** steps with the **students** layer, as shown in the following screenshot:

The imported tables and the associated schema and metadata information will now be visible in DB Manager, as shown in the following screenshot:

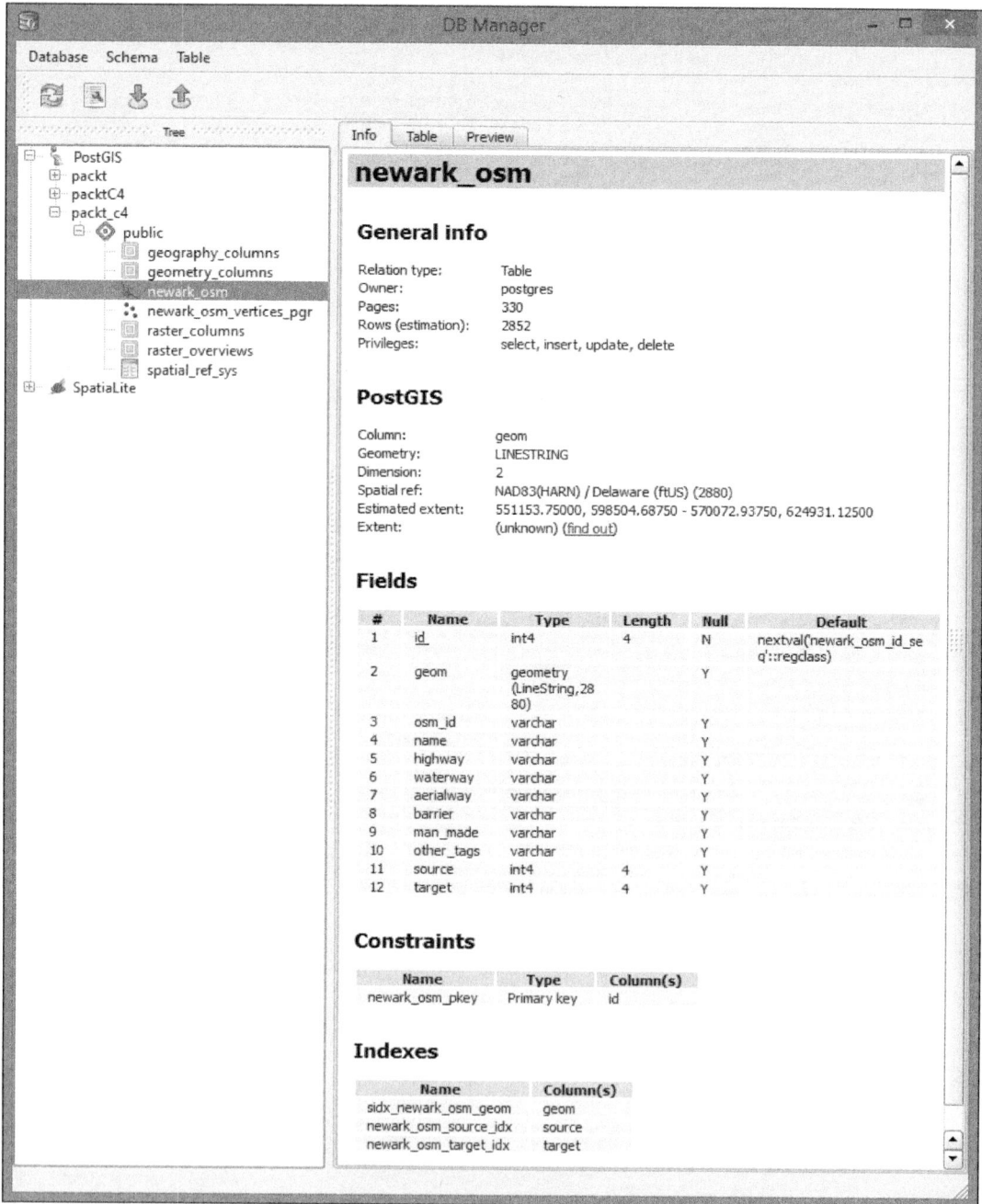

Creating the topological network data

Next, run a query that adds the necessary fields to the newark_osm table, updating these with the topological information, and create the related table of the network vertices, newark_osm_vertices. These field names and types, expected by pgRouting, are added by the alter queries and populated by the pgr_createTopology pgRouting function. The length_m field is populated with the segment length using an update query with the st_length function (and st_transform here to control the spatial reference). This field will be used to help determine the cost of the shortest path (minimum cost) routing. Perform the following steps:

1. Navigate to **Database | DB Manager | DB Manager**.

2. Select the database to be updated.

3. Go to **Database | SQL window**. Enter the following code:

   ```
   alter table newark_osm add column source integer;
   alter table newark_osm add column target integer;
   select pgr_createTopology('newark_osm', 0.0001, 'geom',
     'id');

   alter table newark_osm add column length_m float8;
   update newark_osm set length_m = st_length
     (st_transform(geom,2880));
   ```

An alternate workflow: topology with osm2po

The osm2po program performs many topological dataset preparation tasks that might otherwise require a longer workflow—such as the preceding task. As the name indicates, it is specifically used for the OpenStreetMap data. The osm2po program must be downloaded and installed separately from the osm2po website, http://osm2po.de. Once the program is installed, it is used as follows:

```
[..] > cd c:\packt\c4\data\output
c:\packt\c4\data\output>java -jar osm2po-5.0.0\osm2po-core-5.0.0-
  signed.jar cmd=tj
sp newark_osm.osm
```

This command will create a .sql file that you can run in your database to add the topological table to your database, producing something very similar to what we did in the preceding section.

Using the pgRouting Layer plugin to test

Let's use the pgRouting Layer plugin to test whether the steps we've performed up to this point have produced a functioning topological network to find the shortest path. We will find the shortest path between two arbitrary points on the network: 1 and 1000. Perform the following steps:

1. Install the pgRoutingLayer plugin.
2. If the shortest path panel is not displayed, turn it on under **View | Panels | pgRouting Layer**.
3. Enter the following parameters:
   - **Database**: **packt_c4**.
   - Ensure that you are already connected to the database, as shown in the previous section. You may need to restart QGIS for a new database connection to show up here.
   - **edge_table**: `newark_osm`
   - **geometry**: `geom`
   - **id**: `id`
   - **source**: `source`
   - **target**: `target`
   - **cost**: `length_m`
   - **source_id**: `1`
   - **target_id**: `1000`

Your output will look similar to the following image:

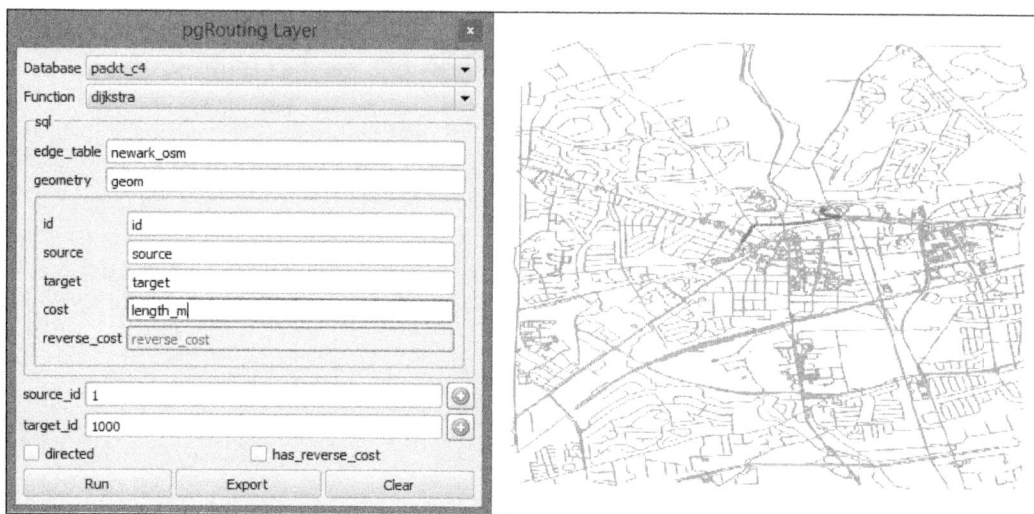

Creating the travel time isochron polygons

Let's say that the school in our study is located at the vertex with an ID of 1 in the newark_osm layer. To visualize the walking time from the students' homes, without releasing sensitive information about where the students actually live, we can create isochron polygons. Each polygon will cover the area that a person can walk from to a single destination within some time threshold.

Generating the travel time for each road segment

We'll use DB Manager to create and populate a column for the travel time on each segment at the walking speed; then, we will create a query layer that includes the travel time from each road segment to our school at vertex 1. Perform the following steps:

1. Navigate to **Database | DB Manager | DB Manager**.

2. Select the database to be updated.

3. Go to **Database | SQL window**.

4. Enter the following code:

```
ALTER TABLE newark_osm ADD COLUMN traveltime_min float8;
UPDATE newark_osm SET traveltime_min = length_m  / 6000.0 *
  60;


SELECT *
FROM pgr_drivingdistance('SELECT id, source, target,
  traveltime_min as cost FROM newark_osm'::text, 1,
  100000::double precision, false, false) di (seq, id1,
  id2, cost)
JOIN newark_osm rd ON di.id2 = rd.id;
```

5. Select the **Load as new layer** option.

6. Select **Retrieve columns**.

7. Select **seq** as your **Column with unique integer values** and **geom** as your **Geometry column**.

8. Click on the **Load now!** button, as shown in the following screenshot:

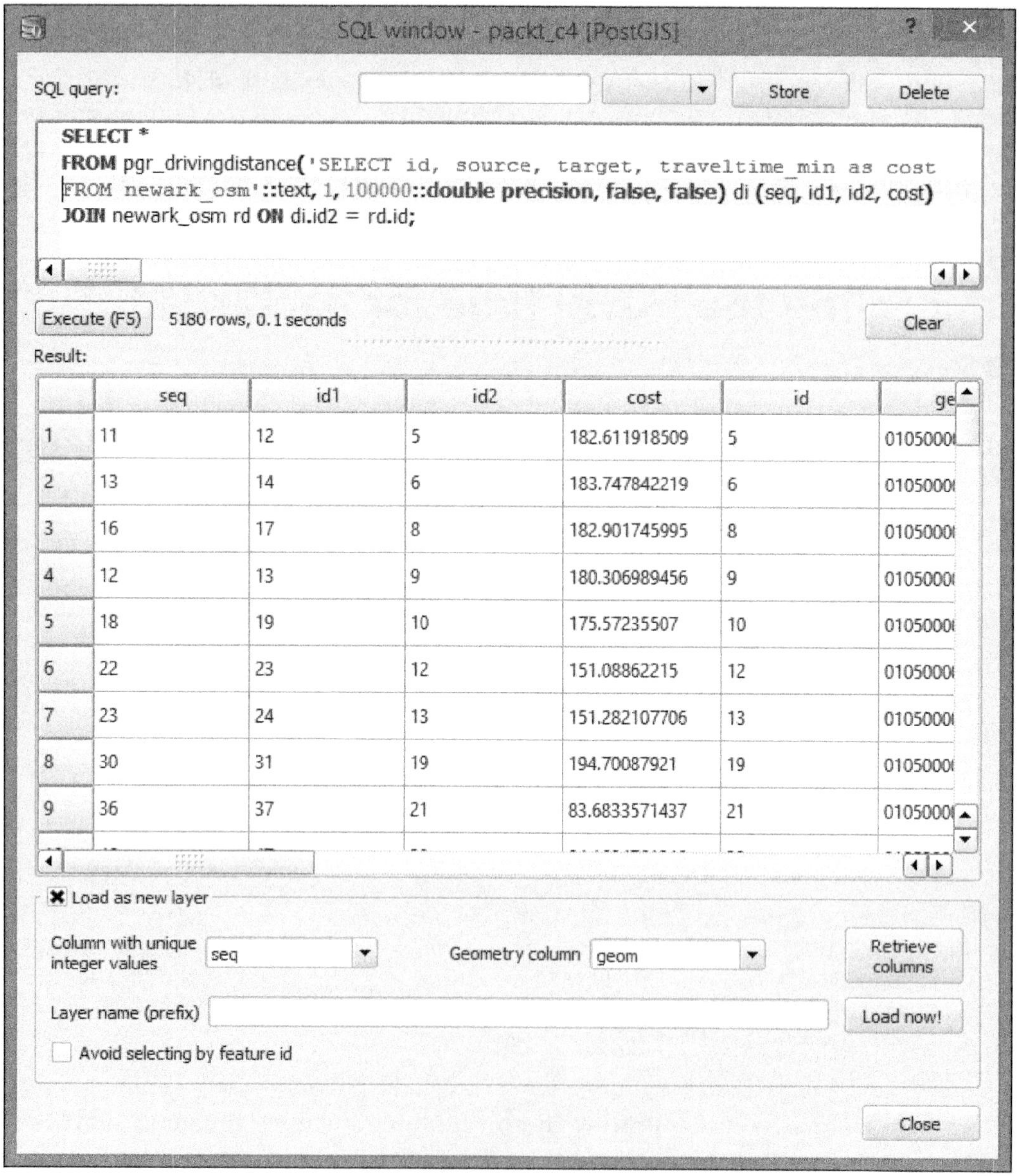

You can now symbolize the segments by the time it takes to get from that location to the school. To do this, use a **Graduated** style type with the `traveltime_min` field. You will see that the network segments with lower values (indicating quicker travel) are closer to vertex 1, and the opposite is true for the network segments with higher values. This method is limited by the extent to which the network models real conditions; for example, railroads are visualized along with other road segments for the travel time. However, railroads could cause discontinuity in our network—as they are not "traversable" by students traveling to school.

Creating isochron polygons

Next, we will create the polygons to visualize the areas from which the students can walk to school in certain time ranges. We can use this technique to characterize the general travel time and keep the student locations hidden.

Converting the travel time lines to points

We will need to first convert our current line-based travel time layer to points (centroids), using the polygons as an intermediate step. Perform the following steps:

1. Save the query layer as a shapefile: `c4/data/output/newark_isochrone.shp`.

2. Navigate to **Vector | Geometry Tools | Line to polygons**. Input the following parameters:

    - **Input line vector layer**: isochron lines
    - **Output polygon shapefile**: `c4/data/output/isochron_polygon.shp`
    - Click on **OK**

3. Navigate to **Vector | Geometry Tools | Polygons to centroid**. Input the following parameters:

    - **Input polygon vector layer**: `c4/data/output/isochron_polygon.shp`
    - **Output point shapefile**: `c4/data/output/isochrons_centroids.shp`
    - Click on **OK**

Selecting the travel time ranges in points and creating convex hulls

Next, we'll create the actual isochron polygons for each time bin. We must select each set of travel time points using a filter expression for the three time periods: 15 minutes or less, 30 minutes or less, and 45 minutes or less. Then, we'll run the **Concave hull** tool on each selection. This will create a polygon feature around each set of points.

You'll perform the following steps three times for each of the three break values, which are 15, 30, and 45:

1. Select **isochron_centroids** from the **Layers** panel.
2. Navigate to **Layer | Query**.
3. Click on **Clear** if there is already a filter expression displayed in the filter expression field of the query dialog.

4. Provide a specific field expression: `cost < [break value]`
   (for example, `cost < 15`).

5. Click on **OK** to select the objects in the layer that matches the expression.

6. Navigate to **Processing Toolbox | Concave hull**.

7. Input the following parameters for **Concave hull**. All other parameters can be left at their defaults:

   ○ **Input point layer**: **isochron_centroids**

   ○ Select **Split multipart geometry into singleparts geometries**

   ○ **Concave hull** (the output file) could be similar to
   `c4/data/output/isochron45.shp`

   ○ Click on **Run**, as shown in the following screenshot:

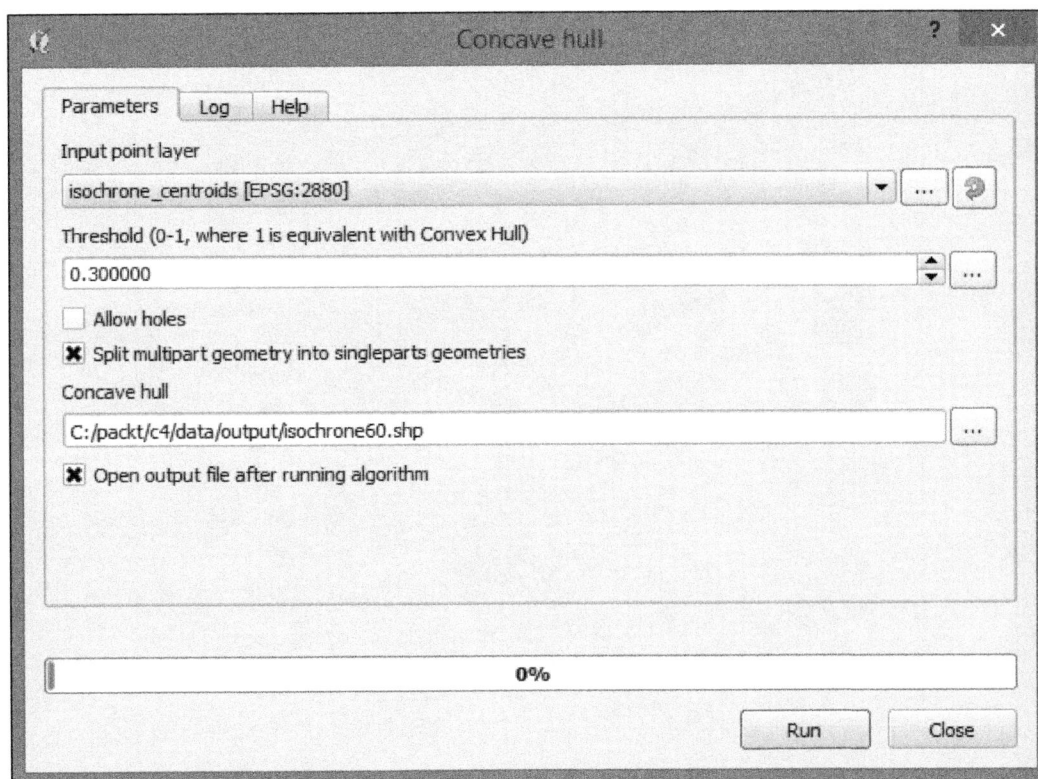

All concave hulls when displayed will look similar to the following image. The "spikiness" of the concave hulls reflects relatively few road segments (points) used to calculate these travel time polygons:

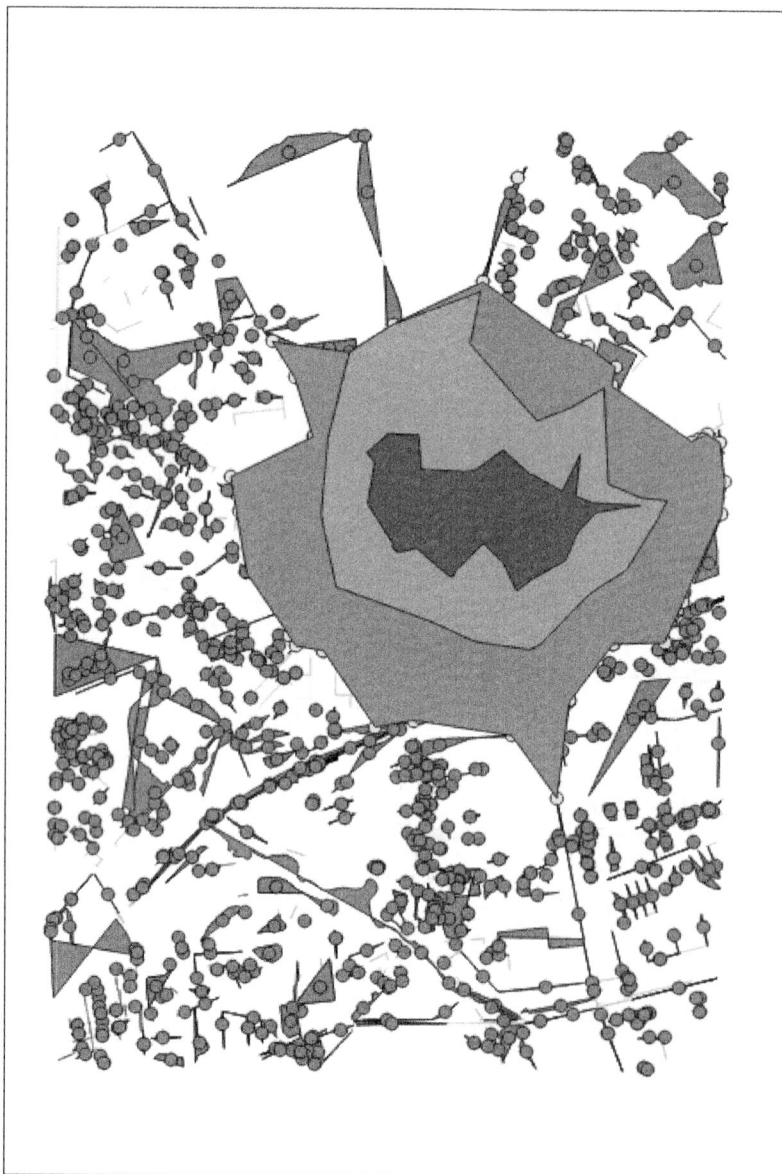

Generating the shortest paths for all students

So far, we have only looked at the shortest path between all the given segments of road in the city. Now, given the student location, let's look at where student traffic will accumulate.

Finding the associated segment for a student location

By following these steps, we will join attributes from the closest road segment—including the associated topological and travel attributes—to each student location. Perform the following steps:

1. Install the NNJoin plugin.
2. Navigate to **Plugins | NNJoin | NNJoin**.
3. Enter the following parameters:
    *   **Input vector layer**: **students**
    *   **Join vector layer**: **newark_osm**
    *   **Output layer**: students_topology
4. Click on **OK**.
5. Import students_topology into the packt_c4 database using Database Manager.

The following image shows the parameters as entered into the NNJoin plugin:

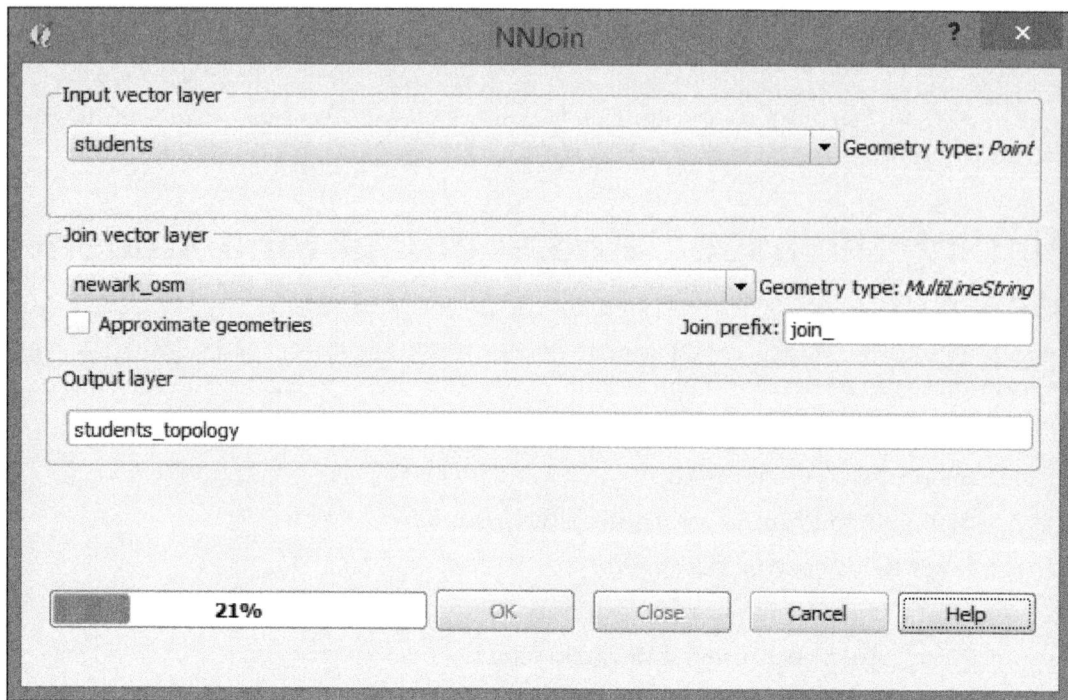

Calculating the accumulated shortest paths by segment

We want to find which routes are the most popular given the student locations, network characteristics, and school location. The following steps will produce an accumulated count of the student traffic along each network segment:

1. Go to **Database | DB Manager | DB Manager**.

2. Select the database to be updated.

3. Navigate to **Database | SQL window**.

4. We want to run a SQL command that will do a shortest path calculation for each student and find the total number of students traveling on each road segment. This query may be very slow. Enter the following code:

```
SELECT id, geom, count(id1)
FROM
(SELECT *
  FROM pgr_kdijkstraPath(
```

```
     'SELECT id, source, target, traveltime_min as cost FROM
newark_osm',
     1, (SELECT array_agg(join_target) FROM students_topology),
false, false
  ) a,
  newark_osm b
WHERE a.id3=b.id) x
GROUP BY id, geom
```

5. Select the **Load as new layer** option.

6. Select **id** as your **Column with unique integer values** and **geom** as your **Geometry column**, as shown in the following screenshot:

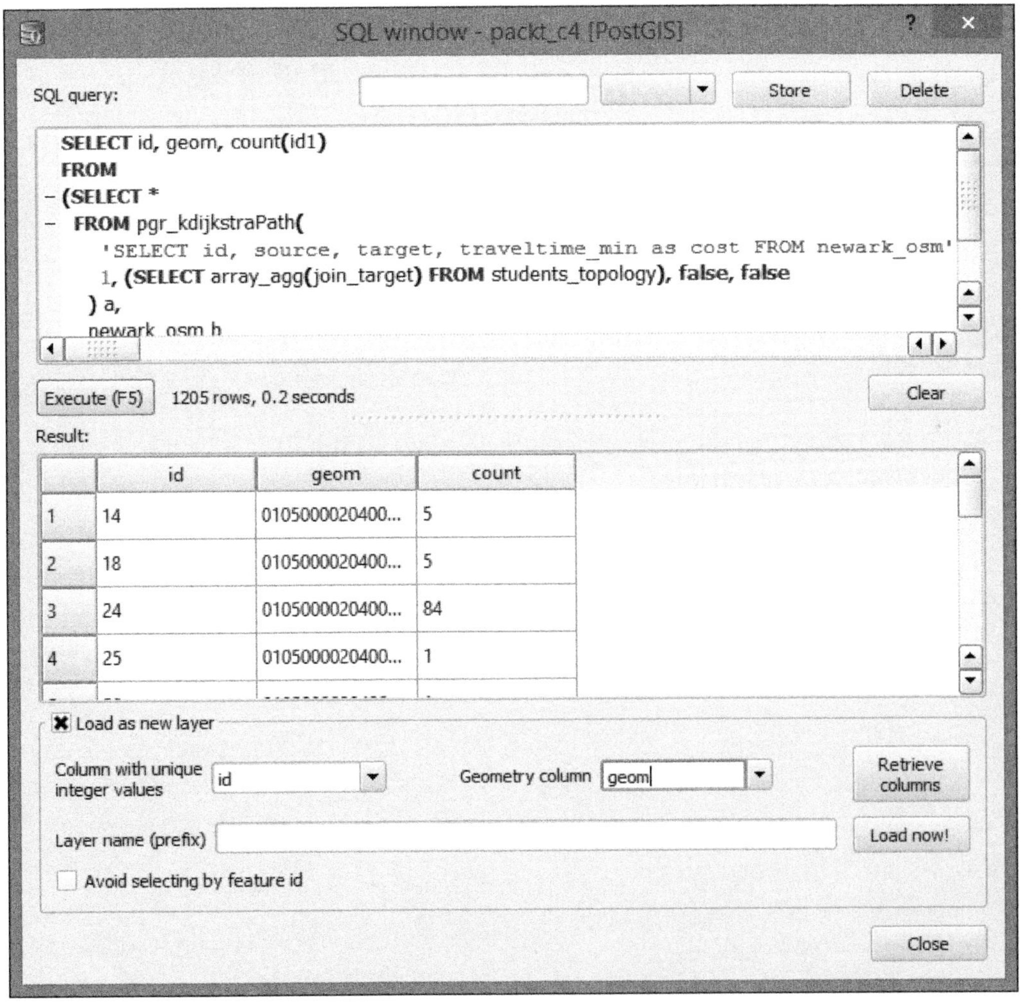

Flow symbology

We want to visualize the number of students on each segment in a way that really accentuates the segments that have a high number of students traveling on them. A great way to do this is with a symbology expression. This produces a graduated symbol as would be found in other GIS packages. Perform the following steps:

1. Navigate to **Layer | Properties | Style**.

2. Click on **Simple line** to access the symbology expressions, as shown in the following screenshot:

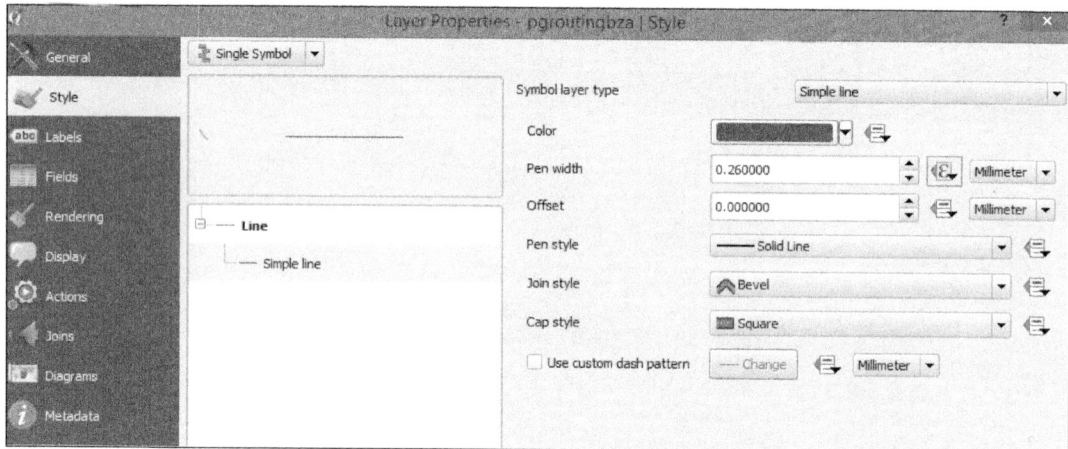

3. In the **Pen width** section, click on the advanced menu to edit the symbology expression.

4. Natural log is a good function to use to get a more linear growth rate when a value grows exponentially. This helps us to produce a symbology that varies in a more visually appealing way. Enter the following expression into the **Expression** string builder dialog:

```
ln("count")
```

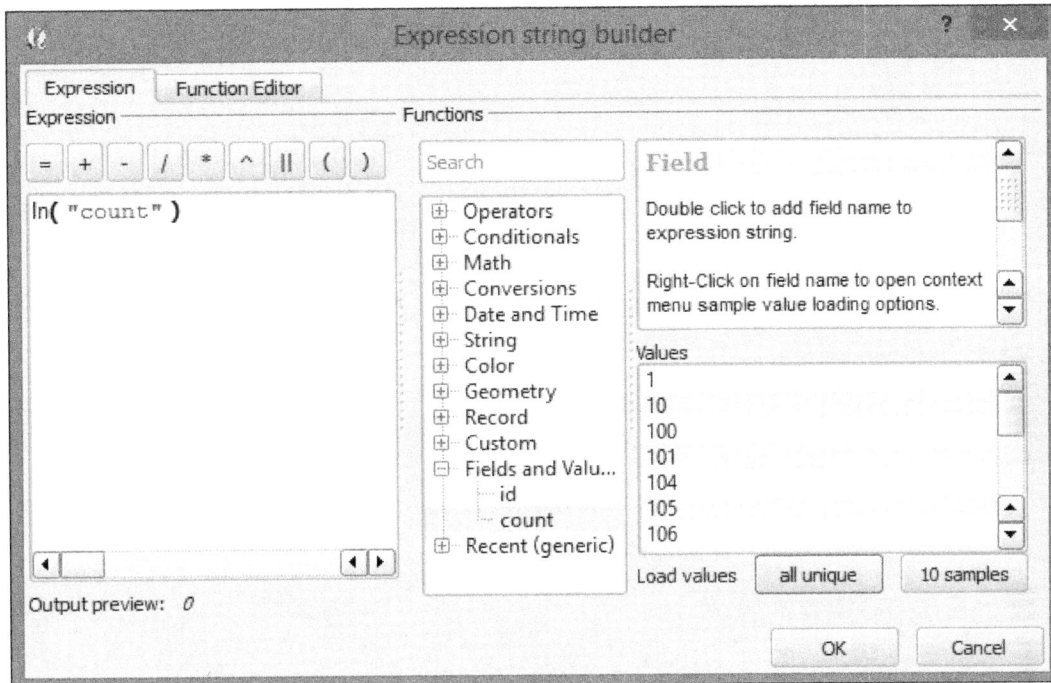

Now that we have mapped the variable sized symbol to the natural log of the count of students traveling on each segment, we will see a pleasing visualization of the "flow" of students traveling on each road segment. The student layer, showing the student locations, is displayed alongside the flow to better illustrate what the flow visualization shows.

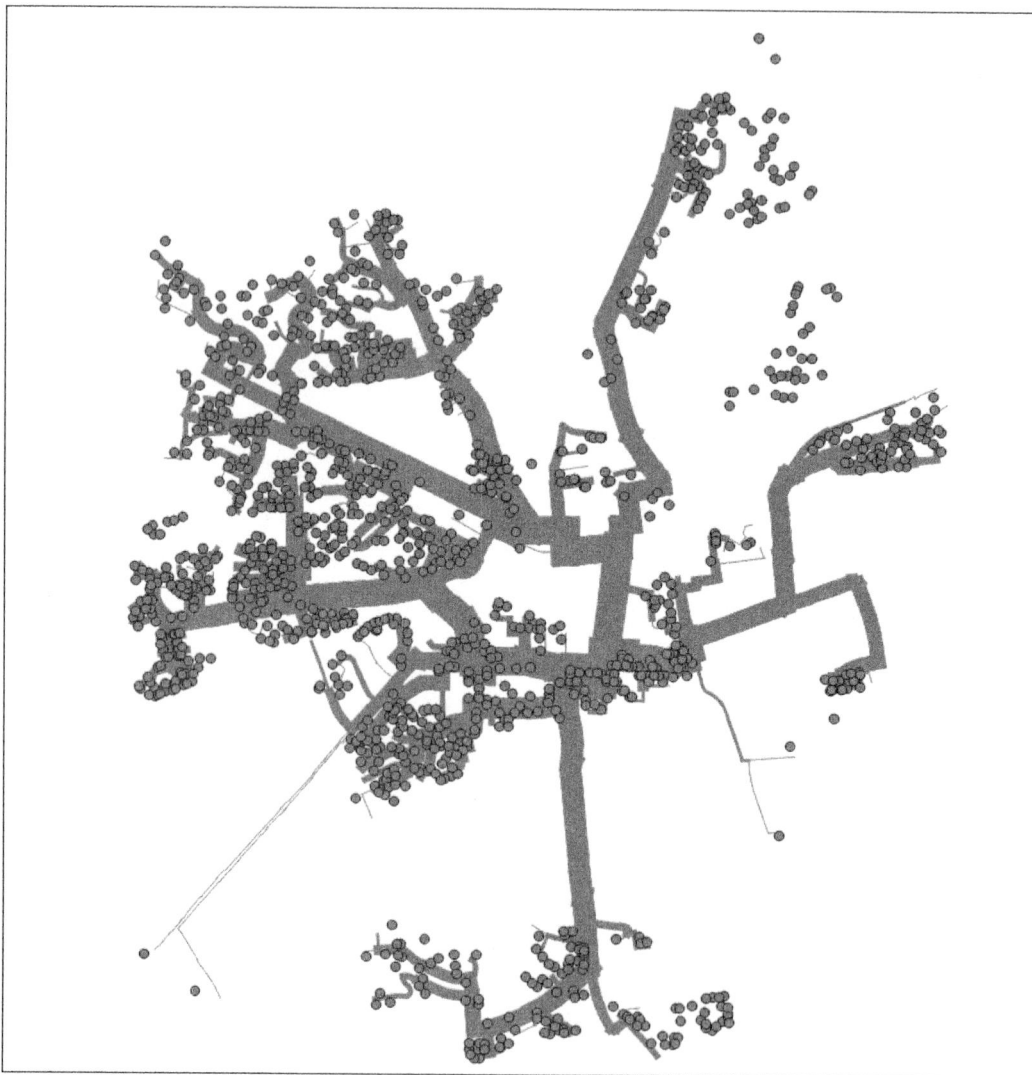

Web applications – creating safe corridors

Decision makers can use the accumulated shortest paths output to identify the busiest paths to the school. They can use this information to communicate with guardians about the safest routes for their children.

Planners can go a step further by investing in safe infrastructure for the most used paths. For example, planners can identify the busy crossings over highways using the "count" attribute (and visualization) from the query layer and the "highways" attribute from newark_osm.

Of course, communication with stakeholders is ideally a two-way process. To achieve this goal, planners could establish a social networking account, such as a Twitter account, for parents and students to report the problems or features of the walking routes. Planners would likely want to look at this data as well to adjust the safe routes to the problem spots or amenities. This highly simplistic model should be adjusted for the other variables that could also be captured in the data and modeled, such as high traffic roads and so on.

Registering a Twitter account and API access

The following instructions will direct you on how to set up a new Twitter account in a web browser and get your community to make geotagged tweets:

1. Create a Twitter account for this purpose (a nonpersonal one). The account will need to be linked to a unique mobile phone and e-mail. If you've already linked your e-mail and mobile phone with an account, there are some hints for getting around this in the following section.

2. Go to https://apps.twitter.com/ and create a new app.

3. You will need to unregister your phone number if it is already registered with another account (Twitter will warn you about this).

4. In **Application Settings**, find **manage keys and access tokens**. Here, you will find your consumer key and secret.

5. You must also create an access token by clicking on **Create my Access Token**.

6. Users who would like to have their tweets added to the system should be directed to use your Twitter handle (@YOURNAME). Retweet the tweets that you wish to add to your map. For a more passive solution, you can also follow all the users who you wish to capture; although, you'll need to find some way to filter out their irrelevant tweets.

Setting up the Twitter Tools API

We must now download and install Python-based Twitter Tools, which leverage the Twitter API. This will allow us to pull down GeoJSON from our Twitter account. Perform the following steps:

1. Download the Twitter Tools API from GitHub: `https://github.com/sixohsix/twitter`.

2. Open the OSGeo4W shell using the **Run as administrator** command via the context menu, or if you're on Mac or Linux, use `sudo` to run it with full privileges. Your OS Account must have administrator privileges. Navigate to `C:\Program Files\QGIS Wien\OSGeo4W.bat`.

3. Extract the Twitter Tools API code and change drive (`cd`) into the directory that you extracted into (for example, `C:\Users\[YOURUSERNAME]\Downloads\twitter-master\twitter-master`), using the following command line:

    ```
    > cd C:\Users\[YOURUSERNAME]\Downloads\twitter-master\twitter-master
    ```

4. Run the following from the command line to install the Twitter Tools software and dependencies:

    ```
    > python setup.py install
    ```
    ```
    > twitter
    ```

    > Running `python setup.py install` in a directory containing the `setup.py` file on a path including the Python executable is the normal way to build (install) a Python program. You will need to install the `setuptools` module beforehand. The instructions to do so can be found on this website: `https://pypi.python.org/pypi/setuptools`.

5. Accept the authorization for the command-line tools. You will need to copy and paste a PIN (as given) from the browser to the command line.

6. Exit the command-line shell and start another OSGeo4W shell under your regular account.

7. You can use `twitter --help` for more options. Execute the following in the command line:

    ```
    > twitter --format json 1> "C:\packt\c4\data\output\twitter.json"
    ```
    ```
    > cd c:\packt\c4
    ```
    ```
    > python
    ```

8. Run the following in the interpreter (refer to the following section to run it noninteractively):

```
import json
f = open('./output/twitter.json', 'r')
jsonStr = f.read()
f.close()
jpy = json.loads(jsonStr)
geojson = ''
for x in jpy['safe']:
    if x['geo'] :
        geojson += '{"type": "Feature","geometry": {"type":
            "Point", "coordinates": [' + str(x['geo']
            ['coordinates'][1]) + ',' + str(x['geo']
            ['coordinates'][0]) + ']}, "properties": {"id": "' +
            str(x['id']) + '", "text": "' + x['text'] + '"}},'
geojson = geojson[:-1]
geojson += ']}'
geojson = '{"type": "FeatureCollection","features": [' +
    geojson
f = open('./data/output/twitter.geojson', 'w')
f.write(geojson)
f.close()
```

Or run the following command:

```
> python twitterJson2GeoJson.py
```

Here is an example of the GeoJSON-formatted output:

```
{"type": "FeatureCollection","features": [{"type":
"Feature","geometry": {"type": "Point", "coordinates":
[-75.75451,39.67434]}, "properties": {"id": "606454366212530177",
"text": "Hello world"}},{"type": "Feature","geometry": {"type":
"Point", "coordinates": [-75.73968,39.68139]}, "properties":
{"id": "606454626456473600", "text": "Testing"}},{"type":
"Feature","geometry": {"type": "Point", "coordinates":
[-75.76838,39.69243]}, "properties": {"id": "606479472271826944",
"text": "Test"}}]}
```

Save this as `c4/output/twitter.geojson` from a text editor and import the file into QGIS as a vector layer to preview it along with the other layers. When these layers are symbolized, you may see something similar to the following image:

Finally, export the web application with qgis2leaf. You will notice some loss of information and symbology here. In addition, you may wish to customize the code to take advantage of the data and content passed through Twitter.

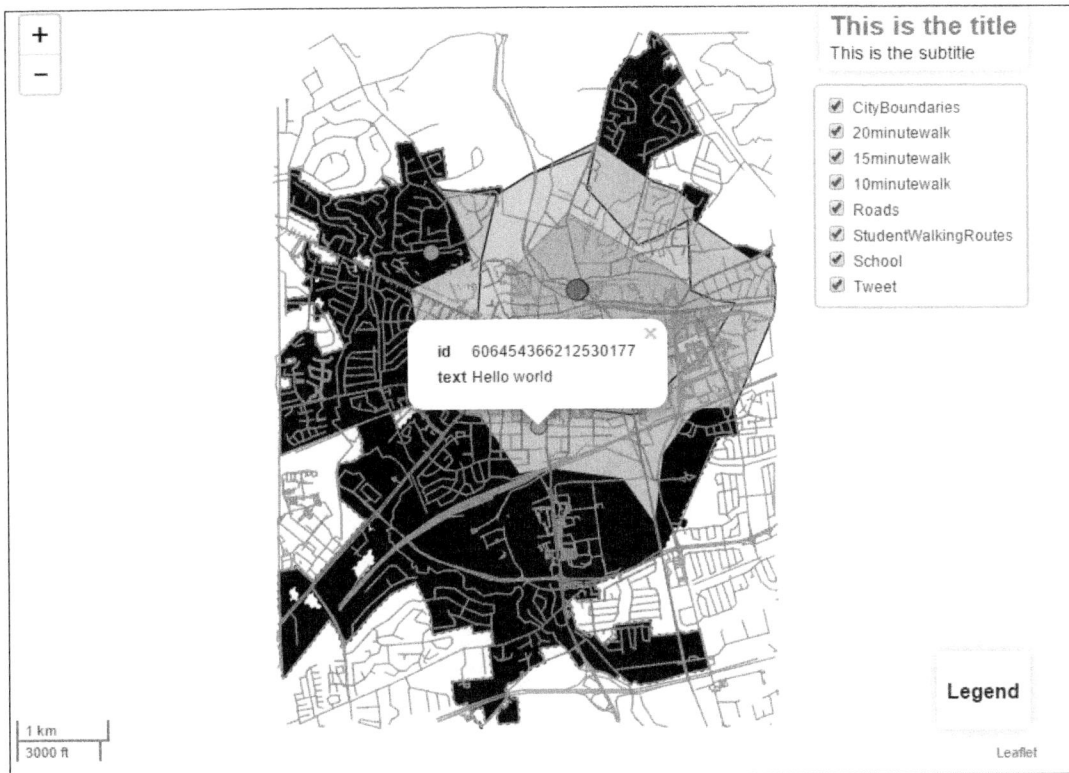

Summary

In this chapter, through a safe route selection example, we built a topological network using OSM data and Postgres with its PostGIS and pgRouting extensions. Using this network, we modeled the travel time to school from different locations on the road network and the students' travel to school, visualizing which routes were more and less frequently used. Finally, we added the contributed social network data on Twitter through a Python-based API, which we built using a typical Python build process. We then exported all the results using the same method as we did in the previous chapters: qgis2leaf. In the next chapter, we will explore the relationship between time and space and visualization through some new libraries.

5
Demonstrating Change

In this chapter, we will encounter the visualization and analytical techniques of exploring the relationships between place and time and between the places themselves.

The data derived from temporal and spatial relationships is useful in learning more about the geographic objects that we are studying—from hydrological features to population units. This is particularly true if the data is not directly available for the geographic object of interest: either for a particular variable, for a particular time, or at all.

In this example, we will look at the demographic data from the US Census applied to the State House Districts, for election purposes. Elected officials often want to understand how the neighborhoods in their jurisdictions are changing demographically. Are their constituents becoming younger or more affluent? Is unemployment rising? Demographic factors can be used to predict the issues that will be of interest to potential voters and thus may be used for promotional purposes by the campaigns.

In this chapter, we will cover the following topics:

- Using spatial relationships to leverage data
- Preparing data relationships for static production
- Vector simplification
- Using TopoJSON for vector data size reduction and performance
- D3 data visualization for API
- Animated time series maps

Leveraging spatial relationships

So far, we've looked at the methods of analysis that take advantage of the continuity of the gridded raster data or of the geometric formality of the topological network data.

For ordinary vector data, we need a more abstract method of analysis, which is establishing the formal relationships based on the conditions in the spatial arrangement of geometric objects.

For most of this section, we will gather and prepare the data in ways that will be familiar. When we get to preparing the boundary data, which is leveraging the State House Districts data from the census tracts, we will be covering new territory — using the spatial relationships to construct the data for a given geographic unit.

Gathering the data

First, we will gather data from the sections of the US Census website. Though this workflow will be particularly useful for those working with the US demographic data, it will also be instructive for those dealing with any kind of data linked to geographic boundaries.

To begin with, obtain the boundary data with a unique identifier. After doing this, obtain the tabular data with the same unique identifier and then join on the identifier.

Boundaries

Download 2014 TIGER/Line Census Tracts and State Congressional Districts from the US Census at `https://www.census.gov/geo/maps-data/data/tiger-line.html`.

1. Select **2014** from the tabs displayed; this should be the default year.
2. Click on the **Download** accordion heading and click on **Web interface**.
3. Under **Select a layer type**, select **Census Tracts** and click on **submit**; under **Census Tract**, select **Pennsylvania** and click on **Download**.

4. Use the back arrow if necessary to select **State Legislative Districts**, and click on **submit**; select **Pennsylvania** for **State Legislative Districts - Lower Chamber (current)** and click on **Download**.

5. Move both the directories to `c5/data/original` and extract them.

> We've only downloaded a single boundary dataset for this exercise. Since the boundaries are not consistent every year, you would want to download and work further with each separate annual boundary file in an actual project.

Tabular data from American FactFinder

Many different demographic datasets are available on the American FactFinder site. These complement the TIGER/Line data mentioned before with the attribute data for the TIGER/Line geographic boundaries. The main trick is to select the matching geographic boundary level and extent between the attribute and the geographic boundary data. Perform the following steps:

1. Go to the US Census American FactFinder site at `http://factfinder.census.gov`.

2. Click on the **ADVANCED SEARCH** tab.

3. In the **topic or table name** input, enter `White` and select **B02008: WHITE ALONE OR IN COMBINATION WITH ONE OR MORE RACES** in the suggested options. Then, click on **GO**.

4. From the sidebar, in the **Select a geographic type:** dropdown in the **Geographies** section, select **Census Tract - 140**.

5. Under **select a state**, select **Pennsylvania**; under **Select a county**, select **Philadelphia**; and under **Select one or more geographic areas and click Add to Your Selections:**, select **All Census Tracts within Philadelphia County, Pennsylvania**. Then, click on **ADD TO YOUR SELECTIONS**.

6. From the sidebar, go to the **Topics** section. Here, in the **Select Topics to add to 'Your Selections'** under **Year**, click on each year available from **2009** to **2013**, adding each to **Your Selections** to be then downloaded.

7. Check each of the five datasets offered under the **Search Results** tab. All checked datasets are added to the selection to be downloaded, as shown in the following screenshot:

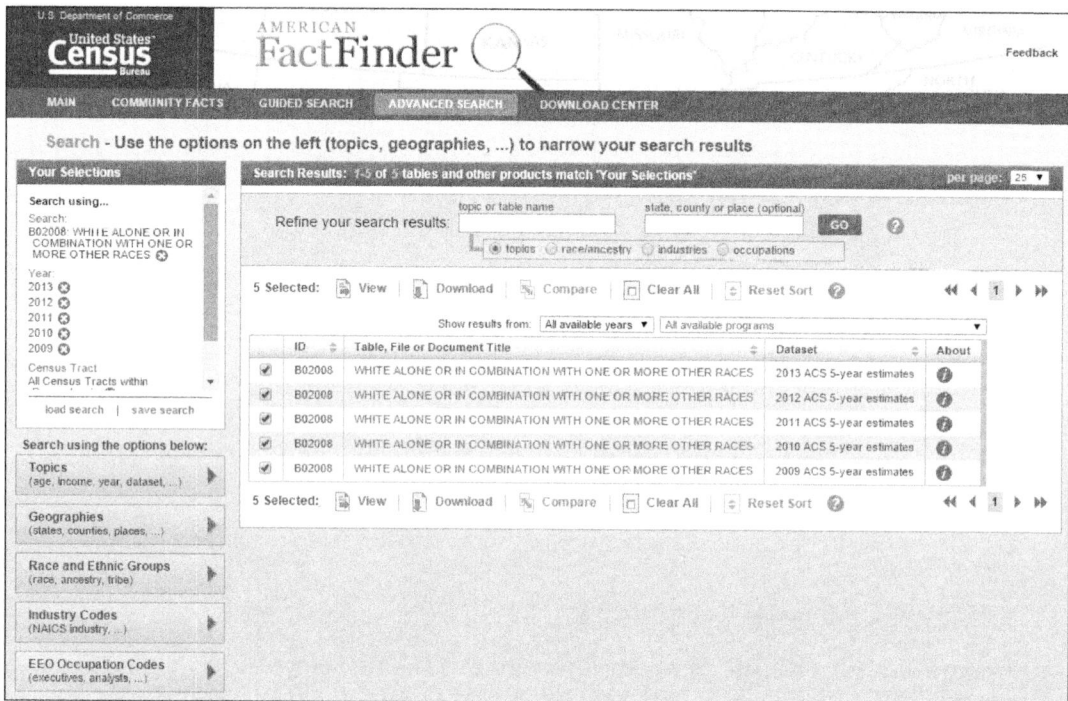

8. Now, remove **B02008: WHITE ALONE OR IN COMBINATION WITH ONE OR MORE RACES** from the search filter showing selections in the upper-left corner of the page.

9. Enter `total` into the **topic or table name** field, selecting **B01003: TOTAL POPULATION** from the suggested datasets, and then click on **GO**.

10. Select the five 2009 to 2013 total population 5-year estimates and then click on **GO**.

11. Click on **Download** to download these 10 datasets, as shown in the preceding screenshot.

12. Once you see the **Your file is complete** message, click on **DOWNLOAD** again to download the files. These will download as a `aff_download.zip` directory.

13. Move this directory to `c5/data/original` and then extract it.

Preparing and exporting the data

First, we will cover the steps for tabular data preparation and exporting, which are fairly similar to those we've done before. Next, we will cover the steps for preparing the boundary data, which will be more novel. We need to prepare this data based on the spatial relationships between layers, requiring the use of SQLite, since this cannot easily be done with the out-of-the-box or plugin functionality in QGIS.

The tabular data

Our tabular data is of the census tract white population. We only need to have the parseable latitude and longitude fields in this data for plotting later and, therefore, can leave it in this generic tabular format.

Combining it yearly

To combine this yearly data, we can join each table on a common GEOID field in QGIS. Perform the following steps:

1. Open QGIS and import all the boundary shapefiles (the tracts and state house boundaries) and data tables (all the census tract years downloaded). The single boundary shapefile will be in its extracted directory with the `.shp` extension. Data tables will be named something similar to `x_with_ann.csv`. You need to do this the same way you did earlier, which was through **Add Vector Layer** under the **Layer** menu. Here is a list of all the files to add:

   - `tl_2014_42_tract.shp`
   - `ACS_09_5YR_B01003_with_ann.csv`
   - `ACS_10_5YR_B01003_with_ann.csv`
   - `ACS_11_5YR_B01003_with_ann.csv`
   - `ACS_12_5YR_B01003_with_ann.csv`
   - `ACS_13_5YR_B01003_with_ann.csv`

2. Select the tract boundaries shapefile, `tl_2014_42_tract`, from the **Layers** panel.

3. Navigate to **Layers | Properties**.

4. For each white population data table (ending in `x_B02008_with_ann`), perform the following steps:

   1. On the **Joins** tab, click on the green plus sign (**+**) to add a join.

   2. Select a data table as the **Join layer**.

   3. Select **GEO.id2** in the **Join field** tab.

   4. **Target field: GEOID**

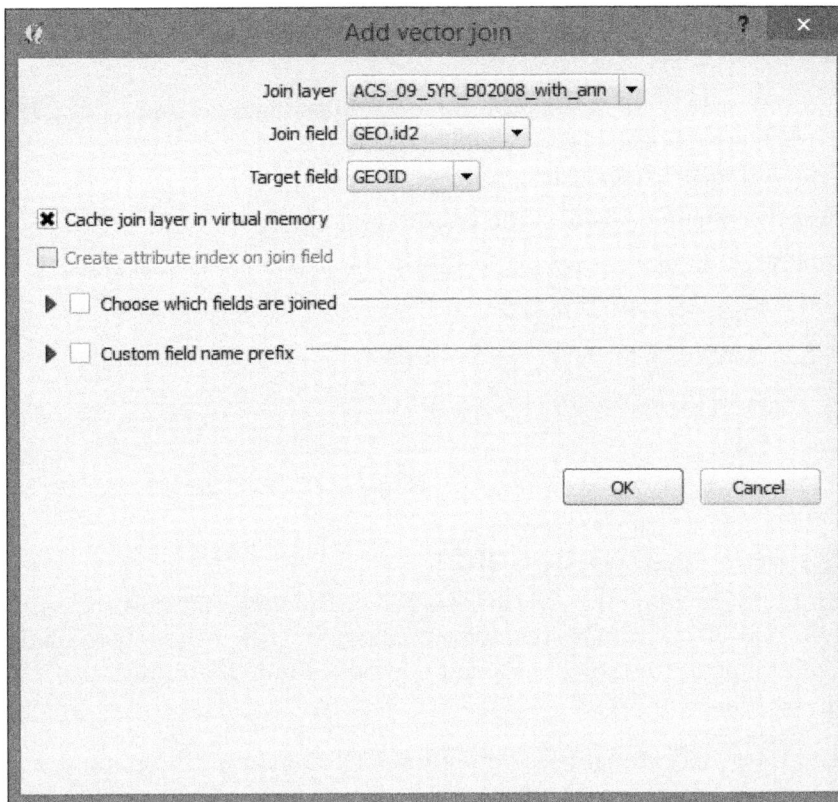

After joining all the tables, you will find many rows in the attribute table containing null values. If you sort them a few years later, you will find that we have the same number of rows populated for more recent years as we have in the Philadelphia tracts layer. However, the year 2009 (`ACS_09_5YR B01003_with_ann.csv`) has many rows that could not be populated due to the changes in the unique identifier used in the 2014 boundary data. For this reason, we will exclude the year 2009 from our analysis. You can remove the 2009 data table from the joined tables so that we don't have any issue with this later.

Now, export the joined layer as a new DBF database file, which we need to do to be able to make some final changes:

1. Ensure that only the rows with the populated data columns are selected in the tracts layer. Attribute the table (you can do this by sorting the attribute table on that field, for example).

2. Select the tracts layer from the **Layers** panel.

3. Navigate to **Layer | Save as**, fulfilling the following parameters:
   - **Format: DBF File**
   - Save only the selected features
   - Add the saved file to the map
   - **Save as**: c5/data/output/whites.dbf
   - Leave the other options as they are by default

Updating and removing fields

QGIS allows us to calculate the coordinates for the geographic features and populate an attribute field with them. On the layer for the new DBF, calculate the latitude and longitude fields in the expected format and eliminate the unnecessary fields by performing the following steps:

1. Open the **Attribute table** for the whites DBF layer and click on the **Open Field Calculator** button.

2. Calculate a new lon field and fulfill the following parameters:
   - **Output field name**: lon.
   - **Output field type: Decimal number (real)**.
   - **Output field width**: 10.
   - **Precision**: 7.
   - **Expression**: "INTPLON". You can choose this from the **Fields** and **Values** sections in the tree under the **Functions** panel.

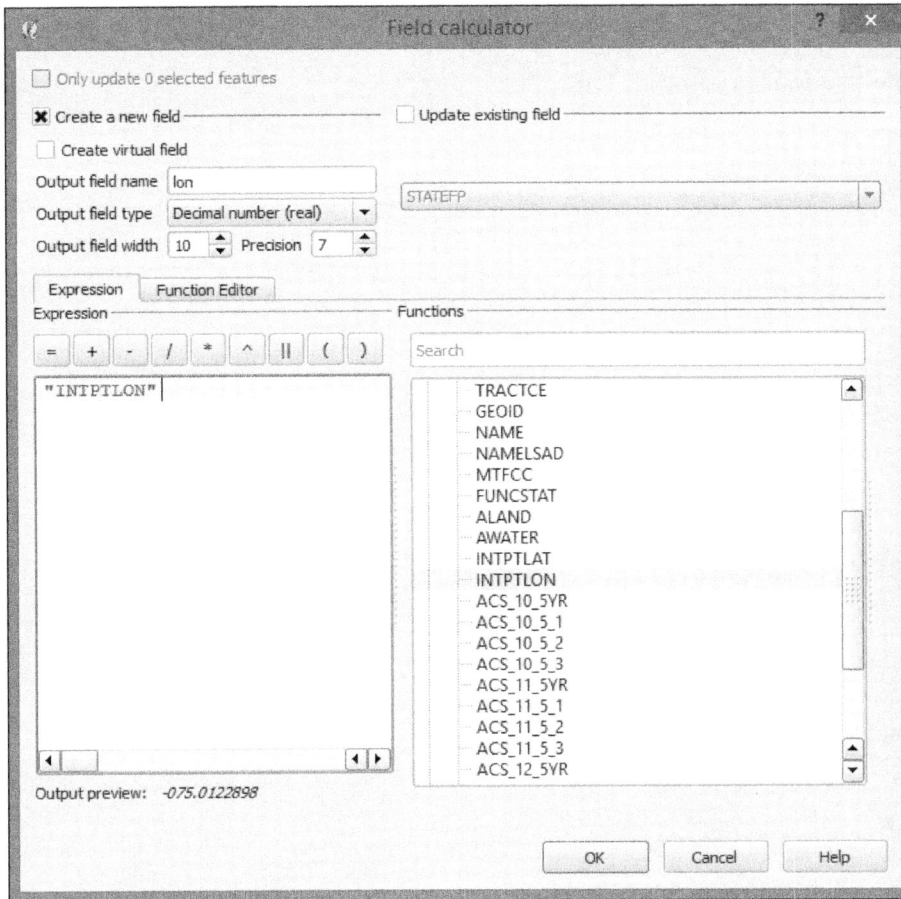

3. Repeat these steps with latitude, making a `lat` field from `INTPLAT`.

4. Create the following fields using the field calculator with the expression on the right:

   ○ **Output field name**: `name`; **Output field type**: Text; **Output field width**: 50; **Expression**: `NAMESLAD`

   ○ **Output field name**: `Jan-11`; **Output field type**: Whole number (integer); **Expression**: `"ACS_11_5_2" - "ACS_10_5_2"`

   ○ **Output field name**: `Jan-12`; **Output field type**: Whole number (integer); **Expression**: `"ACS_12_5_2" - "ACS_11_5_2"`

   ○ **Output field name**: `Jan-13`; **Output field type**: Whole number (integer); **Expression**: `"ACS_13_5_2" - "ACS_12_5_2"`

5. Remove all the old fields (except name, Jan-11, Jan-12, Jan-13, lat, and lon). This will remove all the unnecessary identification fields and those with a margin of error from the table.

6. Toggle the editing mode and save when prompted.

	lon	lat	Jan-11	Jan-12	Jan-13	name
0	-75.0122890	40.1288925	135	-274	-310	Census Tract 365...
1	-75.1804050	39.9497374	13	77	-17	Census Tract 8.01
2	-75.1637160	40.0728148	41	14	-35	Census Tract 263...
3	-75.1021540	40.0249460	113	-113	196	Census Tract 292
4	-75.1638920	40.0248284	20	-135	37	Census Tract 244
5	-75.0448280	40.0439412	-281	4	63	Census Tract 332
6	-75.0443910	40.0714709	-224	62	44	Census Tract 9802
7	-75.1466620	39.9523827	-21	158	-17	Census Tract 1
8	-75.1569770	39.9553999	48	300	-21	Census Tract 2
9	-75.1713010	39.9568346	-600	226	38	Census Tract 3
10	-75.2130770	40.0833122	-92	-69	67	Census Tract 387
11	-75.1982430	40.0571595	-212	-75	-15	Census Tract 388
12	-75.1682760	40.0543431	76	-23	114	Census Tract 389
13	-75.0927150	39.9910899	-102	3	637	Census Tract 379
14	-75.0973640	39.9963741	-133	23	99	Census Tract 382
15	-75.0807870	40.0052270	-193	51	44	Census Tract 380
16	-75.1248980	40.0108630	5	386	179	Census Tract 383
17	-75.0938840	40.0357300	-678	-164	46	Census Tract 390
18	-75.0399560	40.0189334	196	55	23	Census Tract 381
19	-75.1516020	39.9456722	43	86	171	Census Tract 10.01
20	-75.1686950	39.9532973	101	-182	-151	Census Tract 4.02
21	-75.1937460	39.9487129	290	-100	54	Census Tract 369
22	-75.1879360	39.9024981	70	118	240	Census Tract 373
23	-75.1599370	39.9129487	62	8	-4	Census Tract 372
24	-75.2332560	40.0714163	3	-56	-44	Census Tract 384
25	-75.2110910	40.0582762	45	92	-167	Census Tract 386
26	-75.2146230	40.0757528	107	-32	58	Census Tract 385
27	-75.1840640	40.0625796	103	11	236	Census Tract 255
28	-75.1883020	40.0683411	76	172	58	Census Tract 256
29	-75.1962700	40.0724586	242	56	62	Census Tract 257

Attribute table - whites :: Features total: 384, filtered: 384, selected: 0

Show All Features

Finally, export the modified table as a new CSV data table, from which we will create our map visualization. Perform the following steps:

1. Select the whites DBF layer from the **Layers** panel.

2. Navigate to **Layer | Save as** while fulfilling the following parameters:
   - **Format: Comma Separated Value [CSV]**
   - **Save as**: `c5/data/output/whites.csv`
   - Leave the other options as they were by default

The boundary data

Although we have the boundary data for the census tracts, we are only interested in visualizing the State House Districts in our application. Our stakeholders are interested in visualizing change for these districts. However, as we do not have the population data by race for these boundary units, let alone by the yearly population, we need to leverage the spatial relationship between the State House Districts and the tracts to derive this information. This is a useful workflow whenever you have the data at a different level than the geographic unit you wish to visualize or query.

Calculating the average white population change in each census tract

Now, we will construct a field that contains the average yearly change in the white population between 2010 and 2013. Perform the following steps:

1. As mentioned previously, join the total population tables (ending in `B01003_with_ann`) to the joined tract layer, `tl_2014_42_tract`, on the same **GEO. id2**, GEO fields from the new total population tables, and the tract layer respectively. Do not join the 2009 table, because we discovered that there were many null values in the join fields for the white-only version of this.

2. As before, select the 384 rows in the attribute table having the populated join columns from this table. Save only the selected rows, calling the saved shapefile dataset `tract_change` and adding this to the map.

3. Open the **Attribute table** and then open **Field Calculator**.
   - Create a new field.
   - **Output field name**: `avg_change`.
   - **Output field type: Decimal number (real)**.
   - **Output field width: 4, Precision: 2**.

○ The following expression is the difference of each year from the previous year divided by the previous year to find the fractional change. This is then divided by three to find the average over three years and finally multiplied by 100 to find the percentage, as follows:

```
((("ACS_11_5_2" - "ACS_10_5_2")/ "ACS_10_5_2" )+
  (("ACS_12_5_2" - "ACS_11_5_2")/ "ACS_11_5_2" )+
  (("ACS_13_5_2" - "ACS_12_5_2")/ "ACS_12_5_2" ))/3 * 100
```

4. After this, click on **OK**.

The spatial join in SpatiaLite

Now that we have a value for the average change in white population by tract, let's attach this to the unit of interest, which are the State House Districts. We will do this by doing a spatial join, specifically by joining all the records that intersect our House District bounds to that House District. As more than one tract will intersect each State House District, we'll need to aggregate the attribute data from the intersected tracts to match with the single district that the tracts will be joined to.

We will use SpatiaLite for doing this. Similar to PostGIS for Postgres, SpatiaLite is the spatial extension for SQLite. It is file-based; rather than requiring a continuous server listening for connections, a database is stored on a file, and client programs directly connect to it. Also, SpatiaLite comes with QGIS out of the box, making it very easy to begin to use. As with PostGIS, SpatiaLite comes with a rich set of spatial relationship functions, making it a good choice when the existing plugins do not support the relationship we are trying to model.

> SpatiaLite is usually not chosen as a database for live websites because of some limitations related to multiuser transactions—which is why CartoDB uses Postgres as its backend database.

Creating a SpatiaLite database

To do this, perform the following steps:

1. Create a new SpatiaLite database.
2. Navigate to **Layer | Create Layer | New Spatialite Layer**.
3. Using the ellipses button (**...**), browse to and create a database at `c5/data/output/district_join.sqlite`.
4. After clicking on **Save**, you will be notified that a new database has been registered. You have now created a new SpatiaLite database. You can now close this dialog.

Importing layers to SpatiaLite

To import layers to SpatiaLite, you can perform the following steps:

1. Navigate to **Database | DB Manager | DB Manage**.

2. Click on the refresh button. The new database should now be visible under the SpatiaLite section of the tree.

3. Navigate to **Table | Import layer/file** (`tract_change` and `tl_2014_42_sldl`).

4. Click on **Update options**.

5. Select **Create single-part geometries instead of multi-part**.

6. Select **Create spatial index**.

7. Click on **OK** to finish importing the table to the database (you may need to hit the refresh button again for table to be indicated as imported).

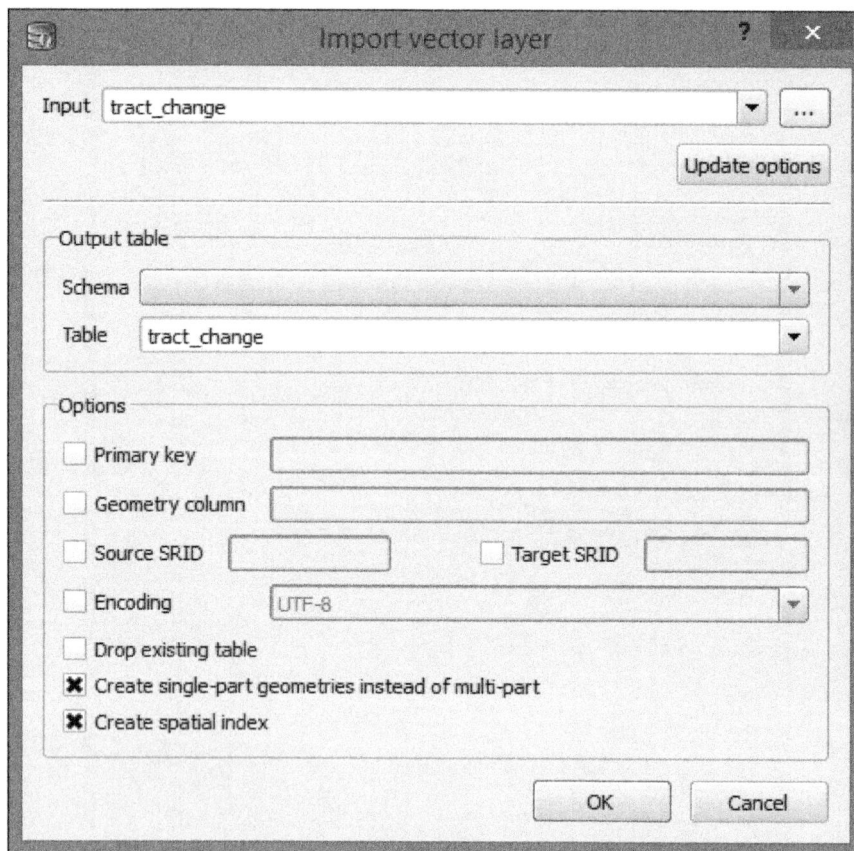

Now, repeat these steps with the House Districts layer (`tl_2014_42_sldl`), and deselect **Create single-part geometries instead of multi-part** as this seems to cause an error with this file, perhaps due to some part of a multi-part feature that would not be able to remain on its own under the SpatiaLite data requirements.

Querying and loading the SpatiaLite layer from the DB Manager

Next, we use the DB Manager to query the SpatiaLite database, adding the results to the QGIS layers panel.

We will use the `MBRIntersects` criteria here, which provides a performance advantage over a regular `Intersects` function as it only checks for the intersection of the extent (bounding box). In this example, we are dealing with a few features of limited complexity that are not done dynamically during a web request, so this shortcut does not provide a major advantage — we do this here so as to demonstrate its use for more complicated datasets.

1. If it isn't already open, open **DB Manager**.

2. Navigate to **Database | SQL window**.

   ○   Fill the respective input fields in the **SQL query** dialog:

- ◦ The following SQL query selects the fields from the `tract_change` and `tl_2014_42_sldl` (State Legislative District) tables, where they overlap. It also performs an aggregate (average) of the change by the State Legislative Districts overlying the census tract boundaries:

```
SELECT t1.pk, t1.namelsad, t1.geom, avg(t2.avg_change)*1.0
  as avg_change
FROM   tl_2014_42_sldl AS t1, tract_change AS t2
WHERE MbrIntersects(t1.geom, t2.geom) = 1
GROUP BY t1.pk;
```

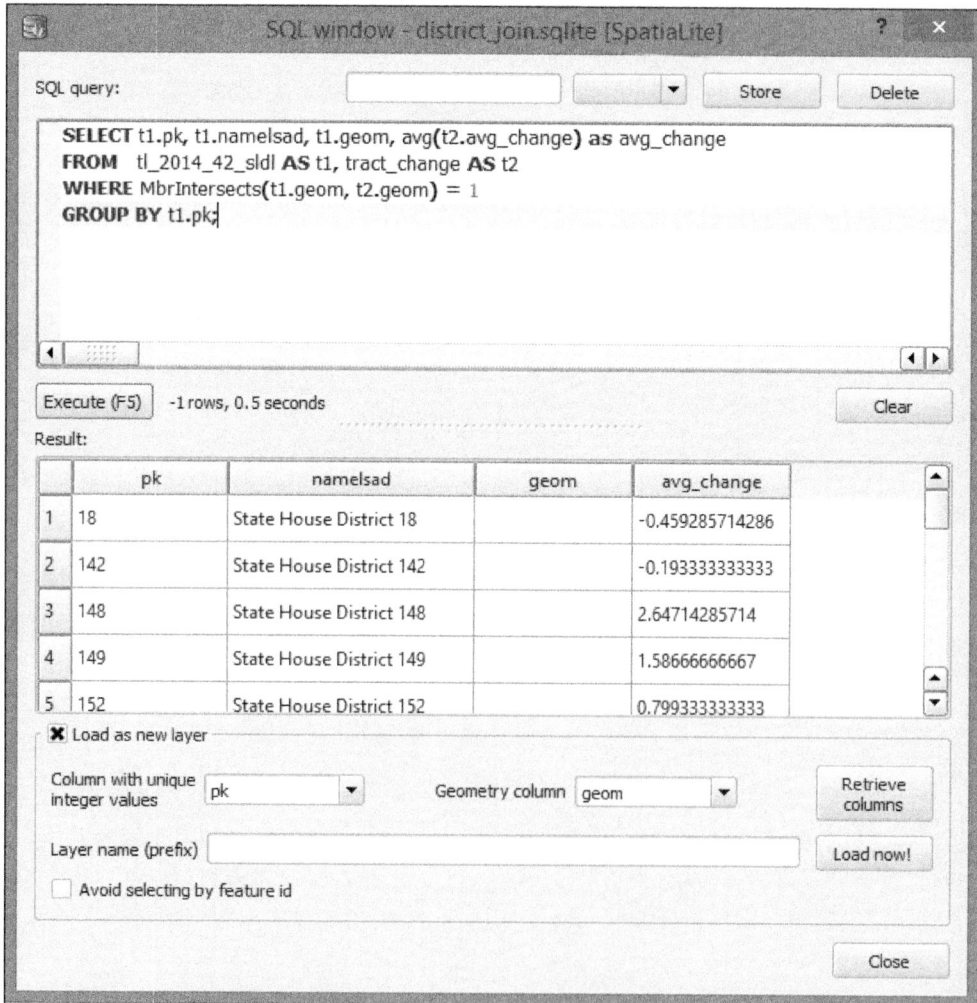

3. Then, click on **Load now!**.

4. You will be prompted to select a value for the **Column with unique integer values** field. For this, select **pk**.

5. You will also be prompted to select a value for the **Geometry column** field; for this, select **geom**.

The symbolized result of the spatial relationship join showing the average white population change over a 4-year period for the State House Districts' census tracts intersection will look something similar to the following image:

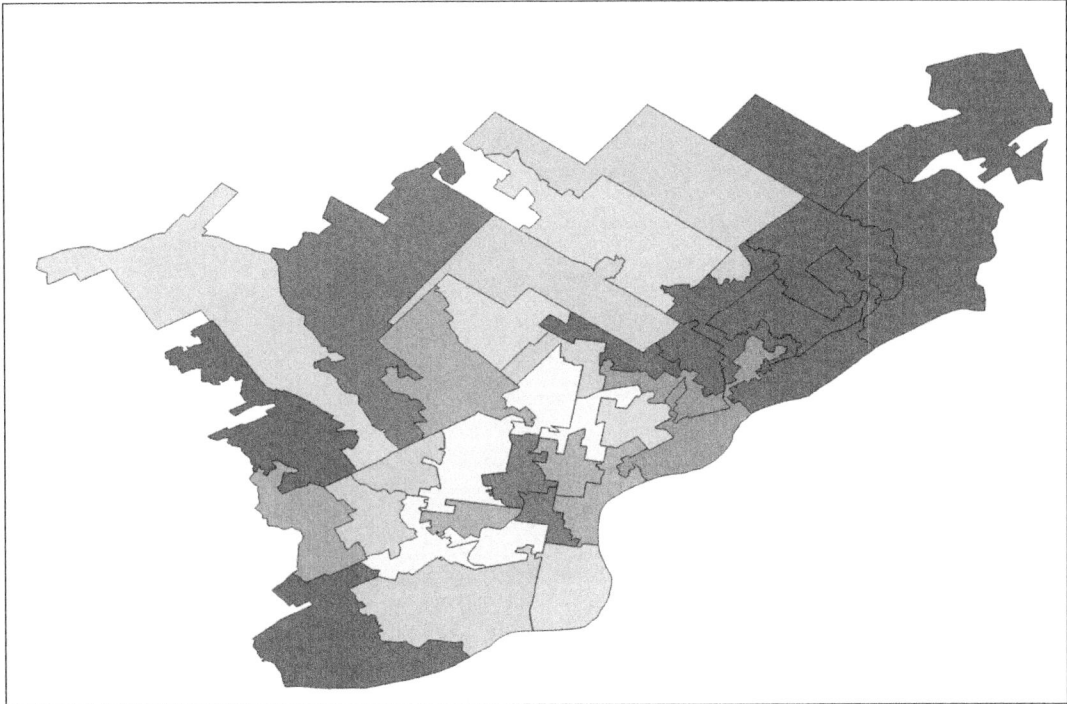

TopoJSON

Next, we will move on to preparing this data relationship for the Web and its spatiotemporal visualization.

TopoJSON is a variant of JSON, which uses the topological relationships between the geometric features to greatly reduce the size of the vector data and thereby improves the browser's rendering performance and reduces the risk of delay due to data transfers.

An example of GeoJSON

The following code is an example of GeoJSON, showing two of our State House Districts. The format is familiar—based on our previous work with JSON—with sets of coordinates that define a polygonal area grouped together. The repeated sections are marked by ellipses (…).

```
{
  "type": "FeatureCollection",
  "crs": { "type": "name", "properties": { "name":
"urn:ogc:def:crs:OGC:1.3:CRS84" } },

  "features": [
    { "type": "Feature", "properties": { "STATEFP": "42", "SLDLST":
"181", "GEOID": "42181", "NAMELSAD": "State House District
181", "LSAD": "LL", "LSY": "2014", "MTFCC": "G5220", "FUNCSTAT":
"N", "ALAND": 8587447.000000, "AWATER": 0.000000, "INTPTLAT":
"+39.9796799", "INTPTLON": "-075.1533540" }, "geometry": { "type":
"Polygon", "coordinates": [ [ [ -75.176782, 39.987337 ], [ … ] ]] } },
{…}]}
```

An example of TopoJSON

The following code is the corresponding representation of the same two State House Districts in TopoJSON, as discussed earlier.

Although this example uses the same coordinate system (WGS84/EPSG:4326) as that used before, it is expressed as simple pairs of abstract space coordinates. These are ultimately transformed into the WGS coordinate system using the scale and translate data in the transform section of the data.

By taking advantage of the shared topological relationships between geometric objects, the amount of data can be drastically reduced from 21K to 7K. That's a reduction of 2/3! You will see in the following code that each polygon is not clearly represented on its own but rather through these topological relationships. The repeated sections are marked by ellipses (…).

```
{"type":"Topology","objects":{"geojson":{"type":"GeometryCollection","
crs":{"type":"name","properties":{"name":"urn:ogc:def:crs:OGC:1.3:CRS
84"}},"geometries":[{"type":"Polygon","properties":{"STATEFP":"42","S
LDLST":"181","GEOID":"42181","NAMELSAD":"State House District 181","LS
AD":"LL","LSY":"2014","MTFCC":"G5220","FUNCSTAT":"N","ALAND":8587447
,"AWATER":0,"INTPTLAT":"+39.9796799","INTPTLON":"-075.1533540"},"arcs-
":[[0,1]]},{"type":"Polygon","properties":{"STATEFP":"42","SLDLST":
"197","GEOID":"42197","NAMELSAD":"State House District 197","LSAD":
"LL","LSY":"2014","MTFCC":"G5220","FUNCSTAT":"N","ALAND":8251026,"A
WATER":23964,"INTPTLAT":"+40.0054726","INTPTLON":"-075.1405813"},"-
arcs":[[-1,2]]}]}},"arcs":[[[903,5300],[…]]]],"transform":{"sca
le":[0.000006659365934984,0.000006594359435944118],"transla
te":[-75.176782,39.961088]}}
```

Vector simplification

Similar to TopoJSON, Vector simplification removes the nodes in a line or polygon layer and will often greatly increase the browser's rendering performance while decreasing the file size and network transfer time.

As the vector shapes can have an infinite level of complexity, in theory, simplification methods can decrease the complexity by more than 99 percent while still preserving the perceivable shape of the geometry. In reality, the level of complexity at which perception becomes significantly affected will almost never be this high; however, it is common to have a very acceptable perception change at 90 percent complexity loss. The more sophisticated simplification methods have improved results.

Simplification methods

A number of simplification methods are commonly in use, each having strengths for particular data characteristics and outcomes. If one does not produce a good result, you can always try another. In addition to the method itself, you will also usually be asked to define a threshold parameter for an acceptable amount of complexity loss, as defined by the percentage of complexity lost, area, or some other measure.

- **Douglas-Peucker**: In this, the threshold affects the distance from which the original lines and edges of the polygons are allowed to change. This is useful when the nodes to be simplified are densely located but can lead to "pointy" simplifications.

- **Visvalingam / effective area**: In this, the point forming the triangle having the least area with two adjacent points is removed. The threshold affects how many times this criterion is applied. This has been described by Mike Bostock, the creator of TopoJSON among other things, as simplification with the criteria of the least perceptible change.

- **Visvalingam / weighted area**: In this, the point forming the vertex with the most acute angle is removed. The threshold affects how many times this criterion is applied. This method provides the "smoothest" result, as it specifically targets the "spikes".

The Visvalingam effective area method is the only method of simplification offered in the TopoJSON command-line tool that we will use. Mapshaper, a web-based tool that we will take a look at offers all these three methods but uses the weighted area method by default.

Other options

Other options affecting the data size are often offered alongside the simplification methods.

- **Repair intersections:** This option will repair the simplifications that cause the lines or polygon edges to intersect.

- **Prevent shape removal:** This option will prevent the simplification that would cause the removal of the (usually small) polygon shapes.

- **Quantization:** Quantization controls the precision of the coordinates. This is easier to think about when we are dealing with the coordinates in linear units. For obvious reasons, you may want to extend the precision to 1/5000 of a mile — getting the approximate foot precision. Also obviously, great precision comes at the cost of greater data size, so you should not overquantize where the application or source does not support such precision.

Simplifying for TopoJSON

Both Web and desktop TopoJSON conversion tools that we will use support these simplification options. That way, you can simplify a polygon at the same time as you reduce the data size through the topological relationship notation.

Simplifying for other outputs

If you wish to produce data other than for TopoJSON, you will need to find another way to do the simplification.

QGIS provides **Simplify Geometries** out of the box (navigate to **Vector | Geometry Tools | Simplify Geometries**), which does a Douglas-Peucker simplification. While it is the most popular method, it may not be the most effective one (see the following section for more).

The Simplify plugin offers a Visalvingam method in addition to Douglas-Peuker.

Converting to TopoJSON

There are a few options for writing TopoJSON. We will take a look at one for the desktop, which requires a software installation, and one via the web browser. As you might imagine, the desktop option will be more stable for doing anything in a customized way, which the web browser does not support, and is also more stable with the more complex feature sets. The web browser has the advantage of not requiring an install.

Web mapshaper

You can use the web-based **mapshaper** software from `http://www.mapshaper.org/` to convert from shapefile and other formats to TopoJSON and vice versa. Perform the following steps to convert the State Legislative Districts shapefile to TopoJSON:

1. Open your browser and navigate to the mapshaper website.

2. Optionally, select a different simplification method or try other options. This is not necessary for this example.

3. Browse to select the Philadelphia State Legislative Districts shapefile (`c5/data/original/tl_2014_42_sldl/tl_2014_42_sldl.shp`) from your local computer or drag a file in. As the page indicates, Shapefile, GeoJSON, and TopoJSON are supported.

4. Optionally, choose a simplification proportion from the slider bar (again, this is not needed for this example).

5. Export as TopoJSON by clicking on the **Export** button at the top.

You will get the following screen in your browser:

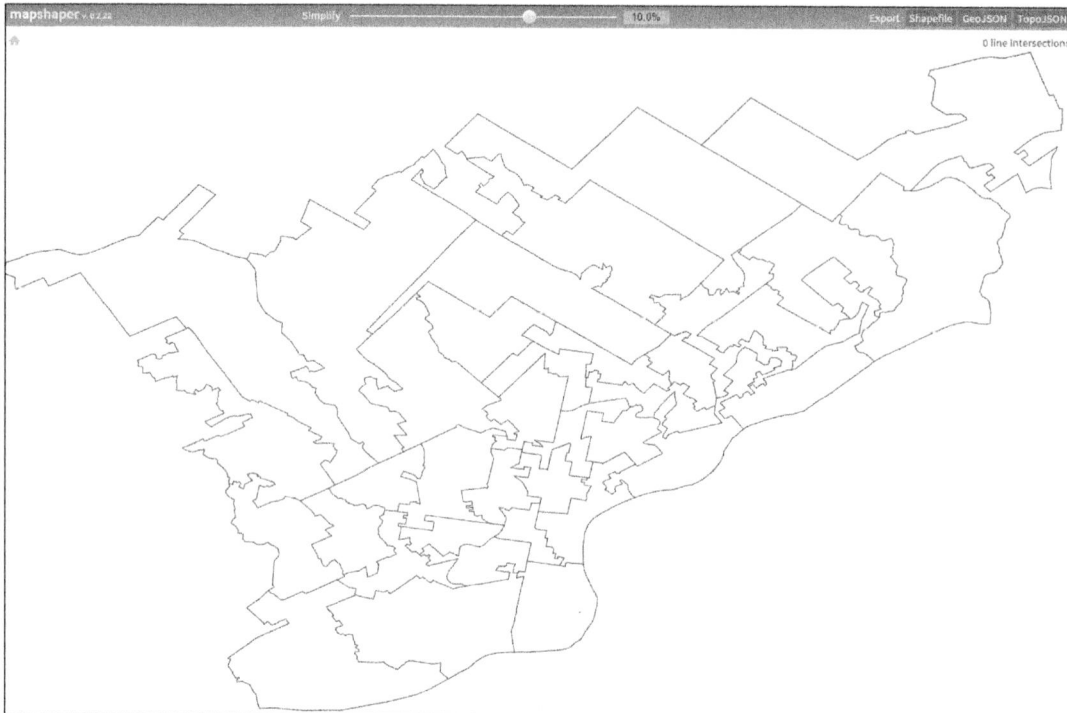

The command-line tool

The command-line tool is useful if you are working with a larger or more complicated dataset. The downside is that it requires that you install Node.js as it is a node package. For our purposes, Node.js is similar to Python. It is an interpreter environment for JavaScript, allowing the programs written in JavaScript to be run locally. In addition, it includes a package manager to install the needed dependencies. It also includes a web server—essentially running JavaScript as a server-side language.

Perform the following steps:

1. Install Node.js from `https://nodejs.org/`.
2. Open your OS command line (for example, on Windows, run cmd).
3. Input the following in the command line:
   ```
   >npm install -g topojson
   ```
4. Navigate to `cd c:\packt\c5\data\output` and input the following:
   ```
   >topojson -p -o house_district.json house_district.shp
   ```

You will now get the following output:

```
c:\packt\c5\data\temp>topojson -p -o house_district.json house_district.shp
bounds: -75.463053 39.848782 -74.869303 40.224734999999995 (spherical)
pre-quantization: 0.0660m (5.94e-7°) 0.0418m (3.76e-7°)
topology: 105 arcs, 16475 points
post-quantization: 6.60m (0.0000594°) 4.18m (0.0000376°)
prune: retained 105 / 105 arcs (100%)
```

Mapshaper also has a command-line tool, which we did not evaluate here.

The D3 data visualization library

D3 is a JavaScript library used for building the visualizations from the **Document Object Model (DOM)** present in all the modern web browsers.

What is D3?

In more detail, D3 manipulates the DOM into abstract vector visualization components, some of which have been further tailed to certain visualization types, such as maps. It provides us with the ability of parsing from some common data sources and binding, especially to the SVG and canvas elements that are designed to be manipulated for vector graphics.

Some fundamentals

There are a few basic aspects of D3 that are useful for you to understand before we begin. As D3 is not specifically built for geographic data, but rather for general data visualization, it tends to look at geographic data visualization more abstractly. Data must be parsed from its original format into a D3 object and rendered into the graphic space as an SVG or canvas element with a vector shape type. It must then be projected using relative mapping between the graphic space and a geographic coordinate system, scaled in relation to the graphic space and the geographic extent, and bound to a web object. This all must be done in relation to a D3 cursor of sorts, which handles the current scope that D3 is working in with keywords like "begin" and "end".

Parsing

We will be parsing through the d3.json and d3.csv methods. We use the callbacks of these methods to wrap the code that we want to be executed after the external data has been parsed into a JavaScript object.

Graphic elements, SVG, path, and Canvas

D3 makes heavy use of the two vector graphic elements in HTML5: SVG and Canvas. **Scaleable Vector Graphics (SVG)** is a mature technology for rendering vector graphics in the browser. It has seen some advancement in cross-browser support recently. Canvas is new to HTML5 and may offer better performance than SVG. Both, being DOM elements, are written directly as a subset of the larger HTML document rendered by the browser. Here, we will use SVG.

Projection

D3 is a bit unusual where geographic visualization libraries are concerned, in that it requires very little functionality specific to geographic data. The main geographic method provided is through the path element, projection, as D3 has its own concept of coordinate space, coordinates of the browser window and elements inside it.

Here is an example of projection. In the first line, we set the projection as Mercator. This allows us to center the map in familiar spherical latitude longitude coordinates. The scale property allows us to then zoom closer to the extent that we are interested in.

```
var projection = d3.geo.mercator()
   .center([-75.166667,40.03])
   .scale(60000);
```

Shape generator

You must configure a shape generator to bind to the d attribute of an SVG. This will tell the element how to draw the data that has been bound to it.

The main shape generator that we will use with the maps is path. Circle is also used in the following example, though its use is more complicated.

The following code creates a path shape generator, assigns it a projection, and stores it all in variable path:

```
var path = d3.geo.path()
   .projection(projection);
```

Scales

Scales allow the mapping of a domain of real data; say you have values of 1 through 100, in a range of possible values, and say you want everything down to numbers from 1 through 5. The most useful purpose of scales in mapping is to associate a range of values with a range of colors. The following code maps a set of values to a range of colors, mapping in-between values to intermediate colors:

```
var color = d3.scale.linear()
  .domain([-.5, 0, 2.66])
    .range(["#FFEBEB", "#FFFFEB", "#E6FFFF"]);
```

Binding

After a data object has been parsed into the DOM, it can be bound to a D3 object through its data or datum attribute.

Select, Select All, Enter, Return, Exit, Insert, and Append

In order to select the potentially existing elements, you will use the Select and Select All keywords. Then, based on whether you expect the elements to already be existent, you will use the Enter (if it is not yet existent), Return (if it is already existent), and Exit (if you wish to remove it) keywords to change the interaction with the element.

Here's an example of Select All, which uses the Enter keyword. The data from the `house_district` JSON, which was previously parsed, is loaded through the d attribute of the path element and assigned the path shape generator. In addition, a function is set on the `fill` attribute, which returns a color from the linear color scale:

```
map.selectAll("path")
  .data(topojson.feature(phila, phila.objects.house_district)
    .features)
  .enter()
    .append("path")
    .attr("vector-effect","non-scaling-stroke")
    .style("fill", function(d) { return color
      (d.properties.d_avg_change); })
    .attr("d", path);
```

Animated time series map

Through the following steps, we will produce an animated time series map with D3. We will start by moving our data to a filesystem path that we will use:

1. Move `whites.csv` to `c5/data/web/csv`.

2. Move `house_district.json` to `c5/data/web/json`.

The development environment

Start the Python HTTP server using the code from *Chapter 1, Exploring Places – from Concept to Interface*, (refer to the *Parsing the JSON data* section from *Chapter 7, Mapping for Enterprises and Communities*). This is necessary for this example, since the typical cross-site scripting protection on the browsers would block the loading of the JSON files from the local filesystem.

You will find the following files and directory structure under `c5/data/web`:

`./`	`index.html`
`./css/`	`main.css`
`./csv/`	`whites.csv` (you moved this here)
`./images/`	Various supporting images
`./js/`	`main.js`
`./json/`	`house_district.json` (you moved this here)
`./lib/`	• `d3.slider.js` • `d3.slider.css` • `d3.v3.min.js` • `topojson.v1.min.js`

Code

The following code, mostly JavaScript, will provide a time-based animation of our geographic objects through D3. This code is largely based on the one found at TIP Strategies' Geography of Jobs map found at `http://tipstrategies.com/geography-of-jobs/`. The main code file is at `c5/data/web/js/main.js`.

Note the reference to the CSV and TopoJSON files that we created earlier: `whites.csv` and `house_district.json`.

main.js

All of the following JavaScript code is in `./js/main.js`. All our customizations to this code will be done in this file:

```javascript
var width = 960,
  height = 600;

//sets up the transformation from map coordinates to DOM
  coordinates
var projection = d3.geo.mercator()
  .center([-75.166667,40.03])
  .scale(60000);

//the shape generator
var path = d3.geo.path()
  .projection(projection);

var svg = d3.select("#map-container").append("svg")
  .attr("width", width)
  .attr("height", height);

var g = svg.append("g");

g.append( "rect" )
  .attr("width",width)
  .attr("height",height)
  .attr("fill","white")
  .attr("opacity",0)
  .on("mouseover",function(){
    hoverData = null;
    if ( probe ) probe.style("display","none");
  })

var map = g.append("g")
  .attr("id","map");

var probe,
  hoverData;

var dateScale, sliderScale, slider;

var format = d3.format(",");

  var months = ["Jan"],
```

```
        months_full = ["January"],
        orderedColumns = [],
        currentFrame = 0,
        interval,
        frameLength = 1000,
        isPlaying = false;

var sliderMargin = 65;

function circleSize(d){
  return Math.sqrt( .02 * Math.abs(d) );
};

//color scale
var color = d3.scale.linear()
  .domain([-.5, 0, 2.66])
    .range(["#FFEBEB", "#FFFFEB", "#E6FFFF"]);

//parse house_district.json TopoJSON, reference color scale and
  other styles
d3.json("json/house_district.json", function(error, phila) {
  map.selectAll("path")
    .data(topojson.feature(phila, phila.objects.house_district)
      .features)
      .enter()
      .append("path")
      .attr("vector-effect","non-scaling-stroke")
      .attr("class","land")
      .style("fill", function(d) { return color(d.properties.
        d_avg_change); })
      .attr("d", path);

  //add a path element for district outlines
  map.append("path")
    .datum(topojson.mesh(phila, phila.objects.house_district,
      function(a, b) { return a !== b; }))
      .attr("class", "state-boundary")
      .attr("vector-effect","non-scaling-stroke")
      .attr("d", path);

  //probe is for popups
  probe = d3.select("#map-container").append("div")
    .attr("id","probe");

  d3.select("body")
```

```
    .append("div")
    .attr("id","loader")
    .style("top",d3.select("#play").node().offsetTop + "px")
    .style("height",d3.select("#date").node().offsetHeight +
      d3.select("#map-container").node().offsetHeight + "px");

//load and parse whites.csv
d3.csv("csv/whites.csv",function(data){
  var first = data[0];
  // get columns
  for ( var mug in first ){
    if ( mug != "name" && mug != "lat" && mug != "lon" ){
      orderedColumns.push(mug);
    }
  }
}

orderedColumns.sort( sortColumns );

// draw city points
for ( var i in data ){
  var projected = projection([ parseFloat(data[i].lon),
    parseFloat(data[i].lat) ])
  map.append("circle")
    .datum( data[i] )
    .attr("cx",projected[0])
    .attr("cy",projected[1])
    .attr("r",1)
    .attr("vector-effect","non-scaling-stroke")
    .on("mousemove",function(d){
      hoverData = d;
      setProbeContent(d);
      probe
      .style( {
        "display" : "block",
        "top" : (d3.event.pageY - 80) + "px",
        "left" : (d3.event.pageX + 10) + "px"
      })
    })
    .on("mouseout",function(){
      hoverData = null;
      probe.style("display","none");
    })
  }
```

```
createLegend();

dateScale = createDateScale(orderedColumns).range([0,3]);

createSlider();

d3.select("#play")
  .attr("title","Play animation")
  .on("click",function(){
    if ( !isPlaying ){
      isPlaying = true;
      d3.select(this).classed("pause",true).attr
        ("title","Pause animation");
      animate();
    } else {
      isPlaying = false;
      d3.select(this).classed("pause",false).attr
        ("title","Play animation");
      clearInterval( interval );
    }
  });

drawMonth( orderedColumns[currentFrame] ); // initial map

window.onresize = resize;
 resize();

d3.select("#loader").remove();

})

});
```

Output

The finished product, which you can view by opening index.html in a web browser, is an animated set of points controlled by a timeline showing the change in the white population by the census tract. This data is displayed on top of the House Districts, colored from cool to hot by the change in the white population per year, and averaged over three periods of change (2010-11, 2011-12, and 2012-13). Our map application output, animated with a timeline, will look similar to this:

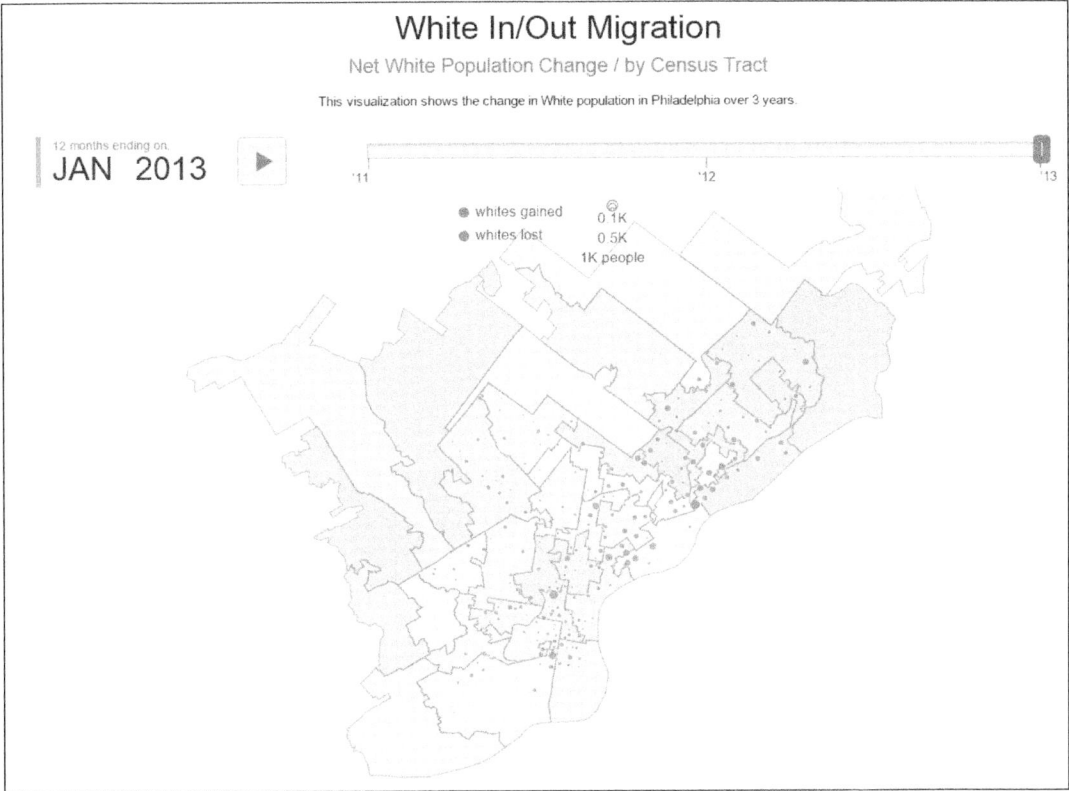

Summary

In this chapter, using an elections example, we covered spatial temporal data visualization and spatial relationship data integration. We also converted the data to TopoJSON, a format associated with D3, which greatly improves performance. We also created a spatial temporal animated web application through the D3 visualization library. In the next chapter, we will explore the interpolation to find the unknown values, the use of tiling, and the UTFGrid method to improve the performance with more complicated datasets.

Estimating Unknown Values

6

In this chapter, we will use interpolation methods to estimate the unknown values at one location based on the known values at other locations.

Interpolation is a technique to estimate unknown values entirely on their geographic relationship with known location values. As space can be measured with infinite precision, data measurement is always limited by the data collector's finite resources. Interpolation and other more sophisticated spatial estimation techniques are useful to estimate the values at the locations that have not been measured. In this chapter, you will learn how to interpolate the values in weather station data, which will be scored and used in a model of vulnerability to a particular agricultural condition: mildew. We've made the weather data a subset to provide a month in the year during which vulnerability is usually historically high. An end user could use this application to do a ground truthing of the model, which is, matching high or low predicted vulnerability with the presence or absence of mildew. If the model were to be extended historically or to near real time, the application could be used to see the trends in vulnerability over time or to indicate that a grower needs to take action to prevent mildew. The parameters, including precipitation, relative humidity, and temperature, have been selected for use in the real models that predict the vulnerability of fields and crops to mildew.

In this chapter, we will cover the following topics:

- Adding data from MySQL
- Using the NetCDF multidimensional data format
- Interpolating the unknown values for visualization and reporting
- Applying a simple algebraic risk model
- Python GDAL wrappers to filter and update through SQLite queries
- Interpolation
- Map algebra modeling

- Sampling a raster grid with a layer of gridded points
- Python CGI Hosting
- Testing and debugging during the CGI development
- The Python SpatiaLite/SQLite3 wrapper
- Generating an **OpenLayers3** (**OL3**) map with the QGIS plugin
- Adding AJAX Interactivity to an OL3 map
- Dynamic response in the OL3 pixel popup

Importing the data

Often, the data to be used in a highly interactive, dynamic web application is stored in an existing enterprise database. Although these are not the usual spatial databases, they contain coordinate locations, which can be easily leveraged in a spatial application.

Connecting and importing from MySQL in QGIS

The following section is provided as an illustration only—database installation and setup are needlessly time consuming for a short demonstration of their use.

> If you do wish to install and set up MySQL, you can download it from `http://dev.mysql.com/downloads/`. MySQL Community Server is freely available under the open source GPL license. You will want to install MySQL Workbench and MySQL Utilities, which are also available at this location, for interaction with your new MySQL Community Server instance. You can then restore the database used in this demonstration using the Data Import/Restore command with the provided backup file (`c6/original/packt.sql`) from MySQL Workbench.

To connect to and add data from your MySQL database to your QGIS project, you need to do the following (again, as this is for demonstration only, it does not require database installation and setup):

1. Navigate to **Layer | Add Layer | Add vector layer**.
   - ° **Source type**: **Database**
   - ° **Type**: **MySQL**, as shown in the following screenshot:

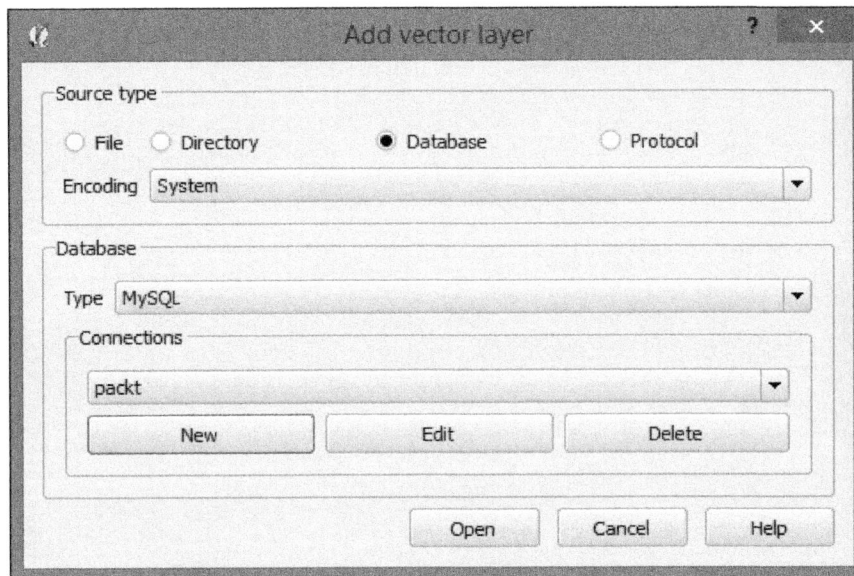

2. Once you've indicated that you wish to add a MySQL Database layer, you will have the option to create a new connection. In **Connections**, click on **New**. In the dialog that opens, enter the following parameters, which we would have initially set up when we created our MySQL Database and imported the .sql backup of the packt schema:
   - ° **Name**: packt
   - ° **Host**: localhost
   - ° **Database**: packt
   - ° **Port**: 3306
   - ° **Username**: packt

◦ **Password**: `packt`, as shown in the following screenshot:

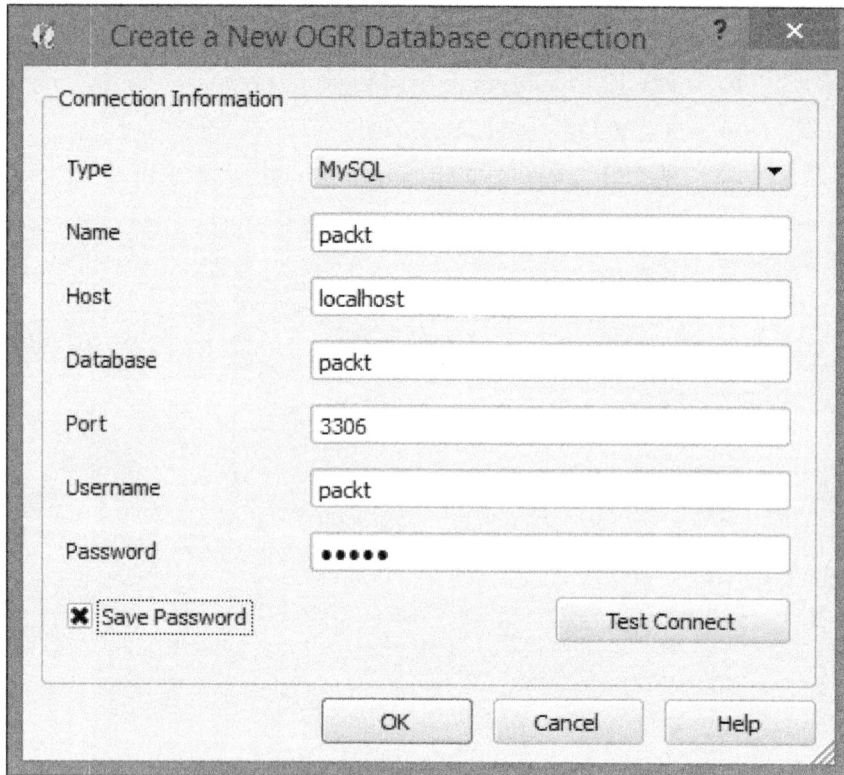

3. Click on **Test Connect**.
4. Click on **OK**.
5. Click on **Open**, and the **Select vector layers to add** dialog will appear.
6. From the **Select vector layers** dialog, click on **Select All**. This includes the following layers:
   ◦ `fields`
   ◦ `precipitation`
   ◦ `relative_humidity`
   ◦ `temperature`
7. Click on **OK**.

The layers (actually just the data tables) from the MySQL Database will now appear in the QGIS Layers panel of your project.

Converting to spatial format

The fields layer (table) is only one of the four tables we added to our project with latitude and longitude fields. We want this table to be recognized by QGIS as geospatial data and these coordinate pairs to be plotted in QGIS. Perform the following steps:

1. Export the fields layer as CSV by right–clicking on the layer under the **Layers** panel and then clicking on **Save as**.

2. In the **Save vector layer as...** dialog, perform the following steps:

    1. Click on **Browse** to choose a filesystem path to store the new .csv file. This file is included in the data under c6/data/output/fields.csv.

    2. For **GEOMETRY**, select **<Default>**.

    3. All the other default fields can remain as they are given.

    4. Click on **OK** to save the new CSV, as shown in the following screenshot:

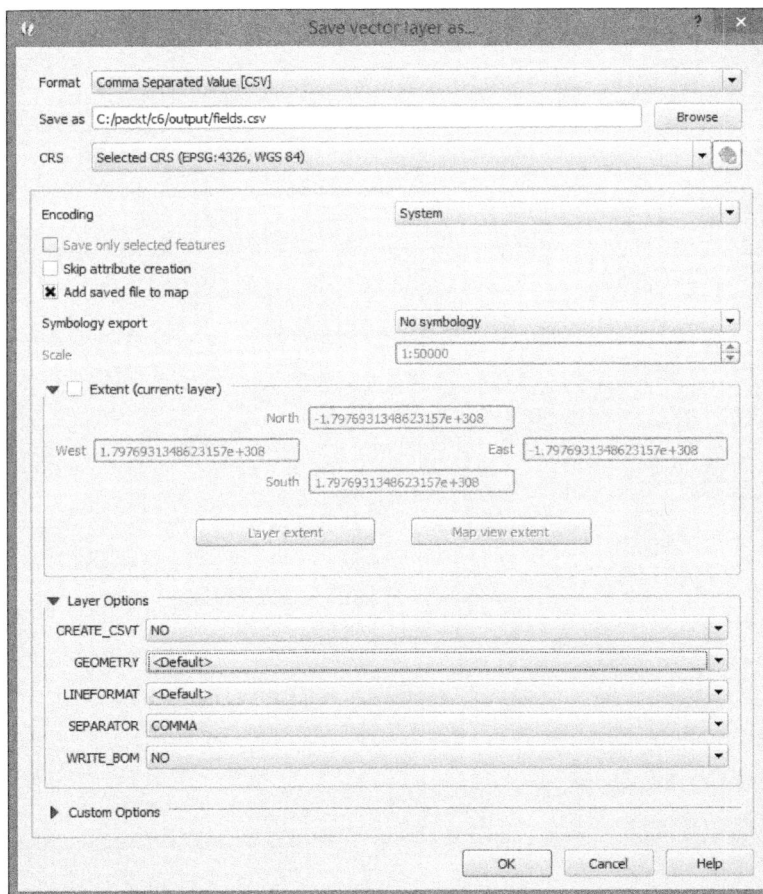

Now, to import the CSV with the coordinate fields that are recognized as geospatial data and to plot the locations, perform the following steps:

1. From the **Layer** menu, navigate to **Add Layer | Add Delimited Text Layer**.

2. **In Create a Layer from the Delimited Text File** dialog, perform the following steps:

    1. Click on the **Browse...** button to browse the location where you previously saved your fields.csv file (for example, `c6/data/output/fields.csv`).

    2. All the other parameters should be correctly populated by default. Take a look at the following image.

    3. Click on **OK** to create the new layer in your QGIS project.

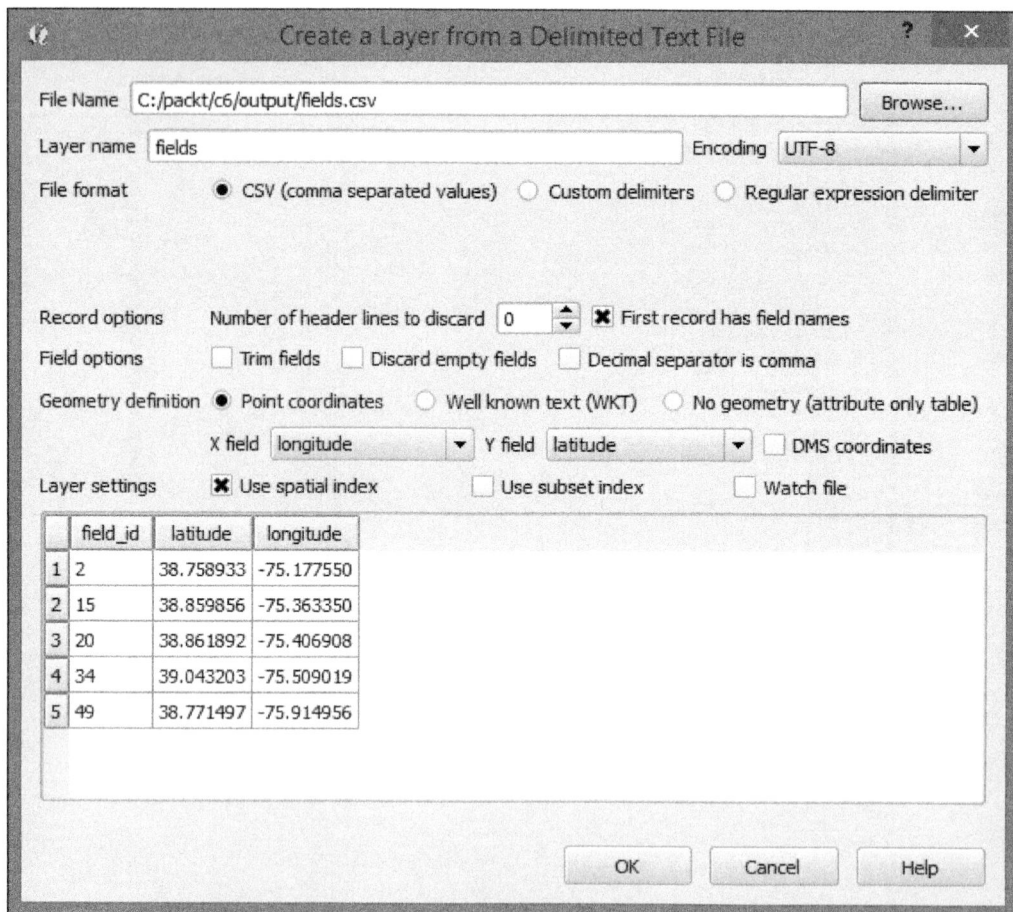

You will receive a notification that as no coordinate system was detected in this file, WGS 1984 was assigned. This is the correct coordinate system in our case, so no further intervention is necessary. After you dismiss this message, you will see the fields locations plotted on your map. If you don't, right–click on the new layer and select **Zoom to Layer**.

Note that this new layer is not reflected in a new file on the filesystem but is only stored with this QGIS project. This would be a good time to save your project.

Finally, join the other the other tables (`precipitation`, `relative_humidity`, and `temperature`) to the new plotted layer (fields) using the `field_id` field from each table one at a time. For a refresher on how to do this, refer to the *Table join* section of *Chapter 1, Exploring Places – from Concept to Interface*. To export each layer as separate shapefiles, right-click on each (`precipitation`, `relative_humidity`, and `temperature`), click on **Save as**, populate the path on which you want to save, and then save them.

The layer/table relations

The newer versions of QGIS support layer/table relations, which would allow us to model the one-to-many relationship between our locations, and an abstract measurement class that would include all the parameters. However, the use of table relationships is limited to a preliminary exploration of the relationships between layer objects and tables. The layer/table relationships are not recognized by any processing functions. Perform the following steps to explore the many-to-many layer/table relationships:

1. Add a relation by navigating to **Project | Project Properties | Relations**. The following image is what you will see once the relationships to the three tables are established:

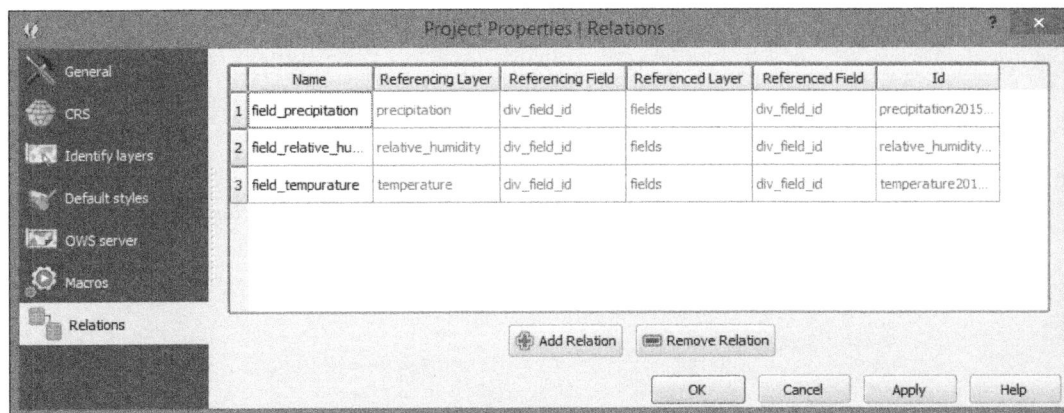

		Name	Referencing Layer	Referencing Field	Referenced Layer	Referenced Field	Id
General	1	field_precipitation	precipitation	div_field_id	fields	div_field_id	precipitation2015...
CRS	2	field_relative_hu...	relative_humidity	div_field_id	fields	div_field_id	relative_humidity...
Identify layers	3	field_tempurature	temperature	div_field_id	fields	div_field_id	temperature201...

Project Properties | Relations

Default styles

OWS server

Macros

Relations

Add Relation   Remove Relation

OK   Cancel   Apply   Help

2. To add a relation, select a nonlayer table (for example, **precipitation**) in the **Referencing Layer (Child)** field and a location table (for example, **fields**) in the **Referenced Layer (Parent)** field. Use the common **Id** field (for example, field_id), which references the layer, to relate the tables. The name field can be filled arbitrarily, as shown in the following screenshot:

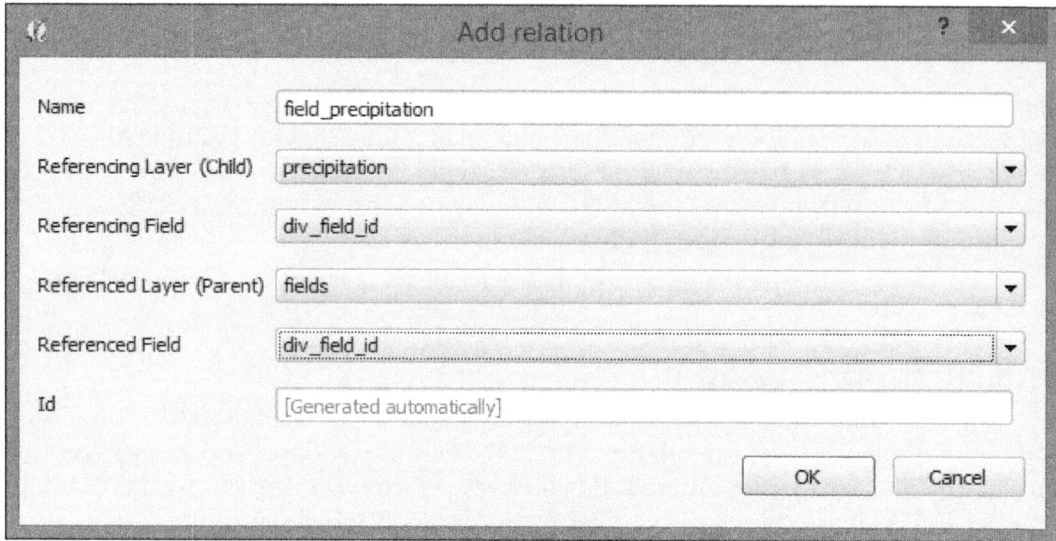

3. Now, to use the relation, click on a geographic object in the parent layer using the identify tool (you need to check **Auto open form** in the identify tool options panel). You'll see all the child entities (rows) connected to this object.

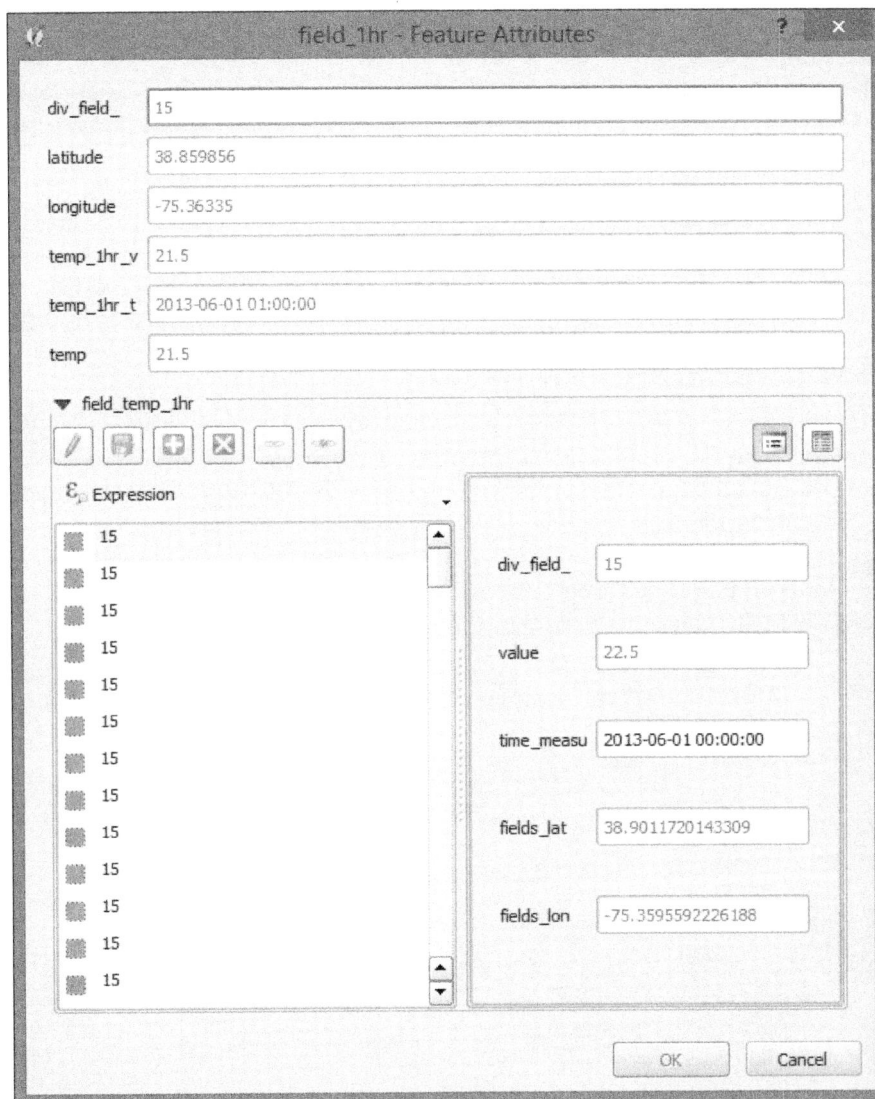

NetCDF

Network Common Data Form (NetCDF) is a standard—and powerful—format for environmental data, such as meteorological data. NetCDF's strong suit is holding multidimensional data. With its abstract concept of dimension, NetCDF can handle the dimensions of latitude, longitude, and time in the same way that it handles other often physical, continuous, and ordinal data scales, such as air pressure levels.

For this project, we used the monthly global gridded high-resolution station (land) data for air temperature and precipitation from 1901-2010, which the NetCDF University of Delaware maintains as part of a collaboration with NOAA. You can download further data from this source at `http://www.esrl.noaa.gov/psd/data/gridded/data.UDel_AirT_Precip.html`.

Viewing NetCDF in QGIS

While there is a plugin available, NetCDF can be viewed directly in QGIS, in GDAL via the command line, and in the QGIS Python Console. Perform the following steps:

1. Navigate to **Layer** | **Add Raster Layer**.

2. Browse to `c6/data/original/air.mon.mean.v301.nc` and add this layer.

3. Use the path **Raster** | **Miscellaneous** > **Information** to find the range of the values in a band. In the initial dialog, click on **OK** to go to the information dialog and then look for `air_valid_range`. You can see this information highlighted in the following image. Although QGIS's classifier will calculate the range for you, it is often thrown off by a numeric nodata value, which will typically skew the range to the lower end.

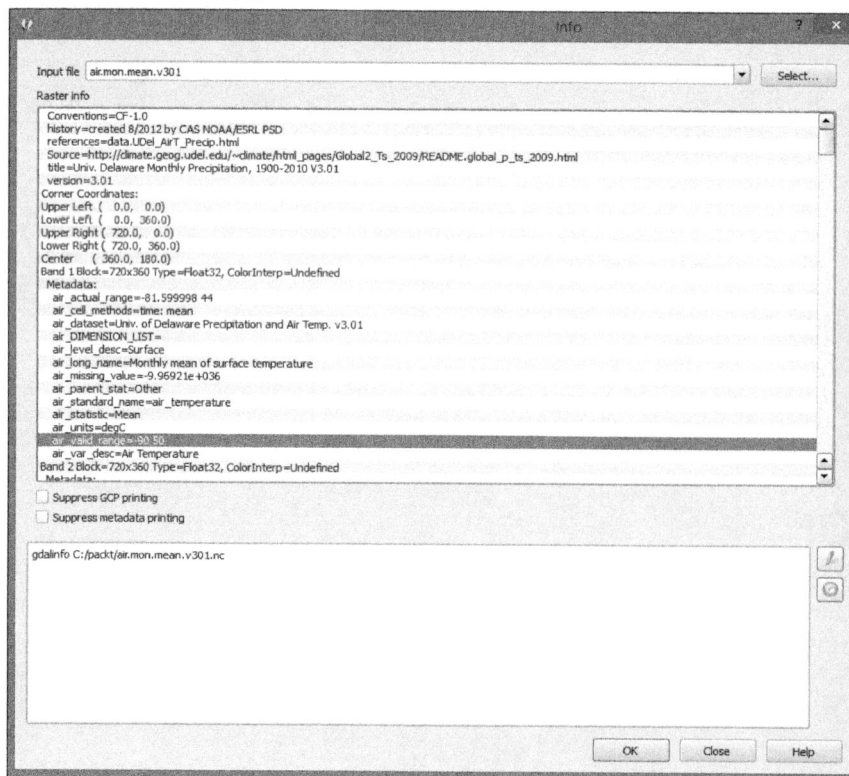

4. Enter the range information (-90 to 50) into the **Style** tab of the **Layer Properties** tab.

5. Click on **Invert** to show cool to hot colors from less to more, just as you would expect with temperature.

6. Click on **Classify** to create the new bins based on the number and color range. The following screenshot shows what an ideal selection of bins and colors would look like:

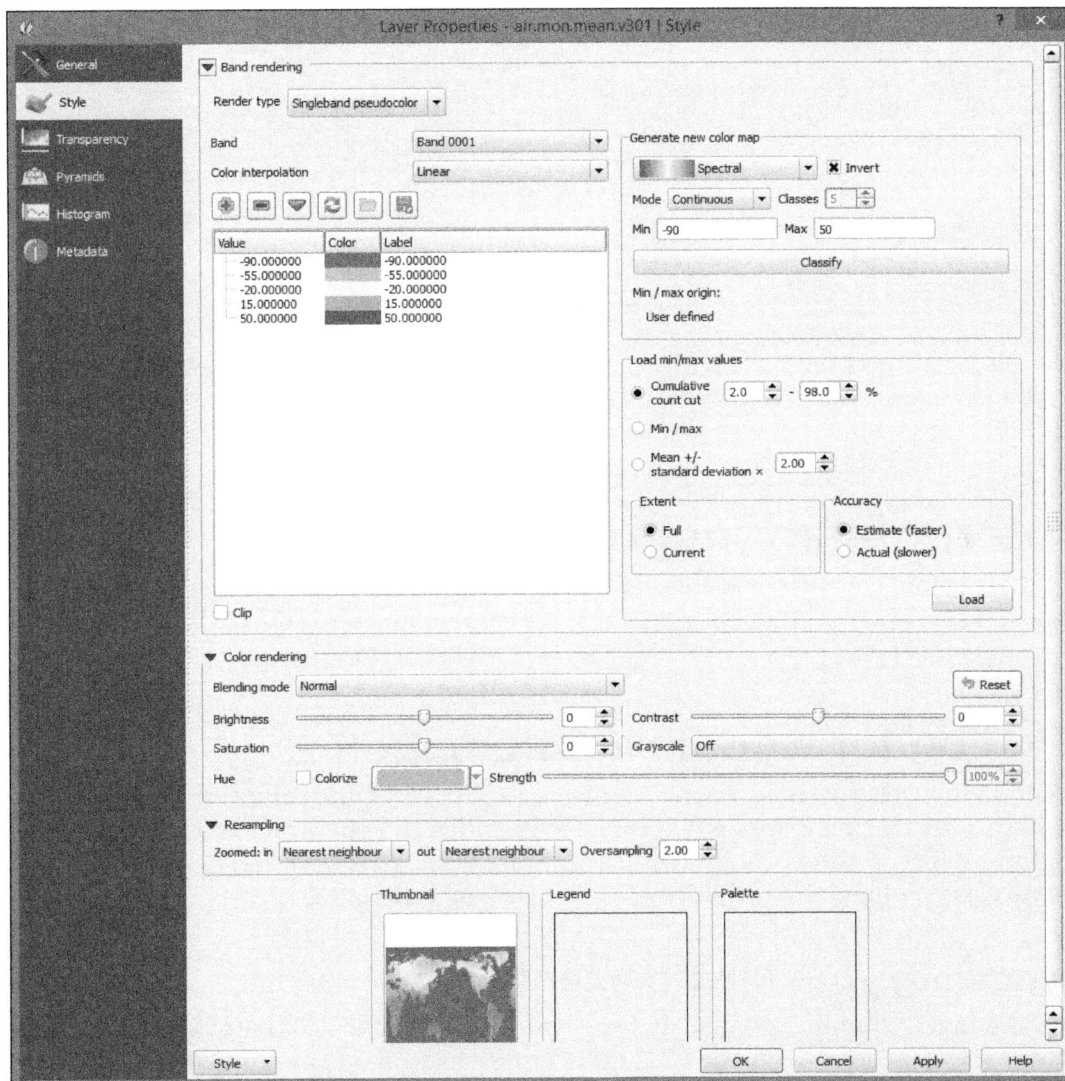

7. Click on **OK**. The end result will look similar to the following image:

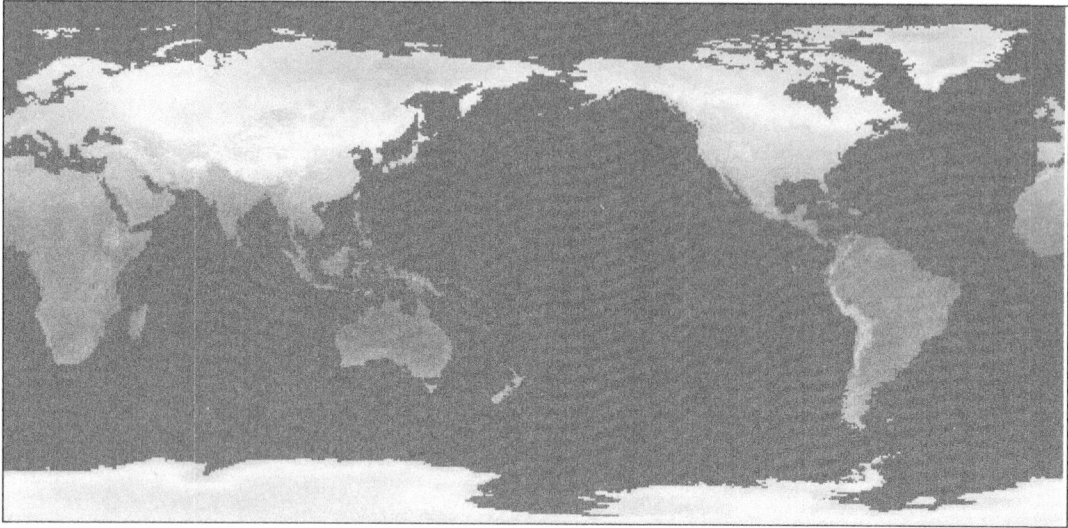

To render the gridded NetCDF data accessible to certain models, databases, and to web interaction, you could write a workflow program similar to the following after sampling the gridded values and attaching them to the points for each time period.

Interpolated model values

In this section, we will cover the creation of new statewide, point-based vulnerability index data from our limited weather station data obtained from the MySQL database mentioned before.

Python for workflow automation

With Python's large and growing number of wrappers, which allow independent (often C written and compiled) libraries to be called directly into Python, it is the natural choice to communicate with other software. Apart from direct API and library use, Python also provides access to system automation tasks.

Knowing your environment

A deceptively simple challenge in developing with Python is of knowing which paths and dependencies are loaded into your development environment.

To print your paths, type out the following in the QGIS Python Console (navigate to **Plugins | Python Console**) or the OSGeo4W Shell bundled with QGIS:

```
import os
try:
    user_paths = os.environ['PYTHONPATH'].split(os.pathsep)
except KeyError:
    user_paths = []
print user_paths
```

To list all the modules so that we know which are already available, type out the following:

```
import sys
sys.modules.keys()
```

Once we know which modules are available to Python, we can look up documentation on those modules and the programmable objects that they may expose.

> Remember to view all the special characters (including whitespace) in whatever text editor or IDE you are using. Python is sensitive to indentation as it relates to code blocks! You can set your text editor to automatically write the tabs as a default number of spaces. For example, when I hit a tab to indent, I will get four spaces instead of a special tab character.

Generating the parameter grids for each time period

Now, we're going to move into nonevaluation code. You may want to take this time to quit QGIS, particularly if you've been working in the Python command pane. If I'm already working on the command pane, I like to quit using Python syntax with the following code:

```
quit()
```

After quitting, start QGIS up again. The Python Console can be found under **Plugins | Python Console**.

By running the next code snippet in Python, you will generate a command-line code, which we will run, in turn, to generate intermediate data for this web application.

What this code does

We will run a Python code to generate a more verbose script that will perform a lengthy workflow process.

- For each parameter (factor), it will loop through every day in the range of days. The range will effectively be limited to 06/10/15 through 06/30/15 as the model requires a 10-day retrospective period.

- We will run it via ogr2ogr — GDAL's powerful vector data transformation tool — and use the SQLite syntax, selecting the appropriate aggregate value (count, sum, and average) based on the relative period.

- It will translate each result by the threshold to scores for our calculation of vulnerability to mildew. In other words, using some (potentially arbitrary) breaks in the data, we will translate the real measurements to smaller integer scores related to our study.

- It will interpolate the scores as an integer grid.

Running a code in Python

Copy and paste the following lines into the Python interpreter. Press *Enter* if the code is pasted without execution. The code also assumes that data can be found in the locations hardcoded in the following (`C:/packt/c6/data/prep/ogr.sqlite`). You may need to move these files if they are not already in the given locations or change the code. You will also need to modify the following code according to your filesystem; Windows filesystem conventions are used in the following code:

```python
# first variable to store commands
strCmds = 'del /F C:\packt\c6\data\prep\ogr.* \n'
# list of factors
factors = ['temperature','relative_humidity','precipitation']
# iterate through each factor, appending commands for each
for factor in factors:
  for i in range(10, 31):
    j = i - 5
    k = i - 9
    if factor == 'temperature':
      # commands use ogr2ogr executable from gdal project
      # you can run help on this from command line for more
      # information on syntax
        strOgr = 'ogr2ogr -f sqlite -sql "SELECT div_field_, GEOMETRY,
AVG(o_value) AS o_value FROM (SELECT div_field_, GEOMETRY, MAX(value)
AS o_value, date(time_measu) as date_f FROM {2} WHERE date_f BETWEEN
date(\'2013-06-{0:02d}\') AND date(\'2013-06-{1:02d}\') GROUP BY div_
field_, date(time_measu)) GROUP BY div_field_" -dialect sqlite -nln
ogr -dsco SPATIALITE=yes -lco SPATIAL_INDEX=yes -overwrite C:/packt/
c6/data/prep/ogr.sqlite C:/packt/c6/data/prep/temperature.shp \n'.
format(j,i,factor)
```

```
        strOgr += 'ogr2ogr -sql "UPDATE ogr SET o_value = 0 WHERE
o_value <=15.55" -dialect sqlite -update C:/packt/c6/data/prep/ogr.
sqlite C:/packt/c6/data/prep/ogr.sqlite \n'
        strOgr += 'ogr2ogr -sql "UPDATE ogr SET o_value = 3 WHERE
o_value > 25.55" -dialect sqlite -update C:/packt/c6/data/prep/ogr.
sqlite C:/packt/c6/data/prep/ogr.sqlite \n'
        strOgr += 'ogr2ogr -sql "UPDATE ogr SET o_value = 2 WHERE o_
value > 20.55 AND o_value <= 25.55" -dialect sqlite -update C:/packt/
c6/data/prep/ogr.sqlite C:/packt/c6/data/prep/ogr.sqlite \n'
        strOgr += 'ogr2ogr -sql "UPDATE ogr SET o_value = 1 WHERE o_
value > 15.55 AND o_value <= 20.55" -dialect sqlite -update C:/packt/
c6/data/prep/ogr.sqlite C:/packt/c6/data/prep/ogr.sqlite \n'
    elif factor == 'relative_humidity':
        strOgr = 'ogr2ogr -f sqlite -sql "SELECT GEOMETRY,
COUNT(value) AS o_value, date(time_measu) as date_f FROM relative_
humidity WHERE value > 96 AND date_f BETWEEN date(\'2013-06-{0:02d}\')
AND date(\'2013-06-{1:02d}\') GROUP BY div_field_" -dialect sqlite
-nln ogr -dsco SPATIALITE=yes -lco SPATIAL_INDEX=yes -overwrite C:/
packt/c6/data/prep/ogr.sqlite C:/packt/c6/data/prep/relative_humidity.
shp \n'.format(j,i)
        strOgr += 'ogr2ogr -sql "UPDATE ogr SET o_value = 0 WHERE o_
value <= 1" -dialect sqlite -update C:/packt/c6/data/prep/ogr.sqlite
C:/packt/c6/data/prep/ogr.sqlite \n'
        strOgr += 'ogr2ogr -sql "UPDATE ogr SET o_value = 3 WHERE o_
value > 40" -dialect sqlite -update C:/packt/c6/data/prep/ogr.sqlite
C:/packt/c6/data/prep/ogr.sqlite \n'
        strOgr += 'ogr2ogr -sql "UPDATE ogr SET o_value = 2 WHERE
o_value > 20 AND o_value <= 40" -dialect sqlite -update C:/packt/c6/
data/prep/ogr.sqlite C:/packt/c6/data/prep/ogr.sqlite \n'
        strOgr += 'ogr2ogr -sql "UPDATE ogr SET o_value = 1 WHERE
o_value > 10 AND o_value <= 20" -dialect sqlite -update C:/packt/c6/
data/prep/ogr.sqlite C:/packt/c6/data/prep/ogr.sqlite \n'
        strOgr += 'ogr2ogr -sql "UPDATE ogr SET o_value = 1 WHERE o_
value > 1 AND o_value <= 10" -dialect sqlite -update C:/packt/c6/data/
prep/ogr.sqlite C:/packt/c6/data/prep/ogr.sqlite \n'
    elif factor == 'precipitation':
        strOgr = 'ogr2ogr  -f sqlite -sql "SELECT GEOMETRY, SUM(value)
AS o_value, date(time_measu) as date_f FROM precipitation WHERE date_f
BETWEEN date(\'2013-06-{0:02d}\') AND date(\'2013-06-{1:02d}\') GROUP
BY div_field_" -dialect sqlite -nln ogr -dsco SPATIALITE=yes -lco
SPATIAL_INDEX=yes -overwrite C:/packt/c6/data/prep/ogr.sqlite C:/
packt/c6/data/prep/precipitation.shp \n'.format(k,i)
        strOgr += 'ogr2ogr -sql "UPDATE ogr SET o_value = 0 WHERE o_
value < 25.4" -dialect sqlite -update C:/packt/c6/data/prep/ogr.sqlite
C:/packt/c6/data/prep/ogr.sqlite \n'
        strOgr += 'ogr2ogr -sql "UPDATE ogr SET o_value = 3 WHERE o_
value > 76.2" -dialect sqlite -update C:/packt/c6/data/prep/ogr.sqlite
C:/packt/c6/data/prep/ogr.sqlite \n'
```

```
        strOgr += 'ogr2ogr -sql "UPDATE ogr SET o_value = 2 WHERE o_
value > 50.8 AND o_value <= 76.2" -dialect sqlite -update C:/packt/c6/
data/prep/ogr.sqlite C:/packt/c6/data/prep/ogr.sqlite \n'
        strOgr += 'ogr2ogr -sql "UPDATE ogr SET o_value = 1 WHERE o_
value > 30.48 AND o_value <= 50.8" -dialect sqlite -update C:/packt/
c6/data/prep/ogr.sqlite C:/packt/c6/data/prep/ogr.sqlite \n'
        strOgr += 'ogr2ogr -sql "UPDATE ogr SET o_value = 1 WHERE o_
value > 25.4 AND o_value <= 30.48" -dialect sqlite -update C:/packt/
c6/data/prep/ogr.sqlite C:/packt/c6/data/prep/ogr.sqlite \n'
        strGrid = 'gdal_grid -ot UInt16 -zfield o_value -l ogr -of
GTiff C:/packt/c6/data/prep/ogr.sqlite C:/packt/c6/data/prep/{0}
Inter{1}.tif'.format(factor,i)
        strCmds = strCmds + strOgr + '\n' + strGrid + '\n' + 'del /F
C:\packt\c6\data\prep\ogr.*' + '\n'

print strCmds
```

Running the printed commands in the Windows command console

Run the code output from the previous section by copying and pasting the result in the Windows command console. You can also find the output of the code to copy in `c6/data/output/generate_values.bat`.

The subprocess module

The subprocess module allows you to open up any executable on your system using the relevant command line syntax.

Although we could alternatively direct the code that we just produced through the subprocess module, it is simpler to do so directly on the command line in this case. With shorter, less sequential processes, you should definitely go ahead and use subprocess.

To use subprocess, just import it (ideally) in the beginning of your program and then use the Popen method to call your command line code. Execute the following code:

```
import subprocess
...
subprocess.Popen(strCmds)
```

Calculating the vulnerability index

GDAL_CALC evaluates an algebraic expression with gridded data as variables. In other words, you can use this GDAL utility to run map algebra or raster calculator type expressions. Here, we will use GDAL_CALC to produce our grid of the vulnerability index values based on the interpolated threshold scores.

Open a Python Console in QGIS (navigate to **Plugins | Python Console**) and copy/paste/run the following code. Again, you may wish to quit Python (using quit()) and restart QGIS/Python before running this code, which will produce the intermediate data for our application. This is used to control the unexpected variables and imported modules that are held back in the Python session.

After you've pasted the following lines into the Python interpreter, press *Enter* if it has not been executed. This code, like the previous one, produces a script that includes a range of numbers attached to filenames. It will run a map algebra expression through gdal_calc using the respective number in the range. Execute the following:

```
strCmd = ''

for i in range(10, 31):
  j = i - 5
  k = i - 9
  strOgr = 'gdal_calc --A C:/packt/c6/data/prep//temperatureInter{0}.
tif -B C:/packt/c6/data/prep/relative_humidityInter{0}.tif -C
C:/packt/c6/data/prep/precipitationInter{0}.tif --calc="A+B+C"
--type=UInt16 --outfile=C:/packt/c6/data/prep/calc{0}.tiff'.format(i)

  strCmd += strOgr + '\n'

print strCmd
```

Now, run the output from this code in the Windows command console. You can find the output code under c6/data/output/calculate_index.bat.

Creating regular points

As dynamic web map interfaces are not usually good at querying raster inputs, we will create an intermediate set of locations—points—to use for interaction with a user click event. The **Regular points** tool will create a set of points at a regular distance from each other. The end result is almost like a grid but made up of points. Perform the following steps:

1. Add c6/data/original/delaware_boundary.shp to your map project if you haven't already done so.

2. In **Vector**, navigate to **Research Tools | Regular points**.
3. Use **delaware_boundary** for the **Input Boundary Layer**.
4. Use a point spacing of `.05` (in decimal degrees for now).
5. Save under `c6/data/output/sample.shp`.

The following image shows these parameters populated:

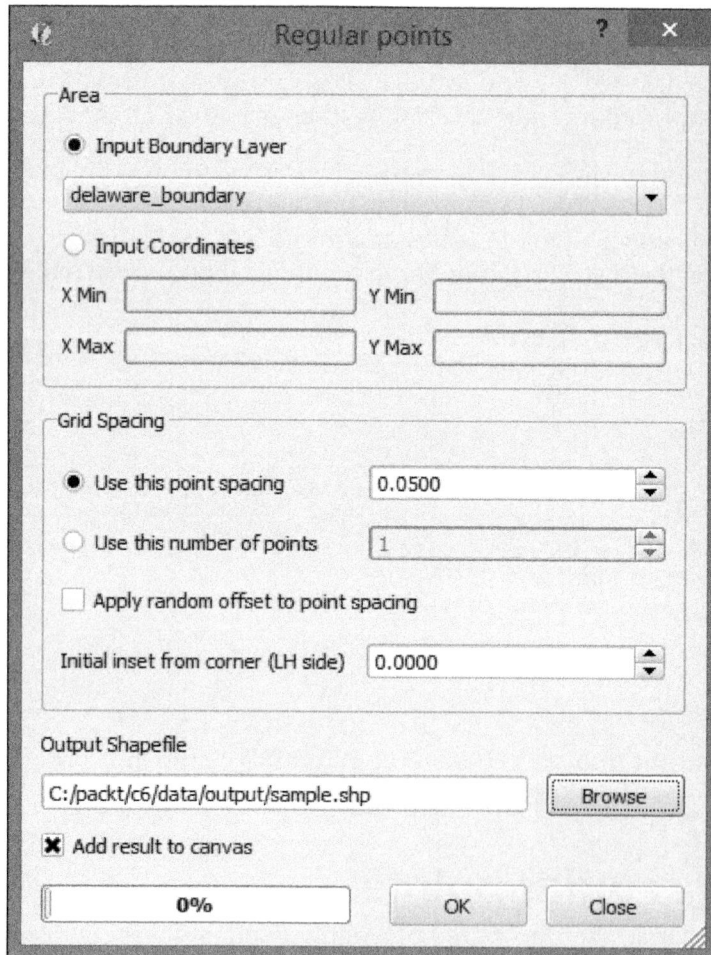

The output will look similar to this:

Sampling the index grid by points

Now that we have regular points, we can attach the grid values to them using the following steps:

1. Add all the calculated grids to the map (`calc10` to `calc30`) if they were not already added (navigate to **Layer | Add Layer | Add Vector Layer**).

2. Search for **points** under the **Processing Toolbox** pane. Ensure that the **Advanced Interface** is selected from the dropdown at the bottom of the pane.

3. Navigate to **SAGA | Shapes - Grid | Add grid values to points**.

4. Select the **sample** layer of regular points, which we just created. Following is a screenshot of this, and you will need to execute the following code:

   ```
   Select all grids (calc10-calc30)
   ```

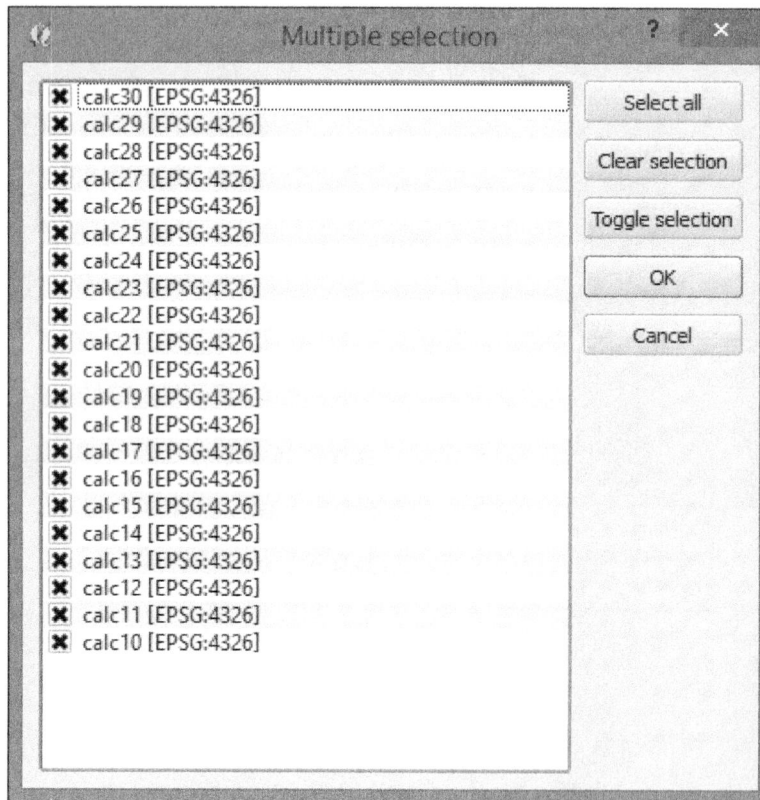

5. Save the output result to `c6/data/output/sample_data.shp`.

6. Click on **Run**, as shown in the following screenshot:

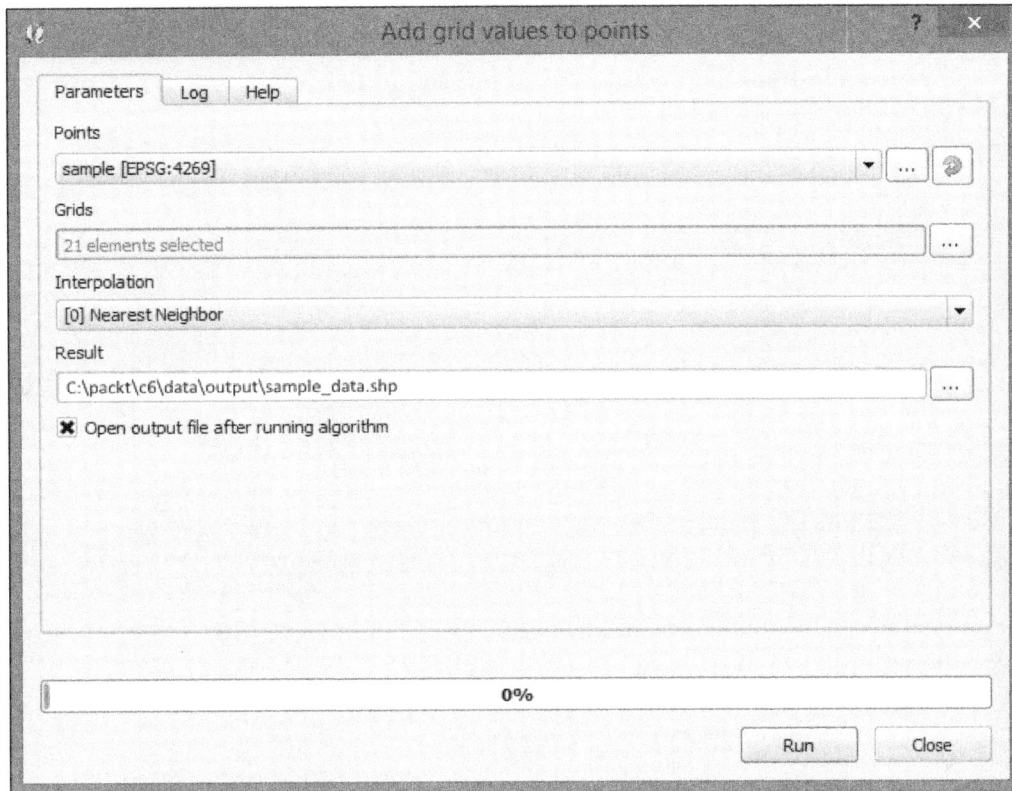

Create SQLite database and import

Next, create a SpatiaLite database at `c6/data/web/cgi-bin/c6.sqlite` (refer to the *Creating a SpatiaLite database* section of *Chapter 5, Demonstrating Change*) and import the `sample_data` shapefile using DB Manager.

DB Manager does not "see" SpatiaLite databases which were not created directly by the **Add Layer** command (as we've done so far; for example, in *Chapter 5, Demonstrating Change*), so it is best to do it this way rather than by saving it directly as a SpatiaLite database using the output dialog in the previous step.

Perform the following steps to test that our nearest neighbor result is correct:

1. Use the coordinate capture to get a test coordinate based on the points in the `sample_data` layer.

2. Create a SpatiaLite database using steps from *Chapter 5, Demonstrating Change* (navigate to **Layer** | **Create Layer**).

3. Open DB Manager (**Database | DB Manager**).

4. Import the `sample_data` layer/shapefile.

5. Run the following query in the DB Manager SQL window, substituting the coordinates that you obtained in step 1, separated by a space (for example, `75.28075 39.47785`):

```
SELECT pk, calc10, min(Distance(PointFromText('POINT (-
    75.28075 39.47785)'),geom)) FROM vulnerability
```

Using the identify tool, click on the nearest point to the coordinate you selected to check whether the query produces the correct nearest neighbor.

A dynamic web application – OpenLayers AJAX with Python and SpatiaLite

In this section, we will produce our web application, which, unlike any so far, involves a dynamic interaction between client and server. We will also use a different web map client API—OpenLayers. OpenLayers has long been a leader in web mapping; however, it has been overshadowed by smaller clients, such as Leaflet, as of late. With its latest incarnation, OpenLayers 3, OpenLayers has been slimmed down but still retains a functionality advantage in most areas over its newer peers.

Server side – CGI in Python

Common Gateway Interface (CGI) is perhaps the simplest way to run a server-side code for dynamic web use. This makes it great for doing proof of concept learning. The most typical use of CGI is in data processing and passing it onto the database from the web forms received through HTTP POST. The most common attack vector is the SQL injection. Going a step further, dynamic processing similar to CGI is often implemented through a minimal framework, such as Bottle, CherryPy, or Flask, to handle common tasks such as routing and sometimes templating, thus making for a more secure environment.

Don't forget that Python is sensitive to indents. Indents are always expressed as spaces with a uniform number per hierarchy level. For example, an `if` block may contain lines prefixed by four spaces. If the `if` block falls within a `for` loop, the same lines should be prefaced by 8 spaces.

Python CGI development

Next, we will start up a CGIHTTPServer hosting instance via a separate Windows console session. Then, we will work on the development of our server-side code— primarily through the QGIS Python Console.

Starting a CGI hosting

Starting a CGI session is simple— you just need to use the -m command line switch directly with Python, which loads the module as you might load a script. The following code starts CGIHTTPServer in port 8000. The current working directory will be served as the public web directory; in this case, this is C:\packt\c6\data\web.

In a new Windows console session, run the following:

```
cd C:\packt\c6\data\web
python -m CGIHTTPServer 8000
```

Testing the CGI hosting

Python (.py) CGI files can only run out of directories named either cgi or cgi-bin. This is a precaution to ensure that we intend the files in this directory to be publically executable.

To test this, create a file at c6/data/web/cgi-bin/simple_test.py with the following content:

> The first line is our shebang, which allows this file to be independently executable through the interpreter listed in the path on Unix systems. While this has no effect on Windows systems, where execution is handled through file associations, we will leave this here for interoperability.

```
#!/usr/bin/python

# Import the cgi, and system modules
import cgi, sys

# Required header that tells the browser how to render the HTML.
print "Content-Type: text/html\n\n"
print "Hello world"
```

You should now see the "Hello world" message when you visit http://localhost:8000/cgi-bin/simple_test.py on your browser. To debug on the client side, make sure you are using a browser-based web development view, plugin, or extension, such as Chrome's Developer Tools toolbar or Firefox's Firebug extension.

Debugging server-side code

Here are a few ways through which you can debug during Python CGI development:

- Use the Python Console in QGIS (navigate to **Plugins | Python Console**). You can run the Python code from your Python CGI Scripts here directly; however, this will fail for the scripts that rely on information passed through HTTP, but you can at least catch syntax errors, and you can populate it with the expected values to compare the result to what you're getting on a web browser. Sometimes, you'll want to quit QGIS to clear out the memory of the Python interpreter.

- A quicker way of doing this is to run your script in the command line with -d (verbose debugging). This will catch any issues that may not come up in interactive use, avoiding the variables that may have inadvertently been set in the same interactive session (substitute index.py with the name of your Python script). Run the following command from your command line shell:

  ```
  python -d C:\packt\c6\data\web\cgi-bin\index.py
  ```

- If your Python CGI script is interacting with a database, you definitely need to test the queries through DB Manager SQL Window (or whichever database interface you prefer). It is often helpful to populate the queries with the expected values.

- Go to the following location in our web browser (substitute index.py with the name of your Python script):

  ```
  localhost:8000/cgi-bin/index.py
  ```

Our Python server-side, database-driven code

Now, let's create a Python code to provide dynamic web access to our SQLite database.

PySpatiaLite

The PySpatiaLite module provides dbapi2 access to SpatiaLite databases. Dbapi2 is a standard library for interacting with databases from Python. This is very fortunate because if you use the dbapi2 connector from the sqlite3 module alone, any query using spatial types or functions will fail. The sqlite3 module was not built to support SpatiaLite.

Add the following to the preceding code. This will perform the following functions:

- Import the PySpatiaLite module and connect to our sqlite3/SpatiaLite database
- Use the connection as a context manager, which automatically commits the executed queries and rolls back in case of an error
- To test that the connection is working, use the SQLITE_VERSION() function in a SELECT query and print the result

The following code, appended to the preceding one, can be found at c6/data/web/cgi-bin/db_test.py. Make sure that the path in the code for the SQLite database file matches the actual location on your system.

```
# Import the pySpatiaLite module
from pySpatiaLite import dbapi2 as sqlite3
conn = sqlite3.connect('C:\packt\c6\data\web\cgi-bin\c6.sqlite')

# Use connection handler as context
with conn:
  c = conn.cursor()
  c.execute('SELECT SQLITE_VERSION()')

  data = c.fetchone()
  print data
  print 'SQLite version:{0}'.format(data[0])
```

You can view the following results in a web browser at http://localhost:8000/cgi-bin/db_test.py.

```
(u'3.7.17',) SQLite version:3.7.17
```

The first time that the data is printed, it is preceded by a u and wrapped in single quotes. This tells us that this is a unicode string (as our database uses unicode encoding). If we access element 0 in this string, we get a nonwrapped result.

The Python code for web access to SQLite through JSON

The following code performs the following functions:

- It connects to the database
- It issues a query to find the minimum distance location and field where the specified location and date are given
- It returns JSON with field value pairs based on the database result field names and values

You can find the code at c6/data/web/cgi-bin/get_json.py:

```python
#!/usr/bin/python

import cgi, cgitb, json, sys
from pySpatiaLite import dbapi2 as sqlite3

# Enables some debugging functionality
cgitb.enable()

# Creating row factory function so that we can get field names
# in dict returned from query
def dict_factory(cursor, row):
  d = {}
  for idx, col in enumerate(cursor.description):
    d[col[0]] = row[idx]
  return d

# Connect to DB and setup row_factory
conn = sqlite3.connect('C:\packt\c6\data\web\cgi-bin\c6.sqlite')
conn.row_factory = dict_factory

# Print json headers, so response type is recognized and correctly
decoded
print 'Content-Type: application/json\n\n'

# Use CGI FieldStorage object to retrieve data passed by HTTP GET
# Using numeric datatype casts to eliminate special characters
fs = cgi.FieldStorage()
longitude = float(fs.getfirst('longitude'))
latitude = float(fs.getfirst('latitude'))
day = int(fs.getfirst('day'))

# Use user selected location and days to find nearest location
(minimum distance)
# and correct date column
query = 'SELECT pk, calc{2} as index_value, min(Distance(PointFrom
Text(\'POINT ({0} {1})\'),geom)) as min_dist FROM vulnerability'.
format(longitude, latitude, day)

# Use connection as context manager, output first/only result row as
json
with conn:
  c = conn.cursor()
  c.execute(query)
  data = c.fetchone()
  print json.dumps(data)
```

You can test the preceding code by commenting out the portion that gets arguments from the HTTP request and setting these arbitrarily.

The full code is available at c6/data/web/cgi-bin/json_test.py:

```
# longitude = float(fs.getfirst('longitude'))
# latitude = float(fs.getfirst('latitude'))
# day = int(fs.getfirst('day'))
longitude = -75.28075
latitude = 39.47785
day = 15
```

If you browse to http://localhost:8000/cgi-bin/json_test.py, you'll see the literal JSON printed to the browser. You can also do the equivalent by browsing to the following URL, which includes these arguments: http://localhost:8000/cgi-bin/get_json.py?longitude=-75.28075&latitude= 39.47785&day=15.

```
{"pk": 260, "min_dist": 161.77454362713507, "index_value": 7}
```

The OpenLayers/jQuery client-side code

Now that our backend code and dependencies are all in place, it's time to move on to integrating this into our frontend interface.

Exporting the OpenLayers 3 map using QGIS

QGIS helps us get started on our project by allowing us to generate a working OpenLayers map with all the dependencies, basic HTML elements, and interaction event handler functionality. Of course, as with qgis2leaf, this can be extended to include the additional leveraging of the map project layers and interactivity elements.

The following steps will produce an OpenLayers 3 map that we will modify to produce our database-interactive map application:

1. Start a new QGIS map or remove all the layers from the current one.
2. Add delaware_boundary.shp to the map. Pan and zoom to the Delaware geographic boundary object if QGIS does not do so automatically.

3. Convert the `delaware_boundary` polygon layer to lines by navigating to **Vector | Geometry Tools | Polygons to lines**. Nonfilled polygons are not supported by **Export to OpenLayers**. The following image shows these inputs populated:

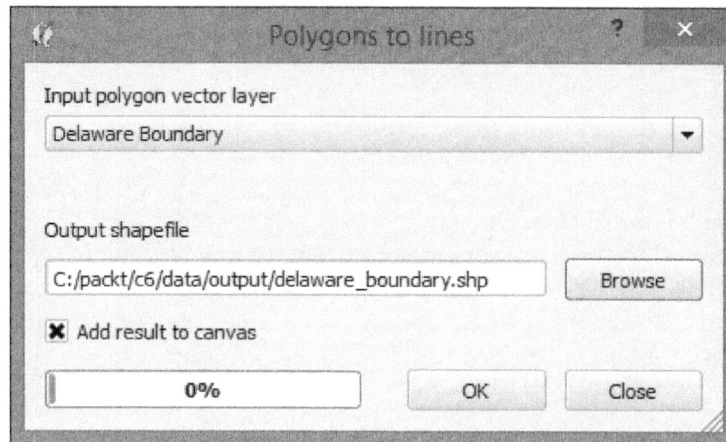

4. After you add the line boundaries, brighten them up and increase the size as well. Clicking on anything outside this boundary may not return a valid result. Rename the layer **Delaware Boundary** in the **Layers** panel.

5. Install the Export to OpenLayers 3 plugin if it isn't already installed.

6. Navigate to **Web | Export to OpenLayers | Create OpenLayers Map**.

7. In the **Export to OpenLayers 3** dialog, use the following parameter values (refer to the following image for clarification):

   ° Ensure that your stylized line boundary for Delaware (which we created in step 4) is checked and visible with no popup. Otherwise, this might obscure the interaction that we will create.

   ° Delete the unused fields. This is an important step, so uncheck this. Otherwise, you may see an error.

   ° If you've already zoomed and panned your canvas to the **Delaware Boundary** layer, you can ignore the **Extent** parameter. Otherwise, set the extent parameter to **Fit to Layers extent**.

   ° **Max zoom level**: 14.

   ° **Min zoom level**: 8.

   ° Select **Restrict to extent**.

- ○ Unselect **Use layer scale dependent visibility**.
- ○ **Base layer**: **MapQuest**, as shown in the following screenshot:

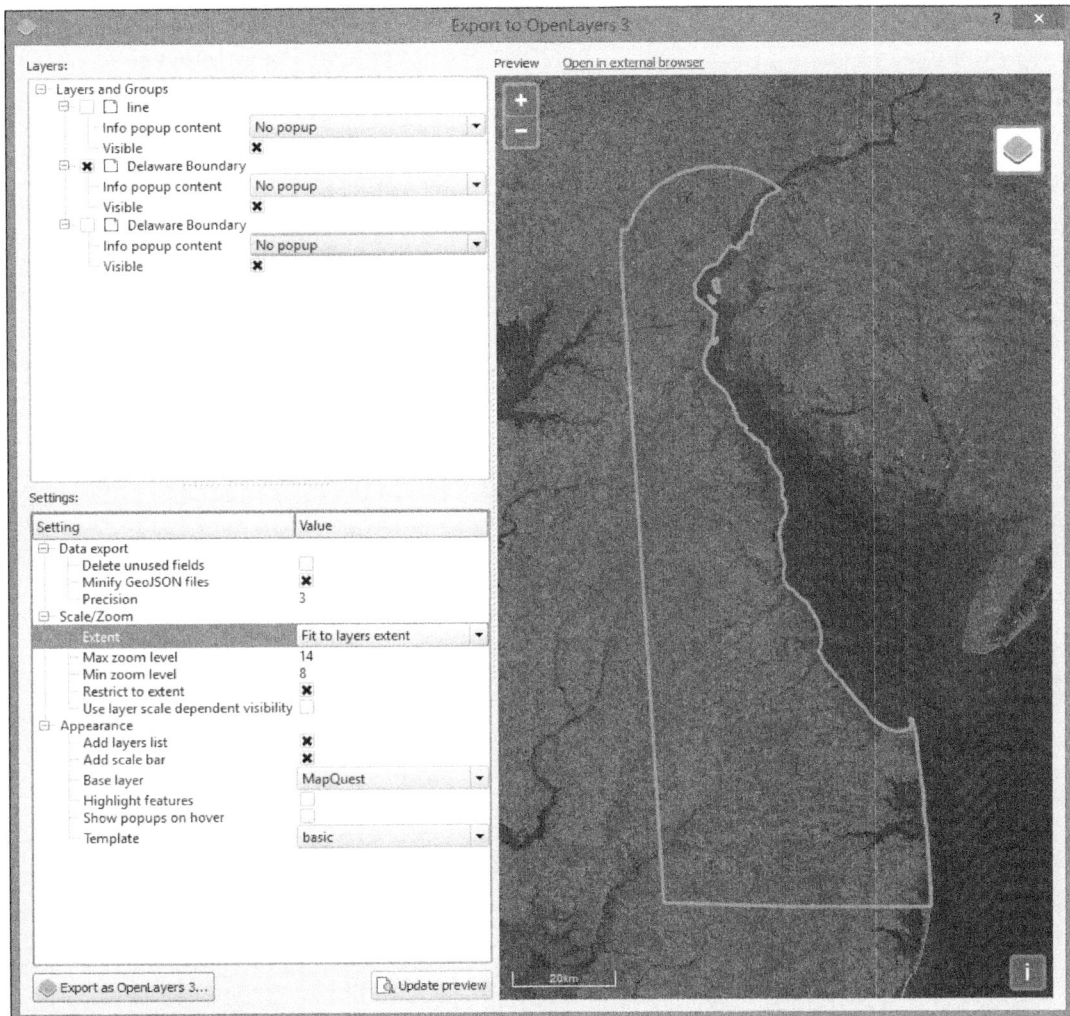

Modifying the exported OpenLayers 3 map application

Now that we have the base code and dependencies for our map application, we can move on to modifying the code so that it interacts with the backend, providing the desired information upon click interaction.

Remember that the backend script will respond to the selected date and location by finding the closest "regular point" and the calculated interpolated index for that date.

Adding an interactive HTML element

Add the following to `c6/data/web/index.html` in the body, just above the `div#id` element.

This is the HTML for the `select` element, which will pass a day. You would probably want to change the code here to scale with your application — this one is limited to days in a single month (and as it requires 10 days of retrospective data, it is limited to days from 6/10 to 6/30):

```html
<select id="day">
  <option value="10">2013-06-10</option>
  <option value="11">2013-06-11</option>
  <option value="12">2013-06-12</option>
  <option value="13">2013-06-13</option>
  <option value="14">2013-06-14</option>
  <option value="15">2013-06-15</option>
  <option value="16">2013-06-16</option>
  <option value="17">2013-06-17</option>
  <option value="18">2013-06-18</option>
  <option value="19">2013-06-19</option>
  <option value="20">2013-06-20</option>
  <option value="21">2013-06-21</option>
  <option value="22">2013-06-22</option>
  <option value="23">2013-06-23</option>
  <option value="24">2013-06-24</option>
  <option value="25">2013-06-25</option>
  <option value="26">2013-06-26</option>
  <option value="27">2013-06-27</option>
  <option value="28">2013-06-28</option>
  <option value="29">2013-06-29</option>
  <option value="30">2013-06-30</option>
</select>
```

This element will then be accessed by jQuery using the `div#id` reference.

AJAX – the glue between frontend and backend

AJAX is a loose term applied specifically to an asynchronous interaction between client and server software using XML objects. This makes it possible to retrieve data from the server without the classic interaction of a submit button, which will take you to a page built on the result. Nowadays, AJAX is often used with JSON instead of XML to the same affect; it does not require a new page to be generated to catch the result from the server-side processing.

jQuery is a JavaScript library which provides many useful cross-browser utilities, particularly focusing on the DOM manipulation. One of the useful features that jQuery is known for is sending, receiving, and rendering results from AJAX calls. AJAX calls used to be possible from within OpenLayers; however, in OpenLayers 3, an external library is required. Fortunately for us, jQuery is included in the exported base OpenLayers 3 web application from QGIS.

Adding an AJAX call to the singleclick event handler

To add a jQuery AJAX call to our CGI script, add the following code to the "singleclick" event handler on SingleClick. This is our custom function that is triggered when a user clicks on the frontend map.

This AJAX call references the CGI script URL. The data object contains all the parameters that we wish to pass to the server. jQuery will take care of encoding the data object in a URL query string. Execute the following code:

```
jQuery.ajax({
    url: http://localhost:8000/cgi-bin/get_json.py,
    data: {"longitude": newCoord[0], "latitude": newCoord[1], "day":
        day}
})
Add a callback function to the jquery ajax call by inserting the
    following lines directly after it.
.done(function(response) {
popupText = 'Vulnerability Index (1=Least Vulnerable, 10=Most
    Vulnerable): ' + response.index_value;
```

Populating and triggering the popup from the callback function

Now, to get the script response to show in a popup after clicking, comment out the following lines:

```
/* var popupField;

    var currentFeature;
    var currentFeatureKeys;
    map.forEachFeatureAtPixel(pixel, function(feature, layer) {
        currentFeature = feature;
        currentFeatureKeys = currentFeature.getKeys();
        var field = popupLayers[layersList.indexOf(layer) - 1];
        if (field == NO_POPUP){
        }
        else if (field == ALL_FIELDS){
            for ( var i=0; i<currentFeatureKeys.length;i++) {
                if (currentFeatureKeys[i] != 'geometry') {
```

```
            popupField = currentFeatureKeys[i] + ': '+
               currentFeature.get(currentFeatureKeys[i]);
            popupText = popupText + popupField+'<br>';
          }
        }
      }
      else{
        var value = feature.get(field);
        if (value){
          popupText = field + ': '+ value;
        }
      }
    }); */
```

Finally, copy and paste the portion that does the actual triggering of the popup in the `.done` callback function. The `.done` callback is triggered when the AJAX call returns a data response from the server (the data response is stored in the response object variable). Execute the following code:

```
.done(function(response) {
  popupText = 'Vulnerability Index (1=Least Vulnerable, 10=Most
    Vulnerable): ' + response.index_value;
  if (popupText) {
    overlayPopup.setPosition(coord);
    content.innerHTML = popupText;
    container.style.display = 'block';
  } else {
    container.style.display = 'none';
   closer.blur();
  }
```

Testing the application

Now, the application should be complete. You will be able to view it in your browser at `http://localhost:8000`.

You will want to test by picking a date from the **Select** menu and clicking on different locations on the map. You will see something similar to the following image, showing a susceptibility score for any location on the map within the study extent (Delaware).

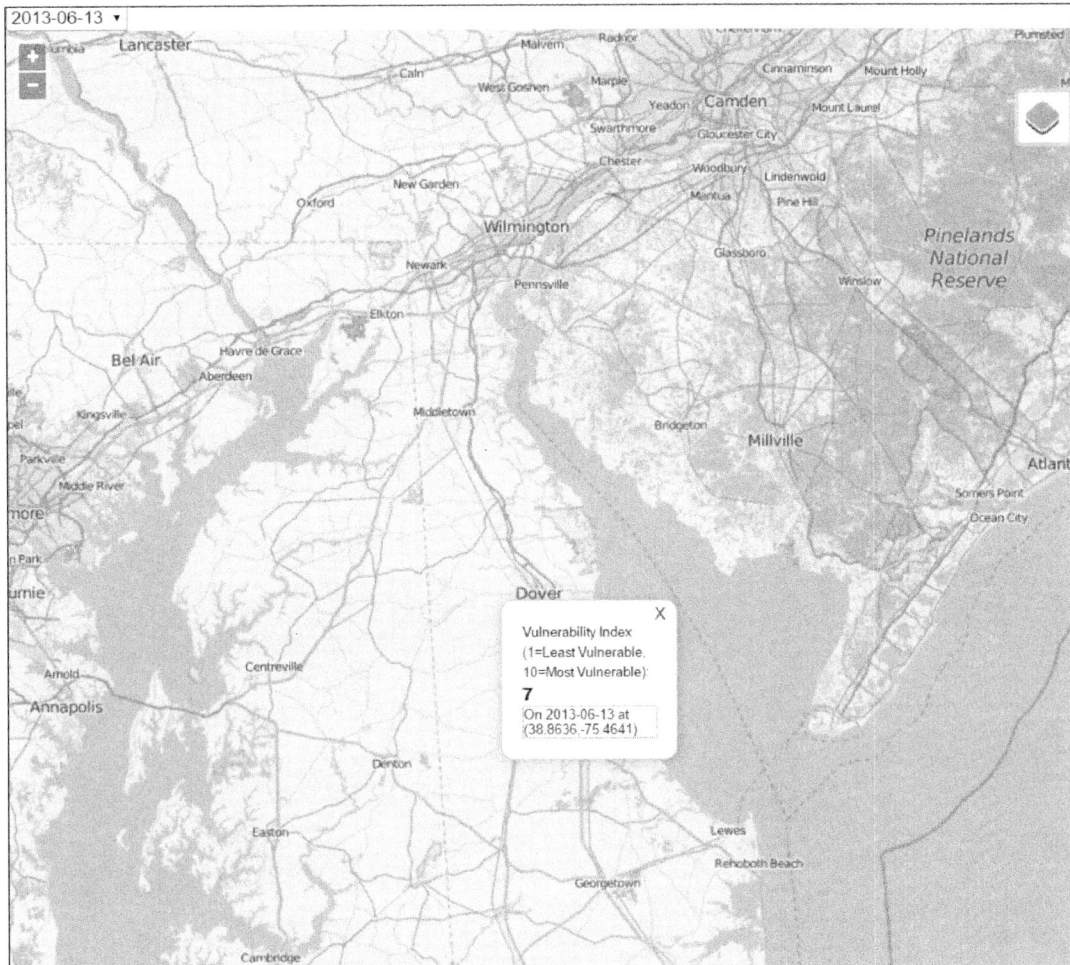

Summary

In this chapter, using an agricultural vulnerability modeling example, we covered interpolation and dynamic backend processing using spatial queries. The final application allows an end user to click on anything within a study area and see a score calculated from the interpolated point data and an algebraic model using a dynamic Python CGI code that queries a SQLite database. In the next chapter, we will continue to explore dynamic websites with an example that provides simple client editing capabilities and the use of the tiling and UTFGrid methods to improve performance with more complicated datasets.

7
Mapping for Enterprises and Communities

In this chapter, we will use a mix of web services to provide an editable collaborative data system.

While the visualization and data viewing capabilities that we've seen so far are a powerful means to reach an audience, we can tap into an audience — whether they are members of our organization, community stakeholders, or simply interested parties out on the web — to contribute improved geometric and attribute data for our geographic objects. In this chapter, you will learn to build a system of web services that provides these capabilities for a university community. As far as editable systems go, this is at the simpler end of things. Using a map server such as GeoServer, you could extend more extensive geometric editing capabilities based on a sophisticated user access management.

In this chapter, we will cover the following topics:

- Google Sheets for collaborative data management and services
- AJAX for web service processing
- OpenStreetMap for collaborative data contribution
- MBTiles and UTFGrid data formats
- Interactive data hosting through Mapbox
- Parsing and mapping JSON to an object
- Mixing web service data
- Setting up an Ubuntu virtual machine with Vagrant
- TileStream for local MBTiles hosting

Google Sheets for data management

Google Sheets provides us with virtually everything we need in a basic data management platform—it is web-based, easily editable through a spreadsheet interface, has fine-grained editing controls and API options, and is consumable through a simple JSON web service—at no cost, in most cases.

Creating a new Google document

To create a new Google document, you'll need to sign up for a Google account at `https://accounts.google.com`. Perform the following steps:

1. Create a new Google Sheets document at `https://docs.google.com/spreadsheets`.

2. Import data from an Excel file.

   1. Navigate to **File | Import**.

   2. Then, navigate to **Upload | ** `c7/data/original/building_export.xlsx`.

Publishing Google Sheets on the Web

By default, Google Sheets will not be publicly viewable. In addition, no web service feed is exposed. To enable access to our data hosted by Google Sheets from our web application, we must publish the sheet. Perform the following steps:

1. Navigate to **File | Publish to the web**.

2. Copy and paste the URL (which appears after clicking on **Published**) to a location that you can refer to later (for example, in your favorite text editor).

3. Select the **Automatically republish when changes are made** checkbox if it is not already selected, as shown in the following screenshot:

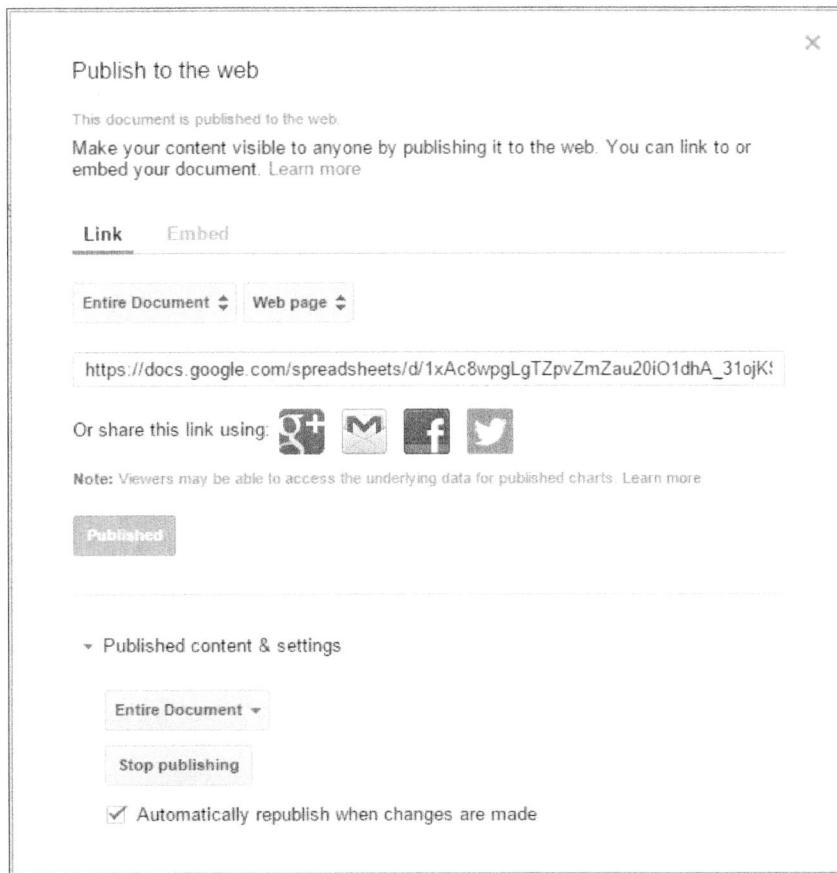

You'll need the section after **d/** (here, it starts with **1xAc8w**). This is the unique identifier referring to your sheet (or as it is sometimes known in documentation, the "key").

Previewing JSON

Now that we've published the sheet, our feed is exposed as JSON. We can view the JSON feed by substituting KEY with our spreadsheet unique identifier in a URL of the format `https://spreadsheets.google.com/feeds/list/KEY/1/public/basic?alt=json`. For example, it would look similar to the following URL:

`https://spreadsheets.google.com/feeds/list/1xAc8wpgLgTZpvZmZau20iO1dhA_31ojKSIBmlG6FMzQ/1/public/basic?alt=json`

This produces the following JSON response. For brevity, the response has been truncated after the first building object:

```
{"version":"1.0","encoding":"UTF-8","feed":{"xmlns":"http://www.
w3.org/2005/Atom","xmlns$openSearch":"http://a9.com/-/spec/opensearc
hrss/1.0/","xmlns$gsx":"http://schemas.google.com/spreadsheets/2006/
extended","id":{"$t":"https://spreadsheets.google.com/feeds/
list/19xiRHxZE4jOnVcMDXFx1pPyir4fXVGisWOc8guWTo2A/od6/public/
basic"},"updated":{"$t":"2012-04-06T13:55:10.774Z"},"category":[{"s
cheme":"http://schemas.google.com/spreadsheets/2006","term":"http://
schemas.google.com/spreadsheets/2006#list"}],"title":{"type":"tex
t","$t":"Sheet 1"},"link":[{"rel":"alternate","type":"application/
atom+xml","href":"https://docs.google.com/spreadsheets/d/19xiRHxZE4j
OnVcMDXFx1pPyir4fXVGisWOc8guWTo2A/pubhtml"},{"rel":"http://schemas.
google.com/g/2005#feed","type":"application/atom+xml","href":"https://
spreadsheets.google.com/feeds/list/19xiRHxZE4jOnVcMDXFx1pPyir4fX
VGisWOc8guWTo2A/od6/public/basic"},{"rel":"http://schemas.google.
com/g/2005#post","type":"application/atom+xml","href":"https://
spreadsheets.google.com/feeds/list/19xiRHxZE4jOnVcMDXFx1pPyir4fXVGi
sWOc8guWTo2A/od6/public/basic"},{"rel":"self","type":"application/
atom+xml","href":"https://spreadsheets.google.com/feeds/list/19xiRHxZE
4jOnVcMDXFx1pPyir4fXVGisWOc8guWTo2A/od6/public/basic?alt\u003djson"}],
"author":[{"name":{"$t":"Ben.Mearns"},"email":{"$t":"ben.mearns@gmail.
com"}}],"openSearch$totalResults":{"$t":"293"},"openSearch$startInde
x":{"$t":"1"},"entry":[{"id":{"$t":"https://spreadsheets.google.com/
feeds/list/19xiRHxZE4jOnVcMDXFx1pPyir4fXVGisWOc8guWTo2A/od6/public/
basic/cokwr"},"updated":{"$t":"2012-04-06T13:55:10.774Z"},"category"
:[{"scheme":"http://schemas.google.com/spreadsheets/2006","term":"h
ttp://schemas.google.com/spreadsheets/2006#list"}],"title":{"type":"
text","$t":"71219005"},"content":{"type":"text","$t":"udcode: NW92,
name: 102 Dallam Rd., type: Housing, address: 102 Dallam Road, _ciyn3:
19716, _ckd7g: 102 Dallam Road 19716, subcampus: WC"},"link":[{"rel"
:"self","type":"application/atom+xml","href":"https://spreadsheets.
google.com/feeds/list/19xiRHxZE4jOnVcMDXFx1pPyir4fXVGisWOc8guWTo2A/
od6/public/basic/cokwr"}]}, …
]}}
```

Parsing the JSON data

To work with the JSON data from this web service, we will use jQuery's AJAX capabilities. Using the attributes of the JSON elements, we can take a look at how the data is rendered in HTML as a simple web page.

Starting up the server

Start up SimpleHTTPServer on port 8000 for c7/data/web on the Windows command line using the following commands:

```
cd c:\packt\c7\data\web
python -m SimpleHTTPServer 8000
```

Test parsing with jQuery

You can take a look at the following code (on the file system at c7/data/web/gsheet.html) to test our ability to parse the JSON data:

```html
<html>
  <body>
    <div class="results"></div>
  </body>
<script src="http://code.jquery.com/jquery-1.11.3.min.js">
  </script>
<script>

  // ID of the Google Spreadsheet
  var spreadsheetID = "1xAc8wpgLgTZpvZmZau20iO1dhA_31ojKSIBmlG6FMzQ";

  // Make sure it is public or set to Anyone with link can view
  var url = "https://spreadsheets.google.com/feeds/list/" +
    spreadsheetID + "/1/public/values?alt=json";

  $.getJSON(url, function(data) {

    var entry = data.feed.entry;

    $(entry).each(function(){
      // Column names are name, type, etc.
      $('.results').prepend('<h2>'+this.gsx$name.$t+
        '</h2><p>'+this.gsx$type.$t+'</p>');
    });

  });

</script>
```

You can preview this in a web browser at `http://localhost:8000/gsheet.html`. You'll see building names followed by types, as shown in the following image:

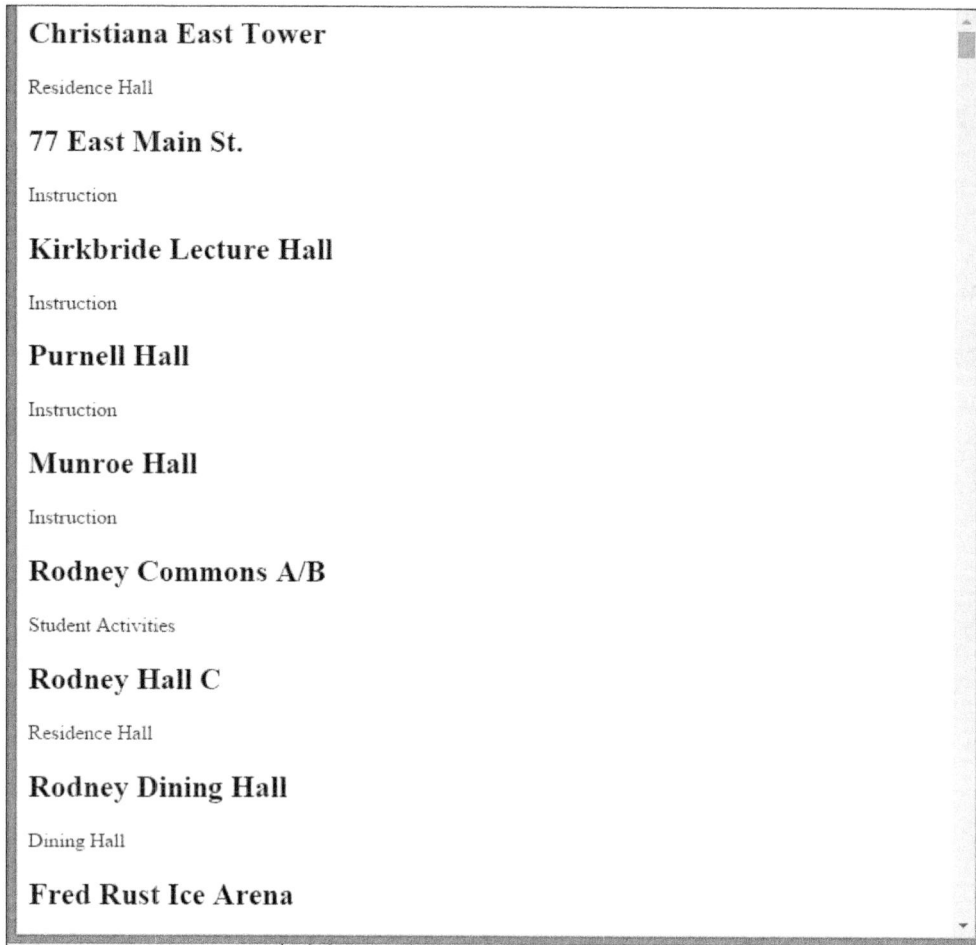

Rollout

Now let's take look at how we would operationalize this system for collaborative data editing.

Assigning permissions to additional users

In the sheet, click on the blue **Share** button in the upper-right corner. Alternatively, from Drive, select the file by clicking on it and then click on the icon that looks like a person with a plus sign on it. Ensure that anyone can find and view the document. Finally, add the address of the people you'd like to be able to edit the document and give them edit permissions, as shown in the following screenshot:

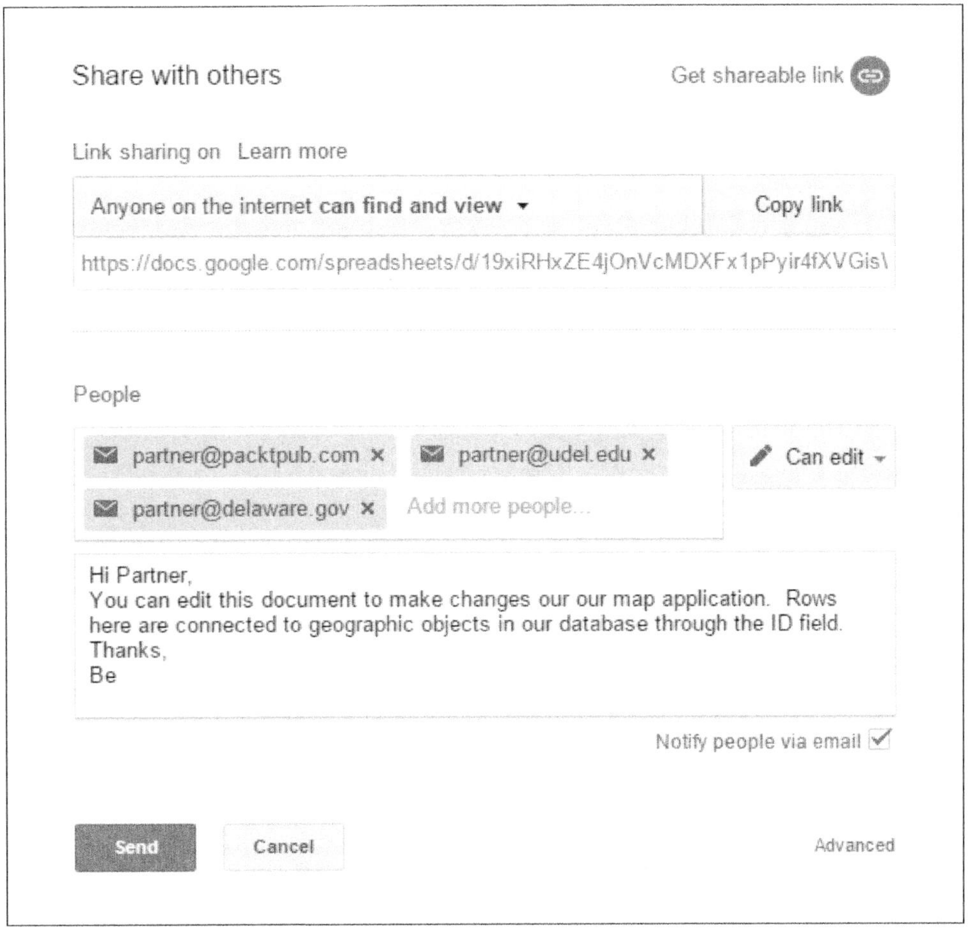

The editing workflow

Now that your collaborators have received an invitation to edit the sheet, they just need to sign in with their Google credentials and make a change to the sheet—the changes will be saved automatically. Of course, if they don't have any Google credentials, they'll need to create an account.

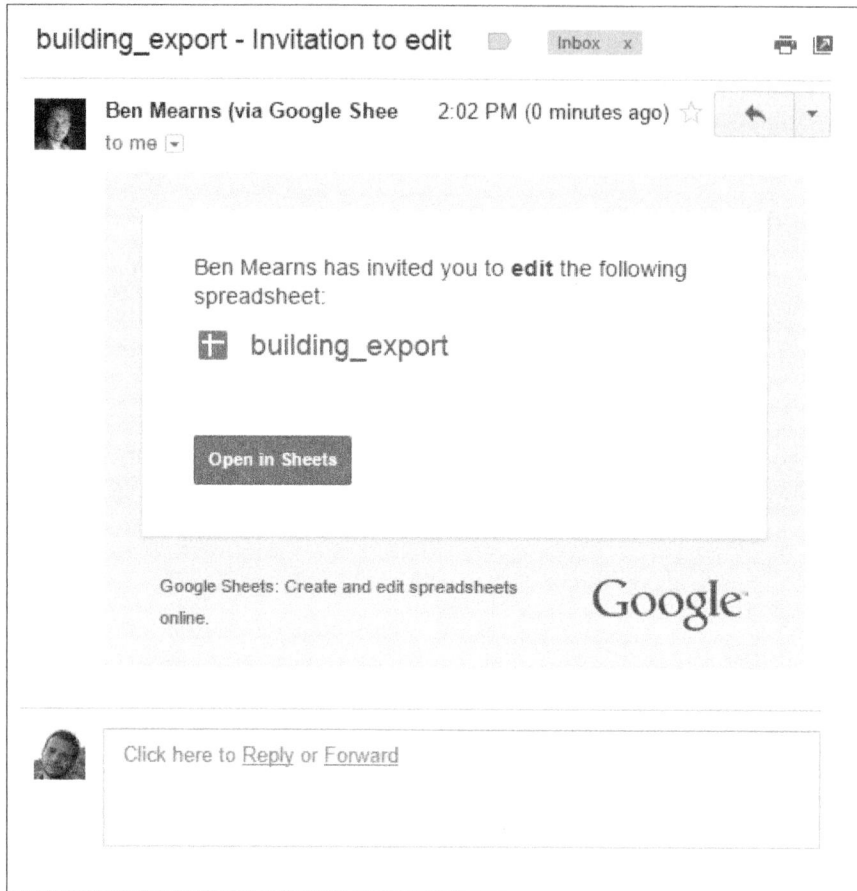

To go to the sheet, your collaborator will just need to click on **Open in Sheets**. The sheet should now also appear under their drive in **Shared with me**.

Here, you can see the type fields for **Christiana Hall**, **Kirkbride Lecture Hall**, and **Purnell Hall** after the changes are made:

	A	B	C	D	E	F	G	H
288	71219153	NW13	Rodney Hall C	Residence Hall	113 Hillside Road	19716	113 Hillside Road 19716	WC
289	71218962	NW17	Rodney Commons A/B	Student Activities	207 Hillside Road	19716	207 Hillside Road 19716	WC
290	71219004	NW26	Munroe Hall	Instruction	46-48 West Delaware Avenue	19716	46-48 West Delaware Avenue 19716	WC
291	71219002	NW35	Purnell Hall	Lecture Hall	42 Amstel Avenue	19716	42 Amstel Avenue 19716	WC
292	71219009	NW65	Kirkbride Lecture Hall	Lecture Hall	114 South College Avenue	19716	114 South College Avenue 19716	WC
293	71219407	NZ16	77 East Main St.	Instruction	77 East Main Street	19716	77 East Main Street 19716	NC
294	71219447	NN39	Christiana East Tower	High Rise	17 Christiana Drive	19716	17 Christiana Drive 19716	LC

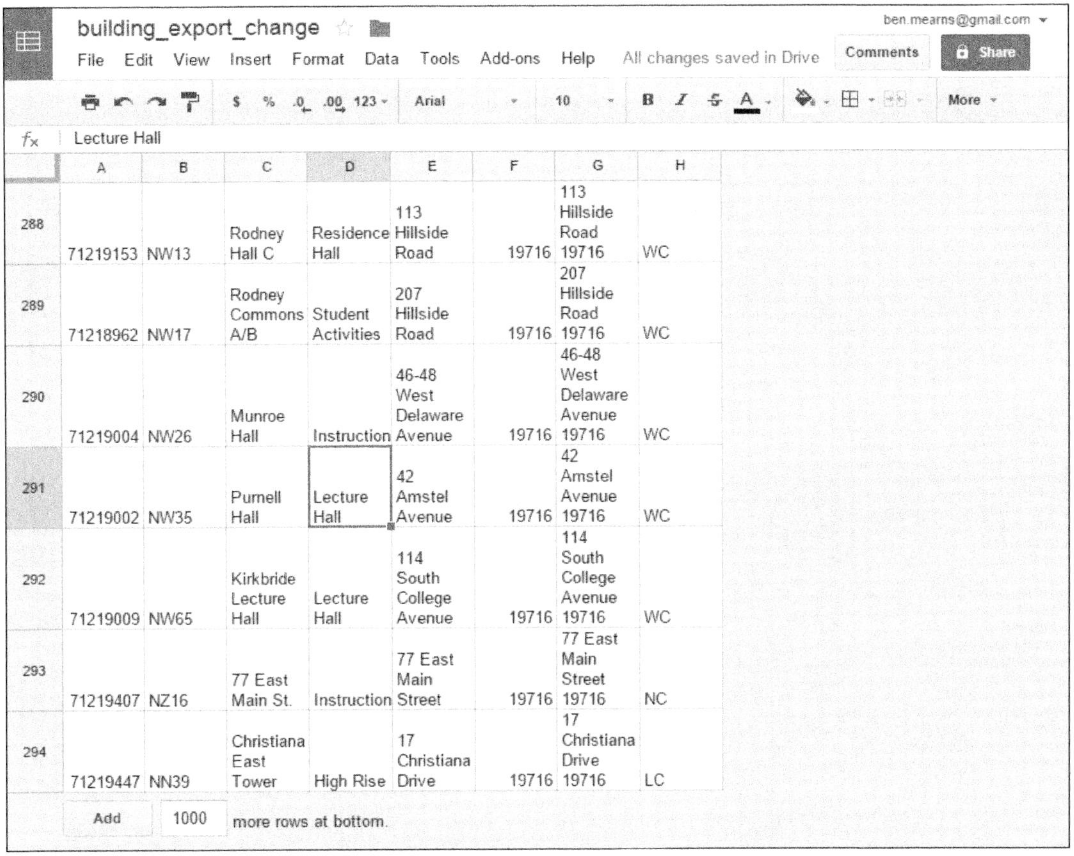

> If you don't require your collaborator to log in with Google, there is always the option of making your document publically editable—although, that comes with its own problems!

The publishing workflow

There is no need for an administrative intervention after the collaborators make changes. Data changed in sheets is automatically republished in the JSON feed, as we selected this option when we published the sheet. If you require more control over the publication of the collaborator edits, you may want to consider unselecting that option and setting up notifications of the changes. This way, you can republish after you've vetted the changes.

You can do a rollback of the changes as needed in the revision history. Perform the following steps:

1. Go to your sheet.

2. Navigate to **File | See revision history**.

3. You can view all the changes color coded by default, as shown in the following screenshot:

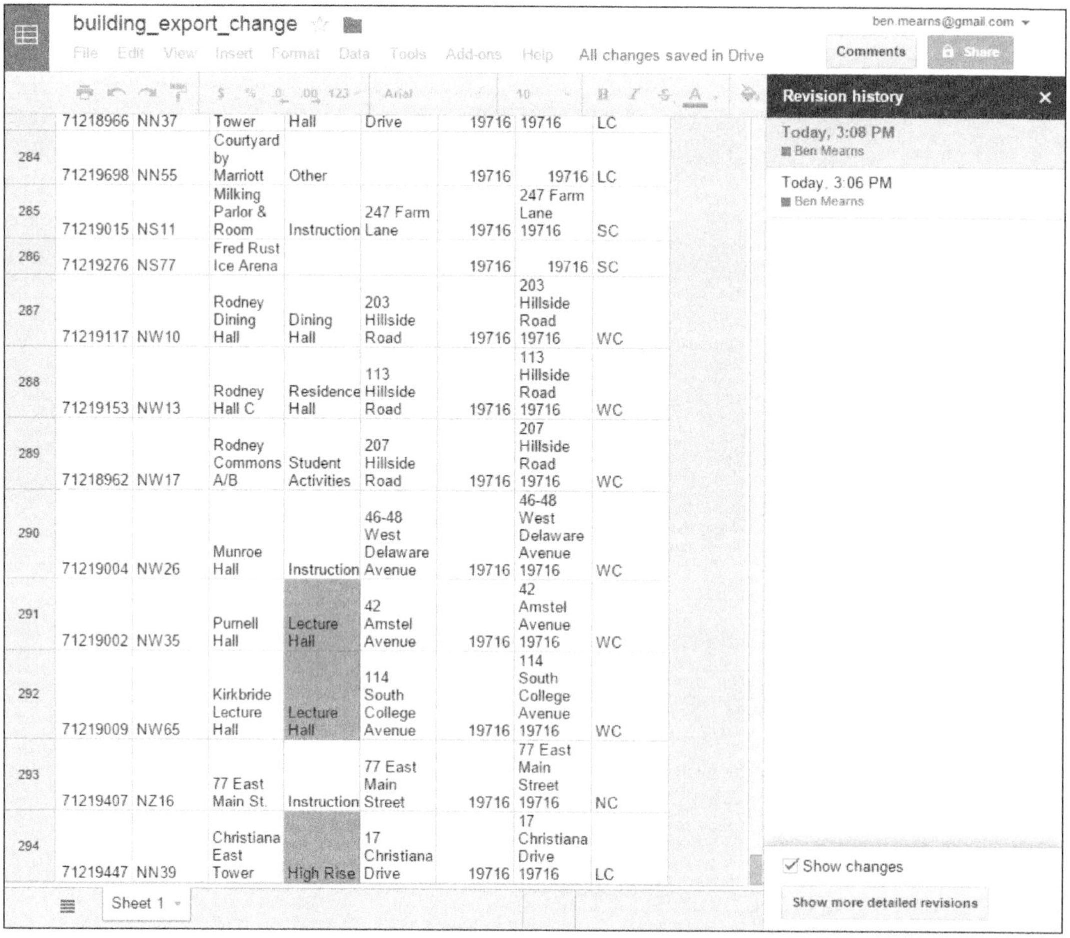

4. If you click on a particular change, you will have the option to restore the revision made to that point, as shown in the following screenshot:

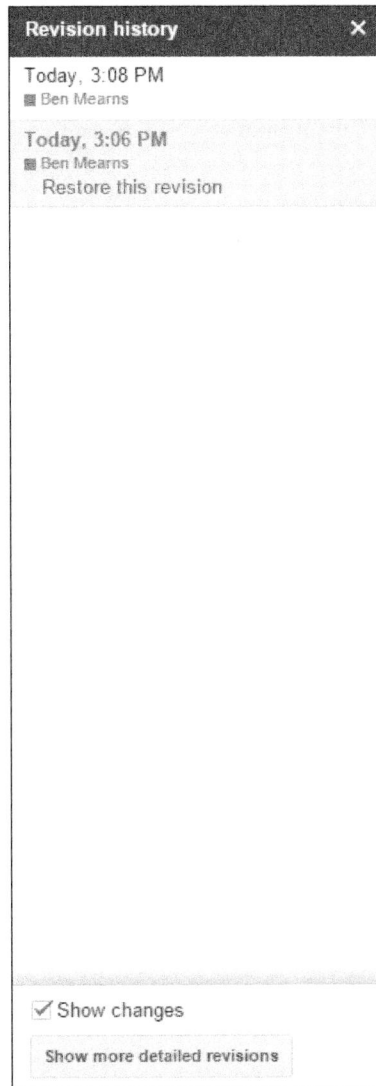

Viewing the changes in your JSON feed

Go to `http://localhost:8000/gsheet.html` again to see how the changes to your sheet affected your JSON feed. Note in the following image the changes we made to the type fields for **Christiana East Tower**, **Kirkbride Lecture Hall**, and **Purnell Hall**:

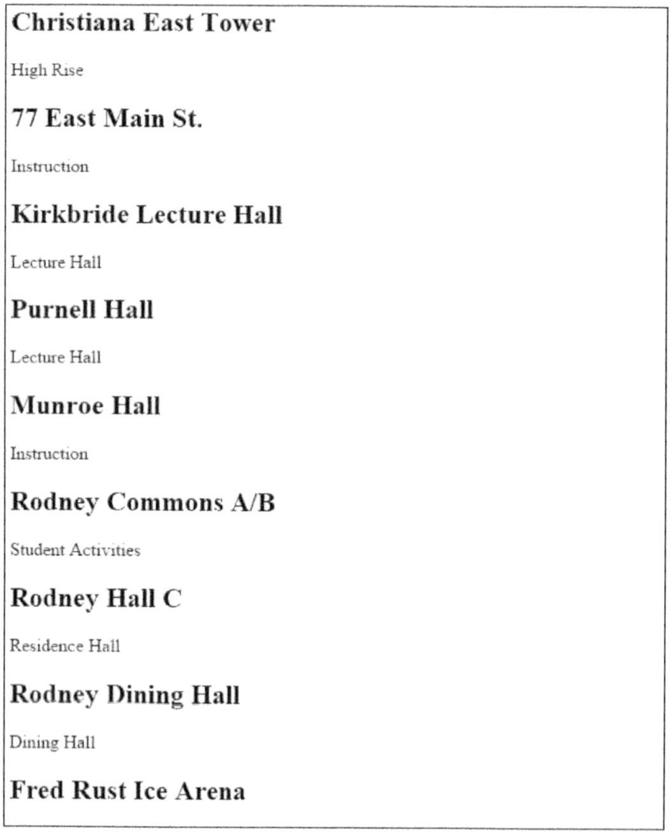

Christiana East Tower

High Rise

77 East Main St.

Instruction

Kirkbride Lecture Hall

Lecture Hall

Purnell Hall

Lecture Hall

Munroe Hall

Instruction

Rodney Commons A/B

Student Activities

Rodney Hall C

Residence Hall

Rodney Dining Hall

Dining Hall

Fred Rust Ice Arena

In the final section of this chapter, we will also take a look at how we can preview this in the map interface.

The cartographic rendering of geospatial data – MBTiles and UTFGrid

At this point, you may be wondering, what about the maps? So far, we have not included any geospatial data or visualization. We will be offloading some of the effort in managing and providing geospatial data and services to OpenStreetMap—our favorite public open source geospatial data repository!

Why do we use OpenStreetMap?

- OSM already provides mirrored map services for quick reproduction in the basemaps
- OSM provides a very extensive and scalable schema for the kind of geographic features that you might find on a campus
- Various web, mobile, and desktop clients have already been written to interact with the OSM API
- OSM provides the databases and other infrastructure, so we don't have to
- OSM has a granular and reliable way to track changes, using the osm_version and osm_user fields, which complement the osm_id unique ID field

OpenStreetMap to SpatiaLite

To use the OSM data, we need to get it in a format that will be interoperable with other GIS software components. A quick and powerful solution is to store the OSM data in a SQLite SpatiaLite database instance, which, if you remember, is a single file with full spatial and SQL functionality.

To use QGIS to download and convert OSM to SQLite, perform the following steps:

1. Obtain the OSM data in the same way that we did in *Chapter 4, Finding the Best Way to Get There*. Use the OpenLayers plugin to zoom into Newark, DE (or use the extent, 39.7009, -75.7195, 39.6542, -75.7784, clockwise from the top of the dialog in the next step):

   1. Navigate to **Vector** | **OpenStreetMap** | **Download Data** to download the OSM data for this extent.

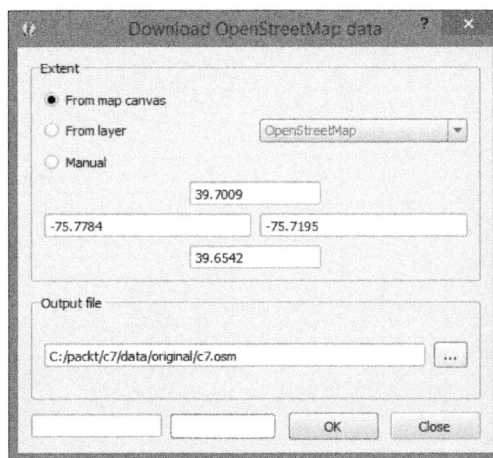

2. Next, export the XML data in the `.osm` file to a topological SQLite database. This could potentially be used for routing; although, we will not be doing so here.

   1. Navigate to **Vector | OpenStreetMap | Import Topology from XML**.

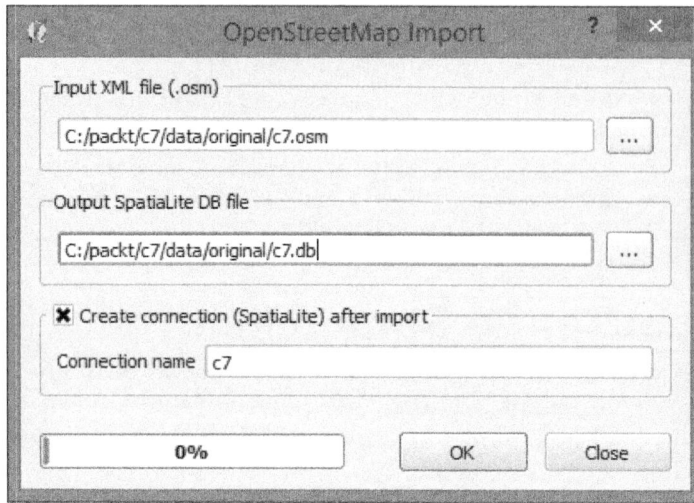

3. Next, export the topological data to normal geospatial data — polygons in this case.

   1. Navigate to **Vector | OpenStreetMap | Export topology to SpatiaLite**.

   2. **Export type**: **Polygons (closed ways)**.

   3. Click on **Load from DB** to populate the list of fields in the data. Select the fields **amenity**, **building**, **name**, and **leisure**, as shown in the following screenshot, as fit allowed:

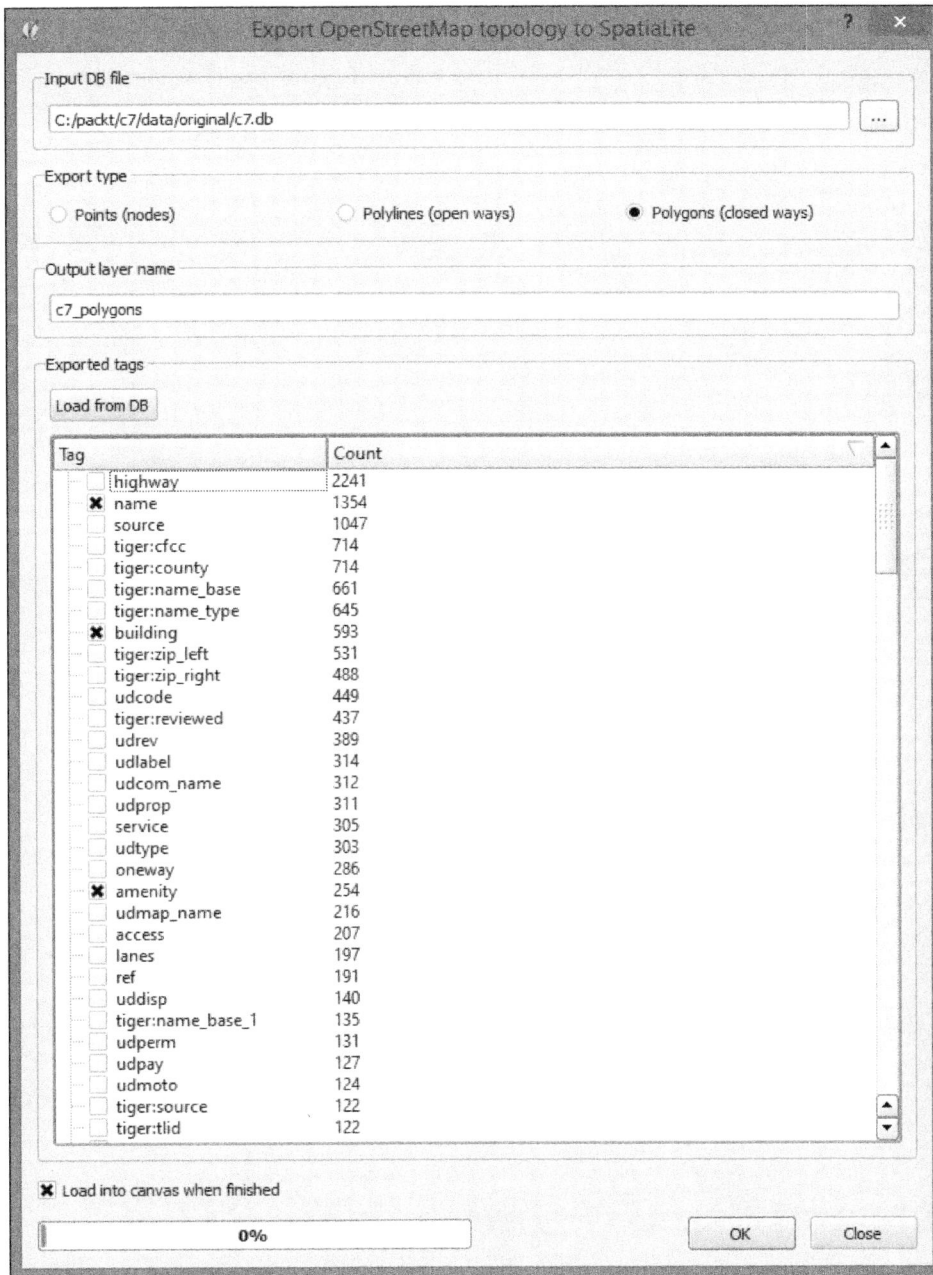

4. Use DB Manager to display the university buildings.

    1. Navigate to **Database** | **DB Manager** | **DB Manager**.

2. Highlight the c7 SQLite database.

3. Execute the following query, ensuring that **Load as new layer** is selected:

```
SELECT * FROM c7_polygons WHERE building = 'yes' and
    amenity = 'university'
```

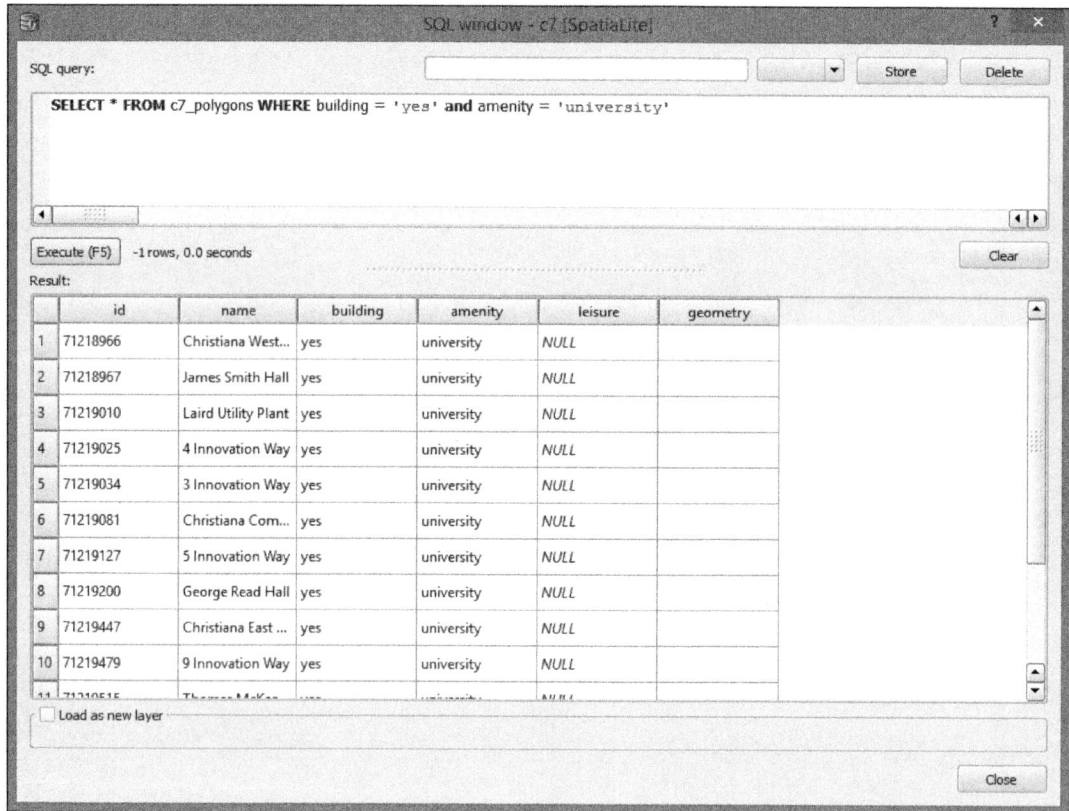

5. Export the query layer to `c7/data/original/delaware-latest-3875/buildings.shp` with the EPSG:3857 projection.

To tile and use UTFGrid with TileMill

Although TileMill is no longer under active production by its creator Mapbox, it is still useful for us to produce MBTiles tiled images rendered by Mapnik using CartoCSS and a UTFGrid interaction layer.

Preparing a basemap from OSM

TileMill requires that all the data be rendered and tiled together and, therefore, only supports vector data input, including JSON, shapefile, SpatiaLite, and PostGIS.

In the following steps, we will render a cartographically pleasing map as a `.mbtiles` (single-file-based) tile cache:

1. Install and open TileMill.

2. Download the Delaware data from the North America section of the Geofabrik OSM extracts site (`http://download.geofabrik.de/north-america.html`) as a shapefile. Alternatively, you can directly download it from `http://download.geofabrik.de/north-america/us/delaware-latest.shp.zip`. Ensure that you expand and copy the zip archive to your project directory after you've downloaded it.

3. Reproject all the data from EPSG:4326 to :3875. If you remember, QGIS can do this in batch as with other **Processing Toolbox** algorithms, as you learned in *Chapter 2, Identifying the Best Places*, making this process a bit quicker.

   Output all the layers to `c7/data/original/delaware-latest-3875`.

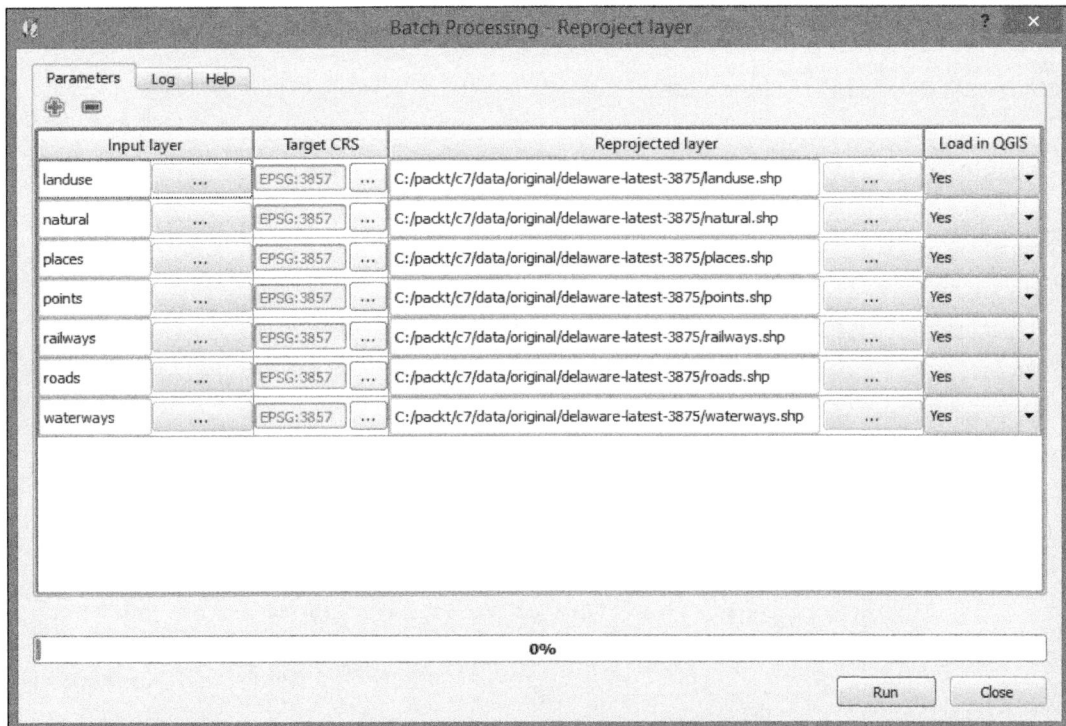

Input layer		Target CRS		Reprojected layer		Load in QGIS	
landuse	...	EPSG:3857	...	C:/packt/c7/data/original/delaware-latest-3875/landuse.shp	...	Yes	▼
natural	...	EPSG:3857	...	C:/packt/c7/data/original/delaware-latest-3875/natural.shp	...	Yes	▼
places	...	EPSG:3857	...	C:/packt/c7/data/original/delaware-latest-3875/places.shp	...	Yes	▼
points	...	EPSG:3857	...	C:/packt/c7/data/original/delaware-latest-3875/points.shp	...	Yes	▼
railways	...	EPSG:3857	...	C:/packt/c7/data/original/delaware-latest-3875/railways.shp	...	Yes	▼
roads	...	EPSG:3857	...	C:/packt/c7/data/original/delaware-latest-3875/roads.shp	...	Yes	▼
waterways	...	EPSG:3857	...	C:/packt/c7/data/original/delaware-latest-3875/waterways.shp	...	Yes	▼

0%

Run   Close

4. Copy the DC example to a new project.

    ○ You will find it in `C:\Program Files (x86)\TileMill-v0.10.1\tilemill\examples\open-streets-dc`

    ○ Copy it to `C:\Users\[YOURUSERNAME]\Documents\MapBox\project\c7`

5. Delete all the files from the `layers` directory.

6. Copy and extract all the shapefiles from `c7/data/original/delaware-latest-3875` into the `layers` directory in the `project` directory of `c7`, which can be found at `C:\Users\[YOURUSERNAME]\Documents\MapBox\project\c7\layers`.

7. Edit the `project.mml` file.

    1. Change all the instances of the `open-streets-dc` string to `c7`.

    2. Change the single instance of `Open Streets, DC` to `c7`.

    3. Substitute the following `bounds` and `center`:

        ```
        "bounds": [
          -75.7845,
          39.6586,
          -75.7187,
          39.71
        ],
        "center": [
          -75.7538,
          39.6827,
          14
        ],
        ```

    4. Change the following layer references to files:

        `Land usages:` Change this layer from `osm-landusages.shp` to `landuse.shp`

        `ocean:` Remove this layer or ignore

        `water:` Change this layer from `osm-waterareas.shp` to `waterways.shp`

        `tunnels:` Change this layer from `osm-roads.shp` to `roads.shp`

        `roads:` Change this layer from `osm-roads.shp` to `roads.shp`

        `mainroads:` Change this layer from `osm-mainroads.shp` to `roads.shp`

        `motorways:` Change this layer from `osm-motorways.shp` to `roads.shp` `bridges`: Change this layer from `osm-roads.shp` to `roads.shp`

`places`: Change this layer from `osm-places.shp` to `places.shp`

`road-label`: Change this layer from `osm-roads.shp` to `roads.shp`

8. Open TileMill and select the `c7` project from the **Projects** dialog, as shown in the following screenshot:

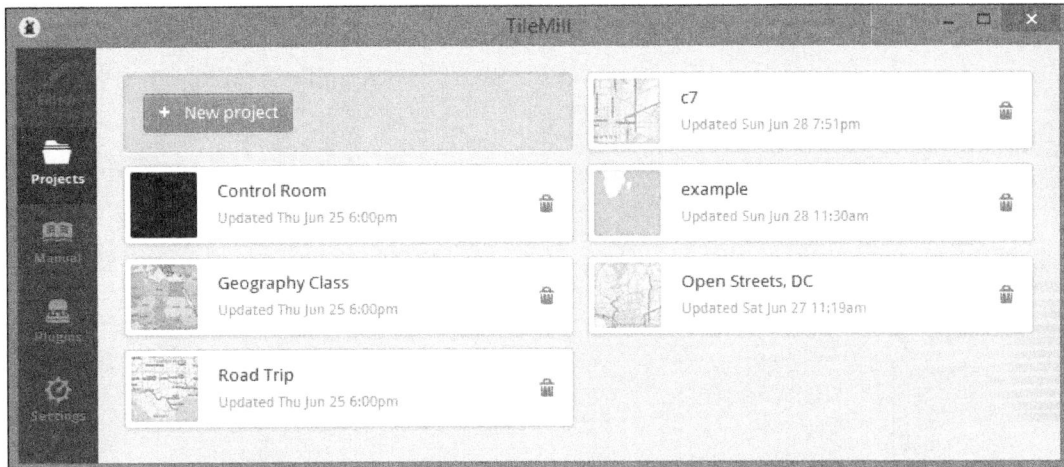

Preparing the operational layer in TileMill

1. Open the **Layers** panel from the bottommost button in the bottom-left corner. Refer to the next image.

2. Click on **+ Add layer**.

3. Populate the parameters with the following values:

    ◦ **ID**: `buildings`.

    ◦ **Datasource**: `c7/data/original/delaware-latest-3875/buildings.shp`.

    ◦ Click on Save & Style. You can return to this dialog later by clicking on the **Editor** button (pencil icon) in the **Layers** panel, by the `#c7` layer, as shown in the next image.

4. If you don't yet see your layer, ensure that you have some style defined in the tab on the right that will be applied to the layer (this should be populated by default with a minimal style). Then, click on **Save** in the top-right corner.

5. Use the CartoCSS syntax to change the style in `style.mss`. TileMill provides a color picker, which we can access by clicking on a swatch color at the bottom of the CartoCSS/style pane. After changing a color, you can view the hex code down there. Just pick a color, place the hex code in your CartoCSS, and save it. For example, consider the following code:

```
#buildings {
  line-color:#eb8f65;
  line-width:0.5;
  polygon-opacity:1;
  polygon-fill:#fdedc9;
}
```

6. Click on **Save** (with the pencil icon) in the upper-right corner of the main screen (above the CartoCSS input) to view the changes, as shown in the following screenshot:

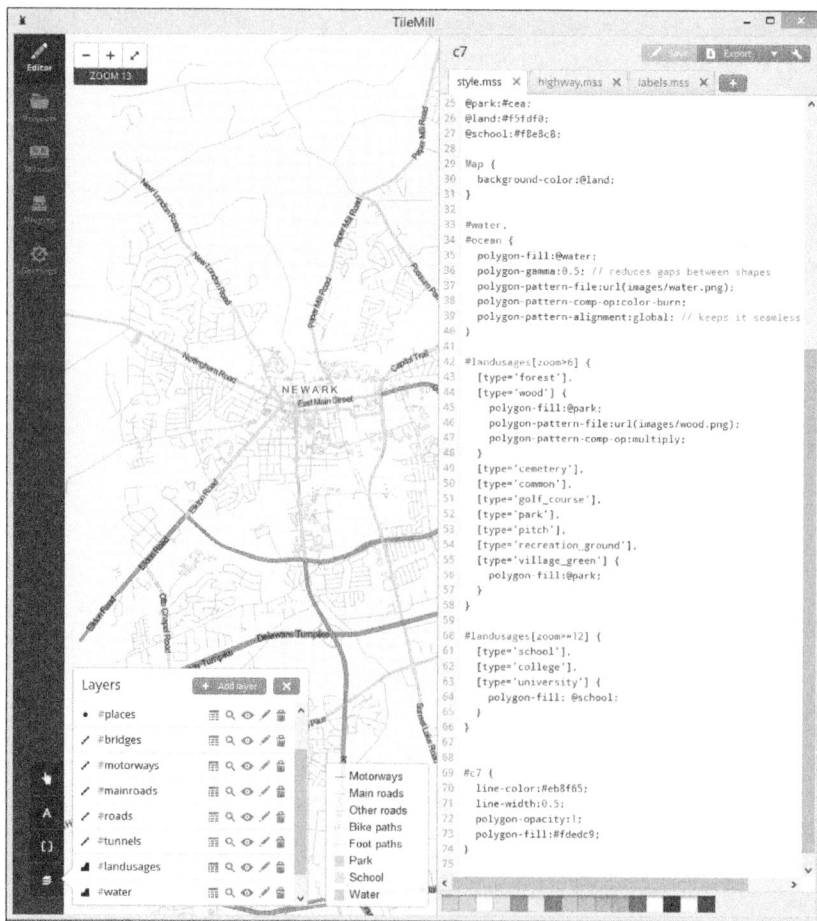

7. Go to the **Templates** tab by clicking on the topmost button in the lower-left corner and change the **Teaser** and **Full** interaction types to use {{{id}}} from buildings, as shown in the following screenshot:

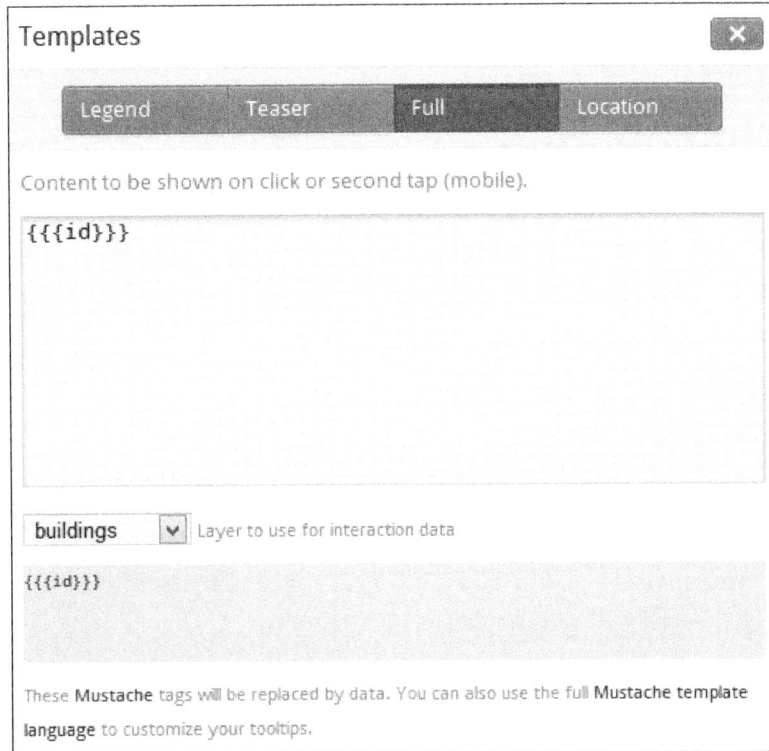

Exporting MBTiles

MBTiles is a format developed by Mapbox to store geographic information. There are two compelling aspects of this format, besides interaction with a small but impressive suite of software and services developed by Mapbox: firstly, MBTiles stores a whole tile store in a single file, which is easy to transfer and maintain and secondly, UTFGrid, which is the use of UTF characters for highly performant data interaction, is enabled by this format.

Uploading to Mapbox

Perform the following steps:

1. Create an account on mapbox.com.

2. Access the **Export** dialog from the **Export** button in the upper-right corner. Select **Upload** from this menu.

3. Sign in to your Mapbox account by clicking on the button at the top of the dialog.

4. Press *Shift*, click on it, and drag to define an extent in the map.

5. Zoom to one level above your intended minimum zoom to preview the extent.

6. Fill in the descriptive information in the export dialog.
    - ◦ **Name**: c7
    - ◦ **Zoom**: 11 to 16

7. Click on the map to establish a **Center** coordinate.

8. Select **Save settings to project**.

9. Upload, as shown in the following screenshot:

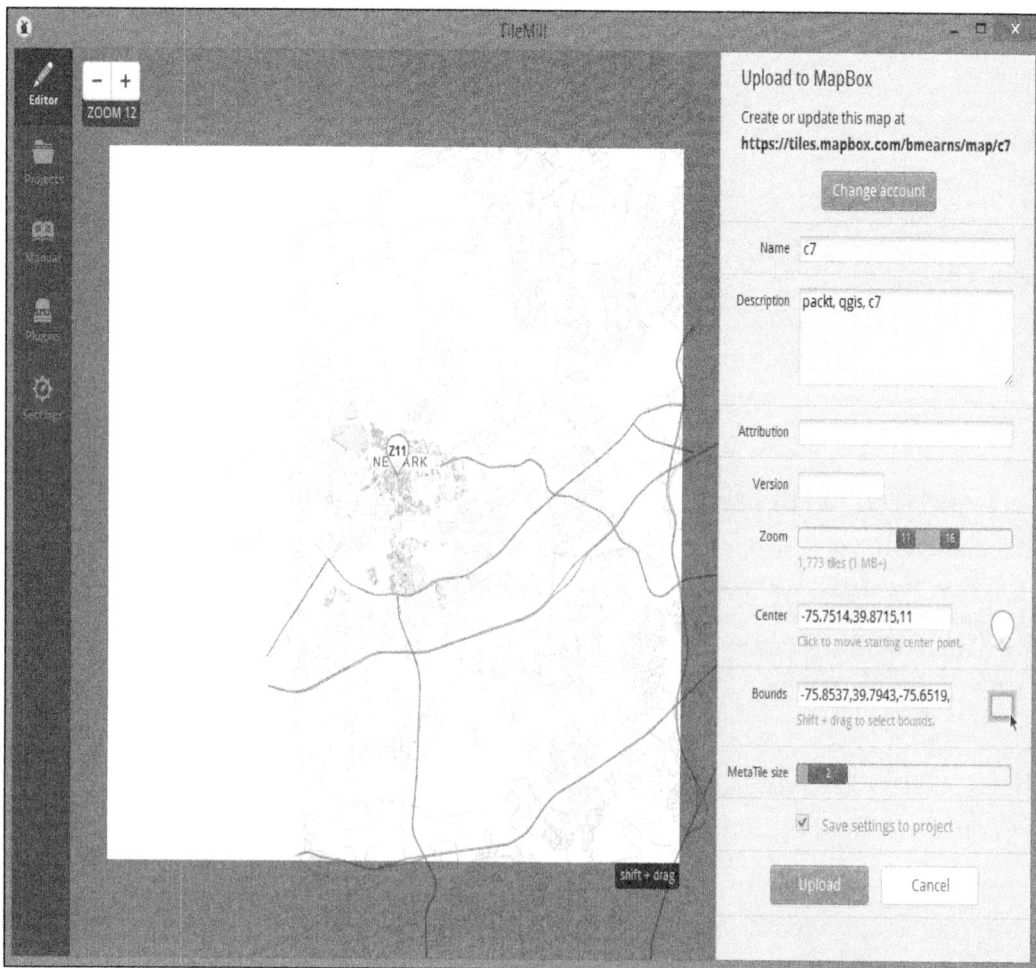

The MBTiles file

The steps for exporting directly to an MBTiles file are similar to the previous procedure. This format can be uploaded to mapbox.com or served with software that supports the format, such as TileStream. Of course, no sign-on is needed.

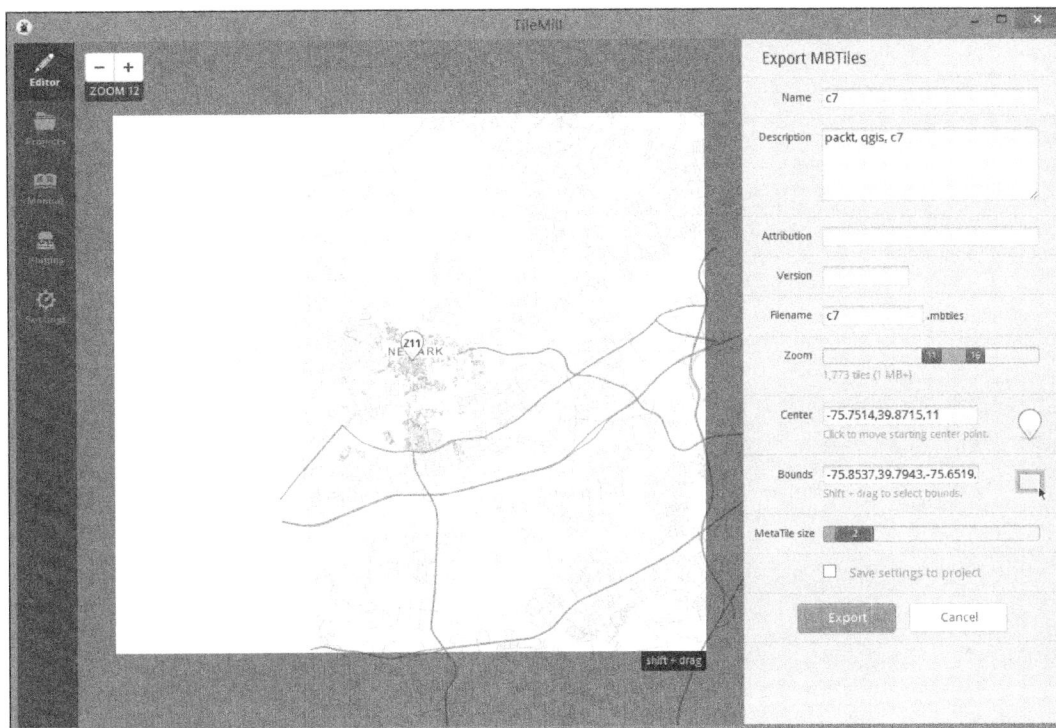

Interacting with Mapbox services

In the last part of the previous section, we uploaded our rendered map to Mapbox in the MBTiles format.

To view the HTML page that Mapbox generates for our MBTiles, navigate to **Export | View Exports**. You'll find the upload listed there. Click on **View** to open it on a web browser.

For example, consider the following URL: `http://a.tiles.mapbox.com/v3/bmearns.c7/page.html#11/39.8715/-75.7514`.

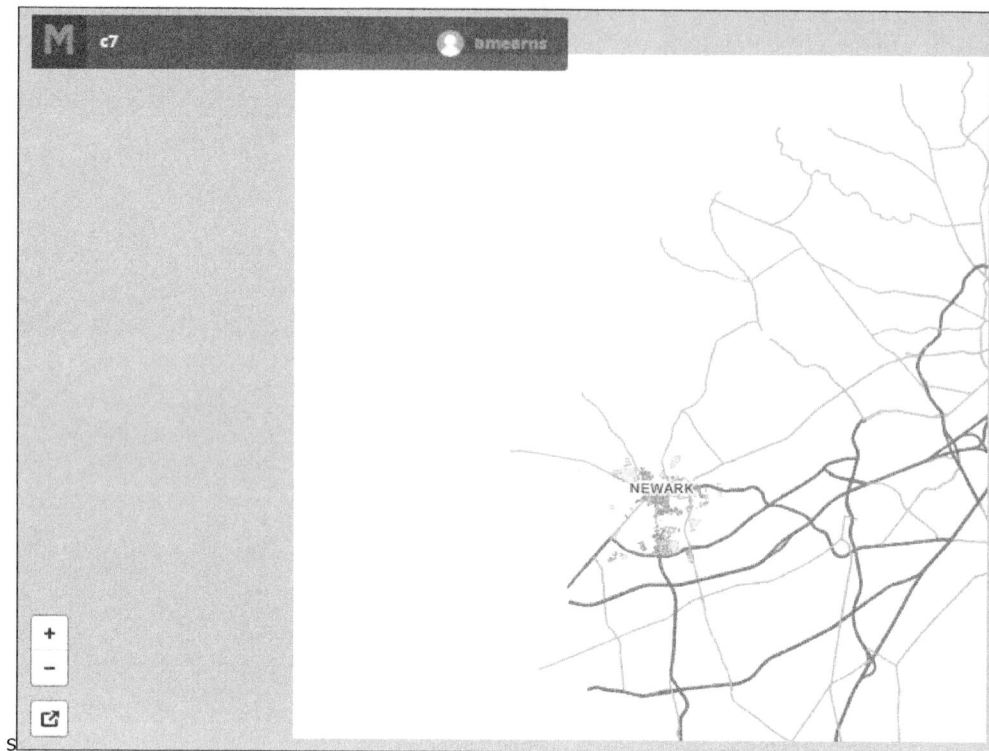

You may also want to preview the TileJSON web service connected to your data. You can do so by adding `.json` after your web map ID (`bmearns.c7`); for example, this is done in `http://a.tiles.mapbox.com/v3/bmearns.c7.json`, which executes the following:

```
{"attribution":"","bounds":[-75.8537,39.7943,-
75.6519,39.9376],"center":[-75.7514,39.8715,11],"description":"p
ackt, qgis, c7","download":"http://a.tiles.mapbox.com/v3/bmearns.
c7.mbtiles","embed":"http://a.tiles.mapbox.com/v3/bmearns.c7.html","f
ilesize":15349760,"format":"png","grids":["http://a.tiles.mapbox.com/
v3/bmearns.c7/{z}/{x}/{y}.grid.json","http://b.tiles.mapbox.com/v3/
bmearns.c7/{z}/{x}/{y}.grid.json"],"id":"bmearns.c7","legend":"","ma
xzoom":16,"minzoom":11,"modified":1435689144009,"name":"c7","private
":true,"scheme":"xyz","template":"{{#__location__}}{{/__location__}}
{{#__teaser__}}{{{id}}}{{/__teaser__}}{{#__full__}}{{{id}}}{{/__full__
}}","tilejson":"2.0.0","tiles":["http://a.tiles.mapbox.com/v3/bmearns.
c7/{z}/{x}/{y}.png","http://b.tiles.mapbox.com/v3/bmearns.c7/{z}/{x}/
{y}.png"],"version":"1.0.0","webpage":"http://a.tiles.mapbox.com/v3/
bmearns.c7/page.html"}
```

Connecting your local app with a hosted service

Now that we can see our tile server via Mapbox-generated HTML and JSON, let's take a look at how we can connect this with a local HTML that we can customize.

The API token

First, you'll need to obtain the API token from Mapbox. The token identifies your web application with Mapbox and enables the use of the web service you've created. As you will be adding this to the frontend code of your application, it will be publically known and open to abuse. Given Mapbox's monthly view usage limitations, you may want to consider a regular schedule for the token rotation (which includes creation, code modification, and deletion). This is also a good reason to consider hosting your service locally with something similar to TileStream, which is covered in the following *Going further – local MBTiles hosting with TileStream* section.

Mapbox.js

`Mapbox.js` is the mapping library developed by Mapbox to interact with its services. As Leaflet is at its core, the code will look familiar. We'll look at the modifications to the `Creating a popup from UTFGrid data` sample app code that you can get at `https://www.mapbox.com/mapbox.js/example/v1.0.0/utfgrid-data-popup/`.

Simple UTFGrid modification

In the following example, we will modify just the portions of code that directly reference the example data. Of course, we would want to change these portions to reference our data instead:

```html
<!DOCTYPE html>
<html>
  <head>
    <meta charset=utf-8 />
    <title>Creating a popup from UTFGrid data</title>
    <meta name='viewport' content='initial-scale=1,maximum-
      scale=1,user-scalable=no' />
    <script src='https://api.tiles.mapbox.com/mapbox.js/v2.2.1/
      mapbox.js'></script>
    <link href='https://api.tiles.mapbox.com/mapbox.js/v2.2.1/
      mapbox.css' rel='stylesheet' />
    <style>
      body { margin:0; padding:0; }
      #map { position:absolute; top:0; bottom:0; width:100%; }
    </style>
  </head>
  <body>
    <div id='map'></div>
    <script>
      // changed token and center coordinate pair/zoom below
      L.mapbox.accessToken = 'YOURMAPBOXTOKEN';
      var map = L.mapbox.map('map', 'mapbox.streets')
        .setView([39.87240,-75.75367], 15);

      // change variable names as appropriate (optional)
      // changed mapbox id to refer to our layer/service
      var c7Tiles = L.mapbox.tileLayer('bmearns.c7').addTo(map);
      var c7Grid = L.mapbox.gridLayer('bmearns.c7').addTo(map);

      // add click handler for grid
      // changed variable name in tandem with change above
      c7Grid.on('click', function(e) {
        if (!e.data) return;
        var popup = L.popup()
          .setLatLng(e.latLng)
          // changed to refer to a field we have here, as seen in
            tilemill interaction tab
          .setContent(e.data.id)
          .openOn(map);
```

```
        });
    </script>
  </body>
</html>
```

Previewing a simple UTFGrid modification

The preceding code will produce the following map view and grid interaction. Note that the value of the `id` attribute is displayed on click:

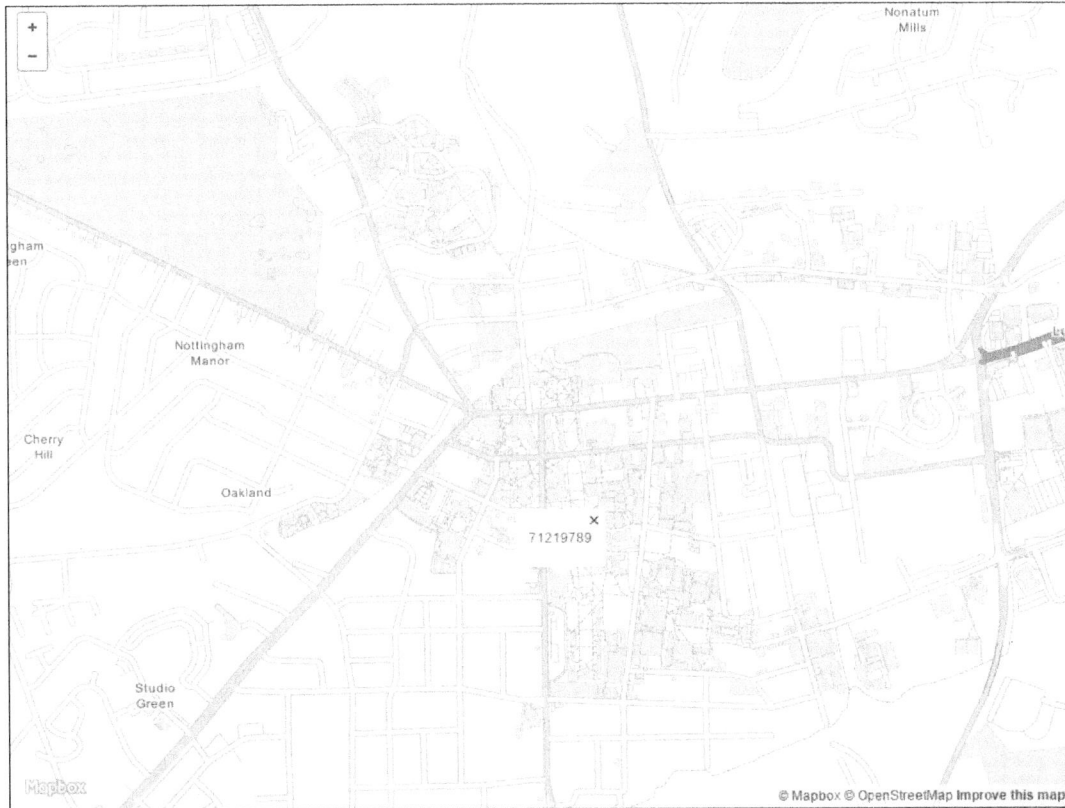

OpenLayers

The OpenLayers project provides a sample UTFGrid web map at
`http://openlayers.org/en/v3.2.1/examples/tileutfgrid.html`.

Code modification

The following is the sample code with the modifications for our data. References to the OpenLayers example (for instance, in the function names) were removed and replaced with generic names. The following example demonstrates a mouseover type event trigger (c7/data/web/utfgrid-ol.html):

```html
<!DOCTYPE html>
<html>
  <head>
  <title>TileUTFGrid example</title>
  <!- dependencies -->
  <script src="https://code.jquery.com/jquery-1.11.2.min.js">
    </script>
  <link rel="stylesheet" href="https://maxcdn.bootstrapcdn.com/
    bootstrap/3.3.4/css/bootstrap.min.css">
  <script src="https://maxcdn.bootstrapcdn.com/bootstrap
    /3.3.4/js/bootstrap.min.js"></script>
  <link rel="stylesheet" href="https://cdnjs.cloudflare.com/ajax/
    libs/ol3/3.6.0/ol.css" type="text/css">
  <script src="https://cdnjs.cloudflare.com/ajax/libs/
    ol3/3.6.0/ol.js"></script>
  </head>
  <body>
    <!-- html layout -->
    <div class="container-fluid">

      <div class="row-fluid">
        <div class="span12">
          <div id="map" class="map"></div>
        </div>
      </div>

      <div style="display: none;">
        <!-- Overlay with target info -->
        <div id="info-info">
          <div id="info-name"> </div>
        </div>
      </div>

    </div>
    <script>
      // new openlayers tile object, pointing to TileJSON object
        from our mapbox service
      var mapLayer = new ol.layer.Tile({
```

```
    source: new ol.source.TileJSON({
      url: 'http://api.tiles.mapbox.com/v3/bmearns.c7.json?
        access_token=YOURMAPBOXTOKENHERE'
    })
  });
  // new openlayers UTFGrid object
  var gridSource = new ol.source.TileUTFGrid({
    url: 'http://api.tiles.mapbox.com/v3/bmearns.c7.json?
      access_token=YOURMAPBOXTOKENHERE'
  });

  var gridLayer = new ol.layer.Tile({source: gridSource});

  var view = new ol.View({
    center: [-8432793.2,4846930.4],
    zoom: 15
  });

  var mapElement = document.getElementById('map');
  var map = new ol.Map({
    layers: [mapLayer, gridLayer],
    target: mapElement,
    view: view
  });

  var infoElement = document.getElementById('info-
    info');
  var nameElement = document.getElementById('info-name');

  var infoOverlay = new ol.Overlay({
    element: infoElement,
    offset: [15, 15],
    stopEvent: false
  });
  map.addOverlay(infoOverlay);

  // creating function to register as event handler, to
  //   display info based on coordinate and view resolution
  var displayInfo = function(coordinate) {
    var viewResolution = /** @type {number} */
      (view.getResolution());
    gridSource.forDataAtCoordinateAndResolution(coordinate,
      viewResolution,
    function(data) {
```

```
        // If you want to use the template from the TileJSON,
        //   load the mustache.js library separately and call
        //   info.innerHTML = Mustache.render(gridSource.
          getTemplate(), data);
        mapElement.style.cursor = data ? 'pointer' : '';
        if (data) {
          nameElement.innerHTML = data['id'];
        }
        infoOverlay.setPosition(data ? coordinate : undefined);
      });
    };

    // registering event handlers
    map.on('pointermove', function(evt) {
      if (evt.dragging) {
        return;
      }
      var coordinate = map.getEventCoordinate(evt.original
        Event);
      displayInfo(coordinate);
    });

    map.on('click', function(evt) {
      displayInfo(evt.coordinate);
    });
  </script>
```

Putting it all together

Now, we'll connect the Google Sheets feed with our Mapbox tiles service in our final application.

Parsing the sheets JSON feed

Previously, we parsed the JSON feed with jQuery for each loop to print two attribute values for each element. Now, we'll remap the feed onto an object that we can use to look up data for the geographic objects triggered in UTFGrid. Review the following code, to see how this done:

```
// Create a data object in public scope to use for mapping
// of JSON data, using id for key
var d = {};

// url variable is set with code from previous section
```

```
// url contains public sheet id

$.getJSON(url, function(data) {
  var entry = data.feed.entry;
  var title = '';

  $(entry).each(function(index, value){
    // Column names are name, type, etc.
    $('.results').prepend('<h2>'+this.gsx$name.$t+'</h2><p>'+
      this.title.$t +'</p>'+'<p>'+this.gsx$type.$t+'</p>');
    title = this.title.$t;
    $.each(this, function(i, n){
      if(!d[title]){
        d[title] = {};
      }
      d[title][i] = n.$t;
    });
  });
});
```

Completing the application

Finally, to complete the application, we need to add the event handler function inside the jQuery AJAX call to the code which handles our feed. This will keep the mapped data variable in a scope relative to the events triggered by the user. The following code is in `c7/data/web/utfgrid-mb.html`:

```
<!DOCTYPE html>
<html>
  <head>
  <meta charset=utf-8 />
  <title>A simple map</title>
  <meta name='viewport' content='initial-scale=1,maximum-
    scale=1,user-scalable=no' />
  <script src="http://code.jquery.com/jquery-1.11.3.
    min.js"></script>
  <script src='https://api.tiles.mapbox.com/mapbox.js/v2.2
    .1/mapbox.js'></script>
  <link href='https://api.tiles.mapbox.com/mapbox.js/v2.2
    .1/mapbox.css' rel='stylesheet' />
  <style>
    body { margin:0; padding:0; }
    #map { position:absolute; top:0; bottom:0; width:100%; }
  </style>
  </head>
  <body>
    <div id='map'></div>
```

```
<script>
  // ID of the Google Spreadsheet
  var spreadsheetID = "1gDPlmvEX0P4raMvTJzcVNT3JVhtL3e
    K1XjqE7u9u4W4";
  // Mapbox ID
  L.mapbox.accessToken = 'pk.eyJlIjoiYmllYXJucyIsImEiO
    iI1NTJhYWZjNmI5Y2IxNDM5M2M0N2M4NWQyMGQ5YzQyMiJ9.q8-
    B7BXtuizGRBcnpREeWw';

  var map = L.mapbox.map('map', 'mapbox.streets')
    .setView([39.87240,-75.75367], 15);

  c7tiles = L.mapbox.tileLayer('bmearns.c7').addTo(map);
  c7grid = L.mapbox.gridLayer('bmearns.c7').addTo(map);

  // Setup click handler, Google spreadsheet lookup
  var d = {};
  // Make sure it is public or set to Anyone with link can
    view
  var url = "https://spreadsheets.google.com/feeds/list/" +
  spreadsheetID + "/od6/public/values?alt=json";
  $.getJSON(url, function(data) {

    var entry = data.feed.entry;
    var title = '';

    // loops through each sub object from the data feed using
      json each function, constructing html from the object
      properties for click handler
    $(entry).each(function(index, value){
      // Column names are name, type, etc.
      $('.results').prepend('<h2>'+this.gsx$name
        .$t+'</h2><p>'+
        this.title.$t +'</p>'+'<p>'+this.gsx$type.$t+'</p>');
      title = this.title.$t;
      $.each(this, function(i, n){
        if(!d[title]){
          d[title] = {};
        }
        d[title][i] = n.$t;
      });
    });
    // register click handler, displaying html constructed
      from object properties/loop
    c7grid.on('click', function(e) {
      if (!e.data) return;
      key = e.data.id;
      content = d[key].content
```

```
            //
            var popup = L.popup()
                .setLatLng(e.latLng)
                .setContent(content)
                .openOn(map);
        });
    });

    </script>
  </body>
</html>
```

After saving this with a .html extension (for example, `c7/data/web/utfgrid-mb.html`), you can preview the application created using this code by opening the saved file in a web browser. When you do so, you will see something similar to the following image:

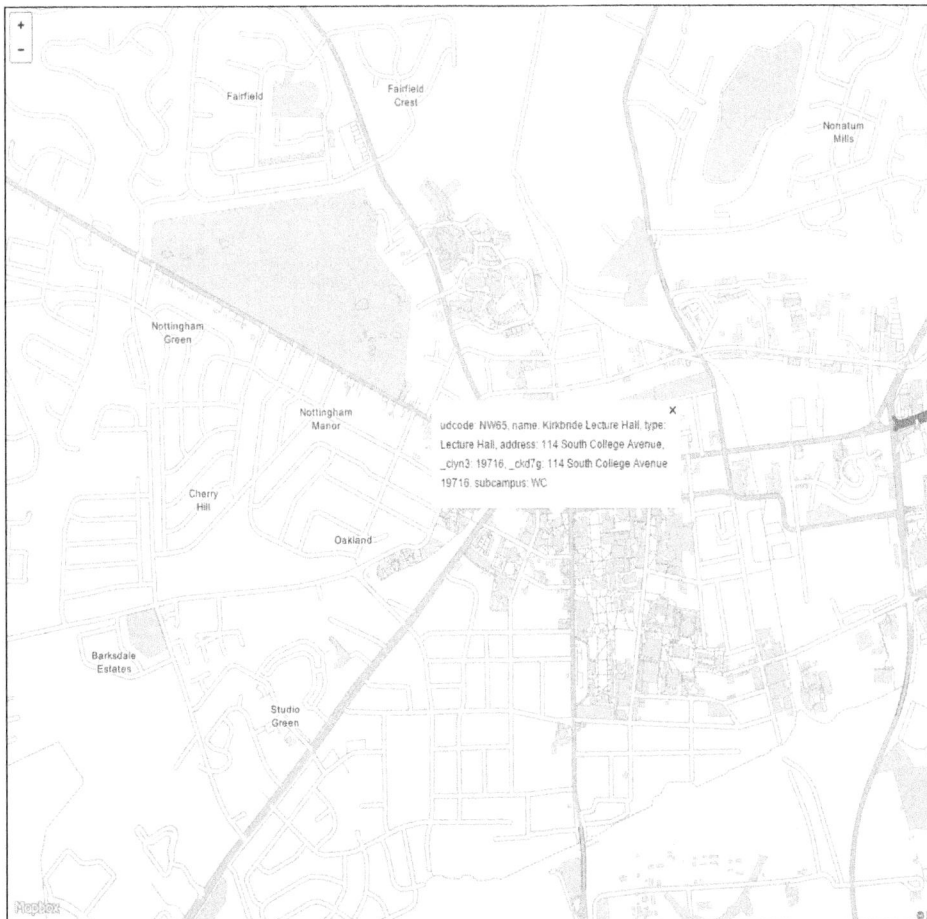

Going further – local MBTiles hosting with TileStream

While Mapbox hosting is very appealing for its relative ease, you may wish to host your own MBTiles, for example, to minimize cost. TileStream is the open source foundation of Mapbox's hosting service. It runs under Node.js.

While TileStream can technically be installed under Windows with a Node.js install, some dependencies may fail to be installed. It is recommended that you perform the following install in a Linux environment. If you are already running Linux on your organization's server, that's great! You can skip ahead to installing Node.js and TileStream. Fortunately, with Virtual Box and Vagrant, it is possible to set up a Linux virtual machine on your Windows system.

Setting up a Vagrant virtual Linux instance

1. Install Virtual Box. You can download Virtual Box from `https://www.virtualbox.org/wiki/Downloads`.

2. Install Vagrant. You can download Vagrant from `https://www.vagrantup.com/`.

3. Create a new directory for your Vagrant instance (for example, `c:\packt\c7\vagrant`).

4. In the Windows command line, run the following:

   `cd c:\packt\c7\vagrant`

5. Create your vagrant instance by running the following in the Windows command line:

   `vagrant init hashicorp/precise32`

   `vagrant up`

6. You should now see a file called Vagrantfile in the present working directory on the Windows command line (for example, `c:\packt\c7\vagrant`). Vagrantfile is the plaintext file that controls the Vagrant configuration. Add the following line to the Vagrantfile to forward the (not yet created) Node.js port to your Windows localhost:

   `config.vm.network "forwarded_port", guest: 8888, host: 8088`

7. Reload Vagrant by running the following in the Windows command line:

   `vagrant reload`

8. Connect to the Vagrant instance through a Windows SSH client.

- ○ If you already have an SSH client on the PATH environment, the `vagrant ssh` variable should start it up and connect it to the instance in this directory

- ○ If not, you can just set the following connection parameters under your Windows SSH client of choice, such as Putty:

  Host: `127.0.0.1`

  Port: `2222`

  Username: `vagrant`

  Password (if needed): `vagrant`

  Private key: `c:/packt/c7/vagrant/.vagrant/machines/default/virtualbox/private_key`

Installing Node.js and TileStream

Use the following commands to install Node.js from the `chris-lea` package archive. This is the Node.js source recommended by Mapbox. The preceding Vagrant setup steps ensure that the dependencies, such as `apt`, are set up as needed. Otherwise, you may install some other dependencies. Also, note that on systems that do not support GNU/Debian, this will not work; you will need to search for the relevant repositories on yum, find RPMs, or build it from the source. However, I'm not sure that any of this will work.

Note that all the following commands are to be run in the Linux instance. If you followed the preceding steps, you will run these through an SSH client such as Putty:

```
sudo apt-add-repository ppa:chris-lea/node.js
sudo apt-get update
sudo apt-get install nodejs
```

Install Git and clone the TileStream source to a new directory. Run the following command line:

```
git clone https://github.com/mapbox/tilestream.git
cd tilestream
npm install
```

Setting up and starting TileStream

You must add your MBTiles file under `/home/vagrant/Documents/MapBox/tiles`. You can use your preferred file transfer client to do this; I like WinSCP. Just use the same SSH connection info you used for SSH.

Finally, start TileStream:

```
./index.js
```

Now, you can preview your TileStream service at `http://localhost:8088`.

Click on the info button to obtain the address to the PNG tiles. You can modify this by removing the reference to the *x*, *y*, and *z* tiles and adding a `.json` extension to get TileJSON such as `http://localhost:8088/v2/c7_8b4e46.json`.

Now, simply modify the OpenLayers example to refer to this `.json` address instead of Mapbox, and you will have a fully nonMapbox use for MBTiles.

The code demonstrating this is at `http://localhost:8000/utfgrid-ts.html`.

Summary

In this final chapter, we looked at a web application built on the web services that provides editing capabilities to our user. This is on the simpler end of collaborative geographic data systems but with an attractive cartographic rendering capability offered by TileMill (and Mapnik) and a highly performant data publishing capability through MBTiles and UTFGrid.

Module 3

QGIS 2 Cookbook

Become a QGIS power user and master QGIS data management,
visualization, and spatial analysis techniques

1

Data Input and Output

In this chapter, we will cover the following recipes:

- ► Finding geospatial data on your computer
- ► Describing data sources
- ► Importing data from text files
- ► Importing KML/KMZ files
- ► Importing DXF/DWG files
- ► Opening a NetCDF file
- ► Saving a vector layer
- ► Saving a raster layer
- ► Reprojecting a layer
- ► Batch format conversion
- ► Batch reprojection
- ► Loading vector layers into SpatiaLite
- ► Loading vector layers into PostGIS

Introduction

If you want to work with QGIS, the first thing you need is spatial data. Whether you want to prepare a nice-looking map layout or perform spatial analysis, you need to open some data to work with. This chapter deals with the basic input and output commands, which will allow you to use data in several different formats and also export to the most convenient format in case you want to use it in different applications or share with others.

Automation is possible for many of the operations that you will see in this cookbook. This chapter contains some recipes that use automation to process a set of input files.

Finding geospatial data on your computer

This recipe shows you how to use the QGIS browser to locate and open spatial data.

Getting ready

Before you start working, make sure that you have copied the sample dataset to your filesystem and you have it located.

How to do it...

There are several ways of locating and opening a data file to open it in QGIS, but the most convenient of these is the QGIS browser:

1. To enable this, go to the **View | Panels** menu and enable the **Browser** checkbox in it. The browser will be shown by default in the left-hand side of the QGIS window, as shown in the following screenshot:

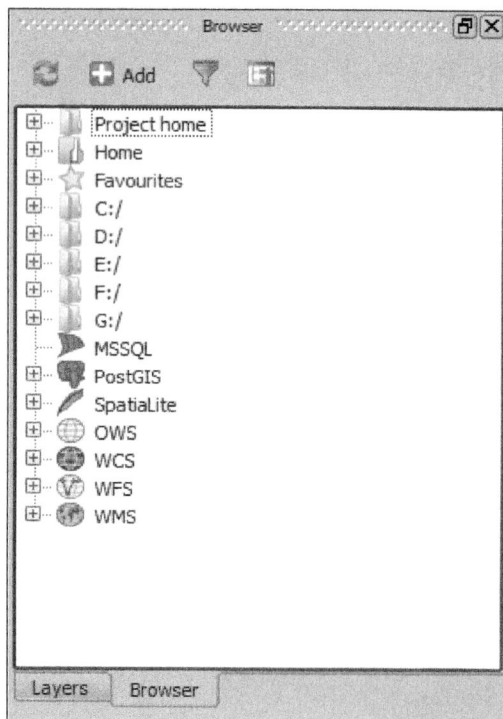

Browser contains a tree with all the available sources of spatial data. This includes data files in your filesystem, databases, and remote services.

2. Navigate to the folder where you copied the sample dataset, and you will see a list of available data files, as shown in the following screenshot:

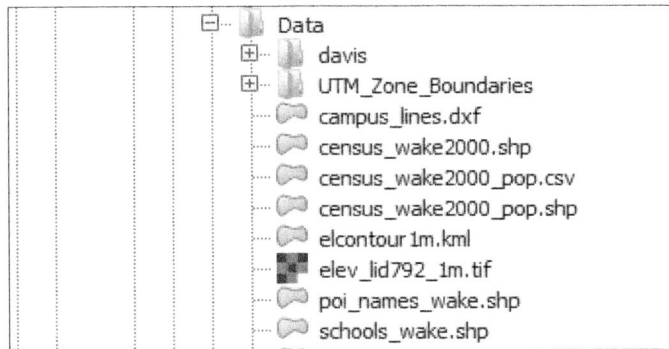

Not all files are shown but just the ones that are identified as valid data sources.

3. To add a file to your project, just right-click on it and select **Add Layer**:

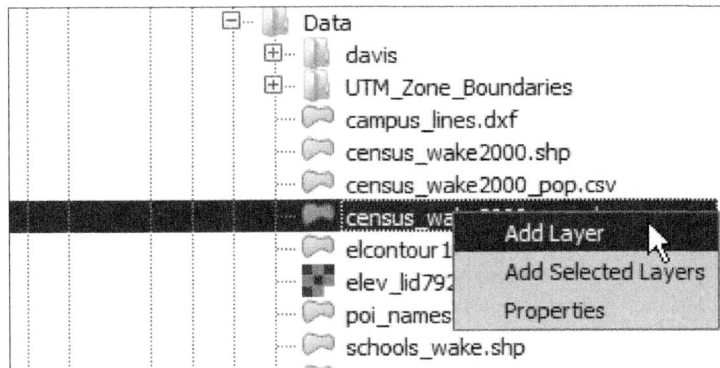

4. Multiple selections are allowed. In that case, select the **Add selected layer** menu.

    Another way of opening a file is by just dragging it and dropping it into the QGIS canvas. Dragging multiple files is allowed, as well, as shown in the following screenshot:

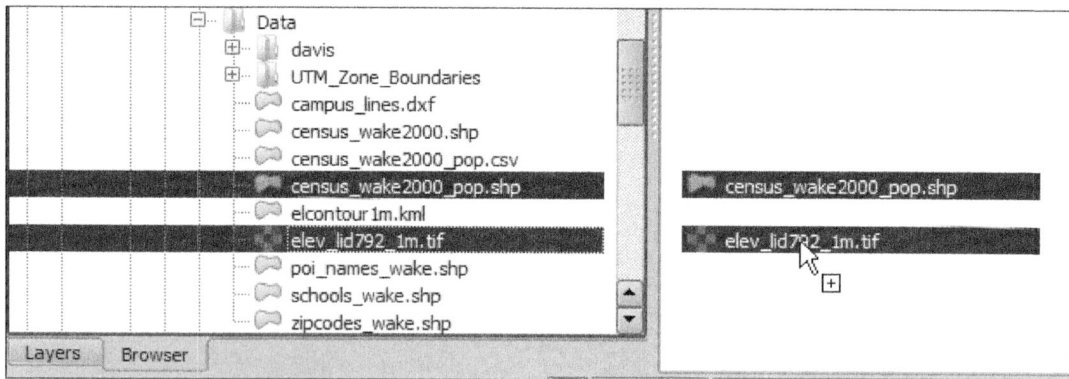

How it works...

The browser acts as a file explorer that is directly linked to QGIS, which only shows valid data files and can be used to easily add them to a QGIS project.

There's more...

There are a few more things that you need to know that are related to this recipe. They are explained in the following sections.

Adding layers with the Layer menu

As an alternative to the browser, the **Layer** menu contains a set of entries. Each of them deals with a different type of data. They give you some additional options, and they might allow you to work with formats that are not directly supported by the browser.

Adding a folder to Favorites

Navigating to the folder where your data is located can be tedious. If you use a given folder regularly, you can right-click on it and select **Add as favorite**. The folder will appear on the **Favorites** section at the top of the browser tree.

Nonfile data sources

The browser also shows non-file data, such as remote services. Services have to be defined before they appear on the corresponding section in the browser. To add a service, right-click on the service name and select **New connection...**. A dialog will appear to define the service connection parameters.

As an example, try adding the following WMS service, using the WMS entry in the browser, as shown in the following screenshot:

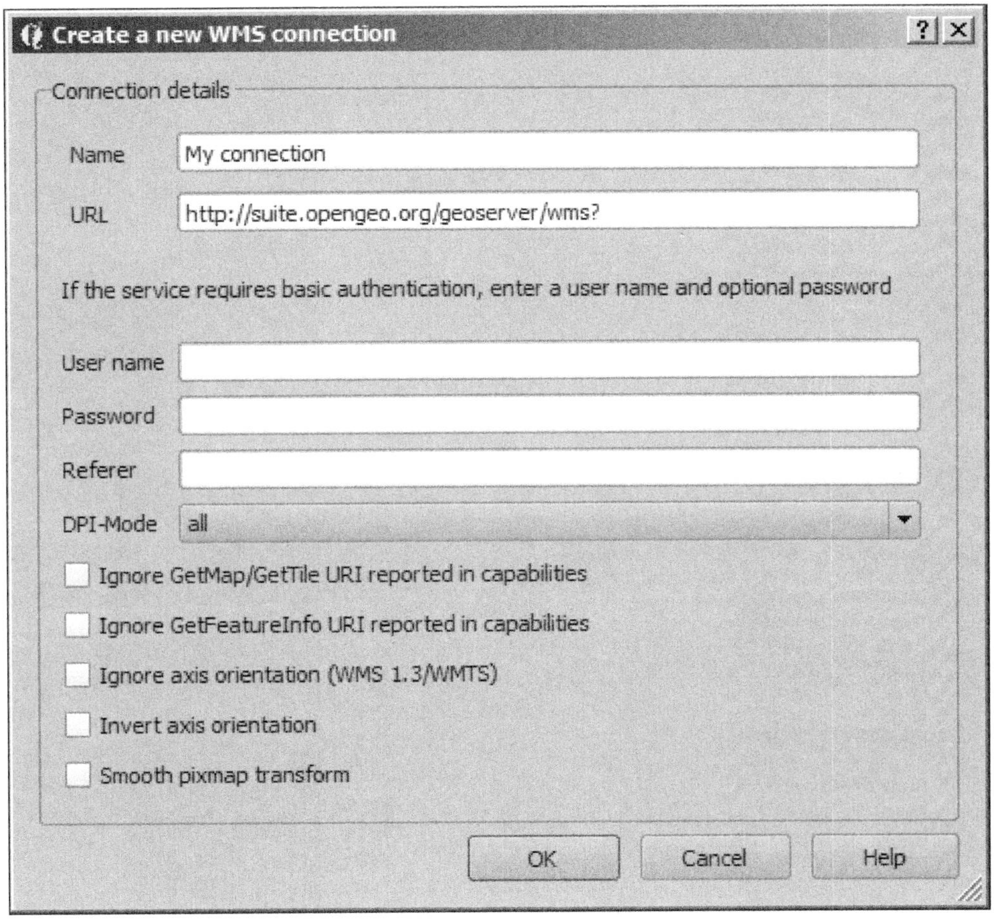

A new entry will appear, containing the layers offered by the service, as shown in the following screenshot:

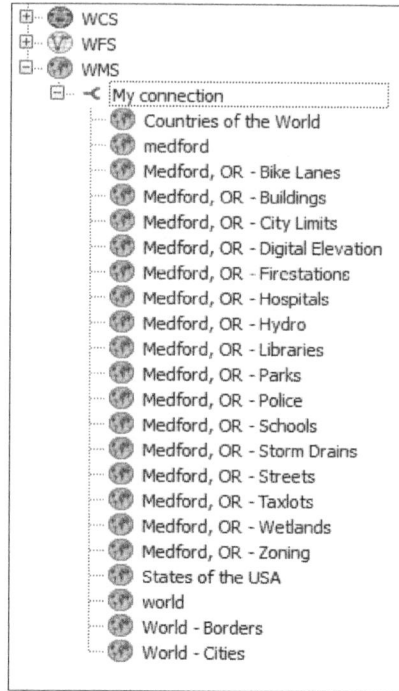

```
⊞ 🌐 WCS
⊞ 🔵 WFS
⊟ 🌐 WMS
     ⊟ ⌐< My connection
          🌐 Countries of the World
          🌐 medford
          🌐 Medford, OR - Bike Lanes
          🌐 Medford, OR - Buildings
          🌐 Medford, OR - City Limits
          🌐 Medford, OR - Digital Elevation
          🌐 Medford, OR - Firestations
          🌐 Medford, OR - Hospitals
          🌐 Medford, OR - Hydro
          🌐 Medford, OR - Libraries
          🌐 Medford, OR - Parks
          🌐 Medford, OR - Police
          🌐 Medford, OR - Schools
          🌐 Medford, OR - Storm Drains
          🌐 Medford, OR - Streets
          🌐 Medford, OR - Taxlots
          🌐 Medford, OR - Wetlands
          🌐 Medford, OR - Zoning
          🌐 States of the USA
          🌐 world
          🌐 World - Borders
          🌐 World - Cities
```

Describing data sources

You can get additional information about a data file before opening it. This recipe shows you how to explore the properties of a data origin.

Getting ready

Before you start working, make sure that you have copied the sample dataset to your filesystem and that you have it located.

How to do it...

1. In the QGIS browser, navigate to the folder with your sample dataset. Select the `elev_lid792_1m` file and right-click on it. In the context menu, select **Properties**. A dialog like the one in the following screenshot will appear:

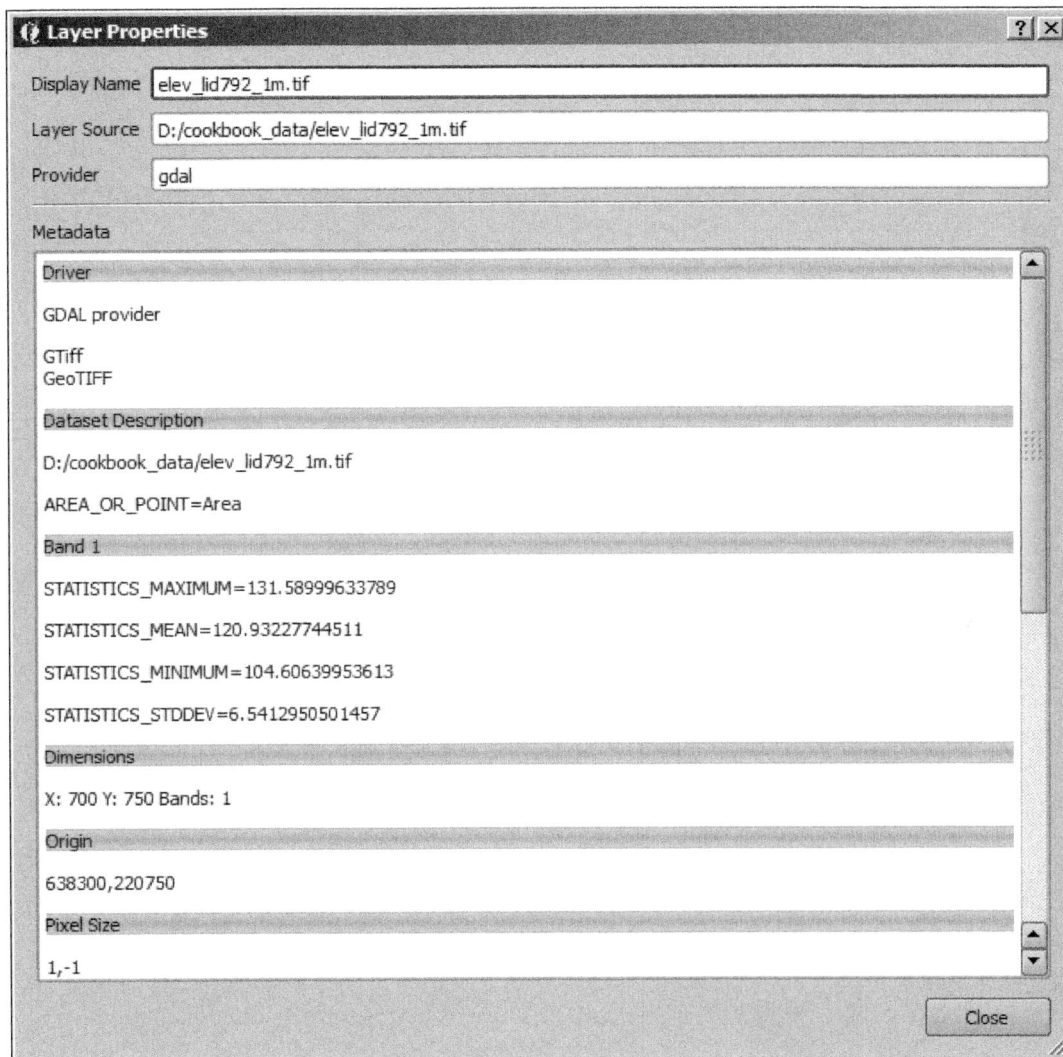

This dialog displays the properties of a raster layer.

2. Now, let's select a vector layer instead. Select the `elev_lid792_randpts.shp` file, right-click on it, and select **Properties**. The information dialog will look like the following:

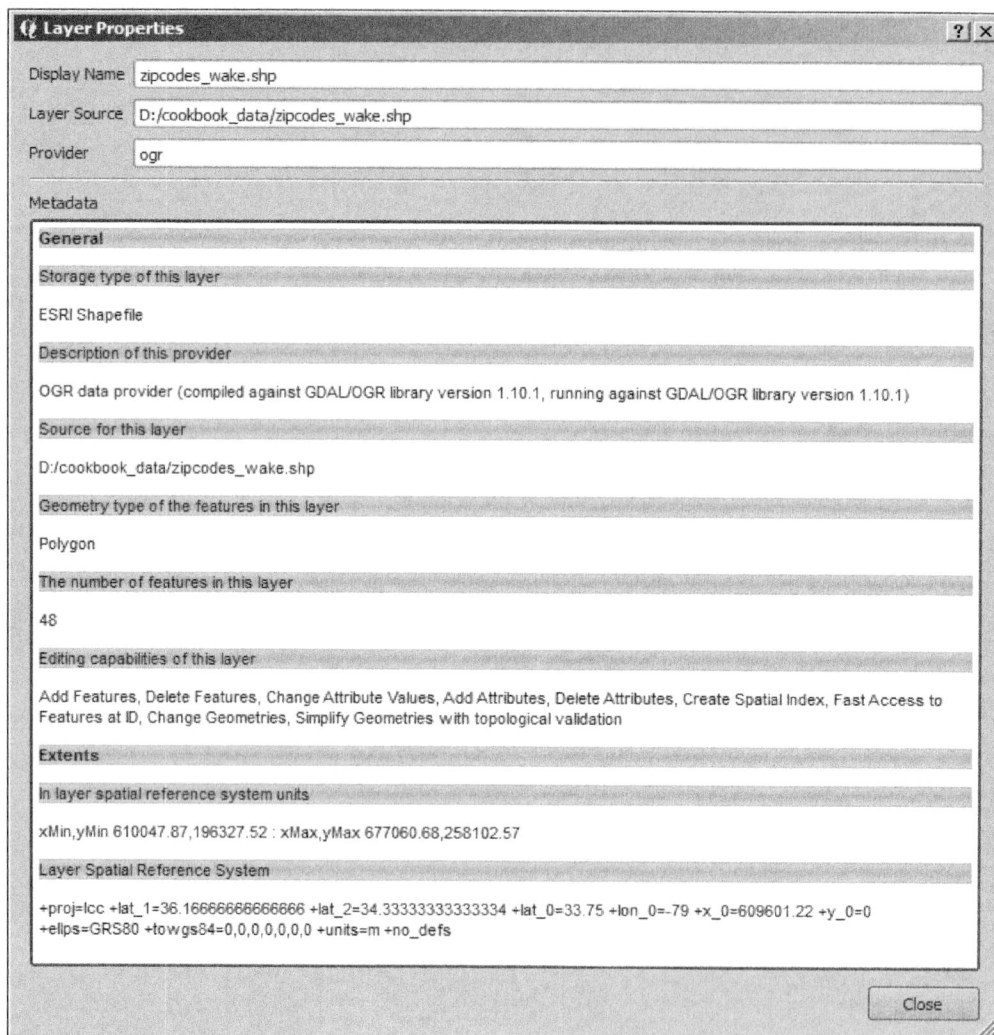

How it works...

In the upper part of the description window, you will see a field named **Provider**. **Provider** defines the type or data origin and who takes care of reading the data and passing it to QGIS. For raster layers, you will see `gdal` as **Provider**. For most file-based vector layers, `ogr` will be the provider that will appear. They refer to the GDAL and OGR libraries, two open-source libraries that are used by many GIS programs to access both raster and vector data.

There's more...

If the data is already loaded in QGIS, you can access the information about it in the **Properties** section of the layer (right-click on the layer name to select the **Properties** entry in the context menu). In the sections displayed in the left-hand side, select the **Metadata** section. You will see a box containing all the information corresponding to the layer data origin:

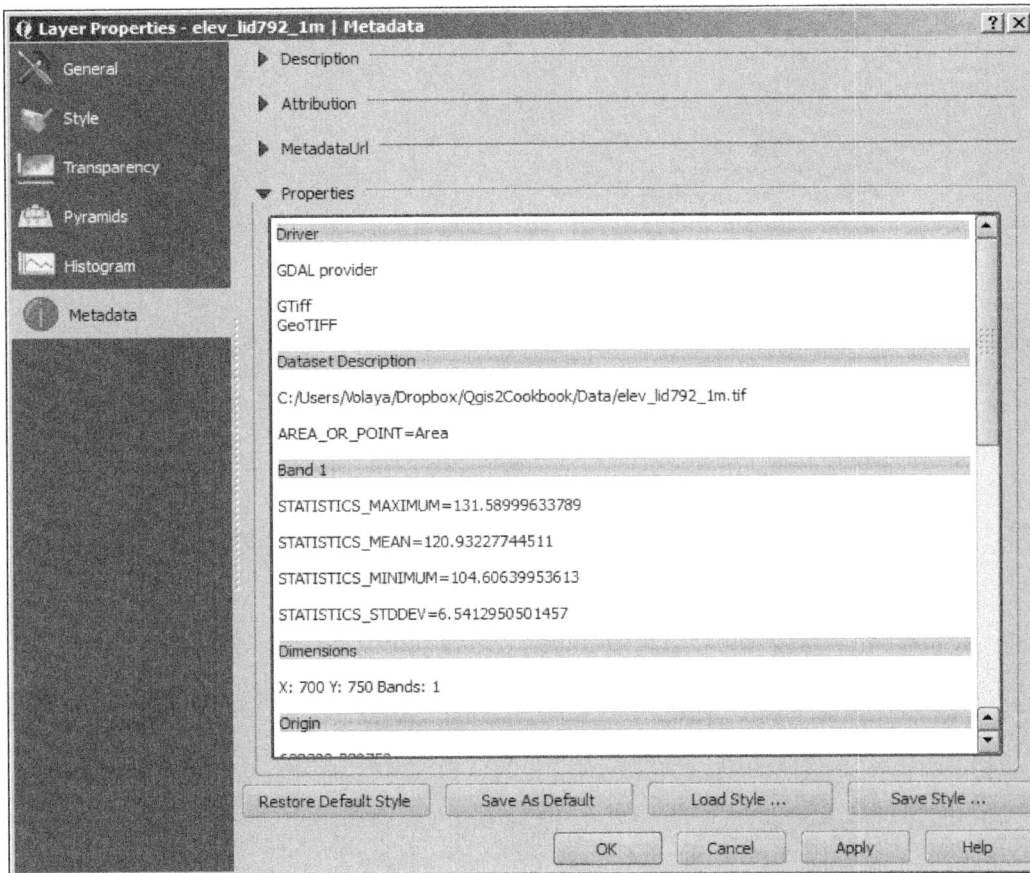

Functionality provided by the GDAL library, which (mentioned earlier) acts as a provider for raster layers, is also available in the **Raster** menu. This includes processing and data analysis methods, but it also includes the information tool that is used to describe a raster data source. You will find it by navigating to **Raster | Miscellaneous | Info**:

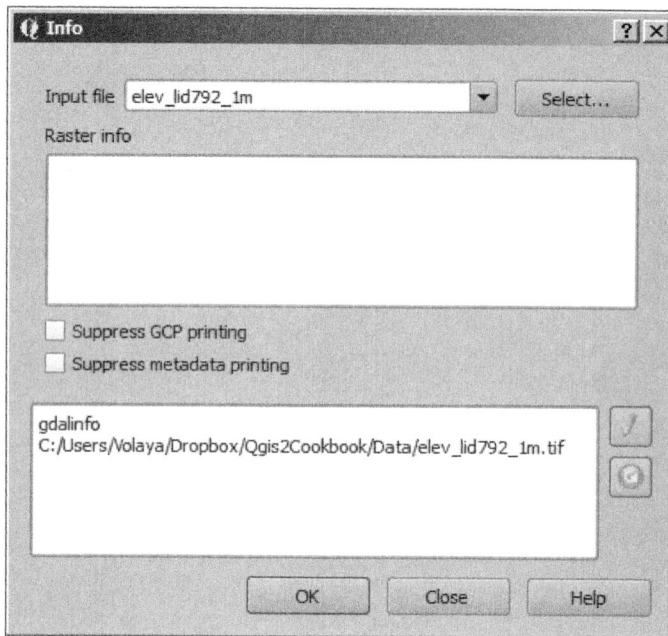

See also

▸ This is a more complex way to retrieve properties as you can call the tool by adjusting the parameters with more details to get additional information. To know more, check the gdalinfo help page at `http://www.gdal.org/gdalinfo.html`.

Importing data from text files

Data can be imported from text files, providing some additional about how the geometry information is stored in the text. This recipe shows you how to create a new points layer, based on a text file.

How to do it...

1. Select the **Add delimited text layer** menu entry from the **Layer** menu. You will see a dialog like the following one:

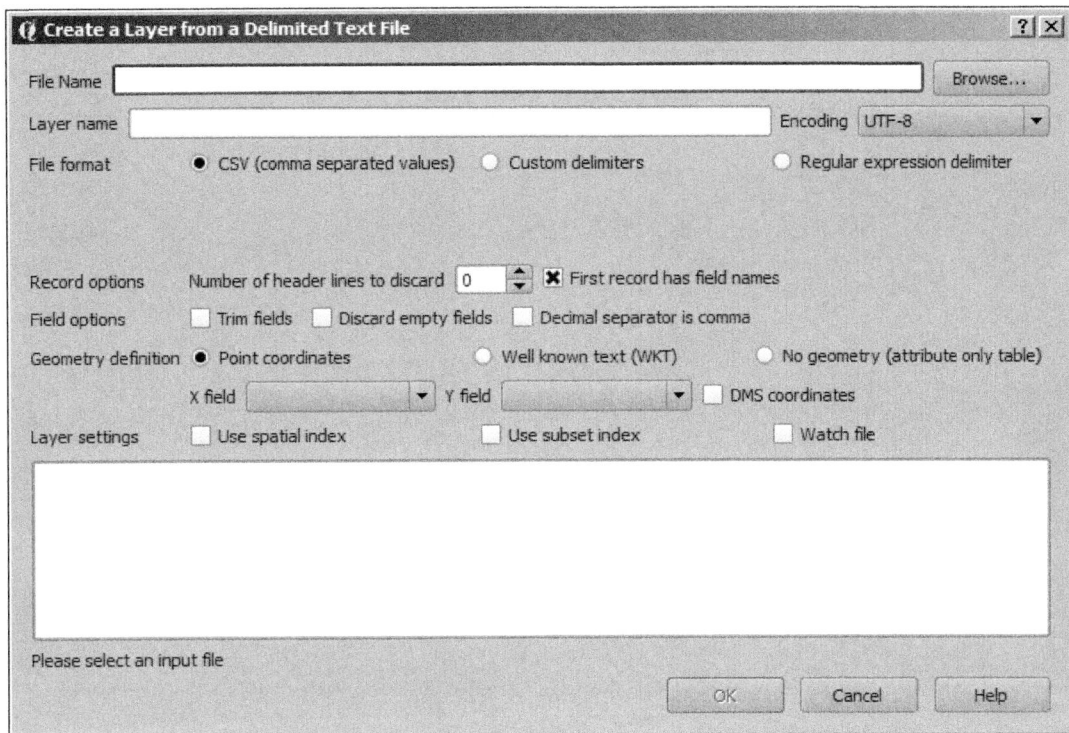

2. In the upper field, enter the path to the `elev_lid792_randpts.csv` file in the sample dataset. That file contains a points layer as text.

3. Once you enter the file path or select it in the file browser that can be opened by clicking on the **Browse** button, the fields in the lower part of the dialog will be filled, as shown in the following screenshot:

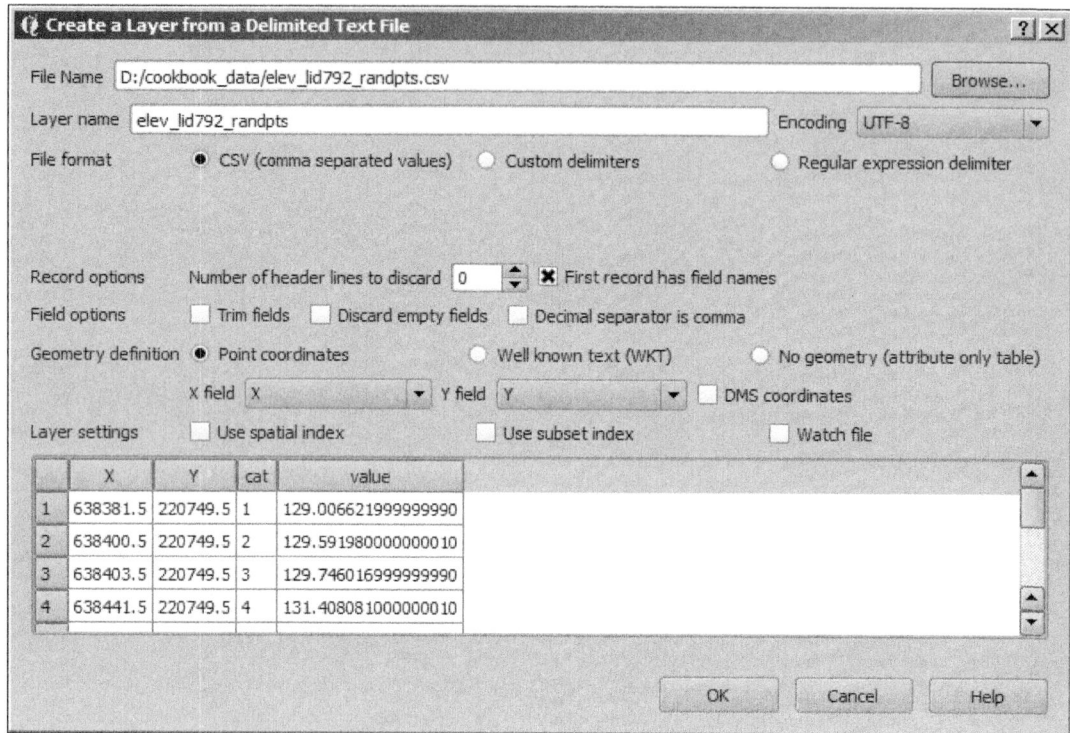

> We are using a CSV file that has values separated by commas, so you must select the **CSV** option in the **Format** field.

The **X field** and **Y field** drop-down lists will be populated with the fields that are available, which are described in the first line of the text file. Select **X** for **X field** and **Y** for **Y field**. Now, QGIS knows how to create the geometries and has enough information to create a new layer from the text file.

4. Enter a name for the layer in the **Layer name** field and click on **OK**. The layer will be added to the QGIS project, as shown in the following screenshot:

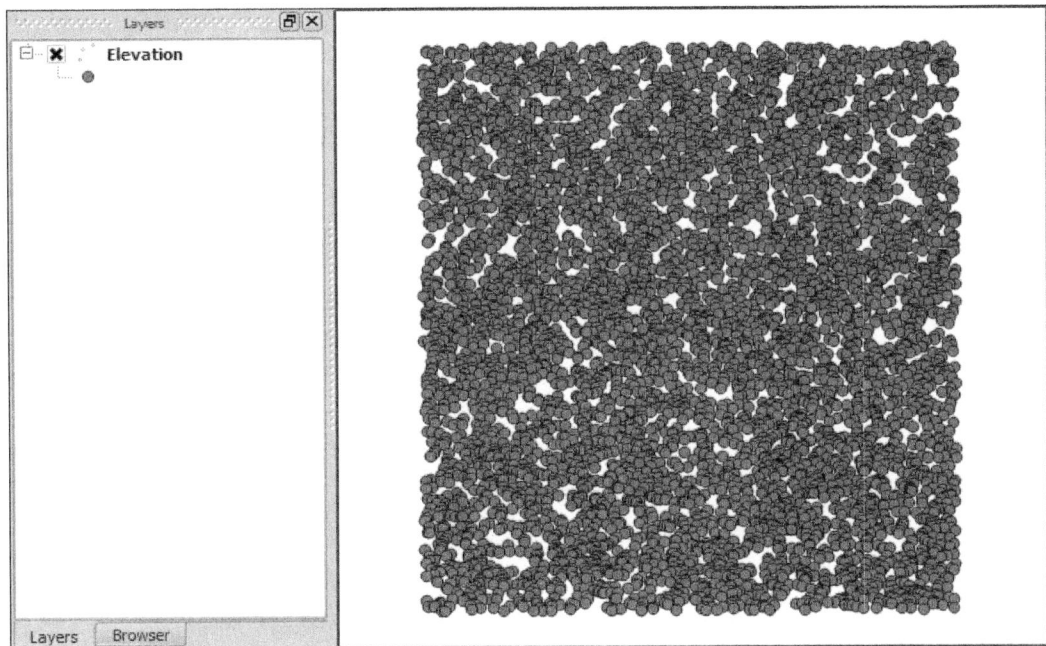

5. No information about the CRS is contained in the text file or entered in the parameters dialog, so it must be added manually. In this case, the CRS used is `EPSG:3358`. To set this as the CRS of the layer, right-click on the layer name and select **Set layer CRS**:

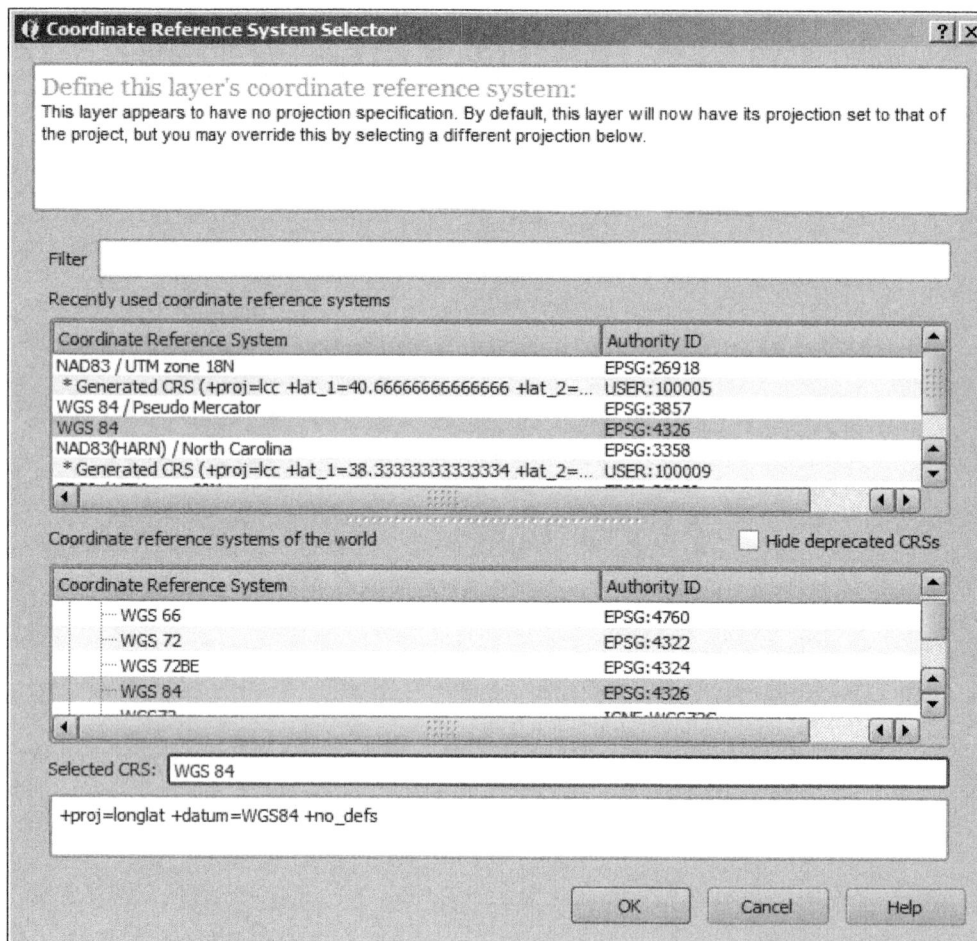

6. In the CRS selection dialog, select the `EPSG:3358` CRS and click on **OK.** The layer now has the correct CRS.

How it works...

Data is read from the text file and processed to create geometries. All the fields in the table (all data in a row in the text file) are also added, including the ones used to create the geometries, as you will see by right-clicking on the layer and selecting **Open attribute table**, as shown in the following screenshot:

	X ▽	Y	cat	value
0	638381.5	220749.5	1	129.006622
1	638400.5	220749.5	2	129.59198
2	638403.5	220749.5	3	129.746017
3	638441.5	220749.5	4	131.408081
4	638469.5	220749.5	5	131.441025
5	638495.5	220749.5	6	130.65657
6	638535.5	220749.5	7	128.474167
7	638591.5	220749.5	8	124.363976
8	638689.5	220749.5	9	124.692833
9	638752.5	220749.5	10	124.022858
10	638935.5	220749.5	11	112.479012

Attribute table - Elevation (6000 Feature(s))

Along with the CSV file, this file may contains a CSVT file, which describes the types of the fields. This is used by QGIS to set the appropriate type for the attributes table of the layer. If the CSVT file is missing, as in our example's case, QGIS will try to figure out the type based on the values for each field.

There's more...

Layers created from text files are not restricted to point files. Any geometry can be created from the text data. However, if it is not a point, instead of selecting two columns, you must place all the geometry information in a single one and enter a text representation of the geometry. QGIS uses the **Well-Known Text** (**WKT**) format, which is a text markup language for vector geometries, to describe geometries as strings. Here is an example of a very simple CSV file with line features and two attributes:

```
geom,id,elevation
LINESTRING(0 1, 0 2, 1 3),1,50
LINESTRING(0 -1, 0 -2, 1 -3),2,60
LINESTRING(0 1, 0 3, 5 4),3,70
```

See also

▶ To know more about the WKT format, you can go to `http://en.wikipedia.org/wiki/Well-known_text`

Importing KML/KMZ files

KML and KMZ files are used and produced by Google Earth and are a popular format. This recipe shows you how to open them with QGIS.

How to do it...

1. To open a KML layer, select **Layer/Add vector layer...**. In the dialog that opens, click on the **Browse** button to open the file selector dialog. Select the **Keyhole Markup Language** (**KML**) format and then select the file that you want to load. In the example dataset, you can find several KML files. Select the `elcontour1m.kml` file. Click on **OK** in the vector layer selector dialog, and the layer will be added to your project, as shown in the following screenshot:

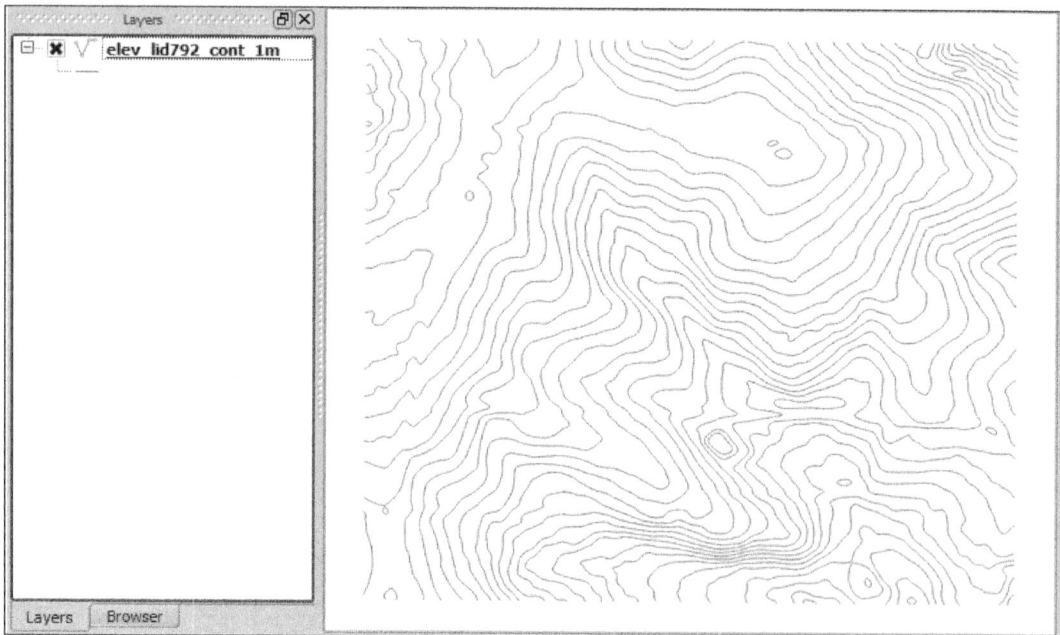

KMZ files can also be opened in QGIS.

2. Go to **Layer | Add vector layer...**. In the dialog that opens, click on the **Browse** button to open the file selector dialog. Select the **All files** option to view all the files and then select the `elcontour1m.kmz` file. There is not a KMZ file type defined in QGIS, but QGIS supports it because the underlying OGR library can read KMZ files as well.

3. Click on **OK** on the open layer dialog to open the selected layer.

From the layers contained in the KMZ file, you must select one of them. In this case, only a layer is contained in the `elcontour1m.kmz` file, so it is loaded automatically. The layer will be added to your QGIS project.

How it works...

KMZ files are compressed files that contain a set of layers. When you select it, the OGR library will unzip the content of this file and then open the layers that it contains.

If just a single layer is contained, you will not see the layer selection dialog. QGIS will automatically open the only layer in the KMZ file.

There's more...

As KMZ is not recognized as a supported format, the KMZ file will not appear in the QGIS browser. However, the browser supports zipped files, and a KMZ file is actually a zipped file with KML files inside it. Unzip it in a folder and then you will be able to use the QGIS Browser to open the layers it contains.

Importing DXF/DWG files

CAD files, such as DXF and DWG files, can be opened with QGIS. This recipe shows you how to do this.

How to do it...

1. To open a DXF layer, select **Add vector layer...** in the **Layer** menu. In the dialog that opens, click on the **Browse** button to open the file selector dialog. Select the **Autocad DXF** format and then the file that you want to load.

2. In the example dataset, you can find several DXF files. Select the `Wake_ApproxContour_100.dxf` file. Click on **OK** in the vector layer selector dialog and the layer will be added to your project, as shown in the following screenshot:

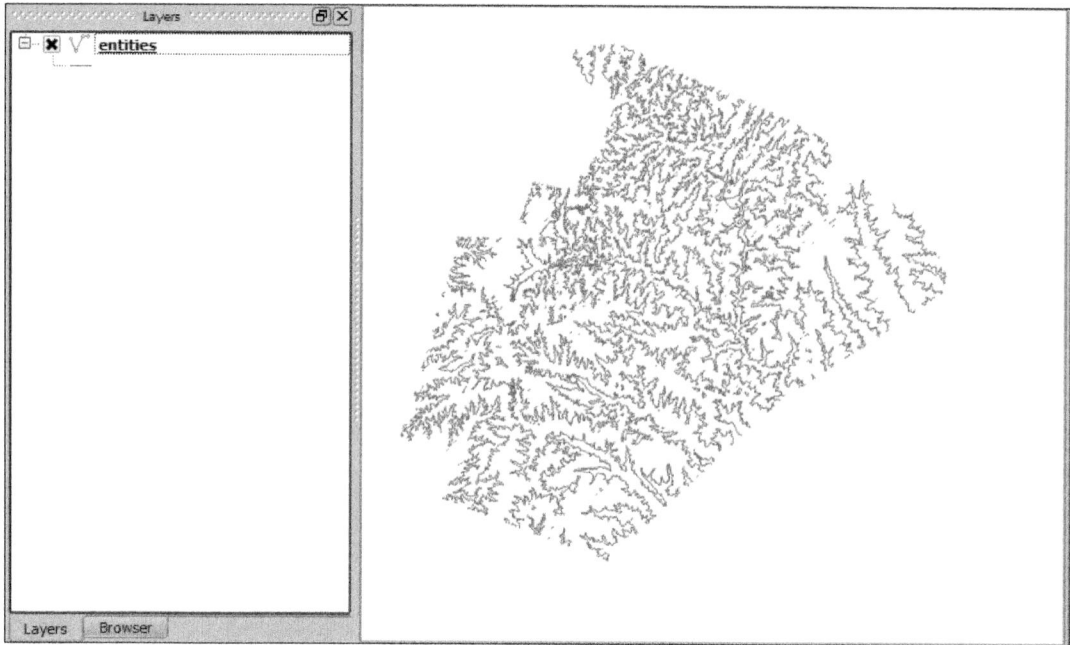

How it works...

DXF files are read as normal vector layers although they do not have the same structure as a regular vector layer as they do not allow adding arbitrary attributes to each geometry.

There's more...

The example DXF file that you opened contained just one type of geometry. DXF files can, however, contain several of them: in this case, they cannot be added to QGIS in one layer. When this happens, QGIS will ask you to select the type of geometry that you want to open.

In the sample dataset, you will find a file named `CSS-SITE-CIV.dxf`. Open it and you will see the following dialog:

Select vector layers to add... ? X

Layer ID	Layer name	Number of features	Geometry type
0	entities	8145	Point
0	entities	43332	LineString
0	entities	111	Polygon
0	entities	1947	GeometryCollection

OK   Select All   Cancel

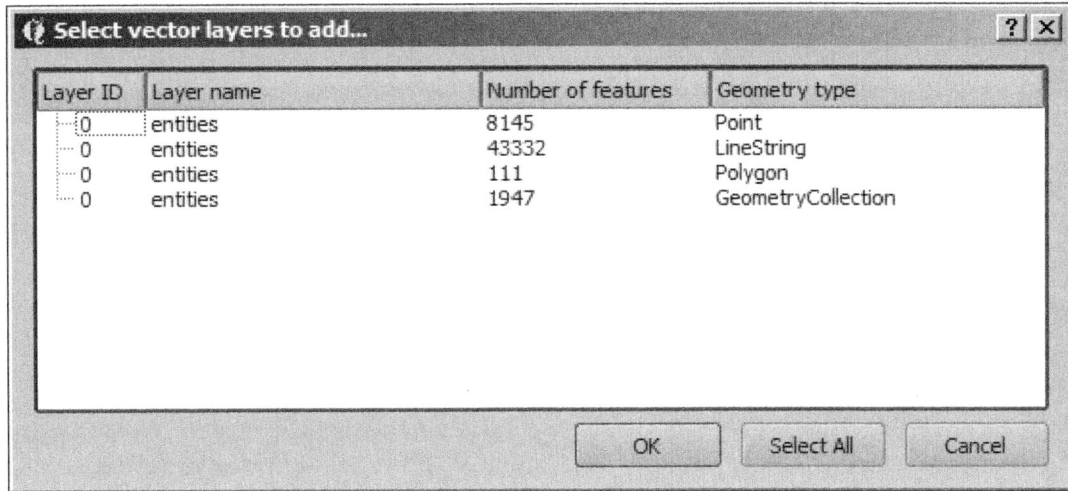

Select one of the available geometries, and a layer will be added to your QGIS project.

Opening DWG files

DWG is a closed format of Autodesk. This means that the specification of the format is not available. For this reason, QGIS, like other open source applications, does not support DWG files. To open a DWG file in QGIS, you need to convert it. Converting it to a DXF file is a good option as this will let you open your file in QGIS without any problem. There are many tools to do this. The Teigha converter can be found at `http://opendesign.com/guestfiles/ TeighaFileConverter` and is a popular and reliable option.

Another option is using the free service offered by Autodesk, called Autocad 360, which can be found at `https://www.autocad360.com/`.

Opening a NetCDF file

The NetCDF data is a data format, which is designed to be used with array-oriented scientific data, and it is frequently used for climate or ocean data, among others. This recipe shows you how to open a NetCDF file in QGIS.

How to do it...

NetCDF files are raster files, and they can be opened using the **Add raster layer** menu. Select `NGMT NetCDF Grid` for CDF as the file format in the file selection dialog that you will see, and select the `rx5dayETCCDI_yr_MIROC5_rcp45_r2i1p1_2006-2100.nc` file from the example dataset. Click on **OK**.

How it works...

The proposed NetCDF file contains a single variable, which is opened as a regular raster layer.

There's more...

A NetCDF file can contain contain multiple layers. In this case, QGIS will prompt you to select the one that you want to add from the ones contained in the specified file.

When only one layer is available, it is opened directly, as in the previously described example.

The NetCDF Browser plugin

Another way of opening NetCDF files is using the NetCDF Browser plugin. Select the **Manage and install plugins...** menu to open the plugin manager. Go to the **Not installed** section and type netcdf in the search field to filter the list of available plugins. Select the **NetCDF Browser** plugin and click on **Install plugin** to install it. Close the plugin manager.

The plugin is now installed, and you can open it by selecting **NetCDF Browser** in the **Plugins** menu:

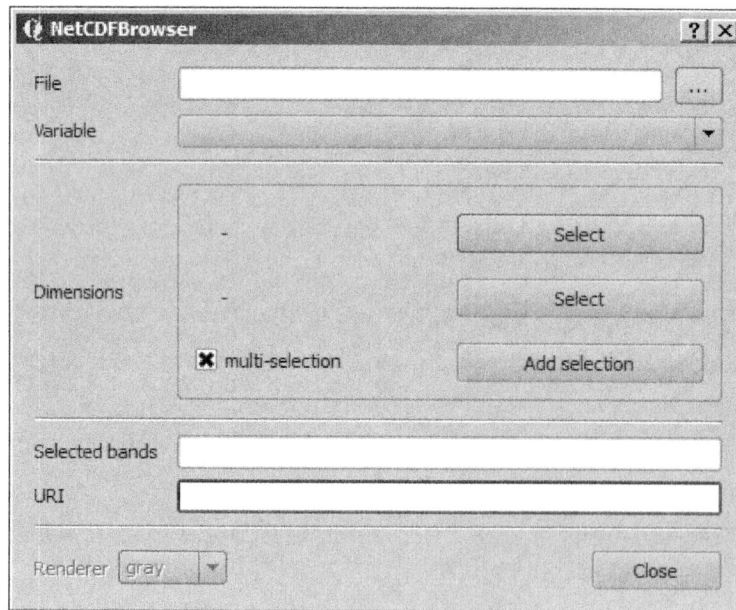

Select the **NetCDF** file in the upper field. The other fields will be updated with the content of the selected file. Select a layer from the available ones and click on **Add** to add the layer to your QGIS project.

Saving a vector layer

QGIS supports multiple formats, not just to read vector layers but to also save them. This recipe shows you how to export a vector layer, converting it to a different format.

Getting ready

You will use the layer named `poi_names_wake.shp` in this recipe. Make sure that it is loaded in your QGIS project.

How to do it...

1. Right-click on the name of the points layer in the QGIS table of contents and select the **Save as...** menu. You will see the following window:

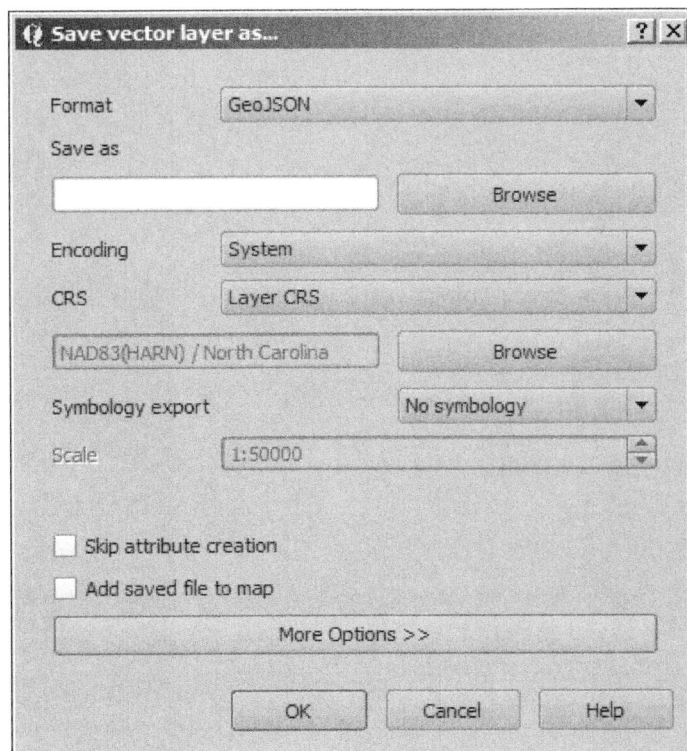

2. Let's suppose that you want to use this layer to create a web map. A popular format supported by libraries, such as Leaflet of OpenLayers 3, is the GeoJSON format. Select **GeoJSON** in the format field and enter a path and filename in the **Save as** field.

3. In the **Save as** dialog, click on **OK**. The GeoJSON file will be created.

How it works...

The OGR library, which is used by QGIS to read and open files, is also used to write them. Not all of the formats that are supported for reading purposes are also supported for writing purposes.

You can export even the layers that are not originally file-based to a file, such as a layer coming from a PostGIS database or a WFS connection. Just select the layer in the table of contents and proceed as just explained.

There's more...

The **Save as** dialog allows additional configuration beyond what you have seen in the example in this recipe.

Fine-tuning the export operation

Depending on the format that you select to export your layer, different options are available to configure how the layer is exported.

The options are shown by clicking on the **More options** button. Select **GeoJSON** as the export format and then display the options for that particular format. The **COORDINATE PRECISION** option controls the number of decimal places to write in the output GeoJSON file. The default precision is too high for almost all cases, and most of the time, having three or four decimal places is more than enough. Set the precision to 4, enter a valid path and filename, and export the layer by clicking on **OK**. Your points layer will now be saved in a smaller GeoJSON file. You can open this with a text editor to verify that the coordinates are expressed with the selected precision or compare its size with the one created without specifying a precision value.

Opening the layer after creating it

If you want to work with the layer after it is created, check the **Add saved file to map** box. The output layer will be opened and added to your current QGIS project.

Saving a raster layer

Raster layers can be exported to a different file. The export process can be used to crop the layer or perform resampling, creating a modified layer. This recipe shows you how to do this.

Getting ready

Open the `elev_lid792_1m` layer in your QGIS project.

How to do it...

1. Right-click on the name of the raster layer in the QGIS table of contents and select the **Save as...** menu. You will see the following window:

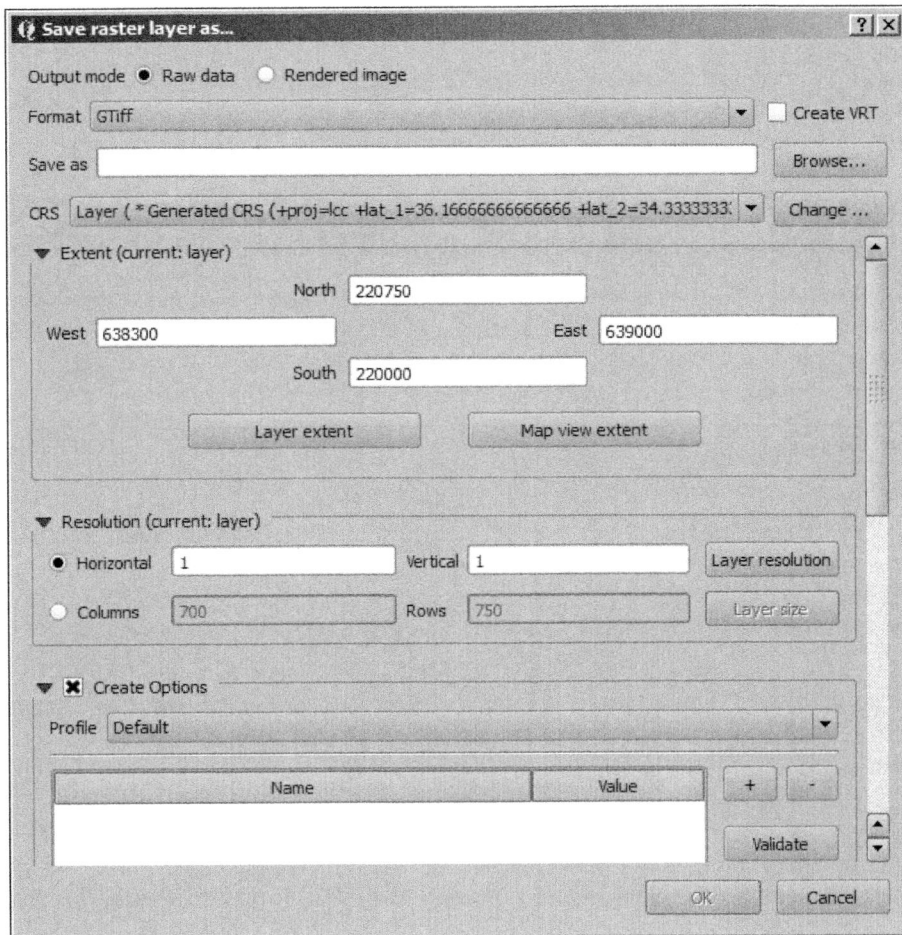

2. In the **Resolution** fields, replace both of them with a value of 2. The original resolution (the size of the cell) is 1, as you saw in a previous recipe.

3. Enter an output file path in the **Save as** field.

4. Click on **OK**. The layer will be saved with a coarser resolution than the original one.

How it works...

The GDAL library is used to save the file. Not all formats supported for input are also supported for output, but the most common ones are supported for both operations.

There's more...

The layer can be exported with a reduced extent. In the QGIS canvas, zoom to a small part of the raster layer. Then open the **Save as** dialog. In the **Extent** section, click on the **Map view extent** button. The bounding coordinates of the current map view will be placed in the four coordinate fields.

Enter a file path to save the file to and click on **OK**. A layer with a reduced extent covering only the region shown in the map view will be exported.

Reprojecting a layer

Layers may be in a CRS other than the one that is best for a given task. Although QGIS supports on-the-fly reprojection when rendering, other tasks, such as performing spatial analysis, may require using a given CRS or having all input layers in the same one. This recipe shows you how to reproject a vector layer.

Getting ready

Open the layer named `Davis_DBO_centerline.shp` from the sample dataset.

How to do it...

The `Davis_DBO_centerline.shp` layer uses a CRS with feet as the unit, which makes this unsuitable for certain operations. We plan to use this layer in future recipes to calculate routes and work in metric units, so including this in a CRS that uses them is then a much better option:

1. Right-click on the layer name in the table of contents and select **Save as...**.
2. Select **Selected CRS** in the drop-down list to specify a different output CRS. Click on the **Browse** button to select a CRS. You will see the **CRS selector** dialog.

3. You will be converting the point to the `EPSG:26911` CRS. Use the filter box to find it among the list of available CRSs and select it. Then click on **OK**.

4. Click on **OK** in the **Save as** dialog to create the layer. A new shapefile will be created with the projected lines.

How it works...

Reprojecting is done by the OGR library when it saves the file because this is one of the options that it supports.

There's more...

Raster layers can be reprojected in a similar way:

1. In the **Save as** dialog, for raster layers, you can find a CRS field with a **Browse** button.

2. Click on it to open the CRS selector, and select the destination CRS.

3. When you click on **OK**, the raster layer will be exported using the selected CRS instead of its original one.

Batch format conversion

The **Save as** dialog can be used to convert the format of a single layer. When several layers have to be converted, it is a better idea to use some automation. This recipe shows you how to easily convert an arbitrary number of layers.

Getting ready

No previous preparation is needed. Batch conversion is not performed based on open layers but performed directly on files, so there is no need to open layers in QGIS before converting them.

How to do it...

1. Open the **Processing Toolbox** menu by selecting **Toolbox** in the **Processing** menu. The **Processing Toolbox** menu is the main element of the QGIS Processing framework, and it is used to call its algorithms:

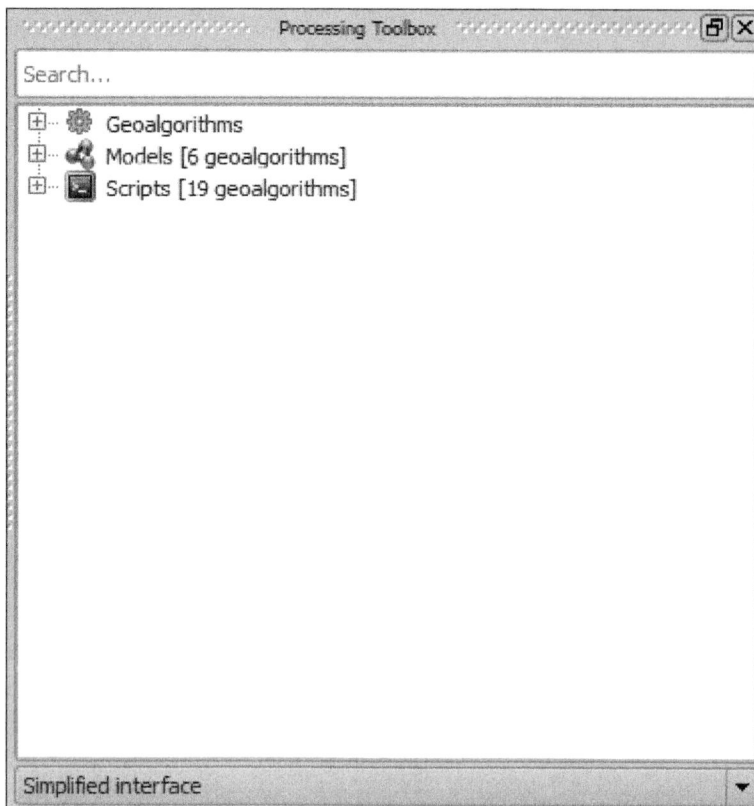

2. In the filter box of the **Processing Toolbox** menu, type `save` to filter the list of available algorithms. Locate the **Save selected features** algorithm, right-click on it, and select **Execute as batch process**. The batch processing interface will be displayed, as shown in the following screenshot:

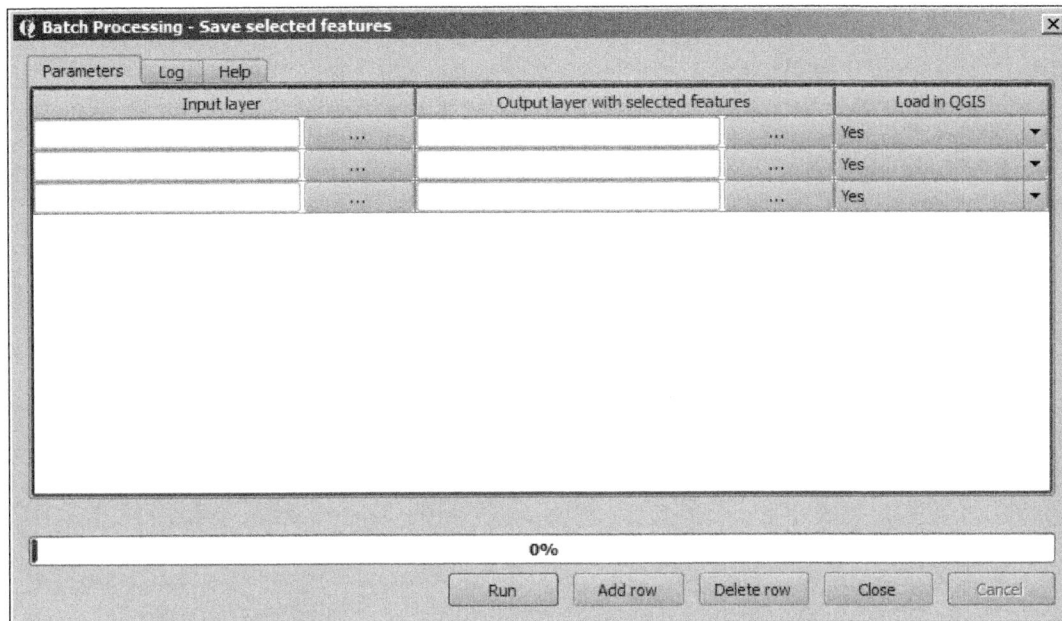

3. In the upper cell in the **Input layer** column, click on the **...** button and select **Select from filesystem**. A file selector dialog will appear. Select the content of the `batch_conversion` folder in the dataset. It should have a total of three files. Click on **OK** on the file selection dialog. The batch processing interface should now have all these selected files, one in each row in the parameters table.

4. In the **Output layer** column, click on the button in the first row. A dialog for saving the file will be opened. Select a file path in your filesystem where you want to save the output files and type `converted.geojson` as the output filename. Click on **OK** and a new dialog like the one shown in the following screenshot will appear:

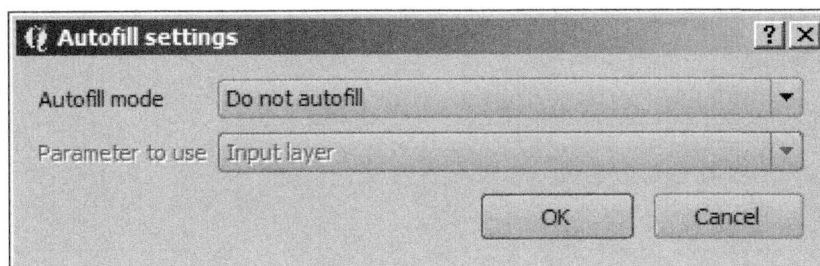

5. Select **Fill with parameter values** in the first field and **Input layer** in the second one. Click on **OK**. All the rows in the table will now have an output value, which was created using the entered filename as a prefix, followed by the name of the input layer.

6. To avoid layers being loaded after they are created, set the first cell in the **Load into QGIS** column to **No**. Then, double-click on the column header to automatically copy this value to all the rows below.

7. With the table already complete, you can launch the batch conversion process by clicking on **Run**. The GeoJSON files will be created in the specified paths.

How it works...

The conversion is performed by an algorithm from the QGIS Processing framework. Processing algorithms can be run either as individual algorithms or, in this case, in a batch process.

Outputs of Processing algorithms can be created in all formats supported by QGIS. The format is selected using the corresponding extension in the filename and, unlike in the case of saving a single layer, does not have to be selected in a field or list. Using geojson as the extension for your output files, you tell processing that you want to generate a file in this format.

Although the algorithm saves only the selected features of the layer, if there is no selection, it will use all the layer features. This is the default behavior of all algorithms in processing. As there is no selection in the layers that you have converted, all of their features will have been used.

When converting files this way, the additional options from the **Save as** dialog are not available, and the default configuration values are used.

There's more...

You can also convert vector layers with another more complex algorithm from the **Processing Toolbox** menu, which allows you to enter the configuration parameters used by the underlying OGR library that takes care of the process. It's called **Export vector**. Find it in the toolbox, right-click on it, and select **Execute as batch process**:

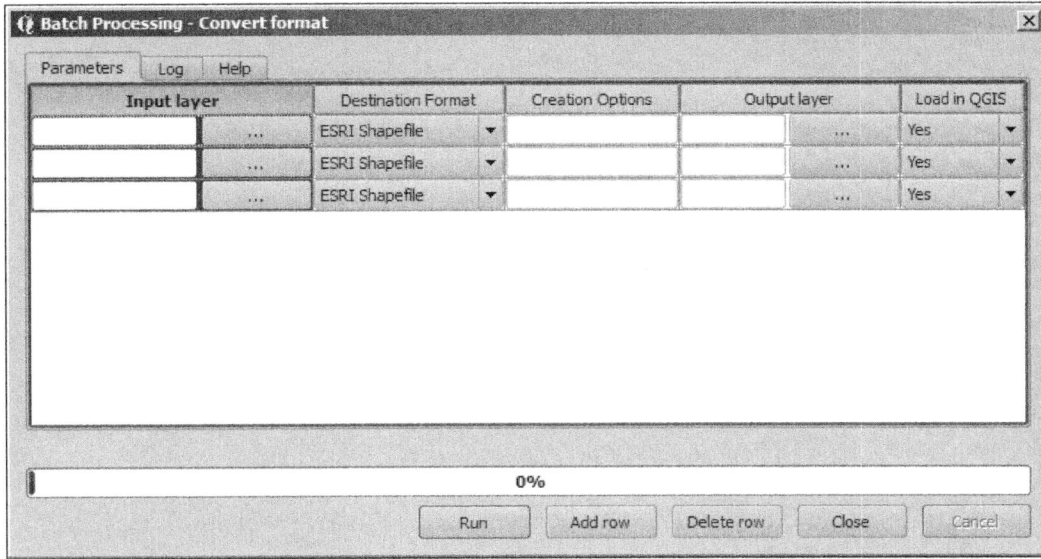

In this case, the output format is not controlled by the extension of the output filename as it happens with other processing algorithms according to what has been already explained.

Batch reprojection

Layers can be reprojected in a batch operation without having to enter parameters individually on the **Save as** dialog. This recipe shows you how to reproject a set of layers to a different CRS using an algorithm from the **Processing Toolbox** menu. You will see how to reproject all the files accompanying the `Davis_DBO_centerline.shp` file that you reprojected in the *Reprojecting a layer* recipe.

How to do it...

1. In the filter box of the **Processing Toolbox** menu, type `Reproject` to filter the list of available algorithms. Locate the **Reproject layer** algorithm, right-click on it, and select **Execute as batch process**. The batch processing interface will be shown, as follows:

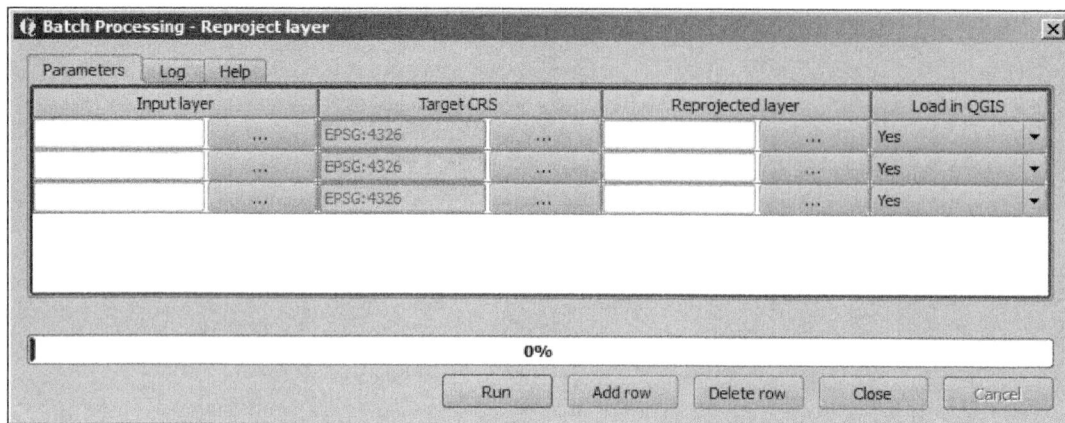

Input layer		Target CRS		Reprojected layer		Load in QGIS	
	...	EPSG:4326	...		...	Yes	▼
	...	EPSG:4326	...		...	Yes	▼
	...	EPSG:4326	...		...	Yes	▼

0%

Run · Add row · Delete row · Close · Cancel

2. In the upper cell of the **Input layer** column, click on the **...** button and select **Select from filesystem**. A file selector dialog will appear. Select the content of the `davis` folder in the dataset and add the files to the table.

3. In the first cell in the **Target CRS** column, click on the **...** button. A CRS selector will appear. Select the `EPSG:26911` CRS, as you did in a previous recipe when converting a single layer. Copy the value to the rest of rows in the column by double-clicking on the column header.

4. Set all the values in the **Reprojected layer** column. Select a file in the first cell, and then use the **Fill with parameter value** option to automatically fill the rest of rows.

5. Once the table is complete, click on **Run** to reproject the layers.

How it works...

The reprojection algorithm is a part of the Processing framework, so you can select the output format by changing the output file extension. You can use this to not only reproject a set of input layers but to also convert their format, all in a single step.

There's more...

Raster layers can also be reprojected with another algorithm from the **Processing Toolbox** menu named **Warp (reproject)**. These inputs are rather similar to the ones in the reprojection tool for vector layers with some additional parameters that are specific to raster layers. Select the algorithm, right-click on it, and select **Execute as batch process** to run it and convert a set of raster layers.

Loading vector layers into SpatiaLite

SpatiaLite is a single file relational database that is built on top of the well-known SQLite database. It can store many layers of various types, including nonspatial tables. Interfaces to the format also allow the ability to run spatial queries of various kinds. It's a highly-flexible and portable format that is great for everyday use, especially when working on standalone projects or with only one user at a time. SpatiaLite works in a similar manner to PostGIS without the need to configure or run a database server.

Getting ready

Pick a vector layer and load it up in QGIS. This step is optional, as you can pick the source layer from the filesystem in a later dialog.

How to do it...

1. Create a SpatiaLite database if you don't already have one and name it `cookbook.db`. The easiest way to do this is with the **Browser** tab, as shown in the following screenshot:

2. Then, pick one of the following methods to import your data. The first option is faster, but the second option gives you more control over the import settings:

    ❑   Import method 1—the fast method

        1. In the QGIS **Browser** tab, find the layer that you want to copy to the database.

        2. Drag and drop this layer on the **Spatialite DB** entry.

> If you have a lot of files listed, this will be quite difficult as the browser doesn't scroll during the drag operation. You can optionally open a second browser window and drag the layer across. Also, note that this defaults to multi-type geometry. If you need to control the options, use the next method.

    ❑   Import method 2—the standard method

        1. Open **DB Manager** from the **Database** menu.

        2. Expand the **Spatialite** item to list your databases. Expand the database that you want to connect to.

        3. Click on the following import layer icon:

        4. A dialog will pop up, providing you with import options.

> SQL databases are usually case insensitive, so you can use all lower case characters. Also, never use spaces or special characters in table names; this can just lead to headaches later. An occasional underscore is okay.

        5. Select the layer to import from the drop-down list.

        6. Fill in a name for the new table.

        7. In most cases, the only thing left to do is check the **Create spatial index** checkbox.

        8. If this works, great. Now, you can load the layer to the map and verify that it's identical to the input.

> This method is more similar to traditional database import and very similar to the *PostGIS* recipe next in this chapter.

How it works...

QGIS converts your geometry to a format that is compatible with SpatiaLite and inserts it, along with the attribute table. Afterwards, it updates the metadata tables in SpatiaLite to register the geometry column and build the spatial index on it. These two postprocesses make the database table appear as a spatial layer to QGIS and speed up the loading of data from the table when panning and zooming.

There's more...

The import dialog contained a few other features that are often useful. You can reproject data as part of the import process if you want, or you can specify the projection if QGIS didn't detect it properly. You can also name the geometry column something different than the default, `geom`; for example, `utmz10n83` (this is normally not recommended). You can specify the character encoding of the text in the event that it's not handled correctly.

You can even use the dialog to append data to an existing table; for example, you have multiple counties with the same data structure that come as two separate files, but you want them all in one layer.

If, for some reason, the layer didn't import the way that you want, delete it and redo the import. If you delete layers, make sure to learn how to vacuum the database to recover the now empty space in the file and shrink its total size (this is not automatic).

> Look for the **Vacuum** option as a button in many graphical tools. If you don't see it, no worries, just run the SQL, `VACUUM;`.

What happens if this fails? Databases can be really picky sometimes. Here are some common issues and solutions:

- It could be character encoding (accents, non-Latin languages), which requires that you specify the encoding.
- It could be picky about mixing multilayers with regular layers. Multilayers is when you have several separate geometries that are part of one record. For example, Hawaii is actually many islands. So, if you only have one row representing Hawaii, you need to cram all the island polygons into one geometry field. However, if you mix this with North Dakota, which is just a polygon, the import will fail. If you have this problem, you'll need to perform the import on the command-line using ogr2ogr and its newish feature, `-nlt PROMOTE_TO_MULTI`, which converts all single items to multi-items to fix this.
- Depending on your original source, you may have a mix of points, lines, and polygons. You'll either need to convert this to a Geometry Collection, or you need to split each type of geometry into a separate layer. Geometry Collections are currently poorly-supported in many GIS viewers, so this is only recommended for advanced users.

See also

If you need more advanced settings or can't get the QGIS tool to work, you may need to use the QspatiaLite Plugin (install this with **Manage Python Plugins** under the **Plugins** menu), the spatialite-gui (download this from `https://www.gaia-gis.it/fossil/spatialite_gui/index`) application, or the ogr2ogr command line (this comes with QGIS, which is part of OSGeo4w shell on Windows, or the terminal on Mac or Linux).

Loading vector layers into PostGIS

PostGIS is the spatial add-on to the popular PostgreSQL database. It's a server-style database with authentication, permissions, schemas, and handling of simultaneous users. When you want to store large amounts of vector data and query them efficiently, especially in a multicomputer networked environment, consider PostGIS. This works fine for small data too, but many users find its configuration too much work when SpatiaLite may be better suited.

Getting ready

Pick a vector layer and load it in QGIS. You will also need to have a working copy of Postgres/PostGIS running, a PostGIS database created, and an account that allows table creation.

> BostonGIS maintains a decent tutorial on installation for Windows, and getting a PostGIS set up for everyone. You can find this at `http://www.bostongis.com/?content_name=postgis_tut01#316`.

You should configure QGIS to be aware of your database and its connection parameters by creating a new database item in the PostGIS load dialog or by right-clicking on **PostGIS** in the **Browser** tab and selecting **New Connection**:

You can find more information about PostGIS at `http://docs.qgis.org/2.8/en/docs/user_manual/working_with_vector/supported_data.html#postgis-layers`.

How to do it...

Now that you can connect to a PostGIS database, you are ready to try importing data:

1. Open **DB Manager** from the **Database** menu.
2. Expand the **PostGIS** item to list your databases. Expand the database that you want to connect to, and you should be prompted to authenticate (if you haven't saved your password in the settings).
3. Expand the list and select the **Public** schema.

> In general, unless you are performing advanced work and understand how Postgres schemas work, place your layers in the **Public** schema. This is the default that everyone expects.

4. Click on the following import layer icon:

5. A dialog will pop up, providing you with import options.

> SQL databases are usually case insensitive, so you can use all lowercase. Also, never use spaces or special characters in table names; this can just lead to headaches later. An occasional underscore is okay.

6. Select the layer to import from the drop-down list.
7. Fill in a name for the new table.
8. Check whether **schema** is set to **public**.
9. In most cases, the only thing left to do is check the **Create spatial index** checkbox:

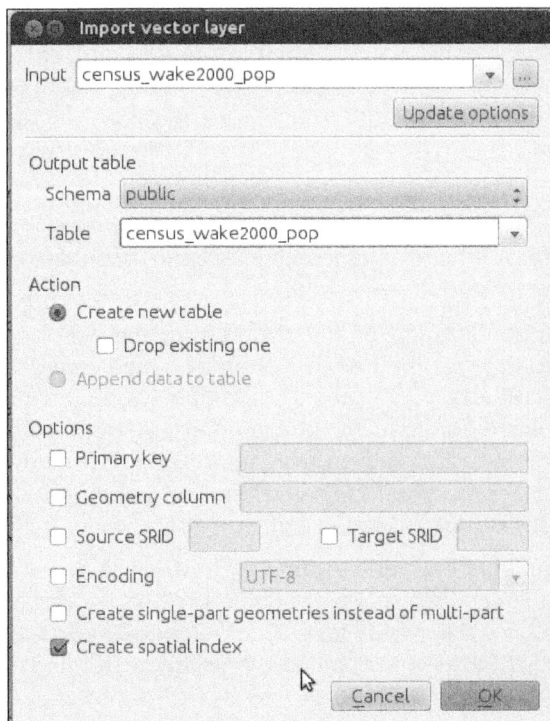

How it works...

QGIS converts your geometries to a format that is compatible with PostGIS, and inserts it, along with importing the attributes. Afterwards, it updates the metadata views in PostGIS to register the geometry column and build the spatial index on it. These two post-processes make the database table appear as a spatial layer to QGIS and speed up the loading of data from the table when panning and zooming.

There's more...

The options presented in the dialog are not all the options that are available. If you need more control or advanced options present, you'll likely be looking at the command-line tools: shp2pgsql (a graphical plugin for pgadmin3 is available on some platforms) and ogr2ogr. The shp2pgsql tool generally only handles shapefiles. If you have other formats, ogr2ogr can handle everything that QGIS is capable of loading. You can also use these tools to develop batch import scripts.

To import large or complicated CSV or text files, you sometimes will need to use the pgadmin3 or psql command-line interface to Postgres.

Need even more control? Then, consider scripting. OGR and Postgres both have very capable Python libraries.

Another option is using the OpenGeo Suite plugin, which has some additional options, such as allowing importing multiple layers into a single table or into one table per layer. To learn more about this, including how to install it, refer to `http://qgis.boundlessgeo.com/static/docs/intro.html`.

What happens if this fails? Databases can be really picky sometimes:

- It could be character encoding (accents, non-Latin languages), which requires specifying the encoding.

- It could be picky about mixing multilayers with regular layers. Multilayers is when you have several separate geometries that are part of one record. For example, Hawaii is actually many islands. So, if you only have one row representing Hawaii, you need to cram all the island polygons into one geometry field. However, if you mix this with North Dakota that is just a polygon, the import will fail. If you have this problem, you'll need to perform the import on the command-line using ogr2ogr and its new feature, `-nlt PROMOTE_TO_MULTI`, which converts all single items to multi-items, to fix this.

- Depending on your original source, you may have a mix of points, lines, and polygons. You'll either need to convert this to a Geometry Collection, or you need to split each type of geometry into a separate layer. Geometry Collections are currently poorly supported in many GIS viewers, so this is only recommended for advanced users.

See also

For more information on PostGIS installation and setup, refer to `http://postgis.net/install`.

For a more in-depth text on using PostGIS, there are many books available, including Packt Publishing's *PostGIS Cookbook*.

2
Data Management

In this chapter, we will cover the following recipes:

- ▶ Joining layer data
- ▶ Cleaning up the attribute table
- ▶ Configuring relations
- ▶ Joining tables in databases
- ▶ Creating views in SpatiaLite
- ▶ Creating views in PostGIS
- ▶ Creating spatial indexes
- ▶ Georeferencing rasters
- ▶ Georeferencing vector layers
- ▶ Creating raster overviews (pyramids)
- ▶ Building virtual rasters (catalogs)

Introduction

One of the reasons to use QGIS is its many features that enable management and analysis preparation of spatial data in a visual manner. This chapter focuses on common operations that users need to perform to get data ready for other uses, such as analysis, cartography, or input into other programs.

In this chapter, you will find recipes to manage vector as well as raster data. These recipes cover the handling of data from both file and database sources.

Joining layer data

We often get data in different formats and information spread over multiple files. Therefore, one important skill to know is how to join attribute data from different layers. Joining data is a way to combine data from multiple tables based on common values, such as IDs or categories.

This exercise shows you how to use the join functionality in **Layer Properties** to join geographic census tract data to tabular population data and how to save the results to a new file.

Getting ready

To follow this exercise, load the census tracts in `census_wake2000.shp` using **Add Vector Layer** (you can also drag and drop the shapefile from the file browser to QGIS) and population data in `census_wake2000_pop.csv` using **Add Delimited Text Layer**.

> You can also load the `.csv` text file using **Add Vector Layer**, but this will load all data as text columns because the `.csv` file does not come with a `.csvt` file to specify data types. Instead, the **Add Delimited Text Layer** tool will scan the data and determine the most suitable data type for each column.

How to do it...

To join two layers, there has to be a column with values/IDs that both layers have in common. If we check the attribute tables of the two layers that we just loaded, we will see that both have the `STFID` field in common. So, to join the population data to the census tracts, use the following steps:

1. Open the **Layer Properties** option of the `census_wake2000` layer (for example, by double-clicking on the layer name in the **Layers** list) and go to **Joins**.

2. To set up a new join action, press the green **+** button in the lower-left corner of the dialog.

3. The following screenshot shows the **Add vector join** dialog, which allows you to configure the join by selecting **Join layer**, which you want to use to join the census tracts and the columns containing the common values/IDs (**Join field** and **Target field**):

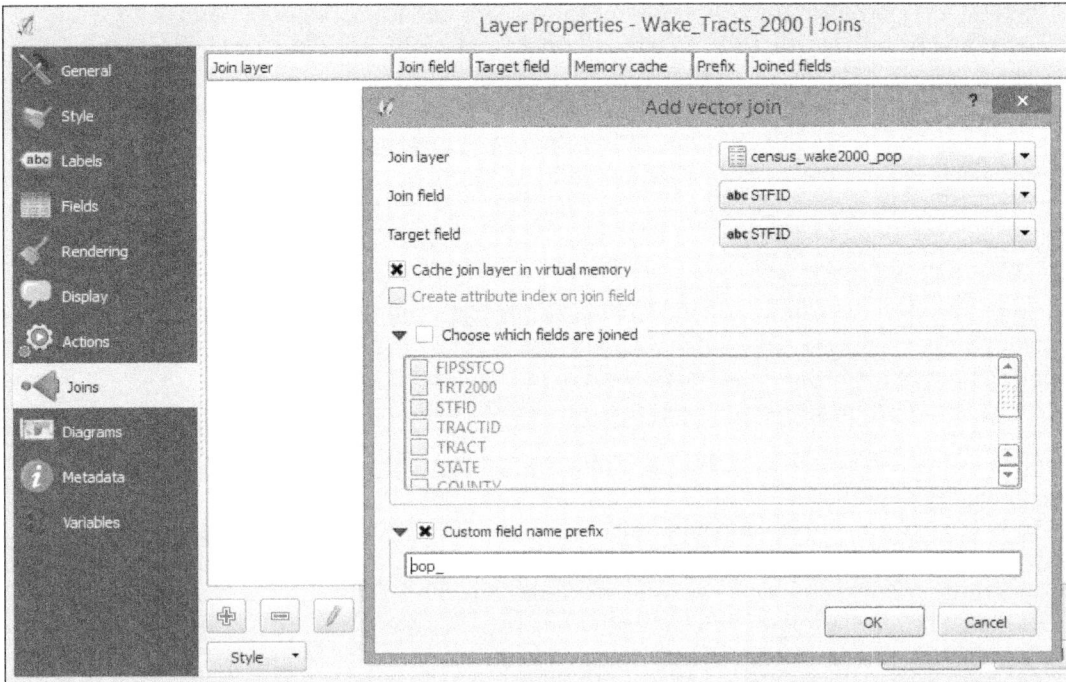

> If you want to change a join, you just need to select the join definition from the list and then press the edit button with the pencil icon, which you find below the list. This will reopen the join definition dialog, and you can make your changes.

4. When you press **OK**, the join definition will be added to the list of joins, as shown in the following screenshot.

5. To verify that you set up the join correctly, close **Layer Properties** and open attribute table to see whether the population columns have been added and are filled with data.

How it works...

Joins can be used to join vector layers and tabular layers from many different file and database sources, including (but not limited to) Shapefiles, PostGIS, CSV, Excel sheets, and more.

When two layers are joined, the attributes of **Join layer** are appended to the original layer's attribute table. If you want, you can use the **Choose which fields are joined** option to select which of the fields from the population layer should be joined to the census tracts. Otherwise, by default, all fields will be added. The number of features in the original layer is not changed. Whenever there is a match between the values in the join and the target field, the new attribute values will be filled; otherwise, there will be NULL values in the new columns.

By default, the names of the new columns are constructed from join layer name with underscore followed by join layer column name. For example, the `STATE` column of `census_wake2000_pop` becomes `census_wake2000_pop_STATE`. You can change this default behavior by enabling the **Custom field name prefix** option, as shown in the previous screenshot. With these settings, the `STATE` column becomes `pop_STATE`, which is considerably shorter and, thus, easier to handle.

There's more...

The join that you've created now only exists in memory. None of the original files have been altered. However, it's possible to create a new file from the joined layers. To do this, just use **Save as ...** from the **Layer** menu or **Context** menu. You can choose between a variety of data formats, including the ESRI shapefile, Mapinfo MIF, or GML.

Shapefiles are a very common choice as they are still the de facto standard GIS data exchange format, but if you are familiar with GIS data formats, you will have noticed that the names of the joined columns are too long for the 10 character-name length limit of the shapefile format. QGIS ensures that all columns in the exported shapefiles have unique names even after the names have been shortened to only 10 characters. To do this, QGIS adds incrementing numbers to the end of, otherwise, duplicate column names. If you save the join from this example as a shapefile, you will see that the column names are altered to `census_w_1`, `census_w_2`, and so on. Of course, these names are less than optimal to continue working with the data. As described in *How it works...* in this recipe, the names for the joined columns are a combination of joined layer name and column name. Therefore, we can use the following trick if we want to create a shapefile from the join: we can shorten the layer name. Just rename the layer in the layer list. You can even have a completely empty layer name! If you change the joined layer name to an empty string, the joined column names will be `_STATE`, `_COUNTY`, and so on instead of `census_wake2000_pop_STATE` and `census_wake2000_pop_COUNTY`. In any case, it is good practice to document your data and provide a description of the attribute table columns in the metadata.

In any case, it is very likely that you will want to clean up the attribute table of the new dataset, and this is exactly what we are going to do in the next exercise.

Cleaning up the attribute table

There are many reasons why we need to clean up attribute tables every now and then. These may be because we receive badly structured or named data from external sources, or because data processing, such as the layer joins that we performed in the previous exercise, require some post processing. This recipe shows us how to use attribute table and the **Table Manager** plugin to rename, delete, and reorder columns, as well as how to convert between different data types using **Field Calculator**.

Getting ready

If you performed the previous recipe, just save the joined layer to a new shapefile; otherwise, load `census_wake2000_pop.shp`. In any case, you will notice that the dataset contains a lot of duplicate information, and the column names could use some love as well. To follow this recipe, you should also install and enable the **Table Manager** plugin by navigating to **Plugins | Manage and Install Plugins**.

How to do it...

1. Our first step to clean up this dataset is to delete duplicated information. From all available columns, we only want to keep `_STATE`, `_COUNTY`, `_TRACT`, `FIPSSTCO`, `TRT2000`, `STFID`, `_POP2000`, `AREA`, and `PERIMETER`.

2. To delete the other columns, enable editing using the **Toggle editing mode** button in the upper-left corner of the attribute table or by pressing *Ctrl + E*. This activates the **Delete column** button.

3. Alternatively, you can also press *Ctrl + L* to open the **Delete attributes** dialog. This dialog allows us to delete multiple columns at once. Just select all the columns that you want to be deleted, press **OK**, and QGIS will display the reduced attribute table.

> It's worth noting that the changes will only be permanent once you use the **Save edits** button or disable the editing mode and confirm that you want to save the changes.

4. Next, we will rename columns to remove the leading underscores in some of the column names. This can be done using the **Table Manager** plugin.

5. When you start the plugin (edit mode should be disabled), you will see a list of the layer columns. The plugin allows you to change the order of columns, as well as rename, insert, clone, and delete columns.

6. To rename a column, just select it in the list and press the **Rename** button. You'll then be asked to provide a new name. Go ahead and remove the leading underscores from `_STATE`, `_COUNTY`, `_TRACT`, and `_POP2000`.

7. Finally, using the **Move up** and **Move down** buttons, you can also rearrange the column order to something more intuitive. We'd suggest moving `STFID` to the first position and `AREA` and `PERIMETER` to the last.

8. If you press **Save**, the changes will be saved back to the layer source file. Alternatively, you can also create a new file using **Save as...**.

How it works...

The steps provided in this exercise are mostly limited to layers with shapefile sources. If you use other input data formats, such as MIF, GML, or GeoJSON files, you will notice that the **Toggle editing** button is grayed out because these files cannot be edited in QGIS. Whether a certain format can be edited in QGIS or not depends on which functionality has been implemented in the respective GDAL/OGR driver.

> The GDAL/OGR version that is used by QGIS is either part of the QGIS package (as in the case of the Windows installers) or QGIS uses the GDAL library existing in your system (on Linux and Mac). To get access to specific drivers that are not supported by the provided GDAL/OGR version, it is possible to compile custom versions of GDAL/OGR, but the details of doing this are out of the scope of this cookbook.

There's more...

Another common task while dealing with attribute table management is changing column data types. Currently, it is not possible to simply change the data type directly. Instead, we have to use **Field Calculator** (which is directly accessible through the corresponding button in the **Attributes** toolbar or from the attribute table dialog) to perform conversions and create a new column for the result.

In our `census_wake2000_pop.shp` file, for example, the tract ID, `TRACT`, is stored in a `REAL` type column with a precision of 15 digits even though it may be preferable to simply have it in a `STRING` column and formatted to two digits after the decimal separator. To create such a column using **Field Calculator**, we can use the following expression:

```
format_number("TRACT",2)
```

Compared to a simple conversion (which would be simple, use `tostring("TRACT")`, `format_number("TRACT",2)` offers the advantage that all values will be formatted to display two digits after the decimal separator, while a simple conversion would drop these digits if they are zeros.

Of course, it's also common to convert from text to numerical. In this case, you can chose between `toint()` and `toreal()`.

See also

▸ Have a look through the conversion functions in the **Field Calculator Function** list to see the other available functions that can deal with date and time data types. Usage of all these functions is explained in **Selected function help** directly in the calculator dialog.

Configuring relations

In the *Joining layer data* recipe, we discussed that joins only append additional columns to existing features (1:1 or n:1 relationships). Using joins, it is, therefore, not possible to model 1:n relationships, such as "one zip code area containing n schools". These kinds of relationships can instead be modeled using relations. This recipe introduces the concept of relations and shows how you can put them to use.

Getting ready

To follow this exercise, load zip code areas and schools from `zipcodes_wake.shp` and `schools_wake.shp`.

How to do it...

Relations are configured in **Project Properties**. The dialog is very similar to the join dialog:

1. Define the two layers (**Referencing/Child** and **Referenced/Parent**), as well as the fields containing the common values/IDs. As you want to model "one zip code area contains n schools," the zip code dataset is the parent layer and the school dataset is the child layer. The connection between both datasets is established based on the zip code fields (**ADDRZIPCOD** and **ZIPNUM**), as shown in the following screenshot:

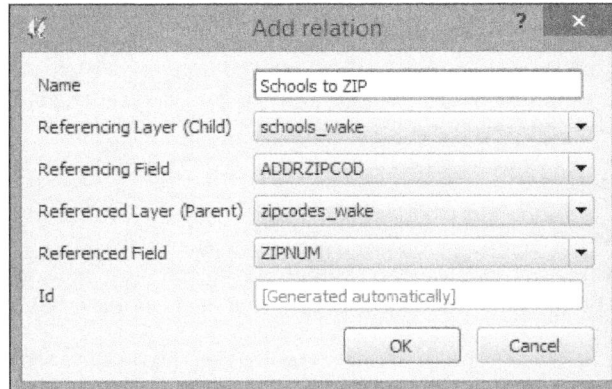

2. To verify that the relation is set up and working, you can either check the attribute table in form view (button in the lower-right corner), as shown in the following screenshot, or open an individual feature form. You will find that the relation information has been appended at the end of the form:

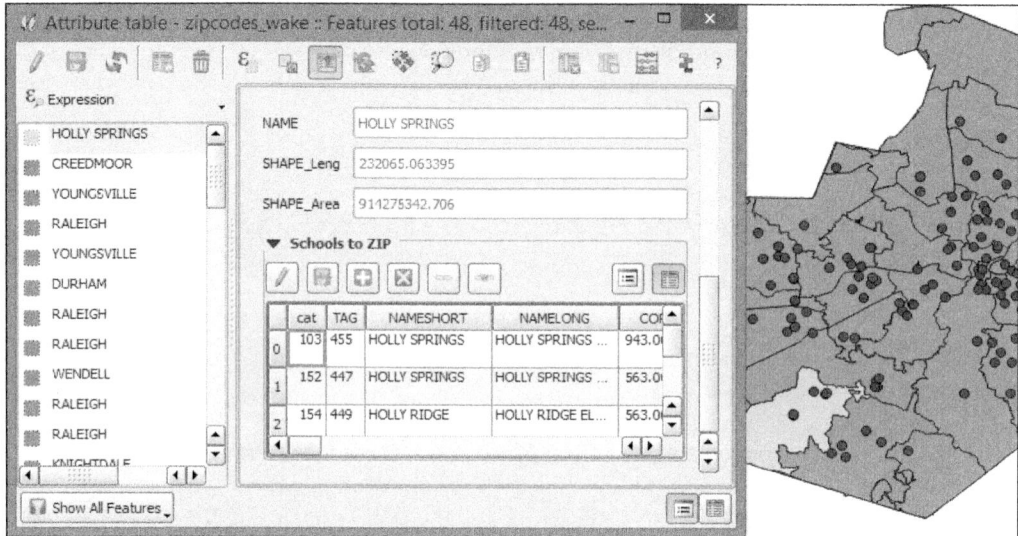

As the preceding screenshot shows, setting up this relation enables you to get access to all schools within a certain zip code in a very convenient way. As the edit button suggests, it is even possible to edit the school data from this view. You can simply edit the values in the table view. You can add and delete schools from the dataset using the **+** and **X** buttons. The next two buttons enable you to quickly add new entries to the relation or to remove them.

How it works...

In this example, removing a school from the dataset works just fine, but adding a school via this dialog makes less sense because you cannot create a point geometry through this process.

If you press the button to add to the relation, you will get a dialog that allows you to choose which existing school you want to add. In the background, the school's ADDRZIPCOD value is updated to match the zip code we just assigned it to.

Similarly, if you select a school and press the button to remove the relation, what actually happens is that the school's ADDRZIPCOD value is set to NULL.

Joining tables in databases

If you use a database (SpatiaLite or PostGIS) to store your data, vector and nonspatial, then you also have the option of using the database and SQL to perform tables joins. The primary advantages of this method include being able to filter data before loading in the map, perform multitable joins (three or more), and have full control over the details of the join via queries.

Getting ready

You'll need at least two layers in either a SpatiaLite or PostGIS database. These two layers need at least one column in common, and the column in common should contain unique values in at least one table. In this case, our example uses the census_wake_2000 polygon layer and census_wake_2000_pop.csv.

How to do it...

1. Open the **DB Manager** plugin that comes with QGIS. You can find this in the **Database** menu.

2. Select your database from the tree on the left-hand side, use cookbook.db in **SpatiaLite** (which was created in *Chapter 1, Data Input and Output*).

> If you don't see this database listed, use **Add SpatiaLite Layer** (the icon or the menu item), or right-click on **SpatiaLite** in the **Browser** window to make a new connection and add it to an existing database.

3. Now, open the SQL window (the second icon from the left in top toolbar of the plugin window).

4. Put in the following SQL code to query and JOIN the tables:
```
SELECT *
FROM census_wake2000 Sas a
JOIN census_wake2000_pop AS b
ON a.stfid = b.stfid;
```

How it works...

SELECT lists all the columns that you want from the source tables; in this case, * means everything. FROM is the first (left) table, as a is an alias, which is used so that there's less typing later. JOIN is the second (right) table, and ON indicates which columns to should be matched between the two tables. The rest of how this works in relational database theory is best explained in other texts.

There's more...

In databases, there's more than one type of join. You can perform a join where you retain only the matches in both tables, or you can retain all content from the left (first table) and any matches from the right. You can also control how a one-to-many relationship is summarized or select specific records instead of aggregating.

If you want to save the results of a query you have two options. You can make a view or a new table. A view is a saved copy of your query. Every time you open it, the query will be rerun. This is great if your data changes because it will always be up-to-date, and this doesn't use any additional disk space. On the other hand, a table is like saving a new file; it becomes a static new copy of the results. This is good to repeatedly access the same answer, and it is usually faster to use, especially for large tables.

See also

▸ Refer to the *Creating views in SpatiaLite* and *Creating views in PostGIS* sections in this chapter to learn how to make views of the query results.

▸ For more general information on writing SQL queries refer to `http://sqlzoo.net/`

▸ Refer to *Chapter 1, Data Input and Output*, about using the `cookbook.db` database

Creating views in SpatiaLite

In a database, view is a stored query. Every time you open it, the query is run and fresh results are generated. To use views as layers in QGIS takes a couple of steps.

Getting ready

For this recipe, you'll need a query that returns results containing a geometry. The example that we'll use is the query from the *Joining tables in databases* recipe (the previous recipe) where attributes were joined 1:1 between the census polygons and the population CSV. The QSpatiaLite plugin is recommended for this recipe.

How to do it...

The GUI method is described as follows:

1. Using the **QspatiaLite** plugin (which is in the **Database** menu, if you've activated it) place the following in the query:

```
SELECT *
FROM census_wake2000 as a
```

```
JOIN census_wake2000_pop as b
ON a.stfid = b.stfid;
```

2. From the **Option** dropdown, select the last choice, **Create Spatial View & Load in QGIS**, and set the **Geometry field** box value to the name of your geometry field from your spatial layer. In this example, this is geom.

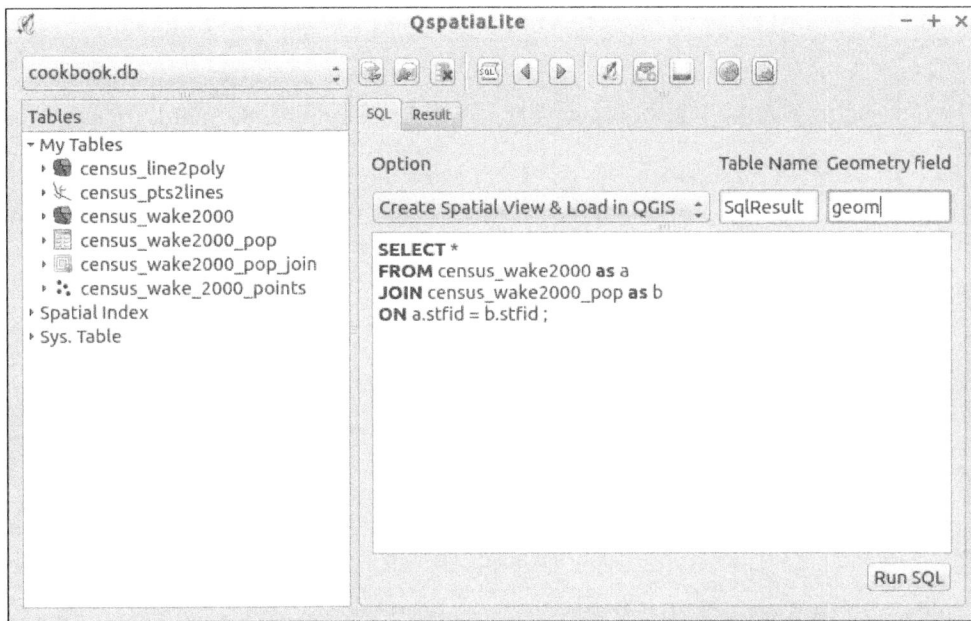

> You can explore your data table fields in the left-hand side to check the name of the fields that you need.

The SQL method is as described, as follows:

1. In **Database | DB Manager**, open **SQL Window**.

2. Write a query. In this example, this is the Join query from the previous recipe.

3. Convert this query to a view by adding CREATE VIEW <name> as SELECT:

```
CREATE VIEW census_wake2000_pop_join AS
SELECT *
FROM census_wake2000 as a
JOIN census_wake2000_pop as b
ON a.stfid = b.stfid;
```

4. Register the view with the SpatiaLite metadata backend with a follow up query. This function is case sensitive:

```
CREATE VIEW census_wake2000_pop_join AS
INSERT INTO views_geometry_columns
(view_name, view_geometry, view_rowid, f_table_name,
f_geometry_column, read_only)
VALUES ('census_wake2000_pop_join', 'geom', 'rowid',
'census_wake2000', 'geom',1);
```

> This only works when the view geometry is based on the geometry of a single table. If you need to generate new geometries, you probably need a table.

5. The pattern is ('name of view','name of view geometry field','A Unique ID','name of table the view gets its geometry from','name of geometry field in the original table',read-only (1) or writable(0)).

6. After running the second query, you should be able to load the view in QGIS and see the same fields as the join query.

How it works...

A view is actually stored in the database and is triggered when you load it. In this way, if you change the original data tables, the view will always be up to date. By comparison, creating new tables makes copies of the existing data, which is stored in a new place, or creates a snapshot or freeze of the values at that time. It also increases the database's size by replicating data. Whereas, a view is just the SQL text itself and doesn't store any additional data.

QGIS reads the metadata tables of SpatiaLite in order to figure out what layers contain spatial data, what kind of spatial data they contain, and which column contains the geometry definition. Without creating entries in the metadata, the tables appear as normal SQLite tables, and you can only load attribute data without spatial representation.

As it's a view, it's really reading the geometries from the original tables. Therefore, any edits to the original table will show up. New in SpatiaLite 4.x series, this makes it easier to create writable views. If you use the spatialite-gui standalone application, it registers all the database triggers needed to make it work, and the changes made will affect the original tables.

There's more...

You don't have to use `ROWID` as unique id, but this is a convenient handle that always exists in SQLite, and unlike an ID from the original table, there's no chance of duplication in an aggregating query.

See also

▸ Read more about writable-view at `https://www.gaia-gis.it/fossil/libspatialite/wiki?name=writable-view`. This recipe is extremely similar to the next one on PostGIS and demonstrates how interchangeable the two can be if you are aware of the slight differences.

Creating views in PostGIS

In a database, a view is a stored query. Every time that you open it, the query is run and fresh results are generated. To use views as layers in QGIS takes a couple of steps.

Getting ready

For this recipe, you'll need a query that returns results containing a geometry. The example that we'll use here is the query from the *Joining tables in databases* recipe where attributes were joined 1:1 between the census polygons and the population CSV.

How to do it...

The SQL method is described as follows:

1. In **Database | DB Manager**, open **SQL Window**.
2. Write a query; in this example, this is the join query that was written in the previous exercise. If you want to see it right away but not necessarily retain it, check the **Load as new layer** checkbox near the bottom:

```
SELECT *
FROM census_wake2000 as a
JOIN census_wake2000_pop as b
ON a.stfid = b."STFID";
```

3. Now, execute the query by clicking on the **Execute (F5)** button:

4. After executing the query, to load it to the map check the **Load as new layer** box, which will expand some additional options. Pick your unique integer (id_0) for **Column with unique integer values** and geom for **Geometry column**. Name your result in the **Layer name (prefix)** textbox and click on **Load now!**.

> If you only needed to see this data in this particular QGIS project, you can stop here. In order to make the database store this query for other projects and users, continue this recipe.

5. Convert this query to a view by adding CREATE VIEW <name> AS SELECT:

```
CREATE VIEW census_wake2000_pop_join AS SELECT *
FROM census_wake2000 as a
JOIN census_wake2000_pop as b
ON a.stfid = b."STFID";
```

6. Go back to **DB Manager** and hit the **Refresh** button (on the left). You should now see your new view listed and be able to add it to the map.

How it works...

QGIS reads the metadata tables or views of PostGIS in order to figure out what layers contain spatial data, what kind of spatial data they contain, and which column contains the geometry definition. Without creating entries in the metadata, the tables appear as normal PostgreSQL tables, and you can only load attribute data without spatial representation.

As this is a view, it's really reading the geometries from the original tables. Therefore, any edits to the original table will also show up.

There's more...

QGIS is really picky about having a unique ID for PostGIS tables and views. There are a few tips to make this always work. Always include a numeric unique ID (as the first column is recommended but not required, IDs must be integer columns (usually int4, but int8 should work now too). Autoincrementing IDs are good idea. When you don't have such an ID field to use from one of the underlying tables, you can add an ID on the fly with the following:

```
SELECT row_number() OVER() AS id_qgis, <add the other fields you
want here> FROM table;
```

The downside of this is that you now have to list out all the fields that you want to use in the view rather than using *. When creating tables, you'll want to turn this id_qgis field into an auto-incrementing field if you plan to add records.

The other big catch is that if you make a new geometry by manipulating existing geometries, QGIS isn't always aware of the results. In the previous example, the geometry is just passed from the original table to the view unchanged, so it is properly registered in the geometry_columns metadata of PostGIS. However, a new geometry doesn't exist in the original table, so the trick is to cast the geometry result, as follows:

```
CREATE VIEW census_wake2000_4326 AS
SELECT id_0,
stfid,tractid,ST_Transform(geom,4326)::geometry(GeometryZ, 4326)
As geom
FROM census_wake2000;
```

QGIS doesn't always think that this is a valid spatial layer but adding to the Canvas should work.

> The more specific you can be, the better. If you're not sure what geometry type it is or if you have 3D (aka Z), check the entries in the geometry_columns view.

Also, keep your eyes on Postgres's relatively new feature called Materialized Views. This is a method of caching view results that don't update automatically, but they also don't require whole new tables.

▸ Finer details from the PostGIS manual can be read at `http://postgis.refractions.net/docs/using_postgis_dbmanagement.html#Manual_Register_Spatial_Column`. This recipe is extremely similar to the previous one and demonstrates how interchangeable these two can be if you are aware of the slight differences.

▸ Read more about *Materialized Views* at `http://www.postgresql.org/docs/9.3/static/rules-materializedviews.html`

Creating spatial indexes

Spatial indexes are methods to speed up queries of geometries. This includes speeding up the display of database layers in QGIS when you zoom in close (it has no effect on viewing entire layers).

This recipe applies to SpatiaLite and PostGIS databases. In the event that you've made a new table or you have imported some data and didn't create a spatial index, it's usually a good idea to add this.

> You can also create a spatial index for shapefile layers. Take a look at **Layer Properties | General** for the **Create Spatial Index** button. This will create a `.qix` file that works with QGIS, Mapserver, GDAL/OGR, and other open source applications. Refer to `https://en.wikipedia.org/wiki/Shapefile`.

Getting ready

You'll need a SpatiaLite and a Postgis database. For ease, import a vector layer from the provided sample data and do not select the **Create spatial index** option when importing. (Not sure how to import data? Refer to *Chapter 1, Data Input and Output*, for how to do this.)

How to do it...

Using the **DB Manager** plugin (in the **Database** menu), perform the following steps:

1. Check whether the index does not exist. In **DB Manager**, open the database and then open the table that you want to check. Looking at the properties on the right, you should see a message just above **Fields** that looks like this:

   ⚠ No spatial index defined (create it)

2. However, what if no index was listed for the geom column? Then, we can make one just by clicking the **create it** link. Or you can do this in a SQL window, as follows:

   ❏ For SpatiaLite, use the following:

   ```
   SELECT CreateSpatialIndex('schools_wake', 'geom');
   ```

   ❏ For PostGIS, use the following:

   ```
   CREATE INDEX sidx_census_wake2000_geom
     ON public.census_wake2000 USING gist(geom);
   ```

3. Verify that the index exists, as follows:

   ❏ For PostGIS (the left-hand side of the following screenshot), on the right-hand side, scroll to the bottom looking for the **Indexes** section

   ❏ For SpatiaLite (the right-hand side of the following screenshot), you can see the idx_nameoftable_geomcolumn listed as a table:

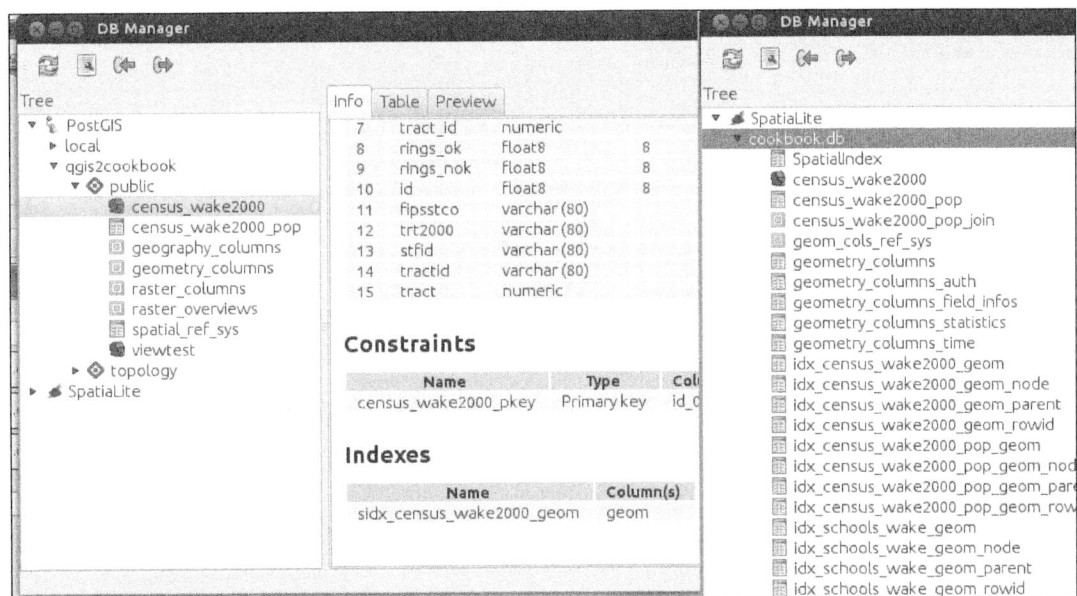

How it works...

When you create a spatial index, the database stores a bounding box rectangle for every spatial object in the geometry column. These boxes are also sorted so that boxes near each other in coordinate space are also near each other in the index.

When queries are run involving a location, a comparison is made against the boxes, which is a simple math comparison. Rows with boxes that match the area in question are then selected to be tested in depth for a precise match, based on their real geometries. This method of searching for intersection is faster than testing complex geometries one by one because it quickly eliminates items that are clearly not near the area of interest.

There's more...

Spatial indexes are really important to speed up the loading time of database spatial layers in QGIS. They also play a critical role in the speed of spatial queries (such as intersects). Note that PostGIS will automatically use a spatial index if one is present. SpatiaLite requires that you write queries that intentionally call a particular spatial index (Refer to Haute Cuisine examples from the *SpatiaLite Cookbook*)

Also, keep in mind that only one spatial index per table can be used in a single query. This really comes into play if you happen to have more than one spatial column or create a spatial index in a different projection than the geometry (check out the *PostGIS Cookbook* by Packt Publishing for more information).

> If you plan to insert many records into a table with an existing spatial index, you may want to disable or drop the index and recreate it after the import is done. Otherwise, the index will be recalculated after each row is inserted. This applies to nonspatial indexes too.

Do you want to check lots of tables at once? You can list all GIST indexes in PostGIS at once:

```
SELECT i.relname as indexname, idx.indrelid::regclass as
  tablename,
  am.amname as typename,
ARRAY(SELECT pg_get_indexdef(idx.indexrelid, k + 1, true)
  FROM generate_subscripts(idx.indkey, 1) as k
  ORDER BY k
  ) as indkey_names
FROM pg_index as idx
JOIN pg_class as i  ON  i.oid = idx.indexrelid
JOIN pg_am as am  ON  i.relam = am.oid
JOIN pg_namespace as ns  ON  ns.oid = i.relnamespace
AND ns.nspname = ANY(current_schemas(false))
Where am.amname Like 'gist';
```

To do something similar in SpatiaLite, use the following:

```
SELECT * FROM geometry_columns WHERE spatial_index_enabled = 1;
```

- ▸ Information on SpatiaLite spatial index implementation can be found at `https://www.gaia-gis.it/fossil/libspatialite/wiki?name=SpatialIndex`

- ▸ More details on using spatial indexes can be found at `https://www.gaia-gis.it/fossil/libspatialite/wiki?name=SpatialIndex`

- ▸ Information about PostGIS implementation is at `http://postgis.net/docs/manual-2.0/using_postgis_dbmanagement.html#gist_indexes`

- ▸ You can also check out *Chapter 10, Maintenance, Optimization, and Performance Tuning*, of *PostGIS Cookbook* by Packt Publishing,

Georeferencing rasters

Sometimes, you have a paper map, an image of a map from the Internet, or even a raster file with projection data included. When working with these types of data, the first thing you'll need to do is reference them to existing spatial data so that they will work with your other data and GIS tools. This recipe will walk you through the process to reference your raster (image) data, called georeferencing.

Getting ready

You'll need a raster that lacks spatial reference information; that is, unknown projection according to QGIS. You'll also need a second layer (reference map) that is known and you can use for reference points. The exception to this is, if you have a paper map that has coordinates marked on it or a spatial dataset that just didn't come with a reference file but you happen to know its CRS/SRS definition. Load your reference map in QGIS.

This book's data includes a scanned USGS topographic map that's missing its `o38121e7.tif` projection information. This map is from Davis, CA, so the example data has plenty of other possible reference layers you could use, for example, the streets would be a good choice.

> Actually, the world file was just renamed to `o38121e7.tfw.orig` so that QGIS wouldn't detect it. You can use this later to compare your georeference quality.

How to do it...

On the **Raster** menu, open the **Georeferencing** tool and perform the following steps:

1. Use the file dialog to open your unknown map in the **Georeferencing** tool.

2. Create a **Ground Control Point** (**GCP**) of matches between your start coordinates and end coordinates.

> 💡 Building corners, street intersections, and things where line features intersect or significant edge features can be found.

3. Add a point in your unknown map with **GCP Add +**. You can now enter the coordinates (that is, if it's a paper map with known coordinates marked on it), or you can select a match from the main QGIS window reference layer.

4. Repeat this process to find at least four matches. If you want to get a really good fit do between 10-20 matches.

5. (Optional) Save your GCPs as a text file for future reference and troubleshooting:

> 💡 Try to spread out your control points so that you have good coverage of the whole map. It's all about averaging the differences.

6. Now, choose **Transformation Settings**, as follows:

7. You have a choice here. Generally, you'll want to use Polynomial. If you set 4+ points for the first order, 6+ points for the second order and 10+ points for the third order, The second order is the currently recommend one. This will be discussed in the *There's more...* section of this recipe.

8. Set **Target SRS** to the same projection as the reference layer. (In this case, this is **EPSG:26910 UTM Zone 10n**)

9. **Output Raster** should be a different name from the original so that you can easily identify it.

> Save your GCP list to the file. If you don't like the results, come back and try a different algorithm or change the number of GCPs used. If you want a reference for comparison, look at the text `o38121e6.tif.points` file in this book's data folder.

10. When you're happy with your list of GCPs click on **Start Georeferencing** in **File** or on the green triangular button.

How it works...

A mathematical function is created based on the differences between your two sets of points. This function is then applied to the whole image, stretching it in an attempt to fit. This is basically a translation or projection from one coordinate system to another.

There's more...

Picking transformation types can be a little tricky, the list in QGIS is currently in alphabetical order and not the recommended order. Polynomial 2 and Thin-plate-spline (TPS) are probably the two most common choices. Polynomial 1 is great when you just have minor shift, zooming (scale), and rotation. When you have old well-made maps in consistent projections, this will apply the least amount of change. Polynomial 2 picks up from here and handles consistent distortion. Both of these provide you with an error estimate as the Residual or **RMSE** (**Root Mean Square Error**). TPS handles variable distortion, varying it's correction around each control point. This will almost always result in the best fit, at least through the GCPs that you provide. However, because it varies at every GCP location, you can't calculate an error estimate and it may actually overfit (create new distortion). TPS is best for hand-drawn maps, nonflat scans of maps, or other variable distorted sources. Polynomial methods are good for sources that had high accuracy and reference marks to begin with.

If you really want a good match, once you have all your points, check the RMSE values in the table at the bottom. Generally, you want this near or less than 1. If you have a point with a huge value, consider deleting it or redoing it. You can move existing points, and a line will be drawn in the direction of the estimated error. So, go back over the high values, zoom in extra close, and use the GCP move option.

Sometimes, just changing your transformation type will help, as shown in the following screenshot that compares Polynomial 1 versus Polynomial 2 for the same set of GCP:

GCP table								
on/off	id	srcX	srcY	dstX	dstY	dX[pixels]	dY[pixels]	residual[pixels]
☑	0	-162100.01	68464.42	599000.00	4275000.00	-1.27	1.65	2.08
☑	1	-161099.60	68430.25	600000.00	4275000.00	-2.41	0.22	2.42
☑	2	-154113.88	68203.95	607000.00	4275000.00	0.76	-1.33	1.53
☑	3	-161493.07	56413.39	600000.00	4263000.00	1.82	-1.25	2.20
☑	4	-153496.71	56161.93	608000.00	4263000.00	-2.87	1.67	3.32
☑	5	-159301.27	62357.43	602000.00	4269000.00	1.16	-0.79	1.40
☑	6	-156178.82	66267.28	605000.00	4273000.00	2.81	-0.16	2.81

Polynomial 1

Note the residual values difference when changing to Polynomial 2 (assuming that you have the minimum number of points to use Polynomial 2):

GCP table								
on/off	id	srcX	srcY	dstX	dstY	dX[pixels]	dY[pixels]	residual[pixels]
☑	0	-162100.01	68464.42	599000.00	4275000.00	0.79	0.36	0.87
☑	1	-161099.60	68430.25	600000.00	4275000.00	-0.96	-0.43	1.05
☑	2	-154113.88	68203.95	607000.00	4275000.00	-0.58	-0.26	0.63
☑	3	-161493.07	56413.39	600000.00	4263000.00	0.19	0.09	0.21
☑	4	-153496.71	56161.93	608000.00	4263000.00	-0.05	-0.02	0.05
☑	5	-159301.27	62357.43	602000.00	4269000.00	-0.74	-0.33	0.81
☑	6	-156178.82	66267.28	605000.00	4273000.00	1.34	0.60	1.46

Polynomial 2

Resampling methods can also have a big impact on how the output looks. Some of the methods are more aggressive about trying to smooth out distortions. If you're not sure, stick with the default nearest neighbor. This will copy the value of the nearest pixel from the original to a new square pixel in the output.

See also

▸ When performing georeferencing in a setting where you need it to be very accurate (science and surveying), you should read up on the different transformations and what RMSE values are good for your type of data. Refer to the general GIS or Remote Sensing textbooks for more information.

▸ For full details of all the features of the QGIS georeferencer, refer to the online manual at `http://docs.qgis.org/2.8/en/docs/user_manual/plugins/plugins_georeferencer.html`.

▸ The QGIS documentation has some basic information about how to pick transformation type at `http://docs.qgis.org/2.8/en/docs/user_manual/plugins/plugins_georeferencer.html#available-transformation-algorithms`.

Georeferencing vector layers

For various reasons, sometimes you have a vector layer that lacks projection information. This is often the case with CAD layers that were created only in local coordinates. When it is possible, try to track down the original projection information. As a last resort, you can attempt to warp the vector layer to match a known reference layer with the recipe described here.

Getting ready

You can open two instances of QGIS (or use one as you'll just be zooming back and forth a lot). In one instance, load a reference layer, something in the projection that you want your data to be in. Activate **Coordinate Capture Plugin** from the **Manage Plugins** menu.

> In Windows, you need the osgeo4w shell for this recipe. If you don't have a start menu item, look for the `OSGeo4W.bat` launcher in your QGIS or OSGeo4w installation folder.

This example uses `cad-lines-only.shp`, which is the line layer extracted from the `CSS-SITE-CIV.dxf` file. This file is a CAD rendering of design plans for Academy St. in the town of Cary, Wake County, North Carolina.

How to do it...

1. Create a list of GCP matches between your unknown layer (`cad-lines-only.shp`) and your reference layer (`CarystreetsND83NC.shp`).

2. Here are some specific adjustments to help with `cad-lines-only.shp` referenced to `CarystreetsND83NC.shp`. These will make it easier to find matches between the two layers:

    1. Load `cad-lines-only.shp`, and adjust its style properties using a rule-based style. Use the "Layer" = 'C-ROAD-CNTR' rule, which will only show you street centerlines.

    2. In your other QGIS session, load `CarystreetsND83NC.shp` in order to find the matching area, open the attribute table, and apply the following select expression: `"Street" LIKE  '%N ACADEMY%' OR "Street" LIKE  '%S ACADEMY%' OR "Street" LIKE '%CHATHAM%'`. The filter here highlights the three main streets of the original project, which is at the intersection of Chatham and N/S Academy streets in the center of the town. This may also be useful to change the color of the selected features to make it easier to find. The traffic circles at either end of the project are good landmarks:

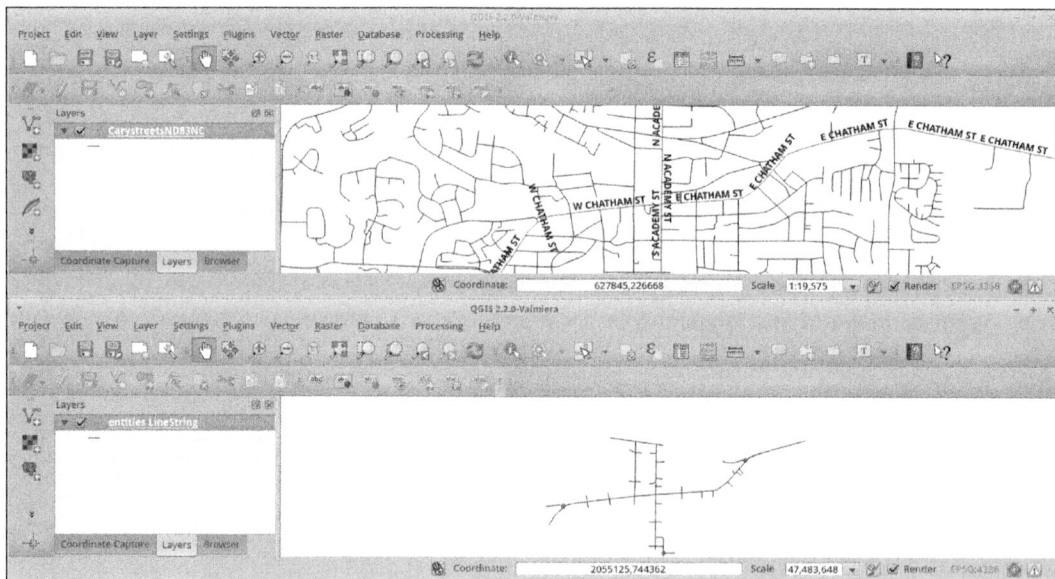

    3. Find an easy-to-identify feature that matches in both layers (street intersections).

4. Use the coordinate capture plugin to copy the x,y value for the point in both layers.

5. Save the coordinates in a text editor while you work.

6. Repeat this procedure until you have at least four pairs of points. Try to pick points spread out across the whole layer:

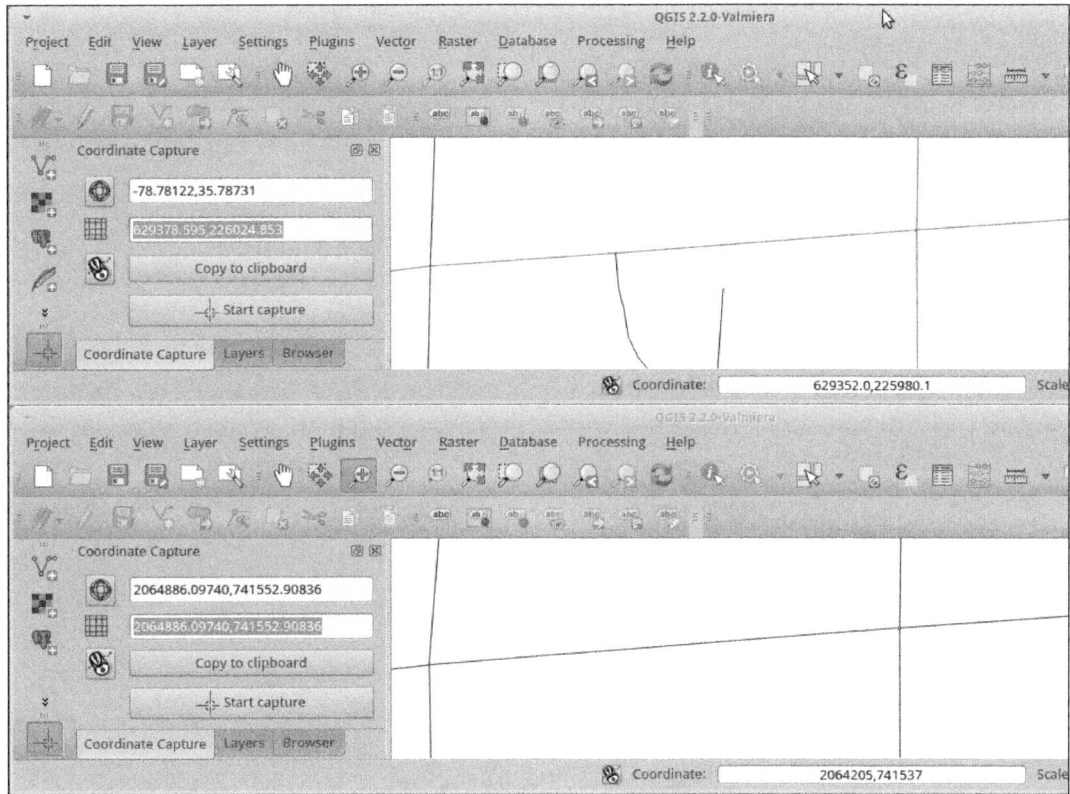

> There is currently no graphical interface in QGIS for the next step, which uses the OGR library that comes with QGIS. Take the list of points and using the ogr2ogr command-line, you're going to apply the GCP to the unknown layer.

3. Each set of coordinate pairs will look as follows:

```
-gcp sourceX sourceY destinationX destinationY
```

4. Open a terminal (Mac or Linux) or an OSGeo4w shell (Windows).

5. Change to the directory where you have the data (Hint: `cd /home/user/Qgis2Cookbook/`):

```
ogr2ogr -a_srs EPSG:3358 -gcp 2064886.09740 741552.90836
629378.595 226024.853 -gcp 2066610.97021 741674.39817
629903.420 226064.049 -gcp 2064904.46214 743055.63847
629384.784 226485.725 -gcp 2062863.85707 741337.65243
628762.587 225960.900 cad_lines_nd83nc.shp cad-lines-only.shp
```

`-a_srs` is the proj code for your reference layer.

The command pattern is `ogr2ogr <options> <destination> <source>`.

> Other useful advanced options include `-order <n>` to indicate polynomial level (default is based on the number of GCPs) or `-tps` to use Thin-plate-spline instead of polynomial. For more options refer to `http://www.gdal.org/ogr2ogr.html`.

6. Now, load your new `cad_lines_nd83nc.shp` file in the same project, as `CarystreetsND83NC.shp`. They should line up without the need to enable projection-on-the-fly:

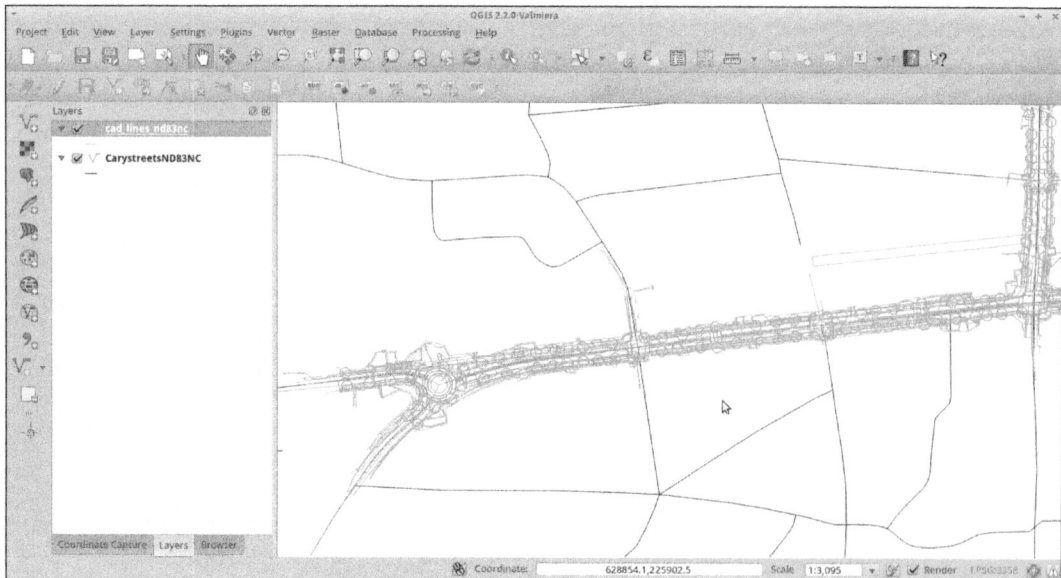

How it works...

Given the list of input coordinates and matching output coordinates, a math formula is derived to translate between the two sets. This formula is then applied to all the points in the original data. The result of this is a reprojected dataset from an unknown projection to a known projection.

> The original data is actually EPSG:102719, but we're pretending that we didn't have this piece of information to demonstrate this example.

There's more...

When picking a reference layer, try to pick something in the projection that you want to use for your maps and analysis. That way you only have to reproject once, as each additional transformation can add an error. There's also more than one way to go about accomplishing this task, including moving the data by hand.

In this particular, example the transformation is autoselected based on the number of GCP point pairs. 4-5 is the first order polynomial, 6-9 is the second order polynomial, and 10+ is the third order polynomial. Refer to the previous recipe in this chapter for more information.

A related topic is *Affine transformations* when you simply want to shift or rotate a vector layer by a known amount. The QgsAffine plugin is great if you already know the parameters, or roughly know how far you want to rotate and shift the vector layer, as it then just needs some math to get the parameters.

> Maybe by the time you read this, all of the difficult things here will be worked in a plugin. Keep an eye open, and try the experimental plugins Vector Bender, vectorgeoref, and Affine Transformations.

See also

- This method is very similar to the *Georeferencing Rasters* recipe and many of the same tips apply to both
- If you want to see how we got the CAD file into an SHP to begin with, look at Importing *DXF/DWG files* in the *Chapter 1, Data Input and Output*
- See the *Using Rule Based Rendering* recipe in *Chapter 10, Cartography Tips*, for tips on how to visualize the resulting CAD import better by applying attribute based rule filtering

- ▸ Too lazy to do the math? You can also just use GvSig to do the math and make a world file; refer to `http://foss4gis.blogspot.com/2011/05/computing-and-applying-affine.html`

- ▸ If you want to do the math yourself see `http://press.underdiverwaterman.com/rotating-a-point-grid-in-qgis/`

Creating raster overviews (pyramids)

Overviews, or pyramids, and resampling are all about making raster layers load faster when zooming and panning in your map canvas, by reducing the amount of data loaded when not zoomed in all the way.

Getting ready

You will need a large raster image.

> Generally, you want to make a copy of the data as this method will likely alter the original file if you choose to make 'internal' pyramids (easy to do on accident).

How to do it...

1. Load your raster in QGIS. `elev_lid792_1m.tif` will work fine for this example.
2. Right-click on the layer name and open **Properties**.
3. Go to the **Pyramids** item on the left:

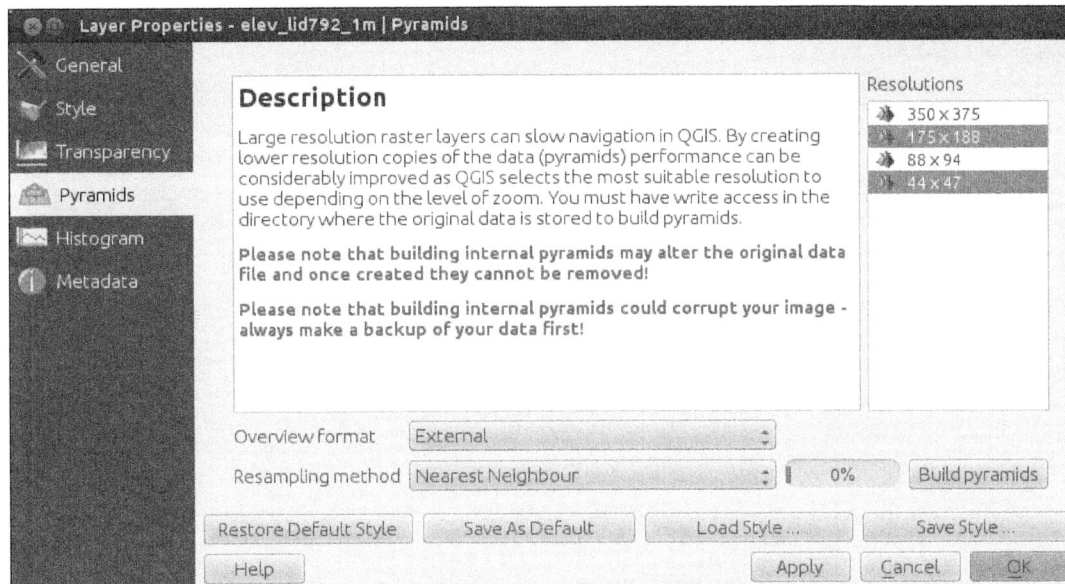

4. Select the image sizes that you want to create pyramids for:

    ❏   Optionally, choose whether to store externally (safer) or internally (less files to keep track of).

    ❏   Optionally, choose a resampling algorithm; **Nearest Neighbor** is the simplest, but other methods may look smoother at the cost of more data manipulation and compute time

5. Click on **Build pyramids**.

6. When this is completed, you'll notice the red X on the sizes that you picked will now show a pyramid.

How it works...

Generating pyramids essentially makes copies of your original data resized for different zoom levels. As you zoom out, the original data is resampled to fit the size of the screen. The pyramids do the same thing, but they let you decide what resampling method to use and generate this overview ahead of time. By generating them ahead of time, QGIS can load the image faster when you change zoom levels.

There's more...

Resampling is a fancy way of saying that at each zoom level that is now 1 pixel is more than 1 pixel from the original data, so they need to be averaged in some way and the result assigned to the 1 pixel that is now available. Each of the different methods uses a different math formula to decide the new value and how much to smooth that value with neighboring pixels (so that it looks aesthetically pleasing). This is the same concept as when you shrink pictures so that you can e-mail them to your friends.

If you chose to save them externally, your overviews are stored in `elev_lid792_1m.tif.ovr`. Some other programs store the same thing in the `.aux` files; however, pyramid formats are not universally compatible between GIS applications.

See also

▸ This is the same effect as using the GDAL `gdaladdo` command; refer to `http://gdal.org/gdaladdo.html`

▸ More details from the QGIS documentation can be found at `https://docs.qgis.org/2.8/en/docs/user_manual/working_with_raster/raster_properties.html`

Building virtual rasters (catalogs)

When you have a lot of rasters (instead of one big raster) that are all part of the same dataset (typically adjacent to each other), you don't want to load each file individually and then style it. It's much easier to load one file and treat it as one layer. This recipe lets you do this without actually creating a single monstrous raster, which can be difficult to work with.

Getting ready

You will need two or more raster files that have adjacent extents or only overlap partially around the edges and are in the same projection. Ideally, the files should be of the same type, such as all elevations, all air photos, and so on. For this recipe, the elevation rasters from the OSGeo EDU (North Carolina) dataset will work.

How to do it...

1. (Optional) Load the elevation rasters to your current map.
2. Go to **Raster Menu | Miscellanous | Build Virtual Raster (Catalog)**.
3. Check the **Use visible raster layers** checkbox or choose **SELECT**, browse to the example data, and select all four.

4. **SELECT** and name an output file using the `.vrt` extension.

5. (Optional) Check the **Load into canvas when finished** checkbox if you want to see the results immediately:

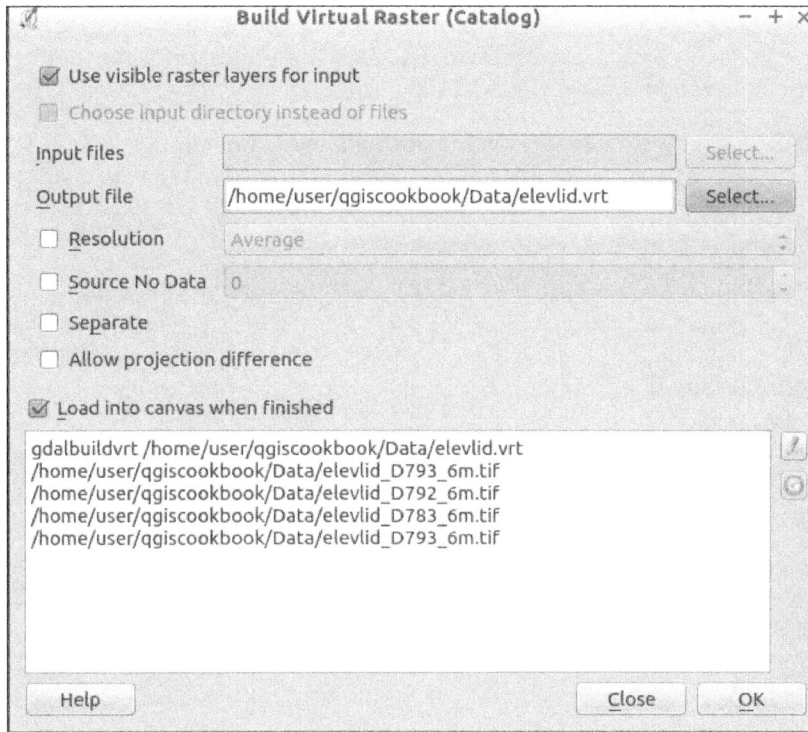

> GDAL command line equivalent: `<command> <output.vrt> <list of inputs... space between each...>`
>
> For example, `gdalbuildvrt elevlid.vrt elevlid_D782_6.tif elevlid_D783_6m.tif elevlid_D792_6m.tif elevlid_D793_6m.tif`.

How it works...

GDAL VRT format is an XML file that defines the location of each raster file relative to an anchor file. It uses the existing spatial extent information of the rasters to figure out their positions relative to each other and then anchors the set in the given coordinate system.

There's more...

Using a VRT is all about saving time. When you have hundreds of raster files for one particular dataset, you can combine them into a single file. However, this file could be gigantic in size and somewhat impossible to work with. This is a quick way to be able use the files as a seamless background layer. If you need to perform analysis, you'll likely need to either combine the layers or loop over them individually.

You could also generate **Tile Index** (also in the **Miscellaneous** menu), which makes a shapefile of the outlines of the rasters and puts the ID and path of the raster in the attribute table. This would allow you to figure out which image you want to load for a given map without having to load them all.

Finally, if you really want to make all of the files a single large file, use the context menu (right-click on the loaded VRT layer and choose **Save As**). If you have overlaps, more complicated situations, or want to merge without loading the files, first use the **Merge** tool (also in the **Miscellaneous** menu). This can be tricky if your files overlap, you'll need to decide how to handle the double data.

See also

- ▸ For another example, please refer to http://manual.linfiniti.com/en/rasters/data_manipulation.html#basic-fa-create-a-virtual-raster
- ▸ GDAL's gdalbuildvrt is the underlying tool; it's documentation can be found at http://gdal.org/gdalbuildvrt.html

3
Common Data Preprocessing Steps

In this chapter, we will cover the following recipes:

- ▶ Converting points to lines to polygons and back – QGIS
- ▶ Converting points to lines to polygons and back – SpatiaLite
- ▶ Converting points to lines to polygons and back – PostGIS
- ▶ Cropping rasters
- ▶ Clipping vectors
- ▶ Extracting vectors
- ▶ Converting rasters to vectors
- ▶ Converting vectors to rasters
- ▶ Building DateTime strings
- ▶ Geotagging photos

Introduction

When working with other people's data, it is often not the exact format that you need for a particular use. This chapter is all about taking the data that you do have and converting it to what you actually need. It covers converting between different types of vectors (points, lines, and polygons), between vectors and polygons, and cutting out only the parts that you need. Taking data from how you get it and converting it to the format and layout that you need in order to work with is often called 'data preprocessing'.

Converting points to lines to polygons and back – QGIS

Sometimes your data is vector formatted (point, line, or polygon), but it is not the right kind of vector for a particular type of analysis. Or perhaps you need to split a vector in a particular way to facilitate some analysis or cartography. Thankfully, all vector formats are related, lines are two or more connected points, polygons are lines whose first and last point are the same, multipolygons are two or more polygons for the same record, and rings are nested polygons where the inner polygon outlines an area to be excluded. This recipe covers how to convert between the different vector types using built-in QGIS methods.

Getting ready

To convert points to lines or polygons, you will need a shapefile with an ID column that has a single value shared between the points of the same line or polygon. In the following example, we will use `census_wake_2000_points.shp`.

You will also need to install and activate the Points2One plugin. Refer to the following website for how install plugins, `http://docs.qgis.org/2.8/en/docs/user_manual/plugins/plugins.html`.

How to do it...

The following instructions show four different conversion methods, depending on the starting data and the end data type. All of the tools are in the **Vector** menu:

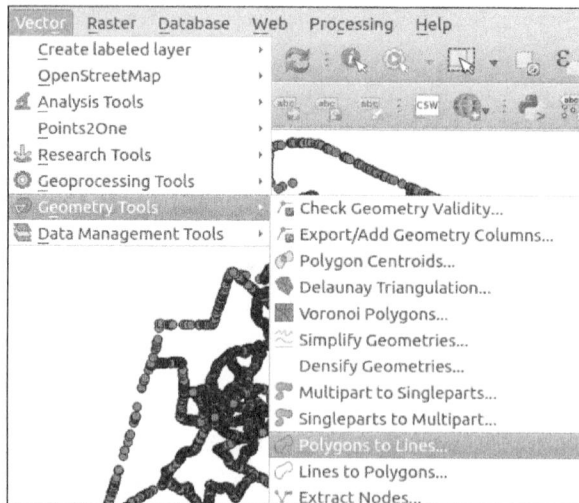

Start by loading the `census_wake_2000_points.shp` layer.

Converting points to lines (or polygons)

1. Go to **Vector** | **Points2One**.

2. Choose to create either lines or polygons.

3. Pick the group ID; in this case, this is STFID.

4. Create the output filename: `census_wake_2000_pt2lines.shp`:

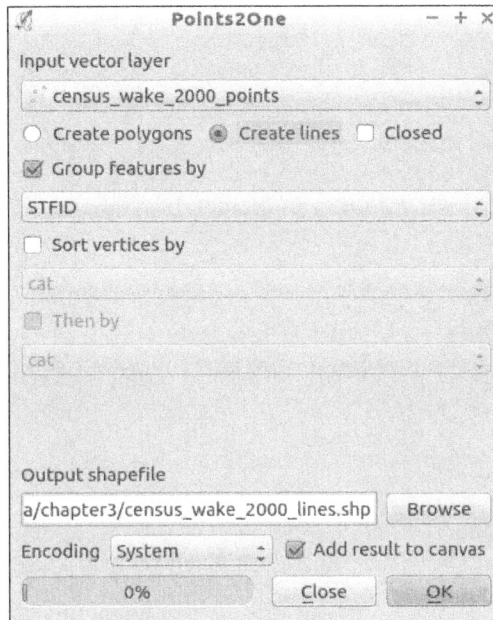

Converting lines to polygons

1. Go to **Vector** | **Geometry Tools** | **Lines to Polygons**.

2. Create the output filename: `census_wake_2000_lines2poly.shp`.

Converting polygons to lines

1. Go to **Vector** | **Geometry Tools** | **Polygons to Lines**.

2. Create the output filename: `census_wake_2000_poly2lines.shp`.

Converting polygons or lines to points

1. Go to **Vector** | **Geometry Tools** | **Extract Nodes**.

2. Create the output filename: `census_wake_2000_poly2pts.shp`.

How it works...

Converting to simpler types from more complex ones is fairly straightforward in simple cases. Lines are just multiple points connected together and polygons are lines that start and end with the same point. So, it's pretty easy to see how to deconstruct one geometry to simpler geometries.

It's building up from points, which is a little trickier. In a line with three or more points, you need to make sure that you have them in the correct order; otherwise, you'll end up with a squiggle. When going to polygons, this can create bigger issues by leaving you with invalid polygons that self-intersect. So, it's really important to order your points in your source table in the same order that they will be combined. Reordering your data can be somewhat tricky. The Points2One plugin now includes a sort order option; to use this, make sure that your attribute table has a numeric column with the order of the points specified per group (you can restart the numbering at 1 for each distinct grouping).

There's more...

You can also split or combine multipolygons with the **Singleparts to Multiparts** and **Multiparts to Singleparts** commands.

When things get really tricky, you may need to switch to editing the shapes by hand or custom scripts. A good example of this is when you want a polygon with a hole in the middle. If you do go the route of editing by hand, make sure to turn on snapping so that your lines are automatically snapped to existing points. The official documentation on snapping can be found at http://docs.qgis.org/2.8/en/docs/user_manual/working_with_vector/editing_geometry_attributes.html#setting-the-snapping-tolerance-and-search-radius.

The **Editing** and **Advanced Editing** toolbars and additional editing related plugins offer the ability to manipulate particularly tricky geometries, one at a time, if you need to.

Converting points to lines to polygons and back – SpatiaLite

The goal of this recipe is identical to the previous recipe, but it covers how to perform the process with data in a SpatiaLite database. You will to turn points into lines and lines into polygons.

Not all methods are available; for those that are not available, you can use the previous recipe. It will also work on a database layer; it just doesn't save the results to the database. So, the results will need to be imported to the database after completion.

You need to load a vector layer of points with a numeric ID indicating order, and an identifier of unique lines or polygons that is shared between points of the same geometry. For example, you can use `census_wake_2000_points` loaded into SpatiaLite with the geometry field called `geom`.

How to do it...

Using **DB Manager Plugin** (comes with QGIS and is in the **Database** menu), the **QspatiaLite** plugin, or an alternate SpatiaLite SQL application (command line or GUI), the following SQL examples will perform the conversions between vector types.

Points to lines

1. Create a table with points grouped by common ID:

```
--Create table grouping points with shared stfid into lines
CREATE Table census_pts2lines AS
SELECT stfid,MakeLine(geom) as geom
FROM census_wake_2000_points
GROUP BY stfid;
```

The following screenshot shows what the screen will look like:

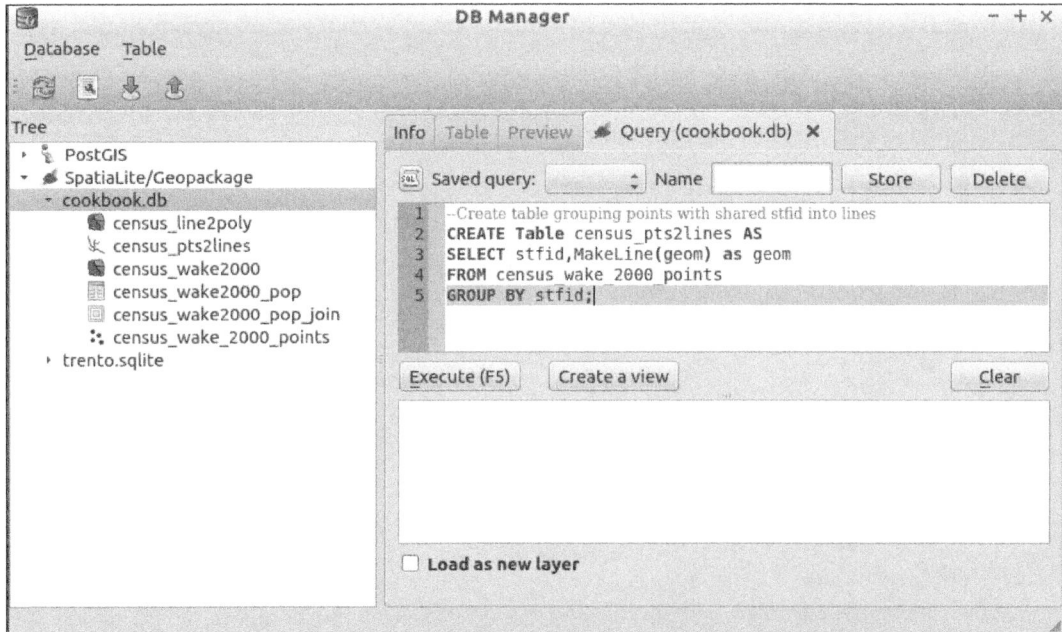

2. Register the new table as spatial:

```
--Register the new table's geometry so QGIS knows its a
spatial layer
SELECT
RecoverGeometryColumn('census_pts2lines','geom',3358,'LINES
TRING',2);
```

> Some SQL interfaces can run multiple SQL statements in a row, separated by a semicolon. However, there are also many interfaces that can only perform one query at a time. Generally, run one query at a time unless you know your software supports multiple queries; otherwise, this may fail or silently only run the first query.

Lines to polygons

1. Create a table with lines grouped by common ID:

```
--Create table grouping lines with shared stfid into polygons
CREATE Table census_line2poly AS
SELECT stfid,ST_Polygonize(geom) as geom
FROM census_pts2lines
GROUP BY stfid;
```

2. Register the new table as spatial:

```
--Register the new table's geometry so QGIS knows its a
spatial layer
SELECT
RecoverGeometryColumn('census_line2poly','geom',3358,'POLYGON',2);
```

> Double dashes (--) is the SQL character for a comment line. It is used to include descriptive text that is ignored in a query.

How it works...

Based on the common identifier specified in GROUP BY, the SQL statement aggregates multiple points into a new geometry of the type specified. After creating the new geometry and saving the results to a table, registration of the spatial metadata allows Spatialite and QGIS to know the table is a spatial layer.

There's more...

In the second example, lines were converted to polygons. You could also go directly from points to polygons with `ST_Polygonize(ST_MakeLine(geom))`.

Under the current versions of SpatiaLite, only aggregation to higher levels is fully supported. If you wish to disaggregate geometries, you can use the QGIS vector tools from the previous recipe.

See also

- ► SpatiaLite does have functions to dump specific points by first, last, or ID, one at a time. Refer to the index of functions (Reference Guide) online for details at `https://www.gaia-gis.it/fossil/libspatialite/index`

- ► The *Converting points to lines to polygons and back – QGIS* recipe in this chapter for nondatabase methods

Converting points to lines to polygons and back – PostGIS

The goal of this recipe is identical to the previous two recipes, but it covers how to perform the process with data in a PostGIS database. You will use it to turn points into lines, and lines into polygons.

Not all methods are available; for those not available, you can use the previous recipe. It will also work on a database layer; it just doesn't save the results to the database. So, the results will need to be imported to the database after completion.

Getting ready

You need to load a vector layer of points with a numeric ID indicating order, and an identifier of unique lines or polygons that is shared between points of the same geometry. For example, you can use `census_wake_2000_points` loaded into PostGIS with the geometry field called `geom`. (Refer to *Chapter 1, Data Input and Output,* the *Loading Vector Data into PostGIS* recipe to see how to load data into PostGIS.)

Import as single not multigeometries. Otherwise, you'll need to carry out some extra steps in the queries to split the multigeometries before they can be converted.

How to do it...

Using **DB Manager Plugin** (this comes with QGIS and is in the **Database** menu) or an alternate PostGIS SQL application (command line—pgsql or GUI—pgadmin III), the following SQL examples will perform the conversions between vector types.

Converting points to lines

1. Run the following query:

```
CREATE VIEW pts2line AS
SELECT ROW_NUMBER() over (order by census_wake_2000_points
.stfid) as id, stfid, ST_MakeLine(geom) as geom
FROM census_wake_2000_points
GROUP BY stfid;
```

The following screenshot shows what the screen will look like:

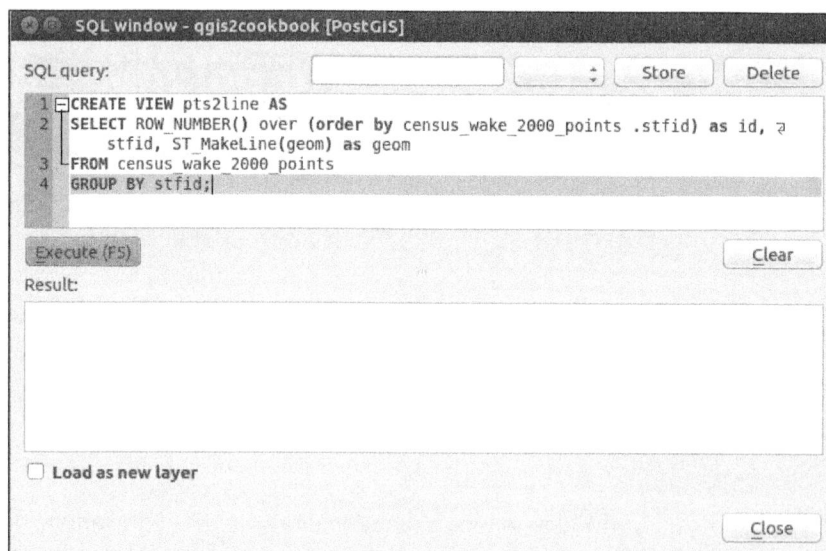

To test the creation of new geometries, wrap the queries in CREATE VIEW, as demonstrated in *Chapter 2, Data Management*. If the data is large or you are happy with the results, you can swap in CREATE TABLE to make a new table for more permanent storage.

Converting lines to polygons

Run the following query:

```
CREATE VIEW line2poly AS
SELECT id,stfid,ST_MakePolygon(geom) as geom
FROM pts2line;
```

> Want to go straight from point to polygons? Try ST_
> MakePolygon(ST_MakeLine(geom)); the rest is
> as shown in the first example: points to lines query.

Converting lines or polygons to points

Run the following query:

```
CREATE VIEW pts AS
SELECT ROW_NUMBER() over (order by a.id_0) as id,id_0 as
grpid,(a.a_geom).path[2] as path,
ST_GeometryType((a.a_geom).geom), ((a.a_geom).geom) as geom
FROM (SELECT id_0,(ST_DumpPoints(geom)) as a_geom FROM
"census_wake2000") as a;
```

> What's ROW_NUMBER() about? This is a trick to ensure a
> unique integer for each row. Some tools complain if you don't
> have this; for example, DB Manager won't preview or load the
> layer, even though direct loading in QGIS works fine.

How it works...

Based on the common identifier specified in GROUP BY, the SQL statement aggregates multiple points into a new geometry of the specified type.

When dumping geometries to points, PostGIS actually dumps an array, including ID information. This is why the example query is actually a nested set of queries. The first is to dump the array of geometry information, and the second to extract the relevant parts of the results in the format that we want them in.

There's more...

PostGIS has a few dump functions with different purposes in mind. Splitting geometries is apparently a difficult concept for databases because aggregation is usually the only direction functions can logically go. Disaggregation is claimed by some to be counter to how SQL conceptually works and would require non-SQL logic.

See also

- ▶ For more details on the dump functions of PostGIS (ST_Dump, ST_DumpPoints, and ST_DumpRings), refer to the PostGIS manual at http://postgis.net/docs/manual-2.1/reference.html

- ▶ Refer to the *Converting points to lines to polygons and back – QGIS* recipe in this chapter for the non-database methods

Cropping rasters

Sometimes, the raster data you have for a theme is just much larger than the actual extent of your study area or map. Or, in the case of scanned maps, you have extra nonmap information around the outside edge. In these cases, you want to cut out a portion of your raster.

Getting ready

You'll need a raster file that you want to cut a portion of. In this example, we will use the North Carolina whole state elevation model (elev_state_500m.tif) and cut it with the outline of Wake County (county_wake.shp). Load both of these files in a fresh QGIS project.

How to do it...

The easiest way to do this is to use a polygon mask layer. The vector mask can be a rectangle, but it doesn't have to be. The outline of a single polygon works best, though.

> An alternate method would be to determine the bounding box (bbox) coordinates of the extent that you want with the Capture Coordinate tool or to draw the rectangle directly on the map.

1. Go to **Raster | Extraction | Clipper**.
2. Set **Input file (raster)** as elev_state_500m.tif.
3. Set **Output file** using the **Select** button to pick a directory, and name the output elev_wake_500m.tif.

4. Set **No data value** to **-9999**.

> Why -9999? Setting **No data value** to something impossible makes it more obvious later to other users. The value 0 is a really bad choice as data can legitimately have a value of zero. As some raster formats only support numbers and, in particular, integers, a large negative number is a common choice.

5. Now change **Clipping mode** to **Mask Layer** and select `county_wake.shp` as **Mask Layer**:

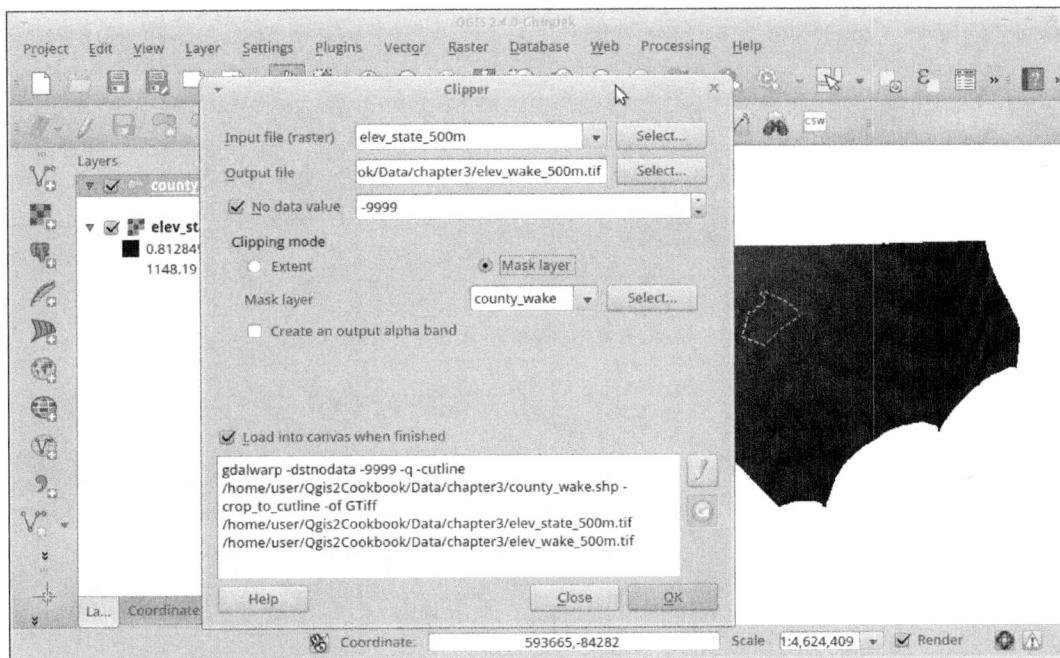

How it works...

The shape of your mask and the size of the raster cells in the source data will determine how pixelated the resulting raster will be. Zoom in to the results and compare the edge of the new raster to the vector outline of the county. You'll notice that because of the 500 m wide pixels, it's hard to exactly match the edge of the county exactly with whole pixels.

Note that this tool, as with all other tools in the GDAL **Tools** menu, is actually a graphical interface to GDAL command-line tools.

There's more...

You'll notice that with this particular example, an issue that arises with converting rasters to nonrectangular shapes; the edges are jagged as compared to the vector. If you need it to be really smooth, there are a few options. You can decrease the pixel size, splitting current pixels into multiple pixels using the `-tr` option. As with other Raster tools, you can use the pencil icon to override the GDAL command-line options to add features not included in the interface. In this case, the `-tr` option inline with the rest of the already formatted command:

```
gdalwarp -tr 100 100
```

This would make each pixel 100 units instead of the current 500 x 500.

> Some important options to remember when saving TIFF files with GDAL are number type (Integer versus Float) and compression. Both of these can greatly impact the final file size. Refer to the *Converting Vectors to Rasters* recipe later in this chapter for an example. Also, if you have a multicore CPU, add `-multi` to take advantage of your CPU cores for faster processing of most raster operations.

See also

▸ For a full list of the gdalwarp options refer to `http://gdal.org/gdalwarp.html`

Clipping vectors

Like rasters, occasionally you only need vector data to cover a certain area of study (area of interest). Also, like rasters, you can use a layer defining the extent that you want to select only for a portion of a vector layer to make a new layer. The tool that is used for this job is Clip; that is, 'Cookie Cutter' because of how the results look afterwards.

Getting ready

For the example in this recipe, we will use `geology.shp` and clip it to the extent of Wake County using `census_wake2000.shp`. Any vector layer with the aggregation of polygons covering all of the county will work.

How to do it...

1. Load the two, `geology.shp` and `census_wake2000.shp`, layers.

2. Open the clipping tool from **Vector | Geoprocessing Tools | Clip**:

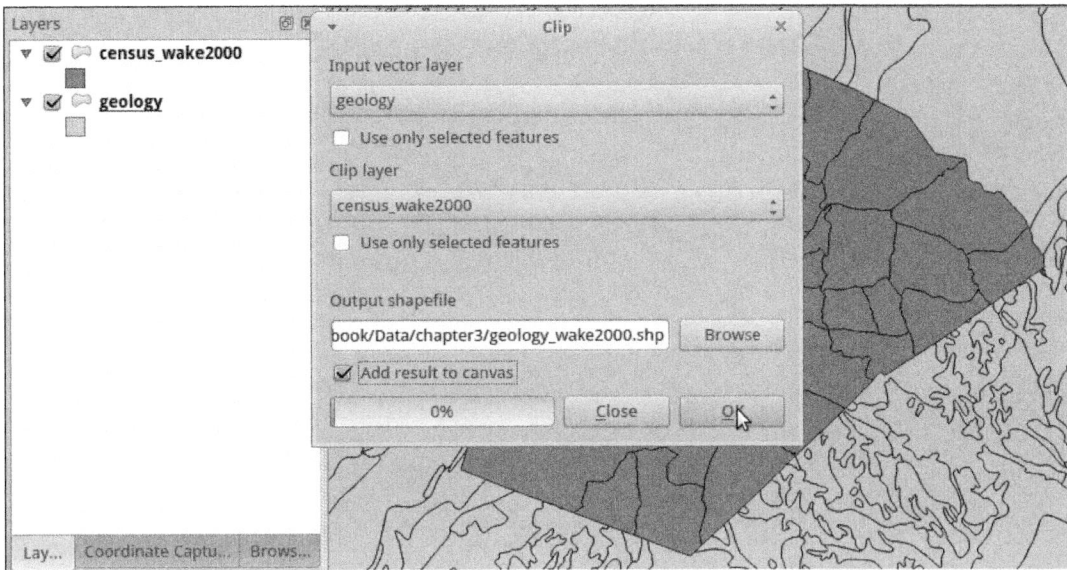

3. Input layer is the layer that has to be cut; this is `geology.shp`.

4. Clip layer defines the boundaries that have to be cut.

> There is no requirement that clip layer be contiguous. You can cut any combination of shapes that you want, circles, squares, triangles, and so on. They just need to be polygons.

5. (Optional) Check **Add result to canvas** so that you see the results immediately.

6. Select **OK** to run the tool:

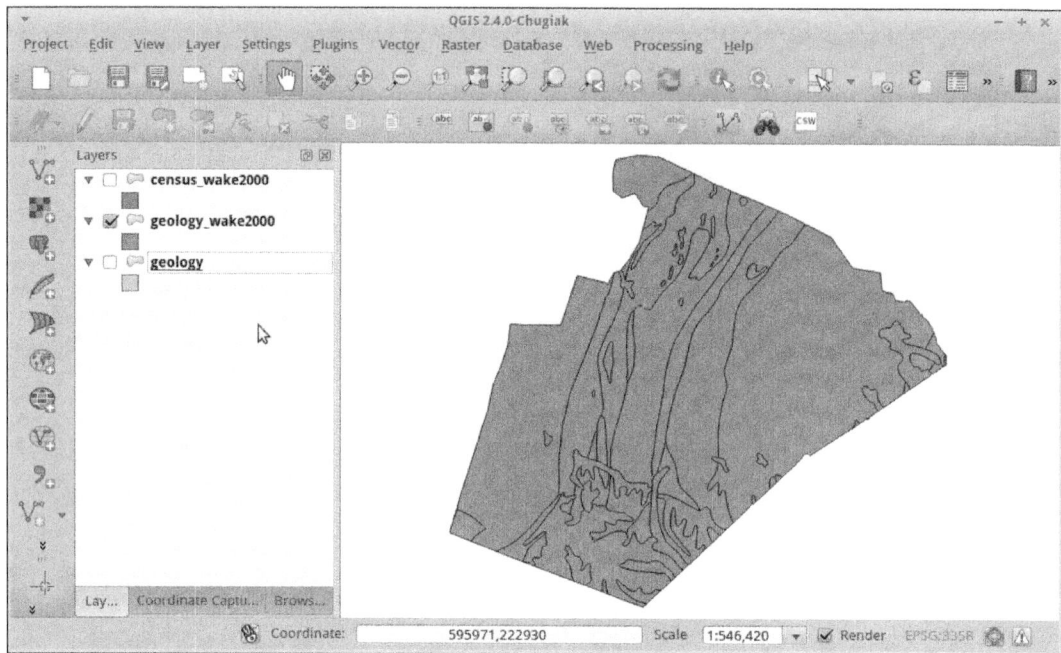

How it works...

All clipping is based on the principle of intersection features. For each feature in Input, the tool checks to see whether it intersects with the overall shape of clip layer. When it does intersect, the algorithm then checks whether any part falls outside the intersection. When a part lands outside, it is cut off.

There's more...

You have to be careful when using clip. If the original table contained columns that included measurements such as area and perimeter, these values are copied from the original. Therefore, they may not reflect the new size of and shapes that were cut.

Generally, all geometry operations and analysis should be done with layers in the same projection in order to ensure consistent results. Also, many tools are not projection aware and won't compensate for two source layers being in different projections.

Tools that create the intersection of objects (for example, in PostGIS's and SpatiaLite's ST_Intersection) can provide you with similar results. However, you may need to perform multiple steps: Intersect, then select by contains or intersection to eliminate unwanted data.

See also

See also

Refer to the next recipe in the chapter if you want a way to limit features without altering the original spatial data

Extracting vectors

Clipping is great, except when you don't want to alter the original geometries, such as when you want to select overlapping features. Or, in other cases, you just want filter the geometries based on nonspatial attributes. To achieve both of these results, you can utilize the Selection tools in combination with **Save Layer As..** to extract just the features of interest. This recipe uses spatial selection methods to extract a subset of original polygons without altering them.

Getting ready

We'll use the same data as the previous recipe, `geology.shp` and `census_wake2000.shp`.

How to do it...

1. Select polygons from `geology.shp` that overlap with Wake County (`census_wake2000.shp`) by navigating to **Vector | Research Tools | Select by location**.

2. Select the feature in **geology**.

3. Intersect the features in `census_wake2000`.

4. Modify the current selection by **creating new selection**.

5. Click on **OK**:

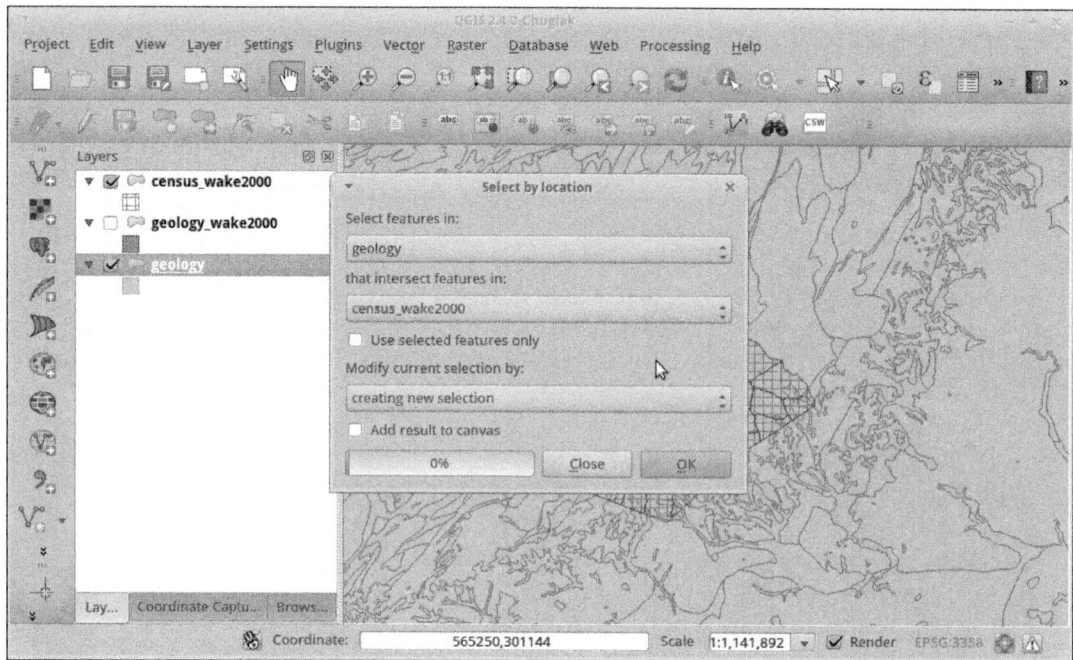

6. Now, you will see the matching features highlighted (by default in yellow):

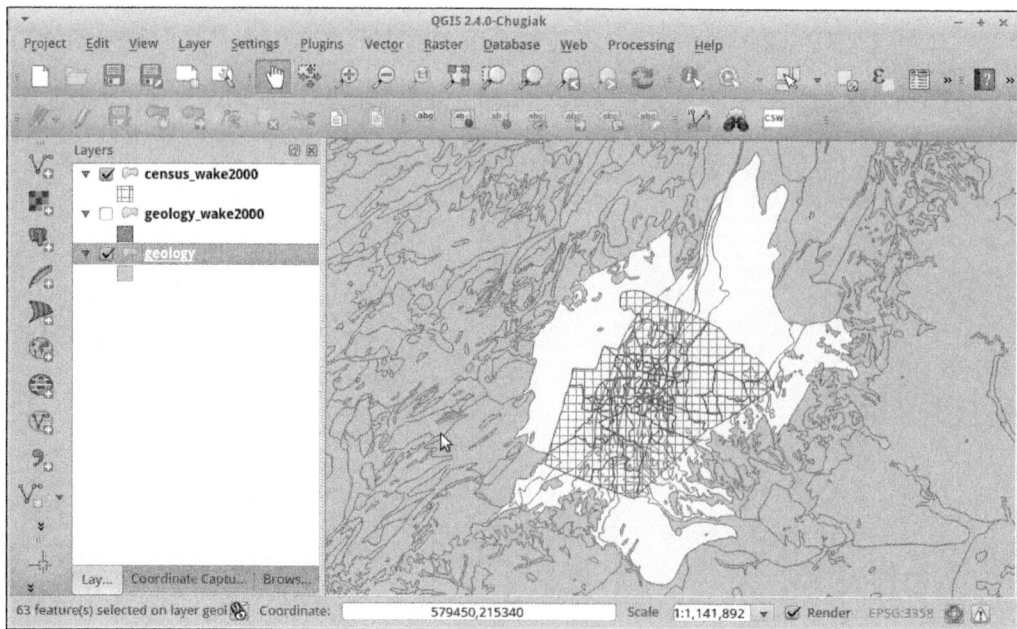

7. If the selection looks good, use the **Layer context** menu, right-click, and click on **Save As...** to create a file containing only the selection.

> When in the **Save As...** (as described in *Chapter 1, Data Input and Output*) dialog make sure to check the box next to **Save only selected features**.

How it works...

This really goes back to the same fundamental concept of Intersection that most vector analysis rely on. When you can test whether two features overlap, there are many different operations possible based on the answer. You can select, deselect, or, as in the previous recipe, select then cut to fit. In these cases, each polygon is tested for at least a partial intersection, and the matches are then highlighted as the results.

There's more...

While this recipe demonstrates how to select a subset of data based on location, you can also do the same thing based on attributes of the features with a query on the attribute table. Or, you can combine attribute based selection, spatial selection, and hand selection graphically on the map—any selection combination that you want can be saved as a new layer.

You may also notice in the **Select by location** tool that vectors can also be added or removed from existing selections in case you want to perform more complicated operations involving more than one type of criteria.

See also

► Refer to the documentation on PostGIS, SpatiaLite, or the *PostGIS Cookbook*, by Packt Publishing, for how to perform similar operations using SQL in PostGIS (SpatiaLite, queries are very similar)

Converting rasters to vectors

Sometimes, you need to convert data that is originally in raster format to a vector format in order to perform vector-based analysis methods. Generally speaking, as rasters are continuous datasets, converting them to polygons is more common than converting them to lines or points.

Getting ready

You need a raster layer, preferably one with groups of the same valued pixels next to each other. For this example, we'll use `geology_30m.tif`, as a 30 meter x 30 meter pixel should give decent results.

> The smaller the pixels, the smoother looking the resulting vector will appear when zoomed out.

How to do it...

1. Load `geology_30m.tif`.

2. Go to **Raster | Conversion | Polygonize**:

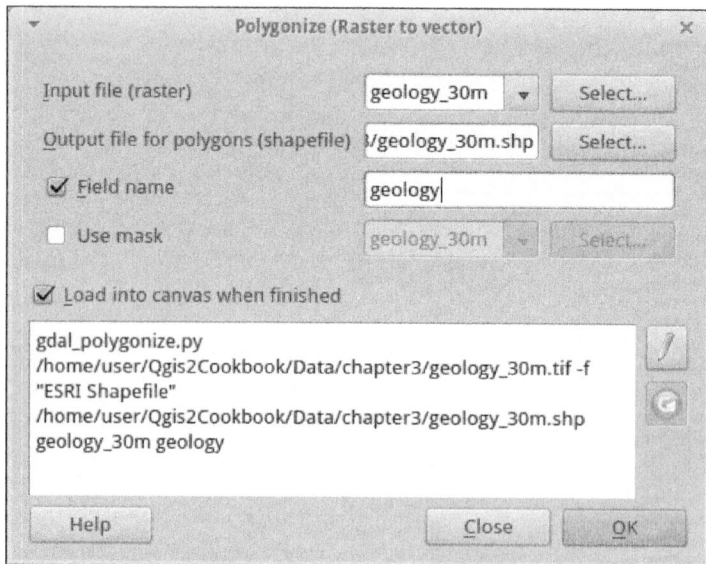

3. Name the output `geology_30m.shp`.

4. (Optional) Name the output column `geology`, `class` or `value`.

5. Press **OK** to run the process.

6. Compare the results (colors are in a similar but different scale):

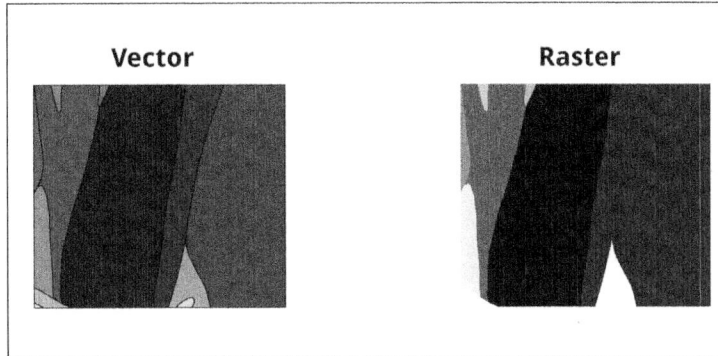

How it works...

For each pixel, the value is compared to its neighbors (there are different neighbor algorithms). When two pixels next to each other have the same value, they are lumped into a polygon. Additional neighbors of the same value get added to the polygon until pixels of differing values are encountered. As it's pixel-based, the edge of the result will usually follow the outline of the pixels, making for a jagged edge. This edge can be smoothed into straight lines with additional options or other tools, such as the QGIS smoothing tool.

There's more...

The minimum number of pixels required to make a polygon or the maximum allowed value difference to be counted as the same can be altered to drop out isolated pixels or to allow for a range of values to be counted together.

Note that if each pixel is unique as compared to its adjacent neighbors, then you'll just end up with a polygon for each pixel. Or if your raster is sufficiently large and varied, this process could take days. You may want to reconsider whether you really need to convert or whether your analysis can be done in raster. Another option would be to resample or reclassify the raster to larger polygons first to decrease the data density. Or, you need to investigate remote sensing type tools that perform classification to create related groupings of pixels based on similarity.

If you want to convert raster data to points, then you probably want to use the points sampling tool. If you want to convert some portion of a raster to lines then you may need more sophisticated feature extraction tools found; for example, in SAGA and GRASS, either through the Processing toolbox or as standalone software. Or, you may even need to result to a mix of pixel extraction and hand digitizing.

See also

▶ *Chapter 7, Raster Analysis I,* and *Chapter 8, Raster Analysis II,* on further raster methods

Converting vectors to rasters

Occasionally, you want to convert vectors to rasters to facilitate using raster analysis tools such as the raster calculator.

Getting ready

You'll need a vector layer; this can be a point, line or polygon layer. The best results generally come from polygon layers. We will use `geology_wake2000reclass.shp`. This file is the result of the earlier clipping vectors recipe with a new column added that codes the geology types as integers. For reference, you'll also use `elev_wake_500m.tif` as a matching raster for the area of interest.

How to do it...

In order to be useful in analysis, here's a checklist:

1. Is the vector data in the same projection as the rest of the raster analysis data? If not, reproject it first. Check the following URL for help, `https://docs.qgis.org/2.8/en/docs/training_manual/vector_analysis/reproject_transform.html`.

2. Clip the vector data to the analysis extent. You may need to convert a raster into a polygon mask to clip it (refer to the clipping vectors recipe earlier in this chapter).

> You can only pick numeric fields as raster formats only store a single number per cell. In order to keep the attribute that you want, you may need to use the field calculator to create a new field that reclassifies categories of text into a numeric scheme (for example, 1 = water, 2 = land, and so on) before performing the conversion. If you copy a unique ID as the attribute, there are some tools later that let you rejoin the original attribute table as a value attribute table (refer to the GRASS functions in **Processing Toolbox**).

3. Load `geology_wake2000reclass.shp` and `elev_wake_500m.tif`.

4. Open **Properties** of `elev_wake_500m.tif`:

    1. In the **Metadata** section, scroll down to **Dimensions**. You will want to match either the dimensions or resolution so that your new raster will match the existing elevation data pixels.

    2. Note that **Dimensions** are X: **134**, Y: **124** and Bands: **1**. The resolution is 499.637,-498.342 pixel size.

    3. Close the dialog.

5. Now, open the conversion dialog by navigating to **Raster | Conversion | Rasterize** and follow these steps:

    1. Input the file as `geology_wake2000reclass`.

    2. Name your output `geology_wake.tif` (you will get a warning to set the size or resolution).

    3. Set the raster size: **Width** to **134** and **Height** to **124**.

    4. Click on **OK** to run the process.

The following screenshot shows how the screen will look:

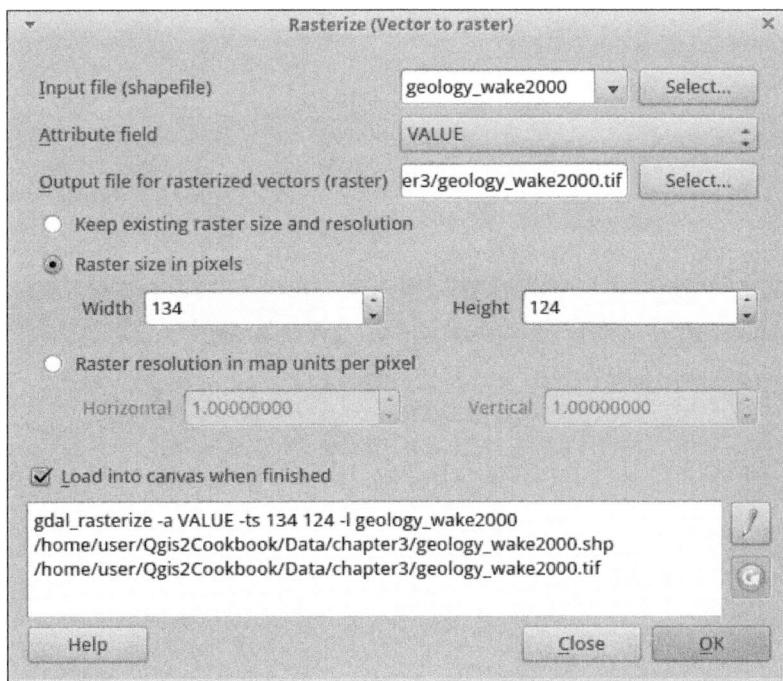

How it works...

A grid of pixels is created at the specified width, height, and extent. For each cell, an intersection is performed with the underlying vector layer. If more than 50% of the cell intersects with the vector, it's designated attribute is assigned to the cell.

There's more...

It's really important to match projection and extent before converting to raster. If you fail to do so, then your pixels in different raster layers won't line up perfectly with each other, and either tools won't work or they will introduce a resampling error. If this looks too pixelated (squares) for your liking, consider creating the raster at a higher pixel density.

If you compare the vector version to the new raster, you'll notice that the area in the middle all came out a similar color. This is due to the values used for classification, where the geology that started with the same major component was given the same starting value (for example, PZ all start with 40, and the last number changes based on the letters after PZ).

Looking at the new layer and want to get rid of the black surrounding the real data? This area is no-data, refer to *Chapter 8, Raster Analysis II*.

See also

▶ There are other methods to calculate the new value of a pixel to make smoother transitions or intermediate values when multiple polygons are with the same pixel. Refer to the GRASS and SAGA methods in Processing Toolbox for more sophisticated alternatives.

Building DateTime strings

Date and time data get stored in all sorts of ways. One of the more frustrating issues is that some common GIS formats (Shapefiles) can't store date and time in the same field without making it a string. This is fine for visual display but terrible for use with tools that use DateTime for their functionality, such as the TimeManager Plugin (refer to *Chapter 4, Data Exploration*).

Getting ready

Use `datetime-example.shp`, which contains a variety of date and time representations to play with.

How to do it...

1. Load `datetime-example.shp`.

2. Open the attribute table of `datetime-example`.

3. Create a new field. As this is a shapefile, we'll need to use a String of length 30 (or you can use the empty field called `calculated`).

4. Turn on layer editing (this is the pencil icon, which is the first icon to the left of the window toolbar).

5. From the drop-down list, select **Calculated**.

6. Now press the **Calculation** button.

> In older versions of QGIS, you'll need to open the Field calculator, which also works in newer versions but has slightly more steps.

7. In the calculator, we'll use the `substr` String operation (that is, Substring) in combination with the `||` concatenation to rearrange the values from existing fields into a valid `DateTime`:

    1. The simplest variant is just to combine `shpDate` with `Time` and put a space in between:

       ```
       "shpdate"  || ' '||  "Time"
       ```

    2. For a bit more of a challenge, use `Date`:

       ```
       substr("Date",7,4) ||'-'||substr("Date",1,2)||'-'||
           substr("Date",4,2) || ' '||  "Time"
       ```

> Note the use of single quotes (') to denote a string as opposed to double quotes ("), which indicate a field name.

8. Experiment with the formulas, checking the results with the calculator preview at the bottom. When satisfied, select **OK**, and then click on the **Update All** button:

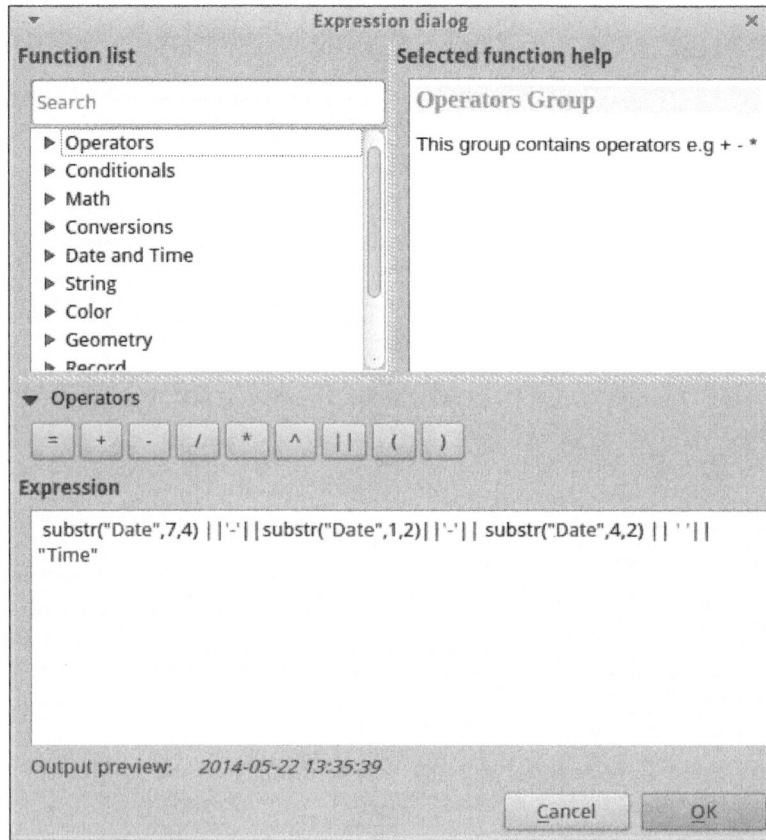

9. If you're happy with the results, save the edits; if not, toggle **editing off** and choose **Close without saving**.

How it works...

Substr takes three arguments: the field name, the starting position, and the number of characters after this to include. The position index starts at 1.

There's more...

Using string manipulation, we've combined multiple fields into an ISO standard format for DateTime, which other tools will recognize and be able to utilize.

The fields included in this example data are as follows:

Field	Type	Explanation
Time	String	This is time in a 24 hour format: hours:minutes:seconds.
datetime	String	This is a DateTime String from a typical GPS GPX file.
calculated	String	This is a String that is long enough to hold date and time with padding characters and a timezone UTC offset.
Date	String	This is a typical date format coming out of a spreadsheet.
shpdate	Date	This is a date format in the Date type within a shapefile, and it can not hold time.

See also

▶ If using database layers, this can all be performed with SQL in SpatiaLite or PostGIS. The ISO date time standard is 8601, and can be found at http://en.wikipedia.org/wiki/ISO_8601.

Geotagging photos

Newer cameras and phones with built-in GPS can be wonderful tools for data collection, as they help keep track of exactly where and when a picture was taken. However, not all cameras have a built-in GPS. You can add geotags afterwards, either with a GPS log from a separate GPS unit or just using a reference map and your memory or notes.

Getting ready

For this recipe, you'll need a some photos and either a GPS log (*.gpx), reference vector, reference raster, or coordinates. We've provided centerofcalifornia.jpg in the geotag folder, and the coordinates are in the image itself but also included as a point in centerofcalifornia.shp.

You will also need the Geotag photos plugin, which requires the exiftool program to be installed on your system. If exiftool didn't come with your install, you can easily get it from the Web at http://www.sno.phy.queensu.ca/~phil/exiftool/ or at package repositories (Linux).

How to do it...

This particular plugin assigns location per folder, so all photos in a folder will get the same coordinates. This works well for batch assigning of general coordinates:

1. Start by loading your GPS log, or creating a new vector layer and digitizing the points that you want to assign to photos. In this case, load `centerofcalifornia.shp`.

    [🔔 Don't have a lot of locations or just have coordinates written down by hand? You can manually enter the information into the plugin interface without an existing layer.]

2. (Optional) Load a background reference layer.

3. Now that you have the layer that you want to associate with photos open the plugin in **Vector | Geotag and import photos | Geotag photos**.

4. Select the layer and then the field (location) that you want to use as the label.

5. Now, click on **Populate Table**. One row should have been added to the interface.

6. Now, pick the photos by clicking under **Path to Folder** in the empty box for the row that you want to assign:

    1. You can type in the path or browse by clicking on **....**

    2. Pick the `geotag` folder.

    3. Make sure to press **Enter** or click outside the box once you are back in the main screen:

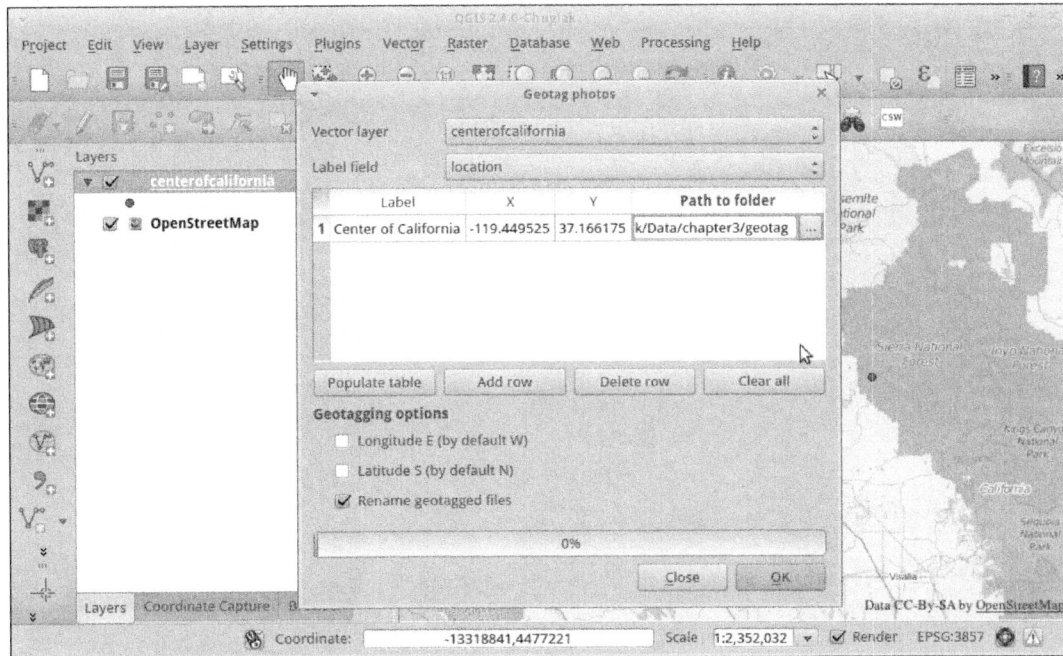

7. (Optional) Check the box to rename geotagged files if you want the geotagged version to be a new copy of the file instead of altering the original files (always keep an original backup).

8. Click on **OK**.

How it works...

Exiftools writes to the built-in metadata of an image file to a section called EXIF. It's a standard in photography to store extra data about photos that many software management tools can easily read from. Latitude and Longitude in WGS 84 coordinates are the standard method of encoding GPS data within the EXIF section.

There's more...

Now that you have a geotagged photo, you can upload it to sites such as Flickr, which will display it on a map, or skip to the recipe *Viewing Geotagged Photos* in *Chapter 4*, *Data Exploration*, for how to make a map in QGIS.

This plugin is very manual and assigns location per folder as it was created to work specifically with camera traps. Instead, if you were travelling between each photo location and have a GPS log, there are other non-QGIS tools to help you match GPS points with your photos. Digikam (a photography management tool) has a function to geotag based on timestamp matches.

See also

▶ The OpenStreetMap wiki lists other free and paid options out there at
  `http://wiki.openstreetmap.org/wiki/Geotagging_Source_Photos`

4
Data Exploration

In this chapter, we will cover the following recipes:

- ▶ Listing unique values in a column
- ▶ Exploring numeric value distribution in a column
- ▶ Exploring spatiotemporal data using Time Manager
- ▶ Creating animations using Time Manager
- ▶ Designing time-dependent styles
- ▶ Loading BaseMaps with the QuickMapServices plugin
- ▶ Loading BaseMaps with the OpenLayers plugin
- ▶ Viewing geotagged photos

Introduction

This chapter focuses on recipes that will help you visually inspect and better comprehend your data. The recipes in this chapter include methods of summarizing, inspecting, filtering, and styling data, based on spatial and temporal attributes so that you can get a better feeling for your data before you perform analysis. The primary goal is to create some visuals or summaries of data that allow you, the human, to utilize your brain's ability to identify patterns of interest. The better you understand your data, the easier it is to pick appropriate analysis methods later.

Listing unique values in a column

When investigating a new dataset, it is very helpful to have a way to quickly check which values a column contains. In this recipe, we will use different approaches using both the GUI and the Python console to list the unique values of POI classes in our sample POI dataset.

Getting ready

To follow this recipe, please load `poi_names_wake.shp`.

How to do it...

If you are simply looking for a solution based on the GUI, the **List unique values** tool is available both in **Vector | Analysis Tools** as well as in the **Processing Toolbox** menu. You can use either one of these to get a list of the unique values in a column. Having this tool available in the **Processing Toolbox** menu makes it possible to include it in processing models and, thus, automate the process. The following steps to list unique values use the **Processing Toolbox** menu:

1. Start **List unique values** from the **Processing Toolbox** menu.

2. Select the `poi_names_wake` layer as **Input layer** and the `class` attribute as **Target field**.

3. Click on **Run** and wait for the tool to finish. The results will be displayed in the **Results** view, which will open automatically.

If you want to further customize this task, for example, by counting how often the values appear in this dataset, it's time to fire up Python console:

1. Start **Python Console**, which you will find in the **Plugins** menu, and click on the **Show editor** button (in the toolbar to the left of Python console) to open the editor window.

2. Paste the following short script into the editor, save it, and then click on the **Run script** button. (Make sure that the POI layer is selected in the layer list.) It loops through all features in the active layer and creates a dictionary object, which contains all unique values and the corresponding counts:

```
import processing
layer = iface.activeLayer()
classes = {}
features = processing.features(layer)
for f in features:
  attrs = f.attributes()
  class_value = f['class']
  if class_value in classes:
```

```
      classes[class_value] += 1
  else:
      classes[class_value] = 1
   print classes
```

The following screenshot shows what the screen looks like:

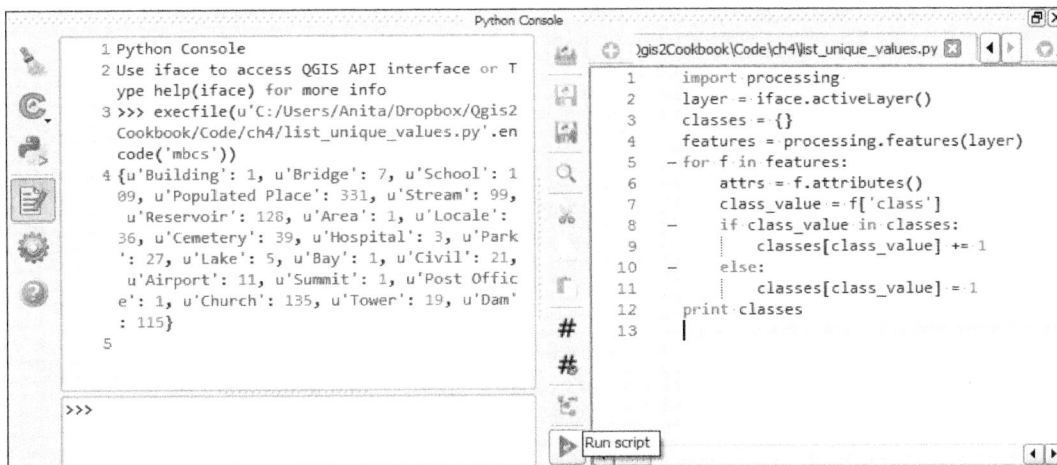

How it works...

In the first line, we use `import processing` because it offers a very handy and convenient function, `processing.features()`, to access layer features, which we use in line 7. It is worth noting that, if there is a selection, `processing.features()` will only return an iterator of the selected features.

In line 3, we get the currently active layer object. Line 5 creates the empty dictionary object, which we will fill with the unique values and corresponding counts.

The `for` loop, starting on line 5, loops through all features of the layer. For each feature, we get the value in the classification field (line 7). You can change the column name to analyze other columns. Then, we only need to check whether this value is already present in the `classes` dictionary (line 8) or whether we have to add it (line 11).

There's more...

If you are using an SQL database, such as Spatialite or PostGIS, you can achieve similar results with a query using the COUNT and GROUP BY functions to count the number of features or records per class:

```sql
SELECT class, COUNT(*)
FROM poi_name_wake
GROUP BY class
```

Exploring numeric value distribution in a column

In this recipe, we will look at how to explore the properties of a column of numeric values. We will look at the tools that QGIS offers and apply them to analyze the elevation values in our sample POI dataset.

Getting ready

To follow this recipe, please load `poi_names_wake.shp`. If you followed the previous recipe, *Listing unique values in a column*, you can continue directly from there.

How to do it...

A good way to get a first impression of the properties of a numeric column is using the **Basic Statistics** tool from **Vector**. This allows you to calculate statistical values, such as the minimum and maximum values, mean and median, standard deviation, and sum.

If you want to examine the distribution of elevation values, there is the handy Statist plugin. Statist generates an interactive histogram representation of the value distribution:

1. Install **Statist** using **Plugin Manager**.

2. Start **Statist** from the **Vector** menu.

3. Specify **Input vector layer** and the attribute that you want to analyze (**Target field**), then click on **OK** to compute the statistics.

4. Using the buttons below the diagram, you can zoom and pan the diagram, as well as save the diagram image.

5. You can even customize the diagram by changing the title and axis labels and ranges. Just use the right-most button with the green tick mark on it to open the customization dialog:

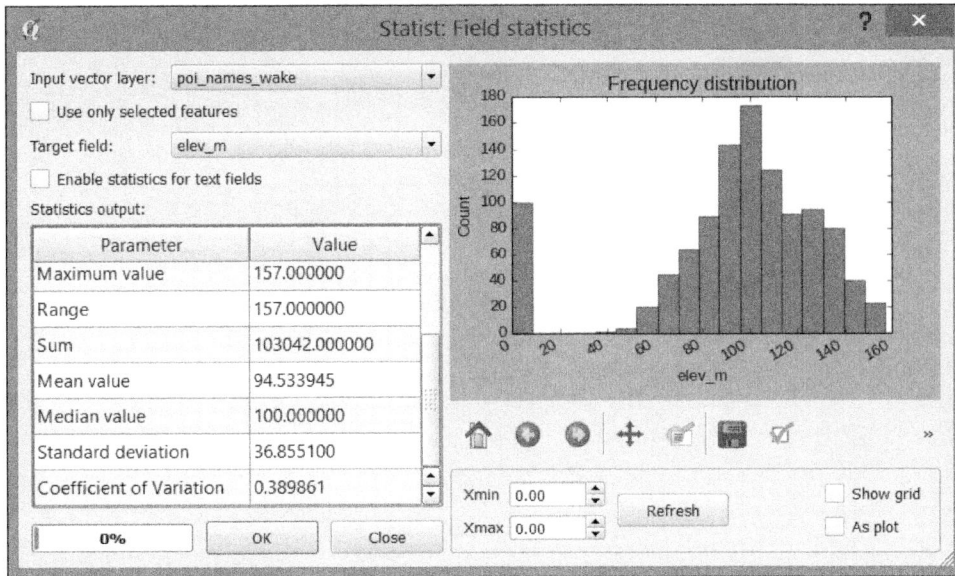

How it works...

Thanks to **Python Console** and the editor, we are not limited to the existing tools and plugins. Instead, we can create or own specialized scripts such as the following one. This script creates a short layer statistics report using HTML and the Google Charts Javascript API (for more information and API docs refer to `https://developers.google.com/chart/`), which it then displays in a `QWebView` window. Of course, you can use any other JavaScript charting API as well. (Note that you need to be connected to the Internet for this script to work because it has to download the Javascript.) We recommend using the editor that was introduced in the previous recipe. Don't forget to select the layer in the legend:

```
import processing
from PyQt4.QtWebKit import QWebView
layer = iface.activeLayer()
values = []
features = processing.features(layer)
for f in features:
  values.append( f['elev_m'])
myWV = wQWebView(None)
html='<html><head><script type="text/javascript"'
html+='src="https://www.google.com/jsapi"></script>'
html+='<script type="text/javascript">'
html+='google.load("visualization","1",{packages:["corechart"]});'
html+='google.setOnLoadCallback(drawChart);'
```

```
html+='function drawChart() { '
  html+='var data = google.visualization.arrayToDataTable(['
    html+='["%s"],' % (field_name)
    for value in values:
      html+='[%f],' % (value)
  html+=']);'
  html+='var chart = new google.visualization.Histogram('
    html+='document.getElementById("chart_div"));'
  html+='chart.draw(data, {title: "Histogram"});}</script></head>'
html+='<body><h1>Layer: %s</h1>' % (layer.name())
html+='<p>Values for %s range from: ' % (field_name)
html+='%d to %d</p>' % (min(values),max(values))
html+='<div id="chart_div"style="width:900px; height:500px;">'
html+='</div></body></html>'
myWV.setHtml(html)
myWV.show()
```

Of course, custom reports such as this one lend themselves to adding more details. For example, we can create separate histograms for each POI class or add other types of charts, such as scatter charts:

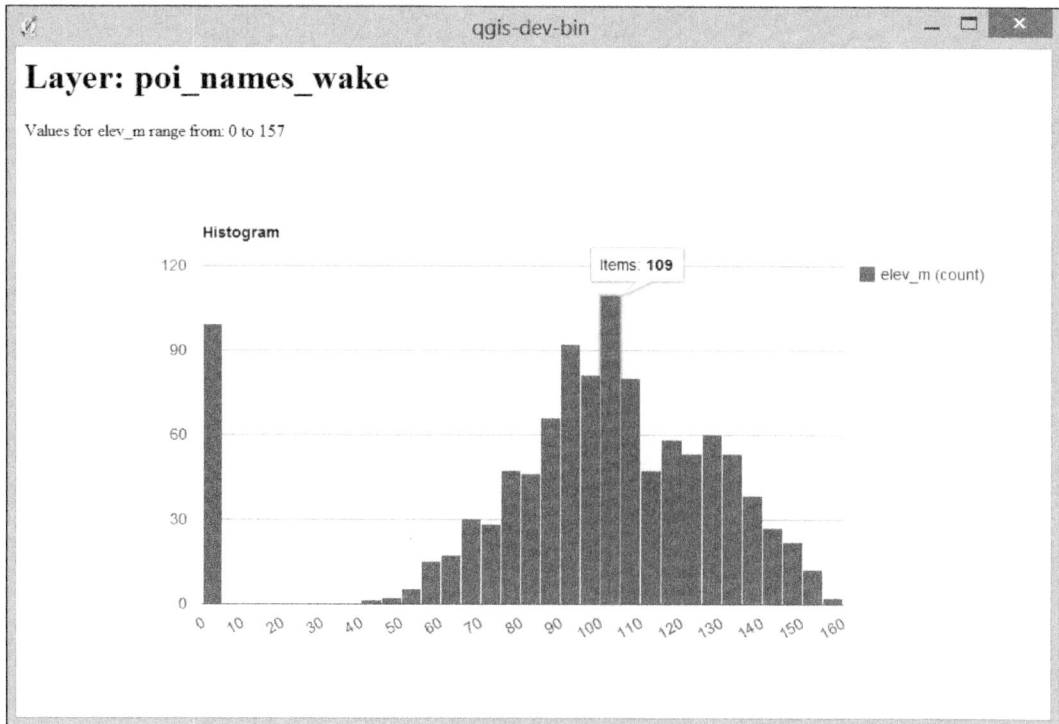

The first part (lines 1 to 12) is very similar to the script explained in the previous recipe, *Listing unique values in a column:* We get the active layer and collect all elevation values in the `values` list.

The `QWebView` created on line 14 enables us to display the HTML content, which we then generate in the following section (lines 16 to 34). First, we load the Google Charts Javascript. The actual magic happens in the `drawChart()` function starting on line 21. Lines 22 to 26 create the `data` object, which is filled with the elevation values from our `values` list. The last three lines of the function (lines 27 to 29) finally create and draw the histogram chart. Finally, lines 30 to 34 contain the HTML body definition with the header stating the layer name and a short introduction text that states the min and max elevation values.

See also

▶ For those who want to perform more advanced graphing and numerical analysis, consider using the matplotlib python library or reading your data sources into R. Aggregate functions in SatialLitetgis PostGIS can also provide you with min, max, average, sum, and other summarization functions. For PostGIS, refer to `http://www.postgresql.org/docs/9.1/static/functions-aggregate.html`.

Exploring spatiotemporal vector data using Time Manager

In this recipe, we will look at exploring spatiotemporal vector data using the Time Manager plugin. We'll use event data from the **ACLED (Armed Conflict Location and Event Data Project)** at `http://www.acleddata.com/about-acled/`.

Getting ready

To follow this recipe, please load `ACLED_africa_fatalities_dec2013.shp`. The layer style that you will see in the following screenshots consists of a simple circle marker at 50% transparency with the data-defined size set to the number of fatalities of the incident. (You can read more about styling in *Chapter 10, Cartography Tips*, and *Learning QGIS* book by Packt Publishing.) If you want some additional geographic context, you can also load `NE_africa.shp`, which contains the outline of Africa.

How to do it...

Once the data is loaded, all event positions will be displayed. The default way to filter the events, for example, to only see the events from December 1, is to use Layer | Query and enter a filter expression or query, such as the following:

```
"EVENT_DATE" >= '2013-12-01' AND "EVENT_DATE" < '2013-12-02'
```

1. It's easy to see that updating this query manually for each day will not be a very convenient way to explore spatiotemporal data. Therefore, we will use the Time Manager plugin (installed using Plugin Manager).

2. The Time Manager panel will be added to the bottom of the QGIS window once the plugin is installed. Click on the **Settings** button to open the **Time manager settings** dialog. We can configure Time Manager here.

3. Click on **Add Layer** to open the **Select layer and column(s)** dialog.

4. Select the **ACLED_africa_fatalities_dec2013** layer and **EVENT_DATE** as starting time and then click on **OK** to add the event point layer to the list of managed layers, as shown in the following screenshot:

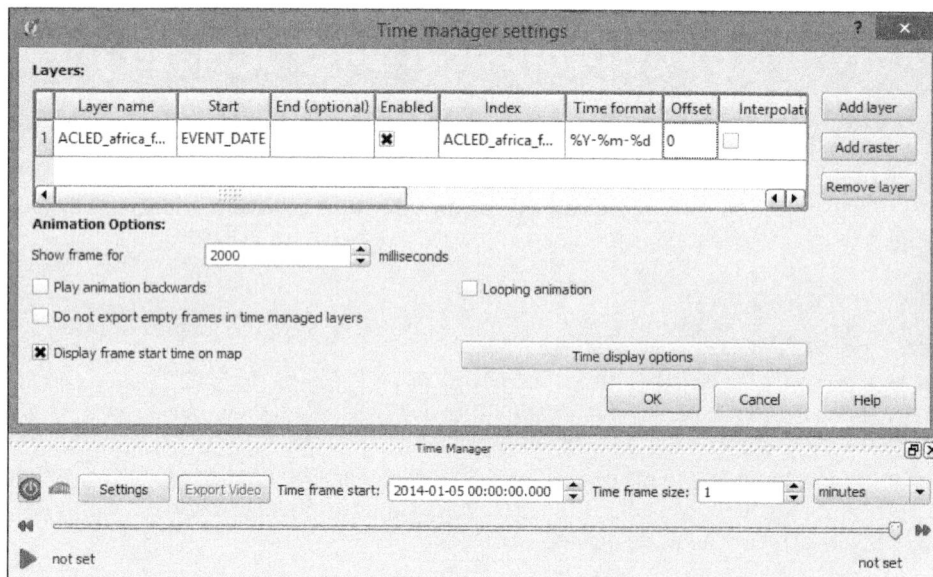

Optionally, you can enable **display frame start time on map** to add a small label with the corresponding timestamp to the rendered map.

5. Click on **OK** when you are done. At this point, Time Manager applies the temporal filter to the dataset, so this can take some time depending on the size of the dataset used.

6. By default, after the first layer has been added, Time Manager will display all the events that occurred during the first day of the dataset. It is easy to adjust the filter by changing the **Time frame size** settings. You can increase the number of days that should be displayed or change to one of the other time units, including seconds, minutes, hours, weeks, and months, as shown in the following screenshot:

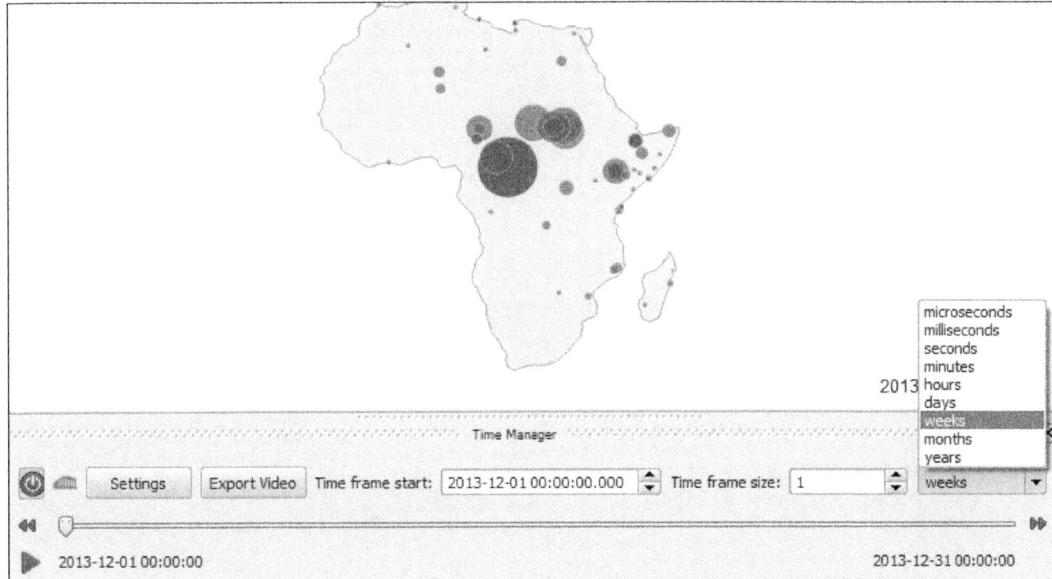

7. Once you are happy with the settings, you have multiple options to navigate through time:

   ❑ Click on the play button in the bottom-left corner of the Time Manager panel to start an automatic animation

   ❑ Move the time slider to the center of the panel like you would do to navigate within a video or music player application

   ❑ Click on the forward or backward button on either side of the slider to advance or go back by one time frame

   ❑ Of course, you can also edit the **Time frame start** setting directly

How it works...

For performance reasons, Time Manager relies on the layer query/filter expression capability of QGIS. This comes with the following limitations:

▶ Time Manager can only be used with data sources that support layer queries or filter expressions. Most notably, this means that it cannot be used with delimited text layers.

▶ As the layer queries or filter expressions have to work with strings, it has to be possible to order the date-time values correctly using text sort. Therefore, the values have to be stored in one of the following formats:

```
%Y-%m-%d %H:%M:%S.%f
%Y-%m-%d %H:%M:%S
%Y-%m-%d %H:%M
%Y-%m-%dT%H:%M:%S
%Y-%m-%dT%H:%M:%SZ
%Y-%m-%dT%H:%M
%Y-%m-%dT%H:%MZ
%Y-%m-%d
%Y/%m/%d %H:%M:%S.%f
%Y/%m/%d %H:%M:%S
%Y/%m/%d %H:%M
%Y/%m/%d
%H:%M:%S
%H:%M:%S.%f
%Y.%m.%d %H:%M:%S.%f
%Y.%m.%d %H:%M:%S
%Y.%m.%d %H:%M
%Y.%m.%d
%Y%m%d%H%M%S
```

> If your data uses a different format, which is ordered correctly as well, you can add it to `timevectorlayer.py` or change the format using Field Calculator.

See also

▶ The following recipes will show you how to create videos and more sophisticated time-dependent styles using Time Manager.

Creating animations using Time Manager

In this recipe, we will use the Time Manager plugin to create an image series out of our spatiotemporal QGIS project and turn it into a video, which is ready to be uploaded on Youtube or added into a presentation using easily available and free tools.

Getting ready

To follow this recipe, it's advisable that you complete the previous recipe, *Exploring spatiotemporal vector data using Time Manager*, to set up this project.

To turn the image series exported by Time Manager into a video, we can use external programs, such as the command-line tool Mencoder, or the free Windows Movie Maker.

Mencoder is a very useful command-line tool to encode videos, which is available from repositories for many Linux distributions and for Mac. Windows users can download it from Gianluigi Tiesi's site at `http://oss.netfarm.it/mplayer-win32.php`.

If you're using Windows, you can also create the video using the free Windows Movie Maker application, which can be downloaded from `http://windows.microsoft.com/en-us/windows/get-movie-maker-download`.

How to do it...

Before starting the export, it is a good idea to check all the settings, as follows:

1. The time slider should be moved to the beginning of the time line, and an appropriate **Time frame size** should be set.

2. Additionally, it can be useful to enable **display frame start time on map** (refer to the screenshots in the previous recipe) if you haven't done so already in the previous recipe because, otherwise, the exported animation frames won't contain any information about the time of the displayed events.

3. When you have found the best settings for your dataset, click on the **Export Video** button. A dialog will open, which will allow you to select the folder that you want to export your video to. After you click on the **Select Folder** button, Time Manager will automatically start to export the video frames. As displayed in the **Export video** information popup, you should now wait for the export to finish. There will be another popup once this process is finished, which looks like the following screenshot:

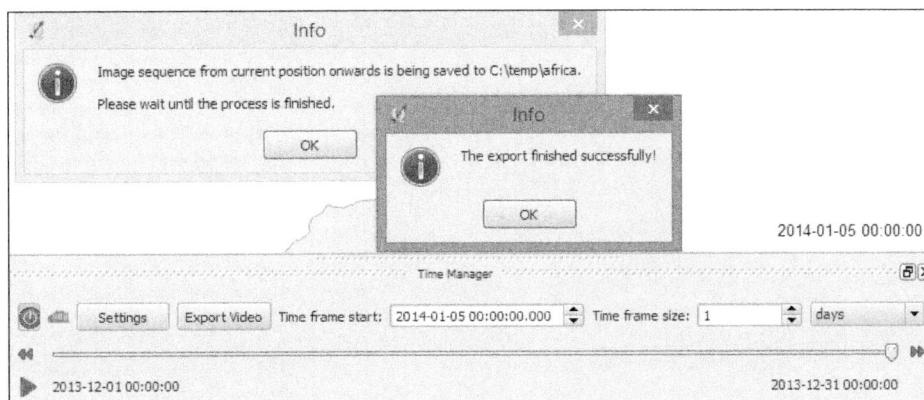

4. If you open the `export` folder, you will see the animation frames that Time Manager just created.

5. This is how you can use Mencoder to create an `.avi` video from all `.png` images in the current working directory. Make sure that you are in the folder containing the images before running the following command:

```
mencoder "mf://*.png" -mf fps=10 -o output.avi -ovc lavc
-lavcopts vcodec=mpeg4
```

6. You can control the speed of the animation using the frames per second (`fps`) parameter. Higher values create a faster animation.

If you're using Windows Movie Maker, perform the following steps:

1. Load the animation frame images.

2. To adjust the speed of the animation, go to **Video Tools | Edit**, and reduce the **Duration** value. Note that you should have all images selected if you want to apply the same duration to all images at once.

3. To save the animation, just go to **File | Save Movie** and select your preferred resolution and quality.

How it works...

Time Manager's Export Video feature uses the `QgsMapCanvas.saveAsImage()` function to export the image series. This means that the images will be of the same size as the map canvas in your QGIS window at the time of clicking on the **Export Video** button.

Designing time-dependent styles

In this recipe, we will use the `animation_datetime()` function, which is exposed by Time Manager to create a time-dependent style for our animation. The style will represent the age of the event feature: the event marker's fill color will fade towards gray the older the event gets.

Getting ready

To follow this recipe, please load `ACLED_africa_fatalities_dec2013.shp` and configure Time Manager, as shown in the *Exploring spatiotemporal vector data using Time Manager* recipe, with the following exception: when adding the layer to Time Manager, set the **End time** value to the `FOREVER` attribute.

How to do it...

To create a time-dependent style, we use the **Data defined properties** option of the Simple marker:

1. In the *Exploring spatiotemporal vector data using Time Manager* recipe, we mentioned that we already used the **FATALITIES** attribute to scale the marker size. For the time-dependent style, we will add a new definition to the **Fill color** property, as shown in the following screenshot:

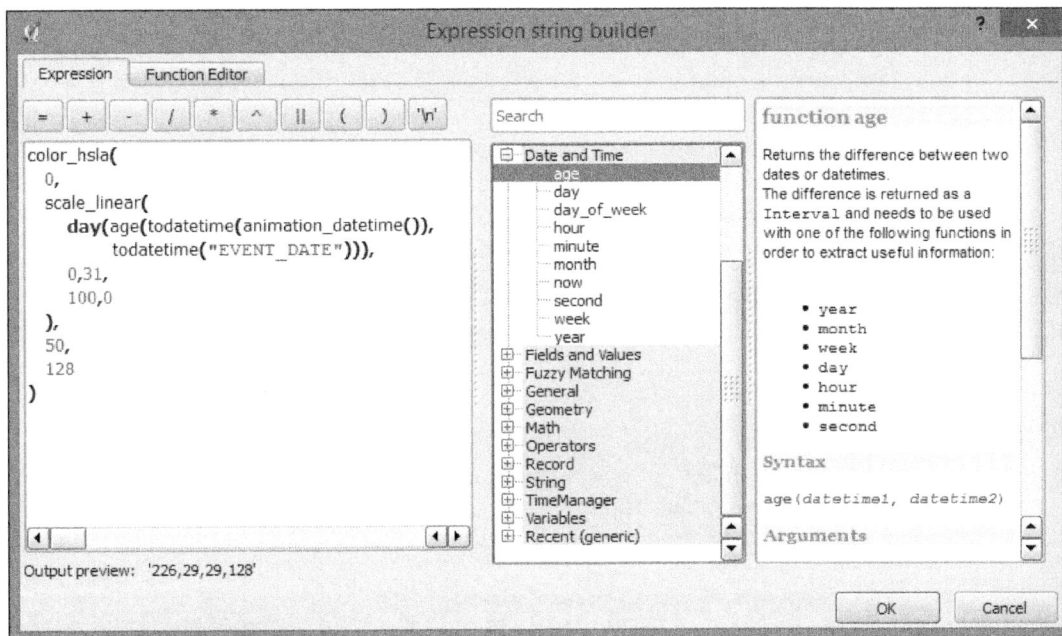

2. Confirm the changes and start the animation to watch the effect.

How it works...

Here is our color expression in more detail:

```
color_hsla(
  0,
  scale_linear(
    day(age(todatetime(animation_datetime()),
    todatetime("EVENT_DATE"))),
    0,31,
```

```
    100,0
  ),
  50,
  128
)
```

The expression consists of multiple parts, as follows:

  ▸ `day(age(todatetime(animation_datetime()),todatetime("EVENT_DATE")))`: This calculates the number of days between the current animation time given by `animation_datetime()` and calculates `EVENT_DATE`

  ▸ `scale_linear`: This transforms the age value (in days between 0 to 31 days) into a value between 100 and 0 which is suitable for the saturation parameter of the following color function

  ▸ `color_hsla`: This is one of many functions that are available in QGIS to create colors. It returns a string representation of a color, based on its attributes for hue (0 equals red), saturation (between 0 and 100 depending on our age function), lightness (50 equals medium lightness) and alpha (128 equals 50% transparency)

You can speed up the fading effect by reducing the `scale_linear` parameter, `domain_max`, from 31 days to a smaller value, such as 7, for a complete fade to gray within one week.

See also

  ▸ If you are interested in learning more about color models, such as the HSL color model used in this recipe, we recommend the Wikibook on color models at `http://en.wikibooks.org/wiki/Color_Models:_RGB,_HSV,_HSL`

Loading BaseMaps with the QuickMapServices plugin

Often, when exploring your data, you may feel somewhat lost. Without the context of the known world, a layer can seem like a blob of information floating in space. By adding an atlas-style map, air photos, or another BaseMap, you can begin to see how your data fits in the on-the-ground reality. However, adding such layers often takes considerable preprocessing work; sometimes, you just don't want to go through this until you know you need it. What's the solution? Use a premade layer, preferably fast-loading tiles, from a web service.

Getting ready

The QuickMapServices plugin works best when you have another dataset that you want to provide extra context for. Start by first loading such a layer and then zooming in to its extent.

You will need the following:

- ▶ A layer of interest to overlay (you can use `Davis_DBO_Centerline-wgs84.shp`)
- ▶ An active Internet connection (this may not work behind corporate proxies)
- ▶ You will need to install and activate the QuickMapServices plugin

How to do it...

Starting with a new QGIS project, follow these instructions to load BaseMap from the web with the QuickMapServices plugin:

1. Start by first loading your local map layers:
2. Verify that the projection definition is correctly identified by QGIS.

> The plugin will not turn on projection-on-the-fly for you unless you change its settings. However, in order for most tile services to work in QGIS, projection-on-the-fly must be enabled and set to EPSG:3857 Psuedo/Web/Popular Mercator. Other data will fail to line up if their projection is not defined or read properly by QGIS.

3. Go to **Web | QuickMapServices** and select a layer to load from the Web. Wait a few seconds for the tiles to be loaded:

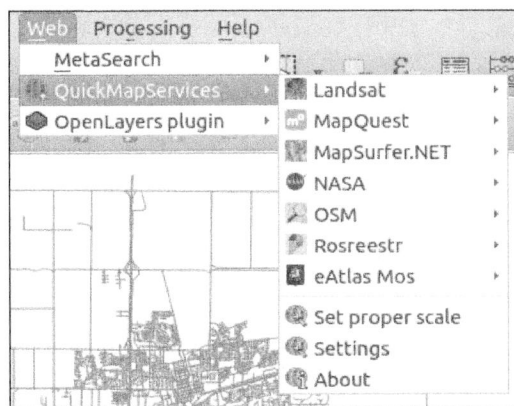

> The default list of services is open and free. If you want to use other services that have more limited licensing restrictions, such as Google and Bing, you need to change some of the plugin's settings. Refer to the *There's more...* section of this recipe.

4. (Optional) Temporarily disable **Rendering** (the checkbox in the bottom panel) to avoid constant redrawing while rearranging the layer order.

5. Rearrange your layers to move the new **QuickMapService** added layer to the bottom of your layer list.

6. Zoom to your original layer's extent.

7. (Optional) If you turned **Rendering** off, reactivate **Rendering** now.

> Are things not lining up? Try zooming in a little more or panning slightly. Most of all, be patient! Depending on your Internet connection, it can take a while to retrieve the tiles.

The following screenshot shows how the screen will look:

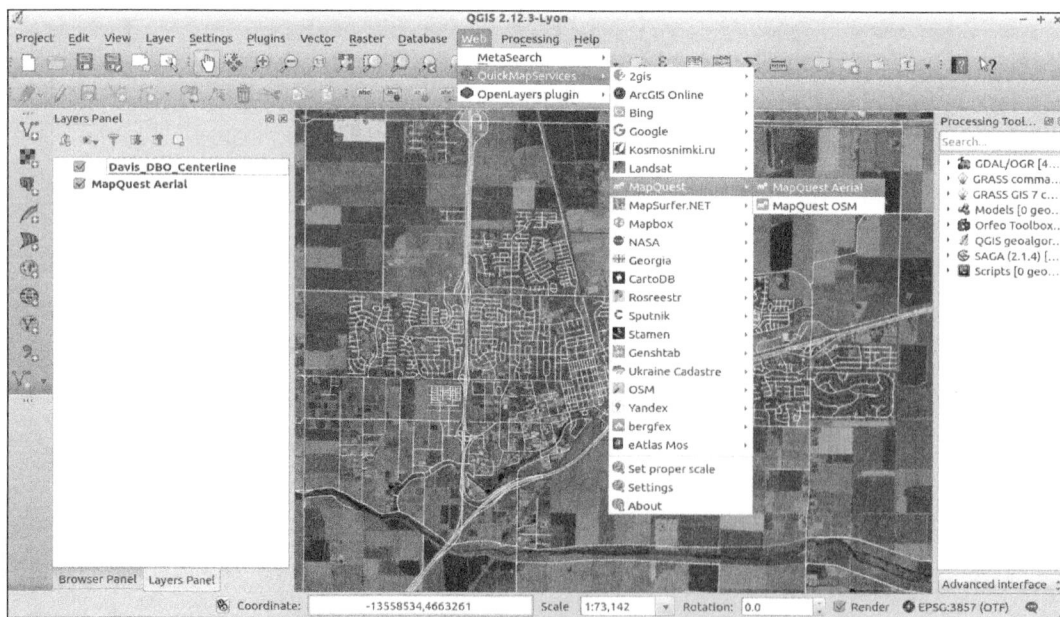

How it works...

The QuickMapServices plugin is a web-based tool. All of the BaseMaps come from the Internet as you pan and zoom; none of the data comes from your computer or QGIS itself.

There are a few things to be cautious of when using the QuickMapServices plugin. It doesn't always line up quite right, especially when zoomed out to big areas. First, check whether your other layers' projections are defined correctly and then try to reset the map by slightly panning to the side. The key idea to remember is that tiled services generally only exist for EPSG:3857 and at a very specific set of scales. QGIS will attempt to pick the closest matching scale and resample the scale to make it fit. This also explains why loading such layers can sometimes be slow.

There's more...

To add more restricted services, such as Google. Bing, and so on, perform the following steps:

1. Go to **Web** | **QuickMapServices** | **Settings** | **Contributed Services**.
2. Click on the **Get contributed pack** button:

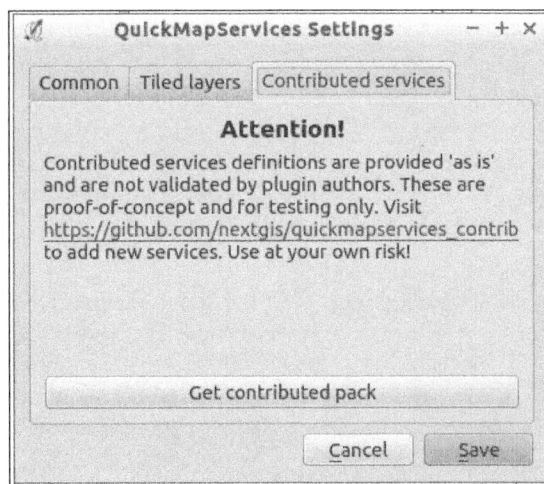

While it may be legal to view the maps (most of the time), depending on layers that are selected, it may not be legal to digitize maps based on them, print them, or, otherwise, save them for offline use. The license varies by data source. So, make sure to check this for the sources you want to use by going online and reading the Terms of Service on their websites. If your use case is outside of generally viewing for quick reference, you will probably need to spend some time obtaining a license or permission for your use.

OpenStreetMap-based sources are often good choices as the licenses typically just require attribution with no restrictions on use. The main layers that originally come with the plugin are there because they have less restrictive licenses.

Finally, you may be wondering how QuickMapServices differs from the OpenLayers plugin mentioned in the next recipe. For starters, this plugin is newer and currently supported. It also solves some long-standing issues, especially in regards to printing. There is also the contributed layers GitHub repository, which should make it easier for people to contribute new layer definitions.

See also

> ► Additional tile services can be added by hacking the plugin code or using a GDAL TMS layer (Refer to *Chapter 9, QGIS and the Web*). You can also substitute in WMS services to serve a similar role without some of the same limitations of tiles. Refer to *Chapter 9, QGIS and the Web*, for information about creating your own web services.

Loading BaseMaps with the OpenLayers plugin

Often, when exploring your data, you may feel somewhat lost. Without the context of the known world, a layer can seem like a blob of information floating in space. By adding an atlas-style map, air photos, or another BaseMap, you can begin to see how your data fits in the on-the-ground reality. However, adding such layers often takes considerable preprocessing work; sometimes, you just don't want to go through this until you know you need it. What's the solution? Use a premade layer from a web service.

> This recipe is almost identical to the previous recipe. QuickMapServices is a replacement for the OpenLayers plugin, which is being discontinued (deprecated). We kept this recipe because it's still a commonly-mentioned plugin and works slightly differently. However, please consider using QuickMapServices.

Getting ready

The Openlayers plugin works best when you have another dataset that you want to provide extra context for. Start by first loading such a layer and then zooming in to its extent.

You will need the following:

- ► A layer of interest to overlay (you can use `Davis_DBO_Centerline-wgs84.shp`)
- ► An active Internet connection (this may not work behind corporate proxies)
- ► You will need to install and activate the OpenLayers plugin

How to do it...

Starting with a new QGIS project, follow these instructions to load BaseMap from the Web with the Openlayers plugin:

1. Start by first loading your local map layers.
2. Verify that the projection definition is correctly identified by QGIS.

> The plugin will set and turn on projection-on-the-fly for you. In order for most tile services to work in QGIS, projection-on-the-fly must be enabled and set to EPSG:3857 Psuedo/Web/Popular Mercator. Other data will fail to line up if their projection is not defined or read properly by QGIS.

3. Go to **Vector | OpenLayers Plugin** and select a layer to load from the Web. Wait a few seconds for the tiles to be loaded.
4. (Optional) Temporarily disable **Rendering** (the checkbox in the bottom panel) to avoid constant redrawing while rearranging layer order.
5. Rearrange your layers to move the new OpenLayers added layer to the bottom of your layer list.
6. Zoom to your original layer's extent.
7. (Optional) If you turned **Rendering** off, reactivate **Rendering** now.

> Are things not lining up? Try zooming in a little more or panning slightly. Most of all, be patient! Depending on your Internet connection, it can take a while to retrieve the tiles.

The following screenshot shows how the screen will look:

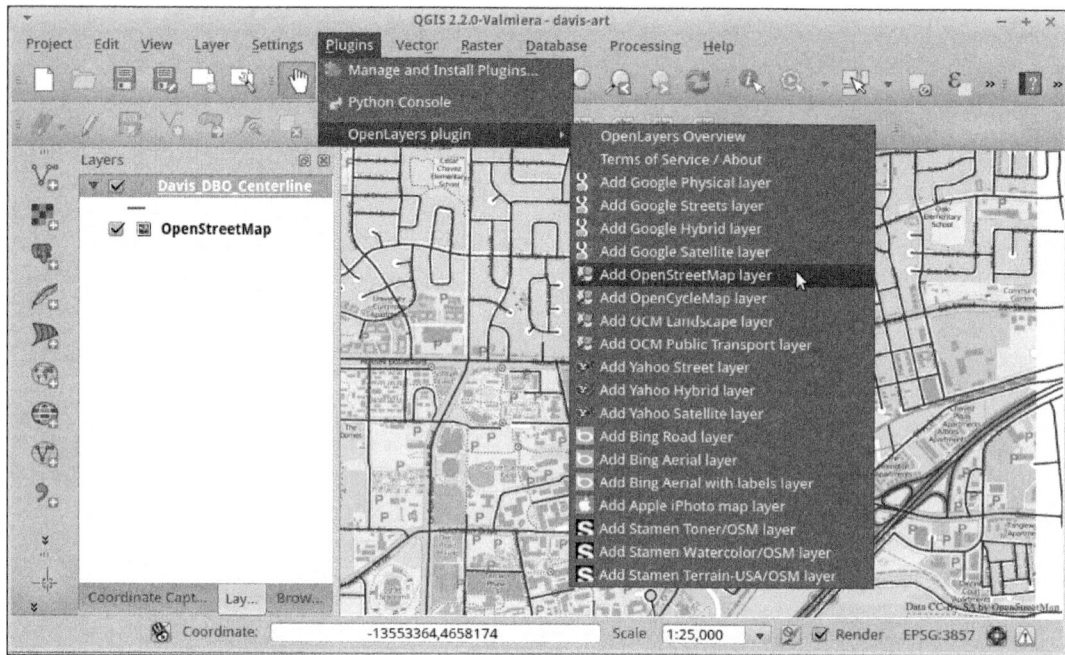

How it works...

The OpenLayers plugin is a web-based tool, based on the similarly named OpenLayers library to create web-based maps in an Internet browser. However, instead of displaying the maps in the browser, this plugin renders them into an active QGIS canvas (that is, a map).

There are a few things to be cautious of when using the OpenLayers plugin. It doesn't always line up quite right, especially when zoomed out to big areas. First, check whether your other layers' projections are defined correctly and then try to reset the map by panning slightly to the side. The key idea to remember is that tiled services generally only exist for EPSG:3857 and at a very specific set of scales. QGIS will attempt to pick the closest matching scale and resample the scale to make it fit. This also explains why loading such layers can sometimes be slow.

There's more...

While it may be legal to view the maps, depending on layers selected, it may not be legal to digitize maps based on them, print them, or, otherwise, save them for offline use. The license varies by data source. So, make sure to check for the sources you want to use by going online and reading the Terms of Service on their websites. If your use case is outside of generally viewing for quick reference, you will probably need to spend some time obtaining a license or permission for your use. OpenStreetMap-based sources are often good choices as the licenses typically just require attribution.

See also

► Additional tile services can be added by hacking the plugin code or using a GDAL TMS layer (Refer to *Chapter 9, QGIS and the Web*). You can also substitute in WMS services to serve a similar role without some of the same limitations of tiles. Refer to *Chapter 9, QGIS and the Web*, for information about creating your own web services.

Viewing geotagged photos

Keeping track of photographs by location can be an extremely useful tool, enabling you to easily pull up relevant photos of a place and time. They provide local context about other data collected in the same place, and they can provide office staff with a view of what people in the field saw. You can think of this as your own personal Street View, which is just more focused than Google's version.

Getting ready

For this recipe, you'll need a set of geotagged photos. We've included a set a photos in this book's data for you to learn with. This is a collection of photos from downtown Davis that highlights the density and variety of public art along several blocks.

This recipe also takes advantage of several plugins, as follows:

► Install and activate **Photo2Shape**

► Activate the core plugin, **eVis** (Event Visualization)

► (Optional) Install and activate OpenLayers Plugin

How to do it...

Follow these steps to view geotagged photo locations in QGIS:

1. In a QGIS project, enable the plugins listed in the *Getting ready* section.

2. (Optional) Load a reference layer to help you see the local context
    (`Davis_DBO_Centerline.shp` and/or `OpenStreetMap/Google Streets`
    via OpenLayers Plugin).

> Keep in mind that GPS locations and geotagged photos are almost
> always in Latitude and Longitude WGS84 coordinates (that is,
> EPSG:4326). So, you'll need to turn on projection-on-the-fly to
> make them line up with your reference layers.

3. Go to the **Vector** menu or locate the icon on the toolbar for **Photo2Shape**:

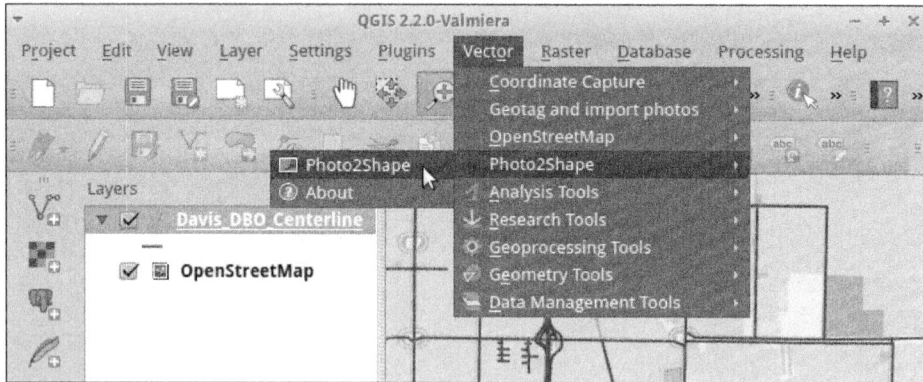

4. This will ask to you select the directory in which you have the geotagged photos and
    set an output shapefile. (Use the `davis-art` folder as the input directory.)

5. You should now get a new shapefile of the point locations of your photos loaded in
    the map. Use **Zoom to Layer Extent** to zoom in on the locations. You should see a
    camera icon at the location of each photo.

6. Looking at the attribute table, you can see all the information about the photos pulled into the table, including the path to the photos on your computer:

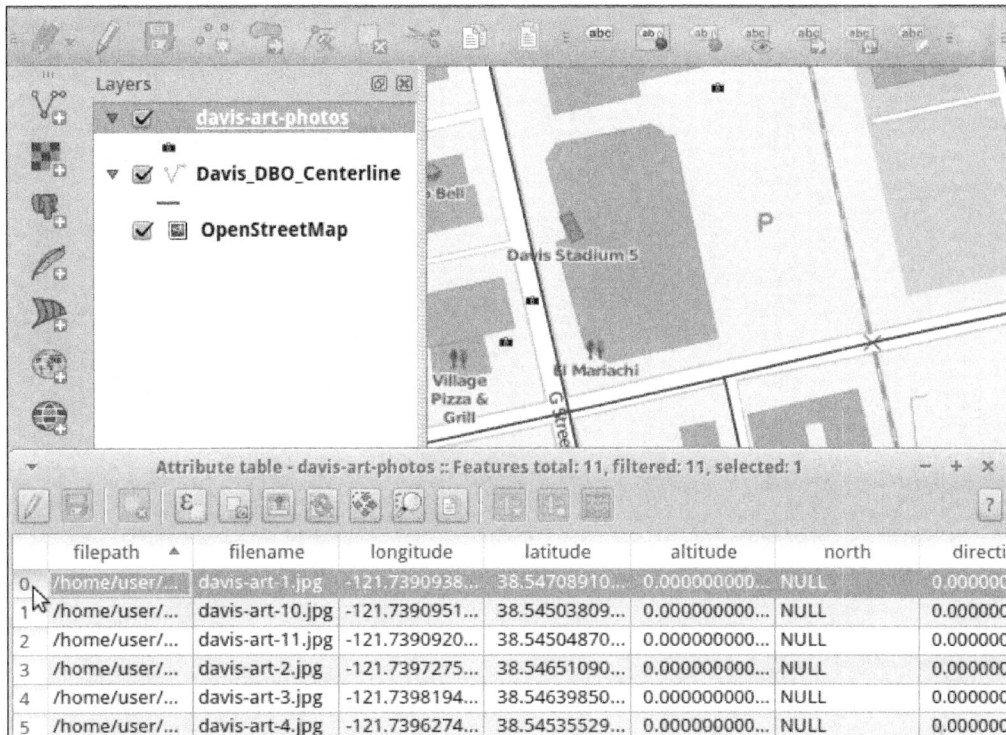

Going a little further

If you want to be able to see the actual photos in QGIS and not just the locations, continue with the next section of steps:

1. Enable the **eVis** plugin.

2. Once activated go to **Database | eVis | eVis Event Browser**.

3. In the new window that pops up, you can see the attributes in the bottom box the photo:

    1. If this is blank, go to the **Options** tab and check whether the correct field is selected for the path to the photo, in this case, this is **filepath**.

2. To make the tool remember this change, check the **Remember This** box and click on the **Save** button at the bottom:

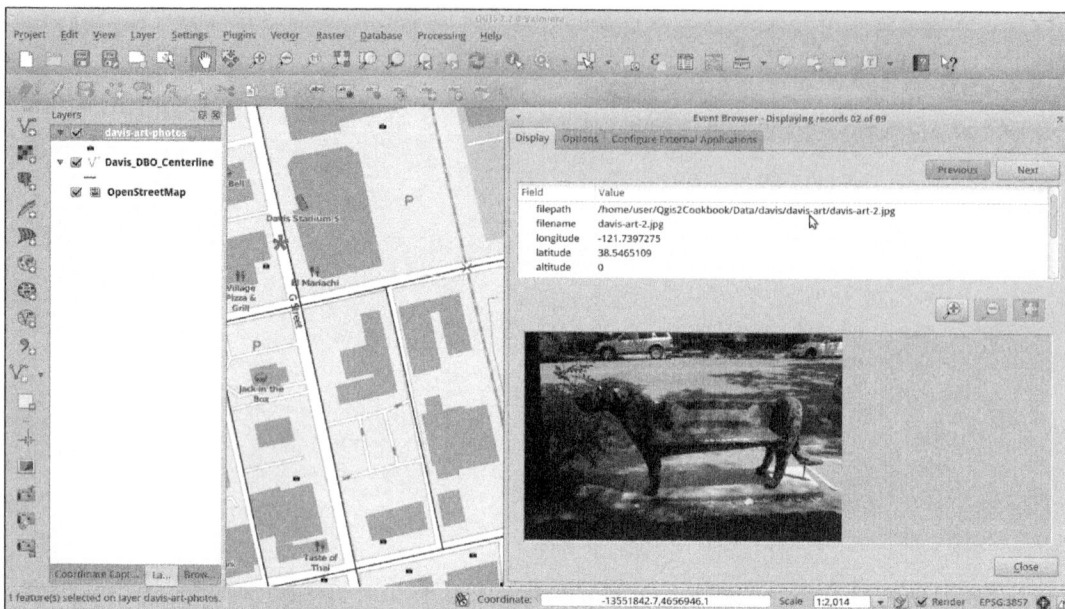

How it works...

In photography, there is a standard metadata format written by most cameras called Exif, which is stored as part of the image file format. Normally, all images store the timestamp, camera model, camera settings, and other general information about an image. When you take a picture with a GPS enabled camera, it should write the latitude and longitude to the photo's metadata. Other programs that are metadata-aware can then read this information at any time. If you happen to touch up these photos, make sure to tell your software to keep or copy the metadata from the original so that you retain the location information.

There's more...

Don't have a camera or phone with built-in geotagging? This is not a problem. There are many ways to add location information by yourself. One such method is with the **Geotag and import photos** plugin that lets you link photo data to known locations, and this can be found at http://hub.qgis.org/projects/geotagphotos/wiki.

If you need something more sophisticated, there are many other tools out there. Digikam, an open source photo management program, includes a geotagging tool that will attempt to automatch a GPX file from a GPS to your photos, based on timestamps.

Geotagged photos are also supported by many online photos services, so you can easily browse a map of the photos that you've uploaded. Flickr is probably the most well-known for this, and it also includes a concept of geo-fences, where you can exclude certain locations from being publicly known.

On the flip-side, you now have an idea about how to remove geotags from photos in case you don't want their locations known if you share them online.

See also

▶ There are other methods of seeing photos in the map besides eVis, including HTML map tips. Refer to Nathan's blog at `http://nathanw.net/2012/08/05/html-map-tips-in-qgis/`.

▶ More information about geotagging with Digikam can be found at `http://docs.kde.org/development/en/extragear-graphics/kipi-plugins/geolocation.html`.

▶ You can also use Flickr to geotag and re-export your images, you can or create online map mash-ups with their API.

5
Classic Vector Analysis

In this chapter, we will cover the following recipes:

- Selecting optimum sites
- Dasymetric mapping
- Calculating regional statistics
- Estimating density using heatmaps
- Estimating values based on samples

Introduction

This chapter will provide you with an introduction to some of the most-common GIS analysis use cases. The recipes focus on step-by-step instructions, as well as a closer explanation of the tools that are used to achieve the desired analysis results. This chapter includes recipes on optimum site selection, using interpolation, and creating heat maps, as well as calculating regional statistics.

Selecting optimum sites

Optimum site selection is a pretty common problem, for example, when planning shop or warehouse locations or when looking for a new apartment. In this recipe, you will learn how to perform optimum site selection manually using tools from the **Processing Toolbox** option, but you will also see how to automate this workflow by creating a Processing model.

In the optimum site selection in this recipe, we will combine different vector analysis tools to find potential locations in Wake County that match the following criteria:

- ▸ Locations are near a big lake (up to 500 m)

- ▸ Locations are close to an elementary school (up to 500 m)

- ▸ Locations are within a reasonable distance (up to 2 km) from a high school

- ▸ Locations are at least 1 km from a main road

Getting ready

To follow this exercise, load the following datasets, `lakes.shp`, `schools_wake.shp`, and `roadsmajor.shp`.

As all datasets in our test data already use the same CRS, we can get right to the analysis. If you are using different data, you may have to get all your datasets into the same CRS first. In this case, please refer to *Chapter 1, Data Input and Output*.

How to do it...

The following steps show you how to perform optimum site selection using the **Processing Toolbox** option:

1. First, we have to filter the lakes layer for big lakes. To do this, we use the **Select by expression** tool from the **Processing** toolbox, select the lakes layer, and enter `"AREA" > 1000000 AND "FTYPE" = 'LAKE/POND'` in the Expression textbox, as shown in the following screenshot:

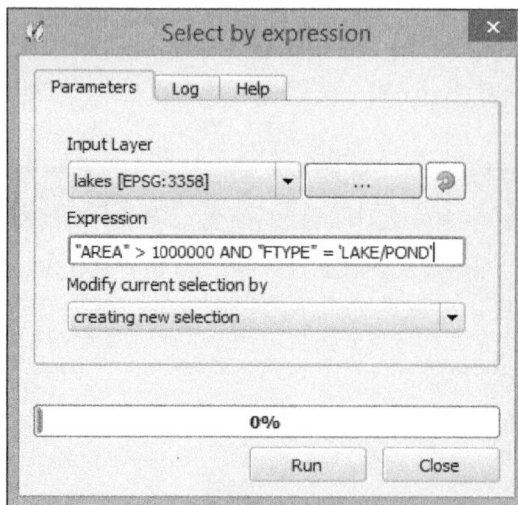

2. Next, we create the buffers that will represent the proximity areas around lakes, schools, and roads. Use **Fixed distance buffer** from the **Processing Toolbox** option to create the following buffers:

   1. For the lakes, select **Distance** of 500 meters and set **Dissolve result** by checking the box as shown in the following screenshot. By dissolving the result, we can make sure that the overlapping buffer areas will be combined into one polygon. Otherwise, each buffer will remain as a separate feature in the resulting layer:

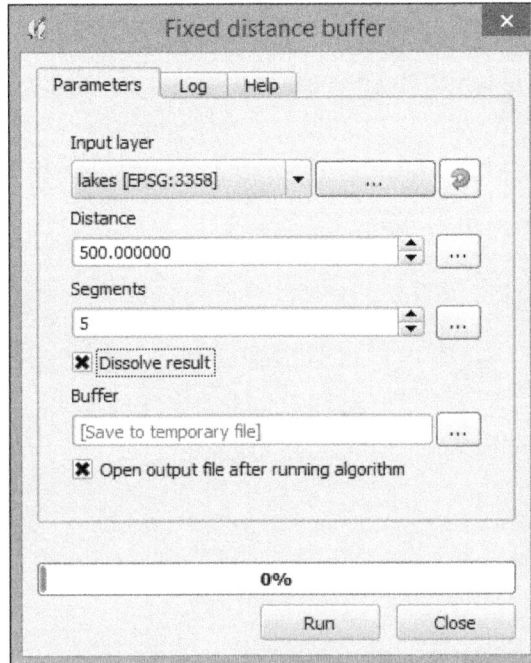

> It's your choice whether you want to save the buffer results permanently by specifying an output file, or you just want to work with temporary files by leaving the Buffer output file field empty.

   2. To create the elementary school buffers, first select only the schools with "GLEVEL" = 'E' using the **Select by Expression** tool like we did for the lakes buffer. Then, use the buffer tool like we just did for the lakes buffer.

   3. Repeat the process for the high schools using "GLEVEL" = 'H' and a buffer distance of 2,000 meters.

   4. Finally, for the roads, create a buffer with a distance of 1,000 meters.

3. With all these buffers ready, we can now combine them to fulfill these rules:

    1. Use the **Intersection** tool from the **Processing Toolbox** option on the buffers around elementary and high schools to get the areas that are within the vicinity of both school types.

    2. Use the **Intersection** tool on the buffers around the lakes and the result of the previous step to limit the results to lakeside areas. Use the **Difference** tool to remove areas around major roads (that is, the buffered road layer) from the result of the previous (Intersection) steps.

4. Check the resulting layer to view the potential sites that fit all the criteria that we previously specified. You'll find that there is only one area close to **WAKEFIELD ELEMENTARY** and **WAKEFIELD HIGH** that fits the bill, as shown in the following screenshot:

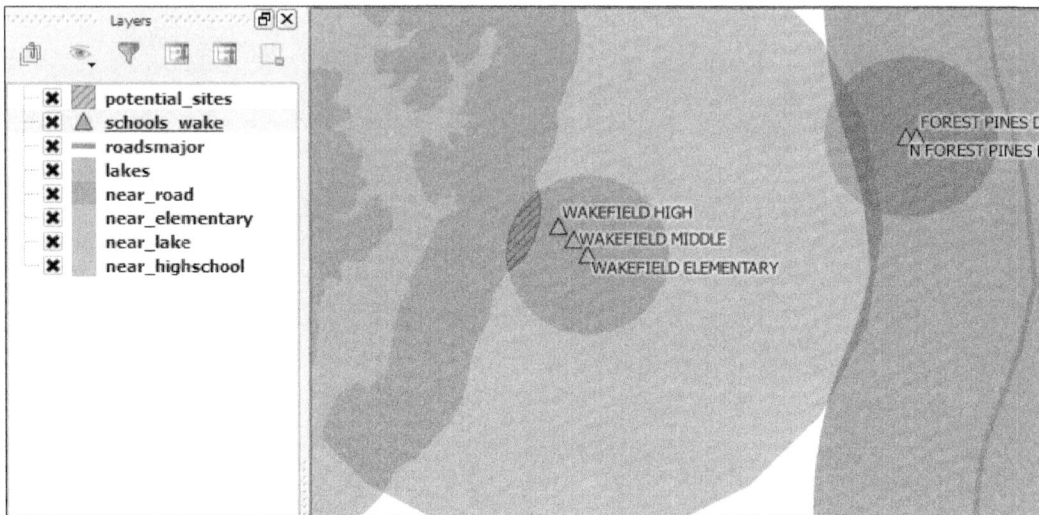

How it works...

In step 1, we used **Intersection** to model the requirement that our preferred site would be near both an elementary and a high school. Later, in step 3, the **Difference** tool enabled us to remove areas close to major roads. The following figure gives us an overview of the available vector analysis tools that can be useful for similar analyses. For example, **Union** could be used to model requirements, such as "close to at least an elementary or a high school". **Symmetrical Difference**, on the other hand, would result in "close to an elementary or a high school but not both", as illustrated in the following figure:

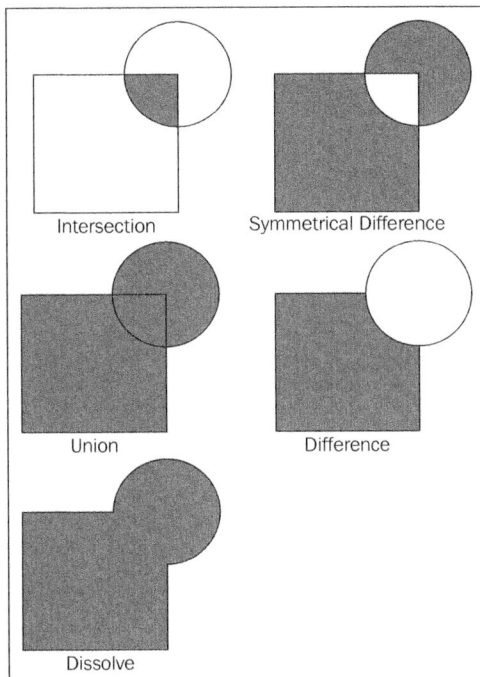

Intersection

Symmetrical Difference

Union

Difference

Dissolve

There's more...

We were lucky and found a potential site that matched all criteria. Of course, this is not always the case, and you will have to try and adjust your criteria to find a matching site. As you can imagine, it can be very tedious and time-consuming to repeat these steps again and again with different settings. Therefore, it's a good idea to create a Processing model to automate this task.

The model (as shown in the following screenshot) basically contains the same tools that we used in the manual process, as follows:

► Use two select by expression instances to select elementary and high schools. As you can see in the following screenshot, we used the descriptions **Select "GLEVEL" = 'E'** and **Select "GLEVEL" = 'H'** to name these model steps.

► For elementary schools, compute fixed distance buffers of 500 meters. This step is called **Buffer "GLEVEL" = 'E'**.

► For high schools, compute fixed distance buffers of 2,000 meters. This step is called **Buffer "GLEVEL" = 'H'**.

► Select the big lakes using Select by expression (refer to the **Select big lakes** step) and buffer them using fixed distance buffer of 500 meters (refer to the **Buffer lakes** step).

▸ Buffer the roads using **Fixed distance buffer** (refer to the **Buffer roads** step). The buffer size is controlled by the number model input called **road_buffer_size**. You can extend this approach of controlling the model parameters using additional inputs to all the other buffer steps in this model. (We chose to show only one example in order to keep the model screenshot readable.)

▸ Use **Intersection** to get areas near schools (refer to the **Intersection: near schools** step).

▸ Use **Intersection** to get areas near schools and lakes (refer to the **Intersection: schools and lakes** step).

▸ Use **Difference** to remove areas near roads (refer to the **Difference: avoid roads** step).

This is how the final model looks like:

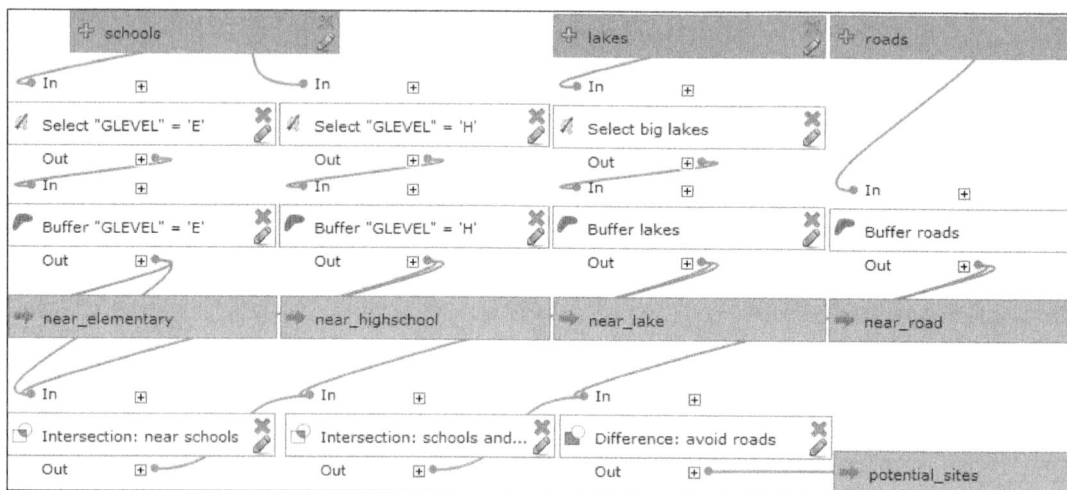

You can run this model from the **Processing Toolbox** option, or you can even use it as a building block in other models. It is worth noting that this model produces intermediate results in the form of buffer results (near_elementary, near highschool, and so on). While these intermediate results are useful while developing and debugging the model, you may eventually want to remove them. This can be done by editing the buffer steps and removing the **Buffer <OutputVector>** names.

Dasymetric mapping

Dasymetric mapping is a technique that is commonly used to improve population distribution maps. By default, population is displayed using census data, which is usually available for geographic units, such as census tracts whose boundaries don't necessarily reflect the actual distribution of the population. To be able to model population distribution better, Dasymetric mapping enables us to map population density relative to land use. For example, population counts that are organized by census tracts can be more accurately distributed by removing unpopulated areas, such as water bodies or vacant land, from the census tract areas.

In this recipe, we will use data about populated urban areas, as well as data about water bodies to refine our census tract population data.

Getting ready

To follow this exercise, please load the population data from `census_wake2000_pop.shp` (the file that we created in *Chapter 2, Data Management*), as well as the urban areas from `urbanarea.shp`, and the lakes from `lakes.shp`.

As all the datasets in our sample data already use the same CRS, we can get right into the analysis. If you are using different data, you may have to first get all datasets into the same CRS. In this case, please refer to *Chapter 1, Data Input and Output*, for details.

How to do it...

To create a new and improved population distribution map, we will first remove the unpopulated areas from the census tracts. Then, we will recalculate the population density values to reflect the changes to the area geometries by performing the following steps:

1. Use **Clip** from the **Processing Toolbox** option (or **Clip** by navigating to **Vector | Geoprocessing tools** if you prefer this option—the results will be identical) on the census tracts and urban area layers to create a new dataset, containing only those parts of the census tracts that are within urban areas.

2. Refine the results of the previous step further by removing the water bodies (the lakes layer) using the **Difference** tool. The following screenshot shows the results of this so far:

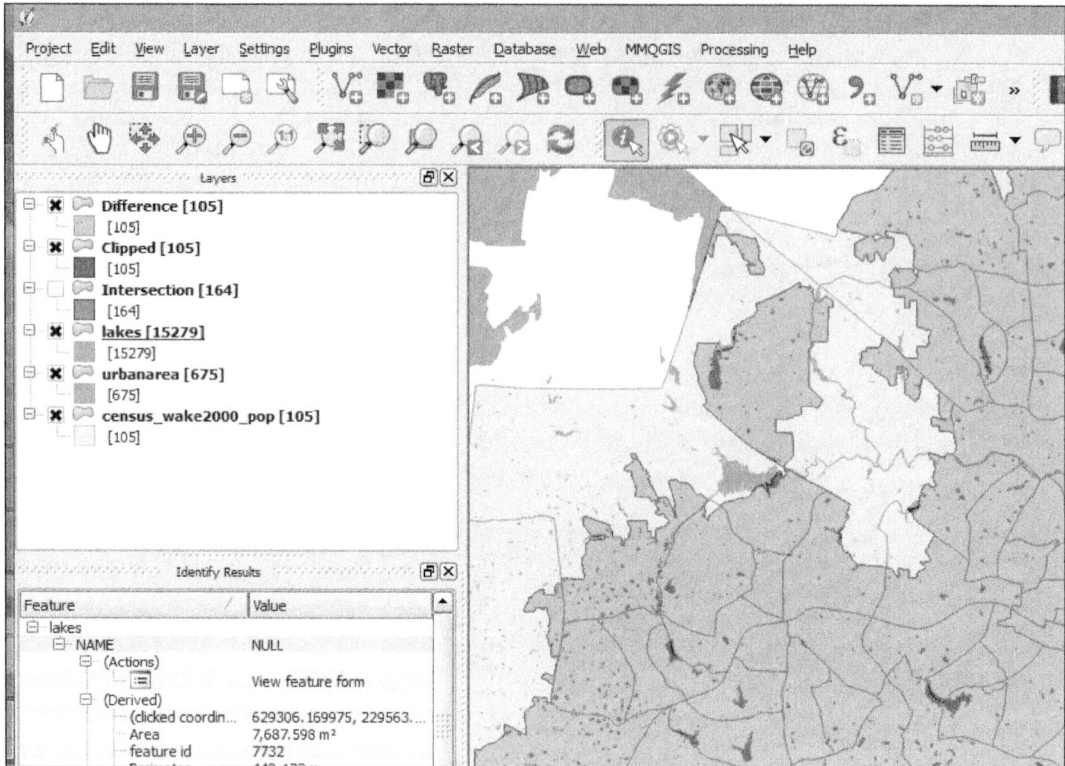

3. Now, we can calculate the population density of the resulting areas, as follows:

   1. Enable editing.
   2. Open **Field calculator**.

3. Calculate a new population density (inhabitants per square km) using the formula, **"_POP2000" / ($area / 1000000)**:

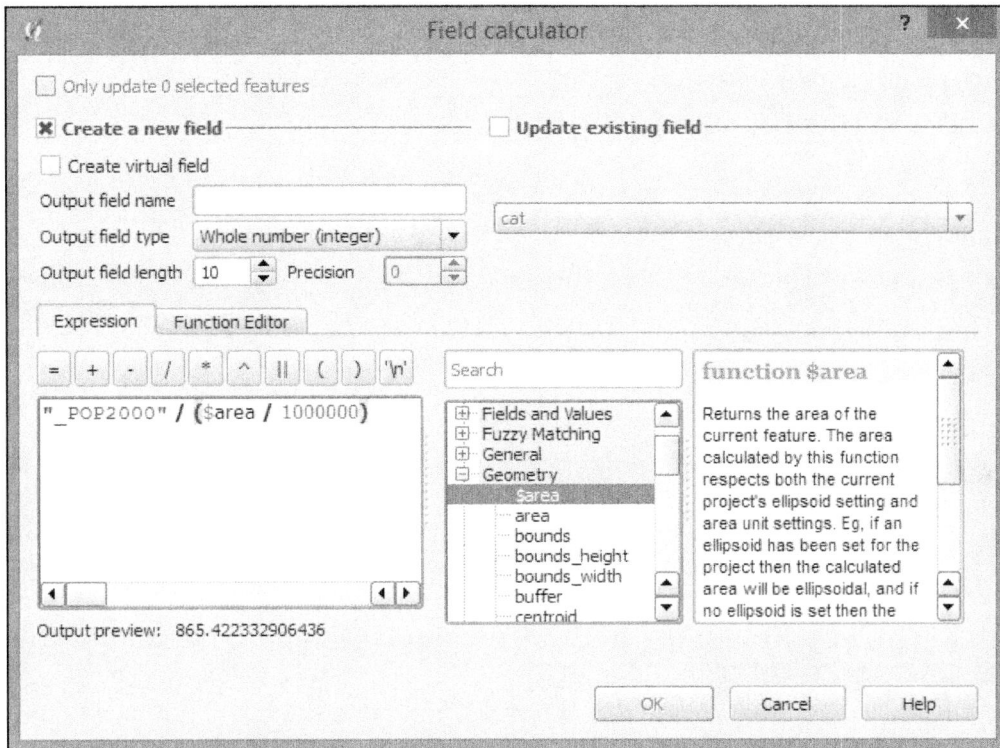

4. Deactivate editing and save the changes.

> It is worth noting that you don't necessarily have to make a new column. If you only want to use the density values for styling purposes, you can also enter the expression directly in the style configuration. On the other hand, if you create a new column, you can inspect the density values in the attribute table, export them, or analyze them further.

We are done, and you can now visualize the results using a Graduated renderer with, for example, the Natural Breaks (Jenks) classification mode. The Jenks Natural Breaks classification is designed to arrange values into "natural" classes by maximizing the variance between different classes while reducing the variance within the generated classes. The following figure shows the population density based on the original census data (on the left) and the results after Dasymetric mapping (on the right):

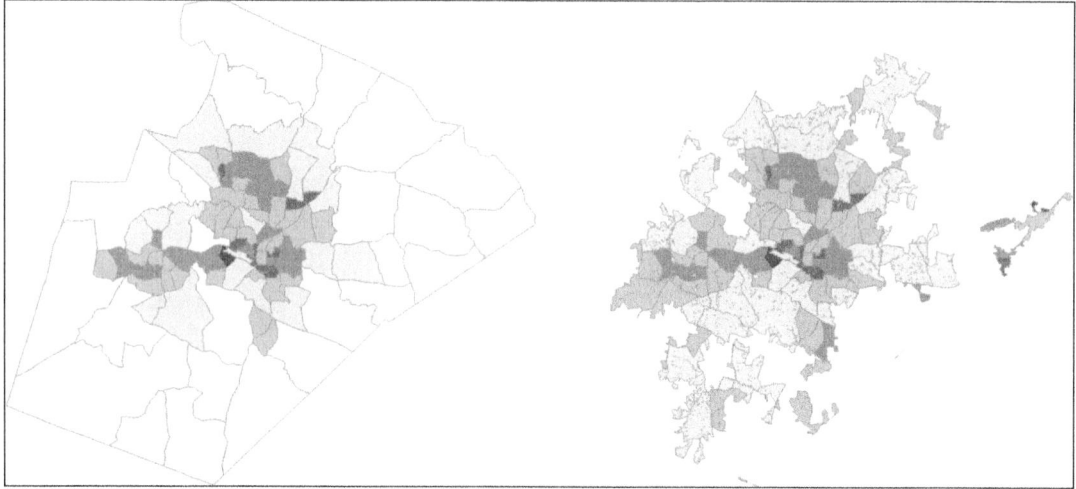

How it works...

In the first step of this recipe, we used the **Clip** operation. As you most likely noticed, the results of a **Clip** operation look very similar to the results of the **Intersection** tool, which we used in the previous recipe of this chapter, *Selecting optimum sites*. Compare both the results, and you will see the following differences:

▶ The layer resulting from an **Intersection** operation contains attributes from both input layers, while the result of a **Clip** operation only contains attributes of the first input layer.

▶ This also means that the layer order is important when using **Clip**, but this does not change the output of **Intersection** (except for the attribute order in the attribute table).

▶ The **Intersection** result is also very likely to contain more features than the **Clip** result (164 instead of 105 if you use our sample data census tracts and urban areas). This is because the **Intersect** tool needs to create a new feature for every combination of intersecting census tracts and urban areas, while the **Clip** tool only removes the parts of the census tracts that are not within any urban area.

A popular way of thinking about the **Clip** operation is to imagine one layer as the cookie cutter and the other layer as the cookie dough.

Calculating regional statistics

Another classic spatial analysis task is calculating the areas of a certain type within regions, for example, the area within a county that is covered by certain land use types, or the share of different crops that is farmed in given municipalities.

In this recipe, we will calculate statistics of geological data for zip code areas. In particular, we will calculate the total area of each type of rock per zip code area.

Getting ready

To follow this recipe, load `zipcodes_wake.shp` and `geology.shp` from our sample data. Additionally, install and activate the **Group Stats** plugin using **Plugin Manager**.

How to do it...

Using the following steps, we can calculate the areas of certain rock types per zip code area:

1. Calculate the intersections between zip code areas and geological areas using the **Intersection** tool in the **Processing Toolbox** option or from the **Vector** menu.
2. Using the **Group Stats** plugin, you can now calculate the total area per rock type and zip code area, as follows:
   1. Select the **Intersection** result layer as the input **Layer**.
   2. Drag the **ZIPCODE** field to the **Rows** input area and the **GEO_NAME** field to the **Columns** input area.
   3. Drag the **sum** function and the **Area** value to the **Value** input area.
   4. Click on **Calculate** to start the calculations.

The following screenshot displays the complete configuration, as well as the results:

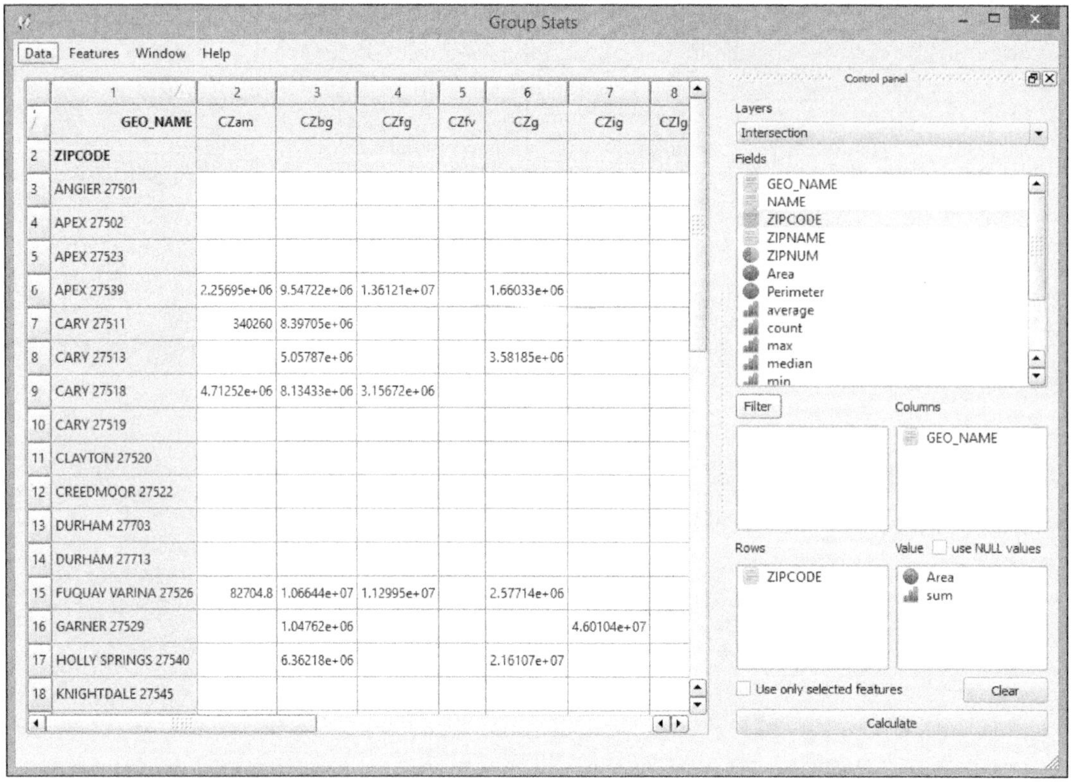

GEO_NAME	CZam	CZbg	CZfg	CZfv	CZg	CZig	CZlg
ZIPCODE							
ANGIER 27501							
APEX 27502							
APEX 27523							
APEX 27539	2.25695e+06	9.54722e+06	1.36121e+07		1.66033e+06		
CARY 27511	340260	8.39705e+06					
CARY 27513		5.05787e+06			3.58185e+06		
CARY 27518	4.71252e+06	8.13433e+06	3.15672e+06				
CARY 27519							
CLAYTON 27520							
CREEDMOOR 27522							
DURHAM 27703							
DURHAM 27713							
FUQUAY VARINA 27526	82704.8	1.06644e+07	1.12995e+07		2.57714e+06		
GARNER 27529		1.04762e+06				4.60104e+07	
HOLLY SPRINGS 27540		6.36218e+06			2.16107e+07		
KNIGHTDALE 27545							

Control panel

Layers: Intersection

Fields: GEO_NAME, NAME, ZIPCODE, ZIPNAME, ZIPNUM, Area, Perimeter, average, count, max, median, min

Filter

Columns: GEO_NAME

Rows: ZIPCODE

Value: Area, sum — use NULL values

Use only selected features — Clear

Calculate

How it works...

The **Group Stats** plugin brings functionality, which is commonly known as pivot tables, to QGIS. A pivot table is a data summarization tool, which is commonly found in applications, such as spreadsheets or business intelligence software. As shown in this example, pivot tables can aggregate data from an input table. Additionally, the **Group Stats** plugin offers extended geometry functions, such as, **Area** and **Perimeter** for polygon input layers, or **Length** for line layers. This makes using the plugin more convenient because it is not necessary to first use **Field calculator** to add these geometric values to the attribute table.

It is worth noting that you always need to put the following two entries into the **Value** input area:

- ▸ An aggregation function, such as sum, average, or count
- ▸ A value field (from the input layer's attribute table) or geometry function, which should be aggregated

Estimating density heatmaps

Whether they are animal sightings, accident locations, or general points of interest, many point datasets can be interpreted more easily by visualizing the point density using a heatmap. In this recipe, we will estimate the density of POIs in Wake county to find areas with a high density.

Getting ready

Load the `poi_names_wake.shp` POI dataset from our sample data. Make sure that the **Heatmap** plugin, which comes with QGIS by default, is enabled in **Plugin Manager**.

How to do it...

Using the following steps, we can calculate the POI heatmap:

1. Start the **Heatmap** plugin from the **Raster** menu.

2. Make sure that **poi_names_wake** is selected as **Input point layer**.

3. Select a location and filename for **Output raster**. You don't need to specify the file extension because this will be added automatically, based on the selected **Output format**. GeoTIFF is usually the first choice.

4. Select a search **Radius** of `1000` **meters**.

5. The **Add generated file to map** option should be activated by default. Click on **OK** to create the default heatmap.

6. By default, the heatmap layer will be rendered using the **Singleband gray** render type. Change the render type to **Singleband pseudocolor** and apply a color ramp that you like to improve the visualization, as show in the following screenshot:

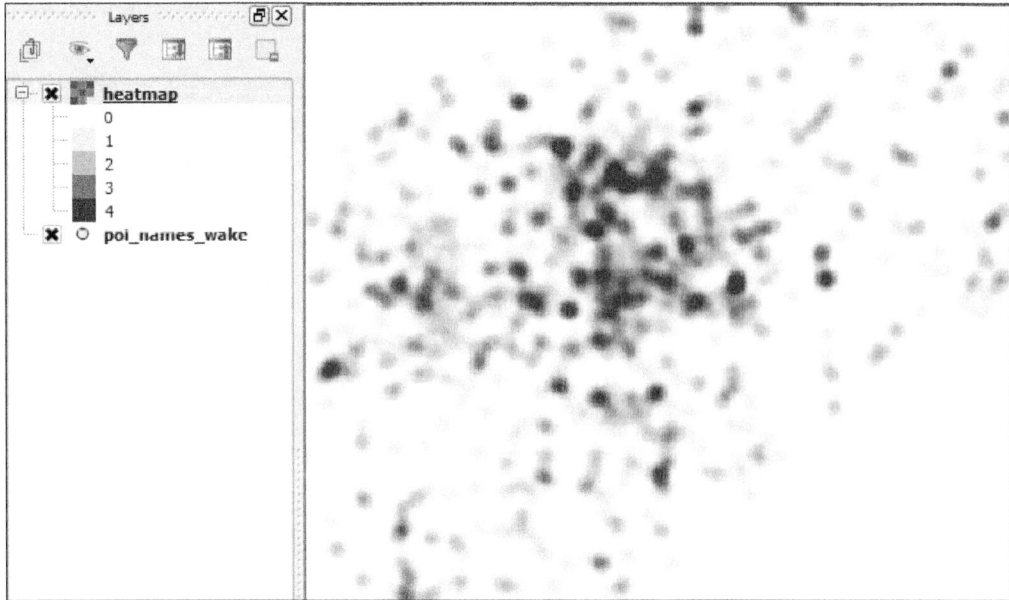

> If you want to control the size of the output raster, just enable the **Advanced** section and adjust the number of **Rows** and **Columns** or **Cell size X** and **Cell size Y**, accordingly. Note that changing rows and columns will automatically recalculate the size of the cell and vice versa.

How it works...

The search radius, which is also known as the kernel bandwidth, determines how smooth the heatmap will look because it sets the distance around each point at which the influence of the point will be felt. Therefore, smaller radius values result in heatmaps that display finer details, while larger values result in smoother heatmaps.

Besides the kernel bandwidth, there are also different kernel shapes to choose from. The kernel shape controls the rate at which the influence of a point decreases with increasing distance from the point. The kernel shapes that are available in the Heatmap plugin can be seen in the following figures. For example, a Triweight kernel (the first on the bottom row) creates smaller hotspots than the Epanechnikov kernel (the second on the bottom) because the Triweight shape gives features a higher influence for distances that are closer to the point:

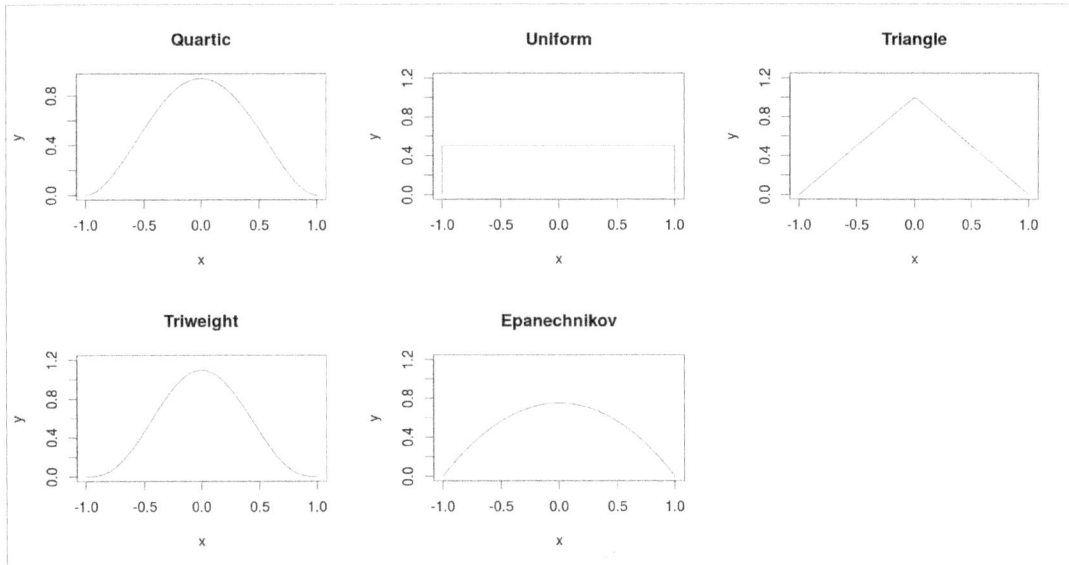

The triangular kernel shape can be further adjusted using the **Decay ratio** setting. In the preceding figure, you can see the shape for ratios of 0 (a solid red line), 0.5 (a dashed black line), and 1 (a dotted black line), which is equal to the uniform kernel shape. You can even specify values greater than 1. In this case, the influence of a feature will increase with the distance from the point.

Estimating values based on samples

Interpolation is the idea that, with a set of known values, you can estimate the values of additional points based on their proximity to these known values. This recipe shows you how to use known values at point locations to create a continuous surface (raster) of value estimates. Classic examples include weather data estimations that are based on weather station data (think temperature or rainfall maps), crop yield estimates that are based on sampling parts of a field, and like in this example in this recipe, elevation estimations that are based on the elevation of sampled points.

Getting ready

Activate **Interpolation Plugin** via **Plugin Manager**.

Load a point layer with numeric columns, representing the feature of interest. For this recipe, use the poi_names_wake.shp, and the elev_m column, which contains elevation in meters for each point.

How to do it...

1. Start by loading poi_name_wake.

2. Zoom to the layer extent.

3. Open the Interpolation tool by navigating to **Raster | Interpolation | Interpolation**.

> Yes, it's on the **Raster** menu; the source data must be a vector, but the results are a raster.

4. Select poi_names_wake for **Input**.

5. Select elev_m for **Interpolation attribute**.

6. Click on the **Add** button, your selection should appear in the box on the left-hand side.

7. Select **Inverse Distance Weighted (IDW)** for **Interpolation Method**.

8. Now, set the **Extent** and **Cell Size** properties. In **Cellsize X** and **Cellsize Y**, enter 100 and 100. This forces the output cells to be 100x100 units of the current projection.

> Generally, if this was for analysis, you would attempt to match the region of interest or other raster layers. In this case, we just want to go for sensibly-sized cells. As the map is in UTM, we will want cells to be integers that represent metric units; 100 meters by 100 meters makes interpreting the results easier.

9. Click on the **Set to current extent** button in the middle.

10. Next to **Output file box**, click on the button labeled **...** to set the output path to save the results:

11. Pick the folder and type in a name with no file extension, such as idw100m (the result will be an ASCII raster .asc file), as shown in the following screenshot:

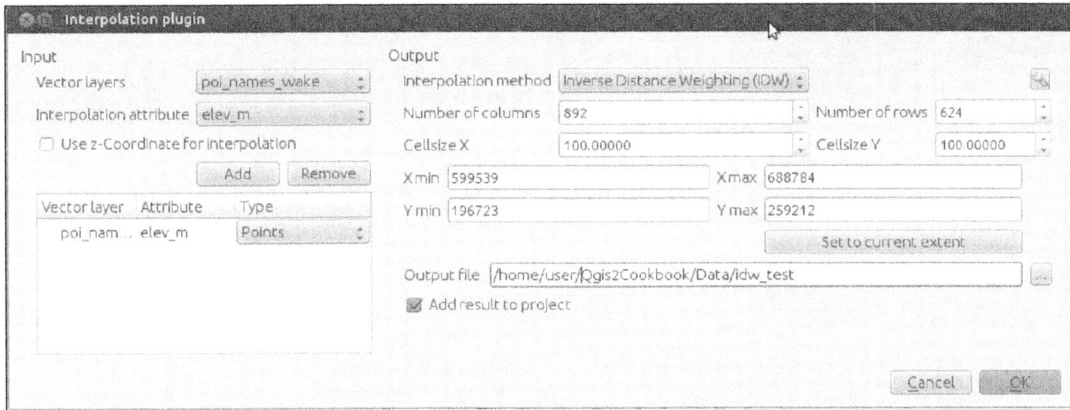

> The wrench tool in the upper-right corner will let you change
> the P value, which is the exponent in the denominator and
> directly sets how much a point influences a nearby location,
> as compared against more distanced points.

12. Check all your settings and then click on the **OK** button.

13. Now, wait patiently for your results, the smaller the size of the cell and the larger the number of columns and data points, the longer the calculation will take, as shown in the following screenshot:

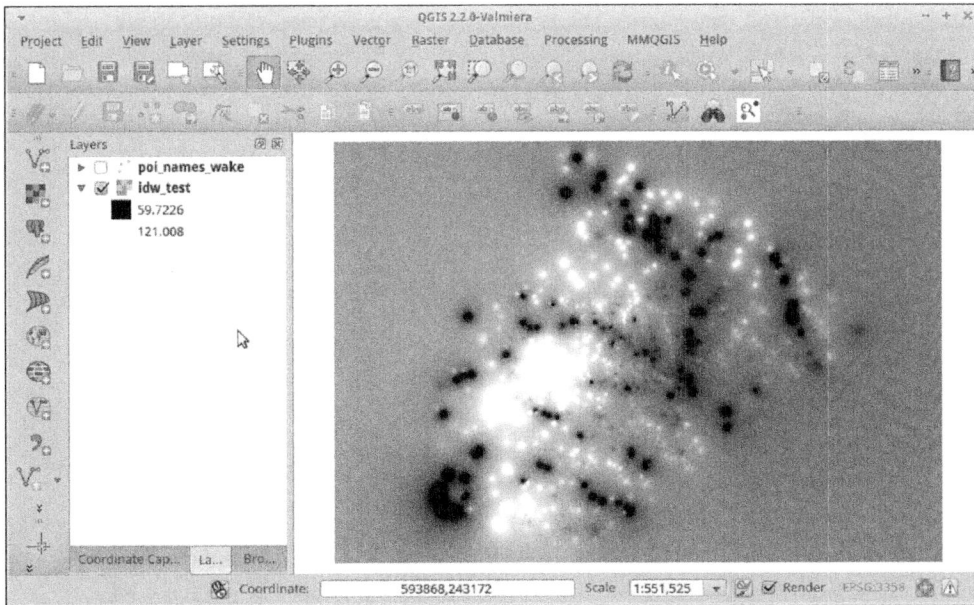

How it works...

The basic idea is that, at a given cell, you take the average of all the nearby points that are weighted by their distance to the cell in order to estimate the value at your current location. **Inverse Distance Weighted** (**IDW**) takes this one step further by giving more weight to values that are closer to the given cell and less weight to values that are further. This function uses an exponent factor P in order to greatly increase the role of closer points over distant points.

There's more...

Are the results not quite what you expected? There are a few parameters that can be adjusted; these are primarily the P value and the size of the cell. Is this still not coming out the way that you want? There are several other Interpolation tools that are accessible in Processing under the SAGA, GRASS, and GDAL toolboxes, which allow you to manipulate more of the formula parameters to refine the results.

Finally, depending on your data, IDW may not do a good job of interpolating. In the example here, you can actually see how there are distinct circles around isolated points. This is generally not a good result, and this needs a smoother transition to nearby points. If you have any control over field sampling to begin with, keep in mind that regularly-spaced grids will usually provide better results.

Do you not have control over the source data or you didn't get good results? Then, you may need to look into other more complicated formulas that compensate for skew, strong directionality, obstructions, and non-regular spacing of samples, such as Splines or Kriging, or **Triangulated Irregular Networks** (**TINs**). There is lot of science and statistics behind the methods and diagnostic tools to determine the best parameters. This is far too complicated a topic for this recipe, but it is well-covered in books on geostatistics.

See also

- ▶ http://docs.qgis.org/2.2/en/docs/user_manual/plugins/plugins_interpolation.html
- ▶ http://en.wikipedia.org/wiki/Inverse_distance_weightinging

6
Network Analysis

In this chapter, we will cover the following recipes:

- ▶ Creating a simple routing network
- ▶ Calculating the shortest paths using the Road graph plugin
- ▶ Routing with one-way streets in the Road graph plugin
- ▶ Calculating the shortest paths with the QGIS network analysis library
- ▶ Routing point sequences
- ▶ Automating multiple route computation using batch processing
- ▶ Matching points to the nearest line
- ▶ Creating a network for pgRouting
- ▶ Visualizing the pgRouting results in QGIS
- ▶ Using the pgRoutingLayer plugin for convenience
- ▶ Getting network data from the OSM

Introduction

This chapter focuses on the common use cases that are related to routing within networks. By far, the most common networks that are used to route are street networks. Other less common cases include networks for indoor routing, that is, through rooms inside buildings, or networks of shipping routes.

Networks and routing are in no way a GIS-only topic. You will find a lot of math literature related to this, called **Graph Theory**. In this chapter, we will use the following terms to talk about networks:

> ▸ A **network** (also known as **graph**) is a collection of connected objects
>
> ▸ These objects are called **nodes** (also known as vertices)
>
> ▸ The connections between nodes are called **links** (also known as **edges**)

The following figure explains these terms:

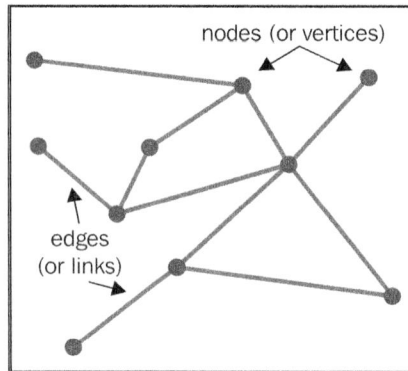

The two routing tools that are commonly used with QGIS are as follows:

> ▸ The Road graph plugin, which is one of the QGIS core plugins; that is, this plugin is available in every QGIS installation, but you may have to activate it in Plugin Manager
>
> ▸ The PostGIS extension pgRouting, which can be used directly through the QGIS DB Manager, or more comfortably through the pgRoutingLayer plugin, which can be installed from the QGIS plugin repository using Plugin Manager

Creating a simple routing network

In this recipe, we will create a routing network from scratch using the QGIS editing tools. Even though more and more open network data is available, there will still be numerous use cases where necessary network data does not exist or is not available for use. Therefore, it is good to know how to create a network and what to pay attention to in order to avoid common pitfalls.

For the task of network creation, the main difference between the Road graph plugin and pgRouting is that pgRouting needs a network node (that is, link start or end node) at each intersection while the Road graph plugin will also use intermediate link geometry nodes to infer intersections if two links share a node. In this recipe, we will create a network, which can be used in both tools.

Getting ready

To follow this recipe, you only need a new empty QGIS project. Additionally, make sure you have the **Digitizing** toolbar enabled (as shown in the following screenshot). We will create an imaginary network, but if you want you can load a background map and digitize this:

How to do it...

Before we can start to create the network, there are a few things that need to be set up first:

1. Create a new shapefile line layer for the network. You don't need to add any extra attributes besides the default ID attribute yet.

> You can read more about creating new shapefiles in the *Learning QGIS* book by Packt Publishing and the QGIS user guide at `http://docs.qgis.org/2.2/en/docs/user_manual/working_with_vector/editing_geometry_attributes.html#creating-a-new-shapefile-layer`.

2. To ensure that we can digitize the network with valid topology, we'll activate snapping next. Go to **Settings | Snapping Options** and activate snapping for your line layer by enabling the checkbox to the left of it. Additionally, set the mode to to vertex and choose a tolerance of at least **5.00000** pixels:

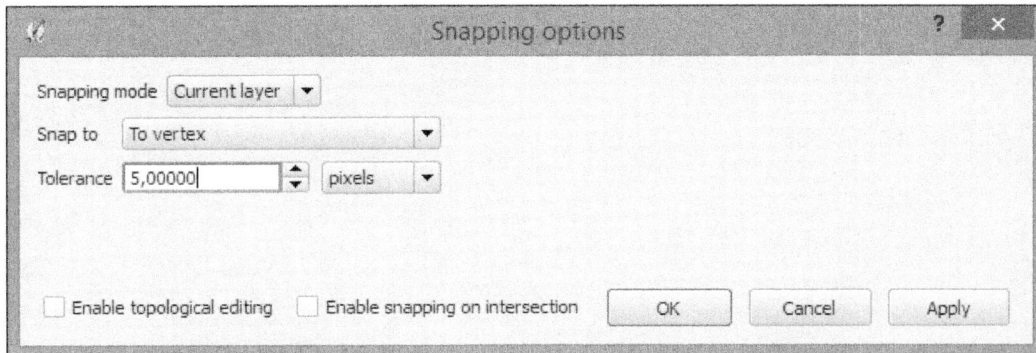

3. Now, we can enable editing for the line layer and then select the **Add Feature** tool from the **Digitizing** toolbar to start digitizing.

4. Create the first line feature now, and give it the ID number **1**. The line can have as many nodes as you wish. We'll create a line with four nodes, as shown in the following screenshot:

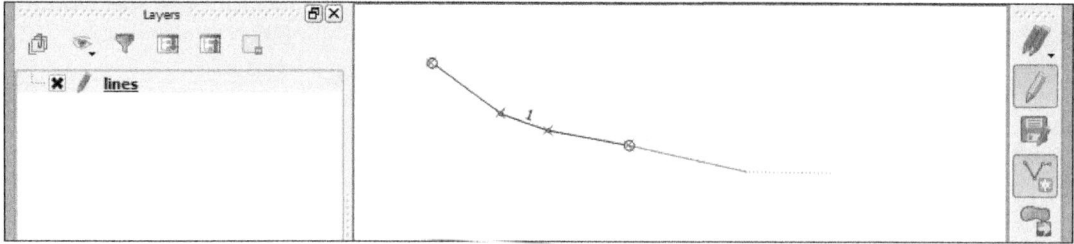

5. To draw the second line feature, start at the first or the last node of line 1. As we have activated snapping, you will see that the node is being highlighted if you hover over it with the mouse cursor. Draw a second line and give it the ID number **2**.

> The line in the preceding screenshot is drawn with a style that has circles on the starting and ending points. You can reproduce this style by adding the **Marker line** symbol levels to the line style or load `network_links.qml` from our sample data. For more details about styling features, please refer to *Chapter 10, Cartography Tips*.

6. Draw a few more lines (around 12 in total) forming a network. Make sure to pay attention to the snapping and assign link IDs:

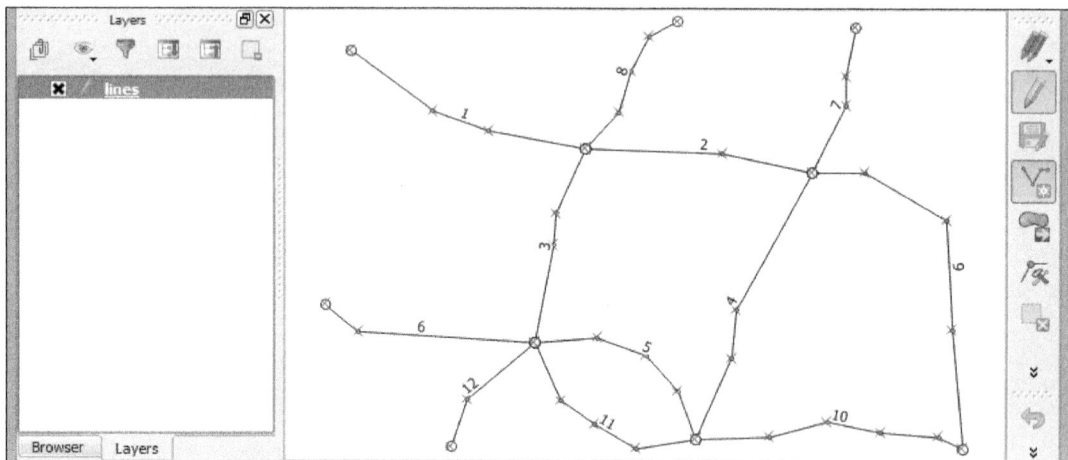

7. Disable editing, and confirm that you want to save the changes.

We will use this basic network as a starting point for the remaining recipes in this chapter.

How it works...

By setting the snapping mode to **to vertex**, we made it possible to digitize the line network in a way that ensures that lines, which should be connected, really contain a node at the exact same position.

There's more...

You can validate the network topology by running the Topology Checker plugin, which is installed with QGIS by default (you can read more about Topology Checker in *Chapter 12, Up and Coming*):

1. Start **Topology Checker** from the **Vector** menu.

2. Click **Configure** to set up a topology rule, as shown in the following screenshot, and click on **Add Rule** to add it to the list of rules to check. Then, close the settings by clicking on **OK**:

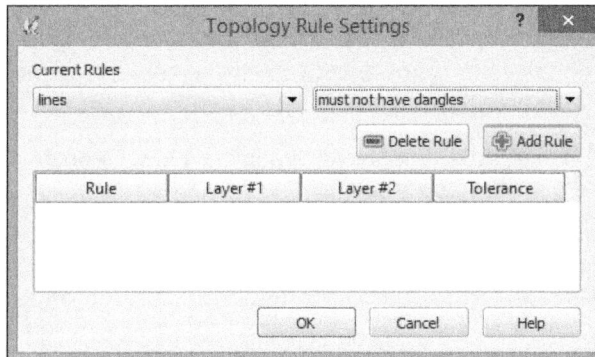

3. Once this tool is configured, click on **Validate All** (the button with the checkmark) to initiate the check. You will see the list of discovered errors displayed in the list above the buttons, as shown in the following screenshot. Additionally, the dangling ends are highlighted in red in the map:

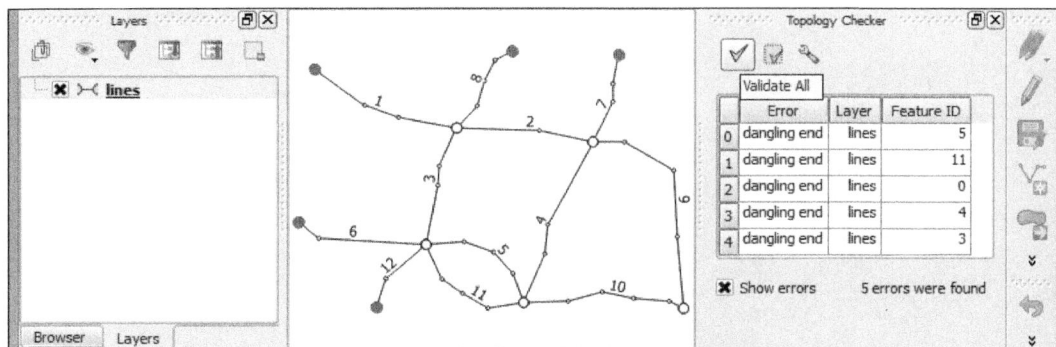

4. You can select the error entries in the list to jump to the line features that failed the check. In our network, only lines with dead-ends should be listed. If you see an error at an intersection, you should zoom closer and try to correct the node positions.

Calculating the shortest paths using the Road graph plugin

This recipe shows you how to use the built-in Road graph plugin to calculate the shortest paths in a network.

Getting ready

To follow this recipe, load `network_pgr.shp` from the sample data. Additionally, make sure that the Road graph plugin is enabled in Plugin Manager.

How to do it...

The Road graph plugin enables us to route between two points that are selected on the map. Before we can use this, we have to configure it first, as follows:

1. Enable the **Shortest path** panel by navigating to **View | Panels**. This should add the plugin panel to the user interface.

2. Go to **Vector | Road graph | Settings** to get to the configuration dialog. For now, the default settings, as shown in the following screenshot, should be fine. Note that the network layer is selected as **Transportation layer**. Click on **OK** to confirm the settings:

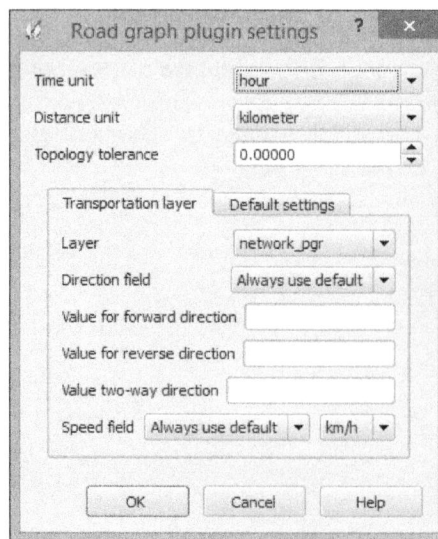

3. Once the settings are configured, we can calculate our first route. Select the **Start** and **Stop** locations using the buttons marked with crosshair icons. Activate the crosshair button and then click in the map to select a location. This location will be marked on the map, and the coordinates will be automatically inserted into the **Start** or **Stop** input field.

4. Click on **Calculate** to initiate route computation. Depending on the size of the network used, this step will either be very fast or it can take much more time. The route will be highlighted in the map, and the route length and travel time will be displayed, as shown in the following screenshot:

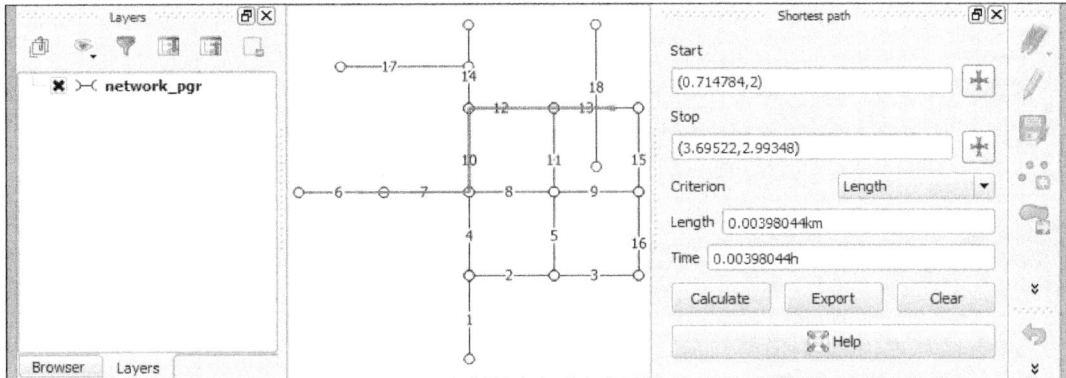

5. If you want to store the computed shortest path, click on **Export** and you will be able to choose whether you want to create a new layer for the path or add the route to an existing line layer.

6. To compute a new route, simply change the start and stop locations and click on **Calculate** again.

7. Click on **Clear** to remove the route highlights when you are done.

How it works...

The Road graph plugin uses the QGIS network analysis library, which implements Dijkstra's algorithm. For a given starting node, the algorithm finds the path with the lowest cost (that is, the shortest path if the cost criterion is length or the fastest path if the cost criterion is time) between this node and every other node in the network. This can also be used to find costs of the shortest paths from a start node to a destination node by stopping the algorithm once the shortest path to the destination node has been determined.

In contrast to many simple routing tools, the Road graph plugin builds the network topology automatically. As our network dataset is topologically sound (that is, there are no tiny gaps where network edges meet), we can set up Road graph plugin settings with **Topology tolerance** as **0**. If you are using a network from a different source, it may not have been created with the same attention to detail, and you may have to increase **Topology tolerance** to get routing to work.

See also

> ▸ If you are interested in learning more about this algorithm, you can start at `http://wiki.gis.com/wiki/index.php/Dijkstra's_algorithm`

Routing with one-way streets in the Road graph plugin

When it comes to vehicle routing, it is often necessary to go into more detail and consider driving restrictions, such as one-way streets. This recipe shows you how to use one-way street information to route with the Road graph plugin.

Getting ready

To follow this recipe, load `network_pgr.shp` from the sample data. Additionally, make sure that the Road graph plugin is enabled in Plugin Manager.

How to do it...

To demonstrate routing with one-way street information, we will first visualize the one-way values, and then we will configure the Road graph plugin to use the one-way information, as follows:

1. Before we start routing with one-way information, it is helpful to visualize the one-way streets. It is worth noting that the one-way direction will depend on the direction of the link geometry (that is, the direction the link was digitized in). The best way to visualize the link direction is by assigning arrow symbols, as shown in the following screenshot. You can load `network_pgr.qml` from our sample data to get the style:

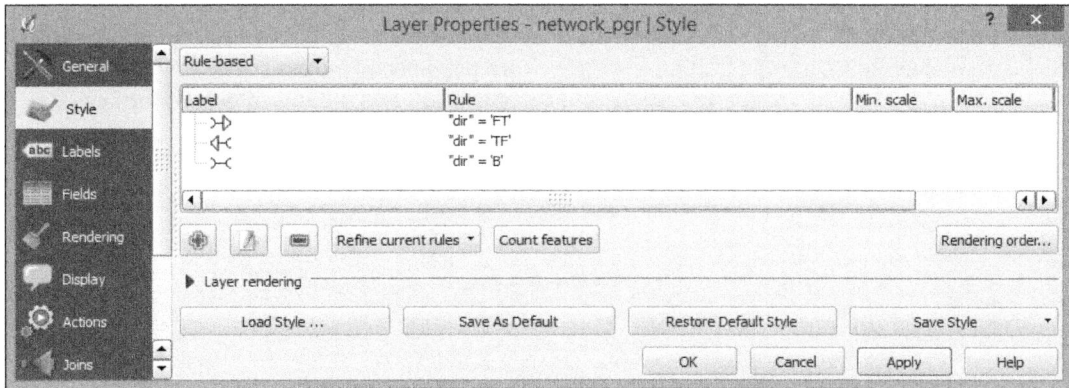

There are many different ways to encode one-way information. In our dataset, a forward direction is encoded as **FT** for "from-to", a backward direction as **TF** for "to-from", and both ways as **B** for "both".

2. Then, we can configure the Road graph plugin to use the one-way information. To do this, we have to choose the **dir** attribute as **Direction field** and enter the values for forward (in link geometry) direction and reverse (against link geometry) direction:

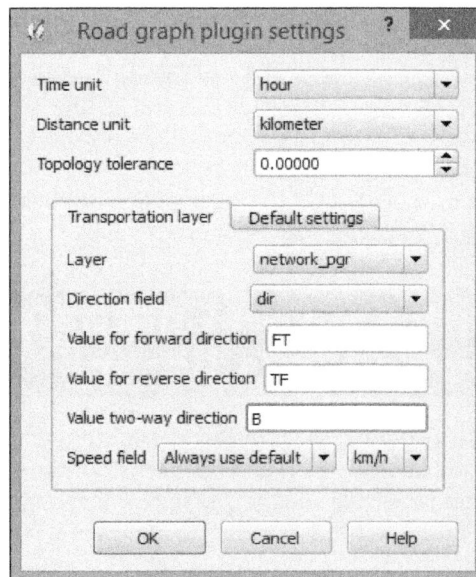

3. Once the plugin is configured, you can compute the shortest path as described in the previous recipe, *Calculating the shortest paths using the Road graph plugin*. You will see how the resulting routes differ from the normal (without one-way restrictions) paths, as shown in the following screenshot where the algorithm avoids the one-way links on the direct route and takes the longer route instead:

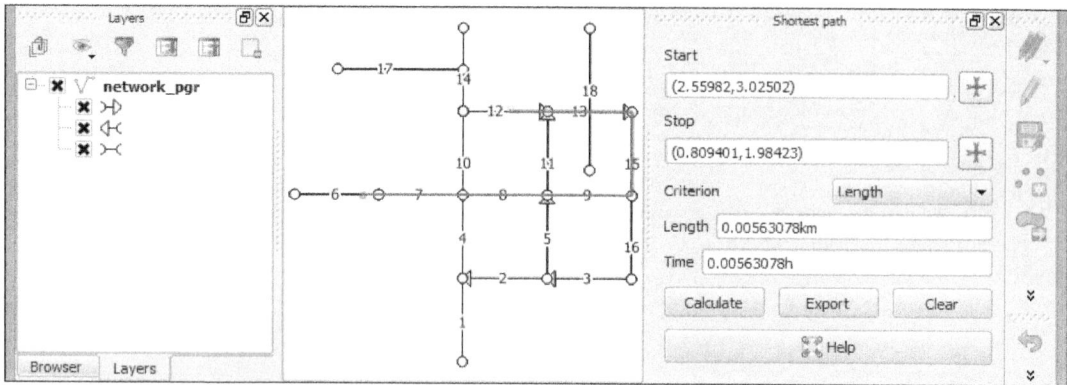

How it works...

When we use the default two-way setting, each network link is interpreted as a connection from the start to end node, as well as a connection from the end to start node. By adding one-way restrictions, this changes and the link is only interpreted as one connection now.

Besides **FT**, **TF**, and **B**, another common way to encode one-ways is **1** for in-link direction, **-1** for against-link direction, and **0** for both ways. In OpenStreetMap, you will find **yes** for the in-link direction, **no** for both ways and **-1** for the against-link direction (refer to http://wiki.openstreetmap.org/wiki/Key:oneway for more details).

Calculating the shortest paths with the QGIS network analysis library

As mentioned in the recipe, *Calculating the shortest paths using the Road graph plugin*, QGIS comes with a network analysis library, which can be used from the Python console, inside plugins, to process scripts, and basically anything else that you can think of. In this recipe, we will introduce the usage of the network analysis to compute the shortest paths in the Python console.

Getting ready

To follow this recipe, load `network_pgr.shp` from the sample data.

How to do it...

Instead of typing or copying the following script directly in the Python console, we recommend opening the Python console editor using the **Show editor** button on the left-hand side of the Python console:

1. Paste the following script into the editor:

```python
import processing
from processing.tools.vector import VectorWriter
from PyQt4.QtCore import *
from qgis.core import *
from qgis.networkanalysis import *

# create the graph
layer = processing.getObject('network_pgr')
director = QgsLineVectorLayerDirector(layer,-1,'','','',3)
director.addProperter(QgsDistanceArcProperter())
builder = QgsGraphBuilder(layer.crs())
from_point = QgsPoint(2.73343,3.00581)
to_point = QgsPoint(0.483584,2.01487)
tied_points =
  director.makeGraph(builder,[from_point,to_point])
graph = builder.graph()

# compute the route from from_id to to_id
from_id = graph.findVertex(tied_points[0])
to_id = graph.findVertex(tied_points[1])
(tree,cost) = QgsGraphAnalyzer.dijkstra(graph,from_id,0)

# assemble the route
route_points = []
curPos = to_id
while (curPos != from_id):
  in_vertex = graph.arc(tree[curPos]).inVertex()
  route_points.append(graph.vertex(in_vertex).point())
  curPos = graph.arc(tree[curPos]).outVertex()
route_points.append(from_point)
```

```
# write the results to a Shapefile
result = 'C:\\temp\\route.shp'
writer = VectorWriter(result,None,[],2,layer.crs())
fet = QgsFeature()
fet.setGeometry(QgsGeometry.fromPolyline(route_points))
writer.addFeature(fet)
del writer
processing.load(result)
```

2. If you are using your own network dataset instead of `network_pgr.shp`, which is provided with this book, adjust the coordinates of `from_point` and `to_point` for the route's starting and ending points.

3. Change the file paths for the result layer depending on your operating system.

4. Make sure that the network layer is loaded and selected in the QGIS layer list.

5. Save the script and run it.

How it works...

On line 8, we created a `QgsLineVectorLayerDirector` object (http://qgis.org/api/classQgsLineVectorLayerDirector.html), which contains the network configuration. The constructor (`QgsLineVectorLayerDirector(layer,-1,'','','',3)`) parameters are as follows:

▶ The network line layer

▶ The ID of the direction field: we set it to `-1` because this script does not consider one-ways

▶ The following three parameters are the values for the in link direction: reverse link direction, and two-way

▶ The last parameter is the default direction: `1` for the in link direction, `2` for the reverse direction, and `3` for the two-way

Line 10 creates the `QgsGraphBuilder` (http://qgis.org/api/classQgsGraphBuilder.html) instance, which will be used to create the routing graph on line 14.

On lines 11 and 12, we defined the starting and ending points of our route. To be able to route between these two points, they have to be matched to the nearest network link. This happens on line 13 in the `makeGraph()` function, which returns the so-called `tied_points`.

The actual route computation takes place on line 18 in the `QgsGraphAnalyzer.dijkstra()` (http://qgis.org/api/classQgsGraphAnalyzer.html) function.

The `while` loop, starting on line 22, is where the script moves through the tree created by Dijkstra's algorithm to collect all the vertices on the way and add them to the `route_points` list, which becomes the resulting route geometry on line 31.

The writer for output route line layer is created on line 29, where we pass the file path, `None` for default encoding, the `[]` for empty fields list, and the `2` for geometry type, which equals to lines as well as the resulting layer CRS. The following lines, 30 to 32, create the route feature and add it to the writer.

Finally, the last line loads the resulting shapefile, and this is displayed on the map, as illustrated by the following screenshot:

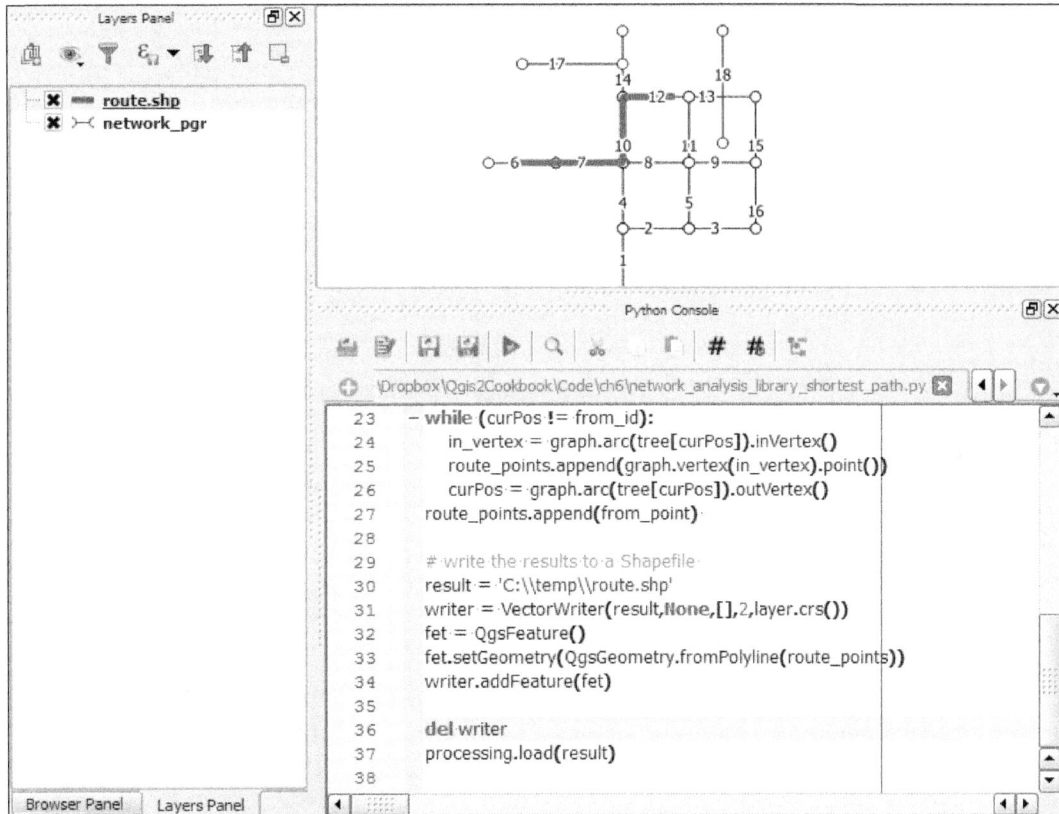

See also

You can read more about QGIS's network analysis library online in the PyQGIS Developer Cookbook at `http://docs.qgis.org/testing/en/docs/pyqgis_developer_cookbook/network_analysis.html`.

Routing point sequences

In the recipes so far, we routed from one starting point to one destination point. Another use case is when we want to compute routes that connect a sequence of points, such as the points in a GPS track. In this recipe, we will use the point layer to route processing script to compute a route for a point sequence. At its core, this script uses the same idea that was introduced in the previous recipe, *Calculating the shortest paths with the QGIS network analysis library*, but this computes several shortest paths one after the other.

Getting ready

To follow this recipe, load `network_pgr.shp` and `sample_pts_for_routing.shp`, which contains a point layer that should be routed from the sample dataset.

Additionally, you need to get the point layer to route script from `https://raw. githubusercontent.com/anitagraser/QGIS-Processing-tools/master/2.6/ scripts/point_layer_to_route.py` and save it in the `Processing` script folder, which is set to `C:\Users\youruser\qgis2\processing\scripts` (on Windows), `/home/ youruser/.qgis2/processing/scripts` (on Linux), and `/Users/youruser/.qgis2/ processing/scripts` (on Mac) by default. Alternatively, save the point layer to route to the folder configured in the **Processing** menu under **Options | Scripts | Scripts folder**.

How to do it...

To compute the route between the input points, you need to perform the following tasks:

1. Load the network and the point layer.

2. If you are using your own data, make sure that both layers are in the same CRS. If they are in different CRS, you need to reproject them (for example, using the **Reproject layer** tool from the **Processing Toolbox** option) before you continue.

3. Start the point layer to route tool from the **Processing Toolbox** option.

4. Pick the **points** and **network** input layers, make sure that **Open output file after running algorithm option** is activated, and click on **Run** to start the route computation. The resulting route layer will be loaded automatically:

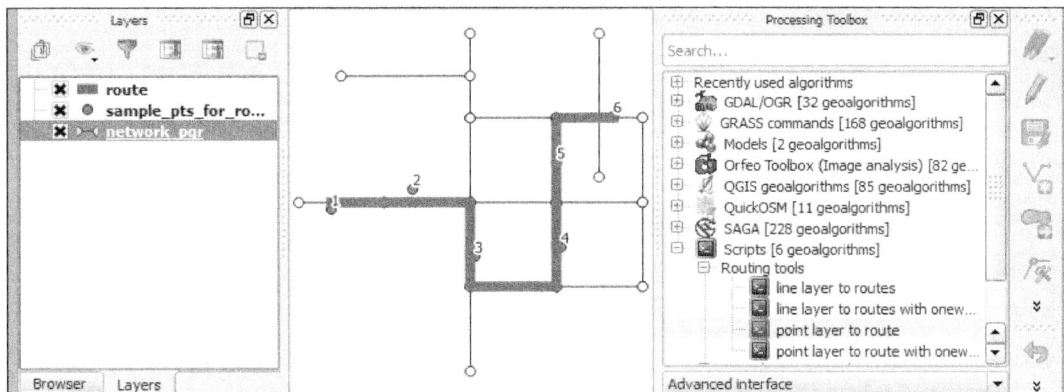

How it works...

The **point layer to route** tool uses the QGIS network analysis library. We already discussed the basic use of this library in the previous recipe, *Calculating the shortest paths with the QGIS network analysis library*. The main difference is that we now have to handle more than two points. Therefore, the script fetches all points from the input point layer and ties or matches them to the graph:

```
points = []
features = processing.features(point_layer)
for f in features:
  points.append(f.geometry().asPoint())
tiedPoints = director.makeGraph(builder, points)
```

For each pair of consecutive points, the script then computes the route between the two points just like we did in the *Calculating the shortest paths with the QGIS network analysis library* recipe:

```
point_count = point_layer.featureCount()
for i in range(0,point_count-1):
  # compute the route between two consecutive points
```

The resulting route line layer contains one line feature for each consecutive point pair.

There's more...

Of course, you can also use the **point layer to route** tool to route between only two points as well.

See also

There is also a version of this script, which takes one-way information into account at `https://raw.githubusercontent.com/anitagraser/QGIS-Processing-tools/master/2.2/scripts/point_layer_to_route_with_oneways.py`.

Automating multiple route computation using batch processing

If you have multiple input point layers, you can use Processing's batch processing capabilities to speed up the process. In this recipe, we will compute routes for two input point layers at once, but the same approach can be applied to many more layers.

Getting ready

To follow this recipe, load `network_pgr.shp` and the two point layers, `sample_pts_for_routing.shp` and `sample_pts_for_routing2.shp`.

How to do it...

To get started, right-click on the **point layer to route** tool in the **Processing Toolbox** option and select **Execute as batch process**. Then perform the following steps:

1. In the **points** column, click the **...** button and use the **Select from open layers** option to select `sample_pts_for_routing` and `sample_pts_for_routing2`.

2. Select and remove the third line using the **Delete row** button at the bottom of the dialog.

3. In the **network** column, click the **...** button and use the **Select from open layers** option to select `network_pgr`. You can avoid having to pick the file twice by double-clicking on the table header entry (where it reads **network**). This will autofill all rows with the same network file path.

4. In the **routes** column, you need to pick a path for the resulting route files. In the **Save file** dialog, which opens when you click on the **...** button, you can specify one base filename and click on **Save**. The following **Autofill settings** dialog lets you specify if and how you want to have the rows filled. Use **Autofill mode Fill with numbers** and Processing will automatically append a running number to the filename that you specified. You can see an example in the following screenshot where we specified route as the base filename.

5. Click on **Run** to execute the batch process. Both routes will be computed and loaded automatically:

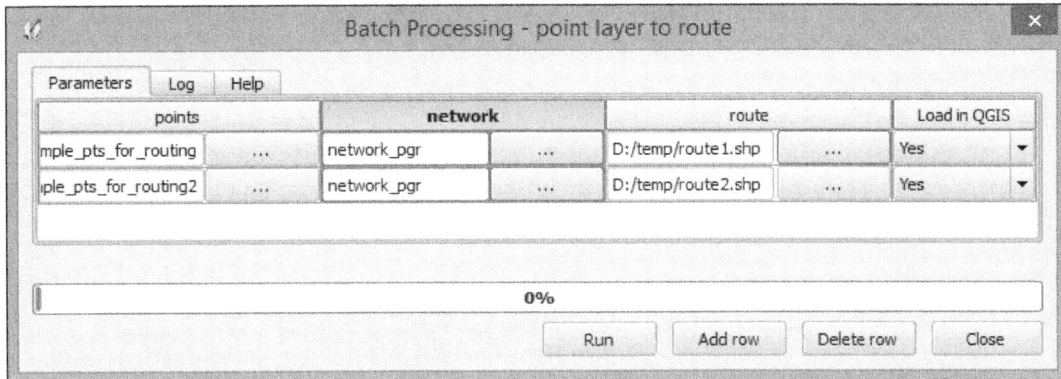

Matching points to the nearest line

In this recipe, we will use the QGIS network analysis library from Python console to match points to the nearest line. This is the simplest form of what is also known as map matching.

Getting ready

To follow this recipe, load `network_pgr.shp` from the sample data.

How to do it...

The following script will match three points, `QgsPoint(3.63715,3.60401)`, `QgsPoint(3.86250,1.58906)`, and `QgsPoint(0.42913,2.26512)`, to the network:

1. Open Python console and its editor and then load or paste the following `network_analysis_match_points.py` script:

```python
import processing
from processing.tools.vector import VectorWriter
from PyQt4.QtCore import *
from qgis.core import *
from qgis.networkanalysis import *

layer = processing.getObject('network_pgr')
director = QgsLineVectorLayerDirector(layer,-1,'','','',3)
director.addProperter(QgsDistanceArcProperter())
builder = QgsGraphBuilder(layer.crs())
additional_points = \
  [QgsPoint(3.63715,3.60401),QgsPoint(3.86250,1.58906),QgsPoi
  nt(0.42913,2.26512)]
```

```
tied_points = director.makeGraph(builder,additional_points)

result = 'C:\\temp\\matched_pts.shp'
writer = VectorWriter(result,None,[],1,layer.crs())
fet = QgsFeature()

for pt in tied_points:
  fet.setGeometry(QgsGeometry.fromPoint(pt))
  writer.addFeature(fet)

del writer
processing.load(result)
```

2. Make sure that the network layer is selected in the layer list.

3. Run the script. The results should be loaded automatically.

How it works...

This script uses the QGIS network analysis library's ability to match points to lines using the `makeGraph()` function. The resulting `tied_points` list contains the coordinates of the points on the network that are closest to the input `points`.

The `1` option on line 15 specifies that the output layer is of type point.

The `for` loop finally goes through all points in the `tied_points` list and creates point features, which are then added to the result `writer`.

Creating a routing network for pgRouting

This recipe shows you how to import a line layer into PostGIS and create a routable network out of it, which can be used by PostGIS's routing library, pgRouting. (For details about pgRouting, please visit the project website at `http://docs.pgrouting.org`.)

The installation of PostGIS with pgRouting won't be covered in detail here because instructions for the different operating systems can be found on the project's website at `http://docs.pgrouting.org/2.0/en/doc/src/installation/index.html`.

If you are using Windows, both PostGIS and pgRouting can be installed directly from the Stack Builder application, which is provided by the standard PostgreSQL installation, as described at `http://anitagraser.com/2013/07/06/pgrouting-2-0-for-windows-quick-guide/`.

Getting ready

To follow this exercise, you need a PostGIS database with pgRouting enabled. In QGIS, you should set up the connection to the database using the **New** button in the **Add PostGIS Layers** dialog. Additionally, you should load `network_pgr.shp` from the sample data.

How to do it...

These steps will create a routable network table in your PostGIS database:

1. Open **DB Manager** by navigating to **Database | DB Manager**.

2. In **Tree** on the left-hand side of the dialog, select the database that you want to load the network to.

3. Go to **Table | Import Layer/File** to load the `network_pgr` layer into your database, as shown in the following screenshot:

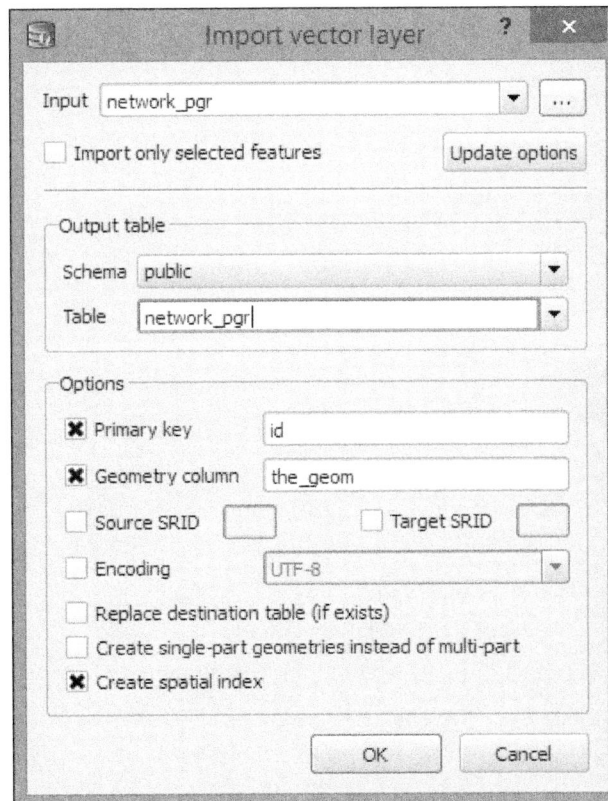

4. After `network_pgr` has been imported successfully, open the SQL window of DB Manager by pressing *F2*, clicking on the corresponding toolbar button, or in the **Database** menu.

5. pgRouting is a little picky when it comes to column data types. You will notice this when you see **Error, columns 'source', 'target' must be of type int4, 'cost' must be of type float8**. When we import `network_pgr` with QGIS's DB Manager, it creates the cost column as numeric. As pgRouting won't accept numeric, we will use **Table | Edit Table** in **DB Manager** to edit the cost column. Click on the **Edit column** button and change **Type** from **numeric** to **double precision** (which equals the required float8).

6. Now that the data is loaded and ready, we can build the network topology. This will create a new `network_pgr_vertices_pgr` table, which contains the computed network nodes:

    ```
    SELECT pgr_createTopology('network_pgr',0.001);
    ```

7. Once this topology is ready, we can test the network by calculating a simple shortest path from the node number 16 to the node number 9:

    ```
    SELECT pgr_dijkstra('SELECT id, source, target, cost
      FROM network_pgr', 16, 9, false, false);
    ```

    This will result in the following:

    ```
    (0,16,6,1)
    (1,17,7,1)
    (2,5,8,1)
    (3,6,9,1)
    (4,11,15,1)
    (5,9,-1,0)
    ```

How it works...

The preceding `pgr_dijkstra` query consists of the following parts:

►   `'SELECT id, source, target, cost FROM network_pgr'`: This is a SQL query, which returns a set of rows with the following columns:

►   `id`: This is the unique edge ID (type int4)

►   `source`: This is the ID of the edge source node (type int4)

►   `target`: This is the ID of the edge target node (type int4)

►   `cost`: This is the cost of the edge traversal (type float8)

►   `16, 9`: These are the IDs of the route source and target nodes (type int4)

- ▸ `false`: This is `true` if the graph is directed
- ▸ `false`: If `true`, the `reverse_cost` column of the SQL-generated set of rows will be used for the cost of the traversal of the edge in the opposite direction

The results of `pgr_dijkstra` contain the list of network links that our route uses to get from the start to the destination. The four values in reach result row are as follows:

- ▸ `seq`: This is the sequence number, which tells us the order of the links within the route starting from O
- ▸ `id1`: This is the node ID
- ▸ `id2`: This is the edge ID
- ▸ `cost`: This is the cost of the link (can be distance, travel time, a monetary value, or any other measure that you chose)

See also

In the following recipe, *Visualizing pgRouting results in QGIS*, we will see how to use the results of `pgr_dijkstra` to visualize the route on a map.

If you are interested in more pgRouting SQL recipes, you will find a whole chapter on this topic in *PostGIS Cookbook* by Packt Publishing.

Visualizing the pgRouting results in QGIS

In the previous recipe, *Creating a routing network for pgRouting*, we imported a network layer, built the topology, and finally tested the routing. Building on these results, this recipe will show you how to visualize the routing results on a map in QGIS.

Getting ready

You should first go through the previous recipe, *Creating a routing network for pgRouting*, to set up the necessary PostGIS tables. Alternatively, you can use your own network tables, but be aware that you may have to alter some of the SQL statements if your table uses different column names.

How to do it...

To visualize the results in QGIS, we can use the DB Manager SQL window, as shown in the following screenshot. The extended query that we use here joins the routing results back to the original network table to get the route link geometries, which we want to display on the map:

1. Open DB Manager by navigating to **Database | DB Manager**.

2. In **Tree** to the left of the dialog, select the database that you want to load the network to.

3. Open the SQL window of DB Manager and configure it, as shown in the following screenshot:

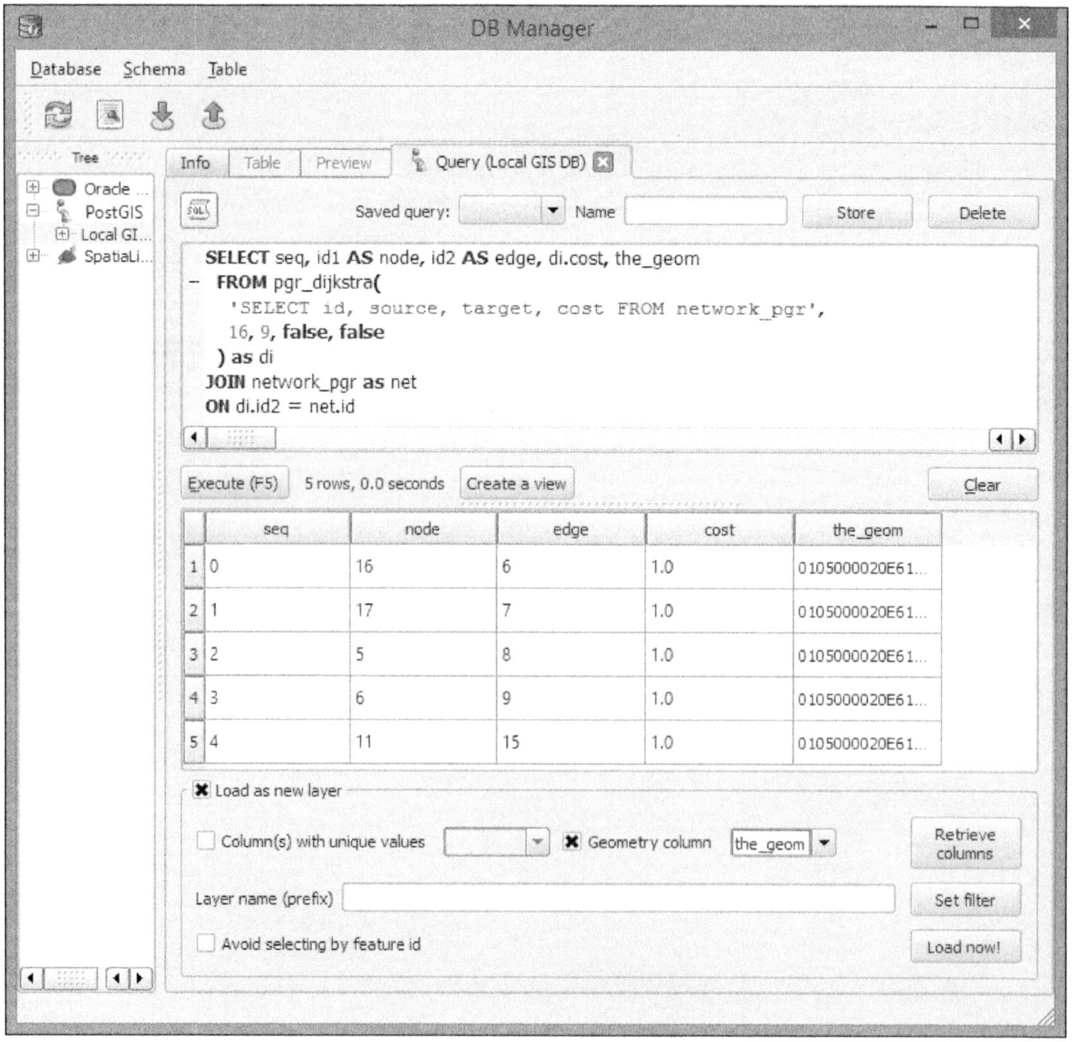

> Note that there must not be a semicolon at the end of the SQL statement. Otherwise, loading the results as a new layer will fail.

4. Make sure that the **Geometry** column is selected correctly and click on the **Load now!** button to load the query result as a new layer, as shown in the following screenshot:

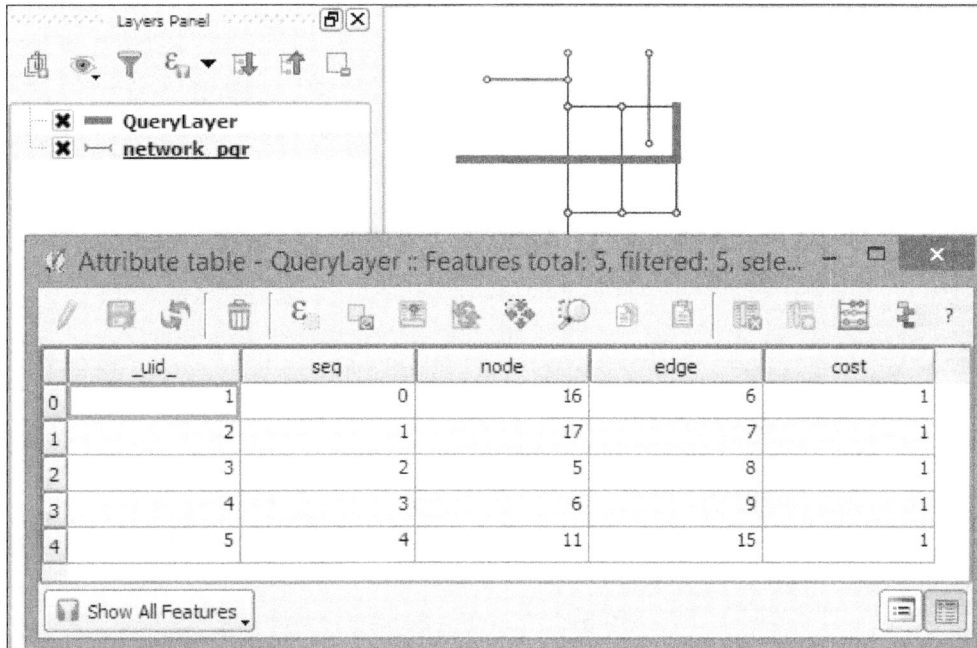

How it works...

As `pgr_dijkstra` only returns a list with the IDs of the route edges, we need to get the edge geometries from the original network table in order to display the route on the map. Therefore, we join the routing results with the network table on `id2` (which contains the edge ID) and the network table's `id` column.

See also

To make using pgRouting from within QGIS more convenient, the pgRoutingLayer plugin provides a GUI to access many of pgRouting's functions. You will find an introduction to this plugin in the *Using the pgRoutingLayer plugin for convenience* recipe.

Using the pgRoutingLayer plugin for convenience

The previous recipe, *Visualizing pgRouting results in QGIS*, showed you how to manually add pgRouting results to the map. In this chapter, we will use the pgRoutingLayer plugin to get more convenient access to the functions that pgRouting offers, including the most basic algorithms, such as Dijkstra's algorithm, which we have used so far, to more complex algorithms, such as `drivingDistance` and `alphashape`, which can be used to visualize catchment zones, also known as service areas.

Getting ready

You should first go through the previous recipe, *Creating a routing network for pgRouting*, to set up the necessary PostGIS tables. Alternatively, you can use your own network tables, but be aware that you may have to alter some of the SQL statements if your table uses different column names.

Additionally, install the pgRoutingLayer plugin from Plugin Installer. You will need to enable experimental plugins in **Settings** to view this.

How to do it...

The pgRoutingLayer plugin adds a new panel to the QGIS GUI, which allows convenient access to the available routing functions. The following steps show you how to use this plugin:

1. First, you should select a database from the **Database** field that contains your routing network table. The drop-down list contains all the configured PostGIS connections.

2. Next, you can select a function from the **Function** field that you want to use. Let's try Dijkstra's algorithm first; select the `dijkstra` function. You will recognize the parameters from the previous recipes where we wrote the pgRouting SQL query manually.

3. Specify the parameters for the network table (`edge_table`) and the **geometry**, **id**, **source**, **target**, and **cost** columns, as shown in the following screenshot:

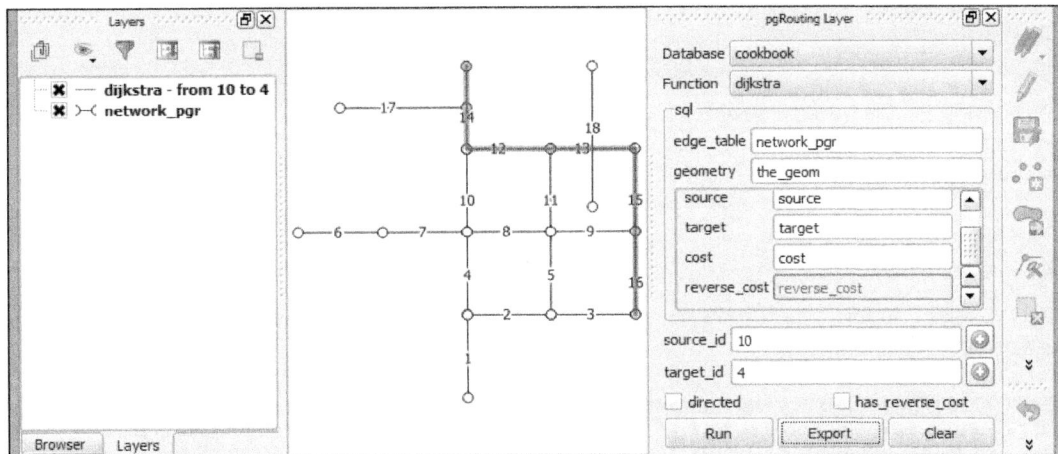

4. Now, you can use the green **+** buttons beside the **source_id** and **target_id** input fields to select the source and target nodes in the map.

5. When everything is configured, you can click on the **Run** button to compute and display the route.

6. Next, you can switch functions and compute a service area. Select the `alphashape` function. The rest of the input fields adapt automatically to the selected function.

7. Now, you can use the green **+** button right beside the **source_id** input field to select the starting or center node of the service area.

8. Then, select the size of the service area by specifying the **distance** limit.

9. Finally, click on the **Run** button to compute and display the service area, as shown in the following screenshot:

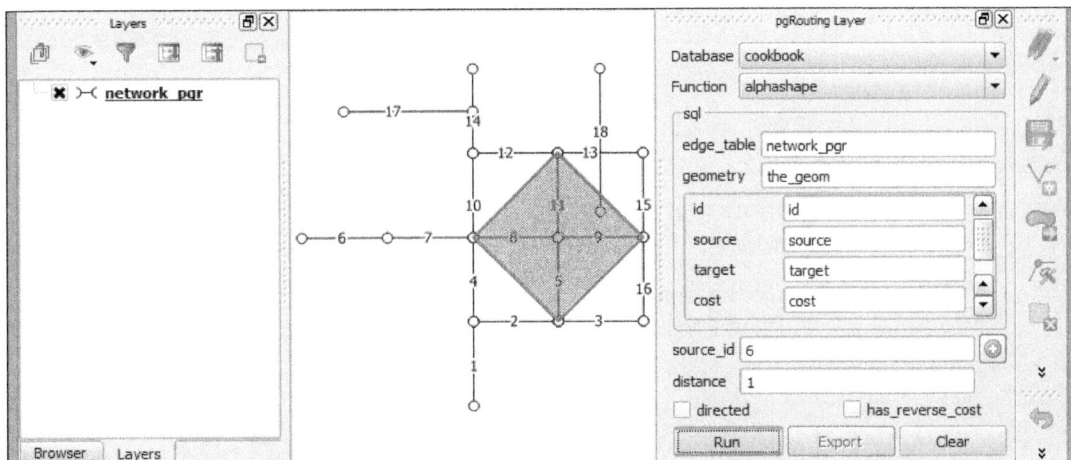

How it works...

When we click on the **Run** button, the query results are visualized as a temporary overlay on the map. If you want to save the output permanently, you can click on the **Export** button. Currently, the **Export** button is only available for the routing functions but not for the service area functions.

See also

For a detailed documentation on the pgRouting algorithms, refer to the project documentation website at `http://docs.pgrouting.org/2.0/en/doc/index.html`.

Getting network data from the OSM

A popular data source for real-world routing applications is **OpenStreetMap** (**OSM**). This recipe shows you how to prepare OSM data for usage with pgRouting using the osm2po command-line tool to convert OSM data to an insert script for PostGIS. Finally, we will test the data import using the pgRoutingLayer plugin.

Getting ready

Download osm2po from `http://osm2po.de` and unpack the download. Note that osm2po requires Java to be installed on your machine.

You also need a pgRouting-enabled database to follow this recipe.

Additionally, you should have the pgRoutingLayer plugin installed and enabled because we will use this to test the OSM data import.

You can use the `wake.pbf` OSM file from our sample data, or download your own data from services such as `http://download.geofabrik.de`.

How to do it...

Open the command line to perform the following steps. If you are working on Windows, we recommend using the osgeo4W Shell:

1. Go to the `osm2po` folder and open `osm2po.config` in a text editor. Look for the following configuration line and remove the # at the beginning of the line to activate the pgRouting export:

    ```
    postp.0.class = de.cm.osm2po.plugins.postp.PgRoutingWriter
    ```

2. Now use osm2po to convert the OSM `.pbf` file to SQL. Adjust the file paths for your system, as follows:

```
D:\osm2po-5.1.0>java -jar osm2po-core-5.1.0-signed.jar prefix=wake
"C:\tmp\OSM_NorthCarolina\wake.pbf"
```

3. When osm2po is finished, you should see the following:

```
INFO Services started. Waiting for requests at
http://localhost:8888/Osm2poService
```

4. You should now find a folder with the name of the prefix (that is, `wake`) inside the `osm2po` folder. This contains a log file, which in turn provides a command-line template to import the OSM network to PostGIS:

```
INFO commandline template:
psql -U [username] -d [dbname] -q -f
"D:\osm2po-5.1.0\wake\wake_2po_4pgr.sql"
```

5. Using this template, we can easily import the `.sql` file into an existing database, as follows:

```
D:\osm2po-5.1.0\wake>psql -U [username] -d cookbook -q -f D:\
osm2po-5.1.0\wake\wake_2po_4pgr.sql
```

6. Now, the data is ready for use in QGIS. When we connect to the cookbook database, we can see the `wake_2po_4pgr` table:

7. Finally, we can use the **pgRouting Layer** plugin to test the OSM data import by calculating a service area of **0.1** hours (the **distance** value) around the **43679** (**source_id**) source node number:

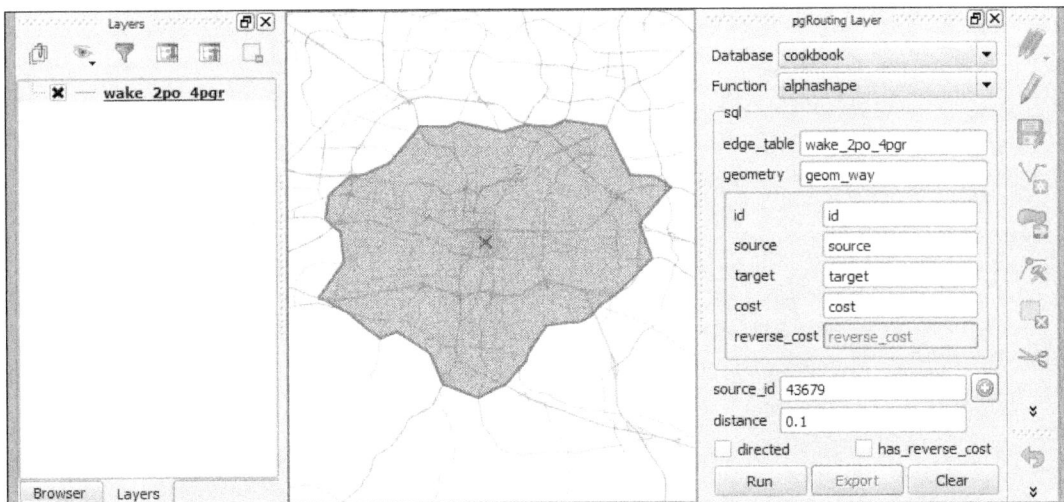

How it works...

The network table created by osm2po contains, among others, the following useful columns:

- ▸ `km`: This is the length of the network edge

- ▸ `kmh`: The is the speed on the edge, depending on the street class and the values specified in the osm2po configuration

- ▸ `cost`: This is the travel time computed using km/kmh

7
Raster Analysis I

In this chapter, we will cover the following recipes:

- ▶ Using the raster calculator
- ▶ Preparing elevation data
- ▶ Calculating a slope
- ▶ Calculating a hillshade layer
- ▶ Analyzing hydrology
- ▶ Calculating a topographic index
- ▶ Automate analysis tasks using the graphical modeler

Introduction

Raster analysis is a classic area in GIS analysis. This chapter shows you some of the most important and common tasks of raster analysis. Elevation data is commonly stored as raster layers, and in this format, it is particularly suitable to run a large variety of analysis. For this reason, terrain analysis has traditionally been one of the main areas of raster analysis, and we will show you some of the most common operations that are related to **Digital Elevation Models** (**DEM**), from simple analysis, such as slope calculation, to more complex ones, such as drainage network delineation or watershed extraction.

Using the raster calculator

The raster calculator is one of the most flexible and versatile tools in QGIS. This allows you to perform algebraic operations based on raster layers, and compute new layers. This recipe shows you how to use it.

Getting ready

Open the `catchment_area.tif` file. The file should look like the following screenshot:

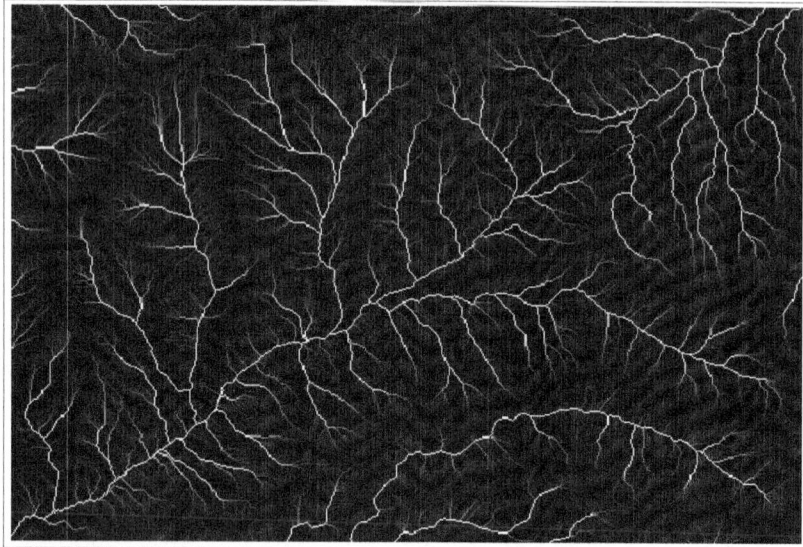

How to do it...

1. Open the **Processing Toolbox** option and find the algorithm called **Raster calculator** by searching for it using the search box. Double-click on the algorithm item to execute it, as shown in the following screenshot:

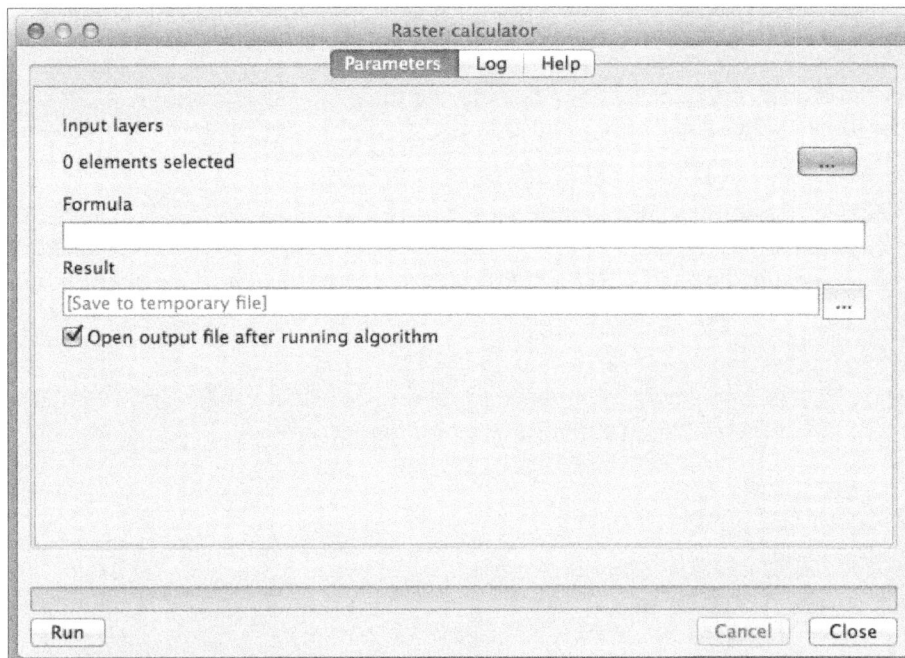

2.   Click on the button in the **Input layers** field to open the layer selector. There is only one layer available: the `catchment_area` layer. Select this layer.

3.   In the **Formula** field, enter `ln(a)`.

4.   Click on **Run** to run the algorithm. The resulting layer will be added to the QGIS project, as follows:

How it works...

The layers selected in the layer selector are referred to using a single letter in alphabetical order (a for the first one, b for the second one, and so on). In this case, we selected just one layer, so we can refer to it as a in the formula.

The formula calculates a natural logarithm of the values in the catchment area layer. The distribution of values in this layer is not homogeneous because it contains a large number of cells with low values and just a few of them with very large values. This causes the rendering of the layer to be not very informative with most of the colors in the color ramp not even being used.

The resulting layer is much more informative because applying the logarithm alters the distribution of values, resulting in a more explicit rendering.

There's more...

QGIS contains a raster calculator module outside of Processing. You can find this by navigating to **Raster | Raster calculator...**:

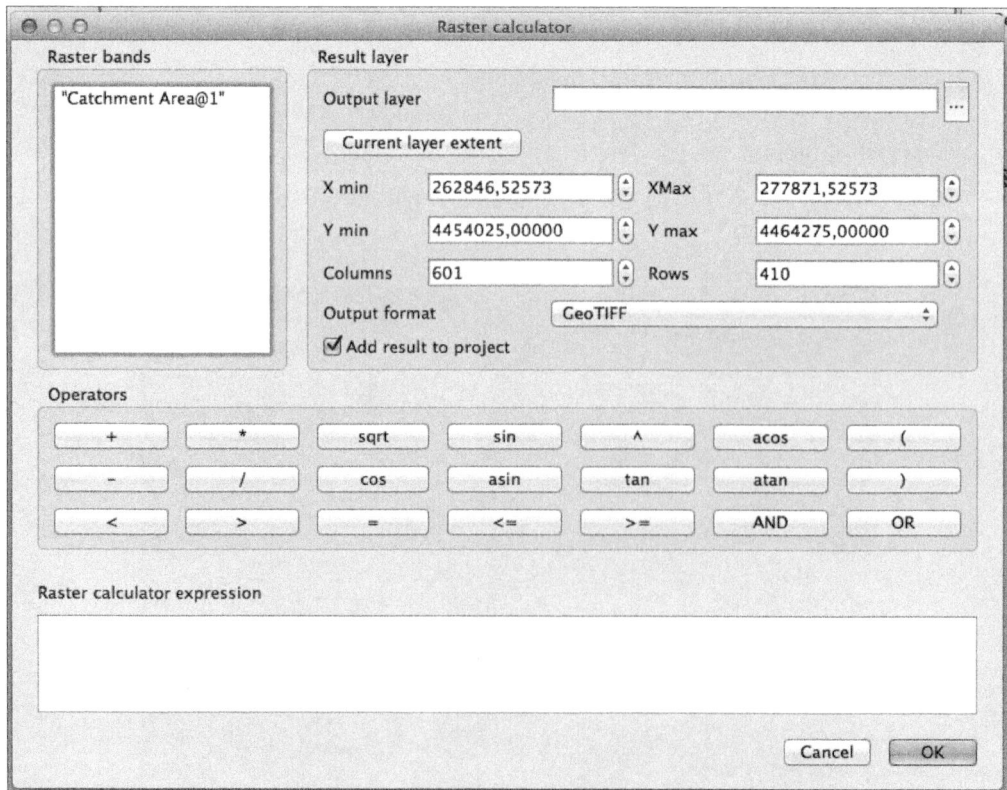

This interface resembles an actual calculator, and it is more intuitive and user friendly. On the other hand, this lacks many of the functions that are available in the Processing raster calculator (the logarithm that we have computed, for instance, is not available). This also cannot be used in automated processes, such as scripts or graphical models, which are only available for the Processing algorithms.

On the other hand, the QGIS built-in calculator supports multiband layers, while the Processing one is limited to single-band ones.

See also

▶ The QGIS raster calculator is described in more detail in the QGIS manual at `http://docs.qgis.org/2.8/en/docs/user_manual/working_with_raster/raster_calculator.html`

Preparing elevation data

In this recipe, we will show you how to perform terrain analysis in QGIS. Terrain analysis algorithms assume certain characteristics in the DEMs that are used as inputs, so it is important to know them and prepare these DEMs if they are needed. This recipe shows you how to do this.

Getting ready

Open the `dem_to_prepare.tif` layer. This layer contains a DEM in the EPSG:4326 CRS and elevation data in feet. These characteristics are unsuitable to run most terrain analysis algorithms, so we will modify this layer to get a suitable one.

How to do it...

1. Reproject the layer to the EPSG:3857 CRS, using the **Save as...** entry in the context menu that appears by right-clicking on the layer name.
2. Open the resulting reprojected layer.
3. Open the Processing raster calculator and select the reprojected layer as the only raster input in the **Input layers** field. Enter a `*` `0.3048` in the **Formula** field. Run the algorithm.

How it works...

Most of the algorithms that we are going to use assume that the horizontal units (the unit used to measure the size of the cell) are the same as the units used in the elevation values that are contained in the layer. If the layer does not meet this requirement, the result of the analysis will be wrong.

Our input layer uses a CRS with geographic coordinates (degrees). As elevation cannot be measured in degrees, the layer cannot have the same units for horizontal and vertical distances, and it is not ready to be used for terrain analysis.

By reprojecting the layer to the EPSG:3857 CRS, we get a new layer in which coordinates are expressed in meters. This is a unit that is more suitable for the type of analysis that we plan to run. Actually, after the reprojection, the units are meters only near the equator, but this gives us enough precision for this case. If more precise calculations are needed, a local projection system should be used.

The next step is converting the elevation values in feet to elevation values in meters. Knowing that 1 foot = 0.3048 meter, we just have to use the calculator to apply this formula and convert the values in the reprojected layer.

There's more...

There are other things that must be taken into account when running a terrain analysis algorithm to ensure that results are correct.

One common problem is dealing with different cell sizes. An assumption that is made by most terrain analysis algorithms (and also most of the ones not related to terrain analysis) is that cells are square. That is, their horizontal and vertical values are the same. This is the case in our input layer (you can verify this by checking the layer properties), but it may not be true for other layers.

In this case, you should export the layer and define the sizes of the cells of the exported layer to have the same value. Right-click on the layer name and select **Save as...**. In the save dialog that will appear, enter the new sizes of the cells in the lower part of the dialog:

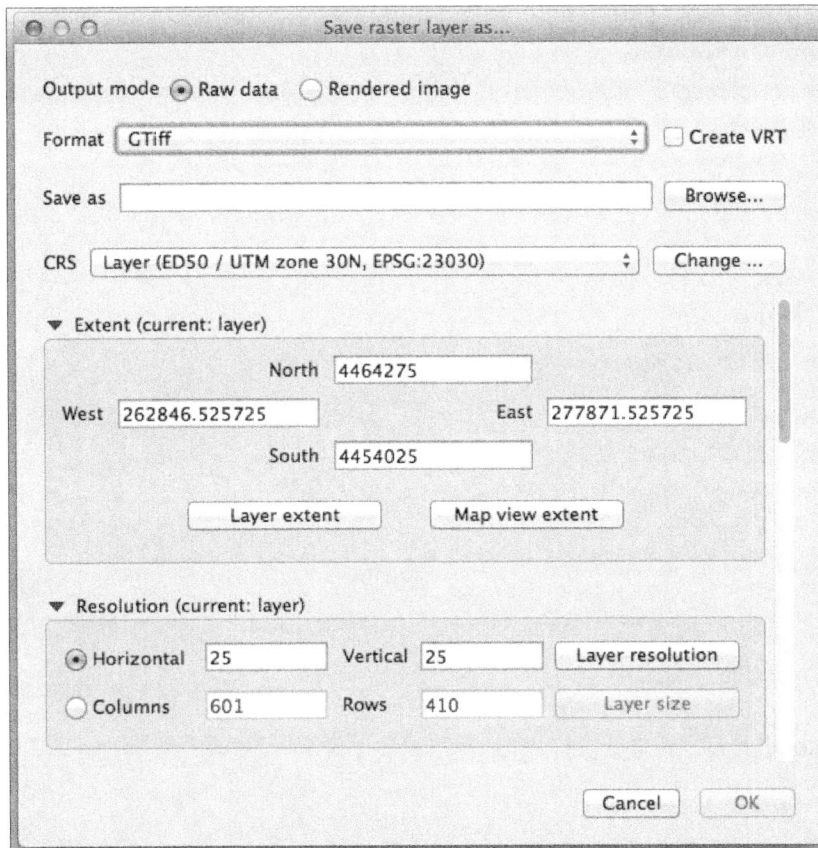

Calculating a slope

Slope is one of the most basic parameters that can be derived from a DEM. It corresponds to the first derivative of the DEM, and it represents the rate of change of the elevation. It is computed by analyzing the elevation of each cell and comparing this with the elevation of the surrounding ones. This recipe shows you how to compute slope in QGIS.

Getting ready

Open the DEM that we prepared in the previous recipe.

How to do it...

1. In the **Processing Toolbox** option, find the **Slope** algorithm and double-click on it to open it:

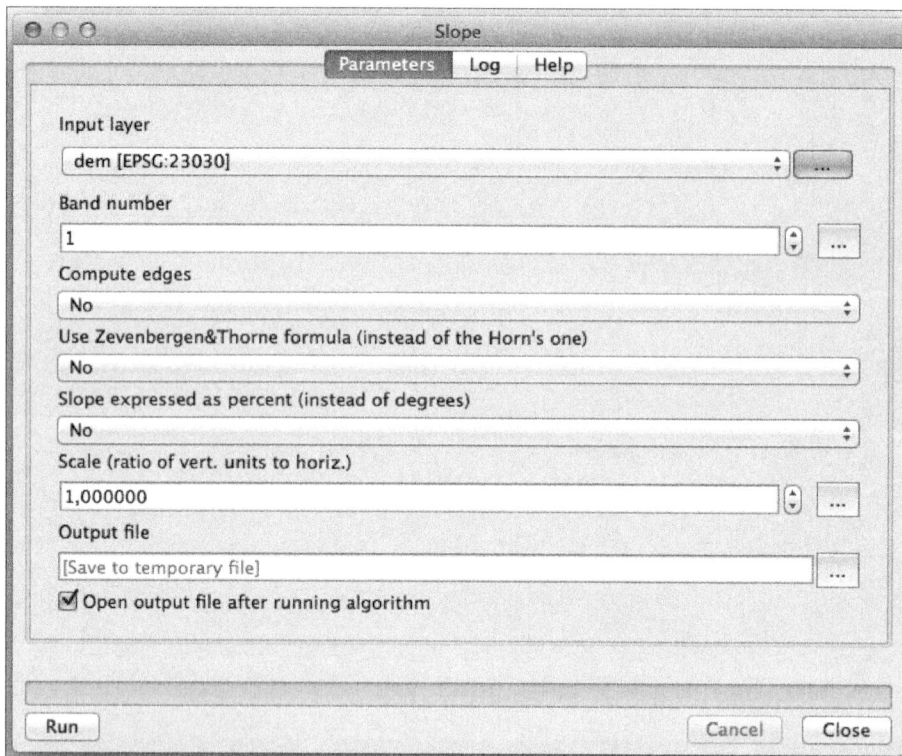

```
⊖ ◯ ◯                          Slope
                    Parameters    Log    Help

  Input layer
  [ dem [EPSG:23030]                              ⇕ ][ ... ]

  Band number
  [ 1                                             ⇕ ][ ... ]

  Compute edges
  [ No                                                 ⇕ ]

  Use Zevenbergen&Thorne formula (instead of the Horn's one)
  [ No                                                 ⇕ ]

  Slope expressed as percent (instead of degrees)
  [ No                                                 ⇕ ]

  Scale (ratio of vert. units to horiz.)
  [ 1,000000                                      ⇕ ][ ... ]

  Output file
  [ [Save to temporary file]                        ][ ... ]
  ☑ Open output file after running algorithm


  [_____]

  [ Run ]                              [ Cancel ]  [ Close ]
```

2. Select the DEM in the **Input layer** field.
3. Click on **Run** to run the algorithm.

The slope layer will be added to the QGIS project.

How it works...

Slope is calculated from a DEM elevation model by analyzing the cells around a given one. This analysis is performed by the slope algorithm from the GDAL library.

There's more...

There are several ways of using the slope algorithms in QGIS. Here are some comments and ideas about this.

Using a ratio for elevation values

If the units of elevation are not the same as the horizontal units, you can convert them, as we did in the previous recipe, using the raster calculator. However, the slope module contains an option to convert them on-the-fly by entering the conversion factor in the Scale field. Note that this option is not available in other terrain analysis modules that we will use, so it's still good practice to create a layer with the correct units, which can be used without any further processing.

Other slope algorithms

The Processing framework contains algorithms that rely on several external applications and libraries. These libraries sometimes contain similar algorithms, so there is more than one option for a given analysis.

If you switch the presentation mode of the toolbox from **simplified** to **advanced** using the lower part of the drop-down list and then type **slope** in the search box, you will see something like the following screenshot:

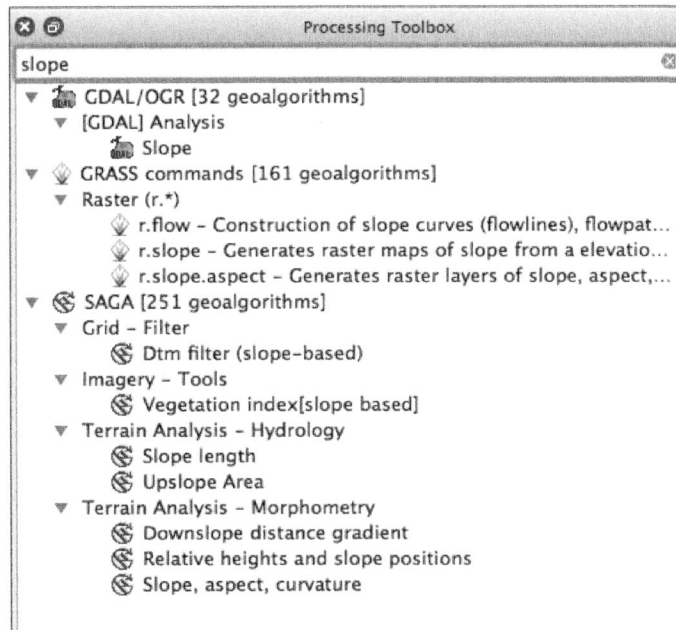

Calculating the slope

Try using the GRASS or SAGA algorithm to calculate the slope. Each of them has different parameters and options, but all of them perform similar calculations and create slope layers.

Apart from Processing, you can also perform analysis using the Raster Terrain Analysis plugin.

See also

▸ The *Using the raster calculator* recipe in the beginning of this chapter

Calculating a hillshade layer

A hillshade layer is commonly used to enhance the appearance of a map and display topography in an intuitive way, by simulating a light source and the shadows it casts. This can be computed from a DEM by using this recipe.

Getting ready

Open the DEM that we prepared in the *Preparing elevation data* recipe.

How to do it...

1. In the **Processing Toolbox** option, find the **Hillshade** algorithm and double-click on it to open it:

2. Select the DEM in the **Input layer** field. Leave the rest of the parameters with their default values.

3. Click on **Run** to run the algorithm.

The hillshade layer will be added to the QGIS project, as follows:

How it works...

As in the case of the slope, the algorithm is part of the GDAL library. You will see that the parameters are very similar to the slope case. This is because slope is used to compute the hillshade layer. Based on the slope and the aspect of the terrain in each cell and using the position of the sun that is defined by the **Azimuth** and **Altitude** fields, the algorithm computes the illumination that the cell will receive. This is based on a focal analysis, so shadows are not considered and are not a real illumination value, but they can be used to render and to display the topography of the terrain.

You can try changing the values of these parameters to alter the appearance of the layer.

There's more...

As in the case of slope, there are alternative options to compute the hillshade. The SAGA one in the **Processing Toolbox** option has a feature that is worth mentioning.

The SAGA hillshade algorithm contains a field named **method**. This field is used to select the method that is used to compute the hillshade value, and the last method that is available. **Raytracing** differs from the other ones as it models the real behavior of light, making an analysis that is not local but that uses the full information of the DEM instead because it takes into account the shadows that are cast by the surrounding relief. This renders more precise hillshade layers, but the processing time can be notably larger.

Enhancing your map view with a hillshade layer

You can combine the hillshade layer with your other layers to enhance their appearance.

As you used a DEM to compute the hillshade layer, it should be already in your QGIS project along with the hillshade itself. However, this will be covered by the hillshade because of the new layers produced by Processing are added on top of the existing ones in the layers list. Move it to the top of the layer list so that you can see the DEM (and not the hillshade layer) and style it to something like the following screenshot:

Lets see the steps to enhance the map view with a hillshade layer:

1. In the **Properties** dialog of the layer, move to the **Transparency** section, and set the **Global transparency** value to **50**%, as shown in the following screenshot:

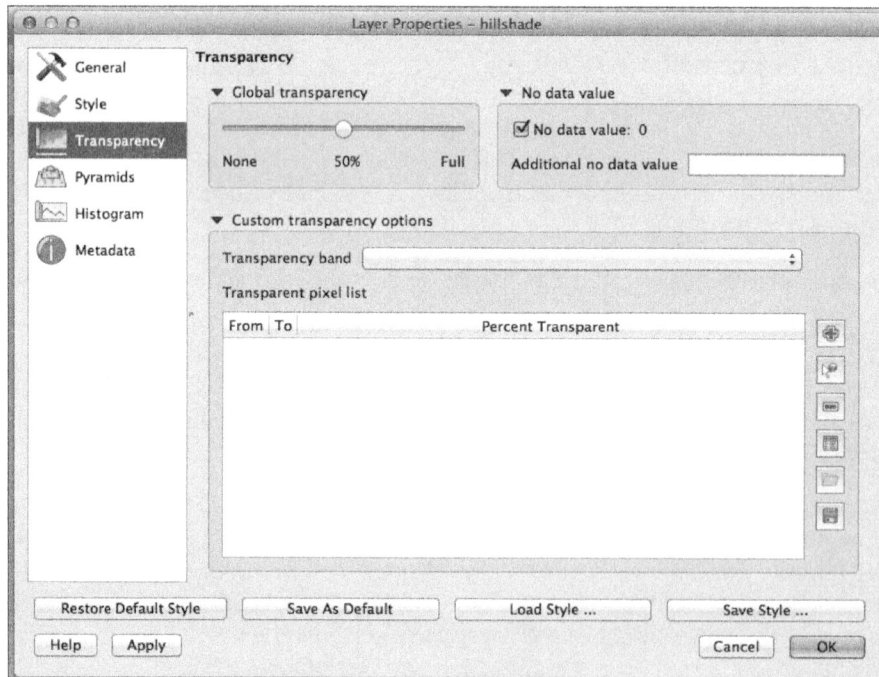

2. Now, you should see the hillshade layer through the DEM, and the combination of both of them will look like the following screenshot:

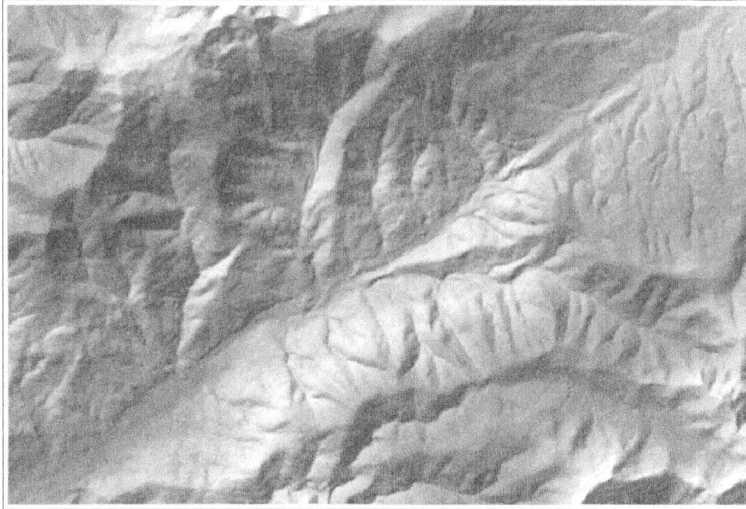

Another way of doing this is using the blending modes in QGIS. You can find more information about this in the recipe, *Understanding the feature and layer blending modes* of *Chapter 10*, *Cartography Tips*, or in the QGIS manual at `http://docs.qgis.org/2.8/en/docs/user_manual/working_with_vector/vector_properties.html#style-menu`.

Analyzing hydrology

A common analysis from a DEM is to compute hydrological elements, such as the channel network or the set of watersheds. This recipe shows you the steps to do these analysis.

Getting ready

Open the DEM that we prepared in the *Preparing elevation data* recipe.

How to do it...

1. In the **Processing Toolbox** option, find the **Fill Sinks** algorithm and double-click on it to open it:

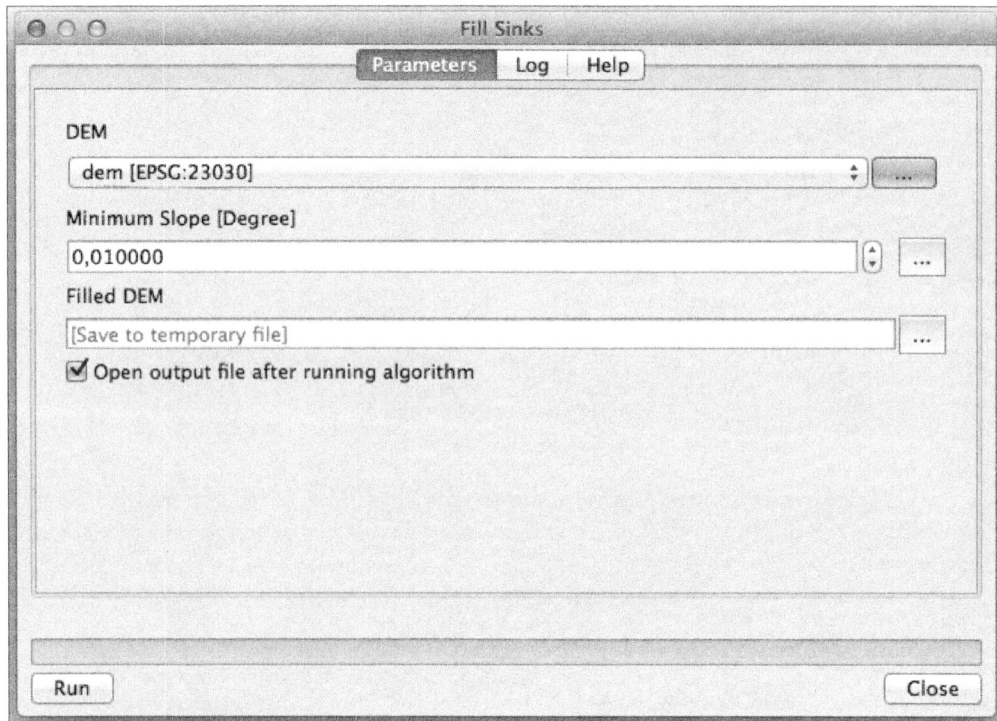

Fill Sinks

Parameters | Log | Help

DEM

dem [EPSG:23030]

Minimum Slope [Degree]

0,010000

Filled DEM

[Save to temporary file]

☑ Open output file after running algorithm

Run | Close

2. Select the DEM in the **DEM** field and run the algorithm. This will generate a new filtered DEM layer. From now on, we will just use this DEM in the recipe and not the original one.

3. Open **Catchment Area** and select the filtered DEM in the **Elevation** field:

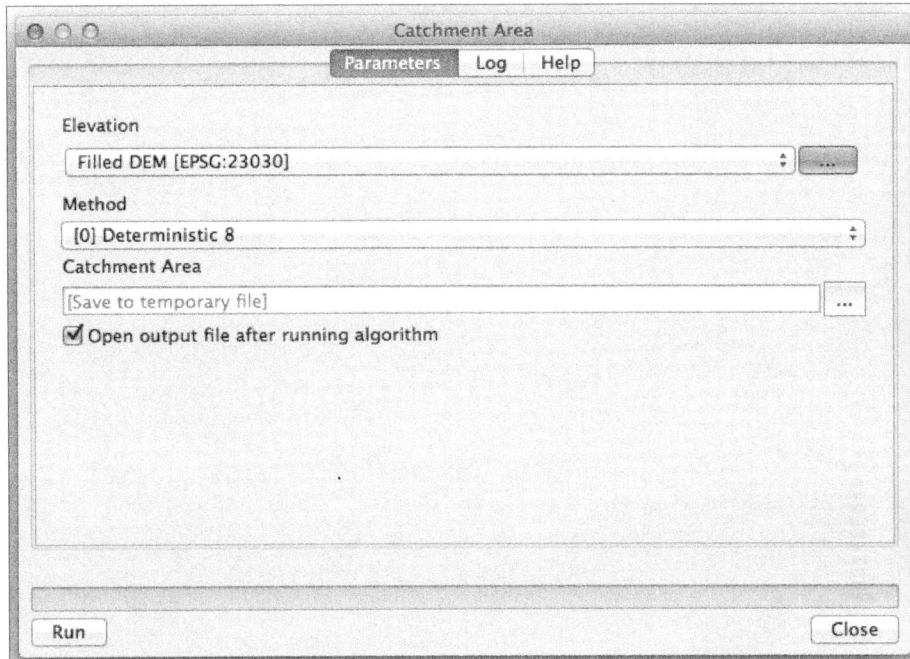

4. Run the algorithm. This will generate a catchment area layer:

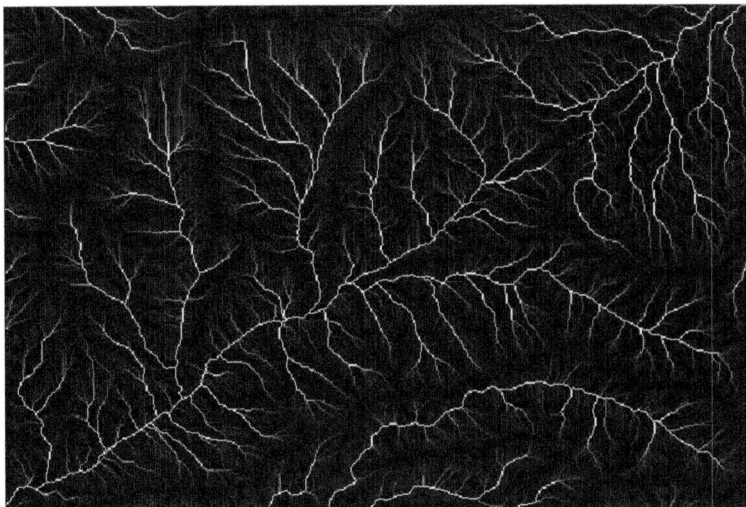

5. Open the **Channel network** algorithm and fill it in, as shown in the following screenshot:

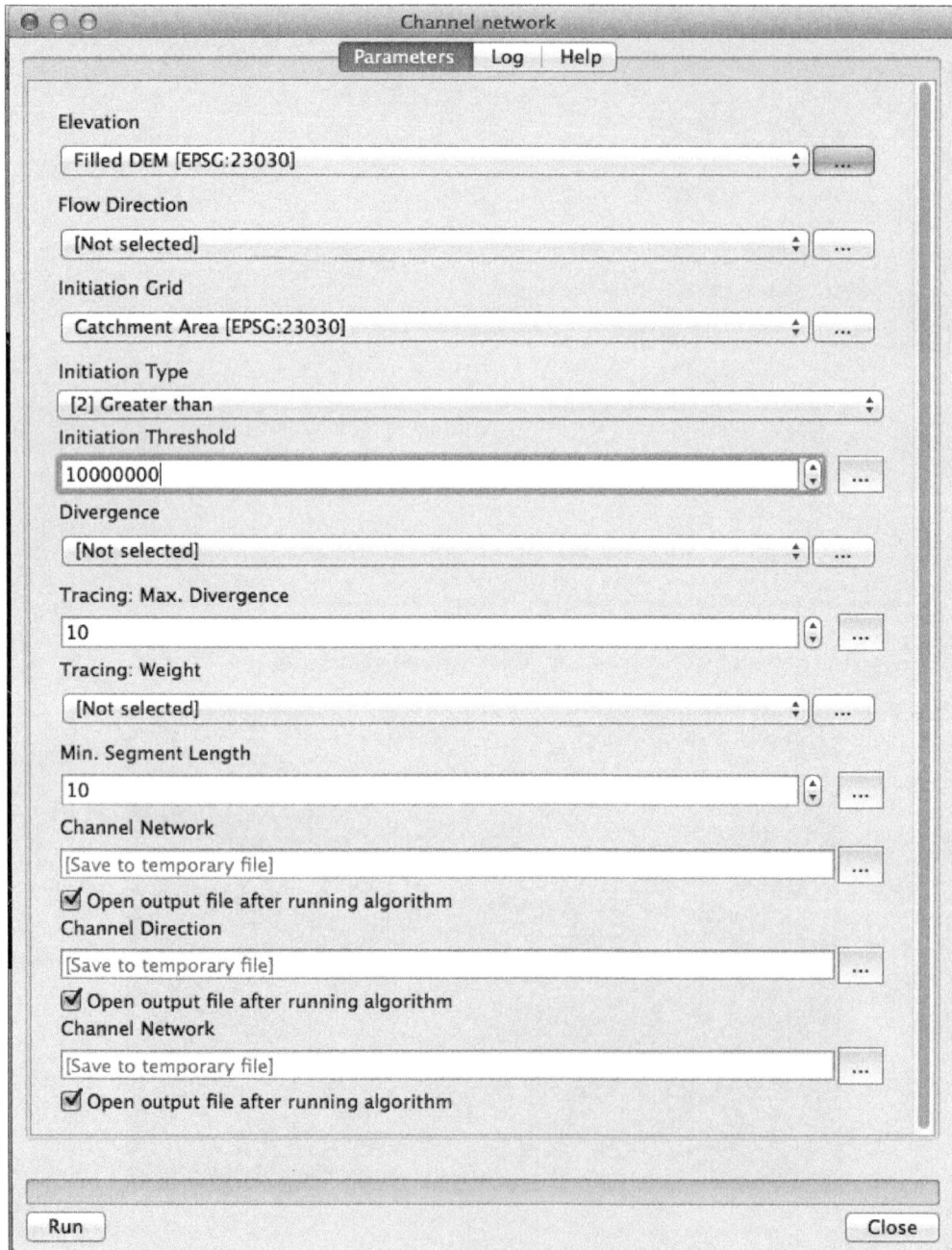

6. Run the algorithm. This will extract the channel network from the DEM, based on the catchment area, and it will then generate it as both a raster and vector layer:

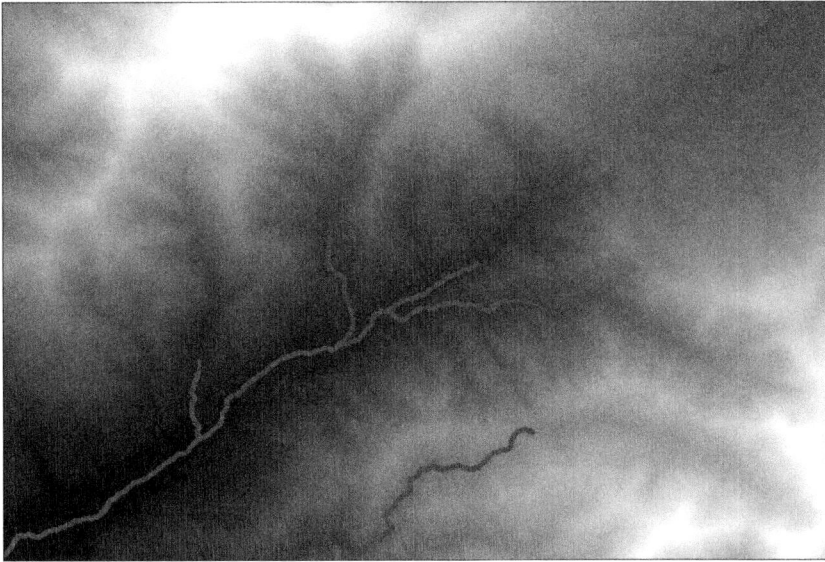

7. Open the **Watershed basins** algorithm and fill it in, as shown in the following screenshot:

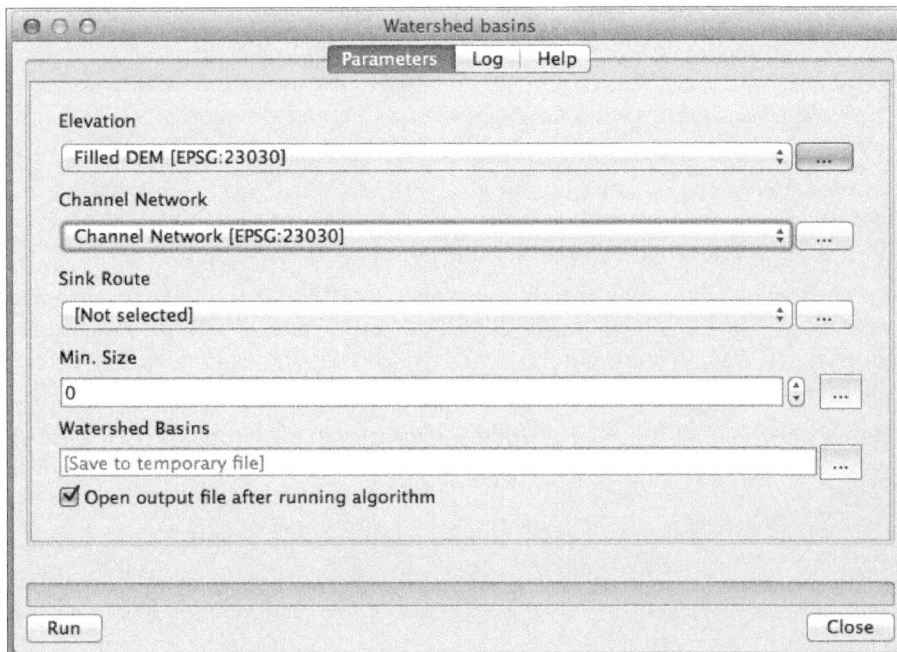

8. Run the algorithm. This will generate a raster layer with the watersheds calculated from the DEM and the channel network. Each watershed is a hydrological unit that represents the area that flows into a junction, which is defined by the channel network:

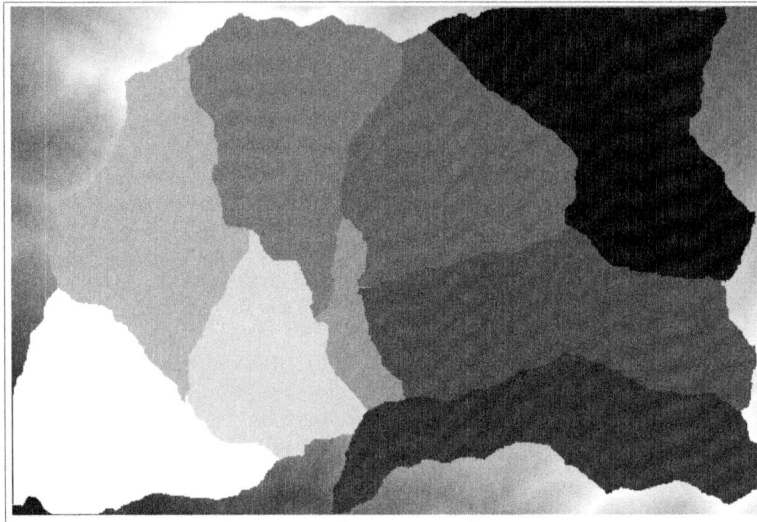

How it works...

Starting from the DEM, the preceding steps follow a typical workflow for hydrological analysis:

▸ First, the sinks are filled. This is a required preparation whenever you plan to perform a hydrological analysis. The DEM may contain sinks where a flow direction cannot be computed, which represents a problem to model the movement of water across these cells. Removing these sinks solves this problem.

▸ The catchment area is computed from the DEM. The values in the catchment area layer represent the area that is upstream of each cell. That is, the total area in which if water is dropped, it will eventually pass through the cell.

▸ Cells with high values of the catchment area will likely contain a river, while cells with lower values will have overland flow. By setting a threshold on the catchment area values, we can separate the river cells (the ones above the threshold) from the remaining ones and extract the channel network.

▸ Finally, we compute the watersheds associated with each junction in the channel network that was extracted in the last step.

There's more...

The key parameter in the preceding workflow is the catchment area threshold. If a larger threshold is used, fewer cells will be considered as river cells, and the resulting channel network will be sparser. As the watershed is computed based on the channel network, this will result in a lower number of watersheds.

You can try this yourself with different values of the catchment area threshold. Here, you can see the result for threshold is equal to 1,000,000 in the following screenshot:

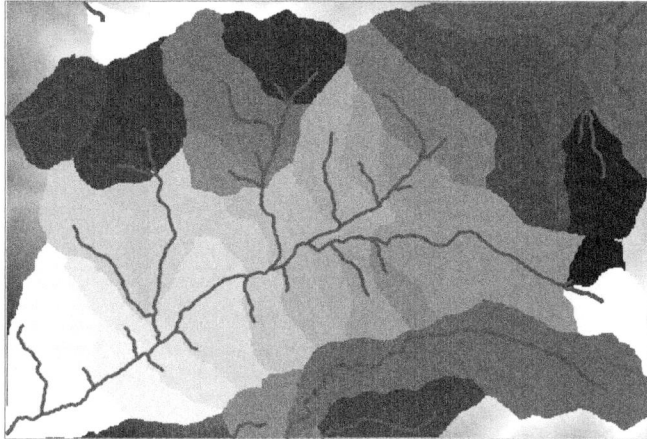

The channel network has been added to help you understand the structure of the resulting set of watersheds.

Here, you can see the result for a threshold of 50,000,000 in the following screenshot:

Note that in this last case, with a higher threshold value, there is only one single watershed in the resulting layer.

The threshold values are expressed in the units of the catchment area which, as the size of the cell is assumed to be in meters, are in square meters.

Calculating a topographic index

As the topography defines and influences most of the processes that take place in a given terrain, the DEM can be used to extract many different parameters, which give us information about these processes. This recipe shows you how to calculate a popular one, which is called the Topographic wetness index, which estimates the soil wetness based on the topography.

Getting ready

Open the DEM that we prepared in the *Preparing elevation data* recipe.

How to do it...

1. Calculate a slope layer using the **Slope, aspect, curvature** algorithm from SAGA in the **Processing Toolbox** option. Calculate a catchment area layer using the **Catchment area** algorithm from the **Processing Toolbox** option. Note that you must use a sink-less DEM, such as the one that we generated in the previous recipe with the **Fill sinks** algorithm.

   Open the **Topographic wetness index** algorithm from the **Processing Toolbox** option and fill it in, as shown in the following screenshot:

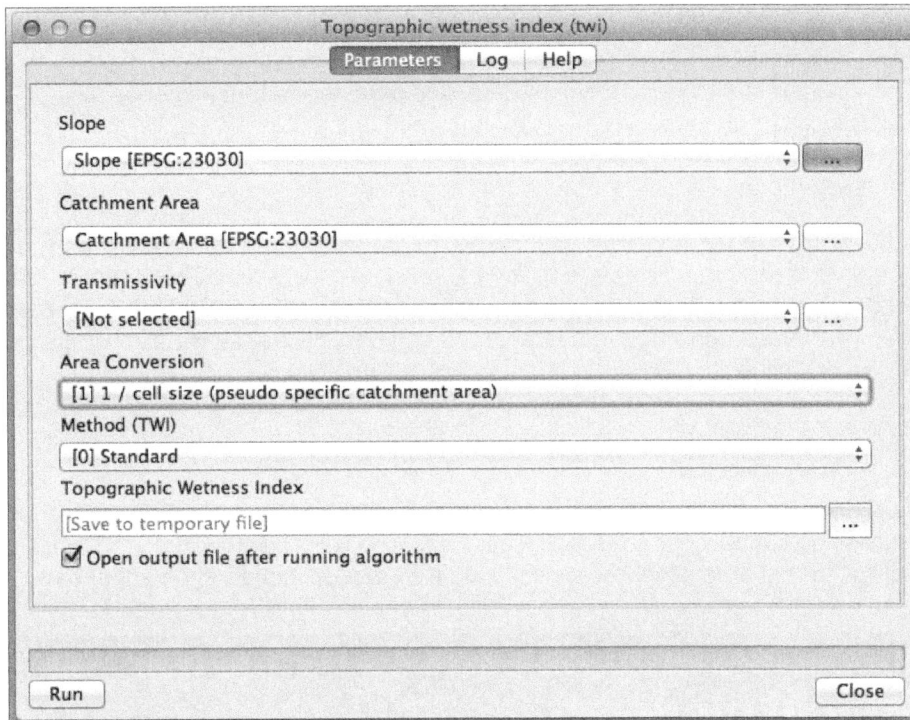

2. Run the algorithm. This will create a layer with the topographic wetness index, indicating the soil wetness in each cell:

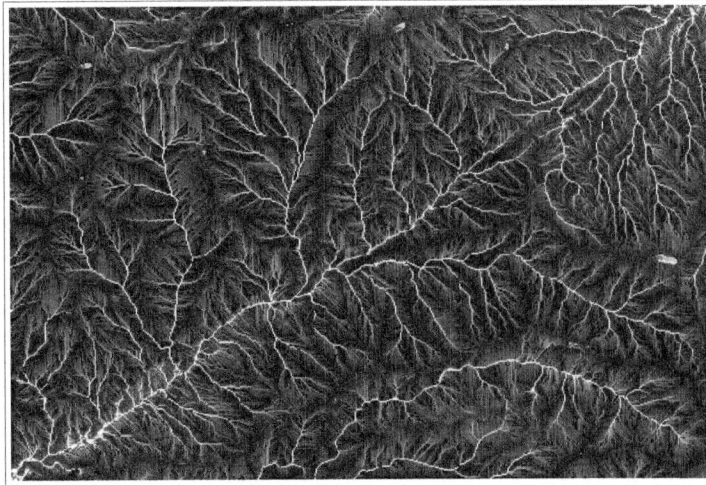

How it works...

The index combines slope and catchment area, two parameters that influence the soil wetness. If the catchment area value is high, this means that more water will flow into the cell, thus, increasing its soil wetness. A low value of slope will have a similar effect because the water that flows into the cell will not flow out of it quickly.

This algorithm expects the slope to be expressed in radians. This is the reason why the **Slope, aspect, curvature** algorithm has to be used because it produces its slope output in radians. The other **Slope** algorithm that you will find, which is based on the GDAL library, creates a slope layer with values expressed in degrees. You can use this layer if you convert its units using the raster calculator.

There's more...

Other indices that are based on the same input layers can be found in different algorithms in the **Processing Toolbox** option. The Stream Power Index and the LS factor both use the slope and catchment area as inputs as well, and they can be related to potential erosion.

Automating analysis tasks using the graphical modeler

Most analysis tasks involve using several algorithms. Repeating the same analysis with a different dataset or different input parameters requires using them one by one, making this task tedious and error-prone. You can automate analysis workflows using the Processing graphical modeler, which allows you to define a workflow graphically and wrap it in a single algorithm. This recipe introduces the main ideas about the modeler and creates a simple model as an example.

Getting ready

No special preparation is needed in QGIS for this recipe, but make sure that you have read the previous recipe about computing a topographic index. This recipe will create a model based on the workflow in that recipe, so it is important that you understand it.

How to do it...

1. Open the graphical modeler by navigating to **Processing | Graphical modeler**:

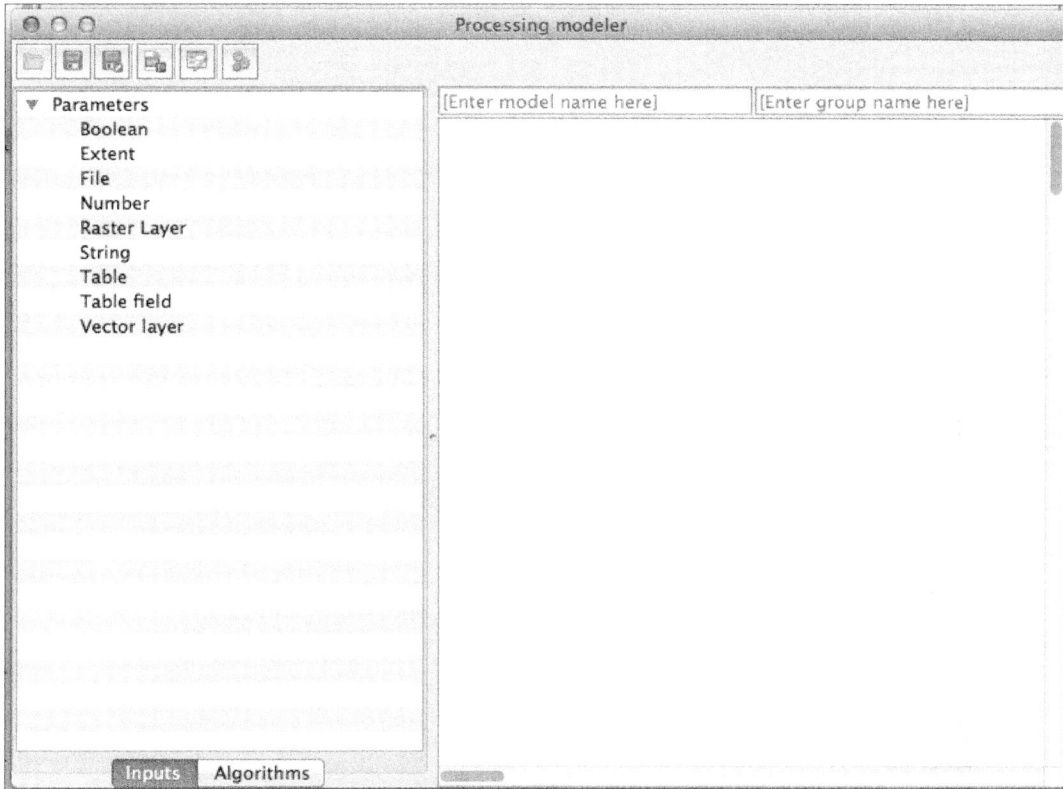

2. Double-click on the **Raster Layer** item to add a raster input. In the dialog that will appear to define the input, name it DEM and set it as mandatory:

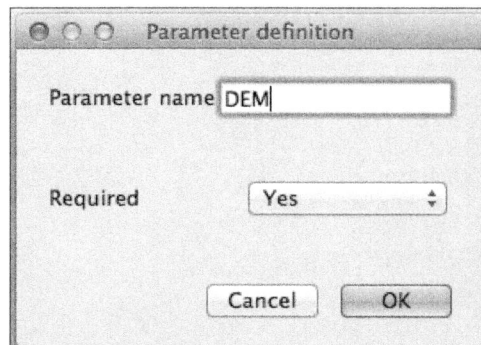

3. Click on **OK** to add the input to the canvas:

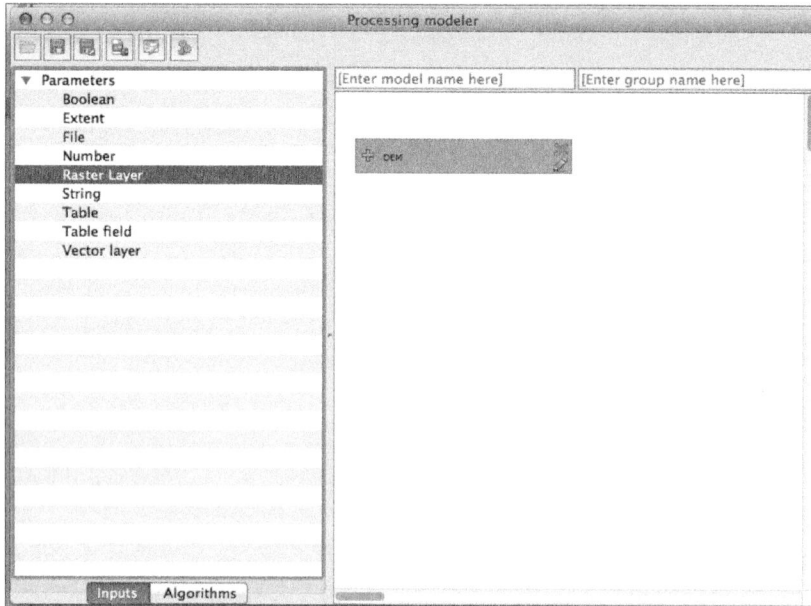

4. Move to the **Algorithms** tab. Double-click on the **Slope, aspect, curvature** algorithm and set the algorithm definition, as shown in the following screenshot:

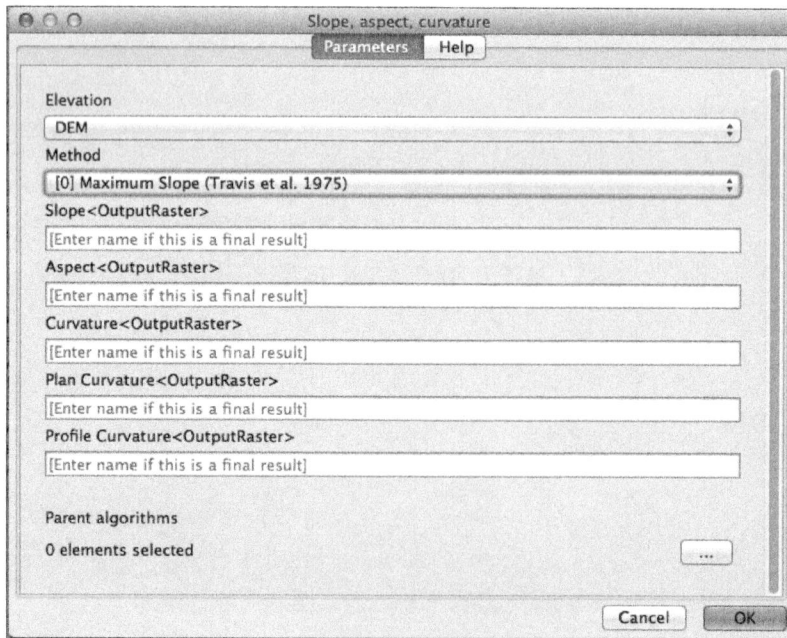

5. Close the dialog by clicking on the **OK** button. This will be added to the modeler canvas, as follows:

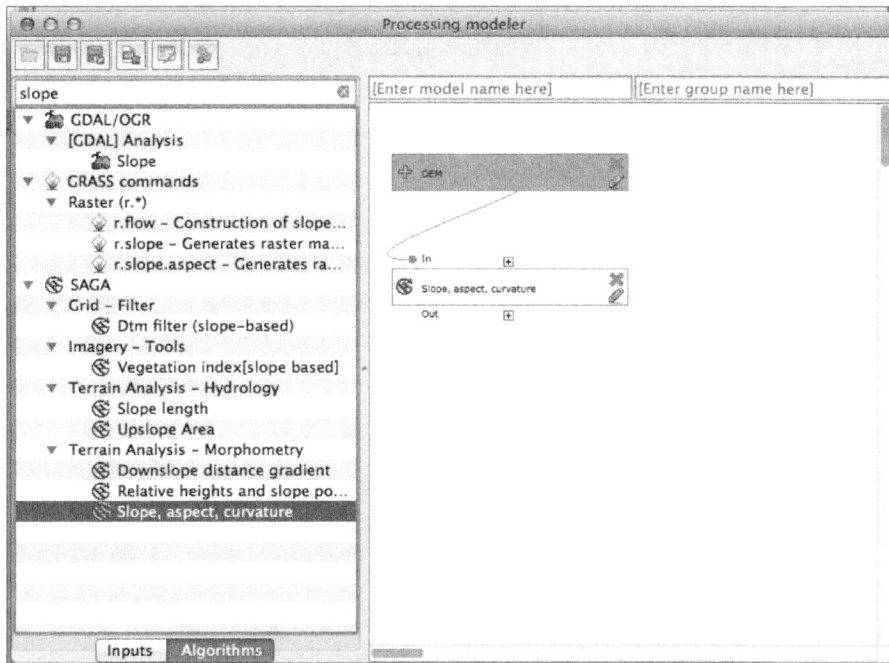

6. Add the **Catchment area** algorithm to the model by double-clicking on it in the algorithm list and filling in the dialog, as shown in the following screenshot:

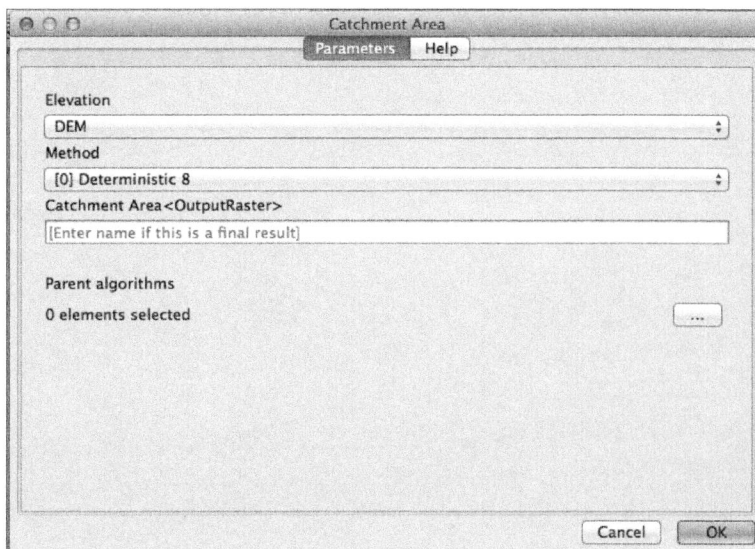

7. Finally, add the **Topographic wetness index** algorithm, defining it as shown in the following screenshot:

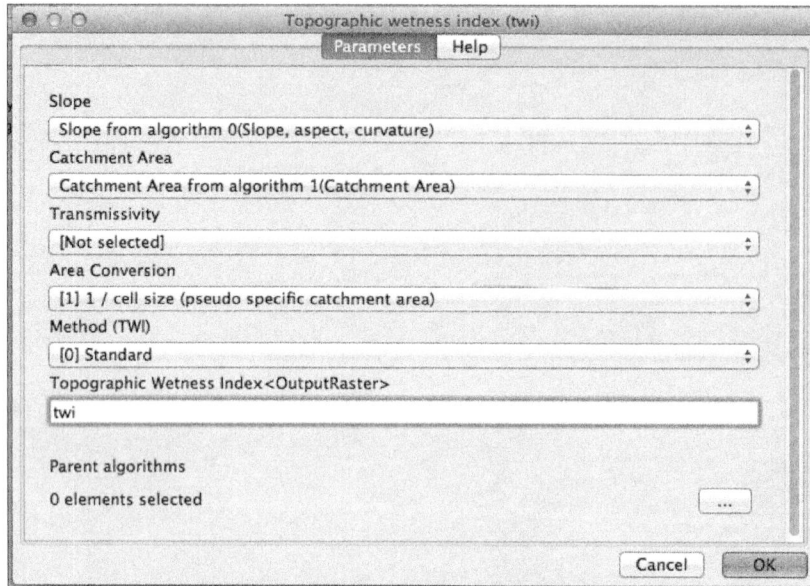

8. The final model should look like the following screenshot:

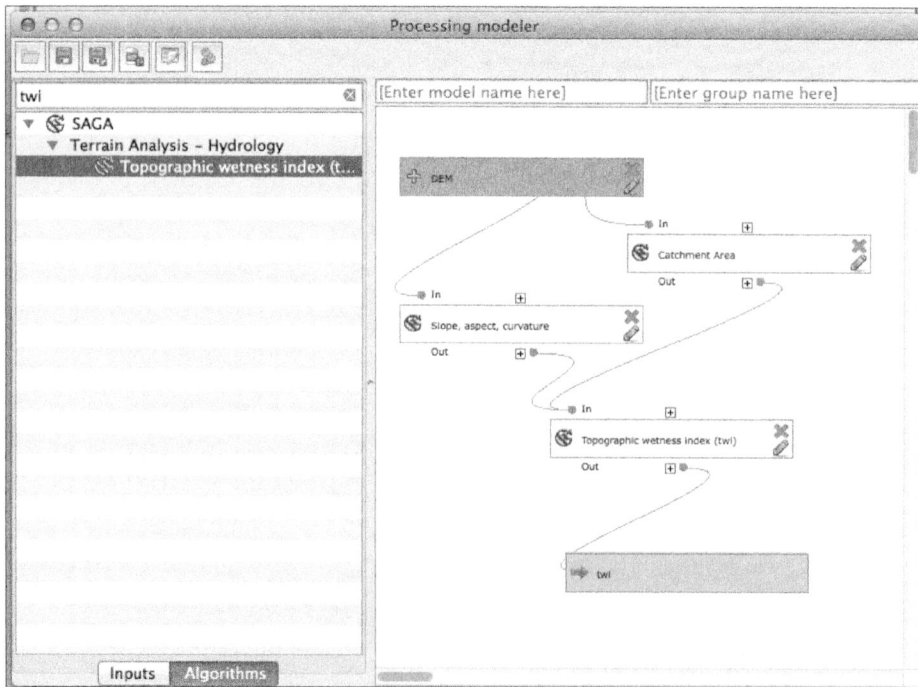

9. Enter a name and a group to identify the model and save it by clicking on the **Save** button. Do not change the save location folder, because Processing will only look for it in the default location, you can however change the name of the model. Close the modeler dialog. If you now go to the **Processing Toolbox** option, you will find a new algorithm in the **Models** section, which corresponds to the workflow that you have just defined:

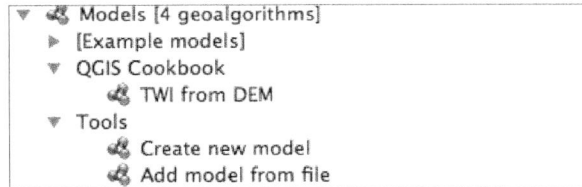

```
▼ 🦾 Models [4 geoalgorithms]
  ▶ [Example models]
  ▼ QGIS Cookbook
      🦾 TWI from DEM
  ▼ Tools
      🦾 Create new model
      🦾 Add model from file
```

How it works...

The model automates the workflow and wraps all the steps into a single one.

By saving the model in the models folder, Processing will see this when updating the toolbox and will include it along with the rest of algorithms so that it can be executed normally.

See also

▶ More information about the graphical modeler can be found in the Processing chapter of the QGIS manual at `http://docs.qgis.org/2.8/en/docs/user_manual/processing/modeler.html`

8
Raster Analysis II

In this chapter, we will cover the following recipes:

- Calculating NDVI
- Handling null values
- Setting extents with masks
- Sampling a raster layer
- Visualizing multispectral layers
- Modifying and reclassifying values in raster layers
- Performing supervised classification of raster layers

Introduction

Following the previous chapter, this chapter introduces some additional techniques for raster analysis. This chapter will show you how to work with images, how to modify raster values and classify them, and how raster layers can be used along with vector layers, thus extending the set of tools that were introduced in the recipes in the previous chapter.

Calculating NDVI

The **Normalized Differential Vegetation Index** is a very popular vegetation index that gives us useful information about the presence or absence of live green vegetation.

Getting ready

NDVI is calculated using a band with red spectral reflectance values, and another one with near-infrared reflectance values. In the sample dataset, you will find two image files named `red.tif` and `nir.tif` that can be used to compute NDVI. A project named `ndvi.qgs` is available, which contains these two layers and a landsat image corresponding to this same area. Open this project.

How to do it...

1. Open the **Processing Toolbox** menu and find the algorithm called **Vegetation index[slope based]**. Double-click on the algorithm item to execute it:

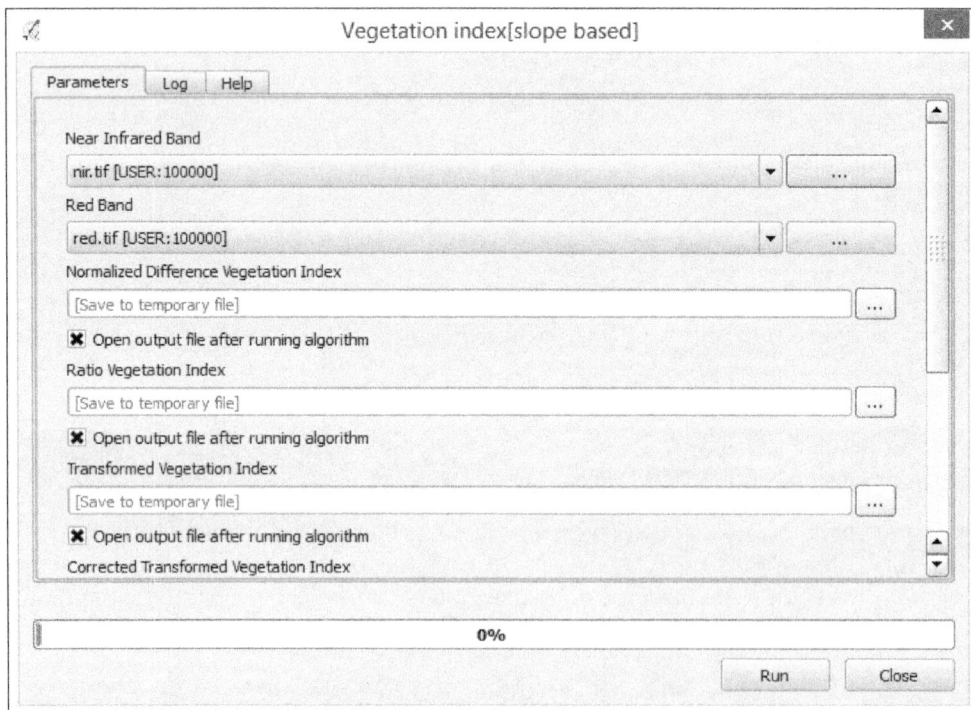

2. Select the `red.tif` layer in the **Red Band** field and the `nir.tif` layer in the **Near Infrared Band** field. Click on **Run** to run the algorithm.

3. The algorithm will produce a set of layers with different vegetation indices, NDVI is among them:

How it works...

All vegetation indices that are computed by the algorithm are based on the relation between red and near-infrared reflectances. Leaf cells scatter solar radiation in the near-infrared reflectance and absorb radiation in the red reflectance, which can be used to predict the location of healthy green vegetation based on these two values.

NDVI is computed with the formula given in the following section.

There's more...

As the formula of the NDVI is rather simple, you can calculate it without using a specific algorithm, just by going to the raster calculator. You can use the one integrated in the Processing Framework or the QGIS built-in on. You can see how you should fill the parameters in the QGIS Raster calculator to compute the NDVI, based on the two proposed sample layers in the following screenshot:

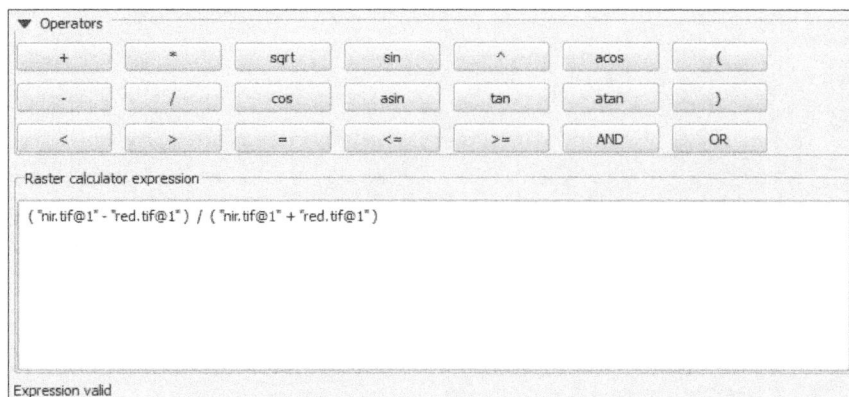

Extracting bands

The vegetation indices algorithm requires the red and infrared values to be in two separate layers, each of them with a single band. However, it's common to have both of them in a multiband image. To be able to use these bands, you must separate them, extracting them into two separate files.

This can be done using the GDAL translate algorithm. The project contains a multiband image named `landsat.tif` with the red band in band number 3 and infrared band in band number 4:

1. Open the **Translate** algorithm in the **Processing Toolbox** menu.
2. Fill its parameters, as shown in the following screenshot, to export the infrared band:

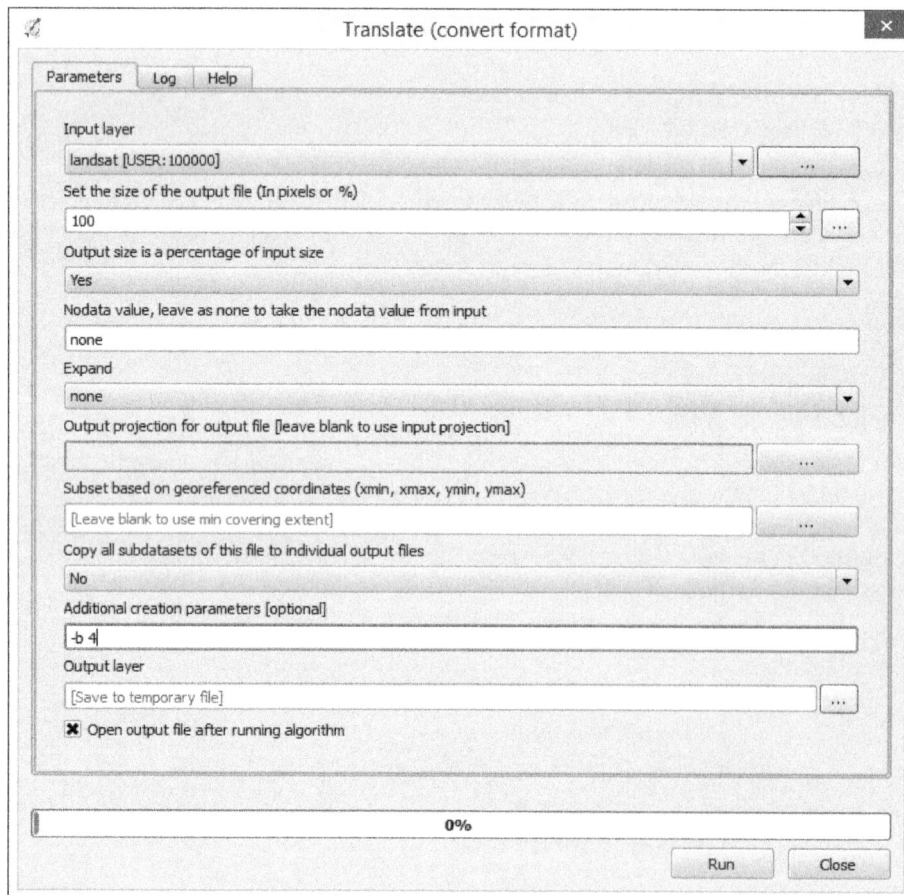

3. Run this again, as shown in the following screenshot, to export the red band:

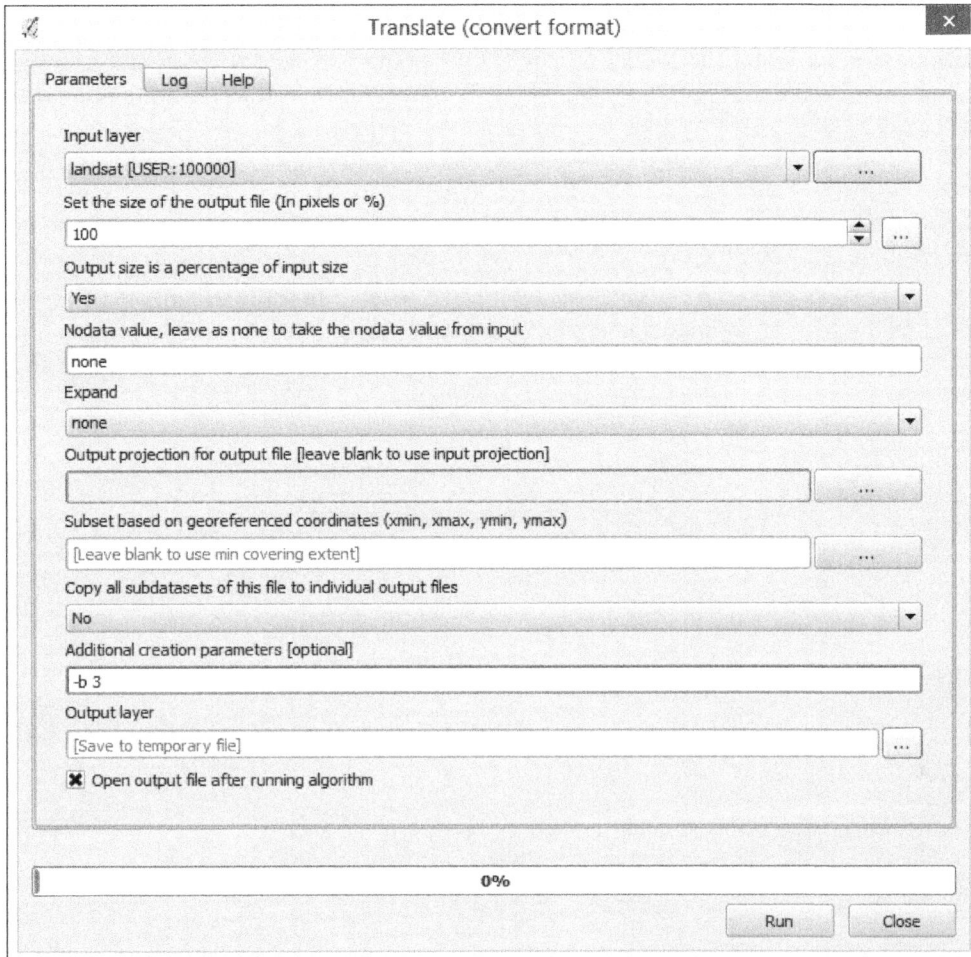

The Translate algorithm uses the GDAL library underneath. You can also use this library as an independent tool from the console. At the lower part of the algorithm dialog, you will find a text field where you will see the equivalent console call to your current algorithm configuration.

Handling null values

Null values are a particular type of values that are used to indicate cells where the value for a given layer is not defined. Understanding how to use them is important to avoid wrong results when performing analyses but also to use them as a tool to get better and more correct results. This recipe explains some of the fundamental ideas about null values in raster layers.

How to do it...

The `watershed.tif` layer contains the area of a watershed. Cells inside the watershed are cells from which water will eventually flow into the outlet point of the watershed. The remaining cells belong to a different watershed. To mask the DEM with the watershed mask, follow these steps:

1. Open the `watershed.tif` layer.

2. Open the identify tool and check whether the cells that belong to the watershed have a value of 1, and the ones outside, have a value of `no data`.

3. Try clicking inside and outside the watershed; in your **Identify Results** dialog, you will see the results, as shown in the following screenshot:

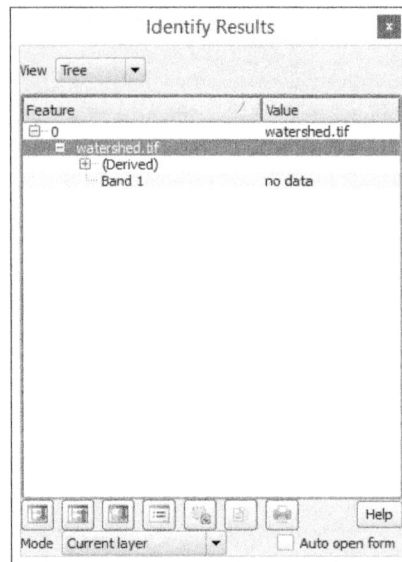

4. Now, let's calculate some statistics of the raster layer. Open the **Raster layer statistics** algorithm in the **Processing Toolbox** menu.

5. Select the watershed layer in the **input layer** field and click on **OK** to run the algorithm. The result is a short text output that looks like the following screenshot:

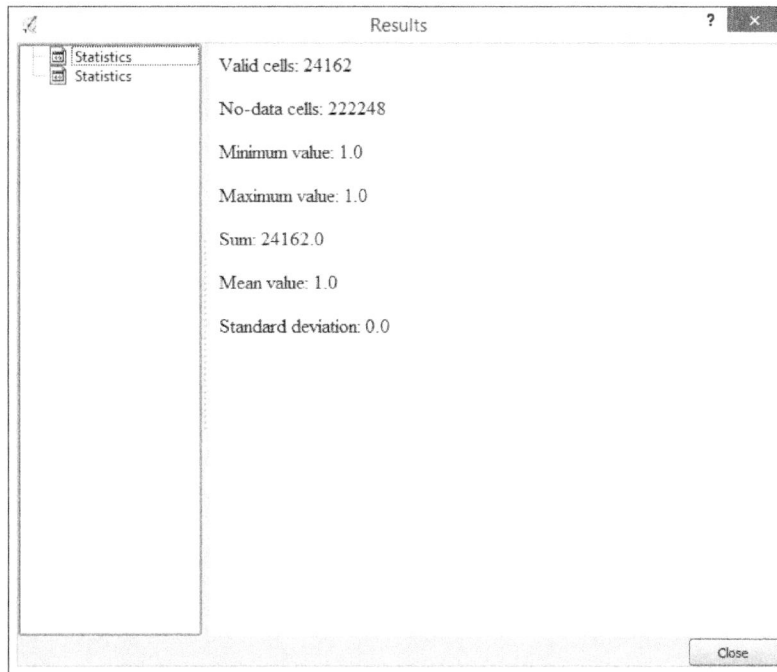

Only the cells with a value of 1 have been considered, and the average value in the layer is equal to 1.

The layer has 610 columns and 401 rows, but the total number of valid cells is much lower than 610 x 410. These are the cells that have been used to compute the statistics.

How it works...

Raster layers always cover a rectangular region. However, in some circumstances, the land object that the layer represents might not be rectangular. This might be due to a purely geophysical reason (imagine a layer with water temperature that contains non-water cells), political ones (a layer with a DEM of a given country with no data available for a neighboring country), or many others. In any case, a value is needed for these cells to indicate that no data is available. An arbitrary value is selected and used. As such, this is usually a value that is not a logical and/or feasible value for the variable that is stored in the layer.

In the case of the example layer, the value used is -99999, which is the default value set for no-data values. This means that, when the identify tool shows **no data**, it has actually selected a value of -99999 in this case.

Algorithms in the Processing framework systematically ignore no-data cells, and do not use their values. You can clearly see this in the preceding example. A large part of the cells in the layer have a value of 1 (the ones that belong to the watershed), but many of them have a value of -99999. The average value of the cells should then be different from 1, but as -99999 is defined as the no-data value, all cells with this value are ignored. The average of the layer is, therefore, equal to 1.

There's more...

Null values should be considered not only when performing an analysis, but also when we just want to render a layer that contains them.

Controlling the rendering of null values

Null values are also considered separately when rendering a raster layer. You can choose to select them using a given color (as set by the current color palette), or to not render them at all. To make all cells with null values transparent, open the layer properties and go to the **Transparency** section. Make sure that the **No data value** checkbox is checked, as shown in the following screenshot:

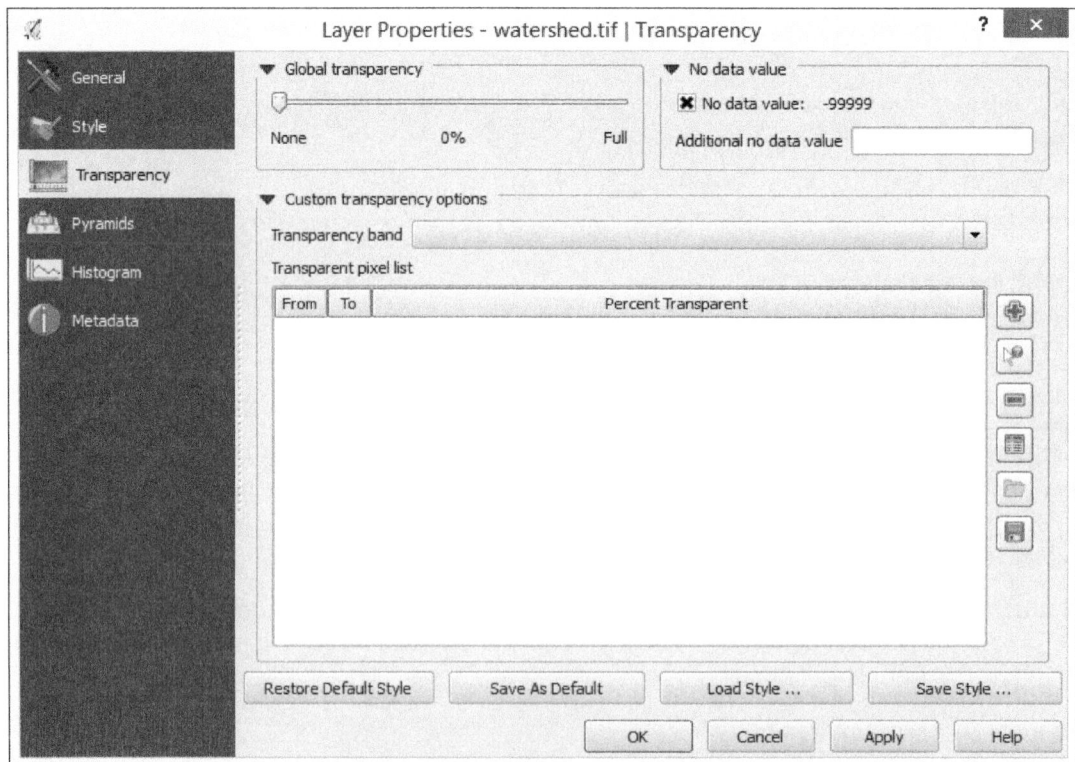

Setting extents with masks

The extent of a layer can be set using a second layer, which acts as a mask. This recipe shows you how to do this.

How to do it...

To mask the DEM with the watershed mask, follow these steps:

1. Open the `watershed.tif` layer and the `dem.tif` layer.
2. Open the **Raster Calculator** algorithm present in the **Processing Toolbox** menu.
3. In **Main input layer**, select the DEM, and in the **Additional layers** field, select the watershed layer.
4. In the **Formula** field, enter the formula, *a*b*.
5. Click on **Run** to run the algorithm. You will get a masked DEM, as follows:

How it works...

When using the raster calculator, all operations involving a no-data value will result in another no-data value. This means that, when multiplying the DEM layer and the mask layer, in the cells that contain no-data values in the mask layer, the value in the resulting layer will be a no-data value, no matter which elevation value is found in the DEM layer for this cell.

As cells inside the watershed in the mask layer have a value of 1, the result is a layer with elevation values for watershed cells and no-data values for the remaining ones.

Here are some additional ideas about masks.

Restricting analysis to a given area

Once we have masked the area of interest (in this case, the watershed), all analysis that we perform will be restricted to this. For instance, let's calculate the average elevation of the watershed:

1. Open the **Basic statistics for raster layers** algorithm.

2. Select the masked DEM in the **Input layer** field and click on **Run** to run the algorithm. You will get the statistics on the **Results** window:

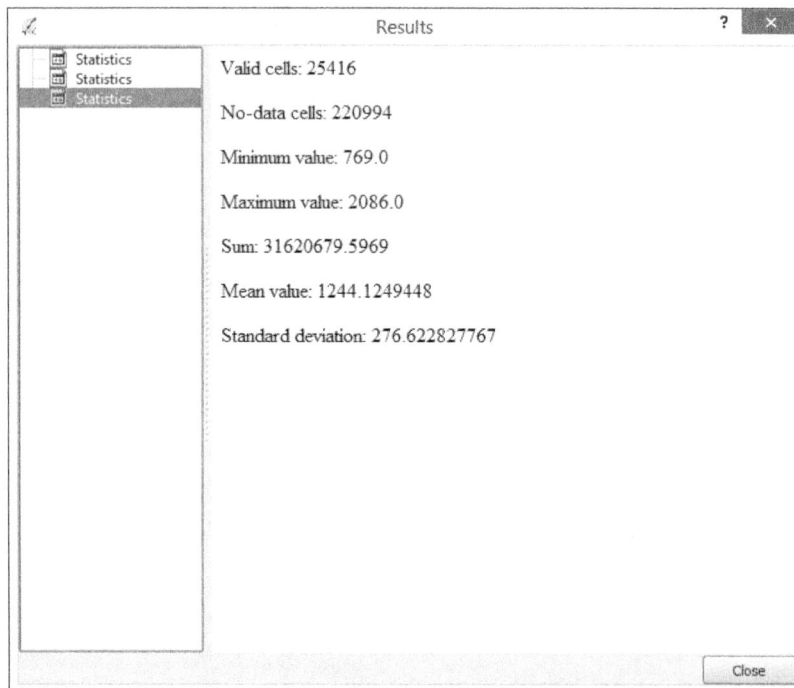

```
                        Results                    ?   ×
  Statistics        Valid cells: 25416
  Statistics
  Statistics        No-data cells: 220994

                    Minimum value: 769.0

                    Maximum value: 2086.0

                    Sum: 31620679.5969

                    Mean value: 1244.1249448

                    Standard deviation: 276.622827767




                                              Close
```

These values have been computed using only valid cell values and ignoring the no-data ones, which means that they refer to the watershed and not the the full extent of the raster layer.

Removing superfluous no-data values

Sometimes, you might have more no-data values that are needed in a raster layer, as in the case of the proposed watershed layer. To reduce the extent of the layer and just have the minimum extent that covers the valid data, you can use the **Crop to data** algorithm:

1. Open the **Crop to data** algorithm in the **Processing Toolbox** menu.
2. Enter the masked DEM in the **Input layer** field and click on **Run** to run the algorithm. The resulting layer should look like this when you disable transparency for no-data values:

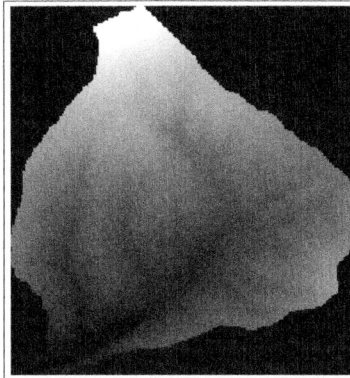

Note that, if you have opted to render no-data cells as transparent pixels, you will see no visual difference between the original and the cropped layer.

Masking using a vector mask

Masking a raster layer can also be done using a polygon vector layer. The `watershed.shp` file contains a single polygon with the area of the watershed that we have already used to mask the DEM. Here is how to use this to mask that DEM without using the raster mask:

1. Open the **Clip** grid with the **polygon** algorithm.
2. Select the DEM in the **Input** field.
3. Select the vector layer in the **Polygons** field.
4. Click on **Run** to run the algorithm. The clipped layer will be added to the QGIS project.

In this case, the clip algorithm automatically reduces the extent of the output layer to the minimum extent defined by the polygon layer, so there is no need to run the **Crop to data** algorithm afterwards.

Sampling a raster layer

Data from a raster layer can be added to a points layer by querying the value of the layer in the coordinates of the points. This process is known as sampling, and this recipe explains how to perform it.

Getting ready

Open the `dem.tif` raster layer and the `dem_points.shp` vector layer:

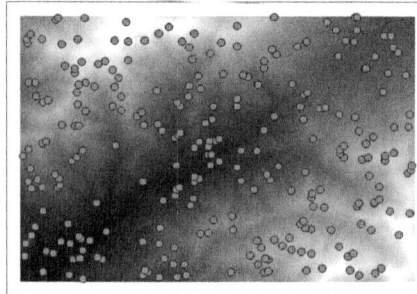

How to do it...

1. In the **Processing Toolbox** menu, find the **Add grid values to points** algorithm and double-click on it to open it:

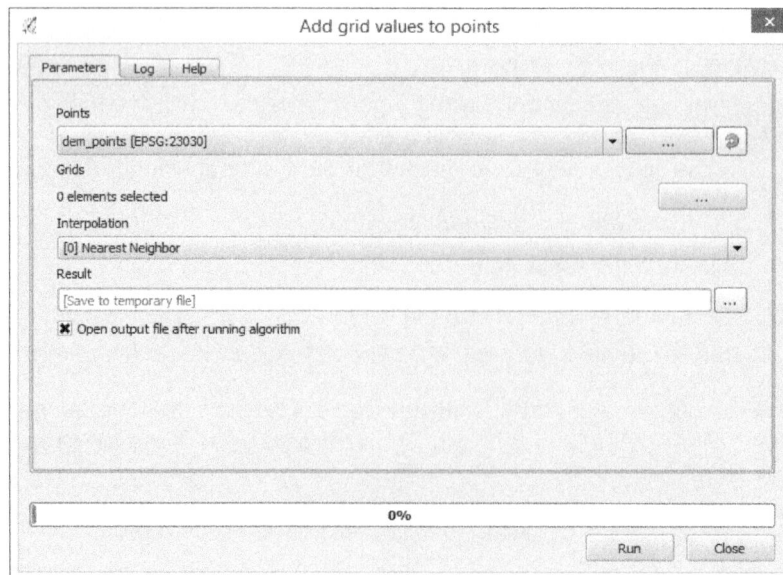

2. Select the DEM in the **Grids** field.

3. Select the point layer in the **Points** field.

4. Click on **Run** to run the algorithm.

A new vector layer will be created. This contains the same points as the input layer, but the attribute table will have an additional field with the name of the selected raster layer and the values corresponding to this layer in each point:

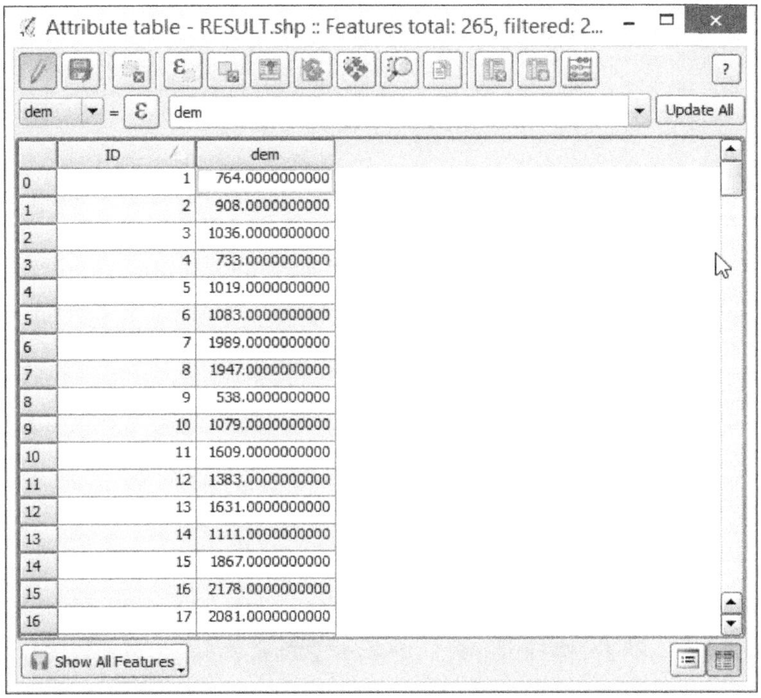

How it works...

The coordinates of the points are taken, and the value of the pixel in which the layer falls is added to the resulting points layer.

This method assumes that the value of a cell is constant in all the area covered by this cell. A different approach is to consider that the value of the cell represents its value only in the center of the cell and perform additional calculations to compute the value at the exact sampling point using the values of the surrounding cells as well. This can be done using several different interpolation methods, which can be selected in the **Interpolation method** selector, changing the default value, which only uses the value of the cell where the sampling point falls.

Layers are assumed to be in the same CRS and no reprojection is performed. If this is not the case, the value added to the vector layer might not be correct.

There's more...

Here, you can find some ideas about how to combine a raster and vector layer in different situations.

Other raster-vector data transfer operations

Data coming from a raster layer can also be added to other types of vector layers. In the case of a vector layer with polygons, the **Grid statistics for polygons** algorithm can be used, as follows:

1. Open the `watershed.shp` file that we used in the previous recipe.

2. Open the **Grid** statistics in the **Polygons** field.

3. Select the raster layer to clip in the **Grids** field.

4. Select the polygon layer with the mask in the **Polygons** field.

5. Select the statistics to be calculated from the remaining parameters. For instance, to calculate just the mean elevation, leave the **Mean** field selected and unselect the others.

6. Click on **Run** to run the algorithm.

The resulting layer is a new polygon layer with the watershed and an additional field in the attributes table, containing the mean elevation value for each polygon.

If more statistics are selected, the result will have a larger number of additional fields added, one for each new parameter computed and each selected grid.

Visualizing multispectral layers

Multispectral layers can be rendered in different ways depending on how bands are used. This recipe shows you how to do this and discusses the theory behind it.

Getting ready

Open the `landsat.qgs` project.

How to do it...

1. The Landsat image, when opened with the default configuration, looks something like the following screenshot:

2. Double-click on the layer to open its properties and move to the **Style** section:

   1. Select the band number 4 in the **Red band** field.

   2. Select the band number 3 in the **Green band** field.

   3. Select the band number 2 in the **Blue band** field.

   Your style configuration should be like the following:

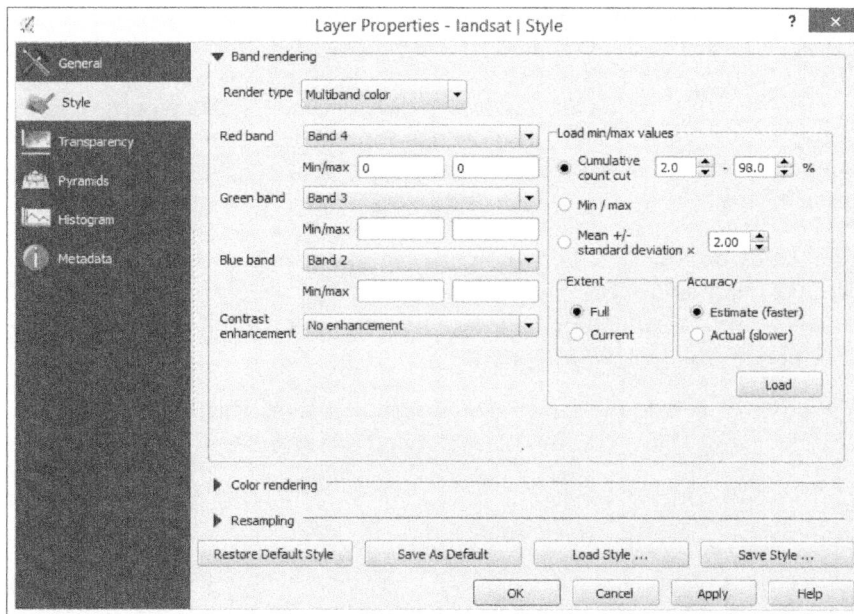

3. Click on **OK**.

The image should now look like the following:

How it works...

Colors representing a given pixel are defined using the RGB color space, which requires three different components. A normal image (such as the one you will get from a digital camera) has three bands containing the intensity for each one of these three components: red, green, and blue.

Multispectral bands, such as the one used in this recipe, have more than three bands and provide more detail in different regions of the electromagnetic spectrum. To visualize these, three bands from the total number of available bands have to be chosen and their intensities have to be used as intensities of the basic red, green, and blue components (although they might correspond to a different region of the spectrum, even outside the visible range). This is known as a *false color* image.

Depending on the combination of the bands that are used, the resulting image will convey a different type of information. The combination chosen is frequently used for vegetation studies, as it allows you to separate coniferous from hardwood vegetation as well as providing information about vegetation health.

The combination is applied, in this case, to a Landsat 7 image, which is taken with the ETM+ sensor. The wavelengths covered by each band are as follows (in micrometers):

- ▶ **Band 1**: 0.45 - 0.515
- ▶ **Band 2**: 0.525 - 0.605
- ▶ **Band 3**: 0.63 - 0.69
- ▶ **Band 4**: 0.75 - 0.90

> ▸ **Band 5**: 1.55 - 1.75
> ▸ **Band 6**: 10.40 - 12.5
> ▸ **Band 7**: 2.09 - 2.35

There's more...

Different combinations are frequently used for Landsat layers. One of them is the following:

> ▸ Select the band number 3 in the **Red band** field
> ▸ Select the band number 2 in the **Green band** field
> ▸ Select band number 1 in the **Blue band** field

This is a natural color combination, as the bands used for the **R**, **G**, and **B** components actually have the wavelengths corresponding to the colors **red**, **green**, and **blue**:

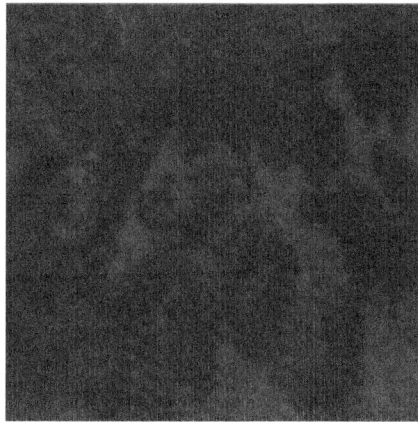

If you are using an image that is not a Landsat 7 one, each band will have a different meaning, and using the same combination of band numbers will yield different results. The meaning of each band must be checked in order to understand the information displayed by the rendered image.

See also

> ▸ Landsat data is freely available. If you want to download Landsat data corresponding to a given region, visit `http://landsat.gsfc.nasa.gov/`. Here, you can find more information about where and how you can download it.

Modifying and reclassifying values in raster layers

A very useful technique to work with raster data is changing their values or grouping them into categories. In this recipe, we will see how to do this.

Getting ready

Open the DEM file that we used in previous recipes.

How to do it...

We will classify the elevation in three groups:

- ▸ Lower than 1,000m
- ▸ Between 1,000 and 2,000m
- ▸ Higher than 2,000m

To do this, follow these steps:

1. Open the **Change grid values** algorithm from the **Processing Toolbox** menu. Set the **Replace condition** parameter to **Low Value <= Grid Value < High Value**.

2. Click on the button in the **Lookup table** parameter and fill the table that will appear, as shown in the following screenshot:

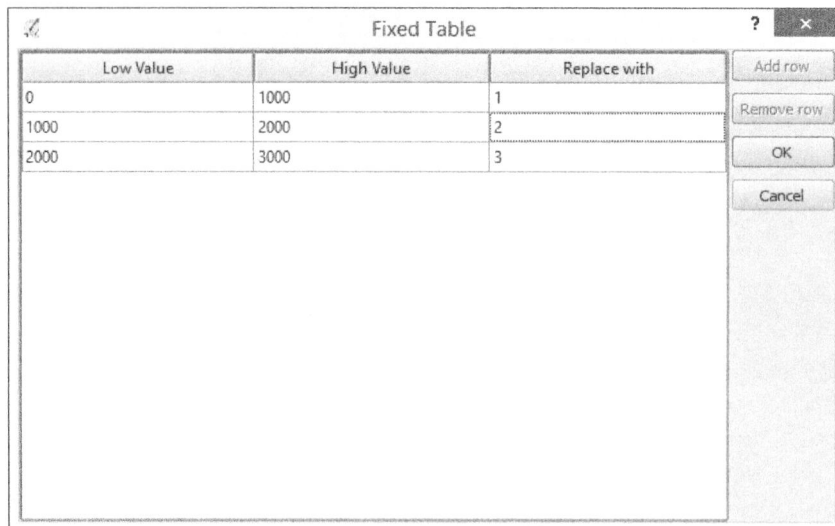

Low Value	High Value	Replace with	
0	1000	1	Add row
1000	2000	2	Remove row
2000	3000	3	OK
			Cancel

Fixed Table

3. Run the algorithm. This will create the reclassified layer:

How it works...

Values for each cell are compared with the range limits in the lookup table, considering the specified comparison criteria. Whenever a value falls into a given range, the class value specified for this range will be used in the output layer.

There's more...

Other strategies can be used to automate a reclassification, especially when this involves dividing the raster layer values into classes with some constant property. Here, we show two of these cases.

Reclassifying into classes of equal amplitude

A typical case of reclassification is dividing the total range of values of the layer into a given number of classes. This is similar to slicing it, and if applied on a DEM, such as our example data, this will have a result similar to that of defining contour lines with a regular interval (although the result is a not vector layer with lines in this case, but a new raster layer).

To reclassify in equal intervals, follow these steps:

1. Open **Raster calculator** from the **Processing Toolbox** menu.

2. Select the DEM as the only layer to use.

3. Enter the formula, *int((a-514)/(2410-514) * 5)*.

The reclassified layer will look like the following:

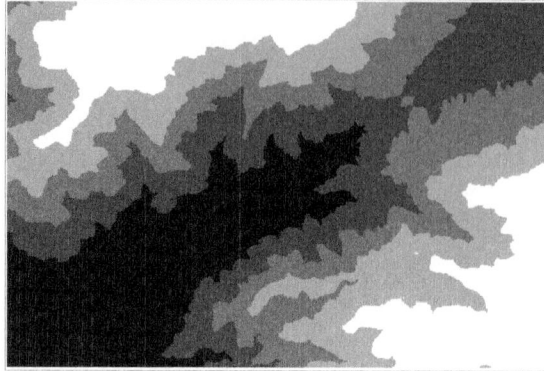

The numerical values in the formula correspond to the minimum and maximum values of the layer. You can find these values in the properties window of the layer.

To create a different number of classes, just use another value instead of 5 in the formula.

Reclassifying into classes of equal area

There is no tool to reclassify into a set of *n* classes, as each of them occupies the same area, but a similar result can be obtained using some other algorithms. To show you how this is done, let's reclassify the DEM into five classes of the same area:

1. Open the **Sort grid** algorithm and enter the DEM as the input layer. Click on **Run** to execute the algorithm.

   The resulting layer has the cells ordered according to their value in the DEM, so the cell with a value of 1 represents the cell with the lowest elevation value, 2 is the second lowest, and so on.

2. Reclassify the ordered layer into five classes of equal amplitude using the procedure described earlier. The final layer should look like the following:

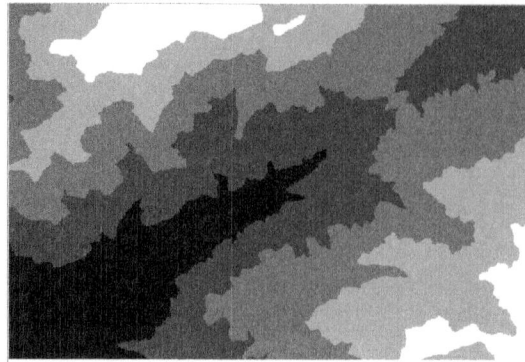

See also

▶ The **Processing Toolbox** menu contains additional classification algorithms, most of them based on SAGA. One algorithm that has a different approach is **Cluster analysis for grids**. This will create a given number of classes in such a way that it minimize the variances in the groups, trying to make them as homogeneous as possible. This is also known as unsupervised classification.

Performing supervised classification of raster layers

In the previous recipes, we saw how to change the values of a raster layer and create classes. When you have several layers, classifying might not be that easy, and defining the patterns to perform this classification might not be obvious. A different technique to be used in this case is to define zones that share a common characteristic and let the corresponding algorithm extract the statistical values that define them so that this can later be applied to perform the classification itself. This is known as **Supervised classification**, and this recipe explains how to do this in QGIS.

Getting ready

Open the `classification.qgs` project. It contains an RGB image and a vector layer with polygons.

How to do it...

1. The image has to be separated into individual bands. Run **Split RGB bands** using the provided image as the input, and you will obtain three layers named R, G, and B.

2. Open the **Supervised classification** algorithm from the **Processing Toolbox** menu.

3. Fill in its parameter window, as shown in the following screenshot:

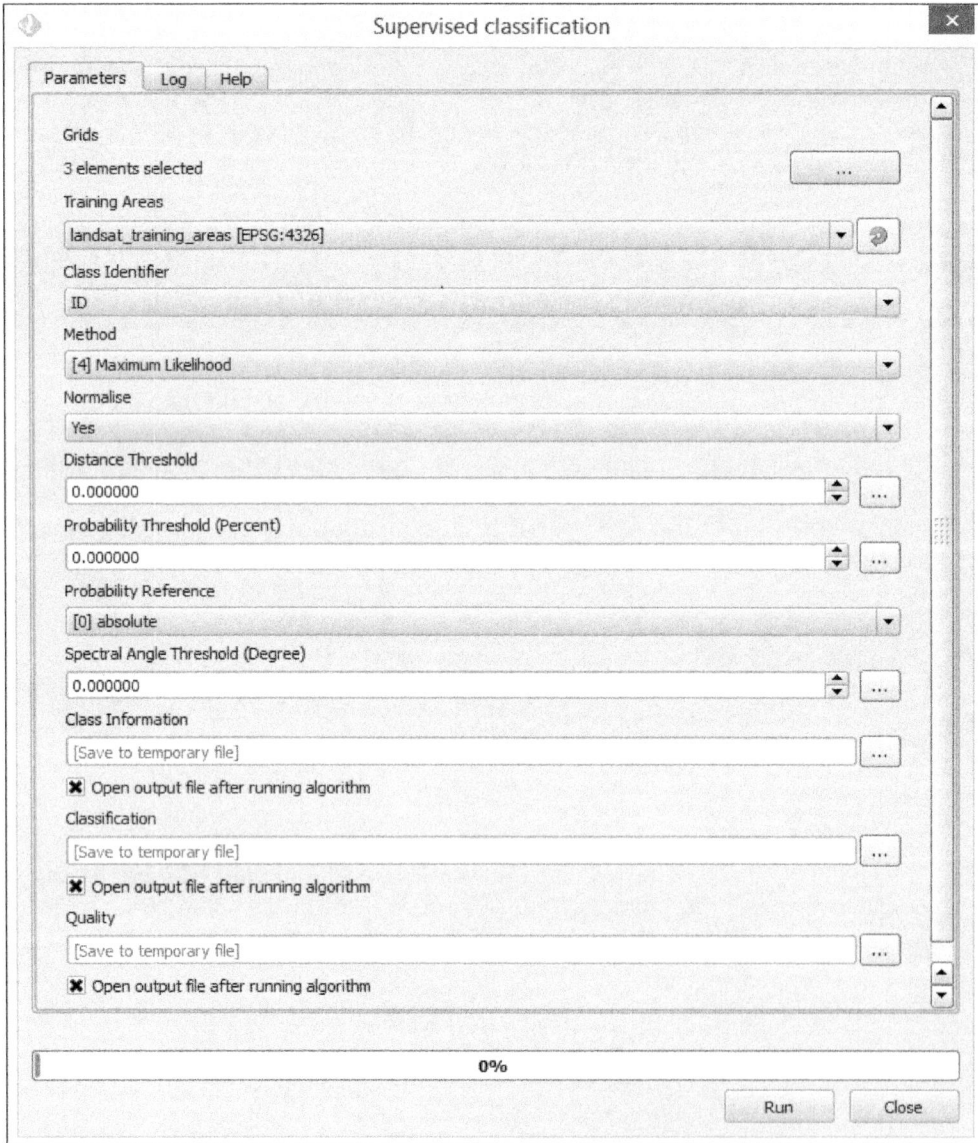

4. In the first field, you should select the three layers resulting from the last step (R, G, and B).

5. Click on **OK** to run the algorithm. Two layers and a table will be created. The layer named **Classification** contains the classified raster layer:

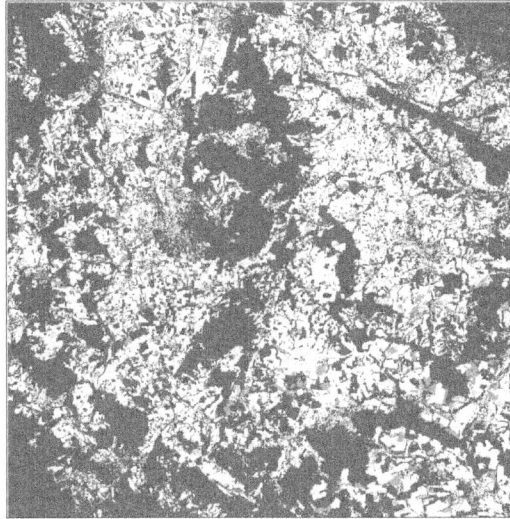

How it works...

The supervised classification needs a set of raster layers and a vector layer with polygons that define the different classes to create. The identifier of the class is defined in the **Class** field in the attributes table. If you open the attributes tables, you will see that it looks something like the following:

	ID	BOTYP
0	1	Forest
1	2	Wheat
2	3	Urban
3	4	Crop
4	5	Crop-clear

There are five different classes, each of them represented by a feature and with a text ID along with a numerical ID. The classification algorithms analyzes the pixels that fall within the polygons of each class and computes statistics for them. Using these statistics assigns a class to each pixel in the image, trying to assign the class that is statistically more similar among the ones defined in the vector layer. The numerical ID is used to identify the class in the resulting raster layer.

There's more...

There are other ways of performing a supervised classification in QGIS. One of them, which allows more control over the different elements in the process, is to use the **QGIS semi-automatic classification** plugin.

Other more sophisticated classification methods can be used from the **Processing Toolbox** menu. They can be found in the **Advanced** interface of the toolbox, under the **Orfeo Toolbox** group, as shown in the following screenshot:

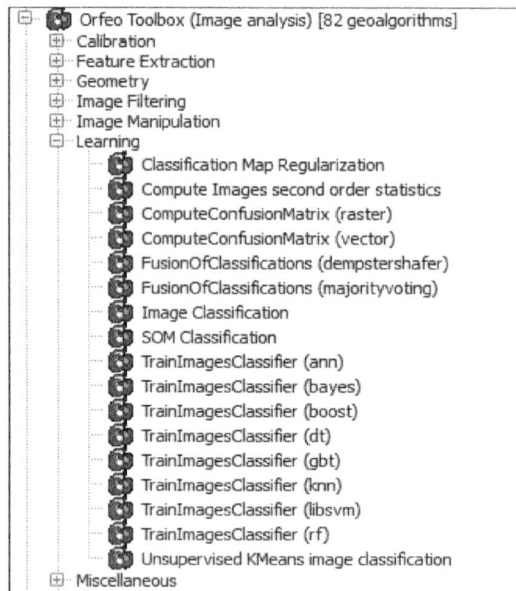

See also

- You can download and install this using the QGIS plugin manager. For more information about how to use the plugin, you can check its website at `http://fromgistors.blogspot.fr/p/semi-automatic-classification-plugin.html`.

9
QGIS and the Web

In this chapter we will cover the following recipes:

- ▸ Using web services
- ▸ Using WFS and WFS-T
- ▸ Searching CSW
- ▸ Using WMS and WMS Tiles
- ▸ Using WCS
- ▸ Using GDAL
- ▸ Serving web maps with the QGIS server
- ▸ Scale-dependent rendering
- ▸ Hooking up web clients
- ▸ Managing GeoServer from QGIS

Introduction

QGIS is a classic desktop **geographic information system** (**GIS**). However, these days only working with local data just isn't enough. You want to be able to freely use data from the web without spending days downloading this data. At the same time, you want to be able to put maps online for a much wider audience than a paper map or PDF. This is where web services come in. QGIS can be both a web service client and a web server, providing you with lots of options to use and share geographic data. This chapter covers the basics of using open web services for geographic data and a few methods to put your maps online.

Using web services

There are quite a few different types of web-based map service that can be loaded in QGIS. Each type of web service provides data; often, this is the same data in different ways. This recipe is about helping you figure out what type of web service you want to consume, and conversely what type of web service you may want to create for others to use.

Getting ready

This recipe is all about thinking, so you don't need anything in particular to start. It does help if you have a project in mind and some type of data you are interested in using or creating. Most, if not all, of these methods require an Internet connection or a local server, providing these services. Of course, if you have the data locally, you should probably just load it directly.

To help with the following section, here's a list of acronyms:

- **CSW**: This is **Catalog Service for the Web**
- **WFS**: This is **Web Feature Service**
- **WFS-T**: This is **Web Feature Service, Transactional**
- **WCS**: This is **Web Coverage Service**
- **WMS**: This is **Web Map Service**
- **WMTS**: This is **Web Map Tile Service**
- **TMS**: This is **Tile Map Service**
- **XYZ**: This is an "X Y Z" Service (there really isn't a formal name for this one because it's not an official standard)

How to do it...

1. Start by answering the following questions with regards to using data over web services:

   - Do you already know where to find the data that you want?
   - Do you need to edit or apply custom styling to this data?
   - Do you care if the data is vector or raster?
   - Do you need the data at its original resolution or quality?
   - Do you need data at specific resolutions or in a specific projection?

2. Use the following decision matrix to pick out which services are appropriate to your use case:

Criteria	CSW	WFS	WFS-T	WCS	WMS	Tiles (WMTS, XYZ, TMS)
Do you already know where to find the data you want?	No	Yes	Yes	Yes	Yes	Yes
Do you need to edit or apply custom styling to the data?		Yes	Yes	Yes	No	No
Do you care if the data is vector or raster?		Vector	Vector	Raster	Raster	Raster
Do you need the data at its original resolution or quality?		Yes	Yes	Yes	No	No
Do you need data at specific resolutions or in a specific projection?		Yes	Yes	Yes	Yes	No
Recipe number in this chapter.	3	2	2	5	4	4, 6

Now that you've found the appropriate recipe for the web service that you want to use, jump to this recipe later in this chapter. If you're still not sure, read on for more hints on how to pick the correct service. This recipe applies both to how you use web services and how to decide what web services to offer (if you put up a web service for other people to use).

Generally speaking, from left (WFS) to right (Tiles) the speed of the service increases. Tiles serve data the fastest to end users but with the most limitations.

How it works...

For each of the services, there is a QGIS tool (built-in or plugin). This tool stores your list of web servers and connection settings for each service. When you go to load a layer from a chosen server for a particular protocol an up-to-date list of layers is requested from the server (that is, the GetCapabilities XML). You then get to pick off this list the layers that you would like to add to the map canvas (and depending on service type, the projection, and the file type).

There's more...

Vector is generally slower, as more data needs to be transmitted as the data grows. Raster formats are a fixed number of pixels onscreen, so it's always approximately the same amount of data per screen load.

> WMS, WMTS, WFS, and WCS are sometimes referred to as W*S as a collective group of related services that behave similarly.

Each situation will have additional considerations. For example, if you need a specific projection, you probably can't use a Tile service because these are usually only in very specific projections (Web/Spherical Mercator). Or perhaps, you want to print large paper maps. Then, you probably want WFS or WCS in order to get the full resolution possible over your entire region.

One of the most common mistakes is to think that you need vector data when you actually just need a background tile that incorporates vector data. A great example of this is road data. If you don't actually need to style, select, or individually manipulate road data, and then a Tile or WMS type layer will be much faster.

See also

▶ For more information, read the standards at the OGC website, `http://opengeospatial.org`

Using WFS and WFS-T

Web Feature Services (**WFS**) is an OGC standard method to access and, in some cases, edit (WFS-T) vector data over the Internet. When you need full attribute tables, local style control, or editing, WFS is the way to go. Like most other web services, the biggest advantage over a local layer is that you don't have to copy or load the whole layer at once.

> If you just need to view the layer, often WMS or a Tile service (described in other recipes within this chapter) are more efficient.

Getting ready

You need the URL of a WFS service to use and a working Internet connection. We will use the public Mapserver demo website (`http://demo.mapserver.org/`).

> To try WFS-T, which involves editing, you will need to get access to a service (typically, password protected) or make one yourself. Do you need a WFS-T test server? This is a great case where OSGeo-Live comes in handy, as you can run your own WFS-T server in a virtual machine at `http://live.osgeo.org`.

How to do it...

1. Find a WFS service that you want to use and copy the GetCapabilities URL. For this example, we will use the Mapserver demo website, `http://demo.mapserver.org/`.

> As with other web services, it's more efficient if you load your local layers and zoom to their extent first. This enables you to not waste time loading data from web services for extents outside your area of interest.

2. Open the add WFS dialog by clicking on the following icon:

3. Create a **New** connection.

4. Assign **Name** of your choosing and paste in the **URL** field for the WFS service, (`http://demo.mapserver.org/cgi-bin/wfs?SERVICE=WFS&VERSION=1.0.0&REQUEST=GetCapabilities`):

Create a new WFS connection	− + ×

Connection details

Name	Mapserver Demo
URL	http://demo.mapserver.org/cgi-bin/wfs?SERVICE=WFS&VERSION=1.0.0&REQUEST=GetCapabilities

If the service requires basic authentication, enter a user name and optional password

User name	
Password	

Help · Cancel · OK

> On future usage of the same service, this will already be in your list of services, so you only have to add it once.

5. Save your edits by clicking on the **OK** button.

6. Now select the service from the drop-down menu.

7. Query for a list of layers by clicking on the **Connect** button.

8. Select the layer or layers that you want to add to the map; either `continents` or `cities` works for this example:

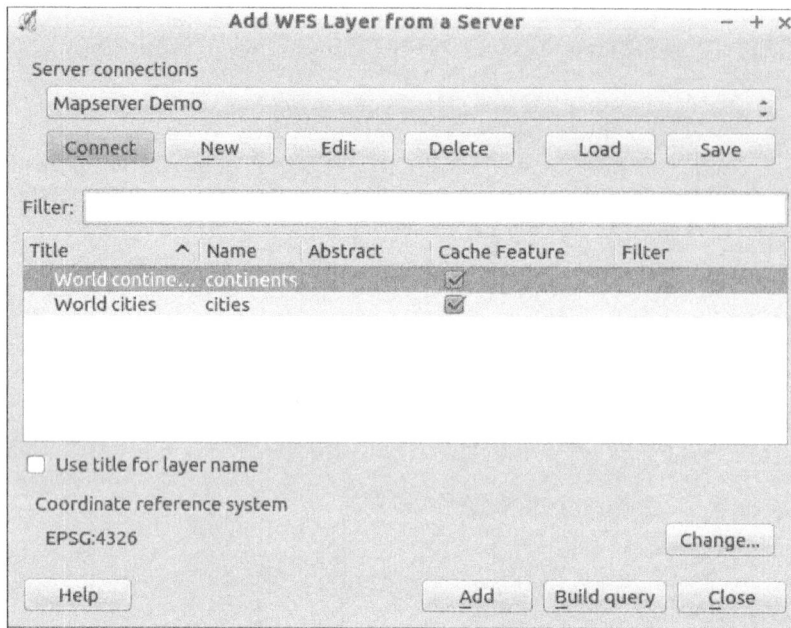

9. When your selection is complete, use the **Add** button to place the layer in the map.

10. Rearrange the render order of the map by dragging layers up and down in the list.

11. Pan and zoom to make fresh requests for WFS data to be loaded to the view.

> WFS layers can be restyled with standard layer properties. Also, the information tool and the attribute table will appear as other vector layers.

How it works...

For each web service, there is a main URL. When you browse to this URL and add the `GetCapabilities` parameter (QGIS does this for you), the returned result is an XML file, which describes the services that are offered by the server. The client, QGIS, parses the list of layers for you to choose from, and once you pick the layer(s), uses the additional information in the XML to look up the data at the specific URL.

Data requests are limited to the visible bounding box of the map canvas. This limits the amount of data that is requested. At least this is how it should work. However, features that go off screen will likely be included in their entirety to maintain geometry integrity. So, expect that loading large vector layers over WFS has the potential to be extremely slow.

There's more...

WFS-T services typically require passwords and are designed to work over the Internet. If you are working within a local network, you may consider just using PostGIS layers. Either way, it should also be noted that versioning and conflict resolution are not automatic, requiring the service backend to be configured to support such features.

Searching CSW

CSW is a catalog web service. Its main function is to provide discoverability of geographic data and link you to usable data either by download or by any other of the web services that are mentioned in this chapter.

Getting ready

This recipe uses the MetaSearch plugin. It requires the pycsw and owslib libraries installed in your system's Python. Refer to the *Adding plugins with Python dependencies* recipe of *Chapter 11, Extending QGIS,* for help on installing pycsw and owslib if you don't know how to do this.

How to do it...

1. Open the MetaSearch plugin by navigating to **Web | MetaSearch | MetaSearch**.

   > If you don't see the **Web** menu, check the plugin manager and ensure that MetaSearch is enabled (checkmark).

2. Pick a service from the dropdown on the right: **UK Location Catalogue Publishing Service**.

   > If you don't see any services in the drop-down list, click on the **Services** tab and use the **Add default services** button.

3. Type a search term in box on the left: Park.

4. (Optional) Set an extent to limit the search. In this case, use **Map Extent**.

> Global searches often return too many results, or they cause the connection to time out while waiting for all the results. As with other web services, it is advisable to load a reference layer and zoom to the area of interest first before trying to search them. The third tab, **Settings**, allows you to adjust the timeout. Increase this if you're getting too many timeout errors.

5. Click on the **Search** button and wait for the results:

   1. Double-click on any of the results to see additional details.

   2. If a selected result is available as a loadable layer, one or more of the service buttons at the bottom of the screen will be enabled. To understand more about how to use each of these choices, refer to the other recipes in this chapter on WMS, WFS, and WCS:

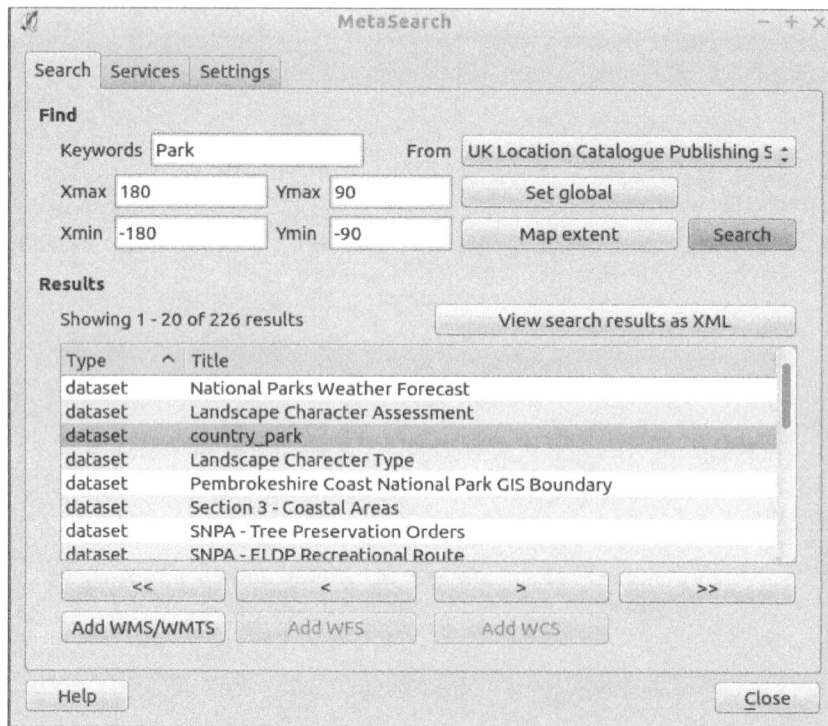

How it works...

MetaSearch queries websites that provide catalogs in the CSW standard, which is defined by the OGC. Once your request parameters are sent, the receiving website queries its online database for matches. If matches are found, metadata about the results is sent back to the client, in this case, QGIS.

CSW currently includes options to search by keyword and spatial extent. Future versions may enable setting time frames.

There's more...

If you pick opening an additional service that is based on the results, Metasearch will create a temporary service registration and open the correct service dialog. Unfortunately, at this time, you need to then scroll through the available layers to find the one that you want and actually add it to the map.

> Additional future CSW searches will ask if you want to override the existing connection. You must say yes. If you find yourself using the same W*S service, consider copying the GetCapabilities URL and making a new permanent entry in the correct service dialog.

You can add more catalogs to search on the **Services** tab within the plugin. You will need to find the CSW GetCapabilities URL on the website that you want to query. Most of the common geoportal-type websites now support CSW, including (but not limited to) Geonode, Geonetwork, and the ESRI Geoportal.

CSW is a relatively new standard when compared to some of the others, and it seems to be hard to find services that consistently work and actually offer WMS, WCS, or WFS of the layers in their catalog.

See also

▸ The *Adding plugins with Python dependencies* recipe of *Chapter 11, Extending QGIS*, for help on installing pycsw and owslib if you don't know how

Using WMS and WMS Tiles

Web Map Services (**WMS**), one of the first OGC web services created, provides a method for dynamic raster generation served over the Web. They are a compromise between the flexibility of WFS and the speed of Tile services.

Getting ready

There are several iterations of WMS, and QGIS supports most of them. To use a WMS, you need to give QGIS the GetCapabilities URL of the service that you want to view data from.

How to do it...

1. Find a WMS service that you want to use and copy the GetCapabilities URL. In this recipe, we can use the Geoserver demo website (`http://demo.opengeo.org/geoserver/web/`).

    > As with other web services, it's more efficient if you load your local layers and zoom to their extent first. This enables you to not waste time loading data from web services for extents outside your area of interest.

2. Open the **Add WMS** dialog.

3. Create a **New** connection.

4. Assign a **Name** of your choosing and paste in the **URL** (`http://demo.opengeo.org/geoserver/ows?service=wms&version=1.3.0&request=GetCapabilities`):

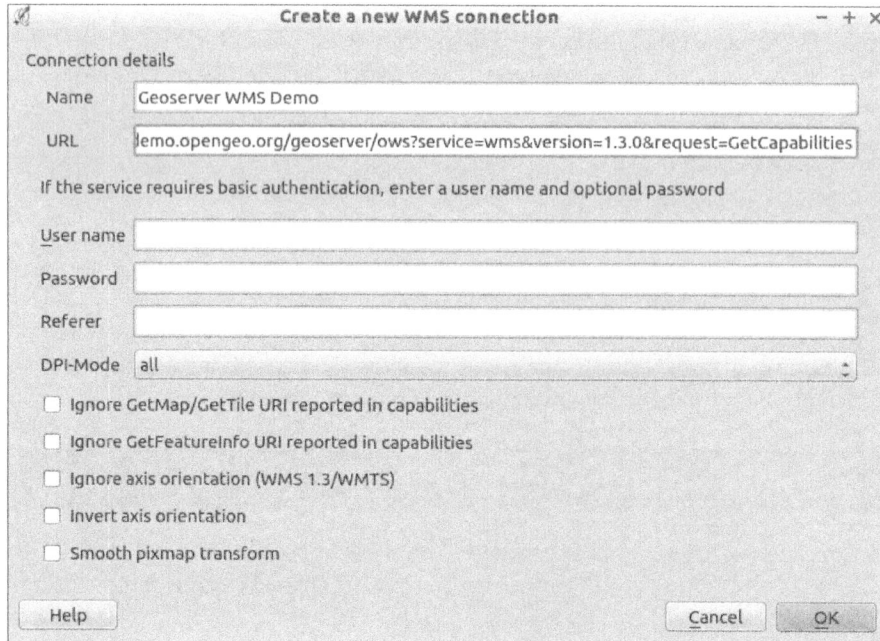

> On future usage of the same service, this will already be in your list of services, so you only have to add it once.

5. Save your edits by clicking on **OK**.

6. Now select the service from the drop-down list.

7. Query for a list of layers using the **Connect** button.

8. Select the layer or layers that you want to add to the map:

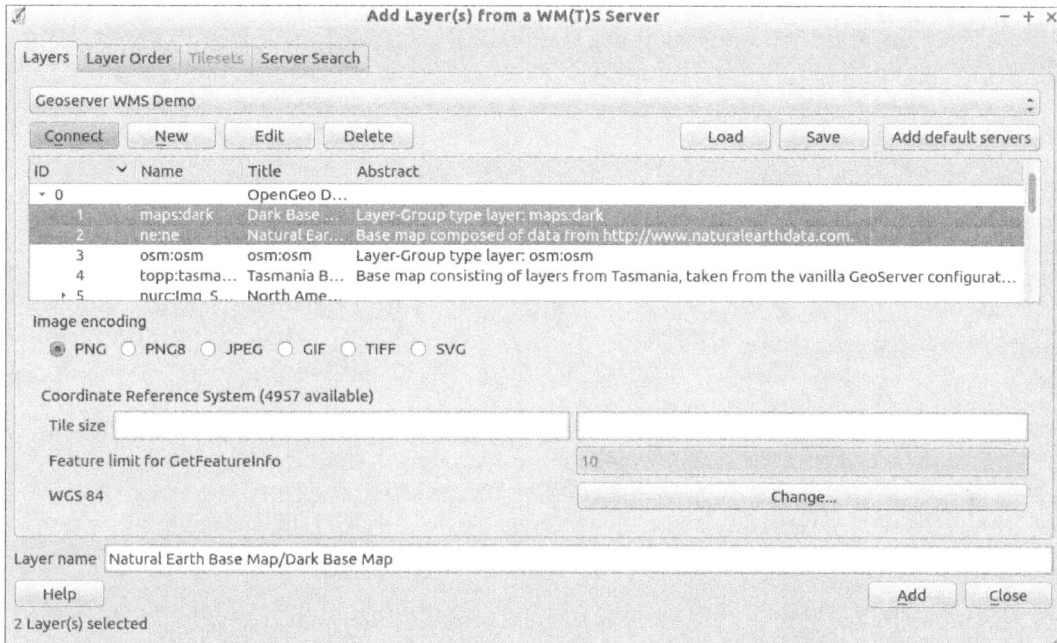

> You can select one or more layers. If you select multiple layers, they will be merged and only appear as a single layer in the QGIS Layers list. The **Layer Order** tab lets you arrange the WMS layers within the combined layer. This is important when one of the layers is opaque and has 100% continuous data, allowing you to put other data on top of it visually.

9. There are several other options, including image type and projection:

   ❑ For an image type, PNG is a good default as it supports lossless compression and transparency. If you don't need transparency and are okay with a little data loss, JPG can be used for smaller files, so they are faster to load.

❑ When picking projection, if you can use the original projection of the data (if you know it), you will get the least resampling. Otherwise, pick something that matches the other data that you plan to use in conjunction with the WMS.

[Not all image types and projections are available; this depends on what the server offers. If one image type doesn't seem to work, try a different one before reporting a bad server.]

10. When your selection is complete, use the **Add** button to place the layer in the map.
11. Rearrange the render order of the map by dragging layers up and down in the list.
12. Pan and zoom to make fresh requests for WMS data to be loaded to the view.

How it works...

When you pan and zoom the map, a request with the bounding box of the viewable extent and scale is sent to the service. The server then renders an image that matches the request and passes it back to the client (in this case, QGIS).

There's more...

Some WMS services now also support tiling under the **Web Map Tiling Service** (**WMTS**) protocol. From the client's perspective, this not really different from WMS in usage. On the server side, after each request the results are cached so that if the same extent and scale is requested, the cached version can be delivered instead of creating the results from scratch. For you, the end user, this should result in faster loading if a service provides WMTS.

When configuring a WMTS, use the WMTS URL instead of the WMS URL. One example would be the Geoserver demo site's WMTS:

```
http://demo.opengeo.org/geoserver/gwc/service/
wmts?REQUEST=GetCapabilities
```

Once successful, this will take you to the **Tilesets** tab, where you can pick which layer and projection of the available options you want to load. As the Tiles are premade or cached, you will usually not have the option to combine multiple layers at once and will need to load them one at a time:

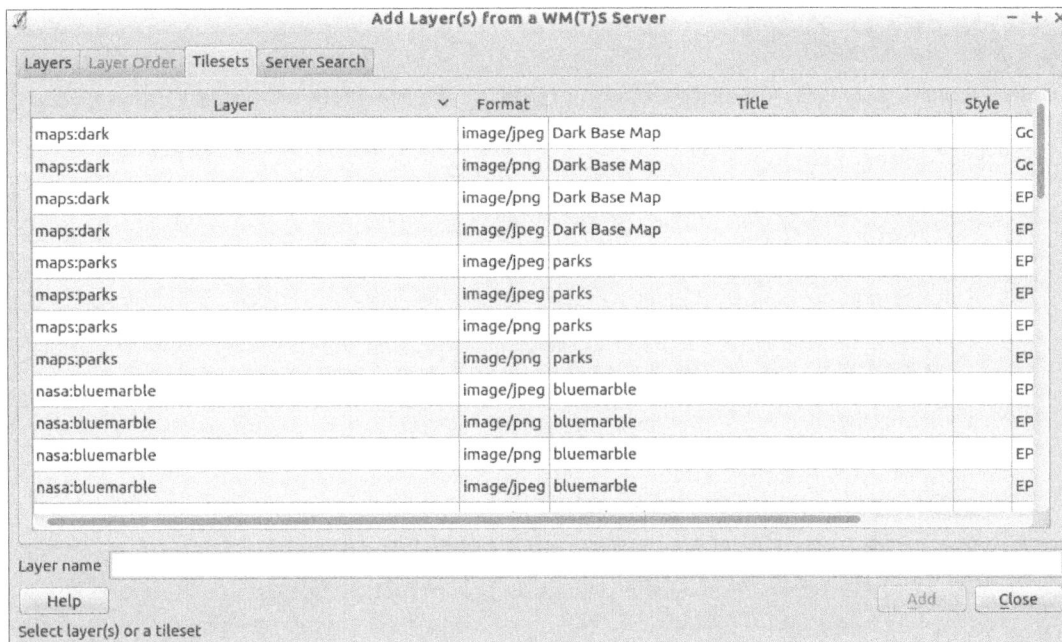

> WMS-C is an earlier version of the WMTS standard. In usage, it's pretty much the same, though the URL pattern may look more similar to the WMS.

See also

▶ See the QGIS documentation for more information about the WMS capabilities of QGIS at `http://docs.qgis.org/2.8/en/docs/user_manual/working_with_ogc/ogc_client_support.html#ogc-wms`

Using WCS

A **Web Coverage Service** (**WCS**) differs greatly in use case from the other services, but it behaves very similarly. The goal of WCS is to allow users to extract a region of interest from a large raster data that is hosted remotely. Unlike a WMS or Tiled set, WCS is a clip of the original data in full resolution and usually in the original projection. This format is ideal if you need the raster data for analysis purposes and not just visualization.

Getting ready

For this recipe, you need a WCS to connect to. Check with your data providers to see whether they offer WCS. For this recipe, we can use the OpenGeo Geoserver Demo site at `http://demo.opengeo.org/geoserver/web/`.

How to do it...

1. Open a web browser and go to `http://demo.opengeo.org/geoserver/web/`.

2. On the right-hand side, you'll see a list of web services that are available; right-click on **WCS 1.1.1** and copy the link.

3. In QGIS, open the WCS dialog.

4. Select **New** to create a new server entry.

5. In the boxes, perform the following:

    1. Provide a name so that you remember which service this is.

    2. Paste the URL that you copied earlier in the URL box (`http://demo.opengeo.org/geoserver/ows?service=wcs&version=1.1.1&request=GetCapabilities`):

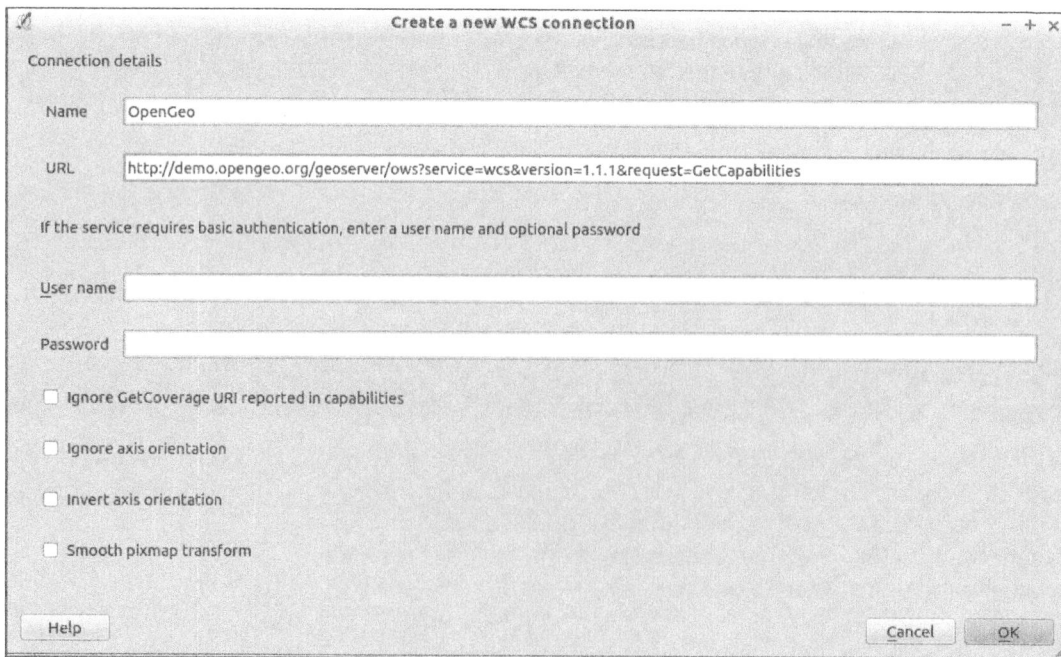

6. Click on the **OK** button.

7. Now, you'll be back on the **Add Layer(s) from a WCS Server** dialog:

   1. Click on the **Connect** button.

   2. After the list is populated, select a layer to add to the map. Click on the **Add** button. Try the Blue Marble layer.

   3. Now, click on the **Close** button to return to your map:

ID	∨	Name	Title	Abstract
0		usgs:ned	National Elevation Dataset	Generated from GeoTIFF
1		usgs:nlcd	National Landcover Dataset	Generated from WorldImage
2		ne:NE1_HR_LC_SR_W_DR	Natural Earth 1	Generated from GeoTIFF
3		nurc:Img_Sample	North America sample imagery	A very rough imagery of North America
4		maps:OB_LR_ti_ov	OB_LR_ti_ov	Generated from GeoTIFF
5		nasa:bluemarble	bluemarble	Generated from GeoTIFF
6		ne:wps4623406955417507685tiff15...	wps4623406955417507685tiff156922...	Generated from GeoTIFF
7		ne:wps4693812227741231645tiff16...	wps4693812227741231645tiff164814...	Generated from GeoTIFF
8		ne:wps5380428517378077718tiff62...	wps5380428517378077718tiff628977...	Generated from GeoTIFF

Add Layer(s) from a WCS Server dialog showing Layers tab with OpenGeo connection, Connect/New/Edit/Delete and Load/Save buttons, layer list, Time, Coordinate Reference System (1 available): WGS 84, Change..., Format: GeoTIFF / GTiff, Cache: Prefer network, Help, Add, and Close buttons.

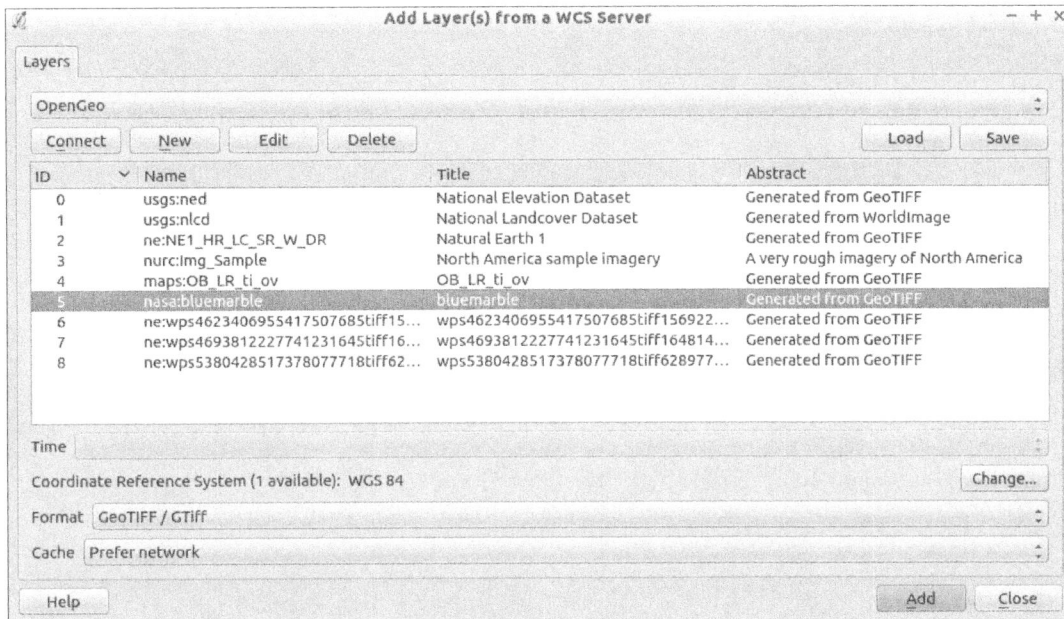

8. You should now see the Blue Marble layer loaded.

> If you zoom in to the level of a US State or a European country, you will see the image start to pixelate. Blue Marble is a low resolution image put together by NASA that roughly shows what the whole world looks like from space, cloud free. It is meant as a general view of the whole world and does not contain fine details.

9. (Optional) Use the **Save As** option to download a portion or the entire WCS layer at its full original resolution.

How it works...

WCS, like other web services, sends a bounding box request to the server, which in turn delivers the raster data to QGIS. Unlike WMS, no rendering is done on the server side, the raw original raster data is sent. This could mean the following:

▶ There was no resampling of the image before it was sent

▶ You can apply your own styling to the data that is delivered

Keep in mind that requesting the full extent of a high resolution raster will result in a large amount of data transfer. This is unlike Tiles or WMS, which at most return the exact number of pixels in the viewable area at the resolution that is requested.

> As with other web services, it is recommended that you zoom in to your area of interest before loading a WCS.

There's more...

Another bonus of WCS over WMS is that because WCS delivers the original data, it is not limited to a 3-band RGB image. You can use WCS to view and download Multi or Hyperspectral data (4+ bands common in remote-sensing applications).

> Currently, QGIS only supports 1.0.x and 1.1.x, not WCS 2.x; at least not yet!

Using GDAL

The QuickMapsServices and OpenLayers plugins, as described in the *Loading BaseMaps with the QuickMapServices plugin* and *Loading BaseMaps with the OpenLayers plugin* recipes in *Chapter 4, Data Exploration*, are awesome as they put a reference layer in your map session. The one downside, however, is that it is a hassle to add new layers. So, if you come across or build your own Tile service and want to use it in QGIS, this recipe will let you use almost any Tile service.

Getting ready

You will need a web browser, text editor, and the URL of a web-based XYZ (sometimes called TMS) service—one that allows you to make requests without an API key. We're going to use the maps at http://www.opencyclemap.org/.

Viewing the JavaScript source (a good tool for this is **Firebug**, or other web-developer tools for the browser), we can view the source URLs for the tiles.

How to do it...

1. Open `http://www.opencyclemap.org/` in a web browser.

2. Now, figure out the URL for the tiles by looking at the source code:

    1. Look in `map.js` and you'll see the layer definition:

        ```
        var cycle = new OpenLayers.Layer.OSM("OpenCycleMap",
          ["https://a.tile.thunderforest.com/cycle/${z}/${x}/${y}.
          png",
          "https://b.tile.thunderforest.com/cycle/${z}/${x}/${y}.
          png",
          "https://c.tile.thunderforest.com/cycle/${z}/${x}/${y}.
          png"],
          { displayOutsideMaxExtent: true,
            attribution: cycleattrib, transitionEffect: 'resize'}
        );
        ```

    2. Or, you can look at the image files your browser downloads. If you put `https://a.tile.thunderforest.com/cycle/13/1325/3143.png` into a browser, it will load that one tile.

3. The pattern is pretty straight forward:

    ```
    <server name>/<layer>/<zoom>/<tile index X>/<tile index
    X>.<image format>
    ```

    > In this particular case, the Tile Index pattern is the TMS style; refer to `http://www.maptiler.org/google-maps-coordinates-tile-bounds-projection/`.

4. To turn this into a layer in QGIS, open up a text editor and paste in the following definition. This definition tells GDAL which driver to use and the server URL pattern with `z`, `x`, and `y` as variables. Save the file as `opencyclemap.xml`:

    ```
    <GDAL_WMS>
      <Service name="TMS">
        <ServerUrl>http://c.tile.thunderforest.com/cycle/${z}/${x}/
          ${y}.png</ServerUrl>
      </Service>
      <DataWindow>
        <UpperLeftX>-20037508.34</UpperLeftX>
        <UpperLeftY>20037508.34</UpperLeftY>
        <LowerRightX>20037508.34</LowerRightX>
        <LowerRightY>-20037508.34</LowerRightY>
        <TileLevel>18</TileLevel>
        <TileCountX>1</TileCountX>
    ```

```
    <TileCountY>1</TileCountY>
    <YOrigin>top</YOrigin>
  </DataWindow>
  <Projection>EPSG:3785</Projection>
  <BlockSizeX>256</BlockSizeX>
  <BlockSizeY>256</BlockSizeY>
  <BandsCount>3</BandsCount>
  <Cache />
</GDAL_WMS>
```

5. You can now load the layer using the Raster dialog or the browser:

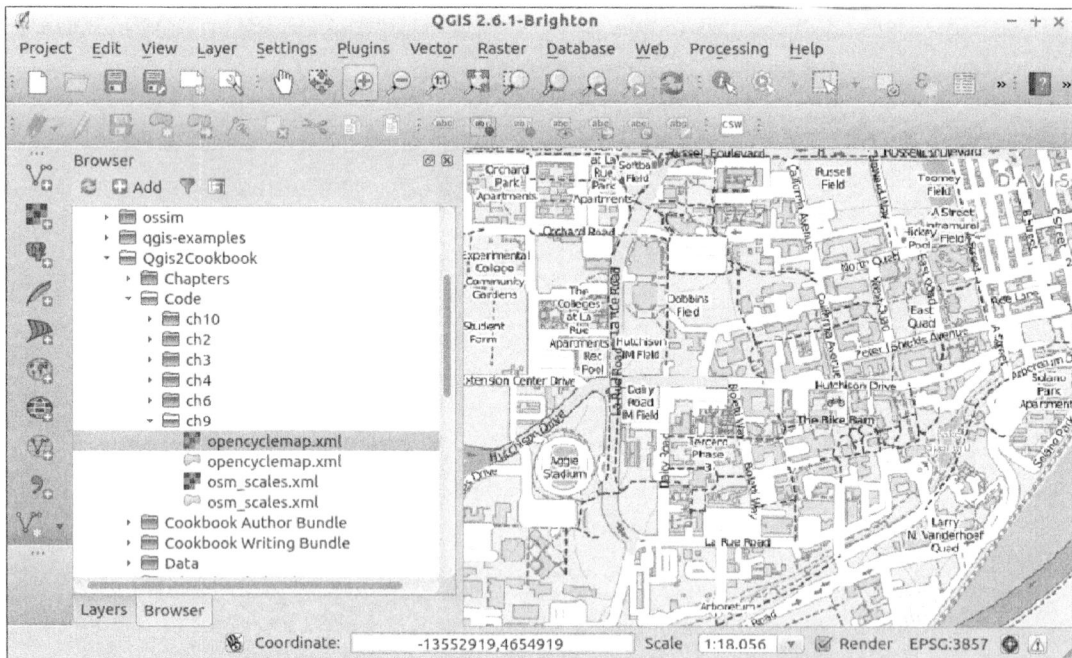

> Note that there are two listings for `opencyclemap.xml`; only the one with the square-shaped icon will work (that is, a raster), as tiles are a raster format.

How it works...

The XML file defines the parameters of the service; however, because XYZ-style servers don't follow a standard, the URL pattern varies slightly for each server and the servers do not have a GetCapabilities function that describes available layers. By telling GDAL how to handle the URL, you are wrapping a nonstandard format into a typical GDAL layer, which QGIS can easily be loaded as a raster.

There's more...

One additional tip when using Spherical Mercator (EPSG:3785) is that you can set a custom list of scales (**Zoom Levels**) in QGIS. The following set of scales can be loaded per QGIS project, and will change the dropdown at the bottom right. These scales match the scales that most servers will provide, so you get the best viewing experience:

1. Go to **File** | **Project Properties**.
2. Select the **General** tab.
3. Check the **Project Scales** checkbox.
4. Load the `scales.xml` file that is provided:

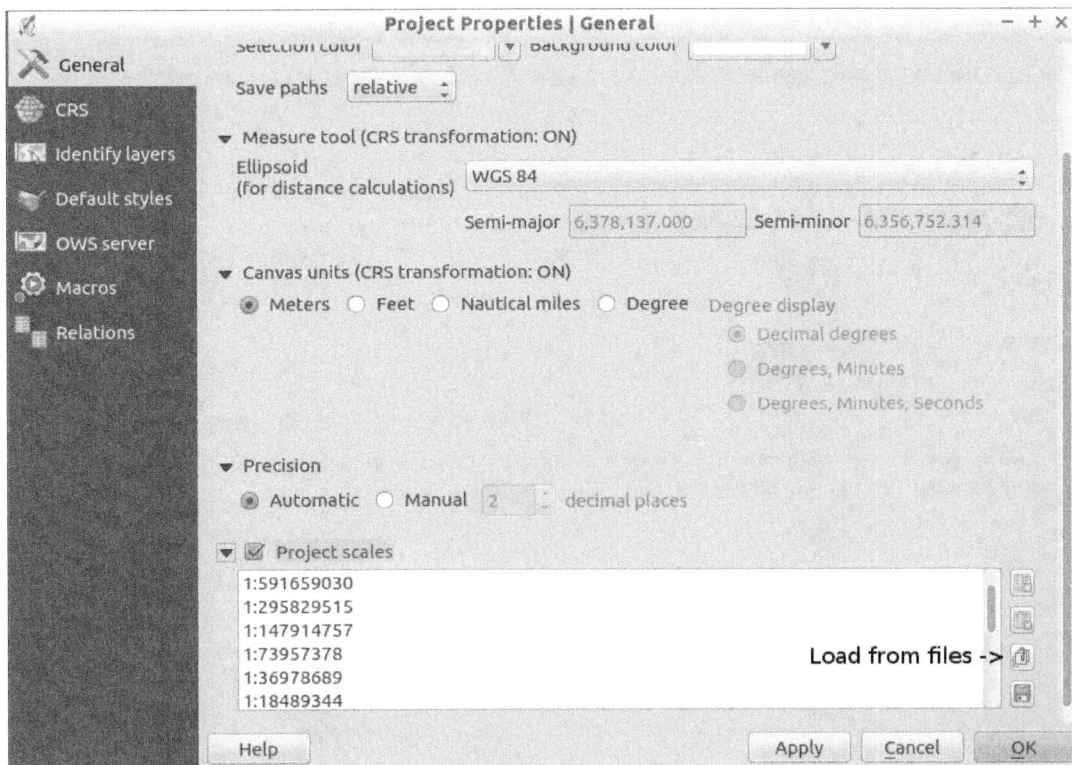

This technique is not limited to just tile services. Many other formats that GDAL works with can be wrapped for easier usage in QGIS. This is a similar method to **Virtual Raster Tables** (**VRT**) layers mentioned in the *Creating raster overviews (pyramids)* recipe in *Chapter 2, Data Management*.

Lastly, you may ask why a new plugin using this method doesn't replace the OpenLayers plugin. Such an idea has been under discussion for a while; the key sticking point is that accessing some layers, such as Google, Bing, and so on, with this method may violate the Terms of Service as they do not keep the Copyright, Trademark, and Logo in the correct place. Also, caching and printing such layers may not be legal. In general, avoid using proprietary data when possible to reduce licensing issues.

See also

> ▶ This recipe and method has actually been known and discussed in many QGIS venues. The most frequently cited example is available at `http://www.3liz.com/blog/rldhont/index.php?post/2012/07/17/OpenStreetMap-Tiles-in-QGIS`.

> ▶ The full explanation of options for GDAL can be found at `http://www.gdal.org/frmt_wms.html`.

Serving web maps with the QGIS server

QGIS and the Web is not all about consuming data, it can also be used to serve data over the Web for others to view online or consume in other web clients (such as QGIS). Keep in mind that setting up your own web service is not the easiest way to make a web map (refer to the *Hooking up web clients* recipe in this chapter). This is, however, a great way to transition all the hard work that you've put into a QGIS project file into something other people can see and use.

Getting ready

For this recipe, you need a working installation of the QGIS server. This involves running a standard web server (such as Apache or Nginx). There are many ways to set up the server, so please see the official documentation at `http://hub.qgis.org/projects/quantum-gis/wiki/QGIS_Server_Tutorial`.

Once you have the QGIS server running, then you just need a QGIS project with the configuration outlined in this recipe.

How to do it...

1. Open QGIS.
2. Load up and style some layers:
   - You need at least one vector layer to offer a WFS.
   - You need at least one raster layer to offer a WCS.
   - WMS can be any combination of layers, you can choose to server each as an independent layer or as a combined layer.
3. Edit the **Project** properties in **File | Project Properties**:
   1. Open the **OWS server** tab.
   2. Check the **Service Capabilities** box to enable GetCapabilities.
   3. Fill out some of the boxes so that end users know what your server is about, who runs it, and how to contact you:

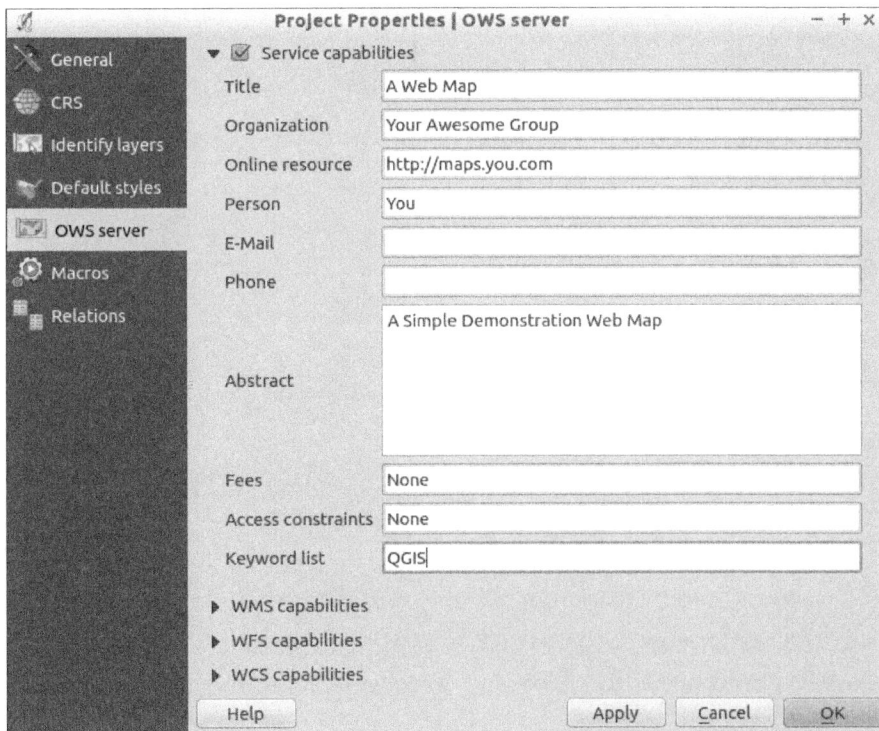

4. Now examine the **WMS capabilities** section:

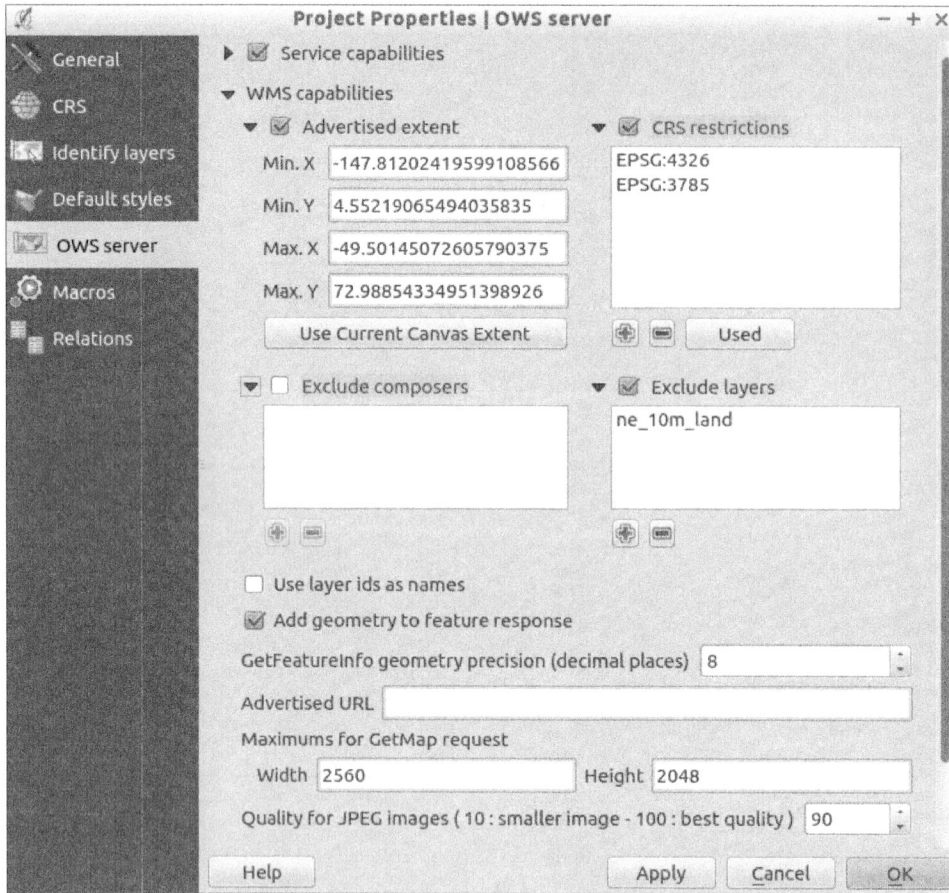

> Most of these features are optional optimizations. Pick and choose what suits your needs.

5. Here, you can set the maximum extent that clients should expect.

6. The **CRS restrictions** option lets you limit what projections are allowed.

7. **Exclude Layers** allows you to have layers in your project that don't show up on the web.

8. **Add geometry to feature response** is an optional enhancement if you are building a web map and you want to be able to work with the actual vectors (if it is a vector to begin with).

9. **GetFeatureInfo** precision is about how close a user has to click to query a location. If you have a lot of data, you probably want this number to be small; but if you have only a few features, making this bigger makes it easier for end users.

10. Set **Maximums for GetMap request** if you want to reduce the load on your server by limiting how much data a user can request at once. This is a good idea for a public server. 2560 x 2048, as shown in the screenshot, is enough pixels for an HD-resolution screen to be filled in a single request.

11. Next, take a look at the **WFS capabilities** section:

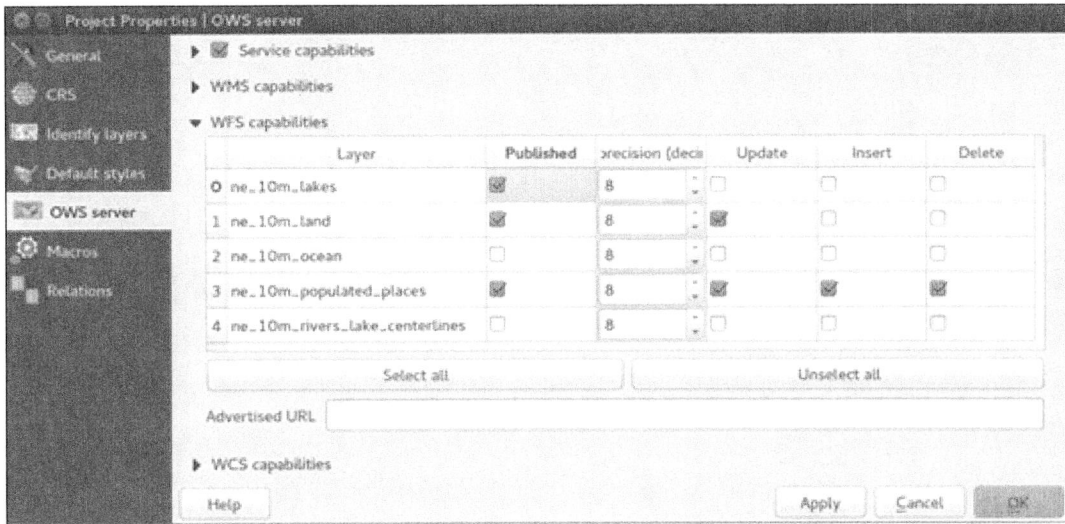

Only enable WFS if you want users to be able to request vector data as vectors. This can be more intensive than WMS on your bandwidth. Also, do not enable WFS-T features unless you secure your server to only permitted users.

1. Check the **Published** box next to any vector layers that you want to be usable over WFS.

2. To enable WFS-T, check the **Update**, **Insert**, and **Delete** checkboxes. As they are separate, you can choose to only allow new data (**Insert**), only allow edits to existing data (**Update**), or only allow removal of data (**Delete**). **Insert** would be the safest option as it prevents editing or deletion of existing data.

12. Finally, take a look at **WCS capabilities**:

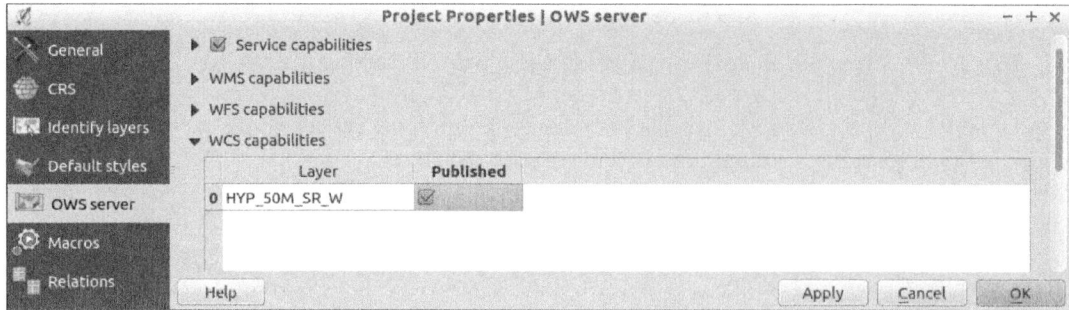

[*This an all or none feature. Don't enable this unless you want users to be able to download the original raster data.*]

13. When you are done setting options, click on the **OK** button.

14. Now, save the project in a place where the QGIS server has access to it.

[*In Apache, this is usually a folder such as* /var/www/.]

15. Once saved, you can test access from any OGC-compliant web client:

   1. For a simple test, use a fresh QGIS project and the **Add WMS** dialog.

   2. The GetCapabilties URL will look something like `http://localhost/cgi-bin/qgis_mapserv.fcgi?map=/usr/local/share/qgis/QGIS-NaturalEarth-Example.qgs`.

[*The key part of this URL that is somewhat unique to QGIS server is the* `map` *parameter, which is followed by the full system path to the QGIS project file.*

This may seem odd, but adding your QGIS server as a WMS in QGIS is a great way to test whether it's working.]

How it works...

The QGIS server is a middleman that takes in web service requests and translates them into QGIS internal calls, returning the requested data or rendered images, which are delivered to the end user via the web server.

There's more...

The QGIS server contains many options that allow you to control which types of service to offer, which layers to offer over each service, and how to style these services. Alternatives to the QGIS server include MapServer and GeoServer (refer to the *Managing GeoServer from QGIS* section in this chapter).

See also

▸ For more details, refer to the main documentation for the QGIS server at `http://hub.qgis.org/projects/quantum-gis/wiki/QGIS_Server_Tutorial`.

▸ Once you create a service, test it by adding your service to a QGIS project. Refer to the previous recipes in this chapter for how to add WMS, WFS, or WCS services.

Scale-dependent rendering

While they are not specifically for web services, being able to change the styling and presence of data based on the scale of the map can have a huge impact on the speed and readability of web services. Unlike printed maps, web maps are viewed at multiple scales. This variation in scales often requires different cartography to keep the map legible and usable.

Getting ready

You'll need a QGIS project, preferably one with a high data density or differing levels of information. A good example is road data, where you have major, minor, local, and other variants of road classification. `caryStreets.shp` converted from CAD in a previous chapter is a good example.

How to do it...

1. Open QGIS and load `caryStreets.shp`.

2. Now, open the attribute table and look for an attribute to filter in. In `caryStreets.shp`, there are several potential columns to use, such as `StreetType`, `Major_Road`, and `Main_Road`.

> `StreetType` appears to be classes, whereas the other two columns appear to be `True` or `False` flags. Any of these are decent candidates for filtering rules.

3. Now, open the **Properties** section for the layer:

    1. Switch to the **Style** tab to edit the symbology.

    2. Change the top-right dropdown to **Rule Based Rendering**.

    3. Create a new rule (green plus sign).

4. In the pop up dialog set **Label** to **Major Roads** and **Filter** to "Major_Road" = 't'.

5. (Optional) You can use the expression builder to build the filter statement and test it. Click on the **...** button to open the dialog.

> You could create two copies of Major with different scale ranges so that as you zoom in, the major roads become thicker at the same time that minor roads are enabled.

This is what your layer looks like before and after you create the first rule:

2118500,722689   Scale :351.407 ▼ ☑ Render

6. Now, add another rule for minor roads by filtering for **"Major_Road" = 'f'**.

7. This time, you're going to enable the **Scale range** option.

8. Set **Minimum (exclusive)** to **1:100,000**. For any scale bigger than this, the features will be hidden. For **Maximum (inclusive)**, type in **1:0**, which will disable the **Max filter**.

9. Pick a different line type and/or color for the minor roads:

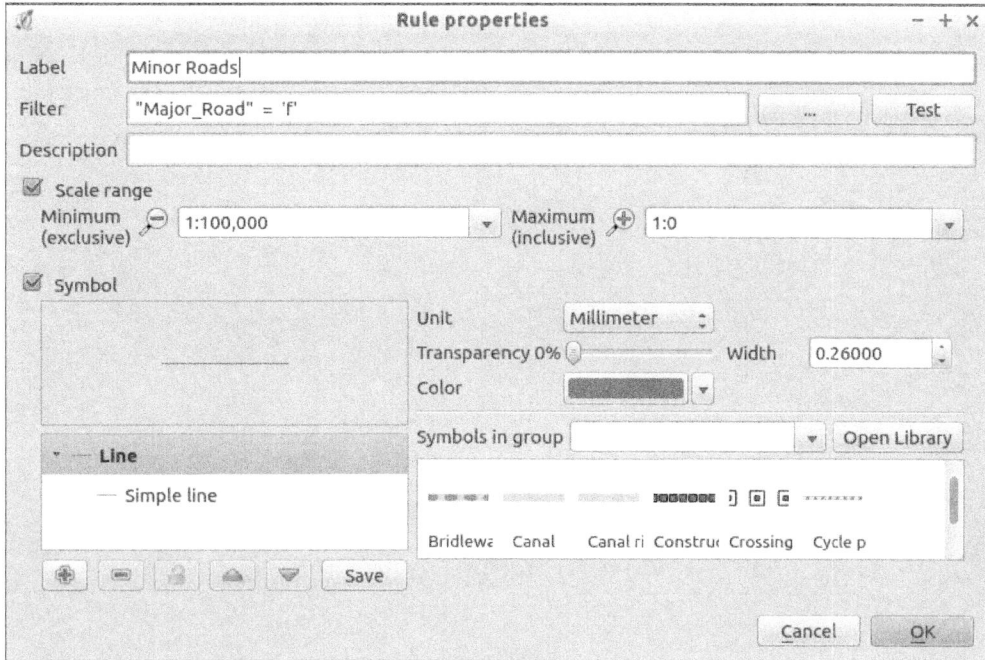

10. You should now have two rules, one for major roads and one for minor roads:

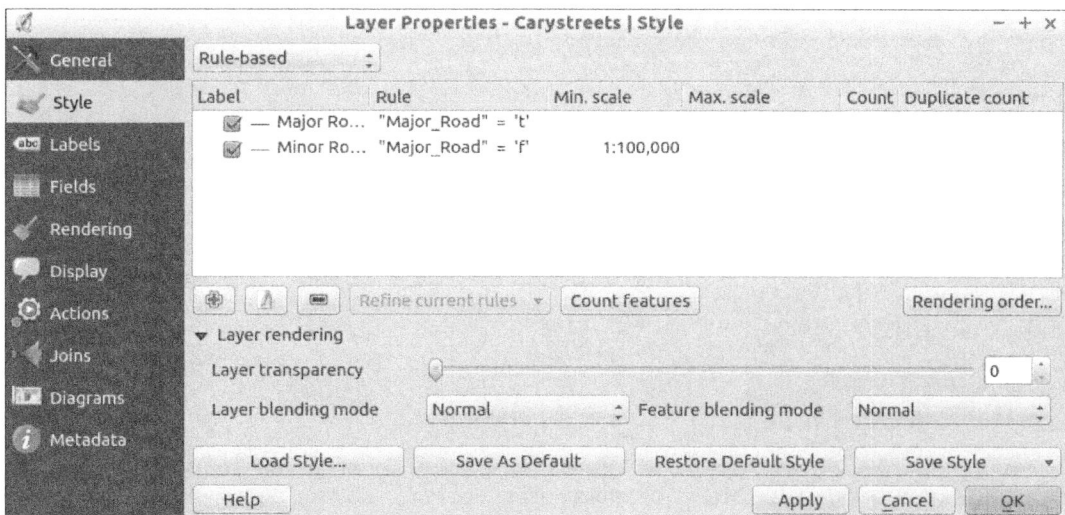

> [💡 You don't have to open the **edit rule** dialog; you can directly modify parts of the rules in the **Rule Based Rendering** page.]

11. Go back to the map and zoom in to **1:50,000**, then zoom out to **1:250,000**. The minor roads should appear and disappear as you change past the **1:100,000** scale:

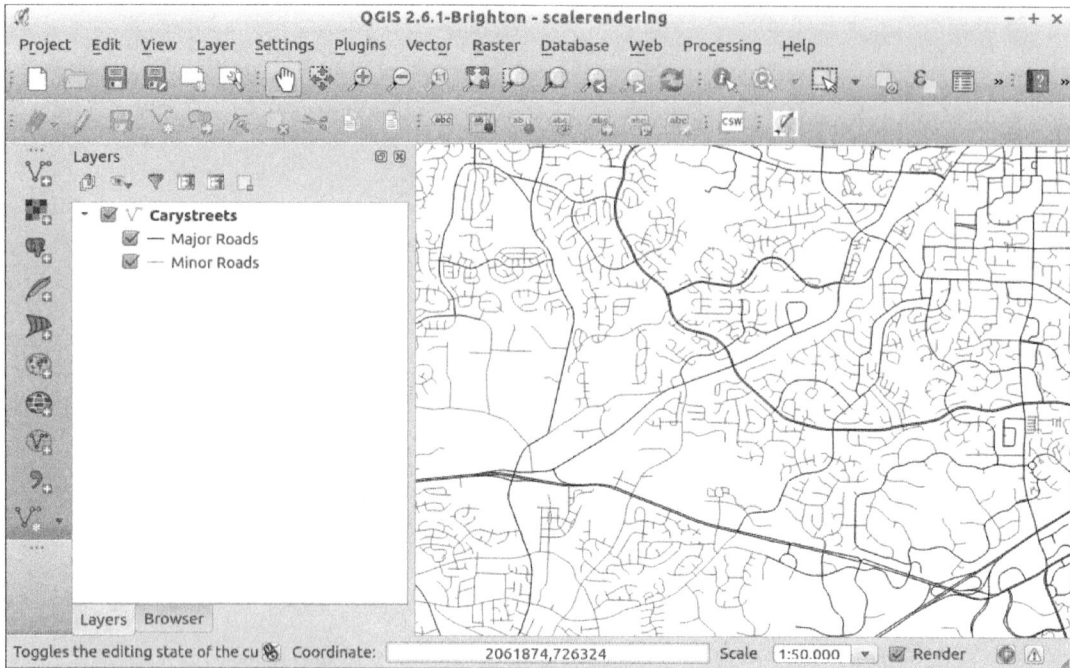

How it works...

The goal with scale-dependent rendering is generally to make your map readable at many different zoom levels. By setting the **Min** and **Max** scales for each layer or subfeatures within a layer, you can declutter a map for readability. The rendering engine just checks the scale against each rule before deciding what to render.

There's more...

Scale-dependent rendering can be used in several ways. This can be used to change the styling based on zoom or hide or reveal data based on the zoom level. However, it's also not limited to just changing styles or layers. You can also perform scale-dependent labeling, which is part of data-driven labeling described in the *Configuring data-defined labels* recipe in *Chapter 10, Cartography Tips*, of this book.

Scale rules also work on raster layers; however, this only allows you to turn a raster on and off. It doesn't allow you to change its appearance.

If you have a QGIS server set up from earlier in this chapter, the scaling rules should apply to your web services (WMS and WFS).

> You probably don't want to use something as complex as a street layer via WFS in a web browser because it's almost guaranteed to crash. Stick to pushing such complex layers as Tiles or WMS.

See also

The Rule Based Rendering has a lot of features crammed into it. However, this is not yet a comprehensive guide to everything that it can do, so you'll need to explore and perform Internet searches for now.

Hooking up web clients

Sometimes, the best way to share a map is to build a website with a map embedded in it. There are many methods to accomplish this goal, ranging from a simple dump of a few layers to a highly-interactive map, which is based on web services. There are many web clients that will work with standard OGC services. This recipe will show you how to build a simple web map using Leaflet—a popular JavaScript library that is used to create web maps.

Getting ready

You will need the qgis2leaf plugin and some sample data. The `schools_wake.shp` (Points) and `census_wake_2000.shp` files make for a good example.

How to do it...

1. Install and enable the qgis2leaf plugin.

> Make sure to check out the qgis2web plugin, which is a newer variant that works similarly but has some different options.

2. Load up some layers to make a map composition.

> Make a copy of your layer and eliminate unnecessary columns that you don't need to show on the web map. Reducing the size of the attribute table will make it easier to read popups with information and speed up web page loading.

3. Style the map as you want it to appear online.

> Styling can be really tricky. Leaflet and other web map libraries don't support 100% of the same options as QGIS. Try making a few maps, changing settings, and re-exporting these maps a few times to figure out how to get it the way that you want. It may not look good in QGIS but look good in the export.

4. (Optional) Configure labels. In this example, label the School names.

> Only black labels are currently supported. Though you can probably customize the CSS and JavaScript (js) after the export if you need labels in a different style.

5. Open the qgis2leaf plugin from its icon on the toolbar or from the **Web** menu:

   1. Click on the **GetLayers** button to add the layers from your map to the export list.

   2. There are lots of options here, and they are optional. Go ahead and check **Create Legend**. If you made labels, also check **Export Labels and labels on hover**.

> **Create Cluster** is a fantastic option if you have a lot of points on the map. This will group points into a circle with a number indicating how many points are near there. As you zoom in, they will split apart into smaller groups, until at some zoom, all the points are in their original spot.

   3. For the frame size, you can pick a size of the page that you want the map to take up (in pixels). However, fullscreen works well if the map is the only thing that you care about.

   4. Go ahead and add a tile-based base layer; **Stamen Terrain** is an interesting choice. Keep in mind that you can only have one of these on at a time, but you can toggle between them.

5. Pick an output folder location and fill in the remaining map information describing how you want it to show up in the results.

6. Export the project:

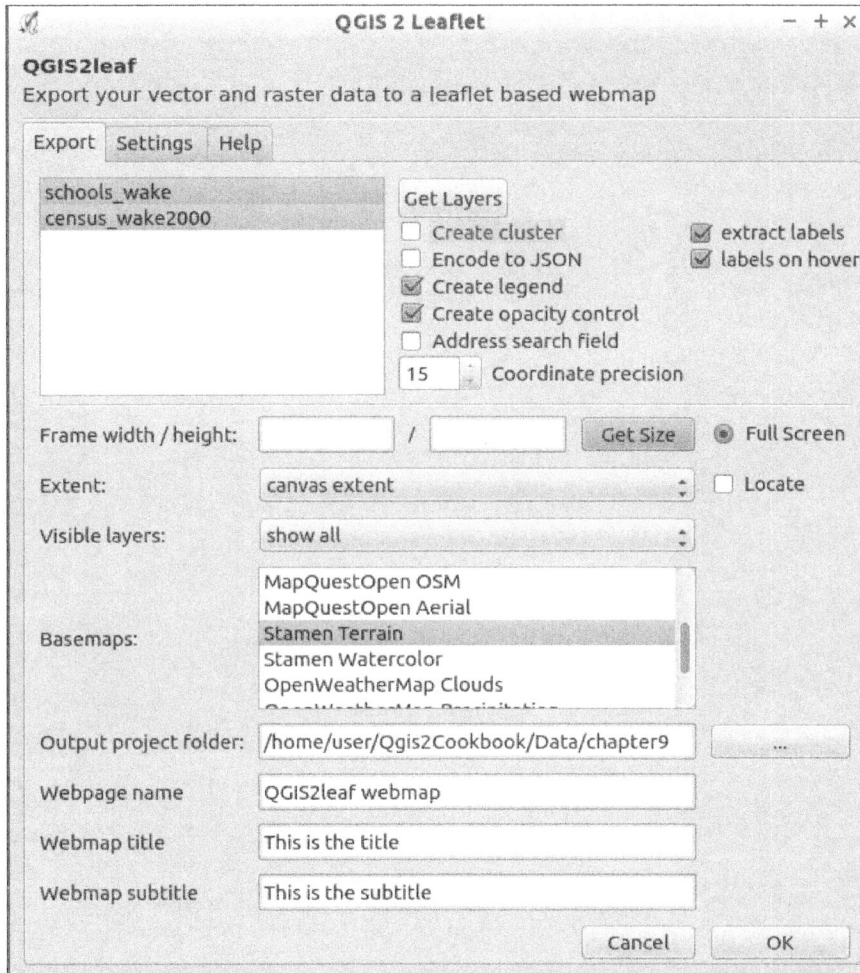

6. After exporting, the map should open in your web browser. If it doesn't, open your operating system file explorer (or web browser) and navigate to the output folder. You should see a new folder called `export_year_month_day_hour_minute_seconds` (for example, `export_2015_02_19_11_34_05`). Inside this folder is `index.html`. Open this file with a web browser to see your map:

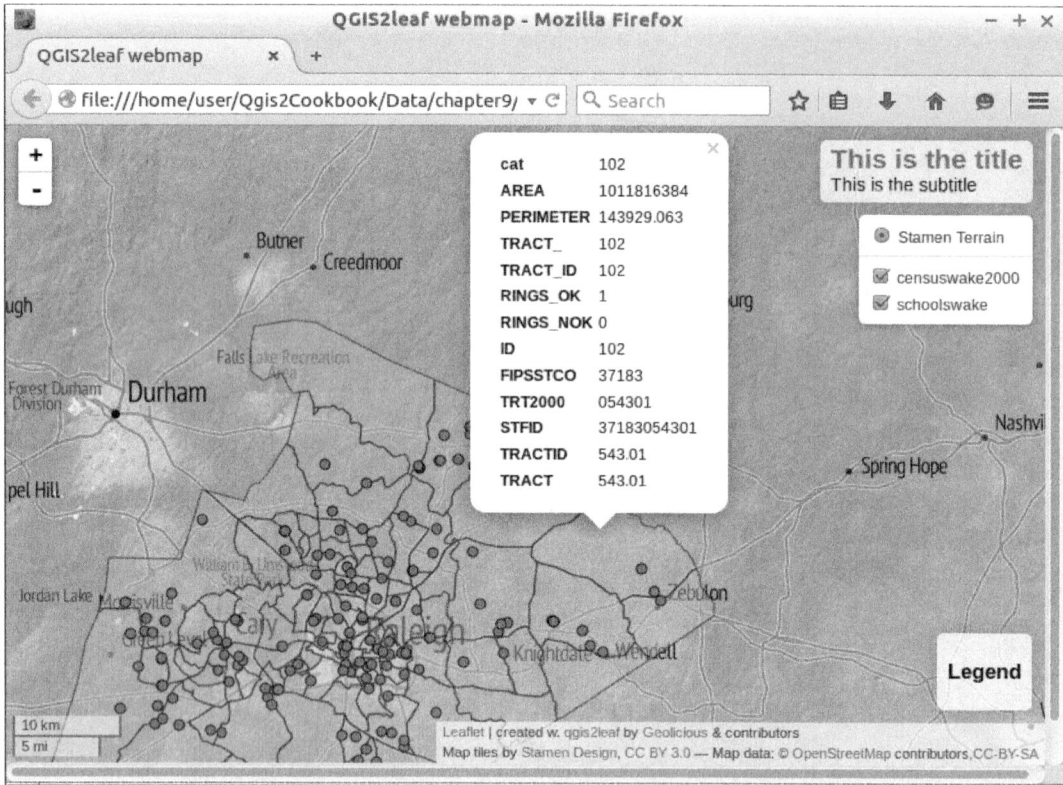

7. Note that all the vectors are clickable, and the popup will display the attribute table information. If you turned on labels and hover, then hovering over a point will display the name.

How it works...

The qgis2leaf plugin converts your map into something that is compatible with the web. Generally, this means converting vector data to the GeoJSON format and generating an HTML page (web page) with some JavaScript to create and populate the map.

Raster layers are trickier, and if you can, try to stick to using Tile or WMS services to serve them. Refer to the next section to see how to use Tiles or WMS.

> If you need host tiles locally, try using the QTiles plugin to generate them.

There's more...

The next logical step is to make the map dynamic based on a web service. To do this, you can swap static files for web services:

1. Add a WMS layer to the map (you can use the previous recipe in this chapter on QGIS server if you have it running). Add an external source WMS, such as the USGS NAIP Airphoto. (Here's the GetCapabilities URL, `http://isse.cr.usgs.gov/arcgis/services/Orthoimagery/USGS_EROS_Ortho_NAIP/ImageServer/WMSServer?request=GetCapabilities&service=WMS`).

2. Re-export with the same settings:

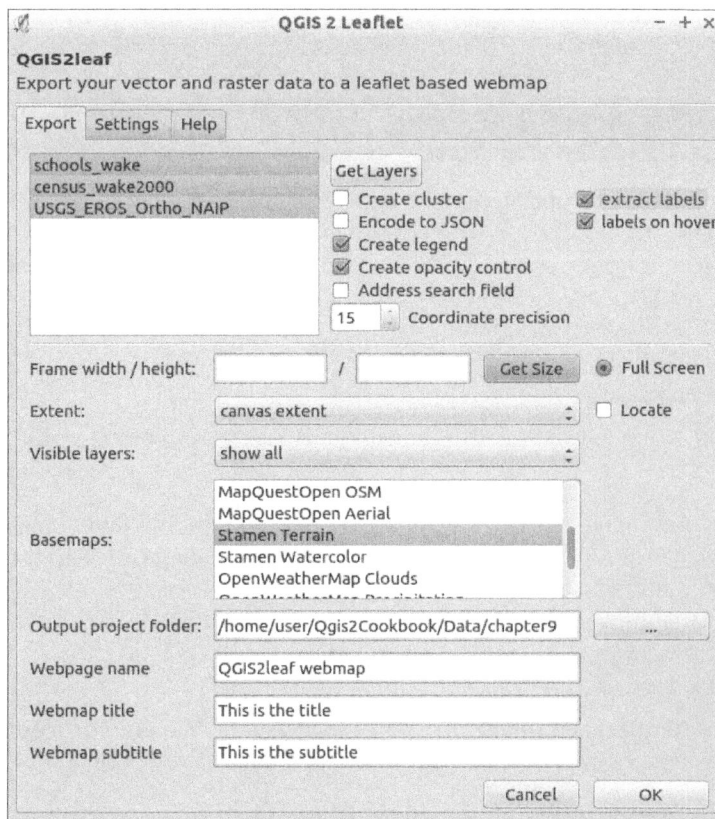

> Now that you've created the Leaflet map, if you wanted to get into JavaScript programming, all of the code that you need is in the directory produced, either directly in `index.html` or in the `js` folder. In particular, you can see exactly how layers are styled and added to the map.

You don't have to use Tiles or WMS for raster layers but this is recommended. If you do want to use a local file, be warned there is a bug currently where some exports fail unless your raster is converted to a `.jpg` format image in EPSG:4326 projection.

See also

▶ Don't forget to look at the documentation for the Leaflet JavaScript library on how to customize your results after the export at `http://leafletjs.com/`.

▶ qgis2web plugin aims to combine qgis2leaflet and qgis2ol3 plugins (`https://plugins.qgis.org/plugins/qgis2web/`), which means it also includes export to OpenLayers 3 that is very similar to Leaflet but uses the OpenLayers JavaScript library. Lizmap (`http://www.3liz.com/en/lizmap.html`) and QGIS Web Client (`https://github.com/qgis/QGIS-Web-Client`) are two more popular options that add more elaborate prebuilt interfaces but require a little more setup.

Managing GeoServer from QGIS

QGIS does not only serve as a frontend for the QGIS server, but it can also serve as a frontend for other similar servers. GeoServer is one of the most popular ones, and you can configure it from QGIS, upload layers, or even edit the style of a GeoServer layer using the QGIS symbology tools.

Getting ready

For this recipe, you will need the GeoServer Explorer plugin. This can be installed using Plugin Manager.

You will also need a running instance of GeoServer. We will assume that you have a local one running on port 8080, but you can replace the corresponding URL with the one of the GeoServer instance that you have available, whether local or remote.

How to do it...

1. Open the **GeoServer Explorer** by navigating to **Web | GeoServer | Geoserver Explorer**. The explorer will appear on the right-hand side of the QGIS window.

2. Click on the **GeoServer Catalogs** item in the explorer tree, and then select the **New catalog** button.

3. Complete the fields in the dialog that will appear to define a new catalog and click on **OK**:

4. The new catalog will be added to the explorer tree, and you can now browse its content.

5. Open the `zipcodes_wake.shp` layer and style it.

6. In the QGIS Layer List, drag the entry corresponding to the `zipcode_wake.shp` layer and drop it on the catalog item in the GeoServer Explorer. The layer will be uploaded and added to the default workspace of the catalog.

7. You can check whether the layer is now in the catalog by opening a web browser and going to the GeoServer web interface at `http://localhost:8080/ geoserver/web/`.

How it works...

The GeoServer Suite plugin communicates with GeoServer using its REST API. By linking QGIS with the GeoServer REST API, it allows you to easily configure many elements that, otherwise, should be configured manually, such as the styling of layers.

There's more...

The Geoserver Explorer plugin has a lot of features to work with GeoServer. Here are some additional ideas so that you can explore them. For more information, check out the plugin help at `http://boundlessgeo.github.io/qgis-geoserver-plugin/`.

Editing a remote style

Once the layer is in the GeoServer catalog, you can edit its style without having to upload the layer again. Just open the **Styles** branch in the explorer tree under the corresponding catalog and double-click on the style to edit, or select the **Edit...** item in the context menu that is shown when right-clicking on the element:

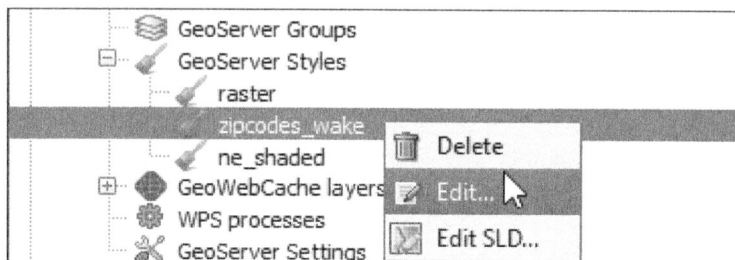

The QGIS symbology dialog will be opened, and you can edit the style in there. Once you close the dialog, the style will be uploaded and updated in the catalog.

Support for multiple formats

The GeoServer REST API only supports shapefiles for vector layers, but you can drag and drop any layer in any format that is supported by QGIS. This plugin will take care of converting it before uploading, in case this is needed.

See also

Don't have a Geoserver instance, it's pretty easy to setup for testing. See `http://geoserver.org/` for details.

10
Cartography Tips

In this chapter, we will cover the following recipes:

- Using Rule Based Rendering
- Handling transparencies
- Understanding the feature and layer blending modes
- Saving and loading styles
- Configuring data-defined labels
- Creating custom SVG graphics
- Making pretty graticules in any projection
- Making useful graticules in printed maps
- Creating a map series using Atlas

Introduction

Cartography has changed quite a bit in the past decade as more people transition to purely electronic map products on a device or on the Web. While some types of visualizations are better suited to different media, many of the underlying tools and techniques can actually be applied across the board. This chapter covers a variety of tools that enable you, the QGIS user, to maximize the readability and beauty of your maps.

Using Rule Based Rendering

In the past, if you wanted to apply a wildly different style to more than one type of data in the same source, the only way to do this was to duplicate or subset a layer. With Rule Based Rendering, you now just have to create rules that are applied on-the-fly. This opens a huge door on cartographic possibilities with different features in the same layer not only having different colors but also different fill types, transparency, line type, and all manner of other customizations. Extending from categorized symbology, rules also allow for mixing and inheritance, allowing for intermediate categories or some shared properties and reducing the amount of work to create elegant symbology.

Getting ready

Rule Based Rendering is built-in to vector symbology. So, you'll need a good complicated vector layer to fully utilize its potential. A road layer is often a good use case, but for this example we'll go slightly simpler with `busroutesall.shp`.

How to do it...

1. Load the `busroutesall.shp` layer.

2. Right-click on the layer name in the **Layers** window, select **Properties**, then pick **Style** on the left-hand side of the new window.

3. Change the symbology drop-down type to **Rule-Based**.

4. Pick the attributes that you want to use to differentiate between groups of features:

    1. In this case, let's edit the initial rule (double-click on the rule or the **Edit** icon between **+** (add) and **-** (remove).

    2. Rules can be based on attribute table values or geometry properties, including on-the-fly calculated values. First let's style routes shorter than 2,000 map units apply here. In the **Filter** box type `$length < 2000` (Do you want to see all the options? Then, open the filter tool with the **...** button). Name your rule and click on **OK**. Back in the main **Style** dialog, apply the rule to see the results in Canvas. Make sure to use the **Test** button to verify that your rule works:

Rule properties — + ×

Label	Under 2000
Filter	$length > 2000

Description

☐ Scale range

Minimum (exclusive) 1:250,000   Maximum (inclusive) 1:50,000

☑ Symbol

Unit   Millimeter

Transparency 0%   Width   0.46000

Color

Symbols in group   Open Library

▾ — **Line**

— Simple line

Bridlewa Canal   Canal ri Construc Crossing Cycle p

Save

Cancel   OK

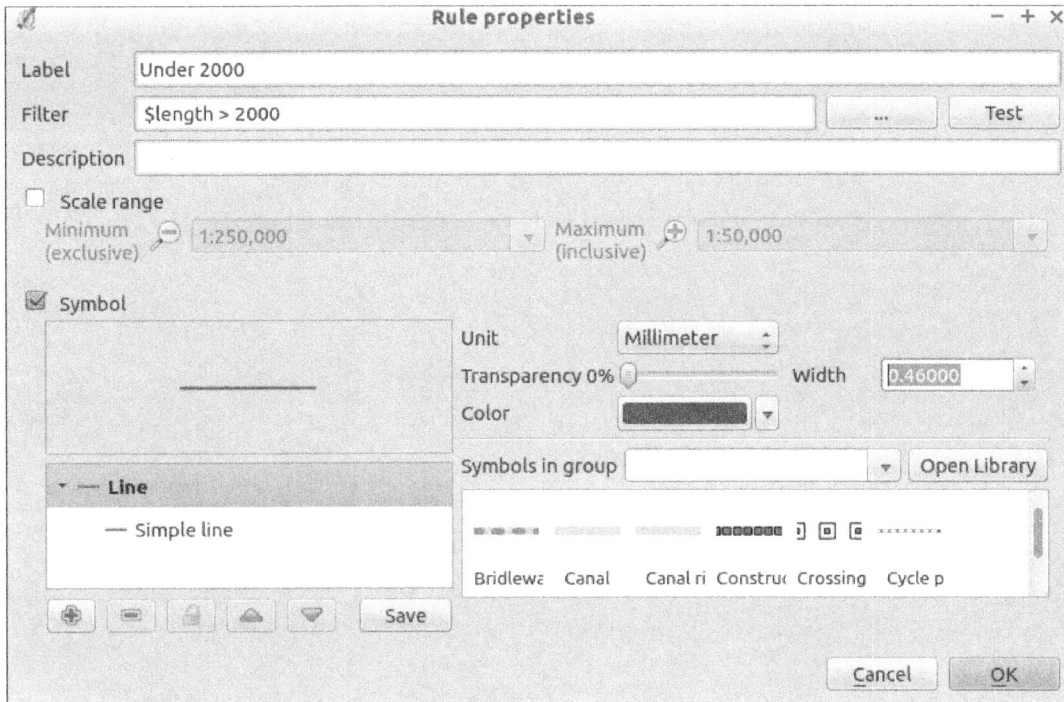

> You can apply more than one rule to objects, the rendering being a combination of the rules and the rendering order.

5. Now to make it more interesting, let's add another rule that's the inverse:

   1. Add a new rule with the green **+** button below the rule list.

   2. For the filter, use `$length > 2000` (don't forget to test this).

   3. Pick some other symbology that differs quite a bit so that it's easy to tell them apart (such as a different line type). Click on **OK** and then click on **Apply** to see to the two rules in action.

6. Now, things get really interesting. Let's add a subrule by either right-clicking on a rule or by highlighting a rule and clicking on the **Refine current rules** dropdown:

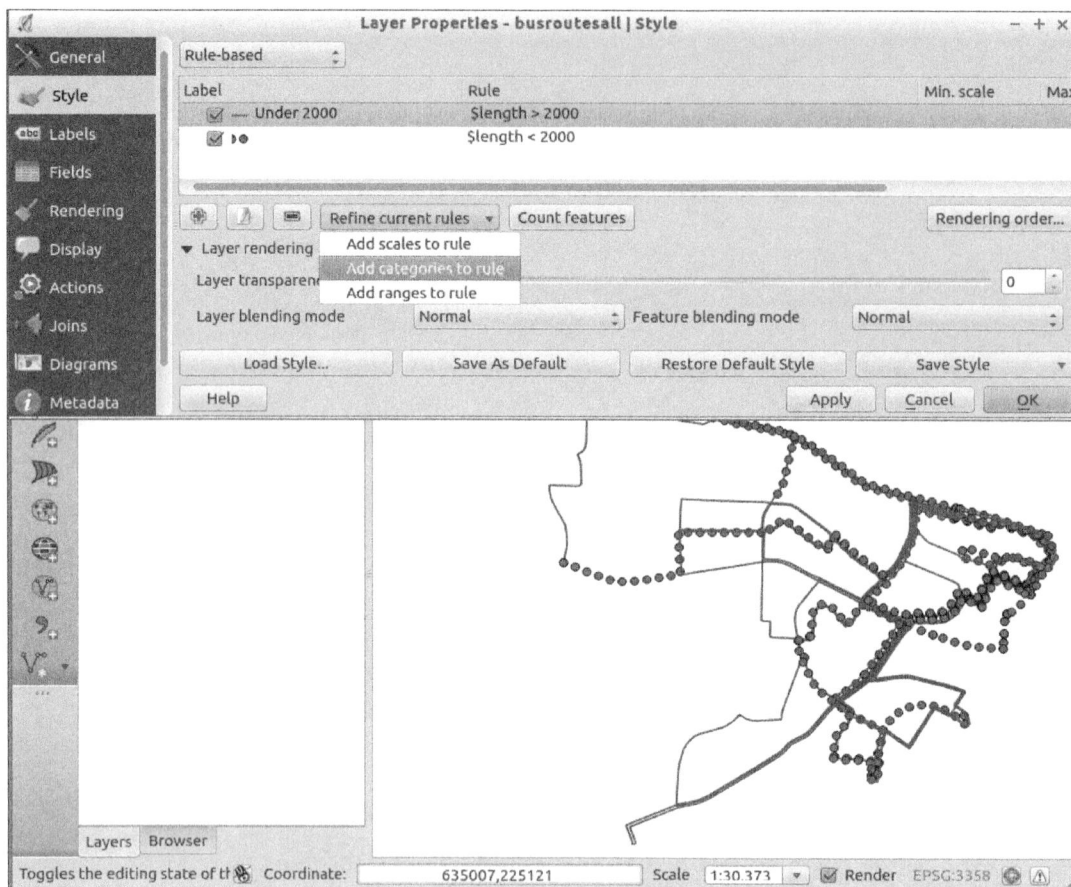

7. Select **Add categories to rule**:

    1. In the subdialog, select **Route**.

    2. Pick a color ramp and/or line style, click on **Classify**, and then click on **OK**:

    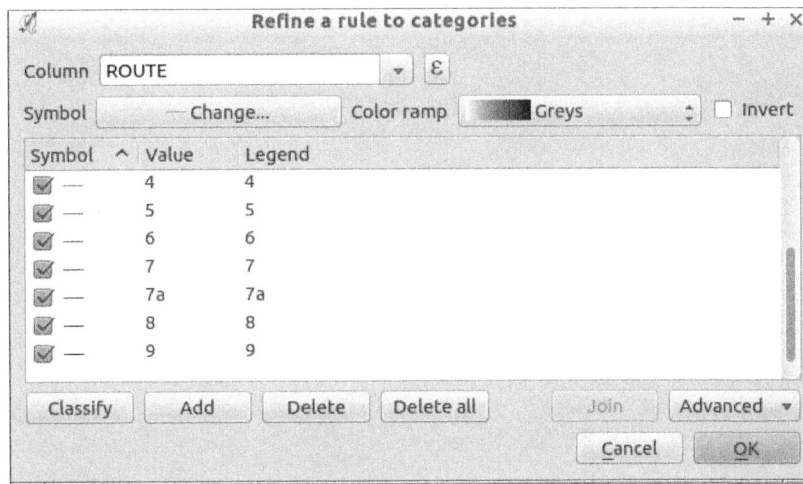

    3. Before you click on **Apply**, edit the main rule and uncheck the **Symbol** box (otherwise, the **Rule** and **Sub Rules** list will be additive, which can be useful in some cases).

8. Now, when you look at the **Rule** list, you will see subrules under their parents.

9. Finally, let's add a third top-level rule that is not based on the length:

   1. Make a rule filter on the ROUTE name that contains a. The rule will look like: `"Route" LIKE '%a'`.

   2. Pick a line symbol that will make these routes stick out even with their current coloring and click on **Apply**:

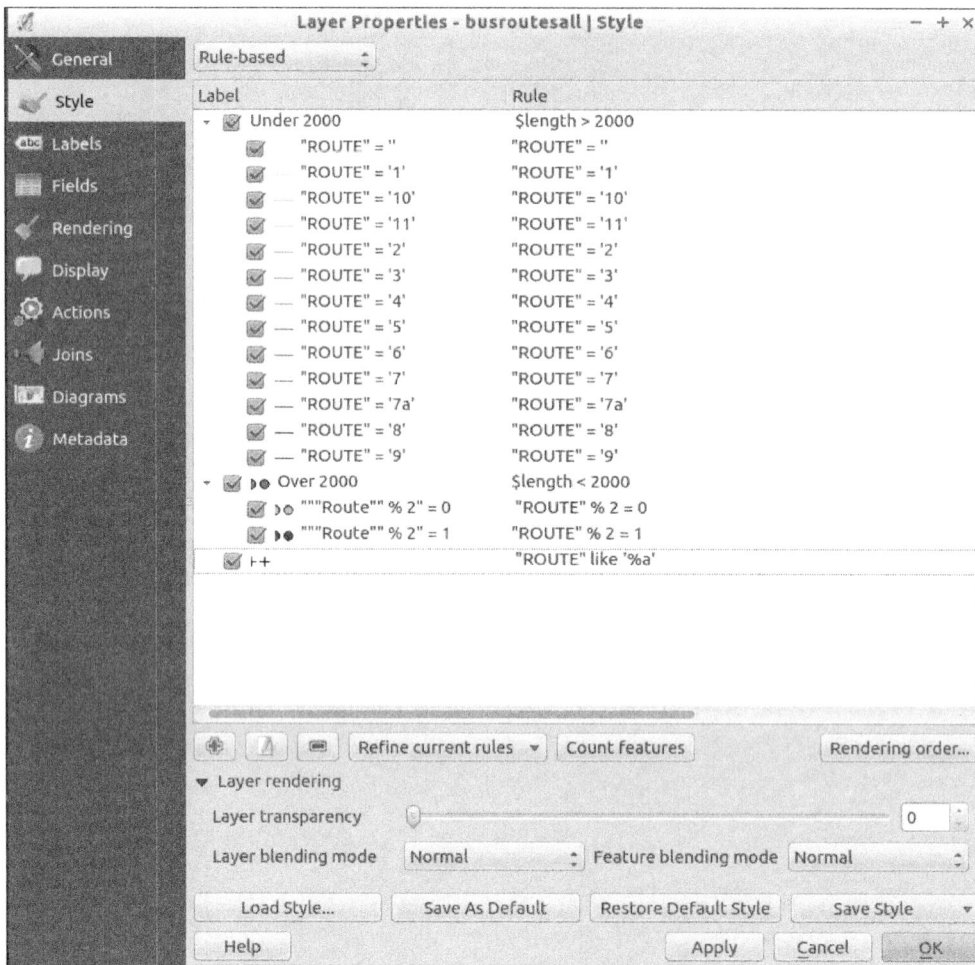

Layer Properties - busroutesall	Style	— + ×

Rule-based

Label	Rule
▾ ☑ Under 2000	$length > 2000
☑ "ROUTE" = ''	"ROUTE" = ''
☑ "ROUTE" = '1'	"ROUTE" = '1'
☑ "ROUTE" = '10'	"ROUTE" = '10'
☑ "ROUTE" = '11'	"ROUTE" = '11'
☑ "ROUTE" = '2'	"ROUTE" = '2'
☑ "ROUTE" = '3'	"ROUTE" = '3'
☑ "ROUTE" = '4'	"ROUTE" = '4'
☑ "ROUTE" = '5'	"ROUTE" = '5'
☑ "ROUTE" = '6'	"ROUTE" = '6'
☑ "ROUTE" = '7'	"ROUTE" = '7'
☑ "ROUTE" = '7a'	"ROUTE" = '7a'
☑ "ROUTE" = '8'	"ROUTE" = '8'
☑ "ROUTE" = '9'	"ROUTE" = '9'
▾ ☑ Over 2000	$length < 2000
☑ """Route"" % 2" = 0	"ROUTE" % 2 = 0
☑ """Route"" % 2" = 1	"ROUTE" % 2 = 1
☑	"ROUTE" like '%a'

Refine current rules ▾   Count features   Rendering order...

▾ Layer rendering

Layer transparency ⬤———————————————— 0

Layer blending mode Normal ⬍   Feature blending mode Normal ⬍

Load Style...   Save As Default   Restore Default Style   Save Style ▾

Help   Apply   Cancel   OK

10. Play around some more; there are all sorts of things you can do, from partial string matching to splitting by even or odd numbers (`"ROUTE" % 2 = 0` is even-numbered).

11. Finally, the map looks like the following:

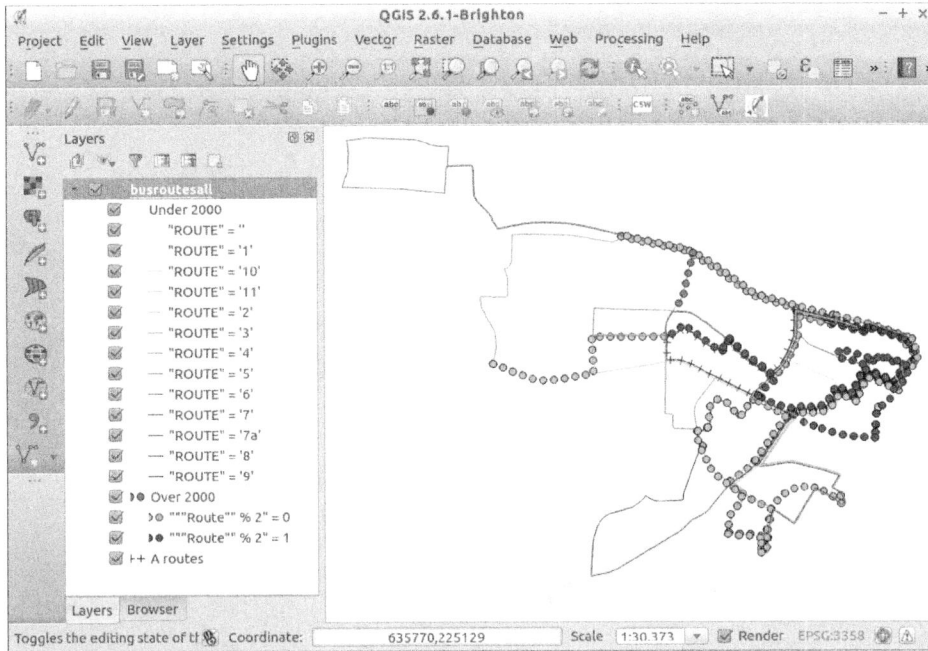

How it works...

Each rule is processed in the rendering order specified from top to bottom, the last rule being drawn last and, therefore, on top. The rules are added to any existing style that is already applied to feature. You can change the rendering order by changing the rule order or by applying a render order. The filters work just like attribute filters in the field calculator or the table search. All of the symbology options are available to vectors and can be applied to one or many rules. You can group rules by scale-rendering rules too.

There's more...

There are way too many possible ways to use Rule Based Rendering than can be described here. You can create rendering groups that inherit rules from their parent and apply their own. Each feature given a unique ID could have a completely different look. The big improvement over using traditional single symbol, categorized, or graduated symbology is that you don't have to edit every possible group, and you can more easily stack rules, mixing and matching all the original methods.

There are some catches. Not everything you do with Rule Based Rendering is possible with web services; so, before you go too crazy, consider your output format and test your ideas before spending too much time on this.

Handling transparencies

Transparency is a lack of pigment or color, such that you can see through one feature to the feature beneath. You can think of this as being similar to tinted or stained glass; some light is allowed to pass through and reflect off what's inside. When used right, transparency can help emphasize or de-emphasize features in a map composition. It can also be used to blend two layers to look as if they are one layer.

Getting ready

This recipe demonstrates transparency for both vectors and rasters, so we'll need an example of each. The `lakes.shp` and `elevlid_D782_6.tif` layers will work well for demonstration purposes. Load both of these layers in a fresh project, putting `lake.shp` on top.

How to do it...

1. With a vector layer loaded, open **Properties** and the **Style** tab.

2. On the right-hand side of the dialog, you will see a **Transparency** slider at 0% (this means 100% solid or opaque).

3. Adjust the slider to the right and apply the changes to see them in the map:

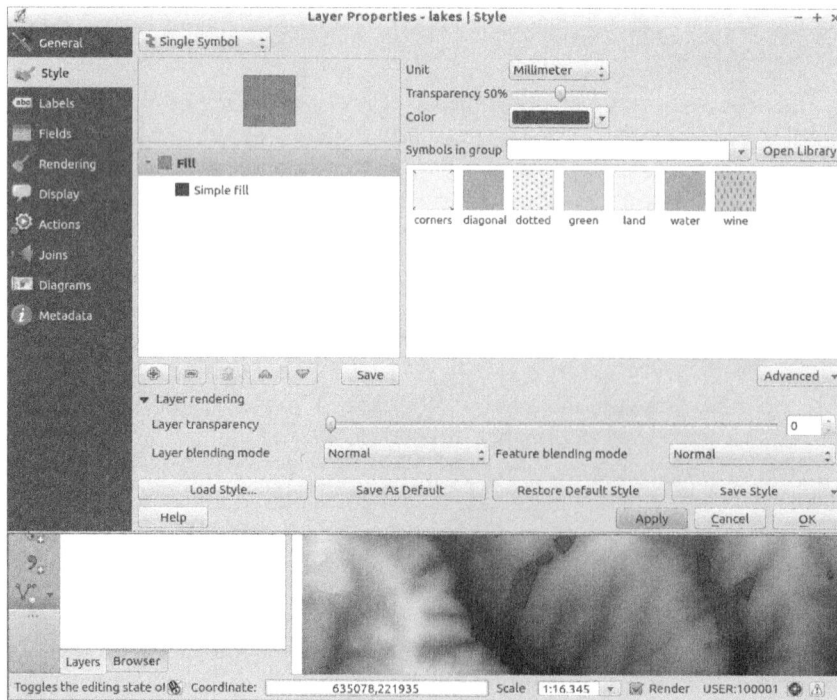

> Using a bold or dark color will make it easier to notice the change. You will also notice that the **Simple fill** option shows the original color.

4. Now to demonstrate this on a raster, first reset the lakes back to 0%.

5. Swap the order in the Layers list so that `elevlid` is on top.

6. Now, open **Properties** of `elevid` and the **Transparency** tab.

7. The **Global transparency** option will change the value evenly for the whole raster. Set it to 50% and apply it. You should now be able to see the lakes layer, which was hidden below:

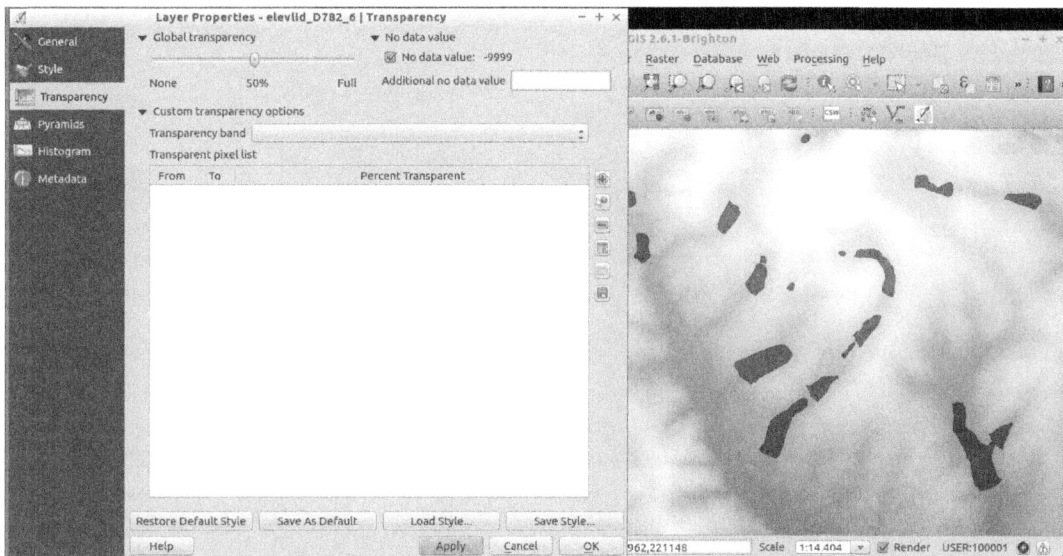

> **No data value** is always 100% transparent no matter what **Global transparency** is set to. Use this to easily eliminate values that you don't want to show up at all.

8. (Optional) You may have noticed that below the **Global transparency** slider is **Custom transparency options**. This will allow you to make particular values more transparent than others. You can either assign specific values to specific transparencies, or you can add a band to the raster (or use a multiband raster), which specifies the amount of transparency to apply to the rest of the raster (some data formats, such as GeoTiff, call this an Alpha Transparency band):

   - Reset the global back to 0% (otherwise, this is applied in too)
   - Use the green **+** sign to add some values

- ❑ From 100 To 125, 25% transparent
- ❑ From 125 To 150, 75% transparent
- ❑ Click **Apply** and notice the lower elevation lakes are harder to see:

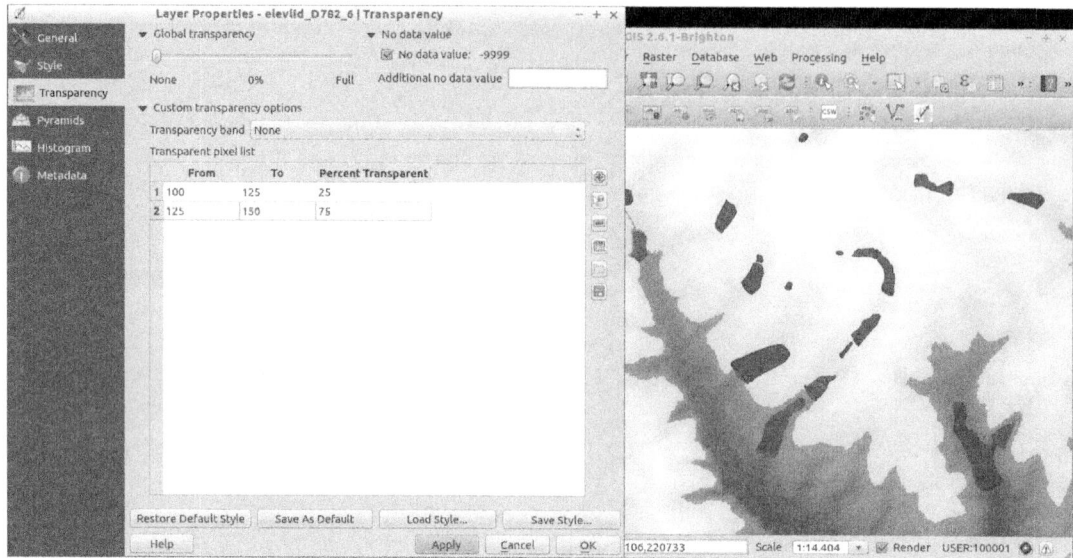

How it works...

This is really a computer graphics thing, but the simplest explanation is that you're telling the computer to combine a percentage of two different layers in the same location instead of the top layer's value covering. Based on the math of the original colors and their transparency, a blended color is calculated for each pixel on the screen.

This doesn't begin to explain all the possible variations of appearance that can be achieved by mixing multiple layers and multiple transparencies, only tinkering can show you this.

There's more...

One classic example of transparencies is to mix hillshades and airphotos. You can place either layer on top and then adjust the transparency to let the other show through. Generally, you would place the hillshade underneath in this case (but either can work). The end result is a landscape that appears to have 3D relief, but it looks like an airphoto.

Another classic example is to create a mask layer with a hole cut out around the region that you want to emphasize. You now place the mask layer on top. Before adding transparency, it blocks everything but the hole. Then, you slowly add transparency so that you can see surrounding regions, but they are muted and stand out less. For this technique, try a black, gray, or white fill for the mask layer. Each will have a slightly different look.

When styling vectors, you can apply different transparencies to different features in the same layer if you use Rule Based Rendering. Each rule can have a different transparency value and the entire layer can have yet another transparency modifier in the **Layer Rendering** section.

Lastly, keep in mind that not all output formats handle transparency well. In particular, be careful using color gradients with transparencies when exporting to PDF. Generally, PNG handles transparency, SVG may work or at least allow to you to edit the transparency after export, unlike image formats.

Understanding the feature and layer blending modes

In this recipe, we will look at the different layer and feature blending modes. Using these tools, we can achieve special rendering effects, which you may already know from other graphics programs.

Getting ready

To follow this recipe, you just need to load `stamen.png` and `effect.png` from our sample data. Make sure that stamen (left-hand side in the following screenshot) is the lower layer and effect (right-hand side in the following screenshot) is the upper layer. To test the feature blending modes, load `blending.shp`:

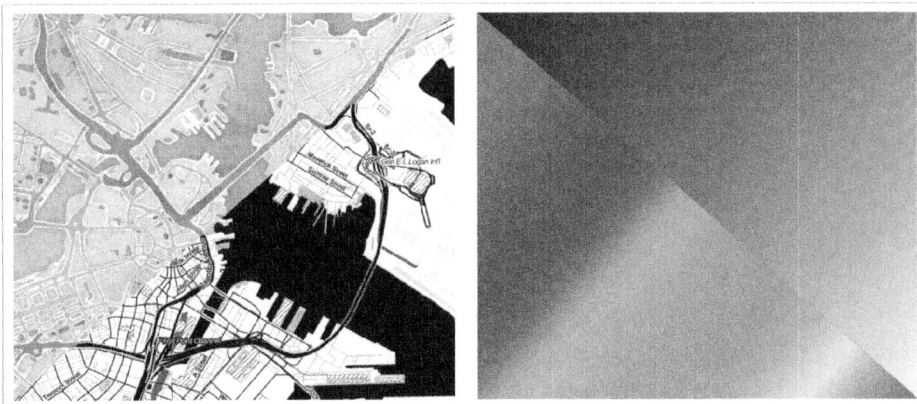

(Background maps "Watercolor" and "Toner" by Stamen Design, under CC BY 3.0. Data by OpenStreetMap, under CC BY SA).

How to do it...

Using the two raster layers, we can try the different blending modes. Of course, this works for vector layers, as well:

1. Double-click on the `effects` layer to open **Layer Properties**.

2. You can find the blending settings by going to **Layer Properties | Style | Color Rendering** together with other helpful controls for **Brightness, Contrast, Saturation,** and more, as shown in the next screenshot:

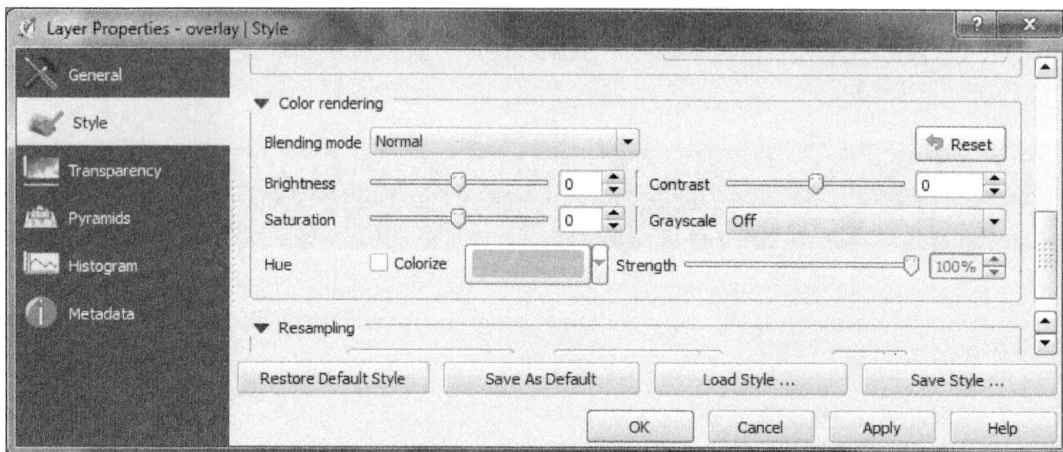

3. Change the **Blending mode** and click on **Apply** to see the results.

4. Similarly, for vector layers, such as our blending layer, we find the blending mode settings by going to **Layer Properties | Style | Layer rendering**, as shown in the following screenshot:

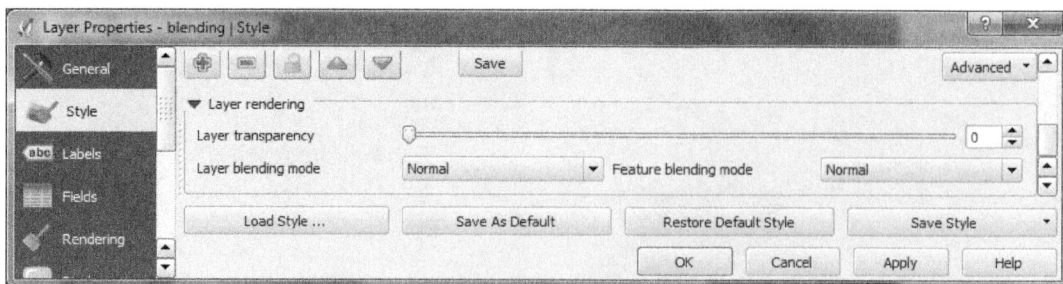

The main difference is that, for vector layers, we can control how features are blended together, and how the result is then blended to the underlying layers using the **Feature blending** and **Layer blending** modes, respectively. The feature blending mode is applied on a per-feature-basis.

The following screenshot shows the differences between feature and layer blending:

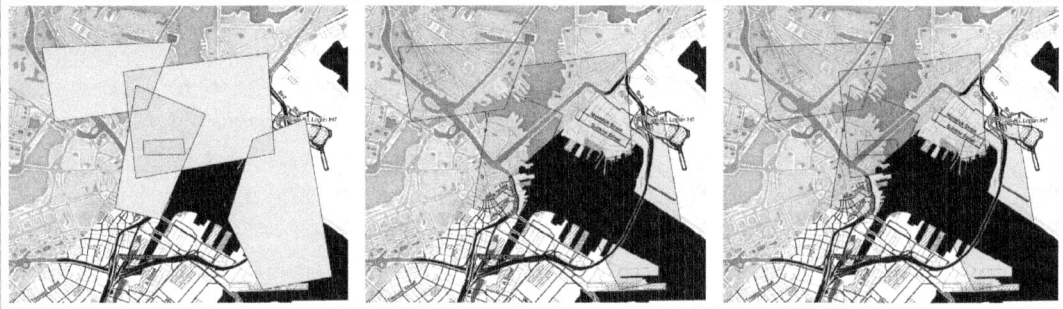

Feature and/or layer blending in action (from left to right): feature blending only, layer blending only, feature and layer blending combined (background maps "Watercolor" and "Toner" by Stamen Design, under CC BY 3.0. Data by OpenStreetMap, under CC BY SA).

The following is an explanation of the preceding screenshots:

▶ The leftmost image shows that **Feature blending** mode is set to **Multiply,** while **Layer blending** mode is set to default, **Normal**. This results in a map where the vector features are rendered on top of each other using the **Multiply** mode before the whole layer is overlaid on top of the lower layer(s).

▶ The center image instead shows **Normal Feature blending** mode combined with **Multiply Layer blending** mode. You can see how the features can block each other out because they are drawn on top of each other.

▶ Finally, the rightmost image shows both **Layer blending** mode and **Feature blending** modes being set to **Multiply**. In this combination, the **Multiply** rule is applied on both the feature and the layer level and, therefore, we can see features and the underlying background layer(s) shining through the features in the upper layer.

How it works...

Based on the selected blending mode, the pixel colors (in the RGB mode) of the lower and upper layers are mixed as described next. For illustration and quick reference, the following figure shows the results of all 12 blending modes (from left to right and top to bottom), except for the **Normal** setting, which does not mix the colors but only uses the alpha channel of the upper layer to blend with the layer below it:

▶ **Lighten**: The **Lighten** mode selects the maximum of each RGB component from the foreground and background pixels. Be aware that the results tend to be jagged and harsh.

▶ **Screen**: The **Screen** mode paints light pixels from the upper layer over the lower layer, but it skips the dark pixels.

- **Dodge**: The **Dodge** mode will brighten and saturate the lower layer based on the lightness of the upper layer. This means that brighter colors in the upper layer cause the saturation and brightness of the lower layer to increase. This works best if the top pixels aren't too bright; otherwise, the effect is quite extreme.

- **Addition**: The **Addition** mode adds the pixel values of both layers. If the result exceeds 1 (in the case of RGB), the respective areas are displayed in white.

- **Darken**: The **Darken** mode creates a result that retains the smallest RGB components of both layers. Therefore, this is the opposite of the Lighten mode and, just as with Lighten, the results tend to be jagged and harsh.

- **Multiply**: The **Multiply** mode multiplies the values of both layers, thus resulting in a darker picture.

- **Burn**: The **Burn** mode causes darker colors in the upper layer to darken the lower layer. **Burn** can be used to tweak and colorize underlying layers.

- **Overlay**: The **Overlay** mode combines the **Multiply** and **Screen blending** modes. As a result, light parts become lighter and dark parts become darker.

- **Soft light**: The **Soft light** mode is very similar to **Overlay**, but it uses a combination of **Burn** and **Dodge**. This is supposed to emulate shining a soft light on an image.

- **Hard light**: The **Hard light** mode is also very similar to **Overlay**. It is supposed to emulate projecting a very intense light on an image.

- **Difference**: The **Difference** mode subtracts the values of the upper layer from the lower layer (or the other way around) to always get a positive value. Blending with black (which has an RGB value of 0,0,0) produces no change.

- **Subtract**: The **Subtract** mode subtracts the values of one layer from the other. In the case of negative values, black is displayed:

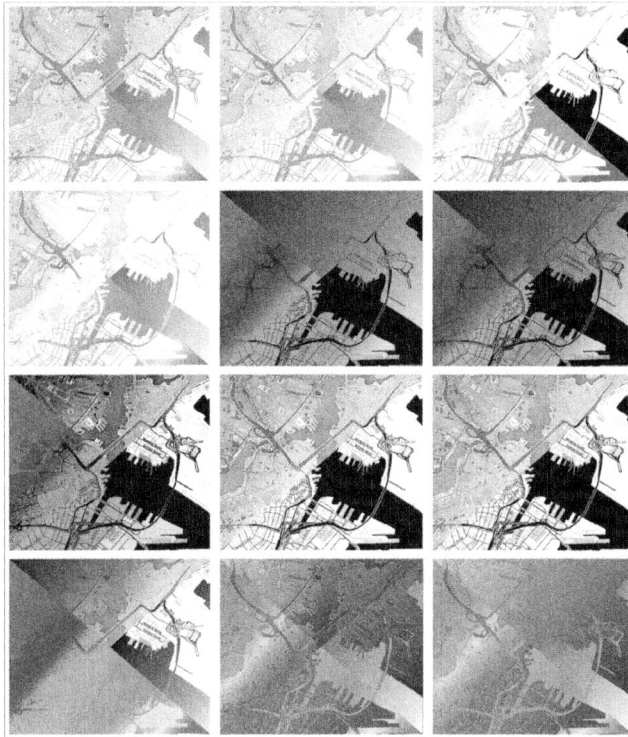

Overview of the 12 blending modes (background maps "Watercolor" and "Toner" by Stamen Design, under CC BY 3.0. Data by OpenStreetMap, under CC BY SA): first row: Lighten, Screen, and Dodge; second row: Addition, Darken, and Multiply; third row: Burn, Overlay, and Soft light; fourth row: Hard light, Difference, and Subtract.

Saving and loading styles

What's better than making an awesome style for your feature layers? Being able to easily share and reuse them. Both vector and raster styles can be saved and reused—however, in slightly different ways.

Getting ready

For this recipe, you need two similar vector layers and a set of two similar raster layers. In the example data that is provided, use two of the bus route shapefiles and two of the elevation rasters (for example, `elevlid_D782_6.tif`).

How to do it...

First we'll start by copying and pasting styles for vector layers:

1. Load up two bus route shapefiles and two elevlid rasters.

2. The simplest method is to copy styles for vectors or rasters. Just right-click on the layer name in the list and select **Copy Style** from the **Style** menu. Then, right-click on the layer that you want to apply this to and select **Paste Style** from the **Style** menu. You can only copy styles between layers of the same type (for example, **Point to Point**):

   Try to copy and paste the style of one bus route to the second bus route using the right-click menus:

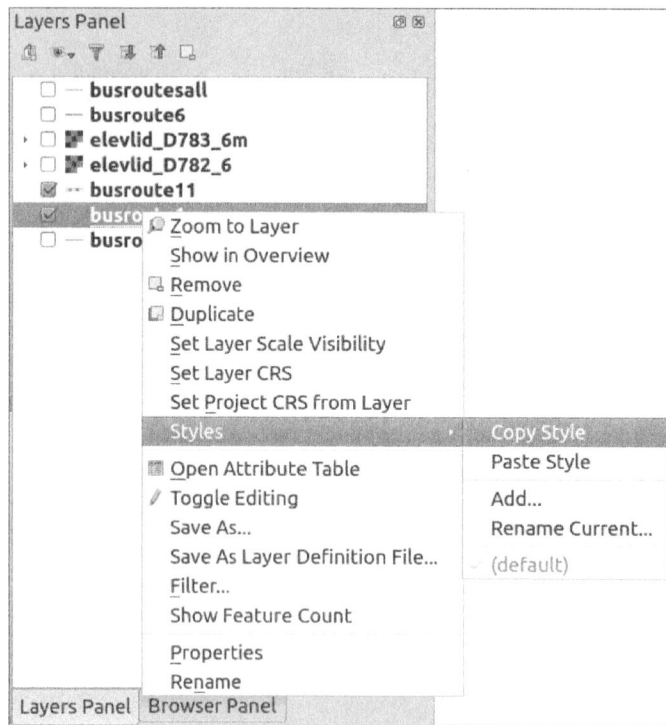

3. Now to export styles for later use, right-click on a layer and navigate to **Properties |
   Symbology**.

4. In the bottom-right, there is a **Save Style** button in the **Style** menu. The output
   choices are **QGIS Layer Style File...** (aka `.qml`) or **SLD File...**. Both formats are
   XML text files, **QGIS Layer Style...** is recommended for maximum compatibility:

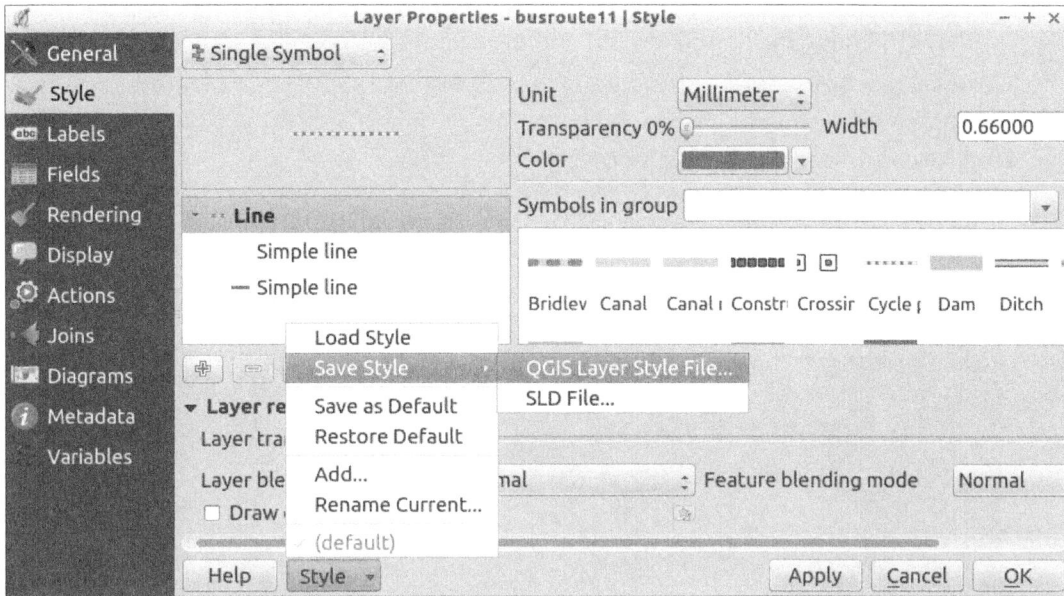

5. SLD is compatible with some other web map systems, but it will not capture your
   QGIS style 100% except in the simplest cases (not all the same options exist in SLD).
   QML is the native QGIS style file. Note the **Load style** option for later usage.

6. Go ahead and apply a new style to one of the bus route layers.

7. Then, save the symbology to **QGIS Layer Style File** (qml).

8. In the property dialog of the second bus route file, click **Load Style...** and pick the file
   that you just saved.

> You can open this file in a text editor and make customizations or,
> for example, batch-find and replace values.

Rasters are slightly trickier in that you can save a symbology file, but you can also save a color table. The color table is a text file that lists raster value ranges and associated color codes. It's a much simpler format to hand-edit than XML (QGIS Layer Style File), but does not retain things like transparency or classification settings:

1. Go ahead and apply a new color gradient to one of the elevlid layers.

2. Save just the color table to a `.txt` file with the disk button (above the color table on the right end of the button row; refer to the screenshot).

3. In the property of the second elevid file, load the color table and pick the file that you just saved.

4. Apply the changes to your layer style:

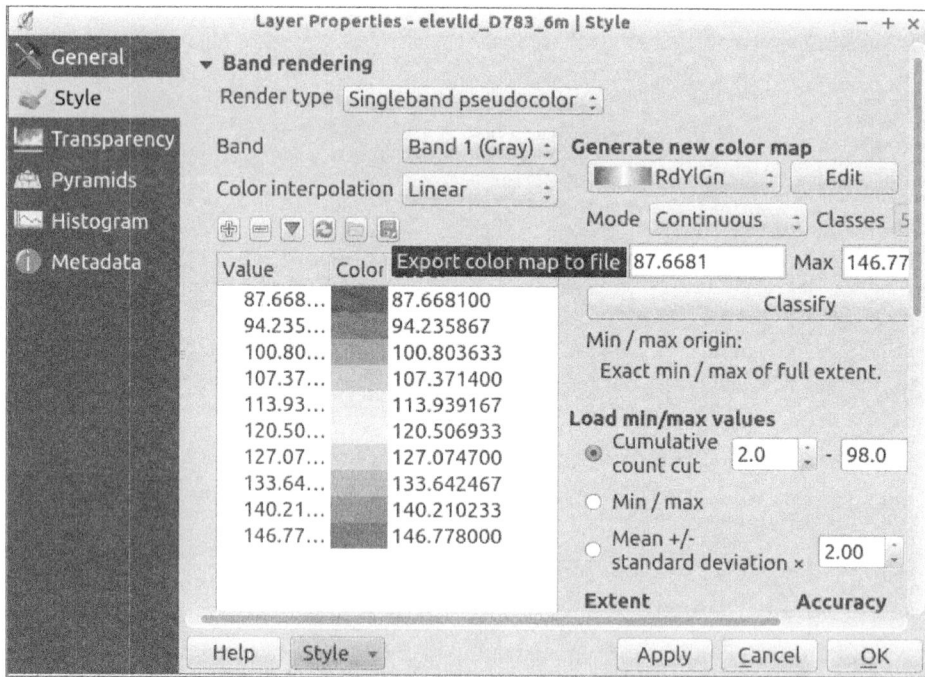

Note that the same **Style** menu is available as was in the vector properties. You can use this to save and load QGIS Layer Style File (.qml) just as we did earlier.

How it works...

Normally the style information for a layer is saved in the `.qgs` (if you save your project) project file. The various export methods just package up the style information for a layer into a separate file in a generic manner (not associated with the original data). This lets you apply similar styles to similar data sources.

Vector symbology is stored in a special XML file that ends in the `.qml` extension. You can read or edit the file if you want, and it can be produced via scripts or copied and pasted to create mashups of multiple styles.

Raster symbology can also be stored in a `.qml` file. However, there's an additional option to export the classification ranges and colors to a simple text file, one value or range of values and one color code per line.

There's more...

The second format **SLD** (**Style Layer Descriptors**) is very common in web services. While not all features of QGIS styling have equivalents in SLD, it's still a good starting point to share your style across software platforms such as Mapserver or Geoserver.

Configuring data-defined labels

If there was a list of top features of QGIS, data-defined labels would be high on that list. They offer the ease of automatic labeling with the customization of freehand labeling. You can mix and match automatic and custom edits, storing the values in a table for later reference.

Getting ready

There are a couple of useful plugins for data-defined labeling which will add the extra attribute fields that you need to either an existing layer or make a new layer just for labels. Download and install **Layer to labeled layer** and **Create labeled layer**.

How to do it...

1. Open QGIS and load `census_wake2000.shp`.
2. Create a copy of the layer using the **Save As** dialog, and save the layer as `census_wake2000_label.shp`. (You don't always have to do this but this process does modify the table, so it's a good idea to make a backup.)
3. Highlight `census_wake2000_label.shp` in the layer list.

4. Run the **Layer to labeled layer** plugin (**Plugins | Layer to Labeled layer** plugin):

    1. Set **Label Field** to STFID.

    2. Click on **OK**:

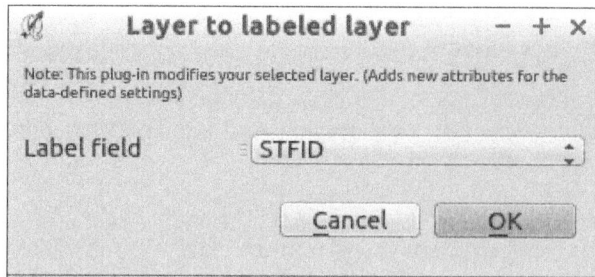

5. If you look at the attribute table now, you will see a whole bunch of new fields, starting with the **Lbl** prefix, which are NULL:

	LblSize	LblColor	LblBold	LblItalic	LblUnderl	LblStrike	LblFont
0	NULL	NULL	NULL	NULL	NULL	NULL	NULL
1	NULL	NULL	NULL	NULL	NULL	NULL	NULL
2	NULL	NULL	NULL	NULL	NULL	NULL	NULL
3	NULL	NULL	NULL	NULL	NULL	NULL	NULL
4	NULL	NULL	NULL	NULL	NULL	NULL	NULL
5	NULL	NULL	NULL	NULL	NULL	NULL	NULL
6	NULL	NULL	NULL	NULL	NULL	NULL	NULL
7	NULL	NULL	NULL	NULL	NULL	NULL	NULL
8	NULL	NULL	NULL	NULL	NULL	NULL	NULL
9	NULL	NULL	NULL	NULL	NULL	NULL	NULL
10	NULL	NULL	NULL	NULL	NULL	NULL	NULL
11	NULL	NULL	NULL	NULL	NULL	NULL	NULL
12	NULL	NULL	NULL	NULL	NULL	NULL	NULL

6. Now, ensure that you have the **Label** toolbar open (**View | Toolbars | Label**):

7. Either in the layer (by navigating to **Properties | Labels**) or using the first button on **Label Toolbar, Layer Labeling Options**, open the label management dialog.

8. Throughout the dialogs, you will see markers next to each field. A yellow one indicates a data-defined attribute, a white marker is the same setting for all:

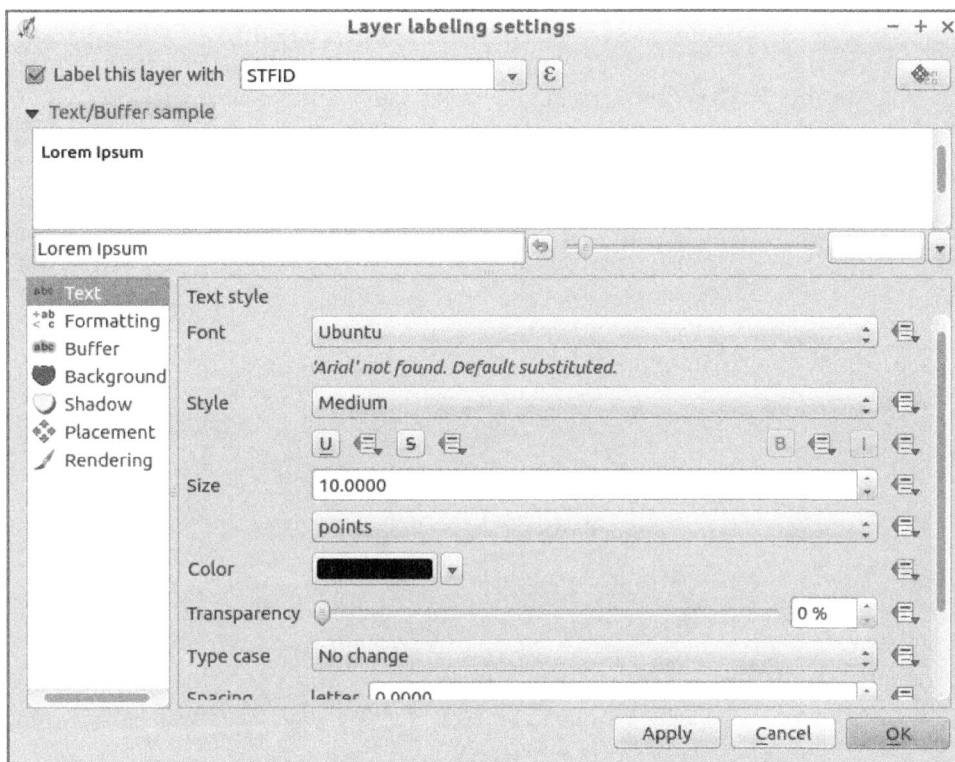

> If you want to control additional attributes at this point, add a new field to the layer. Then, return to this dialog and select the white icon to pick the name of the field to use.

9. Now, you are ready to make custom edits to various labels and have the table store the settings. Depending on the setting, there are a couple of ways to make the edits. Note that you must toggle editing on the layer before you can change the labels:

    1. You can edit the field directly in the table either by hand, or you can use the field calculator to automate repetitive patterns (for example, give all major roads the same **Font** and **Color** label).

    2. For some attributes, such as X,Y and rotation, you can also edit by hand in the map using the **Label Toolbar** option.

Example: moving and rotating a label

1. Toggle editing by clicking on the following icon:

2. On the **Label Toolbar** menu, select the **Move Label** button. Now, click on a label and drag it to a new location, releasing the mouse button when you are done moving the label. Note that you must ensure that the X and Y fields in step 38 are set for this tool to be usable:

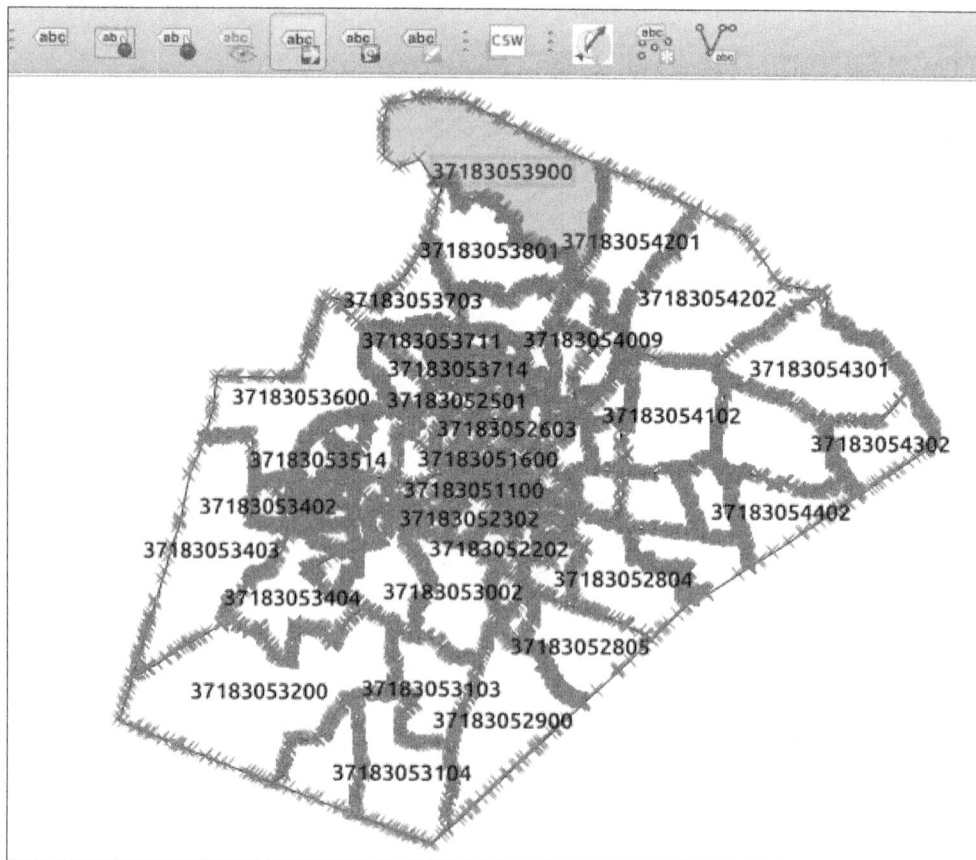

> If you check the attribute table you will see that in the **LblX** and **LblY** fields, the values have now been saved for the labels that you moved.

3. Now, try the **Rotate Label** button. See if you can make some of the labels fit inside their polygons using the move and rotate:

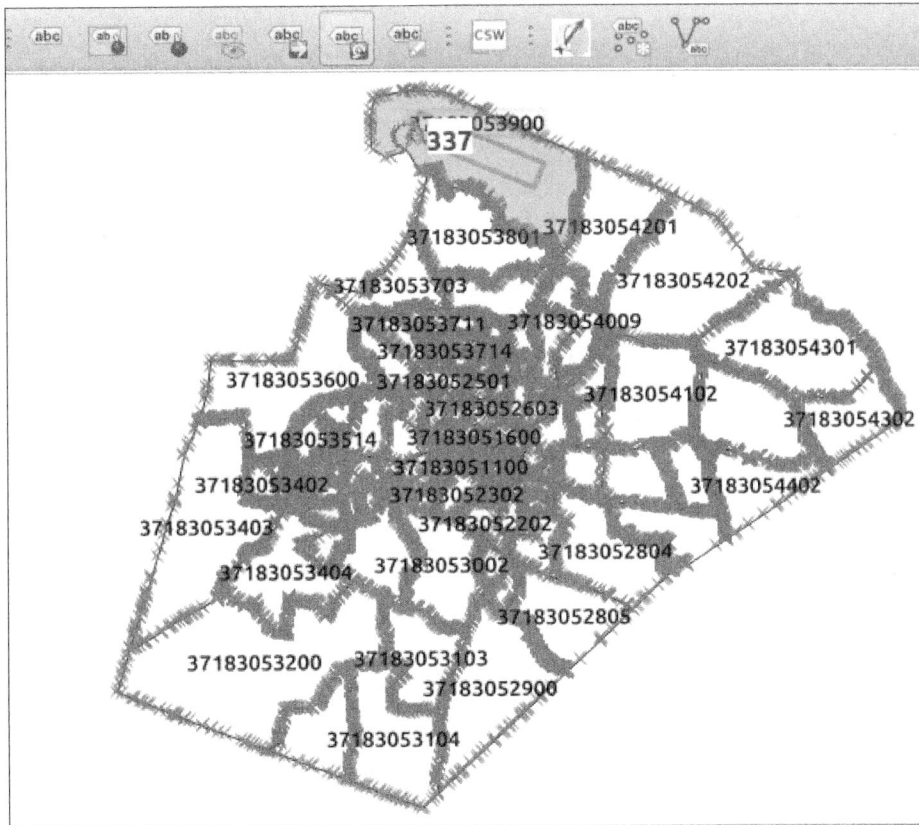

You can also use the **Change Label** button to edit the other properties of a specific label that you select. This is really nice when you just need some fine-tuning.

4. Save your edits and toggle editing off to keep your changes.

How it works...

The basic premise is that you keep an extra set of attributes in a table often as additional fields to your existing table.

> You could add fields to your attribute table by hand, and assign them to label properties. Using the **Layer to Labeled Layer** plugin does this for you.

These fields if you set them are used in determining the location, size, font, color, angle, and so on, of the label for the given row. If you don't set them, then the automatic settings from the labeling engine are kept.

There's more...

Data-defined labels are powerful in that you can combine automated, calculated, and custom-edited values. They are automated from the built-in labeling engine and calculated using the field calculator to populate the data-defined fields (for example, with `if` statements or calculations that are based on other attributes). Lastly, by just making these little hand tweaks, you can fix a few not-quite labels that misbehave.

Note that you don't have to use data-defined labeling on an existing layer. You can create just a label layer with the **Create labeled layer** plugin. In other software, user-defined labeling is often called Annotation layers. QGIS also has annotation layers. These are layers where you click to add a label to the map and then write and style it however you want. The biggest problem is that these layers are not associated with the data that they label. You can't easily give them to someone else, and if a label name or style changes, you have to chase down and hand-edit every fix. In QGIS, data-defined labeling solves almost all the shortcomings of annotation layers because it actually saves to a shapefile with all its properties as fields.

Creating custom SVG graphics

This recipe is all about making your map unique by creating custom icons, north arrows, or even fill patterns.

You will need a vector illustration program (for example, Inkscape or Adobe Illustrator).

> Don't have one? There are several free and open source options available on all platforms. Many people in the QGIS community use Inkscape (`http://inkscape.org`), but you can also use LibreOffice Draw or OpenOffice Draw. The most common proprietary software equivalent is Adobe Illustrator.

You will also need a text editor, such as TextEdit (Mac), Notepad, Notepad++ (Windows).

How to do it...

1. Open up your vector illustration program.

2. Set the canvas to a reasonable size to work with. Square ratios tend to work well because the icon will eventually be used to mark points in QGIS; 100x100 pixels is fine.

3. Draw a simple shape such as a square, circle, or star. Make sure you go most of the way towards the edges and fill the whole page.

> Remember that you will be using this drawing at sizes closer to 8-32 pixels; it's just really annoying to work at these scales. when creating and editing illustrations

4. Save the drawing as an `.svg` file.

5. Now, open the `.svg` file in a text editor, search and find the style line of your object, and replace it with the following lines:

```
stroke-width="param(outline-width) 1"
stroke="param(outline) #000"
fill="param(fill) #FFF"
```

> If working with a complex icon, set your line to a specific color code that is different from all other colors in the drawing. Make a note of the color code so that you can use it to search the .svg file in your text editor.

The before-after scenario when this code has been incorporated is shown in the following table:

Before	After
``<rect
style="color:#000000;display
:inline;overflow:visible;vis
ibility:visible;opacity:1;fi
ll:"param(fill)
#000000";fill-
opacity:1;stroke:"param(outl
ine) #ff0000";stroke-
width:"param(outline-width)
4";stroke-
miterlimit:4;stroke-
dasharray:none;stroke-
opacity:1;marker:none;enable
-background:accumulate"
id="rect3336"
width="301.61023"
height="308.96658"
x="30.651445"
y="725.00476" />```	```<rect
stroke-width="param(outline-
width) 1"
stroke="param(outline) #000"
fill="param(fill) #FFF"
id="rect3336"
width="301.61023"
height="308.96658"
x="30.651445"
y="725.00476" />```

6. Save your changes.

7. Now, start up QGIS and load a point layer.

8. Go to **Properties | Style**.

9. In the symbology options, there are two levels of objects that make a symbol: the marker and then a sublevel of actual symbols that combine to make it.

10. Select the subobject, which is usually labeled **Simple Marker** by default.

11. Now, change the dropdown in the upper-right to SVG Marker.

12. Below the box displaying the symbol options look for the **...** button and select to load an SVG from file. Use this to select the `.svg` file that you previously created.

13. Once imported, you should be able to change the fill color of the symbol (if you performed Step 5):

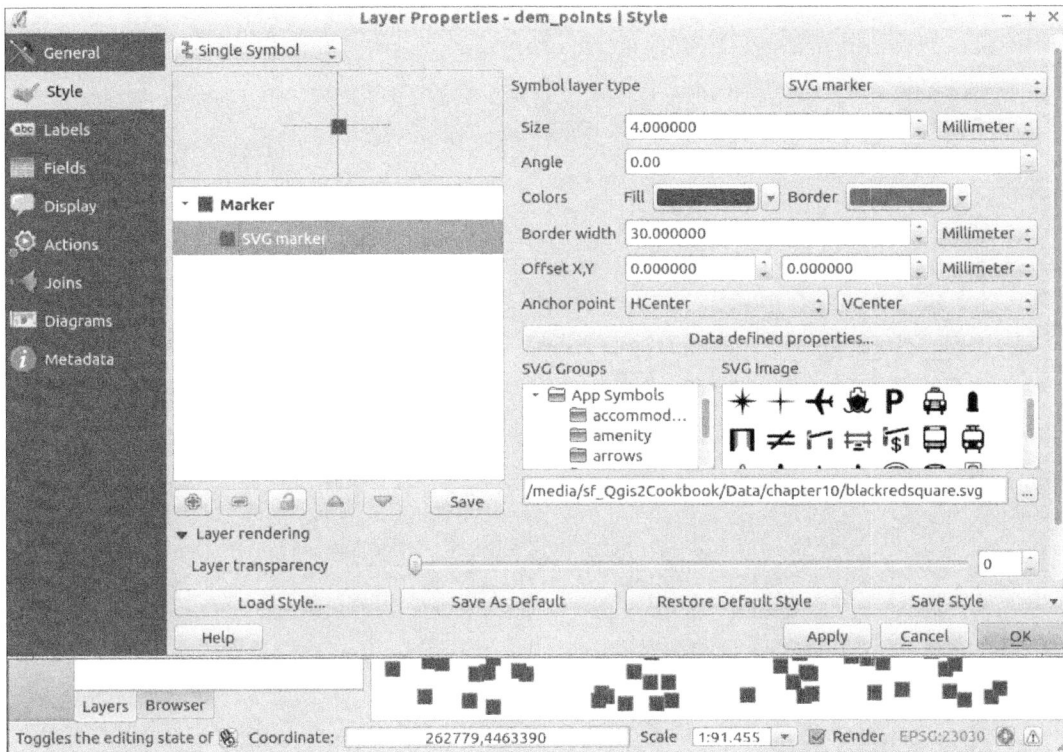

> You may need to adjust the size and widths in large amounts for changes to be apparent. Make use of the **Apply** button to see the changes in the map but keep the dialog open for easy adjustment.

How it works...

The special text that you add to the `.svg` file is a marker or placeholder. QGIS looks for these particular words and then utilizes them to insert symbol changes on-the-fly as the SVG is read into the program.

There's more...

While this recipe demonstrated a very simple SVG, this method applies to more complicated symbols.

Also note that in **Settings | Options | System**, you can set paths to folders of SVGs so that all of them will be available in the symbology dialogs all the time.

See also

QGIS also lets you customize fill patterns using SVG symbols. The QGIS *Training Manual* has a good example of this at `http://docs.qgis.org/2.8/en/docs/training_manual/basic_map/symbology.html#hard-fa-creating-a-custom-svg-fill`.

Making pretty graticules in any projection

A graticule is a set of reference lines on a map that help orient a map reader. They are often set at, and labeled, with the coordinates. The tricky part about using graticules, however, is projections. If you don't make them correctly, instead of smooth curves between the line intersections, you get awkward unusual shapes (mostly straight lines). The default QGIS graticule creator is not projection-friendly, so in this recipe, you'll see an add-on processing algorithm that does this. This recipe is about ensuring you get nice, smooth, and properly-labeled graticules.

Getting ready

You don't really need much for this recipe other than a bounding box and a coordinate interval that you want to space the lines at. Usually, these will be in Latitude, Longitude WGS 84 (EPSG:4326), and decimal degrees, respectively, since the whole point of a graticule is to add reference lines that help orient a user.

How to do it...

1. Start by downloading a **Processing Toolbox** algorithm specifically for this task called **Lines Graticule**:

    1. Open the **Processing Toolbox**.

    2. Go to **Scripts | Tools | Get scripts from on-line scripts collection**:

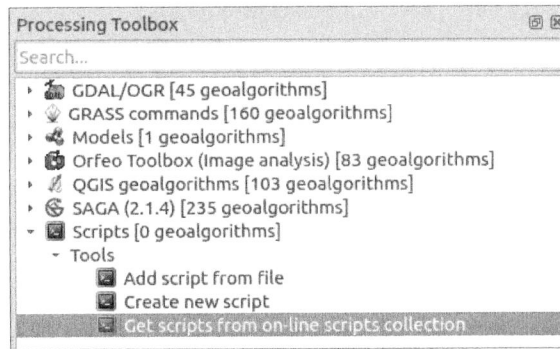

3. In the **Not Installed** section, check the box for the **Lines Graticule** algorithm.

4. Click on the **OK** button to install the algorithm.

> Every time that you use a tool, it's good to check for updates.

You will see something like the following screenshot:

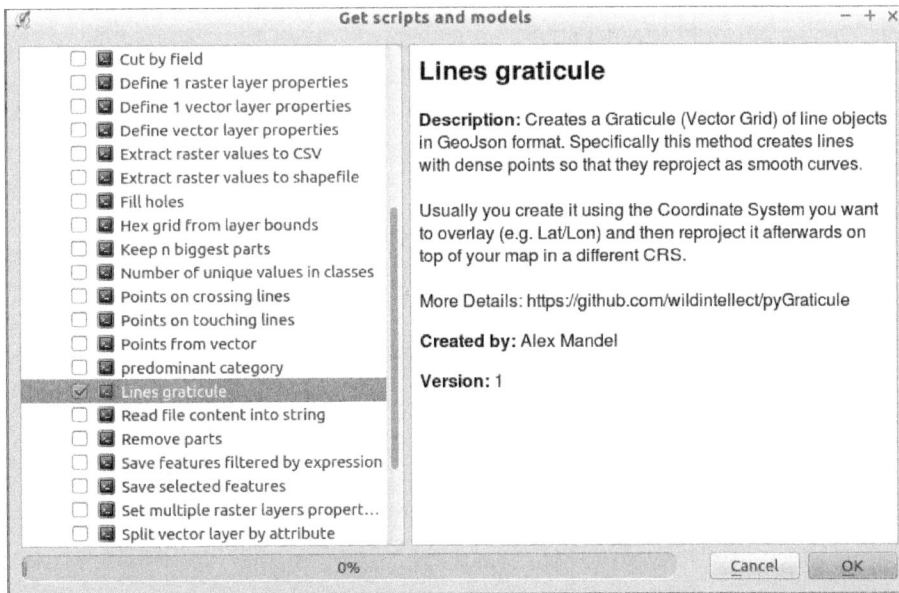

2. Now that you've downloaded the algorithm, open it by navigating to **Scripts | Vector** (it's called **Lines graticule** though the code is actually pygraticule.py):

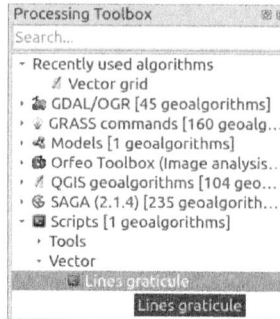

3. You can fill in the parameters by hand if you know them or use the **...** button to get values from your existing project.

4. For now, you can use the defaults that will make a graticule for the whole world. The outputs are determined by outfile and graticule. These parameters are optional, you can choose to pick one, both, or neither. If you want a GeoJSON file, set the outfile. If you want a shapefile, set the graticule (if you want the results to autoload afterwards, make sure that the second output is set to temporary or a real file, just not blank). Refer to the **Help** tab for details about each parameter. There are two really important values to control the graticule:

   1. The **spacing** value denotes how often to draw a line (when doing world-scale maps, 20 or 30 degrees works well).

   2. The **density** value denotes how often to put nodes:

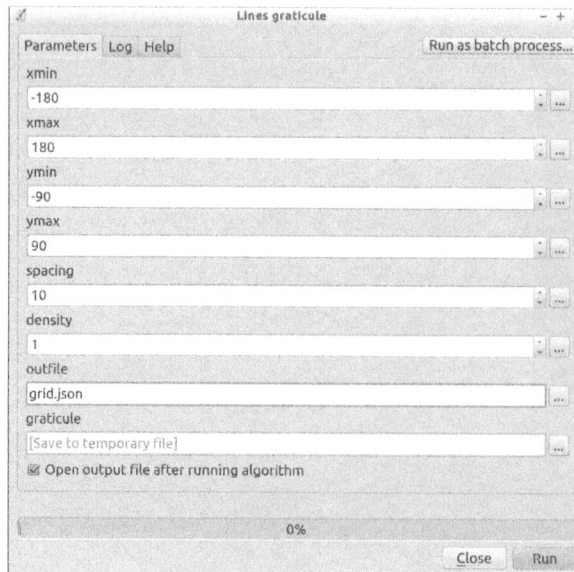

> The more nodes, the smoother the curves; however, you get a bigger file that takes longer to make. Picking the right density may require trial and error to find the largest density before you notice the lines stop curving smoothly for a given map scale.

5. Once you've chosen your settings, click on **Run**.

6. After it runs, a vector layer should get loaded with the results. This won't look all that exciting, just straight lines making a grid.

7. The real magic is to now enable projection on-the-fly with one of the many decent world-wide projections such as "World Robinson (EPSG:54030):

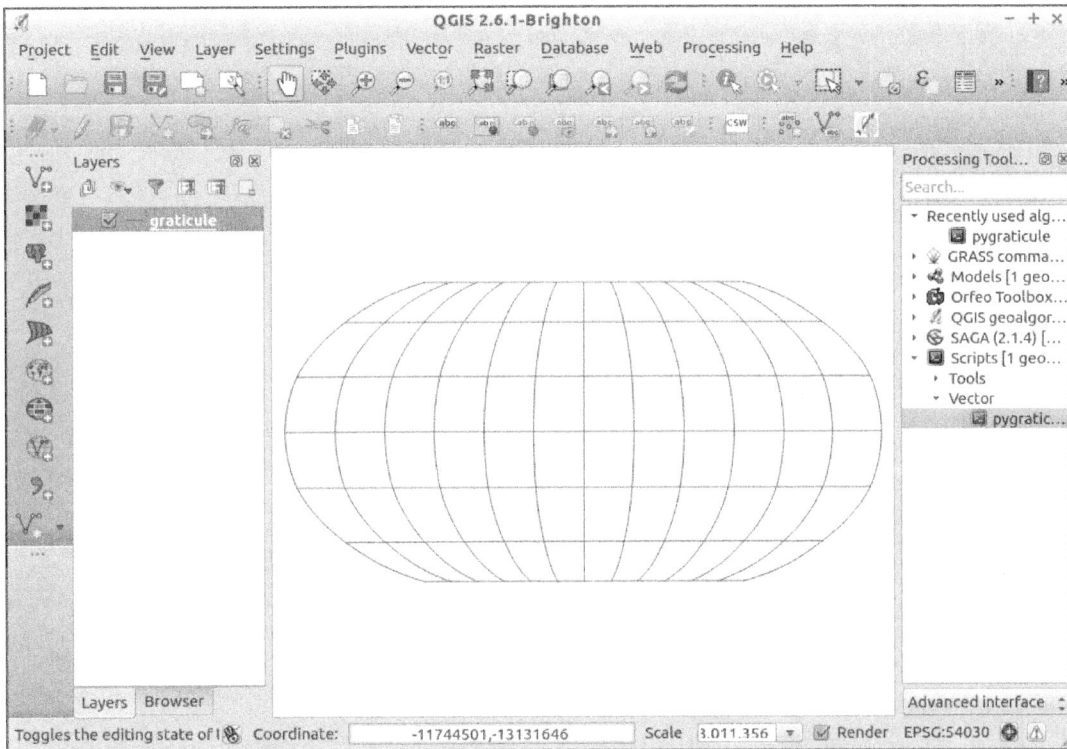

8. (Optional) If it doesn't look like the image, but instead still has straight lines that are oddly spaced, you need to disable the QGIS rendering simplification:

    1. Pick the layer from **Properties** | **Rendering**.

    2. Make sure that **Simplify geometry** is disabled:

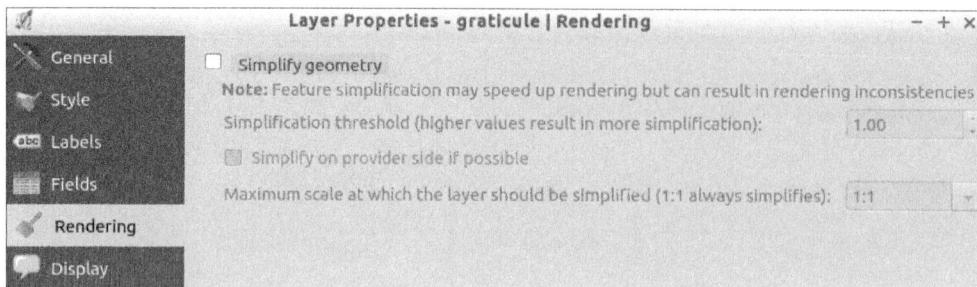

9. (Bonus) Generate a vector grid from **Vector** | **Research tools**. The difference looks like the following:

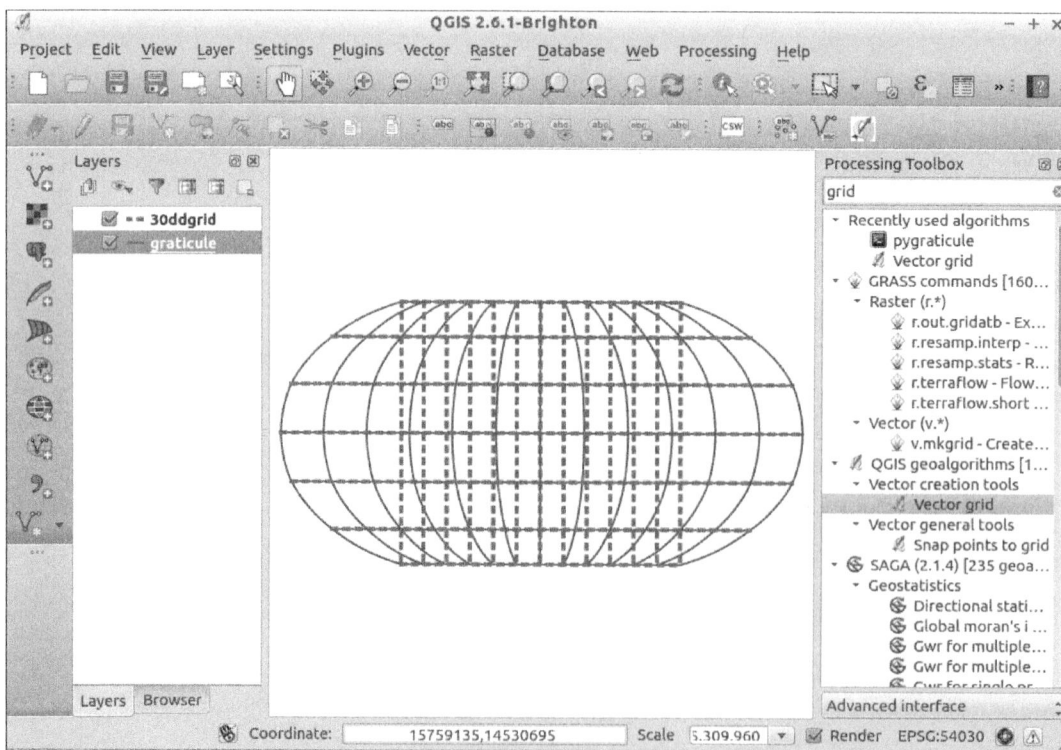

How it works...

Graticules are basically line layers (though sometimes they are also polygons). If you draw a grid with nodes only at the points where two lines intersect, you can easily see how distorting the grid will lead to blocky shapes. The key to smooth graticules is adding additional line nodes in between the intersections (that is, increase the node density).

It's important to note that, when using projections that don't cover the whole world (for example, polar or stereographic projections), pick bounding box values that fall within the projection limits; otherwise, you may get errors when trying to reproject.

There's more...

The primary advantages of graticules in the main map canvas are that you can use them as references while working in QGIS, include them in web and digital maps, and have full control of the labels and symbology. The method used here differs from other graticule (grid) tools in QGIS because it focuses on putting Latitude/Longitude lines with smooth curves as references into any projection. Other grid tools focus more on making regular squares across a map to subdivide a region.

The main advantages of the print composer method (next recipe) are its ability to make multiple coordinate systems easily and to add tick marks around the outside edge of a map. Tick marks are what you commonly see on navigation-oriented maps, such as USGS Topo quads, and other printed maps.

See also

Lines graticule (aka Pygraticule) can also be used as a pure Python script; for updates and more information, refer to `https://github.com/wildintellect/pyGraticule`.

To learn how to write your own processing toolbox algorithms, refer to the *Writing processing algorithms* recipe in *Chapter 11, Extending QGIS*.

Making useful graticules in printed maps

A graticule is a set of reference lines on a map that help orient a map reader. They are often set at and labeled with the coordinates. For traditional printed maps that are intended for navigation and surveying tasks where you want to mark the geographic coordinates, sometimes in multiple coordinate systems. This recipe is about adding such reference lines to a Print Composer map.

Getting ready

You will need a map, typically of a small area (several miles or km across). For this recipe, `elevlid_D782_6.tif` works well.

How to do it...

1. Load `elevlid_D782_6.tif`.

2. Turn on **Projection on-the-fly** by selecting **UTM Zone 17 N, WGS 84 (EPSG:32617)**.

3. Now create **New Print Composer**.

4. In **Print Composer**, select **Add New Map**, and then draw a rectangle on the canvas.

5. Now that you have the map, in the dialogs on the right-hand side of the screen select the **Item Properties** tab.

6. Scroll down or collapse sections until you see the **Grids** section.

7. Use the green plus (**+**) symbol to add a new grid.

8. Now, edit **Interval X** and **Interval Y** to 1,000 map units. (Make sure to tab to the next field or click on **Enter** for the values to stick.):

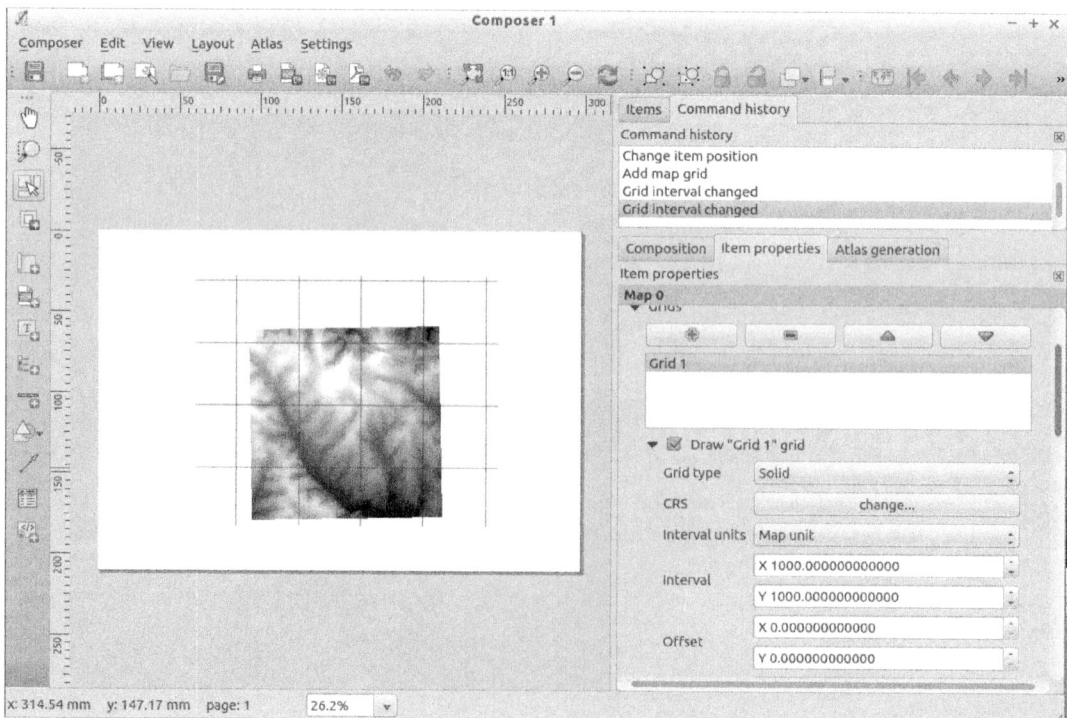

> The current map units are UTM-based, meters, which means the lines will be 1,000 meters or 1 km apart.

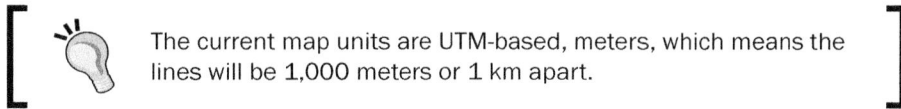

9. Just below the **Interval** section, change **Line Style** and make the lines red so that they are easier to see.

10. Now, scroll down even further to the **Draw coordinates** section and check the box to enable labels for the grid lines:

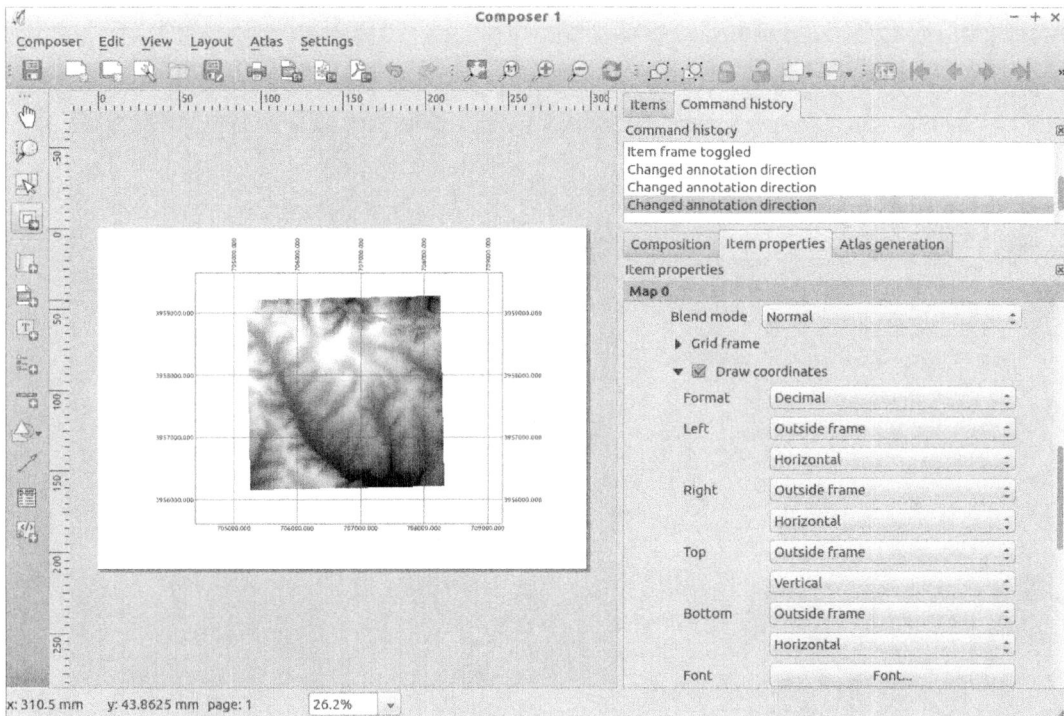

11. Once this is enabled, change the top and bottom orientation to vertical, and change the font color to red.

12. Now, to create a second grid, scroll back up to the **Grids** section and click the green plus sign (**+**) again to add a second grid.

13. This time, change the **CRS** (**Coordinate Reference System**) to **WGS 84 (EPSG:4326)**, which is the most common Latitude and Longitude system that people use.

14. Make this grid be spaced 0.01 map units (that is, degrees in this case) and change the style to blue to contrast with the other grid.

15. Now, scroll down and add **Draw coordinates**. Also, make the top and bottom vertical-oriented so that they avoid the first grid. You can also change the font color to match the lines:

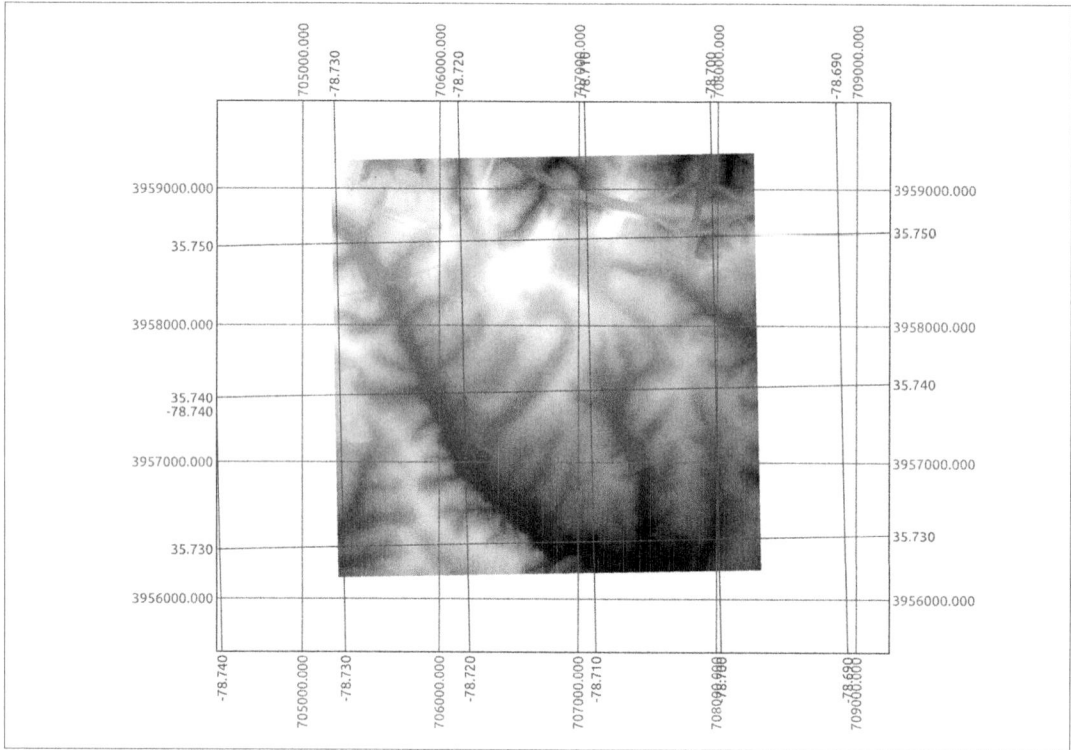

How it works...

Reference graticules are evenly spaced lines with marked coordinates. Based on your settings the composer calculates the positioning of the lines from the map data coordinates. The key to making useful graticules in the print composer is to select intervals that are often enough to provide reference but not so often that they cover a large portion of the map. It's also important to pick intervals that have nice rounded numbers, so that it's easy to calculate the value half way between two lines.

There's more...

There are two ways to make grids/graticules in QGIS: the print composer for printed maps or as a layer in QGIS for printed web maps as an internal usage.

The main advantages of the print composer method are the ability to do multiple coordinate systems easily and to add tick marks around the outside edge of a map. Tick marks are what you commonly see on navigation oriented maps, such as USGS Topo quads.

The primary advantages of graticules in the main map canvas are that you can use them as references while working with QGIS and have full control of the labels and symbology. Refer to the *Making pretty graticules in any projection* recipe in this chapter for how to make graticules in the main map interface.

Creating a map series using Atlas

In this recipe, we will use the **Print Composer Atlas** functionality to automatically create a PDF map book with a series of maps.

Getting ready

To follow this recipe, load `zipcodes_wake.shp` and `geology.shp` from our sample data. In the following screenshots, the `zipcodes_wake` layer was styled with a simple white border, while the geology layer is styled with random colors.

How to do it...

The **Print Composer Atlas** feature will create one map for each feature in the so-called **Coverage** layer. In this recipe, the zipcodes layer will serve as a **Coverage** layer, and we will create one map for each zipcode feature:

1. Click on the **New Print Composer** button or press *Ctrl + P* to get started. You will be prompted to set a title for the new composer. This can be left empty if you want QGIS to generate a title automatically.

2. Click on the **Add new map** button and drag open a rectangle on the composer page to create a map item for the main map.

3. To activate the Atlas functionality, we enable the map item's **Controlled by atlas** checkbox. The following screenshot shows the fully configured map's item properties. In the **Controlled by atlas** section, we can select which zoom mode Atlas should use:

    1. **Margin around feature**: This is the most flexible option, which tells Atlas to zoom to the feature while keeping the specified margin percentage around the feature.

    2. **Predefined scale (best fit)**: This tells Atlas to use the one predefined project scale (configurable in **Project Properties | General | Project scales**) where the feature best fits in.

3. **Fixed scale**: This keeps the same scale for all maps of the series; the scale is configured in the map's **Main properties**, that is, 100,000 in the following screenshot:

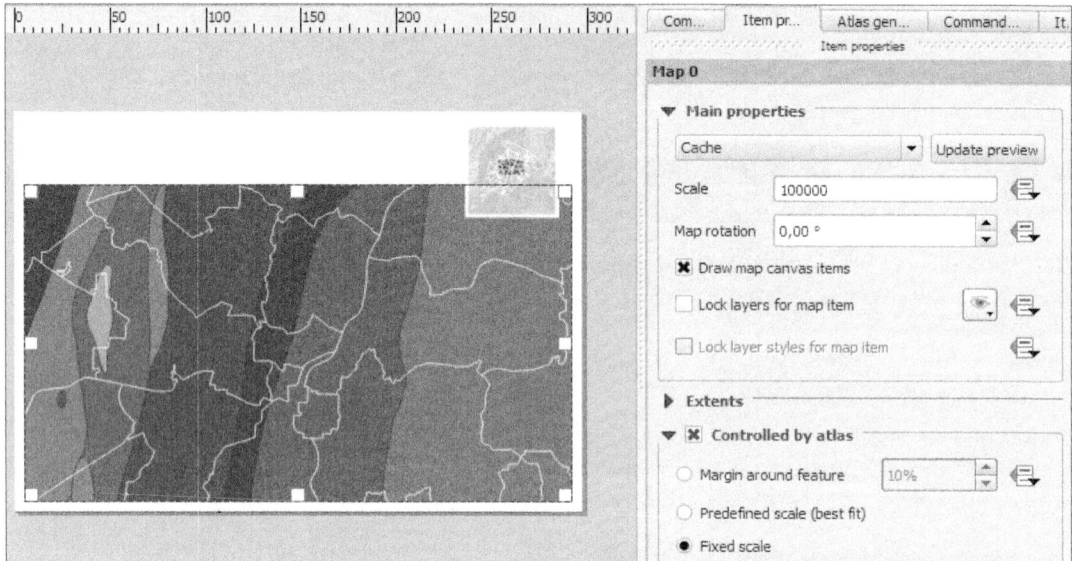

4. Next, we add a label for the title using the **Add new label** button. This title label will display the zip code polygon feature's NAME value which will be automatically updated by Atlas for each map in the series. To achieve this, we insert the following expression in the input field of the label item's **Main properties**:

```
[%attribute( @atlas_feature, 'NAME' ) %]
```

5. To finalize the Atlas configuration, we need to go to the **Atlas generation** tab. There, we first have to enable the **Generate an atlas** checkbox. This activates the **Configuration** section, where we can pick the **Coverage** layer and set it to the zipcodes_wake layer, as shown in the following screenshot.

6. To preview the Atlas output, we can now click on the **Preview Atlas** button. This button is only active if the **Generate an atlas** checkbox in the **Atlas generation** tab is enabled. Once the preview mode is active, you can step through the map series using the arrow buttons right besides the **Preview Atlas** button.

7. When we are happy with the preview, we can export the map series. The output behavior is controlled by the configuration in the **Atlas generation** tab's **Output** section, which you can also see in the following screenshot. Atlas supports exporting to separate image, SVG, or PDF files. Activate the **Single file export when possible** option to combine all maps into one PDF and click on the **Export Atlas as PDF** button, as shown in the following screenshot:

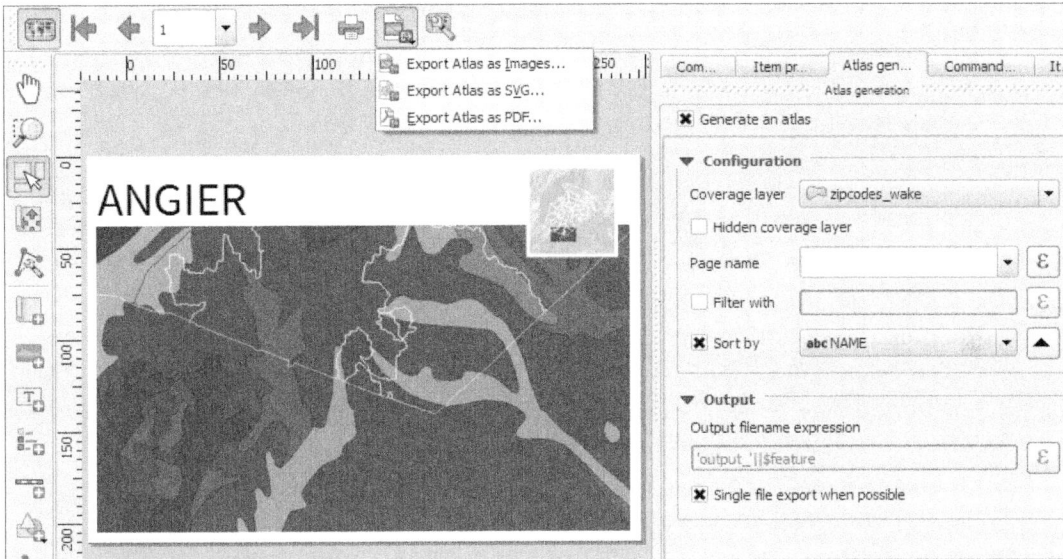

How it works...

The Atlas feature provides access to a series of variables related to the current feature. We already used this to display the NAME value of the current feature in the title label using the [%attribute(@atlas_feature, 'NAME') %] expression. Besides @atlas_feature, you have access to the following variables:

- ► @atlas_feature: This is the feature ID of the current Atlas feature. This makes it possible to use this information in rules to, for example, hide or highlight features based on their ID.

- ► @atlas_geometry: This is the geometry of the current Atlas feature and can be used in rules to, for example, only show features of other layers if their geometry intersects the Atlas feature geometry.

- ► @atlas_featurenumber: This is the number of the current Atlas feature.

- ► @atlas_totalfeatures: This is the total number of features in the Atlas coverage layer.

There's more...

Overview maps are a great way to provide context to more detailed main maps. To add an overview map (as shown in the upper-right corner of the composition in the following screenshot), you need to add a second map item to the composition. To turn this map item into an overview map, go to **Item properties | Overviews** and click on the button with the green plus sign. This will add an `Overview 1` entry and enable the **Draw "Overview 1" overview** configuration GUI:

- ▸ **Map frame**: The **Map frame** drop-down list enables us to define the main map that should be referenced by the overview map. By default, the map items are named `Map 0`, `Map 1`, `Map 2`, and so on, depending on the order they were added to the composition. Therefore, we will select the `Map 0` entry if the main map was the first item that was added to the composition.

- ▸ **Frame style**: The **Change ...** button can be used to choose a style for the overview frame. Usually, this will be a simple fill with transparency.

- ▸ **Blending mode**: These are supported by overview frames, as explained in detail in the *Understanding the feature and layer blending modes* recipe.

- ▸ **Invert overview**: Enable the **Invert overview** checkbox if you want to apply the overview frame style to the areas outside the extent of the main map.

- ▸ **Center on overview**: Enable the **Center on overview** checkbox if you want the overview map to automatically pan to center on the extent of the main map.

11
Extending QGIS

In this chapter, we will cover the following topics:

- ▸ Defining custom projections
- ▸ Working near the dateline
- ▸ Working offline
- ▸ Using the QSpatiaLite plugin
- ▸ Adding plugins with Python dependencies
- ▸ Using the Python console
- ▸ Writing Processing algorithms
- ▸ Writing QGIS plugins
- ▸ Using external tools

Introduction

QGIS can do many things on its own. However, as with all software, there are limits to its default abilities. The great news is there are many ways to extend QGIS to do even more through built-in customization options, existing add-on plugins, creating new analysis algorithms, creating your own plugins, and using external software that compliments QGIS. This chapter covers just a few of the common customizations and plugins that haven't been mentioned in other chapters, and how you can get started with making your own add-ons to share with others.

Defining custom projections

Map projections stump just about everybody at some point in their GIS career, if not more often. If you're lucky, you just stick to the common ones that are known by everyone and your life is simple. Sometimes though, for a particular location or a custom map, you just need something a little different that isn't in the already vast QGIS projections database. (Often, these are also referred to as **Coordinate Reference System (CRS)** or **Spatial Reference System (SRS)**.)

I'm not going to cover what the difference is between a Projection, Projected Coordinate System, and a Coordinate system. From a practical perspective in QGIS, you can pick the one that matches your data or your intended output. There's lots of little caveats that come with this, but a book or class is a much better place to get a handle on it.

Getting ready

For this recipe, we'll be using a custom graticule, a grid of lines every 10 degrees (`10d_graticule.json.geojson`), and the Natural Earth 1:10 million coastline (`ne_10m_coastline.shp`).

How to do it...

1. Determine what projection your data is currently in. In this case, we're starting with EPSG:4236, which is also known as Lat/Lon WGS84.

2. Determine what projection you want to make a map in. In this example, we'll be making an Oblique Stereographic projection centered on Ireland.

3. Search the existing QGIS projection list for a match or similar projection. If you open the **Projection** dialog and type `Stereographic`, this is a good start.

4. If you find a similar projection and just want to customize it, highlight the `proj4` string and copy the information. **NAD83(CSRS) / Prince Edward Isl. Stereographic (NAD83)** is a similar enough projection.

> If you don't find anything in the QGIS projection database, search the Web for a `proj4` string for the projection that you want to use. Sometimes, you'll find `Projection WKT`. With a little work, you can figure out which `proj4` slot each of the WKT parameters corresponds to using the documentation at `https://github.com/OSGeo/proj.4/wiki/GenParms`. A good place to research projections is provided at the end of this recipe.

5. Under **Settings**, open the **Custom CRS** option.

6. Click on the **+** symbol to add a new definition.

7. Put in a name and paste in your projection string, modifying it in this case with coordinates that center on Ireland. Change the values for the `lat_0` and `lon_0` parameters to match the following example. This particular type of projection only takes one reference point. For projections with multiple standard parallels and meridians, you will see the number after the underscore increment:

```
+proj=sterea +lat_0=53.5 +lon_0=-7.8 +k=0.999912
+x_0=400000 +y_0=800000 +ellps=GRS80 +towgs84=0,0,0,0,0,0,0
+units=m +no_defs
```

The following screenshot shows what the screen will look like:

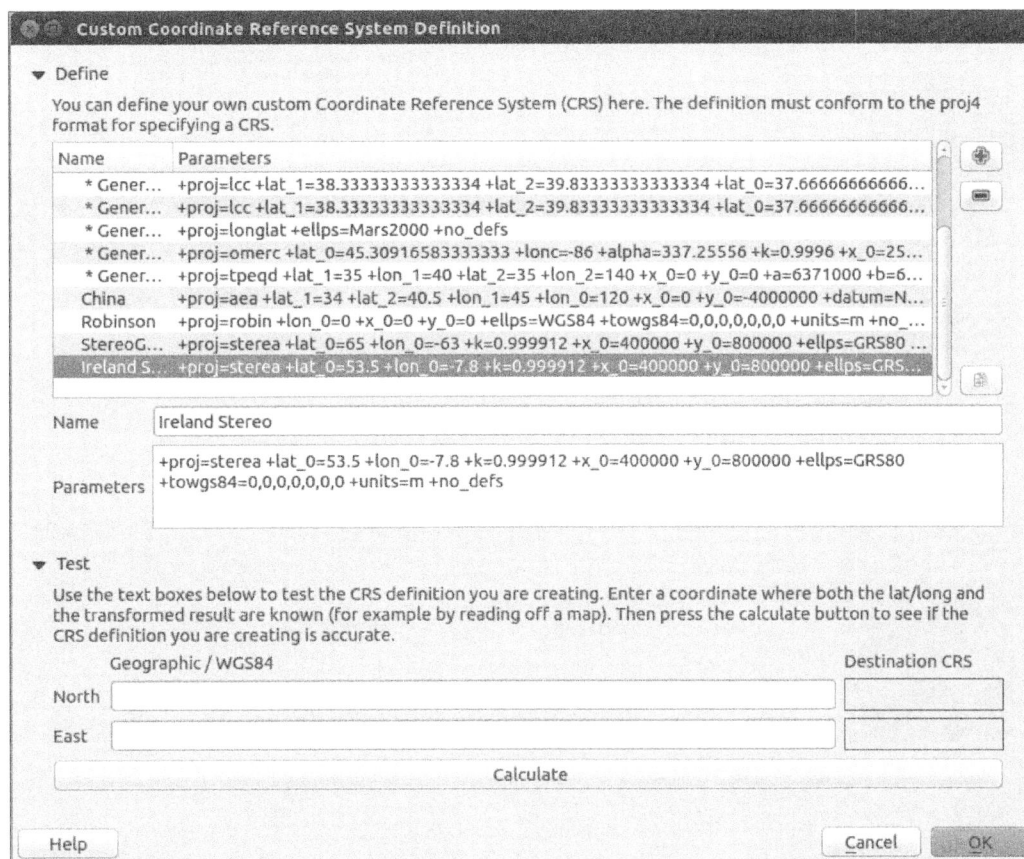

8. Now, click on another projection in the list of custom projections. There's currently a quirk where if you don't toggle off to another projection, then it doesn't save when you click on **OK**.

9. Now, go to the map, open the projection manager and apply your new projection with OTF on to check whether it's right. You'll find your new projection in the third section, **User Defined Coordinate Systems**:

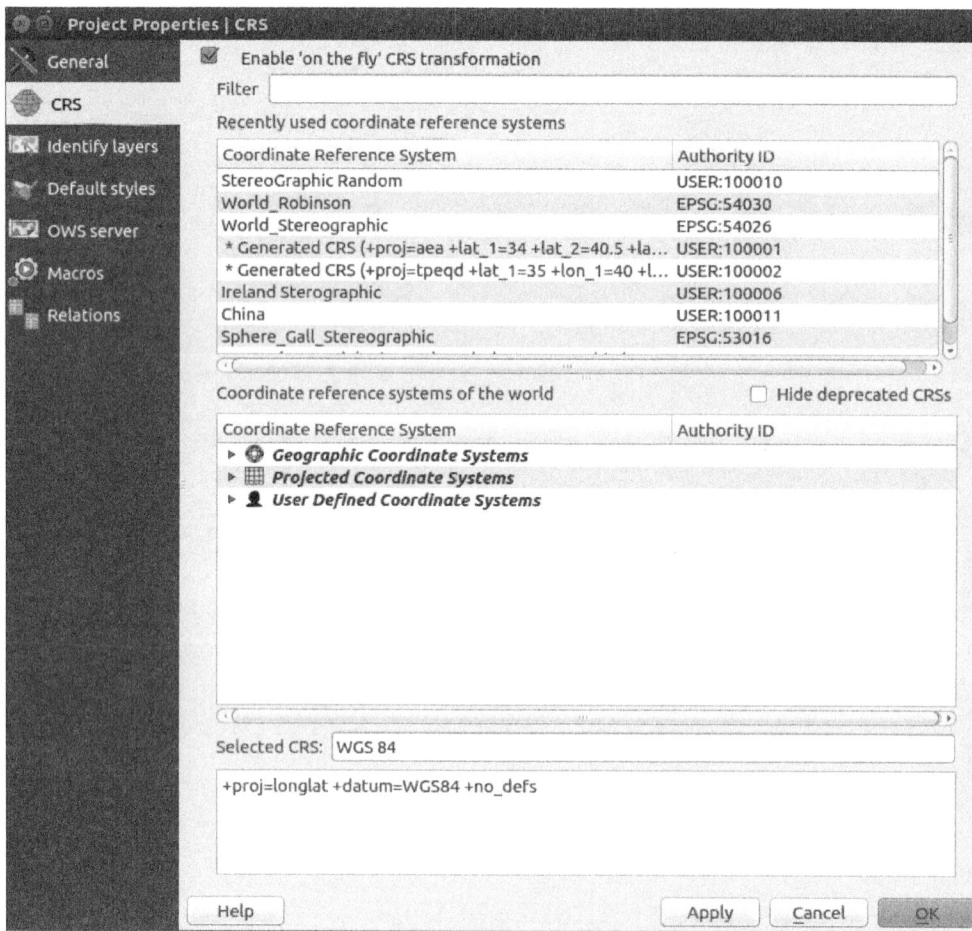

The following screenshot shows the projection:

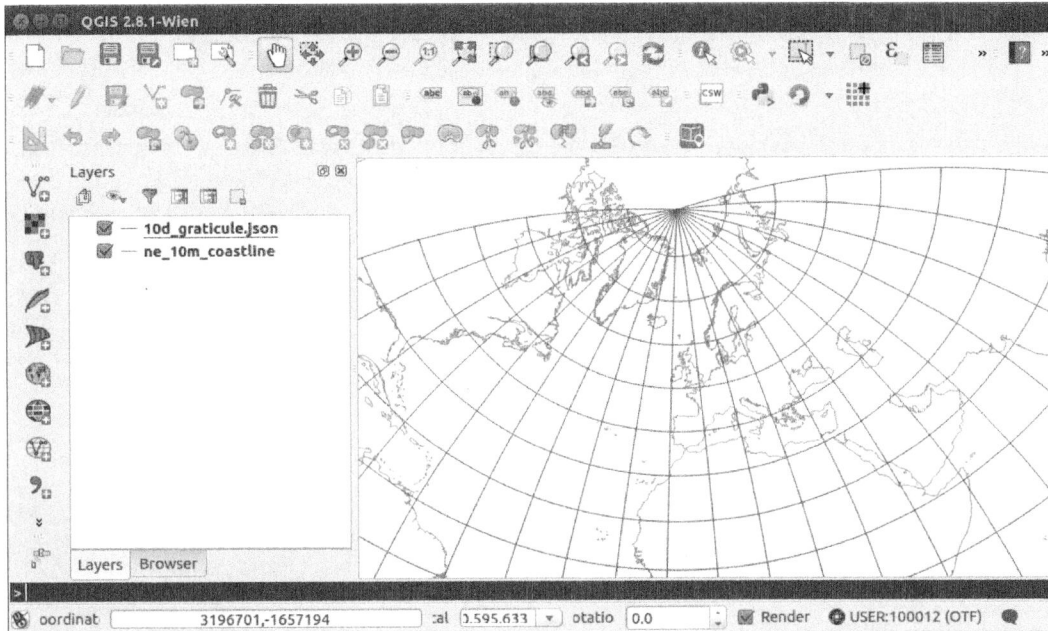

How it works...

Projection information (in this case, a `proj4` string) encodes the parameters that are needed by the computer to pick the correct math formula (projection type) and variables (various parameters, such as parallels and the center line) to convert the data into the desired flat map from whatever it currently is. This library of information includes approximations for the shape of the earth and differing manners to squash this into a flat visual.

You can really alter most of the parameters to change your map appearance, but generally, stick to known definitions so that your map matches other maps that are made the same way.

There's more...

QGIS only allows forward/backward transformation projections. Cartographic forward-only projections (for example, Natural Earth, Winkel Tripel (III), and Van der Grinten) aren't in the projection list currently; this is because these reprojections are not a pure math formula, but an approximate mapping from one to the other, and the inverse doesn't always exist. You can get around this by reprojecting your data with the `ogr2ogr` and `gdal_transform` command line to the desired projection, and then loading it into QGIS with **Projection-on-the-fly** disabled. While the `proj4` strings exist for these projections, QGIS will reject them if you try to enter them.

> [💡 If you disable **Projection-on-the-fly**, make sure that all layers are in the
> same projection; otherwise, they won't line up. Also, perform all analysis
> steps before converting to a projection that is intended for cartography,
> as the units of measurement may become messy.]

Geometries that cross the outer edge of projections don't always cut off nicely. You will often
see this as an unexpected polygon band across your map. The easiest thing to do in this case
is to remove data that is outside your intended mapping region. You can use a clip function or
simply select what you want to keep and **Save Selection As** a new layer.

There are other common projection description formats (prj, WKT, and proj4) out there.
Luckily, several websites help you translate. There are a couple of good websites to look up
the existing Proj4 style projection information available at http://spatialreference.
org and http://epsg.io.

See also

> ▸ Need more information on how to pick an appropriate projection for the type of
> map you are making? Refer to the USGS classic map projections poster available at
> http://egsc.usgs.gov/isb/pubs/MapProjections/projections.html.
> Much of this is also used in the Wikipedia article on the topic available at
> http://en.wikipedia.org/wiki/Map_projection. The https://www.
> mapthematics.com/ProjectionsList.php link also has a great list of
> projections, including unusual ones with pictures.

Working near the dateline

If you read the previous recipe about custom projections, you might have noticed the note
about data that crosses the edge of projections and how it doesn't usually render properly.
When working on data near -180 or 180 degrees longitude, you are going to have this issue.
Maps showing far Eastern Russia, Fiji, New Zealand, and the South Pacific, to name a few
places, will often contend with this issue.

The required solution really depends on what you're trying to do. If you just need a map of
such areas, pick a locally suitable projection. If you have existing data from other sources,
it may be cut along the edge and you might need to stitch it back together. As for worldwide
maps, sometimes you have to trim .01 degrees of the edge of your data so that it doesn't
display oddly.

Getting ready

To follow this recipe, you will need the honolulu-flights.shp layer and the SpatiaLite
database new-zealand.sqlite from the sample data.

How to do it...

Load the `honolulu-flights.shp` layer in QGIS. This layer represents great circles flight lines from the Honolulu airport. As you can see, it is displayed in a very strange manner, as some flight lines cross the dateline meridian:

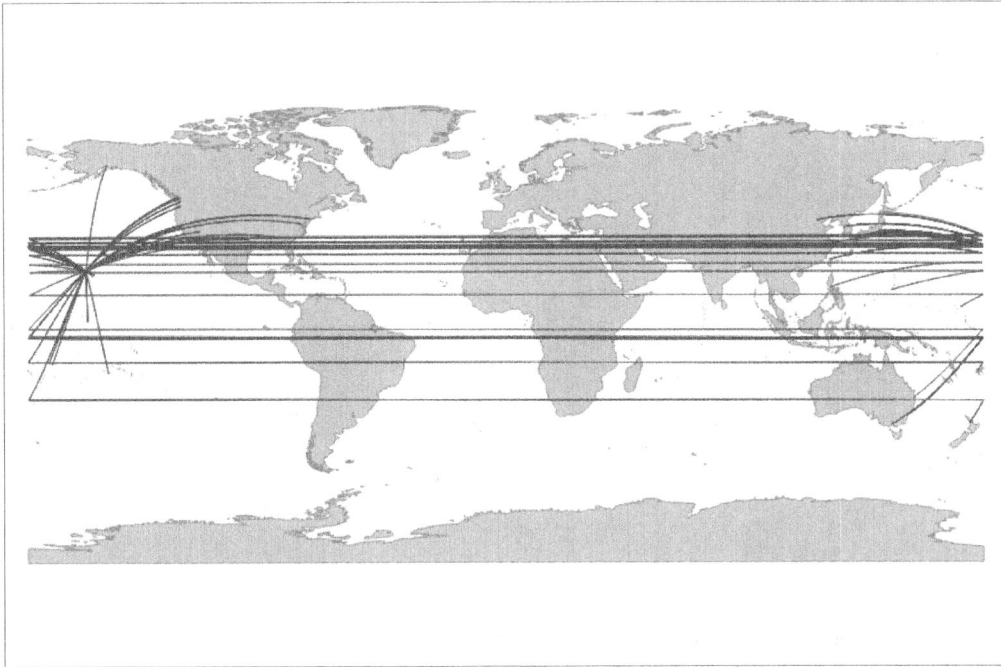

To display this layer correctly, we can select a suitable projection for your map. To do this, perform the following steps:

1. Open the **Project Properties** dialog by clicking on the *Ctrl + Shift + P* keyboard shortcut or navigating to **Project | Project Properties**.
2. Go to the **CRS** tab and activate the **Enable 'on the fly' CRS transformation** checkbox.
3. Select projection suitable for location. In our case, this is WGS84/PDC Mercator (EPSG:3832).

> Note that for different locations, different projections should be used.

4. Click on the **OK** button to save changes and close the dialog. Now, our data is displayed correctly:

Another option is to clip data to the dateline meridian. This can be done with the `ogr2ogr` tool from the GDAL toolset. To do this, perform the following steps:

1. Open the OSGeo4W command prompt if you are a Windows user, or the terminal window if you are a Linux or Mac OS user.

2. Change the directory to the folder where `honolulu-flights.shp` is located, for example, the following directory:

   ```
   cd c:\data
   ```

3. Enter the following command in the command prompt. Note that we first specify the output file and then the input file:

   ```
   ogr2ogr -wrapdateline honolulu-flights-wrapped.shp
   honolulu-flights.shp
   ```

4. After loading the newly-created `honolulu-flights-wrapped.shp` layer into QGIS, you will now see that flights wrapped on the dateline meridian are displayed correctly:

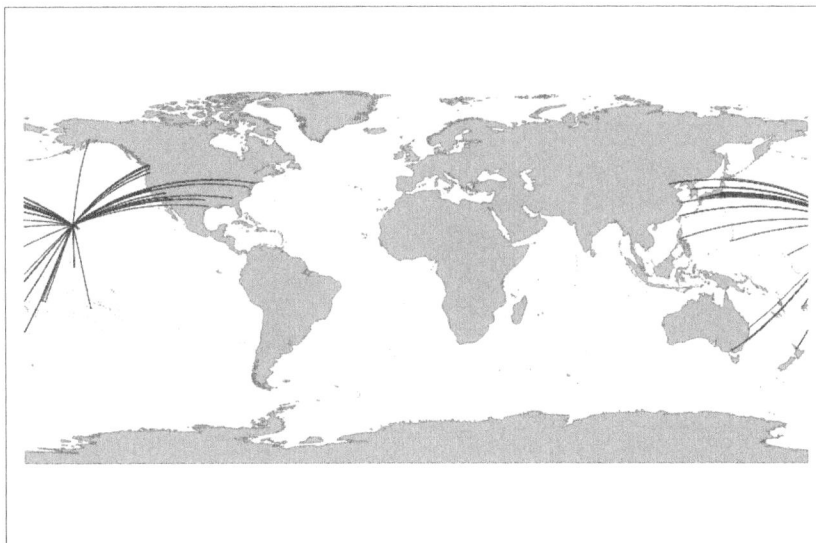

5. Now load the `nz-coastlines-and-islands` layer from the `new-zealand.sqlite` database. You should see two sets of polygons far from each other. This is New Zealand and Chatham islands, which should be located nearby:

To display them correctly, we can use the `ST_Shift_Longitude` function available in the SpatiaLite. To do this, perform the following steps:

1. Open the **DB Manager** plugin by clicking on its button on the toolbar or navigating to **Database | DB Manager | DB Manager**.

2. Expand the **SpatiaLite** group in the connections tree on the left-hand side of the dialog, and select the `new-zealand` database.

3. Open **SQL Window** and run the following query:

```
UPDATE "nz-coastlines-and-islands" SET
Geometry=ST_Shift_Longitude(Geometry)
```

4. Remove the `nz-coastlines-and-islands` layer from QGIS and add it again. Now, New Zealand and Chatham islands will be displayed correctly, as follows:

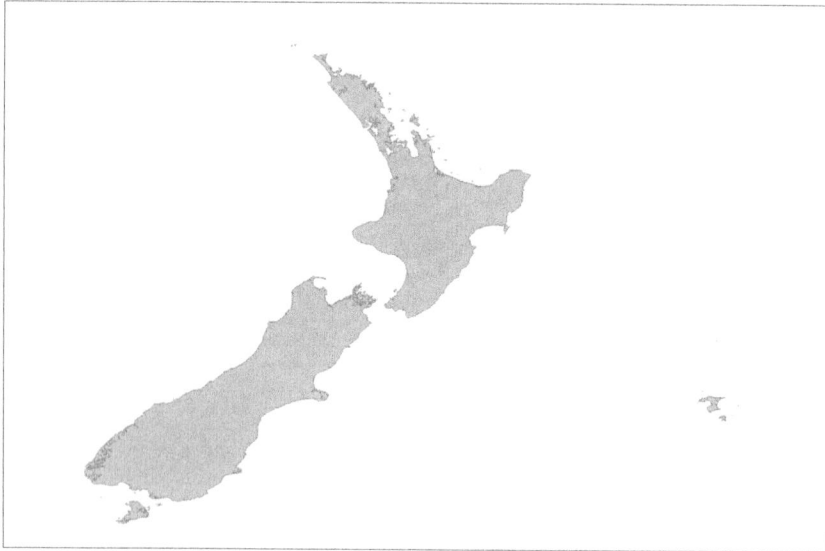

It is worth mentioning that the `ST_Shift_Longitude` function is also available in PostGIS.

How it works...

When we enable **'on the fly' CRS transformation**, every geometry is reprojected to the given CRS (in our case Pacific centered) so that coordinates now have the same sign.

The `ogr2ogr` tool with the `-wrapdateline` option splits all geometries that cross the dateline and write them to the output file. Geometries that do not cross the dateline are copied without changes.

The `ST_Shift_Longitude` function translates negative longitudes by 360 and as a result, all the data will be in the range of 0-360 degrees and displayed correctly.

See also

▶   http://docs.qgis.org/2.2/en/docs/user_manual/working_with_
    vector/supported_data.html#vector-layers-crossing-180-degrees-
    longitude

Working offline

The Internet is an awesome resource, but sometimes you just don't have access to it. For field work, in places with intermittent services, on an airplane, or even in a meeting room, you just might not be able to access all the stuff that you need. By stuff, we're referring to documentation (user and developer), but more importantly database layers (for example, PostGIS) and web service-based layers (for example, WMS, WFS, the OpenLayers plugin, and so on).

This recipe is about caching local copies of the files that you need on your computer before you leave for an unconnected place.

Getting ready

For this recipe, you will need to open a PostGIS database or WFS and enable the **Offline Editing** plugin that ships with QGIS.

How to do it...

1. Load your layer from PostGIS or WFS.

2. Make sure to activate the **Offline Editing** option.

3. In the **Database** menu, you should see **Offline Editing**, choose **Convert to offline project**:

4. Choose the local file to use to store the data.

5. Then, select all of the layers to convert (vector layers only):

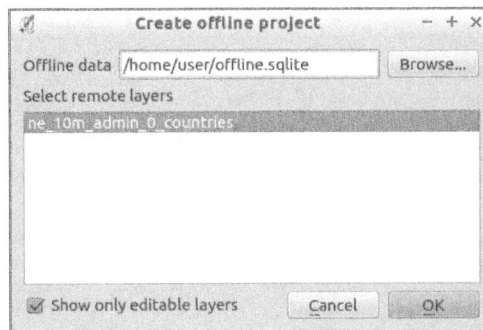

6. You can now use your PostGIS layers without a network connection to the online database. Go ahead and try to make some edits. (We recommend that you do this on a copy of database or table until you know what you're doing.)

7. When you come back to your network, you can now send your changes to the database by choosing the **Synchronize** option:

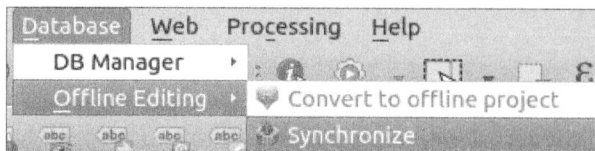

How it works...

The basics are straightforward, a copy of you data is saved into a SpatiaLite database locally on your computer. The project file records the change, and you are good to go as SpatiaLite can do anything any other vector data source in QGIS can do.

Be careful when working in a multiuser environment, this does not handle dealing with editing conflicts if multiple users have been modifying the same dataset independently.

There's more...

Also, there are all sorts of ways to create offline caches of Raster datasets (network files or web services) including gdalwmscaching or mbtiles. If you plan to need to work away from the Internet for periods of time, plan ahead, and test solutions before actually needing to go offline. No amount of plugins makes up for good planning.

Please remember to check the legality of caching web services (for example, Google and Bing) before doing so. OpenStreetMap is a reliable source of tiles for offline usage without restrictions.

See also

▶ GDAL WMS Cache options are available at http://www.gdal.org/frmt_wms.html

▶ A discussion of mbtiles usage is available at http://blogs.terrorware.com/geoff/2012/11/17/offline-map-tiles-in-qgis/

▶ A recent plugin to help you set this up is available at https://plugins.qgis.org/plugins/MBTiles2img/

Using the QspatiaLite plugin

Sometimes, you may not need to load a whole layer into QGIS, but only some subset of it, or perform some calculations on the fly. In such situations, the ability to run complex SQL queries and display their results in QGIS will be very useful.

This recipe shows you how to execute SQL code with the QspatiaLite plugin and load data in QGIS.

Getting ready

To follow this recipe, you need to create connection to the `cookbook.db` database created in the *Loading vector layers into SpatiaLite* recipe in *Chapter 1, Data Input and Output*. Alternatively, you can use your own SpatiaLite database, but be aware that you might have to alter some of the following SQL statements to match your tables.

Additionally, install the **QspatiaLite** plugin from **Plugin Manager**.

How to do it...

Make sure that you created a connection to `cookbook.db`. Start the **QspatiaLite** plugin by navigating to **Database | SpatiaLite | QspatiaLite**:

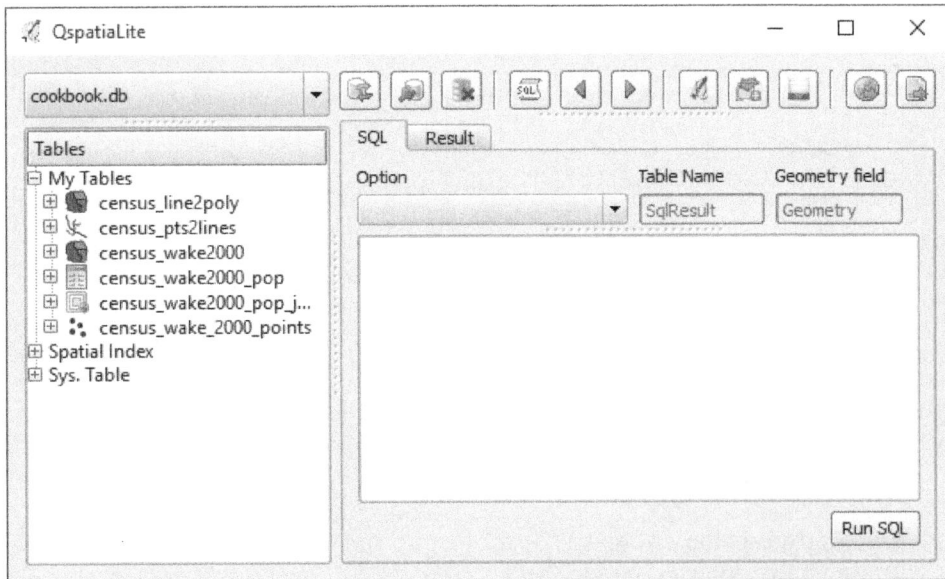

To execute the SQL query, perform the following steps:

1. Select database you want to use from the combobox in the top-left corner of the plugin dialog.

2. In the **SQL** tab, enter following query:

```
SELECT "census_wake2000".'pk' AS id,
"census_wake2000".'geom' AS Geometry,
"census_wake2000".'area', "census_wake2000".'perimeter'
FROM "census_wake2000" WHERE "census_wake2000".'perimeter >
100000;
```

   You can easily insert the table and column names by double-clicking on them in the **Tables** tree on the left-hand side of the dialog.

3. Click on the **Run** button at the bottom of the dialog to execute the query. The **Result** tab will open automatically and you can examine the query results in the table representation, as follows:

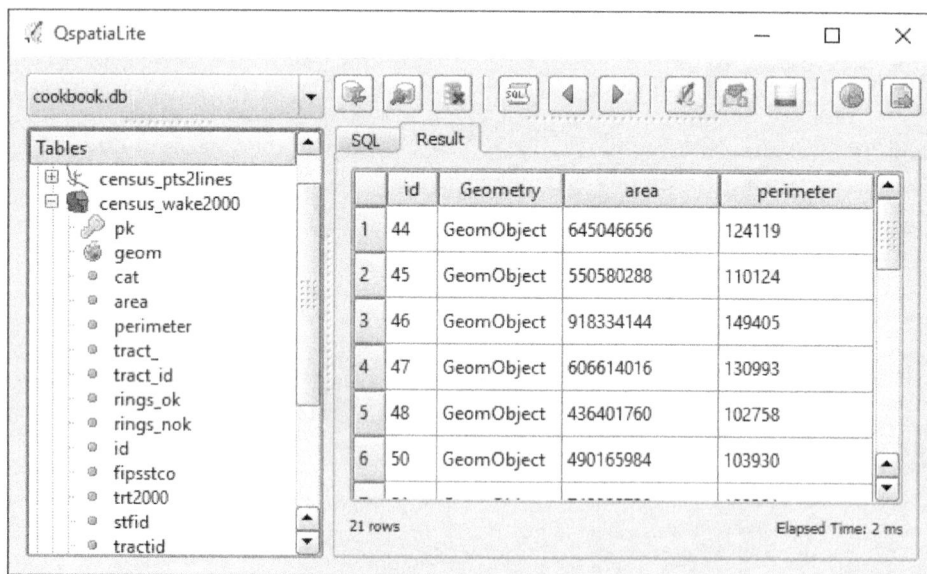

If the query results contain geometry information (the so-called geometry column), you can display them in QGIS. To do this, perform the following steps:

1. Switch back to the **SQL** tab.

2. In the **Option** combobox, select the action that you want to perform, for example, **Create Spatial View & Load in QGIS**.

3. In the **Table** field, enter name of the resulting view, for example, `above100k`.

4. Ensure that you entered the correct name of the geometry column in the **Geometry** field.

5. Click on the **Run** button at the bottom of the dialog.

6. A dialog will pop up asking for the source geometry table. Select table that you used in the query and click on **OK**.

7. A new view will be created and added to the QGIS as a new layer.

How it works...

When we click on the **Run** button, the query is passed to the SpatiaLite database engine for execution, and the results are returned to the plugin and displayed in the table. If you want to store results permanently, you can export them in a text file or in an OGR-compatible format using the corresponding buttons in the plugin dialog.

There's more...

You can also use the **DB Manager** plugin (which is bundled with QGIS) to execute SQL-queries directly and load them as layers.

See also

▶ A very good introduction to SpatiaLite and SQL can be found at `https://www.gaia-gis.it/fossil/libspatialite/wiki?name=misc-docs`. Also, a full list of the supported spatial SQL functions is available at `http://www.gaia-gis.it/gaia-sins/spatialite-sql-4.3.0.html`.

Adding plugins with Python dependencies

While the most common and widely-used Python packages are shipped with QGIS, and they can be used by plugins without any additional actions, some QGIS plugins need third-party Python packages, which are not available with the default QGIS installation.

This recipe shows you how to add missing Python packages to the QGIS installation.

Getting ready

To follow this recipe, you may need administrator rights if you are a Windows user, and QGIS is installed in the system drive.

How to do it...

This steps will install pip — a Python package management tool:

1. Download the `get-pip.py` file from `https://raw.githubusercontent.com/pypa/pip/master/contrib/get-pip.py` and save it somewhere on your hard drive, for example in `D:\Downloads`.

2. Open the OSGeo4W command prompt as administrator. Right-click on the **OSGeo4W Shell** shortcut on your Desktop and select **Run as Administrator** from the context menu. If you cannot find this shortcut on your Desktop, look for it in the Windows **Start** menu.

3. In the OSGeo4W command prompt, type `python D:\Downloads\get-pip.py`. Don't forget to replace `D:\Downloads` with the correct path to the `get-pip.py` file. Wait while the command execution completes.

Now, when pip is ready, you can easily download and install third-party Python packages. To do this, perform the following steps:

1. Open the OSGeo4W command prompt as administrator. Right-click on the **OSGeo4W Shell** shortcut on your desktop and select **Run as Administrator** from the context menu. If you cannot find this shortcut on the desktop, look for it in the Windows **Start** menu.

2. In the OSGeo4W command prompt, type `pip install package_name`. Don't forget to replace `package_name` with the name of the package that you want to install. For example, if you want to install the PySAL package, use this command: `pip install pysal`.

If you are a Linux user, use your package manager to install pip. For example, under Debian and Ubuntu, use the `sudo apt-get install python-pip` command to install pip. After doing this, you can use pip to download and install packages as described in the preceding paragraph.

Mac OS users can install pip via Homebrew using the `brew install pip` command.

Using pip, you also can view installed packages, update, and remove them. For more information please look at the pip documentation available at `https://pip.pypa.io/en/stable/`.

How it works...

pip downloads the requested package with all necessary dependencies from the Python Package Index (`https://pypi.python.org/`) and installs them into Python bundled with QGIS.

There's more...

You can also register Python bundled with QGIS in the Windows registry as the system default Python version. After this, you can use usual Windows installers to install the required packages. More information on this topic can be found at `https://trac.osgeo.org/ osgeo4w/ticket/114`.

Using the Python console

QGIS has a built-in Python console, where you can enter commands in the Python programming language and get results. This is very useful for quick data processing.

Getting ready

To follow this recipe, you should be familiar with the Python programming language. You can find a small but detailed tutorial in the official Python documentation at `https://docs. python.org/2.7/tutorial/index.html`.

Also load the `poi_names_wake.shp` file from the sample data.

How to do it...

QGIS Python console can be opened by clicking on the **Python Console** button at toolbar or by navigating to **Plugins | Python Console**. The console opens as a non-modal floating window, as shown in the following screenshot:

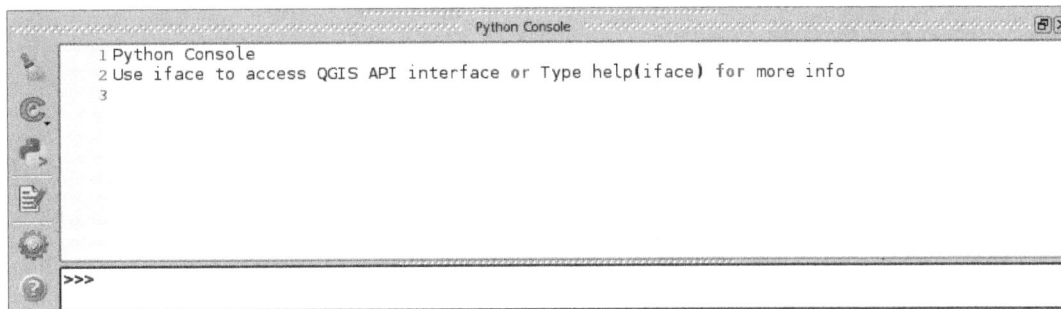

Let's take a look at how to perform some data exploration with the QGIS Python console:

1. First, it is necessary to get a reference to the active (selected in the layers tree) layer and store it in the variable for further use by running this command:

```
layer = iface.activeLayer()
```

2. After acquiring a reference to the layer, we can examine some of its properties. For example, to get the number of features in the layer, execute the following command:

```
layer.featureCount()
```

> At any time, you can use the `dir()` function to list all the available methods of the object. Try to execute `dir(layer)` or `dir(QgsFeature)`.

3. You can also loop over layer features and print their attributes using the following code snippet:

```
for f in layer.getFeatures():
    print f["featurenam"], f["elev_m"]
```

> Note that you need to press *Enter* twice after entering this code to exit the loop definition and start executing commands.

You can also use the Python console for more complex tasks, such as exporting features with some attributes to a text file. Here is how to do this:

1. Open the **Python Console** editor using the **Show editor** button on the left-hand side of the Python console.

2. Paste the following code into the editor (make sure to change path to file according to your system):

```
import csv
layer = iface.activeLayer()
with open('c:\\temp\\export.csv', 'wb') as outputFile:
    writer = csv.writer(outputFile)
    for feature in layer.getFeatures():
        geom = feature.geometry().exportToWkt()
        writer.writerow([geom, feature["featurenam"],
feature['elev_m"]])
```

3. If you are using your own vector layer instead of `poi_names_wake.shp`, which is provided with this book, adjust attribute names in line 8.

4. Change the file paths for the result file in line 4 depending on your operating system.

5. Save the script and run it. Don't forget to select the vector layer in the QGIS layer tree before running the script.

How it works...

In line 1, we imported the `csv` module from the standard Python library. This module provides a convenient way to read and write comma-separated files. In line 3, we obtained a reference to the currently selected layer, which will be used later to access layer features.

In line 3, an output file opened. Note that here we use the `with` statement so that later there is no need to close the file explicitly, context manager will do this work for us. In line 5, we set up the so-called writer—an object that will write data to the CSV file using specified format settings.

In line 6, we started iterating over features of the active layer. For each feature, we extracted its geometry and converted it into a **Well-Known Text** (**WKT**) format (line 7). We then wrote this text representation of the feature geometry with some attributes to the output file (line 8).

It is necessary to mention that our script is very simple and will work only with attributes that have ASCII encoding. To handle non-Latin characters, it is necessary to convert the output data to the unicode before writing it to file.

There's more...

Using the Python console, you also can invoke Processing algorithms to create complex scripts for automated analysis and/or data preparation.

To make the Python console even more useful, take a look at the Script Runner plugin. Detailed information about this plugin with some usage examples can be found at `http://spatialgalaxy.net/2012/01/29/script-runner-a-plugin-to-run-python-scripts-in-qgis/`.

See also

▶ If you are new to Python and QGIS API, don't forget to look at the following documentation:

  ❏ Official Python documentation and tutorial can be found at `https://docs.python.org/2/`

  ❏ *QGIS API Documentation* can be found at `http://qgis.org/api/2.8/`

  ❏ *PyQGIS Developer Cookbook* can be found at `http://docs.qgis.org/2.8/en/docs/pyqgis_developer_cookbook/`

> ▸ Another great resource to learn programming with QGIS is *QGIS Python Programming Cookbook, Joel Lawhead,* published by Packt Publishing

Writing Processing algorithms

You can extend the capabilities of QGIS by adding scripts that can be used within the Processing framework. This will allow you to create your own analysis algorithms and then run them efficiently from the toolbox or from any of the productivity tools, such as the batch processing interface or the graphical modeler.

This recipe covers basic ideas about how to create a Processing algorithm.

Getting ready

A basic knowledge of Python is needed to understand this recipe. Also, as it uses the Processing framework, you should be familiar with it before studying this recipe.

How to do it...

We are going to add a new process to filter the polygons of a layer, generating a new layer that just contains the ones with an area larger than a given value. Here's how to do this:

1. In the **Processing Toolbox** menu, go to the **Scripts/Tools** group and double-click on the **Create new script** item. You will see the following dialog:

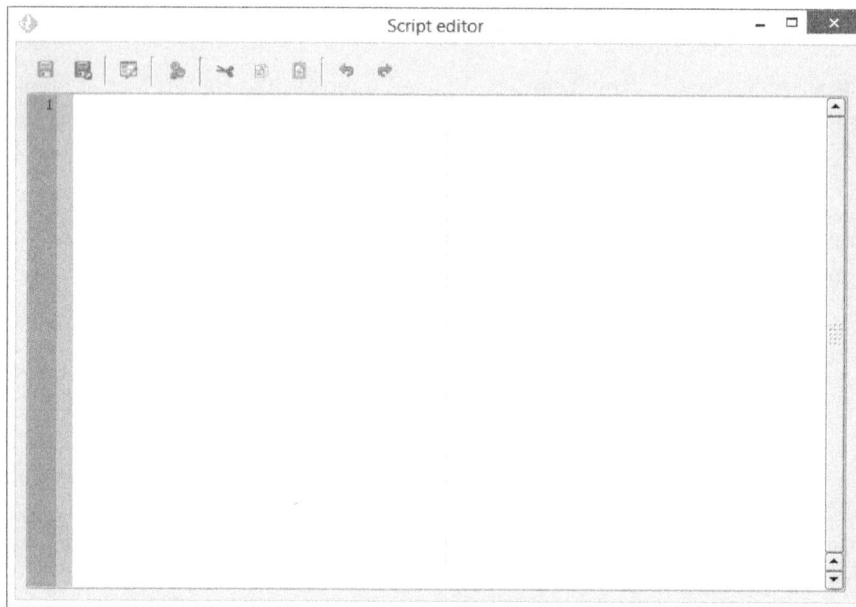

2. In the text editor of the dialog, paste the following code:

```
##Cookbook=group
##Filter polygons by size=name
##Vector_layer=vector
##Area=number 1
##Output=output vector

layer = processing.getObject(Vector_layer)
provider = layer.dataProvider()
writer = processing.VectorWriter(Output, None,
  provider.fields(), provider.geometryType(), layer.crs())
for feature in processing.features(layer):
  print feature.geometry().area()
  if feature.geometry().area() > Area:
    writer.addFeature(feature)
del writer
```

3. Select the **Save** button to save the script. In the file selector that will appear, enter a filename with the `.py` extension. Do not move this to a different folder. Make sure that you use the default folder that is selected when the file selector is opened.

4. Close the editor.

5. Go to the **Scripts** groups in the toolbox, and you will see a new group called **Cookbook** with an algorithm called `Filter polygons by size`.

6. Double-click on it to open it, and you will see the following parameters dialog, similar to what you can find for any of the other Processing algorithms:

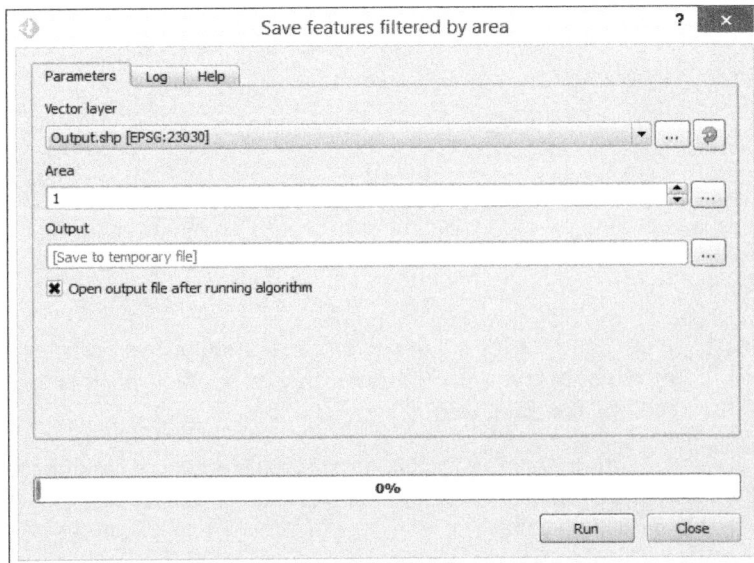

How it works...

The script contains mainly two parts:

▸ A part in which the characteristics of the algorithm are defined. This is used to define the semantics of the algorithm, along with some additional information, such as the name and group of the algorithm.

▸ A part that takes the inputs entered by the user and processes them to generate the outputs. This is where the algorithm itself is located.

In our example, the first part looks like the following:

```
##Cookbook=group
##Filter polygons by size=name
##Vector_layer=vector
##Area=number 1
##Output=output vector
```

We are defining two inputs (the layer and the area value) and declaring one output (the filtered layer). These elements are defined using the Python comments with a double Python comment sign (#).

The second part includes the code itself and looks like the following:

```
layer = processing.getObject(Vector_layer)
provider = layer.dataProvider()
writer = processing.VectorWriter(Output, None,
  provider.fields(), provider.geometryType(), layer.crs())
for feature in processing.features(layer):
  print feature.geometry().area()
  if feature.geometry().area() > Area:
    writer.addFeature(feature)
del writer
```

The inputs that we defined in the first part will be available here, and we can use them. In the case of the area, we will have a variable named `Area`, containing a number. In the case of the vector layer, we will have a `Layer` variable, containing a string with the source of the selected layer.

Using these values, we use the PyQGIS API to perform the calculations and create a new layer. The layer is saved in the file path contained in the `Output` variable, which is the one that the user will select when running the algorithm.

Apart from using regular Python and the PyQGIS interface, Processing includes some classes and functions because this makes it easier to create scripts, and that wrap some of the most common functionality of QGIS.

In particular, the `processing.features(layer)` method is important. This provides an iterator over the features in a layer, but only considering the selected ones. If no selection exists, it iterates over all the features in the layer. This is the expected behavior of any Processing algorithm, so this method has to be used to provide a consistent behavior in your script.

There's more...

Some of the core algorithms that are provided with Processing are actually scripts, such as the one we just created, but they do not appear in the scripts section. Instead, they appear in the **QGIS algorithms** section because they are a core part of Processing.

Other scripts are not part of processing itself but they can be installed easily from the toolbox using the **Tools/Get scripts from on-line collection** menu:

You will see a window like the following one:

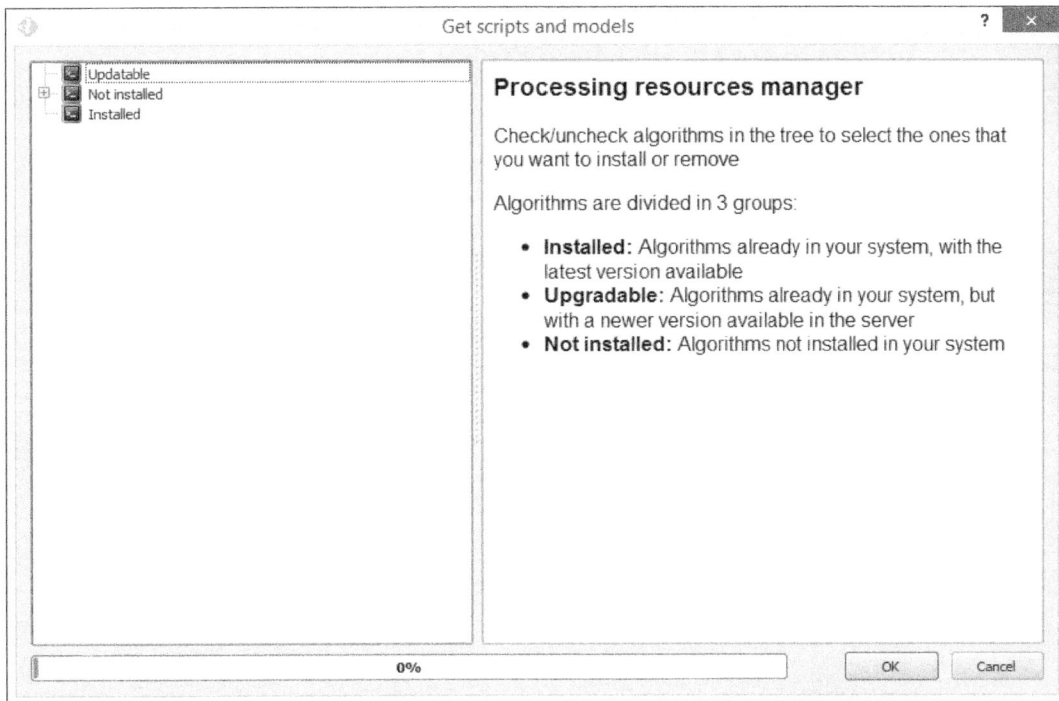

Just select the scripts that you want to install and then click on **OK**. The selected scripts will now appear in the toolbox. You can use it as you use any other Processing algorithm.

See also

► All the information about creating scripts and running Processing code from the QGIS Python console can be found in the corresponding section in the QGIS manual.

Writing QGIS plugins

One of the main reasons of the popularity of QGIS is its extensibility. Using the basic tools and features provided by the QGIS API, new functionality can be implemented and added as a new plugin that can be shared by contributing it to the QGIS plugins repository.

Getting ready

To be able to develop a new QGIS plugin, you should be familiar with the Python programming language. If the plugin has a graphical interface, you should have some knowledge of the Qt framework, as this is used for all UI elements, such as dialogs. To access the QGIS functionality, it is required that you know the QGIS API.

A very handy resource for all these (plus a few others) is the GeoAPIs website, which is created by SourcePole at `http://geoapis.sourcepole.com/`.

To simplify the creation of a plugin, we will use an additional plugin named Plugin Builder. It should be installed in your QGIS application.

How to do it...

The following steps create a new plugin that will print out detailed information about the layers currently loaded in your QGIS project:

1. Open Plugin Builder by navigating to **Plugin | Plugin Builder**.

2. Fill out the dialog that will appear, as shown in the following screenshot:

3. Click on **OK**.

4. In the folder selector dialog that will appear, select the folder where you want to store your plugin. Click on **OK** and the plugin skeleton will be created. In the selected folder, you will now have a subfolder named `LayerInfoPlugin`, with the following content (items in square brackets indicate folders):

```
[help]
[i18n]
[scripts]
[test]
icon.png
layerinfo.py
layerinfo_dialog.py
layerinfo_dialog_base.ui
Makefile
metadata.txt
pb_tool.cfg
```

```
plugin_upload.py
pylintrc
README.html
README.txt
resources.qrc
__init__.py
```

5. Open the `layerinfo.py` file in a text editor. At the end of it, you will find the `run()` method, with the following code:

```
def run(self):
    """Run method that performs all the real work"""
    # show the dialog
    self.dlg.show()
    # Run the dialog event loop
    result = self.dlg.exec_()
    # See if OK was pressed
    if result: pass
```

6. Replace the `run` method with the following code:

```
def run(self):
    layers = self.iface.legendInterface().layers()
    print "---LAYERS INFO---"
    for layer in layers:
        print "Layer name: " + layer.name()
        print "Layer source " + layer.source()
        print "Extent: " + layer.extent().asWktCoordinates()
        print
```

7. Install the `pb_tool` application by opening a terminal and running `easy_install pb_tool` (you can also use `pip install pb_tool` or any other way of installing a library from PyPI).

8. Open a terminal in the folder where you have the plugin code and run `pb_tool` and compile. Then, run `pb_tool deploy` to install the plugin in your local QGIS.

9. Open QGIS. Go to **Plugin Manager** and make sure that the new plugin we have created is there and is enabled:

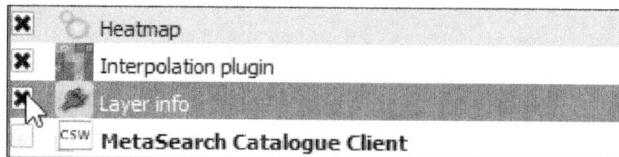

10. In the **Plugins** menu, you will now have the entry corresponding to the plugin:

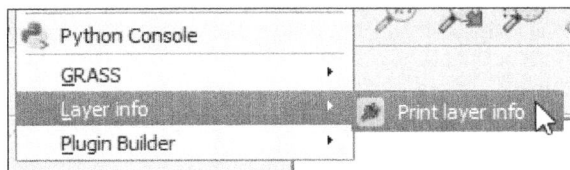

11. Populate your project with some layers so that the plugin can display information about them.
12. Open the QGIS Python console.
13. Run the plugin by selecting its menu entry. Information about the layers in the project will be shown in the console:

How it works...

The Plugin Builder plugin takes some basic information about the plugin to create it, and uses it to create its skeleton. By default, it includes a menu entry, which becomes the entry point to the plugin from the QGIS interface.

When the menu item is selected, the corresponding action in the plugin code is executed. In this case, it runs the `run()` method, where we have added our code.

The plugin will always have a reference to the QGIS instance (an object of class `QgsInterface`), which can be used to access the QGIS API and connect with the elements in the current QGIS session. In our case, this is used to access the legend, which contains a list of all the layers loaded in the current project. Calling the corresponding methods in each one of these layers, the information about them is retrieved and printed out.

The standard output is redirected to the QGIS Python console, so printing a text using the built-in Python print command will cause the text to appear in the console in case it is open.

QGIS stores its plugins in the `.qgis2/python/plugin` folder under the current user folder. For instance, this is when you download a new plugin using Plugin Manager. Each time you start QGIS, it will look for plugins there and load them. Copying the folder is done by the deploy task that we have run, and this allows QGIS to discover the plugin and add it to the list of available plugins when QGIS is started.

There's more...

The following are some ideas to create better plugins and manage them.

Creating plugins with more complex UI elements

The plugin that we have created has no UI elements. However, among the files created by the plugin builder, you can find a basic dialog file with the `.ui` extension. You can edit this to create a dialog that can later be used, by calling it from your plugin code. To know more about how to create and use UI elements from the Qt framework (QGIS is built on top of this framework), check out the PyQt documentation.

Documenting you plugin

Another thing that is created by the Plugin Builder is a Sphinx documentation project where you can write the usage documentation of your plugin using RestructuredText. To know more about Sphinx, you can visit the Sphinx official site at `http://www.sphinx-doc.org/en/stable/`.

The documentation project is built when the deploy task is run, and will create HTML files and place them in the plugin folder.

Releasing your plugin

Once your plugin is finished, it would be a good idea to share it and let other people use it. If you upload your plugin to the QGIS plugin server, it would be easy for all QGIS users to get it using Plugin Manager and also get the latest updates.

To upload the plugin, you first need to create a ZIP file containing all its code and resources. There is a `pb_tool` task for this, and you just have to run `pb_tool zip` in a terminal. With the resulting ZIP file, you can start the release process. More information about it can be found at `http://docs.qgis.org/2.6/en/docs/pyqgis_developer_cookbook/releasing.html`.

Using external tools

While QGIS itself is a great and functional program, sometimes it is better to use more suitable tools to perform some simple or complex actions. This recipe shows you how to use some of these third-party tools.

Getting ready

To follow this recipe, you will need a `btnmeatrack_2014-05-22_13-35-40.nmea` file from the book dataset. We will also use the `cookbook.db` SpatiaLite database that we created in the *Loading vector layers into SpatiaLite* recipe in *Chapter 1, Data Input and Output*, and the PostgreSQL database, which we developed in *Chapter 6, Network Analysis*.

Besides this, don't forget to install GPSBabel (usually this comes with QGIS), spatialite-gui, and pgAdmin (these should be installed manually).

How to do it...

First we will convert NMEA data to GPX format with GPSBabel, then learn how to use SpatiaLite GUI tools and pgAdmin to work with databases.

GPSBabel

GPSBabel is a command-line tool to manipulate, convert, and process GPS data (waypoints, tracks, and routes) in different formats.

To convert a file from the NMEA format to more common GPX, follows these steps:

1. Open the command prompt and go to the directory where the `btnmeatrack_2014-05-22_13-35-40.nmea` file is located. Usually, this can be done with the `cd` command, for example, if the file is located in the `data` directory on the `C:` drive, use this command:

   ```
   cd c:\data
   ```

2. In the command prompt, enter the following command to convert the NMEA file to the GPX file:

   ```
   gpsbabel -i nmea -f btnmeatrack_2014-05-22_13-35-40.nmea -o
   gpx -F 2014-05-22_13_35-40.gpx
   ```

spatialite-gui

spatialite-gui is a GUI tool supporting SpatiaLite. This is lightweight and very useful when you need to quickly perform some queries or just check contents of the SQLite/SpatiaLite database.

To explore spatial or nonspatial tables in the SpatiaLite database, perform these steps:

1. Start `spatialite-gui` by double-clicking on its executable file.

2. Connect to the database that you want to explore by navigating to **Files | Connecting an existing SQLite DB** or clicking on the corresponding button on the toolbar.

3. Select the table you want to explore in the table tree on the left-hand side of the **spatialite-gui** dialog, open its context menu by clicking on the right mouse button, and select the **Edit table rows** menu entry.

4. If your table contains spatial data, it is possible to view geometry in different representations. Select the field with the geometry information in the row, open the context menu by clicking the right mouse button and select the **BLOB Explore** menu entry:

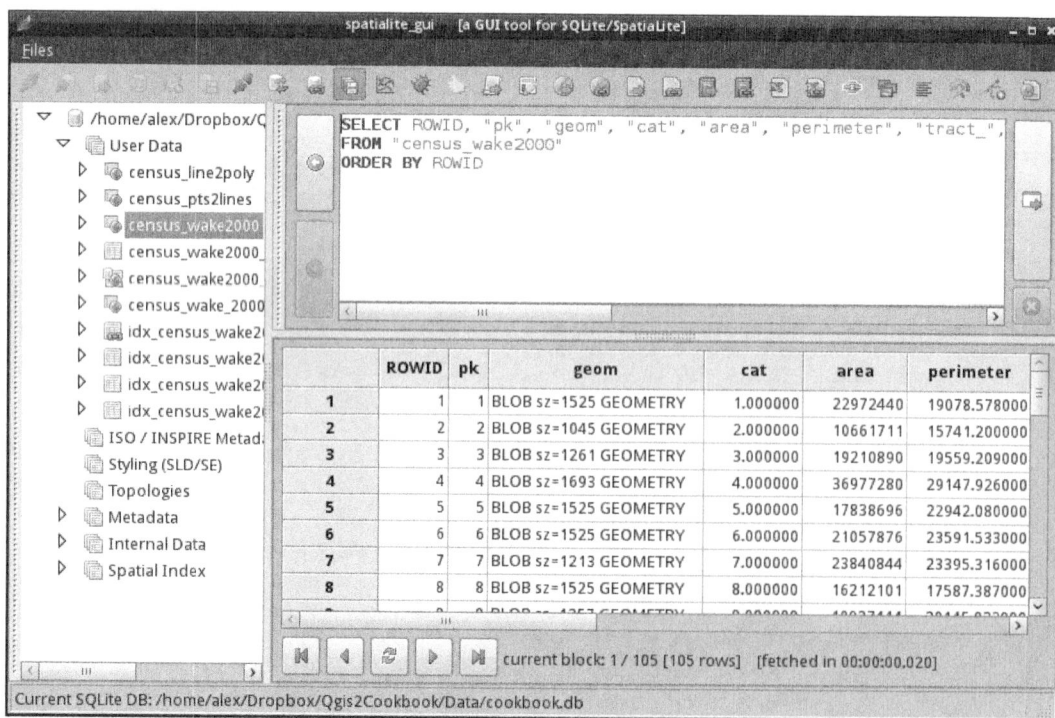

After massive edits, especially when tables were altered or deleted, it is recommended to run VACUUM command to rebuild the database. To do this, perform these steps:

1. Start `spatialite-gui` by double-clicking on its executable file.

2. Connect to the database that you want to explore by navigating to **Files | Connecting an existing SQLite DB** or clicking on the corresponding button on the toolbar.

3. Navigate to **Files | Optimizing current SQLite DB [VACUUM]** or click on the corresponding button on the toolbar.

pgAdmin

pgAdmin is an administration tool and development platform for PostgreSQL databases. It allows you to perform administrative tasks (such as backup and restore), run simple queries as well as develop new databases from scratch.

To create a backup of the database with pgAdmin, follow these steps:

1. Start pgAdmin by clicking on its desktop shortcut or by finding it in the **Start** menu.

2. Create a connection to your database server if it does not exist by navigating to **File | Add Server...** or clicking on the corresponding button on the toolbar.

3. Connect to the database server where your database is located by double-clicking on its name in **Object Browser** on the left-hand side of the **pgAdmin** window.

4. Select the database that you want to back up, open its context menu by clicking the right mouse button, and select **Backup**. A backup settings dialog will be opened, as shown in the following screenshot:

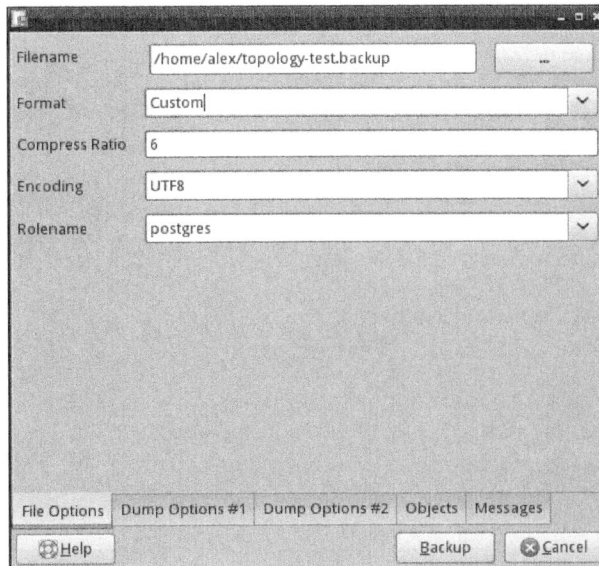

5. Choose a location where your backup will be saved, adjust the backup options according to your needs, and click on the **Backup** button to start the backup process. The progress will be displayed in the **Messages** tab.

To restore the database from the backup, perform the following steps:

1. Start pgAdmin by clicking on its desktop shortcut or by finding it in the **Start** menu.

2. Create a connection to your database server if it does not exist by navigating to **File | Add Server...** or clicking on the corresponding button on the toolbar.

3. Connect to the database server where you want to restore the backup and double-click on its name in **Object Browser** on the left-hand side of the **pgAdmin** window.

4. Select database that should be restored, open its context menu by clicking the right mouse button, and select **Restore**. A restore options dialog will be opened, as shown in the following screenshot:

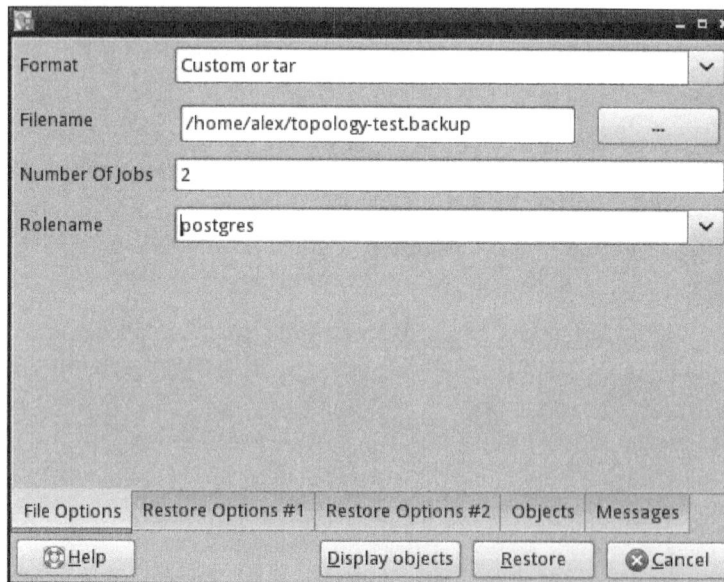

It is worth mentioning that the `pg_restore` tool used by pgAdmin to restore cannot create the database that has to be restored. It is necessary to create a new empty database manually and then start the restoration with this freshly created database.

5. Select the location of the backup file and adjust the restore options according to your needs.

> Note that you can restore single table or schema, just click on the **Display objects** button after selecting the backup file and choose desired objects on the **Objects** tab.

6. Click on the **Restore** button to start restoring. The progress will be displayed in the **Messages** tab.

How it works...

All of the tools here work on the same file formats as QGIS. This allows for greater flexibility when working by being able to use the best tool at the right time.

There's more...

There are many other different tools that can be useful in various situations, for example, exiv2 can be used to manipulate the EXIF tags of the photos, ImageMagic to process rasters, and so on.

12
Up and Coming

In this chapter, we will cover the following topics:

- ▶ Preparing LiDAR data
- ▶ Opening File Geodatabases with the OpenFileGDB driver
- ▶ Using Geopackages
- ▶ The PostGIS Topology Editor plugin
- ▶ The Topology Checker plugin
- ▶ GRASS Topology tools
- ▶ Hunting for bugs
- ▶ Reporting bugs

Introduction

The software landscape is constantly changing and QGIS is no exception. There are new features added weekly, and a huge, growing library of plugins. This chapter highlights some of the newer features at the time of writing. These are features that we think will be around for some time due to their usefulness. Keep in mind, however, that they are still in development and can easily change at any moment; hopefully, this is for the better. Included in this chapter are the handling of some more recent and additional formats that were not covered earlier, such as LIDAR, File Geodatabases, and Geopackages. Also included are several recipes on topology usage, editing, and fixing. Finally, there are a few recipes on how you can become part of the community that helps evolve QGIS through bug hunting and reporting.

Preparing LiDAR data

LiDAR data is becoming more available, and it represents a fundamental source of detailed elevation data. This chapter will show you how to work with LiDAR data in QGIS.

Getting ready

We will use the Processing framework, so you should be familiar with it.

We will also use LASTools, which is not included with QGIS. Download LASTools binaries from `http://lastools.org/download/LAStools.zip` and install them on your computer.

Processing has to be configured so that it can find and execute LASTools. Open the Processing configuration by going to the **Processing | Options** menu and move to the **Tools for LiDAR data** section, as shown in the following screenshot:

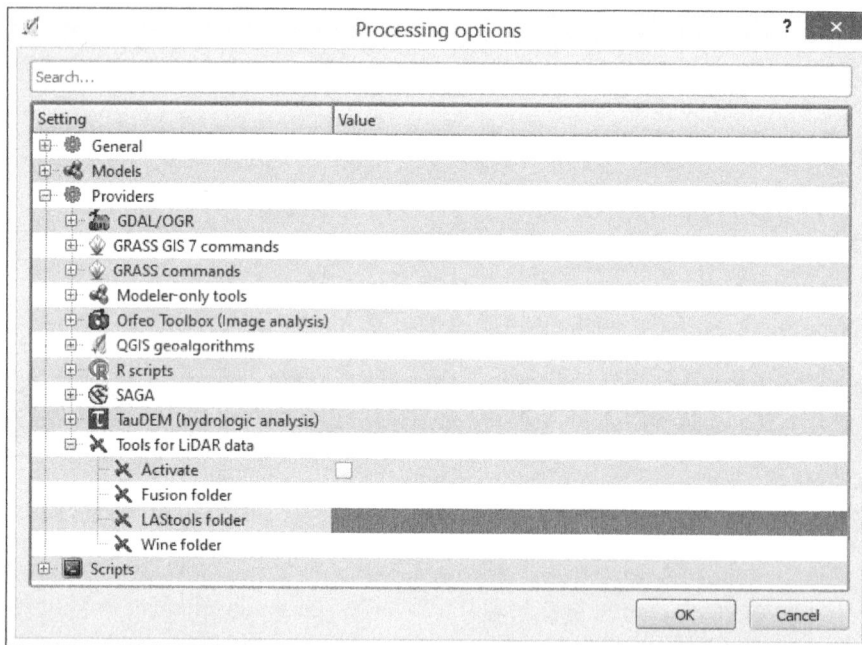

In the **LAStools folder** field, type the path to the folder where you have installed the LASTools executables.

How to do it...

In the data corresponding to this recipe, you will find a `las` file with LiDAR data. This cannot be opened in QGIS, but we will convert it so that it can be opened and rendered as part of a normal QGIS project.

Follow these steps:

1. Open the **Processing Toolbox** menu.

2. In the **Tools for LiDAR data/LASTools** branch, double-click on the **las2shp** algorithm. The parameters dialog of the algorithm looks like the following:

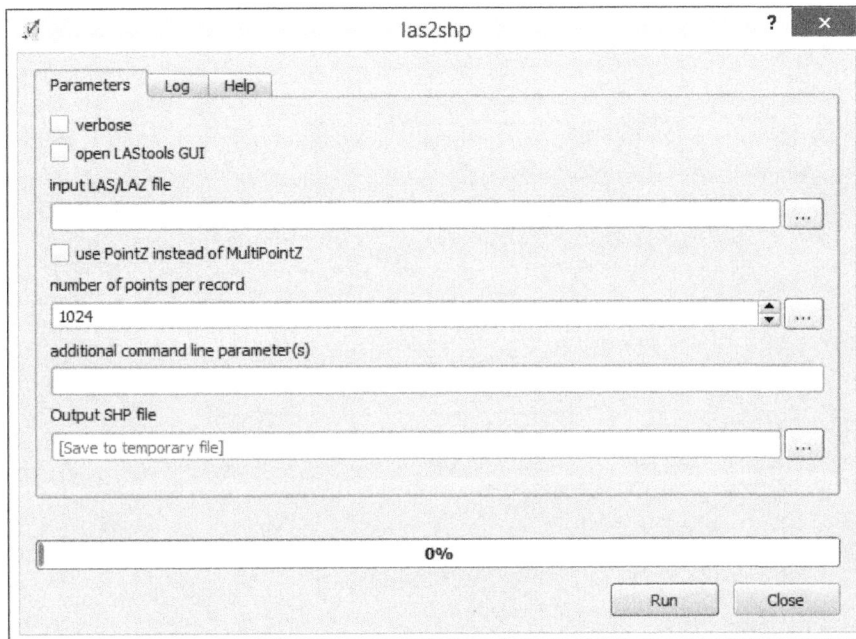

3. Enter the path to the sample LAS file provided with this recipe in the **Input LAS/LAZ file** field.

4. Enter the path to the output shapefile in the **Output SHP file** field.

5. Leave the remaining parameters as they are and click on **OK** to run the algorithm.

6. The resulting shapefile with the point cloud will be added to your QGIS project.

How it works...

The las2shp tool converts a LAS file into a SHP file. Processing calls las2shp using the provided parameters, and then loads the resulting layer into your QGIS project.

There's more...

You can also convert a LAS file into a raster layer using the las2dem algorithm instead.

In the **Tools for LiDAR data/LASTools** branch, double-click on the **las2dem** algorithm. The **Parameters** dialog of the algorithm looks like the following:

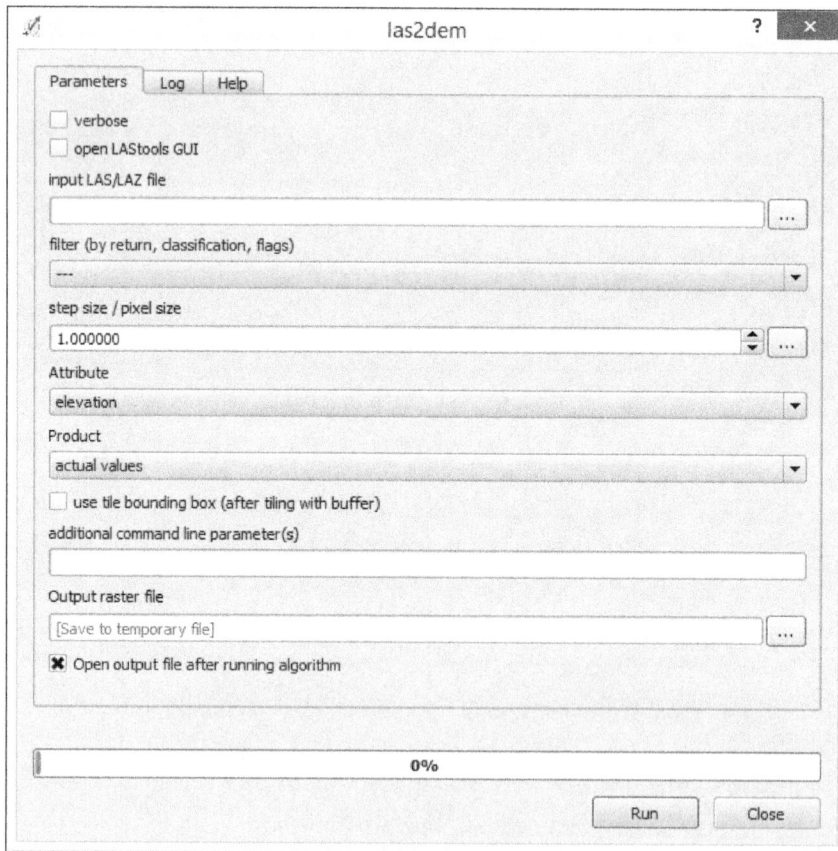

1. Enter the path to the sample LAS file that is provided with this recipe in the **Input LAS/LAZ file** field.

2. Enter the path to the output TIFF file in the **Output file** field.

3. Enter `0.005` in the **step size/pixel size** field.

4. Leave the remaining parameters as they are and click on **OK** to run the algorithm.

5. The resulting raster layer will be added to your QGIS project.

Opening File Geodatabases with the OpenFileGDB driver

File **Geodatabases** (**GDB**) are a relatively new format compared to shapefiles, and they were created by Esri for their Arc product line. They allow the storage of multiple vector and raster layers in a single database. Some government agencies release data officially in this format. However, only in the last few years has it been possible to open this data with open source tools.

Getting ready

For this recipe, you will need a File Geodatabase, `naturalearthsample.gdb.zip`, which is included in the sample data, and GDAL 1.11 or a newer version.

> Check your GDAL version by navigating to **Help** | **About** | **About**. If your GDAL is a lower number, upgrading your QGIS should get you a new enough version. Refer to `http://qgis.org/en/site/forusers/download.html` for more options, especially if on Linux where you may need third-party repositories for a newer version of GDAL.

File Geodatabases are actually folders full of all sorts of binary files. Typically, you will get them zipped and must extract the zip to a real system folder before you can use it.

How to do it...

1. Unzip the `naturalearthsample.gdb.zip` file so that you have a folder called `naturalearthsample.gdb`.

2. Select the **Add Vector** dialog.

3. Select **Directory** instead of **File** for the **Source type** option.

4. From the **Type** dropdown, pick **OpenFileGDB**.

5. Now, choose **Browse** and navigate to the `naturalearthsample.gdb` folder (if you haven't unzipped this already you need to do this first).

> Yes, it's a little odd to have `.gdb` on the end of a folder as this makes it look like a file. This just seems to be the standard convention.

6. Select the folder (not the contents), and then select **Open**.

7. Once back in the main dialog, choose **Open**, as shown in the following screenshot:

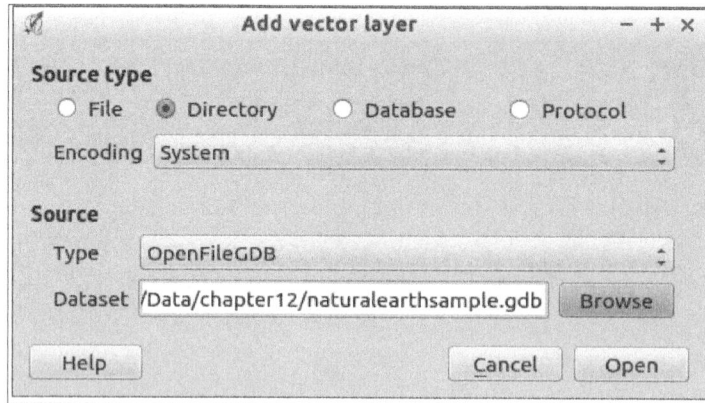

	Add vector layer	− + ×

Source type

    ○ File   ● Directory   ○ Database   ○ Protocol

    Encoding System

Source

    Type   OpenFileGDB

    Dataset /Data/chapter12/naturalearthsample.gdb Browse

    Help   Cancel   Open

8. You should be prompted with a list of available layers. Select the ones that you want, and click **OK**. You can select multiple layers to add at the same time:

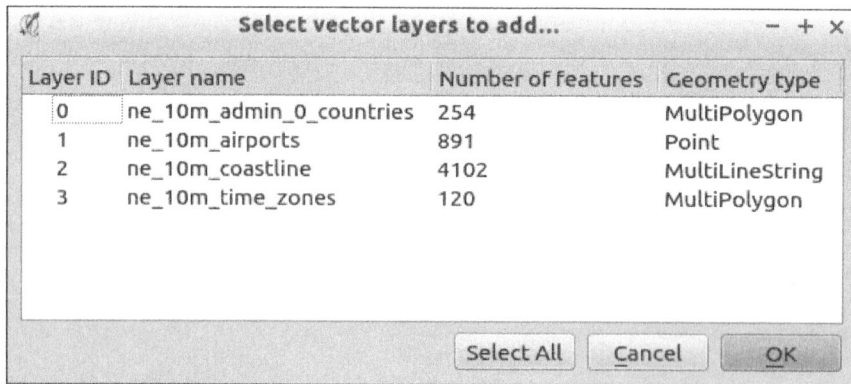

Layer ID	Layer name	Number of features	Geometry type
0	ne_10m_admin_0_countries	254	MultiPolygon
1	ne_10m_airports	891	Point
2	ne_10m_coastline	4102	MultiLineString
3	ne_10m_time_zones	120	MultiPolygon

Select All   Cancel   OK

How it works...

This is fairly straightforward. You tell QGIS the root folder of the File Geodatabase, and it can figure out how to use all the files inside of the folder appropriately. As long as GDAL has a driver for a given format, then you should be able to open the data with QGIS. Support for additional formats is always ongoing and being refined.

There's more...

The key limitation to File Geodatabase drivers currently are that raster layers are not supported and that there is limited write ability for vectors. There are actually two different drivers. One is an open source project, which is built by the community, and is the default driver. The other is based on a development library, which is released publicly by ESRI that has specific license restrictions.

OpenFileGDB, the open source community-built driver, can open multiple versions of GDB (9 and 10), is read only, and comes with most versions of GDAL 1.11+.

The ESRIFileGDB driver can read and write vector layers (this has some limitations, which are discussed in the link in the *See also* section). However, it often can only open the version of GDB it was built for (the newest version only reads newer GDB formats, for example, 10). Sometimes, it requires you to build the GDAL driver from the SDK code provided by ESRI. (This is done for Windows users as part of osgeo4w; Linux, and Mac users at this time need to compile GDAL with the FileGDB SDK 1.4.)

To use this driver, pick a different type in the dialog as **ESRIFileGDB**. If you don't see it listed, you don't have a version of GDAL that includes this, and you will need to compile GDAL yourself.

If you get a database in this format, consider batch converting it to Spatialite, which will maintain most of the same information and give you full read, write, query, and edit capabilities in QGIS. You'll need the ogr2ogr command for now until someone writes a plugin (or you could load them one by one with the DB Manager):

```
ogr2ogr -f SQLite naturalearthsample.sqlite naturalearthsample.gdb -skip-
failures -
nlt PROMOTE_TO_MULTI -dsco SPATIALITE=YES
```

See also

▶ The GDAL/OGR information pages about the two formats can be found at http://gdal.org/drv_filegdb.html vs http://gdal.org/drv_openfilegdb.html

Using Geopackages

Geopackage is a new open standard for geospatial data exchange from the **Open Geospatial Consortium** (**OGC**), an industry standards organization. It is intended to allow users to bundle multiple layers of various types into a single file that can easily be passed to others. This recipe demonstrates how to utilize this new data format and what to expect in the future.

Getting ready

For this recipe, you will need a Geopackage file, often the extension is `.gpkg`. There should be a `naturalearthsample.gpkg` file in the provided sample data.

You'll also need GDAL 1.11 or newer; if you have QGIS 2.6 or newer, this probably came with a new enough GDAL. If you don't have a new enough GDAL, consider upgrading QGIS, which usually bundles newer versions.

[🔆 Want to check what versions you have? In QGIS, open **Help | About | About**.]

How to do it...

1. Open the **Add Vector** dialog.
2. Click on the **Browse** button and select the `naturalearthsample.gpkg` file:

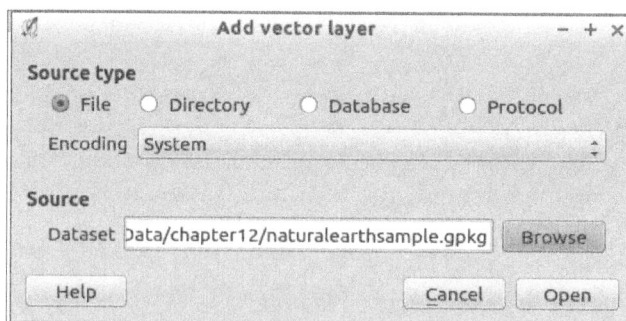

3. Now, back in the main dialog, click on **Open**.
4. This should prompt you, asking which layers you want to add from the database:

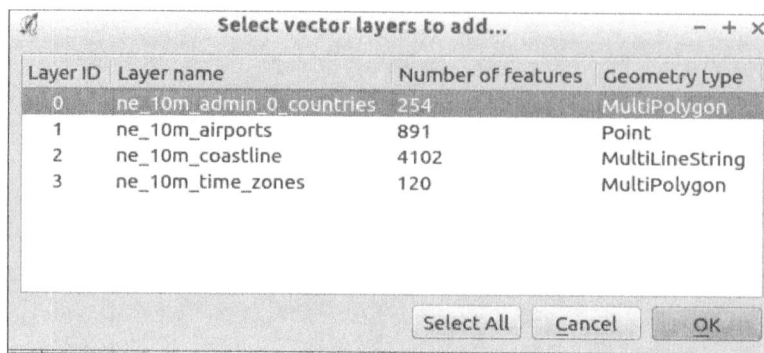

> Note that the QGIS browser can detect and read Geopackage files. Just navigate to the file and double-click on it to get the same layer selector, as shown in the preceding screenshot.

How it works...

Consider Geopackage more of a read-only format. Even though it is not, its whole purpose is to exchange collections of data between systems with a single file, especially mobile systems. Due to this, once you have loaded layers, consider saving them to another format. Keep in mind that saving to Shapefiles may cause data loss in the attribute table. Spatialite or PostGIS are the recommend formats; refer to recipes *Loading vector layers into SpatiaLite and Loading vector layers into PostGIS* in *Chapter 1, Data Input and Output*.

There's more...

Geopackage is also a database that is based on SQLite and it is compatible with SpatiaLite. If you open it with SpatiaLite tools, you should be able to query the tables. Geopackage and SpatiaLite store geometries differently, so not all functions or spatial index methods are available to Geopackages, but they are very easy to convert.

QGIS 2.10 introduces the ability to write a single layer to a Geopackage. It's expected that QGIS 2.12 will add the ability to write multiple layers to the same Geopackage (as well as SpatiaLite). In the meantime, you can use `ogr2ogr` on the command line to manage layers in a Geopackage.

If you want to batch convert a Geopackage to SpatiaLite, this can be done on the command line (OSGeo4W Shell on Windows, and a Terminal on Mac or Linux), as follows:

```
ogr2ogr -f SQLite naturalearthsample.sqlite naturalearthsample.gpkg
-skip-failures -nlt
PROMOTE_TO_MULTI -dsco SPATIALITE=YES
```

You can also perform the reverse to create a Geopackage:

```
ogr2ogr -f GPKG naturalearthsample.gpkg naturalearthsample.sqlite
```

Keep your eyes out for future implementation of raster support. The Geopackage specification does include limited raster support, which is primarily targeted at including imagery or tiles in the database for use on mobile devices.

See also

▶ For more information about the format, visit `http://www.geopackage.org/`

The PostGIS Topology Editor plugin

Maintaining topology in the vector layers is very important; this results in greater data integrity and leads to more accurate analysis results. This recipe shows you how to edit PostGIS topology layers (in other words, layers with topology objects, such as edges, faces, and nodes) with QGIS.

> Installation of PostGIS with topology support won't be covered in detail here because instructions for the different operating systems can be found on the project website at http://postgis.net/docs/manual-2.1/postgis_installation.html. If you are using Windows, PostGIS can be installed directly from the Stack Builder application, which is provided by the standard PostgreSQL installation, as described at http://www.bostongis.com/PrinterFriendly.aspx?content_name=postgis_tut01.

Getting ready

To follow this exercise, you need a PostGIS database with topology enabled. In QGIS, you should set up the connection to the database using the **New** button in the **Add PostGIS Layers** dialog.

Also, it is necessary to install and activate the **PostGIS Topology Editor** plugin.

How to do it...

These steps will create a topology-enabled vector layer in your PostGIS database:

1. Open **DB Manager** by navigating to **Database | DB Manager**.
2. In the tree to the left-hand side of the dialog, select the database that you want to create the topology in.

3. Go to **Database | SQL window** to open SQL-editor, as shown into following screenshot:

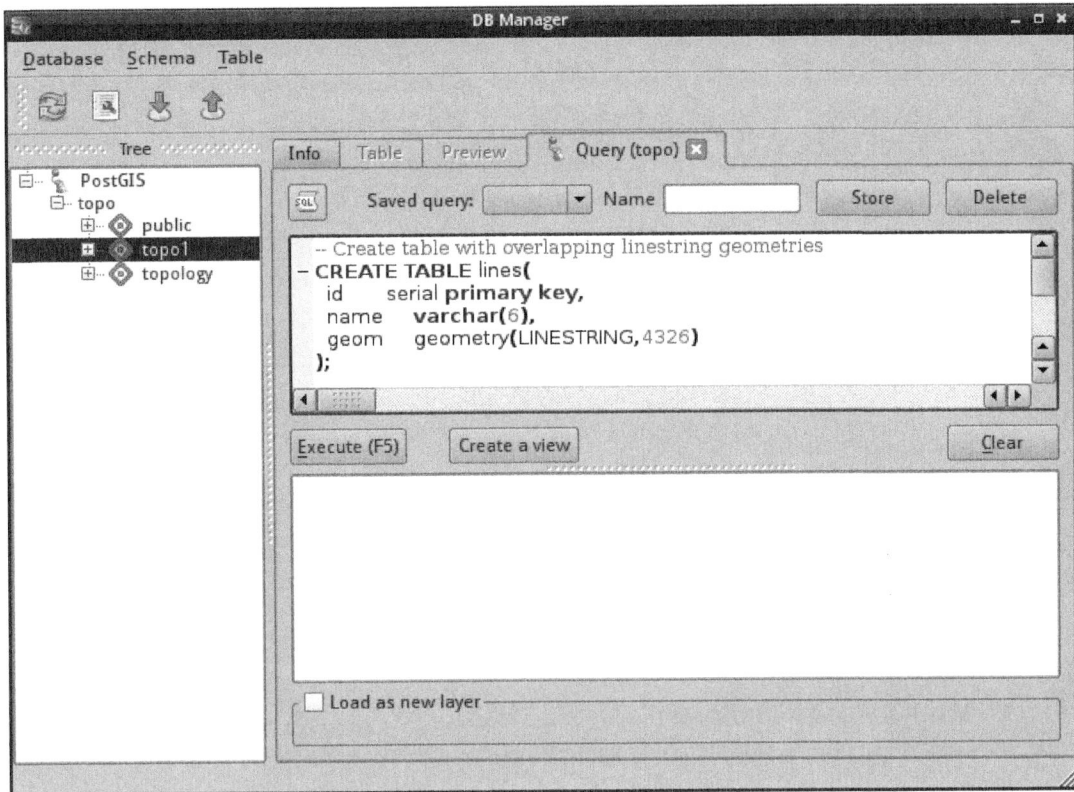

4. In the editor, paste the contents of the `topology.sql` file and click on **Execute (F5)** to run the queries.

5. After the topology has been created, click on the **Refresh** button on the **DB Manager** toolbar to reload the list of available tables. You should see a new `topo1` table in **Tree**.

6. Select the newly created `topo1` table in **Tree** and go to **Schema | TopoViewer** to load all the topology layers into QGIS. The result should look like the following:

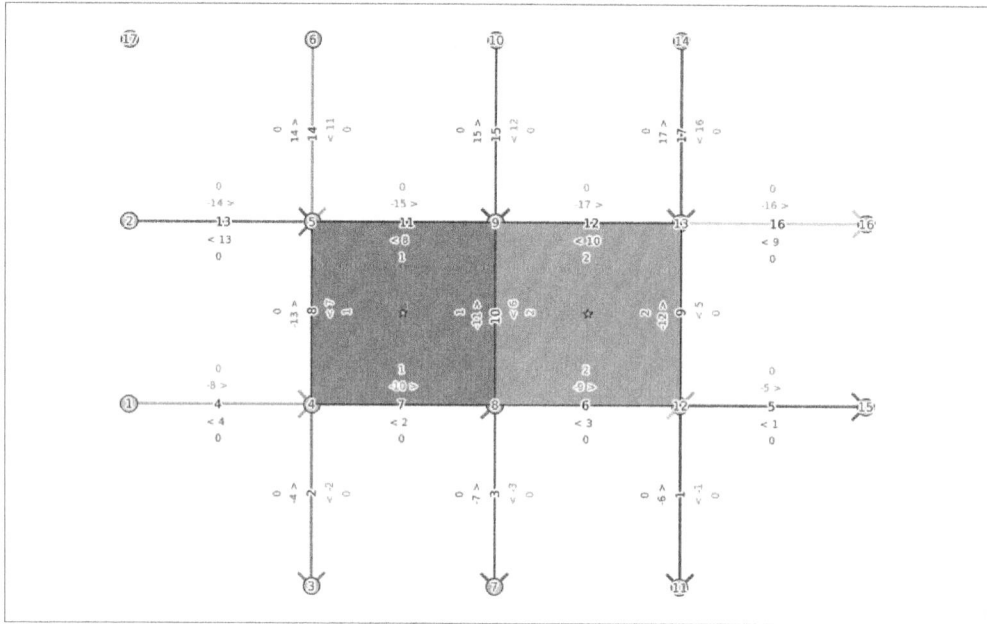

Once the topology is ready and loaded into QGIS, we can edit it with the **PostGIS Topology Editor** plugin. It is worth mentioning that, currently, the plugin allows us only to delete nodes and edges. Other editing operations are not supported.

To delete a node, perform the following steps:

1. In **Layers Panel**, expand the `Nodes` group and select the `topo1.node` layer.
2. Using the **Select features by area or single click** tool, select the QGIS canvas isolated node that you want to delete, for example node 17.
3. Click on the **Remove node** button, and the node will be deleted. In case of any error, you will see an error message with a possible reason.

> Remember that the **PostGIS Topology Editor** plugin operates on the database level and all actions performed by it can not be reverted.

To delete edges, perform the following steps:

1. In **Layers Panel**, expand the `Edges` group and select the edge layer that you want to edit, for example, the `topo1.edge` layer.

2. Using the **Select features by area or single click** tool, select the edges that you want to delete.

3. Click on the **Remove edge** button to remove the edges, and they will be deleted. In case of any error, you will see an error message with a possible reason.

As QGIS currently does not support dynamic updates of topology, it is necessary to reload topology layers with TopoViewer to reflect our edits:

1. Create a new project by clicking on the **New** button on the QGIS toolbar.

2. Open **DB Manager** by navigating to **Database | DB Manager**.

3. In the tree to the left-hand side of the dialog, find the database with your topology layers.

4. Select the `topo1` table in the tree, and go to **Schema | TopoViewer** to load all topology layers into QGIS:

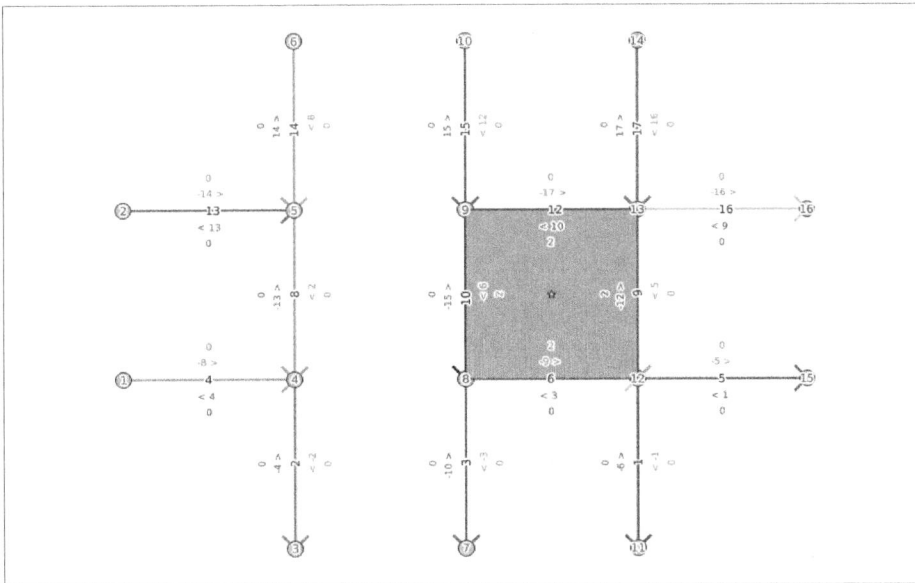

You will see that the previously deleted nodes and edges now disappear.

How it works...

The PostGIS Topology Editor plugin issues SQL queries directly to the corresponding topology tables in the PostGIS database to remove edges and nodes.

See also

▸ More information about PostGIS topology support can be found in the official PostGIS documentation at `http://postgis.net/docs/manual-2.1/Topology.html`

The Topology Checker plugin

Topology is a set of rules that defines the spatial relationship between adjacent features, and it also defines and enforces data integrity and validity.

This recipe shows you how to use the built-in Topology Checker plugin to find topology errors in vector layers.

Getting ready

To follow this recipe, load the `census_wake2000_topology.shp` and `roadsmajor.shp` layers from the sample data. Additionally, make sure that the **Topology Checker** plugin is enabled in **Plugin Manager**.

How to do it...

The Topology Checker plugin allows us to test a vector layer or its part for different topology errors. Before we can use this, we should load all the layers that we want to test in QGIS and then configure topology rules:

1. Enable the **Topology Checker** panel in the **View | Panels** menu. This should add the plugin panel to the user interface, as shown in the following screenshot:

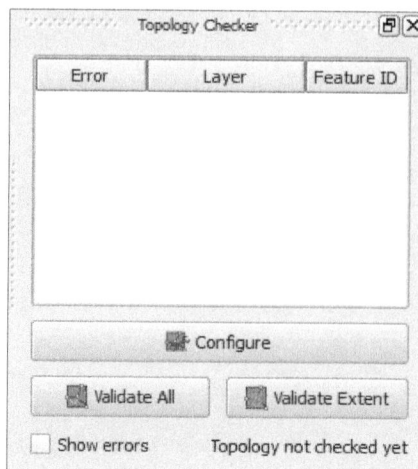

2. Click on the **Configure** button at the bottom of the plugin panel to open the **Topology Rule Settings** dialog:

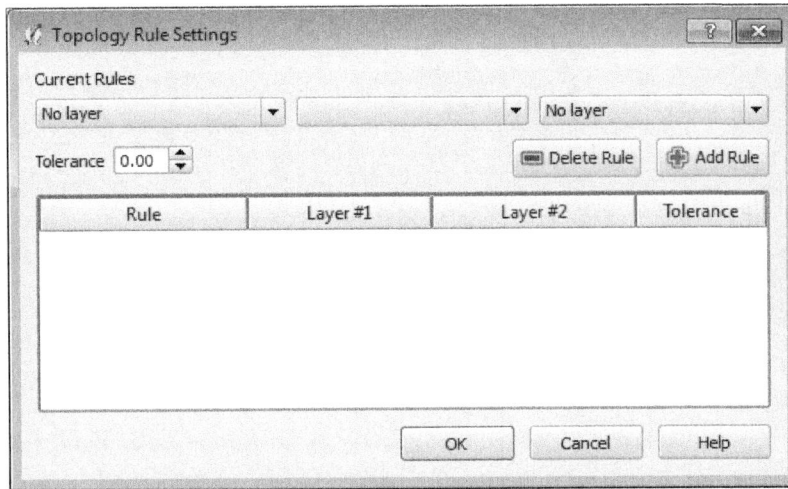

3. To set a rule, choose a layer that you want to check in the first combobox. Select the `roadsmajor` layer.

4. Then, select the rule from the second combobox, for example, **must not have dangles**. As this rule needs only one layer, the third combobox disappears.

5. Note that the list of available rules depends on the geometry type of the target layer; also, some rules allow the testing of the spatial relationship between two layers.

6. Click on the **Add Rule** button to add rule to the list of current rules:

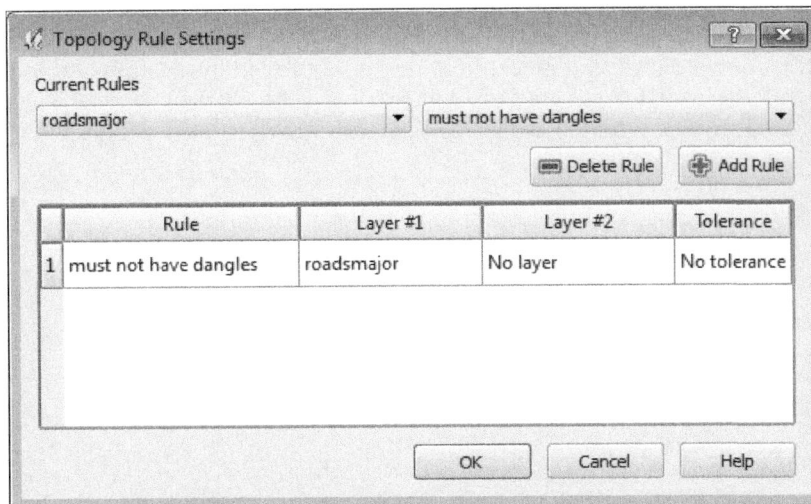

7. Let's add another rule, this time to check the polygonal layer. Select `census_wake2000_topology` as the target layer.

8. Select **must not overlap** as the rule and click on the **Add Rule** button to create a new rule.

9. Using the same approach, add another two rules to check this layer: **must not have gaps** and **must not have duplicates**:

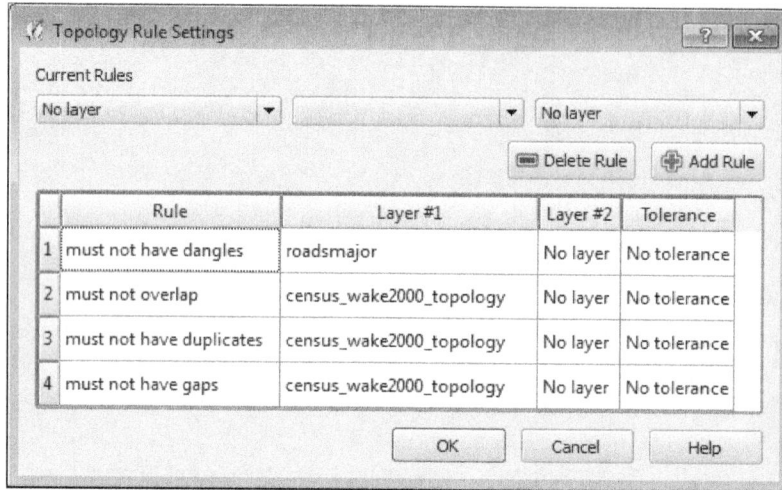

	Rule	Layer #1	Layer #2	Tolerance
1	must not have dangles	roadsmajor	No layer	No tolerance
2	must not overlap	census_wake2000_topology	No layer	No tolerance
3	must not have duplicates	census_wake2000_topology	No layer	No tolerance
4	must not have gaps	census_wake2000_topology	No layer	No tolerance

10. Click on the **OK** button to save your settings and close the dialog.

11. Now, when we have defined the rules, we can check topology of the whole layers by clicking on the **Validate All** button or only features within visible area by clicking on the **Validate Extent** button. For this recipe, we will validate all layers, so click on the **Validate All** button.

12. After some time (this depends on the number of the features in the layer and computer speed), all detected topology errors will be displayed in the plugin panel, as shown in the following screenshot:

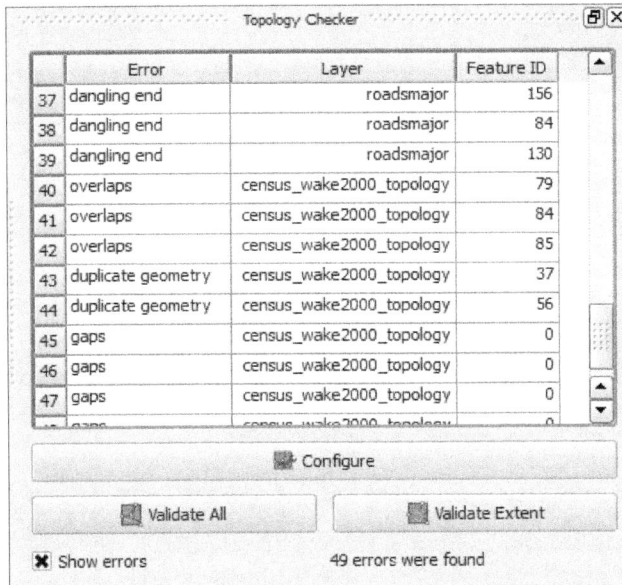

13. If the **Show errors** checkbox is activated (this is the default setting), topology errors that can be visualized will also be highlighted in red on the map:

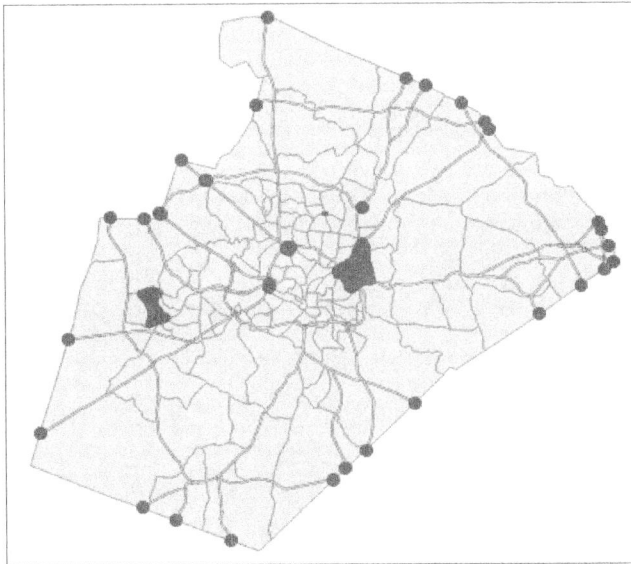

14. Selecting the error in the plugin panel will center the QGIS map canvas on the problematic feature and highlight it in green if possible.

How it works...

The Topology Checker plugin uses the GEOS library as well as its own algorithms to check spatial relationships between features in the vector layer.

See also

▸ A short introduction to vector topology can be found in the Gentle GIS introduction at `https://docs.qgis.org/2.2/en/docs/gentle_gis_introduction/topology.html`

▸ More information about the available rules of the Topology Checker plugin can be found in the QGIS User Guide at `http://docs.qgis.org/2.8/en/docs/user_manual/plugins/plugins_topology_checker.html`

GRASS Topology tools

Having vector data without topology errors is important for further analysis, as these errors may lead to incorrect results.

This recipe shows you how to use the built-in GRASS tools to fix various topology errors in vector layers.

Getting ready

QGIS has very good integration with GRASS GIS; there is a **GRASS** plugin that provides access to the GRASS GIS database and functionality. GRASS algorithms are also available from the **Processing** plugin. The latter is simpler because you don't need to bother with setting up GRASS locations and mapsets and importing and exporting data.

To follow this recipe, load the `nonbreak.shp`, `dangles.shp`, and `nosnap.shp` layers from the sample data. Additionally, make sure that the **Processing** plugin is enabled in **Plugin Manager**.

How to do it...

The following steps show you how to fix various topology errors with the GRASS v.clean toolset using the Processing toolbox:

First, we will learn how to remove dangling lines. Dangling lines are lines that have no connection with other lines on one or either end nodes:

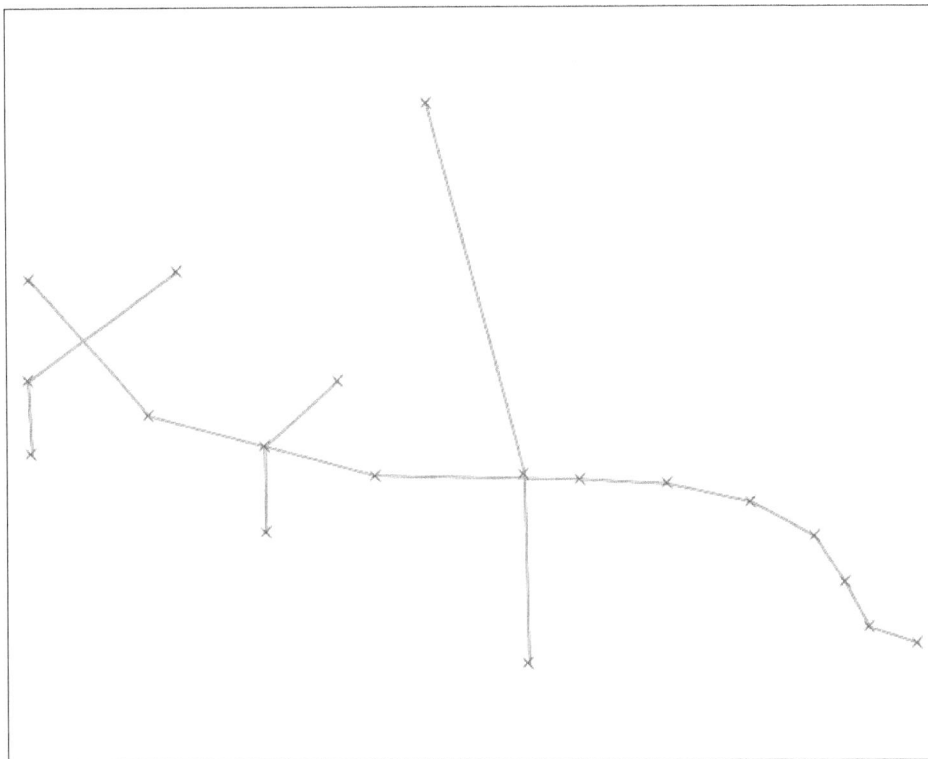

To remove them, perform the following steps:

1. In the **Processing Toolbox** menu, find the **v.clean** algorithm by typing its name in the **filter** field at the top of the toolbox. Double-click on the algorithm name to open its dialog.

2. In the **Layer to clean** combobox, select the dangling layer.

3. In the **Cleaning tool** combobox, select **rmdangle**—a tool for the removal of dangles.

4. The **Threshold** field is used to define the maximum length of the dangling line. For our example, enter **6.000000**:

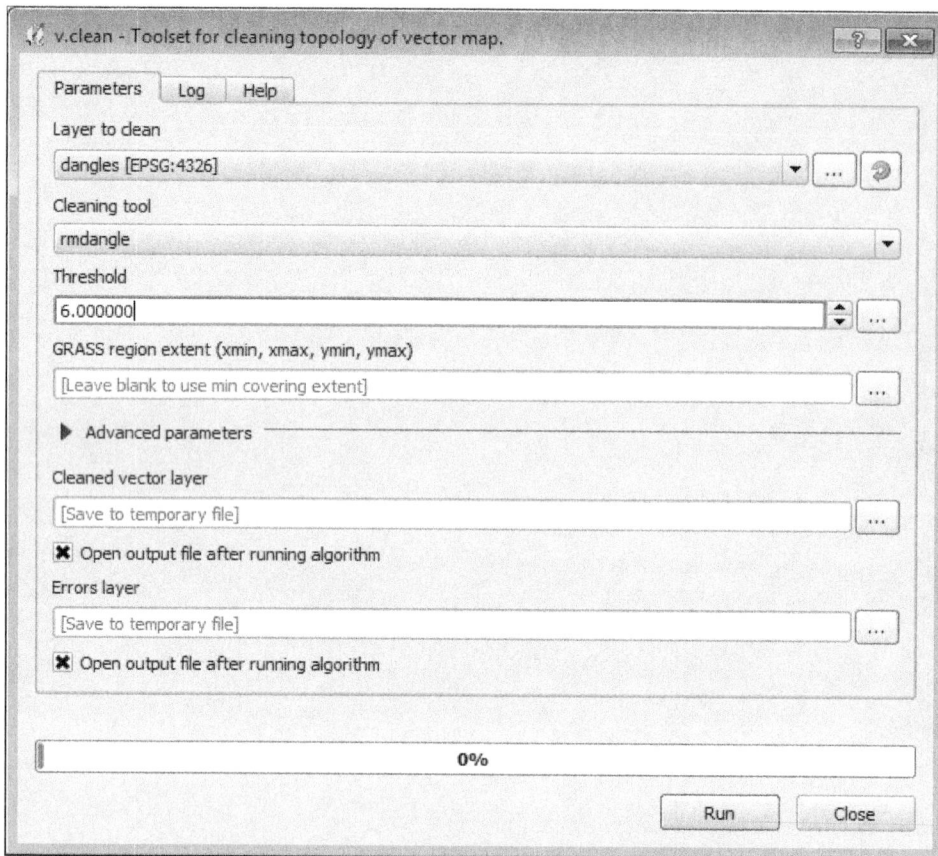

5. Click on the **Run** button to remove dangles. When the algorithm is finished, two new layers will be added to QGIS: the `Cleaned` layer contains cleaned geometries (shown in green) and the `Errors` layer contains dangles that were removed (shown in red):

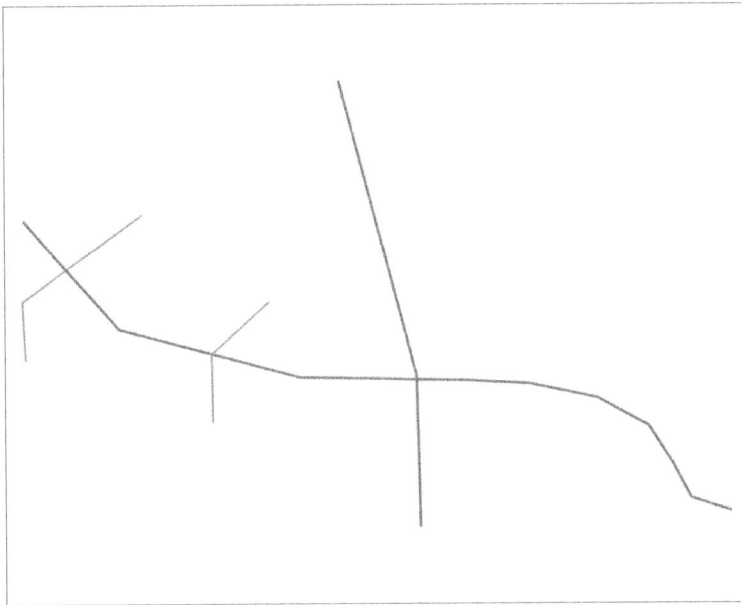

Another topology issue is missed line breaks in the intersection nodes. To add break at intersections, perform the following steps:

1. In the **Processing Toolbox** menu, find the **v.clean** algorithm by typing its name in the **filter** field at the top of the toolbox. Double-click on the algorithm name to open its dialog.

2. In the **Layer to clean** combobox, select the `nobreaks` layer.

3. In the **Cleaning tool** combobox, select **break**.

4. Leave all other parameters unchanged and click on the **Run** button to break lines on intersections. When the algorithm is finished, a new layer will be added to QGIS. You can easily verify that now lines are split at the intersection point.

Another very common topology issue is undershots, which happen when the line feature is not connected with another one at the intersection point and overshoots, which happens when the line ends beyond another line instead of connecting to it. Such errors often appear after inaccurate digitizing. To fix them, perform the following steps:

1. In the **Processing Toolbox** menu, find the **v.clean** algorithm by typing its name in the **filter** field at the top of the toolbox. Double-click on the algorithm name to open its dialog.

2. In the **Layer to clean** combobox, select the `nosnap` layer.

3. In the **Cleaning tool** combobox, select **snap**.

4. The **Threshold** field is used to define the snapping tolerance in map units. For our example, you can leave this unchanged.

5. Click on the **Run** button to remove overshoots and undershots. When the algorithm is finished, two new layers will be added to QGIS: the `Cleaned` layer contains features with fixed errors and the `Errors` layer contains original invalid features.

How it works...

The rmdangle tool simply sequentially removes all dangling lines with length less than the given threshold. If the threshold is less than 0, then all dangles will be removed.

The break tool breaks lines at intersections, so all lines will have a common node. This tool does not need a threshold value to be specified.

The snap tool tries to snap vertices to another one within the given threshold, if no appropriate vertices are found, then no snapping is done. It is worth mentioning that large threshold values may break the topology of polygonal features.

There's more...

If you need more control over the topology cleaning process, try to use **v.clean.advanced** from the **Processing Toolbox** menu or consider using the GRASS plugin.

Also, there are other ways to clean vector topology, for example, using the lwgeom functions or external tools such as prepair and pprepair. Both tools are available as **Processing** plugins, and they can be installed via **Plugin Manager**.

See also

▶ More information about the GRASS v.clean toolset can be found at `http://grass.osgeo.org/grass64/manuals/v.clean.html`

Hunting for bugs

While QGIS developers do their best to make every QGIS release as stable as possible, sometimes you may encounter bugs or even crashes. To get them fixed in the future, it is necessary to inform the developers about issues.

This recipe shows you how to perform basic debugging and collect information that will help developers understand the problem better and help to fix it.

Getting ready

As the QGIS development process is very quick, bugs that are present in older versions are very likely already fixed in the latest version. So, it is necessary to ensure that you have the most recent QGIS version. If you use the development version of QGIS (so called "nightly" builds), upgrade to the last available build. If you prefer stable releases, then ensure that you have the latest stable version.

How to do it...

1. Repeat the same actions again using the same data and settings to ensure that this is not an accidental error.

2. Test your vector data (if any) with geometry checking tools to ensure that data is valid and has no geometry errors. If the data has geometry errors, then try to reproduce the bug with valid data.

3. Check whether the same error happens with other data to ensure that this is not related to the specific dataset.

4. If the error happens only on some specific features, extract them into a separate layer and make a small self-containing test dataset that allows you to reproduce bug. The same approach should be used if the dataset is large.

5. Sometimes, errors may be caused by third-party plugins. Disable all plugins and try to reproduce the error. If you cannot reproduce the bug with the disabled plugins, probably this bug is somehow related to some plugin. To find this problematic plugin, activate the plugins one by one and try to reproduce the error.

6. Look in the QGIS message log, it may contain useful debug and/or error messages that are related to your problem:

7. To open the **Log Messages** window, click on the **Messages** button located in the right corner of the QGIS status bar.

8. If QGIS crashes, try to create a backtrace and/or collect debug messages (refer to the following sections). This will be extremely useful if your bug is not reproducible on the developer's computer.

Creating a backtrace under Linux

Under Linux, QGIS automatically tries to use gdb to produce a backtrace when crashed.

> To see the backtrace, it is necessary to start QGIS from the terminal emulator.

If you see no backtrace after the crash, this may mean that the possibility to connect debugger to the running processes is disabled in your distribution (for example, Ubuntu after version 10.10). This behavior is controlled by the `ptrace_scope` sysctl value. If it equals to 1 ptrace calls from external processes are not allowed. A value that equals to 0 allows external processes to examine memory of the other process.

In such cases, to enable a backtrace creation, temporarily open the root shell and execute the following command:

```
echo 0 > /proc/sys/kernel/yama/ptrace_scope
```

If you want to enable a backtrace creation permanently, you need to edit the `/etc/sysctl.d/10-ptrace.conf` file as root, and set the value to 0. Then, run as root to reload sysctl settings, as follows:

```
sysctl -p
```

After this, repeat the steps to reproduce the crash, copy the backtrace, and attach it to your bug report or e-mail.

Capturing debug output with DebugView under Windows

DebugView is a small program for the Windows operating system that allows you to view and save the debug output of programs. With its help, you can easily get the QGIS debug output and add it to your bug report.

> Note that you will see no debug output if your QGIS compiled without debugging support. Official packages from the OSGeo4W installer and the QGIS standalone installer are built with the debugging output.

To get the debug output with DebugView, follow these steps:

1. Download DebugView from the Microsoft site at `https://technet.microsoft.com/en-us/sysinternals/bb896647.aspx`.

2. Extract the archive to some folder on your hard drive and launch `Dbgview.exe`.

3. Start QGIS and perform the actions that lead to a crash or an error:

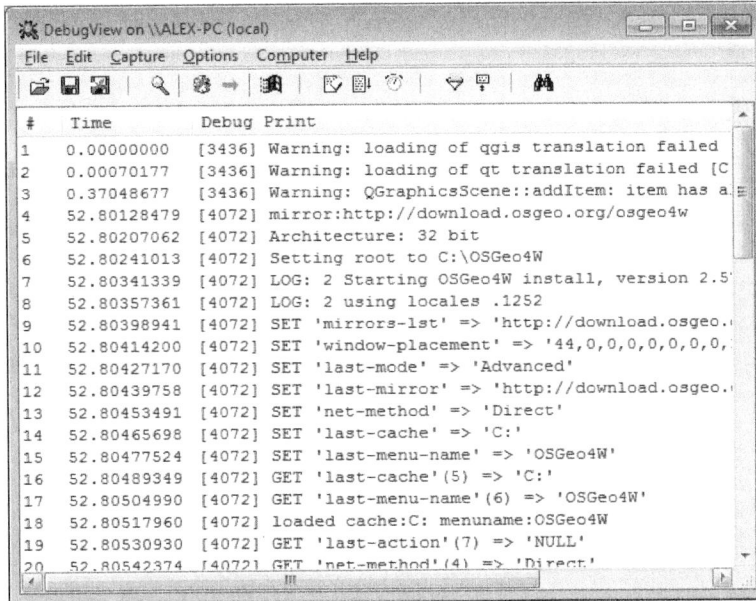

4. Save the log to a file using the **Save** button on the **DebugView** toolbar.

5. Attach the saved file to your bug report or e-mail.

Also, if QGIS crashes, it produces a minidump file (usually these files are created in your Temp directory and have the tmp.mdmp extension), as shown in the following screenshot:

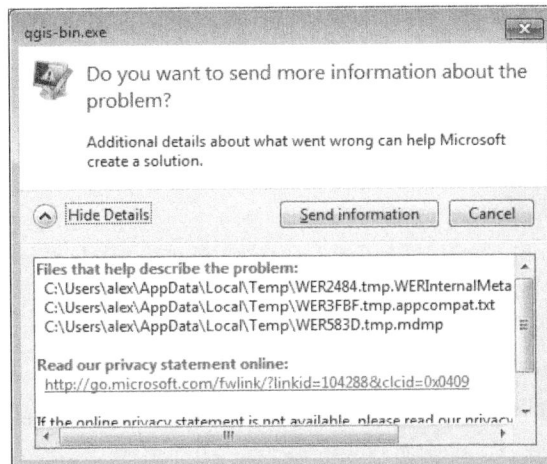

6. This file should also be attached to the bug report, as it allows developers to understand the problem better even if they cannot reproduce the crash on their computers.

How it works...

A backtrace is a summary of program functions that are still active. In other words, it shows all nested functions and calls from the program's start to the crash point. With the help of a backtrace, developers can isolate place where the bug is.

There's more...

If you have access to computers with different operating systems, it would be good to check whether this error is reproduced in different environments.

Almost all modern computers and laptops have enough performance to run virtual machines. The snapshots feature is available in the most popular virtual machines. You can have a clean and up-to-date system with recent QGIS for testing and debugging purposes.

See also

  ▶ More information about backtrace creation can be found on the QGIS site at `http://qgis.org/en/site/getinvolved/development/index.html#creating-a-backtrace`

Reporting bugs

Once you have found a bug and collected all the potentially useful information about its occurrence, it is time to create a bug report.

This recipe shows you how to file a bug report in a right way.

Getting ready

While QGIS project hosts its own bugtracker, you still need an OSGeo User ID to use it. If you don't have an OSGeo account, create one by filling in the form at `https://www.osgeo.org/cgi-bin/ldap_create_user.py`.

How to do it...

Go to the QGIS bugtracker at `http://hub.qgis.org/projects/quantum-gis/issues` and use your OSGeo User ID and password to log in. The **Login** link is located in the top-right corner of the page.

Before creating a new bug report, it is necessary to make sure this bug has not yet been reported. To do this, perform the following steps:

1. Go to the **Issues** tab.

2. In the **Filters** group, add and configure the necessary filters. For example, the following filters:

    ❏ **Status**: Configure this to find only open issues

    ❏ **Subject**: Configure this to find issues with the given substring in the **Subject** field

3. Click on the **Apply** link above the issues list to apply your filters:

4. Check whether the resulting list contains issues that are similar to one that you found.

All tickets that match your criteria will be listed in the table.

Also, it makes sense to try to find similar issues with the ordinal search functionality:

1. Open the **Search** page at `https://hub.qgis.org/search/index/quantum-gis`.

2. Enter the keywords in the field.

3. Select **QGIS Application** from the combobox.

4. If necessary, perform the search only in ticket titles by activating the corresponding checkbox.

5. Deactivate all checkboxes under the search field except **Issues** to find only issues with given keywords.

6. Click on the **Submit** button to start the search.

Results will be displayed as a raw list of all existing tickets (open and closed), which contain keywords in their titles and description:

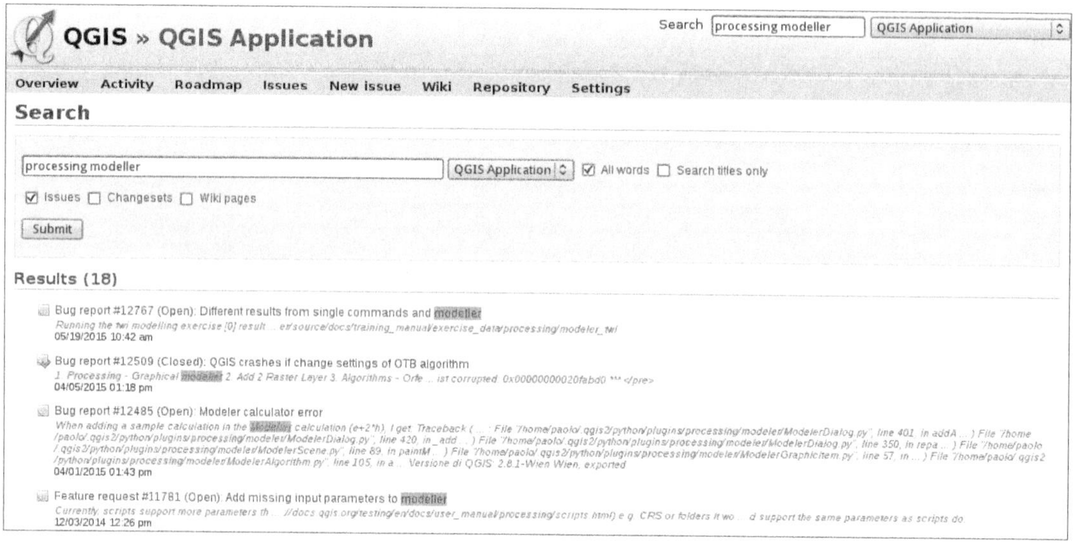

If your issue is already reported, add your observations to it. If you cannot find anything similar to your problem, it is time to submit a bug report. To do this, perform the following steps:

1. Log in to the QGIS bugtracker with your OSGeo user ID and password.

2. Go to the QGIS Application project at `http://hub.qgis.org/projects/quantum-gis`.

3. Open the **New issue** tab by clicking on the corresponding link in the menu and populate the form with the requested information:

This form contains many fields, the most important ones are listed as follows:

- **Tracker**: This defines the ticket type. For bug reports, select **Bug Report**.

- **Subject**: This is a short and clear description of the problem. It will be used as the ticket title.

- **Description**: This is a full description of the issue. Describe your problem in detail and provide steps to reproduce it. If there are any debug messages in the console, backtraces, or minidumps, include or attach them, as well as the sample dataset. If you suspect that bug is related to the specific platform version or a specific version of the third-party dependency package (for example, GDAL, GEOS, SpatiaLite, and so on) provide this information too.

- **Priority**: This is where you set the anticipated importance of the bug. Currently, the following classification is used:

  - **Low**: This is used for bugs that does not affect day-to-day usage of QGIS

  - **Normal**: This is the default value for all new bug reports and feature requests

- **High**: This is used for bugs that have a significant impact on QGIS usability in some cases, but at the same time, they do not block QGIS usage in other tasks

- **Blocker**: This is used for bugs that make QGIS totally unusable, leads to data loss or corruption, or for regressions from previous QGIS versions

▶ **Component**: This chooses the most appropriate subsystem of QGIS, which is closely related to the issue.

▶ **Platform and Platform version**: This specifies the operating system and its version, respectively.

▶ **Causes crash or corruption**: This activates the checkbox if the bug causes a QGIS crash or data loss or corruption.

Check the formatting of the bug report by clicking on the **Preview** link at the bottom. To submit a bug report, click on the **Submit** button.

How it works...

Bug Tracker is a database with information about bugs. Developers look over bug queue and arrange them according to priorities, available resources, and fix them. Fixes usually go to the development version (the so-called "master"), but fixes for regressions and important bugs also go to the long-term release branch.

There's more...

Using the QGIS Bug Tracker, you also can leave feature requests and submit patches. However, for the latter, creating a pull-request at GitHub is preferable.

See also

▶ More information about OSGeo User ID can be found at `http://www.osgeo.org/osgeo_userid`.

▶ Additional information about using QGIS Bug Tracker can be found at the following wiki page `https://hub.qgis.org/wiki/17/Bugreports`.

▶ Also, the BUGS document in the QGIS source tree contains some useful tips. You can find it in the QGIS GitHub repository at `https://github.com/qgis/QGIS/blob/master/BUGS`.

Bibliography

This course is a blend of text and quizzes, all packaged up keeping your journey in mind. It includes content from the following Packt products:

- *Learning QGIS, Third Edition, Anita Graser*

- *QGIS Blueprints, Ben Mearns*

- *QGIS 2 Cookbook, Alex Mandel, Víctor Olaya Ferrero, Anita Graser, Alexander Bruy*

Index

B

C

W

web application
about 309, 368
API access 309
testing 378
Twitter account, registering 309
Twitter Tools API, setting up 310-313
web browser
opening, actions used 162
web clients
hooking up 669-674
Web Coverage Service (WCS)
about 31, 642, 653
using 653-656
Web Feature Services (WFS)
about 31, 33, 642, 644
using 644-647
Web Feature Service, Transactional (WFS-T)
about 642-644
using 644-646
web maps
3D web map, exporting 156, 157
about 153
exporting 153, 154
map tiles, creating 155, 156
serving, with QGIS server 660-665

Web Map Services (WMS) 31, 642, 649-653
web mapshaper
about 335
reference 335
Web Map Tile Service (WMTS) 642, 652
web publishing 191
web services
using 642-644
Well Known Text (WKT) 191, 433, 735
Windows
about 3
QGIS, installing on 4-9
WinPython
reference 175
WMS capabilities
reference 653
WMS Tiles
using 649-652
working offline 727, 728
writable-view
reference 469

Z

zonal statistics
about 242-245
computing 92-94

Packt>

Thank you for buying
QGIS: Becoming a GIS Power User

About Packt Publishing

Packt, pronounced 'packed', published its first book, *Mastering phpMyAdmin for Effective MySQL Management*, in April 2004, and subsequently continued to specialize in publishing highly focused books on specific technologies and solutions.

Our books and publications share the experiences of your fellow IT professionals in adapting and customizing today's systems, applications, and frameworks. Our solution-based books give you the knowledge and power to customize the software and technologies you're using to get the job done. Packt books are more specific and less general than the IT books you have seen in the past. Our unique business model allows us to bring you more focused information, giving you more of what you need to know, and less of what you don't.

Packt is a modern yet unique publishing company that focuses on producing quality, cutting-edge books for communities of developers, administrators, and newbies alike. For more information, please visit our website at www.packtpub.com.

Writing for Packt

We welcome all inquiries from people who are interested in authoring. Book proposals should be sent to author@packtpub.com. If your book idea is still at an early stage and you would like to discuss it first before writing a formal book proposal, then please contact us; one of our commissioning editors will get in touch with you.

We're not just looking for published authors; if you have strong technical skills but no writing experience, our experienced editors can help you develop a writing career, or simply get some additional reward for your expertise.

Printed in Great Britain
by Amazon